September 16–20, 2015
Vienna, Austria

I0047350

Association for Computing Machinery

Advancing Computing as a Science & Profession

RecSys'15
Proceedings of the 9th ACM Conference on
Recommender Systems

Sponsored by:
ACM SIGCHI

In cooperation:
ACM SIGAI, SIGIR, SIGWEB, SIGMOD and SIGecom

Supported by:
amazon, booking.com, Netflix, Pandora, Xing, contentwise, criteolabs, IBM Research, OpenTable, YAHOO! Labs, WKO Wien, Stadt Wien, YOOCHOOSE, TU Wien, Alpen-Adria-Universität Klagenfurt, informatik austria, Austrian Airlines

Association for Computing Machinery

Advancing Computing as a Science & Profession

The Association for Computing Machinery
2 Penn Plaza, Suite 701
New York, New York 10121-0701

Notice to Past Authors of ACM-Published Articles

ACM intends to create a complete electronic archive of all articles and/or other material previously published by ACM. If you have written a work that has been previously published by ACM in any journal or conference proceedings prior to 1978, or any SIG Newsletter at any time, and you do NOT want this work to appear in the ACM Digital Library, please inform permissions@acm.org, stating the title of the work, the author(s), and where and when published.

ISBN: 978-1-4503-3692-5 (Digital)

ISBN: 978-1-4503-4029-8 (Print)

Additional copies may be ordered prepaid from:

ACM Order Department
PO Box 30777
New York, NY 10087-0777, USA

Phone: 1-800-342-6626 (USA and Canada)
+1-212-626-0500 (Global)
Fax: +1-212-944-1318
E-mail: acmhelp@acm.org
Hours of Operation: 8:30 am – 4:30 pm ET

Printed in the USA

RecSys 2015 Chairs' Welcome

Our very warm welcome to the 9th ACM Recommender Systems Conference (ACM RecSys 2015), held between September 16th and 20th, in Vienna, Austria. The RecSys conference series has clearly established itself as the premier international forum for research and development in the field of Recommender Systems, where leading researchers and practitioners from academia and industry meet to share their challenges, solutions, research results, and experiences in the field.

The maturity of the conference is clearly demonstrated by the high quality of the submitted research work. This year RecSys received again clearly more than 200 submissions (131 long papers and 84 short papers) and the review process was extremely selective. The Program Committee worked very hard to ensure that every paper got at least three careful and fair reviews and one metareview. All papers, particularly those at the borderline, were also reviewed and thoroughly discussed by a Senior Program Committee member and by the PC Chairs. This process finally led to the acceptance of 28 long papers for oral presentation (acceptance rate 21.4%) and 22 short papers for poster presentation (acceptance rate 26.2%). We are therefore extremely grateful to our 131 Program Committee members (34 senior and 97 regular) and to our 57 additional reviewers for producing more than 875 detailed and insightful reviews and meta-reviews. Furthermore, we would like to particularly thank those Senior Program Committee members, who assisted the program chairs in identifying those distinguished papers who received awards.

Besides the technical paper program consisting of oral presentations and a poster and demo session, the core conference program also includes two keynote speakers, two industry sessions and a panel discussion. In order to accommodate the program in a two and a half day format technical papers are presented in two parallel tracks for the first time in this conference series. In addition the conference includes four tutorials and a challenge as a pre-conference program and nine workshops as well as a doctoral symposium as post-conference events.

We also would like to take this opportunity to thank all our colleagues, who volunteered their time to contribute to the success of this conference, as well as to acknowledge the support from our sponsors and network partners, who generously provided funds and services which are crucial for the organization of this event. This conference would also not be possible without the dedication, devotion and hard work of the members of our organizing committee. Our special thanks extend to all of them. Finally, we want to acknowledge the EasyChair infrastructure for the management of the review process.

Please join us at RecSys 2015 to interact with experts from academia and industry on topics related to recommender systems and to experience and share new research findings, best practices, state-of-the-art systems and applications of recommender systems.

Hannes Werthner and Markus Zanker
RecSys'15 General Co-Chairs

Jennifer Golbeck and Giovanni Semeraro
RecSys'15 Program Co-Chairs

Werner Geyer and Domonkos Tikk
RecSys'15 Industry Co-Chairs

Table of Contents

Invited Keynote

Session 1a: The User in the Loop

Session 1b: Recommender Systems and Social Networks

Session 2a: Contextual Challenges

Session 2b: Cold Start and Hybrid Recommender Systems

Session 3: Distinguished Papers

Session 4a: Novel Setups

Session 4b: Algorithms

Session 5a: News and Media

Session 5b: E-Commerce & Ads

Industry Session 1: Media and TV, People and Skills

Industry Session 2: Generic Platforms and Location-based Application Domains

Short Papers

Demonstrations

Workshops and Challenge

Tutorials

Doctoral Symposium

RecSys 2015 Conference Organization

General Co-Chairs: Hannes Werthner *(TU Wien, Austria)*
Markus Zanker *(Alpen-Adria-Universität Klagenfurt, Austria)*

Program Co-Chairs: Jennifer Golbeck *(University of Maryland, USA)*
Giovanni Semeraro *(University of Bari Aldo Moro, Italy)*

Poster and Demo Chair: Pablo Castells *(Universidad Autónoma de Madrid, Spain)*

Workshop Co-Chairs: Tsvi Kuflik *(University of Haifa, Israel)*
Alan Said *(Recorded Future, Sweden)*

Tutorial Co-Chairs Francesco Ricci *(Free University of Bozen-Bolzano, Italy)*
Alexander Tuzhilin *(New York University, USA)*

Doctoral Symposium Co-Chairs Gedas Adomavicius *(University of Minnesota, USA)*
Dietmar Jannach *(TU Dortmund, Germany)*

Proceedings Chair: Marco de Gemmis *(University of Bari Aldo Moro, Italy)*

Publicity Co-Chairs: Pasquale Lops *(University of Bari Aldo Moro, Italy)*
Alexandros Karatzoglou *(Telefonica Research, Spain)*

Industry Co-Chairs Werner Geyer *(IBM Research, USA)*
Domonkos Tikk *(Gravity R&D, Hungary)*

Treasurer: Natascha Zachs *(TU Wien, Austria)*

**Local Arrangements and
Student Volunteer Co-Chairs:** Marion Scholz *(TU Wien, Austria)*
Christoph Grün *(TU Wien, Austria)*

Web Chair: Benedikt Loepp *(University of Duisburg-Essen, Germany)*

Senior Program Committee: Gediminas Adomavicius *(University of Minnesota)*

Xavier Amatriain *(Netflix)*

Shlomo Berkovsky *(NICTA)*

Peter Brusilovsky *(University of Pittsburgh)*

Robin Burke *(DePaul University)*

Iván Cantador *(Universidad Autónoma de Madrid)*

Pablo Castells *(Universidad Autónoma de Madrid)*

Li Chen *(Hong Kong Baptist University)*

Paolo Cremonesi *(Politecnico di Milano)*

Marco de Gemmis *(University of Bari Aldo Moro)*

Martin Ester *(Simon Fraser University)*

Boi Faltings *(EPFL)*

Alexander Felfernig *(Graz University of Technology)*

Jill Freyne *(CSIRO)*

Werner Geyer *(IBM T.J. Watson Research)*

Ido Guy *(Yahoo! Israel)*

Alan Hanjalic *(TU Delft)*

Dietmar Jannach *(TU Dortmund)*

Alexandros Karatzoglou *(Telefonica Research)*

George Karypis *(University of Minnesota)*

Alfred Kobsa *(University of California, Irvine)*

Yehuda Koren *(Google)*

Pasquale Lops *(University of Bari Aldo Moro)*

Bamshad Mobasher *(DePaul University)*

Wolfgang Nejdl *(L3S and University of Hannover)*

Pearl Pu *(Swiss Federal Institute of Technology)*

Francesco Ricci *(Free University of Bozen-Bolzano)*

Lior Rokach *(BGU)*

Lars Schmidt-Thieme *(University of Hildesheim)*

Bracha Shapira *(Ben-Gurion University)*

Harald Steck *(Netflix)*

Domonkos Tikk *(Gravity)*

Alexander Tuzhilin *(Stern School of Business, New York University)*

Yong Yu *(Shanghai Jiao Tong University)*

Program Committee: Amr Ahmed *(Google Research)*
Jussara Almeida *(UFMG)*
Sarabjot Anand *(Algorithmic Insight)*
Linas Baltrunas *(Telefonica Research)*
Alejandro Bellogin *(Universidad Autonoma de Madrid)*
Maria Bielikova *(Slovak University of Technology in Bratislava)*
Derek Bridge *(University College Cork)*
Sylvain Castagnos *(LORIA)*
Enhong Chen *(University of Science & Technology of China)*
Maurice Coyle *(Heystaks)*
Elizabeth M. Daly *(IBM Research)*
Ernesto William De Luca *(Potsdam University of Applied Sciences)*
Toon De Pessemier *(Ghent University)*
Arjen de Vries *(CWI)*
Tommaso Di Noia *(Politecnico di Bari)*
Ernesto Diaz-Aviles *(IBM Reseach)*
Simon Dooms *(Ghent University)*
Hendrik Drachsler *(Open University of the Netherlands)*
Gideon Dror *(The Academic College of Tel-Aviv-Yaffo)*
Casey Dugan *(IBM T.J. Watson Research)*
Michael Ekstrand *(Texas State University)*
Abdulmotaleb El-Saddik *(University of Ottawa)*
Zeno Gantner *(Nokia gate5 GmbH)*
Florent Garcin *(EPFL)*
Franca Garzotto *(Politecnico di Milano)*
Yong Ge *(University of North Carolina at Charlotte)*
Fatih Gedikli *(adesso AG)*
Marcos Goncalves *(Federal University of Minas Gerais)*
Derek Greene *(University College Dublin)*
Jiawei Han *(University of Illinois at Urbana-Champaign)*
Frank Hopfgartner *(University of Glasgow)*
Andreas Hotho *(University of Wuerzburg)*
Rong Hu *(Swiss Federal Institute of Technology)*
Neil Hurley *(University College Dublin)*
Alejandro Jaimes *(Yahoo! Research)*
Mohsen Jamali *(Walmart Labs)*
Robert Jäschke *(L3S Research Center)*
Yexi Jiang *(Florida International University)*
Bart Knijnenburg *(University of California, Irvine)*
Noam Koenigstein *(Microsoft R&D)*
Tsvi Kuflik *(The University of Haifa)*
Paul Lamere *(The Echo Nest)*
Martha Larson *(Delft University of Technology)*

RecSys 2015 Sponsors & Supporters

Sponsor:

SIGCHI

In cooperation:

acm SIGAI

SIGIR
Special Interest Group
on Information Retrieval

sig web

ACM SIGMOD

acm SIGecom

Diamond Supporter:

amazon

Platinum Supporters:

Booking.com

NETFLIX

PANDORA®

XING

Gold Supporters:

IBM Research

Silver Supporters:

Supporters:

A (Persuasive?) Speech on Automated Persuasion

Oliviero Stock

FBK-irst

Via Sommarive 18

38100 Povo, Trento, Italy

stock@fbk.eu

General Terms

Design

Keywords

Intelligent persuasion systems; computational creativity; computational ethics

ABSTRACT

Philosophers of language have taught us that at the basis of language production there is the intention to change the state of the world by intervening linguistically on other agents. Persuasion, being the process of influencing attitudes, beliefs, behaviors, mood of a target, is a matter of stronger emphasis. Argumentation is just one resource to persuasion; it has been studied since the times of Aristotle and now for quite some time in artificial intelligence. The peripheral route to persuasion [1] is a different modality, one that is based on indirect, evocative, aesthetic aspects of the message. Automated intelligent persuasion of this sort (and also defense from inappropriate persuasion) is a research area close to producing usable results, both through creative production of language expressions, and through other forms of communication.

The traditional goal of human-oriented information technology is mostly to offer services. With intelligent persuasive interfaces, instead, the overall goal is to produce an effect on humans, to influence their beliefs, their attitudes and eventually their actions and overall behavior. The area of intelligent persuasion has the potential to change the picture radically in the world of advertising and of social influencing.

Computer-based systems can be flexible, and starting from goals they have to pursue, they can take into account the situation and the specific target, adapt the messages in appropriate ways and assess the outcome. In addition, the availability of very large amounts of data which can be exploited also in real time provides

RecSys '15, September 16-20, 2015, Vienna, Austria

ACM 978-1-4503-3692-5/15/09.

http://dx.doi.org/10.1145/2792838.2799503

unprecedented possibilities. It is easy now to predict the following developments for the advertising sector:

- reduction in time to market and extension of possible occasions for advertisement;
- overall reduction of off target messages, eliminating the less relevant for the individual in a given situation;
- more attention to the wearing out of the message and to the need for planning variants and connected messages across time and space;
- contextual personalization, on the basis of audience profile and dynamic model (emotional state, beliefs, goals, etc.) and situational information;
- interactivity;
- audience reaction monitoring and system feedback on message effectiveness.

In the Per Te project we have explored several areas concerned with intelligent persuasion. One topic is concerned with getting the attention and evoking a desired concept by means of original linguistic expressions. A main theme is the automatic production of flexible creative messages [2]. The approach is based on developing specific techniques, mostly corpus based, for producing variations of given expressions [3].

Another theme is concerned with ambient intelligence and peripheral displays. A novel technology is able to indirectly but purposefully impact on the behavior of a co-located group of people. Continuous recognition of each individual's focus of attention and activity is used to drive a tabletop interface aimed at facilitating group interaction during a brainstorming-style activity [4].

We believe one of the ultimate criteria for interactive systems' acceptability is going to be the moral implications of their actions. Persuasion is a sensitive topic and we believe ethics has to be studied from now, in view of granting systems will be accepted by users. We have conducted experiments based on the approach of moral dilemmas, so to understand what persuasion means are acceptable in stressed contexts [5].

In conclusion the potential of intelligent persuasion systems is great, not only for commercial applications but also with a societal view: for influencing social attitudes of people and leading to better social behavior.

SHORT BIO

Oliviero Stock has been at IRST since 1988 and has been its director from 1997 to 2001. His activity is mainly in artificial intelligence, natural language processing, intelligent user interfaces, cognitive technologies, computational creativity. He is the author of over two hundred and fifty peer-reviewed papers and author or editor of twelve volumes, and has been a member of the editorial board of a dozen scientific journals. He has been Chairman of the European Coordinating Committee for Artificial Intelligence (ECCAI), President of the Association for Computational Linguistics and of the Italian AI Association and is an ECCAI and a AAAI Fellow. Since 2012 he has been directing the Per Te project concerned with various aspects of intelligent persuasion technologies.

REFERENCES

[1] Petty, R. E. and Cacioppo, J. T. 1986 *Communication and persuasion: Central and peripheral routes to attitude change.* New York: Springer.

[2] Gatti, L., Guerini, M., Stock, O. and Strapparava, C. 2014 Sentiment Variations in Text for Persuasion Technology *Proceedings of PT-2014 Persuasive Technologies* (Padova, 2014).

[3] Gatti, L., Ozbal, G., Guerini, M., Stock, O. and Strapparava, C. 2015 Slogans are not Forever: Adapting Linguistic Expressions to the News *Proceedings of of IJCAI-2015, the Twentyfourth International Joint Conference on Artificial Intelligence,* (Buenos Aires, 2015).

[4] Schiavo, G., Cappelletti, A., Mencarini, E., Stock, O. and Zancanaro, M. 2014 Overt or Subtle? Supporting Group Conversations with Automatically Targeted Directives *Proceedings of IUI-2014, International Conference on Intelligent User Interfaces* (Haifa, 2014).

[5] Guerini, M., Pianesi, F. and Stock, O. 2015 Is it morally acceptable for a system to lie to persuade me? *Proceedings of AAAI Workshop on AI and Ethics, AAAI-2015*, 53-60, ISBN 978-1-57735-713-1, WS-15-02 (Austin, 2015).

Putting Users in Control of their Recommendations

F. Maxwell Harper, Funing Xu, Harmanpreet Kaur,
Kyle Condiff, Shuo Chang, Loren Terveen
GroupLens Research
University of Minnesota
Minneapolis, MN, USA
{harper, xuxx0572, kaurx090, cond0155, schang, terveen}@cs.umn.edu

ABSTRACT

The essence of a recommender system is that it can recommend items *personalized* to the preferences of an individual user. But typically users are given no explicit control over this personalization, and are instead left guessing about how their actions affect the resulting recommendations. We hypothesize that any recommender algorithm will better fit some users' expectations than others, leaving opportunities for improvement. To address this challenge, we study a recommender that puts some control in the hands of users. Specifically, we build and evaluate a system that incorporates user-tuned popularity and recency modifiers, allowing users to express concepts like "show more popular items". We find that users who are given these controls evaluate the resulting recommendations much more positively. Further, we find that users diverge in their preferred settings, confirming the importance of giving control to users.

Categories and Subject Descriptors

H.5.3 [**Group and Organization Interfaces**]: Computer-supported cooperative work; H.1.2 [**User/Machine Systems**]: Human factors; H.3.3 [**Information Search and Retrieval**]: Information filtering

Keywords

recommender systems; collaborative filtering; social computing; user control; personalization; user study; simulation study; MovieLens

1. INTRODUCTION

Recommender systems are usually not user-configurable. Recommendation algorithms personalize their responses for users by measuring behaviors (ratings, clicks, purchases, survey questions, etc.), sometimes matching these with content attributes (popularity, price, author, etc.) Typically, users are given no explanation of how their behaviors affect their recommendations[1]; the system is a "black box". Therefore, while users may *want* a recommender to behave differently ("my recommendations are too obscure", or "my recommendations show too many expensive things"), they are not given any means to *tell* the system to behave differently.

In this research, we explore the idea of giving users control over their recommender. What if the user could tell the recommender to de-emphasize obscure content, or to prioritize affordable content? We hypothesize that such a system could leave users feeling more satisfied with their recommendations and more in control of the process.

To this end, we evaluate a system that gives users control over a single variable that is external to (or subsumed by) the recommendation algorithm. By examining a single variable, we allow users to control the recommender through simple actions like "show less expensive items".

Our recommendation method uses a linear weighted combination of a *personalization variable* (the output of a recommender algorithm such as item-item collaborative filtering) and a *blending variable* (a non-personalized content attribute such as price); we give users control over the weights. This approach has a number of advantages. It can be incorporated into any existing item-ranking recommender system by simply re-ranking result lists. It is computationally cheap, both to recommend items, and to change the recommender's weights. It is simple to understand, both from a user perspective and from a data analytics perspective.

We structure this work around the following research questions:

- RQ1: Do users like having control over their recommendations?

- RQ2: Given control, how different are users' tuned recommendations from their original recommendations?

- RQ3: Do users converge to a common "best tuning" setting?

We focus our analysis on two attributes available in most recommender systems: item *popularity*, and item *age*. Item popularity — the number of users who have interacted with the item — may be operationalized by measuring data such as clicks, ratings, and mentions. Item age may be operationalized by the time when the item was added to the system, or when the item was created/released.

RecSys'15, September 16–20, 2015, Vienna, Austria.
© 2015 ACM. ISBN 978-1-4503-3692-5/15/09 ...$15.00.
DOI: http://dx.doi.org/10.1145/2792838.2800179.

---

[1]Some users will try to reverse engineer the algorithm [12]

To deepen our understanding of the impact of using popularity and age in item recommendations, we conduct an offline simulation study and an online user study in MovieLens (http://movielens.org), a movie recommendation web site with several thousand active monthly users. MovieLens members rate movies on a 5 star scale (with half-star increments). They expect that rating more movies will help the system deliver better recommendations.

We make several research contributions. We describe a functional, computationally efficient recommendation method that can add user-configurability into any existing item recommendation framework. Through a simulation study, we develop several insights concerning popularity and age — two widely-available, easily understood variables for user manipulation. We determine, via a user study, that users who are given control over their recommender evaluate the resulting recommendations more positively.

2. RELATED WORK

There has been substantial research effort on optimizing recommender algorithms for system-determined outcome measures such as prediction accuracy, click-through rate, purchase dollars, and return visits. Some of the best-known approaches are based on nearest-neighbor (e.g., item-item collaborative filtering [19]) or matrix factorization approaches (e.g., SVD++ [14]).

Recently, there has been an emphasis on learning to rank [15], a family of machine learning techniques that are trained on a ranking-oriented loss function. There are several related approaches to this idea that seek to maximize ranking outcomes while remaining computationally feasible (e.g., [6, 4]). Learning to rank has the potential for optimizing recommendation lists by examining many sources of behavioral input, including implicit feedback such as clicks and purchases [18]. Algorithms will continue to improve in their ability to optimize system-determined outcomes. We build on this fact by seeking a method that lets users decide their own outcomes. Our recommendation method can extend any algorithm that scores or ranks items.

In this work, we develop a *hybrid* recommender — an ensemble of multiple recommender algorithms. Hybrid recommenders have been widely applied to improve prediction and recommendation accuracy [3, 13, 23, 21]. Weighted ensembles — linear combinations of multiple recommendation algorithms — are one of the most popular methods in this area [3]. For example, [1] describes introducing a simple linear ensemble model in Netflix, incorporating predicted ratings with many other features. We build on this literature by allowing the user to vary the weights, and by conducting a user study to measure user perceptions of different weights.

We are interested in more than just offline optimizations; we want happy users. Statistical accuracy metrics (e.g., accuracy, recall, and fallout) are not necessarily a good approximation of the recommendation quality perceived by users [8]. Other factors, such as transparency [22] and user control [16, 5] also affect the user experience [9].

Especially relevant to this work are systems that give users more control over their recommended items. Critiquing recommender systems [7, 17] allow users to quickly build a highly-customized, task-specific, transparent taste profile. These systems rely on content attributes and are task-specific; in this work we aim to provide users with control over longer-lived, general-purpose, content-agnostic recommendation algorithms. Research on Tasteweights [2], an interactive recommender system that allows users to directly manipulate many attributes, found that users were more satisfied when they were given control. We extend this idea by evaluating a recommendation method that works on top of existing recommendation methods, and that allows simple user manipulation.

3. RECOMMENDATION METHOD

To build a top-N recommendation list for each user, we build a personalized blending score ($s_{u,i}$) for each item, then sort by that score. The mechanism for computing these scores is kept simple so that we can learn from the results, and flexible so that we can experiment with different blending strategies.

Equation 1 shows the general form of our method — a weighted linear combination of input variables. $r_{u,i}$ is the recommender's score of item i for user u; $f_i^1, ..., f_i^n$ are numeric representations of item features, and $w_u^0, ... w_u^n$ are weights that determine the relative importance of the features.

$$s_{u,i} = w_u^0 \cdot r_{u,i} + w_u^1 \cdot f_i^1 + ... + w_u^n \cdot f_i^n \qquad (1)$$

We operationalize this general method as shown in Equation 2.

$$s_{u,i} = w_u^0 \cdot pred_{u,i} + w_u^1 \cdot pop_i + w_u^2 \cdot age_i \qquad (2)$$

The specific variables used are:

- $pred_{u,i}$: a prediction of the rating that user u will assign item i, as generated by an item-item collaborative filtering algorithm. We use Lenskit [10], configured to use cosine similarity scoring and a neighborhood size of 20. We clamp the output values to the range of 0.5-5 to match the values used in the live system.

- pop_i: the number of times item i was rated in the past year.[2]

- age_i: 50 minus the number of years since item i was released, clamped to the range of 0-50. We subtract from 50 so that newer items have higher values, which is more consistent with typical user preferences.

Weights $\{w^0, w^1, w^2\}$ may take any value; we experiment with weights in the range of 0-1. In addition, we examine only one of $\{w^1, w^2\}$ at a time, which we accomplish by setting the other variable's weight to zero.

We scale $pred_{u,i}$, pop_i, and age_i to the range of 0-1 by computing their percentile rank before combining them, in order to make their weights comparable. For example, to scale $pred_{u,i}$, we first compute the user's predicted rating for each item on a 0.5-5 scale, then calculate the percentile of each of those scores. In this way, we flatten the distributions in a consistent manner (as compared with simple normalization, which would preserve the existing shape of the distribution). This flattening step is critical for ratings data, such as those found in MovieLens, where the normal-shaped distribution of rating values ($\mu = 3.53, \sigma = 1.05$) causes many closely-clustered predicted rating values, thus dramatically over-weighting differences in other parameters

---

[2]In our offline analysis, we varied the popularity window across 3, 6, 12, and 24 months, and found no major differences in outcomes.

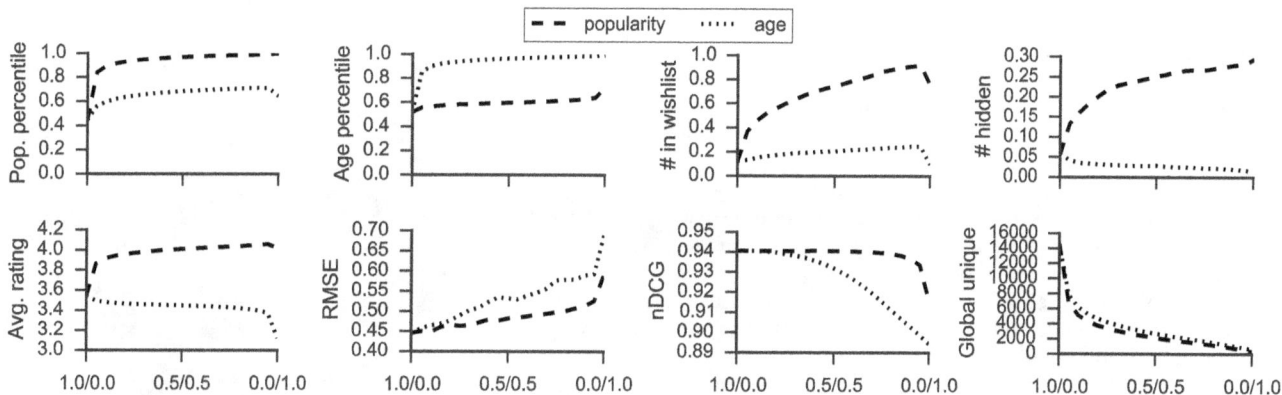

Figure 1: Simulated effects from the offline experiments that blend predicted rating with one of two non-personalized blending variables: popularity and age. The x-axis shows the algorithm weights; values range from (1.0 * predicted rating + 0.0 * blending variable) on the left to (0.0 * predicted rating + 1.0 * blending variable) on the right. That is, the leftmost point represents the unadjusted behavior of the item-item CF algorithm; as the line travels right, it shows the effect of diminishing the importance of CF while increasing the importance of the blending variable. The outcome variables (on the y-axis) are discussed in the text.

for movies in this prediction range. We note that percentile-adjusted distributions are not perfectly flat, since percentiles may have ties.

4. OFFLINE ANALYSIS

To establish the feasibility of our recommendation method, and to guide the design of our user-facing experiment, we use an offline simulation study to understand the impact of different weighting values.

4.1 Methods

This study is based on a dataset of user ratings and movie rating statistics drawn from the MovieLens database on April 2, 2015. We sample users who joined MovieLens in the six months preceding that date. We include users with at least 40 ratings, to ensure that all users could have at least 20 ratings in both their training and test sets. The resulting sample consists of 4,976 users; these users had visited Movie-Lens a median of 35 times and had rated a median of 253 movies.

We conduct an offline simulation study using a rating-holdout methodology [11] to simulate users' top-N recommendation lists. Specifically, we conduct 5-fold cross-validation experiments, using the LensKit evaluation framework [10], which partitions by user. In each fold, we use four groups of users to train the item-item similarity model; we measure outcomes for the remaining group. For users in that group, we choose 20 ratings at random as their training data (their simulated ratings profile), while their remaining ratings are treated as their test data.

We run two groups of simulations, one to measure the impact of each of the two blending variables: popularity ("pop") and age. For both pop and age, we test simulated outcomes with differently configured recommenders that span the range of weighting. The recommenders' weights span the following values, where the first number in the tuple is the weight assigned to predicted rating, and the second number is the weight assigned to the blending variable (pop

or age):

$$(1.00, 0.00), (0.95, 0.05), ..., (0.00, 1.00)$$

We only experiment with one blending variable at a time (the other blending variable is held constant at 0) to isolate its effect.

For each configuration, and for each user, we simulate generating a top-20 list of recommendations. Using the test data for that user, we can then evaluate their ability to interact with those recommendations (e.g., to add the item to their wishlist). All reported metrics only concern these top-20 recommendations (e.g., RMSE is measured on rated items in users' top-20 simulated recommendations).

4.2 Results

See Figure 1 for a visualization of the results of this simulation. Each plot in this figure shows the simulated results in both experiments — popularity and age — on a single outcome variable, averaged across users. The x-axis represents the full range of relative weighting: the far-left point is the result of sorting by predicted rating, while the far-right point is the result of sorting by the blending variable (pop or age). The intermediate points on the x-axis span the range of weighting values as discussed above. Though the far-right point represents a recommendation algorithm that is 0% predicted rating, it is still semi-personalized because we assume in this experiment, as we do in the live system, that we do not display already-rated movies to users.

Manipulation checks. Blending a small amount of popularity strongly increases the average `pop percentile` of top-N lists; blending a small amount of age strongly increases the average `age percentile`. These effects are expected, and are included mostly as sanity checks. However, these charts also show that even small weights on the blending variable will have a dramatic influence on the resulting recommendations.

Actionable items. MovieLens users add items to a "wishlist" to express interest, and "hide" items to express a lack of interest. We simulate the presence of these items in users' top-20 lists with `# in wishlist` and `# hidden`. We find, interestingly, that increasing popularity simultaneously increases both actions, though they express opposite responses to the content. Possibly, this is due to increased familiarity with the items in the list — a user may have stronger preferences for items they have heard of. Increasing the weighting of age has the property of increasing the number of wishlisted items and decreasing the number of hidden items, though the effect is more subtle than with popularity.

Item quality. `Average rating` is a non-personalized proxy for item quality, which we measure on a 0-5 star scale. Adding a small amount of popularity dramatically increases the average rating, while adding age slightly lowers the average rating of items in users' top-20 lists.

Recommender quality. `RMSE` is a prediction accuracy metric; `nDCG` is a rank quality metric [20]. We find that both pop and age have worsening effects on both metrics, though the effects are minimal at low blending values.

Impact on personalization. By blending non-personalized factors into a recommender algorithm, we expect the system to become less personalized. We quantify this cost using `global unique`, which shows the number of unique movies recommended across all users in our sample. We find that even small weights cause a large decline in this metric — even blending in 5% popularity drops the number of unique top-20 movies from 14.5k to 6.8k, while blending 5% age drops the number to 7.7k.

5. USER EXPERIMENT

Offline analysis gives us some general understanding of the effects of blending on top-N recommendations, but does not tell us how users perceive these effects and what amount of popularity or age (if any) they choose to blend in. We therefore conduct a user experiment in which users are able to control the blending themselves.

Our user experiment has two main parts. First, we ask users to "tune" a list of recommendations using a small set of controls. Then, we ask users to complete two surveys (in random order): one about their original list of recommendations, and another (with the same questions) about their adjusted list.

5.1 Methods

We invited 2,023 existing MovieLens users to participate in the user study between March 26 and April 16, 2015. This set of users was chosen randomly among a larger set of users who (a) had logged in during the previous six months, (b) had rated at least 15 movies, and (c) had consented to receive emails from MovieLens.

Our study has a 2x2 design with random assignment. The first variable, *condition*, determines if the user will be given control over the popularity ("pop") variable or the age variable in their recommendations. The second variable, *order*, determines the order of the surveys shown, to test and control for order effects.

Subjects first see the *recommender tuner* interface — a top-24 list of movies and several buttons for changing the contents of the list (see Figure 2). The instructions read:

> Your task is to find your favorite list of recommendations by picking a **position** in a spectrum of values. Use the **left** and **right** buttons to adjust your position one direction or the other. Use the **reset** button to return to the neutral posi-

personalize your recommendations

Your task is to find your favorite list of recommendations by picking a *position* in a spectrum of values. Use the **left** and **right** buttons to adjust your position one direction or the other. Use the **reset** button to return to the neutral position. When you are satisfied with your recommendations, click **I'm done!** You can exit to MovieLens at any time.

← left   reset   right →   I'm done!

what changed

we removed these movies ...

... and replaced them with these

your new recommendations

Figure 2: A screenshot of the experimental recommender tuner interface. Users click *left* or *right* to explore different recommender configurations. Each click changes the list by four movies — these are emphasized visually in the "what changed" section.

tion. When you are satisfied with your recommendations, click **I'm done!**

These instructions intentionally do not reveal how their actions control the recommendations in order to remove any cognitive bias. E.g., a user who believes "I want to watch new releases" may use the feature differently if the controls are labelled "older" and "newer" rather than the more neutral "left" and "right". Note that the offline analysis above evaluates top-20 lists; we choose 24 for this experiment because it matches the system interface.

By clicking the *left*, *right*, and *reset* buttons, the user is able to change the movies shown in the list. At the time the page is loaded (i.e., the *origin*), the top-24 list is the result of 100% predicted rating from MovieLens's item-item CF algorithm. Each subsequent click "farther" from the origin increases the weight of the blending variable (pop or age) relative to the personalization variable. Values to the "right" of the origin represent positive weights on the blending variable. As in the offline analysis, moving farther from the origin simultaneously increases the weight on the blending variable and decreases the weight on the personalization variable (to a maximum of 1.0 blending, 0.0 personalization). Values to the left of the origin represent negative weights (to a maximum of -1.0 blending, 0.0 personalization). Note that the offline analysis above does not model negative weights; we include these so that users can express "more obscure" or "older" if they wish.

Each *step* — a *right* or *left* click — changes four items in the user's top-24 list. This means that the specific amount

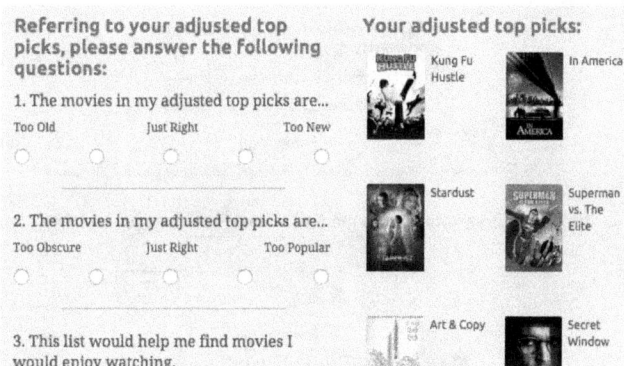

Figure 3: A screenshot of the survey that asks users to evaluate their top-24 list. Subjects take this survey twice in random order — once for their original recommendations, and once for their hand-tuned recommendations.

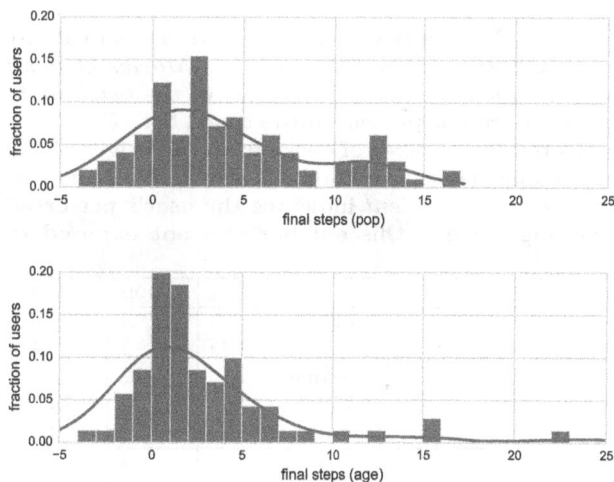

Figure 4: A histogram with a smoothed density overlay (red line) of users' final recommender selections, represented in the number of steps (i.e., clicks) away from the origin of 100% item-item CF. Each step represents a change of four movies out of the 24 shown. Negative values represent final selections with negative weights for the variable (i.e., biasing the list towards obscure or old content).

by which the weights change per step varies by user. Early testing of the interface revealed that it was difficult to set an increment that worked well for all users (a given change in weights may affect half of the items in the recommendation list for one user, and not change the list for another user). Thus, we pre-computed a set of weights for each subject that would correspond to replacing four items — enough to feel the list changing, but not enough to be overwhelming. We locate a value for each step using a binary search algorithm.

To assist users in determining whether the list is better before or after the change, we show two boxes, one showing the movies that were just removed, and one showing the movies that were just added. We also call attention to the new items in the top-24 list by highlighting them.

After clicking *I'm done!*, we ask survey questions about the subject's original and tuned recommendations (see Figure 3). These questions are designed to assess their perceptions of the differences between the two lists. Several of these questions are derived from [5]. We conclude the survey with several questions concerning the general feasibility of this interface as a permanent feature in MovieLens.

5.2 Results

We consider two groups for analysis. First, for examining use of the recommender tuner interface, we look at users who (a) used both the left and the right buttons, (b) took three or more actions, and (c) clicked *I'm done!* (N=168, 8.3% of those emailed). Second, for examining survey results, we look at users from the first group who also completed the survey (N=148, 7.3% of those emailed). Both groups come from a pool of 381 users (19% of those emailed) who clicked on the email link and were assigned to an experimental condition. These samples skew towards highly-active users (e.g., users who finished the survey have a median of 186 logins and 626 ratings vs. the broader sample of emailed users who have a median of 48 logins and 254 ratings).

Overall, subjects used a median of 10 actions in tuning their list of recommendations (pop condition: median=12; age condition: median=10). 15% of subjects chose the original recommender as their favorite configuration, while the remaining 85% chose a configuration one or more steps from the initial setting. See Figure 4 for a histogram of these

subjects' final choices (measured in number of clicks left or right from the initial configuration) and Table 1 for descriptive statistics of three outcome measures.

See Table 2 for an overview of how the top-24 movies themselves changed in terms of popularity, age, and average rating. Subjects in the pop condition tuned their recommendations to become more popular (average ratings, last year: $22 \Rightarrow 100$), newer (average release date: $1993 \Rightarrow 1998$), and more highly-rated (average rating: $3.58 \Rightarrow 3.85$). Subjects in the age condition tuned their recommendations to become newer (average release date: $1995 \Rightarrow 2002$); there were not statistically significant differences in the other metrics.

Of the 148 subjects who completed the survey, 85 are in the pop condition, 63 are in the age condition. 72 users took the *original list* survey first, while 76 users took the *tuned list* survey first. We found no order effects in any of the statistical tests described below.

Subjects in both the pop condition and the age condition responded more favorably concerning the properties of the tuned list, as compared with the original list. These results are summarized in Figure 5 and Figure 6. All differences shown in those figures concerning the distributions of responses between *original* and *tuned* are statistically significant (p<0.001) using a Wilcoxon rank sum test.

Subjects responded that the tuned list contained more movies they had heard of, and more movies they wanted to watch (Wilcoxon test, p<0.001). See Table 3 for descriptive statistics. These differences remain statistically significant when looking only at subjects in the pop condition (p<0.001) and the age condition (p<0.001).

6. DISCUSSION

RQ1: Do users like having control over their recommendations? Subjects strongly preferred their top-24 recommen-

Table 1: Descriptive statistics of users' tuned list of recommendations, by condition. *Movies changed from original* indicates how many of the original 24 movies were not present in the tuned list. *Final step* indicates the number of clicks from the origin of the final choice (negative numbers are "left" of the origin). *Final coefficient* indicates the user's preferred blending weight (this number was not exposed to users).

		pop	age
movies changed from original	min	0	0
	25%	5	4
	median	12	7
	75%	20	14.5
	max	24	24
final step	min	-4	-4
	25%	0	0
	median	3	1
	75%	6	4
	max	16	25
final coefficient	min	-0.052	-0.012
	25%	0.000	0.000
	median	0.021	0.002
	75%	0.193	0.014
	max	0.990	1.000

dation lists after using the experimental controls to adjust the popularity or age. Subjects in the popularity condition were more likely to say that their recommendations were "just right" in terms of popularity; subjects in the age condition were more likely to say that their recommendations were "just right" in terms of recency. Across both conditions, subjects reported that their adjusted lists better represent their preferences, and would better help them find movies to watch.

Subjects responded positively to a survey question asking if they would use a feature like this if it were a permanent part of the system (median "agree" on a likert scale). However, subjects responded negatively to a survey question asking if they found the interface easy to use (median "disagree" on a likert scale). Based on user feedback, we attribute a large part of this usability problem to our decision to obfuscate the experimental controls (e.g., labeling a button with "right" instead of "newer", asking them to pick "a position in a spectrum of values" instead of "a popularity setting"). Given the strongly positive feedback towards the tuned lists of recommendations, we feel it is worth investing effort in

Table 2: Average statistics of subjects' original and tuned top-24 recommendation lists by condition. * denotes a statistically significant difference ($p < 0.001$) using a paired t-test.

condition	metric	original	tuned
pop	pop. percentile	0.80	0.91*
	age percentile	0.51	0.57*
	avg. rating	3.58	3.85*
age	pop. percentile	0.77	0.79
	age percentile	0.53	0.65*
	avg. rating	3.49	3.47

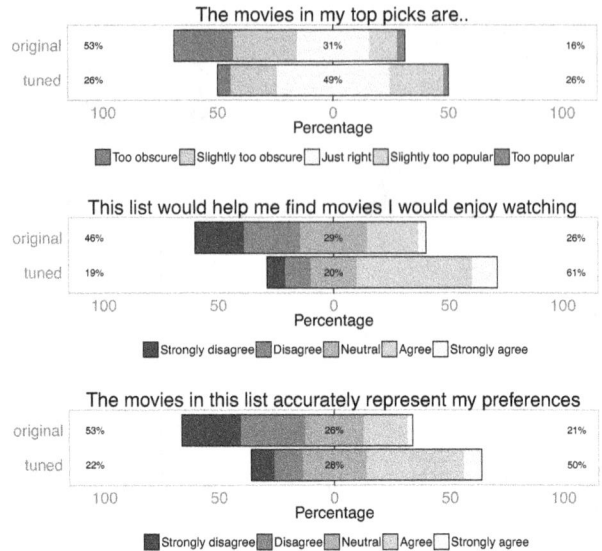

Figure 5: User survey responses from the *popularity* condition. Note that the first plot uses a custom scale where the best values are in the middle ("just right"), while the other two plots use a conventional agree/disagree scale. All differences between original and tuned are statistically significant (Wilcoxon test, p<0.001).

building usable interfaces for recommender tuning, but this remains future work.

RQ2: Given control, how different are users' tuned recommendations from their original recommendations? Different users used the controls in different ways. The median user in the pop condition changed out 12 (50%) of their original top-24 recommendations, while the median user in the age condition changed out 7 (29%). There were some users who changed out all of their movies (N=13, 7.7%), and some users who did not change any movies (N=13, 7.7%).

Offline simulation predicts several effects of our recommendation method on resulting lists. We are able to measure several of these same effects using data from the user study — popularity percentile, age percentile, and average rating — and find that subjects' recommendation lists moved in the predicted direction. These results show some striking differences in the tuned recommendation. For example, users in

Table 3: User responses concerning their familiarity with and desire to watch the movies in the original and tuned top-24 lists. The difference between original and tuned is statistically significant (Wilcoxon test, p<0.001).

		original	tuned
# heard of	25%	3	7
	median	7	13
	75%	12	18
# want to watch	25%	2	5
	median	5	9
	75%	10	15

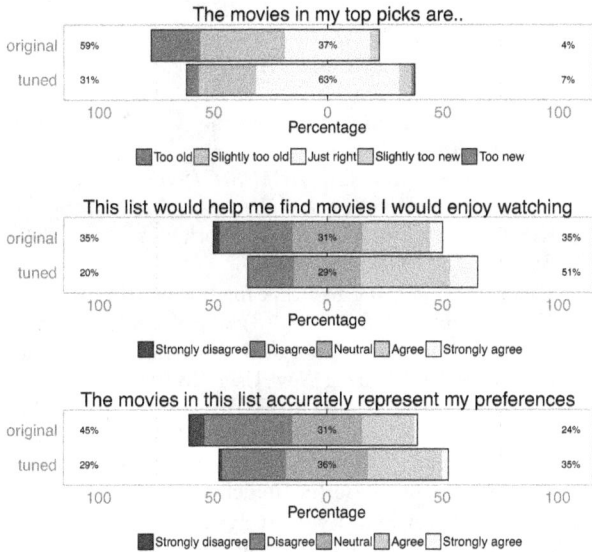

Figure 6: User survey responses from the *age* condition. Note that the first plot uses a custom scale where the best values are in the middle ("just right"), while the other two plots use a conventional agree/disagree scale. All differences between original and tuned are statistically significant (Wilcoxon test, p<0.001).

the popularity condition tuned their lists to contain movies that were rated nearly five times as often in the past year (100 vs. 22), on average.

RQ3: Do users converge to a common "best tuning" setting? There does not appear to be a "one size fits all" tuning value where users converge in their preferences, in either condition. In fact, 15% of users in the pop condition chose weights below 0.0 (to the "left" of the origin, in the interface) to encourage less popular items to appear; 17% of users in the age condition chose negative weights to encourage older items to appear. Given that the majority of user feedback in MovieLens (outside this experiment, in day-to-day operation) indicates recommendations that skew too old or too obscure, the number of users who chose negative value weights is surprising, which underscores the importance of giving the users control.

6.1 Limitations

Our algorithm uses item-item collaborative filtering as the baseline personalization algorithm. This algorithm, optimized for accuracy in the prediction task, may behave extremely differently from other algorithms [9], content-based or machine-learning algorithms in particular. It is possible that user controls would have a more subtle effect in the context of a recommender that was on average better oriented with user goals (e.g., optimized to predict movies that will be added to the wishlist).

Our experiments examine just two attributes — popularity and age — in a single context — movie recommendations. Therefore, our findings may or may not generalize to a broader pool of entity attributes in different domains; different systems will probably need to experiment to find the most useful attributes for providing users with control. In addition, our method lends itself most naturally to attributes that may be linearly scaled; categorical variables (e.g., movie genre) do not fit naturally into this framework.

Our user study was taken by power users of MovieLens. These users may have responded more favorably to our experimental interface than more typical users would have, but we cannot know. We must consider the possibility that a typical user would not be nearly as sensitive to the differences in top-24 recommended items.

Our experimental interface was poorly rated for its usability, and we received several comments about the difficulty of the task. Again, this biases the experimental sample towards users who have a higher tolerance for complexity or navigating unclear tasks.

6.2 Future Work

In this research, we address only item-level recommendations. Our method does not naturally generalize to different types of recommendation tasks, such as recommending categories ("top dark comedies") or recommending similar items ("more movies like this"). Developing and evaluating the feasibility of user-tuned recommenders for these tasks is future work.

We make the assumption that users have relatively static preferences, but in reality, a user's context is always changing (e.g., changing moods, social contexts, or physical locations). A recommender tuning that works one day may be less appropriate the next day. Understanding the relationship between context-sensitive recommenders and user-tuned recommenders — and developing interfaces that merge the two — is an interesting next step.

7. CONCLUSION

In this paper, we build and evaluate a recommender system that incorporates user-tuned popularity and recency modifiers. We find that users who are given these controls evaluate the resulting recommendations much more positively than their original recommendations: they rated the tuned recommendations to be more personalized, and identified more movies that they hoped to watch. Further, we find that there is no globally optimal setting that works for all users. Some used the experimental controls to change out every movie in their recommendation list, while others responded that their original list was optimal.

These results underscore the importance of user control — based on these data, any globally-optimized hybrid recommender we deploy will not match the desires of a large fraction of our users. Recommender systems traditionally offer no explicit control to users, and leave users guessing about the relationship between their actions and the resulting recommendations. Based on the results of this study, we want this to change — users will be happier if they are given control.

8. ACKNOWLEDGMENTS

We would like to thank Joseph Konstan and Daniel Kluver for their contributions, and MovieLens users for their participation. This material is based on work supported by the National Science Foundation under grants IIS-0808692, IIS-0964695, IIS-0968483, and IIS-1111201. This project was supported by the University of Minnesota's Undergraduate Research Opportunities Program.

9. REFERENCES

[1] X. Amatriain. Mining Large Streams of User Data for Personalized Recommendations. *SIGKDD Explor. Newsl.*, 14(2):37–48, Apr. 2013.

[2] S. Bostandjiev, J. O'Donovan, and T. Hãűllerer. TasteWeights: A Visual Interactive Hybrid Recommender System. In *Proceedings of the Sixth ACM Conference on Recommender Systems*, RecSys '12, pages 35–42, New York, NY, USA, 2012. ACM.

[3] R. Burke. Hybrid Web Recommender Systems. In P. Brusilovsky, A. Kobsa, and W. Nejdl, editors, *The Adaptive Web*, number 4321 in Lecture Notes in Computer Science, pages 377–408. Springer Berlin Heidelberg, 2007.

[4] Z. Cao, T. Qin, T.-Y. Liu, M.-F. Tsai, and H. Li. Learning to Rank: From Pairwise Approach to Listwise Approach. In *Proceedings of the 24th International Conference on Machine Learning*, ICML '07, pages 129–136, New York, NY, USA, 2007. ACM.

[5] S. Chang, F. M. Harper, and L. Terveen. Using Groups of Items for Preference Elicitation in Recommender Systems. In *Proceedings of the 18th ACM Conference on Computer Supported Cooperative Work and Social Computing*, CSCW '15, pages 1258–1269, New York, NY, USA, 2015. ACM.

[6] O. Chapelle and S. S. Keerthi. Efficient algorithms for ranking with SVMs. *Information Retrieval*, 13(3):201–215, Sept. 2009.

[7] L. Chen and P. Pu. Critiquing-based recommenders: survey and emerging trends. *User Modeling and User-Adapted Interaction*, 22(1-2):125–150, Oct. 2011.

[8] P. Cremonesi, F. Garzotto, S. Negro, A. V. Papadopoulos, and R. Turrin. Looking for "Good" Recommendations: A Comparative Evaluation of Recommender Systems. In P. Campos, N. Graham, J. Jorge, N. Nunes, P. Palanque, and M. Winckler, editors, *Human-Computer Interaction - INTERACT 2011*, number 6948 in Lecture Notes in Computer Science, pages 152–168. Springer Berlin Heidelberg, 2011.

[9] M. D. Ekstrand, F. M. Harper, M. C. Willemsen, and J. A. Konstan. User Perception of Differences in Recommender Algorithms. In *Proceedings of the 8th ACM Conference on Recommender Systems*, RecSys '14, pages 161–168, New York, NY, USA, 2014. ACM.

[10] M. D. Ekstrand, M. Ludwig, J. A. Konstan, and J. T. Riedl. Rethinking the Recommender Research Ecosystem: Reproducibility, Openness, and LensKit. In *Proceedings of the Fifth ACM Conference on Recommender Systems*, RecSys '11, pages 133–140, New York, NY, USA, 2011. ACM.

[11] J. L. Herlocker, J. A. Konstan, L. G. Terveen, and J. T. Riedl. Evaluating Collaborative Filtering Recommender Systems. *ACM Trans. Inf. Syst.*, 22(1):5–53, Jan. 2004.

[12] M. Honan. I Liked Everything I Saw on Facebook for Two Days. Here's What It Did to Me, Aug. 2014.

[13] M. Jahrer, A. Toscher, and R. Legenstein. Combining Predictions for Accurate Recommender Systems. In *Proceedings of the 16th ACM SIGKDD International Conference on Knowledge Discovery and Data Mining*, KDD '10, pages 693–702, New York, NY, USA, 2010. ACM.

[14] Y. Koren. Factorization Meets the Neighborhood: A Multifaceted Collaborative Filtering Model. In *Proceedings of the 14th ACM SIGKDD International Conference on Knowledge Discovery and Data Mining*, KDD '08, pages 426–434, New York, NY, USA, 2008. ACM.

[15] T.-Y. Liu. Learning to Rank for Information Retrieval. *Found. Trends Inf. Retr.*, 3(3):225–331, Mar. 2009.

[16] S. M. McNee, S. K. Lam, J. A. Konstan, and J. Riedl. Interfaces for Eliciting New User Preferences in Recommender Systems. In P. Brusilovsky, A. Corbett, and F. d. Rosis, editors, *User Modeling 2003*, number 2702 in Lecture Notes in Computer Science, pages 178–187. Springer Berlin Heidelberg, 2003.

[17] P. Pu and L. Chen. User-Involved Preference Elicitation for Product Search and Recommender Systems. *Ai Magazine*, 29(4):93–103, 2008.

[18] S. Rendle, C. Freudenthaler, Z. Gantner, and L. Schmidt-Thieme. BPR: Bayesian Personalized Ranking from Implicit Feedback. In *Proceedings of the Twenty-Fifth Conference on Uncertainty in Artificial Intelligence*, UAI '09, pages 452–461, Arlington, Virginia, United States, 2009. AUAI Press.

[19] B. Sarwar, G. Karypis, J. Konstan, and J. Riedl. Item-based Collaborative Filtering Recommendation Algorithms. In *Proceedings of the 10th International Conference on World Wide Web*, WWW '01, pages 285–295, New York, NY, USA, 2001. ACM.

[20] G. Shani and A. Gunawardana. Evaluating Recommendation Systems. In F. Ricci, L. Rokach, B. Shapira, and P. B. Kantor, editors, *Recommender Systems Handbook*, pages 257–297. Springer US, 2011.

[21] J. Sill, G. Takacs, L. Mackey, and D. Lin. Feature-Weighted Linear Stacking. *arXiv:0911.0460 [cs]*, Nov. 2009. arXiv: 0911.0460.

[22] R. Sinha and K. Swearingen. The Role of Transparency in Recommender Systems. In *CHI '02 Extended Abstracts on Human Factors in Computing Systems*, CHI EA '02, pages 830–831, New York, NY, USA, 2002. ACM.

[23] L. Tang, Y. Jiang, L. Li, and T. Li. Ensemble Contextual Bandits for Personalized Recommendation. In *Proceedings of the 8th ACM Conference on Recommender Systems*, RecSys '14, pages 73–80, New York, NY, USA, 2014. ACM.

Letting Users Choose Recommender Algorithms: An Experimental Study

Michael D. Ekstrand[1], Daniel Kluver[2], F. Maxwell Harper[2], and Joseph A. Konstan[2]

[1]Dept. of Computer Science
Texas State University
San Marcos, TX, USA
ekstrand@txstate.edu

[2]GroupLens Research
Dept. of Computer Science
University of Minnesota
Minneapolis, MN, USA
{kluver,harper,konstan}@cs.umn.edu

ABSTRACT

Recommender systems are not one-size-fits-all; different algorithms and data sources have different strengths, making them a better or worse fit for different users and use cases. As one way of taking advantage of the relative merits of different algorithms, we gave users the ability to change the algorithm providing their movie recommendations and studied how they make use of this power. We conducted our study with the launch of a new version of the MovieLens movie recommender that supports multiple recommender algorithms and allows users to choose the algorithm they want to provide their recommendations. We examine log data from user interactions with this new feature to understand whether and how users switch among recommender algorithms, and select a final algorithm to use. We also look at the properties of the algorithms as they were experienced by users and examine their relationships to user behavior.

We found that a substantial portion of our user base (25%) used the recommender-switching feature. The majority of users who used the control only switched algorithms a few times, trying a few out and settling down on an algorithm that they would leave alone. The largest number of users prefer a matrix factorization algorithm, followed closely by item-item collaborative filtering; users selected both of these algorithms much more often than they chose a non-personalized mean recommender. The algorithms did produce measurably different recommender lists for the users in the study, but these differences were not directly predictive of user choice.

Categories and Subject Descriptors

H.1.2[**User/machine systems**]: Human factors;
H.3.3[**Information storage and retrieval**]: Retrieval models

General Terms

Human Factors, Algorithms

Keywords

Recommender systems; experiment; field study

1. INTRODUCTION

Recommender systems generally keep their algorithms "behind the scenes" and do not offer users a choice of algorithm. In this paper, we report on a field study where we deployed a recommender that offered users the choice of different algorithms. In this study, we investigate both how users explore and/or switch among algorithms and the preferences they reveal when given the chance to experience multiple algorithms.

This experiment takes place in the context of the release of a new version of the MovieLens movie recommendation service[1]. The new release adds support for multiple recommender algorithms and gives users the ability to switch their algorithm. Users are randomly assigned to one of the algorithms as their initial condition. This gives us the opportunity to study three things: the ways in which users take advantage of the ability to switch the algorithm providing their recommendations, the algorithm or algorithms users prefer, and the impact of the assigned algorithm on user behavior.

Within this setting, we seek to answer several research questions:

1. Do users take advantage of a means to switch recommender algorithms?
2. What algorithm(s) do users prefer to use? Is there a clear favorite, or do different users prefer different algorithms?
3. How do users explore the algorithm options?
4. How stable are user selections? Do they experiment for a little while, pick a recommender, and leave it alone, or do they change recommenders often throughout their use of the application?
5. How do the recommendations users receive from the algorithms differ?
6. Can we predict the user's choice of algorithm, or do we need to keep them in control in order to identify the algorithm with which they will be most satisfied?
7. Does the algorithm with which a user starts affect their use of the system, final choice of algorithm, or likelihood to continue using the system?

We use three primary algorithms in this study: a baseline using user and item mean ratings, an item-item collaborative filter, and a matrix factorization recommender. These were selected for broad usability (the baseline recommender), continuity with the system's previous behavior and widely-deployed algorithms (item-item CF) and to have an algorithm representative of the current state of the art in collaborative filtering (matrix factorization).

In the remainder of this paper, we describe our experimental setup, our key findings, and conclusions and lessons for the design and deployment of recommender applications.

---

[1] http://movielens.org

2. BACKGROUND AND RELATED WORK

It is well-understood that different recommender algorithms, even ones that have quantitatively similar behavior on common accuracy metrics, produce recommendations that differ in ways that users can perceive [7, 18] and that may impact their ability to meet different user needs, or the needs of different users.

One way of making use of the advantages of different algorithms to improve recommendation for particular users is through hybrid recommenders [2]. Hybrids can blend the strengths of different approaches, even tuning the blend on a per-user or per-item basis to use each algorithm the most where it has the most to offer [27], or attempting to detect the best algorithm for each user [9]. We can view the goal of such hybrids as that of building a *meta-recommender*, identifying the particular algorithm (or combination of algorithms) that will best meet the needs of a particular user in a particular context.

Another approach, which we explore in this paper, is to involve the users in the process of selecting their recommender. Many recommenders take explicit feedback from their users to form the basis of the recommendations [23], or to set up an initial context for new users [5, 17, 24]. Relevance feedback incorporates user responses — either explicit or implicit — into a feedback loop to improve future iterations of the recommender [1, 13]. In this work, we take a very basic approach to incorporating users' explicit feedback into the recommender selection process: we invite users to try different recommender algorithms and pick the one they want to use. This is similar to the work of Dooms, where users were given some control over their recommendations [6]; some results in that work parallel ours.

Many previous studies have examined the impact of different recommendation techniques on users' subjective perceptions of recommendations [7, 14, 25], and it is common practice in industrial applications to measure the impact of recommendations on user behavior using A/B trials and similar experimental models [15]. In this work, we examine user response to different recommendation approaches when the action they can take is to switch recommender algorithms, rather than simply to accept or reject algorithms or discontinue use of the service. Our motivations are similar to those behind the idea of user studies: providing ratings and other actions in response to a single recommendation approach is an inadequate expression of the user's thoughts and preferences as to how their recommendations should be provided, and there is value in listening to what users say they want to do, not just optimizing the system for particular user responses that we the system's creators and analysts deem indicative of usefulness. In user studies, we solicit users' subjective impressions and stated preferences with regards to an algorithm; in this work, we examine the choices users make when they can select the recommender suggesting movies to them.

There has been previous work on providing users with insight into, and in some cases control over, the system's model of their preferences [4, 12]. Some commercial recommenders support some version of this, through explicit interest profiles often used in a new user onboarding process (exemplified by Twitter or Microsoft Cortana) or by allowing the user to view and correct profile information that will feed into their recommendations (a model adopted by Amazon.com). One of the goals of recommender explanation is also to provide some transparency to users into the source of their recommendations [28]. Ziegler et al. proposed a user-adjustable control for the amount of diversification applied to a recommendation list [30], and the retrieval models of Tapestry were entirely user-guided [10]. But there is comparatively little

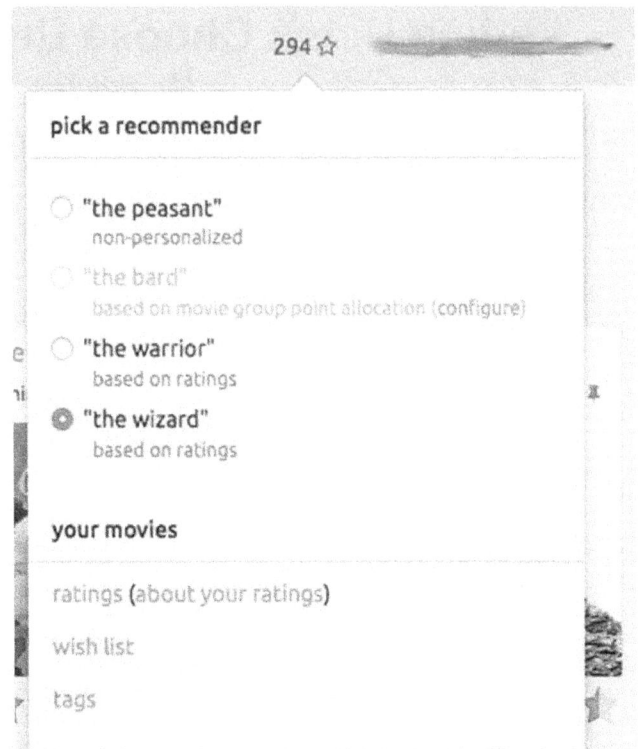

Figure 1: Recommender Switching Control

work on allowing users to control *what algorithm* provides their recommendations, as opposed to refining the algorithm's input data or re-tuning a structurally static algorithm.

3. EXPERIMENTAL SETUP

We studied the behavior of users of MovieLens, a non-commercial movie recommendation service, as they interacted with the recommender switching capabilities deployed as a part of an overhaul of the service. The new version of the service supports multiple recommender algorithms, selectable on a per-user basis, and gives users a control to pick the algorithm that they are using. When an existing user signed in to the new version of the service, or returned to it after the feature was deployed, they were randomly assigned one of the algorithms as their initial condition. They were also shown a brief interstitial informing them that the service now supports multiple algorithms, and pointing to the control for changing algorithms. In this study, we only consider previously-existing users who signed in to the new site.[2]

We consulted with our IRB on this study, and they determined that the research was exempt and did not require specific user consent beyond users' general agreement to use our service and acceptance of its terms of use.

The service supports four algorithms. Each algorithm was identified to users using a code name, derived from common role-playing character classes, so that they could be memorable but would not disclose to users exactly what algorithm they were using; a very brief description accompanied each algorithm name.

---

[2] New users who first signed up with the new site participated in a different experiment, so they could not be considered in the data analysis for this study.

- The *Baseline* algorithm predicts ratings using a user-item personalized mean. This algorithm was called the *Peasant*, and was described as "non-personalized".
- The *Pick-Groups* recommender is an item-item collaborative filter that uses synthetic item ratings derived from the user's choice of different movie groups [3]. It is intended to provide an improved user experience for new users of the system. No existing users started with this algorithm, but they could try it out if they wished. This algorithm was called the *Bard*, and was described as "based on movie group point allocation".
- The *Item-Item* recommender [26], called the *Warrior* and described as "based on ratings", is an item-item collaborative filter. It uses cosine similarity over item-mean-centered rating vectors, a maximum neighborhood size of 20, minimum neighborhood of 2, and a neighborhood similarity weight threshold of 0.1.[3] Item-item CF was the only recommender available in the service prior to deploying the recommender-switching feature.
- The *SVD* recommender, called the *Wizard* and also described as "based on ratings", is a matrix factorization recommender using the FunkSVD algorithm [19, 22] with 50 features, 125 training epochs per feature, and subtracting the user-item personalized mean prior to factorizing the matrix.

All algorithms are built with the LensKit toolkit [8]. To compute top-N lists, the algorithm's predicted rating is the primary ranking factor, but it is blended with the popularity of the item:

$$\widehat{s_{ui}} = 0.9 \cdot rank(s_{ui}) + 0.1 \cdot rank(p_i)$$

s_{ui} is the score; p_i is the number of ratings the item received in the last 365 days; and $rank(x)$ normalizes its input to a rank, returning 1 for the largest value (across all items) and 0 for the smallest value. This blending is the result of empirical evidence that balancing popularity with prediction rank leads to greater satisfaction with top-N recommendation lists.

Full LensKit configurations for each algorithm are available as a supplement in the ACM Digital Library.

Once in the system, users could change their algorithm by clicking a widget in the site's top bar, as show in Figure 1. This took effect immediately; once the user selected a different recommender, the system would reload the list of movies on the current page (if they were viewing a movie recommendation page) and show the results from the freshly-selected recommender. The system's interface is organized around three major functions:

1. Movie recommendations: the default view shows a set of movie recommendations with relevant images, usually a movie poster, and the predicted rating.
2. Movie details: clicking on a movie image brings up more details such as production metadata, tags, average rating statistics, etc.
3. Search: a keyword-based search feature, with additional options to search by various movie attributes. Search results are displayed in the same fashion as recommendations, and the recommender's predicted rating is a component of the search result ranking function.

The user's choice of recommender algorithm persisted throughout the application, affecting all use of predictions for display or movie ranking.

Table 1: Summary of Experiment Data

Users	3005
Users switching at least once	748 (24.9%)
Recommender change events	11,423
Median changes per user w/ at least 1 change	3
Median account age	1653 days
Median ratings per user (at end of study)	354

Our reporting here is based on logs of the feature's use from its deployment in November 4, 2014 through March 31, 2015. Table 1 summarizes the data we collected. 3005 users used the system, of which 748 changed recommenders at least once; the median account age upon signing in to the new system was 1653 days (min 0, max 6086). Our logs have 11,423 change events.

In addition to using the logs of user interactions, we also used the ratings database to run an offline evaluation to measure the accuracy of the algorithms on each user's recent history prior to entering the experiment. Starting with a current dump of the ratings database, we put all ratings from all users not in our experiment into a training set. For each user in our experiment, we did the following:

- Discarded all ratings after entering the experiment
- Put the 5 most recent ratings prior to entering the experiment into a set of test ratings
- Put the user's remaining ratings into the training set

We then ran each algorithm (with the exception of *Pick-Groups*; it is difficult to do historical recreations of that algorithm outside of a running instance of the recommendation service) and measured the following:

- Prediction accuracy (RMSE) for the test ratings.
- Top-*N* accuracy (Recall) for finding the user's recent ratings among the top 24 recommendations.[4]
- Diversity (intra-list similarity [30], with cosine similarity over descriptive attribute data [29] as the movie similarity metric) of a 24-item recommendation list. Not all movies have sufficient data for a similarity computation, so we normalized the intra-list similarity by dividing it by the ILS that would be achieved if all pairs of genome movies recommended had a similarity of 1.
- Popularity (mean popularity rank, where 1 is the most popular movie) of movies in a 24-item list.

We used 24 items for each recommendation list because that is the length of a single page of recommendations in the recommender application's web interface.

4. RESULTS

In this section, we describe our findings from this study. We have organized this section in order of our research questions, though more than one question may be addressed in a section.

---

[3] This means that it would only recommend items for whom it could find a neighborhood with a total similarity of at least 0.1.

[4] We also measured reciprocal rank and average precision, but the recommenders found users' rated items so infrequently that these did not provide very meaningful comparisons. They effectively compare how well less than a third of the algorithms/user pairs do at ranking items for the user. Whether the algorithm was able to find one (or more) of the user's items is a question that can be meaningfully answered for all algorithm/user pairs.

4.1 RQ1: Users Switch Algorithms

Of the 3005 users in our study, 748 (24.9%) changed recommenders at least once. This does not count the 31 users whose only interaction with the control was to select their current recommender. These users' activity was likely the result of an interface artifact; the control indicated the user's current algorithm (with a filled radio button) but did not disable that algorithm, and some users may have thought that clicking the algorithm would provide more information on it.

While the feature was certainly not used universally, it was tried by a significant fraction of users. 539 users (72.1% of the users who tried the control) settled on a different algorithm than they had been assigned. This answers RQ1 in the affirmative: users did make use of the ability to change recommenders.

Of the users who entered the experiment before March 1, 2015 (so we have data on them for at least a month since they entered), users who switched recommenders were more likely to sign in again at least a week later (83.4% vs. 54.5%; p<0.001). This is not necessarily a causal relationship, but may indicate that more active users in the system are more particularly interested in the recommender-switching feature. This finding is consistent with those of Dooms [6].

4.2 RQ2: User Algorithm Preferences

Among users who tried different algorithms, SVD was the most favored algorithm, followed by Item-Item and finally the Pick-Groups and Baseline recommenders. Figure 2 shows how many users who switched recommenders at least once selected each of the algorithms as their final choice (their active recommender as of close of data collection).

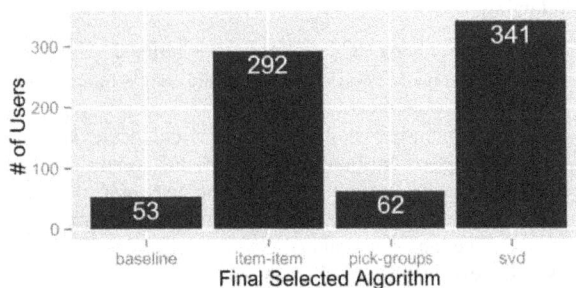

Figure 2: User Choice of Algorithm

We can see that users clearly favor the personalized algorithms over the baseline, and over the group-based recommender. Since users knew that the baseline was non-personalized, and that the pick-groups recommender was based on movie groups, we cannot infer from this data that users preferred the recommendations provided by the personalized algorithms (as opposed to the idea of personalization). We can, however, observe that, given the choice,

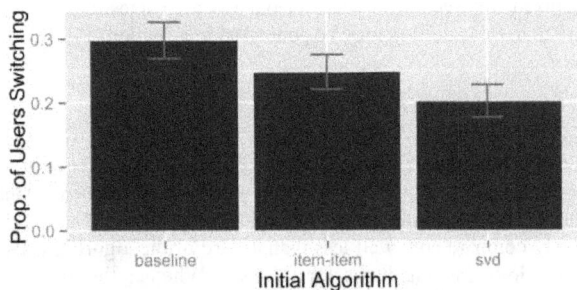

Figure 3: Likelihood to Switch Recommenders

most users will choose to use recommendations they know (or at least believe) to be personalized. This result is not surprising, but does provide more data to support the idea that users believe the work of recommender systems to be useful.

4.2.1 Response to Initial Algorithm

Users who were assigned to the non-personalized condition were more likely to try other recommenders. Item-item users were the next most likely to use the switcher. Figure 3 shows the fraction of users in each initial algorithm condition who tried a different recommender; all differences are significant (,   with Bonferroni correction for multiple tests). Analyzing this result shares the confound discussed previously: users knew that the baseline algorithm was non-personalized. They did have to access (but not necessarily use) the control in order to obtain this information, but all logging is server-side, so we do not have log data on how many users viewed the switcher control but did not use it.

Integrating users' final choices and whether they switched at all indicates that more users find the SVD-based recommendations to be most satisfactory; item-item the next most satisfactory; and finally the baseline algorithm.

We did not find any effect of the user's initial algorithm on their final choice if the user tried different algorithms; users settled on each algorithm at similar rates irrespective of the algorithm they started with. The only measurable impact of initial algorithm on final choice was via its impact on whether users experimented with different algorithms in the first place.

In addition to refining our answer to RQ2 (users are most satisfied with SVD, followed by item-item, we make two observations with respect to RQ7: the initial algorithm affects the likelihood that a user will try other recommenders, but once they decide to experiment, it has little bearing on their final choice.

4.3 RQ3&4: Switching Behavior

The vast majority (97.3%) of users switched recommenders no more than 20 times (although one user recorded 7296 transitions). Most users switched just a few times; only 21.4% switched more than 5 times. Figure 4 shows the distribution of user transition counts (for users switching no more than 20 times).

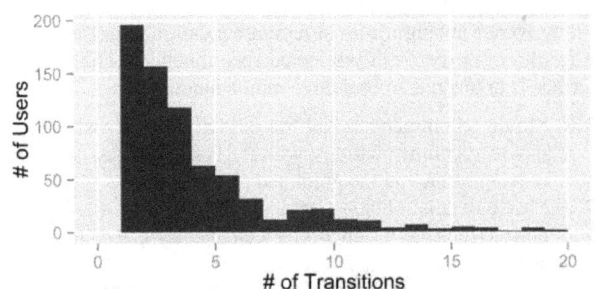

Figure 4: Transition Count Distribution

The most common switching patterns were for a user to switch away to a different algorithm, or try two or three algorithms and then settle down. The median number of transitions is 3, after which there is a marked drop-off; this is enough transitions for a user to try each of the personalized algorithms and return to their favorite.

4.3.1 Transition Sequences

We examine the transitions in more detail, looking to see the relative likelihood of different state transition sequences. Table 2 shows the common transition patterns among users who switched at least once. Percentages are the percentage of users who started with that algorithm and transitioned at least once. Patterns not shown appeared less than 5% of the time. Transition chains are complete: II → SVD means that the user started with item-item, transitioned to SVD, and did not switch recommenders again.

Users generally experimented with the personalized algorithms, trying each at most once and sometimes returning to an earlier good algorithm. Behavior of users starting with the baseline was somewhat more diffuse than users starting with one of the personalized algorithms; the most users switched from the baseline to one of the personalized recommenders (29.6%, evenly split between the two of them), with an additional 7.9% trying both and staying with SVD, and 6.5% trying both and selecting item-item.

Table 2: Common Transition Sequences

Sequence	Count	%	Cum %
II → SVD	52	21.1%	21.1%
II → SVD → II	23	9.3%	30.4%
SVD → II	30	15.2%	15.2%
SVD → II → SVD	21	10.0%	25.2%
BL → II	45	14.8%	14.8%
BL → SVD	45	14.8%	29.6%
BL → II → SVD	24	7.9%	37.5%
BL → II → SVD → II	12	3.9%	41.4%
BL → SVD → II	8	2.6%	44.0%

4.3.2 Transition Time and Other Events

26.2% of users who switched recommenders only did so within their first hour of using the new system. The median user performed their first transition in the first 10 minutes or 16 logged actions[5] (viewing a page, changing recommenders, or taking an action on a movie or a tag), and their last transition within the first 18 hours.

We also broke user actions down into *sessions*, considering a session to end when the user is inactive for at least 60 minutes [11]. As implied by the timing data in the previous paragraph, the median user first switched recommenders in the first session. 44.1% of users only switched recommenders during their first session; these users had a median of 2 and mean of 9 further sessions after the one in which they changed recommenders. 63% of users only switched recommenders in a single session, even if it was not their first, and 80.7% of users only switched recommenders in 2 different sessions.

Users also interacted with the recommender changer without very many intervening events. They would change recommenders, see the results, and if they switched recommenders again, they usually did so quickly. The median user viewed one page between recommender changes within a single session.

4.3.3 Summary

To answer RQs 3 and 4, users tended to experiment with the recommender switching control early in their use. Most users flipped the switch a small number of times, usually in one or two distinct sessions and without much other intervening activity, and then left the recommender setting alone.

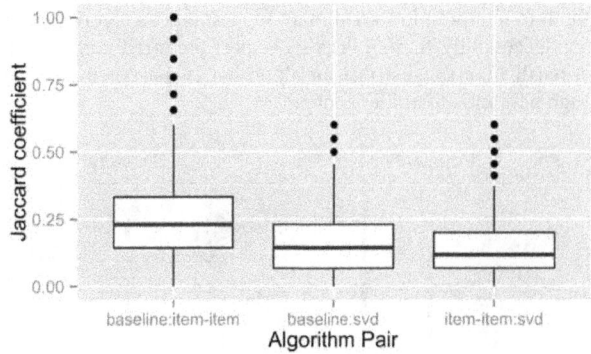

Figure 5: Overlap in Recommendations

4.4 RQ5: Recommendation Properties

Our offline simulation of the recommenders the users interacted with allow us to examine how different the output of the different recommender algorithms are in terms of various objectively measurable characteristics. In addition to providing insight for interpreting user behavior, these results also provide some measurement of the recommendations that are seen by actual active users in the system, rather than the mix of inactive and active users seen in typical offline evaluations over entire data sets. This does not take into account changes resulting from users adding ratings to the system after joining the experiment, but captures the behavior of the recommender immediately before they entered the study.

374 of the users participating in our study did not have sufficient data for the offline analysis (they had 5 or fewer ratings prior to joining the experiment), so they are excluded from the analysis in this section.

First, the algorithms did produce different lists of items. The three recommenders (baseline, item-item, and SVD) produced an average of 53.8 unique items per user (out of a maximum of 72 for three 24-item lists). Figure 5 shows the Jaccard similarity of each pair of recommendation lists for each user. Baseline and item-item were the most similar, with SVD producing results that were more divergent from them.

The algorithms also had differing prediction and recommendation accuracy (measured against the user's 5 most recent ratings prior to entering the experiment), shown in the left side of Figure 6. The patterns in objective accuracy track with those in user preference, with SVD being the most accurate, followed by item-item and finally baseline.

The second shows Boolean recall, the fraction of users for which each algorithm produced at least one of the user's test ratings in the first 24 recommendation results. This metric tracks differently from user's choice of algorithms: even though item-item found the user's rated item for more items, more users preferred the

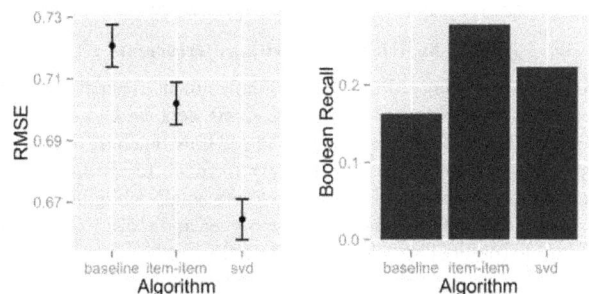

Figure 6: Algorithm Accuracy

SVD recommender. We recognize that the effects of recall can be difficult to interpret; low recall may suggest that an algorithm that is not successfully finding the user's most preferred items, while high-recall may suggest that an algorithm is not recommending enough new and unfamiliar content.

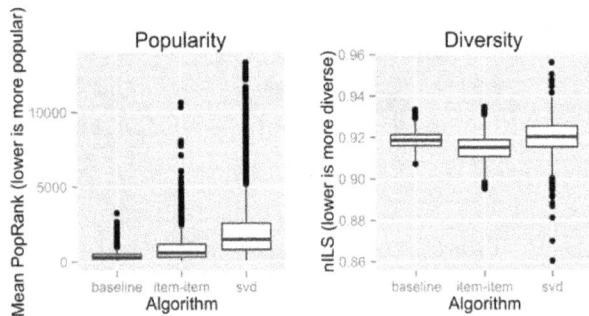

Figure 7: Popularity and Diversity of Recommendation Lists

Figure 7 shows the popularity and diversity of recommendations achieved by each recommender. SVD produced the most novel (least popular) recommendations. Item-item produced the most diverse recommendations, with SVD having the greatest variance in diversity, although the differences in diversity are small.

The charts so far have all considered the performance of the algorithms without accounting for their relative performance within the user experience. For any particular user, it is unlikely to matter whether one algorithm tends produce more diverse recommendation lists than another; rather, when comparing algorithms, they will notice if one algorithm produces more or less diverse results than another *for them*. To address this question, Figure 8 shows the relative performance of the two personalized algorithms, normalized to the performance of the baseline algorithm on each user. For example, an RMSE of 0.03 for a user means that the algorithm in question had an RMSE that was 0.03 better than that of the baseline algorithm for that particular user. We averaged the relative performance across all users, and show the results with standard error bars. Recall in this chart is the ordinary recall, the fraction of relevant items retrieved, rather than Boolean recall.

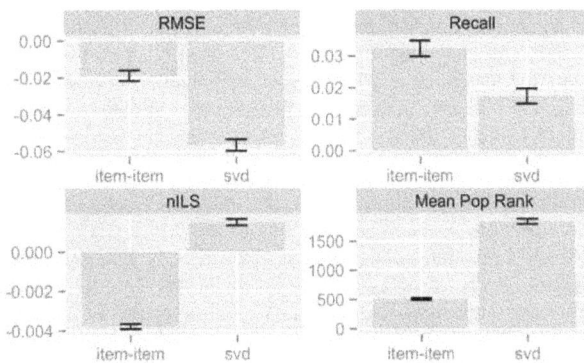

Figure 8: Relative Algorithm Performance

We note significant differences in algorithm performance on all metrics. These differences are trend-consistent with the overall differences previously, but allow us to see how much difference in e.g. diversity each algorithm is likely to make for an individual user. The differences in diversity are quite small, while the differences in popularity and accuracy are bigger and more likely to be noticeable (particularly the popularity difference).

Our offline metrics do not predict which algorithm users will prefer, or if they will switch algorithms in the first place, beyond the predictive power of the algorithm's identity. That is, the popularity of a recommender's results is no more powerful of a predictor of user switching and selection behavior than 'is the algorithm SVD?'. The most-preferred recommender – SVD – produces less popular (and therefore more likely to be novel) results than the other recommenders, but do not have direct evidence that this difference in novelty is the reason that users prefer SVD. The fact that the relative popularity of recommendations from the three algorithms is rank-consistent with users' tendency to choose those algorithms, whereas their relative diversity is not, suggests that popularity or novelty may play a larger role in user preference than diversity, at least as we have measured it here, but is not conclusive evidence.

4.5 RQ6: Predicting User Behavior

We built logistic regressions to attempt to predict switching behavior. The most significant predictor of whether a user would try a different algorithm was the algorithm they started with. The significant differences in metrics between algorithms induced multicolinearities that made a single regression incorporating both identity and metrics infeasible.

To work around this problem, we built separate logistic regression models for users starting with each algorithm. With these models, we found that for users starting with the baseline algorithm, increased diversity in the list of recommendations increased the likelihood that they would try another algorithm (   ), and users starting with item-item were more likely to try another if the list of recommendations was more novel (   ).

We have similarly been unable to predict the user's final choice of recommender beyond the fact that it is a particular recommender. Comparing the popularity of the items recommended by user's initial and final recommenders, we saw that users tended to choose final recommenders with less popular items, but that seems to be linked to the fact that they tended to prefer SVD.

We also examined several properties of users to look for predictors of either behavior or of final preferred algorithm, but did not find any significant predictors. We considered the user's account age, the number of ratings they had provided, and the diversity of the movies they had rated, but none were effective for predicting the user's activity.

4.6 RQ7: Initial Algorithm and Retention

As noted in section 4.2.1, the user's initial recommender influenced whether or not a they changed algorithms, but did not directly affect their final choice of algorithm.

In section 4.1, we noted that users who make use of the recommender switching control were more likely to come back to the site. We also examined whether, for users who did not switch recommenders, the initial recommender condition affected retention, but found no effect. The initial recommender the user encountered in the new site did not, for our experiment, affect the user's likelihood to continue using the service.

To summarize our answer to RQ7, the primary effect of initial algorithm that we could observe was that it influenced whether the user would use the recommender selection control.

5. DISCUSSION

Users used the recommender-switching feature, and often changed to a different recommender than their initially-assigned one, even if they were already using a personalized recommender. While we have not seen any conclusive effect on user retention in our system, and do not have significant qualitative feedback on from users on the recommender-switching feature, it seems to have enough use to warrant continued inclusion and development. Other systems may also want to consider allowing the user to have more control over the way in which their recommendations are computed.

Users in the user forums did express interest in knowing what algorithms were used, or understanding the difference between the *Wizard* and *Warrior* recommenders; this information was withheld for experimental purposes, but we will be considering how best to present more information about the meaning of the user's choice.

Users who made use of the recommender selection control usually experimented with it a little bit early in their use of the system, and then left it set for the duration of their usage. They also came back for multiple sessions after leaving it set, suggesting some degree of satisfaction with their choice.

It is instructive to compare our results with those in our previous user study [7]. In that study, users did not have a measurable preference between item-item and SVD, in the context of reviewing a single 10-item recommendation list. Our results here suggest that more users do prefer SVD when they have the opportunity to interact with the algorithms in a longer-term context. However, many users still preferred the item-item recommender; there was no clear (near-unanimous) winner. Further, while we have noted a strong correlation between novelty and the user's preference (stronger than diversity), as was found in the aforementioned user study, the directionality of this correlation is reversed: users were more likely to stick with the algorithm that was also more novel (recommended less popular items). This provides additional evidence that negative impact of novelty is primarily concentrated in users' initial reactions, and that after they gain experience it may even be a positive influence in the user's satisfaction.

We tried several different ways to predict whether the user would switch from properties of the recommendations produced by their initial algorithm, and properties of the user (user account age, rating count, diversity of their rated items), but found very few significant predictors. If there are identifiable characteristics of users that predict the usefulness of different algorithms for providing their recommendations, we have yet to find them (or at least to demonstrate conclusively that identifiable differences are, indeed, the reason for particular user preferences).

6. CONCLUSIONS AND FUTURE WORK

We have reported on an experiment in which we gave users the ability to select the algorithm that would be providing their recommendations in a movie recommender application. We found that users made use of the control, typically experimenting with the different options to find a satisfactory recommender early on and keeping their choice for the remainder of their use of the system. We also found that SVD is the most preferred algorithm, followed somewhat closely by item-item, and finally the baseline and group-based recommenders. This shows that users do have a preference for personal recommendations, and while the preference between item-item and SVD was close, SVD was preferred by more users. We also observe a correlation between users taking advantage of the feature and long-term user retention. Giving users choice may promote their long-term use of the system.

This is an initial investigation of the dynamics of giving users control of the means by which their recommendations are computed. Previous systems have given users some control of their recommendations, such as Amazon's feature whereby users can

indicate that they want certain items excluded from the data Amazon uses to provide recommendations. However, we are not aware of other services that allow end users to switch the entire recommender algorithm, or published research on how users interact with such a feature, aside from the implied ability to re-shop recommendation techniques in decentralized architectures such as the original GroupLens architecture [23].

There are a number of things needed to build on this work and carry it forward. First, it should be examined in other domains: do users benefit from the ability to select recommenders in other types of applications, such as book recommenders or tools for finding health information?

Second, we would like to consider more effective tools for allowing users to preview the recommendations. In our application, users could switch recommenders, but could not view recommendations side-by-side or 'try out' a recommender other than by selecting it and switching back. Users may use the feature in different ways if they can directly compare the output of different recommenders.

Thirdly, our switching mechanism was very course, allowing the user to swap out one recommender for another. But choice of recommender algorithm does not need to be an either-or decision, and there are many more nuanced decisions that could be made. There could be great potential in an interface that allows users to adjust the blend between different algorithms, and tweak the behavior of algorithms in other ways (e.g. adjusting the minimum neighbor count for a k-NN collaborative filtering, making it more or less conservative in its recommendations). Ziegler et al. [30] suggested a knob to allow users to adjust the amount of diversity they wanted added to their recommendations; we envision a panel of options that allow users to fine-tune their recommendations, ideally viewing the impact of these changes in real time. In order to make this feasible, we will not only need to develop useful interfaces, but identify the user-visible impact of different recommender tweaks so that the controls can be labeled in a manner that is understandable to end users, rather than 'Number of Latent Features'.

Providing users with control over the recommendation has the potential to significantly improve the user experience, and the sense of investment that users feel in the system, leading to better user retention and engagement. The control, and sense of transparency that comes with it, may also make users more comfortable with the system. A current popular complaint about recommender systems is that they are opaque algorithms with limited transparency and accountability for their outputs. User push-back against such algorithms changing and affecting their experience has been particularly pronounced in reactions to the Facebook emotional contagion study [16], or in concerns about the potential isolating effects of personalized information filtering [21]. Even if such concerns are not well-founded or even contrary to available evidence [20], users still need to feel that they can trust the system, and that trust may be damaged. Providing opportunities for the user to inspect and/or control the means by which their recommendations are computed may be valuable tool for the system to build and maintain their trust.

This paper represents our initial investigation into what happens when we give users the ability to control their recommendations. We look forward to further results, from our own work and that of others, on how to provide compelling, customizable recommendation experiences.

7. ACKNOWLEDGMENTS

This work was supported by the National Science Foundation under grants IIS 0808692 and IIS 1017697.

8. REFERENCES

[1] Balabanović, M. and Shoham, Y. 1997. Fab: content-based, collaborative recommendation. *Commun. ACM.* 40, 3 (1997), 66–72.

[2] Burke, R. 2002. Hybrid Recommender Systems: Survey and Experiments. *User Modeling and User-Adapted Interaction.* 12, 4 (Nov. 2002), 331–370.

[3] Chang, S., Harper, F.M. and Terveen, L. 2015. Using Groups of Items for Preference Elicitation in Recommender Systems. In *Proc. ACM CSCW '15* (2015), 1258–1269.

[4] Cook, R. and Kay, J. 1994. The justified user model: a viewable, explained user model. *Proceedings of the Fourth International Conference on User Modelling* (1994).

[5] Cremonesi, P., Garzottto, F. and Turrin, R. 2012. User Effort vs. Accuracy in Rating-based Elicitation. In *Proc. RecSys 2012* (2012), 27–34.

[6] Dooms, S. 2014. *Dynamic Generation of Personalized Hybrid Recommender Systems.* Ph.D thesis, Universiteit Gent.

[7] Ekstrand, M.D., Harper, F.M., Willemsen, M.C. and Konstan, J.A. 2014. User Perception of Differences in Recommender Algorithms. In *Proc. RecSys '14* (2014).

[8] Ekstrand, M., Ludwig, M., Konstan, J.A. and Riedl, J. 2011. Rethinking the Recommender Research Ecosystem: Reproducibility, Openness, and LensKit. In *Proc. RecSys '11* (2011), 133–140.

[9] Ekstrand, M. and Riedl, J. 2012. When recommenders fail: predicting recommender failure for algorithm selection and combination. In *Proc. RecSys '12* (2012), 233–236.

[10] Goldberg, D., Nichols, D., Oki, B.M. and Terry, D. 1992. Using collaborative filtering to weave an information tapestry. *Commun. ACM.* 35, 12 (1992), 61–70.

[11] Halfaker, A., Keyes, O., Kluver, D., Thebault-Spieker, J., Nguyen, T., Shores, K., Uduwage, A. and Warncke-Wang, M. 2014. User Session Identification Based on Strong Regularities in Inter-activity Time. *arXiv:1411.2878 [cs].* (Nov. 2014).

[12] Kay, J. 2006. Scrutable Adaptation: Because We Can and Must. *Adaptive Hypermedia and Adaptive Web-Based Systems.* V.P. Wade, H. Ashman, and B. Smyth, eds. Springer Berlin Heidelberg. 11–19.

[13] Kelly, D. and Belkin, N.J. 2001. Reading Time, Scrolling and Interaction: Exploring Implicit Sources of User Preferences for Relevance Feedback. In *Proc. SIGIR '01* (2001), 408–409.

[14] Knijnenburg, B., Willemsen, M., Gantner, Z., Soncu, H. and Newell, C. 2012. Explaining the user experience of recommender systems. *User Modeling and User-Adapted Interaction.* 22, 4-5 (Oct. 2012), 441–504.

[15] Kohavi, R., Longbotham, R., Sommerfield, D. and Henne, R.M. 2008. Controlled experiments on the web: survey and practical guide. *Data Mining and Knowledge Discovery.* 18, 1 (Jul. 2008), 140–181.

[16] Kramer, A.D.I., Guillory, J.E. and Hancock, J.T. 2014. Experimental evidence of massive-scale emotional contagion through social networks. *Proceedings of the National Academy of Sciences.* 111, 24 (Jun. 2014), 8788–8790.

[17] Levi, A., Mokryn, O., Diot, C. and Taft, N. 2012. Finding a Needle in a Haystack of Reviews: Cold Start Context-based Hotel Recommender System. In *Proc. RecSys '12* (2012), 115–122.

[18] McNee, S., Kapoor, N. and Konstan, J.A. 2006. Don't Look Stupid: Avoiding Pitfalls When Recommending Research Papers. In *Proc. CSCW '06* (2006), 171.

[19] Netflix Update: Try This at Home: 2006. *http://sifter.org/~simon/journal/20061211.html.* Accessed: 2010-04-08.

[20] Nguyen, T.T., Hui, P.-M., Harper, F.M., Terveen, L. and Konstan, J.A. 2014. Exploring the Filter Bubble: The Effect of Using Recommender Systems on Content Diversity. In *Proc. WWW '14* (2014), 677–686.

[21] Pariser, E. 2011. *The Filter Bubble: How the New Personalized Web Is Changing What We Read and How We Think.* Penguin.

[22] Paterek, A. 2007. Improving regularized singular value decomposition for collaborative filtering. In *Proc. KDD Cup and Workshop 2007* (Aug. 2007).

[23] Resnick, P., Iacovou, N., Suchak, M., Bergstrom, P. and Riedl, J. 1994. GroupLens: an open architecture for collaborative filtering of netnews. In *Proc. ACM CSCW '94* (1994), 175–186.

[24] Rich, E. 1979. User modeling via stereotypes. *Cognitive Science.* 3, 4 (Oct. 1979), 329–354.

[25] Said, A., Fields, B., Jain, B.J. and Albayrak, S. 2013. User-centric Evaluation of a K-furthest Neighbor Collaborative Filtering Recommender Algorithm. In *Proc. ACM CSCW '13* (2013), 1399–1408.

[26] Sarwar, B., Karypis, G., Konstan, J. and Reidl, J. 2001. Item-based collaborative filtering recommendation algorithms. In *Proc. WWW '01* (2001), 285–295.

[27] Sill, J., Takacs, G., Mackey, L. and Lin, D. 2009. Feature-Weighted Linear Stacking. *arXiv:0911.0460.* (Nov. 2009).

[28] Tintarev, N. 2007. Explanations of recommendations. In *Proc. RecSys '07* (2007), 203–206.

[29] Vig, J., Sen, S. and Riedl, J. 2012. The Tag Genome: Encoding Community Knowledge to Support Novel Interaction. *ACM Trans. Interact. Intell. Syst.* 2, 3 (Sep. 2012), 13:1–13:44.

[30] Ziegler, C.-N., McNee, S., Konstan, J.A. and Lausen, G. 2005. Improving Recommendation Lists through Topic Diversification. In *Proc. WWW '05* (2005), 22–32.

"I like to explore sometimes": Adapting to Dynamic User Novelty Preferences

Komal Kapoor[1*]   Vikas Kumar[1*]   Loren Terveen[1]   Joseph A. Konstan[1]   Paul Schrater[2]

[1] Dept. of Computer Science
University of Minnesota
Minneapolis, MN 55455, USA
{kapoor,vikas,terveen,konstan}@cs.umn.edu

[2] Dept. of Psychology & Computer Science
University of Minnesota
Minneapolis, MN-55455, USA
schrater@umn.edu

ABSTRACT

Studies have shown that the recommendation of unseen, novel or serendipitous items is crucial for a satisfying and engaging user experience. As a result, recent developments in recommendation research have increasingly focused towards introducing novelty in user recommendation lists. While, existing solutions aim to find the right balance between the similarity and novelty of the recommended items, they largely ignore the user needs for novelty. In this paper, we show that there are large individual and temporal differences in the users' novelty preferences. We develop a regression model to predict these dynamic novelty preferences of users using features derived from their past interactions. Finally, we describe an adaptive recommender, *adaNov-R*, that adapts to the user needs for novel items and show that the model achieves better recommendation performance on a metric that considers both novel and familiar items.

Categories and Subject Descriptors:
H.1.2 [User/Machine System]:Human Information processing; H.3.3 [Information Search and Retrieval]:Information filtering

General Terms: Recommendation Systems

Keywords: recommendation systems; dynamic user preferences; novelty; diversity

1. INTRODUCTION

The internet supports a giant ecosystem of independent content providers (such as Amazon, Netflix, Last.fm, YouTube etc.) and consumers (web users). Faced with the needle in the haystack problem, online users rely on recommender systems to find more relevant content. Thus, the personalized recommender systems play a crucial role in making web services more usable and engaging for their

---

*Both authors have contributed equally.

RecSys'15, September 16–20, 2015, Vienna, Austria.
ACM 978-1-4503-3692-5/15/09.
DOI: http://dx.doi.org/10.1145/2792838.2800172.

users, directly impacting the success and revenue of such businesses [15].

The common recommendation models are based on either finding items similar to those preferred by the users in the past (content-based) or those consumed by the users most similar to them (collaborative filtering), or a hybrid of these techniques [13, 15]. However, these methods have accrued criticism over time due to their disproportionate emphasis on similarity alone, producing recommendations that are often obvious and redundant. For instance, recommending other songs from the same artist the user liked in the past can be quite accurate but often less useful than identifying unknown artists for the user to try. Over time, the self-reinforcing emphasis on similarity is seen to produce the undesirable filter bubble effect [14] associated with decreased content diversity at the user level. Instead, studies reveal that quality and usefulness of recommendations depend to a large extent on how novel, unique and serendipitous they are and how often they include items that the users would not have arrived at on their own [6].

However, a major bottleneck for efforts to introduce novelty in user recommendation lists is that they inadvertently reduce the accuracy of the system. Methods which have found success, jointly optimize both the recommendation novelty and similarity (ex: [7]) to find an appropriate combination of these factors to better fulfill the needs of the user. The goal of a typical novelty recommender system can be generalized as:

$$R_u = \frac{S_u + \lambda * N_u}{1 + \lambda}; \qquad (1)$$

where, S_u, N_u represents the similarity and novelty criteria for the recommendation list R for user u. Furthermore, λ denotes the trade-off between similarity and novelty, identified by the system to be appropriate for its users. A further appeal of such a formulation is that once defined as such, one can leverage a plethora of optimization tools to determine a domain based λ.

Recommender systems research has not, so far, considered the problem of attempting to estimate different user specific and time-dependent λ's based on users' past behaviors. Assuming a fixed λ predicts that users have the same and constant appetite for novel items. However, we believe that it is far more likely for user behavior to vary, seeking familiar (or known) options at some times and being open to explore newer options at others. For instance, users who just started listening to a new artist 'A', are likely to appreciate other recommendations of songs from the artist 'A'. The same users may however, be more open to trying newer bands, once they have listened to band 'A' several times, favoring more novel recommendations at that point. We define the extent to which the exploratory mode is prominent in users' behaviors at any moment, as their novelty preference ($nvPref_t^u$).

In this work, we postulate that a recommender's emphasis on novelty should depend on each user's dynamic novelty preferences. Thus, we propose user and time dependent λ_t^u's which are a function of users' dynamic novelty preferences at time t i.e. $\lambda_t^u = f(nvPref_t^u)$. To realize such an adaptive novelty recommender, we first develop a regression model to predict users' time-variant novelty preferences. We use features derived from the users' past interactions with the system, based on two specific insights from behavioral psychology on this subject — (a) individual attitudinal differences in user novelty seeking tendencies [19], and (b) that user novelty seeking desires are associated with disengagement and boredom with their current environment [9]. We consider features based on both these factors and show that we can achieve good predictive performance using our model.

We further propose an elegant framework to combine the novelty predictor with existing recommendation techniques to develop an *adaptive* novelty recommender (*adaNov-R*) for the users. Our system design allows us to optimize our recommendation performance towards novel recommendations for users with high novelty preferences, and focus on familiar items for users with low novelty preferences. This further allows us to test the impact of dynamic novelty preference prediction on actual recommendation performance. By leveraging off-the-shelf collaborative filtering techniques, we make our system easily assessable to existing systems.

2. CONCEPTUAL BACKGROUND

In this section we provide a brief overview of related research from the field of behavioral psychology and recommender systems, relevant to our work.

2.1 Psychological Bases for Novelty Seeking

Several common day experiences, reveal a prominent desire in individuals for novel, varied and complex stimuli [4] even at physical, social and monetary costs to oneself. Studies have shown that users have individualized preferences for novelty and variety that vary over time [21, 20]. For example, users' variety seeking behaviors differ based on the product category level [21] and display format [20], and user current satiation level with the product attributes [9]. However, most of these studies were conducted from controlled experiments and user surveys. User online multimedia consumptions can provide a new lens for studying user novelty and variety seeking behaviors using unobtrusive empirical analysis and modeling methods.

To the best of our knowledge, the only study of this kind has been the recent work by Zhang et al. [25] which measures novelty seeking levels for users from their check-ins and online shopping traces. A major distinction of our work from theirs is that they assume a static multinomial distribution for user novelty levels whose mean reflects the novelty seeking trait of the user, while we focus on predicting the dynamics in user novelty preferences. From our experiments we show that in addition to the general propensity towards

novelty, the current level of boredom is equally important to predict novelty preference of the user.

2.2 Novelty in Recommendation Systems

Recommendation novelty and diversity has been conceptualized, measured and evaluated by researchers in different ways [22]. Diversity based metrics focus on how dissimilar the recommended items are from each other [2, 14, 26]. Novelty, on the other hand focuses on the novelty of the items for the users [8]. In this work, we focus on the novelty metric but we expect the learnings from here to carry over to recommendation diversity as well.

Novelty of an item can be relative to user's perspective or system's perspective. An item can be novel to a user in three ways — (a) *new to system* : item is novel for the system and thus for every user in the system (b) *new to user*: item is known to system but unknown to the user (c) *oblivious/forgotten item*: item was known to the user in the past but has become somewhat unfamiliar due to the length of time elapsed since its last consumption. Repetition of forgotten items in future consumptions has been shown to produce increased diversity and emotional excitement [17, 3]. In this work, we only consider the type (b) and (c) as novel items for evaluation and do not discuss items of type (a), often referred as coldstart problem [10]. We consider a strict boolean definition of novelty where item is either considered novel by the above definitions or not, for the sake of simplicity. However, our work can be extended to incorporate more relaxed definitions e.g. based on how dissimilar an item is from those seen by the user in the past [22].

Plenty of approaches have been developed to improve the novelty and diversity of recommendation lists such as topic diversification [29], use of item taxonomy [23], bubble declustering [27] etc. Others have looked at both the accuracy and the diversity of recommendations and suggested approaches for dealing with the apparent trade-off between the two, such as multi-criterion optimization [26], item re-ranking and re-weighting [7] and heat spreading algorithms [28]. However, none of these approaches measure their performance in terms of their ability to provide the right amount of novelty as actually *desired* by the user. Different novelty requirements of users make the existing *one-size-fits-all* approaches insufficient. Instead, in this work, we develop recommendation system that can adapt the novelty provided by the system to the user's need for novelty.

3. TERMINOLOGIES

We now formalize the terms used in this paper.

Item (i): An item corresponds to the unit of resource in the system. This definition includes both individual commodities like songs, books, movies etc. or their categories such as artist, genre and style. As a result, one can consider recommendation of novel songs, artists or genres using the same methodologies as discussed in this work.

Session (S) A session is defined as a continuous period of user activity during which, a user consumes one or more items within a small time gap (identified using a minimum duration threshold). The history of a user u is represented as a sequential list of sessions — $H^u = \{S_{t_1}^u, S_{t_2}^u, \dots\}$, where $S_{t_x}^u$ denotes the x-th session of the user starting at time t_x.

Familiar Set ($famSet$) **and Novel Set** ($nvSet$) For a user u, the familiar set $famSet_t^u$ at some time t constitutes the set of unique items consumed in sessions falling in the last time window $[t - T, t)$. To eliminate noise, items which are consumed less than a threshold number of times in the last time window are eliminated from the familiar set. Similarly, a user's novel set at time t, $nvSet_t^u$ constitutes the set of items that do *not* belong to the user's familiar set at time t i.e. $nvSet_t^u = I - famSet_t^u$, where I is the set of all the items in the system (see Figure 2a).

Novelty Preference ($nvPref$) To define a user's novelty preference for a session starting at time t we use the fraction of novel items (items from set $nvSet_t^u$) consumed over the total number of items consumed by the user in that session.

$$nvPref_t^u = \frac{|S_t^u \cap nvSet_t^u| + c}{|S_t^u| + 2 * c} \quad (2)$$

The parameter c is a Laplacian correction for small sessions.

4. DATASET

For our analysis we use music consumption logs from two popular online music streaming websites. The first is a publicly available dataset from the online music service Last.fm[1]. The other is a more recent (proprietary) dataset from an online music service. Both music services let users either chose specific songs or listen to a radio. We do not have any explicit ratings, or feedback signals (e.g. clicks and likes) other than the act of listening, present in these datasets.

We perform our experiments at both the song and the artist level with similar findings. We only report artist level results due to space constraints. The plots and results for song level results can be found online[2]. To remove inactive users from our analysis, we only consider users with more than 20 distinct items listened. The threshold for the gap between sessions is set to 6 hours based on a visual examination of the gap distribution. The time window (T), determines how quickly we update our models to incorporate recent changes in the user interest. We use small time window lengths as music listeners change their music preferences frequently. We use one months and three weeks for the Last.fm dataset and the proprietary dataset respectively. For each user, their first time window (session) is used as the burn-in period, the second is used for training and the third is used for testing. For both datasets we include only those items in a user's *famSet* that were repeated more than 2 times during the time window T. Finally, a Laplace correction $c = 3$ is used throughout. We summarize the partitions and basic statistics on the datasets in the Table 1.

5. USER NOVELTY PREFERENCES

Surprisingly little has been said in existing recommendation literature, about the actual nature of user consumption of novel items while interacting with system. Via our empirical analysis we aim to understand the temporal novelty preferences of the users and thus verify the following two hypotheses:

H1: Users have different novelty preferences

H2: Users have dynamic novelty preferences

We therefore look at the variance (measured using standard deviation) in the novelty preference scores across users

[1]www.last.fm
[2]http://www.cs.umn.edu/~vikas/

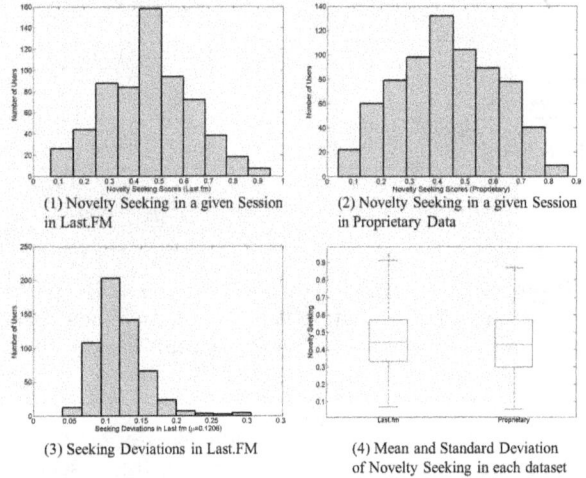

Figure 1: novelty deviations across and within users for the datasets

and within users, respectively. Figures 1 (1,2) shows the distribution of the session novelty preferences of the users in the first session of the training period. As apparent from the plots, users prefer a substantial amount of novelty in a session. Users consume on an average around 43% and 46% new artists per session in the Last.fm and the proprietary data respectively ($\mu(nvPref_t^u)_{Last.fm} = 0.4599$, $\mu(nvPref_t^u)_{Proprietary} = 0.434$). Furthermore, the across users standard deviations for the Last.fm and the proprietary datasets is found to be 0.1718 and 0.176, respectively. Both measures are significantly higher than 0 (p-value ~ 0, obtained using one-sided chi-squared test for variance). This suggests that users have significantly different novelty preferences - **Empirical evidence supports H1**.

We then study within users differences in novelty preferences. For our analysis, we consider the session novelty preference scores of each user as a separate random variable and estimate its standard deviation across sessions in the training period. To obtain a reliable estimate, we only consider users with more than 10 sessions during the training period (Last.fm dataset). Figure 1(3) shows the distribution of the within users standard deviations in novelty preferences. The mean of the distribution (0.1206) is significantly greater than 0 (p-value ~ 0, obtained using one-sided t-test). This shows that users have significantly changing novelty preferences - **Empirical evidence supports H2**.

The individualized and time-varying user novelty preferences render existing novelty recommendation approaches as insufficient, making it critical for new strategies to adapt to the novelty needs of the users for better user satisfaction.

6. NOVELTY PREFERENCE PREDICTION

The ability to predict user novelty preferences is crucial for designing an adaptive novelty recommender system. Here, we propose a model that utilizes user's *recent* consumption behaviors for predicting user preference for novelty. We consider two features for this task.

Feature 1: *Diversity of their familiar set.* Users may have different predilections for novelty and diversity. This

	Last.fm				Proprietary Data			
	Burn	Train	Test	**Total**	Burn	Train	Test	**Total**
Duration	1st month	2nd month	3rd month	3 months	1st-3rd week	4th week	5th week	5 weeks
Number of Users	882	758	733	882	1,642	1,209	933	1,642
Avg. Session/User	21	20	20	56	7	3	3	11
Avg. Session Length (# items)	40	39	38	39	24	23	23	24

Table 1: Dataset statistics.

distinguishes users who repeat favorites on a loop from those who listen to top 10 radio. We identify such differences among users using a simple measure for the diversity of their recently consumed items as follows: $div_t^u = \frac{|famSet_t^u|}{\text{\# of consumptions of } famSet_t^u \text{ in } [t-T,t]}$

Feature 2: *Cumulative **negative** preference for items in the familiar set.* Users novelty needs are further associated with the lack of stimulation in their respective environments or boredom [9]. This is equivalent to the users desiring newer items once they have exhausted their collection of known items. In a recent work, Kapoor et. al. [12, 11] propose techniques for quantifying user changing preferences for known items given past repetitions and boredom. They use a semi-Markov model for modeling two states of engagement with an item - sensitization state (when users consume the item in short gaps) or the boredom state (when users take longer gaps to consume the item). Using their model, they compute item's *dynamic preference* score (or $dpref_t^{(i,u)}$) which is based on the user state for the item and time since the last consumption. We use the negative transform of this dynamic preference score to quantify a user's current boredom with the item. The overall boredom of the user with the familiar set at time t is obtained by summing over the negative dynamic preference scores for each item in the familiar set. $negCumPref_t^u = \sum_{i \in famSet_t^u} -dpref_t^{(i,u)}$

Model	Last.fm	Proprietary Dataset
Constant	0.1686	0.1809
Logistic Model(diversity feature)	0.1574	0.1620
Logistic Model (*diversity+boredom* feature)	0.1420	0.1549

Table 2: Novelty preference prediction performance evaluated using the RMSE metric at artist level.

	Last.fm	Proprietary Dataset
Feature	**Coefficient**	**Coefficient**
div_t^u	4.7886 **	3.0963 **
$negCumPref_t^u$	0.0124 **	0.0071 *

Table 3: Feature importance for the logistic regression model for novelty preference. Significance indicators- <0.00001 **, <0.0001 *

6.1 Regression & Evaluation

We apply a logistic regression model for predicting $nvPref_t^u$. The logistic regression model ensures that our estimate $\widehat{nvPref}_t^u$ falls within $[0,1]$.

$$\widehat{nvPref}_t^u = Logistic_\theta(D_t^u, negCumPref_t^u,) \qquad (3)$$

The novelty preference prediction model is evaluated using Root Mean Squared Error (or RMSE) between the predicted and actual novelty preference scores for user sessions in the test period. We evaluate our model against a constant baseline $\overline{nvPref}$ to show the benefits of individualized and dynamic novelty seeking prediction. The results are summarized in Table 2. The logistic models (*diversity* and *diversity + boredom* model) perform better than the constant model for both datasets. The improvement in performance are significant (p-value ~ 0 computed using the deviance test chi-squared statistic).

We further analyze our model parameters. Table 3 shows the regression coefficient and the significance level for each feature. Both the div_t^u and the $negCumPref_t^u$ features are found to be significant for the prediction task. A positive value of the coefficient for diversity indicates that novelty preference increases with diversity in the familiar set. The boredom related feature $negCumPref_t^u$ has a positive coefficient which further indicates that users display higher preferences for novelty when their preferences for the familiar set are low and vice-versa.

Finally, we measure how different our novelty preferences predictions are across the users. The standard deviation of the predicted user novelty preferences for the test data ($\sigma_{Last.fm} = 0.0874$, $\sigma_{Proprietary} = 0.1034$) were significantly higher than 0 (p-value ~ 0, obtained using one-sided chi-squared test for variance). This suggests that our model predicts significantly different novelty preferences for different users. This coupled with the improvement in accuracy suggests that our model can well estimate the individualized and time-variant novelty preference scores for the users.

7. ADAPTIVE RECOMMENDATION

We now propose an adaptive novelty recommender (*adaNov-R*) to allow existing recommendation techniques to include dynamic user preferences for novelty. Our framework (*adaNov-R*) has three main modules, namely - (1) Novelty Preference Prediction module, (2) Item Ranking Module, and (3) Adaptive Recommendation module. We summarized these modules in Figure 2b and explain them in details below.

Novelty Preference Prediction Module: The purpose of this module is to predict novelty preference scores for a user session. The logistic regression model, described in the previous section, is used for this purpose.

Item Ranking Module: This module produces a preference ranking list for novel and familiar items for each user based on their past interactions (ex: frequency of consumption or ratings for an item). Several specialized algorithms can be used for generating novel (N_t^u) [7, 27] and familiar recommendations (F_t^u) [12], respectively.

In our implementation of the module, we use off-the-shelf *item-based* collaborative filtering technique. The item-based

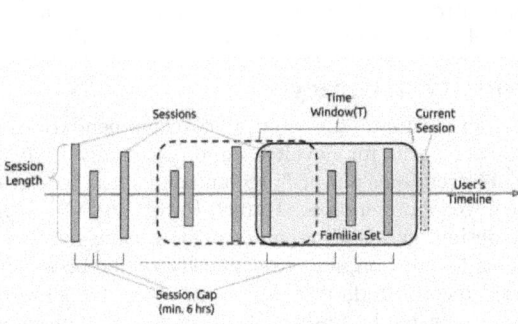

(a) A user timeline illustrating the different terminologies defined by us.

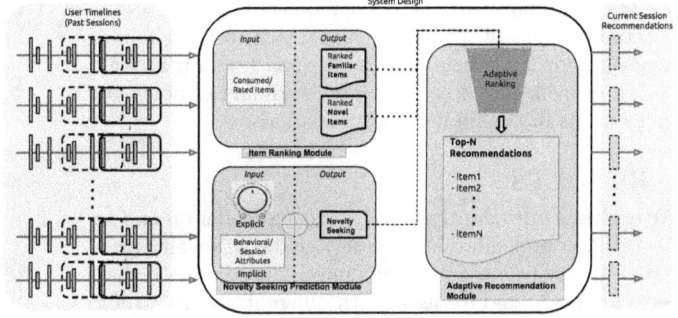

(b) Adaptive Novelty Preference Recommender System design.

Figure 2: Adaptive Novelty Recommendation

recommender computes preference scores for items based on their similarity to the items already rated by the user. This approach is easy to train and has been shown to achieve good performance in several real world systems [15]. Since, we do not have explicit ratings in our dataset, we modify the item-based recommendation algorithm to include the dynamic preference score $dpref_t^{(i,u)}$ (defined in last sub-section) instead of ratings for generating preference scores for items. The modified item scoring function is formulated as:

$$dpref_t^{(j,u)} = \frac{\sum_{i \in Neighbors(j)} sim(i,j) * dpref_t^{(i,u)}}{\sum_{i \in Neighbors(j)} sim(i,j)}; \quad (4)$$

where, j is an item for which the dynamic preference score is predicted, i is an item whose preference score is already known, $sim(i,j)$ is the similarity between i and j computed using cosine similarity and $Neighbors(j)$ are the nearest neighbors (top 50) of item j.

We use this scoring function to generate the ranking list and then extract the ranking lists N_t^u and F_t^u.

Adaptive Recommendation Module: The Adaptive Recommendation module integrates the other two modules to determine the final top-N recommendations for the user session optimized for the user novelty preference score. The module uses the following scheme to optimize the final preferred list for user:

$$R_t^u = \frac{(1 - nvPref_t^u) * F_t^u + nvPref_t^u * \alpha * N_t^u}{(1 - nvPref_t^u) + nvPref_t^u * \alpha}. \quad (5)$$

The dynamic weight used by us for novel items is determined by (a) novelty preference of the user ($nvPref_t^u$) (b) a proportionality constant α which allows us to incorporate domain specific emphasis for novelty. For example, recommenders systems for music may value novelty more than those for holiday destinations as users are more likely to experiment more with the former than latter. The dynamic weight for familiar items is proportional to the user's preference for familiarity $(1 - nvPref_t^u)$. After suitable transformation, $\frac{nvPref_t^u * \alpha}{(1-nvPref_t^u)+nvPref_t^u * \alpha}$ corresponds to the dynamic λ_t^u we motivated in the introduction section. Further, such an objective function has close resemblance to the value function used in weighted multi-class learning literature [16].

One can use various novelty and similarity (or familiarity) criteria based on their application. Refer to [5, 8] for a comprehensive survey of the various novelty and similarity metrics. Here, we use *f-measure*, a standard metric for evaluating how well a system can recommend preferred items to the users and is defined as the harmonic mean of the precision (p) and recall (r) scores. However, vanilla f-measure does not distinguish between recommendation of novel and familiar items. We instead, compute precision, recall and f-measure accuracy metrics, separately for novel and familiar items as follows:

$$p_t^u(Z) = \frac{|R_t^u \cap S_t^u \cap ZSet_t^u|}{|R_t^u|} \quad ; \quad p(Z) = Avg_{u,t} \ p_t^u(Z) \quad (6)$$

$$r_t^u(Z) = \frac{|R_t^u \cap S_t^u \cap ZSet_t^u|}{|S_t^u \cap ZSet_t^u|} \quad ; \quad r(Z) = Avg_{u,t} \ r_t^u(Z) \quad (7)$$

Where, Z can be $\{fam, nv\}$.

We define the overall performance metric as the weighted sum of the performance scores on novel and familiar items using our dynamic weights defined above, as follows:

$$wp_t^u = \frac{nvPref_t^u * \alpha * p_t^u(nov) + (1 - nvPref_t^u) * p_t^u(fam)}{(1 - nvPref_t^u) + nvPref_t^u * \alpha} \quad (8)$$

$$wr_t^u = \frac{nvPref_t^u * \alpha * r_t^u(nov) + (1 - nvPref_t^u) * r_t^u(fam)}{(1 - nvPref_t^u) + nvPref_t^u * \alpha} \quad (9)$$

$$wp = Avg_{u,t} \ wp_t^u \ ; \ wr = Avg_{u,t} \ wr_t^u \ ; \ wF1 = \frac{2 * wp * wr}{wp + wr} \quad (10)$$

We follow a greedy approach for learning the right proportion of novel and familiar items to include in the final recommendation. Our approach is based on optimizing our weighted performance metric using the training data. We first segregate users into ten different partitions based on their novelty preference scores such that $[[0 - 0.1] \rightarrow partition_1, \ldots, [0.9 - 1] \rightarrow partition_{10}]$. We then learn a rule-based novelty introduction function $partition_i \rightarrow x_i$ for partitions 1-10 where x_i is fraction of novel items in the recommendation list for the best weighted f-measure for partition i. For example, $partition_i \rightarrow 0.4$ suggests that inclusion of 4 novel items in the top 10 recommendation list provides the optimal weighted f-measure for $partition_i$. Having once trained our novelty introduction function, the Adaptive Recommendation module first uses the predicted novelty preference score to identify the partition in which the user falls in a future session and then uses the learned fraction for that partition to incorporate an appropriate amount of novel and familiar items in the final recommendations.

8. RESULTS

We evaluate our adaptive novelty recommender on two aspects (a) Recommendation Accuracy, and (b) Novelty accuracy i.e. ability to meet the user's novelty needs. Both these aspects are evaluated for users with different novelty preferences and different choices of $\alpha = \{1, 2, 5, 10, 20, 30, 40, 50\}$.

We compare our model against alternative strategies for novelty recommendation. We first consider the two extreme models *PureN* - which recommends only novel items and *PureF* - which recommends only familiar items. We then compare our model against a constant novelty recommender (*CN*) that recommends a constant number of novel items in topN to the users, optimized using the training data. Finally we compare ourselves against the standard *item-based* recommendation approach (Item Based CF) which only considers users' static item preferences.

8.1 Recommendation Accuracy

We first compare the models on the weighted $f-measure$ metric (Figure 3a). First, we see that for $\alpha = 1$, PureF, Item based CF, CN and adaNov-R have an equivalent performance, which decreases as user novelty preferences increase. This is because when α is set to one, we do not incentivize novel recommendations at all and the system naturally favors the recommendation of more accurate familiar items. However, as α increases ($>=2$), interesting differences emerge. We see that the performance of PureF and item based CF are quite identical and decrease as user novelty preferences increase. The performance of PureN on the other hand, increases as user novelty preferences increase. The performance of CN is similar to PureF for low values of α ($\alpha <= 20$) and to that of PureN for high values of α ($\alpha > 20$), as this model picks the winning side. However, adaNov-R, is seen to adapt it's performance based on user novelty preferences and is better than PureN for low novelty preferences and better than PureF for higher novelty preferences.

We further look at the f-measure metric for familiar and novel items separately. We also show the vanilla f-measure (which does not differentiate between novel and familiar items) for completeness (Figure 3b). Due to space constraints, we only show the results for $\alpha = 10$. We see that similarity based methods PureF and Item based CF, and the CN perform well in terms of f-measure (familiar) metric, while PureN works well in terms of F-measure (novel) metric. Only adaNov-R maintains good performance for both the metrics. Further, comparing against similarity based methods - PureF and Item-based CF, it performs much better on F-measure (novel) and is not too worse on f-measure (familiar). Also, as expected, the adaNov-R does not do very well as compared to PureF, Item based CF, CN on the vanilla F-measure metric. But this can be easily related to the fact that none of these baselines focus much on novel recommendation (seen from their dismal performance on the F-measure (novel) metric). Instead, adaNov-R provides performance guarantees in terms of weighted F-measure and

ensures decent performance on f-measure. Further, a system can control the decrease in the overall f-measure, by appropriately choosing the α that work best for them.

8.2 Novelty Accuracy

To further evaluate the ability of recommendations to adapt to user needs for novelty, we look specifically at the *number* of novel items out of N recommended to the user for different novelty preferences. PureN, PureF and CN, based on their design, can only recommend the same number of novel items for all ranges of user novelty preferences, while item-based recommends very few novel items (as shown in Figure 3c). Instead, adaNov-R recommends more novel items when a user has a higher novelty preference (for $\alpha >= 2$). Further, we find that the number of novel items recommended is dependent on the domain specific α i.e. for low α, the system still largely focuses on familiar items only. We therefore recommend using α greater than 2 for such datasets.

The ability of adaNov-R to modulate the number of novel and familiar items based on users' needs while guaranteeing performance in terms of weighted accuracy (weighted f-measure) make it a much better approach for novelty recommendation than the current non-adaptive systems. Further, we see that although there is an impact on the overall f-measure metric, the impact can be modulated by choosing the right α for the system.

9. DISCUSSIONS AND FUTURE WORK

To our knowledge, this is the first work of its kind to consider dynamics in user needs for novelty. We show that users had varied and dynamic preferences for novelty and therefore require specialized adaptive techniques for addressing their novelty needs. We develop a model for predicting the variable novelty preferences of the users with good predictive performance. We also propose an adaptive novelty recommendation *adaNov-R* framework that adapted to the novelty preferences of the users while maintaining a tight control over accuracy using weighted f-measure. We also show how our model successfully caters personalized recommendations to users with different novelty needs.

At the same time, there are certain limitations to this work that we can address in the future. Our current approach ignores users' external context and environmental factors such as time of day, mood, social company and whether they are engaging simultaneously in other activities such as working, running or driving etc. which can potentially impact their acceptance and need for novel recommendations. We believe that detailed user evaluation would clearly benefit our approach to further understand the role of external contextual factors for novelty recommendation. We would also like to explore novelty preferences of users for other multimedia content like movies, videos, news etc. going forward.

10. ACKNOWLEDGEMENT

This work was supported in part by the National Science Foundation under grants IIS 08-08692 and IIS 09-64695, the UMN SOBACO grant and the Doctoral Dissertation Fellowship.

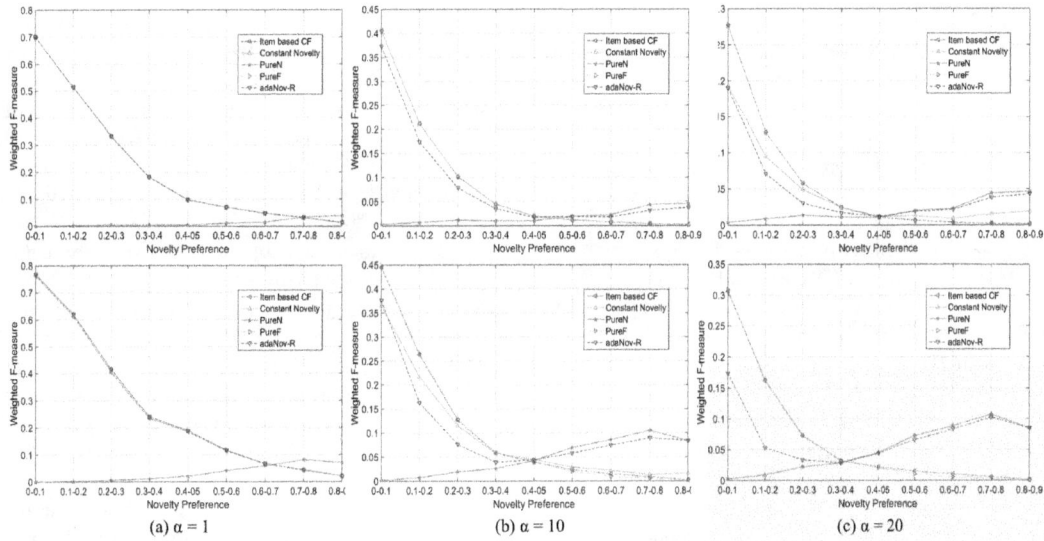

(a) Weighted f-measure for different novelty preference scores of the user and α. Last.fm(top); Proprietary data (bottom).

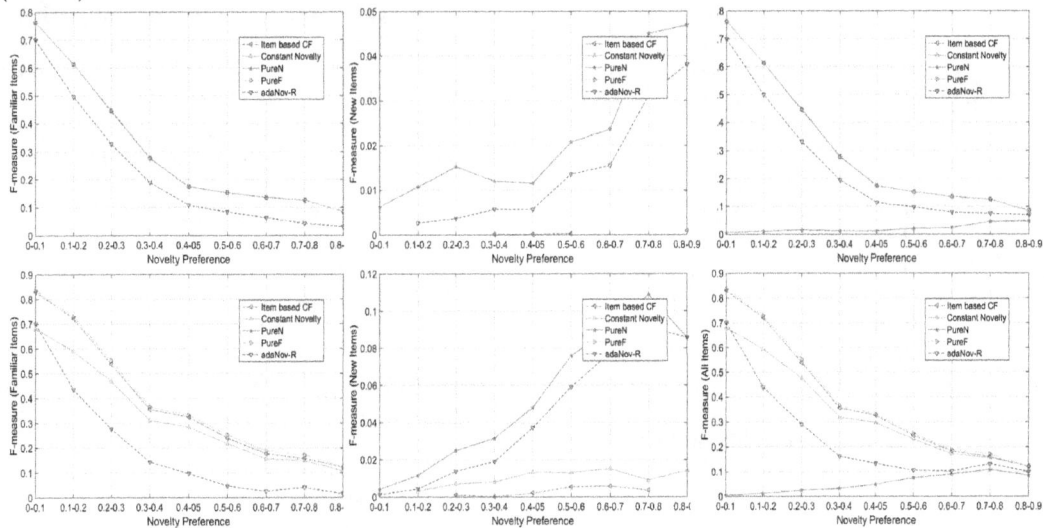

(b) F-measure (familiar), f-measure (novel) and overall f-measure for different novelty preference scores of the user and $\alpha = 10$. Last.fm(top); Proprietary data (bottom).

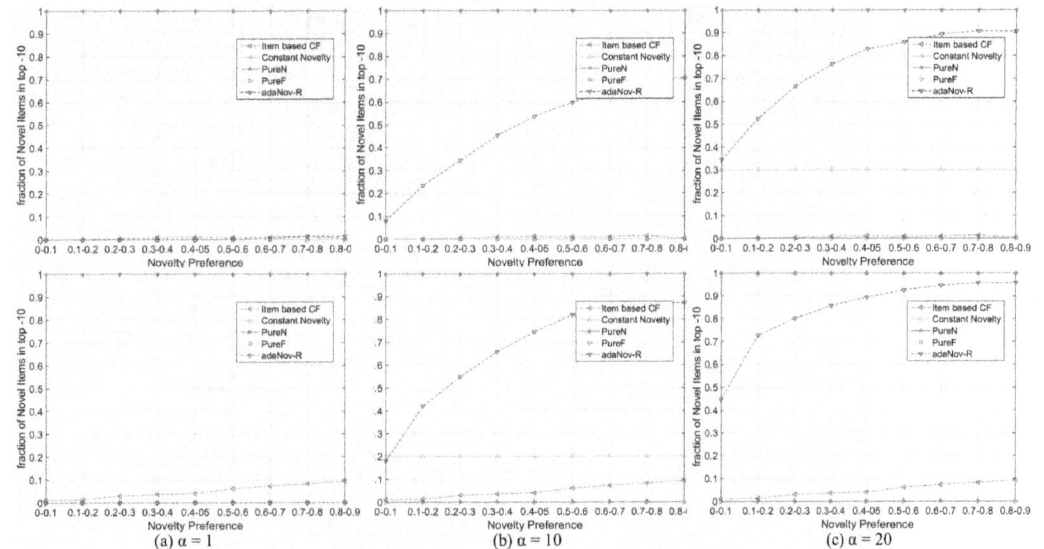

(c) Fraction of novel items introduced for different *novelty preference scores* and α. Last.fm(top); Proprietary data (bottom).

Figure 3: Recommendation and Novelty Accuracy Results

11. REFERENCES

[1] G. Adomavicius and Y. Kwon. Toward more diverse recommendations: Item re-ranking methods for recommender systems. In *Workshop on Information Technologies and Systems*, 2009.

[2] G. Adomavicius and Y. Kwon. Maximizing aggregate recommendation diversity: A graph-theoretic approach. In *Proc. of the 1st International Workshop on Novelty and Diversity in Recommender Systems (DiveRS 2011)*, pages 3–10. Citeseer, 2011.

[3] A. Anderson, R. Kumar, A. Tomkins, and S. Vassilvitskii. The dynamics of repeat consumption. In *Proceedings of the 23rd international conference on World wide web*, pages 419–430. International World Wide Web Conferences Steering Committee, 2014.

[4] D. E. Berlyne. Novelty, complexity, and hedonic value. *Perception & Psychophysics*, 8(5):279–286, 1970.

[5] P. Castells, S. Vargas, and J. Wang. Novelty and diversity metrics for recommender systems: choice, discovery and relevance. In *International Workshop on Diversity in Document Retrieval (DDR 2011) at the 33rd European Conference on Information Retrieval (ECIR 2011)*, pages 29–36. Citeseer, 2011.

[6] J. L. Herlocker, J. A. Konstan, L. G. Terveen, and J. T. Riedl. Evaluating collaborative filtering recommender systems. volume 22, pages 5–53, New York, NY, USA, Jan. 2004. ACM.

[7] Y. Hijikata, T. Shimizu, and S. Nishida. Discovery-oriented collaborative filtering for improving user satisfaction. In *Proceedings of the 14th international conference on Intelligent user interfaces*, pages 67–76. ACM, 2009.

[8] N. Hurley and M. Zhang. Novelty and diversity in top-n recommendationŰanalysis and evaluation. *ACM Transactions on Internet Technology (TOIT)*, 10(4):14, 2011.

[9] J. J. Inman. The role of sensory-specific satiety in attribute-level variety seeking. *Journal of Consumer Research*, 28(1):105–120, 2001.

[10] T. Jambor and J. Wang. Optimizing multiple objectives in collaborative filtering. In *Proceedings of the fourth ACM conference on Recommender systems*, pages 55–62. ACM, 2010.

[11] K. Kapoor, N. Srivastava, J. Srivastava, and P. Schrater. Measuring spontaneous devaluations in user preferences. In *Proceedings of the 19th ACM SIGKDD international conference on Knowledge discovery and data mining*, pages 1061–1069. ACM, 2013.

[12] K. Kapoor, K. Subbian, J. Srivastava, and P. Schrater. Timing matters! - modeling dynamics of boredom in activity streams. In *due In Proceedings of the eigth ACM conference on Web Search and Data Mining*. ACM, 2015.

[13] Y. Koren, R. Bell, and C. Volinsky. Matrix factorization techniques for recommender systems. *Computer*, 42(8):30–37, 2009.

[14] N. Lathia, S. Hailes, L. Capra, and X. Amatriain. Temporal diversity in recommender systems. In *Proceedings of the 33rd international ACM SIGIR conference on Research and development in information retrieval*, pages 210–217. ACM, 2010.

[15] G. Linden, B. Smith, and J. York. Amazon. com recommendations: Item-to-item collaborative filtering. *Internet Computing, IEEE*, 7(1):76–80, 2003.

[16] X.-Y. Liu and Z.-H. Zhou. The influence of class imbalance on cost-sensitive learning: An empirical study. In *Data Mining, 2006. ICDM'06. Sixth International Conference on*, pages 970–974. IEEE, 2006.

[17] E. H. Margulis. *On Repeat: How Music Plays the Mind*. Oxford University Press, 2014.

[18] C. Martindale and K. Moore. Priming, prototypicality, and preference. *Journal of Experimental Psychology: Human Perception and Performance*, 14(4):661, 1988.

[19] R. K. Ratner, B. E. Kahn, and D. Kahneman. Choosing less-preferred experiences for the sake of variety. *Journal of Consumer Research*, 26(1):1–15, 1999.

[20] I. Simonson and R. S. Winer. The influence of purchase quantity and display format on consumer preference for variety. *Journal of Consumer Research*, pages 133–138, 1992.

[21] H. C. Van Trijp, W. D. Hoyer, and J. J. Inman. Why switch? product category: level explanations for true variety-seeking behavior. *Journal of Marketing Research*, pages 281–292, 1996.

[22] S. Vargas and P. Castells. Rank and relevance in novelty and diversity metrics for recommender systems. In *Proceedings of the fifth ACM conference on Recommender systems*, pages 109–116. ACM, 2011.

[23] L.-T. Weng, Y. Xu, Y. Li, and R. Nayak. Improving recommendation novelty based on topic taxonomy. In *Web Intelligence and Intelligent Agent Technology Workshops, 2007 IEEE/WIC/ACM International Conferences on*, pages 115–118. IEEE, 2007.

[24] R. B. Zajonc. Mere exposure: A gateway to the subliminal. *Current directions in psychological science*, 10(6):224–228, 2001.

[25] F. Zhang, N. J. Yuan, D. Lian, and X. Xie. Mining novelty-seeking trait across heterogeneous domains. In *Proceedings of the 23rd international conference on World wide web*, pages 373–384. International World Wide Web Conferences Steering Committee, 2014.

[26] M. Zhang and N. Hurley. Avoiding monotony: improving the diversity of recommendation lists. In *Proceedings of the 2008 ACM conference on Recommender systems*, pages 123–130. ACM, 2008.

[27] Y. C. Zhang, D. Ó. Séaghdha, D. Quercia, and T. Jambor. Auralist: introducing serendipity into music recommendation. In *Proceedings of the fifth ACM international conference on Web search and data mining*, pages 13–22. ACM, 2012.

[28] T. Zhou, Z. Kuscsik, J.-G. Liu, M. Medo, J. R. Wakeling, and Y.-C. Zhang. Solving the apparent diversity-accuracy dilemma of recommender systems. volume 107, pages 4511–4515. National Acad Sciences, 2010.

[29] C.-N. Ziegler, S. M. McNee, J. A. Konstan, and G. Lausen. Improving recommendation lists through topic diversification. In *Proceedings of the 14th international conference on World Wide Web*, pages 22–32. ACM, 2005.

Overlapping Community Regularization for Rating Prediction in Social Recommender Systems*

Hui Li, Dingming Wu, Wenbin Tang, Nikos Mamoulis
Department of Computer Science
The University of Hong Kong, Hong Kong
{hli2,dmwu,wbtang,nikos}@cs.hku.hk

ABSTRACT

Recommender systems have become de facto tools for suggesting items that are of potential interest to users. Predicting a user's rating on an item is the fundamental recommendation task. Traditional methods that generate predictions by analyzing the user-item rating matrix perform poorly when the matrix is sparse. Recent approaches use data from social networks to improve accuracy. However, most of the social-network based recommender systems only consider direct friendships and they are less effective when the targeted user has few social connections. In this paper, we propose two alternative models that incorporate the overlapping community regularization into the matrix factorization framework. Our empirical study on four real datasets shows that our approaches outperform the state-of-the-art algorithms in both traditional and social-network based recommender systems regarding both cold-start users and normal users.

1. INTRODUCTION

Recommender systems have become essential tools for suggesting items of potential interest to users and they have successfully been deployed in the industry, with applications such as movie recommendations (Netflix), product recommendations (Amazon), and music recommendations (Last.fm).

The various definitions of the recommendation problem all boil down to predicting the ratings of a *target* user on items (e.g., movies) that the user has not rated before (e.g., unwatched movies). Specifically, consider a set of m users and a set of n items in a rating-based recommender system: each user u can rate any item by giving it a score. Given a target user u, for each item i that u has not rated, the system predicts the rating, based on the existing ratings of other users. Then, the unrated items with high predicted rating scores are offered as suggestions to u.

Traditional recommender systems [9, 3, 11, 24, 10, 5, 26, 31, 14] are effective for target users who have rated many items, since it is easy to find other users that have rated these items. However, they perform poorly for *cold-start* users who have very few ratings; in this case, it becomes hard to find similar users to the target user, in order to generate recommendations based on their ratings.

The increasing popularity of online social networks offer chances to improve the accuracy of rating predictions; as sociologists postulate, people tend to relate to people with similar preferences and people that influence each other become more similar [27]. [2] also confirm that a social network provides an independent source of information which can be exploited to improve the quality of rating predictions. Based on the rationale that a user's interest is similar to or influenced by her/his friends, several social-based recommender systems [17, 16, 7, 18, 15, 30, 12] have recently been proposed. Experiments demonstrate that making recommendations based on the ratings of the users socially connected to the target user improves traditional techniques, especially when the user-item rating matrix is sparse. However, in the literature, the most effective social-based recommenders systems [7, 18, 30] only consider direct friendships in the network. As shown in our empirical study, they become less effective for target users who have few ratings (*rating-cold-start* users) or few social connections (*social-cold-start* users).

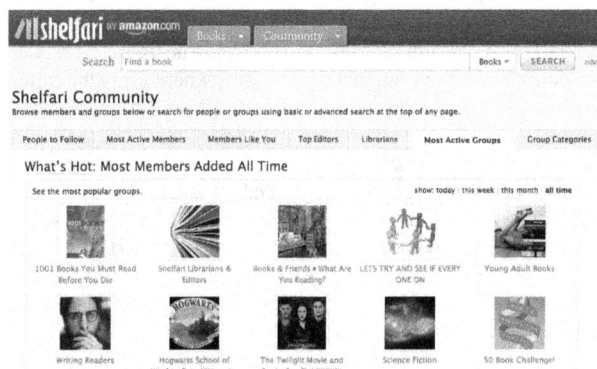

Figure 1: Communities in Shelfari

In this paper, we exploit information about the communities formed by users in social networks, to improve the recommendation accuracy. Social network users tend to establish relationships with people who share similar interests with them. For example, Figure 1 illustrates user communities in a book recommender system[1], based on different topics. The members in the same community usually share characteristics and can be an alternative of direct friends for social recommender systems. Aiming at solving the problems of social-based recommenders discussed in the previous paragraph, we propose two models that incorporate the overlapping community regularization into the matrix factorization framework differently. The communities are detected based on the social network structure; a user may belong to multiple communities with differ-

---

*Work supported by grant HKU 715413E from Hong Kong RGC.

[1] http://www.shelfari.com

(a) Social Graph

	u_1	u_2	u_3	u_4	u_5
u_1	0	0.8	0	0.1	0
u_2	0	0	0.3	0	0
u_3	0.1	0	0	0	0.1
u_4	0	0	0.7	0	0
u_5	0.4	0	0	0.8	0

(b) Adjacency Matrix

	v_1	v_2	v_3	v_4	v_5
u_1	5	?	3	1	?
u_2	2	?	?	4	?
u_3	?	5	?	?	?
u_4	?	?	2	?	?
u_5	4	3	2	?	?

(c) Rating Matrix

	v_1	v_2	v_3	v_4	v_5
u_1	5	3.3	3	1	4.6
u_2	2	4	3.2	4	2.8
u_3	4	5	2.4	4.9	1.7
u_4	3	4.3	2	4.7	2.3
u_5	4	3	2	3.2	4.3

(d) Output

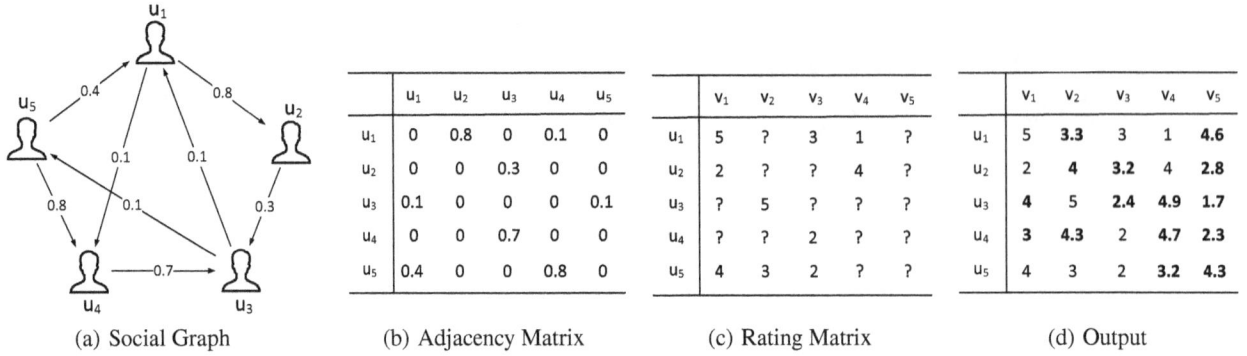

Figure 2: An Example of Social Recommender System

ent interests. One of our models (MFC) ensures that the distance between the latent feature vectors of users u and u' is low if u and u' belong to the same community c. Our other model (MFC$^+$) forces the user latent feature vectors to be close to those of her/his communities. Empirical studies on four real datasets show that our approaches outperform the state-of-the-art traditional and social-based recommenders by 6%-42% for general users. Moreover, we put emphasis on *cold-start* users. While the problem of rating-cold-start users is studied in previous research on social recommender systems, *social-cold-start* users are ignored by previous work. Our methods consider both cases and beat baselines by 7%-32% for *rating-cold-start* users and 4%-37% for *social-cold-start* users.

The rest of the paper is organized as follows. Section 2 formally defines the problem. Section 3 reviews major rating prediction approaches in the literature. Section 4 introduces our MFC and MFC$^+$ models. The results of our empirical study are reported in Section 5. We conclude in Section 6.

2. PROBLEM DEFINITION

In a traditional ratings-based recommender system, there are m users $\{u_1, \cdots u_m\}$ and n items $\{v_1, \cdots v_n\}$. The users' ratings on items form a $m \times n$ rating matrix $R = [r_{ij}]$ where r_{ij} is the rating of user u_i on item v_j. Typically, 5-scale or 10-scale rating systems are used.

In a social recommender system, we have a social network graph where each node represents a user and edges model the social relationships between users (e.g., friendship or influence). The social graph can also be modeled by a $m \times m$ *adjacency* matrix $S = [s_{ij}]$, where s_{ij} represents the similarity between users u_i and u_j or how much user u_i trusts user u_j. Figure 2 shows a toy example of a social recommender system with 5 users and 5 items. Figure 2(a) is the social network graph and Figure 2(b) is the corresponding adjacency matrix $S = [s_{ij}]$ where a positive s_{ij} indicates a social edge between user u_i and user u_j. Figure 2(c) is an exemplary user-item rating matrix where questionmarks are unknown ratings. Figure 2(d) illustrates the possible output of the social recommender system where any unknown ratings are predicted.

The basic task of a social recommender is as follows: given the user-item rating matrix $R = [r_{ij}]$ and the adjacency matrix $S = [s_{ij}]$, predict an unknown rating r_{ij} for user u_i on item v_j.

3. RELATED WORK

This section reviews important rating prediction approaches in traditional and social-based recommender systems.

3.1 Traditional Approaches

One of the most commonly-used and successfully-deployed rating prediction approaches in traditional recommender systems is collaborative filtering (CF). Two classes of CF methods are widely used. *Memory-based* methods predict ratings for the target user based on the ratings of similar users [9] or the computed information of items similar to those chosen by the target user [3, 24]. *Model-based* methods make predictions using a trained compact model from the user-item rating matrix. Various training models have been investigated, such as the clustering model [10], the aspect models [5, 26], the Bayesian hierarchical model [31], and the ranking model [14]. None of these traditional approaches take social network data into account.

3.2 Social-based Approaches

Most of the social-based approaches [17, 16, 7, 18, 15, 30] follow the matrix factorization (MF) framework [11, 23], due to its effectiveness and efficiency in dealing with large user-item rating matrices. Let R be an $m \times n$ matrix with the ratings of m users on n items. The basic MF method shown in Figure 3(a) predicts the rating matrix R by multiplying a d-rank user-specific matrix $U \in \mathbb{R}^{d \times m}$ with a d-rank item-specific matrix $V \in \mathbb{R}^{d \times n}$, i.e., $R \approx U^T V$, where $d \ll \min(m, n)$. Column vectors U_i and V_i represent the d-dimensional latent feature vectors of user u_i and item v_j, respectively. The latent vectors can be learnt by minimizing the following sum-of-squared-errors objective function with two quadratic regularization terms to avoid overfitting:

$$\frac{1}{2} \sum_{i=1}^{m} \sum_{j=1}^{n} I_{ij}^R (R_{ij} - U_i^T V_j)^2 + \frac{\lambda_U}{2} \|U\|_F^2 + \frac{\lambda_V}{2} \|V\|_F^2,$$

where $\|\cdot\|_F^2$ denotes the Frobenius norm and I_{ij}^R is equal to 1 if user u_i rated item v_j and equal to 0 otherwise. Gradient descent can be applied to find a local minimum. Having latent feature vectors U_i and V_j, the unknown rating on item v_j for user u_i is predicted as $\hat{R}_{ij} = U_i^T V_j$.

SoRec [17] extends the basic MF model by integrating the social network, as shown in Figure 3(b). T is the matrix representation of the social network; $I_{ik}^T = 1$ if users u_i and u_k are friends and $I_{ik}^T = 0$ otherwise. Matrix T is factorized into a user-specific matrix U and a factor-specific matrix W. The latent feature vectors of users are learnt based on both the rating and social network matrices. The objective function to be minimized is:

$$\frac{1}{2} \sum_{i=1}^{m} \sum_{j=1}^{n} I_{ij}^R (R_{ij} - U_i^T V_j)^2 + \frac{\lambda_T}{2} \sum_{i=1}^{m} \sum_{k=1}^{m} I_{ik}^T (T_{ik} - U_i^T W_k)^2$$
$$+ \frac{\lambda_U}{2} \|U\|_F^2 + \frac{\lambda_V}{2} \|V\|_F^2 + \frac{\lambda_W}{2} \|W\|_F^2.$$

Later, as shown in Figure 3(c), STE [16] modified the basic MF model so that each rating R_{ij} in the user-item matrix R reflects (i)

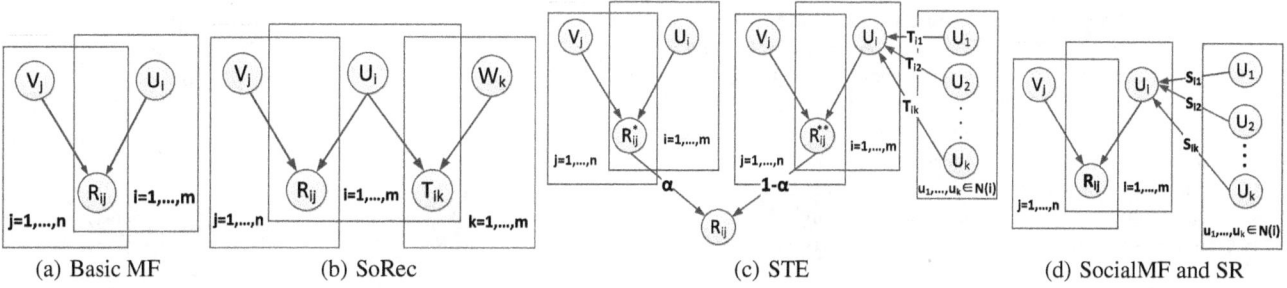

(a) Basic MF   (b) SoRec   (c) STE   (d) SocialMF and SR

Figure 3: Matrix Factorization (MF) Based Models

user u_i's favor on item v_j and (ii) the favors of user u_i's friends ($N(i)$ indicates u_i's friends) on item v_j. The objective function is:

$$\frac{1}{2}\sum_{i=1}^{m}\sum_{j=1}^{n}I_{ij}^{R}\Big(R_{ij}-\big(\alpha U_i^T V_j+(1-\alpha)\sum_{u_k\in N(i)}T_{ik}U_k^T V_j\big)\Big)^2$$
$$+\frac{\lambda_U}{2}\|U\|_F^2+\frac{\lambda_V}{2}\|V\|_F^2,$$

where T is the matrix representation of the social network, $N(i)$ is the friend set of user u_i, and α controls the effect of friends on the rating estimation.

A recent model, SocialMF [7], learns the latent feature vectors of users based on the latent feature vectors of their friends, as shown in Figure 3(d). SR model [18] improves SocialMF by treating friends with dissimilar tastes differently, so as to consider the diversity of each user's friends. SR's objective function is:

$$\frac{1}{2}\sum_{i=1}^{m}\sum_{j=1}^{n}I_{ij}^{R}(R_{ij}-U_i^T V_j)^2+\frac{\lambda_U}{2}\|U\|_F^2+\frac{\lambda_V}{2}\|V\|_F^2$$
$$+\frac{\beta}{2}\sum_{i=1}^{m}\sum_{u_k\in N(i)}S_{ik}\|U_i-U_k\|_F^2,$$

where S_{ik} is the similarity between users u_i and his/her friend u_k. Concerning the social-cold-start users who have few friends in the social network, in the SR^+ model [15], the latent feature vectors of users depend on the latent feature vectors of both their friends and the users with high similarities. However, SR^+ requires an a priori similarity threshold. The CircleCon model [30] refines SocialMF by considering category-specific friends and the intuition is that a user may trust different subsets of users regarding different domains. GSBM [8] extends the mixed membership stochastic blockmodel [1] to capture both the social relations and the rating behavior for groups of users and items. However, its rating prediction accuracy is worse than that of SocialMF.

PSLF [25] is a unified probabilistic model for social recommendation. It extracts the social factor vectors of users from the social network based on the mixture membership stochastic blockmodel [1] and integrates them into the user-item space.

In summary, most of the social-based approaches only consider direct friendships in the social network. They become less effective when a user has few social connections.

4. OVERLAPPING COMMUNITY REGULARIZATION

We propose two models, MFC and MFC^+, that incorporate the overlapping community information as regularization terms into the widely used MF framework. We first introduce the concept of overlapping community in Section 4.1. The two models MFC and

MFC^+ are presented in Sections 4.2 and 4.3. The time complexity is analyzed in Sections 4.4.

4.1 Overlapping Community

Community structures are quite common in social networks. The users in the same community share characteristics (e.g., they may have common locations, interests, occupations, etc.). In some real applications (e.g., Douban which is an online recommender system for book, movie and music and Shelfari which is a recommender system for book), there are some manually formed communities which represents members' interests. It is natural that a user may belong to multiple communities and overlapping communities can represent the users' diverse characteristics. For example, a user may join a group for mystery novels and a group for historical novels at the same time.

We derive the rating vector of a community as the mean vector of the rating vectors of all the users in the community. We adopt the widely used Pearson Correlation Coefficient (PCC) [22] to measure the similarity S_{ij} between two users based on their rating vectors. The interest Z_{ih} of a user u_i on community c_h is the PCC between the rating vectors of user u_i and community c_h. We map PCC into range $[0, 1]$ using function $f(x)=(x+1)/2$. PCC is defined as:

$$sim_{ij}=\frac{\sum_{p\in P}(x_{ip}-\overline{x}_i)(x_{jp}-\overline{x}_j)}{\sqrt{\sum_{p\in P}(x_{ip}-\overline{x}_i)^2}\sqrt{\sum_{p\in P}(x_{jp}-\overline{x}_j)^2}},$$

where P is the intersection of the two vectors.

4.2 MFC Model

The SR model [18, 15] improves ratings prediction by imposing similarity constraints between users and their friends. Given the social network, model SR can be easily extended by considering all the members in the community where the target user belongs to. However, taking the individual influence based on the user-to-user similarity constraints may cause overfitting.

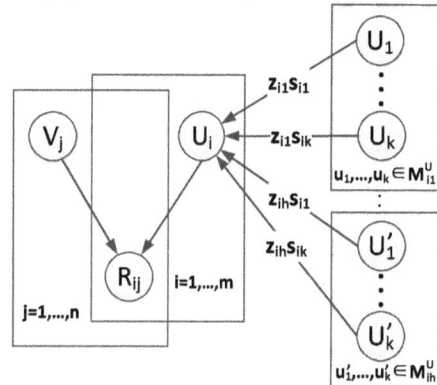

Figure 4: MFC Model

29

Our proposed MFC model, shown in Figure 4, injects community interest constraints into the SR model. Our motivation is that users who belong to different communities should be treated differently, as opposed to the SR model, which treats them equally. If the target user is more interested in music than sports, users belonging to the music community should be weighed higher. In MFC, the latent feature vector of user u_i depends on the users belonging to the same communities as u_i. The regularization term in MFC considers both the user similarity S_{ik} and the community interest Z_{ih}:

$$\frac{\lambda_Z}{2} \sum_{i=1}^{m} \sum_{h=1}^{l} I_{ih}^Z Z_{ih} \sum_{u_w \in M_{ih}^U} S_{iw} \| U_i - U_w \|_F^2,$$

where M_{ih}^U contains the users in the same community c_h as user u_i, I_{ih}^Z equals 1 if user u_i belongs to c_h and equals 0 otherwise. The objective function E to be minimized is

$$E = \frac{1}{2} \sum_{i=1}^{m} \sum_{j=1}^{n} I_{ij}^R (R_{ij} - U_i^T V_j)^2 + \frac{\lambda_U}{2} \|U\|_F^2 + \frac{\lambda_V}{2} \|V\|_F^2$$
$$+ \frac{\lambda_Z}{2} \sum_{i=1}^{m} \sum_{h=1}^{l} I_{ih}^Z Z_{ih} \sum_{u_w \in M_{ih}^U} S_{iw} \| U_i - U_w \|_F^2.$$

A local minimum of the above function E can be found by performing gradient descent in U_i and V_j:

$$\frac{\partial E}{\partial U_i} = \sum_{j=1}^{n} I_{ij}^R (U_i^T V_j - R_{ij}) V_j + \lambda_U U_i$$
$$+ \lambda_Z \sum_{h=1}^{l} I_{ih}^Z Z_{ih} \sum_{u_w \in M_{ih}^U} S_{iw} (U_i - U_w)$$
$$- \lambda_Z \sum_{u_p \in G} \sum_{c_h \in F} Z_{ph} S_{pi} (U_p - U_i),$$

$$\frac{\partial E}{\partial V_j} = \sum_{i=1}^{m} I_{ij}^R (U_i^T V_j - R_{ij}) U_i + \lambda_V V_j,$$

where $G = \{u_p | \exists h, u_i \in M_{ph}^U \ \& \ I_{ph}^Z = 1\}$ and $F = \{c_h | u_i \in M_{ph}^U \ \& \ I_{ph}^Z = 1\}$.

4.3 MFC$^+$ Model

In real life, it is common for users to seek advice from members in different groups and summarize suggestions as an overall view of a group. For example, John, who joined two groups *Comedy* and *Romance* in a social-based movie recommender system, wants to watch a movie on the weekend. After reading comments, he chooses *Four Weddings and a Funeral* with high average ratings in these two groups.

Model MFC$^+$, shown in Figure 5, learns the latent feature vector of the target user u_i based on the latent feature vectors of the communities where u_i belongs. The latent feature vector C_h of community c_h is defined based on the latent feature vectors of the users that belong to c_h and the interests of these users for c_h. A user with high interest in community c_h contributes more to the latent feature vector of c_h. Also, each user's latent feature vector can contribute to multiple community latent feature vectors. The latent feature vector of a community is calculated as:

$$C_h = \frac{\sum_{u_w \in M_h^C} Z_{wh} U_w}{\sum_{u_w \in M_h^C} Z_{wh}},$$

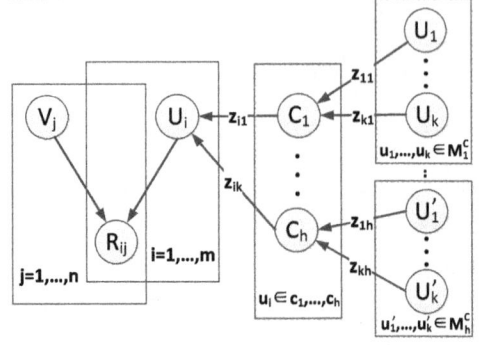

Figure 5: MFC$^+$ Model

where M_h^C contains the users belonging to community c_h. Note that C_h is a latent feature vector, while the community vector we used in Section 4.1 to calculate Z is a ratings vector. The overlapping community-based regularization term in the MFC$^+$ model is $\frac{\lambda_Z}{2} \sum_{i=1}^{m} \sum_{h=1}^{l} I_{ih}^Z Z_{ih} \| U_i - C_h \|_F^2$. The objective function E in MFC$^+$ is:

$$E = \frac{1}{2} \sum_{i=1}^{m} \sum_{j=1}^{n} I_{ij}^R (R_{ij} - U_i^T V_j)^2 + \frac{\lambda_U}{2} \|U\|_F^2 + \frac{\lambda_V}{2} \|V\|_F^2$$
$$+ \frac{\lambda_Z}{2} \sum_{i=1}^{m} \sum_{h=1}^{l} I_{ih}^Z Z_{ih} \left\| U_i - \frac{\sum_{u_w \in M_h^C} Z_{wh} U_w}{\sum_{u_w \in M_h^C} Z_{wh}} \right\|_F^2.$$

A local minimum of objective function E can be found by performing gradient descent in U_i and V_j:

$$\frac{\partial E}{\partial U_i} = \sum_{j=1}^{n} I_{ij}^R (U_i^T V_j - R_{ij}) V_j + \lambda_U U_i$$
$$+ \lambda_Z \sum_{h=1}^{l} I_{ih}^Z Z_{ih} \left(U_i - \frac{\sum_{u_w \in M_h^C} Z_{wh} U_w}{\sum_{u_w \in M_h^C} Z_{wh}} \right)$$
$$- \lambda_Z \sum_{u_p \in G} \sum_{c_h \in F} \left(\frac{Z_{ph} Z_{ih}}{\sum_{u_w \in M_h^C} Z_{wh}} \left(U_p - \frac{\sum_{u_w \in M_h^C} Z_{wh} U_w}{\sum_{u_w \in M_h^C} Z_{wh}} \right) \right),$$

$$\frac{\partial E}{\partial V_j} = \sum_{i=1}^{m} I_{ij}^R (U_i^T V_j - R_{ij}) U_i + \lambda_V V_j,$$

where $G = \{u_p | \exists h, u_i \in M_h^C \ \& \ I_{ph}^Z = 1\}$ and $F = \{c_h | u_i \in M_h^C \ \& \ I_{ph}^Z = 1\}$.

4.4 Time Complexity

Let d be the dimensionality of the latent space, m be the number of users, n be the number of items, $\bar{r}$ be the average number of ratings per user gave, $\bar{f}$ be the average number of communities where to each user belongs, and $\bar{w}$ be the average number of members per community. The complexity of evaluating the objective function is $O(\bar{r}md + \bar{f}\bar{w}md)$, while the cost of computing the gradients is $O(\bar{r}nd + \bar{f}\bar{w}md)$. These costs are linear with respect to $\bar{r}$ and $\bar{f}\bar{w}$. Since the rating matrix is very sparse, $\bar{r}$ is relatively small. According to the analysis of real networks including information network (Wikipedia), content-sharing network (Flickr) and social networks (Facebook, Google+ and Twitter) [29], $\bar{f}$ and $\bar{w}$ are also small.

5. EMPIRICAL STUDY

We conducted an empirical study using four public datasets, Yelp, Flixster, Douban and Dianping, to evaluate MFC and MFC$^+$ compared to the state-of-the-art approaches.

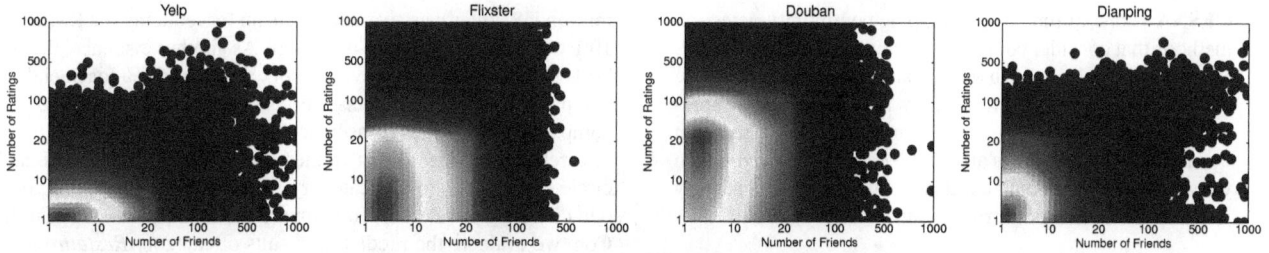

Figure 6: Distributions of Four Datasets

5.1 Data

Datasets Yelp, Flixster, Douban are widely used in previous studies of social recommender systems. We crawled Dianping from a social recommender system.

- **Yelp**[2] is provided by the fourth round of the Yelp Dataset Challenge. It is a local business recommendation platform with a social networking feature.

- **Flixster**[3] [7] is a social networking service where users can rate movies.

- **Douban**[4] [18] is an online community service, providing recommendations for movies, books and music.

- **Dianping** was crawled from the real social network-based recommender system Dianping[5], which is a leading local business search and review platform in China. The dataset contains business items in Shanghai, a social network of users, and the ratings from April 2003 to November 2013.

General statistics of the four datasets are shown in Table 1. Rating sparsity is defined as $1 - |R|/mn$ and edge sparsity is calculated as $1 - 2|E|/[m(m-1)]$, where $|R|$ is the number of ratings and $|E|$ is the number of social connections. In each dataset, every user has at least one friend and has rated at least one item. Each item has at least one rating. Figure 6 illustrates the relationship between the number of friends and the number of ratings per user in the four datasets and the intensity of color shows the density of users. In general, more than half of the users have few ratings and few social connections. The number of users in red regions are shown in Table 1. The whole social network and randomly selected 80% ratings are used for training. The remaining 20% ratings are held out for testing. The random selection was carried out 5 times independently and we report the average results.

Table 1: General Statistics of Four Datasets

Statistics	Yelp	Flixster	Douban	Dianping
Users	123,369	137,925	111,210	147,918
Users in Red Region	69,393	61,382	39,957	75,366
Items	41,958	48,758	57,934	11,123
Ratings	804,791	8,071,979	15,221,584	2,149,675
Social Connections	956,020	1,269,373	855,901	629,618
Rating Sparsity	99.98%	99.88%	99.76%	99.87%
Edge Sparsity	99.99%	99.99%	99.99%	99.99%

[2] http://www.yelp.com/dataset_challenge
[3] http://www.flixster.com
[4] http://www.douban.com
[5] http://www.dianping.com

5.2 Performance Metric

We adopt the *Root Mean Square Error* (RMSE) to measure the accuracy of the predicted ratings because it is widely used in the evaluation of rating-based recommendations [4]. RMSE is defined as follows:

$$RMSE = \sqrt{\frac{1}{|N|} \sum_{u_i, v_j} (R_{ij} - \hat{R}_{ij})^2},$$

where $|N|$ denotes the number of tested ratings, R_{ij} is a real rating, and $\hat{R}_{ij}$ is a predicted rating.

5.3 Competitors

To evaluate the effectiveness of our proposals, we compare with the following state-of-the-art approaches:

- **SCF** [13] is a social collaborative filtering method. Unlike the traditional user-based collaborative filtering (CF) that considers the top-k similar users, SCF makes predictions based on users' direct friends. SCF has been reported superior to CF.

- **BaseMF** [23] is the basic matrix factorization based approach that does not take the social network into account.

- **SR** [18] is a social regularization model, which adopts the individual-based regularization.

- **SR$^+$** [15]: an improved version of SR by using similar users (i.e., users' similarity is larger than θ) regarding to the target user rather than just direct friends in SR.

- **CircleCon** [30] is an extension of SocialMF and uses category-specific friends.

5.4 Community Detection

In some applications, it may be difficult to obtain the structure information of communities. To the best of our knowledge, there are no public datasets for the research of social recommender systems including such information. As a replacement, we use three prominent overlapping community detection methods to identify overlapping communities.

- **CPM** is the *clique percolation method* [20] based on k-clique. A k-clique is the complete subgraph of k nodes (e.g., a 3-clique is equivalent to a triangle), such that every two nodes in the subset are connected by an edge. Two k-cliques are adjacent if they share $k-1$ nodes. A community is a maximal set of cliques, such that every clique can be reached from every other clique through a series of adjacent cliques. CPM only considers the structure of social network.

- **BIGCLAM** is the *cluster affiliation model for big networks* [28] based on a novel observation that overlaps between communities are densely connected. It is efficient and scale to large networks but only considers the structure of social network.

- **CESNA** is one of the few overlapping community detection methods that consider both structure and node attributes [29]. Since CESNA also takes user attributes into account, we use a binary category vector from users to rated items to represent each user's attributes. For example, if user u_i rated item v_j of which the categories are *Fast Food* and *Ice Cream* then we set the corresponding entities of his/her binary category vector to 1. It has a linear runtime in the network size.

We use the fast clique percolation algorithm[6] introduced in [21] for CPM and the implementations from Stanford Network Analysis Project[7] for BIGCLAM and CESNA. For each user who does not belong to any community, we form a simple community by taking the user and all his/her direct friends.

5.5 Parameter Settings

We performed 5-fold cross-validation on the training set to empirically tune parameters, so that each method achieves its own best result.

λ_U and λ_V are set to 0.01 for all methods. In SR and SR^+, β is set to 0.35, 1.1, 0.6 and 0.55 on Yelp, Flixster, Douban, and Dianping, respectively. SR^+ requires an additional parameter θ which is hard to know a priori and we adopt 0.75, used in the original paper, in our evaluation. For CircleCon, β are set to 20 for Yelp and Dianping. For MFC, λ_Z is set to 0.0001 on Douban dataset and 0.001 on other datasets. For MFC^+, λ_Z is set to 0.1 for Douban, 0.5 for other datasets. We list the results for $d = 10$ where d is the dimensionality of the latent space. As d varies, our methods outperform the competitors consistently.

For community detection approaches BIGCLAM and CESNA, default parameters are used. For CPM, we report the results when $k = 3$. When k is less than 6, our methods beat SR method and achieve their best result when $k = 3$. When k exceeds 6, the number of communities that can be detected begins to decline sharply and our methods degrade to BaseMF.

5.6 Performance on All Users

We report the results of all tested users in Table 2. The standard deviations of the results are around 0.0015. The notation p, b, c denote that community structures are generated from CPM, BIGCLAM and CESNA, respectively. The percentages are the highest improvements of MFC or MFC^+ over the competitors. For example, the best results in Flixster (1.0134) is achieved by MFC_b^+ and the percentages in that row mean the percentages of the improvements of MFC_b^+ over the baselines. Note that datasets Douban and Flixster do not contain additional information about item category. Therefore, CESNA cannot be used in Douban and Flixster and the corresponding results are denoted by "None".

Our proposed models beat all competitors in all the four datasets, since the community information plays a positive role in rating predictions. The SR model only considers direct friends, hence the predictions for the users having few friends may not be accurate. Also, some of the friends may have inconsistent interest with the target user, causing the SR model to make inaccurate predictions. Although the SR^+ model takes highly similar users into account, our approaches further refine the similarities using community interest. The effectiveness has been proved by the result. Our proposals beat the state-of-the-art SR model by 7%-16% and SR^+ model by 5%-11% on four datasets. As an indication about the significance of this improvement, the well-known Netflix Prize[8] of one

million US dollar was awarded to a team for reducing the RMSE by 10% compared to the state-of-the-art. As another evidence, the improvements reported in previous work are around 5% for SocialMF compared with STE in dataset Flixster and 1.42%-2.33% for SR compared with STE in dataset Douban.

CircleCon divides direct friends into different circles and each circle corresponds to one category. When making prediction, only one circle is considered. To compare our approaches with CircleCon, we evaluate the prediction results of category *Restaurants* in datasets Yelp and Dianping since datasets Douban and Flixster do not have the information about item category. *Restaurants* is the largest category in both two datasets. Table 3 displays the results for *Restaurants* category. According to the results, our approaches outperform CircleCon, since CircleCon has the same limitation as does SR that only direct friends are considered.

From experiment results, we can also find that our methods outperform baselines no matter which overlapping community detection methods is employed. MFC_b and MFC_b^+ are slightly better than MFC_p and MFC_p^+. When additional information about users is available, MFC_c and MFC_c^+ perform much better than MFC_b, MFC_b^+, MFC_p and MFC_p^+. It is reasonable because CESNA considers both node attributes and structure while CPM and BIGCLAM only take structure into account. Our methods are independent of the communitiy detection methods and the reduction of RMSE may go up if better community detection method is used. When explicit community structure is known, our models are expected to perform even better since they outperform baselines though current community structure is generated from community detection methods.

5.7 Performance on Cold-Start Users

In this section, we consider two types of cold-start users in order to evaluate the performance of our approaches: *rating cold-start* users, who have few ratings, and *social cold-start* users, who have few social connections. Recommender systems must be capable of matching the characteristics of an item against relevant features in the user's profile. In order to do this, it must first construct a sufficiently-detailed model of the user's tastes and preferences through preference elicitation. Rating cold-start users is challenging for traditional recommender systems, because there is not enough information about them that can be utilized to generate a recommendation. A motivation behind social recommender systems is to utilize social information to improve prediction accuracy for rating cold-start users. Previous studies [17, 7] illustrate the effectiveness of taking direct friendships into account when making predictions for rating cold-start users. However, social cold-start users are ignored in most evaluations of social recommender systems. On average, 44.70% of users are rating cold-start users and 50.62% of them are social cold-start users in four datasets used in our experiments (i.e., users in red regions in Figure 6). Due to the significant number of both rating cold-start and social cold-start users, the effectiveness of any social recommendation approach is important for both of these two types of users.

We assess the performance of our approaches for rating cold-start users with less than 5 ratings (following the setting in [7, 19, 6]) and the results are reported in Table 4. We also evaluate the performance for soical cold-start users (with less than 5 direct friends) and the result is reported in Table 5. CircleCon cannot model circle influence when user does not have enough friends who have rated items belonging to a specific category. CESNA fails to identify community for cold-start users due to the lack of their ratings. Hence, their results are omitted. As expected, all methods perform worse compared to the results in Table 2. However, our proposed methods still reduce RMSE by 5%-10% for rating cold-start users

---

[6]http://github.com/aaronmcdaid/MaximalCliques
[7]http://snap.stanford.edu/snap
[8]http://www.netflixprize.com

Table 2: Performance Comparison

Dataset	SCF	BaseMF	SR	SR$^+$	MFC$_p$	MFC$_p^+$	MFC$_b$	MFC$_b^+$	MFC$_c$	MFC$_c^+$
Yelp	1.4730 24.35%	1.2498 10.84%	1.2216 8.78%	1.2032 7.39%	1.1618	1.1617	1.1543	1.1602	1.1324	**1.1143**
Flixster	1.1761 13.83%	1.1853 14.50%	1.1041 8.21%	1.0823 6.37%	1.0427	1.0436	1.0325	**1.0134**	None	None
Douban	1.2788 31.37%	1.0478 16.24%	0.9441 7.04%	0.9322 5.86%	0.8952	0.8961	**0.8776**	0.8823	None	None
Dianping	1.3642 41.86%	1.0598 25.16%	0.9449 16.05%	0.9012 11.98%	0.8678	0.8748	0.8812	0.8721	**0.7932**	0.8211

Table 3: Performance Comparison with CircleCon

Dataset	CircleCon	MFC$_p$	MFC$_p^+$	MFC$_b$	MFC$_b^+$	MFC$_c$	MFC$_c^+$
Yelp	1.1907 7.71%	1.1332	1.1345	1.1287	1.1333	1.1001	**1.0989**
Dianping	0.8234 14.84%	0.7754	0.7801	0.7562	0.7612	0.7122	**0.7012**

Table 4: Performance on Rating Cold-start Users

Dataset	SCF	BaseMF	SR	SR$^+$	MFC$_p$	MFC$_p^+$	MFC$_b$	MFC$_b^+$
Yelp	1.7832 28.9%	1.4270 11.16%	1.3769 7.92%	1.3865 8.56%	1.3082	1.3079	**1.2678**	1.2867
Flixster	1.6086 27.42%	1.3573 13.98%	1.2589 7.25%	1.2321 5.23%	1.1747	1.1769	**1.1676**	1.1832
Douban	1.2194 23.90%	1.1198 17.13%	1.0373 10.54%	0.9823 5.53%	**0.9280**	0.9287	0.9331	0.9423
Dianping	1.6098 31.71%	1.3344 17.62%	1.1868 7.37%	1.2012 8.48%	1.1331	1.1197	1.1023	**1.0993**

Table 5: Performance on Social Cold-start Users

Dataset	SCF	BaseMF	SR	SR$^+$	MFC$_p$	MFC$_p^+$	MFC$_b$	MFC$_b^+$
Yelp	1.6472 25.2%	1.3902 11.44%	1.3521 8.94%	1.3234 6.97%	1.2938	1.2935	1.2421	**1.2312**
Flixster	1.4080 24.34%	1.2160 12.39%	1.1911 10.56%	1.1342 6.07%	1.0953	1.0956	1.0732	**1.0653**
Douban	1.4320 36.29%	1.1432 20.20%	1.0119 9.84%	1.0012 8.88%	0.9432	0.9234	**0.9123**	0.9321
Dianping	1.3724 35.00%	1.1027 19.10%	0.9847 9.40%	0.9321 4.29%	0.9109	0.9246	**0.8921**	0.9012

and 4%-10% for social cold-start users, compared with SR and SR$^+$ indicating that community regularization handles both rating cold-start users and social cold-start users better than baselines.

5.8 Impact of parameter λ_Z

Parameter λ_Z controls the influence of communities in the prediction process of MFC and MFC$^+$. A large λ_Z indicates strong influence of communities. Figure 7(a) show the impact of λ_Z over dataset Dianping when CPM is employed and similar trends can be observed over other datasets. MFC$^+$ achieves its best performance when $\lambda_Z = 0.5$, while the best results of MFC are when λ_Z is small (0.001).

The two models exhibit different behaviors because MFC$^+$ minimizes the distance between the target user and her/his interested communities, while MFC tries to minimize the distances between the target user and the users in the same communities. This means that λ_Z is considered more times for MFC than for MFC$^+$ in the calculation of gradient descent, since the number of communities to which the target user belongs is generally much smaller than the numbers of users in these communities. Thus, a large λ_Z can help MFC$^+$ achieve a good result, while a small λ_Z can avoid the over-influence of communities to MFC.

5.9 Comparison between MFC and MFC$^+$

From the experimental results, we can see that MFC and MFC$^+$ have similar performance. Intuitively, MFC should perform better when the communities include diverse users since it minimizes the distance between community members, while MFC$^+$ should outperform MFC when community members have consistent tastes, because it minimizes the distances between members and community center. To analyze differences in the performance of these two methods for different kinds of communities, we use Root Mean Square Distance (RMSD) for comparison. RMSD is defined as:

$$\bar{S}_h = \frac{2 \sum_{u_i, u_j \in c_h} S_{ij}}{|C_h| (|C_h| - 1)},$$

$$RMSD = \sqrt{\frac{2 \sum_{u_i, u_j \in c_h} (S_{ij} - \bar{S}_h)^2}{|C_h| (|C_h| - 1)}},$$

where $|C_h|$ is the number of users in community c_h and S_{ij} is the PCC defined in Section 4.1. Small RMSD means community members have consistent tastes.

Take for example dataset Dianping, where CPM is employed. From Figure 7(b), we can see that MFC$^+$ performs better than MFC for users in communities with small RMSD. When RMSD exceeds 0.3, the results of MFC are superior.

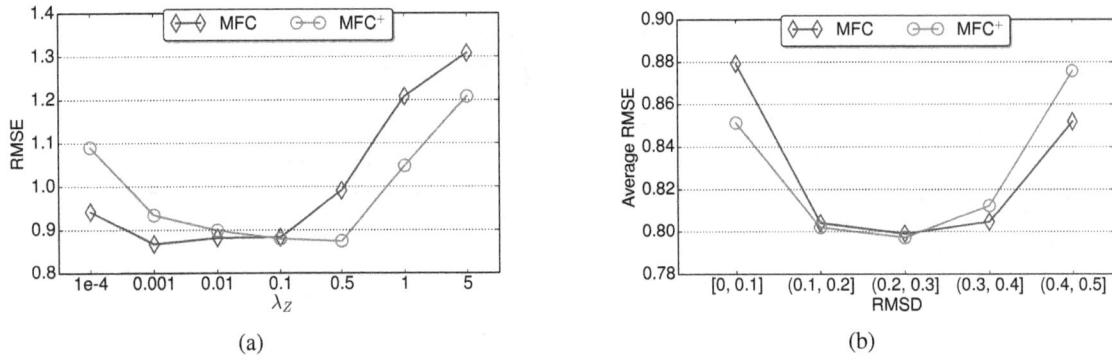

Figure 7: (a) Impact of parameter λ_Z on RMSE (Dianping) when CPM is employed. (b) Performance of MFC and MFC$^+$ over different kinds of communities in Dianping when CPM is employed.

6. DISCUSSION

In this paper, we improved the effectiveness of social-network based recommendation, by proposing two models that incorporate the overlapping community regularization into the matrix factorization framework differently.

The idea of utilizing communities to enhance the accuracy of rating prediction should not be confined to social network based recommender systems. When more information is available, it is also possible to consider *communities of items* and plug item-community regularization into our models. Communities of items can be obtained via item clustering based on the item features or the user-item bipartite network. In addition, explicit relationships (e.g., similar tastes and frequent interactions) can also be taken into consideration instead of only considering implicit social relationships. By considering information from both the implicit relationships and item network, traditional recommender systems without a supporting social network can benefit from social recommendation models and the idea of social collaborative filtering can be applied in a much broader context. Besides the above possible enhancements, in our future work, we also intend to further analyze the relationship between different community members and explore how these relationships affect users' rating behaviors, and, in turn, improve our approaches based on these results.

7. REFERENCES

[1] E. Airoldi, D. M. Blei, S. E. Fienberg, and E. P. Xing. Mixed membership stochastic blockmodels. In *NIPS*, pages 33–40, 2008.

[2] D. J. Crandall, D. Cosley, D. P. Huttenlocher, J. M. Kleinberg, and S. Suri. Feedback effects between similarity and social influence in online communities. In *KDD*, pages 160–168, 2008.

[3] M. Deshpande and G. Karypis. Item-based top-*N* recommendation algorithms. *ACM Trans. Inf. Syst.*, 22(1):143–177, 2004.

[4] J. L. Herlocker, J. A. Konstan, L. G. Terveen, and J. Riedl. Evaluating collaborative filtering recommender systems. *ACM Trans. Inf. Syst.*, pages 5–53, 2004.

[5] T. Hofmann. Collaborative filtering via gaussian probabilistic latent semantic analysis. In *SIGIR*, pages 259–266, 2003.

[6] M. Jamali and M. Ester. Trustwalker: a random walk model for combining trust-based and item-based recommendation. In *KDD*, pages 397–406, 2009.

[7] M. Jamali and M. Ester. A matrix factorization technique with trust propagation for recommendation in social networks. In *RecSys*, pages 135–142, 2010.

[8] M. Jamali, T. Huang, and M. Ester. A generalized stochastic block model for recommendation in social rating networks. In *RecSys*, pages 53–60, 2011.

[9] R. Jin, J. Y. Chai, and L. Si. An automatic weighting scheme for collaborative filtering. In *SIGIR*, pages 337–344, 2004.

[10] A. Kohrs and B. Mérialdo. Clustering for collaborative filtering applications. In *CIMCA*, 1999.

[11] Y. Koren, R. M. Bell, and C. Volinsky. Matrix factorization techniques for recommender systems. *IEEE Computer*, 42(8):30–37, 2009.

[12] H. Li, D. Wu, and N. Mamoulis. A revisit to social network-based recommender systems. In *SIGIR*, pages 1239–1242, 2014.

[13] F. Liu and H. J. Lee. Use of social network information to enhance collaborative filtering performance. *Expert Syst. Appl.*, 37(7):4772–4778, 2010.

[14] N. N. Liu and Q. Yang. Eigenrank: a ranking-oriented approach to collaborative filtering. In *SIGIR*, pages 83–90, 2008.

[15] H. Ma. An experimental study on implicit social recommendation. In *SIGIR*, pages 73–82, 2013.

[16] H. Ma, I. King, and M. R. Lyu. Learning to recommend with social trust ensemble. In *SIGIR*, pages 203–210, 2009.

[17] H. Ma, H. Yang, M. R. Lyu, and I. King. Sorec: social recommendation using probabilistic matrix factorization. In *CIKM*, pages 931–940, 2008.

[18] H. Ma, D. Zhou, C. Liu, M. R. Lyu, and I. King. Recommender systems with social regularization. In *WSDM*, pages 287–296, 2011.

[19] P. Massa and P. Avesani. Trust-aware recommender systems. In *RecSys*, pages 17–24, 2007.

[20] G. Palla, I. Derényi, I. Farkas, and T. Vicsek. Uncovering the overlapping community structure of complex networks in nature and society. *Nature*, 435(7043):814–818, 2005.

[21] F. Reid, A. F. McDaid, and N. J. Hurley. Percolation computation in complex networks. In *ASONAM*, pages 274–281, 2012.

[22] P. Resnick, N. Iacovou, M. Suchak, P. Bergstrom, and J. Riedl. Grouplens: An open architecture for collaborative filtering of netnews. In *CSCW*, pages 175–186, 1994.

[23] R. Salakhutdinov and A. Mnih. Probabilistic matrix factorization. In *NIPS*, pages 1257–1264, 2007.

[24] B. M. Sarwar, G. Karypis, J. A. Konstan, and J. Riedl. Item-based collaborative filtering recommendation algorithms. In *WWW*, pages 285–295, 2001.

[25] Y. Shen and R. Jin. Learning personal + social latent factor model for social recommendation. In *KDD*, pages 1303–1311, 2012.

[26] L. Si and R. Jin. Flexible mixture model for collaborative filtering. In *ICML*, pages 704–711, 2003.

[27] S. Wasserman and K. Faust. *Social Network Analysis*. Cambridge Univ. Press, 1994.

[28] J. Yang and J. Leskovec. Overlapping community detection at scale: a nonnegative matrix factorization approach. In *WSDM*, pages 587–596, 2013.

[29] J. Yang, J. J. McAuley, and J. Leskovec. Community detection in networks with node attributes. In *ICDM*, pages 1151–1156, 2013.

[30] X. Yang, H. Steck, and Y. Liu. Circle-based recommendation in online social networks. In *KDD*, pages 1267–1275, 2012.

[31] Y. Zhang and J. Koren. Efficient bayesian hierarchical user modeling for recommendation system. In *SIGIR*, pages 47–54, 2007.

Preference-oriented Social Networks: Group Recommendation and Inference

Amirali Salehi-Abari
Department of Computer Science
University of Toronto
abari@cs.toronto.edu

Craig Boutilier[*]
Department of Computer Science
University of Toronto
cebly@cs.toronto.edu

ABSTRACT

Social networks facilitate a variety of social, economic, and political interactions. Homophily and social influence suggest that preferences (e.g., over products, services, political parties) are likely to be correlated among people whom directly interact in a social network. We develop a model, *preference-oriented social networks*, that captures such correlations of individual preferences, where preferences take the form of rankings over a set of options. We develop probabilistic inference methods for predicting individual preferences given observed social connections and partial observations of the preferences of others in the network. We exploit these predictions in a *social choice* context to make group decisions or recommendations even when the preferences of some group members are unobserved. Experiments demonstrate the effectiveness of our algorithms and the improvements made possible by accounting for social ties.

Categories and Subject Descriptors

H.3.3 [**Information Storage and Retrieval**]: Information Search and Retrieval—*Information filtering, Retrieval models, Selection process*

General Terms

Algorithms, Experimentation, Measurement

Keywords

Group recommendation; social networks; preferences; probabilistic models; probabilistic inference

1. INTRODUCTION

Social networks play a crucial role in many social and economic interactions [17], including discovery of job opportunities [15], the products we consume [13], or even weight

---

[*]Currently on leave at Google, Inc. Mountain View.

RecSys'15, September 16–20, 2015, Vienna, Austria.
© 2015 ACM. ISBN 978-1-4503-3692-5/15/09 ...$15.00.
DOI: http://dx.doi.org/10.1145/2792838.2800190.

gain [10]. Due to such factors, it is widely recognized that individuals' behaviors and preferences are correlated with those of their friends or connections (e.g., music tastes [21]).

Because of this, and increasing availability of user preference and behavioral data, it is essential to study the interplay of social network structure and individual behaviour, attitudes, and preferences. This has lead to research focused on inferring individual attributes and behaviour using social connections, e.g., inference of ratings over items [23, 24, 18], latent group membership [19], or latent "social positions" [16]. Yet surprisingly, using social networks to infer individual preferences—in the form of rankings of alternatives—has received little attention. Methods for inference and learning of preference rankings are studied in econometrics, psychometrics, statistics, and machine learning and data mining; in the latter case, they find application to recommender systems, information retrieval and group decision/recommendation problems (i.e., social choice), especially when faced with partial information. In contrast to cardinal utilities, preference rankings (or ordinal preferences) are of special interest in social choice and group recommendation, since they help circumvent, to some extent, the problem of interpersonal comparisons of utilities [2, 36].

In this work, we address how to use *social network structure* to support more accurate inference of preference rankings and to make group decisions when some individual preferences are unknown. Specifically, we exploit the fact that *homophily* or *social selection*—association with similar individuals—and *social influence*—adoption of properties and attitudes of those to whom one is connected—can be used to infer individual preferences more efficiently and with less data. This can in turn support more accurate group decision making with partial preferences.

To capture correlations of preference rankings over social networks, we introduce *preference-oriented social networks (POSNs)*, a generative model in which the similarity of the preference rankings of two individuals determines the odds with which they are connected. We exploit this model to infer unobserved individual preferences given observed preferences of others in the network. Intuitively, if we know something about the preferences of an individual's friends, family or colleagues—or their friends, etc.—we should be able to more accurately predict their preference ranking if homophily or social influence shapes network dynamics. Moreover, we demonstrate how network structure, by allowing such predictions, can be used to support effective group recommendations/decisions with incomplete preferences.

2. PREFERENCE-ORIENTED NETWORKS

We start by outlining our basic model (we contrast it with existing network generation models in Sec. 3). A *preference-oriented social network (POSN)* consists of: (i) a social network, where nodes represent individuals, and edges represent some social relationship; and (ii) a finite set of options over which individuals have preferences, where these preferences take the form of an ordering or ranking. The model also includes a probabilistic generative process used to generate individual preferences and connections that induce correlated preferences.

The network in a POSN is an undirected graph $G = (\mathcal{N}, E)$ over individuals $\mathcal{N} = \{1, \ldots, n\}$. We use a binary adjacency matrix $[e_{ij}]$ where $e_{ij} = 1$ iff $(i, j) \in E$. We assume a finite set of *alternatives (or options)* $\mathcal{A} = \{a_1, \ldots, a_m\}$, e.g., a set of products, political candidates, policies, genre of movies, etc. over which individuals have preferences. The preference of node i is a *ranking* (or strict total order) r_i over $\mathcal{A}$. Let $\Omega(\mathcal{A})$ denote the set of all $m!$ rankings over $\mathcal{A}$.

The generative process for POSNs has two stages: first, individual preferences are drawn from a ranking distribution; then individuals form connections with a probability increasing with the *similarity* of their preferences. Each node i's preference ranking r_i is drawn independently from some distribution $\rho(r|\boldsymbol{\eta})$ over $\Omega(\mathcal{A})$ with parameters $\boldsymbol{\eta}$. Many ranking distributions can be used, e.g., Plackett-Luce, Bradley-Terry, etc. [25]. Here, we focus on the *Mallows ϕ-model*, characterized by a "modal" *reference ranking* σ and a *dispersion parameter* $\phi \in [0, 1)$, with the probability of a ranking r decreasing exponentially with its τ-*distance* from σ:

$$\rho(r|\sigma, \phi) = \frac{1}{z(\phi)} \phi^{d_\tau(r,\sigma)}, \qquad (1)$$

where $d_\tau(r, \sigma)$ is Kendall's τ distance between r and σ (see below) and $z(\phi)$ is a normalization constant.

To compute connection probabilities, we define the similarity of two rankings using the τ metric, frequently used in psychometrics and social choice:

$$d_\tau(r_i, r_j) = \sum_{k \neq l} I[r_i(a_k) > r_i(a_l) \text{ and } r_j(a_k) < r_j(a_l)],$$

Intuitively, $d_\tau(r_i, r_j)$ measures the number of pairwise swaps needed to transform r_i to r_j.[1] A strictly decreasing *connection probability function* $c(d) : [0, \infty) \to [0, 1]$ specifies the probability that two nodes i, j are connected given the distance $d_\tau(r_i, r_j)$ between their corresponding rankings. We use the following connection function [38]:

$$c(d|\boldsymbol{\lambda}) = \gamma \left(1 + \frac{d}{\beta}\right)^{-\alpha}. \qquad (2)$$

Here β controls average node degree and $\alpha > 1$ determines the extent of homophily (greater α implies more homophily). We use $\gamma \in (0, 1]$ to control the odds of connecting nodes with the same ranking (accounting for the discrete nature of ranking space). We sometimes write the connection probability as $c(r_i, r_j)$. Denote the parameters of c by $\boldsymbol{\lambda} = (\alpha, \beta, \gamma)$; the parameters of the ranking distribution by $\boldsymbol{\eta} = (\sigma, \phi)$; and all POSN parameters by $\boldsymbol{\theta} = (\boldsymbol{\lambda}, \boldsymbol{\eta})$. Fig.1 illustrates a small POSN, where individuals have preferences over three options; nodes with similar preferences are more

---

[1]Other distance metrics for rankings can be used as well, e.g., Spearman's rho or footrule, or Hamming distance.

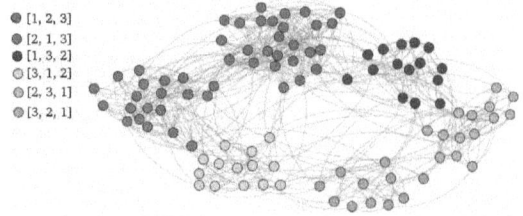

Figure 1: A POSN ($\alpha : 2; \gamma : 0.5; \beta : 0.5; m : 3; n : 100; \phi : 0.7$).

densely connected. Our POSN model is an instance of a more general notion of a *ranking network*, a latent space network model (see Sec. 3), in which latent attributes are generic rankings over options. We analyze general topological properties of this model in [33]; here we focus directly on inference and group recommendation.

3. INFERENCE AND SOCIAL CHOICE

We now address two tightly connected problems, *preference inference* and *single-option group recommendation* (or consensus decision making). While preference inference is interesting in its own right, it plays a vital role in group recommendation when preferences of some group members are unobserved.

3.1 Preference Inference

We assume that individuals are partitioned into two sets: $O \subseteq \mathcal{N}$, whose complete preference rankings are observed (e.g., elicited or otherwise revealed); and $U = \mathcal{N} \setminus O$, whose preferences are unknown or "missing." Let $R^O = \{r_i | i \in O\}$ be the set of observed rankings and $R^U = \{r_i | i \in U\}$ be the set of random variables associated with unknown preferences. In this work, we assume that the network G and model parameters $\boldsymbol{\theta}$ are known. Learning model parameters given observed preferences is an important problem (and the subject of ongoing research); but learning can exploit our solution to the inference problem (e.g., when using EM).

Our goal in preference inference is to compute the posterior distribution over unobserved preferences $\Pr(R^U | G, R^O, \boldsymbol{\theta})$ given observed preferences R^O. We discuss sampling methods for approximating the posterior distribution in Sec. 5. Other inference problems include the *most probable explanation (MPE)*, i.e., finding the instantiation of R^U which maximizes the posterior:

$$R^{MPE} = \arg\max_{R^U} \Pr(R^U | G, R^O, \boldsymbol{\theta}).$$

We may also be interested in the posterior over the preferences of a single individual $i \in U$:

$$\Pr(r_i | G, R^O, \boldsymbol{\theta}) = \sum_{R^U \setminus \{r_i\}} \Pr(R^U | G, R^O, \boldsymbol{\theta})$$

and as well as the "individual MPE:"

$$r_i^{MPE} = \arg\max_{r \in \Omega(\mathcal{A})} \Pr(r_i = r | G, R^O, \boldsymbol{\theta}).$$

3.2 Group Recommendation

A key goal in this work is to exploit social network structure to make higher quality group decisions with incomplete preference information. Suppose we need to select an option from $\mathcal{A}$ for a group or "subpopulation" $\mathcal{S} \subseteq \mathcal{N}$ using some preference aggregation method (i.e., a *social choice function*, for example, a voting rule). We distinguish the subsegment

$\mathcal{S}$ (e.g., friends planning an activity, the electorate in a small district) from the larger society $\mathcal{N}$ (e.g., users of an online social network, eligible voters in a country): while many group decisions are local, they can be supported by knowledge of the preferences of individuals outside that group. We focus on the choice of a single option with an emphasis on "social welfare maximization" relative to a *scoring rule* $g : (\mathbb{N}, \mathbb{N}) \to \mathbb{R}^+$ where $g(k, m)$ is the positional score of an option ranked k^{th} relative to m options (the Borda and plurality score are common examples, we define Borda in Sec. 6). Define the *social welfare* of $a \in \mathcal{A}$:

$$sw(a, \mathcal{S}) = \sum_{i \in \mathcal{S}} g(r_i(a), m),$$

with the goal of selecting $a^* \in \mathcal{A}$ that maximizes $sw(., \mathcal{S})$.

In general, we will not know the preferences of all individuals in $\mathcal{S}$, requiring that we *infer* the social welfare of an option a given the observations at hand. Define $sw(a, \mathcal{S}|R^O, G, \boldsymbol{\theta})$ to be this *inferred social welfare*, which varies depending on the method of inference (we sometimes omit mention of G and $\boldsymbol{\theta}$). Assuming each individual's contribution to social welfare is independent, it can be decomposed into a *revealed component* $sw_{rev}(a, R_{\mathcal{S}}^O)$ (corresponding to observed preferences) and an *inferred component* $sw_{inf}(a, R_{\mathcal{S}}^U|R^O)$ (for unobserved preferences):

$$sw(a, \mathcal{S}|R^O) = sw_{rev}(a, R_{\mathcal{S}}^O) + sw_{inf}(a, R_{\mathcal{S}}^U|R^O).$$

The revealed component is straightforward:

$$sw_{rev}(a, R_{\mathcal{S}}^O) = \sum_{r \in R_{\mathcal{S}}^O} g(r(a), m).$$

But there are various ways to define the inferred component.
Expected Score (ES). The most natural, principled way to define inferred component is the *expected score*:

$$sw_{inf}^E\left(a, R_{\mathcal{S}}^U|G, R^O\right) = \sum_{R_{\mathcal{S}}^U} \Pr(R_{\mathcal{S}}^U|G, R^O) \sum_{i \in U_{\mathcal{S}}} g(r_i(a), m),$$

which can be computed in $O(m!^{|U_{\mathcal{S}}|}|U_{\mathcal{S}}|)$ time (where $U_{\mathcal{S}}$ are those individuals with unobserved preferences). If $\Pr(r_i|G, R^O)$ is pre-computed for each $i \in U_{\mathcal{S}}$, we can write

$$sw_{inf}^E\left(a, R_{\mathcal{S}}^U|G, R^O\right) = \sum_{i \in U_{\mathcal{S}}} \sum_{r_i} \Pr(r_i|G, R^O) g(r_i(a), m),$$

which can be computed in $O(m!|U_{\mathcal{S}}|)$ time.
Joint Most Probable Explanation Score (JMPES). This uses the unobserved preferences, R^{MPE}, which maximizes the joint posterior $\Pr(R^U|G, R^O, \boldsymbol{\theta})$:

$$sw_{inf}^{JM}(a, R_{\mathcal{S}}^{MPE}) = \sum_{r \in R_{\mathcal{S}}^{MPE}} g(r(a), m).$$

It can be computed in $O(|U_{\mathcal{S}}|)$ time if R^{MPE} is given.
Individual Most Probable Explanation Score (IMPES). This uses the instantiation r_j^{MPE} for each $j \in U$ that maximizes the posterior $\Pr(r_j|G, R^O, \boldsymbol{\theta})$:

$$sw_{inf}^{IM}(a, \{r_j^{MPE}\}) = \sum_{j \in U_{\mathcal{S}}} g(r_j^{MPE}(a), m).$$

It is computable in $O(|U_{\mathcal{S}}|)$ time if the r_j^{MPE} are given.

3.3 Related Work and Models

We review the related work on group recommendation, network formation models, nodal attribute inference, preference ranking learning, collaborative filtering methods using social networks, and decision making on social networks.

Group Recommendation. Group recommendation can be broadly categorized as follows: (i) *Virtual/artificial profile methods* (see, e.g., [29]), where joint artificial user profiles for each group of users are created to keep track of their joint revealed/elicited preferences; (ii) *Profile-merging methods* (see, e.g., [42, 5]), which merge group member profiles to form a group profile, based on which recommendations are made; (iii) *Recommendation/scoring aggregation methods* (see, e.g., [27, 3, 1, 35, 12]), which aggregate the recommendations (or inferred preferences) for each group member into single group recommendation list (or recommended option). This aggregation is usually conducted by a *group consensus function* (or social choice function). Our method falls into this third category.

Network Formation Models. Our POSN model lies in the class of random, static network formation models [31]. It is also a *spatial (or latent space) networks* [16, 4], where nodes possess *latent attributes* and are connected with odds determined by these attributes. The *Waxman model* [39] distributes nodes uniformly at random on the plane with node connection probabilities decreasing exponentially with Euclidean distance. Hoff *et al.* [16] develop a similar model where nodes are points in a d-dimensional "social space". The *hidden variable model* [7] generalizes the Waxman model, giving nodes a hidden (real-valued or integer) random attribute drawn independently from a specified distribution.

Nodal Attribute Inference. Inference of nodal attributes, given social network structure, has also received attention. Hoff *et al.* [16] develop inference and learning methods for spatial models. Kim and Leskovec [19] propose a *variational EM* method for learning model parameters given network structure and node attributes, and for inferring latent attributes. Other related work includes *collective classification* [37] and active learning over networks [6].

Learning Preference Rankings. Distributional models of rankings are widely studied in statistics, psychometrics and machine learning, though accounting for social network structure has been unaddressed. EM has been used to learn model parameters of mixtures of distance-based ranking models given completely or partially observed individual rankings [30, 9, 22]. Our model is distinct from those above as it models preference correlations induced by social ties, requiring new sampling and inference methods.

Collaborative Filtering and Social Networks. Collaborative Filtering (CF) methods which exploit social networks for rating prediction have recently become popular (see for example, [23, 18, 24, 41, 14, 26, 20] and [40] for a recent survey). These methods—along with traditional CF methods—fall into two broad categories, *memory-based* [14, 26, 20] and *model-based* [23, 18, 24, 41] approaches. In memory-based approaches, the social network structure is usually taken into account when computing the pairwise similarity scores (or trust values) between users [14, 26]. These scores are then used for prediction of missing ratings. Model-based approaches focus largely on latent space probabilistic models in which users and items are embedded in a low-dimensional latent feature space, and ratings are generated by combining these feature vectors while accounting for social network structure. Our model differs in that it considers preference ranking correlations rather than ratings correlations over social networks, and in its focus on group rather than individual recommendation.

Group Recommendation using Social Factors. Group recommendations based on social factors or interaction patterns have recently drawn a fair amount of attention. Masthoff and Gatt [28] analyse the effect of group member relationship types on their emotional conformity and contagion in a group recommendation task. Social relationship strength has been considered in a group collaborative filtering context [32]. Salehi-Abari and Boutilier [34] study *empathetic social choice* in social networks, in which individuals derive benefit based on both their own intrinsic preferences and empathetic preferences, the latter determined by the satisfaction of their neighbors.

4. TARGET DISTRIBUTIONS

We describe the form and structure of the joint distribution induced by POSNs. Assuming that the preference distribution parameters η are given, the joint over R^U is:

$$\Pr(R^U|\eta) = \prod_{r \in R^U} \rho(r|\eta), \qquad (3)$$

where $\rho(r|\eta)$ is the preference distribution. To specify the distribution over G, given θ, we first focus on the probability $\Pr(e_{ij} = 1)$ with which an edge occurs between two nodes i and j in G. We define it under three conditions: (1) the preferences of both i and j are unobserved (and drawn independently from $\rho(r|\eta)$); (2) one is observed and the other unobserved; and (3) both are observed.

Unobserved preferences for both nodes. In this case, $\Pr(e_{ij} = 1|\theta)$ is the chance of an edge between two nodes whose preferences are drawn independently from $\rho(r|\eta)$:

$$\mathcal{E}(\theta) = \sum_{r \in \Omega(\mathcal{A})} \sum_{r' \in \Omega(\mathcal{A})} \rho(r|\eta)\rho(r'|\eta)c\left(d_\tau(r', r)|\lambda\right), \quad (4)$$

(The expected number of edges in a POSN is $\binom{n}{2}\mathcal{E}(\theta)$.)

Unobserved preference for one node. When only one node's preference is observed (say i) $\Pr(e_{ij} = 1|r_i, \theta)$ is:

$$\mathcal{D}(r, \theta) = \sum_{r' \in \Omega(\mathcal{A})} \rho(r'|\eta)c\left(d_\tau(r', r)|\lambda\right). \qquad (5)$$

$\mathcal{D}(r, \theta)$ also determines the expected degree of a node with ranking r, which is simply $(n-1)\mathcal{D}(r, \theta)$.

Observed preferences for both nodes. The edge probability between i and j when both r_i and r_j are observed is $\Pr(e_{ij} = 1|r_i, r_j, \theta) = c(d_\tau(r_i, r_j)|\lambda)$.

Using these edge probabilities, the probability $\Pr(G|R^O, \theta)$ of graph structure G given observed preferences R^O is:

$$\Pr(G|R^O, \theta) = \prod_{i,j \in U; i<j} \mathcal{E}(\theta)^{e_{ij}} (1 - \mathcal{E}(\theta))^{1-e_{ij}} \times$$

$$\prod_{i \in O, j \in U} \mathcal{D}(r_i, \theta)^{e_{ij}} (1 - \mathcal{D}(r_i, \theta))^{1-e_{ij}} \times$$

$$\prod_{i,j \in O; i<j} c(r_i, r_j|\lambda)^{e_{ij}} (1 - c(r_i, r_j|\lambda))^{1-e_{ij}}. \qquad (6)$$

We formulate $\Pr(G|R^U, R^O)$ by focusing on the probability $\Pr(e_{ij}|r_i, r_j)$ of an edge between i and j. Since $\Pr(e_{ij}|r_i, r_j) = c(r_i, r_j)^{e_{ij}}(1 - c(r_i, r_j))^{1-e_{ij}}$, we have:

$$\Pr(G|R^O, R^U) = \prod_{\substack{i,j \in \mathcal{N} \\ i<j}} c(r_i, r_j)^{e_{ij}} (1 - c(r_i, r_j))^{1-e_{ij}} \qquad (7)$$

Using Bayes rule, the posterior over R^U given observed preferences R^O and network G is given by:

$$\Pr(R^U|G, R^O, \theta) = \frac{\Pr(G|R^U, R^O) \Pr(R^U|\eta)}{\Pr(G|R^O, \theta)}, \qquad (8)$$

where one can use Eq. 3, Eq. 6, and Eq. 7 for computation of $\Pr(R^U|\eta)$, $\Pr(G|R^O, \theta)$, and $\Pr(G|R^U, R^O)$, respectively.

5. SAMPLING METHODS

For both preference inference and group recommendation, we must compute the joint posterior $\Pr(R^U|G, R^O, \theta)$. Exact computation is, not surprisingly, computationally expensive. So we develop sampling methods to approximate the posterior. At a high level, we sample L *preference profiles* $R^{(1)}, \ldots, R^{(L)}$ from the posterior, where each profile consists of a preference ranking for each individual $i \in U$. Let $R_i^{(t)}$ denote the sampled preference ranking of individual $i \in U$ in the tth profile. We approximate the posterior preference of any individual $i \in U$, $\Pr(r_i = l|G, R^O, \theta)$, $\forall l \in \Omega(\mathcal{A})$, and the expected score of the inferred component of social welfare $sw_{inf}^E(a, G, R^O, O)$ as follows:

$$\Pr(r_i = l|G, R^O, \theta) \approx \frac{1}{L} \sum_{t=1}^{L} I[R_i^{(t)} = l], \text{and}$$

$$sw_{inf}^E\left(a, G, R^O\right) \approx \frac{1}{L} \sum_{t=1}^{L} \sum_{i \in U} g(R_i^{(t)}(a), m)$$

Here $g(R_i^{(t)}(a), m)$ is the positional score of option a in i's preference ranking for the tth sample. L must be sufficiently large to ensure a good approximation. More critically, we must be able to draw independent samples from the (unknown) posterior. To do this, we use an MCMC algorithm, specifically, *Gibbs sampling*, where individual variables are in turn sampled using *Metropolis sampling*.

We use iterative Gibbs sampling to sample unobserved preferences R^U. It begins with an initial preference profile $R^{(0)}$, completing the rankings for all unobserved preferences. At each iteration l, we sample $r_i^{(l)}$ for each $i \in U$ from the conditional distribution

$$\Pr(r_i|R_1^{(l)}, \ldots, R_{i-1}^{(l)}, R_{i+1}^{(l-1)}, \ldots, R_{|U|}^{(l-1)}, R^O).$$

The order in which preferences are sampled can impact the efficiency of the method. The order can be deterministic or stochastic, and may be based on node degree or the number of observed preferences of their neighbors. In our experiments, we use a fixed arbitrary ordering.

To sample r_i from the distribution $\Pr(r_i|R_{\setminus i})$ we use *Metropolis sampling*. By Eqs. 6–8 and 3, the probability of r_i given all other individual preferences is $\Pr(r_i|R_{\setminus i}) \propto \tilde{p}(r_i)$, where

$$\tilde{p}(r_i) = \prod_{j \in U} \Pr(e_{ij}|r_i, r_j) \prod_{j \in O} \Pr(e_{ij}|r_i, r_j)\phi^{d_\tau(\sigma, r_i)},$$

which can be computed in $O(n)$ time. To sample r_i at iteration l of Gibbs, we sample r^* from a *conditional proposal* *distribution*

$$q(r^*|R_i^{(l-1)}) = \frac{1}{z(\hat{\phi_i})} \hat{\phi_i}^{d_\tau(r_i,\sigma)},$$

which is a Mallows distribution that uses the previous sample of i's preference $R_i^{(l-1)}$ as its reference ranking and a dispersion parameter $\hat{\phi_i}$ (below we fix $\hat{\phi_i} = \phi$, preference dispersion parameter). We accept proposal r^* as $R_i^{(l)}$ (i.e., set $R_i^{(l)} = r^*$) with probability

$$A(r^*, R_i^{(l-1)}) = \min\left(1, \frac{\tilde{p}(r^*)}{\tilde{p}(R_i^{(l-1)})}\right);$$

otherwise, we set $R_i^{(l)} = R_i^{(l-1)}$. To sample from the Mallows model $q(.)$, we use the *repeated insertion model* [11]. One can sample L preference profiles given $|R^U|$ unobserved preferences in $O(L|R^U|nm)$ time using our proposed method. Assuming $|R^U|$ is a constant fraction of n, our sampling methods runs in $O(Ln^2m)$ time, which may prove intractable for very large networks. Designing more scalable sampling methods is an important future direction.

6. EMPIRICAL ANALYSIS

We conduct experiments to assess the effectiveness of our inference and group recommendation algorithms. We measure the accuracy of preference inference, and more importantly, assess the quality of the group decisions reached when exploiting network structure to better deal with missing preferences of certain group members.

Experimental Setup. We experiment on three types of data sets: *two-sided synthetic data* in which both preferences and networks are randomly generated; *one-sided real-world data* in which preferences are derived from Irish electoral data, but networks are synthetically generated; and *two-sided real-world data* in which both preferences and network structure are derived from Flixster. We assume the model parameters $\boldsymbol{\theta}$ are known (e.g., learned from a similar population). Unless otherwise noted, we set $(\alpha, \gamma, \beta) = (2, 0.7, 1)$ and $n = 200$. We use Borda as our scoring rule where $g(r(a), m) = m - r(a)$. While other rules can be used, Borda is a useful surrogate for random utility models [8] and serves to illustrate the value of the POSN model.

We vary the degree to which preferences are observed with parameter $\psi \in [0, 1]$, the probability that any node's ranking is observed. By varying ψ, we can assess the impact of preference observability on the efficiency of our methods. We select the *decision making group* $\mathcal{S} \subseteq \mathcal{N}$ (with n_s members), for whom a group recommendation is to be made, using one of three methods. *RSA (Random Selection from All)* selects n_s individuals uniformly at random from $\mathcal{N}$. *RSU (Random Selection from Unobserved)* select n_s individuals uniformly at random from U (e.g., reflecting a company with access to a social network and the preferences of existing customers, and wanting to market to new prospects without knowing their preferences). *RSC (Random Selection from Community)* selects a connected community: it first selects a "seed" individual at random, then extends the group by selecting $n_s - 1$ friends of this seed at random; if this set is smaller than $n_s - 1$, friends of these friends are selected at random to complete the group.

Performance Metrics. To measure prediction accuracy, we determine how close inferred preferences are to the *true*

$m\,/\,\psi$	$\psi = 0.5$	$\psi = 0.6$	$\psi = 0.7$	$\psi = 0.8$
$m = 3$	0.000	0.000	0.000	0.000
$m = 4$	0.009	0.008	0.007	0.006
$m = 5$	0.168	0.158	0.152	0.148
$m = 6$	0.378	0.367	0.349	0.335

Table 1: Avg. MSEK (10 instances), various m, ψ.

unobserved preferences from a held out test set. We measure closeness using *mean scaled expected Kendall-τ (MSEK)*:

$$MSEK = \frac{1}{\binom{m}{2}|U|} \sum_{i \in U} \sum_{r \in \Omega(\mathcal{A})} \Pr(r|G, R^O, \boldsymbol{\theta}) d_\tau(r, \hat{r}_i),$$

where $\hat{r}_i$ is the true preference of i and $\binom{m}{2}$ is maximum τ-distance between two rankings over m options. MSEK lies in $[0, 1]$: $MSEK = 0$ if all preferences are inferred correctly, while $MSEK = 1$ implies maximum "inaccuracy."

To examine the decision/recommendation quality using inferred preferences, we compare its social welfare with that of *the decision that would be made had actual preferences been observed*. Let $sw(\cdot)$ denote social welfare with true preferences, and a^* and a_{inf}^* be the optimal options under given actual and inferred preferences. Rather than directly comparing social welfare, we define *relative social welfare loss (RSWL)* to be $[sw(a^*) - sw(a_{inf}^*)]/sw(a^*)$ (we report it as a percentage).

Benchmarks. We consider several other ways of dealing with missing preferences in decision making, and use these as benchmarks. In ϕ-*mallows inference (PM)*, we assume that all unobserved preferences are independent and are drawn from a ϕ-mallows model (with parameters identical to those in the POSN model). We calculate the same inferred social welfare functions as in our model, namely, ES, JMPES, IMPES. Note that ES will be the same for all unobserved preferences and can be computed once. Moreover, JMPES and IMPES must be the same as the reference ranking σ. Another approach to missing preferences, dubbed *Discard Unobserved (DU)*, is to ignore them and make a decision using only observed preferences.

For each fixed setting, we generate 10 partially observed POSNs. In each, we burn-in 1000 samples, then collect 1000 samples using our Gibbs-Metropolis method. We report MSEK averaged over the 10 instances. For each instance, we also randomly select 40 decision making groups of fixed sizes $\{3, 5, 10, 15, 20\}$ using RSA, RSU, or RSC, giving 400 social choice instances per an experimental setting. RSWL is reported as the average over these 400 instances.

Two-sided synthetic. We set $\phi = 0.85$, $\sigma = (1, \ldots, m)$, and $\boldsymbol{\lambda}$ as stated above. Table 1 shows average MSEK for various ψ and m. Unsurprisingly, MSEK increases with m and decreases with ψ. As m increases, the number of rankings increases factorially, as does the the support of the ranking distribution. In such cases, lower MSEK requires more information for accurate prediction. When $m = 3$, $n = 200$ is sufficient to push MSEK to almost 0. With $m = 4$, it remains very low. To examine the effect of n on MSEK, we fix $m = 6$ and $\psi = 0.8$ but vary n: Table 2 shows that MSEK decreases with n as expected. Decision quality of our methods in this setting is qualitatively similar to those discussed below. Our ES and IMPES methods outperform the other benchmark methods in most settings, including over all group sizes, group selection methods, and various m (even for $m = 6$ with relatively high MSEK).

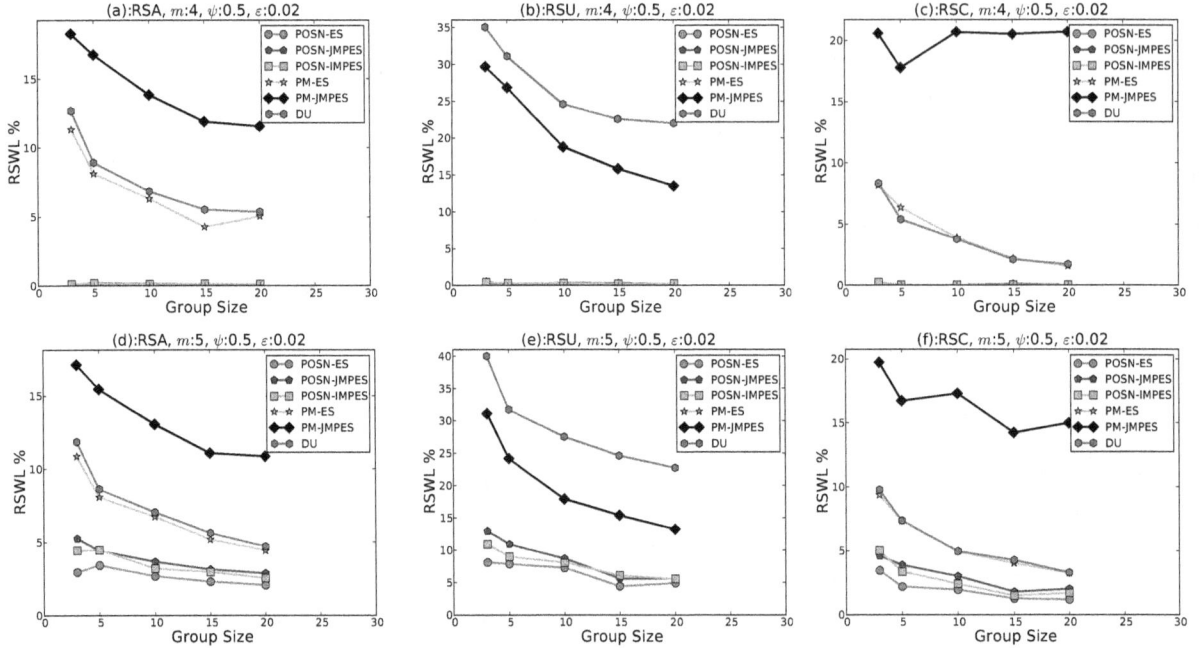

Figure 2: Avg. RSWL (over 400 instances) for various group sizes n_s, group selection methods, and m but fixed $\psi = 0.5$, $\varepsilon = 0.2$.

n	200	400	600	800	1000
MSEK	0.335	0.2474	0.185	0.141	0.106

Table 2: Avg. MSEK (10 instances), $\psi = 0.8$, $m = 6$.

m / ε	$\varepsilon = 0.0$	$\varepsilon = 0.01$	$\varepsilon = 0.02$	$\varepsilon = 0.05$
$m = 4$	0.007	0.009	0.009	0.022
$m = 5$	0.172	0.198	0.214	0.274

Table 3: Avg. MSEK, $\psi = 0.5$, $n = 200$, Irish data set.

Irish data. We test our methods using real-world preferences from the 2002 Irish Election, Dublin West Constituency, with 9 candidates and 29, 989 ballots of the top-t form, of which 3800 are complete rankings. We created preference data sets with various values m from these complete preferences, by choosing m candidates with highest aggregate Borda score, and limiting each individual's preferences to these m options.

For each m, we learn ϕ and σ from its corresponding filtered data set and used those parameters in our methods (hence we have a loose prior over preferences, but not a precise prior for specific group , see below). For each experimental setting, we generate 10 partially observed POSNs with $\psi = 0.5$ and 200 individuals with preferences drawn from the filtered Irish data set. We then generate the POSN using our model, but with additional noise: we randomly change the parity of each e_{ij} (i.e., delete or add an edge) with probability ε. Though we create a synthetic social network using our POSN model, adding noise in this fashion reflects scenarios in which the social network is not generated using our specific model, or when learned model parameters provide a less-than-ideal fit to the underlying data.

Table 3 reports average MSEK when ε varies ($m = 4, 5$). Unsurprisingly, MSEK increases with both m and ε when n and ψ are fixed. MSEK is very low when $m = 4$, even with high $\varepsilon = 0.05$ (10 edge flips per node in expectation). Tables 1 and 3 show comparable MSEK values for $m = 4, 5$, suggesting that that even in scenarios where the preference

distribution $\rho(.)$ is not known a priori, but is a learned ϕ-mallows model, POSNs support effective inference.

Fig. 2 shows average RSWL with $\psi = 0.5$ and $\varepsilon = 0.02$ (400 expected edge flips in the network). We vary m, the group selection method and the inference method. Our POSN-ES and POSN-IMPES approaches outperform the other benchmarks in most settings, including: all situations in which no group preferences are observed (see Fig. 2(b) and 2(e)); and even with $m = 5$ (see Fig. 2(d)-2(f)) despite its relatively high MSEK (see Table 3). RSWL in all benchmark methods (PM-ES, PM-JMPES, DU) is very sensitive to group size, increasing dramatically as group size decreases (see Fig. 2(a)-(f)). However, POSN-ES and POSN-IMPES are more robust to group size (see Fig. 2(a)-(f)). POSN-IMPES approximates POSN-ES reasonably well, while POSN-JMPES also performs well.

Flixster data. The Flixster dataset [18] consists of a social network of movie watchers and their ratings of movies, and allows a test of our methods using both real-world network and preference data. Because movie ratings are sparse, we aggregate them into preferences over movie genres (genres were determined automatically using the Rotten Tomatoes and IMDB web sites). Let $\tilde{r}_{um}$ be the rating of user u for movie m where $\tilde{r}_{um} \in \{0.5, 1, \cdots, 5\}$ if u has rated m otherwise 0 (for missing ratings). For each user u and genre g, we define a *user-genre* score

$$S_{ug}^C = \frac{1}{\hat{I}_u} \sum_m \text{sign}(\tilde{r}_{um}) A_{mg},$$

where $\hat{I}_u = \sum \text{sign}(\tilde{r}_{um})$ is the number of movies rated by u, and $A_{mg} = 1$ if movie m has genre g (and $A_{mg} = 0$ otherwise). This score reflects the relative number of movies of each genre watched by a specific user. This is converted into a ranking of genres for each user u by ordering genres according to their scores S_{ug}^C. We limit our focus to four diverse genres—Comedy, Drama, Kids/Family

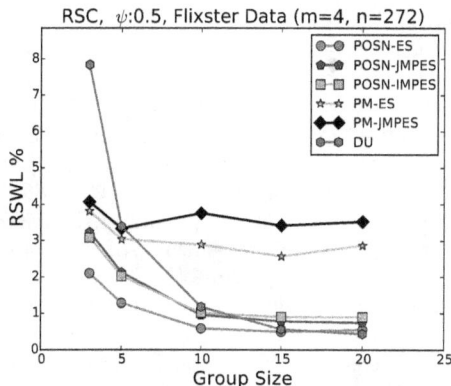

RSC, ψ:0.5, Flixster Data (m=4, n=272)

Figure 3: Avg. RSWL (400 instances), Flixster.

	$n_s=3$	$n_s=5$	$n_s=10$	$n_s=15$	$n_s=20$
POSN-ES	**7.34**	**5.04**	**2.86**	**2.57**	2.66
POSN-JMPES	9.89	7.67	4.33	3.69	3.29
POSN-IMPES	9.59	7.09	4.34	3.89	3.77
PM-ES	9.36	8.07	7.56	6.76	6.73
PM-JMPES	9.72	8.54	8.63	7.84	7.48
DU	20.61	12.07	5.31	2.92	**2.12**

Table 4: Std. RSWL in percentage (Flixster, ψ=0.5)

and Mystery/Suspense.[2] We run our methods on a 272-node subgraph of the Flixster data set, with 924 edges. We estimate a ϕ-Mallows model and POSN model parameters using maximum likelihood methods on this sub-network; the learned parameters are $(\alpha, \beta, \gamma, \phi) = (2.05, 1.06, 0.07, 0.33)$. For each run, we test our methods on 10 instances of a partially observed network, censoring each individual's genre preference with probability $\psi = 0.5$ or $\psi = 0.3$.

Average MSEK is 0.242 and 0.256 for $\psi = 0.5$ and $\psi = 0.3$ (resp.). This suggests that genre preferences are reasonably predictable using the POSN model. Fig. 3 shows decision making performance, i.e., average RSWL, for the various methods described above using RSC to select groups. Each of our POSN-sensitive methods—ES, IMPES, and JMPS—outperform the ϕ-Mallows benchmark for all group sizes, and outperform DU significantly for small groups. DU performs comparably to methods that account for network structure when groups are larger (15 or 20 individuals) since, in expectation, the preferences of 7–10 group members are observed: this is sufficient to make a good decision without estimating missing preferences explicitly due to normal sampling bounds from the underlying Mallows model. This, in addition to the fact that homophily across a large group makes it likely that the missing preferences are similar to those observed, means that making a group decision based only on observed preferences usually results in near-optimal decisions. Table 6 reports the std. dev. for these results when $\psi = 0.5$. ES has the smallest variance in RSWL in general, implying more robustness in the decisions made. Overall, ES is the most reliable method of those analyzed here. (Results for $\psi = 0.3$ are qualitatively similar).

---

[2] We focus on these four genres in part to increase data "density." Our choice of these genres may impact the results below; future investigation is needed to assess this impact.

7. CONCLUDING REMARKS

We introduced preference-oriented social networks (POSNs) to capture the correlation of preference rankings between individuals who interact in social networks. We developed effective inference methods to predict an individual's preferences by exploiting these correlations. We also developed methods for group recommendation when the preferences of some (or even all) group members are unobserved. Our experiments showed the value of accounting for social ties in inference and group recommendation when faced with missing preferences.

This work is a starting point for the deeper modeling of preferences in a social network context. Interesting future directions include: empirical investigation of preference correlations in real-world networks; scalable learning methods for estimating model parameters; more efficient sampling methods based on network topology; studying other aggregation functions (e.g., other social choice functions, voting rules, bargaining solution concepts, etc.), and extensions to other social choice problems (e.g., matchings, assignments).

Of practical importance is investigating the extent to which preference rankings are correlated and play a role in shaping connections in real-world social networks. Developing scalable methods for learning model parameters is essential; such learning techniques can exploit our inference methods as important building block (e.g., in EM-based algorithms). More efficient sampling methods can be designed by taking into account the presence or absence of subsets of possible edges. Our model can provide the basis for more effective preference elicitation. As decision making using MPE seems to provide a reasonable approximation to optimal decisions, studying how MPE can be computed or approximated without the use of sampling remains of interest. Similar to active learning methods [6], the tighter integration of inference and decision making methods would also be of value.

There are a number of potential extension to our POSN model. This includes accommodating partial information about the preferences of specific users (e.g., a small set of pairwise comparisons); and incorporating both the strength and types of relationships between individuals. Such generalizations may offer greater performance in certain preference inference and group recommendation settings.

Acknowledgements. This research was supported by NSERC.

8. REFERENCES

[1] S. Amer-Yahia, S. B. Roy, A. Chawlat, G. Das, and C. Yu. Group recommendation: Semantics and efficiency. *Proc. VLDB Endow.*, 2(1):754–765, 2009.

[2] K. Arrow. *Social Choice and Individual Values.* 1951.

[3] L. Baltrunas, T. Makcinskas, and F. Ricci. Group recommendations with rank aggregation and collaborative filtering. *Proc. 4th ACM Conf. on Recommender Systems (RecSys-10)*, pp.119–126, 2010.

[4] M. Barthélemy. Spatial networks. *Physics Reports*, 499(1):1–101, 2011.

[5] S. Berkovsky and J. Freyne. Group-based recipe recommendations: Analysis of data aggregation strategies. *Proc. 4th ACM Conf. on Recommender Systems (RecSys-10)*, pp.111–118, 2010.

[6] M. Bilgic, L. Mihalkova, and L. Getoor. Active learning for networked data. *Proc. 27th Intl. Conf. on Mach. Learn. (ICML-10)*, pp.79–86, 2010.

[7] M. Boguñá and R. Pastor-Satorras. Class of correlated random networks with hidden variables. *Physical Review E*, 68:036112, Sep 2003.

[8] C. Boutilier, I. Caragiannis, S. Haber, T. Lu, A. D. Procaccia, O. Sheffet. Optimal social choice functions: A utilitarian view. *Proc. 13th ACM Conf. on Electronic Commerce (EC-12)*, pp.197–214, 2012.

[9] L. M. Busse, P. Orbanz, J. M. Buhmann. Cluster analysis of heterogeneous rank data. *Proc. 24th Intl. Conf. on Mach. Learn.*, pp.113–120, 2007.

[10] N. A. Christakis and J. H. Fowler. The spread of obesity in a large social network over 32 years. *New England J. Medicine*, 357(4):370–379, 2007.

[11] J.-P. Doignon, A. Pekec, and M. Regenwetter. The repeated insertion model for rankings: Missing link between two subset choice models. *Psychometrika*, 69(1):33–54, 2004.

[12] M. Gartrell, X. Xing, Q. Lv, A. Beach, R. Han, S. Mishra, K. Seada. Enhancing group recommendation by incorporating social relationship interactions. *Proc. 16th Intl. Conf. on Supp. Group Work*, pp.97–106, 2010.

[13] M. Gladwell. *The Tipping Point: How Little Things can Make a Big Difference*. Little Brown, 2000.

[14] J. Golbeck and J. Hendler. Filmtrust: Movie recommendations using trust in web-based social networks. *Proc. IEEE Consumer Communications and Networking Conf.*, Vol. 96, pp.282–286, 2006.

[15] M. S. Granovetter. The strength of weak ties. *American J. Sociology*, 78(6):1360–1380, 1973.

[16] P. D. Hoff, A. E. Raftery, and M. S. Handcock. Latent space approaches to social network analysis. *J. American Statistical Assoc.*, 97(460):1090–1098, 2002.

[17] M. Jackson. *Social and Economic Networks*. 2008.

[18] M. Jamali, M. Ester. A matrix factorization technique with trust propagation for recommendation in social networks. *Proc. 4th ACM Conf. on Recommender Systems (RecSys-10)*, pp.135–142, 2010.

[19] M. Kim and J. Leskovec. Latent multi-group membership graph model. *Proc. 29th Intl. Conf. on Machine Learning (ICML-12)*, pp.1719–1726, 2012.

[20] I. Konstas, V. Stathopoulos, J. Jose. On social networks and collaborative recommendation. *Proc. 32nd Intl. Conf. on R&D in Info. Retr. (SIGIR)*, pp.195–202, 2009.

[21] K. Lewis, M. Gonzalez, and J. Kaufman. Social selection and peer influence in an online social network. *PNAS*, 109(1):68–72, 2012.

[22] T. Lu and C. Boutilier. Learning mallows models with pairwise preferences. *Proc. 28th Intl. Conf. on Machine Learning (ICML-12)*, pp.145–152, 2011.

[23] H. Ma, I. King, M. Lyu. Learning to recommend with social trust ensemble. *Proc. 32nd Intl. Conf. on R&D in Info. Retr. (SIGIR)*, pp.203–210, 2009.

[24] H. Ma, H. Yang, M. R. Lyu, and I. King. SoRec: Social recommendation using probabilistic matrix factorization. *Proc. 17th ACM Conf. on Information and Knowledge Mgmt.*, pp.931–940, 2008.

[25] J. I. Marden. *Analyzing and Modeling Rank Data*. Chapman and Hall, London, 1995.

[26] P. Massa, P. Avesani. Controversial users demand local trust metrics: An experimental study on epinions.com community. *Proc. 20th National Conf. on Artificial Intelligence (AAAI-05)*, pp.121–126, 2005.

[27] J. Masthoff. Group modeling: Selecting a sequence of television items to suit a group of viewers. *User Model. & User-Adapted Interact.*, 14(1):37–85, 2004.

[28] J. Masthoff and A. Gatt. In pursuit of satisfaction and the prevention of embarrassment: Affective state in group recommender systems. *User Model. & User-Adapted Interact.*, 16(3-4):281–319, 2006.

[29] J. F. McCarthy, T. D. Anagnost. Musicfx: An arbiter of group preferences for computer supported collaborative workouts. *Proc. 1998 ACM Conf. on Computer-supported Coop. Work*, pp.363–372, 1998.

[30] T. Murphy, D. Martin. Mixtures of distance-based models for ranking data. *Comp. Stats. & Data Anal.*, 41(3):645–655, 2003.

[31] M. Newman. *Networks: An Intro.* Oxford, 2010.

[32] L. Quijano-Sanchez, J. Recio-Garcia, B. Diaz-Agudo, G. Jimenez-Diaz. Social factors in group recommender systems. *ACM Trans. Intel. Sys. & Tech.*, 4(1):8, 2013.

[33] A. Salehi-Abari and C. Boutilier. Ranking networks. *NIPS-13 Workshop on Frontiers of Network Analysis: Methods, Models, and Applications*, 2013.

[34] A. Salehi-Abari and C. Boutilier. Empathetic social choice on social networks. *Proc. 13th Intl. Conf. on Autonomous Agents and Multiagent Systems (AAMAS-14)*, pp.693–700, 2014.

[35] S. Seko, T. Yagi, M. Motegi, and S. Muto. Group recommendation using feature space representing behavioral tendency and power balance among members. *Proc. Fifth ACM Conf. on Recommender Systems (RecSys-11)*, pp.101–108, 2011.

[36] A. K. Sen. *Collective Choice and Social Welfare*. North-Holland, 1970.

[37] P. Sen, G. M. Namata, M. Bilgic, L. Getoor, B. Gallagher, and T. Eliassi-Rad. Collective classification in network data. *AI Magazine*, 29(3):93–106, 2008.

[38] M. A. Serrano, D. Krioukov, and M. Boguñá. Self-similarity of complex networks and hidden metric spaces. *Physical Review Letters*, 100:078701, Feb 2008.

[39] B. M. Waxman. Routing of multipoint connections. *IEEE J. Selected Areas in Communications*, 6(9):1617–1622, Dec. 1988.

[40] Y. Xiwang, Y. Guo, Y. Liu, and H. Steck. A survey of collaborative filtering based social recommender systems. *Computer Communications*, 41:1–10, 2014.

[41] X. Yang, H. Steck, Y. Liu. Circle-based recommendation in online social networks. *Proc. 18th Intl. Conf. on Knowl. Disc. and Data Mining*, pp.1267–1275, 2012.

[42] Z. Yu, X. Zhou, Y. Hao, and J. Gu. TV program recommendation for multiple viewers based on user profile merging. *User Model. & User-Adapted Interact.*, 16(1):63–82, 2006.

A Probabilistic Model for Using Social Networks in Personalized Item Recommendation

Allison J.B. Chaney
Princeton University
achaney@cs.princeton.edu

David M. Blei
Columbia University
blei@cs.columbia.edu

Tina Eliassi-Rad
Rutgers University
eliassi@cs.rutgers.edu

ABSTRACT

Preference-based recommendation systems have transformed how we consume media. By analyzing usage data, these methods uncover our latent preferences for items (such as articles or movies) and form recommendations based on the behavior of others with similar tastes. But traditional preference-based recommendations do not account for the social aspect of consumption, where a trusted friend might point us to an interesting item that does not match our typical preferences. In this work, we aim to bridge the gap between preference- and social-based recommendations. We develop *social Poisson factorization* (SPF), a probabilistic model that incorporates social network information into a traditional factorization method; SPF introduces the social aspect to algorithmic recommendation. We develop a scalable algorithm for analyzing data with SPF, and demonstrate that it outperforms competing methods on six real-world datasets; data sources include a social reader and Etsy.

Keywords

Recommender systems; probabilistic models; social networks.

1. INTRODUCTION

Recommendation has become a core component in our online experience, such as when we watch movies, read articles, listen to music, and shop. Given information about what a user has consumed (e.g., items viewed, marked as "favorites," or rated), the goal of recommendation is to suggest a set of unobserved items that she will like.

Most recommendation systems aim to make personalized suggestions to each user based on similar users' histories. To solve this problem, matrix factorization algorithms are the workhorse methods of choice [20, 32]. Factorization algorithms use historical data to uncover recurring patterns of consumption, and then describe each user in terms of their varying preferences for those patterns. For example, the discovered patterns might include art supplies, holiday decorations, and vintage kitchenware; and each user has different preferences for each category. To perform recommendation, factorization algorithms find unmarked items of each user that are characteristic of her preferences.

RecSys'15, September 16–20, 2015, Vienna, Austria.
Copyright is held by the owner/author(s). Publication rights licensed to ACM.
ACM 978-1-4503-3692-5/15/09 ...$15.00.
DOI: http://dx.doi.org/10.1145/2792838.2800193.

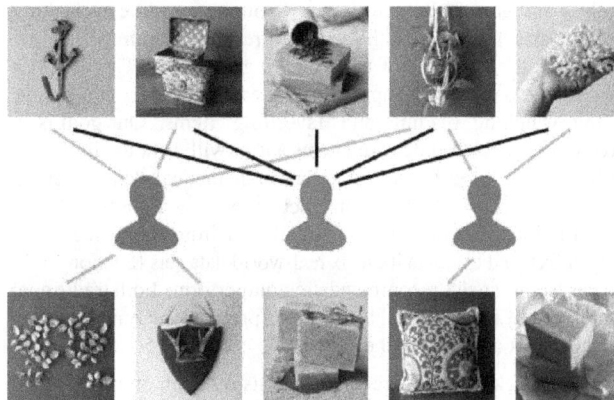

Figure 1: Observed and recommended items[1] for an Etsy user. The user is shown in the center, with friends on the sides. The top row is training items and the bottom row is the top recommendations from our model (SPF). Some items are recommended because they are favorites of the friends, and others because they match the general preferences of the user.

Many applications of recommendation contain an additional source of information: a social network. This network is increasingly available at the same platforms on which we read, watch, and shop. Examples include Etsy, Instagram, and various social readers. Researchers have found that users value the opinions of their friends for discovering and discussing content [18, 33], and online access to their network can reinforce this phenomenon.

Factorization approaches, however, cannot exploit this information. They can capture that you may enjoy an item because it matches your general preferences, but they cannot capture that you may enjoy another because your friend enjoyed it. Knowing your connections and what items your friends like should help better predict what you will enjoy.

In this paper we develop *social Poisson factorization* (SPF), a new Bayesian factorization method that accounts for the social aspect of how users consume items. (SPF is based on Poisson factorization [11], a new model that is particularly suited for implicit data.) SPF assumes that there are two signals driving each user's clicks: her latent preferences for items (and the latent attributes of each) and the latent "influence" of her friends.[2] From observed

---

[1]Etsy product images courtesy of Amber Dubois and Ami Lahoff. Used with permission.

[2]There is a large body of research literature on peer influence [22, 6, 30]. In this work we use the term to indicate the latent change in consumption due to social connections.

data—which contains both click histories and a social network—SPF infers each user's preferences and influences. Subsequently, it recommends items relating both to what a user is likely to be interested in and what her friends have clicked.

Figure 1 gives the intuition. The user is in the center. She clicked on items (on the top, connected to the user), has friends (to either side), and those friends have clicked on items too (top and bottom, connected to each friend). From this data, we can learn both about her preferences (e.g., for handmade soap) and about how much she is influenced by each of her friends (e.g., more strongly by the friend on the left). SPF recommends items on the bottom, based on both aspects of the data. It is important to be able to explain the origins of recommendations to users [15], and SPF can tell the user why an item was recommended: it can indicate friends ("you always trust Sally") and general item attributes ("you seem to like everything about ninjas") to describe the source of recommendations.

We use the language of users clicking on items. This is just a convenience—our model applies just as easily for users purchasing, rating, watching, reading, and "favoriting" items. Our goal is to predict which of the unclicked items a user will want to click.

In the following, we develop the mathematical details behind the model (Section 2), derive an efficient learning algorithm (based on variational inference) for estimating it from data (Section 2, Appendix), and evaluate it on six real-world data sets (Section 3). In all cases, our social recommendation outperforms both traditional factorization approaches [11, 29] and previous recommendation methods that account for the network [14, 17, 24, 25, 34].

Related work. We first review previous research on using social networks to help recommend items to users. A crucial component of SPF is that it infers the influence that users have with each other. In previous work, some systems assume that user influence (sometimes called "trust") is observed [27]. However, trust information beyond a binary yes/no is onerous for users to input, and thus observing trust beyond "following" or "friending" is impractical in a large system. Others assume that trust is propagated [2] or computed from the structure of the network [10]. This is limited in that it ignores user activity, which can reveal the trust of a user for some parts of the network over others; SPF captures this idea. Information diffusion [8, 12] also relies on user activity to describe influence, but focuses on understanding the widespread flow of information. A final alternative is to compute trust from rating similarities between users [9]. However, performing this computation in advance of fitting the model confounds general preference similarity with instances of influence—two people with the same preferences might read the same books in isolation.

Other research has included social information directly into various collaborative filtering methods. Ref. [36] incorporates the network into pairwise ranking methods. Their approach is interesting, but one-class ranking methods are not as interpretable as factorization, which is important in many applications of recommender systems [15]. Refs. [25, 28, 34] have explored how traditional factorization methods can exploit network connections. For example, many of these models factorize both user-item data and the user-user network. This brings the latent preferences of connected users closer to each other, reflecting that friends have similar tastes. Refs [24, 35] incorporate this idea more directly by including friends' latent representations in computing recommendations made for a user.

Our model has a fundamentally different approach to using the network to form recommendations. It seeks to find friends with different preferences to help recommend items to a user that are outside of her usual taste. For example, imagine that a user likes an item simply because many of her friends liked it too, but that it falls squarely outside of her usual preferences. Models that adjust their friends' overall preferences according to the social network do not allow the possibility that the user may still enjoy this anomalous item. As we show in Section 3, using the social network in this way performs better than these previous approaches.

2. SOCIAL POISSON FACTORIZATION

In this section we develop social Poisson factorization (SPF). SPF is a model for recommendation; it captures patterns in user activity using traditional signals—latent user preferences and latent item attributes—and estimates how much each user is influenced by his or her friends' observed clicks. From its estimate of influence, SPF recommends clicked items by influential friends even when they are not consistent with a user's factorization-based preferences.

We first review Poisson factorization and give the intuition on our model. Then, we formally specify our model, describe how to form recommendations, and discuss how we learn the hidden variables.

Background: Poisson factorization. SPF is based on Poisson factorization (PF) [11], a recent variant of probabilistic matrix factorization for recommendation. Let r_{ui} be the count of how many times user u clicked item i.[3] PF assumes that an observed count r_{ui} comes from a Poisson distribution. Its rate is a linear combination of a non-negative K-vector of user preferences θ_u and a non-negative K-vector of item attributes β_i,

$$r_{ui} \sim \text{Poisson}(\theta_u^\top \beta_i).$$

The user preferences and item attributes are hidden variables with Gamma priors. (Recall that the Gamma is an exponential family distribution of positive values.) Given a matrix of observed clicks, posterior inference of these hidden variables reveals a useful factorization: latent attributes describe each item and latent preference describe each user. These inferences enable personalized recommendations.

PF relates to the GaP topic model [5], and can be viewed as a type of Bayesian non-negative matrix factorization [21]. Ref. [11] shows that PF realistically captures patterns of user behavior, lends itself to scalable algorithms for sparse data, and outperforms traditional matrix factorization based on Gaussian likelihoods [11, 29].

Social Poisson factorization. In many settings, users are part of an online social network that is connected to the same platforms on which they engage with items. For some, such as Etsy, these networks are innate to the site. Others may have external data, e.g., from Facebook or LinkedIn, about the network of users.

We build on PF to develop a model of data where users click on items and where the same users are organized in a network. Social Poisson factorization (SPF) accounts for both the latent preferences of each user and the click patterns of her neighbors.

Consider the user whose items are shown in Figure 1. The intuition behind SPF is that there can be two reasons that a user might like an item. The first reason is that the user's general preferences match with the attributes of the item; this is the idea behind Poisson factorization (and other factorization approaches). For example, the user of Figure 1 may inherently enjoy handmade soap. A second reason is that the user has a friend who likes the item, or perhaps a collection of friends who all like it. This possibility is not exposed by factorization, but captures how the user might find items that are outside of her general preferences. Without learning the influence of friends in Figure 1, the system could easily interpret the woven box as a general preference and recommend more boxes, even if the user doesn't usually like them.

---

[3]The theory around PF works on count data, but Ref. [11] shows that it works well empirically with implicit recommendation data, i.e., censored counts, as well.

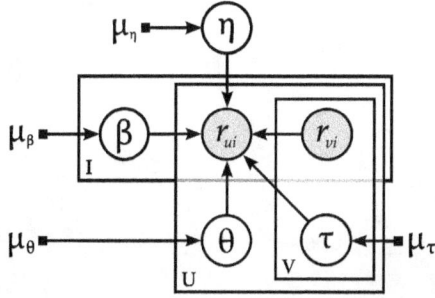

Figure 2: A conditional directed graphical model of social Poisson Factorization (SPF) to show considered dependencies. For brevity, we refer to the set of priors a and b as μ; for example, $\mu_\theta = (a_\theta, b_\theta)$. These hyperparameters are fixed.

SPF captures this intuition. As in PF, each user has a vector of latent preferences. However, each user also has a vector of "influence" values, one for each of her friends. Whether she likes an item depends on both signals: first, it depends on the affinity between her latent preferences and the item's latent attributes; second, it depends on whether her influential friends have clicked it.

Model specification. We formally describe SPF. The observed data are user behavior and a social network. The behavior data is a sparse matrix $\mathbf{R}$, where r_{ui} is the number of times user u clicked on item i. (Often this will be one or zero.) The social network is represented by its neighbor sets; $N(u)$ is the set of indices of other users connected to u. Finally, the hidden variables of SPF are per-user K-vectors of non-negative preferences θ_u, per-item K-vectors of non-negative attributes β_i, and per-neighbor non-negative user influences τ_{uv}. Loosely, τ_{uv} represents how much user u is influenced by the clicks of her neighbor, user v. (Note we must set the number of components K. Section 3 studies the effect of K on performance; usually we set it to 50 or 100.)

Conditional on the hidden variables and the social network, SPF is a model of clicks r_{ui}. Unlike many models in modern machine learning, we specify the joint distribution of the entire matrix $\mathbf{R}$ by the conditionals of each cell r_{ui} given the others,

$$r_{ui} \mid r_{-u,i} \sim \text{Poisson}\left(\theta_u^\top \beta_i + \sum_{v \in N(u)} \tau_{uv} r_{vi}\right), \quad (1)$$

where $r_{-u,i}$ denotes the vector of clicks of the other users of the ith item.[4] This equation captures the intuition behind the model, that the conditional distribution of whether user u clicks on item i is governed by two terms. The first term, as we said above, is the affinity between latent preferences θ_u and latent attributes β_i; the second term bumps the parameter up when trustworthy neighbors v (i.e., those with high values of τ_{uv}) also clicked on the item. Figure 2 shows the dependencies between the hidden and observed variables as a conditional graphical model.

To complete the specification of the variables, we place gamma priors on all of the hidden variables. We chose the hyperparameters of the gammas so that preferences, attributes, and influences are sparse. (See Section 3 for details.)

Forming recommendations with SPF. We have specified a probabilistic model of hidden variables and observed clicks. Given a $U \times I$ click matrix $\mathbf{R}$ and a $U \times U$ social network $\mathbf{N}$, we analyze

the data by estimating the posterior distribution of the hidden preferences, attributes, and influences $p(\theta_{1:U}, \beta_{1:I}, \tau_{1:U} \mid \mathbf{R}, \mathbf{N})$. This posterior places high probability on configurations of preferences, attributes, and influence values that best describe the observed clicks within the social network.

From this posterior, we can form predictions for each user and each of their unclicked items. For a user u and an unclicked item j, we compute

$$\text{E}\left[r_{uj}\right] = \text{E}\left[\theta_u\right]^\top \text{E}\left[\beta_j\right] + \sum_{v \in N(u)} \text{E}\left[\tau_{uv}\right] r_{vj}, \quad (2)$$

where all expectations are with respect to the posterior. For each user, we form recommendation lists by making predictions for the user's set of unclicked items and then ranking the items by these continuous-valued predictions. This is how we can use SPF to form a recommendation system.

Learning the hidden variables with variational methods. Social PF enjoys the benefits of Poisson factorization and accounts for the network of users. However, using SPF requires computing the posterior. Conditioned on click data and a social network, our goal is to compute the posterior user preferences, item attributes, and latent influence values.

As for many Bayesian models, the exact posterior for SPF is not tractable to compute; approximating the posterior is our central statistical and computational problem. We develop an efficient approximate inference algorithm for SPF based on variational methods [4, 19], a widely-used technique in statistical machine learning for fitting complex Bayesian models.[5] With our algorithm, we can approximate posterior expectations with very large click and network data (see Section 3).

Variational inference approximates the posterior by solving an optimization problem. We define a freely parameterized distribution over the hidden variables, and then fit its parameters to be close to the posterior distribution. We measure "closeness" by the Kullback-Leibler divergence, which is an assymetric measure of distance between distributions. Finally, we use the fitted variational distribution as a proxy for the posterior, for example to compute the expectations we need on the right-hand side of Eq. 2.

We use the *mean-field* variational family, where each latent variable is independent and governed by its own varitional parameter. The latent variables are the user preferences θ_u, item attributes β_i, and user influences τ_{uv}. The variational family is

$$q(\theta, \beta, \tau) = \prod_{u,k} q(\theta_{uk} \mid \lambda_{uk}^\theta) \prod_{i,k} q(\beta_{ik} \mid \lambda_{ik}^\beta) \prod_{u,v} q(\tau_{uv} \mid \lambda_{uv}^\tau). \quad (3)$$

This is a flexible family. For example each cell of each user's preference vector θ_{uk} is associated with its own variational parameter λ_{uk}^θ. Thus, when fit to be close to the model's posterior, the variational parameters can capture each user's unique interests, each item's unique attributes, and each friend's unique influence value.

With the family in place, variational inference solves the following optimization problem,

$$q^*(\theta, \beta, \tau) = \arg\min_q \text{KL}\left(q(\theta, \beta, \tau) \| p(\theta, \beta, \tau \mid \mathbf{R}, \mathbf{N})\right). \quad (4)$$

Note that the data—the clicks and the network—enter the variational distribution through this optimization. Finally, we use the resulting variational parameters of $q^*(\cdot)$ as a proxy for the exact posterior. This lets us use SPF to perform recommendation.

In the appendix we describe the details of how we solve the problem in Eq. 4 to find a local optimum of the KL divergence. We

---

[4]We are specifying an exponential family model conditionally. This leads to a well-defined joint if and only if the natural parameters for each conditional are sums and products of the sufficient statistics of the corresponding conditionals of the conditioning set [3]. In our case, this is satisfied.

[5]Source code available at https://github.com/ajbc/spf.

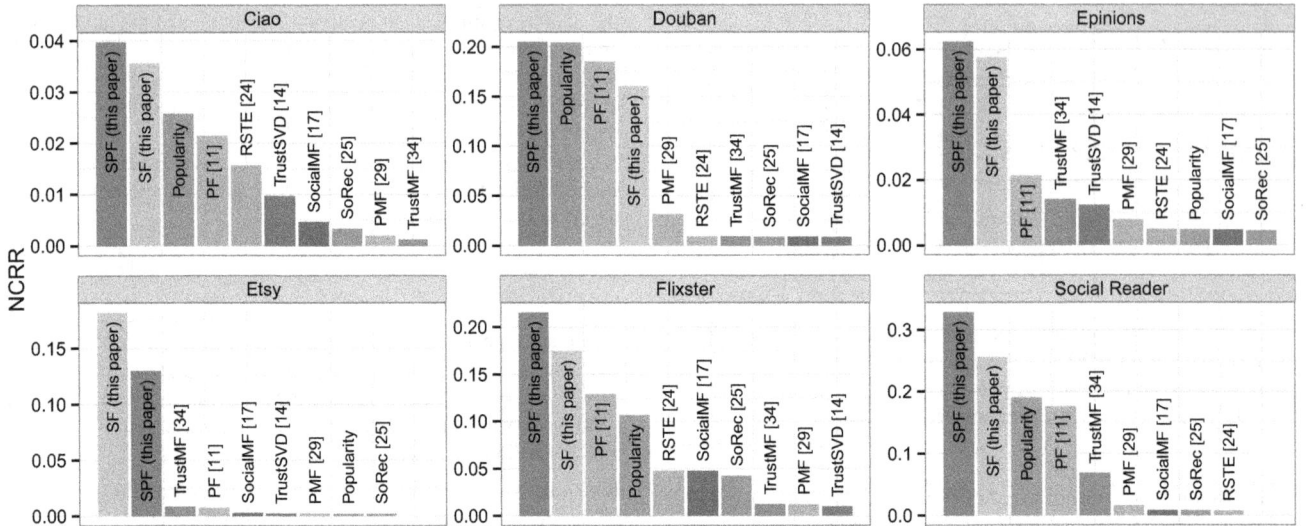

Figure 3: Performance of various methods on all six datasets, measured as NCRR averaged over users with held-out data. The Poisson-based factor models (PF and SPF) use $K = 40$ on Ciao, $K = 125$ on Epinions, $K = 100$ on Etsy, and $K = 50$ on Flixster, Douban, and Social Reader. Similar K values are used for competing models, but some perform best with lower K, in which case those settings are used. Models are sorted by performance. RSTE was omitted on Etsy data due to long run time and TrustSVD was omitted on Social Reader data due to difficulty in finding appropriate parameter settings. SPF outperforms all competing methods, except on Etsy, where our alternate model SF achieves top performance.

use a form of alternating minimization, iteratively minimizing the KL divergence with respect to each of the variational parameters while holding the others fixed. This leads to a scalable iterative algorithm, where each iteration runs on the order of the number of non-zero entries of the matrix. (In Section 3 we empirically compare the runtime of SPF with competing methods.) We now turn to an empirical study of SPF.

3. EMPIRICAL STUDY

In this section we study the performance of SPF. We compared SPF to five competing methods that involve a social network in recommendation [14, 17, 24, 25, 34] as well as two traditional factorization approaches [11, 29]. Across six real-world datasets, our methods outperformed all of the competing methods (Figure 3). We also demonstrate how to use SPF to explore the data, characterizing it in terms of latent factors and social influence. Finally, we assess sensitivity to the number of latent factors and discuss how to set hyperparameters on the prior distributions.

3.1 Datasets, methods, and metrics

Datasets and preprocessing. We studied six datasets. Table 1 summarizes their attributes. The datasets are:

- *Ciao* (ciao.co.uk) is a consumer review website with an underlying social network. Guo et al. [13] crawled DVD ratings and trust values for a small dataset of 7K users and 98K items.

- *Epinions* (epinions.com) is another consumer reviews website where users rate items and mark users as trustworthy. Our data source was Massa and Avesani [27]; the dataset consists of 39K users and 131K items.

- *Flixster* (flixster.com) is a social movie review website crawled by Jamali and Ester [17]. We binarized ratings, thresholding at 3 or above, resulting in 132K users and 42K items.

- *Douban* (douban.com) is a Chinese social service where users record ratings for music, movies, and books; it was crawled by Ma et al. [26]. It contains 129K users and 57K items.

- *Etsy* (etsy.com) is a marketplace for handmade and vintage items, as well as art and craft supplies. Users may follow each other and mark items as favorites. This data was provided directly by Etsy, and culled to users who have favorited at least 10 items and have at least 25% of their items in common with their friends; we omitted any items with fewer than 5 favorites. This is a large dataset of 40K users and 5.2M items.

- *Social Reader* is a dataset from a large media company that deployed a reader application on a popular online social network. The data contains a friendship network and a table of article clicks. We analyzed data from April 2-6, 2012, only including users who read at least 3 articles during that time. It contains 122K users and 6K items.

These datasets include both explicit ratings on a star scale and binary data. Content consumption is binary when the data is implicit (a news article was viewed) or when the system only provides a binary flag (favoriting). With implicit data, non-Poisson models require us to subsample 0's so as to differentiate between items; in these instances, we randomly sampled negative examples such that each user has the same number of positive and negative ratings. Note that Poisson-based models implicitly analyze the full matrix without needing to pay the computational cost of analyzing the zeros [11].

For each dataset, we preprocessed the network. We removed network connections where the users have no items in common. Note this advantages both SPF and comparison models (though SPF can learn the relative influence of the neighbors).

Our studies divided the data into three groups: approximately 10% of 1000 users' data are held-out for post-inference testing, 1% of all users' data are used to assess convergence of the inference algorithm (see Appendix), and the rest is used to train. One exception is Ciao, where we used 10% of all users' data to test.

	Ciao	Epinions	Flixster	Douban	Social Reader	Etsy
# of users	7,375	39,307	131,542	129,097	121,950	39,862
# of items	97,540	130,786	41,878	56,862	6,153	5,201,879
# user-item interactions	270,427	639,775	6,740,332	16,207,151	489,735	18,650,632
% user-item interaction matrix	0.038%	0.012%	0.122%	0.221%	0.065%	0.009%
interaction type	5-star	5-star	binary (thresholded)	5-star	binary (clicks)	binary (favoriting)
network type	directed	directed	undirected	undirected	undirected	directed
# network connections	56,267	176,337	488,869	1,323,828	100,175	4,761,437
network edge density	0.103%	0.011%	0.006%	0.016%	0.001%	0.300%
% shared	25.0%	36.0%	62.3%	51.0%	50.1%	30.8%

Table 1: Attributes of each data source, post-curation. User-item interactions are non-zero clicks, favorites, or ratings. Percent shared is the average percentage of items users have in common with their friends. Data sources were chosen for their diversity of attributes.

Competing methods. We compared SPF to five competing models that involve a social network in recommendation: RSTE [24], TrustSVD [14], SocialMF [17], SoRec [25], and TrustMF [34].[6] We also include probabilistic Gaussian matrix factorization (PMF) [29], because it is a widely used recommendation method. For each of these, we used the parameter settings that achieved best performance according to the example fits published on the LibRec website.

We can think of SPF having two parts: a Poisson factorization component and a social component (see Eq. 1). Thus we also compared SPF to each of these components in isolation, Poisson factorization [11] (PF) and *social factorization* (SF). SF is the influence model without the factorization model.[7] We note that SF is a contribution of this paper.

Finally, we compare to two baselines, ordering items randomly and ordering items by their universal popularity.

Metrics. We evaluate these methods on a per-user basis. For each user, we predict clicks for both held-out and truly unclicked items, and we rank these items according to their predictions. We denote the user-specific rank to be rank_{ui} for item i and user u. A better model will place the held-out items higher in the ranking (giving smaller rank_{ui} values on held-out items). We now introduce the *normalized cumulative reciprocal rank* (NCRR) metric to gauge this performance.

Reciprocal rank (RR) is an information retrieval measure; given a query, it is the reciprocal of the rank at which the first relevant document was retrieved. (Larger numbers are better.) Users "query" a recommender system similarly, except that each user only has one query (e.g., "what books should I read?") and they care not just about the first item that's relevant, but about finding as many relevant items as possible.

Suppose user u has held out items $\mathcal{D}_u$.[8] We define the cumulative reciprocal rank to be:

$$\text{CRR}_u = \sum_{i \in \mathcal{D}_u} \frac{1}{\text{rank}_{ui}}.$$

CRR can be interpreted as the ease of finding all held-out items, as higher numbers indicate that the held-out items are higher in the list. For example, a CRR of 0.75 means that the second and fourth items are in the held-out set, or are relevant to the user.

CRR behaves similarly to discounted cumulative gain (DCG), except it places a higher priority on high-rank items by omitting the log factor—it can be thought of as a harsher variant of DCG. Like DCG, it can be also be normalized. The normalized cumulative reciprocal rank (NCRR) is

$$\text{NCRR}_u = \frac{\text{CRR}_u}{\text{ideal } \text{CRR}_u},$$

where the ideal variant in the denominator is the value of the metric if the ranking was perfect. To evaluate an entire model, we can compute average NCRR over all users, $\frac{1}{U}\sum_u \text{NCRR}_u$. We will use this metric throughout this section.

Performance measured by NCRR is consistent with performance measured by NDCG, but NCRR is more interpretable—simple reciprocals are easier to understand than the reciprocal of the log.

Note we omit root-mean-square error (RMSE) as a metric. Improvements in RMSE often do not translate into accuracy improvements for ranked lists [1, 7, 23, 31], especially with binary or implicit data. Our end goal here is item recommendation and not rating prediction—"which movie should I watch next?" is inherently a ranking problem—thus we treat the predictions as means to an end.

3.2 Performance and exploration

We evaluate SPF by considering overall performance and performance as a function of user degree. We also show how to explore the data using the algorithm.

Performance. Figure 3 shows the performance of SPF against the competing methods: the previous methods that account for the social network, social factorization (SF), Poisson factorization (PF), and the popularity baseline. (We do not illustrate the random baseline because it is far below all of the other methods.) SPF achieves top performance on five of the datasets. On the one remaining dataset, Etsy, the social-only variant of our model (SF) performs best.

Notice the strong performance of ranking by popularity. This highlights the importance of social factorization. It is only social Poisson factorization that consistently outperforms this baseline.

We measured runtime with the Ciao data set to get a sense for the relative computational costs. Figure 4 shows the runtime for all of the methods at various values of K. The Poisson models are average in terms of runtime.

Finally, using the Ciao and Epinions data, we break down the performance of SPF, SF, and PF as a function of the degree of each user; the results are shown in Figure 5.[9] All models perform better on high-degree users, presumably because these are higher activity users as well. Overall, SPF performs better than SF because of its advantage on the large number of low-degree users.

---

[6] We used the LibRec library (librec.net) for all competing methods.

[7] Social factorization has a technical problem when none of a user's friends has clicked on an item; the resulting Poisson cannot have a rate of zero. Thus we add a small constant $\epsilon = 10^{-10}$ to the rate in social factorization's model of clicks.

[8] With binary data this is simply the full set of heldout items. When items have non-binary ratings, we threshold the set such to include only highly rated items (4 or 5 in a 5-star system).

[9] Smoothed with GAM. http://www.inside-r.org/r-doc/mgcv/gam

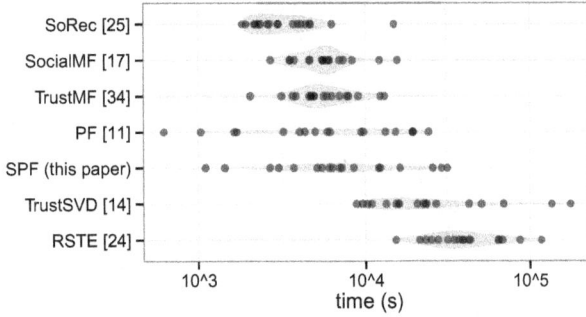

Figure 4: Training and testing runtimes for multiple models on Ciao data, with the number of latent factors K ranging from 1 to 500. Each dot represents a full cycle of training and evaluating. SPF performs with average runtime.

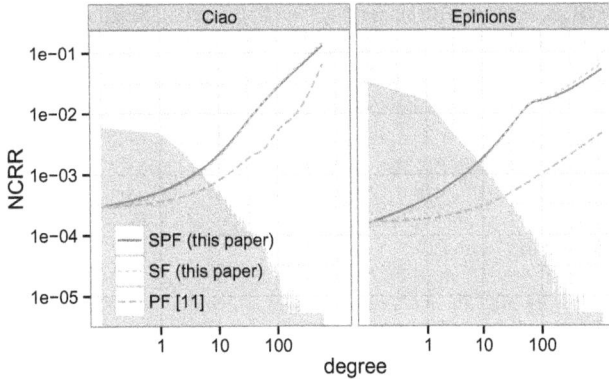

Figure 5: Performance on Ciao and Epinions broken down as a function of degree; grey in background indicates density of users. SPF and SF perform similarly, with SPF doing slightly better on a large number of low-degree users and SF doing better on a low number of high-degree users.

Interpretability. It is important to be able to explain the origins of recommendations to users [15]. Items recommended with SPF have the advantage of interpretability. In particular, we use auxiliary variables (see Appendix) to attribute each recommendation to friends or general preferences; we then use these attributions to explore data.

When items are recommended because of social influence, the system may indicate a friend as the source of the recommendation. Similarly, when items are recommended because of general preferences, the system may indicate already clicked items that exhibit that preference. On the Etsy data, learned item factors included coherent groupings of items such as mugs, sparkly nail polish, children's toys, handmade cards, and doll clothes. Thus, SPF explains the recommended the handmade soap in Figure 1 as coming from general preferences and the others items as coming from social influence. The social and preference signals will not always be cleanly separated; SPF attributes recommendations to sources probabilistically.

Figure 6 shows how the proportion of social attribution (as opposed to general preference attribution) changes as a function of user degree on Ciao and Epinions. We observe that Epinions attributes a larger portion of behavior to social influence, controlled for user degree. Similarly, we can compute the contribution of users to their friends' behavior. Figure 7 shows social contribution as a function of indegree; here we see that Epinions users with higher indegree have lower social contribution than low-indegree users.

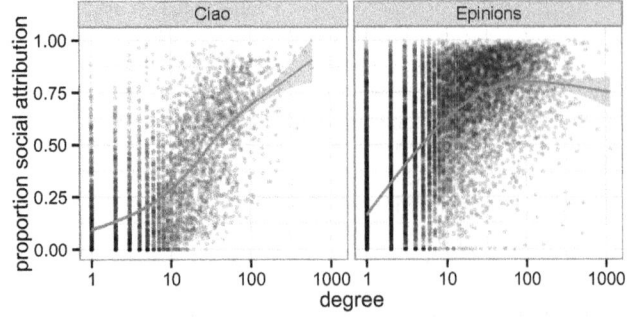

Figure 6: The proportion of social attribution (vs. general preference attribution) as a function of user degree. Attributions are calculated on all training data from Ciao and Epinions. Epinions attributes a larger portion of rating to social influence.

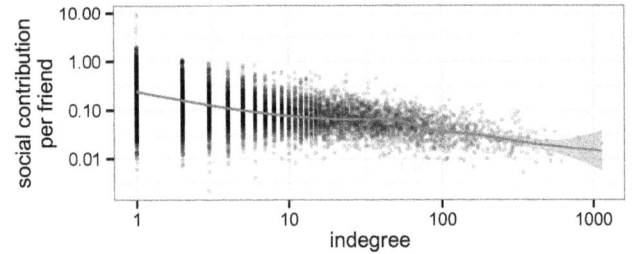

Figure 7: Contribution to friends' behavior as a function of indegree, calculated on all Epinions training data. Users with higher indegree have lower social contribution.

3.3 Experimental details

The details of our methods requires some decisions: we must choose the number of latent factors K and set the hyperparameters.

Choosing the number of latent factors K. All factorization models, including SPF, require the investigator to select of the number of latent factors K used to represent users and items. We evaluated the sensitivity to this choice for the Ciao dataset. (We chose this dataset because of its smaller size; ranking millions of items for every user is computationally expensive for any model.) Figure 8 shows per-user average NCRR K varies from 1 to 500; SPF performs best on the Ciao dataset with $K = 40$, though is less sensitive to this choice than some other methods (such as PF).

Hyperparameters. We also must set the hyperparameters to the gamma priors on the latent variables. The gamma is parameterized by a shape and a rate. We followed [11] and set them to 0.3 for the priors on latent preferences and attributes. We set the hyperparameters for the prior on user influences to $(2, 5)$ in order to encourage the model to explore explanation by social influence. In a pilot study, we found that the model was not sensitive to these settings.

Does learning influence matter? We can easily fix each user-friend influence at 1, giving us local popularity among a user's social connections. We compared fitted influence against fixed influence on both Ciao and Epinions and found that SPF with fitted influence performs best on both datasets.

In the case of cold-start users, where we know the user's social network but not their click counts on items, SPF will perform equivalently to SF with fixed influence. SPF in this cold-start user scenario performs better than competing models.

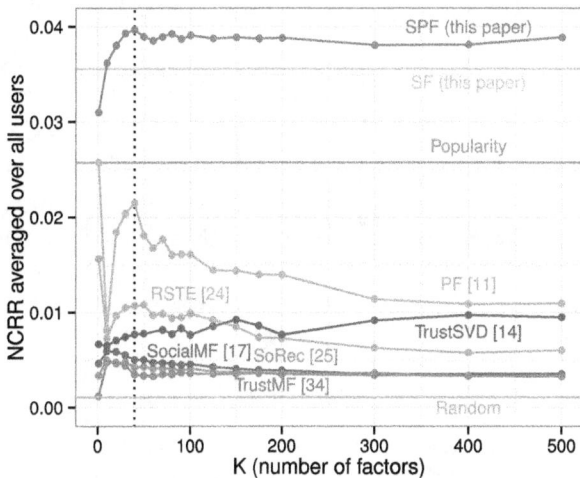

Figure 8: Model performance on Ciao data (measured as NCRR averaged over all users) as a function of number of latent factors K. The dotted vertical line at $K = 40$ indicates the best performance for Poisson family models.

4. DISCUSSION

We presented social Poisson factorization, a Bayesian model that incorporates a user's latent preferences for items with the latent influences of her friends. We demonstrated that social Poisson factorization improves recommendations even with noisy online social signals. Social Poisson factorization has the following properties: (1) It discovers the latent influence that exists between users in a social network, allowing us to analyze the social dynamics. (2) It provides a source of explainable serendipity (i.e., pleasant surprise due to novelty). (3) It enjoys scalable algorithms that can be fit to large data sets.

We anticipate that social Poisson factorization will perform well on platforms that allow for and encourage users to share content. Examples include Etsy, Pinterest, Twitter, and Facebook. We note that our model does not account for time—when two connected users both enjoy an item, one of them probably consumed it first. Future work includes incorporating time, hierarchical influence, and topical influence.

5. ACKNOWLEDGMENTS

We thank Prem Gopalan, Jake Hofman, Chong Wang, Laurent Charlin, Rajesh Ranganath, and Alp Kucukelbir for their insights and discussions. We thank Etsy, Diane Hu in particular, for sharing data. We also thank LibRec's creator, Guibing Guo. DMB is supported by NSF BIGDATA NSF IIS-1247664, ONR N00014-11-1-0651, and DARPA FA8750-14-2-0009. TER is supported by NSF CNS-1314603, by DTRA HDTRA1-10-1-0120, and by DAPRA under SMISC Program Agreement No. W911NF-12-C-0028.

6. REFERENCES

[1] X. Amatriain, P. Castells, A. de Vries, and C. Posse. Workshop on recommendation utility evaluation: Beyond RMSE. In *RecSys*, pages 351–352, 2012.

[2] R. Andersen, C. Borgs, J. Chayes, U. Feige, A. Flaxman, A. Kalai, V. Mirrokni, and M. Tennenholtz. Trust-based recommendation systems: an axiomatic approach. In *WWW*, pages 199–208, 2008.

[3] B. C. Arnold, E. Castillo, and J. M. Sarabia. *Conditional specification of statistical models*. Springer, 1999.

[4] C. Bishop. *Pattern Recognition and Machine Learning*. Springer New York, 2006.

[5] J. Canny. GaP: a factor model for discrete data. In *SIGIR*, pages 122–129, 2004.

[6] D. Crandall, D. Cosley, D. Huttenlocher, J. Kleinberg, and S. Suri. Feedback effects between similarity and social influence in online communities. In *KDD*, pages 160–168, 2008.

[7] P. Cremonesi, Y. Koren, and R. Turrin. Performance of recommender algorithms on top-n recommendation tasks. In *RecSys*, pages 39–46, 2010.

[8] N. Du, L. Song, H. Woo, and H. Zha. Uncover topic-sensitive information diffusion networks. In *AISTATS*, pages 229–237, 2013.

[9] S. Fazeli, B. Loni, A. Bellogin, H. Drachsler, and P. Sloep. Implicit vs. explicit trust in social matrix factorization. In *RecSys*, pages 317–320, 2014.

[10] J. Golbeck and J. Hendler. FilmTrust: Movie recommendations using trust in web-based social networks. *TOIT*, 6(4):497–529, Jan. 2006.

[11] P. Gopalan, J. M. Hofman, and D. M. Blei. Scalable recommendation with hierarchical Poisson factorization. In *UAI*, pages 326–335, 2015.

[12] A. Guille, H. Hacid, C. Favre, and D. A. Zighed. Information diffusion in online social networks: A survey. *SIGMOD Record*, 42(2):17–28, July 2013.

[13] G. Guo, J. Zhang, D. Thalmann, and N. Yorke-Smith. Etaf: An extended trust antecedents framework for trust prediction. In *ASONAM*, pages 540–547, 2014.

[14] G. Guo, J. Zhang, and N. Yorke-Smith. TrustSVD: Collaborative filtering with both the explicit and implicit influence of user trust and of item ratings. *AAAI*, pages 123–129, 2015.

[15] J. L. Herlocker, J. A. Konstan, and J. Riedl. Explaining collaborative filtering recommendations. In *CSCW*, pages 241–250, 2000.

[16] M. Hoffman, D. Blei, C. Wang, and J. Paisley. Stochastic variational inference. *Journal of Machine Learning Research*, 14(1303–1347), 2013.

[17] M. Jamali and M. Ester. A matrix factorization technique with trust propagation for recommendation in social networks. In *RecSys*, pages 135–142, 2010.

[18] J. Johnstone and E. Katz. Youth and popular music: A study in the sociology of taste. *Journal of Sociology*, 62(6):563–568, May 1957.

[19] M. I. Jordan, Z. Ghahramani, T. S. Jaakkola, and L. K. Saul. An introduction to variational methods for graphical models. *Machine Learning*, 37(2):183–233, Nov. 1999.

[20] Y. Koren, R. Bell, and C. Volinsky. Matrix factorization techniques for recommender systems. *IEEE Computer*, 42:30–37, 2009.

[21] D. D. Lee and H. S. Seung. Algorithms for non-negative matrix factorization. In *NIPS*, pages 556–562, 2000.

[22] J. Leskovec, A. Singh, and J. Kleinberg. Patterns of influence in a recommendation network. In *PAKDD*, pages 380–389, 2006.

[23] D. Loiacono, A. Lommatzsch, and R. Turrin. An analysis of the 2014 recsys challenge. In *RecSysChallenge*, page 1, 2014.

[24] H. Ma, I. King, and M. R. Lyu. Learning to recommend with social trust ensemble. In *SIGIR*, pages 203–210, 2009.

[25] H. Ma, H. Yang, M. R. Lyu, and I. King. SoRec: Social recommendation using probabilistic matrix factorization. In *CIKM*, pages 931–940, 2008.

[26] H. Ma, D. Zhou, C. Liu, M. R. Lyu, and I. King. Recommender systems with social regularization. In *WSDM*, pages 287–296, 2011.

[27] P. Massa and P. Avesani. Trust-aware recommender systems. In *RecSys*, pages 17–24, 2007.

[28] S. Purushotham, Y. Liu, and C.-C. J. Kuo. Collaborative topic regression with social matrix factorization for recommendation systems. *CoRR*, abs/1206.4684, 2012.

[29] R. Salakhutdinov and A. Mnih. Probabilistic matrix factorization. In *NIPS*, pages 1257–1264, 2007.

[30] S. Shang, P. Hui, S. R. Kulkarni, and P. W. Cuff. Wisdom of the crowd: Incorporating social influence in recommendation models. In *ICPADS*, pages 835–840, 2011.

[31] P. Singh, G. Singh, and A. Bhardwaj. Ranking approach to recsys challenge. In *RecSysChallenge*, page 19, 2014.

[32] X. Su and T. M. Khoshgoftaar. A survey of collaborative filtering techniques. *Advances in Artificial Intelligence*, page 4, Jan. 2009.

[33] I. P. Volz. The impact of online music services on the demand for stars in the music industry. In *WWW*, pages 659–667, 2006.

[34] B. Yang, Y. Lei, D. Liu, and J. Liu. Social collaborative filtering by trust. In *IJCAI*, pages 2747–2753, 2013.

[35] M. Ye, X. Liu, and W.-C. Lee. Exploring social influence for recommendation: A generative model approach. In *SIGIR*, pages 671–680, 2012.

[36] T. Zhao, J. McAuley, and I. King. Leveraging social connections to improve personalized ranking for collaborative filtering. In *CIKM*, pages 261–270, 2014.

APPENDIX

In this appendix, we describe the details of the variational inference algorithm for SPF. This algorithm fits the parameters of the variational distribution in Eq. 3 so that it is close in KL divergence to the posterior. We use coordinate ascent, iteratively updating each parameter while holding the others fixed. This goes uphill in the variational objective and converges to a local optimum [4].

To obtain simple updates, we first construct auxiliary latent variables z. These variables, when marginalized out, leave the original model intact. Recall the additive property of the Poisson distribution. Specifically, if $r \sim \text{Poisson}(a + b)$ then $r = z_1 + z_2$, where $z_1 \sim \text{Poisson}(a)$ and $z_2 \sim \text{Poisson}(b)$. We apply this decomposition to the conditional click count distribution in Eq. 1. We define Poisson variables for each term in the click count:

$$z_{uik}^M \sim \text{Poisson}(\theta_{uk}\beta_{ik}) \quad z_{uiv}^S \sim \text{Poisson}(\tau_{uv}r_{vi}).$$

The M and S superscripts indicate the contributions from matrix factorization (general preferences) and social factorization (influence), respectively. Given these variables, the click count is deterministic,

$$r_{ui} \mid r_{-u,i} = \sum_{k=1}^{K} z_{uik}^M + \sum_{v=1}^{V} z_{uiv}^S,$$

where $V = |N(u)|$ and the index v selects a friend of u (as opposed to selecting from the set of all users).

Coordinate-ascent variational inference is derived from the complete conditionals, i.e., the conditional distributions of each variable given the other variables and observations. These conditionals define both the form of each variational factor and their updates. For the Gamma variables—the user preferences, item attributes, and user influence—the conditionals are

$$\theta_{uk} \mid \beta, \tau, z, \mathbf{R}, \mathbf{N} \sim \text{Gam}\left(a_\theta + \sum_i z_{uik}^M, b_\theta + \sum_i \beta_{ik}\right) \quad (5)$$

$$\beta_{ik} \mid \theta, \tau, z, \mathbf{R}, \mathbf{N} \sim \text{Gam}\left(a_\beta + \sum_u z_{uik}^M, b_\beta + \sum_u \theta_{uk}\right) \quad (6)$$

$$\tau_{uv} \mid \theta, \beta, z, \mathbf{R}, \mathbf{N} \sim \text{Gam}\left(a_\tau + \sum_i z_{uiv}^S, b_\tau + \sum_i r_{vi}\right). \quad (7)$$

The complete conditional for the auxiliary variables is $z_{ui} \mid \theta, \beta, \tau, \mathbf{R}, \mathbf{N} \sim \text{Mult}(r_{ui}, \phi_{ui})$ where

$$\phi_{ui} \propto \left\langle \theta_{u1}\beta_{i1}, \cdots, \theta_{uK}\beta_{iK}, \tau_{u1}r_{1i}, \cdots, \tau_{uV}r_{Vi} \right\rangle. \quad (8)$$

(Intuitively, these variables allocate the data to one of the factors or one of the friends.) Each variational factor is set to the same family as its corresponding complete conditional.

Given these conditionals, the algorithm sets each parameter to the expected conditional parameter under the variational distribution. (Thanks to the mean field assumption, this expectation will not involve the parameter being updated.) Note that under a gamma distribution, $\text{E}[\lambda] = \lambda_a/\lambda_b$, where λ_a and λ_b are shape and rate parameters. For the auxiliary variables, the expectation of the indicator is the probability, $\text{E}[z_{ui}] = r_{ui} * \phi_{ui}$.

Algorithm 1 shows our variational inference algorithm. It is $O(N(K+V))$ per iteration, where N is the number of recorded user-item interactions (click counts, ratings, etc.). K is the number of latent factors, and V is the maximum user degree. (Note that both K and V are usually small relative to N.) We can modify the algorithm to sample users and update the variables stochastically [16]; this approach scales to much larger datasets than competing methods.

Algorithm 1 Mean field variational inference SPF

1: initialize $\text{E}[\theta]$, $\text{E}[\beta]$ randomly
2: **for** each user u **do**
3:     **for** each friend $v \in N(u)$ **do**
4:         $\lambda_{u,v}^{\tau,b} \leftarrow$ prior $b_\tau + \sum_i r_{vi}$ ▷ see Eq. 7
5: **while** $\Delta \log \mathcal{L} > \delta$ **do**   ▷ check for model convergence
6:     init. global $\lambda^{\beta,a}$ to prior a_β for all items and all factors
7:     **for** each user u **do**
8:         **while** $\Delta[\theta_u] + \Delta[\tau_u] > \delta'$ **do**   ▷ user convergence
9:             init. local $\lambda^{\beta,a}$ to 0 for all items and factors
10:            init. preferences $\lambda_u^{\theta,a}$ to prior a_θ for all factors
11:            $\lambda_u^{\theta,b} \leftarrow$ prior $b_\theta + \sum_i \text{E}[\beta_i]$ ▷ see Eq. 5
12:            init. influence $\lambda_{user}^{\tau,a}$ to prior a_τ for all friends
13:            **for** each (item i, click count r) $\in clicks_u$ **do**
14:                set ϕ_{ui} from $\text{E}[\theta_u], \text{E}[\beta_i], \text{E}[\tau_u]$, and r_i (Eq. 8)
15:                $\text{E}[z_{ui}] = r * \phi_{ui}$
16:                update $\lambda_u^{\theta,a} \mathrel{+}= \text{E}[z_{ui}^M]$ ▷ see Eq. 5
17:                update $\lambda_u^{\tau,a} \mathrel{+}= \text{E}[z_{ui}^S]$ ▷ see Eq. 7
18:                update local $\lambda_i^{\beta,a} \mathrel{+}= \text{E}[z_{ui}^M]$ ▷ see Eq. 6
19:            $\text{E}[\theta_u] = \lambda_u^{\theta,a}/\lambda_u^{\theta,b}$
20:            $\text{E}[\tau_u] = \lambda_u^{\tau,a}/\lambda_u^{\tau,b}$
21:            global $\lambda^{\beta,a} \mathrel{+}= $ local $\lambda^{\beta,a}$
22:     $\lambda^{\beta,b} = $ prior $b_\beta + \sum_u \text{E}[\theta_u]$ ▷ see Eq. 6
23:     $\text{E}[\beta] = \lambda^{\beta,a}/\lambda^{\beta,b}$

To assess convergence, we use the change in the average click log likelihood of a validation set.

PushTrust: An Efficient Recommendation Algorithm by Leveraging Trust and Distrust Relations

Rana Forsati
Computer Science &
Engineering
Michigan State University
forsati@cse.msu.edu

Iman Barjasteh
Electrical & Computer
Engineering
Michigan State University
barjaste@msu.edu

Farzan Masrour
Department of Statistics &
Probability
Michigan State University
masrour@msu.edu

Abdol-Hossein Esfahanian
Computer Science &
Engineering
Michigan State University
esfahanian@cse.msu.edu

Hayder Radha
Electrical & Computer
Engineering
Michigan State University
radha@egr.msu.edu

ABSTRACT

The significance of social-enhanced recommender systems is increasing, along with its practicality, as online reviews, ratings, friendship links, and follower relationships are increasingly becoming available. In recent years, there has been an upsurge of interest in exploiting social information, such as trust and distrust relations in recommendation algorithms. The goal is to improve the quality of suggestions and mitigate the data sparsity and the cold-start users problems in existing systems. In this paper, we introduce a general *collaborative social ranking* model to rank the latent features of users extracted from rating data based on the social context of users. In contrast to existing social regularization methods, the proposed framework is able to simultaneously leverage trust, distrust, and neutral relations, and has a linear dependency on the social network size. By integrating the ranking based social regularization idea into the matrix factorization algorithm, we propose a novel recommendation algorithm, dubbed `PushTrust`. Our experiments on the Epinions dataset demonstrate that collaboratively ranking the latent features of users by exploiting trust and distrust relations leads to a substantial increase in performance, and to effectively deal with cold-start users problem.

Categories and Subject Descriptors

H.3.3 [**Information Search and Retrieval**]: Relevance feedback; D.2.8 [**Software Engineering**]: Metrics—*complexity measures, performance measures*

General Terms

Algorithms, Measurement, Performance, Experimentation

Keywords

Collaborative filtering; Matrix factorization; Social regularization; Collaborative social ranking

RecSys'15, September 16–20, 2015, Vienna, Austria.
© 2015 ACM. ISBN 978-1-4503-3692-5/15/09 ...$15.00.
DOI: http://dx.doi.org/10.1145/2792838.2800198.

1. INTRODUCTION

Recommender systems have become ubiquitous in recent years, and are applied in a variety of applications [12]. Typically, the recommendation system selects a small set from the underlying pool of items (e.g., products, news, movies, books) to recommend to an active user. The user can either like (e.g., read, click, buy, etc.) or dislike the items in the list, or take no action. Content-based filtering (CB) and collaborative filtering (CF) are well-known examples of recommendation approaches. As demonstrated in KDD Cup [5] and Netflix competition [2], the most successful recommendation technique used is collaborative filtering which exploits the users' opinions (e.g., movie ratings) and/or purchasing (e.g., watching, reading) history in order to extract a set of interesting items for each user. In fictionalization based CF methods, both users and items are mapped into a latent feature space based on observed ratings that are later used to make predictions.

Despite significant improvements on recommendation approaches, and in particular collaborative filtering based methods, these systems suffer from a few inherent limitations that must be addressed. In particular, these techniques suffer from data sparsity in real-world scenarios and fail to address users who rated few or no items or items that have not been rated by any user– commonly known as cold-start users and items problems, respectively. For instance, according to [24], the density of extant ratings in most commercial recommender systems is often much less than one.

In recent years there has been an upsurge of interest in exploiting social information such as trust relations among users along with rating data to improve the performance of recommender systems and resolve sparsity and cold-start problems (see e.g. [29, 25, 6] for more recent surveys). A well-known example is the `FilmTrust` system [7]. This is an online social network that provides movie rating and review features to its users. The social networking component of the website requires users to provide a trust rating for each person they add as a friend. The main motivation for exploiting trust information in recommendation process stems from the observation that the ideas we are exposed to and the choices we make are significantly influenced by our social context. For example, in [26] it was pointed out that people tend to rely more on recommendations from others they trust more than recommendations based on anonymous people similar to them. This observation, combined with the growing popularity of open social networks, has generated a rising interest in trust-enhanced recommendation systems. Based on this intuition, a few trust-aware recommendation methods have been proposed [15, 19, 10].

Recently, online networks where two opposite kind of relationships can occur have become common. For instance, the Epinions [8], an e-commerce site for reviewing and rating products, allows users to evaluate others based on the quality of their reviews, and make trust and distrust relations with them. Similar patterns can be found in online communities such as Slashdot in which millions of users post news and comment daily and are capable of tagging other users as friends/foes or fans/freaks. Additionally, users on Wikipedia can vote for or against the nomination of others to adminship [4]. When more users issuing distrust statements, the more important it will become to exploit this new information source in recommender systems.

It is acknowledged that along with the trust relationships, also distrust can play an important role in boosting the accuracy of recommendations [29, 28, 6]. Recently, some attempts have been made to explicitly incorporate the distrust relations in recommendation process [8, 16, 28]. This demonstrated that the recommender systems can benefit from the proper incorporation of distrust relations in social networks. However, despite these positive results, there are some unique challenges involved in distrust-enhanced recommender systems. In particular, it has proven challenging to model distrust propagation in a manner which is both logically consistent and psychologically plausible. Furthermore, the naive modeling of distrust as negative trust raises a number of challenges- both algorithmic and philosophical. Finally, it is an open challenge how to best incorporate trust and distrust relations in model-based methods, e.g., matrix factorization, simultaneously. In memory based recommender systems, the simultaneous exploitation of trust and distrust has been investigated in [30, 27].

An attempt to simultaneously exploit trust and distrust relations in factorization based method has been made very recently in [6]. In particular, a ranking model was proposed to rank the latent features of users, from the perspective of individual users, that respects their social context. Despite the encouraging improvements that has been brought by simultaneous exploitation of trust and distrust relations, the proposed algorithm suffers from two issues. First, as the number of constraint triplets imposed from social regularization of latent features can increase cubically in the number of users in the social network, it is computationally difficult to make their idea scalable to large social graphs. Second, the algorithm proposed in [6] only considers the trusted and distrusted friends of each user in order to regularize the latent features. Thus, it ignores the neutral friends – the users who has no relation to the user. As a result, the neutral friends might appear before the trusted friends in the ranked list. Therefore neutral friends might become more influential than trusted friends and impact the recommendation negatively.

In this paper we describe and analyze a fairly general and flexible method to learn and infer from rating data, along with trust and distrust relationships between users. The main building block of our proposed algorithm, dubbed PushTrust, is an efficient algorithm to rank the latent features of users by leveraging their social context. In ranking of latent features, we wish to make sure that the top portion of the list includes the trusted friends and the distrusted friends are pushed to the bottom of list. Also, we would like the neutral friends appear after trusted and before distrusted friends in the list. Compared to the method proposed in [6], the key features of the PushTrust algorithm are: (i) its quadratic time complexity in the number of users, and (ii) its ability to take the neutral friends of users into the consideration in regularizing the latent features of users. Thorough experiments on on the Epinions dataset demonstrate the merits of the proposed algorithm in boosting the quality of recommendations and dealing with data sparsity and cold-start users problems.

Outline. The paper is organized as follows. In Section 2 we give a formal definition of our setting and briefly review the existing social enhanced matrix factorization methods. The PushTrust algorithm and its associated optimization method are presented in Section 3. Experiments are provided in Section 4 and concluding remarks with few directions as future work are given in Section 5.

2. SOCIAL ENHANCED MATRIX FACTORIZATION

In this section we establish the notation used throughout the paper and formally describe our problem setting.

We adopt the following notation throughout the paper. Scalars are denoted by lower case letters and vectors by bold face lower case letters such as $\mathbf{u}$. We use bold face upper case letters such as $\mathbf{A}$ to denote matrices. The Frobenius norm of a matrix $\mathbf{A} \in \mathbb{R}^{n \times m}$ is denoted by $\|\mathbf{A}\|_{\mathrm{F}}$, i.e, $\|\mathbf{A}\|_{\mathrm{F}} = \sqrt{\sum_{i=1}^{n} \sum_{j=1}^{m} |\mathbf{A}_{ij}|^2}$ and its (i, j)th entry is denoted by $\mathbf{A}_{i,j}$. The transpose of a vector and a matrix denoted by $\mathbf{u}^\top$ and $\mathbf{U}^\top$, respectively. We use $[n]$ to denote the set on integers $\{1, 2, \cdots, n\}$. The set of non-negative real numbers is denoted by $\mathbb{R}_+$. The indicator function is denoted by $\mathbb{I}[\cdot]$. For a vector $\mathbf{u} \in \mathbb{R}^p$ we use $\|\mathbf{u}\|_1 = \sum_{i=1}^{p} |u_i|$, $\|\mathbf{u}\|_2 = \left(\sum_{i=1}^{p} |u_i|^2\right)^{1/2}$, and $\|\mathbf{u}\|_\infty = \max_{1 \leq i \leq p} u_i$ to denote its ℓ_1, ℓ_2, and ℓ_∞ norms, respectively. The dot product between two vectors $\mathbf{u}$ and $\mathbf{u}'$ is denoted by either $\langle \mathbf{u}, \mathbf{u}' \rangle$ or $\mathbf{u}^\top \mathbf{u}'$. We use $[z]_+ = \max(0, z)$ to denote the positive component of a scalar.

2.1 Matrix factorization for recommendation

In collaborative filtering we assume that there is a set of n users $\mathcal{U} = \{u_1, \cdots, u_n\}$ and a set of m items $\mathcal{I} = \{i_1, \cdots, i_m\}$ where each user u_i expresses opinions about a set of items. In this paper, we assume opinions are expressed through an explicit numeric rating (e.g., scale from one to five), but other rating methods such as hyperlink clicks are possible as well. We are mainly interested in recommending a set of items for an active user such that the user has not rated these items before. To this end, we are aimed at learning a model from the existing ratings, i.e., *offline phase*, and then use the learned model to generate recommendations for active users, i.e., *online phase*. The rating information is summarized in an $n \times m$ matrix $\mathbf{R} \in \mathbb{R}^{n \times m}, 1 \leq i \leq n, 1 \leq j \leq m$ where the rows correspond to the users and the columns correspond to the items and (p, q)th entry is the rate given by user u_p to the item i_q. We note that the rating matrix is partially observed and it is sparse in most cases.

An efficient and effective approach to recommender systems is to factorize the user-item rating matrix $\mathbf{R}$ by a multiplicative of k-rank matrices $\mathbf{R} \approx \mathbf{U}\mathbf{V}^\top$, where $\mathbf{U} \in \mathbb{R}^{n \times k}$ and $\mathbf{V} \in \mathbb{R}^{m \times k}$ utilize the factorized user-specific and item-specific matrices, respectively, to make further missing data prediction. There are two basic formulations to solve this problem: these are optimization based (see e.g., [22, 14, 17, 13]) and probabilistic [20]. Let $\Omega_\mathbf{R}$ be the set of observed ratings in the user-item matrix $\mathbf{R} \in \mathbb{R}^{n \times m}$, i.e., $\Omega_\mathbf{R} = \{(i, j) \in [n] \times [m] : \mathbf{R}_{ij} \text{ has been observed}\}$, where

n is the number of users and m is the number of items to be rated. In optimization based matrix factorization, the goal is to learn the latent matrices $\mathbf{U}$ and $\mathbf{V}$ by solving the following optimization problem:

$$\mathcal{F}(\mathbf{U}, \mathbf{V}) = \frac{1}{2} \sum_{(i,j) \in \Omega_{\mathbf{R}}} \left(\mathbf{R}_{i,j} - \mathbf{u}_i^\top \mathbf{v}_j \right)^2 + \lambda_{\mathbf{U}} \|\mathbf{U}\|_F^2 + \lambda_{\mathbf{V}} \|\mathbf{V}\|_F^2$$

(1)

The optimization problem in Eq. (1) constitutes of three terms: the first term aims to minimize the inconsistency between the observed entries and their corresponding value obtained by the factorized matrices. The last two terms regularize the latent matrices for users and items, respectively. The parameters $\lambda_{\mathbf{U}}$ and $\lambda_{\mathbf{V}}$ are regularization parameters that are introduced to control the regularization of latent matrices $\mathbf{U}$ and $\mathbf{V}$, respectively.

2.2 Matrix factorization with social regularization

In this section we briefly review the existing factorization methods that are capable of exploiting social context of users. The general theme in these methods is to regularize the latent features of users based on their social context.

To incorporate the trust relations in the optimization problem formulated in Eq. (1), few papers [16, 11, 18, 14] proposed the social regularization method which aims at keeping the latent vector of each user similar to his/her trusted neighbors in the social network. The proposed models force the user feature vectors to be close to those of their neighbors to be able to learn the latent features of users with no or very few ratings [11]. More specifically, the optimization problem becomes as:

$$\mathcal{F}(\mathbf{U}, \mathbf{V}) = \frac{1}{2} \sum_{(i,j) \in \Omega_{\mathbf{R}}} \left(\mathbf{R}_{ij} - \mathbf{u}_i^\top \mathbf{v}_j \right)^2 + \frac{\lambda_{\mathbf{U}}}{2} \|\mathbf{U}\|_F + \frac{\lambda_{\mathbf{V}}}{2} \|\mathbf{V}\|_F$$
$$+ \frac{\lambda_{\mathbf{S}}}{2} \sum_{i=1}^{n} \left\| \mathbf{u}_i - \frac{1}{|\mathcal{N}^+(i)|} \sum_{j \in \mathcal{N}^+(i)} \mathbf{u}_j \right\|,$$

(2)

where $\lambda_{\mathbf{S}}$ is the social regularization parameter and $\mathcal{N}^+(i) \subseteq \mathcal{V}$ is the subset of users who have trust relationships with ith user in the social graph.

In a similar way one can exploit the distrust relations by forcing the latent features of each user to be as far as possible from the average of latent features of his/her distrusted friends formulated by:

$$\mathcal{F}(\mathbf{U}, \mathbf{V}) = \frac{1}{2} \sum_{(i,j) \in \Omega_{\mathbf{R}}} \left(\mathbf{R}_{ij} - \mathbf{u}_i^\top \mathbf{v}_j \right)^2 + \frac{\lambda_{\mathbf{U}}}{2} \|\mathbf{U}\|_F + \frac{\lambda_{\mathbf{V}}}{2} \|\mathbf{V}\|_F$$
$$- \frac{\lambda_{\mathbf{S}}}{2} \sum_{i=1}^{n} \left\| \mathbf{u}_i - \frac{1}{|\mathcal{N}^-(i)|} \sum_{j \in \mathcal{N}^-(i)} \mathbf{u}_j \right\|,$$

(3)

where $\mathcal{N}^-(i) \subseteq \mathcal{V}$ is the subset of users who have distrust relationships with ith user in the social graph.

It is remarkable that while intuition and experimental evidence indicate that trust is somewhat transitive, distrust is certainly not transitive. Therefore, the distrust can not be considered as the negative of trust relations in social network [28]. As a result, simultaneous exploitation of trust and distrust relationships is not as straightforward as exploiting either trust or distrust relations. In a very recent work [6], the authors proposed the first matrix factorization based recommender algorithm that is able to exploit both types of relationships in factorization. The main idea is to learning

the latent features for each user u such that users trusted by u in the social network (with positive edges) are close and users which are distrusted by u (with negative edges) are more distant. Learning latent features in this way basically induces a ranking of latent features of each user's neighbors where the trusted friends appear on the top of the list and distrusted friends move to the bottom of the list.

To formalize the ranking idea in learning the latent features, let $\Omega_{\mathbf{S}}$ denote the set of triplets (i, j, k) where ith user trust jth user and distrusts kth user in the social relations, i.e., $\Omega_{\mathbf{S}} = \{(i, j, k) \in [n] \times [n] \times [n] : \mathbf{S}_{ij} = 1 \ \& \ \mathbf{S}_{ik} = -1\}$. Then the objective of factorization becomes:

$$\mathcal{F}(\mathbf{U}, \mathbf{V}) = \frac{1}{2} \sum_{(i,j) \in \Omega_{\mathbf{R}}} \left(\mathbf{R}_{ij} - \mathbf{u}_i^\top \mathbf{v}_j \right)^2 + \frac{\lambda_{\mathbf{U}}}{2} \|\mathbf{U}\|_{\mathbf{F}} + \frac{\lambda_{\mathbf{V}}}{2} \|\mathbf{V}\|_{\mathbf{F}}$$
$$+ \frac{\lambda_{\mathbf{S}}}{2} \sum_{(i,j,k) \in \Omega_{\mathbf{S}}} \left[1 - \|\mathbf{u}_i - \mathbf{u}_j\|^2 + \|\mathbf{u}_i - \mathbf{u}_k\|^2 \right]_+,$$

(4)

where the third term is introduced to regularize the latent features of users who violate the ranking constraints.

As mentioned earlier, the simultaneous exploitation of trust and distrust has been investigated in memory based recommender systems too [30, 27]. The main rational behind the algorithm proposed in [30] is to employ the distrust information to debug or filter out the users' propagated web of trust. It is also has been realized that the debugging methods must exhibit a moderate behavior in order to be effective. [27] addressed the problem of considering the length of the paths that connect two users for computing trust-distrust between them, according to the concept of *trust decay*. This work also introduced several aggregation strategies for trust scores with variable path lengths.

3. THE PUSHTRUST ALGORITHM

In this section we introduce the collaborative social ranking framework for social recommendation which, in contrast to social regularization based methods, is able to incorporate both trust and distrust relationships in the social network along with the partially observed rating matrix.

3.1 Collaborative social ranking

Before delving into the mathematical formulation, we first discuss the main idea behind the proposed PushTrust algorithm. As discussed earlier, to incorporate the social context of users in the factorization model, the appropriate latent features for users must be found such that each user is brought closer to the users she/he trusts and separated from the users that she/he distrusts and have different interests. We note that simply incorporating this idea in matrix factorization, by naively penalizing the similarity of each user's latent features to his distrusted friends' latent features, fails to reach the desired goal. The main reason is that distrust is not as transitive as trust and can not directly replace trust in trust propagation approaches. Therefore, simultaneously utilizing distrust and trust relations in matrix factorization requires careful consideration (trust is transitive, i.e., if user u trusts user v and v trusts w, there is a good chance that u will trust w, but distrust is certainly not transitive, i.e., if u distrusts v and v distrusts w, then w may be closer to u than v or maybe even farther away). This observation implies that distrust should not be used as a way to reverse deviations. This statement is consistent with the preliminary experimental results in [28] for memory-based CF methods which revealed that taking distrust as the negative of trust relations is not the correct way to incorporate distrust in recommender systems.

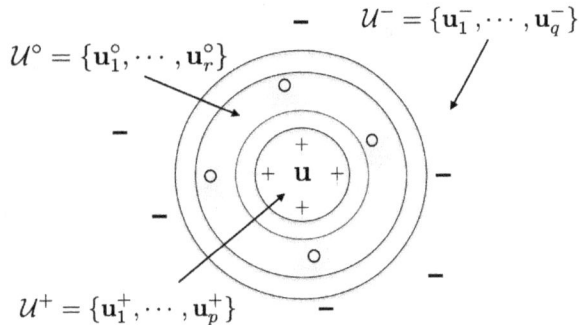

$\mathcal{U}^\circ = \{\mathbf{u}_1^\circ, \cdots, \mathbf{u}_r^\circ\}$

$\mathcal{U}^- = \{\mathbf{u}_1^-, \cdots, \mathbf{u}_q^-\}$

$\mathcal{U}^+ = \{\mathbf{u}_1^+, \cdots, \mathbf{u}_p^+\}$

Figure 1: **The ultimate goal is to extract latent features from the rating matrix R in a way that respects the social context of users in social network S. In particular, from each user's perspective, say user u, the goal is to find latent features for u's neighbors such that when ranked based on their similarity to the latent features of the user u, i.e., $\mathbf{u} \in \mathbb{R}^k$, the trusted friends $\mathcal{N}^+(u)$ are pushed to the top portion of the list, the distrusted friends $\mathcal{N}^-(u)$ are pushed to the bottom of the list, and the neutral friends $\mathcal{N}^\circ(u)$ appear in the middle of ranked list.**

Motivated by this negative result, in [6] the ranking of latent features of neighbors of users based on the type of their relations has been shown as a suitable solution to incorporate both trust and distrust relations. The goal was to construct a ranking of latent features of all users based on their similarity such that trusted friends get a higher rank/score than the distrusted friends. In particular, from a ranking perspective, the similarity of latent features induce an ordering over all users where trusted users are pushed to top of the list.

However, the ranking method proposed in [6] suffers from two main issues. First, when the neighbors of a specific user u are considered in the ranking model based on the similarity of their latent features to latent features of u, the neutral users who have no relation to u are ignored. This might cause the neutral friends to appear any place in the ranking (e.g., above the trusted friends or below the distrusted friends). This affects the quality of recommendations significantly. More specifically, this contradicts our basic assumption on the effectiveness of social information, which relies on the fact that people tend to rely more on recommendations from people they trust than recommendations based on anonymous people. Therefore, in sharp contrast to [6] which excludes the users who have no relation to a specific user, we also model these users in learning the latent features by forcing them to appear in the ranked list after the trusted friends yet before the distrusted friends. This matches our intuition as we expect neutral friends' contribution to the prediction not to be better than the contribution of trusted friends and worse than the contribution distrusted friends.

Moreover, the number of constraints imposed by social regularization in the ranking model proposed in [6] increases cubically with the number of users in the network. This growth limits the applicability of their method to small scale social networks. To resolve this issue, we introduce a novel raking model that only introduces a quadratic number of constraints into the factorization objective, thus making it more favorable for large scale social networks.

The main intuition behind the ranking model utilized in the `PushTrust` algorithm is shown in Figure 3.1. To keep our discussion simple and easy to follow, we consider the social regularization for a single user u with latent features vector $\mathbf{u} \in \mathbb{R}^k$. Let $\mathcal{N}^+(u) = \{v \in [n] \mid \mathbf{S}_{uv} = +1\}$, $\mathcal{N}^-(u) = \{v \in [n] \mid \mathbf{S}_{uv} = -1\}$ be the set of trusted and distrusted neighbors of u in the social network, respectively. Also let $\mathcal{N}^\circ(u) = \mathcal{V} \setminus (\mathcal{N}^+(u) \cup \mathcal{N}^-(u))$ be the set of users for whom the user u is not socially connected, i.e, $\mathcal{N}^\circ(u) = \{v \in [n] \mid \mathbf{S}_{uv} = 0\}$. If we rank the latent features of users from the viewpoint of user u, we wish the trusted friends $\mathcal{N}^+(u)$ have the maximum similarity to u and are pushed to the top portion of the ranked list. Similarly, the distrusted friends $\mathcal{N}^-(u)$ are expected to have less similarity to $\mathbf{u}$ and appear at the bottom portion of the ranked list. The set of neutral users who are not connected to user u, i.e., $\mathcal{N}^\circ(u)$ are potentially either trusted or distorted. As a result, a conservative decision is to place the latent features of neutral users after trusted and before distrusted friends. To accomplish this goal, we introduce a social regularization term for each user $u \in \mathcal{U}$, where the the latent features of the user $\mathbf{u}$ is penalized based on the deviation of ranking of u's neighbors from the optimal ranking discussed above.

3.2 A convex formulation for social ranking

To simplify the analysis we rewrite the social regularized matrix factorization problem as:

$$\mathcal{F}(\mathbf{U}, \mathbf{V}) = \frac{1}{2} \sum_{(i,j) \in \Omega_\mathbf{R}} \left(\mathbf{R}_{ij} - \mathbf{u}_i^\top \mathbf{v}_j\right)^2 + \frac{\lambda_\mathbf{V}}{2} \|\mathbf{V}\|_\mathrm{F}$$
$$+ \frac{\lambda_\mathbf{U}}{2} \|\mathbf{U}\|_\mathrm{F}^2 + \lambda_\mathbf{S} \sum_{i=1}^n \mathcal{P}(\mathbf{u}_i),$$

where $\mathcal{P} : \mathbb{R}^k \mapsto \mathbb{R}_+$ is the social regularization of latent features of individual users.

The formalization of discussed intuition on social regularization of latent features of users is as follows. Let $\mathcal{U}^+ = \{\mathbf{u}_1^+, \mathbf{u}_2^+, \cdots, \mathbf{u}_p^+\}$, $\mathcal{U}^- = \{\mathbf{u}_1^-, \mathbf{u}_2^-, \cdots, \mathbf{u}_q^-\}$, and $\mathcal{U}^\circ = \{\mathbf{u}_1^\circ, \mathbf{u}_2^\circ, \cdots, \mathbf{u}_r^\circ\}$ be the set of latent features of users in $\mathcal{N}^+(u)$, $\mathcal{N}^-(u)$, and $\mathcal{N}^\circ(u)$, respectively, where $p = |\mathcal{N}^+(u)|$, $q = |\mathcal{N}^-(u)|$, and $r = |\mathcal{N}^\circ(u)|$. The similarity between the latent features of u and their neighbor v in the network is measured by $\langle \mathbf{u}, \mathbf{u}_v \rangle$. A naive implementation of ranking idea is to consider the triplet of latent features which yields a large number of constraints to be satisfied. However, here we rely on the recent methods that assist with rank learning to rank, such as p-norm push, infinite push, and reverse-height push [23, 1], to order the latent features based on their similarity to the latent features of u. In particular, we define the following ranking function that tries to put as many possible trusted friends before the most similar distrusted and neutral friends. As it will be revealed later in this section, this formulation results in a significant decrease in the number of constraints that only linearly depends on the number of users in the social network. Formally, for user u we define the following objective as its social regularization:

$$\mathcal{P}(\mathbf{u}) = \frac{1}{p} \sum_{i=1}^p \mathbb{I}\left[\langle \mathbf{u}, \mathbf{u}_i^+ \rangle \leq \max_{1 \leq j \leq q} \langle \mathbf{u}, \mathbf{u}_j^- \rangle\right]$$
$$+ \frac{1}{p} \sum_{i=1}^p \mathbb{I}\left[\langle \mathbf{u}, \mathbf{u}_i^+ \rangle \leq \max_{1 \leq j \leq r} \langle \mathbf{u}, \mathbf{u}_j^\circ \rangle\right] \quad (5)$$
$$+ \frac{1}{r} \sum_{i=1}^r \mathbb{I}\left[\langle \mathbf{u}, \mathbf{u}_i^\circ \rangle \leq \max_{1 \leq j \leq q} \langle \mathbf{u}, \mathbf{u}_j^- \rangle\right],$$

Algorithm 1 `PushTrust Algorithm`

1: **Input: R** $\in \mathbb{R}^{n \times m}$: the partially observed rating matrix, $\Omega_{\mathbf{R}} \subseteq [n] \times [m]$: the set of observed ratings in **R**, **S** $\in \{-1, 0, +1\}^{n \times n}$: the social graph between users
1: $\lambda_{\mathbf{U}}, \lambda_{\mathbf{V}}, \lambda_{\mathbf{S}} \in \mathbb{R}_+$: the regularization parameters
2: **for** $t = 1, \ldots, T$ **do**
3:    **for** $i = 1, \ldots, n$ **do**
4:       Compute the gradient $\mathbf{g}^t_{\mathbf{u}_i}$ using Eq. (8)
5:       Set $\mathbf{u}^{t+1}_i = \mathbf{u}^t_i - \eta_t \mathbf{g}^t_{\mathbf{u}_i}$
6:    **end for**
7:    **for** $j = 1, \ldots, m$ **do**
8:       Compute the gradient $\mathbf{g}^t_{\mathbf{v}_j}$ using Eq. (9)
9:       Set $\mathbf{v}^{t+1}_j = \mathbf{v}^t_j - \eta_t \mathbf{g}^t_{\mathbf{v}_j}$
10:   **end for**
11: **end for**
12: **Output:** $\tilde{\mathbf{R}} = \mathbf{U}_T \mathbf{V}^\top_T$, where $\mathbf{U}_T = [\mathbf{u}^T_1, \ldots, \mathbf{u}^T_n]$ and $\mathbf{V}_T = [\mathbf{v}^T_1, \ldots, \mathbf{v}^T_m]$

---

where $\mathbb{I}[\cdot]$ is the indicator function which returns 1 when the input is true and 0 otherwise.

The social regularization in Eq. (5) consists of four terms. The first term is the standard regularization of latent features which is included to simplify the derivation of the objective. The second and third terms aim to put trusted friends at top of the ranked list based on their similarity to the latent features of u. Finally, the last term attempts to put neutral friends before the distrusted friends. Clearly, by minimizing the social regularization for each user; $\min_{\mathbf{u} \in \mathbb{R}^k} \mathcal{P}(\mathbf{u})$, it is guaranteed that the extracted latent features respect the social context of individual users discussed in section 4.1.

The above optimization problem is intractable due to the non-convex indicator function. To design practical learning algorithms, we replace the indicator function in Eq. (5) with its convex surrogate. To this end, define the convex loss function $\ell : \mathbb{R} \mapsto \mathbb{R}_+$ as $\ell(x) = [1 - x]_+$. This is the widely used hinge loss in SVM classification (see e.g., [3]) [1]. This loss function reflects the amount by which the constraints are not satisfied. By replacing the non-convex indicator function with this convex surrogate leads to the following tractable convex optimization problem:

$$
\begin{aligned}
\mathcal{P}(\mathbf{u}) = \quad & \frac{1}{p} \sum_{i=1}^{p} \ell \left(\langle \mathbf{u}, \mathbf{u}^+_i \rangle - \max_{1 \le j \le q} \langle \mathbf{u}, \mathbf{u}^-_j \rangle \right) \\
+ \quad & \frac{1}{p} \sum_{i=1}^{p} \ell \left(\langle \mathbf{u}, \mathbf{u}^+_i \rangle - \max_{1 \le j \le r} \langle \mathbf{u}, \mathbf{u}^\circ_j \rangle \right) \quad (6) \\
+ \quad & \frac{1}{r} \sum_{i=1}^{r} \ell \left(\langle \mathbf{u}, \mathbf{u}^\circ_i \rangle - \max_{1 \le j \le q} \langle \mathbf{u}, \mathbf{u}^-_j \rangle \right).
\end{aligned}
$$

Equipped with the social regularization of individual users, we now turn to the final matrix factorization objective. To do so, Let $\mathbf{U}^-_i = [\mathbf{u}^-_{i,1}, \cdots, \mathbf{u}^+_{i,q}]^\top$, and $\mathbf{U}^\circ_i = [\mathbf{u}^\circ_{i,1}, \cdots, \mathbf{u}^\circ_{i,r}]^\top$ denote the matrix of latent features of distrusted and neutral friends of ith user in the social network, respectively. Here $\mathbf{u}^-_{i,j}$ and $\mathbf{u}^\circ_{i,j}$ is the latent features of jth distrusted and neutral friends of the ith user, respectively.

---

[1] We note that other convex loss functions such as exponential loss $\ell(x) = \exp(-x)$, and logistic loss $\ell(x) = \log(1 + \exp(-x))$ also can be used as the surrogates of indicator function, but for the simplicity of derivation we only consider the hinge loss here.

Then, we have:

$$
\begin{aligned}
\mathcal{F}(\mathbf{U}, \mathbf{V}) = & \frac{1}{2} \sum_{(i,j) \in \Omega_{\mathbf{R}}} \left(\mathbf{R}_{ij} - \mathbf{u}^\top_i \mathbf{v}_j \right)^2 + \frac{\lambda_{\mathbf{V}}}{2} \|\mathbf{V}\|_{\mathrm{F}} + \frac{\lambda_{\mathbf{U}}}{2} \|\mathbf{U}\|^2_{\mathrm{F}} \\
& + \lambda_{\mathbf{S}} \sum_{i=1}^{n} \left(\frac{1}{p} \sum_{j \in \mathcal{N}^+(i)} \ell \left(\langle \mathbf{u}_i, \mathbf{u}^+_{i,j} \rangle - \|\mathbf{U}^-_i \mathbf{u}_i\|_\infty \right) \right) \\
& + \lambda_{\mathbf{S}} \sum_{i=1}^{n} \left(\frac{1}{p} \sum_{j \in \mathcal{N}^+(i)} \ell \left(\langle \mathbf{u}_i, \mathbf{u}^+_{i,j} \rangle - \|\mathbf{U}^\circ_i \mathbf{u}_i\|_\infty \right) \right) \\
& + \lambda_{\mathbf{S}} \sum_{i=1}^{n} \left(\frac{1}{r} \sum_{j \in \mathcal{N}^\circ(i)} \ell \left(\langle \mathbf{u}_i, \mathbf{u}^\circ_{i,j} \rangle - \|\mathbf{U}^-_i \mathbf{u}_i\|_\infty \right) \right).
\end{aligned}
$$

$$(7)$$

3.3 Optimization procedure

We now turn to solving the optimization problem in Eq. (7). We note that by excluding the ranking constraints from the formulation in Eq. (7), we get the standard matrix factorization objective as formulated in Eq. (1) which is non-convex jointly in both **U** and **V**. However, despite its non-convexity, it is widely used in practical collaborative filtering applications as the performance is competitive (or better) when compared to trace-norm minimization, while scalability is much better. For example, as indicated in [13], to address the Netflix problem, Eq. (1) has been applied with a fair amount of success to factorize datasets with 100 million ratings. To find a local solution one can stick to the standard gradient descent method to find a solution in an iterative manner.

The detailed steps of the proposed `PushTrust` algorithm in its most basic form are shown in Algorithm 1. The optimization is done by alternating minimization, i.e., updating **U** while keeping **V** fixed, and then updating **V** while keeping **U** fixed. The objective function is bi-convex, i.e., convex in one argument while keeping the other fixed. The updates of the latent factors for each user and each item can be done using gradient descent. In particular, a local minimum of the objective function can be found by performing gradient descent in feature vectors $\mathbf{u}_i$ and $\mathbf{v}_j$. To do so, we first compute the (sub)gradient of objective function $\mathcal{F}(\mathbf{U}, \mathbf{V})$ with respect to $\mathbf{u}_i$ and $\mathbf{v}_j$ as:

$$
\mathbf{g}_{\mathbf{u}_i} = \frac{\partial \mathcal{F}}{\partial \mathbf{u}_i} = \sum_{j=1}^{m} \mathbb{I}_{ij} (\mathbf{R}_{ij} - \mathbf{u}^\top_i \mathbf{v}_j) \mathbf{v}_j + \lambda_{\mathbf{U}} \mathbf{u}_i \quad (8)
$$

$$
+ \frac{\lambda_{\mathbf{S}}}{p} \sum_{j=1}^{p} \mathbb{I} \left[\langle \mathbf{u}_i, \mathbf{u}^+_{i,j} \rangle - \|\mathbf{U}^-_i \mathbf{u}_i\|_\infty \le 1 \right] \left(\partial \|\mathbf{U}^-_i \mathbf{u}_i\|_\infty - \mathbf{u}^+_{i,j} \right)
$$

$$
+ \frac{\lambda_{\mathbf{S}}}{p} \sum_{j=1}^{p} \mathbb{I} \left[\langle \mathbf{u}_i, \mathbf{u}^+_{i,j} \rangle - \|\mathbf{U}^\circ_i \mathbf{u}_i\|_\infty \le 1 \right] \left(\partial \|\mathbf{U}^\circ_i \mathbf{u}_i\|_\infty - \mathbf{u}^+_{i,j} \right)
$$

$$
+ \frac{\lambda_{\mathbf{S}}}{r} \sum_{j=1}^{r} \mathbb{I} \left[\langle \mathbf{u}_i, \mathbf{u}^\circ_{i,j} \rangle - \|\mathbf{U}^-_i \mathbf{u}_i\|_\infty \le 1 \right] \left(\partial \|\mathbf{U}^-_i \mathbf{u}_i\|_\infty - \mathbf{u}^\circ_{i,j} \right)
$$

and

$$
\mathbf{g}_{\mathbf{v}_j} = \frac{\partial \mathcal{F}}{\partial \mathbf{v}_j} = \sum_{i=1}^{n} \mathbb{I}_{ij} (\mathbf{R}_{ij} - \mathbf{u}^\top_i \mathbf{v}_j) \mathbf{u}_i + \lambda_{\mathbf{V}} \mathbf{v}_j. \quad (9)
$$

where $\mathbb{I}_{ij}$ is the indicator function of observed entries in the rating matrix **R**, i.e., $\mathbb{I}_{ij} = 1$ if $(i, j) \in \Omega_{\mathbf{R}}$ and 0 otherwise, and $\partial \|\mathbf{U}^-_i \mathbf{u}_i\|_\infty$ is the subdifferential of the function $\|\mathbf{U}^-_i \mathbf{u}_i\|_\infty$ at point $\mathbf{u}_i$. Since the subdifferential of the maximum of functions is the convex hull of the union of subdifferentials of the active functions at point $\mathbf{u}$ [21], we have:

$$\partial \|\mathbf{U}_i^- \mathbf{u}_i\|_\infty = \partial \max_{1 \le j \le q} \langle \mathbf{u}_i, \mathbf{u}_j^- \rangle$$
$$= \text{conv} \left\{ \mathbf{u}_j^- | \langle \mathbf{u}_i, \mathbf{u}_j^- \rangle = \|\mathbf{U}_i^- \mathbf{u}_i\|_\infty, j \in [q] \right\}.$$

In a similar way, we can compute the $\partial \|\mathbf{U}_i^\circ \mathbf{u}\|_\infty$. Having computed the gradients, we iteratively update the latent features at iteration $t + 1$ by:

$$\mathbf{u}_i^{t+1} \leftarrow \mathbf{u}_i^t - \eta_t \mathbf{g}_{\mathbf{u}_i}^t, \quad \mathbf{v}_i^{t+1} \leftarrow \mathbf{v}_i^t - \eta_t \mathbf{g}_{\mathbf{v}_i}^t.$$

Here, η_t is the learning rate, and $\mathbf{g}_{\mathbf{u}_i}^t$ and $\mathbf{g}_{\mathbf{v}_i}^t$ are the subgradients of the objective with respect to $\mathbf{u}_i$ and $\mathbf{v}_i$ at iteration t, respectively. We observe that, due to the non-smooth max operator in the social regularization term, one needs to use to sub-gradient descent methods to optimize the above objective.

Comparing the objective in Eq. (7) with objective Eq. (4) that is introduced in [6], a few comments are in order. First, here the neutral friends of users are also incorporated in ranking the latent features. This is more conservative than the formulation in Eq. (4) which ignores these types of relations. In particular, in Eq. (4) the neutral friends may appear any place in the ranking even before the trusted friends. However, in Eq. (7) neutral friends are pushed to the middle of ranked list which is more reasonable under real world assumptions. Second, as it will become more clear in the dual formation of objective Eq. (7), the number of constraints in Eq. (7) increases quadratically $O(n^2)$ with the number of users because of the maximum norm used in formulation, while in Eq. (4) the number of constrains is cubic $O(n^3)$ in the number of users due to the pairwise ranking used to rank the neighbors of each user. This provides a significant computational advantage when we tackle social recommendation problems with large number of users.

REMARK 3.1. *We note that for large-scale networks, the computation of gradient at each step of Algorithm 1 might be computationally expensive and one can use stochastic methods to replace the expensive full gradient computation with cheap stochastic gradient computation. This can be done by sampling a user and only updating his/her latent features.*

4. EXPERIMENTS

In this section, we conduct several experiments to compare the recommendation qualities of our `PushTrust` algorithm with other state-of-the-art recommendation methods. We begin with a brief description of the Epinions dataset and the evaluation metrics, and then introduce the baseline methods, followed by discussion of our experimental results.

4.1 The Epinions dataset

To evaluate the proposed algorithm on trust- and distrust-aware recommendations, we use the Epinions dataset, the only social rating network dataset publicly available. Moreover, an important reason why we choose the Epinion dataset is that user trust and distrust information is included in this dataset. Epinions allows users to evaluate other users based on the quality of their reviews. It additionally provides trust and distrust evaluations in addition to ratings. The social relations in in Epinions are directed.

Table 4.1 shows the statistics of the Epinions dataset used in our experiments. To conduct the coming experiments, we sampled a subset of Epinions dataset with $n = 121,240$ users and $m = 685,621$ different items. The total number of observed ratings in the sampled dataset is 12,721,437 which

Statistic	Quantity
Number of users	121,240
Number of items	685,621
Number of ratings	12,721,437
Number of trust relations	481,799
Number of distrust relations	96,823

Table 1: Statistics of rating data and social network in the sample Epinions dataset used in our experiments.

approximately includes 0.02% of all entries in the rating matrix $\mathbf{R}$. This demonstrates the sparsity of the rating matrix. The social network includes 481,799 and 96,823 trust and distrust relations between users, respectively.

4.2 Evaluation metrics

We adopt the widely used the Mean Absolute Error (MAE) and Root Mean Squared Error (RMSE) [9] metrics for prediction accuracy. The MAE metric is very appropriate and useful measure for evaluating prediction accuracy in offline tests [9]. Let $\mathcal{T}$ denote the set of ratings to be predicted, i.e., $\mathcal{T} = \{(i,j) \in [n] \times [m], \mathbf{R}_{ij}$ needs to be predicted$\}$ and let $\widehat{\mathbf{R}}$ denote the prediction matrix obtained by a recommendation algorithm. Then, the MAE and RMSE metrics are defined as:

$$\text{MAE} = \frac{1}{|\mathcal{T}|} \sum_{(i,j) \in \mathcal{T}} |\mathbf{R}_{ij} - \widehat{\mathbf{R}}_{ij}|,$$

and

$$\text{RMSE} = \sqrt{\sum_{(i,j) \in \mathcal{T}} \left(\mathbf{R}_{ij} - \widehat{\mathbf{R}}_{ij} \right)^2 / |\mathcal{T}|}.$$

The first measure (MAE) considers every error of equal value, while the second one (RMSE) emphasizes larger errors.

4.3 Baseline algorithms

In order to demonstrate the benefits of our approach, we compare our model with the following factorization based methods with and without social regularization.

- **MF** (matrix factorization based recommender): This algorithm is the basic matrix factorization in Eq. (1), which does not take the social data into account.

- **MF-T** (matrix factorization with trust information): The matrix factorization algorithm which exploits the trust relations between users in factorization [16] as formulated in Eq. (2).

- **MF-D** (matrix factorization with distrust information): The algorithm proposed in [16] to only exploit distrust relations as formulated in Eq. (3).

- **MF-TD** (matrix factorization with trust and distrust information): The algorithm proposed in [6] to incorporate both trust and distrust relationships as formulated in Eq. (4).

- **PushTrust**: The algorithm proposed in this paper.

Experimental setup. For testing our algorithm, we perform 5-fold cross validation in our experiments. In each fold

k	Method	MAE	RMSE
5	MF	0.9512	1.2612
	MF-T	0.8735	1.2030
	MF-D	0.9137	1.2230
	MF-TD	0.8312	1.1023
	PushTrust	**0.8010**	**1.0802**
10	MF	0.9763	1.2725
	MF-T	0.8930	1.2134
	MF-D	0.9234	1.2300
	MF-TD	0.8432	1.1450
	PushTrust	**0.8216**	**1.1230**

Table 2: Comparison with other popular methods in terms of MAE and RMSE errors.

80% of the rating data was randomly selected as the training set and the remaining 20% as the test data. After optimization over training data, the extracted latent models are used to predict the test data.

4.4 Comparison to baseline algorithms

We now focus on check how do the trust, distrust and neutral relationships between users affect the recommendation accuracy. In other words, we would like to experimentally evaluate whether incorporating different social relationships can indeed enhance the trust-based recommendation process. In this section, we present results on accuracy of rating prediction in terms of RMSE and MAE. We compare our approach with the four state-of-the-art algorithms discussed above: MF, MF-T, MF-D, and MF-TD on the Epinions.

We run the algorithms with different latent vector dimensions, $k = 5$ and $k = 10$. We evaluate these algorithms by measuring both MAE and RMSE errors. The parameters of all algorithms are tuned to achieve the best performance. Table 2 reports the MAE and RMSE of all comparison algorithms on the Epinions dataset. We unsurprisingly observed that the performance of algorithms exploiting social information are better than the pure matrix factorization based algorithm. Additionally the proposed algorithm outperforms the other baseline algorithms in all cases. It is also surprising to see that increasing k in the Epinions dataset did not improve the results while we know that by increasing k, the flexibility of the algorithm will be increased which should yield more accurate results. The Epinions dataset is small and increasing k creates more parameters in the model which leads to overfitting. We also note that MF-T performs better than the MF-D due to large number of trust relations in dataset compared to the number of distrust relations.

4.5 Experiments on handling cold-start users

Handling cold-start users (i.e., users with few ratings or new users) is one the main challenges in existing recommender systems. For example, more than 50 % of users in the Epinions are cold-start users. Hence efficiency of any recommendation algorithm for cold-start users becomes very important. In this set of experiments, the performance of proposed algorithm is evaluated on clod-start users and compared to baseline algorithms. To evaluate different algorithms we randomly select 30%, 20%, and 10% of the users, to be cold-start users. For cold-start users, we do not include any rating in the training data and consider all ratings made by cold-start users as testing data.

Table 3 shows the performance of above mentioned algorithms. As it is clear from the Table 3, when the number of cold-start users is high, exploiting the trust and distrust relationships significantly improves the performance of recommendation. This result is interesting as it reveals that the lack of rating information for cold-start and new users can be alleviated by incorporating the social relations of users. The improvement becomes significant by exploiting both trust and distrust relationships which amplifies the importance of social data when exploited in an appropriate way.

The results reported in that Table 3 imply that PushTrust is able to handle cold-start users more effectively than other algorithms. We also note that PushTrust outperforms the recently developed MF-TD algorithm. This is because the MF-TD ignores the neutral friends but PushTrust is designed to push these users to appear after the trusted friends and before the distrusted friends in the ranked list of latent features. We note that without considering neutral friends, their latent features might become even closer than the trusted friends of a specific user and consequently influence the predictions negatively. This crucial difference shows significant improvement in the performance as revealed by the results in Table 3.

5. CONCLUSIONS AND FUTURE WORK

In this paper, we have presented a novel approach for recommendation with social information by collaboratively ranking the latent features of users in matrix factorization by exploiting the social context of users. In contrast to social regularization based methods which are able to exploit either trust or distrust relations, and exclude the neutral friends in regularization, the proposed PushTrust algorithm is able to simultaneously exploit the trust and distrust relationships between users and considers neutral friends in ranking. Finally, the potential of distrust as a side information to improve accuracy of recommender systems and overcome the cold-start problems in traditional recommender systems is experimentally investigated on Epinions dataset. In summary, our results showed that more accurate recommendations can be obtained with trust/distrust incorporation and distrust information can indeed be beneficial for the recommendation process.

We believe that the proposed collaborative ranking framework leaves few interesting directions as future work. As an interesting direction, we are interested in devising more efficient optimization procedures for the proposed algorithm by solving the dual problem. Since the objective in the primal form presented in this paper is not differentiable, by turning the objective into its dual form, the objective becomes smooth and consequently faster optimization algorithms such as accelerated gradient methods can be utilized. Also, through comparison to other recommendation methods with social information and in particular memory-based recommenders with trust and distrust information [30, 27] is left for future work which may help judge the significance of proposed method in a larger scope. Finally, although the proposed ranking method has a linear dependency on the network size, empirical investigation of stochastic optimization methods and in particular stochastic gradient descent algorithm to investigate the scalability of the proposed algorithm to large-scale social networks would be interesting.

6. ACKNOWLEDGMENTS

This work was supported in part by the National Science Foundation under Awards IIS-096849, CCF-1117709, and 1331852. The authors would like to thank the anonymous reviewers for their insightful comments and suggestions. We also acknowledge valuable technical discussions with Mehrdad Mahdavi and Dennis Ross during this work.

% Cold-start Users	Measure	MF	MF-T	MF-D	MF-TD	PushTrust
30%	MAE	0.9923	0.9124	0.9721	0.8603	0.8345
	RMSE	1.7211	1.5562	1.6433	1.4602	1.3362
20%	MAE	0.9812	0.8905	0.9405	0.8542	0.8268
	RMSE	1.6962	1.4339	1.5250	1.2630	1.2430
10%	MAE	0.9634	0.8802	0.9233	0.8480	0.8204
	RMSE	1.3222	1.2921	1.3105	1.1688	1.1207

Table 3: The accuracy of handling cold-start users and the effect of social relations. The number of latent features in this set of experiments is set to $k = 5$.

7. REFERENCES

[1] S. Agarwal. The infinite push: A new support vector ranking algorithm that directly optimizes accuracy at the absolute top of the list. In *SDM*, pages 839–850. SIAM, 2011.

[2] R. M. Bell and Y. Koren. Lessons from the netflix prize challenge. *ACM SIGKDD Explorations Newsletter*, 9(2):75–79, 2007.

[3] C. J. Burges. A tutorial on support vector machines for pattern recognition. *Data mining and knowledge discovery*, 2(2):121–167, 1998.

[4] M. Burke and R. Kraut. Mopping up: modeling wikipedia promotion decisions. In *Proceedings of the 2008 ACM conference on Computer supported cooperative work*, pages 27–36. ACM, 2008.

[5] G. Dror, N. Koenigstein, Y. Koren, and M. Weimer. The yahoo! music dataset and kdd-cup'11. In *KDD Cup*, pages 8–18, 2012.

[6] R. Forsati, M. Mahdavi, M. Shamsfard, and M. Sarwat. Matrix factorization with explicit trust and distrust side information for improved social recommendation. *ACM Transactions on Information Systems (TOIS)*, 32(4):17, 2014.

[7] J. Golbeck and J. Hendler. Filmtrust: Movie recommendations using trust in web-based social networks. In *Proceedings of the IEEE Consumer communications and networking conference*, volume 96. Citeseer, 2006.

[8] R. Guha, R. Kumar, P. Raghavan, and A. Tomkins. Propagation of trust and distrust. In *WWW*, pages 403–412. ACM, 2004.

[9] J. L. Herlocker, J. A. Konstan, L. G. Terveen, and J. T. Riedl. Evaluating collaborative filtering recommender systems. *ACM Transactions on Information Systems (TOIS)*, 22(1):5–53, 2004.

[10] M. Jamali and M. Ester. A matrix factorization technique with trust propagation for recommendation in social networks. In *ACM RecSys*, pages 135–142. ACM, 2010.

[11] M. Jamali and M. Ester. A transitivity aware matrix factorization model for recommendation in social networks. In *AAAI*, pages 2644–2649, 2011.

[12] D. Jannach, M. Zanker, A. Felfernig, and G. Friedrich. *Recommender systems: an introduction*. Cambridge University Press, 2010.

[13] Y. Koren, R. Bell, and C. Volinsky. Matrix factorization techniques for recommender systems. *Computer*, 42(8):30–37, 2009.

[14] J. Liu, C. Wu, and W. Liu. Bayesian probabilistic matrix factorization with social relations and item contents for recommendation. *Decision Support Systems*, 2013.

[15] H. Ma, I. King, and M. R. Lyu. Learning to recommend with social trust ensemble. In *ACM SIGIR*, pages 203–210. ACM, 2009.

[16] H. Ma, M. R. Lyu, and I. King. Learning to recommend with trust and distrust relationships. In *ACM RecSys*, pages 189–196. ACM, 2009.

[17] H. Ma, H. Yang, M. R. Lyu, and I. King. Sorec: social recommendation using probabilistic matrix factorization. In *ACM CIKM*, pages 931–940. ACM, 2008.

[18] H. Ma, D. Zhou, C. Liu, M. R. Lyu, and I. King. Recommender systems with social regularization. In *ACM WSDM*, pages 287–296. ACM, 2011.

[19] P. Massa and P. Avesani. Trust-aware collaborative filtering for recommender systems. In *On the Move to Meaningful Internet Systems 2004: CoopIS, DOA, and ODBASE*, pages 492–508. Springer, 2004.

[20] A. Mnih and R. Salakhutdinov. Probabilistic matrix factorization. In *NIPS*, pages 1257–1264, 2007.

[21] Y. Nesterov. *Introductory lectures on convex optimization*, volume 87. Springer, 2004.

[22] J. D. Rennie and N. Srebro. Fast maximum margin matrix factorization for collaborative prediction. In *ICML*, pages 713–719. ACM, 2005.

[23] C. Rudin. The p-norm push: A simple convex ranking algorithm that concentrates at the top of the list. *JMLR*, 10:2233–2271, 2009.

[24] B. Sarwar, G. Karypis, J. Konstan, and J. Riedl. Item-based collaborative filtering recommendation algorithms. In *WWW*, pages 285–295. ACM, 2001.

[25] Y. Shi, M. Larson, and A. Hanjalic. Collaborative filtering beyond the user-item matrix: A survey of the state of the art and future challenges. *ACM Computing Surveys (CSUR)*, 47(1):3, 2014.

[26] R. R. Sinha and K. Swearingen. Comparing recommendations made by online systems and friends.

[27] N. Verbiest, C. Cornelis, P. Victor, and E. Herrera-Viedma. Trust and distrust aggregation enhanced with path length incorporation. *Fuzzy Sets and Systems*, 202:61–74, 2012.

[28] P. Victor, C. Cornelis, M. D. Cock, and A. Teredesai. Trust- and distrust-based recommendations for controversial reviews. *IEEE Intelligent Systems*, 26(1):48–55, 2011.

[29] P. Victor, C. Cornelis, and M. De Cock. Trust and distrust-based recommendations. In *Trust Networks for Recommender Systems*, pages 109–153. Springer, 2011.

[30] P. Victor, N. Verbiest, C. Cornelis, and M. D. Cock. Enhancing the trust-based recommendation process with explicit distrust. *ACM Transactions on the Web (TWEB)*, 7(2):6, 2013.

Top-N Recommendation for Shared Accounts

Koen Verstrepen   Bart Goethals

University of Antwerp
Antwerp, Belgium
{koen.verstrepen,bart.goethals}@uantwerp.be

ABSTRACT

Standard collaborative filtering recommender systems assume that every account in the training data represents a single user. However, multiple users often share a single account. A typical example is a single shopping account for the whole family. Traditional recommender systems fail in this situation. If contextual information is available, context aware recommender systems are the state-of-the-art solution. Yet, often no contextual information is available. Therefore, we introduce the challenge of recommending to shared accounts in the absence of contextual information. We propose a solution to this challenge for all cases in which the reference recommender system is an item-based top-N collaborative filtering recommender system, generating recommendations based on binary, positive-only feedback. We experimentally show the advantages of our proposed solution for tackling the problems that arise from the existence of shared accounts on multiple datasets.

Categories and Subject Descriptors: H.3.3 [Information Storage and Retrieval]: Information filtering

Keywords: Collaborative filtering, recommender systems, nearest neighbors, explaining recommendations, shared account.

1. INTRODUCTION

Typical recommender systems assume that every user-account represents a single user. However, multiple users often share a single account. An example is a household in which all people share one video-streaming account, one music-streaming account, one online-shopping account, one loyalty card for a store they make purchases in, etc.

Three problems arise when multiple users share one account. First, the *dominance problem* arises when all recommendations are relevant to only some of the users that share the account and at least one user does not get any relevant recommendation. We say that these few users dominate the account. Consider, for example, a family that often purchases household items. Once in a while they also purchase

toys for the children together with the household items. Now, it is likely that all recommendations will be based on the numerous household items and the recommender system will be essentially useless for the children.

Second, the *generality problem* arises when the recommendations are only a little bit relevant to all users in the shared account, but are not really appealing to any of them. When the diverse tastes of multiple users are merged into one account, the recommender system is more likely to recommend overly general items that are preferred by most people, regardless their individual tastes.

Third, if the recommender system would be able to generate relevant recommendations for every user in the shared account, how does every user know which recommendation is meant for her? We call this the *presentation problem*.

If contextual information such as time, location, buying intent, item content, session logs, etc. is available, context aware recommender systems are the state-of-the-art solution to split accounts into multiple users and detect the identity of the active user at recommendation time.

However, often no contextual information is available for splitting the accounts. A first example concerns the case of the numerous organizations that simply did not keep records of any contextual information in the past, not even time stamps. A second example are families that shop together in a hypermarket: they have one loyalty card account and bundle their purchases when they visit the store. In this case, the context is exactly the same for every family member and cannot be used to split the family account into its members. Therefore, we introduce the challenge of *top-N recommendation for shared accounts in the absence of contextual information,* in which the above three shared account problems are tackled without using any contextual information.

Formally, we consider the setting of collaborative filtering with binary, positive-only preference feedback. We represent the available data as a preference matrix in which the rows represent the users and the columns represent the items. Every value in this preference matrix is 1 or 0, with 1 representing a known preference and 0 representing the unknown. Pan et al. [12] call this setting one-class collaborative filtering (OCCF) but it is also referred to as top-N recommendation based on binary, positive-only preference data [2]. This kind of data is typically associated with implicit feedback [5]. However, it can also be the result of explicit feedback. Likes on social networking sites for example, are explicit, binary and positive-only. Other applications that correspond to this version of the collaborative filtering problem are tags for photo's, words for documents, articles bought by a customer etc.

Despite the significance of *top-N recommendation for shared accounts in the absence of contextual information*, we know of no prior research on tackling this challenge. We give a start to filling this gap by proposing a solution for all cases in which the reference recommender system is an item-based top-N collaborative filtering recommender system, generating recommendations based on binary, positive-only feedback [2]. In this way, we cover a large number of applications since item-based top-N collaborative filtering recommender systems are very popular. Multiple authors attribute this popularity to the combination of favorable properties such as simplicity, stability, efficiency, reasonable accuracy, the ability for intuitively explaining their recommendations, and the ability for immediately taking into account newly entered feedback [3, 8, 6, 9].

Central to our approach, we show a property of item-based top-N collaborative filtering recommender systems that allows us to compute a recommendation score in $\mathcal{O}(n \log n)$ instead of exponential time.

The main contributions of this work are:

- We formally introduce the challenge of *top-N recommendation for shared accounts in the absence of contextual information* (Sec. 2).

- We propose a solution to this challenge for all cases in which the reference recommender system is an item-based top-N collaborative filtering recommender system, generating recommendations based on binary, positive-only feedback [2] (Sec. 5-8).

- Most importantly, we show an essential property of item-based top-N collaborative filtering recommender systems that allows us to keep the time complexity of our proposed solution within practically feasible limits (Sec. 6).

- We experimentally show on multiple datasets that our proposed solution is able to detect preferences of individual users in shared accounts and has therefore significant advantages for tackling the dominance, generality and presentation problems (Sec. 9).

After formalizing the definitions of the challenge (Sec. 2) and the reference recommender system (Sec. 3) we first give further insight in how the reference recommender system suffers from the shared account problems (Sec. 4). Afterwards we sequentially solve the generality problem (Sec. 5), the dominance problem (Sec. 7) and the presentation problem (Sec. 8). Furthermore, we inserted a section on the efficient computation of our solution to the generality problem (Sec. 6). Finally, we discuss the experimental evaluation of our proposed solution (Sec. 9).

2. PROBLEM DEFINITION

Let $\mathcal{U}$ be the set of users, $\mathcal{A}$ the set of accounts and $\mathcal{I}$ the set of items. Furthermore, let $U(a) \subseteq \mathcal{U}$ be the set of users that share account a, i.e. the userset of account a, and let $a(u) \in \mathcal{A}$ be the account that user u belongs to. Notice that in this problem setting every user belongs to exactly one account.

First, consider the user-rating-matrix $\mathbf{T} \in \{0,1\}^{|\mathcal{U}| \times |\mathcal{I}|}$. $\mathbf{T}_{ui} = 1$ indicates that there exists a preference of user $u \in \mathcal{U}$ for item $i \in \mathcal{I}$. $\mathbf{T}_{ui} = 0$ indicates that there is no such preference.

We are given a reference recommender system R_{ref} that produces the desired recommendations given $\mathbf{T}$. Consequently, we say that an item i is **relevant** to a user u if i is in the top-N recommendations for u as computed by the reference recommender system $R_{ref}(\mathbf{T})$ on the user-rating-matrix $\mathbf{T}$.

Unfortunately, in our problem setting $\mathbf{T}$ is unknown. Instead we are given the account-rating-matrix $\mathbf{R} \in \{0,1\}^{|\mathcal{A}| \times |\mathcal{I}|}$. $\mathbf{R}_{ai} = 1$ indicates that there is a known preference of account $a \in \mathcal{A}$ for item $i \in \mathcal{I}$. $\mathbf{R}_{ai} = 0$ indicates that there is no such information.

Now, the challenge of *top-N recommendation for shared accounts in the absence of contextual information* is to devise a shared account recommender system $R_{sa}(\mathbf{R})$ that, based on the account-rating-matrix $\mathbf{R}$, computes for every account a the top N_a recommendations such that:

- Ideally, this top-N_a contains all top-N items for every user in the userset of a, with $N = \frac{N_a}{|U(a)|}$. Practically, the goal is to avoid the dominance and the generality problem by maximizing the number of users with at least one item from its top-N.

- It is clear for a user in the userset of a which items in the top-N_a are meant for her, i.e. the presentation problem gets solved.

Notice that in the above definition, the shared account recommender system does **not** get the number of users sharing every account as an input. Furthermore, no assumption is made about the shared interests of the users sharing an account. They can have totally different interests, partially overlapping interests or fully overlapping interests.

Finally, notice that this problem definition is orthogonal to a typical group recommendation problem [10]. First, in group recommendation, the individual profiles of the users in the shared account are typically known. Here, they are unknown. Second, in group recommendation, it is typically assumed that the recommendations will be consumed by all users in the shared account together. Here, it is assumed that every user in the shared account can identify the recommendations meant for her and consumes these recommendations individually.

3. THE REFERENCE RECOMMENDER SYSTEM

Typically, recommender systems find the top-N recommendations for a user u by first computing the recommendation scores $s(u, i)$ for every candidate recommendation i and afterwards selecting the N recommendations i for which $s(u, i)$ is the highest.

One of the most popular classes of recommender systems for binary, positive-only feedback are the item-based collaborative filtering recommender systems which Deshpande et al. discussed in detail [2]. These item-based recommender systems are rooted in the intuition that good recommendations are similar to the items already preferred by the target user, where the similarity between two items is measured using any set similarity measure between the respective sets of users preferring the items. Thus, for a target user u, this recommender system first finds $KNN(j)$, the k most similar items to j, for every preferred item j ($\mathbf{T}_{uj} = 1$) by using a similarity measure $sim(j,i)$. Next, every preferred item independently increases the recommendation score for its k most similar items $i \in KNN(j)$ with the similarity value $sim(j,i)$. Thus, the item-based recommendation score of a candidate recommendation i for user u is given by [2]:

$$s_{IB}(u,i) = s_{IB}(I(u),i)$$
$$= \sum_{j \in I(u)} sim(j,i) \cdot |KNN(j) \cap \{i\}|, \quad (1)$$

with $I(u) = \{j \in \mathcal{I} \mid \mathbf{T}_{uj} = 1\}$, the set of items preferred by u.

A typical choice for $sim(j,i)$ is the cosine similarity. Furthermore, Deshpande et al. report that normalizing the similarity scores improves the performance [2]. This comes down to defining $sim(j,i)$ in Equation 1 as:

$$sim(j,i) = \frac{cos(j,i)}{\sum_{l \in KNN(j)} cos(j,l)}.$$

We will use this recommender system as the reference recommender system R_{ref}.

4. SHARED ACCOUNT PROBLEMS OF THE REFERENCE RECOMMENDER SYSTEM

Simply applying the reference recommender system (Sec. 3) to the account-rating-matrix $\mathbf{R}$ leads to inferior results because the reference recommender system suffers from all three shared account problems. We illustrate this with two toy examples. In both examples we consider the two users u_a and u_b that share the account s. User u_a has a known preference for the items a_1 and a_2 and user u_b has a known preference for the items b_1, b_2 and b_3. There are five candidate recommendations: $r_a^1, r_a^2, r_b^1, r_b^2$ and r_g. r_a^1 and r_a^2 are good recommendations for u_a. r_b^1 and r_b^2 are good recommendations for u_b. r_g is an overly general recommendation to which both users feel neutral.

Tables 1 and 2 summarize some intermediate computations on the first and second example respectively. The left hand side of both tables lists for every candidate recommendation (rows) the similarity to the known preferences of the shared account s (columns). The right hand side of both tables lists for every candidate recommendation (rows) three recommendation scores (columns). These scores are computed using Equation 1 and the similarity values on the left hand side of the respective row. The first two scores are for u_a and u_b respectively if they would not share an account. The third score is for s, the account shared by u_a and u_b.

The first example, corresponding to Table 1, illustrates that the item-based reference recommender system can suffer from the generality problem. From Table 1 we learn that if u_a would not share an account with u_b, the item-based reference recommender system would correctly assign the highest scores to r_a^1 and r_a^2 for u_a and to r_b^1 and r_b^2 for u_b. However, if u_a and u_b share the account s, the overly general item r_g receives the highest score. In this case, the item-based reference recommender system suffers from the generality problem because it does not discriminate between a recommendation score that is the sum of a few large contributions and a recommendation score that is the sum of many small contributions.

Table 1: Item similarities and resulting scores for Example 1.

	sim					s_{IB}		
	$(a_1,*)$	$(a_2,*)$	$(b_1,*)$	$(b_2,*)$	$(b_3,*)$	$(u_a,*)$	$(u_b,*)$	$(s,*)$
r_a^1	5	5	1	0	0	10	1	11
r_a^2	4	4	1	0	0	8	1	9
r_b^1	1	0	5	5	2	1	12	13
r_b^2	1	0	4	4	2	1	10	11
r_g	3	3	3	3	3	6	9	15

Table 2: Item similarities and resulting scores for Example 2.

	sim					s_{IB}		
	$(a_1,*)$	$(a_2,*)$	$(b_1,*)$	$(b_2,*)$	$(b_3,*)$	$(u_a,*)$	$(u_b,*)$	$(s,*)$
r_a^1	5	5	0	0	1	10	1	11
r_a^2	4	4	1	0	0	8	1	9
r_b^1	0	1	5	5	5	1	15	16
r_b^2	1	0	4	4	4	1	12	13
r_g	2	1	2	1	2	3	5	8

The second example, corresponding to Table 2, illustrates that the item-based reference recommender system can suffer from the dominance problem. From Table 2 we learn that if u_a would not share an account with u_b, the item-based reference recommender system would correctly assign the highest scores to r_a^1 and r_a^2 for u_a and to r_b^1 and r_b^2 for u_b. However, if u_a and u_b share the account s, all recommendations for u_b receive a higher score than any recommendation for u_a. Hence, the recommendations for u_b dominate the account at the expense of u_a. In this case, the item-based reference recommender system suffers from the dominance problem because it does not take into account that u_b has more known preferences than u_a (3 vs. 2).

Both examples are suitable to illustrate that the reference recommender system suffers from the presentation problem. As an example, consider the first row of Table 1. The recommendation score $s(s, r_a^1) = 11$ is the sum of $sim(a_1, r_a^1) = 5$, $sim(a_2, r_a^1) = 5$ and $sim(b_1, r_a^1) = 1$. Therefore, it can be explained by a_1, a_2 and b_1. This is however a bad explanation because due to the presence of b_1, u_a will have difficulties to identify with the explanations and u_b might wrongly conclude that the recommendation is meant for her.

In our experimental evaluation (Sec. 9), we show that similar problems also arise for multiple large, real-life datasets.

5. SOLVING THE GENERALITY PROBLEM

The previous section showed that the generality problem arises because the item-based reference recommender system (Eq. 1) does not discriminate between a score that is the sum of a few large similarities and a score that is the sum of many small similarities. Therefore, our first step is to adapt the item-based recommendation score (Eq. 1) into the *length-adjusted* item-based recommendation score:

$$s_{LIB}(u,i) = s_{LIB}(I(u),i)$$
$$= \frac{1}{|I(u)|^p} \cdot s_{IB}(I(u),i), \quad (2)$$

with the hyperparameter $p \in [0, 1]$. Although this adjustment does not immediately solve the generality problem, it does provide a way to differentiate between the sum of a few large similarities and the sum of many small similarities. By choosing $p > 0$, we create a bias in favor of the sum of a few large similarities. The larger p, the larger the bias.

Since the factor $\frac{1}{|I(u)|^p}$ is the same for all candidate recommendations i, the top N items for user u according to s_{LIB} and s_{IB} are the same. However, when we compare the scores of two different users, s_{LIB} also takes into account the the total amount of items preferred by the user.

To avoid the generality problem we ideally want to recommend an item i if it is highly relevant to one of the users in the userset of the shared account a. Hence, we want to compute the recommendation score of an item i for every individual user $u \in U(a)$, and use the highest one. Formally, we want to rank all items i according to their ideal recommendation score

$$\max_{u \in U(a)} s_{LIB}(I(u), i).$$

Unfortunately, we cannot compute this ideal recommendation score because $U(a)$ and consequently $I(u)$ are unknown. Instead, we only know $I(a) = \{j \in \mathcal{I} \mid \mathbf{R}_{aj} = 1\}$, the set of items preferred by account a.

We can, however, approximate the ideal recommendation score with its upper bound:

$$\max_{S \in 2^{I(a)}} s_{LIB}(S, i) \geq \max_{u \in U(a)} s_{LIB}(I(u), i),$$

in which $2^{I(a)}$ is the powerset of $I(a)$, i.e. the set containing all possible subsets of $I(a)$. The proposed approximation is an upper bound of the ideal score because every set of items $I(u)$ for which $u \in U(a)$ is also an element of $2^{I(a)}$. This approximation is based on the assumption that of all possible subsets of $I(a)$, the ones that correspond to users are more likely to result into the highest recommendation scores than the ones put together at random.

Consequently, we propose to solve the generality problem with the *disambiguating* item-based (DAMIB) recommender system, according to which the DAMIB recommendation score of an account a for an item i is given by:

$$s_{DAMIB}(a, i) = \max_{S \in 2^{I(a)}} s_{LIB}(S, i). \quad (3)$$

Every score $s_{DAMIB}(a, i)$ corresponds to an optimal subset $S_i^* \subseteq I(a)$:

$$S_i^* = \operatorname*{argmax}_{S \in 2^{I(a)}} s_{LIB}(S, i). \quad (4)$$

Hence, $s_{DAMIB}(a, i) = s_{LIB}(S_i^*, i)$. As such, the DAMIB recommender system not only computes the recommendation scores, but also finds the subset S_i^* that maximizes the length-adjusted item-based recommendation score of a for i. This subset serves as the sharply defined, intuitive explanation for recommending i to a.

In other words, the DAMIB-recommender system implicitly splits the shared account a into (possibly overlapping) subsets S_i^* based on the intuitive and task-specific criterium that every S_i^* maximizes s_{LIB} for one of the candidate recommendations i. When $s_{LIB}(S_i^*, i)$ is high, we expect that S_i^* corresponds well to an individual user. When $s_{LIB}(S_i^*, i)$ is low, there is no user in the shared account for whom i is a strong recommendation and we expect S_i^* to be a random

subset. As such, we avoid the error prone task of estimating the number of users in the shared account and explicitly splitting the account a into its alleged users, based on a general clustering criterium [15].

Furthermore, since subsets can potentially overlap, the DAMIB recommender system does not care whether the known preferences of the users in a shared account are strongly, slightly or not at all overlapping.

Finally, notice that for $p = 0$ it always holds that $s_{DAMIB} = s_{LIB} = s_{IB}$. Hence, the item based recommender system is a special case of the DAMIB recommender system.

6. EFFICIENT COMPUTATION

Finding the maximum in Equation 3 in a direct way requires to compute s_{LIB} an exponential number of times, namely $2^{|I(a)|}$. Consequently, computing s_{DAMIB} in a direct way is intractable.

Fortunately, we are able to show a property of s_{LIB} that allows us to compute s_{DAMIB} in $\mathcal{O}(n \log n)$ time, with $n = |I(a)|$. This property is given by Theorem 6.1.

THEOREM 6.1. *Let a be an account that prefers the set of items $I(a)$. Furthermore, let i be a candidate recommendation. If we rank all items $j, l \in I(a)$ such that $rank(j) < rank(l) \iff sim(j, i) > sim(l, i)$, then the subset $S_i^* \subseteq I(a)$ that maximizes $s_{LIB}(S, i)$ over all $S \in 2^{I(a)}$ is a prefix of that ranking.*

PROOF. Given any $S \subseteq I(a)$. Initialize $P = S$. While P is not a prefix, remove r, the worst ranked item from P, and add a, the best ranked item that is not in P to P. As long as P is not yet a prefix, it holds that $sim(a, i) \geq sim(r, i)$. Therefore, every such item replacement increases (or keeps equal at least) $s_{LIB}(P, i)$ since the factor $1/|I(a)|^p$ does not change and a smaller term in the sum $\sum_{j \in I(a)} sim(j, i) \cdot |KNN(j) \cap \{i\}|$ is replaced by a larger term. Hence, for every $S \subseteq I(a)$ that is not a prefix of the ranking, we can always find a prefix $P \subseteq I(a)$ for which $s_{LIB}(P, i) \geq s_{LIB}(S, i)$. Therefore, the subset S_i^* that maximizes $s_{LIB}(S, i)$ over all $S \in 2^{I(a)}$ must always be a prefix of the ranking. $\square$

Since the optimal subset is a prefix, we can find it with one scan over the ranked items of $I(a)$ in linear time. The logarithmic factor in the time complexity comes from ranking the $|I(a)|$ items.

This theorem is central to our approach because it allows us to compute s_{DAMIB} in $\mathcal{O}(n \log n)$ instead of exponential time.

7. SOLVING THE DOMINANCE PROBLEM

The DAMIB recommender system allows us to detect when the dominance problem arises. This is because every recommendation i provided by DAMIB comes with a clear explanation in the form of the optimal subset $S_i^* \subseteq I(a)$. Therefore, if the union $\bigcup_{i \in top-N_a} S_i^*$ is only a small subset of $I(a)$, we know for sure that this small subset dominates the generation of the top N_a recommendations for account a.

Solving the dominance problem is done by choosing $ALG = $ DAMIB in Algorithm 1, called COVER. As such, our final algorithm for recommending to shared accounts is DAMIB-COVER, with DAMIB-COVER$(a) = $ COVER$(a, $DAMIB$)$.

The DAMIB-COVER algorithm uses the DAMIB scores to find the N_a highest scoring candidate recommendations

Algorithm 1: COVER(a,ALG)

input : $a \in \mathcal{A}$, ALG
output: top-N_a recommendations for account a
1 Compute $s_{ALG}(a,i)$ for all $i \in \mathcal{I} \setminus I(a)$
2 Rank all $i \in \mathcal{I} \setminus I(a)$ according to $s_{ALG}(a,i)$ in descending order with $t_a[r]$ the item at position r in the tuple of ranked items t_a
3 $C(a) \leftarrow \{\}$
4 $r \leftarrow 1$
5 $top\text{-}N_a \leftarrow \{\}$
6 **while** $|top\text{-}N_a| < N_a$ **do**
7     $c \leftarrow t_a[r]$
8   compute S_c^*
9   **if** $D(S_c^*, C(a)) \geq \theta_D$ **then**
10       $top\text{-}N_a \leftarrow top\text{-}N_a \cup \{c\}$
11       $C(a) \leftarrow C(a) \cup S_c^*$
12   remove c from t_a
13   **if** $C(a) = I(a)$ **then**
14         $C(a) \leftarrow \{\}$
15         $r \leftarrow 1$
16   **else**
17       $r \leftarrow r + 1$
18   **if** $r > |t_a|$ **then**
19         $C(a) \leftarrow \{\}$
20         $r \leftarrow 1$

and removes a candidate recommendation c from the top N_a if its explanation S_c^* is not sufficiently different from the explanations of the higher ranked candidates. The explanation-difference condition $D(S_c^*, C(a)) \geq \theta_D$ measures whether the explanation of a candidate (S_c^*) and the union of the explanations of the higher ranked candidates ($C(a)$) are sufficiently different.

Possible heuristic definitions of the explanation-difference condition are $|S_c^* \setminus C(a)| \geq 0.5 \cdot |S_c^*|$, and $|S_c^* \setminus C(a)| = |S_c^*|$. However, our experiments showed that $|S_c^* \setminus C(a)| \geq 1$ works better than the other two. We therefore use the latter heuristic in the remainder of this work.

8. SOLVING THE PRESENTATION PROBLEM

Generating the $top\text{-}N_a$ recommendations for a shared account a with DAMIB-COVER is insufficient because the users that share the account don't know which recommendation belongs to which user. This is the presentation problem.

Our solution to the presentation problem is to present every recommendation $i \in top\text{-}N_a$ together with its explanation S_i^* as defined by Equation 4. We expect that for a large majority of the items i in the $top\text{-}N_a$, the explanation S_i^* is a subset of the preferences $I(u)$ of u, one of the user that shares the account a. We empirically validate this hypothesis in the experimental section (Sec. 9).

Hence, we can present the recommendations as *the item r is recommended to the person that prefers the items s_1, s_2 and s_3*. Then, a user will recognize s_1, s_2 and s_3 as her preferences, and know that r is recommended to her.

9. EXPERIMENTAL EVALUATION

All datasets used are publicly available, readily or upon request to the owner. Furthermore, both the source code

of our algorithms and links to the datasets are available on *https://bitbucket.org/BlindReview/rsa*. Besides, this website contains scripts to automatically run every experiment in this section after compiling our source code and retrieving the datasets. As such, all our results can be reproduced with minimal effort, and the way in which we obtained the results can be thoroughly inspected by inspecting the scripts.

9.1 Datasets

Ideally, we would use a dataset that contains real life shared account information. The CAMRa 2011 dataset, for example, contains household membership information for a subset of the users that rated movies [15]. As such we could construct realistic shared accounts with this dataset. Unfortunately, the owner did not wish to distribute the dataset anymore and we have no knowledge of other datasets that contain shared account information. However, from the CAMRa 2011 dataset we learn that most household accounts consist of two users (272 out of 290 households) and some consist of three (14 out of 290) or four users (4 out of 290). Therefore, we will follow the approach of Zhang et al. and create 'synthetic' shared accounts by randomly grouping users in groups of two, three or four [15]. Although this approach is not perfect, Zhang et al. showed that the properties of the 'synthetic' shared accounts were similar to the properties of the real shared accounts from the CAMRa 2011 dataset [15].

We evaluated our proposed solution on four datasets: the *Yahoo!Music* [13], *Movielens1M* [4], *Book-Crossing* [16] and the *Wiki10+* [17] datasets.

The *Yahoo!Music* dataset contains ratings of 14382 users on 1000 songs on a 1 to 5 scale [13]. Since we consider the problem setting with binary, positive-only data we binarize the ratings. We convert the ratings 4 and 5 to preferences and ignore all other ratings. On average, a user has 8.7 preferences.

The *Movielens1M* dataset contains ratings of 6038 users on 3533 movies on a 1 to 5 scale [4]. Again, we convert the ratings 4 and 5 to preferences and ignore all other ratings. On average, a user has 95.3 preferences.

The *Book-Crossing* dataset contains two sorts of information [16]. First, there are ratings of users for books on a 1 to 10 scale. Analogously to the previous two datasets, we convert the ratings 8,9 and 10 to preferences and ignore all other ratings. Secondly, there are also binary preferences that we simply add to our list of preferences. In total, there are 87 835 users, 300695 books and every user has on average 11 preferences.

The *Wiki10+* dataset contains 99162 tags assigned to 20 751 Wikipedia articles [17]. In this case we consider the recommendation of tags to articles, hence the articles take the role of 'users' and the tags take the role of 'items'. If an article a was tagged at least once with a tag t, we consider a 'preference' of article a for tag t. In this context, a shared account is a big article on a wider topic containing multiple smaller 'articles' on subtopics. On average, every article has 22.1 tags.

Due to space restrictions we only show numerical results for the *Yahoo!Music* dataset. However, the results for the three other datasets can be consulted on *https://bitbucket.org/BlindReview/rsa*, and lead to the same conclusions.

9.2 Competitive Algorithms

We compare our novel algorithm, DAMIB-COVER, with two competitive algorithms. The first one is IB, simply the item-based reference recommender system applied to the account-rating-matrix, essentially ignoring the existence of the shared account problems. This is our baseline. The second competitive algorithm is IB-COVER, which is defined as $IB\text{-}COVER(a) = COVER(a, IB)$. IB-COVER is similar to one of the algorithms already proposed by Yu et al. in a different context [14].

9.3 Performance

First, consider the recall of a user that shares an account a with $|U(a)|$ other user. This is the percentage of its individual top-5 recommendations that is also present in the top-N_a recommendations for its shared account, with $N_a = 5 \cdot |U(a)|$. Formally, we define the recall of user u as:

$$rec(u) = \frac{|top\text{-}5(u) \cap top\text{-}N_a(a)|}{5}.$$

Ideally, the recall of all users in a shared account is 1, meaning that the top-N_a for the shared account is the union of the individual top-5's of the $|U(a)|$ users sharing the account.

Now, to investigate how many users genuinely suffer from sharing an account, we measure the fraction of users that does not get any relevant recommendation, i.e. that does not find a single one of its top-5 individual recommendations in the top-N_a recommendations of the shared account it belongs to. We denote this number as $rec_0^{\mathcal{U}}$, the fraction of users for which the recall is zero. Formally, we define

$$rec_0^{\mathcal{U}} = \frac{|\{u \in \mathcal{U} \mid rec(u) = 0\}|}{|\mathcal{U}|}.$$

An illustrative example of a user that genuinely suffers from sharing an account is depicted in Table 3. This table shows two real users from the *Movielens1M* dataset with their respective known preferences $I(u)$ and item-based individual top-5 recommendations. Their item-based individual top-5 recommendations look reasonable given their known preferences and it is not unrealistic that these two users would be part of the same household and therefore share an account. Consequently, Table 3 also shows the recommendations for the 'synthetic' account shared by both users for two cases: $R_{sa} = IB$ and $R_{sa} = DAMIB\text{-}COVER$. In case $R_{sa} = IB$, $rec(562) = 0$, i.e. user 562 does not get a single recommendation and genuinely suffers from sharing an account. In case $R_{sa} = DAMIB\text{-}COVER$, $rec(562) = 0.6$, i.e. user 562 gets 3 good recommendation and there is no serious problem. Obviously, this is just one example and we need to look at all users in the dataset for comparing the different algorithms.

Figure 1 displays $rec_0^{\mathcal{U}}$ for the *Yahoo!Music* dataset. The number of nearest neighbors, k, is a parameter of the item-based reference recommender system (Eq 1). There are multiple ways of choosing k. Amongst others, examples are accuracy in an off-line experiment, subjective quality judgment of the recommendations, accuracy in an on-line A/B test, computational efficiency, etc. Therefore, we present our results for a variation of reference recommender systems, i.e. item-based collaborative filtering recommender systems that differ in their choice of k. Consequently, every plot in Figure 1 shows the results for a different k.

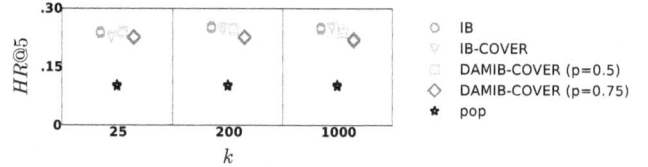

Figure 2: HR@5 as a function of k for different recommender systems. Higher is better.

For every choice of k and the individual top-5 recommendations corresponding to this choice we consider four experiments: an account shared by one, two, three or four users respectively. Notice that an account shared by one user is actually not shared. Every horizontal axis indicates the number of users that share the account, every vertical axis indicates the resulting $rec_0^{\mathcal{U}}$. The four different markers show the results for four different shared account recommender systems R_{sa}: the baseline algorithm IB, the competitor IB-COVER and two variations of the proposed DAMIB-COVER algorithm. These two variations differ in their choice of the parameter p (Eq. 2): $p = 0.5$ and $p = 0.75$. Since we repeat every experiment 5 times with other randomizations, every plot contains $5 \times 4 = 20$ markers of the same kind. However, because of the low spread, most markers are plotted on top of each other, forming dense marker clouds. Furthermore, since the 95% confidence intervals for the mean are more narrow than the marker-clouds of 5 datapoints, we do not draw them. Consequently, two marker clouds that are visually well separated, are also significantly different at the 5% significance level.

We make four observations from Figure 1. First, we observe that the baseline performance is not good. Up to 19% of the users get no relevant recommendation when they share their account with another user. This confirms that shared accounts can cause significant problems for recommender systems.

Secondly, our proposed solution, the DAMIB-COVER algorithm, can significantly improve $rec_0^{\mathcal{U}}$. In some cases the improvement is even drastic. One example is for the case that $|U(a)| = 2$ and that the individual top-5 is generated with $k = 200$. In this case, 12% of the users does not get any relevant recommendation when using the baseline algorithm IB. By using DAMIB-COVER ($p = 0.75$), this number is reduced with a factor four ($rec_0^{\mathcal{U}} = 0.03$).

Thirdly, sometimes IB-COVER already improves over IB. There are however multiple cases in which DAMIB-COVER further improves over IB-COVER. Furthermore, the advantages of DAMIB-COVER over IB-COVER will become even more evident in the evaluation of the presentation problem in Section 9.5.

Finally, when $|U(a)| = 1$, i.e. when the accounts are not shared, $rec_0^{\mathcal{U}} = 0$ by definition for the baseline algorithm IB. However, we observe that also for the IB-COVER and the variants of the DAMIB algorithms $rec_0^{\mathcal{U}}$ can be kept sufficiently low. Hence, the proposed DAMIB algorithm does not fail when accounts are not shared.

9.4 Limited Trade-Off

To emphasize the point that the DAMIB-COVER algorithm still performs well in a traditional setting when no accounts are shared, we also discuss the results of DAMIB-COVER on a more established experimental setup that was

Table 3: Example of user 562 suffering from sharing an account with user 4385.

user ID	562	4385
$I(u)$	Wes Craven's New Nightmare, The Exorcist III, Serial Mom, Scream, Scream 2, The Blair Witch Project, Good Will Hunting, Misery, Interview with the Vampire, Candyman, Freddy's Dead: The Final Nightmare	American Beauty, The Shawshank Redemption, Being John Malkovich, L.A. Confidential, Boys Don't Cry, Croupier, Dogma, Cider House Rules, Girl Interrupted, Saving Grace, The Talented Mr. Ripley
individual top-5: IB, $k = 25$	A Nightmare on Elm Street, Halloween, Halloween:H20, The Shining, Seven	Pulp Fiction, Fargo, The Sixth Sense, The Silence of the Lambs, Shindler's List
R_{sa} = IB	The Silence of the Lambs, Fargo, Pulp Fiction, The Sixth Sense, **Saving Private Ryan, The Usual Suspects,** Shindler's List, **Shakespeare in Love, Star Wars: Episode V, The Matrix**	
R_{sa} = DAMIB-COVER (p=0.75)	The Silence of the Lambs, Fargo, Schindler's List, A Nightmare on Elm Street, Halloween:H20, Pulp Fiction, Shakespeare in Love, The Shining, **The Exorcist, Sleepy Hollow**	

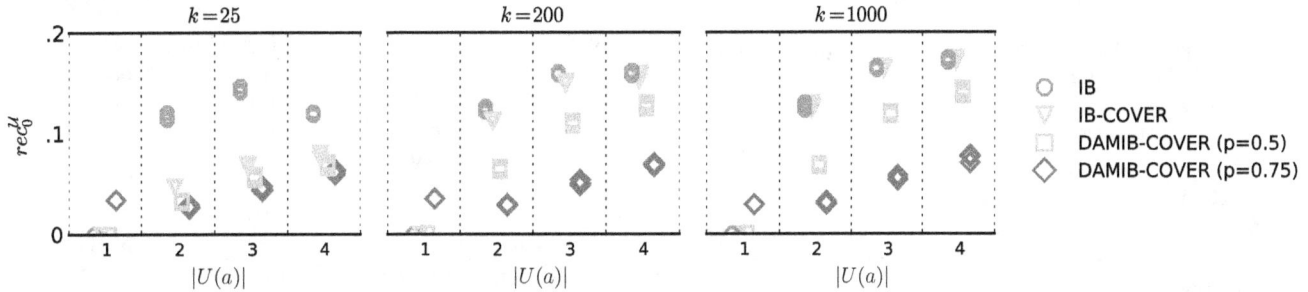

Figure 1: $rec_0^{\mathcal{U}}$ as a function of the number of merged users, $|U(a)|$, for different k and shared account recommender systems R_{sa}. **Lower is better.** 95% confidence intervals are more narrow than the marker clouds and are therefore not drawn.

used by Deshpande et al. [2], amongst many others. To avoid all confusion: this experimental setup has nothing to do with shared accounts. In this experimental setup, one preference of every user is randomly chosen to be the test preference h_u for that user. If a user has only one preference, no test preference is chosen. The remaining preferences are represented as a 1 in the training matrix $\mathbf{R}$ (which is in this case exactly the same as $\mathbf{T}$ because no accounts are shared). All other entries of $\mathbf{R}$ are zero. We define $\mathcal{U}_t$ as the set of users with a test preference. For every user $u \in \mathcal{U}_t$, every algorithm ranks the items $\{i \in \mathcal{I} \mid \mathbf{R}_{ui} = 0\}$ based on $\mathbf{R}$. Following Deshpande et al. we evaluate every ranking using hit rate at 5 [2]. Hit rate at 5 is given by

$$HR@5 = \frac{1}{|\mathcal{U}_t|} \sum_{u \in \mathcal{U}_t} |\{h_u\} \cap top5(u)|,$$

with $top5(u)$ the 5 highest ranked items for user u. Hence $HR@5$ gives the percentage of test users for which the test peference is in the top 5 recommendations. The results of the experiment for the *Yahoo!Music* dataset are shown in Figure 2. Additionally to the algorithms discussed earlier, Figure 2 also contains the results for the baseline-algorithm POP, the non-personalized algorithm that ranks all items according to their popularity, i.e. the number of users in the training set that prefer the item. Also in this case we repeated every experiment five times with a different randomization. Again, the five data points are often plotted on top of each other because of the low spread. Figure 2 shows that $HR@5$ is very similar for DAMIB-COVER and IB. Hence, there is almost no trade-off in terms of global accuracy measured as $HR@5$.

9.5 Presentation

In Section 8 we proposed to solve the presentation problem by presenting every recommendation together with its explanation. If then, a user in the shared account recognizes an explanation as a subset of her preferences, this user can identify with the recommendation and therefore knows the recommendation is meant for her. For this proposed solution to work, it is crucial that the recommendation is identifiable, i.e. that its explanation is a subset of the preferences of one of the users in the shared account. We quantify the identifiability of a recommendation i, with explanation S_i^*, for a shared account a as:

$$ident(S_i^*) = \max_{u \in U(a)} \frac{|S_i^* \cap I(u)|}{|S_i^*|}.$$

Ideally, $ident(S_i^*) = 1$, i.e. every item in the explanation is a preference of one and the same user. In the worst case, $ident(S_i^*) = 1/|U(a)|$, i.e. the explanation contains an equal amount of preferences from all users in the shared account and therefore none of the users can identify herself with the recommendation.

Figure 3 shows histograms of the identifiability of the top-10 recommendations for $|U(a)| = 2$ on the *Yahoo!Music* dataset for multiple shared account recommender systems R_{sa}. From Figure 3a we learn that if one simply applies the item-based reference algorithm to the shared account data of the *Yahoo!Music* dataset, the presentation problem arises: very few recommendations can be identified with one of the users in the shared account, i.e. $ident(S_i^*) = 1$ for only 10% of the explanations. Figure 3b shows that using IB-COVER instead of IB does not improve the situation. However, figure 3c shows that using DAMIB-COVER dras-

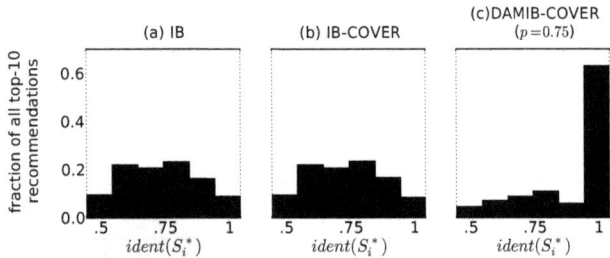

Figure 3: Histograms of identifiability of top-10 recommendations for $|U(a)| = 2$ on the *Yahoo!Music* dataset. $R_{ref} = $ IB, $k = 200$

tically increases the identifiability of the recommendations, i.e. $ident(S_i^*) = 1$ for approximately 60% of the explanations. Hence, the DAMIB explanations are superior to the item-based explanations.

10. RELATED WORK

Although we did not find prior art tackling the same challenges as we do, there are some works that have commonalities with ours.

First, Palmisano et al. [11] consider a problem setting in which the contextual information is *sometimes* missing. However, their proposed solution draws upon all training data for which they do know the context to devise a 'context predictor'. Hence, their solution relies on contextual information.

Second, Anand et al. [1] do not use explicit contextual information. However, their solution assumes that the preferences of every account are grouped into transactions. Our solution does not assume that this kind of extra data is available.

Third, Zhang et al. [15] study the extent to which it is possible to explicitly split shared accounts into their individual users without contextual information. They are able to split certain shared accounts very nicely, but find that in general, explicitly splitting accounts into their users is very error prone. Fortunately, by means of s_{DAMIB}, we are able to avoid this explicit split of accounts into users and perform a softer, implicit split instead.

Fourth, Yu et al. [14] propose to use the explanations of item-based recommendations to generate diversified top-N recommendation lists. Where they focus on the diversity of the explanations, we focus on covering all items preferred by the account with the different explanations. Furthermore, in our experimental evaluation (Sec. 9) we showed that the explanations provided by our DAMIB-COVER algorithm are superior to those that can be extracted from an item-based algorithm.

Finally, the NLMF algorithm might be an alternative to solve the generality problem [7]. However, in that case it is not clear how to solve the dominance an presentation problems.

11. CONCLUSIONS AND FUTURE WORK

We showed that the widely used item-based recommender systems fails when it makes recommendations for shared accounts. Therefore, we introduced the challenge of Top-N recommendation for shared accounts in the absence of con-

textual information. Furthermore, we proposed the DAMIB-COVER algorithm, our solution to this challenge. Central to our approach, we showed a theorem that allowed us to compute a recommendation score in $\mathcal{O}(n \log n)$ instead of exponential time. Finally, we experimentally validated that our proposed solution has important advantages.

As future work, we plan to generalize our proposed solution to a wider range of reference recommender systems.

12. REFERENCES

[1] S. Anand and B. Mobasher. Contextual recommendation. In *WebMine*, pages 142–160, 2006.

[2] M. Deshpande and G. Karypis. Item-based top-n recommendation algorithms. *TOIS*, 22(1):143–177, 2004.

[3] C. Desrosiers and G. Karypis. A comprehensive survey of neighborhood-based recommendation methods. In F. Ricci, L. Rokach, B. Shapira, and P. Kantor, editors, *Recommender Systems Handbook*. Springer, Boston, MA, 2011.

[4] Grouplens. ml-1m.zip. http://grouplens.org/datasets/movielens/.

[5] Y. Hu, Y. Koren, and C. Volinsky. Collaborative filtering for implicit feedback datasets. In *ICDM*, pages 263–272, 2008.

[6] D. Jannach, M. Zanker, A. Felfernig, and G. Frierich. *Recommender Systems: An Introduction*. Cambridge University Press, New York, NY, 2011.

[7] S. Kabbur and G. Karypis. Nlmf: Nonlinear matrix factorization methods for top-n recommender systems. In *ICDMW*, pages 167–174. IEEE, 2014.

[8] Y. Koren and R. Bell. Advances in collaborative filtering. In F. Ricci, L. Rokach, B. Shapira, and P. Kantor, editors, *Recommender Systems Handbook*. Springer, Boston, MA, 2011.

[9] G. Linden, B. Smith, and J. York. Amazon.com recommendations: Item-to-item collaborative filtering. *Internet Comp.*, 7(1):76–80, 2003.

[10] J. Masthoff. Group recommender systems: Combining individual models. In F. Ricci, L. Rokach, B. Shapira, and P. Kantor, editors, *Recommender Systems Handbook*. Springer, Boston, MA, 2011.

[11] C. Palmisano, A. Tuzhilin, and M. Gorgolione. Using context to improve predictive modeling of customers in personalization applications. *TKDE*, 20(11):1535–1549, 2008.

[12] R. Pan, Y. Zhou, B. Cao, N. Liu, R. Lukose, M. Scholz, and Q. Yang. One-class collaborative filtering. In *ICDM*, pages 502–511, 2008.

[13] Yahoo!Research. Yahoo_webscope_r3.tgz. http://research.yahoo.com/Academic_Relations.

[14] C. Yu, L. Lakshmanan, and S. Amer-Yahia. Recommendation diversification using explanations. In *ICDE*, pages 1299–1302, 2009.

[15] A. Zhang, N. Fawaz, S. Ioannidis, and A. Montanari. Guess who rated this movie: Identifying users through subspace clustering. In *UAI*, pages 944–953, 2012.

[16] C.-N. Ziegler, S. M. McNee, J. A. Konstan, and G. Lausen. Improving recommendation lists through topic diversification. In *WWW*, pages 22–32, 2005.

[17] A. Zubiaga. Enhancing navigation on wikipedia with social tags. arXiv:1202.5469, 2012.

Exploiting Geo-Spatial Preference for Personalized Expert Recommendation

Haokai Lu
Texas A&M University
hlu@cse.tamu.edu

James Caverlee
Texas A&M University
caverlee@cse.tamu.edu

ABSTRACT

Experts are important for providing reliable and authoritative information and opinion, as well as for improving online reviews and services. While considerable previous research has focused on finding topical experts with broad appeal – e.g., top Java developers, best lawyers in Texas – we tackle the problem of *personalized expert recommendation*, to identify experts who have special personal appeal and importance to users. One of the key insights motivating our approach is to leverage the geo-spatial preferences of users and the variation of these preferences across different regions, topics, and social communities. Through a fine-grained GPS-tagged social media trace, we characterize these geo-spatial preferences for personalized experts, and integrate these preferences into a matrix factorization-based personalized expert recommender. Through extensive experiments, we find that the proposed approach can improve the quality of recommendation by 24% in precision compared to several baselines. We also find that users' geo-spatial preference of expertise and their underlying social communities can ameliorate the cold start problem by more than 20% in precision and recall.

Categories and Subject Descriptors

H.2.8 [**Database Applications**]: Data Mining

Keywords

expert recommendation; geospatial preference; GPS-tagged social media

1. INTRODUCTION

Finding and recommending *experts* is a critical component for many important tasks. For example, the quality of movie recommenders can be improved by biasing the underlying models toward the opinions of experts [1]. Making sense of mobile and social information streams such as the Facebook newsfeed and the Twitter stream can be improved by focusing on content contributed by experts. Along these lines, companies like Google and Yelp are actively soliciting *expert reviewers* to improve the coverage and reliability of their services [8]. More generally and in contrast to sea-rch engines and question-answer systems, experts can provide ongoing help for evolving and ill-specified needs, as well as personalized access to knowledge and experience that only experts possess.

Indeed, there has been considerable effort toward expert finding and recommendation, e.g., [2, 3, 6, 7, 14, 17, 20, 22]. These efforts have typically sought to identify topical experts with broad appeal, e.g., the top Java developer in an enterprise, the best lawyer in Texas. However, there is a research gap in our understanding of both (i) identifying *personal experts*, that is experts who are of significance and importance to me, but perhaps not viewed so more broadly. For example, I may be interested in the expert opinions of nearby local foodies, but less interested in the opinions of globally popular celebrity chefs; and (ii) how spatial preference for personally-valuable expertise varies across topics, across regions, and based on different underlying social communities. For example, technologists in Houston, TX may be more interested in the opinions of experts in nearby Austin and in more distant Silicon Valley, but less so in the opinions of experts from New York. Similarly, the reach of experts may vary by location, so that tech experts from Silicon Valley have a larger footprint than do experts from other regions.

Hence, in this paper, we are interested to study the problem of *personalized expert recommendation* by integrating the geo-spatial preferences of users and the variation of these preferences across different regions, topics, and social communities. These geo-spatial preferences are increasingly being revealed through the fine-grained geo-spatial footprints of Instagram, Foursquare, and Twitter, among other mobile location sharing platforms. Concretely, we opportunistically leverage a collection of GPS-tagged Twitter users and their relationships in Twitter lists, a form of crowd-sourced knowledge whereby user A may label user B with a descriptor (like "technology"). In isolation these lists allow a user to organize a personal Twitter stream; in aggregate, the many labels applied to a target user in many lists can provide a crowdsourced expertise profile of the target user. Specifically, we propose and evaluate a matrix factorization-based personalized expert recommender that leverages three key factors:

- *Region-based locality*, reflecting the variation in spatial preference from region to region. For example, Figure 1b and Figure 1c shows that the preference of users for food experts varies greatly based on the location of the user (in essence, local users prefer local foodies). How can these regional differences be captured and incorporated into a personalized expert recommender?

- *Topic-based locality*, reflecting the variation in spatial preference across different topics. For example, Figure 1b and Figure 1e demonstrate that spatial preference is much less local for the topic technology than for food. How can this topical variation be integrated into a personalized expert recommender?

RecSys'15, September 16–20, 2015, Vienna, Austria.
© 2015 ACM. ISBN 978-1-4503-3692-5/15/09 ...$15.00.
DOI: http://dx.doi.org/10.1145/2792838.2800189.

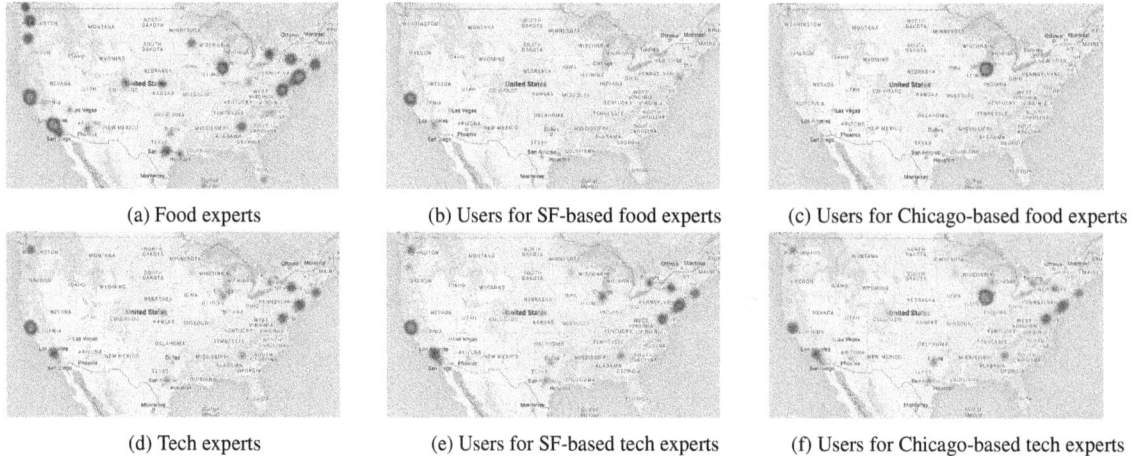

| (a) Food experts | (b) Users for SF-based food experts | (c) Users for Chicago-based food experts |
| (d) Tech experts | (e) Users for SF-based tech experts | (f) Users for Chicago-based tech experts |

Figure 1: Spatial distribution of experts (a,d) and for the users who have listed experts (b,c,e,f) based on geo-tagged Twitter lists.

- *Social-based locality*, reflecting the social connections between users and experts. For example, are users who are connected in an underlying social network more "similar" in their preferences for experts? Are experts who are more tightly coupled in the underlying social network preferred by the same set of users?

Through extensive experimental validation, we find that each of these factors – region, topic, and social-based locality – improves the quality of personalized expert recommendation. And together, the proposed model achieves around 24% improvement in precision and 21% improvement in recall versus both a collaborative filtering and a baseline matrix factorization based recommender. Furthermore, we also find that the proposed approach can ameliorate the cold start problem when users have few experts on their lists, leading to more than 20% improvement over the baseline in precision and recall.

2. RELATED WORK

Many previous works [2, 3, 14, 22] have focused on finding general topic experts in many domains (e.g., enterprise corporate, email networks), with a recent emphasis on social media and microblogging sites [7, 17, 20]. Weng et al. [20] proposed a PageRank-based approach to find topic experts by taking advantage of both topical similarity between users and social link structure. Pal and Counts [17] introduced a probabilistic clustering followed by a within-cluster Gaussian ranking framework to find topic authorities using nodal and topical features on Twitter. Ghosh et al. [7] proposed and built a system called Cognos to find topic experts by relying on Twitter Lists (though not with any geo-spatial information, as in this work). Recently, Cheng et al. [6] addressed the problem of identifying local experts on Twitter. Our work extends on these prior efforts by focusing on *personalized* experts and in investigating the impact of region-based, topic-based, and social community-based locality on personalized expert recommendation.

With the rapid growth of location-based social networks in recent years, many applications [5, 9, 12, 13, 15, 21] have started to take advantage of geo footprints such as point-of-interest (POI) recommendation on social networks. Ye et al. [21] explored the spatial clustering phenomenon and proposed a unified POI recommendation framework combining user preference, geographical influence, and social influence. Cheng et al. [5] proposed a multi-center Gaussian model to model user's check-in behavior, which is used as input for a generalized matrix factorization framework. Liu et al. [13] proposed a geographical probabilistic factor analysis

framework, which jointly models the effect of geographical distance, user preference, POI popularity and user mobility. Another different application that utilizes geographical footprints is the rating prediction problem in Yelp [9], where Hu et al. observed weak positive correlation between a business's ratings and its neighbor's ratings, and used this observation to improve rating predictions. In contrast, we are focused on preferences for experts, rather than on particular POIs or venues.

3. PERSONALIZED EXPERT RECOMMENDATION: OVERVIEW

In this section, we introduce the problem of personalized expert recommendation and outline our core approach.

3.1 Problem Statement

We assume there exists a set of users $U = \{u_1, u_2, ..., u_N\}$, where N is the total number of users. From this set U, there are a number of recognized experts denoted as $E = \{e_1, e_2..., e_M\}$, where M is the total number of experts. Each user has a preference over some of these experts, expressed as a *personalized expertise list*. For example, Alice may prefer Beth to Candace in the topic of "Java programming", but have no opinion on Doug. We then define the problem of *personalized expert recommendation* as: Given a user u_i, identify the top-n personally relevant experts to u_i. That is, can we further identify experts Eva and Frank that are of personal interest to Alice?

3.2 Recommendation by Matrix Factorization

We tackle *personalized expert recommendation* using latent factor matrix factorization [10]. We assume there is a factor p_i associated with each user u_i and a factor q_j associated with each expert e_j. The model defines a rating score between the list and the expert, denoted as y_{ij}, and factors the score into a latent space through p_i and q_j as follows:

$$y_{ij} = p_i^T q_j + b_j \tag{1}$$

Through this factorization, we can think of q_j as the latent properties for expert e_j, p_i as the latent preference of user u_i and b_j as the popularity bias for e_j. However, unlike the standard recommendation task, we do not have a rating score for each expert on the lists. Instead, we only have the implicit feedback for a list, which assumes a user prefers an expert who is already on the list to an expert who is not. Accordingly, the learning objective should be based on the pair-wise ranking between experts. In recommendations when only implicit feedback is available, the one-class collaborative filtering approach [4, 18, 23] can be used for learning a rank order among items. Similar efforts have been targeted at tag recommendation [19], tweet recommendation [4], and event-based groups [11, 23]. Here, we adapt the Bayesian Personalized Ranking (BPR) criterion proposed by Rendle et al. in [18] to our problem.

Formally, for a user u_i, an expert e_k and an expert e_h, suppose u_i puts e_k on the list while not e_h, we denote this pair as $e_k^{u_i} \succeq e_h^{u_i}$, and the likelihood for this preference under BPR can be written as:

$$p(e_k^{u_i} \succeq e_h^{u_i}) = \sigma(y_{ik} - y_{ih}) \text{ where } \sigma(x) = \frac{1}{1 + e^{-x}}$$

Therefore, the likelihood for all users could be written as:

$$p(R|\Theta) = \prod_{e_k^{u_i} \in \mathcal{P}^{u_i}, e_h^{u_i} \in \mathcal{N}^{u_i}, u_i \in U} p(e_k^{u_i} \succeq e_h^{u_i})$$

where R is the set of all preference pairs, Θ is the set of all parameters, $\mathcal{P}^{u_i}$ is the set of experts included on u_i's list and $\mathcal{N}^{u_i}$ is the set of absent experts for u_i. If Θ has a prior density $p(\Theta)$, we can derive a bayesian version of the likelihood, where the prior is used to prevent the overfitting of the parameters as a form of regularization. Thus, the posterior log-likelihood to maximize is

$$p(R|\Theta) = \sum_{e_k^{u_i} \in \mathcal{P}^{u_i}, e_h^{u_i} \in \mathcal{N}^{u_i}, u_i \in U} ln(\sigma(y_{ik} - y_{ih})) - \text{regularization}$$

which can be learned through stochastic gradient descent (SGD) by iterating each of the preference pairs and updating the corresponding parameters.

4. REGION, TOPIC, AND SOCIAL-BASED LOCALITY

While promising, the baseline matrix factorization approach ignores the geo-spatial preferences of users and the variation of these preferences across different topics, regions, and social communities (as suggested by Figure 1's intuitive support for these notions). Hence, we turn in this section to demonstrating how these factors manifest in real-world Twitter-based data and how each of these factors can be incorporated into a new personalized expert recommendation matrix factorization framework.

4.1 Data and Metrics

We begin by highlighting the data used here and two statistical measures – expert entropy and expert spread – to characterize region and topic-based locality. We then turn to the social properties of the dataset to demonstrate social-based locality.

Data. We use the geo-tagged Twitter lists collected in [6]. In total, there are about 12 million crowd-generated lists and 14 million geo-tagged listings, where a geo-tagged listing indicates a direct link from a list creator to an expert where both of their geo-locations are known. That is, each user $u_i \in U$ is associated with geographical coordinates $coord_{u_i}$. Furthermore, for each list, there exist associated labels that list creators use to indicate the topic of that list. In the following analysis, we selected lists which include the most frequent unigram labels indicating typical topics as follows: news, music, tech, sports, celebs, and food. Additionally, we randomly sampled lists which include any unigram occurring more than 200 times in list labels. We denote this randomly sampled list data as "general". Furthermore, we excluded experts who have only occurred in one list and also excluded lists which includes only one expert. After filtering, we have the geo-tagged Twitter list data

Table 1: Geo-tagged Twitter list data.

topic	# of lists	# of experts	# of listings	sparsity(%)
news	35,539	20,295	287,321	0.04
music	17,945	7,896	160,286	0.11
sports	16,018	5,395	139,838	0.16
food	10,476	5,485	96,661	0.17
celebs	9,783	4,090	104,004	0.26
tech	13,046	10,760	125,178	0.26
general	30,000	36,217	289,528	0.03

statistics shown in Table 1. In the following sections, we refer to list creators as *users* and list members as *experts*.

Metrics. We discretize the continental US surface with a $1°$ by $1°$ geodesic grid to map the coordinates to discrete regions.[1] Formally, we have a total number of K grids, which we call regions. We denote K regions as $R = \{r_i | i = 1, 2, ..., K\}$, to which each coordinate inside the US can be mapped. Furthermore, we assume for an expert e, there are totally n_e users who put e on their lists. Among them, we let U^e be the set of users for expert e, and $U_{r_i}^e$ be the set of users from the region r_i. Thus, the probability of expert e's user from the region r_i can be defined as $p_{r_i}^e = \frac{|U_{r_i}^e|}{\sum_{r_i \in R} |U_{r_i}^e|}$. With these preliminaries, we quantity the geographical characteristics of expertise with:

Expert entropy. The *expert entropy* is defined as

$$H(e) = -\sum_{r_i \in R} p_{r_i}^e log(p_{r_i}^e)$$

This measure indicates the degree of randomness in spatial distribution of the users for an expert. It ranges from 0 when all users for the expert are only from one region, to $log K$ when user's distribution is uniform across all regions. Thus, it implicitly reflects the level of an expert's recognizability across the entire country.

Expert spread. While entropy provides insights into the spatial distribution of users, it lacks explicit consideration for the distance between a user and an expert. Hence, we define another measure called *expert spread* as follows:

$$S(e) = Median_{u_i \in U^e}(d(coord_e, coord_{u_i}))$$

where d is the distance between two locations, computed with Haversine function to account for the shape of the earth. The expert spread indicates how far a typical user is from an expert, thus can be considered as the localness of an expert.

4.2 Region-Based Locality

In Figure 1b and 1c, we observed that food experts from San Francisco and Chicago are preferred by users nearby. How does this observation manifest according to our statistical measures? To that end, we select experts from the following cities: San Francisco (SF), New York (NY), Chicago, Houston, Denver and Seattle. We first show the average expert entropy for these cities with respect to different topics in Table 2. As can be observed from the table: (i) Experts from different geo-locations have different levels of recognizability across the country; and (ii) Generally, experts from SF and NY are popular in more regions than those from other geo-locations, indicating that SF and NY have a greater impact on expertise curation for users on Twitter.

In Figure 2a, we examine expert spread for these cities. We can see that generally, experts from different geo-locations have different levels of locality, with experts from Chicago and SF having the

---

[1] $1°$ by $1°$ is approximately 70 miles by 50 miles at latitude $40°$. We also tested a finer mesh of $0.1°$ by $0.1°$, which gave quantitatively similar results.

Table 2: Average expert entropy for different cities.

topic	SF	NY	Houston	Chicago	Seattle	Denver
news	**2.461**	2.342	2.021	1.950	1.836	1.884
music	**2.514**	2.386	1.946	1.996	2.105	2.162
sports	2.518	**2.703**	1.956	2.281	2.217	2.060
food	1.689	**2.105**	1.315	1.172	1.439	1.327
celebs	**3.274**	2.777	3.013	2.781	2.950	2.842
tech	2.323	**2.400**	2.262	2.249	2.098	1.917
general	**1.954**	1.932	1.645	1.610	1.606	1.585

Table 3: Average expert entropy and expert spread (miles) when $CDF = 0.5$ for different topics.

topic	food	news	tech	sports	music	celebs
entropy	1.661	2.048	2.235	2.247	2.267	**2.868**
spread	290	630	950	580	830	**1060**

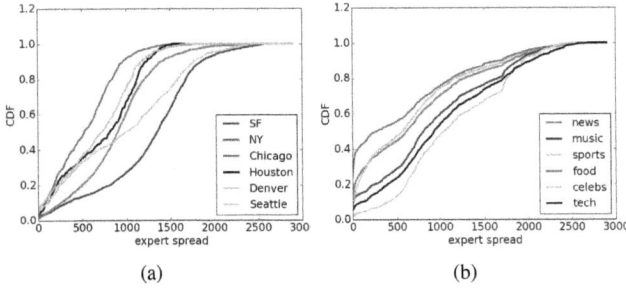

Figure 2: CDF of expert spread (a) for different cities and (b) for different topics.

smallest and largest expert spread. This indicates that compared to other cities, Chicago has the most local influence on expertise curation while SF reaches the farthest. Combined with the observations from Table 2, we conclude that *experts from different regions may have different levels of locality*, i.e., some may reach a wider geographical scope but others may be only locally popular.

Integrating region-based locality. Since the observed region-based locality reflects collective opinion, how can we integrate it into personalized expert recommendation? That is, if we know the geo-location of a user, can we recommend experts who are popular around the user's geo-location? As can be observed in Figure 1, an expert's popularity is not necessarily linear in the distance between user and expert; rather, it is often in the form of "clusters", i.e., experts may be popular in one region but not in other regions. Thus, we introduce the concept of "regional popularity", where we parameterize the popularity of each expert by regions, with the regional popularity to be learned from training.

Concretely, we assume the geographical space is partitioned into K regions. For an expert e_j and a region r_i, we assume there is a popularity parameter s_{ij} associated with r_i and e_j. This parameter is used to capture the degree of popularity that expert e_j receives in region r_i. Thus, if we have a total of M experts, the popularity parameters constitute the matrix S of dimension K by M, which represents regional popularity for all experts. Each column $s_{.j}$ represents the popularity e_j receives in all regions. Then, given a user u_i, the popularity e_j receives at the region where u_i is from is denoted as $s_{c(u_i)j}$, where $c(x)$ is a function mapping a user to its region. We use s_{c_ij} instead of $s_{c(u_i)j}$ for convenience. By integrating the matrix S to the original matrix factorization, we have:

$$y_{ij} = p_i^T q_j + s_{c_ij} \qquad (2)$$

We denote Equation 2 as the Geo-Enhanced factorization (GEF). Note that GEF is reduced to Equation 1 when $K = 1$. The GEF approach has the advantage over the baseline matrix factorization of explicitly capturing and learning expert regional popularity.

4.3 Topic-Based Locality

In the previous analysis of expertise, we observed that expert entropy can be impacted by geo-locations (see Table 2). Additionally, this table also implies that expert entropy can be impacted by the choice of topic. To further observe the geo-spatial distribution of expertise for different topics, we list the average expert entropy for the six sample topics in Table 3. As we can see, celebs has the largest entropy, which indicates that users interested in celebrity are most widely spread across the country; while food has the smallest entropy, indicating that users interested in food experts are most concentrated in certain regions. This is intuitively reasonable since a celebrity is very likely to have a better chance of being known in the whole country than a food expert from a certain location.

In Figure 2b, we show the cumulative density function against expert spread for different topics. We can see that, for a fixed spread value, the topic food gives the largest cumulative probability, indicating that users interested in food are closest to the experts; while users interested in celebrity are farthest. We also show the expert spread when the CDF is 0.5 in Table 3. We can see that the topics with increasing expert spread are ordered as: food < sports < news < music < tech < celebs, with food having the smallest expert spread of 290 miles, and celebs having the largest expert spread of 1060 miles, which is almost half the distance from the west coast to east coast of the US. Combined with the previous observation on expert entropy, we can conclude that the topic food is the most local among all, with users mostly concentrated in local regions of experts, while the topic celebs is the least local, with users scattered across the country. In another word, users interested in food tend to select food expert nearby, while users interested in celebrity do not have such geographical constraints, and users interested in other topics fall in between.

Overall, we can conclude that *expert's regional popularity can vary by topic*; in other words, users may have different regional preference for experts because of their topic interests.

Integrating topic-based locality. Now that we have observed that topic locality can influence user's preference for experts, it is important that user's interests should be aligned with the interests of the experts to be recommended. Since each Twitter list is labeled with certain keywords, we can aggregate all of the labels for an expert in all lists he appears. As a result, an expert e_j has a description d_{e_j} consisting of the aggregated labels. We then introduce a user latent topic factor t_{u_i}, representing u_i's topical preference, and expert topic factor $\bar{t}_{e_j}$, representing the topical property of e_j. Thus, the inner product $t_{u_i}^T \bar{t}_{e_j}$ indicates an affinity score of user u_i and expert e_j with respect to topic. Here, $\bar{t}_{e_j}$ is treated as known through d_{e_j}, and t_{u_i} is treated as unknown to be learned. The reason to model in this way is that labels for lists often have only one term, e.g., lists with one term label "food" occupy about 60% percent of total lists with any "food" in its labels. But often, a list is very focused on finer aspects of a topic. For example, a list labeled with "food" may include many "wine" experts, implying that we should also consider expert candidates labeled with "wine". By making t_{u_i} unknown, we are forcing the model to learn topic aspects of a user from those of experts she selected. For convenience, we use t_i instead of t_{u_i} and $\bar{t}_j$ instead of $\bar{t}_{e_j}$ afterwards. Thus, our

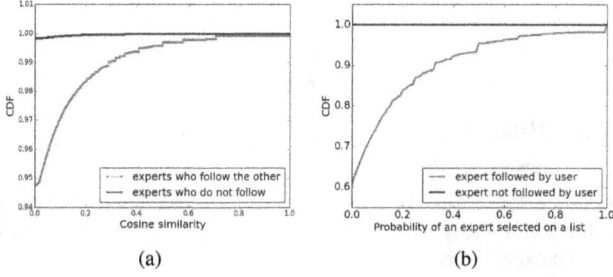

(a)   (b)

Figure 3: (a): CDF for similarity between experts; (b) CDF for the probability of an expert on a list.

Topic-Enhanced factorization (TEF) can be written as:

$$y_{ij} = p_i^T q_j + t_i^T \bar{t}_j \qquad (3)$$

Here, we treat each label as a dimension of $\bar{t}_j$. Through the explicit handling of each user's topic aspects, it is expected that user's interests are aligned with the interests of the experts to be recommended.

Fusion of region and topic-based locality. Naturally, we can integrate both region and topic-based locality into the model. We adopt a linear model for the integration of Equation 2 and Equation 3, resulting in our Geo-Topic Enhanced factorization (GTEF):

$$y_{ij} = p_i^T q_j + s_{c_i j} + t_i^T \bar{t}_j \qquad (4)$$

The intuition is when we know the region of a user and her topic aspects (by looking at the labels of her selected experts), we can recommend an expert both topically and geographically relevant.

4.4 Social-Based Locality

In addition to the modeling of region and topic based locality, we are also interested to explore if social connections among users and experts can improve expert recommendation. Our intuition is that (i) people who are connected by social ties have a higher probability to have similar interests; (ii) people who are socially related may have a higher probability to select who they follow as experts.

As evidence of social-based locality, in Figure 3a, we compare the similarity of experts for two cases: (i) when one expert follows the other; (ii) when no tie exists between two experts. Here, similarity of experts is defined as the cosine similarity computed by viewing each expert as a vector of all users, with each element being a value indicating whether the expert is listed by the user or not. Thus, a large similarity of two experts indicates that they often occur on the same list. We can observe that experts who follow the other generally have a larger similarity. We also compare the probability of an expert selected on a list in Figure 3b for two cases: (i) when experts are followed by the user; and (ii) when experts are not followed by the user. We can see that the chance for an expert to be listed by a user is boosted significantly when that expert is already followed by the user. Based on these observations, we individually model three kinds of social relationships:

User-user relationship. In this case, the following relationship is from a list creator to another list creator. When one user follows another, we assume that their preference is more similar to each other than those who do not. In terms of modeling, we adopt the approach of regulating their latent factors as in [16]. Formally, suppose there are user u_i and u_j, assume $\mathcal{F}_i^u$ is the set of users u_i follows, the social regularization incurred by user user relationship can be written as:

$$\sum_{i=1}^{N} \sum_{f \in \mathcal{F}_i^u} w(u_i, u_f)||p_i - p_f||^2$$

where $w(u_i, u_f)$ represents the similarity between u_i and u_f. Thus, if u_i and u_f is more similar, the latent preference factor p_i and p_f is also closer. Here, we use cosine similarity of users as the weighting scheme. The cosine similarity of users is computed by viewing each user as a vector of all experts, with each element taking a value — 1 if the expert is on the list, 0 if not.

Expert-expert relationship. In this case, the following relationship is from an expert to another expert. Using a similar approach as in the previous case, we regulate their latent factors so that experts following the other have similar latent factors. Formally, assume $\mathcal{F}_i^e$ is the set of experts e_i follows, the social regularization incurred by expert expert relationship can be written as:

$$\sum_{j=1}^{M} \sum_{f \in \mathcal{F}_j^e} w(e_j, e_f)||q_j - q_f||^2$$

where $w(e_j, e_f)$ represents the similarity between e_j and e_f. Here, we also use cosine similarity of experts as the weighting scheme.

User-expert relationship. In this case, the following relationship is from a user to an expert. Unlike the previous two kinds of social ties, this relationship links two different entities, and so the regularization approach is ill-suited here. Instead, we explicitly model these relationships with a bias term added to Equation 4 as follows:

$$y_{ij} = p_i^T q_j + s_{c_i j} + t_i^T \bar{t}_j + \theta_i b_{ij} \qquad (5)$$

where b_{ij} takes a boolean value 1 if u_i follows e_j, and 0 if not. θ_i is a weighting parameter to be learned. Thus, by adding a personalized bias term for each user, the model can take advantage of the following ties between user and expert.

4.5 Model Training

Combining the social regularization and Equation 5, the final objective function to maximize can be written as:

$$\sum_{e_k^{u_i} \in \mathcal{P}^{u_i}, e_h^{u_i} \in \mathcal{N}^{u_i}, u_i \in U} ln(\frac{1}{1 + e^{-(y_{ik} - y_{ih})}})$$

$$-\frac{\beta_1}{2} \sum_{i=1}^{N} \sum_{f \in \mathcal{F}_i^u} w(u_i, u_f)||p_i - p_f||^2$$

$$-\frac{\beta_2}{2} \sum_{j=1}^{M} \sum_{f \in \mathcal{F}_j^e} w(e_j, e_f)||q_j - q_f||^2 - regularization$$

where L_2-norm regularization is adopted, with β_1 and β_2 as the corresponding regularization parameters. In summary, the parameter set Θ to be learned through SGD is $\{p_i, q_j, t_i, \theta_i, s_{.j}\}$. For each iteration of SGD, we need to sample a user u_i, and from u_i's list, an expert e_k. Due to the large size of absent experts for each user, we also need to sample the set $\mathcal{N}^{u_i}$. Here, we adopt the strategy of random sampling. Then, for each sampled triplet $< l_i, e_k, e_h >$, we update each parameter value by taking a step along its gradient ascending:

$$\Theta^{t+1} = \Theta^t + \epsilon \frac{\partial L_{ikh}}{\partial \Theta}$$

where L_{ikh} is the posterior log-likelihood for the triplet $< l_i, e_k, e_h >$, and ϵ is the step size.

Update of S. For expert e_k and e_h, the corresponding parameters to update are $s_{.k}$ and $s_{.h}$. If the region of u_i is c_i, then the parameter $s_{.k}$ and $s_{.h}$ can be updated with

$$\frac{\partial L_{ikh}}{\partial s_{jk}} = -I(j = c_i)\hat{e} + \beta s_{c_i k}, \quad \frac{\partial L_{ikh}}{\partial s_{jh}} = I(j = c_i)\hat{e} + \beta s_{c_i h}$$

where $\hat{e} = \frac{e^{-(y_{ik}-y_{ih})}}{1+e^{-(y_{ik}-y_{ih})}}$, $I(j = c_i)$ is a Kronecker delta function that gives value 1 if and only if $j = c_i$, for $j = 1, ..., K$, and β is a regularization parameter.

Update of t_i and θ_i. Similarly, we have the gradient for t_i and θ_i as follows:

$$\frac{\partial L_{ikh}}{\partial t_i} = -\hat{e}(\bar{t}_k - \bar{t}_h) + \beta t_i, \frac{\partial L_{ikh}}{\partial \theta_i} = -\hat{e}(b_{ik} - b_{ih}) + \beta\theta_i$$

Update of p_i, q_k and q_h. Since p and q are socially regularized, we have the following socially regularized gradients:

$$\frac{\partial L_{ikh}}{\partial p_i} = -\hat{e}(p_k - p_h) + \beta p_i + \beta_1 \sum_{f \in \mathcal{F}_i^u} w(u_i, u_f)(p_i - p_f)$$

$$\frac{\partial L_{ikh}}{\partial q_k} = -\hat{e}p_i + \beta q_k + \beta_2 \sum_{f \in \mathcal{F}_i^e} w(e_k, e_f)(q_k - q_f)$$

The gradient for q_h can be obtained similarly as q_k.

5. EXPERIMENTAL EVALUATION

In this section, we report on experiments to evaluate the proposed Geo-Topic Enhanced Factorization with Social ties (GTEF-S) for personalized expert recommendation. Specifically, we seek answers to the following questions:

- How well does the proposed method perform compared to alternative baselines? Does region, topic and social-based locality give improvement individually, and if they do, do they complement each other?

- How well does it perform in cold-start situation, i.e., for users who have very few experts on their lists?

- Does the number of regions affect performance? If so, how?

5.1 Data Preparation and Experimental Setup

For evaluation, we randomly partition experts for a user into 50% for training and 50% for testing. To determine the number of negative experts for each user, we experimented with {50, 100, 150, 200, 250} and selected 150 for a tradeoff between accuracy and computational efficiency. For latent factor dimension, we empirically select 20 for all methods. For regularization parameters β, β_1 and β_2, we use cross-validation for tuning and select 0.02, 0.01 and 0.015, respectively. For gradient step, we initialize it with the step size 0.025, and decrease it to its 98% after each pass throughout all triples. This strategy is shown to be effective in reducing the number of iterations for the method to converge [9].

In the modeling of region locality, it is assumed that the continental US has been partitioned into K regions. Instead of using a gridding approach, we resort to k-means clustering to obtain the partitions by clustering the geo-locations of the entire set of users U. We choose a clustering approach based on Euclidean distance because the geo-spatial distribution of users exhibits a clustering effect, as shown in Figure 1, and can be satisfactorily captured by k-means clustering. In section 5.5, we evaluate the effect of the number of regions K. For other experiments, we select K to be 80.

For evaluation metrics, we adopt Precision@k (Prec@k) and Recall@k (Rec@k). Prec@k represents the percentage of correctly recommended experts out of the top k recommendations, while Rec@k represents what percentage of experts can emerge in the top k recommendations. Formally, if we define $Test(u)$ as the set of experts selected by user u and $Reco(u)$ as the set of top k recommended experts, we have

$$Prec@k = \frac{1}{N} \sum_{i=1}^{N} \frac{|Test(u_i) \cap Reco(u_i)|}{k}$$

$$Rec@k = \frac{1}{N} \sum_{i=1}^{N} \frac{|Test(u_i) \cap Reco(u_i)|}{|Test(u_i)|}$$

In our experiments, we evaluate k at 5, 10 and 15.

5.2 Baselines

We consider the following baselines:

- Expert Popularity (EP). In this baseline, we recommend experts for each user by ranking experts according to the number times each expert is listed by users.

- User-based Collaborative Filtering (UCF). Collaborative filtering method can be used to discover user's implicit preference by aggregating similar users. Formally, let a_{ij} take a boolean value, where $a_{ij} = 1$ represents expert e_j is selected by u_i, while $a_{ij} = 0$ means the opposite. Thus, according to UCF, the prediction score $\bar{c}_{ij}$ of u_i selecting e_j can be obtained by $\bar{c}_{ij} = \frac{\sum_k w_{ik} \cdot c_{kj}}{\sum_k w_{ik}}$, where w_{ik} is computed with cosine similarity. We then rank the candidate experts according to $\bar{c}_{ij}$ and select the top k experts for recommendation. We select the number of neighbors for each user to be 100.

- MF. This is the basic pair-wise latent factor model shown in Equation 1 trained by BPR.

- GEF. This model only considers region-based locality manifested through users' geographical footprints, shown in Equation 2.

- TEF. This model only considers topic-based locality manifested through experts' labels, shown in Equation 3.

- GTEF. This model is the fusion of GEF and TEF, considering both region and topic-based locality as shown in Equation 4.

- Social MF. This model considers three different kinds of social ties. If the model only considers user user relationship, it is denoted as MF-S1; if the model only considers expert expert relationship, it is denoted as MF-S2; and if the model only considers user expert relationship, it is denoted as MF-S3. We denote the model as MF-S if it considers all three kinds of social ties.

5.3 Comparison with Baselines

How well does the proposed method compare to alternative approaches? To answer this question, we first show the performance comparison in Figure 4, where we report Prec@k and Rec@k for all topics. As we can see, overall, the proposed GTEF-S generally gives the best performance for different k. Specifically, it gives an average improvement of 24.6% over the best of EP, UCF and MF for precision, and 21.3% for recall. GTEF-S generally performs better than either GTEF or MF-S, indicating the superiority of enhanced pair-wise matrix factorization by considering region, topic and social-based locality, and that these three factors are able to complement each other.

Comparison for MF, GEF, TEF and GTEF. By comparing these methods, we can examine if the explicit modeling of region and topic-based locality can provide any improvement. In Figure 4, we can see that GEF, TEF and GTEF perform consistently better than MF. Specifically, GEF gives an average improvement of 3.73% for precision and 3.43% for recall over MF for all datasets. This indicates that the introduction of the regional popularity matrix S for modeling expert's regional popularity can help distinguish regionally popular experts if we know the geo-location of the user.

Furthermore, we can see that TEF also performs consistently better than MF, specifically, giving an average improvement of 3.91% for precision and 3.16% for recall. This indicates that modeling user topic factor through the labels of experts can help find experts with similar topic aspect.

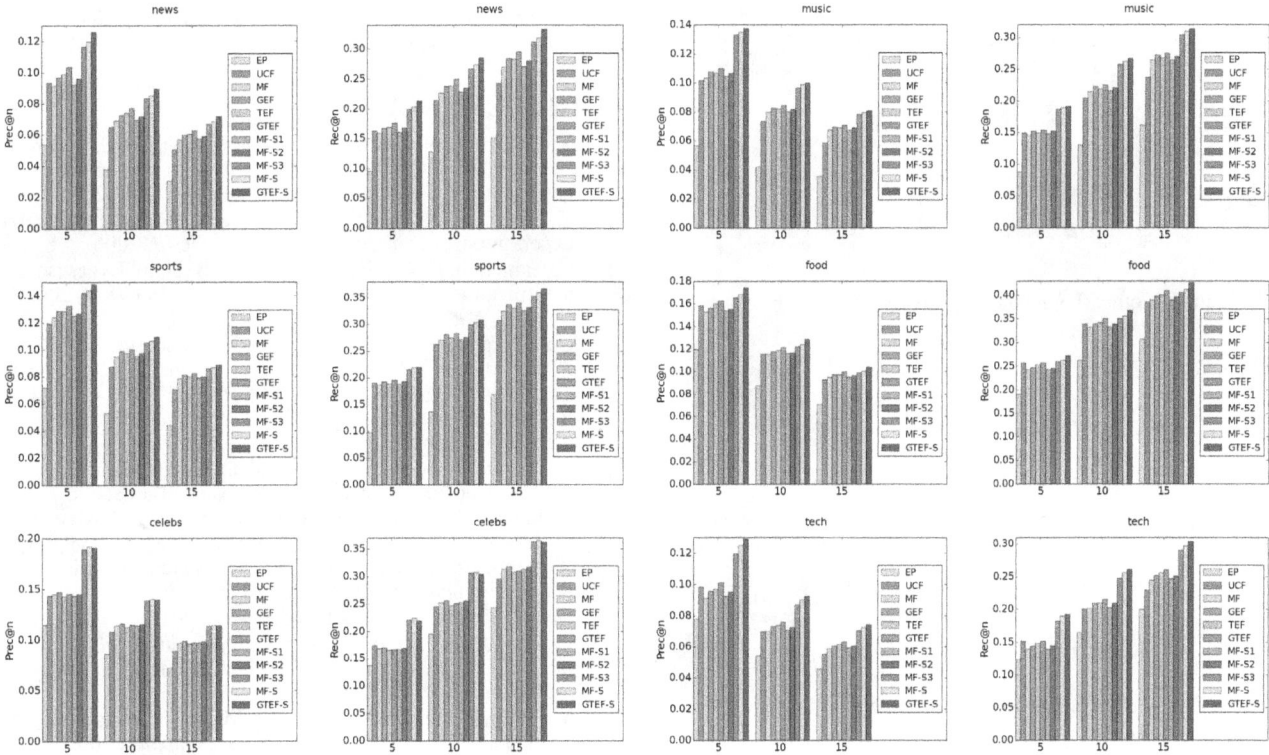

Figure 4: Evaluating personalized expert recommendation: Precision and Recall at 5, 10, and 15 for six different topics across 11 approaches.

Finally, we can see that GTEF gives the best performance among all (an average improvement of 7.35% for precision and 6.28% for recall over MF). These improvements are very close to the additive improvements of both GEF and TEF, thus indicating geographical influence is complementary to topic influence in modeling expert's regional popularity, and that they should be considered together for recommendation. Note that for topic celebs, the improvement of GEF (1.44% for precision) is not as good as those for other topics. This is probably because celebrities are heavily concentrated in the region of Los Angeles, and since its expert entropy is very high, it would not be very useful to model expert regional popularity. Also, TEF performs slightly worse than MF. Upon further examining the labels for experts and user's topic preference factors, we found that the labeling information for experts is scarce and most experts are only labeled with "celebs", without finer topic aspects.

Comparison for MF-S1, MF-S2, MF-S3 and MF-S. By comparing these methods, we can examine if the modeling of social-based locality can help recommend experts. Specifically, we have explored three kinds of relations: user following user (S1), expert following expert (S2) and user following expert (S3). From Figure 4, we can see that MF-S1 gives only slightly better performance than MF (0.43% for precision and 0.35% for recall), indicating that social ties between users barely provide additional information for recommending experts. For MF-S2, we see that it provides descent improvement over MF (5.02% for precision and 4.92% for recall), confirming that if an expert is similar to another expert, i.e., if they often co-occur on other lists, it is likely that the other expert can be recommended to this user. For MF-S3, it is shown to be rather effective. On average, it gives an improvement of 16.6% for precision and 14.4% for recall over MF, which confirms that if a user is already following this expert, it is very likely that this user will include this expert on the list. MF-S, modeling the previ-

ous three social relationships together, gives the best improvement of all (21.4% for precision and 18.8% for recall), indicating three kinds of social ties complement each other.

5.4 Recommendation for Cold-Start Lists

Previously, we found that the introduction of geographical, topical and social influence in pair-wise MF can improve expert recommendation. In this section, we examine how the proposed methods perform in the cold-start situation. When there is only limited number of experts on a list, there is little positive feedback for training, making it hard to obtain accurate latent factors of users' preferences. In consideration of this, we perform experiments to investigate the recommendation performance of the proposed methods for lists with few experts. Specifically, we select only lists which have fewer than 3 experts on the list to examine the performance. In Figure 5, we report the prec@5 and rec@5 for the method MF, GTEF, MF-S and GTEF-S. As we can see, GTEF, MF-S and GTEF-S consistently give better performance than MF for all topics, with GTEF-S showing the best improvement on average (23.7% for precision and 22.3% for recall). This indicates that the knowledge of user's region, topic preference and social relations can help relieve the cold-start problem. Also, MF-S gives better performance than GTEF, indicating that social relation is a stronger signal than user's geo-topic preference. Additionally, note that GTEF-S brings the best improvement over MF-S for news and food. This implies that modeling region and topic-based locality works best when users demonstrate strong regional preference (see Table 3).

5.5 Effect of Number of Regions

In this section, we study the effect of the number of regions K chosen to cluster the geographical coordinates of users. To that end, we select the number of regions from the set $\{10, 20, 40, 60, 80, 100\}$,

73

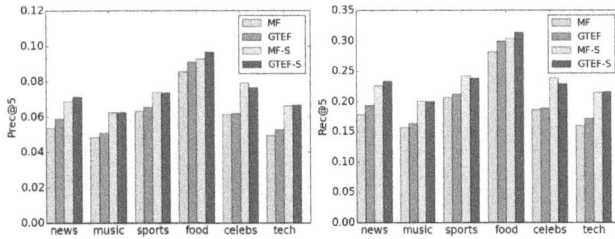

Figure 5: Comparing recommenders for cold start lists.

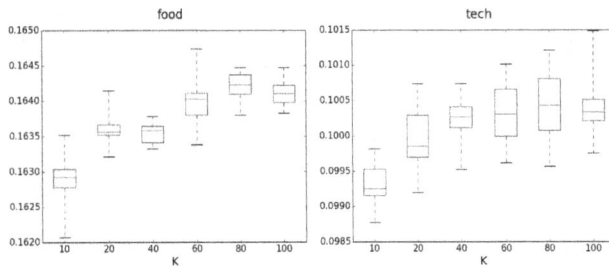

Figure 6: Effect of number of regions.

and run GTEF with each number for ten random initializations for topic food and tech (we ignore plots for other topics since they show similar trends). In Figure 6, we show how prec@5 changes with K. We can see that as the number of regions increases, the precision also generally increases, although the value of K varies for two topics when the performance reaches saturation. Specifically, for tech, the precision reaches almost the best at a smaller K, while for food, the precision gradually increases and reaches the best at a larger K. This can be explained by the observation from the previous analysis about topic locality. Specifically, topics such as food and news are relatively more local, i.e., experts of these topics are listed by local people more often. Also, experts of these topics are usually concentrated in many regions across the country, as shown in Figure 1a. As a result, a finer clustering of regions would separate two close regions. For example, it would separate the region of NY and Washington D.C. in Figure 1a, so that a user interested in food in NY can be recommended with popular food experts from NY instead of popular food experts from Washington D.C. On the other hand, topics such as tech and celebs are less local, and considering most of these experts are concentrated in fewer regions, it is not necessary to use a finer clustering.

6. CONCLUSION

In this paper, we tackled the problem of personalized expert recommendation in GPS-enabled social media. Specifically, we investigated the geo-spatial preferences of users and the variation of these preferences across different regions, topics and social communities. We proposed a matrix factorization-based personalized expert recommender that leverages region, topic and social-based locality. Through experimental evaluation over a Twitter list dataset, we found that the proposed approach achieves more than 20% in precision and recall and can ameliorate the cold start problem compared to several baselines. This confirmed users' geo-spatial preference of expertise and their underlying social communities have great potential for personalized expert recommendation.

7. ACKNOWLEDGMENTS

This work was supported in part by NSF grant IIS-1149383 and Google Research Award. Any opinions, findings and conclusions or recommendations expressed in this material are the author(s) and do not necessarily reflect those of the sponsors.

8. REFERENCES

[1] X. Amatriain, N. Lathia, J. M. Pujol, H. Kwak, and N. Oliver. The wisdom of the few: A collaborative filtering approach based on expert opinions from the web. In *SIGIR*, 2009.

[2] K. Balog, L. Azzopardi, and M. De Rijke. Formal models for expert finding in enterprise corpora. In *SIGIR*, 2006.

[3] C. Campbell, P. Maglio, A. Cozzi, and B. Dom. Expertise identification using email communications. In *CIKM*, 2003.

[4] K. Chen, T. Chen, G. Zheng, Q. Jin, E. Yao, and Y. Yu. Collaborative personalized tweet recommendation. In *SIGIR*, 2012.

[5] C. Cheng, H. Yang, I. King, and M. R. Lyu. Fused matrix factorization with geographical and social influence in location-based social networks. In *AAAI*, 2012.

[6] Z. Cheng, J. Caverlee, H. Barthwal, and V. Bachani. Who is the barbecue king of texas?: A geo-spatial approach to finding local experts on twitter. In *SIGIR*, 2014.

[7] S. Ghosh, N. Sharma, F. Benevenuto, N. Ganguly, and K. Gummadi. Cognos: Crowdsourcing search for topic experts in microblogs. In *SIGIR*, 2012.

[8] Google. Overview of local guides, April 2015.

[9] L. Hu, A. Sun, and Y. Liu. Your neighbors affect your ratings: On geographical neighborhood influence to rating prediction. In *SIGIR*, 2014.

[10] Y. Koren, R. Bell, and C. Volinsky. Matrix factorization techniques for recommender systems. *Computer*, 2009.

[11] A. Krohn-Grimberghe, L. Drumond, C. Freudenthaler, and L. Schmidt-Thieme. Multi-relational matrix factorization using bayesian personalized ranking for social network data. In *WSDM*, 2012.

[12] D. Lian, C. Zhao, X. Xie, G. Sun, E. Chen, and Y. Rui. Geomf: joint geographical modeling and matrix factorization for point-of-interest recommendation. In *SIGKDD*, 2014.

[13] B. Liu, Y. Fu, Z. Yao, and H. Xiong. Learning geographical preferences for point-of-interest recommendation. In *SIGKDD*, 2013.

[14] X. Liu, B. Croft, and M. Koll. Finding experts in community based question-answering services. In *CIKM*, 2005.

[15] Y. Liu, W. Wei, A. Sun, and C. Miao. Exploiting geographical neighborhood characteristics for location recommendation. In *CIKM*, 2014.

[16] H. Ma, D. Zhou, C. Liu, M. Lyu, and I. King. Recommender systems with social regularization. In *WSDM*, 2011.

[17] A. Pal and S. Counts. Identifying topical authorities in microblogs. In *WSDM*, 2011.

[18] S. Rendle, C. Freudenthaler, Z. Gantner, and L. Schmidt-Thieme. Bpr: Bayesian personalized ranking from implicit feedback. In *UAI*, 2009.

[19] S. Rendle and L. Schmidt-Thieme. Pairwise interaction tensor factorization for personalized tag recommendation. In *WSDM*, 2010.

[20] J. Weng, E.P. Lim, J. Jiang, and Q. He. Twitterrank: Finding topic-sensitive influential twitterers. In *WSDM*, 2010.

[21] M. Ye, P. Yin, W.C. Lee, and D.L. Lee. Exploiting geographical influence for collaborative point-of-interest recommendation. In *SIGIR*, 2011.

[22] J. Zhang, M. S. Ackerman, and L. Adamic. Expertise networks in online communities: structure and algorithms. In *WWW*, 2007.

[23] W. Zhang, J. Wang, and W. Feng. Combining latent factor model with location features for event-based group recommendation. In *SIGKDD*, 2013.

Risk-Hedged Venture Capital Investment Recommendation

Xiaoxue Zhao, Weinan Zhang,[*] Jun Wang
Department of Computer Science, University College London
{x.zhao, w.zhang, j.wang}@cs.ucl.ac.uk

ABSTRACT

With the increasing accessibility of transactional data in venture finance, venture capital firms (VCs) face great challenges in developing quantitative tools to identify new investment opportunities. Recommendation techniques have the possibility of helping VCs making data-driven investment decisions by providing an automatic screening process of a large number of startups across different domains on the basis of their past investment data. A previous study has shown the potential advantage of using collaborative filtering to catch and predict the VCs' investment behaviours [17]. However, two fundamental challenges in venture finance make conventional recommendation techniques difficult to apply. First, risk factors should be cautiously considered when making investments: for a potential startup, a VC needs to specifically estimate how well this new investment can fit into its *holding* investment portfolio in such a way that investment risk can be *hedged*. Second, The investment behaviours are much sparser than conventional recommendation applications and a VC's investments are usually limited to a few industry categories, making it impossible to use a topic-diversification method to hedge the risk. In this paper, we solve the startup recommendation problem from a risk management perspective. We propose 5 risk-aware startup selection and ranking algorithms to catch the VCs' investment behaviours and predict their new investments. Apart from the contribution on the new risk-aware recommendation model, our experiments on the collected CrunchBase dataset show significant performance improvements over strong baselines.

Keywords

Recommendation Diversification, Recommender Systems, Portfolio Theory, Venture Finance

1. INTRODUCTION

Early-stage investment is a key driving force of technological innovation and is vitally important to the wider economy, especially in high-growth and hi-tech industries, such as life sciences, clean-tech and information technology. Traditionally, investment opportunities are either referred or identified through manual technology scans [18]. The main stages of an investor's decision making process involve deal origination, screening, evaluation, structuring and post investment activities. These stages align with those identified by other research into venture capital (VC) investment [7]. In recent years, the traditional venture financing landscape has also shown signs of evolving. Some commentators [2] depict an industry "trifurcating" with (i) top-tier firms, e.g., Sequoia Capital, (ii) incubators and accelerators, e.g., Y Combinator, and, finally, (iii) firms that are taking a more quantitative approach to funding, e.g., Correlation Ventures. There is potentially a fourth factor in the emergence of entirely new funding sources such as "crowdfunding" which generally operate through online platforms, e.g., AngelList. Shifts towards more quantitative and data driven approaches along with new opportunities for online private investment provide additional impetus and scope for applying data mining and intelligent recommendations to this domain [17].

Whilst recommendation is useful in helping make investment decisions, this new domain, however, is quite distinct from existing applications of recommender systems (e.g., for movies and music) and represents unique cha-llenges. First, an essential question about venture finance is to estimate and control the risk, which is not well modelled for traditional recommender systems. Specifically, in a recent work where the collaborative filtering method is applied to the startup recommendations [17], the authors purely explored the similarity between new investment opportunities and VCs' holding investments. Promoting similar opportunities may be attractive to the VCs at the first sight, but such similarity-based methods fail to catch VCs' underlying main investment intention, which is to examine how well the new investment will fit into the current investment portfolio to hedge the risk and increase the return [9]. Figure 1 further illustrates our motivation by employing a latent-factor model on our collected dataset from CrunchBase (https://www.crunchbase.com/). This figure compares the mean and variance between the probabilistic matrix factorisation (PMF) [14] recommendations and VCs' groundtruths (detailed in Section 3). The PMF recommendations are made to contain the same number of items as the groundtruths for each VC in order to make comparison. We can see that for 76.3% VCs, PMF recommendations have higher mean values, but in 83.5% cases, the VCs' true investments have lower variances and thus lower risk.

Furthermore, investments usually involve a long term process, which is different from content consumption behaviours such as movie watching. It is because a VC's decision on more investments does not necessarily indicate terminations of previous holding investments, but adding them into the existing portfolio. This emphasises the need that instead of

---

[*] Joint first authorship.

RecSys'15, September 16–20, 2015, Vienna, Austria.
© 2015 ACM. ISBN 978-1-4503-3692-5/15/09 ...$15.00.
DOI: http://dx.doi.org/10.1145/2792838.2800181

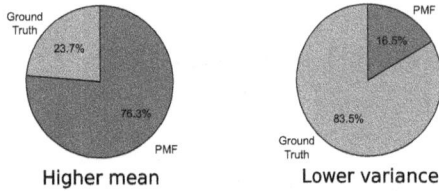

Figure 1: Mean and variance comparisons between PMF recommendations and groundtruth investments in CrunchBase. Left: percentage of higher mean for individual VCs. Right: percentage of lower variance for individual VCs.

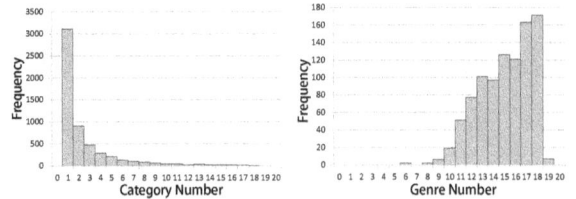

(a) CrunchBase   (b) MovieLens

Figure 2: Behaviour comparison by category/genre distribution.

diversifying the recommendation list alone, as many personalised recommendation systems have studied [16, 24, 22], it is more sensible to diversify the *joint* investment portfolio including both the VCs' holding investments and potential future ones. In other words, the recommended investment opportunities should be able to potentially hedge some risk of the portfolio the investor has already held. This point makes the VC investment recommendation significantly different from traditional recommendation tasks.

Finally, from the analysis of the CrunchBase data, we can find some unique characteristics in the VC investment behaviours (see Section 3). The dataset is much sparser as each VC usually only invests in a small number of investments. Meanwhile, a VC usually only focuses on a few industry categories, making the previous recommendation methods based on topic diversification, e.g., [27, 8], infeasible here.

In this paper, we address the above issues by integrating risk management into recommender systems and tailoring it for venture finance. Our contributions are fourfold. (i) We find that with advances in recommender systems, particularly collaborative filtering, it is possible to envision an automatic startups screening process according to the expectation and risk revealed by the VC-startup relationships. (ii) Based on the estimated risk, we propose 5 algorithms to systematically optimise the startup recommendations in a risk-aware manner. (iii) We conduct comprehensive experiments which show significant improvements on various measures, proving the effectiveness of our algorithms in recommending future investments and predicting VC investment behaviours. (iv) We publicise our collected Crunch-Base venture finance dataset used in this paper, in an effort to facilitate scientific research on investment behaviours and recommendations in venture finance.

The rest of this paper is organised as follows. Related work is discussed in Section 2. In Section 3, we describe and analyse the CrunchBase dataset. In Section 4 we present the proposed risk-aware solutions for startup recommendations. Our experimental evaluation is reported in Section 5 and Section 6 summarises and concludes this paper.

2. RELATED WORK

Venture Finance. Venture finance refers to the financing of private companies through the use of venture capital. Venture capital is a form of private equity, a medium to long-term form of finance provided in return for an equity stake in potentially high growth companies. Early-stage investment is typified by venture capital firms who deploy capital towards high-risk ventures. Venture capital has five main characteristics [13]: is a financial intermediary; invests only in private companies; takes an active role in monitoring and helping portfolio companies; primary goal is to maximise financial return by exiting investments through sale or an initial public offering (IPO); invests to fund the internal growth of companies. Whilst there have been some

applications of recommender systems to the broader domain of finance, including microfinance [3], there has seemingly been little previous academic research in applying such techniques directly to venture finance. To our knowledge, [17] is the first and the only one that has studied collaborative filtering on venture finance recommendation. However, [17] only showed some empirical results of a direct application of recommendation algorithms to venture finance, lacking a more sophisticated consideration or adjustment of recommendation methods to the unique domain, where the risk is a major concern. It is worth mentioning that [25] also considered risk in recommendation optimisation for a P2P lending investment recommendation problem. However, the authors failed to address the correlations between investments or to analyse the investors' risk-averse levels, making it significantly different from our paper.

Diversification in Recommender Systems. Recommendation diversification has become a hot research topic recently, and there are mainly two types of solutions. The first type of work tries to diversify the recommendation result explicitly [27, 22, 11]. For example, the authors of [27] explicitly introduced an intra-list similarity metric based on content-based features of the items and increased topic diversification by reducing the intra-list similarity. The authors of [22] defined an item set diversity based on averaged item-pair distances in a learnt latent space, and formulated the diversification problem into a binary optimisation problem to balance the accuracy and diversity. In [11], the authors discussed the diversification of recommended items as a temporal process so that the system delivers novel items with respect to the recommendations made in the past. And [19] discussed several evaluation metrics for diversification and novelty of the recommendation result. Generally, this type of work first defines a diversity metric, e.g., item category coverage or item distance in a latent space, and then proposes solutions to increase the measured diversity.

The second type of work achieves diversification by introducing the risk management concept from finance [9], where the investors can combine negatively or weakly correlated investments to diversify the risk of deficit using quantitative methods such as the modern portfolio theory [5]. In the recommendation scenario, items with the same topics or attributes usually have positive correlations with respect to users' preferences on them, making it higher risk to include them in one recommendation list. Thus by controlling the risk in the recommendation list, diversification of topics and results can be naturally achieved [16, 24, 4]. The authors of [16] first introduced the idea of portfolio theory to the mean-variance analysis of user-item preference modelling and then proposed a re-ranking algorithm to balance between the uncertainty and expectation of user preferences. The authors found that by increasing the risk-averse level, the item category diversification in the recommended ranked list can be improved. The authors of [24] studied a bi-portfolio scenario, where the recommendation lists from personalised and non-personalised methods were modelled as two portfolios. By proposing a risk-aware switching algorithm, they answered the dilemma of whether the personalised or non-personalised recommendations should be used. In [4], a contextual bandit algorithm is proposed to control the risk in mobile recommendations which dynamically address the user's risk levels. However, there has been no academic research how to address risk control in venture finance recommendation, which is the main focus of this paper.

3. THE CRUNCHBASE DATASET

CrunchBase is a repository of startup companies, individual partners, and financial institutes focusing on the US high-tech sectors [1]. With its self-description as a "free database of technology companies, people and investors that anyone can edit", CrunchBase maintains the investment events between investors (including financial institutes and individual partners) and investment opportunities (usually startup companies) associated with the total amount of raised funding[1] and time. According to [17], financial organisations and individual partners are significantly different in their investment behaviours. Thus in search of consistent properties, in this work we focus on only the financial organisations. We crawled the CrunchBase data from its official API[2] in May 2014. In total, we collected 62,926 investment events between 7,706 VCs and 18,026 startups from 1987 to 2014. We publicise the dataset online for research use[3].

By comparing the statistics between CrunchBase and the MovieLens 1M dataset (a well-known dataset for collaborative filtering research), we have identified quite different characteristics. First, as shown in Figure 2, VCs in the CrunchBase dataset tend to invest in a small number of industry categories, whereas users in the MovieLens dataset tend to rate a variety of movies, which often span more than 15 different genres. The reasons could be that, on one hand, VC's investment numbers in CrunchBase are generally much lower than the user rating numbers in MovieLens, due to the severe sparsity of the CrunchBase dataset (detailed below); on the other hand, VCs may be cautious in investing in unfamiliar industry categories to avoid risk.

Second, the CrunchBase dataset is much sparser than conventional recommendation data. The rating ratio of the MovieLens 1M dataset is about 4.46%, and it is 1.17% for another well-known movie-rating dataset Netflix. These ratios are already very low, but the observed investment ratio of CrunchBase is even lower: only 0.045%, about 1/97 of MovieLens 1M's and 1/25 of Netflix's. Such sparsity is reasonable since private investment activity is not as commonplace as simply watching movies. Also, the final investment decision will require the consent of both the company and VCs and usually involves a lengthy due diligence process [6].

The distinct characteristics of the venture finance investment behaviours revealed by the CrunchBase data motivate us to build new risk-aware recommendation algorithms tailored for the unique investor-investment ecosystem:

- From Figure 1, VCs tend to invest in opportunities with risk concerns rather than pure recommendations based on similarity.
- VCs usually cannot make extremely large numbers of investments. For each new investment opportunity, the VC may consider how it can fit into its holding portfolio. This motivates us to optimise the portfolio

[1]It is the total raised money in one round for a startup instead of indicated for each funding party. Therefore we choose not to use the funding amount information in this work.
[2]CrunchBase API: http://developer.crunchbase.com
[3]http://www0.cs.ucl.ac.uk/staff/w.zhang/cb.html

including both the invested startups and those to be recommended together.
- VCs normally focus on a small number of industry categories, unlike the wide range of genres in users' movie watching behaviours. This suggests that we cannot simply use a topic-diversification method commonly used for recommendation list diversification [27].

4. METHODOLOGY
4.1 Problem Formulation

Let us denote a VC (venture capital firm) as u and the available startup (investment opportunity) pool as $\mathcal{I}$. Suppose that VC u has already invested in m startups from the pool, and the recommender system is to seek another n startups from the pool for this VC to invest in. Without loss of generality, we denote the m holding investments (startups that the VC has already invested in) as $\boldsymbol{i} = (i_1, i_2, \ldots, i_m)$, and denote the startups to recommend as $\boldsymbol{j} = (j_1, j_2, \ldots, j_n)$ where $\boldsymbol{j} \subset \mathcal{I} \backslash \boldsymbol{i}$. We will also refer to the available startup set for VC u as $\mathcal{I}^u$ ($\mathcal{I}^u = \mathcal{I} \backslash \boldsymbol{i}$) in the sequel.

We define a joint portfolio $p(\boldsymbol{j})$ as a linear combination of the $m + n$ startups (m invested startups and n recommendations) with normalised weights:

$$p(\boldsymbol{j}) = \{(i_1, w_{i_1}), \ldots (i_m, w_{i_m}), (j_1, w_{j_1}), \ldots (j_n, w_{j_n})\} \quad (1)$$

with $\sum_{\alpha=1}^{m} w_{i_\alpha} + \sum_{\beta=1}^{n} w_{j_\beta} = 1$. Here the weights stand for estimated importance of each startup in the portfolio and will finally determine the ranking of the recommendation list [24]. Note that $\boldsymbol{i}$ is omitted in this notation for the sake of simplicity because the holding startups denoted by $\boldsymbol{i}$ are always contained in the joint portfolio.

We further denote VC u's preference on the joint portfolio $p(\boldsymbol{j})$ as $R_{u,p(\boldsymbol{j})}$, which is a weighted linear combination of the preferences on its component, as will be discussed later. According to PMF, $R_{u,p(\boldsymbol{j})}$ can be modelled as a random variable [14]. The utility function $U[R_{u,p(\boldsymbol{j})}]$ based on the random variable $R_{u,p(\boldsymbol{j})}$ is defined as a trade-off between the expected reward $\mathbb{E}[R_{u,p(\boldsymbol{j})}]$ and the associated risk. The risk is usually defined as the variance of the reward $\text{Var}[R_{u,p(\boldsymbol{j})}]$ [12, 21, 24]. In the risk-averse case, it is subtracted from the expected reward $\mathbb{E}[R_{u,p(\boldsymbol{j})}]$ to form the utility function.

The objective function is thus to find n startups (with rankings) to recommend to the VC so that the VC's utility over the joint portfolio is optimised:

$$j^* = \underbrace{\arg\max_{\boldsymbol{j}}}_{\text{startup selection}} \underbrace{\left[\max_{\boldsymbol{w_i}, \boldsymbol{w_j}} \left(\mathbb{E}[R_{u,p(\boldsymbol{j})}] - b \, \text{Var}[R_{u,p(\boldsymbol{j})}] \right) \right]}_{\text{portfolio optimisation}}. \quad (2)$$

Here we have already used vectors $\boldsymbol{w_i}$ and $\boldsymbol{w_j}$ to denote the weight vector of startups $\boldsymbol{i}$ and startups $\boldsymbol{j}$ respectively. The n recommended startups are then ranked according to their weights optimised in the process. Parameter b is the VC's risk-averse level. A higher b means that the VC is more risk-averse and is willing to sacrifice the expected reward to hedge the risk. It can be optimised globally (for all the VCs) or personally (adapted for each individual VC) from the data. We will show in the experiment section how b is determined and calibrated from the data.

We can see that there are two sub-problems in the objective function:
- **Portfolio optimisation**: given a candidate recommendation set of startups $\boldsymbol{j}$, to find the optimally allocated weights to maximise the utility of the joint portfolio $p(\boldsymbol{j})$. This part is discussed in Section 4.2.
- **Startup selection and ranking**: given a pool of available startups $\mathcal{I}^u$, to select a subset $\boldsymbol{j} \subseteq \mathcal{I}^u$ ($|\boldsymbol{j}| = n$) to form the joint portfolio $p(\boldsymbol{j})$. This part is discussed in Section 4.3.

Algorithm 1 Sampling-based Startup Selection (Sampling)

Require: VC u, current invested startups $i_1, \ldots, i_m$, candidate startup set $\mathcal{I}^c$, risk-averse parameter b, recommendation size n, utility function U, sampling time T.

  Initialise $j^* \leftarrow \emptyset$

  for $t = 1 \ldots T$ **do**

    Sample $\boldsymbol{j}_t = (j_1, j_2, \ldots, j_n)$ from $\mathcal{I}^c$

    Build portfolio $p(\boldsymbol{j}_t)$ based on the joint set $(i_1, \ldots, i_m, j_1, j_2, \ldots, j_n)$ via Eq. (1)

    Calculate the maximum utility $U[R_{u,p(\boldsymbol{j}_t)}]$ via Eq. (3)

    if $U[R_{u,p(\boldsymbol{j}_t)}]$ is the largest utility so far **then**

      Update $\boldsymbol{j}^* \leftarrow \boldsymbol{j}_t$

    end if

  end for

  return Rank list $\boldsymbol{j}^*$

The two sub-problems are inter-connected. To optimise the portfolio we need to provide the selected startup subset, and to determine the optimal startups to recommend, we need to optimise each joint portfolio and compare between different startup selections.

4.2 Portfolio Optimisation

We first focus on the portfolio optimisation problem:

$$\max_{\boldsymbol{w}_i, \boldsymbol{w}_j} U[R_{u,p(j)}] = \max_{\boldsymbol{w}_i, \boldsymbol{w}_j} \mathbb{E}[R_{u,p(j)}] - b \operatorname{Var}[R_{u,p(j)}]. \quad (3)$$

To further simplify the notations, we will use $\boldsymbol{w}$ as the concatenation $(\boldsymbol{w}_i, \boldsymbol{w}_j)$ in the sequel. We will also denote the startups contained in the joint portfolio as $\boldsymbol{\kappa}$ which is a concatenation $(\boldsymbol{i}, \boldsymbol{j})$. A startup in the joint portfolio is thus denoted by a single symbol κ ($\kappa \in \boldsymbol{\kappa}$). Now, the optimisation problem is simplified as $\max_{\boldsymbol{w}} \mathbb{E}[R_{u,p(j)}] - b \operatorname{Var}[R_{u,p(j)}]$. Here we allow flexible weights $\boldsymbol{w}_i$ of existing startups in the portfolio optimisation process as we assume the VC can adjust importance and priorities of them.

4.2.1 Portfolio-Level Preference

As mentioned before, we associate weights as the importance of startups in the portfolio. We also define the ranking order of startups by the importance (weight) order among all recommended items. Now that the problem is translated into a ranking problem, and thus we adopt a generalised definition of weight which can be either positive or negative [24]. An advantage of this treatment also lies in its analytical solution for weight optimisation.

As mentioned before, a VC u's preference on a portfolio is a random variable $R_{u,p(j)}$, which is a linear combination of the preference random variables of individual startups denoted by $r_{u,\kappa}$:

$$R_{u,p(j)} = \sum_\kappa w_\kappa r_{u,\kappa} = \boldsymbol{w}^T \boldsymbol{r}, \quad (4)$$

where $\boldsymbol{r}$ is the vector representation of the VC's preferences of startups in the portfolio. By denoting the mean and variance of the preference $r_{u,\kappa}$ as $\mu_{u,\kappa}$ and $\sigma_{u,\kappa}^2$, the expectation and variance of $R_{u,p(j)}$ are calculated as:

$$\mathbb{E}[R_{u,p(j)}] = \sum_\kappa w_\kappa \mathbb{E}[r_{u,\kappa}] = \boldsymbol{w}^T \boldsymbol{\mu}, \quad (5)$$

$$\operatorname{Var}[R_{u,p(j)}] = \sum_\kappa \sum_{\kappa'} w_\kappa w_{\kappa'} \operatorname{Cov}(\kappa, \kappa') = \boldsymbol{w}^T \boldsymbol{\Sigma} \boldsymbol{w}. \quad (6)$$

Here we have used $\boldsymbol{\mu}$ to denote the vector of the preference expectations, and $\boldsymbol{\Sigma}$ to denote the covariance matrix whose (κ, κ')-th element is given by the covariance $\operatorname{Cov}(\kappa, \kappa') = \rho_{\kappa,\kappa'} \sigma_{u,\kappa} \sigma_{u,\kappa'}$, where $\rho_{\kappa,\kappa'}$ is the correlation between startup κ and κ' [12, 21] and can be estimated via industry category overlap [17] or latent factor vector cosine [24].

In this paper, we follow [26, 24] and use the PMF model [14] to obtain the probabilistic representations of the VC-startup preferences. Assuming that uncertainty in the preference originates from the uncertainty of the user latent factor estimation [26], we can estimate the expectation and variance of $r_{u,\kappa}$ as follows:

$$\mu_{u,\kappa} = \mathbb{E}[\boldsymbol{p}_u]^T \boldsymbol{q}_\kappa, \quad (7)$$

$$\sigma_{u,\kappa}^2 = \boldsymbol{q}_\kappa^T \operatorname{Cov}[\boldsymbol{p}_u] \boldsymbol{q}_\kappa. \quad (8)$$

Here $\boldsymbol{p}_u$ and $\boldsymbol{q}_\kappa$ can be estimated by the MAP solution of $p(r_{u,i} | \boldsymbol{p}_u, \boldsymbol{q}_i, \sigma^2) = \mathcal{N}(r_{u,i} | \boldsymbol{p}_u^T \boldsymbol{q}_i, \sigma^2)$. Due to space limit, the technical details are omitted here and we refer to the PMF setting in [26, 24].

4.2.2 Portfolio Weight Optimisation

Integrating Eqs. (5) and (6) into Eq. (3), we translate the portfolio optimisation problem into the portfolio weight optimisation problem:

$$\max_{\boldsymbol{w}} \boldsymbol{w}^T \boldsymbol{\mu} - b \boldsymbol{w}^T \boldsymbol{\Sigma} \boldsymbol{w}, \quad (9)$$

which is a standard quadratic optimisation problem. In the case when $\boldsymbol{w}$ can take any value in $\mathbb{R}^{m+n}$, there is an analytic solution explicitly given in [24]. Without loss of generality we assume an optimised portfolio is ranked according to the item weight such that

$$w_{i_1} > w_{i_2} > \cdots > w_{i_m}, \text{ and } w_{j_1} > w_{j_2} > \cdots > w_{j_n},$$

i.e., elements in $\boldsymbol{i}$ and $\boldsymbol{j}$ are ranked by their importance.

4.3 Startup Selection and Ranking

In Section 4.2, we discussed the model to estimate the maximum investment utility $U[R_{u,p(j)}]$ given the recommended startups $\boldsymbol{j}$. In this section, we discuss the algorithms to efficiently find the optimal recommendation set $\boldsymbol{j}$ from a large candidate corpus $\mathcal{I}^u$.

Considering the fact that the possible startup combination space is extremely large ($C_{|\mathcal{I}^u|}^n$), we need to first reduce the candidate set by pre-selecting a size-N candidate startup set $\mathcal{I}^c \subseteq \mathcal{I}^u$ ($|\mathcal{I}^c| = N$) with the highest expected preferences $\mu_{u,\kappa}$ estimated from PMF (Eq. (7)). Then within the candidate set $\mathcal{I}^c$ we determine the final ranked list of startups $\boldsymbol{j}$. All of our proposed algorithms share the procedure of first choosing the size-N candidate set and then determining the final size-n ranked recommendations.

With the candidate set $\mathcal{I}^c$ we propose the following 5 different algorithms to find the optimal selections and their ranking.

4.3.1 Startup Selection by Sampling

A straightforward solution is to use a sampling method to approximate the optimal solution, which greatly reduces the computational cost. The details are presented in Algorithm 1. By sampling n-sized startup combinations among the N candidates for T times and picking the combination with the highest utility, we can get a globally $1/T$ best combination in expectation. As $T \to C_{|\mathcal{I}^c|}^n$, the performance of the sampling-based method will converge to the globally optimal solution, i.e., the portfolio $p(\boldsymbol{j}^*)$ leading to the highest utility $U[R_{u,p(\boldsymbol{j}^*)}]$.

4.3.2 Startup Selection by Individual Score Ranking

This is a simple ranking algorithm that ranks the startup utility by considering individual startups joining the current portfolio. We denote the joint portfolio including one candidate startup j as $p(j)$, and the maximum utility $U[R_{u,p(j)}]$ with j will act as the ranking score of j. Based on the score of each candidate startup, we can rank them and choose the

Algorithm 2 Individual Startup Selection (Idv)

Require: VC u, current invested startups $i_1, \ldots, i_m$, candidate startup set $\mathcal{I}^c$, risk-averse parameter b, recommendation size n, utility function U.
  for each candidate startup j in $\mathcal{I}^c$ **do**
    Build portfolio $p(j)$ based on the joint set $(i_1, \ldots, i_m, j)$ via Eq. (1)
    Calculate the maximum utility $U[R_{u,p(j)}]$ via Eq. (3)
  end for
  return Rank list $\boldsymbol{j}^*$ of n startups with highest $U[R_{u,p(j)}]$

Algorithm 3 Sequential Startup Selection (Seq)

Require: VC u, current invested startups $i_1, \ldots, i_m$, candidate startup set $\mathcal{I}^c$, risk-averse parameter b, recommendation size n, utility function U.
  Initialise startup set $\boldsymbol{j}^* \leftarrow \emptyset$
  for $l = 1 \ldots n$ **do**
    Select the optimal startup j_l^* in $\mathcal{I}^c$ such that

$$j_l^* = \arg\max_{j_l \in \mathcal{I}^c} U[R_{u,p(\boldsymbol{j}^*, j_l)}]$$

    where the portfolio $p(\boldsymbol{j}^*, j_l)$ is built based on startups $\{i_1, \ldots, i_m, j_1^*, j_2^*, \ldots, j_{l-1}^*, j_l\}$ via Eq. (1)
    $\boldsymbol{j}^* \leftarrow \boldsymbol{j}^* \cup \{j_l^*\}$
    $\mathcal{I}^c \leftarrow \mathcal{I}^c \backslash j_l^*$
  end for
  return Rank list $\boldsymbol{j}^*$ with the selection order

---

top-n startups with the highest scores. This procedure is given in Algorithm 2.

As we can see, Algorithm 2 is quite straightforward: selecting each startup based on the utility it brings. However, this algorithm fails to consider the correlation among the n recommended startups.

4.3.3 Sequential Startup Selection

Inspired by [21, 16], we select the startups incrementally to approximate the optimal solution with a large computational cost reduced. For each iteration, in a greedy fashion, we select one startup which can bring the highest increase in the utility function when being added into the current portfolio. This procedure is described in Algorithm 3.

Sequential methods have been adopted in previous work on top-N recommendation [16] and webpage ranking [21]. Though it is a greedy method, it has shown high efficiency and good empirical performances.

4.3.4 Startup Selection by Weight Ranking

With the candidate startup set $\mathcal{I}^c$, we can build a portfolio p_g with all the candidate startups and the invested startups $\boldsymbol{i}$. Then we can apply the portfolio optimisation according to Eq. (3) to obtain the optimal weights for all the candidates. We rank their weights and select the top n. This algorithm is illustrated in Algorithm 4.

This algorithm takes into account the inter-relationship between each pair of candidate startups in $\mathcal{I}^c$. However, by selecting the top n candidates with the highest portfolio weights, the resulting portfolio is already different from the global portfolio p_g. In other words, the top n candidates are selected based on a globally learnt weight ranking rather than a direct optimisation on the joint portfolio with only these n candidates added, which is a discrepancy.

4.3.5 Startup Selection by Weight Filtering

Here we implement a backward sequential method shown in Algorithm 5. In each iteration, we build the global portfolio p_g based on the invested startups and the startups

Algorithm 4 Weight-based Startup Selection (Weight)

Require: VC u, current invested startups $i_1, \ldots, i_m$, candidate startup set $\mathcal{I}^c$, risk-averse parameter b, recommendation size n, utility function U.
  Build the portfolio p_g based on the joint set $\boldsymbol{g} = \{i_1, \ldots, i_m\} \cup \mathcal{I}^c$ via Eq. (1)
  Calculate the optimal weights $\boldsymbol{w_g}$ via Eq. (3)
  Sort the candidate startups by their weight in $\boldsymbol{w_g}$
  return Rank list $\boldsymbol{j}^*$ of n startups with highest weights

---

Algorithm 5 Filtering-based Startup Selection (Filtering)

Require: VC u, current invested startups $i_1, \ldots, i_m$, candidate startup set $\mathcal{I}^c$, risk-averse parameter b, recommendation size n, utility function U.
  while $|\mathcal{I}^c| > n$ **do**
    Build portfolio p_g based on the joint startup set $\boldsymbol{g} = \{i_1, \ldots, i_m\} \cup \mathcal{I}^c$ via Eq. (1)
    Obtain the optimal weights $\boldsymbol{w_g}$ via Eq. (3)
    Obtain j_f with the lowest weight in $\boldsymbol{w_g}$
    Update $\mathcal{I}^c \leftarrow \mathcal{I}^c \backslash j_f$
  end while
  return Rank list of startups in $\mathcal{I}^c$ by the optimal weights

---

in the candidate set, optimise the portfolio to obtain the optimal weights according to Eq. (3), and remove the candidate startup with the lowest weight from the candidate startup set. This process iterates until the resulting candidate startup set shrinks to the size of n. Similar to the weight ranking algorithm, the weight filtering algorithm is also based on the weights obtained by optimising the portfolio constructed by the overall startup set rather than the selected subset, and thus suffers from the same discrepancy.

4.4 Adaptive Risk-Averse Level

With different industry category focuses and investment strategies, different VCs may have different risk-averse levels, represented as the parameter b in our model Eq. (3). All the above discussed algorithms take b as a model parameter, yet b can also be learnt for each VC u and thus the portfolio can be optimised in a personalised manner.

In order to adaptively learn this parameter for each VC, we conduct a cross validation on the training data, tune the parameter b_u for each VC u and pick its optimal value for each VC which maximises the startup ranking evaluation measure (e.g., NDCG) on the validation data. Then the learnt b_u for VC u will be used in the test phase.

5. EXPERIMENTS

After describing the experiment setup in Section 5.1, we present the experimental results in three parts. (i) In Section 5.2, we focus on the case of recommending the next startup, i.e., $n = 1$. With only one startup to be recommended, the correlation between the recommended startup and the existing portfolio plays the key role in the decision process. (ii) In Section 5.3, we study the cases where multiple recommendations are made, i.e., $n = 3, 5, 10$. In these cases, not only the correlation between each of the new items and the existing investments, but also correlations among the recommended ones are important. (iii) In Section 5.4, we further perform a statistical data analysis on the optimal risk-averse level b among the VCs.

5.1 Experimental Setup

5.1.1 Data Processing

As described in Section 3, we base our experiments on the CrunchBase dataset that we collected. We first divide the CrunchBase dataset into training set and test set with 2:1 ratio for each VC according to investment time. Splitting this way, the total investment number is 69,422 in the training set and 24,138 in the test set.

We label a recorded investment from a VC to a startup as 1, i.e., a positive observation. Since it is a one-class training data [15], we follow [15] to perform a user-oriented negative item sampling process, i.e., for each VC, we sample the same number of negative data points as its observed positive points and label them with 0. We train the PMF model to obtain the latent factors for the VCs and startups as well as the probabilistic representation of the VC latent factors (as discussed in Section 4.2). Note that our focus in this paper is not on the performance comparison against the state-of-the-art recommendation methods, but on investigating how the proposed portfolio-based algorithms can *improve* the recommendation results. The choice of PMF enables a coherent view of the effectiveness of the proposed method as it enables pure model-based mean/variance/covariance estimation for building portfolios.

5.1.2 Compared Algorithms

Three types of state-of-the-art algorithms are compared: the conventional recommendation algorithms, portfolio-based algorithms and adaptive-b portfolio-based algorithms. As described in Section 4.3, we always first determine a candidate item set $\mathcal{I}^c$ obtained as the top-N items from PMF, before applying any item selection and ranking algorithm.

Random sampling (Random). As a baseline, we compare our results with randomly-chosen n startups from the candidate set.

PMF. PMF method directly gives the top-n startup determined by the maximum a posteriori (MAP) estimation of the VC's preference regarding each startup.

Portfolio-based methods. These methods include Sampling, Sequential Selection (Seq), Individual Score Ranking (Idv), Weight Ranking (Weight), and Weight Filtering (Filtering). Details of each algorithm are described in Section 4.3.

Adaptive-b portfolio-based methods. These methods adopt a personalised risk-averse level b for each VC, as described in Section 4.4. We denote them with '-A' following the algorithm's name.

5.1.3 Evaluation Measures

As the task falls into the category of top-N recommendation based on implicit data, we follow previous work [26, 23] to evaluate the recommendation performances with the following ranking evaluation measures: Precision (P@n), Normalised Discounted Cumulative Gain (NDCG@n) [10], and Mean Reciprocal Rank (MRR@n) [20]. For each algorithm, we calculate the recommendation performances (with respect to these three measures) in regard to each test VC, then average for all test VCs to get the average performances.

5.2 Next Startup Recommendation

In this subsection, we focus on the case of $n = 1$, i.e., only one startup is recommended for each test VC. In this case, Sampling, Idv, and Seq are essentially the same, denoted as Portfolio. We compare Portfolio and its adaptive-b version Portfolio-A with the baseline algorithm PMF. As P@1, NDCG@1 and MRR@1 provide exactly the same result in the case $n = 1$, we only use P@1 as the measure here.

Figure 3 shows the result comparison between PMF, Portfolio and the adaptive-b version Portfolio-A, for different latent space dimensions ($k = 25$ and $k = 50$). The candidate size N and the risk-averse level b are both tuned to optimal to obtain the Portfolio performance.

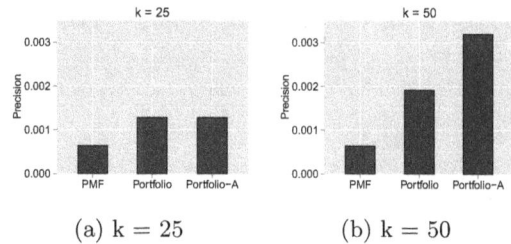

(a) k = 25 (b) k = 50

Figure 3: Precision comparison when $n = 1$.

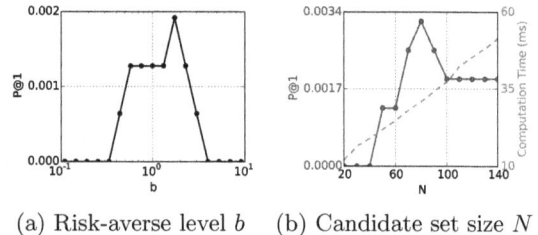

(a) Risk-averse level b (b) Candidate set size N

Figure 4: Performance against parameters when $n = 1$. The computation time is calculated as per test VC.

From Figure 3, we have the following observations. (i) For both cases ($k = 25$ and $k = 50$), Portfolio and Portfolio-A perform significantly better than PMF. (ii) Comparing between $k = 25$ and $k = 50$, the performance of PMF keeps unchanged, whilst the performance improvements by Portfolio and Portfolio-A are even higher when $k = 50$. (iii) In the case of $k = 50$, Portfolio is outperformed by Portfolio-A. These facts show the effectiveness of our proposed algorithms over PMF, indicating that recommendations with risk concerns are superior in catching the VCs' investment behaviour, and different VCs have different risk-averse levels. We will extend these discussions in Section 5.4.

In Figure 4, we show the effect of parameters b and candidate size N. From Figure 4(a), we can see that the performance peaks when the global risk-averse level $b = 1$. The global b reflects the overall risk-averse level for all test VCs, and the peak value indicates that a certain risk-averse level optimally catches the VCs' overall investment behaviour and leads to the best recommendation result. In Figure 4(b), we show the effect of tuning the candidate size N with the corresponding computational time shown as a reference. We can see that when the candidate set gets larger, the performance first increases and then drops to a lower level. It indicates that though an increasing candidate size N adds more options for the algorithm to choose, an oversized candidate set may also mislead the algorithm due to overfitted estimation of latent factors from PMF. The computation time increases linearly as the candidate set enlarges, so one may find a trade-off between the candidate size N and the computation speed as desired.

5.3 Top-N Startup Recommendation

Here we present the results for multiple item recommendations. In this task, ranking measures NDCG@n and MRR@n are also used in addition to P@n. In Table 1, we compare the results between baseline algorithms Random and PMF, portfolio-based algorithms and adaptive-b portfolio-based algorithms. All the (hyper)parameters are optimised with cross-validation. From Table 1, we can make the following observations. (i) All the proposed algorithms have great improvements over the results of PMF for all three measures (with a few exceptions for Weight and Filtering), showing the effectiveness of our algorithms in a multiple item recommendation task generally. (ii) Among the (non-adaptive) portfolio-based methods, Sampling, Seq and Idv

Table 1: Performance comparison by different algorithms. The improvement(-A) is calculated from the best Portfolio(-A) algorithm over PMF for each measure. (All the numbers except the percentages are in the unit of 0.001.)

n	@3			@5			@10		
Rec \ Measure	Pre	NDCG	MRR	Pre	NDCG	MRR	Pre	NDCG	MRR
Random	0.746	0.849	1.662	0.665	0.646	1.452	0.659	0.647	1.859
PMF	0.853	0.829	1.492	0.895	0.87	1.939	0.703	0.748	2.288
Sampling	1.492	1.729	3.41	1.279	1.235	3.218	0.959	0.955	3.177
Seq	1.279	1.429	2.771	1.151	1.126	2.931	0.831	0.871	2.931
Idv	1.279	1.239	2.451	1.151	1.105	2.771	0.959	0.987	2.937
Weight	1.066	1.279	2.558	0.767	0.946	2.558	0.703	0.741	2.835
Filtering	1.066	1.35	2.771	0.895	0.927	2.398	0.767	0.781	2.394
Improvement	74.9%	108.6%	128.6%	42.9%	42.0%	66.0%	36.4%	32.0%	38.9%
Sampling-A	5.968	6.126	11.509	5.243	5.395	12.479	3.964	4.112	12.293
Seq-A	1.705	1.879	3.73	1.662	1.74	3.986	1.087	1.299	4.276
Idv-A	1.705	1.768	3.41	1.662	1.616	3.89	1.087	1.304	4.452
Weight-A	1.066	1.279	2.558	0.767	1.008	2.685	0.703	0.786	2.92
Filtering-A	1.705	1.807	3.41	1.407	1.391	3.325	1.023	1.163	3.773
Improvement-A	599.6%	639.0%	671.4%	485.8%	520.1%	543.6%	463.9%	449.7%	437.3%

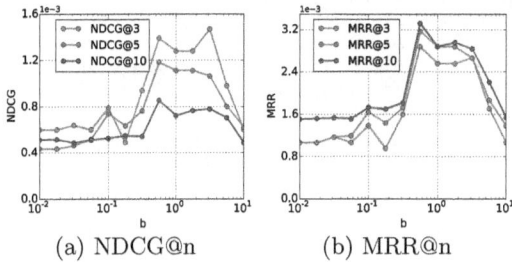

(a) NDCG@n   (b) MRR@n

Figure 5: Performance against risk-averse level b.

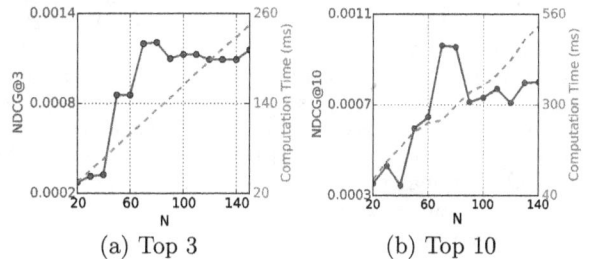

(a) Top 3   (b) Top 10

Figure 6: Impact of candidate size N on performance and computational time for Seq. The computation time is calculated as per test VC.

perform better than Filtering or Weight. This fact indicates that top-down algorithms like Filtering and Weight, which filter out items according to the *direct* portfolio optimisation weight for the *overall* joint portfolio (invested startups plus *all* the candidate startups), do not work as well as the group-selection-based Sampling, or the bottom-up Seq and Simple. This is due to the discrepancy between the weights learnt by a global optimisation and the weights learnt directly for the chosen group, as mentioned in Section 4.3. (iii) Adaptive-b portfolio-based algorithms perform better than non-adaptive ones, showing that each VC's risk-averse level is indeed different, so by adaptively fitting the VC's own risk-averse level, the performance can be further improved. (iv) Sampling(-A) outperforms all other algorithms. Again we ascribe its superior performances to its group-selection nature, as according to Eq. (3), a group selection method can achieve the best results. The other methods Seq(-A), Idv(-A), Weight(-A) and Filtering(-A) are further approximations than Sampling to approach the exact solution. (iv) Among the two baselines, PMF performs better than Random, indicating the effectiveness of the PMF model to catch the latent factors of VCs and startups.

5.3.1 Parameter Tuning

In Figure 5 we present the influence of b evaluated by NDCG and MRR, with different $n = 3, 5, 10$. From Figure 5, we can see that for each n and each measure, the performance has a peak around $b = 1$, which is consistent with the case of P@1 in Section 5.2. Furthermore, comparing different top-n tasks, as n increases, NDCG@n decreases whilst MRR@n increases. This can be explained by the sparsity of the dataset. When only a small number of recommendations are made (e.g., 3), only a smaller number of VCs are provided with the correct recommendations within the recommendation list. Whereas when the number of recommendations is enlarged (e.g., 10), more users are provided with correct recommendation within the longer recommendation list. According to the definition of MRR [20],

only the first correct recommendation counts. Thus, the result of MRR always increases with n in this case. On the other hand, NDCG considers the whole ranking list in a discounted manner, and, due to the sparseness of the dataset, it naturally decreases as n increases.

In Figure 6, we plot the influence of the candidate size N for the algorithm Seq, when $n = 3$ and $n = 10$. We can see that the performance first increases as the candidate size gets larger, then slightly drops after peaking around $N = 70$. This result may be due to the overfitting of PMF as mentioned before. Meanwhile, we plot the computation time for each N accordingly. We can see the computation time increases linearly with the candidate size N. Similar to the case when $n = 1$, we may trade off some performance for the computation speed by choosing a smaller candidate set than optimal.

In Figure 7, we plot the influence of the sampling time T in Algorithm 1 on the performances for both the non-adaptive and the adaptive-b cases. We can see that the performance peaks around $T = 120$ for both cases. The decrease of performance after the peak in Figure 7(b) may also be caused by the overfitting of the PMF model. Again, for the sampling method, we may also seek a trade-off between the ranking performance and efficiency by tuning the sampling time T.

5.4 Risk-Averse Level Analysis

In Figure 8(a), we plot the distribution of b optimised for individual VCs. We can see that VCs generally form two clusters: a risk-sensitive group whose risk-averse levels b are larger than 0.1 and a risk-neutral group whose risk-averse levels are much smaller. We also have interesting findings on the relationship between the number of investments made by a VC and its optimal risk-averse level b, shown in Figure 8(b). Here we applied a log-scale on the investment number, because the VCs' investment activity distribution is power-

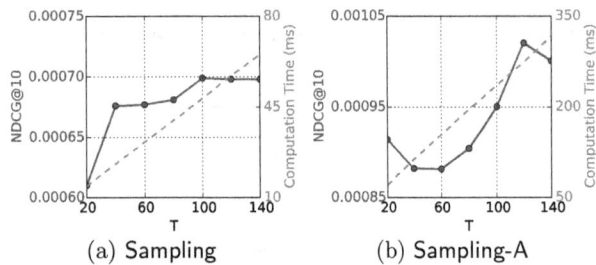

(a) Sampling   (b) Sampling-A

Figure 7: Impact of sampling time T on the performance of Sampling(-A) and computational time. The computation time is calculated as per test VC.

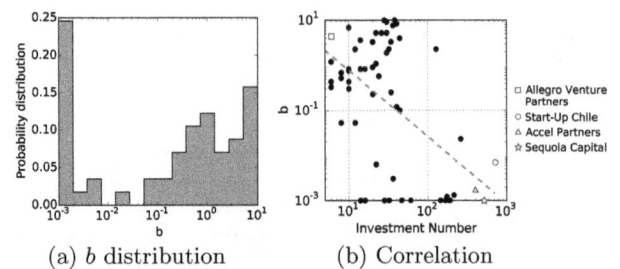

(a) b distribution   (b) Correlation

Figure 8: Data analysis on the personalised b. (a) Distribution of personalised b. (b) Correlation between VC's investment number and b for majority VCs.

law [17]. We can find that on the log-log plot, the correlation of the two is negative: companies holding a large number of investments tend to be more risk-neutral, whilst companies with smaller investment scales tend to have higher risk-averse levels (more risk-sensitive). By inspecting company names, we can find some of the largest VCs in the world, such as Start-Up Chile, Sequoia Capital and Accel Partners, fall in the category of the risk-neutral group, whereas smaller VCs, such as Allegro Venture Partners, are more risk-averse. These companies are tagged on Figure 8(b) for reference. These observations coincide with the intuition that the fewer investments held by a VC, the more careful it should be in making new investments, whereas, for a VC with a great number of investments, the risk may have already been diversified in its holding portfolio, and thus there is less risk concerns in making new investments compared to smaller VCs.

6. CONCLUSIONS

In this paper, we proposed a portfolio optimisation framework to solve the information filtering problem in venture finance, specifically by optimising the joint portfolio of VC's holding investments and potential investment opportunities. We exploited the variance defined on latent factors using a probabilistic matrix factorisation model, and optimised the joint portfolio towards a trade-off between expected preference and uncertainty. We divided the problem into two connected sub-problems including an item selection problem and a portfolio optimisation problem, and proposed five different algorithms to solve it. Through the experiments, we demonstrated significant improvement by using our portfolio-based algorithms and adaptive-b portfolio-based algorithms, compared with a direct PMF approach. In addition, we discussed the influence of the risk-averse level b, and conducted a data analysis over the distribution of risk-averse levels among the VCs.

For future work, we are interested in investigating the relation between the users' past investment scales and their levels of risk appetite, and how this can affect the portfolio optimisation process. Also, we will investigate the dynamic portfolio optimisation problem where the portfolio is optimised over time. Finally, we are also interested in including more features to our model, such as the amount of investment, investment actions (e.g., buying back or reinvesting) and how these can facilitate the model.

7. REFERENCES

[1] O. T. Alexy, J. H. Block, P. Sandner, and A. L. Ter Wal. Social capital of venture capitalists and start-up funding. *Small Business Economics*, 39(4):835–851, 2012.

[2] S. Anthony. Is venture capital broken? *Harvard Business Review Blog*, 2012.

[3] T. Bhaskar and G. Subramanian. Loan recommender system for microfinance loans: Increasing efficiency to assist growth. *Journal of Financial Services Marketing*, 15(4):334–345, 2011.

[4] D. Bouneffouf. R-ucb: a contextual bandit algorithm for risk-aware recommender systems. *arXiv:1408.2195*, 2014.

[5] E. J. Elton and M. J. Gruber. *Modern portfolio theory and investment analysis*. J. Wiley and Sons, 2006.

[6] B. Flyvbjerg. Quality control and due diligence in project management: Getting decisions right by taking the outside view. *International Journal of Project Management*, 31(5):760–774, 2013.

[7] V. H. Fried and R. D. Hisrich. Toward a Model of Venture Capital Investment Decision Making. *Financial Management*, 23(3):28–37, 1994.

[8] R. Hu and P. Pu. Enhancing recommendation diversity with organization interfaces. In *IUI*, 2011.

[9] J. Hull. *Risk Management and Financial Institutions,+ Web Site*, volume 733. John Wiley & Sons, 2012.

[10] K. Järvelin and J. Kekäläinen. Cumulated gain-based evaluation of ir techniques. *TOIS*, 20(4):422–446, 2002.

[11] N. Lathia, S. Hailes, L. Capra, and X. Amatriain. Temporal diversity in recommender systems. In *SIGIR*, 2010.

[12] H. Markowitz. Portfolio selection. *The journal of finance*, 7(1):77–91, 1952.

[13] A. Metrick and A. Yasuda. *Venture capital and the finance of innovation,2nd Edition*. John Wiley and Sons, Inc, 2010.

[14] A. Mnih and R. Salakhutdinov. Probabilistic matrix factorization. In *NIPS*, 2007.

[15] R. Pan, Y. Zhou, B. Cao, N. N. Liu, R. Lukose, M. Scholz, and Q. Yang. One-class collaborative filtering. In *ICDM*, 2008.

[16] Y. Shi, X. Zhao, J. Wang, M. Larson, and A. Hanjalic. Adaptive diversification of recommendation results via latent factor portfolio. In *SIGIR*, 2012.

[17] T. Stone, W. Zhang, and X. Zhao. An empirical study of top-n recommendation for venture finance. In *CIKM*, 2013.

[18] T. T. Tyebjee and A. V. Bruno. A Model of Venture Capitalist Investment Activity. *Management Science*, 30(9):1051–1066, 1984.

[19] S. Vargas and P. Castells. Rank and relevance in novelty and diversity metrics for recommender systems. In *RecSys*, 2011.

[20] E. M. Voorhees et al. The trec-8 question answering track report. In *TREC*, 1999.

[21] J. Wang and J. Zhu. Portfolio theory of information retrieval. In *SIGIR*, 2009.

[22] M. Zhang and N. Hurley. Avoiding monotony: improving the diversity of recommendation lists. In *RecSys*, 2008.

[23] W. Zhang, T. Chen, J. Wang, and Y. Yu. Optimizing top-n collaborative filtering via dynamic negative item sampling. In *SIGIR*, 2013.

[24] W. Zhang, J. Wang, B. Chen, and X. Zhao. To personalize or not: A risk management perspective. In *RecSys*, 2013.

[25] H. Zhao, L. Wu, Q. Liu, Y. Ge, and E. Chen. Investment recommendation in p2p lending: A portfolio perspective with risk management. In *ICDM*, 2014.

[26] X. Zhao, W. Zhang, and J. Wang. Interactive collaborative filtering. In *CIKM*, 2013.

[27] C.-N. Ziegler, S. M. McNee, J. A. Konstan, and G. Lausen. Improving recommendation lists through topic diversification. In *WWW*, 2005.

ExcUseMe: Asking Users to Help in Item Cold-Start Recommendations

Michal Aharon
Yahoo Labs, Haifa, Israel
michala@yahoo-inc.com

Oren Anava
Technion, Haifa, Israel
oanava@tx.technion.ac.il

Noa Avigdor-Elgrabli
Yahoo Labs, Haifa, Israel
noaa@yahoo-inc.com

Dana Drachsler-Cohen
Technion, Haifa, Israel
ddana@cs.technion.ac.il

Shahar Golan
Yahoo Labs, Haifa, Israel
shaharg@yahoo-inc.com

Oren Somekh
Yahoo Labs, Haifa, Israel
orens@yahoo-inc.com

ABSTRACT

The item cold-start problem is of a great importance in collaborative filtering (CF) recommendation systems. It arises when new items are added to the inventory and the system cannot model them properly since it relies solely on historical users' interactions (e.g., ratings). Much work has been devoted to mitigate this problem mostly by employing hybrid approaches that combine content-based recommendation techniques or by devoting a portion of the user traffic for exploration to gather interactions from random users.

We focus on pure CF recommender systems (i.e., without content or context information) in a realistic online setting, where random exploration is inefficient and smart exploration that carefully selects users is crucial due to the huge flux of new items with short lifespan. We further assume that users arrive randomly one after the other and that the system has to immediately decide whether the arriving user will participate in the exploration of the new items.

For this setting we present *ExcUseMe*, a smart exploration algorithm that selects a predefined number of users for exploring new items. *ExcUseMe* gradually excavates the users that are more likely to be interested in the new items and models the new items based on the users' interactions. We evaluated *ExcUseMe* on several datasets and scenarios and compared it to state-of-the-art algorithms. Experimental results indicate that *ExcUseMe* is an efficient algorithm that outperforms all other algorithms in all tested scenarios.

1 Introduction

Recommendation systems aim to present users with the most relevant items (e.g., movies, songs, advertisements, etc.) by predicting the user interest. Typically, they base their predictions on predefined features and user activity. User activity refers to numerical ratings or binary interactions users provide that reflect their interest in certain items. Techniques that rely on features are known as *content-based* [23] while techniques that rely solely on user activity are known as *collaborative filtering* (CF). CF is widely-used in recommenders due to its high accuracy, good scalability, and ability to execute without content analysis for feature extraction.

Though CF is employed in many industrial recommenders, there is still active research on the question of how to cope with new users

or items [2, 3, 4, 15, 22]. This challenge, known as *the cold-start problem*, arises since the system does not have relevant interactions for the new entity (user or item) and thus cannot model it properly. The user cold-start problem, in which a new user joins the system, is commonly addressed by interviewing the new user and asking her to rate several key items [9, 14, 24]. Unfortunately, the item cold-start problem is trickier because items cannot be interviewed and typically there are no users willing to rate every new item.

To model new items, CF recommenders select users for exploration and record their interactions with the new items. However, recommender systems typically have only a handful of slots to present items, for both exploration and recommendation, and since their goal is to present recommendations, the exploration process must be: (i) efficient, namely require a few impressions for new items, and (ii) accurate, namely obtain good results under some quality measure, for example under the *root mean squared error* (RMSE). Not only are CF recommenders expected to meet these two goals but they also face the challenge that users arrive in an online fashion, namely systems do not know which users will arrive and when. This enforces the exploration process to decide whether to present to users new items immediately upon their arrival.

In this paper, we present *ExcUseMe*, an algorithm for selecting users in online explorations of CF recommenders that rely on binary interactions. *ExcUseMe* aims to select users that are likely be interested in the new item and are thus expected to provide feedback. To detect such users, *ExcUseMe* attempts to **exc**avate the interested **use**rs' **me**an characteristics. It begins with selecting users with distinct tastes until obtaining the first feedback. Once a user provides feedback, *ExcUseMe* selects users that are similar to this user and are thus more likely to provide feedback on the new item.

We compare *ExcUseMe* to state-of-the-art algorithms on several datasets and scenarios. Our scenarios simulate real-world settings by varying the number of users available for exploration and the number of participants. Experimental results indicate that *ExcUseMe* obtains the best RMSE in all tested scenarios namely it is an efficient and accurate algorithm. In addition, results show that *ExcUseMe* converges towards selecting users that are interested in the new items, thus *ExcUseMe* also provides better user experience during exploration compared to the other algorithms.

Main Contributions The contributions of this paper are:

- Definition of an online exploration framework for selecting users for the item cold-start problem, inspired by real-world settings (Sec. 3). To the best of our knowledge, we are the first to consider such realistic framework for this problem.

- An efficient and accurate algorithm, named *ExcUseMe*, for selecting users in online explorations (Sec. 4).

- Evaluation of the exploration framework and the *ExcUseMe* algorithm. Experiments show that *ExcUseMe* is an efficient and accurate algorithm that outperforms state-of-the-art algorithms in several datasets and scenarios (Sec. 5).

The rest of the paper is organized as follows. Sec. 2 provides background and related work, Sec. 3 presents the problem definition and the exploration framework, Sec. 4 describes the *ExcUseMe* algorithm, Sec. 5 presents evaluation results, and Sec. 6 concludes.

2 Background and Related Work

In this section, we provide background and survey related work. We first describe the collaborative filtering recommendation technique (Sec. 2.1), then its inherent cold-start problem (Sec. 2.2), and finally we discuss related aspects of online algorithms (Sec. 2.3).

2.1 Collaborative Filtering

Collaborative filtering (CF) is one of the most widely-used approaches for constructing recommender systems, commonly implemented via *latent factor models* (LFM) or *neighborhood methods*. The difference between these techniques is that LFM models users and items in the same (latent factor) space and predicts whether a user is interested in an item based on their relationship in that space, whereas neighborhood methods predict the interest based on the relationship of the user to other users or the relationship of the item to other items [15]. For example, the item-item approach [19, 26] predicts the tendency of a user to an item by inspecting her ratings of items that tend to be rated similarly by other users.

Latent Factor Models In this paper, we follow the LFM approach. In this approach, items and users are associated with *latent factor vectors* and *biases* [17]. The vectors capture the users' and items' characteristics through latent factors, and the biases capture either the likelihood that the user will be interested in an arbitrary item (the *user bias*) or the likelihood that an arbitrary user will be interested in the item (the *item bias*). The latent factor vectors and biases are inferred from the observed interactions, which are assumed to be drawn from patterns reflecting the users' tastes.

Matrix Factorization To infer the vectors and biases we employ a common realization of the LFM which is based on low-rank matrix factorization [17]. This approach is appealing due to its high predictive accuracy and good scalability and it provides a substantial expressive power that allows modeling specific data characteristics such as temporal effects [16], item taxonomy [6], and attributes [1].

2.2 The Cold-Start Problem

An inherent requirement of CF is to have historical user-item interactions. Thus, when a new entity (user or item) appears and there is no relevant historical interactions, the CF recommender cannot model the new entity reliably. This is known as the *user cold-start problem* if the new entity is user, or the *item cold-start problem*, otherwise. While users and items are represented similarly in the latent vector space (usually), these two problems are essentially different. The main difference is that new users can be interviewed by the recommender to bootstrap their modeling. Another difference is that in most settings the number of users is much larger than the number of items, hence a typical item usually gets more ratings than an individual user provides, which may affect the modeling. We next review past work that has addressed these challenges.

The User Cold-Start Problem Modeling new users' preferences is typically obtained by short interviews during which the users rate several items from carefully constructed *seed sets*. Seed sets may be constructed based on *popularity*, *contention*, and *coverage* [10, 14, 24, 25]. In [24] the idea of constructing seed sets adaptively based on user responses (in adaptive interviews) was recognized as beneficial. Since then it was employed in many works, commonly using decision trees [9, 18, 25].

The Item Cold-Start Problem A common approach to mitigate the item cold-start problem is by providing additional attributes of the new items to the recommender systems [1, 11, 12, 21]. This approach is known as the *hybrid* approach since it combines CF with content based methods. The authors of [11, 12] propose a hybrid approach based on *Boltzmann machines*. The authors of [1] propose a regression-based latent factor model in which the items' and users' latent vectors are obtained from low-rank matrix decomposition of a matrix whose products are weight matrices and attribute matrices. The authors of [21] improve this work by solving a convex optimization problem to estimate the weight matrices.

Other works have addressed a different setting in which there are few ratings to the new items but there is no item content or context information. They showed that new items' latent factor vectors could be estimated by a linear combination of the raters' latent factor vectors and their ratings (without retraining the model) [2, 3, 15, 22]. A common approach to obtain these ratings for new items to bootstrap their modeling, applied by large-scale commercial recommenders, devotes a portion of the user traffic for *random exploration* of the new items. A recent work [4] addresses this problem of obtaining few ratings for new items in an offline setting in which all users are available for selection and their modeling is known. The authors first showed how to estimate the new item's latent vector and bias from ratings and the raters' latent vectors and biases to obtain the optimal RMSE. They then formalized the problem of selecting the raters as an optimization problem where the goal was to minimize the RMSE obtained by the estimated new item's vector and bias. This problem was solved via an *optimal design approach* and the solution was shown to be an approximation of the optimal solution. While this work considers a different setting than ours since it was applied in an offline setting and considered only positive interactions (ratings) while ignoring missing interactions, to the best of our knowledge, it is the closest work to ours.

2.3 Online Algorithms

In this paper, we consider the setting of online explorations and thus we apply *online computations*. In online computation settings, the input sequence is unknown and must be processed upon its arrival. A well-studied problem in this field is the *secretary problem* in which an unknown series of secretaries arrive one by one where each is assigned with a value revealed upon her arrival, and the goal is to pick the secretary with the highest value. However, the algorithm must decide upon the arrival of a new secretary whether to hire her (and end the process) or decline her (which is an irrevocable decision) and wait for a future, possibly better, secretary. Due to this limitation, the goal in such algorithms is to obtain a *good* secretary, e.g., one whose value is guaranteed not to be too far from the best secretary's value.

The secretary problem has been extensively studied as well as its variants. A relevant variant to our setting is the k *secretary problem* [5, 8, 13] in which the k best secretaries need to be hired. Our work can be phrased as the k-secretary problem: the series of secretaries are the series of users arriving and available to present them the new item; the value of k is the predefined number of users that may be selected; and the value of the users (the secretaries) is determined by the *ExcUseMe* algorithm. To select the k users (secretaries) we follow the work of [5] that showed that it is beneficial to split the set of arriving users to k portions and select one user from each portion; further details are provided in Sec. 3.

3 Definitions and Exploration Framework

In this work, our goal is to compute latent factor vectors and biases for new items by carefully selecting a few users to present them with the new items and then computing the vectors and biases from their interactions (feedback or lack of feedback). We begin this section with a formal definition of this problem. Then, we explain how to optimally compute such a vector from users' interactions. Thereby, the problem at hand boils down to selecting users to provide interactions for the new item (which is the problem *ExcUseMe* addresses). Finally, we describe the online exploration framework which resembles realistic online recommender settings.

The Item Cold-Start Problem We assume we are given a recommender system whose data is:

- N users: $\mathbf{U} = \{u_1, u_2, \ldots, u_N\}$,
- M "old" items: $\mathbf{Q} = \{q_1, q_2, \ldots, q_M\}$, and
- $N \cdot M$ interactions: $I : \mathbf{U} \times \mathbf{Q} \to \{0, 1\}$, where $I(u, q)$ equals 1 if u provided feedback to q, or 0 otherwise.

We further assume that the system has learned from these interactions a CF-model that captures characteristics of users and items via real-valued column vectors of dimension d (where d is typically small) and real-valued biases. Based on this model, the system estimates the interest of a user u in an item q as follows:

$$\widetilde{I}(u, q) = V_u^T \cdot V_q + b_u + b_q + \mu \qquad (1)$$

where V_u and V_q are the latent vectors, b_u and b_q are the biases, and μ is the average feedback rate: $\mu = \frac{1}{|\mathbf{U} \times \mathbf{Q}|} \cdot \sum_{u \in \mathbf{U}, q \in \mathbf{Q}} I(u, q)$.

In this setting we define the item cold-start problem. Given:

- a new item i,
- a candidate set U_A ($\subseteq \mathbf{U}$) revealed in an online fashion, and
- a budget of k users for exploring i,

select k users from U_A to provide interactions with i and accordingly compute a latent factor vector and bias for i obtaining the lowest root mean squared error (RMSE), where:

$$\mathrm{RMSE} = \sqrt{\frac{1}{|\mathbf{U}|} \cdot \sum_{u \in \mathbf{U}} (\widetilde{I}(u, i) - I(u, i))^2} \qquad (2)$$

Computing Vectors and Biases from Interactions To compute the new item's latent factor vector V_i and bias b_i from a set of interactions we assume we are given k users $\mathbf{U_i} = \{u_{j_1}, \ldots, u_{j_k}\}$, their vectors, biases, and interactions with the new item: $I_i : \mathbf{U_i} \to \{0, 1\}$. We then follow the approach in [4] and define V_i and b_i to be those minimizing the mean squared error, namely:

$$(V_i, b_i) = \operatorname*{argmin}_{V_i', b_i'} \sum_{u \in \mathbf{U_i}} ((V_u^T \cdot V_i' + b_u + b_i' + \mu) - I_i(u))^2 \quad (3)$$

This equation can be solved analytically, yielding the solution:

$$(V_i, b_i) = \left(\sum_{u \in \mathbf{U_i}} V_u' \cdot V_u'^T \right)^{-1} \left(\sum_{u \in \mathbf{U_i}} (I_i(u) - b_u - \mu) \cdot V_u' \right) \quad (4)$$

where V_u' is the concatenated column vector $(1, V_u)$. As noted in [4], the left term in Eq. (4) might be non-invertible, however, in practice a regularization term $\lambda \cdot (||V_i'||^2 + b_i'^2)$ is added to Eq. (3) resulting in a different and invertible term: $(\lambda \cdot \mathcal{I} + \sum_{u \in \mathbf{U_i}} V_u' \cdot V_u'^T)^{-1}$.

The Online Exploration Framework To model realistic settings we assume that the candidate set U_A is revealed in an online fashion, i.e., users arrive one by one. Upon the arrival of a user, an immediate decision is required on whether she is chosen for exploring the new item. If a user u is selected, a binary interaction $I_i(u)$ is revealed, indicating if u is interested in the new item i.

Algorithm 1: The Item Cold-Start Exploration Framework

Input: A new item i, a candidate set U_A, a budget k, and a score function F_s.
Output: The set of selected users and their interactions D_i.

1   $D_i = \emptyset$
2   phase$= 0.5 \cdot |U_A|/k$
3   initialize the auxiliary data structure A
4   **for** $i = 0; i < k; i\texttt{++}$ **do**
5      $s_m = -\infty$
6   **for** $j = 0; j < phase; j\texttt{++}$ **do** // The learning phase
7   Upon the arrival of a new user u from U_A:
8         $s_m = \max(s_m, F_s(u, A))$
9   **for** $j = 0; j < phase; j\texttt{++}$ **do** // The selection phase
10   Upon the arrival of a new user u from U_A:
11   **if** $F_s(u, A) \geq s_m$ *or* $j == phase - 1$ **then**
12           $I_i(u) = \mathrm{getInteraction}(u, i)$
13           $D_i = D_i \cup \{(u, I_i(u))\}$
14   update the auxiliary data structure A
15   break

16   **return** D_i

To select users in such online setting, we follow the approach presented in [5]. In this approach, k users are selected in k intervals where each interval is divided into a *learning phase* and a *selection phase*. During the learning phase, users are not selected but instead evaluated via a score function, F_s, and the best score is recorded. After the learning phase is completed, the selection phase begins and the first user whose score is not lower than the recorded score is selected. If no such user arrives, the last user of the selection phase is selected. Once a user is selected, the next interval begins. The size of each interval is at most U_A/k thus enabling equal intervals.

Algorithm 1 summarizes this approach. It receives the new item i, the candidate set U_A that is revealed in a stream, the budget k, and the score function F_s. The algorithm's goal is to select k users from U_A and return the set D_i of selected users and their interactions with i. In case F_s requires an auxiliary data structure A, A is initialized at the beginning and updated after each user selection.

4 The ExcUseMe Approach

In this section, we present the *ExcUseMe* algorithm that evaluates users for exploring new items. It is defined by its score function and auxiliary data structure required by the exploration framework.

The Score Function F_s ***and the*** **UseMe** ***Vector*** *ExcUseMe* aims to discover (*excavate*) the mean latent vector of the users that are interested in the new item. To this end, it maintains a vector that converges to this average latent vector, which we call the *UseMe* vector, and it is the auxiliary data structure described in the previous section. The *UseMe* vector, denoted by V_{UseMe}, is initialized with zeros and after users provide interactions it is updated to the vector V_i computed in Eq. (4) (Sec. 3) based on all revealed interactions.

The score function F_s returns the sum of the user bias and the dot product of the user's latent factor vector and V_{UseMe}, namely: $F_s(u, V_{UseMe}) = V_u^T \cdot V_{UseMe} + b_u$. The dot product captures the similarity of u to the *UseMe* vector and thus the likelihood that u will provide feedback to i, while the user's bias captures the likelihood that u will provide feedback to an arbitrary item, as the bias is positively correlated to the number of old items for which u provided feedback. In the first iteration, F_s boils down to the user bias, namely it guides to select users who tend to provide feedback.

The Rationale Behind **ExcUseMe** *ExcUseMe* is guided by two principles: (i) to excavate the new item's vector it is required to reveal as much feedback as possible (because user feedback is sparse), and (ii) the user whose score is maximal is assumed to be

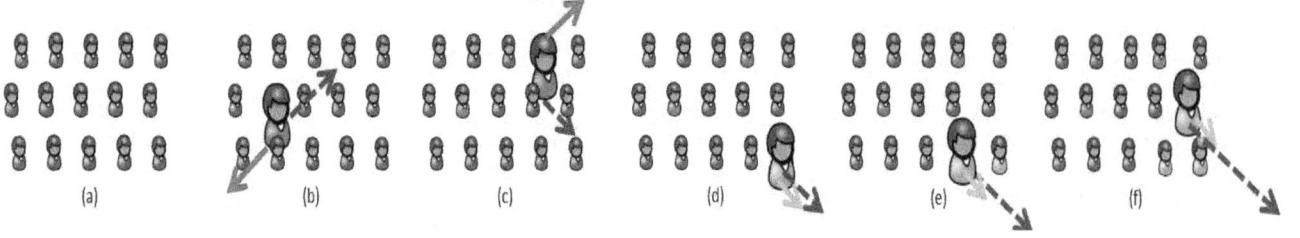

Figure 1: A schematic illustration of ExcUseMe converging toward users who show interest in the new item (see Section 4 for details).

the most interested in the new item. Driven by these two guidelines, *ExcUseMe* selects the users that are believed to be more likely to provide feedback and thus will help to excavate the *UseMe* vector. In addition, *ExcUseMe* leverages the co-existence of the users' and items' latent vectors in the same latent space by computing V_{UseMe} as if it were the new item's vector while treating it as capturing the mean latent vector of the interested users. Hence, since V_{UseMe} and the estimated latent vector of the new item's are computed in the same manner (see Eq. 4), not only does *ExcUseMe* converge towards selecting the interested users but also it is a semi-greedy algorithm to estimate the new item's vector.

Example To illustrate why *ExcUseMe* converges towards selecting the interested users, consider Figure 1. To simplify presentation, assume an offline setting. In 1(a), a set of candidates is revealed and in 1(b) the first selected user is the one with the maximal positive interactions. Assume this user does not provide feedback to the new item. The *UseMe* vector (in dashed arrow) is updated to capture this negative interaction, and the next user with the highest score is in the opposite direction of that user's vector. Then, in 1(c), the second selected user does not provide feedback either and the *UseMe* vector is updated to be orthogonal to the two users' vectors. In 1(d), the third selected user is the first to provide feedback and thus the *UseMe* vector roughly remains in the same direction as this user's vector. The following selected users are assumed to have vectors roughly in the same direction as well. In 1(e) and 1(f), the two selected users are also assumed to provide feedback, which strengthens the direction of the *UseMe* vector towards the interested users, thus converging towards the mean vector of the interested users.

Complexity We next show that *ExcUseMe* complexity is $O(1)$. A single score computation of F_s in *ExcUseMe* is $O(d)$ where d is the dimension of the latent factor vectors. The *UseMe* vector is updated incrementally: after selecting a user, the terms $V'_u \cdot V'^T_u$ and $(I_i(u) - b_u - \mu) \cdot V'_u$ are computed and added to the two terms in Eq. (4) (Sec. 3), then the left factor inverse is computed, and finally the dot product is computed. Computing these two terms is $O(d)$, computing the inverse is $O(d^2)$ since this term is a symmetrical matrix, and the final dot product is also $O(d^2)$. Since d is constant (and typically small), *ExcUseMe* overall complexity is $O(1)$.

5 Evaluation

In this section, we evaluate the effectiveness of *ExcUseMe* using several datasets. For each dataset we define 200 randomly selected items as "new items". The remaining items are used to train the initial model. After obtaining a mature initial latent factor model, we evaluate the performance of the different exploration algorithms: we execute them under the exploration framework for all 200 new items (independently), where users selected by the algorithms return interactions based on the datasets (these interactions are not used during the initial model training), then the new items' latent

vectors and biases are computed as described in Eq. (4), and finally they are evaluated based on three metrics. Experiments were implemented in Java and ran on a Sony Vaio with Intel(R) Core(TM) i7-3612QM processor and 8GB RAM.

We next provide more details on the evaluation and present experimental results. We begin with describing the datasets (Sec. 5.1), then explain how the initial model is constructed (Sec. 5.2), continue with providing the evaluation metrics (Sec. 5.3), then list the baseline algorithms (Sec. 5.4), and finally describe in more detail the experiments and present their results (Sec. 5.5).

5.1 Datasets

Here, we describe the datasets and the data pre-processing steps.

Datasets The datasets we use are: (i) *MovieLens1M* from `grouplens.org`, (ii) *Netflix* from `netflixprize.com`, and (iii) *Yahoo! Music* from `webscope.sandbox.yahoo.com`. *MovieLens1M* and *Netflix* contain movie ratings in a 1–5 scale, and *Yahoo! Music* contains song ratings in a 0–100 scale.

Data Filtering To avoid entities which are less indicative as they have too few ratings, we consider only users with at least 10 ratings and items with at least 20 ratings. Also, to avoid users which are noisy and unreliable we removed those with more than 300 ratings.

Data Statistics After filtering the data, *MovieLens1M* contained $488,616$ rates from $5,085$ users to $2,388$ items; *Netflix* contained $638,343$ rates from $6,657$ users to $6,685$ items; and *Yahoo! Music* contained $441,954$ rates from $9,458$ users to $2,640$ items.

Obtaining Binary Interactions Since all datasets contain numerical ratings while we require binary interactions, we interpreted the ratings as follows. We say user u provided feedback on item i if the dataset contains a numerical rating u provided to i. Otherwise, we say u did not provide feedback. This definition considers also low rates as feedback. We believe this interpretation is valid since even a low rate indicates that the user chose to interact with that item, in contrast to items she ignored and did not provide feedback at all.

5.2 Constructing the Initial Model

We next describe how we constructed the initial latent factor model that captures the characteristics of the users and the "old" items.

The Model To model the users and old items, we apply regularized matrix factorization [27] where the goal is to minimize the mean squared error. Namely, given the interactions $I : \mathbf{U} \times \mathbf{Q} \rightarrow \{0,1\}$, the estimated interest $\widetilde{I} : \mathbf{U} \times \mathbf{Q} \rightarrow \{0,1\}$ (see Eq. (1), Sec. 3), and a regularization parameter λ, the goal is to minimize:

$$\sum_{\substack{u \in \mathbf{U} \\ q \in \mathbf{Q}}} \left(\widetilde{I}(u,q) - I(u,q) \right)^2 + \lambda \left[\sum_{u \in \mathbf{U}} (||V_u||^2 + b_i^2) + \sum_{q \in \mathbf{Q}} (||V_q||^2 + b_q^2) \right]$$

$$(5)$$

where the variables are the average feedback rate, μ, the latent factor vectors, and the biases.

Model Training To optimize the cost function (Eq. (5)) we set the latent factor dimension d to 10 and λ to 0.1 (these parameters were optimized using a grid search over a validation set), and applied stochastic gradient descent (SGD) [17]. The SGD step sizes were determined according to the AdaGrad approach [7] that adapts the steps based on the aggregated gradient of each factor in the vectors. SGD was executed for 1000 iterations, after which further iterations would negligibly improve the cost function.

RMSE Model for Binary Interactions Typically, in settings considering binary interactions models are optimized based on the *logistic regression* approach [20] that minimizes the log-loss function instead of RMSE. We implemented both approaches to construct the model and observed they achieved similar results for our purposes. Since RMSE allows to analytically compute the new item's latent vector and bias (see Sec. 3), we chose it over the log-loss.

5.3 Evaluation Metrics

We next present the evaluation metrics.

RMSE Measures the root mean squared error between the estimated and actual scores. RMSE was described in Eq. (2) (Sec. 3) and considered all users in the system. However, it is common to consider only a test set of users and we follow this approach in the experiments. Namely, given a test set of users, $\mathbf{U}'(\subseteq \mathbf{U})$, the new item i's interactions $I_i : \mathbf{U}' \rightarrow \{0, 1\}$ and the estimated scores $\widetilde{I}_i : \mathbf{U}' \rightarrow \{0, 1\}$, RMSE equals: $\sqrt{\frac{1}{|\mathbf{U}'|} \cdot \sum_{u \in \mathbf{U}'} (\widetilde{I}_i(u) - I_i(u))^2}$.

Probability of Receiving Positive Interactions To estimate accurately a new item's latent factor vector from binary interactions it is crucial to receive positive interactions. Positive interactions are strong indications to the new items' characteristics and thus having only negative interactions is likely to result in inaccurate estimated latent vectors. Thus, we measure the probability of revealing positive interactions, namely the fraction of new items for which the algorithm revealed at least one positive interaction.

Number of Positive Interactions While revealing one positive interaction is crucial for estimating the new item's vector, having multiple positive interactions is typically more desirable. Having only few users that provided positive interactions may lead to estimating a vector biased towards these users and thus the estimated vector would not capture accurately the new item's characteristics. Moreover, an algorithm that selects on average more interested users provides better *user experience* because in real recommender systems users are unaware that they participate in exploration and expect to receive only recommendations. Thus, we measure the average positive interactions the algorithm reveals for new items.

5.4 Baseline Algorithms

We next describe the algorithms compared to *ExcUseMe* by describing their score functions required by the exploration framework (none of them require auxiliary data structures). We consider two algorithms commonly used by recommenders (*Random* and *Frequent Users*), a state-of-the-art approach in an offline setting (*Anava et al.*), and a complementary approach to ours (*Distance*).

Random Users are randomly picked with a probability of $k/|U_A|$ where k is the number of users that participate in the exploration and U_A is the set of available users.

Frequent Users In this approach, users that provided more positive interactions to "old" items (items that were already modeled) are believed to be more likely to provide positive interactions to new items. Thus, the score is the number of items to which the user provided positive interactions, namely: $F_s(u) = \sum_{q \in \mathbf{Q}} I(u, q)$.

Anava et al. This approach, proposed by [4], is an approximation algorithm for an offline setting in which *all* users in the recommender system may be considered and when selecting the next user *all* users may be examined. This algorithm was adapted to our online setting by defining F_s to be the function used in [4] to select the next user: $F_s(u) = 1/\text{Trace}\left(\left(\mathcal{P}_{B \setminus u} \mathcal{P}_{B \setminus u}^\top\right)^{-1}\right)$, where B is the set of users not selected yet and $\mathcal{P}_{B \setminus u}$ is a matrix whose columns are the latent factor vectors of the users in $B \setminus \{u\}$. This approach was shown to outperform other well-known offline approaches, and thus we consider this approach as the representative of offline approaches.

Distance This approach picks the first user randomly and afterwards selects the user with the farthest vector from the selected users' vectors, namely: $F_s(u) = min\{||V_u - V_{u'}||^2 \mid u' \in S\}$, where S is the set of selected users and the distance is the L^2 norm. This approach is in some sense complementary to *ExcUseMe* because it explores the user space by locating the user which is the most different from the previously selected users. This is in contrast to *ExcUseMe* that converges towards selecting users which are very similar to each other.

5.5 Experimental Setting and Results

Here, we describe the experiments that evaluate all algorithms.

Experimental Setting In each experiment, we fix a new item i and a budget k and let the algorithms select k candidates to learn i's latent vector and bias. As described in Sec. 3, users are revealed gradually and after a user is revealed the algorithms have to decide immediately whether to ask her for feedback on i.

Simulating Real-World Scenarios In real-world scenarios, not only do recommendation systems have to decide immediately upon the user arrival whether to ask for feedback, but they are also exposed to only $n\%$ users. This is because they wish to model the new item's quickly and thus cannot wait for all users to arrive.

To simulate this, in each experiment we randomly selected $n\%$ users, shuffled them, and let the algorithms select users from this set of users. The values of n were 10, 25, 50, and 100. Since we select the available users randomly, to increase the statistical significance of the results, we repeated each experiment 15 times.

RMSE Evaluation To evaluate the estimated items' latent vectors and biases, we measured RMSE (Sec. 5.3). To this end, before each experiment, 10% of the users were put aside as a test set to compute RMSE and were not selected to the $n\%$ available users.

Figure 2 shows the RMSE obtained on the different datasets and different values of n. The graphs show the RMSE as a function of the budget k where each point is the average RMSE of the 200 new items' latent vectors and biases, where the RMSE of a single new item is the average RMSE over the 15 repeating experiments.

Figure 2 shows that in all tested scenarios *ExcUseMe* outperforms all other approaches. The improvement of *ExcUseMe* over other approaches is most significant for low budgets and when there are more available users to consider for exploration (large n). Thus, we conclude that (i) *ExcUseMe* allows a fast exploration that expedites the convergence towards the new item's latent factor vector, and that (ii) *ExcUseMe* provides a score function that is adaptable to the number of available users (n) and as this number increases, the RMSE may only decrease. This is in contrast to other approaches which do not demonstrate this property. To illustrate it, consider the graphs showing the RMSE of the *Netflix* dataset, when the budget is $k=20$, and the percentage of available users is $n=50$ and $n=100$: only the *ExcUseMe* approach obtains a better RMSE when there are 100% available users. These two conclusions imply that recommender systems may obtain a short exploration with

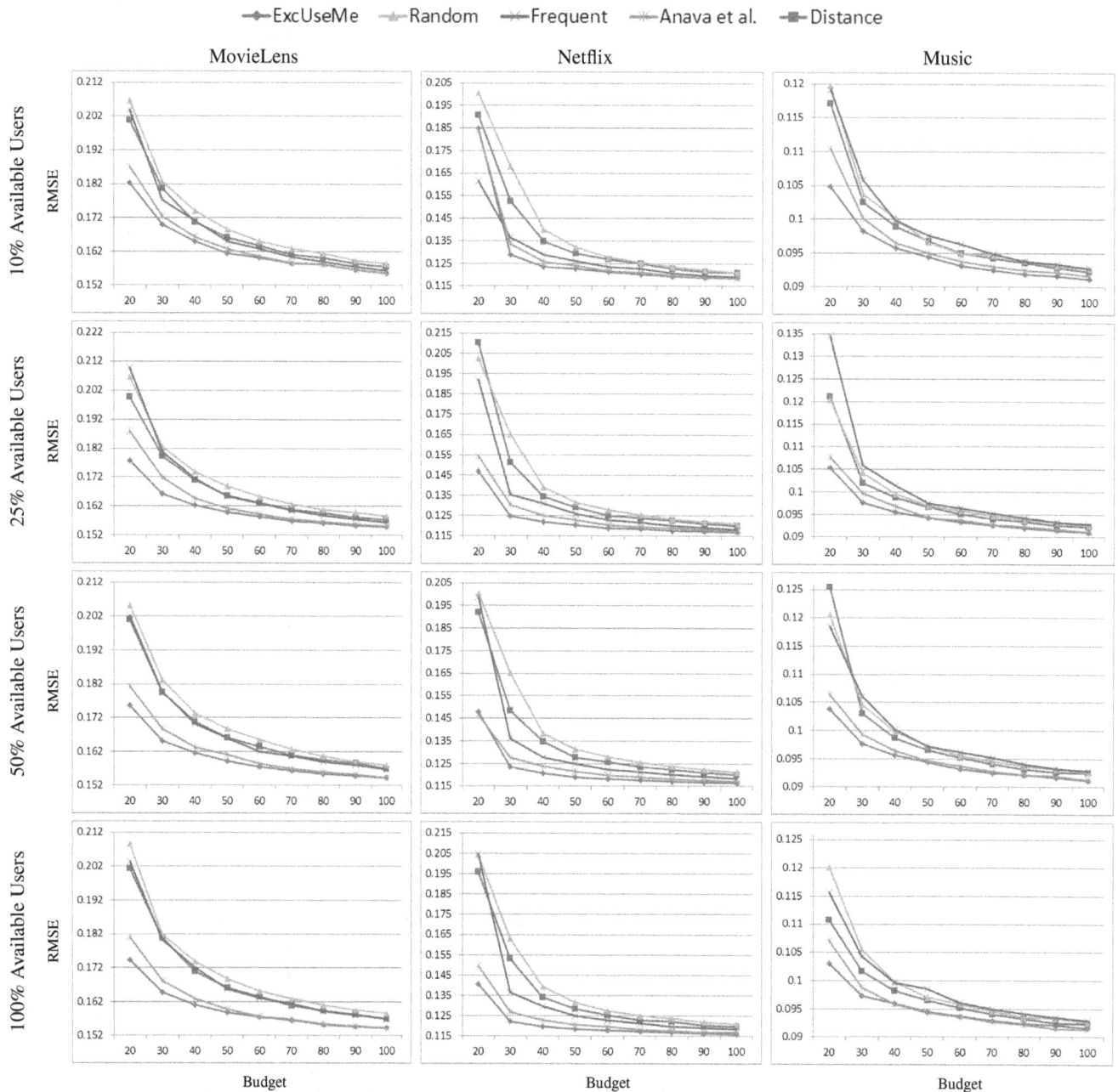

Figure 2: The RMSE value on all datasets for different percentages of available users.

ExcUseMe, both in terms of the number of available users, thus not having to wait until enough candidates arrive, and in terms of the budget size. In addition, *ExcUseMe* adapts well to the size of available users which may be beneficial for recommenders in which at certain times (e.g., evenings) users connect more frequently and then more users are available (i.e., *n* increases).

Probability of Receiving Positive Interactions We next study how well the different algorithms succeed in selecting users that provide positive interactions. As discussed in Sec. 5.3, having at least one positive interaction for new items is crucial to learn their characteristics accurately. Figure 3 shows the results for the *MovieLens1M* dataset for different percentages of available users. The results for the other datasets were similar and are thus omitted. The graphs

show the average probability of receiving at least one positive interaction for the new items averaged over 15 repeating experiments.

The results indicate that *ExcUseMe*, *Frequent*, and *Anava et al.* behave similarly which explains why they obtain better RMSE than *Random* and *Distance*. In addition, as expected, the results show that as the budget increases the probability of receiving positive interactions increases consistently for all approaches. Results also indicate that as the number of available users (*n*) increases, the probability to receive positive interactions increases for all approaches except *Random*. We believe this is the result of longer learning and selection phases in the exploration framework that help to select better users, a property relevant to all approaches but *Random*.

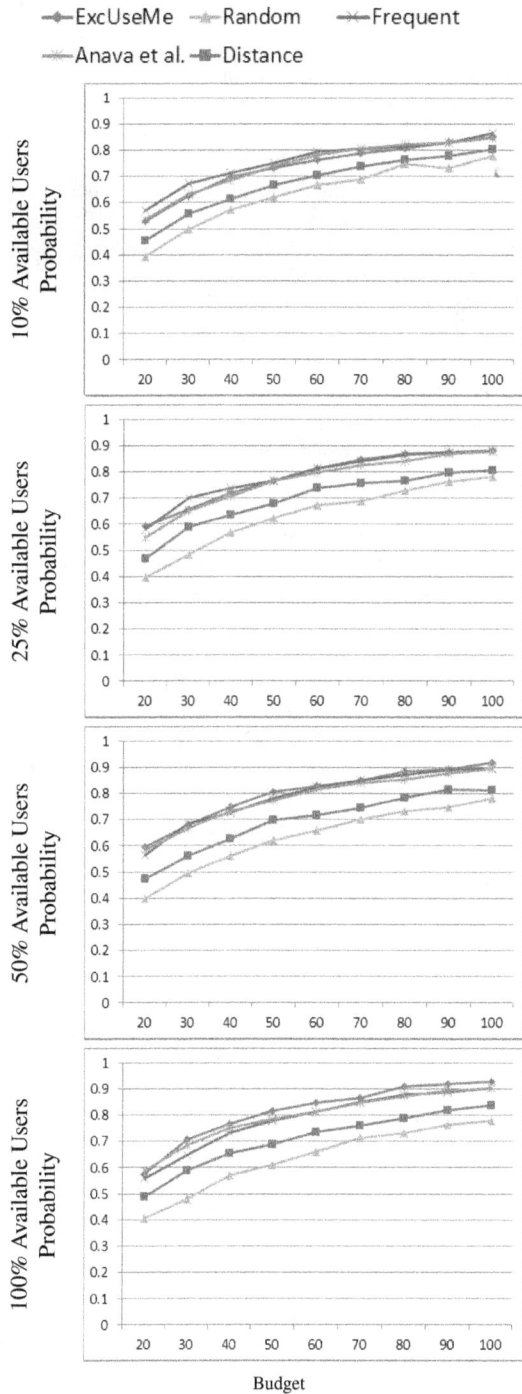

Figure 3: Probability of receiving positive interactions.

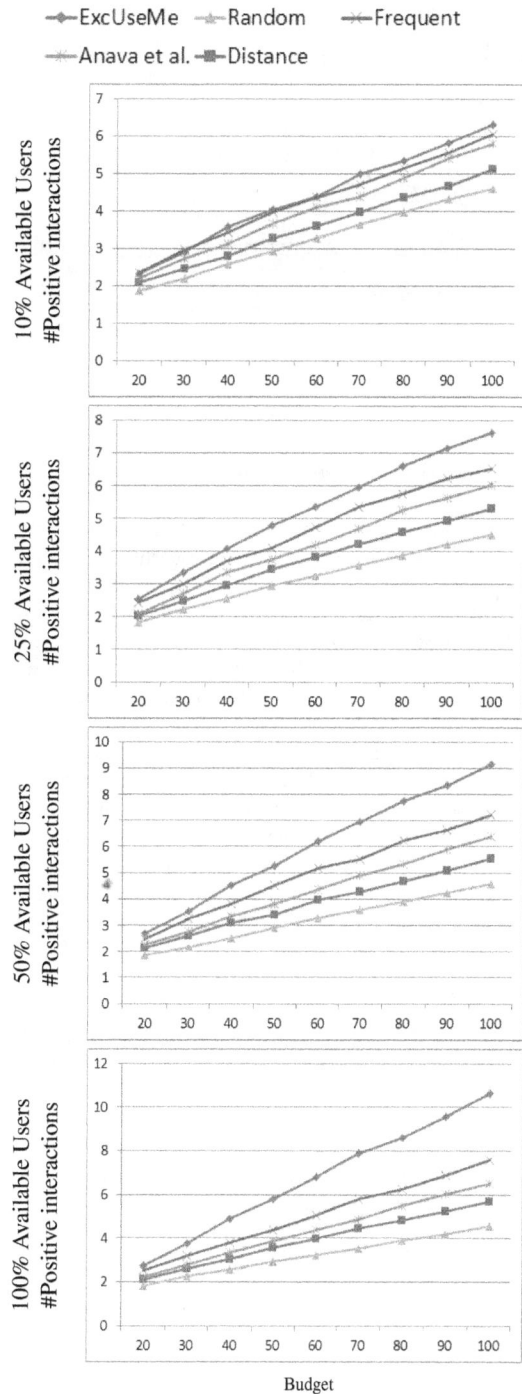

Figure 4: Number of positive interactions for items.

Average Number of Positive Interactions Lastly, we study the average number of positive interactions the approaches reveal for the new items. As discussed in Sec. 5.3, revealing many positive interactions is important to accurately model the new items and it also provides better user experience. Figure 4 shows the average number of positive interactions revealed for the new items on the *MovieLens1M* dataset for different percentages of available users (experiments on the other datasets obtained similar results).

Results indicate that *ExcUseMe* consistently and significantly reveals more positive interactions compared to all other approaches under all budgets for all percentages of available users. Further, as the budget increases and/or when there are more candidates available, the number of positive interactions that *ExcUseMe* reveals increases more significantly than the other approaches. Namely, *ExcUseMe* provides better user experience than the other approaches.

In addition, we believe that the fact that *ExcUseMe* reveals more positive interactions than the other approaches is the reason for obtaining better RMSE. Specifically, this explains why *ExcUseMe* outperforms *Frequent* and *Anava et al.*, which demonstrated a similar behaviour to *ExcUseMe* in revealing at least one positive interaction for new items.

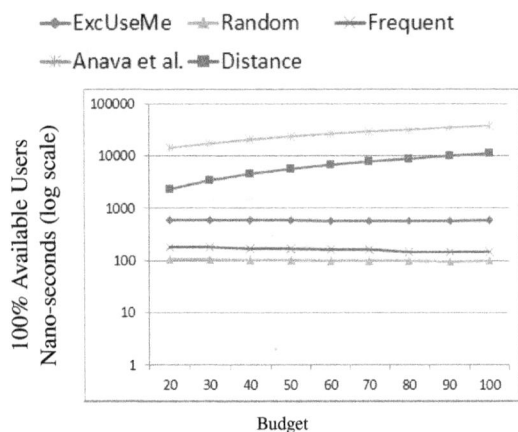

Figure 5: Computational Time.

Computational Complexity To evaluate the computational complexity of the *ExcUseMe* score function, we measured the time a single computation takes. The computational time may be affected by the budget (for example, the *Anava et al.* and *Distance* approaches base their scores on previously selected users), and thus we measured time as a function of the budget. However, the computational time is unaffected by the dataset or the number of available users and thus we only show the results on the *MovieLens1M* dataset where all users are available for selection (i.e., $n = 100$). Results are presented in Figure 5 that shows the average time in a *log scale* when time was measured in nano-seconds. Results indicate that while *ExcUseMe* requires longer computations compared to *Random* or *Frequent* (as expected), it is only by a factor of less than 4 compared to *Frequent* and less than 5 compared to *Random*. In contrast, *Distance* and *Anava et al.* require expensive computations and their performance becomes worse as budget increases.

6 Conclusions

We presented *ExcUseMe*, a novel and simple algorithm for selecting users to cope with the item cold-start problem, an inherent problem in collaborative filtering recommender systems. *ExcUseMe* assumes an initial model capturing the characteristics of the users and accordingly selects the users that are most likely to be interested in the new items. To evaluate *ExcUseMe*, we applied it in an online setting that captures two realistic aspects: a limited number of available users and a limited number of users that may participate in the exploration. We compared *ExcUseMe* against state-of-the-art algorithms and experimental results show that *ExcUseMe* is efficient and obtains the best RMSE in all tested scenarios. In addition, *ExcUseMe* converges towards selecting users that are likely to be interested in the new items, thus provides better user experience while smartly exploring the new items.

7 References

[1] D. Agarwal and B.-C. Chen. Regression-based latent factor models. In *KDD '09*.

[2] M. Aharon, A. Kagian, Y. Koren, and R. Lempel. Dynamic personalized recommendation of comment-eliciting stories. In *RecSys '12*.

[3] N. Aizenberg, Y. Koren, and O. Somekh. Build your own music recommender by modeling internet radio streams. In *WWW '12*.

[4] O. Anava, S. Golan, N. Golbandi, Z. Karnin, R. Lempel, O. Rokhlenko, and O. Somekh. Budget-constrained item cold-start handling in collaborative filtering recommenders via optimal design. In *WWW '15*.

[5] M. Bateni, M. Hajiaghayi, and M. Zadimoghaddam. Submodular secretary problem and extensions. *ACM Trans. Algorithms*, 9(4), 2013.

[6] G. Dror, N. Koenigstein, and Y. Koren. Yahoo! music recommendations: Modeling music ratings with temporal dynamics and item. In *RecSys '11*.

[7] J. C. Duchi, E. Hazan, and Y. Singer. Adaptive subgradient methods for online learning and stochastic optimization. *Journal of Machine Learning Research*, 12, 2011.

[8] M. Feldman, J. Naor, and R. Schwartz. Improved competitive ratios for submodular secretary problems (extended abstract). In *APPROX-RANDOM '11*.

[9] N. Golbandi, Y. Koren, and R. Lempel. Adaptive bootstrapping of recommender systems using decision trees. In *WSDM '11*.

[10] N. Golbandi, Y. Koren, and R. Lempel. On bootstrapping recommender systems. In *CIKM '10*.

[11] A. Gunawardana and C. Meek. Tied boltzmann machines for cold start recommendations. In *RecSys '08*.

[12] A. Gunawardana and C. Meek. A unified approach to building hybrid recommender systems. In *RecSys '09*.

[13] A. Gupta, A. Roth, G. Schoenebeck, and K. Talwar. Constrained non-monotone submodular maximization: Offline and secretary algorithms. In *WINE '10*.

[14] A. Kohrs and B. Mérialdo. Improving collaborative filtering for new-users by smart object selection. In *ICME '01*.

[15] Y. Koren. Factorization meets the neighborhood: a multifaceted collaborative filtering model. In *KDD '08*.

[16] Y. Koren. Collaborative filtering with temporal dynamics. *Commun. of the ACM*, 53(4), 2010.

[17] Y. Koren, R. M. Bell, and C. Volinsky. Matrix factorization techniques for recommender systems. *Computer*, 42(8), 2009.

[18] S.-L. Lee. Commodity recommendations of retail business based on decision tree induction. *Expert Systems with Applications*, 37(5), 2010.

[19] G. Linden, B. Smith, and J. York. Amazon. com recommendations: Item-to-item collaborative filtering. *Internet Computing, IEEE*, 7(1), 2003.

[20] P. McCullagh and J. A. Nelder. Generalized linear models (Second edition). 1989.

[21] S.-T. Park and W. Chu. Pairwise preference regression for cold-start recommendation. In *RecSys '09*.

[22] A. Paterek. Improving regularized singular value decomposition for collaborative filtering. In *KDD '07*.

[23] M. J. Pazzani and D. Billsus. Content-based recommendation systems. *The Adaptive Web*, 4321, 2007.

[24] A. M. Rashid, I. Albert, D. Cosley, S. K. Lam, S. M. McNee, J. A. Konstan, and J. Riedl. Getting to know you: Learning new user preferences in recommender systems. In *IUI '02*.

[25] A. M. Rashid, G. Karypis, and J. Riedl. Learning preferences of new users in recommender systems: an information theoretic approach. *SIGKDD Explor. Newsl.*, 10(2), 2008.

[26] B. Sarwar, G. Karypis, J. Konstan, and J. Riedl. Item-based collaborative filtering recommendation algorithms. In *WWW '01*.

[27] G. Takacs, I. Pilaszy, B. Nemeth, and D. Tikk. Investigation of various matrix factorization methods for large recommender systems. In *ICDMW '08*.

Cold-Start Item and User Recommendation with Decoupled Completion and Transduction

Iman Barjasteh
Electrical & Computer Eng.
Michigan State University
barjaste@msu.edu

Rana Forsati
Computer Science & Eng.
Michigan State University
forsati@cse.msu.edu

Farzan Masrour
Statistics & Probability
Michigan State University
masrour@msu.edu

Abdol-Hossein Esfahanian
Computer Science & Eng.
Michigan State University
esfahanian@cse.msu.edu

Hayder Radha
Electrical & Computer Eng.
Michigan State University
radha@egr.msu.edu

ABSTRACT

A major challenge in collaborative filtering based recommender systems is how to provide recommendations when rating data is sparse or entirely missing for a subset of users or items, commonly known as the *cold-start* problem. In recent years, there has been considerable interest in developing new solutions that address the cold-start problem. These solutions are mainly based on the idea of exploiting other sources of information to compensate for the lack of rating data. In this paper, we propose a novel algorithmic framework based on matrix factorization that simultaneously exploits the similarity information among users and items to alleviate the cold-start problem. In contrast to existing methods, the proposed algorithm *decouples* the following two aspects of the cold-start problem: (a) the completion of a rating sub-matrix, which is generated by excluding cold-start users and items from the original rating matrix; and (b) the transduction of knowledge from existing ratings to cold-start items/users using side information. This crucial difference significantly boosts the performance when appropriate side information is incorporated. We provide theoretical guarantees on the estimation error of the proposed two-stage algorithm based on the richness of similarity information in capturing the rating data. To the best of our knowledge, this is the first algorithm that addresses the cold-start problem with provable guarantees. We also conduct thorough experiments on synthetic and real datasets that demonstrate the effectiveness of the proposed algorithm and highlights the usefulness of auxiliary information in dealing with both cold-start users and items.

Categories and Subject Descriptors

H.3.3 [**Information Search and Retrieval**]: Miscellaneous

Keywords

Matrix factorization; Sparsity; Cold-start Problem

RecSys'15, September 16–20, 2015, Vienna, Austria.
© 2015 ACM. ISBN 978-1-4503-3692-5/15/09 ...$15.00.
DOI: http://dx.doi.org/10.1145/2792838.2800196.

1. INTRODUCTION

The ever-growing popularity of e-commerce sites and exponential growth of online users and huge collections of items have created a compelling demand for efficient recommender systems to guide users toward items (e.g., products, books, movies, etc). In the past decade, there has been a vast amount of research in this field, mostly focusing on designing novel algorithms for generating high quality suggestions (see e.g. [1], for a more recent survey). For instance, Collaborative filtering (CF) aims to predict preferences of a given "user" for some "objects" based on her previously revealed preferences– typically in the form of purchases or ratings– as well as the revealed preferences of other users.

Despite significant improvements, recommendation systems suffer from a few inherent limitations and weaknesses that need to be addressed and have captured the attention of researchers. Among such limitations are *data sparsity* and *cold-start* problems. For instance, for many applications the rating data is usually very sparse or there is no available rating for a subset of users or items (known as cold-start user and cold-start item, respectively)– making standard collaborative filtering algorithms infeasible. Therefore, it is of significant interest to develop algorithms that alleviate the data sparsity challenge and solve the cold-start problem.

Due in part to its importance, there has been an active line of work to address difficulties associated with cold-start users and items, and several researchers have considered a variety of techniques [16, 22, 21, 24, 27, 8, 26, 28, 14, 17], where a common theme among them is to exploit auxiliary information about users or items besides the rating data that are usually available. The main motivation behind these techniques stems from the following observation: other sources of data could potentially provide useful information about the underlying model and complement the rating data. For instance, users' decisions on item ratings are very likely to be influenced by other users with whom they have social connections (friends, families, etc). As a result, the availability of auxiliary information such as users' profile information [2], social context (trust and distrust relations) of users [4], information embedded in the review text [8], and features of items [5] would definitely benefit the recommendations. Therefore, an interesting research question, which is the main focus of this paper is: *how to effectively incorporate the side information about users and items to overcome the cold-start problem.*

The aim of this paper is to propose an efficient matrix factorization algorithm with similarity information to answer the above question. In fact, we study a somewhat more general problem where both cold-start users and cold-start items are present simultaneously and address these two challenges in combination. The dominant paradigm in existing methods such as shared subspace learning [22] and kernelized matrix factorization [28] is to augment the existing methods with side information and perform (a) the *completion* of rating matrix and (b) the *transduction* of knowledge from existing ratings to cold-start items/users simultaneously. While this recipe can generate good results in practice, it has a notable drawback: these methods propagate the completion and transduction errors repetitively and in an uncontrolled way. Therefore, we propose a two-stage algorithm that *decouples* completion from transduction. In particular, in the first step we exclude the cold-start users and items from the rating matrix and recover the obtained sub-matrix in a perfect way. Then, the recovered sub-matrix along with available similarity side information about users and items will be utilized to transduct the knowledge to cold-start users/items. We provide theoretical performance guarantees on the estimation error of the proposed algorithm while most of the existing methods do not provide any theoretical support. We also conduct a set of through experiments to demonstrate the merits of the proposed algorithm and complement our theoretical results. Finally, we compare our algorithm with several other specialized algorithms for cold-start user and item recommendation to demonstrates the superiority of our proposed framework over existing methods.

Outline. The remainder of the paper is organized as follows. In Section 2, we begin by establishing notation and providing background on matrix factorization, noting a few of its deficiencies for our setting. We then in Section 3 describe the proposed algorithm and state our main theorem on its estimation error. The experimental results are provided in Section 4 and concluding remarks are given in Section 5.

2. THE SETTING

Before proceeding to the proposed algorithm, in this section we establish the notations which are used throughout the paper and formally describe our problem setting.

The set of non-negative real numbers is denoted by $\mathbb{R}_+$. We use $[n]$ to denote a set on integers $\{1, 2, \cdots, n\}$. Scalars are denoted by lower case letters and vectors by bold face lower case letters such as $\mathbf{u}$. We use bold face upper case letters such as $\mathbf{M}$ to denote matrices. The Frobenius and spectral norms of a matrix $\mathbf{M} \in \mathbb{R}^{n \times m}$ is denoted by $\|\mathbf{M}\|_F$, i.e, $\|\mathbf{M}\|_F = \sqrt{\sum_{i=1}^{n} \sum_{j=1}^{m} |\mathbf{M}_{ij}|^2}$ and $\|\mathbf{M}\|_2$, respectively. The transpose of a vector and a matrix denoted by $\mathbf{m}^\top$ and $\mathbf{M}^\top$, respectively. We use $(\mathbf{M})^\dagger$ to denote the Moore-Penrose pseudo inverse of matrix $\mathbf{M}$. The dot product between two vectors $\mathbf{m}$ and $\mathbf{n}$ is denoted by $\mathbf{m}^\top \mathbf{n}$.

In collaborative filtering we assume that there is a set of n users $\mathcal{U} = \{u_1, \cdots, u_n\}$ and a set of m items $\mathcal{I} = \{i_1, \cdots, i_m\}$ where each user u_i expresses opinions about a subset of items. In this paper, we assume opinions are expressed through an explicit numeric rating (e.g., scale from one to five), but other rating methods such as hyperlink clicks are possible as well. We are mainly interested in recommending a set of items for an active user such that the user has not rated these items before. The rating information is summarized in an $n \times m$ matrix $\mathbf{R} \in \mathbb{R}^{n \times m}, 1 \leq i \leq n, 1 \leq j \leq m$ where the rows correspond to the users and the columns correspond to the items and (p, q)th entry is the rate given by user u_p to the item i_q. We note that the rating matrix is partially observed and it is sparse in most cases.

An efficient and effective approach for recommender systems is to factorize the user-item rating matrix $\mathbf{R}$ by a multiplicative of k-rank matrices $\mathbf{R} \approx \mathbf{U}\mathbf{V}^\top$, where $\mathbf{U} \in \mathbb{R}^{n \times k}$ and $\mathbf{V} \in \mathbb{R}^{m \times k}$ utilize the factorized user-specific and item-specific matrices, respectively, to make further missing data prediction. There are two basic formulations to solve this problem: these are optimization approaches(see e.g., [19, 9, 11, 7]) and probabilistic approach [15]. Let $\Omega_\mathbf{R}$ be the set of observed ratings in the user-item matrix $\mathbf{R} \in \mathbb{R}^{n \times m}$, i.e., $\Omega_\mathbf{R} = \{(i, j) \in [n] \times [m] : \mathbf{R}_{ij} \text{ has been observed}\}$, where n is the number of users and m is the number of items to be rated. In optimization based matrix factorization, the goal is to learn the latent matrices $\mathbf{U}$ and $\mathbf{V}$ by solving the following optimization problem:

$$\mathcal{L}(\mathbf{U}, \mathbf{V}) = \min_{\mathbf{U}, \mathbf{V}} \frac{1}{2} \sum_{(i,j) \in \Omega_\mathbf{R}} \left(\mathbf{R}_{i,j} - \mathbf{u}_i^\top \mathbf{v}_j\right)^2 + \lambda_\mathbf{U} \|\mathbf{U}\|_F^2 + \lambda_\mathbf{V} \|\mathbf{V}\|_F^2 \tag{1}$$

The optimization problem in Eq. (1) has three main terms: the first term aims to minimize the inconsistency between the observed entries and their corresponding values obtained by the factorized matrices. The last two terms regularize the latent matrices for users and items, respectively. The parameters $\lambda_\mathbf{U}$ and $\lambda_\mathbf{V}$ are regularization parameters that are introduced to control the regularization of latent matrices $\mathbf{U}$ and $\mathbf{V}$, respectively. After learning the latent features for users and items, the prediction of each missing entry can be computed by the inner product of latent vectors of the corresponding row and the corresponding column.

For new users or items in the system, since there is no observed rating data in $\mathbf{R}$, the corresponding rows and columns in the rating matrix is fully unobserved which results in an inability to draw inferences to either recommend existing items to new users or new items to existing users. In particular, it is not feasible for standard Matrix Factorization formulation to fill in a row or a column that is entirely missing in the original rating matrix. In this paper, we assume that there is a sub-matrix $\mathbf{M} \in \mathbb{R}^{p \times q}, 1 \leq p \leq n, 1 \leq q \leq m$ which includes enough rating data to be fully recovered via standard methods such as matrix factorization or matrix completion. We call the rest of items and users for which the rating data is entirely missing and are not present in $\mathbf{M}$ as cold-start. To make recommendations to cold-start users/items we assume that besides the observed entries in the matrix $\mathbf{M}$, there exist two auxiliary similarity matrices $\mathbf{A} \in \mathbb{R}^{n \times n}$ and $\mathbf{B} \in \mathbb{R}^{m \times m}$ that capture the pairwise similarity between users and items, respectively as shown in Figure 1. The similarity matrices can be computed from

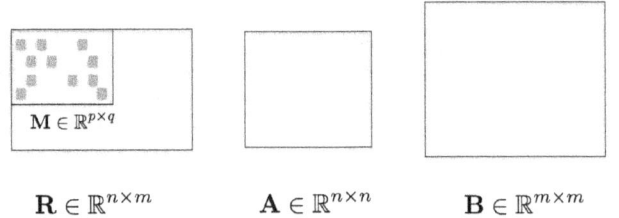

$$\mathbf{R} \in \mathbb{R}^{n \times m} \qquad \mathbf{A} \in \mathbb{R}^{n \times n} \qquad \mathbf{B} \in \mathbb{R}^{m \times m}$$

Figure 1: In our setting we assume that there are many fully unobserved rows and columns in the input rating matrix $\mathbf{R} \in \mathbb{R}^{n \times m}$ and only a small sub-matrix $\mathbf{M} \in \mathbb{R}^{p \times q}$ has enough information to be recovered by the off-the-shelf methods such as matrix factorization or completion. Besides, the similarity matrices $\mathbf{A} \in \mathbb{R}^{n \times n}$ and $\mathbf{B} \in \mathbb{R}^{m \times m}$ about users and items are provided, respectively, that could potentially benefit the recommendation.

the available information such as users' profile or social context or items' features. The main focus of this paper is on exploiting available side information to improve the accuracy of recommendations and resolve the cold-start items and users problems.

3. MATRIX FACTORIZATION WITH SIMILARITY INFORMATION

We now focus on describing our algorithm and the assumptions underlying it. We assume that the rating matrix and the side information matrices are correlated and to some extent. This will be formalized later to share the same latent information; that is, the row and column vectors in $\mathbf{R}$ share an underlying subspace spanned by the leading eigen-vectors in the similarity matrices $\mathbf{A}$ and $\mathbf{B}$, respectively. This assumption follows from the fact that the similarity matrices provide auxiliary information about the users/items, otherwise there would not be any chance to benefit from these information in addressing the cold-start problems.

Before delving into the algorithm, we discuss two alternative methods to exploit the similarity information in matrix factorization and motivate our own algorithm. A straightforward approach to exploit and transfer knowledge from similarity matrices to the rating data is to cast the problem as a shared subspace learning framework based on a joint matrix factorization to jointly learn a common subset of basis vectors for the rating matrix $\mathbf{R}$ and the corresponding similarity matrices $\mathbf{A}$ and $\mathbf{B}$ for users and items. In particular, the goal is is to factorize the matrices $\mathbf{R}$ and $\mathbf{A}$ with equal number of rows and the matrices $\mathbf{R}$ and $\mathbf{B}$ with equal number of columns into four subspaces: two are shared between rating matrix and each of two similarity matrices, and two are specific to the matrices as formulated in the following optimization problems:

$$
\begin{aligned}
\min_{\substack{\mathbf{U} \in \mathbb{R}^{n \times r}, \mathbf{V} \in \mathbb{R}^{m \times r}, \\ \mathbf{W} \in \mathbb{R}^{n \times r}, \mathbf{Z} \in \mathbb{R}^{m \times r}}} &\frac{1}{2} \|\mathbf{R} - \mathbf{U}\mathbf{V}^\top\|_{\mathrm{F}}^2 + \lambda \left(\|\mathbf{U}\|_{\mathrm{F}}^2 + \|\mathbf{V}\|_{\mathrm{F}}^2 \right) \\
&+ \frac{1}{2} \|\mathbf{A} - \mathbf{U}\mathbf{W}^\top\|_{\mathrm{F}}^2 + \frac{1}{2} \|\mathbf{B} - \mathbf{Z}\mathbf{V}^\top\|_{\mathrm{F}}^2 \\
&+ \lambda \left(\|\mathbf{W}\|_{\mathrm{F}}^2 + \|\mathbf{Z}\|_{\mathrm{F}}^2 \right)
\end{aligned}
\tag{2}
$$

with λ as the regularization parameter for the norms of the solution matrices and common latent space representation is achieved by using the same matrices $\mathbf{W} \in \mathbb{R}^{n \times r}$ and $\mathbf{Z}$.

An alternative approach is to kernelize the matrix factorization by assessing the similarity of latent features using the available similarity matrices [28]. In particular, instead of directly solving the optimization problem in Eq. (1), we optimize the following objective

$$
\begin{aligned}
\mathcal{L}(\mathbf{U}, \mathbf{V}) = \min_{\mathbf{U}, \mathbf{V}} &\frac{1}{2} \sum_{(i,j) \in \Omega_{\mathbf{R}}} \left(\mathbf{R}_{i,j} - \mathbf{u}_i^\top \mathbf{v}_j \right)^2 \\
&+ \lambda_{\mathbf{U}} \sum_{i=1}^n \mathbf{u}_i^\top \mathbf{A} \mathbf{u}_i + \lambda_{\mathbf{V}} \sum_{i=1}^m \mathbf{v}_i^\top \mathbf{B} \mathbf{v}_i,
\end{aligned}
\tag{3}
$$

where the similarity matrices are explicitly used to regularize the latent features.

However, in our setting there are many rows and columns in the rating matrix $\mathbf{R}$ that are fully unobserved, which makes the subspace learning and kernelized factorization methods inapplicable. The main issue with these approaches is that the *completion* of the unobserved entries in rating matrix $\mathbf{R}$ and *transduction* of knowledge from these entries to cold-start users/items via similarity matrices is carried out simultaneously. Therefore, the completion and transduction errors are propagated repetitively and in a uncontrolled way. The issue with error propagation becomes even worse due to

---

Algorithm 1 Matrix Factorization with Decoupled Completion and Transduction (DCT)

1: **Input:**
- $\mathbf{R} \in \mathbb{R}^{n \times m}, r$: the partially observed rating matrix and its rank
- $\mathbf{A} \in \mathbb{R}^{n \times n}$: the auxiliary users' similarity matrix
- $\mathbf{B} \in \mathbb{R}^{m \times m}$: the auxiliary items' similarity matrix
- $\mathbf{M} \in \mathbb{R}^{p \times q}$: the maximal recoverable rating sub-matrix

2: Complete the sub-matrix $\mathbf{M}$ to get $\widehat{\mathbf{M}}$ [Completion]

3: Decompose $\widehat{\mathbf{M}}$ as $\widehat{\mathbf{M}} = \sum_{i=1}^r \widehat{\mathbf{u}}_i \widehat{\mathbf{v}}_i^\top$

4: Extract subspaces $\mathbf{U_A}$ and $\mathbf{U_B}$ by spectral clustering from similarity matrices $\mathbf{A}$ and $\mathbf{B}$, respectively

5: Compute $\widehat{\mathbf{a}}_i = \left(\widehat{\mathbf{U}}_{\mathbf{A}}^\top \widehat{\mathbf{U}}_{\mathbf{A}} \right)^\dagger \widehat{\mathbf{U}}_{\mathbf{A}}^\top \widehat{\mathbf{u}}_i, i = 1, 2, \cdots, r$

6: Compute $\widehat{\mathbf{b}}_i = \left(\widehat{\mathbf{U}}_{\mathbf{B}}^\top \widehat{\mathbf{U}}_{\mathbf{B}} \right)^\dagger \widehat{\mathbf{U}}_{\mathbf{B}}^\top \widehat{\mathbf{v}}_i, i = 1, 2, \cdots, r$

7: Compute $\widehat{\mathbf{R}} = \mathbf{U_A} \left(\sum_{i=1}^r \widehat{\mathbf{a}}_i \widehat{\mathbf{b}}_i^\top \right) \mathbf{U_B}^\top$ [Transduction]

8: **Output:** $\widehat{\mathbf{R}}$

---

the non-convexity of optimization problems in Eq. (2) and Eq. (3)– jointly in parameters $\mathbf{U}$ and $\mathbf{V}$.

In effort to alleviate this difficulty, in this section we propose an alternative approach that diverges from these algorithms and transfers information from similarity matrices to rating matrix via the fully recoverable sub-matrix $\mathbf{M}$. In particular, the proposed algorithm **decouples** the *completion* from *transduction* and constitutes of two stages: (i) completion of the sub-matrix $\mathbf{M}$ which can be done perfectly with zero completion error, and (ii) transduction of rating data from the recovered sub-matrix to cold-start items and users using similarity matrices. This crucial difference greatly boosts the performance of the proposed algorithm when appropriate side information is incorporated.

With our assumption concerning the correlation of rating and similarity matrices in place, we can now describe our algorithm. To this end, we construct an orthogonal matrix $\mathbf{U_A} = [\mathbf{u}_1^{\mathbf{A}}, \cdots, \mathbf{u}_s^{\mathbf{A}}] \in \mathbb{R}^{n \times s}$ whose column space subsumes the row space of the rating matrix. We also construct another orthogonal matrix $\mathbf{U_B} = [\mathbf{u}_1^{\mathbf{B}}, \cdots, \mathbf{u}_s^{\mathbf{B}}] \in \mathbb{R}^{m \times s}$ whose column space subsumes the column space of the rating matrix. To construct subspaces $\mathbf{U_A}$ and $\mathbf{U_B}$ we use the first s eigen-vectors corresponding to the s largest eigen-values of the provided similarity matrices $\mathbf{A}$ and $\mathbf{B}$, respectively.

We note that the extent to which the extracted subspaces $\mathbf{U_A}$ and $\mathbf{U_B}$ from similarity matrices subsume the corresponding row and column spaces of the rating matrix, depends on the richness of the similarity information. To formalize this, first from the low-rank assumption of the rating matrix $\mathbf{R}$, it follows that it can be decomposed as $\mathbf{R} = \sum_{i=1}^r \mathbf{u}_i \mathbf{v}_i^\top$ where r is the rank of the matrix. Now we note that the ith latent features vector $\mathbf{u}_i$ can be decomposed in a unique way into two parallel and orthogonal parts as $\mathbf{u}_i = \mathbf{u}_i^{\|} + \mathbf{u}_i^{\perp}$, where $\mathbf{u}_i^{\|}$ is the part that is spanned by the subspace $\mathbf{U_A}$ extracted from the similarity information about users and $\mathbf{u}_i^{\perp}$ is the part orthogonal to $\mathbf{U_A}$.

In a similar way, for the latent features vector of jth item, i.e., $\mathbf{v}_j$, we have the following similar decomposition as $\mathbf{v}_i = \mathbf{v}_i^{\|} + \mathbf{v}_i^{\perp}$, where $\mathbf{v}_i^{\|}$ is the part that is spanned by the subspace $\mathbf{U_B}$ extracted from the similarity information about users and $\mathbf{v}_i^{\perp}$ is the part orthogonal to $\mathbf{U_B}$. We note that the orthogonal components of left and singular vectors $\mathbf{u}_i^{\perp}$ and $\mathbf{v}_i^{\perp}$ captures the extent to which the similarity matrices do not provide information about rating data and can not be recovered using these auxiliary information.

To build intuition for the algorithm we propose, we first relate the rating matrix to the similarity matrices. Having decomposed the latent features as above into two parallel and orthogonal components, we can rewrite the rating matrix $\mathbf{R}$ as:

$$
\begin{aligned}
\mathbf{R} &= \sum_{i=1}^{r} \mathbf{u}_i \mathbf{v}_i^\top = \sum_{i=1}^{r} (\mathbf{u}_i^\| + \mathbf{u}_i^\perp)(\mathbf{v}_i^\| + \mathbf{v}_i^\perp)^\top \\
&= \sum_{i=1}^{r} \mathbf{u}_i^\| \mathbf{v}_i^{\|\top} + \sum_{i=1}^{r} \mathbf{u}_i^\| \mathbf{v}_i^{\perp\top} + \sum_{i=1}^{r} \mathbf{u}_i^\perp \mathbf{v}_i^{\|\top} + \sum_{i=1}^{r} \mathbf{u}_i^\perp \mathbf{v}_i^{\perp\top} \\
&= \mathbf{R}_* + \mathbf{R}_\mathrm{L} + \mathbf{R}_\mathrm{R} + \mathbf{R}_\mathrm{E},
\end{aligned}
\tag{4}
$$

where $\mathbf{R}_*$ is the part of the rating matrix that is fully spanned by the subspaces $\mathbf{U_A}$ and $\mathbf{U_B}$, the matrix $\mathbf{R}_\mathrm{L}$ is the part where only the left singular vectors are spanned by $\mathbf{U_A}$ and the right singular vectors are orthogonal to the subspace spanned by $\mathbf{U_B}$, and the matrix $\mathbf{R}_\mathrm{R}$ is the part that the left singular vectors are orthogonal to the subspace spanned by $\mathbf{U_A}$ and the right singular vectors are spanned by $\mathbf{U_B}$. Finally, the matrix $\mathbf{R}_\mathrm{E}$ is the error matrix where both left and singular vectors are orthogonal to the subspaces spanned by $\mathbf{U_A}$ and $\mathbf{U_B}$, respectively, which does not benefit form the side information at all. In particular, the error matrix $\mathbf{R}_\mathrm{E}$ can not be recovered from the side information as the extracted subspaces provide no information about the orthogonal parts $\mathbf{u}_i^\perp$ and $\mathbf{v}_i^\perp$ of the singular vectors. Therefore, the error contributed by this matrix into the estimation error of final recovered rating matrix is unavoidable.

In the following subsections, we first devise an effective method to recover the rating matrix $\mathbf{R}$ from the sub-matrix $\mathbf{M}$ and subspaces $\mathbf{U_A}$ and $\mathbf{U_B}$, and then provide theoretical guarantees on the estimation error in terms of the magnitude of the error matrix $\|\mathbf{R}_\mathrm{E}\|_\mathrm{F}$.

The Completion Stage. The first step in Algorithm 1 is to complete the sub-matrix $\mathbf{M}$ to create the fully recovered matrix $\widehat{\mathbf{M}}$. To do so, we use the matrix factorization formulation in Eq. (1) which has achieved great success and popularity among the existing matrix completion techniques [25, 15, 23]. We note that based on matrix completion theory, it is guaranteed that the recovery of the low-rank matrix $\mathbf{M}$ is perfect provided the number of observed entries is sufficiently high.

The Transduction Stage. We now turn to recovering the matrix $\mathbf{R} = \sum_{i=1}^{r} \mathbf{u}_i \mathbf{v}_i^\top$ from the submatrix $\widehat{\mathbf{M}}$ and the subspaces $\mathbf{U_A}$ and $\mathbf{U_B}$ extracted from the similarity matrices $\mathbf{A}$ and $\mathbf{B}$ about users and items, respectively. The detailed steps of the proposed completion algorithm are shown in Algorithm 1.

In the second step, the rating information in the recovered matrix $\widehat{\mathbf{M}}$ is transducted to the cold-start users and items. To motivate the transduction step, let us focus on the $\mathbf{R}_*$ matrix as defined in Eq. (4). Since $\mathbf{u}_i^\|$ and $\mathbf{v}_i^\|$ are fully spanned by the subspaces $\mathbf{U_A}$ and $\mathbf{U_B}$ following our construction above, we can write them as:

$$
\mathbf{u}_i^\| = \mathbf{U_A} \mathbf{a}_i, \quad \mathbf{v}_i^\| = \mathbf{U_B} \mathbf{b}_i, \quad i = 1, 2, \cdots, r
\tag{5}
$$

where $\mathbf{a}_i \in \mathbb{R}^s, i = 1, 2, \cdots, r$ and $\mathbf{b}_i \in \mathbb{R}^s, i = 1, 2, \cdots, r$ are the orthogonal projection of the singular vectors to the corresponding subspaces. By substituting the equations in Eq. (5) into the decomposition of $\mathbf{R}_*$ we get:

$$
\mathbf{R}_* = \sum_{i=1}^{r} \mathbf{u}_i^\| \mathbf{v}_i^{\|\top} = \sum_{i=1}^{r} \mathbf{U_A} \mathbf{a}_i \mathbf{b}_i^\top \mathbf{U_B^\top} = \mathbf{U_A} \left(\sum_{i=1}^{r} \mathbf{a}_i \mathbf{b}_i^\top \right) \mathbf{U_B^\top}
\tag{6}
$$

From above derivation, we observe that the key to recover the matrix $\mathbf{R}_*$ is to estimate the vectors $\mathbf{a}_i, \mathbf{b}_i, i = 1, 2, \cdots, r$. In the following we show how the recovered rating sub-matrix $\widehat{\mathbf{M}}$ along with the subspaces extracted from the similarity matrices can be utilized to estimate these vectors perfectly under some mild condition on the number of cold-start users and items. To this end, first consider the decomposition of the recovered matrix as $\widehat{\mathbf{M}} = \sum_{i=1}^{r} \widehat{\mathbf{u}}_i \widehat{\mathbf{v}}_i^\top$. The estimation of vectors $\mathbf{a}_i, \mathbf{b}_i, i = 1, 2, \cdots, r$ in Eq. (6) and equivalently the matrix $\mathbf{R}_*$ is as follows. First, let $\widehat{\mathbf{U}}_\mathbf{A} \in \mathbb{R}^{p \times s}$ be a random submatrix of $\mathbf{U_A}$ where the sampled rows correspond to the subset of rows in the matrix $\widehat{\mathbf{M}}$. Similarly, we construct a submatrix of $\mathbf{U_B}$ denoted by $\widehat{\mathbf{U}}_\mathbf{B} \in \mathbb{R}^{q \times s}$ by sampling the rows of $\mathbf{U_B}$ corresponding to the columns in $\widehat{\mathbf{M}}$. An estimation of $\mathbf{a}_i, \mathbf{b}_i, i \in [r]$ vectors is obtained by orthogonal projection of left and right singular vectors of $\widehat{\mathbf{M}}$ onto the sampled subspaces $\widehat{\mathbf{U}}_\mathbf{A}$ and $\widehat{\mathbf{U}}_\mathbf{B}$ by solving following optimization problems:

$$
\begin{aligned}
\widehat{\mathbf{a}}_i &= \arg\min_{\mathbf{a} \in \mathbb{R}^s} \left\| \widehat{\mathbf{u}}_i - \widehat{\mathbf{U}}_\mathbf{A} \mathbf{a} \right\|_2^2, \\
\widehat{\mathbf{b}}_i &= \arg\min_{\mathbf{b} \in \mathbb{R}^s} \left\| \widehat{\mathbf{v}}_i - \widehat{\mathbf{U}}_\mathbf{B} \mathbf{a} \right\|_2^2.
\end{aligned}
\tag{7}
$$

Then, we estimate the $\mathbf{R}_*$ by:

$$
\begin{aligned}
\widehat{\mathbf{R}}_* &= \mathbf{U_A} \left(\sum_{i=1}^{r} \widehat{\mathbf{a}}_i \widehat{\mathbf{b}}_i^\top \right) \mathbf{U_B^\top} \\
&= \mathbf{U_A} \left(\widehat{\mathbf{U}}_\mathbf{A}^\top \widehat{\mathbf{U}}_\mathbf{A} \right)^\dagger \widehat{\mathbf{U}}_\mathbf{A}^\top \left(\sum_{i=1}^{r} \widehat{\mathbf{u}}_i \widehat{\mathbf{v}}_i^\top \right) \widehat{\mathbf{U}}_\mathbf{B} \left(\widehat{\mathbf{U}}_\mathbf{B}^\top \widehat{\mathbf{U}}_\mathbf{B} \right)^\dagger \mathbf{U_B},
\end{aligned}
$$

where in the last equality we used the fact that $\left(\widehat{\mathbf{U}}_\mathbf{A}^\top \widehat{\mathbf{U}}_\mathbf{A} \right)^\dagger \widehat{\mathbf{U}}_\mathbf{A}^\top \widehat{\mathbf{u}}_i$ and $\left(\widehat{\mathbf{U}}_\mathbf{B}^\top \widehat{\mathbf{U}}_\mathbf{B} \right)^\dagger \widehat{\mathbf{U}}_\mathbf{B}^\top \widehat{\mathbf{v}}_i$ are the optimal solutions to the ordinary least squares regression problems in Eq. (7). Here $(\cdot)^\dagger$ denotes the Moore-Penrose pseudo inverse of a matrix. The final estimated rating matrix $\widehat{\mathbf{R}}$ is simply set to be $\widehat{\mathbf{R}} = \widehat{\mathbf{R}}_*$.

An upper bound on estimation error. In order to see the impact of similarity information on recovering the rating matrix, we theoretically analyze the estimation error. In particular, the performance of proposed algorithm on estimating the rating matrix is stated in the following theorem.

THEOREM 3.1. *Let $\mathbf{R} \in \mathbb{R}^{n \times m}$ be a low-rank matrix with coherence parameter μ. Let $\mathbf{M} \in \mathbb{R}^{p \times q}$ be a sub-matrix of $\mathbf{R}$ where the rows and columns are uniformly sampled with*

$$
p \geq 8\mu r \log \left(\frac{r}{\delta} \right) \quad \text{and} \quad q \geq 8\mu r \log \left(\frac{r}{\delta} \right)
$$

where r is the rank of the original matrix $\mathbf{R}$. Let $\widehat{\mathbf{R}}$ be the recovered matrix by Algorithm 1 using similarity matrices $\mathbf{A}$ and $\mathbf{B}$ about users and items, respectively. Then with probability $1 - \delta$, it holds:

$$
\|\mathbf{R} - \widehat{\mathbf{R}}\|_\mathrm{F} \leq \left(1 + \frac{4nm}{pq} + \frac{2n}{p} + \frac{2m}{q} \right) \|\mathbf{R}_\mathrm{E}\|_\mathrm{F}.
$$

We note that in above inequality the parameter μ is known as incoherence [3, 18] which is the prevailing assumption in analysis of matrix completion algorithms. This parameter states that the singular vectors of $\mathbf{R}$ should be de-localized so that they have a small inner product with the standard basis making a full recovery possible.

REMARK 3.2. *Let us pause to make some remarks concerning the results given above. First, one can observe that* *the recovery error is stated in terms of the norm of error matrix $\mathbf{R}_E$ which captures the extent to which the similarity matrices $\mathbf{A}$ and $\mathbf{B}$ fail to capture the rating data. This error is unavoidable even if there is no cold-start item or users, $p = n$ and $q = m$ which yields $O(1) \|\mathbf{R}_E\|_F$ error bound. Also, the error decreases by reducing the number of cold-start items and users as expected.*

4. EXPERIMENTS

In this section, we conduct exhaustive experiments to demonstrate the merits and advantages of the proposed algorithm. We conduct the experiments on synthetic and two well-known NIPS [1] and MovieLens [2] datasets, aiming to accomplish and answer the following fundamental questions:

- **Prediction accuracy:** How does the proposed algorithm perform in comparison to the state-of-the-art algorithms with incorporating side information of users/items. And to what degree the available side information could help in making more accurate recommendations?
- **Dealing with cold-start users:** How does exploiting similarity relationships between users affect the performance of recommending existing items to cold-start users?
- **Dealing with cold-start items:** How does exploiting similarity information between items affect the performance of recommending cold-start items to existing users?
- **Dealing with cold-start users and items simultaneously:** How does exploiting similarity information between users and items affect the performance of recommending cold-start items to cold-start users?

In the following subsections, we intend to answer these questions. First we introduce the datasets that we use in our experiments and then the metrics that we employ to evaluate the results, followed by our detailed experimental results on both synthetic and real datasets.

4.1 Metrics

We adopt the widely used the Mean Absolute Error (MAE) and the Root Mean Squared Error (RMSE) [6] metrics for prediction accuracy [6, 13]. Let $\mathcal{T}$ denote the set of ratings that we want to predict, i.e., $\mathcal{T} = \{(i,j) \in [n] \times [m], \mathbf{R}_{ij}$ needs to be predicted$\}$ and let $\widehat{\mathbf{R}}$ denote the prediction matrix obtained by a recommendation algorithm. Then,

$$\text{MAE} = \frac{\sum_{(i,j) \in \mathcal{T}} |\mathbf{R}_{ij} - \widehat{\mathbf{R}}_{ij}|}{|\mathcal{T}|},$$

The RMSE metric is defined as:

$$\text{RMSE} = \sqrt{\frac{\sum_{(i,j) \in \mathcal{T}} \left(\mathbf{R}_{ij} - \widehat{\mathbf{R}}_{ij}\right)^2}{|\mathcal{T}|}}.$$

We would like to emphasize that even *small improvements* in RMSE are considered valuable in the context of recommender systems. For example, the Netflix prize competition offered a $1,000,000 reward for only 10% reduction of RMSE.

To measure the effectiveness of the order of the recommended users/items based on their predicted rating, we employ Mean Average Precision (MAP) [12] and Normalized Discount Cumulative Gain (NDCG) measures. Given an item i, let r_i be the relevance score of the item ranked at position i, where $r_i = 1$ if the item is relevant to the i and

[1] http://www.cs.nyu.edu/~roweis/data.html
[2] http://www.grouplens.org/node/73/

Table 1: Statistics of MovieLens dataset

Statistic	Quantity
Number of users	6,040
Number of items	3,706
Number of ratings	1,000,209
Range of ratings	1 to 5
Maximum number of ratings by users	2314
Maximum number of ratings for items	3428
Average number of ratings by users	165.59
Average number of ratings for items	257.58

$r_i = 0$ otherwise. Then we can compute the Average Precision (AP) as

$$\text{AP} = \frac{\sum_i r_i \times \text{Precision@}i}{\text{\# of relevant items}}.$$

where Precision is defined as the number of relevant items (users) divided by the number of items (users) in the dataset. MAP is the average of AP over all the users in the network.

The NDCG measure is a normalization of the Discounted Cumulative Gain (DCG) measure. DCG is a weighted sum of the degree of relevancy of the ranked users. The value of NDCG is between $[0, 1]$ and at position k is defined as:

$$\text{NDCG@}k = Z_k \sum_{i=1}^{k} \frac{2^{r_i} - 1}{\log(i+1)}$$

where k is also called the scope, which means the number of top-ranked items presented to the user and Z_k is chosen such that the perfect ranking has a NDCG value of 1.

4.2 Datasets and configuration

MovieLens dataset. As our first dataset, we use the well known MovieLens dataset, which has side information about both users and items that makes it ideal for our setting. This dataset consists of 1000K ratings made by 6040 users for 3706 movies. In addition to rating data, this dataset also contains features for both users and movies. For each movie we used features such as title, year, genre, etc. For each user we extracted features such as gender, age, occupation, and location. The statistics of the dataset is given in Table 4.1.

NIPS dataset. We have also applied our algorithm to paper-author and paper-word matrices extracted from the co-author network at the NIPS conference [20]. This dataset has only side information about items. The number of users (i.e., authors) and items (i.e., papers) are 2037 and 1740, respectively. The length of feature vector of each paper is 13649, which is the size of the vocabulary in NIPS (i.e., unique tokens in all articles). The content of the papers is preprocessed such that all words are converted to lower case and stemmed and stop-words are removed. We compute the cosine similarity of the vector representation weighted with TD-IDF of papers with the ones of all other papers.

Experiments setup. We separated the dataset into two subsets, a training set that used for training the model and a test set that used for evaluating it. We partition the data into 5 equal subsets and then use one for testing and the rest for training, giving a ratio of testing to training data 1:4, and we repeat the experiment for each of the partitions.

To better evaluate the effect of utilizing the features of users and items in dealing with cold-start problem, we employ different cold-start scenarios.

- I [Existing items/Cold-start users]: Often, in a recommender system a vast majority of the users are comprised of new users. To simulate the cold-start user scenario, we divide the users into a disjoint training set and a test set. The representative items are selected only based on the ratings by the users in the training set. Then for the users in the test set, we make predictions only based on their ratings on the representative items.

- II [Existing users/Cold-start items]: Similarly, for cold-start item scenario, we divide the items into a training and a test set. The representative users are determined based on the training set only. Then for the test set of items, we try to predict the interests level of existing users on new items

- III [Cold-start items/Cold-start users]: In this scenario we divide both users and items into two subsets of existing and cold-start users and items, respectively. We aim to recommend the cold-start items to the cold-start users, which is the most challenging form of cold-start problems.

The first scenario happens in systems when new users request for recommendations while the second and third scenarios usually happen in newly-launched systems, new item advertisements, news or where a recommender is always forced to recommend new items.

4.3 The baseline algorithms

To evaluate the performance of our proposed DCT algorithm, we consider a variety baseline approaches. The baseline algorithms are chosen from three types of categories: (i) those that can only deal with cold-start users, (ii) ones that can deal with cold-start users, and (iii) algorithms that are capable of dealing with both cold-start items and users. In particular, we consider the following basic algorithms:

- **RS** (Random Strategy) [10]: A simple baseline that selects at random a subset of users or items. The recommendation for cold-start users and items is a challenging case, where RS is one of the baseline methods.

- **MP** (Most Popular) [16]: Another typical cold-start recommendation algorithm is to select the most popular item. For cold-start users without historical ratings, MP recommends the highly-rated items. MP provides the same recommendation to all users based on global popularity of items. To compute the global popularity of an item we utilized the scoring method introduced in [16].

- **CBF** (Content Based Filtering) [22]: Can effectively recommend new items to existing users based on the users' historical ratings and features of items. This algorithm builds a profile for each user based on the properties of the past users's preferred items.

- **LCE** (Local Collective Embeddings) [22]: Is a matrix factorization method that exploits items' properties and past user preferences while enforcing the manifold structure exhibited by the collective embeddings. We use LCE-I and LCE-U to refer the algorithm when LCE is fed with items' and users' features, respectively. We also conduct experiments with a version of LCE without laplacian regularization which will be referred by LCE-NL [22].

- **KMF** (Kernelized Matrix Factorization) [28]: Is a matrix completion based algorithm, which incorporates external side information of the users or items into the matrix factorization process. In comparison with Probabilistic Matrix Factorization (PMF), it imposes a Gaussian Process (GP) prior over all rows of the matrix, hence the learned model explicitly captures the underlying correlation among the rows.

4.4 Experiments on synthetic dataset

In this section we present the results of our proposed algorithm on one synthetic dataset. We generated a syn-

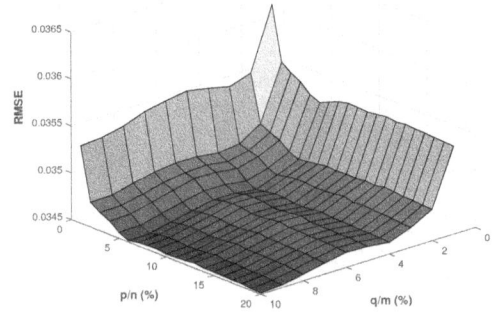

Figure 2: The RMSE of test data for different p and q values

thetic dataset to evaluate our approach before moving forward to real datasets. First we generate two matrices $\mathbf{U} \in [0,1]^{4000 \times r}$ and $\mathbf{V} \in [0,1]^{2000 \times r}$. Then by using $\mathbf{U}$ and $\mathbf{V}$ we generated a rating matrix $\mathbf{R}^{4000 \times 2000} = \mathbf{UV}^\top$ that includes 4000 users and 2000 items. Then we generated a similarity matrix $\mathbf{A}^{4000 \times 4000} = \mathbf{UU}^\top$ for users and a similarity matrix $\mathbf{B}^{2000 \times 2000} = \mathbf{VV}^\top$ for items. Then we added random noise to the all elements of $\mathbf{A}$ and $\mathbf{B}$ where the noise follows a Gaussian distribution $\mathcal{N}(0, 0.5)$. We consider $\mathbf{A}$ and $\mathbf{B}$ as two similarity matrices between users and items, respectably.

In this study we tried different values for p within the range of 100 to 2000 with step-size of 100 and different values for q within the range of 100 to 1000 with same step-size. To generate cold-start users and items in our dataset, we divided the dataset into 4 partitions. We divided users into two groups of p existing users and $n - p$ cold-start users. We also selected q items as existing items and $m - q$ as cold-start items. Hence Partitions 1 and 2 have p users and partitions 3 and 4 have $n - p$ cold-start users; partitions 1 and 3 have q items and partitions 2 and 4 have $m - q$ cold-start items.

The statistics of the dataset is given in Table 2. The RMSE of test data for different combinations of p and q values is shown in Figure 2. It shows that by increasing p and q, the RMSE decreases. Hence, the fewer unobserved elements we have, the lower the error is. Considering the fact that our theoretical upper bound of error decreases by increasing $\frac{p}{m}$ or $\frac{q}{n}$, this observation is completely consistent with our theoretical upper bound.

For our synthetic dataset, we added noise to similarity matrices that follows a zero mean Gaussian distribution with variance of 0.5. To observe the effects of noise variance, we changed the variance from 0.1 to 1 with step size of 0.1and calculated the accuracy of our algorithm. As Figure 3 shows, by increasing the noise variance, both RMSE and MAE of the results on test dataset increase.

Table 3: Cold-start users on MovieLens dataset

	MAE	RMSE	MAP	NDCG
RS	0.7423	0.6734	0.1234	0.4240
MP	0.7213	0.5800	0.107	0.5890
LCE-NL-U	0.7014	0.5409	0.1746	0.6047
LCE-U	0.7004	0.5400	0.1798	0.6147
KMF-U	0.6620	0.4217	0.1587	0.6214
DCT	0.5862	0.4018	0.1749	0.6223

Table 2: Synthetic DataSet

Setting	Algorithm	Training (10%)		Training (20%)		Training (30%)		Training (40%)		Training (50%)	
		MAE	RSME	MAE	RSME	MAE	RSME	MAE	RSME	MAE	RSME
Scenario I	DCT	0.0353	0.0020	0.0345	0.0018	0.0345	0.0018	0.0341	0.0018	0.0340	0.0018
Scenario II	DCT	0.0345	0.0010	0.0342	0.0019	0.0342	0.0019	0.0343	0.0019	0.0342	0.0019
Scenario III	DCT	0.0349	0.0019	0.0340	0.0018	0.0346	0.0019	0.0343	0.0019	0.0344	0.0018

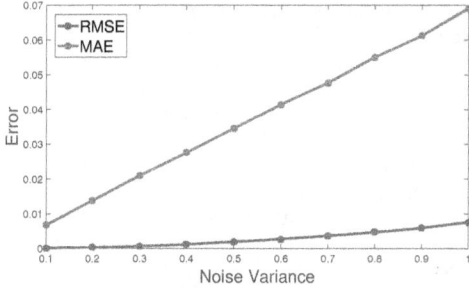

Figure 3: RMSE and MAE of test dataset for different noise variances

Table 5: Experiments with cold-start items on MovieLens and NIPS datasets.

Dataset	Algorithm	Measure			
		MAE	RMSE	MAP	NDCG@2
MovieLens	CBF	0.7008	0.5418	0.0016	0.3800
	LCE-I	0.7088	0.5535	0.0091	0.4287
	LCE-NL-I	0.7087	0.5535	0.0085	0.4281
	KMF-I	0.5067	0.3176	0.0708	0.5087
	DCT	0.5143	0.3070	0.0800	0.5133
NIPS	CBF	0.8810	0.7944	0.1291	0.3862
	LCE-I	0.8576	0.7593	0.1656	0.4240
	LCE-NL-I	0.8663	0.7633	0.1623	0.4187
	KMF-I	0.8804	0.7657	0.1466	0.4219
	DCT	0.6805	0.5111	0.1954	0.4626

Table 4: Cold-start items and cold-start users on MovieLens

	MAE	RMSE	MAP	NDCG
RS	0.9326	1.3820	0.0070	0.0652
KMF	0.8442	0.9730	0.0171	0.1834
DCT	0.7162	0.8524	0.1943	0.2783

4.5 Experiments of cold-start users

To simulate cold-start user scenario, we divide the users into two training and test disjoint subsets. We use 80% of the users for training and the remaining 20% of users for testing. Then we apply baseline algorithms to predict ratings of cold-start users for different items and evaluate the results using the ground truth, which is the complete rating matrix.

We compared our proposed approach to five alternative recommendation methods: RS, MP, KMF-U and two variations of the LCE algorithm. Since NIPS dataset does not have any information (features) about users, for testing this scenario we only apply these methods on MovieLens dataset. Table 3 shows the average performance of each method across the MovieLens dataset for the first scenario.

Considering the RMSE measure, we observed that DCT and KMF-U behave similarly and outperform others algorithms. DCT has also the highest MAP and outperforms others on MovieLens dataset. The LCE-U performs better than MP and the differences between two version of LCE are not significant, but always LCE performs better than LCE-NL. As expected, RS is the least accurate recommender.

4.6 Experiments of cold-start items

To simulate cold-start item scenario, we divide the items into two training and test disjoint subsets. We use 80% of the items for training and the remaining 20% of items for testing. We compared our algorithm to four alternative recommendation methods: CBF, KMF-I, LCE and LCE-NL on NIPS and MovieLens datasets. In the scenarios that we have cold-start items, since there is no historical ratings, MP cannot work. Table 5 shows the average performance

of each method across the MovieLens and NIPS datasets for cold-start item scenario.

In terms of NDCG, MAP and RMSE measures, DCT outperforms all other approaches on MovieLens and NIPS datasets. Only the MAE of KMF-I is lower than DCT on MovieLensIn. Based on the evaluation measure one can conclude that DCT generally outperforms other approaches. We also observed that DCT works better for cold-start items than cold-start users on MovieLens; and that is because features of movies are much more richer than those of users in MovieLens dataset.

4.7 Experiments of cold-start items and cold-start users

In this scenario, since there is not any historical information for nor users neither items, we can only compare our algorithm with RS and KMF on MovieLens. Table 4 shows the results of applying these three algorithms on MovieLens. It is shown that DCT outperforms both RS and KMF in all measures. Hence, DCT is a novel algorithm that can deal with all three types of cold-start problems. We would like to note that DCT is able to predict an initial guess of an item popularity for cold-start items in online recommenders.

The results of Tables 3, 4 and 5 reveal the following findings:

1) RS generally performs significantly worse than the other algorithms in all scenarios for all datasets, which confirms that it is necessary to carefully use similarity information of users and items to have a more accurate recommendations.

2) The DCT outperformed all other methods by a significant margin in almost all scenarios and datasets except for the cold-start users on the NIPS dataset, in which it attained similar performance as KMF-U.

4) The results for MovieLens are generally better than the results for NIPS for all methods, possibly because of the fact that the items in MovieLens have more and richer features, while the items in NIPS are all papers with just keywords. Another explanation for the better results on MovieLens could be that MovieLens is a richer dataset than NIPS since there are more features and ratings per user/item.

5. CONCLUSIONS

In this paper, we proposed a novel factorization model to explicitly exploit similarity information about users and items to alleviate corresponding cold-start problems. In contrast to exiting methods such as subspace sharing and kernelized factorization methods, in the proposed method the completion of unobserved ratings and transduction of knowledge to cold-start items/users is decoupled. In particular, we first perform a full recovery of the sub-matrix obtained by excluding cold-start items and users, and then exploit the similarity matrices to transduct recovered ratings to cold-start users/items. The performance of the proposed algorithm is theoretically analyzed and empirically verified on synthetic and real datasets. Our results demonstrated that the proposed decoupling idea significantly improves the quality of the recommendations and alleviates the cold-start problem when rich side information about users and items is provided.

6. ACKNOWLEDGMENT

This work was supported in part by the National Science Foundation under Awards IIS-096849, CCF-1117709, and 1331852. The authors would like to thank the anonymous reviewers for their insightful comments and suggestions. We also acknowledge valuable technical discussions with Mehrdad Mahdavi and Dennis Ross during this work.

7. REFERENCES

[1] Gediminas Adomavicius and Alexander Tuzhilin. Toward the next generation of recommender systems: A survey of the state-of-the-art and possible extensions. *IEEE Transactions on Knowledge and Data Engineering*, 17(6):734–749, 2005.

[2] Gediminas Adomavicius and Alexander Tuzhilin. Toward the next generation of recommender systems: A survey of the state-of-the-art and possible extensions. *Knowledge and Data Engineering, IEEE Transactions on*, 17(6), 2005.

[3] Jian-Feng Cai, Emmanuel J Candès, and Zuowei Shen. A singular value thresholding algorithm for matrix completion. *SIAM Journal on Optimization*, 20(4):1956–1982, 2010.

[4] Rana Forsati, Mehrdad Mahdavi, Mehrnoush Shamsfard, Mohamed Sarwat. Matrix factorization with explicit trust and distrust side information for improved social recommendation. *ACM Transactions on Information Systems*, 32(4):17, 2014.

[5] Zeno Gantner, Lucas Drumond, Christoph Freudenthaler, Steffen Rendle, and Lars Schmidt-Thieme. Learning attribute-to-feature mappings for cold-start recommendations. In *Data Mining (ICDM), 2010 IEEE 10th International Conference on*. IEEE, 2010.

[6] Jonathan L Herlocker, Joseph A Konstan, Loren G Terveen, and John T Riedl. Evaluating collaborative filtering recommender systems. *ACM Transactions on Information Systems (TOIS)*, 22(1):5–53, 2004.

[7] Yehuda Koren, Robert Bell, and Chris Volinsky. Matrix factorization techniques for recommender systems. *Computer*, 42(8):30–37, 2009.

[8] Guang Ling, Michael R Lyu, and Irwin King. Ratings meet reviews, a combined approach to recommend. In *ACM Conference on RecSys*, pages 105–112. ACM, 2014.

[9] Juntao Liu, Caihua Wu, and Wenyu Liu. Bayesian probabilistic matrix factorization with social relations and item contents for recommendation. *DSS*, 2013.

[10] Nathan N Liu, Xiangrui Meng, Chao Liu, and Qiang Yang. Wisdom of the better few: cold start recommendation via representative based rating elicitation. In *ACM RecSys*, pages 37–44. ACM, 2011.

[11] Hao Ma, Haixuan Yang, Michael R Lyu, and Irwin King. Sorec: social recommendation using probabilistic matrix factorization. In *Proceedings of the 17th ACM conference on Information and knowledge management*, pages 931–940. ACM, 2008.

[12] Christopher D Manning, Prabhakar Raghavan, and Hinrich Schütze. *Introduction to information retrieval*, volume 1. Cambridge university, 2008.

[13] Paolo Massa and Paolo Avesani. Trust-aware collaborative filtering for recommender systems. In *On Move to Meaningful Internet Systems 2004: CoopIS, DOA, and ODBASE*, pages 492–508. Springer, 2004.

[14] Aditya Krishna Menon, Krishna-Prasad Chitrapura, Sachin Garg, Deepak Agarwal, Nagaraj Kota. Response prediction using collaborative filtering with hierarchies and side-information. In *Proceedings of the 17th ACM SIGKDD, KDTM,* pages 141–149, 2011.

[15] Andriy Mnih and Ruslan Salakhutdinov. Probabilistic matrix factorization. In *NIPS*, pages 1257–1264, 2007.

[16] Seung-Taek Park and Wei Chu. Pairwise preference regression for cold-start recommendation. In *Proceedings of the third ACM conference on Recommender systems*, pages 21–28. ACM, 2009.

[17] Ian Porteous, Arthur U Asuncion, and Max Welling. Bayesian matrix factorization with side information and dirichlet process mixtures. In *AAAI*, 2010.

[18] Benjamin Recht. A simpler approach to matrix completion. *The Journal of Machine Learning Research*, 12:3413–3430, 2011.

[19] Jasson DM Rennie and Nathan Srebro. Fast maximum margin matrix factorization for collaborative prediction. In *Proceedings of the 22nd ICML*, pages 713–719. ACM, 2005.

[20] S Roweis. Nips dataset (2002). *URL http://www. cs. nyu. edu/~ roweis*.

[21] Laila Safoury and Akram Salah. Exploiting user demographic attributes for solving cold-start problem in recommender system. *Lecture Notes on Software Engineering*, 1(3):303–307, 2013.

[22] Martin Saveski and Amin Mantrach. Item cold-start recommendations: learning local collective embeddings. In *Proceedings of the 8th ACM Conference RecSys*, pages 89–96. ACM, 2014.

[23] Hanhuai Shan and Arindam Banerjee. Generalized probabilistic matrix factorizations for collaborative filtering. In *ICDM*, pages 1025–1030. IEEE, 2010.

[24] Le Hoang Son. Dealing with the new user cold-start problem in recommender systems: A comparative review. *Information Systems*, (0):–, 2014.

[25] Nathan Srebro, Jason Rennie, and Tommi S Jaakkola. Maximum-margin matrix factorization. In *NIPS*, pages 1329–1336, 2004.

[26] Michele Trevisiol, Luca Maria Aiello, Rossano Schifanella, Alejandro Jaimes. Cold-start news recommendation with domain-dependent browse graph. In *ACM RecSys*, volume 14, 2014.

[27] Ke Zhou, Shuang-Hong Yang, and Hongyuan Zha. Functional matrix factorizations for cold-start recommendation. In *ACM SIGIR*, pages 315–324. ACM, 2011.

[28] Tinghui Zhou, Hanhuai Shan, Arindam Banerjee, and Guillermo Sapiro. Kernelized probabilistic matrix factorization: Exploiting graphs and side information. In *SDM*, volume 12, pages 403–414. SIAM, 2012.

HyPER: A Flexible and Extensible Probabilistic Framework for Hybrid Recommender Systems

Pigi Kouki
UC Santa Cruz
pkouki@soe.ucsc.edu

Shobeir Fakhraei
University of Maryland
shobeir@cs.umd.edu

James Foulds
UC Santa Cruz
jfoulds@ucsc.edu

Magdalini Eirinaki
San Jose State University
magdalini.eirinaki@sjsu.edu

Lise Getoor
UC Santa Cruz
getoor@soe.ucsc.edu

ABSTRACT

As the amount of recorded digital information increases, there is a growing need for flexible recommender systems which can incorporate richly structured data sources to improve recommendations. In this paper, we show how a recently introduced statistical relational learning framework can be used to develop a generic and extensible hybrid recommender system. Our hybrid approach, HyPER (HYbrid Probabilistic Extensible Recommender), incorporates and reasons over a wide range of information sources. Such sources include multiple user-user and item-item similarity measures, content, and social information. HyPER automatically learns to balance these different information signals when making predictions. We build our system using a powerful and intuitive probabilistic programming language called probabilistic soft logic [1], which enables efficient and accurate prediction by formulating our custom recommender systems with a scalable class of graphical models known as hinge-loss Markov random fields. We experimentally evaluate our approach on two popular recommendation datasets, showing that HyPER can effectively combine multiple information types for improved performance, and can significantly outperform existing state-of-the-art approaches.

Keywords

Hybrid recommender systems, graphical models, probabilistic programming, probabilistic soft logic.

1. INTRODUCTION

Recent work on hybrid recommender systems has shown that recommendation accuracy can be improved by combining multiple data modalities and modeling techniques within a single model [2, 3, 4, 5, 6]. Existing hybrid recommender systems are typically designed for a specific problem domain, such as movie recommendations, and are limited in their ability to generalize to other settings or make use of any further information. As our daily lives become increas-ingly digitally connected, the list of data sources available for recommendations continues to grow. There is a need for general-purpose, extensible frameworks that can make use of arbitrary data modalities to improve recommendation.

The challenge of custom model-building has been extensively studied in the fields of probabilistic programming [7] and statistical relational learning (SRL) [8], which provide programming language interfaces for encoding knowledge and specifying models. Probabilistic programs can be used to encode graphical models for reasoning with graph-structured probabilistic dependencies. Graphical models are a natural approach to recommendations given that the user-item rating matrix can be interpreted as a graph, with weighted edges between users and items corresponding to the respective ratings [4].

In modern recommendation contexts, a bipartite user-item graph is insufficient to represent all available information, such as user-user and item-item similarity, content, social information, and metadata. For example, neighborhood-based collaborative filtering techniques can be interpreted as predicting ratings based on an extension of the user-item graph with additional edges between pairs of similar users or similar items (Figure 1). We need a more general representation to reason over this richly structured information.

In this paper, we propose a general hybrid recommender framework, called HyPER (HYbrid Probabilistic Extensible Recommender), which leverages the flexibility of probabilistic programming in order to build adaptable and extensible hybrid recommender systems which reason over complex data. In particular, we use a modeling language called *probabilistic soft logic* (PSL) [9]. PSL is especially well-suited to collaborative-filtering based recommendation graphs as it is able to fuse information from multiple sources and it was originally designed as a flexible framework for reasoning and combining similarities [10]. It provides a general declarative framework for combining entity similarities, attribute similarities, and information from additional sources including the predictions of other algorithms. The models defined by PSL programs, called *hinge-loss Markov random fields* (HL-MRFs), are amenable to efficient and scalable inference, which is crucial in a recommendation context.

Our contributions include (1) a general and extensible hybrid recommender system with a probabilistic programming interface, (2) a method for learning how to balance the different input signals in the hybrid system, and (3) extensive experimental studies using several information sources which validate the performance of the proposed framework and highlight contribution of each source to the final pre-

RecSys'15, September 16–20, 2015, Vienna, Austria.
© 2015 ACM. ISBN 978-1-4503-3692-5/15/09 ...$15.00.
DOI: http://dx.doi.org/10.1145/2792838.2800175

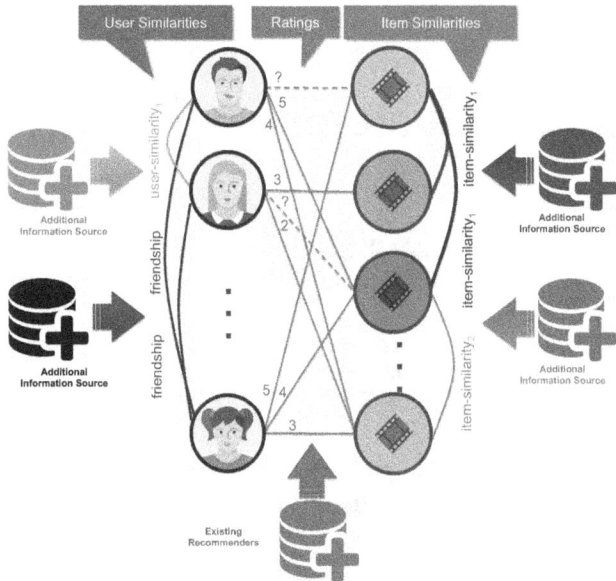

Figure 1: Example recommendation graph.

diction. To the best of our knowledge, our proposed HyPER framework is the first which provides a mechanism to extend the system by incorporating and reasoning over currently unspecified additional information types and similarity measures. We evaluate our system on two rich datasets from the local business and music recommendation domains (Yelp and Last.fm) comparing our model to state-of-the-art recommendation approaches. Our results show that HyPER is able to effectively combine multiple information sources to improve recommendations, resulting in significantly improved performance over the competing methods in both datasets.

2. BACKGROUND

Recommender systems play a significant role in many everyday decision-making processes which affect the quality of our lives, from the restaurant we have lunch at, to the hotel for our vacation, to the music we listen to. Traditional recommender systems primarily leverage underlying similarities between users and items in order to make predictions based on observed ratings. Content-based filtering (CB) approaches compute these similarities by using features extracted from content to build user profiles, which are compared with content features of items. While content-based approaches can recommend newly added items, they are limited by a lack of serendipity. The recommendations are limited to the user's known likes and do not generally include items out of the user's (recorded) comfort zone [11].

Collaborative filtering (CF) techniques address this by identifying similar users or items based on their rating patterns instead of content, using methods such as neighborhood-based approaches and matrix factorization models. However, collaborative filtering methods typically do not perform well in "cold-start" settings, where there are few ratings for a user or an item [12]. Moreover, pure rating-based collaborative filtering approaches cannot take advantage of data which may be available in addition to ratings.

To address these shortcomings, hybrid recommender systems (HRSs) were introduced, combining content-based and

collaborative-filtering techniques (e.g. [2, 3, 4]). HRS techniques can improve performance over content-based and collaborative filtering methods alone, especially in the case where the ratings matrix is sparse [2]. However, existing HRSs have their own limitations. First, they are problem- and data-specific. Each HRS is typically motivated by a specific problem domain (e.g. movie recommendations) and the solution is fine-tuned to solve a specific problem with datasets of specific characteristics. Hence, HRSs typically cannot be generalized to different problem domains or input data, or be easily expanded to incorporate knowledge from richer datasets.

As the web has evolved into a participatory, user-driven platform, additional information is increasingly becoming available. Users form social networks, give verbal feedback on items via reviews, endorse or down-vote items or other users, form trust relationships, "check-in" at venues, and perform many other social actions that may potentially be leveraged to better understand users in order to improve recommendations. A flexible and extensible hybrid recommender system which can make use of this wealth of information is increasingly important.

The remainder of the paper is structured as follows. In Section 3 we introduce HyPER, a general hybrid recommendation framework which is extensible and customizable using a probabilistic programming interface. We systematically evaluate our framework in Section 4, and place our system in the context of related work in Section 5. Finally, we conclude with a discussion in Section 6.

3. PROPOSED APPROACH

We propose HyPER, a general hybrid framework that combines multiple different sources of information and modeling techniques into a single unified model. HyPER offers the capability to extend the model by incorporating additional sources of information as they become available. Our approach begins by viewing the recommendation task as a bipartite graph, where users $\mathcal{U}$ and items $\mathcal{I}$ are the vertices, and ratings are edges between users and items [4]. Using PSL [1], a flexible statistical relational learning system with a probabilistic programming interface, this graph is then augmented to construct a probabilistic graphical model with additional edges to encode similarity information, predicted ratings, content and social information, and metadata. We then train the graphical model to learn the relative importance of the different information sources in the hybrid system, and make predictions for target ratings, using graphical model learning and collective inference techniques.

Figure 1 shows an overview of our modeling approach. In the figure, items and users are nodes, and green edges represent the ratings that users gave to items, with edge weights corresponding to the rating values. The goal is to predict the edge weights for unobserved edges, denoted as dashed lines. Neighborhood-based approaches find the k most similar users or similar items, and use their ratings to make these predictions. In our graph-based representation, we interpret these k-nearest neighbor relationships as k edges which are added to the graph. In Figure 1, blue edges encode user similarities and red edges correspond to item similarities.

We can further encode additional sources of information and outputs of other recommendation algorithms within this graph-based representation in a similar way, i.e. in the form of additional links or nodes. For instance, latent factor methods identify latent representations which can be used to augment the graph with weighted edges encoding predictions of user-item ratings based on the latent space. The latent representations can also be used to construct additional user-user and item-item edges by identifying similar users and similar items in the latent space. Content information and metadata, such as demographics and time information, can be incorporated in the graph representation by identifying further similarity links, or by adding nodes with attribute values, and edges to associate these values with users and items. Furthermore, social information from digital social media is inherently relational, and can readily be incorporated into a graph-based representation.

Having encoded all available information in the graph, the next step is to reason over this graph to predict unobserved user-item rating edges. We view the prediction task as inference in a graphical model, the structure of which is defined by our graph representation. As scalability is important for recommendation tasks in practice, we use a hinge-loss Markov random field (HL-MRF) formulation [9]. HL-MRFs are highly scalable as they admit exact inference by way of efficient parallel algorithms. In the next section we briefly review HL-MRFs. We then describe our unified recommender system modeling framework in detail in Section 3.2, and we show how to learn the relative importance of the information sources for our hybrid model in Section 3.3.

3.1 Hinge-loss Markov Random Fields

Hinge-loss Markov random fields (HL-MRFs) [9] are a general class of conditional probabilistic models over continuous random variables which admit tractable and efficient inference. The key to the tractability of these models is the use of hinge-loss feature functions. More formally, a hinge-loss Markov random field defines a conditional probability density function over random variables $\mathbf{Y}$ conditioned on $\mathbf{X}$,

$$P(\mathbf{Y}|\mathbf{X}) \propto \exp\left(-\sum_{j=1}^{m} w_j \phi_j(\mathbf{Y}, \mathbf{X})\right) , \qquad (1)$$

where ϕ_j is a *hinge-loss* potential function, of the form

$$\phi_j(\mathbf{Y}, \mathbf{X}) = (max\{\ell_j(\mathbf{X}, \mathbf{Y}), 0\})^{p_j} . \qquad (2)$$

Here, ℓ is linear function of $\mathbf{X}$ and $\mathbf{Y}$, and $p_j \in \{1, 2\}$ optionally squares the potential. The variables in $\mathbf{X}$ and $\mathbf{Y}$ are in the unit interval [0,1]. Each ϕ_j is associated with a weight w_j which determines its importance in the model. We learn the weights from the data, as discussed later in Section 3.3. Note that Equation 1 is log-concave in $\mathbf{Y}$, so maximum a posteriori (MAP) inference to find the optimal $\mathbf{Y}$ in HL-MRFs can be solved exactly via convex optimization. We use the alternating direction method of multipliers (ADMM) approach of Bach et al. [9] to perform this optimization efficiently and in parallel.

HL-MRFs can be specified using a probabilistic programming language called *Probabilistic Soft Logic (PSL)* [1], and this is the language we use to specify our unified recommendation framework. PSL is a declarative first-order logical language where logical rules are composed of continuous relaxations of Boolean logical operators. These rules define templates for hinge-loss potential functions, which are instantiated to construct an HL-MRF model. For example, $a \Rightarrow b$ corresponds to the hinge function $\max(a - b, 0)$, and $a \wedge b$ corresponds to $\max(a + b - 1, 0)$. We refer the reader to [1] for a detailed description of PSL operators.

To illustrate PSL in a movie recommendation context, the following rule encodes that users tend to rate movies of their preferred genres highly:

$$LikesGenre(U, G) \wedge IsGenre(M, G) \Rightarrow Rating(U, M) ,$$

where $LikesGenre(U, G)$ is a binary observed predicate, $IsGenre(M, G)$ is a continuous observed predicate in the interval [0, 1] capturing the affinity of the movie to the genre, and $Rating(U, M)$ is a continuous variable to be inferred, which encodes the star rating as a number between 0 and 1, with higher values corresponding to higher star ratings. For example, we could instantiate $U = Jim$, $G = classics$ and $M = Casablanca$. This instantiation results in a hinge-loss potential function in the HL-MRF,

$$\begin{aligned} \max(&LikesGenre(Jim, classics) \\ &+ IsGenre(Casablanca, classics) \\ &- Rating(Jim, Casablanca) - 1, 0) . \end{aligned}$$

3.2 Hybrid Framework

The strengths of the HyPER framework include the ability to extensibly incorporate multiple sources of information in a unified hybrid recommendation model, as well as learning how to balance these signals from training data. HyPER models are specified using a collection of PSL rules which encode graph-structured dependency relationships between users, items, ratings, content and social information. Additionally, the model provides the flexibility to incorporate prior predictions, such as mean-centering predictors and the results of other recommendation algorithms. In what follows, we present the rules that define the HL-MRF model for the core of the HyPER framework. We emphasize that while this set of rules covers a breadth of input sources, the model can be readily extended to incorporate other sources of information such as time, implicit feedback, and social interactions, with the introduction of new PSL rules. Moreover, additional similarity measures and recommendation algorithms can straightforwardly be included with analogous rules. HyPER builds upon the ideas of Fakhraei et al. [13], which is an important precursor to this work.

3.2.1 User-based Collaborative Filtering

Motivated by the basic principles of the neighborhood-based approach, we can define PSL rules of this form:

$$SimilarUsers_{sim}(u_1, u_2) \wedge Rating(u_1, i) \Rightarrow Rating(u_2, i) .$$

This rule captures the intuition that similar users give similar ratings to the same items. The predicate $Rating(u, i)$ takes a value in the interval [0, 1] and represents the normalized value of the rating that a user u gave to an item i, while $SimilarUsers_{sim}(u_1, u_2)$ is binary, with value 1 iff u_1 is one of the k-nearest neighbors of u_2. The similarities can be calculated with any similarity measure sim, as we will describe in Section 3.2.3. The above rule represents a template for hinge functions which reduce the probability of predicted ratings as the difference between $Rating(u_2, i)$ and $Rating(u_1, i)$ increases, for users that are neighbors.

3.2.2 Item-based Collaborative Filtering

Similarly, we can define PSL rules to capture the intuition of item-based collaborative filtering methods, namely that similar items should have similar ratings from the same users:

$$SimilarItems_{sim}(i_1, i_2) \wedge Rating(u, i_1) \Rightarrow Rating(u, i_2) .$$

The predicate $SimilarItems_{sim}(i_1, i_2)$ is binary, with value 1 iff i_1 is one of the k-nearest neighbors of i_2 (using similarity measure sim), while $Rating(u, i)$ represents the normalized value of the rating of user u to item i, as discussed above.

3.2.3 Combining Collaborative Filtering Measures

By including both types of rules described in Sections 3.2.1 and 3.2.2 we can define an HL-MRF model that combines user-based and item-based techniques to predict ratings. There exist many measures available to compute similarities between entities for user-based and item-based methods, and these different measures capture different notions of similarity. For instance, in neighborhood-based approaches, vector-based similarity measures are broadly used, whereas in latent factor approaches other similarities, applicable to the low dimensional space, are preferred. While most existing recommender systems are designed to use a single similarity measure, HyPER allows for the simultaneous incorporation of multiple similarity measures, and can automatically adjust the importance of each based on training data.

In this instantiation of our HyPER framework we use the most popular similarity measures in the neighborhood-based recommendations literature [4]. More specifically, we apply Pearson's correlation and cosine similarity measures to calculate similarities between users and items; for the items we additionally apply the adjusted cosine similarity measure. To incorporate matrix-factorization collaborative filtering, and inspired by Hoff et al. [14], we compute similar users and items in the low-dimensional latent space using two popular distance measures in that space, namely, cosine and Euclidean. The user similarities are identified using the following rules:

$$SimilarUsers_{cosine}(u_1, u_2) \land Rating(u_1, i) \Rightarrow Rating(u_2, i)$$
$$SimilarUsers_{pearson}(u_1, u_2) \land Rating(u_1, i) \Rightarrow Rating(u_2, i)$$
$$SimilarUsers_{\substack{latent \\ cosine}}(u_1, u_2) \land Rating(u_1, i) \Rightarrow Rating(u_2, i)$$
$$SimilarUsers_{\substack{latent \\ euclidean}}(u_1, u_2) \land Rating(u_1, i) \Rightarrow Rating(u_2, i) .$$

Analogous rules are introduced to identify similar items, but are omitted due to space limitations. As noted earlier, this initial set of similarity measures can be readily expanded by adding the corresponding rules, in the same form as above.

3.2.4 Mean-Centering Priors

Each individual user considered in a recommender system has her own biases in rating items (e.g. some users tend to be stricter than others). Moreover, each item's rating is influenced by its overall quality and popularity (e.g. a popular blockbuster may get higher ratings on average than a low-budget movie). To address such biases, a recommender system needs to incorporate a normalization mechanism, both per user, and per item. Using mean-centering normalization for neighborhood-based approaches, or including intercept terms in probabilistic latent factor models, addresses this issue and generally improves performance [4]. In our HyPER framework we encode this intuition with rules that encourage the ratings to be close to the average, per-user and per-item:

$$AverageUserRating(u) \Rightarrow Rating(u, i)$$
$$\neg AverageUserRating(u) \Rightarrow \neg Rating(u, i)$$

$$AverageItemRating(i) \Rightarrow Rating(u, i)$$
$$\neg AverageItemRating(i) \Rightarrow \neg Rating(u, i) .$$

The predicate $AverageUserRating(u)$ represents the average of the ratings over the set of items that user u provided in the training set. Similarly, $AverageUserRating(i)$ represents the average of the user ratings an item i has received. The pair of PSL rules per-user and per-item corresponds to a "V-shaped" function centered at the average rating, which penalizes the predicted rating for being different in either direction from this average.

In order to capture cases where we have no information about a user or an item, we use a general prior rating centered at the average value of all of the ratings in the system (i.e. the average over all items rated by all users). We encode this prior with the following rules:

$$PriorRating \Rightarrow Rating(u, i)$$
$$\neg PriorRating \Rightarrow \neg Rating(u, i) .$$

The real-valued predicate $PriorRating$ represents the average of all of the ratings.

3.2.5 Using Additional Sources of Information

Incorporating other sources of information pertaining to the items, the users, and the respective ratings to our framework is straightforward. In the present instantiation of our framework, we use the content of the items to find similar items:

$$SimilarItems_{Content}(i_1, i_2) \land Rating(u, i_1) \Rightarrow Rating(u, i_2) .$$

In this rule, the predicate $SimilarItems_{Content}(i_1, i_2)$ represents items that have similar content-based features (e.g. in the movie recommendation domain such features are the genre, actor, director, etc.), instead of similar ratings.

The HyPER framework can also incorporate social information, when this is available. For instance, in the present instantiation of the system, we leverage social network friendship links as follows:

$$Friends(u_1, u_2) \land Rating(u_1, i) \Rightarrow Rating(u_2, i) .$$

Note that our framework is flexible and can incorporate many other sources of information that are available. For instance, we can leverage demographic information by computing similarity neighborhood relationships in demographic feature space and employing the rule:

$$SimilarUsers_{Demo}(u_1, u_2) \land Rating(u_1, i) \Rightarrow Rating(u_2, i) .$$

3.2.6 Leveraging Existing Recommendation Algorithms

Every recommendation algorithm has strengths and weaknesses which may depend on data-specific factors such as the degree of sparsity or the shape of the data matrix. This imposes a big limitation in the recommendation process, as choosing one algorithm as the core of a recommender system limits its strength to a particular set of domains. In this work, our motivation is to provide a flexible framework that can be used as-is to generate accurate recommendations for any domain and data regime. Therefore, instead of selecting a single recommendation algorithm, we propose to incorporate the predictions from different methods into our unified model. These predictions are further augmented with any other available information, using the rules discussed above. For example, the predictions from matrix factorization (optimizing regularized squared error via stochastic gradient descent) (MF), Bayesian probabilistic matrix factorization

(BPMF) [15], and item-based collaborative filtering can be incorporated in the model via the following rules:

$$Rating_{MF}(u,i) \Rightarrow Rating(u,i)$$
$$\neg Rating_{MF}(u,i) \Rightarrow \neg Rating(u,i)$$

$$Rating_{BPMF}(u,i) \Rightarrow Rating(u,i)$$
$$\neg Rating_{BPMF}(u,i) \Rightarrow \neg Rating(u,i)$$

$$Rating_{\substack{item \\ based}}(u,i) \Rightarrow Rating(u,i)$$
$$\neg Rating_{\substack{item \\ based}}(u,i) \Rightarrow \neg Rating(u,i) \ .$$

Additional algorithms can be easily incorporated in a similar manner.

3.3 Balancing the Information Sources

An important task of any hybrid recommender system is to trade off and balance the different information sources according to their informativeness for predicting ratings. Each of the first-order rules introduced above corresponds to a different information source in our hybrid model, and is associated with a non-negative weight w_j in Equation 1. These weights determine the relative importance of the information sources, corresponding to the extent to which the corresponding hinge function ϕ_j alters the probability of the data under Equation 1, with higher weight w_j corresponding to a greater importance of information source j. For each rule we learn a weight using Bach et al. [9]'s approximate maximum likelihood weight learning algorithm for templated HL-MRFs. The algorithm approximates a gradient step in the conditional likelihood,

$$\frac{\partial log P(\mathbf{Y}|\mathbf{X})}{\partial w_j} = \mathbb{E}_w[\phi_j(\mathbf{Y},\mathbf{X})] - \phi_j(\mathbf{Y},\mathbf{X}) \ , \quad (3)$$

by replacing the intractable expectation with the MAP solution based on w, which can be rapidly solved using ADMM.

3.4 Scaling to Large Datasets

Due to the hinge-loss formulation, inference and learning are relatively scalable via ADMM, which can be performed in parallel. The UMD/UCSC implementation of PSL uses a single-machine multi-threaded ADMM algorithm, and we use this implementation for our experiments on datasets with around 100,000 ratings. For deployment in industrial applications with millions of users, items, and ratings, the main bottleneck for scalability is memory to store the ground model. This can be addressed simply in the current implementation of PSL by dividing the graph into densely connected subgraphs, e.g. a subgraph per city, that are inferred independently and in parallel on different machines. Alternatively, a fully distributed implementation of ADMM would straightforwardly facilitate the scaling of HyPER to the big data setting via model parallelism.

4. EXPERIMENTAL VALIDATION

In this section we evaluate our HyPER framework with comparison to state-of-the-art recommender algorithms. We report experimental results on two popular datasets for both the complete hybrid model and for each individual component of our hybrid models.[1]

---

[1]Code is available at https://github.com/pkouki/recsys2015

Table 1: Dataset Description

Dataset	Yelp	Last.fm
No. of users	34,454	1,892
No. of items	3,605	17,632
No. of ratings	99,049	92,834
Content	514 business categories	9,719 artist tags
Social	81,512 friendships	12,717 friendships
Sparsity	99.92%	99.72%

4.1 Datasets and Evaluation Metrics

For our experimental evaluation we used the Yelp academic dataset and the Last.fm dataset.[23] Our goal with Yelp is to recommend local businesses to users by predicting the missing ratings of businesses based on previous ratings. For our experiments, we used all businesses, users, and ratings from Scottsdale, Arizona, one of the largest cities in the dataset. Since we employ user and item similarities as well as social information, it makes sense to focus those relationships within the subgroup of the businesses of one physical location. Additionally, we used the categories of each business as content information and the explicit user friendships provided as social information. Yelp users give ratings from 1 to 5 stars, which we linearly scaled into the [0,1] range that PSL operates over for the purposes of our model.

For the Last.fm dataset our goal is to recommend artists to users. As Last.fm does not provide explicit user-artist ratings we leverage the number of times a user has listened to an artist to construct implicit ratings. We use a simple model-based approach, where the repeated-listen counts for each user across artists are modeled with a negative-binomial distribution. We used this distribution as it is appropriate for count data where the sample variance is greater than the sample mean, which is typically the case for Last.fm. For each user, we fit a negative binomial to their counts via maximum likelihood estimation, and we calculate the user's implicit rating for an artist as the cumulative distribution function (CDF) of the distribution, evaluated at the artist's count. This corresponds to the proportion of hypothetical artists that a user would listen to less than the given artist, under the model. The Last.fm dataset also includes tags on artists that we use for content-based information, as well as user friendship data that we use for social recommendation.

We deliberately selected two datasets with a similar total number of ratings but a different ratio of users to items. Different recommendation methods may perform better with more users than items or vice versa, and hybrid systems must account for this. We provide the summary statistics of the two datasets in Table 1.

To learn the appropriate balance between information sources for HyPER, i.e. to learn the weights of each rule in the model, we train using the approximate maximum likelihood method described in Section 3.3, with 20% of the training folds treated as the prediction target variables $\mathbf{Y}$. During testing, we performed MAP inference to make predictions using ADMM. We report the root mean squared error (RMSE) and the mean absolute error (MAE). We compute these metrics by performing 5-fold cross-validation and reporting the average cross-validated error.

---

[2]https://www.yelp.com/academic_dataset
[3]http://grouplens.org/datasets/hetrec-2011/

Table 2: Overall Performance of Different Recommender Systems on Yelp and Last.fm.

	Model	Yelp		Last.fm	
		RMSE (SD)	MAE (SD)	RMSE (SD)	MAE (SD)
Base models	Item-based	1.216 (0.004)	0.932 (0.001)	1.408 (0.010)	1.096 (0.008)
	MF	1.251 (0.006)	0.944 (0.005)	1.178 (0.003)	0.939 (0.003)
	BPMF	1.191 (0.003)	0.954 (0.003)	1.008 (0.005)	0.839 (0.004)
Hybrid models	Naive hybrid (averaged predictions)	1.179 (0.003)	0.925 (0.002)	1.067 (0.004)	0.857 (0.004)
	BPMF-SRIC	1.191 (0.004)	0.957 (0.004)	1.015 (0.004)	0.842 (0.004)
	HyPER	**1.173** (0.003)	**0.917** (0.002)	**1.001** (0.004)	**0.833** (0.004)

4.2 Experimental Results

We report overall results with comparison to a selection of competing algorithms in Table 2, and show more detailed results for the individual components of our hybrid models in Table 3. The following sections discuss these results.

4.2.1 Overall Performance Comparison

We study the performance of HyPER in comparison to several state-of-the-art models. We considered the following baselines:

- **Item-based:** The method in Equation 4.16 from [4], using Pearson's correlation with a mean-centering correction, as implemented in Graphlab.[4]

- **Matrix factorization (MF):** MF optimizing for regularized squared error using stochastic gradient descent [12], as implemented in Graphlab.

- **Bayesian probabilistic matrix factorization (BPMF):** The Bayesian variant of probabilistic matrix factorization, trained using Gibbs sampling [15].

- **Naive hybrid:** A simple hybrid approach where the predictions of the above models are averaged.

- **BPMF with social relations and items' content (BPMF-SRIC):** A hybrid model that extends BPMF with social and content information [5].

The performance of our model is statistically significantly better than the baselines at $\alpha = 0.05$ for both datasets and evaluation metrics when using paired t-test. We denote with bold the numbers that are statistically significantly better. These results confirm our initial intuition that by incorporating a wide variety of information sources and balancing them appropriately, the HyPER framework manages to perform very well with rich and diverse datasets. We explore HyPER components in more detail in the following section.

4.2.2 Performance per Information Type

For each type of information, we further evaluated our approach by building simple HyPER models with each rule individually, and comparing these to combined hybrid sub-models comprising all of the corresponding rules of that type. Each sub-model also included the corresponding mean-centering rules (e.g. the user-average rating rule for the user-based models). To balance the effect of each rule, we performed weight learning within each training fold to learn rule weights. We report the results in Table 3. The results show that for each information type, the HyPER model

---

[4]http://www.dato.com

which combines all of the corresponding components performs significantly better than each component, considered in isolation. We denote with bold the cases where the performance of each HyPER model is statistically significantly better than all the individual models in the same category at $\alpha = 0.05$ using paired t-test. The final HyPER model shown in the last line, which combines all of the available information into a single hybrid model, also performs statistically significantly better than all sub-models and baselines.

Mean-Centering Priors: We created simple HyPER models using only the average rating of each user, or the average rating of each item, or the average overall rating, as well as a combined model. In the case of Yelp, the item-average model had a lower error compared to the user average rule, while the opposite was true for Last.fm (Table 3(a)). This may be because the ratio of users to items is different in the two datasets. The combined model performed better than the individual models in both datasets.

Neighborhood-Based Collaborative Filtering: We constructed individual models based on the similarities described in Section 3.2.1. The number of neighbors is typically set to between 20 and 50 in the literature [4], and so we used 50 neighbors for users/item in all experiments. We also employed a mean-centered approach by providing each of these models with the corresponding average-rating mean-centering rules (e.g. the average user-rating rule for user-based collaborative filtering). As in the previous experiment, user-based techniques perform poorly on Yelp, but have better performance on Last.fm (Tables 3(b) and 3(c)). The opposite is true for the item-based techniques, which perform poorly on Last.fm, but better on Yelp. The performance varied between the different similarity measures, with distances computed in the latent space usually performing the best individually. Again, the HyPER combination of all similarity measures improves performance.

Additional Sources of Information: We constructed individual and hybrid models using friendship information, as well as content similarity between items based on the business category and the tags of artists for Yelp and Last.fm respectively. We used Jaccard similarity for both datasets. In each sub-model we also provided additional rules for mean centering using both average user and item ratings. Content and friendship information help performance in both datasets, and the model that combines both content and social information matched and often improved on the best individual models' performance (Table 3(d)).

Leveraging Existing Algorithms: As discussed in section 3.2.6, our framework is able to combine predictions from a number of different models. In Table 3(e) we show the performance of three baseline recommenders, and in the fourth line we present the results of a HyPER ensemble which com-

Table 3: Performance of HyPER sub-models on Yelp and Last.fm.

	Model	Yelp RMSE (SD)	Yelp MAE (SD)	Last.fm RMSE (SD)	Last.fm MAE (SD)
(a) Mean-centering	User average rating	2.313 (0.008)	1.656 (0.008)	1.043 (0.004)	0.873 (0.004)
	Item average rating	1.215 (0.003)	0.932 (0.001)	1.399 (0.009)	1.092 (0.008)
	Overall average rating	1.280 (0.005)	1.030 (0.004)	1.792 (0.004)	1.464 (0.004)
	HyPER (all mean-centering rules)	**1.199** (0.003)	0.952 (0.002)	**1.032** (0.004)	**0.861** (0.004)
(b) User-based	Similar users (Pearson)	2.313 (0.008)	1.656 (0.008)	1.043 (0.004)	0.874 (0.004)
	Similar users (cosine)	2.313 (0.008)	1.657 (0.008)	1.043 (0.004)	0.873 (0.004)
	Similar users (latent, cosine)	2.227 (0.007)	1.597 (0.007)	1.025 (0.004)	0.862 (0.004)
	Similar users (latent, Euclidean)	2.226 (0.009)	1.596 (0.008)	1.025 (0.004)	0.863 (0.004)
	HyPER (all user-based rules)	**2.194** (0.008)	**1.573** (0.008)	1.025 (0.004)	**0.861** (0.004)
(c) Item-based	Similar items (Pearson)	1.213 (0.004)	0.931 (0.002)	1.397 (0.008)	1.098 (0.006)
	Similar items (cosine)	1.211 (0.003)	0.928 (0.001)	1.396 (0.008)	1.100 (0.007)
	Similar items (adjusted cosine)	1.210 (0.004)	0.924 (0.002)	1.405 (0.008)	1.092 (0.007)
	Similar items (latent, cosine)	1.212 (0.003)	0.923 (0.001)	1.379 (0.009)	1.080 (0.008)
	Similar items (latent, Euclidean)	1.212 (0.003)	0.931 (0.001)	1.379 (0.008)	1.081 (0.008)
	HyPER (all item-based rules)	**1.208** (0.004)	0.923 (0.002)	**1.362** (0.007)	**1.070** (0.006)
(d) Content &Social	Similar items (content)	1.200 (0.003)	0.939 (0.002)	1.029 (0.004)	0.867 (0.004)
	Friends	1.199 (0.003)	0.932 (0.002)	1.013 (0.004)	0.853 (0.004)
	HyPER (content + social rules)	**1.195** (0.003)	**0.927** (0.002)	1.013 (0.004)	**0.857** (0.004)
(e) Base models	Item-based	1.216 (0.004)	0.932 (0.001)	1.408 (0.010)	1.096 (0.008)
	MF	1.251 (0.006)	0.944 (0.005)	1.178 (0.003)	0.939 (0.003)
	BPMF	1.191 (0.003)	0.954 (0.003)	1.008 (0.005)	0.839 (0.004)
	HyPER (baseline rules)	**1.179** (0.003)	**0.926** (0.002)	**1.005** (0.005)	**0.836** (0.004)
	HyPER (all rules)	**1.173** (0.003)	**0.917** (0.002)	**1.001** (0.004)	**0.833** (0.004)

bines the results of those recommenders, without any additional rules. The combined model performed better than the individual baselines.

Relative Importance of Information Sources: When performing weight learning (Section 3.3), the learned weights of the rules are indicative of the relative importance of the signals. For Last.fm, average user ratings had a high rule weight while average item ratings did not, while the reverse was true for Yelp, suggesting a difference in the importance of user judiciousness versus item popularity between the data sets. Item similarities had a high weight for Last.fm, while MF predictions had a high weight for Yelp. Negated rules, which decrease predicted ratings, were typically weighted lower than their non-negated counterparts. In general, the rules for BPMF predictions had high weights.

5. RELATED WORK

There is a large body of work on recommender systems; see Ricci et al. [16] for an overview. We focus our related work discussion on hybrid recommender systems, and particularly systems that can incorporate multi-relational and heterogeneous data as well as graphical modeling approaches. In Burke [17]'s taxonomy of hybrid recommender systems our work falls into the "feature augmentation" category.

Hybrid systems typically combine two or more approaches in order to provide better recommendations, usually content-based and collaborative filtering approaches [18, 19] or variations of collaborative filtering approaches [20]. Gunawardana and Meek [18] present a domain-agnostic hybrid approach for using content to improve item-item modeling. After the Netflix Prize competition, ensemble methods [21] have gained popularity. Factorization Machines [22] are a general matrix factorization method that can be applied to design hybrid factorization models. Recently, as user-generated content has become available, researchers have studied how to leverage information such as social relationships [5, 6], reviews [23, 24], tags [25], and feedback [26] to improve recommendations. Incorporating additional information for users and/or items is especially beneficial in cold-start settings [27]. Dooms [28] argues that a flexible recommendation system that automatically generates good hybrid models would be very valuable as information sources increase. Our model provides such flexibility, allowing for the combination of as many information sources as are available. Fakhraei et al. [13] use PSL to reason over multiple similarity measures for predicting drug-target interactions. Our approach extends this model in several important ways for the recommender systems domain.

Chen at al. [29] learn the strength of ties between users based on multi-relational network information. The learned network is combined with item-based collaborative filtering to improve recommendation results. Burke et al. [30, 31] integrate different dimensions of data about users in a heterogenous network by using metapaths to create multiple two-dimensional projections representing relationships between entities (e.g. users-tags) and then linearly combining these projections. Also using metapaths, Yu et al. [32] propose a global and a personalized recommendation model. In their approach, implicit feedback is incorporated into metapaths and latent features for users and items are generated using matrix factorization.

De Campos et al. [3] propose a probabilistic graphical modeling recommendation approach using Bayesian networks. Their approach combines individual predictions from content-based and user-based collaborative filtering components. Hoxha and Rettinger [33] also discuss a probabilistic graphical modeling representation, using Markov Logic Networks (MLNs) [34] to combine content with collaborative filtering. Both MLNs and HL-MRFs operate on undirected graphical models using a first-order logic as their template language, while Bayesian networks are directed. We chose HL-MRFs because they can represent ordered data such as ratings, and due to their scalability with parallel convex optimization for inference. Speed and scalability is of paramount importance in recommender systems and in particular when we run the prediction task collectively over multiple types of input data with a variety of similarity measures.

6. CONCLUSION

In this paper we presented HyPER, a new hybrid recommender system which is flexible, problem-agnostic, and is easily extensible via a probabilistic programming interface. HyPER uses a hinge-loss MRF formulation, allowing scalable and accurate inference. Our comprehensive experiments demonstrate that HyPER can learn to appropriately balance many information sources, resulting in improved performance over previous state-of-the-art approaches on two benchmark datasets.

Acknowledgements

We would like to thank Ben London and Alex Ntoulas for insightful discussions. We thank Juntao Liu for sharing the code of their approach [5], George Karypis, Christian Desrosiers, Chris Meek, Asela Gunawardana, and Robin Burke for their help. This work was partially supported by NSF grant IIS1218488 and by the IARPA via DoI/NBC contract D12PC00337. The U.S. Government is authorized to reproduce and distribute reprints for governmental purposes notwithstanding any copyright annotation thereon. Disclaimer: The views and conclusions contained herein are those of the authors and should not be interpreted as necessarily representing the official policies or endorsements, either expressed or implied, of NSF, IARPA, DoI/NBC, or the U.S. Government.

7. REFERENCES

[1] S.H. Bach, M. Broecheler, B. Huang, and L. Getoor. Hinge-loss markov random fields and probabilistic soft logic. *ArXiv:1505.04406 [cs.LG]*, 2015.

[2] G. Adomavicius and A. Tuzhilin. Toward the next generation of recommender systems: A survey of the state-of-the-art and possible extensions. *Transactions on Knowledge and Data Engineering*, 17(6), 2005.

[3] L. de Campos, J. Fernández-Luna, J. Huete, and M. Rueda-Morales. Combining content-based and collaborative recommendations: A hybrid approach based on Bayesian networks. *International Journal of Approximate Reasoning*, 51(7), 2010.

[4] C. Desrosiers and G. Karypis. A comprehensive survey of neighborhood-based recommendation methods. In *Recommender Systems Handbook*. Springer, 2011.

[5] J. Liu, C. Wu, and W. Liu. Bayesian probabilistic matrix factorization with social relations and item contents for recommendation. *Decision Support Systems*, 55(3), 2013.

[6] H. Ma, D. Zhou, C. Liu, M. R. Lyu, and I. King. Recommender systems with social regularization. In *WSDM*, 2011.

[7] N. Goodman, V. Mansinghka, D.M. Roy, K. Bonawitz, and J. Tenenbaum. Church: a language for generative models with non-parametric memoization and approximate inference. In *UAI*, 2008.

[8] L. Getoor and B. Taskar. *Introduction to statistical relational learning*. MIT press, 2007.

[9] S. H. Bach, B. Huang, B. London, and L. Getoor. Hinge-loss Markov random fields: Convex inference for structured prediction. In *UAI*, 2013.

[10] M. Broecheler, L. Mihalkova, and L. Getoor. Probabilistic similarity logic. In *UAI*, 2010.

[11] P. Lops, M. Gemmis, and G. Semeraro. Content-based recommender systems: State of the art and trends. In *Recommender Systems Handbook*. Springer, 2011.

[12] Y. Koren, R. Bell, and C. Volinsky. Matrix factorization techniques for recommender systems. *IEEE Computer*, 42(8), 2009.

[13] S. Fakhraei, B. Huang, L. Raschid, and L. Getoor. Network-based drug-target interaction prediction with probabilistic soft logic. *Transactions on Computational Biology and Bioinformatics*, 11(5), 2014.

[14] P. D. Hoff, A. E. Raftery, and M. S. Handcock. Latent space approaches to social network analysis. *Journal of the American Statistical Association*, 97, 2001.

[15] R. Salakhutdinov and A. Mnih. Bayesian probabilistic matrix factorization using Markov chain Monte Carlo. In *ICML*, 2008.

[16] F. Ricci, L. Rokach, B. Shapira, and P. B. Kantor. *Recommender Systems Handbook*. Springer, 2011.

[17] R. Burke. Hybrid web recommender systems. In *The Adaptive Web*. Springer, 2007.

[18] A. Gunawardana and C. Meek. A unified approach to building hybrid recommender systems. In *RecSys*, 2009.

[19] P. Forbes and M. Zhu. Content-boosted matrix factorization for recommender systems: Experiments with recipe recommendation. In *RecSys*, 2011.

[20] Y. Koren. Factorization meets the neighborhood: A multifaceted collaborative filtering model. In *KDD*, 2008.

[21] M. Jahrer, A. Töscher, and R. Legenstein. Combining predictions for accurate recommender systems. In *KDD*, 2010.

[22] S. Rendle. Factorization machines with libFM. *ACM Transactions on Intelligent Systems and Technology*, 3(3), 2012.

[23] J. McAuley and J. Leskovec. Hidden factors and hidden topics: Understanding rating dimensions with review text. In *RecSys*, 2013.

[24] G. Ling, M. R. Lyu, and I. King. Ratings meet reviews, a combined approach to recommend. In *RecSys*, 2014.

[25] I. Guy, N. Zwerdling, I. Ronen, D. Carmel, and E. Uziel. Social media recommendation based on people and tags. In *SIGIR*, 2010.

[26] S. Sedhain, S. Sanner, D. Braziunas, L. Xie, and J. Christensen. Social collaborative filtering for cold-start recommendations. In *RecSys*, 2014.

[27] Z. Gantner, L. Drumond, C. Freudenthaler, S. Rendle, and L. Schmidt-Thieme. Learning attribute-to-feature mappings for cold-start recommendations. In *ICDM*, 2010.

[28] S. Dooms. Dynamic generation of personalized hybrid recommender systems. In *RecSys*, 2013.

[29] J. Chen, G. Chen, H. Zhang, J. Huang, and G. Zhao. Social recommendation based on multi-relational analysis. In *WI-IAT*, 2012.

[30] R. Burke, F. Vahedian, and B. Mobasher. Hybrid recommendation in heterogeneous networks. In *User Modeling, Adaptation, and Personalization*. Springer, 2014.

[31] J. Gemmell, T. S., B. Mobasher, and R. Burke. Resource recommendation in social annotation systems: A linear-weighted hybrid approach. *Journal of Computer and System Sciences*, 78(4), 2012.

[32] X. Yu, X. Ren, Y. Sun, Q. Gu, B. Sturt, U. Khandelwal, B. Norick, and J. Han. Personalized entity recommendation: A heterogeneous information network approach. In *WSDM*, 2014.

[33] J. Hoxha and A. Rettinger. First-order probabilistic model for hybrid recommendations. In *ICMLA*, 2013.

[34] M. Richardson and P. Domingos. Markov logic networks. *Machine Learning*, 62(1-2), 2006.

Applying Differential Privacy to Matrix Factorization

Arnaud Berlioz, Arik Friedman,
Mohamed Ali Kaafar, Roksana Boreli
NICTA,* Australia
{firstname.lastname}@nicta.com.au

Shlomo Berkovsky
CSIRO
shlomo.berkosvky@csiro.au

ABSTRACT

Recommender systems are increasingly becoming an integral part of on-line services. As the recommendations rely on personal user information, there is an inherent loss of privacy resulting from the use of such systems. While several works studied privacy-enhanced neighborhood-based recommendations, little attention has been paid to privacy preserving latent factor models, like those represented by matrix factorization techniques. In this paper, we address the problem of privacy preserving matrix factorization by utilizing differential privacy, a rigorous and provable privacy preserving method. We propose and study several approaches for applying differential privacy to matrix factorization, and evaluate the privacy-accuracy trade-offs offered by each approach. We show that input perturbation yields the best recommendation accuracy, while guaranteeing a solid level of privacy protection.

Keywords

Differential privacy; matrix factorization

1. INTRODUCTION

In the last decade, recommender systems have become a fundamental tool in on-line services. One of the dominant recommendation approaches is collaborative filtering (CF), which can be partitioned into two families. Neighborhood methods learn correlations between items or users [5] and generate predictions based on their similarity. In contrast, latent factor models [12] derive models that characterize users and items with respect to a set of latent factors.

Matrix factorization (MF) methods [12] have evolved as the state-of-the-art latent factor technique. There, the rating matrix is decomposed into two low-dimensional matrices, capturing latent factors of users and items, respectively. MF has been shown to provide a higher predictive accuracy than the neighborhood methods, it is computationally cheaper, and easier to extend, for example, to consider temporal effects or ratings with varying levels of confidence.

Recommender systems rely on personal user information and raise privacy concerns related to the misuse of the collected data for inferring personal information [10]. The raw user ratings, even if anonymized, pose a privacy risk: the data can be de-anonymized using information obtained from other sources and then be used to infer sensitive information [18], e.g., gender, political views, or sexual orientation. Moreover, it was shown that even without direct access to user ratings, personal user information could be inferred from recommendations provided by the system to other users [2]. These inherent privacy risks of recommender systems motivated research of privacy-preserving recommenders [8, 10]. However, this body of research has mainly focused on neighborhood methods, with limited work on privacy preserving latent factor recommenders [14, 15].

In this paper, we approach the problem of privacy preserving MF by utilizing the concept of *differential privacy* [7], a rigorous and provable approach to privacy in statistical databases, previously applied to neighborhood based CF [13, 14]. While differential privacy sets constraints on privacy preserving computations, these computations can be carried out in various ways, which result in different privacy-accuracy trade-offs. We propose a number of approaches to alter MF, such that it maintains differential privacy guarantees. We study the privacy guarantees that can be achieved by the following approaches: (i) obfuscating the input data before applying the MF algorithm; (ii) adding noise within a stochastic gradient descent solver of the MF problem; and (iii) obfuscating the output of an alternating least squares MF mechanism. For these approaches, we provide a theoretical analysis of the (calibrated) noise level introduced in the algorithms, and empirically evaluate the resulting privacy-accuracy trade-offs by observing the effect of the noise on the computed rating predictions.

The contributions of our work are three-fold. We provide an analysis and evaluation of **three differentially private MF approaches**. The evaluation demonstrates that the best performing method, yielding the highest predictive accuracy while still ensuring a solid level of privacy protection, is input obfuscation. We further conduct an investigation of the **design choices** that affect the privacy-accuracy trade-off, showing the impact of the data pre-processing, the dependencies between the characteristics of a dataset (size,

*NICTA is funded by the Australian Government through the Department of Communications and the Australian Research Council through the ICT Centre of Excellence Program.

density, number of user/item ratings) and the choice of the algorithm, and the influence of the privacy constraints on parameter tuning. Finally, we **compare the accuracy** of the predictions generated by differentially private MF with that of privacy-preserving neighborhood based methods. Our experiments demonstrate that neighborhood methods are more resilient to the noise introduced by the differential privacy constraints, and are more appropriate when high levels of privacy protection are required. However, when weaker privacy levels are acceptable, privacy preserving MF techniques achieve higher levels of predictive accuracy than neighborhood based methods.

2. RELATED WORK

Personalization and recommender systems inherently bring to the fore the issue of privacy [8, 11]. Privacy hazards in recommender systems are aggravated by the fact that generation of quality recommendations requires large amounts of user data. For instance, the accuracy of CF recommendations is correlated with both the number of users in the system and the number of their ratings [5]. Hence, there is a trade-off between the accuracy of recommendations provided to users and the degree of user privacy.

We divide prior works on privacy enhanced recommender systems into two categories: distributed recommenders and data modification techniques. In the distributed group, user profiles are stored across several repositories. Canny proposed a decentralized storage of user profiles, which requires the adversary to compromise multiple systems when attacking a distributed recommender [3]. Vallet et al. [17] have shown how MF techniques can be leveraged to allow a central server to provide accurate recommendations without retention of user data, storing it on the client side instead.

Data modification techniques include approaches such as encryption [15], obfuscation [1], and randomization [16]. Polat and Du proposed to add uncertainty to user ratings through randomized data perturbation [16]: users substitute ratings in their profiles with modified ratings, resembling the real ones. Hence, if user data is exposed to an adversary, only the modified ratings will leak. Nikolaenko et al. showed how secure multiparty computation could be utilized in MF [15], so that the recommender learns only the item profiles, but not the user ratings. Such techniques, however, do not prevent the inference of user ratings from the output of MF, and are orthogonal to the techniques studied in this paper, as they address a different threat model.

Calandrino et al. [2] studied the privacy risks imposed by recommenders, such as Hunch, Last.fm, and Amazon. In item-to-item CF, when a user makes a transaction involving an item, this results in an increase of the similarity of the item to other items in the user's transaction history. Therefore, the attacker can track the similarity lists of items associated with a target user, and identify new items in the lists. When the same item appears in a number of tracked lists, the attacker can infer that the item was added to the target user's record. The authors pointed to differential privacy as a possible solution to this problem.

Differential privacy has drawn much research attention; it makes no assumptions about the adversary's background knowledge and computation power, and provides formally provable privacy guarantees [7]. To the best of our knowledge, only two works have investigated the application of differential privacy to recommender systems, although not in the immediate context of MF.

Machanavajjhala et al. studied the problem of privacy-preserving social recommendations on the basis of a graph linking between users and items, e.g., items purchased by users [13]. A utility vector derived from the graph captures the utility of each item for the target user, and the goal is to induce a probability distribution over the items, such as to maximize the user's utility, while keeping the vector private. It was found that good recommendations were achievable only under weak privacy parameters, or only for a small fraction of users.

McSherry and Mironov applied differential privacy to CF [14]. They used the Laplace mechanism to compute a differentially-private item-to-item covariance matrix, which was used to find neighbors and compute SVD recommendations. Their solution involved breaking the recommendation process into a learning phase, in which the private covariance matrix was derived, and a recommendation phase, in which the predictions were computed. In contrast, we consider direct privacy-preserving derivation of the latent factor models. Overall, our work explores additional approaches beyond those investigated in [14], and compares their performance.

3. PRELIMINARIES

3.1 MF Recommendations

The input to MF is typically a sparse rating matrix $R_{n \times m}$, containing the ratings of n users for m items. Each matrix element r_{ui} reflects the rating of user u for item i. MF factorizes $R_{n \times m}$ into two latent matrices of a lower dimension d: user-factor matrix $P_{n \times d}$ and item-factor matrix $Q_{m \times d}$. The factorization is done such that R is approximated as a product of P and Q, i.e., each known rating r_{ui} is approximated by $\hat{r}_{ui} = p_u \cdot q_i^\mathsf{T}$. To obtain P and Q, MF minimizes the regularized squared error:

$$\min_{P,Q} \sum_{r_{ui} \in R} \left[(r_{ui} - p_u q_i^\mathsf{T})^2 + \lambda(||p_u||^2 + ||q_i||^2) \right] \ , \quad (1)$$

where λ regularizes the factors and prevents overfitting.

Two common ways to solve the resulting non-convex optimization problem are stochastic gradient descent (SGD) and alternating least squares (ALS). In SGD, the factors are learned by iteratively evaluating the error $e_{ui} = r_{ui} - p_u q_i^\mathsf{T}$ for each rating r_{ui}, and updating the user and item vectors by taking a step in the direction opposite to the gradient of the regularized loss function:

$$p_u \leftarrow p_u + \gamma(e_{ui} q_i - \lambda p_u) \ , \quad (2)$$
$$q_i \leftarrow q_i + \gamma(e_{ui} p_u - \lambda q_i) \ .$$

The constant γ determines the rate of minimizing the error and is often referred to as the learning rate.

In ALS, the optimization problem is solved iteratively. In each iteration, one latent matrix (say, P) is fixed, resulting in a convex optimization problem, where the solution (for Q) can be found efficiently. Then, the other matrix (Q) is fixed, and the optimization problem is solved again (this time for P). These steps are repeated until convergence.

3.2 Differential Privacy

Differential privacy is based on the principle that the output of a computation should not allow inference about any particular record in the input [7]. This is achieved by requiring that the probability of any computation outcome is insensitive to small input changes. We denote two datasets A and B as *adjacent*, $A \approx B$, if they are identical in all records but one. Formally, there exist a user u and an item i such that $A = B \setminus \{r_{ui}\} \cup \{r'_{ui}\}$, where r'_{ui} and r_{ui} are the ratings that u assigned to i in A and B, respectively. The guaranteed privacy level is measured by a parameter ϵ. Formally, a randomized computation K maintains ϵ-differential privacy if for any two datasets $A \approx B$, and any subset S of possible outcomes in Range(K),

$$Pr[K(A) \in S] \le exp(\epsilon) \times Pr[K(B) \in S] \ , \quad (3)$$

where the probability is over the randomness of K. Low values of ϵ correspond to a high degree of privacy. Setting the bounds for the acceptable value of ϵ is an open question. In the literature, privacy settings of $\epsilon = \ln 2$ or $\epsilon = \ln 3$ are considered as providing acceptable levels of privacy, although Dwork suggested that in some cases much higher values of ϵ could provide meaningful guarantees [6].

A common way to obtain differential privacy is by applying random noise to the measurement. The amount of noise added depends on the L_1-sensitivity of the evaluated function, which is the largest possible change in the measurement given a change in a single record in the dataset. In general, the L_k-sensitivity of a function g is given by:

$$S_k(g) = \max_{A \approx B} ||g(A) - g(B)||_k \ , \quad (4)$$

where $|| \cdot ||_k$ denotes the L_k-norm.

The *Laplace mechanism* [7] obtains ϵ-differential privacy by adding noise sampled from Laplace distribution, with a calibrated scale b. The probability density function of Laplace distribution with mean 0 and scale b ($x \sim Laplace(b)$) is $f_b(x) = \frac{1}{2b} \exp(-\frac{|x|}{b})$. Given a function $g : \mathcal{D} \to \mathbb{R}^d$, the following computation maintains ϵ-differential privacy [7]:

$$K(x) = g(x) + (Laplace(S_1(g)/\epsilon))^d \ . \quad (5)$$

For example, consider the function $\text{COUNT}_c(A)$, which counts the number of records in dataset A that satisfy condition c. It has sensitivity 1, since changing a single record affects the count by at most 1. Hence, $K(A) = \text{COUNT}_c(A) + Laplace(1/\epsilon)$ maintains ϵ-differential privacy. Consider also the function $\text{SUM}(A)$, where $a_i \in [0, \Lambda]$. It has sensitivity Λ, which is the maximal change in the sum by changing one element of A. Hence, $K(A) = \text{SUM}(A) + Laplace(\Lambda/\epsilon)$ maintains ϵ-differential privacy.

We also rely in this work on the K-norm mechanism [9], which allows to calibrate noise to the L_2-sensitivity of the evaluated function. Given a function $g : \mathcal{D} \to \mathbb{R}^d$, the computation $K(x) = g(x) + r\alpha$ maintains ϵ-differential privacy, where r is a d-dimensional vector uniformly sampled from a d-dimensional sphere with radius 1, and $\alpha \sim \Gamma(d, S_2(g)/\epsilon)$.

4. DIFFERENTIALLY PRIVATE MF

Differential privacy sets the conditions that should be maintained to preserve privacy, but within these constraints it is often possible to implement various mechanisms that evaluate the same computation, resulting in different privacy-accuracy trade-offs. Considering the stages of the MF process, we highlight a number of possible approaches for adding differentially private noise, as shown in Figure 1.

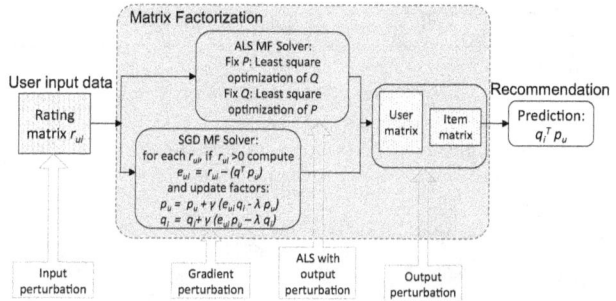

Figure 1: Various noise application points in regards to the input, output and the solver within the MF mechanism

Input Perturbation. The original MF input ratings are perturbed with a calibrated noise, and then the algorithm is trained using the noisy input ratings. Since input perturbation is performed before training the recommender, it can be followed by any recommendation algorithm, and in particular by (any variant of) MF.

In-process Mechanisms. In this approach, the algorithms used to decompose the rating matrix R into the latent matrices P and Q are adapted to maintain differential privacy. We focus in this work on two MF algorithms, and propose their differentially private variants:

SGD. In the training process of MF with SGD, in each iteration, the gradient of the regularized loss function determines the direction of the update and its magnitude. In the gradient perturbation approach the gradient is perturbed with noise in each iteration.

ALS with Output Perturbation. In each step of ALS, two optimization problems are solved to update the matrices P and Q. These empirical risk minimization problems can be solved in a differentially-private manner using the techniques proposed in [4]. In particular, we apply the output perturbation approach to obtain noisy versions of P and Q.

Output Perturbation. In this approach, a non-private MF algorithm is executed, and then the resulting latent factors are perturbed to maintain differential privacy. Unfortunately, the optimization problem in MF is non-convex, and a small change in the input could lead to a large change in the factors. Consequently, the sensitivity of the optimization problem would require introducing large noise, potentially resulting in poor utility.

Hence, in this work we restrict the evaluation to three variants of differentially private MF—input perturbation, SGD perturbation, and ALS with output perturbation—and do not consider the output perturbation approach, where noise is added to the latent factors, after a non-private MF. We first outline the data pre-processing steps that were taken before applying these approaches. For the pre-processing, we utilize the private versions of the following aggregate values, based on the training dataset (will be described in detail in Section 5.1): *global average* $GAvg(R)$ – average of all the ratings for all items; *item average* $IAvg(i)$ – average rating for item i; and *user average* $UAvg(u)$ – average rating of user u. We will now describe the three aforementioned differentially private MF approaches.

4.1 Private Preprocessing and Global Effects

Prior to applying differential privacy to MF, we preprocess the inputs as in [14]. A notable exception is that we

---

Algorithm 1: Evaluation of item averages

Input:

$R = \{r_{ui}\}$ – ratings of n users for m items,

β_i – stabilization parameter,

ϵ_1 – global average privacy parameter,

ϵ_2 – item average privacy parameter

Output:

Item averages IAvg(i)

1: GAvg $= \frac{(\sum_R r_{ui}) + \text{Laplace}(\Delta r / \epsilon_1)}{|R|}$

2: **for** $j = 1$ *to* m **do**

3: $\quad$ Let $R_j = \{r_{ui} \in R | i = j\}$

4: $\quad$ IAvg(j) $= \frac{(\sum_{R_j} r_{ui}) + \beta_i \cdot \text{GAvg} + \text{Laplace}(\Delta r / \epsilon_2)}{|R_j| + \beta_i}$

5: $\quad$ Clamp IAvg(j) to $[r_{\min}, r_{\max}]$.

Algorithm 2: Evaluation of users effects

Input:

$R = \{r_{ui}\}$ – ratings of n users for m items,

β_u – stabilization parameter,

ϵ_1 – global average privacy parameter,

ϵ_2 – user average privacy parameter

Output:

User averages UAvg(u)

1: Let $R' = \{r_{ui} - \text{IAvg}(i) | r_{ui} \in R\}$

2: GAvg$' = \frac{(\sum_{R'} r'_{ui}) + \text{Laplace}(\Delta r / \epsilon_1)}{|R'|}$

3: **for** $v = 1$ *to* n **do**

4: $\quad$ Let $R_v = \{r'_{ui} \in R' | u = v\}$

5: $\quad$ UAvg(v) $= \frac{(\sum_{R_v} r'_{ui}) + \beta_u \cdot \text{GAvg}' + \text{Laplace}(\Delta r / \epsilon_2)}{|R_v| + \beta_u}$

6: $\quad$ Clamp UAvg(v) to $[-2, 2]$

Algorithm 3: Differentially Private Input Perturbation

Input:

$R = \{r_{ui}\}$ – preprocessed user ratings,

d – number of factors,

λ – regularization parameter,

B – clamping parameter,

ϵ – privacy parameter

Output:

Latent factor matrices $P_{n \times d}$ and $Q_{m \times d}$

1: Let $R' = \{r_{ui} + \text{Laplace}(\frac{\Delta r}{\epsilon}) | r_{ui} \in R\}$

2: Clamp the ratings in R' to the range $[-B, B]$

3: $(P, Q) = \min_{P,Q} \sum_{R'} [(r'_{u,i} - p_u q_i^{\mathsf{T}})^2 + \lambda(\|q_i\|^2 + \|p_u\|^2)]$

4: **return** P and Q

---

lower magnitude of noise being introduced in the differentially private computation. We denote the clamping parameter B (set to 1 in the experiments), i.e., $r_{ui} \in [-B, B]$. The pre-processed matrix R is passed to the MF algorithm to derive the matrices P and Q. Predicted ratings are then obtained through $\hat{r}_{ui} = \text{IAvg}(i) + \text{UAvg}(u) + p_u q_i^{\mathsf{T}}$.

Differential privacy maintains the composability property: if each computation in a series of computations is ϵ_i-differentially private, then the overall algorithm is $\sum_i \epsilon_i = \epsilon$-differentially private. Accordingly, the overall privacy budget ϵ is divided between the computation of global averages, item effects, user effects, and, lastly, MF. Note that it is possible to predict ratings using only the user and item averages, $\hat{r}_{ui} = \text{IAvg}(i) + \text{UAvg}(u)$, which is referred to as *Global Effects* (see Comparison Baselines in Section 5.1). This leads to its differentially-private counterpart, as described in the above three pre-processing steps. In this case, as MF is not applied, the privacy budget is divided between three computations: global averages, item averages and user averages. We refer to this technique as *Private Global Effects*.

4.2 Private Input Perturbation

In input perturbation the Laplace mechanism is applied directly to each input rating. Following data pre-processing, the sensitivity of the inputs is $\Delta r = r_{\max} - r_{\min} = 2B$, and perturbing each rating with noise sampled from the distribution Laplace$(\Delta r / \epsilon)$ ensures ϵ-differential privacy.[2] The noisy ratings can then be clamped again, to limit the influence of excessive noise. Algorithm 3 summarizes this process.

4.3 Private SGD

The gradient perturbation approach, outlined in Algorithm 4, guarantees privacy throughout the MF process by introducing noise in the SGD step in each iteration of the algorithm. The error calculation conducted in each step is carried out with the Laplace mechanism to maintain differential privacy, and consequently the SGD step maintains differential privacy. Optionally, the noisy error can be clamped to constrain the effect of noise (in our experiments we used $e_{\max} = 2$). The number of iterations k should be known in advance, so the noise introduced in each iteration is calibrated to maintain ϵ/k-differential privacy. Composability ensures that the k iterations maintain the overall bound of ϵ-differential privacy.

incorporate the user averages in rating predictions, as this allows to derive more accurate predictions when using MF. The preprocessing consists of the following three steps.

Firstly, we compute the (differentially-private) average item ratings according to the process described in Algorithm 1. We add a number of fictitious ratings β_i with the global average GAvg to stabilize the item averages—this limits the effect of noise for items with few ratings, while only slightly affecting the average for items with many ratings. If the added noise causes an item average to go beyond the range of ratings $[r_{\min}, r_{\max}]$, the average is clamped to fit the range. Differential privacy is guaranteed by adding noise calibrated to the L_1-sensitivity of ratings, given by $\Delta r = r_{\max} - r_{\min}$.

Secondly, we follow the same technique to compute the user averages, as outlined in Algorithm 2. The basis for the user averages is the ratings after the item average discounting. We stabilize the user effects with the addition of β_u fictitious ratings with the newly computed global average. The user averages are also clamped to a bounded range (in the experiments[1] we used $[-2, 2]$ for user averages).

Finally, the item and user averages are discounted from the rating matrix R, and the resulting ratings are clamped. The clamping reduces the L_1-sensitivity of the computations conducted during the MF process, and results in a

---

[1] In the evaluation we used the MovieLens dataset with the rating scale of 1 to 5 stars.

[2] Proofs of the differential privacy properties of algorithms in Sections 4.2-4.4 are omitted due to space limitations.

Algorithm 4: Differentially Private SGD

Input:
$R = \{r_{ui}\}$ – preprocessed user ratings,
d – number of factors,
γ – learning rate parameter,
λ – regularization parameter,
k – number of gradient descent iterations,
$e_{\max}$ – upper bound on per-rating error,
ϵ – privacy parameter

Output:
Latent factor matrices $P_{n \times d}$ and $Q_{m \times d}$

1: Initialize random factor matrices P and Q.
2: **for** k *iterations* **do**
3:     **for** *each* $r_{ui} \in R$ **do**
4:        $e'_{ui} = r_{ui} - p_u q_i^{\mathsf{T}} + \text{Laplace}(k\Delta r/\epsilon)$
5:        Clamp e'_{ui} to $[-e_{\max}, e_{\max}]$
6:        $q_i \leftarrow q_i + \gamma(e'_{ui} \cdot p_u^{\mathsf{T}} - \lambda \cdot q_i)$
7:        $p_u \leftarrow p_u + \gamma(e'_{ui} \cdot q_i^{\mathsf{T}} - \lambda \cdot p_u)$
8: **return** P and Q.

4.4 Private ALS with Output Perturbation

The basic idea of ALS is to alternately fix one of the latent matrices P and Q, and optimize the regularized loss function for the other matrix. Once one matrix is fixed, the optimization problem becomes convex and can be solved analytically. For example, once Q is fixed, the overall regularized loss function can be minimized by considering for each user u the following loss function defined over the subset of ratings $R_u = \{r_{vi} \in R | v = u\}$:

$$J_Q(p_u, R) = \Big[\sum_{R_u} (r_{ui} - p_u q_i^{\mathsf{T}})^2 \Big] + n_u \lambda \|p_u\|^2 \ , \quad (6)$$

where $n_u = |R_u|$. Each user vector p_u is then obtained by solving the risk minimization problem

$$p_u(R, Q) = \arg\min_{p_u} J_Q(p_u, R) \ . \quad (7)$$

The problem of differentially private empirical risk minimization (ERM) was studied by Chaudhuri et al. [4]. An adaptation of their techniques shows that the L_2-sensitivity of $p_u(R, Q)$ in Equation 7, is $\Delta p_u = \frac{q_{\max}\Delta r}{n_u \lambda}$, where $q_{\max}$ is the upper bound on the L_2-norm of each row q_i in Q. Similarly, when fixing P and optimizing Q based on the regularized loss function $J_P(q_i, R) = [\sum_{R_i} (r_{ui} - p_u q_i^{\mathsf{T}})^2] + n_i \lambda \|q_i\|^2$, the L_2-sensitivity of each row q_i is $\frac{p_{\max} \cdot \Delta r}{\lambda n_i}$. For the preprocessed ratings, we have $\Delta r = 2B$, where B is the clamping parameter. Since we calculated the L_2-sensitivity of the user-vector p_u and item-vector q_i, the noise added to these vectors is taken from the Gamma distribution.

Following the above analysis, Algorithm 5 outlines a differentially-private ALS algorithm with output perturbation. Similarly to the SGD approach, we calibrate the noise so that each optimization problem is $\epsilon/2k$-differentially private and the overall ALS computation is ϵ-differentially private due to composability.

5. EVALUATION

In this section, we present the results of the evaluation of the proposed differentially private MF approaches.

Algorithm 5: Differentially Private ALS with Output Perturbation

Input:
$R = \{r_{ui}\}$ – preprocessed user ratings,
d – number of factors,
λ – regularization parameter,
k – number of ALS iterations,
ϵ – privacy parameter,
$p_{\max}$ – upper bound on $\|p_u\|_2$,
$q_{\max}$ – upper bound on $\|q_i\|_2$

Output:
Latent factor matrices $P_{n \times d}$ and $Q_{m \times d}$

1: Initialize random factor matrices P and Q.
2: **for** k *iterations* **do**
3:     **for** *each user* u, *given* Q **do**
4:        Sample noise vector b with pdf
$$f(b) \propto \exp\left(-\frac{\epsilon \cdot \|b\|_2}{2k} \cdot \frac{n_u \lambda}{p_{\max} \cdot \Delta r}\right)$$
5:        $p_u \leftarrow \arg\min_{p_u} J_Q(p_u, R_u) + b$
6:        **if** $\|p_u\|_2 > p_{\max}$ **then** $p_u \leftarrow p_u \cdot \frac{p_{\max}}{\|p_u\|_2}$
7:     **for** *each item* i, *given* P **do**
8:        Sample noise vector b with pdf
$$f(b) \propto \exp\left(-\frac{\epsilon \cdot \|b\|_2}{2k} \cdot \frac{n_i \lambda}{q_{\max} \cdot \Delta r}\right)$$
9:        $q_i \leftarrow \arg\min_{q_i} J_P(q_i, R_i) + b$
10:       **if** $\|q_i\|_2 > q_{\max}$ **then** $q_i \leftarrow q_i \cdot \frac{q_{\max}}{\|q_i\|_2}$
11: **return** P and Q.

	ML-100K	ML-1M	ML-10M
Users	943	6040	71567
Movies	1682	3952	65133
Density	6.3%	4.19%	0.21%
Average rating	3.5299	3.5816	3.5124
Variance of ratings	1.2671	1.2479	1.1245
Avg. ratings per user	106	165.6	139.7
Avg. ratings per item	59.4	253	153.5

Table 1: Statistical properties of the MovieLens datasets

5.1 Experimental Setting

We use in the evaluation the 100K, 1M and 10M MovieLens datasets. Table 1 summarizes selected statistical properties of the datasets.

We use 10-fold cross validation[3] to train and evaluate the recommender system. We measure the accuracy of the predicted ratings $\hat{r}_{ui}$ using the Root Mean Square Error (RMSE) metric (averaged over all the ratings), computed by $\text{RMSE} = \left(\sum_R (r_{ui} - \hat{r}_{ui})^2 / |R|\right)^{\frac{1}{2}}$. Due to the possible discrepancies in the introduction of noise, the reported RMSE is averaged across multiple runs.

We compare the performance of the privacy-preserving MF approaches against the following baselines:

Global average: the average rating is computed over the entire training set, and used as the prediction for all the ratings in the test set, i.e., $\hat{r}_{ui} = GAvg(R)$. We treat the global average RMSE as the upper bound for error.

Item average: the average rating for each item is computed over all the available training item ratings, and used as the prediction for all the ratings for that item in the test

---

[3]We used Matlab and, specifically, *crossvalind*.

	ML-100K	ML-1M	ML-10M
Parameter settings			
Number of factors	3	5	7
Regularizer	0.06	0.045	0.03
Baseline RMSE			
Global average	1.1256	1.1171	1.0604
Item average (IA)	1.0278	0.9795	0.9436
Global effects (GE)	0.9571	0.9161	0.8738
ALS	0.9198	0.8604	0.8013
Private Global Effects			
IA ϵ-crossing	0.5	0.2	0.18
Input Perturbation (ISGD)			
IA ϵ-crossing	2	0.9	0.7
GE ϵ-crossing	5	2.7	2.1
Stochastic Gradient Perturbation (PSGD)			
IA ϵ-crossing	2	0.8	0.6
GE ϵ-crossing	20	8	5.5
ALS with Output Perturbation (PALS)			
IA ϵ-crossing	2	0.8	0.6
GE ϵ-crossing	19	8	6

Table 2: Summary of the experimental settings and results.

(a) MovieLens-1M

(b) MovieLens-10M

Figure 2: Differentially-private MF approaches

set, i.e., $\hat{r}_{ui} = IAvg(i)$. This baseline reflects the RMSE score attainable without personalization.

Global effects: the average ratings $IAvg(i)$ for each item i and $UAvg(u)$ for each user u are computed over the entire training set. The item and user biases are both used when predicting the test ratings, $\hat{r}_{ui} = IAvg(i) + UAvg(u)$. We treat this baseline as the most simple way to obtain personalization, and we consider RMSE scores below this baseline to represent effective personalization.

Clean MF: ALS is executed to solve the MF problem without any noise. These RMSE scores reflect the lower bound for error attainable with no privacy constraints.

We use the item average and global effects baselines to assess the privacy-accuracy trade-off offered by the private approaches. To this end, we measure the values of the privacy parameter ϵ for which the RMSE scores attained by each algorithm *cross the RMSE* scores of these baselines, where low values of ϵ indicate that the algorithm can provide the same level of accuracy as the baseline with a low cost in privacy. Thus, the focus is on the privacy-accuracy trade-offs of the approaches, rather than on evaluating their performance for certain values of ϵ. Also, we investigate several factors that may affect the system performance.

5.2 Comparison of MF Approaches

In each experiment, given the overall ϵ-differential privacy constraint, we allocated 0.3ϵ to pre-processing. Out of this, 0.02ϵ was used to compute the global averages (split between the user and item average calculations), whereas the user and item averages were computed with 0.14ϵ each. The remaining privacy budget of 0.7ϵ was allocated to MF. This distribution of the privacy budget is based on an offline optimization, which is beyond the scope of the paper.

Where applicable, we bounded the L_2-norm of the user vectors to $p_{max} = 0.4$, and of the item vectors to $q_{max} = 0.5$. In both the SGD and ALS experiments, we set the number of iterations to $k = 5$. The number of iterations for input perturbation was set to $k = 20$. Table 2 details several other dataset specific parameters, which were set in an offline optimization. We note that the selected number of factors and the number of iterations were lower than typical for these algorithms, to limit the amount of noise introduced by

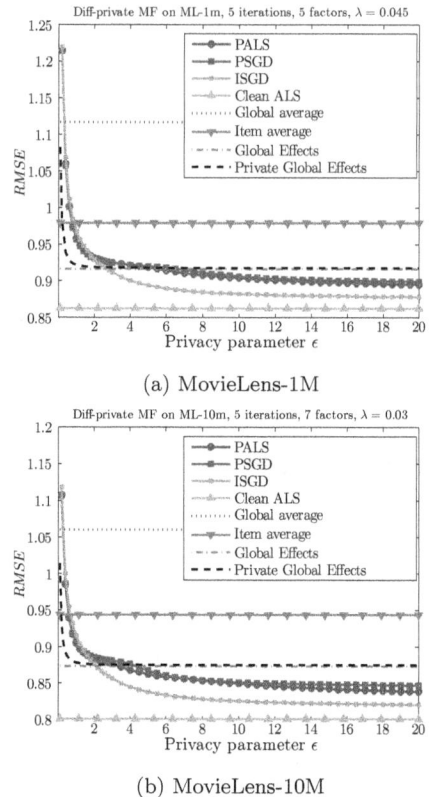

differential privacy. Table 2 shows also the baseline RMSE scores measured for each dataset, and the values of ϵ for which each approach crossed those baselines.

Figures 2a and 2b show the privacy-accuracy trade-offs for all the approaches observed for the MovieLens-1M and MovieLens-10M datasets, respectively.[4] In addition to the aforementioned baselines, the figures show the results for the Input Perturbation approach followed by a non-private SGD algorithm (ISGD), the Private SGD approach (PSGD), and the Private ALS approach (PALS).

In general, the performance of all the approaches improves with the size of the dataset. For example, ISGD crosses the IA baseline for MovieLens-100K, MovieLens-1M, and MovieLens-10M at $\epsilon = 2$, $\epsilon = 0.9$ and $\epsilon = 0.7$, respectively. This is not surprising; the larger the dataset, the more resilient it is to the noise introduced through differential privacy. Since the noise is calibrated to mask the effect of a single rating, larger datasets provide a higher signal-to-noise ratio, thereby allowing better performance with respect to the baseline for any value of ϵ.

As expected, crossing of the IA is observed for lower values of ϵ than crossing of the GE baseline. This is explained by the lower degree of personalization offered by IA, which is achievable with higher levels of noise and, therefore, a higher degree of privacy. For all the datasets, the IA crossing values of the approaches are similar, but there is a substantial difference between the GE crossings. Specifically, the IA crossings of PSGD and PALS are very close, and both are

---

[4]Results obtained for MovieLens-100K exhibit a similar trend and are not shown, but are summarized in Table 2.

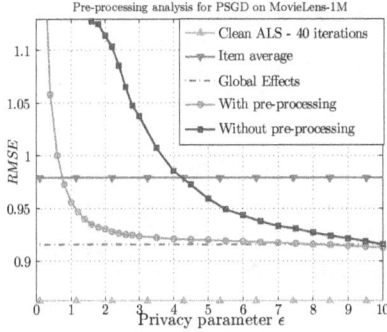

Figure 3: The effect of pre-processing

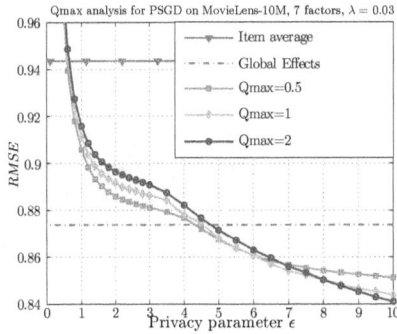

Figure 4: The effect of factor vector $L2$-norm bounds

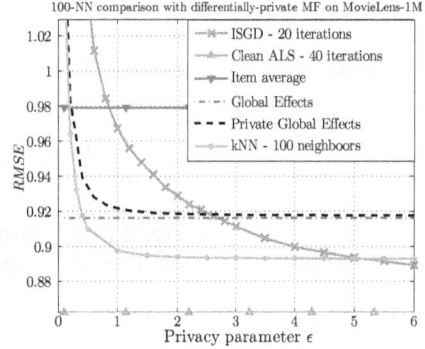

Figure 5: Comparison of private MF and kNN algorithms

slightly lower than that of ISGD. However, the GE crossing of ISGD is much lower than those of PSGD and PALS.

For example, consider the MovieLens-10M dataset. The PSGD and PALS approaches both cross the IA baseline at $\epsilon = 0.6$, whereas ISGD crosses it at $\epsilon = 0.7$. This is explained by the fact that the matrices P and Q in PALS and PSGD are bounded with $L2$-norm bounds p_{max} and q_{max}. Bounding the $L2$-norm provides a small improvement for low values of ϵ and gives PALS and PSGD a slightly earlier crossing. However, for higher ϵ, ISGD achieves a better performance; it crosses the GE baseline at $\epsilon = 2.1$, whereas PSGD and PALS cross it at $\epsilon = 5.5$ and $\epsilon = 6$, respectively. Similar trade-offs were observed also for other datasets.

5.2.1 Impact of pre-processing and L2-norm bounds

Figure 3 shows two variants of the PSGD approach, evaluated using the MovieLens-1M dataset: the RMSE curve of PSGD extracted from Figure 2a and the curve of PSGD with exactly the same parameters but with no data pre-processing. Data pre-processing has a substantial effect on the RMSE, as it reduces the sensitivity and the required levels of noise—in particular for low ϵ, when the IA baseline crossing is considered. Similar trends were observed also for the PALS and ISGD approaches, and for other datasets.

We also demonstrate the effect of bounding q_{max} in PSGD. Specifically, we set p_{max} to 80% of the q_{max} value, while the regularizer λ and the number of factors d are fixed to $\lambda = 0.03$ and $d = 7$. We conduct the experiment using three values of q_{max}: $q_{max} = 0.5$, $q_{max} = 1$, and $q_{max} = 2$. Figure 4 shows the results obtained for MovieLens-10M. While the value of q_{max} does not affect much the crossing of the IA baseline, it changes the value of the GE crossings and

the accuracy achieved for higher values of ϵ. In PSGD, the $L2$-norm bounds do not affect the noise added to P and Q and are used only to control the $L2$-norm of the latent vectors. For low ϵ, more noise is added and a small bound is preferable over greater bounds, since it removes the noisy elements. However, for higher values of ϵ, a small bound prevents MF from fully realizing the potential of the seven factors, and, therefore, a higher bound achieves a better predictive accuracy when less noise is added.

5.3 Comparison to other CF Approaches

In this experiment we compare the results of the privacy-preserving MF approach to two other privacy preserving CF algorithms: a private version of the GE baseline and private k-Nearest Neighbors (kNN) algorithm [5].

For private GE, we used the following allocation for the privacy budget: 0.02ϵ for the global average, 0.54ϵ for item average and 0.44ϵ for user average. For the private kNN recommendation algorithm, we followed the approach of McSherry and Mironov [14].[5] We applied a different privacy budget allocation: 0.9ϵ was allocated to data pre-processing, out of which 0.02ϵ was used for the global average, while the item and user averages were computed with 0.44ϵ each, and the remaining 0.1ϵ was used for the identification of nearest neighbors. It should be highlighted that kNN combines the differentially private item-to-item covariance matrix with the private user ratings, giving it an *a-priori* advantage over the proposed differentially private MF algorithms.

Figure 5 shows the comparison of the private versions of MF and kNN for the MovieLens-1M dataset.[6] For low values of ϵ, computing only the private GE was more effective than the MF approaches (both kNN and private GE cross the IA baseline at $\epsilon = 0.18$), since it makes the smallest number of computations and introduces the lowest amount of noise. However, this approach cannot outperform the GE baseline, and therefore cannot take advantage of weaker privacy constraints, when available.

While latent factors models typically outperform neighborhood based approaches in terms of predictive accuracy [5, 12], surprisingly this is not the case in the presence of privacy constraints. For lower values of ϵ, the improved ac-

---

[5] The differentially private implementation of kNN outlined in [14] is not publicly available, such that we were not able to reproduce the exact results reported therein.

[6] Due to memory limitations, kNN implementation for the MovieLens-10M dataset was not feasible.

curacy offered by MF in the non-private settings does not compensate for the higher noise required to meet the privacy constraints. However, for higher ϵ and weaker privacy, the predictive accuracy advantage of MF becomes apparent, and it outperforms the private kNN algorithm.

We posit that the superiority of private neighborhood based approaches over the MF approaches is explained by their better resilience to the noise introduced by differential privacy. Linking the average number of user ratings (Table 1) with the number of latent factors (Table 2), we observe that each factor relies, on average, on a few dozens of ratings. Hence, applying even moderate noise deteriorates the signal-to-noise ratio and affects the predictions. In contrast, the private item-to-item covariance matrix relies on thousands of ratings and is more resilient to noise. Due to this, kNN outperforms MF for lower values of ϵ (stringent privacy constraints). However, higher values of ϵ (lenient privacy constraints) allow decreasing the level of noise applied, such that MF approaches outperform kNN.

6. DISCUSSION

To address privacy concerns of recommender systems, we investigated the application of differential privacy to MF, the state-of-the-art recommendation approach. Differential privacy does not dictate a specific way to conduct a computation, but is rather a property that should be maintained. Hence, it is possible to design various approaches that carry out the same computation in a differentially private manner, with different levels of effectiveness. We proposed and evaluated three approaches reflecting the stages of MF: input perturbation, and differentially private variants of ALS and SGD. We also analyzed the sensitivity of the proposed approaches and compared private MF to other privacy preserving recommender approaches, namely, GE and kNN.

We showed that input perturbation yields the best performance amongst the three evaluated private MF approaches. However, when privacy is a priority and high degree of noise is applied, private kNN outperforms MF. We believe this observation is inherent to sparse datasets and stringent privacy requirements, as kNN is not as sensitive to noise as MF. On the other hand, when weaker privacy settings are acceptable, MF offers a better alternative: in that case, the predictive accuracy of the private algorithms gets closer to that of the respective non-private variants, and MF is shown to outperform other private recommendation approaches.

Following our evaluation, we identified the following design choices that should be considered when applying differential privacy to recommender systems.

Contextual considerations. Data characteristics, such as size, density and the distribution of ratings, may affect the privacy-accuracy trade-offs of the approaches. Beyond these, additional factors need to be considered. For example, the scalability and flexibility of the model-based approaches may outweigh the advantage of neighborhood methods in privacy protection, making privacy-preserving MF algorithm a viable option. Also, methods like input perturbation may be more amenable to the processing of streaming data, since each new rating can be perturbed independently, whereas for other approaches further work is required to adapt incremental learning models to the private setting.

Mind your parameters. Typically, MF parameters such as the number of factors, the regularizer, and the learning rate are tuned to increase prediction accuracy, while pre-

venting over-fitting and ensuring convergence. In the private setting, these considerations should be augmented to incorporate their impact on the introduced noise. For example, increasing the number of factors results in larger L_2-norms of the latent vectors, and requires larger magnitudes of noise to obtain the same level of privacy. This noise abolishes the increased accuracy driven by the additional factors, and parameter tuning is needed to balance these effects.

7. REFERENCES

[1] S. Berkovsky, T. Kuflik, and F. Ricci. The impact of data obfuscation on the accuracy of collaborative filtering. *Expert Syst. Appl.*, 39(5):5033–5042, 2012.

[2] J. A. Calandrino, A. Kilzer, A. Narayanan, E. W. Felten, and V. Shmatikov. "You might also like:" privacy risks of collaborative filtering. In *IEEE S&P*, pages 231–246, 2011.

[3] J. Canny. Collaborative filtering with privacy. In *IEEE S&P*, pages 45–57, 2002.

[4] K. Chaudhuri, C. Monteleoni, and A. D. Sarwate. Differentially private empirical risk minimization. *Journal of Mach. Learn.*, 12:1069–1109, 2011.

[5] C. Desrosiers and G. Karypis. A comprehensive survey of neighborhood-based recommendation methods. In *Rec. Sys. Handbook*, pages 107–144. 2011.

[6] C. Dwork. Differential privacy: a survey of results. In *TAMC*, pages 1–19, 2008.

[7] C. Dwork, F. Mcsherry, K. Nissim, and A. Smith. Calibrating noise to sensitivity in private data analysis. In *TOC*, pages 265–284, 2006.

[8] A. Friedman, B. Knijnenburg, K. Vanhecke, L. Martens, and S. Berkovsky. Privacy aspects of recommender systems. In *Rec. Sys. Handbook*. 2015.

[9] M. Hardt and K. Talwar. On the geometry of differential privacy. In *STOC*, pages 705–714, 2010.

[10] A. J. Jeckmans, M. Beye, Z. Erkin, P. Hartel, R. L. Lagendijk, and Q. Tang. Privacy in recommender systems. In *Social Media Retrieval*. 2013.

[11] A. Kobsa. Privacy-enhanced web personalization. In *The Adaptive Web*, pages 628–670, 2007.

[12] Y. Koren, R. Bell, and C. Volinsky. Matrix factorization techniques for recommender systems. *Computers*, 42(8):30–37, Aug. 2009.

[13] A. Machanavajjhala, A. Korolova, and A. D. Sarma. Personalized social recommendations - accurate or private? *PVLDB*, 4(7):440–450, 2011.

[14] F. McSherry and I. Mironov. Differentially private recommender systems: Building privacy into the netflix prize contenders. In *KDD*, pages 627–636, 2009.

[15] V. Nikolaenko, S. Ioannidis, U. Weinsberg, M. Joye, N. Taft, and D. Boneh. Privacy-preserving matrix factorization. In *CCS*, pages 801–812, 2013.

[16] H. Polat and W. Du. Achieving private recommendations using randomized response techniques. In *PAKDD*, pages 637–646, 2006.

[17] D. Vallet, A. Friedman, and S. Berkovsky. Matrix factorization without user data retention. In *PAKDD*, 2014.

[18] U. Weinsberg, S. Bhagat, S. Ioannidis, and N. Taft. BlurMe: inferring and obfuscating user gender based on ratings. In *RecSys*, pages 195–202, 2012.

Gaussian Ranking by Matrix Factorization

Harald Steck
Netflix Inc.
Los Gatos, California
hsteck@netflix.com

ABSTRACT

The ranking quality at the top of the list is crucial in many real-world applications of recommender systems. In this paper, we present a novel framework that allows for pointwise as well as listwise training with respect to various ranking metrics. This is based on a training objective function where we assume that, for given a user, the recommender system predicts scores for all items that follow approximately a *Gaussian* distribution. We motivate this assumption from the properties of implicit feedback data. As a model, we use matrix factorization and extend it by non-linear activation functions, as customary in the literature of artificial neural networks. In particular, we use non-linear activation functions derived from our Gaussian assumption. Our preliminary experimental results show that this approach is competitive with state-of-the-art methods with respect to optimizing the Area under the ROC curve, while it is particularly effective in optimizing the head of the ranked list.

Categories and Subject Descriptors

H.2.8 [**Database Management**]: Database Applications—*Data Mining*

Keywords

Recommender Systems; Collaborative Filtering; Matrix Factorization; Learning to Rank

1. INTRODUCTION

In many applications, the recommendation quality at the head of the ranked list of items is crucial. There has been a large body of work on training collaborative filtering approaches as to maximize various ranking metrics, see eg [5, 8, 17, 2, 18, 10, 20, 21, 14, 13, 12]. This is a difficult optimization problem, as recommender systems typically predict a continuous-valued score for each item, based on which the items are then ranked for a given user. The mapping from scores to ranks is not smooth, however, which makes

RecSys'15, September 16–20, 2015, Vienna, Austria.
ACM 978-1-4503-3692-5/15/09.
DOI: http://dx.doi.org/10.1145/2792838.2800185

it hard to optimize ranking metrics directly during training. For this reason, most approaches make smooth approximations to the ranking metric as to enable gradient descent for computationally efficient training. In many cases, a specific training method has been developed for each particular ranking metric, eg [18, 10, 20, 14, 13, 12].

In this paper, we develop an approach for training a recommender system toward various ranking metrics, as chosen by the researcher. We illustrate its flexibility in terms of ranking metrics by optimizing normalized Discounted Cumulative Gain (nDCG), which emphasizes the top of the ranked list, as well as the Area Under the ROC Curve (AUC), which gives equal importance to the ranking of items across the entire list. Moreover, we develop a pointwise variant as well as a listwise one. While the listwise variant requires a more involved training algorithm, we find in our experiments that it yields improved results when optimizing toward the head of the ranked list, while the required computation time is comparable to the one of the pointwise approach.

In our approach, we take advantage of two well-known properties of implicit feedback data, namely that it is typically *binary* and *sparse*. Binary implicit feedback data are ubiquitous in many applications of recommender systems, like clicks on links, purchases of goods, or plays of songs and movies. Moreover, the data are typically extremely sparse, as each user provides feedback on only a small number of items, and no feedback on the vast majority. Usually, the density of the data is around 1% for many publicly available data sets, while it is often orders of magnitudes lower in industrial settings.

Moreover, we specifically focus on the matrix factorization (MF) model (see Section 2). MF has been found to be one of the best single models for collaborative filtering in the literature, see eg [6]. In this paper, we take advantage of the fact that it predicts the score for an item by summing over numerous latent dimensions. This fact, combined with the central limit theorem in statistics, as well as with the properties of implicit feedback data mentioned above, motivated us to approximate the distribution of the predicted scores by a *Gaussian* distribution in this paper (see Section 3). Furthermore, we present several approximations to this Gaussian assumption, which results in different *activation functions*–some of which are also commonly used in artificial neural network models (see Section 4.2). We also present a novel activation function that is particularly efficient and simple, as it is only slightly different from the root mean squared error (RMSE), which is perhaps the most popular accuracy metric in the recommender literature. We use these activation functions as to map between the scores of the items as predicted by the MF model, and the corresponding ranks of the items. The obtained ranks can then be used in various ranking metrics–we use nDCG and AUC in this paper (see Section 4.1). The resulting training objective function and algorithm are outlined in Section 5. In Section 6, we compare our approach to related work in the literature, and point out its advantages. In our experiments on a publicly available data set as well as on a proprietary one (see Section 7), we find that the presented approach is competitive with state-of-the-art ranking methods regarding AUC, while it is particularly effective in optimizing the head to the ranked list.

In summary, the contributions of this paper are as follows:

- We present a novel training approach for ranking problems, tailored to sparse binary data and the MF model,

- which allows for different ranking metrics like AUC or nDCG.

- This approach can also be understood from the perspective of training neural networks–but with the difference that we use a ranking metric as objective.

- We developed a pointwise as well as listwise variant, where the latter is particularly effective for optimizing the head of the ranked list in our experiments.

2. MATRIX FACTORIZATION MODEL

Matrix factorization (MF) has proven to be one of the most accurate approaches to collaborative filtering in the literature of recommender systems, eg see [6] and references therein. For a given user u, the score $s_{u,i}$ of an item i is determined by the dot product of the latent item and user vectors, $\vec{p}_i$ and $\vec{v}_u$, respectively:

$$s_{u,i} = \vec{p}_i^\top \vec{v}_u = \sum_k p_{i,k} v_{u,k} \qquad (1)$$

where $k = \{1, ..., K\}$ is the index over the latent dimensions. In matrix notation, this reads $\vec{s}_u = P\vec{v}_u$ with score vector $\vec{s}_u = [s_{u,1}, ..., s_{u,N}]^\top$ and matrix $P = [\vec{p}_1, ..., \vec{p}_N]^\top$ regarding all items $i \in \{1, ..., N\}$.

Concerning implicit feedback data, one typically distinguishes between *positive* and *negative* items. *Positive* items are defined as the ones for which the user provided (positive) implicit feedback. In contrast, all other items are typically considered *negative* items. Note that the items in the negative class may be further subdivided into items that the user truly does not like, items that the user may like but did not have time yet to provide feedback on, etc. Even though a single negative class is a simplification, it makes practical approaches feasible, and has been adopted as the common approach in the literature, eg [5, 8, 10, 17]. In the remainder of this paper, the number of positive and negative items of a given user u is denoted by $N_u^{(+)}$ and $N_u^{(-)} = N - N_u^{(+)}$, respectively.

In this paper, we use the asymmetric matrix factorization model (AMF) introduced by [9] and later extended to SVD++ in [6]: the latent user-vector is defined as the sum of the latent item-vectors $\vec{q}_j$ of the positive items j of the user:

$$\vec{v}_u = \frac{1}{\sqrt{N_u^{(+)}}} \sum_{j \in I(u)} \vec{q}_j = Q\vec{h}_u \qquad (2)$$

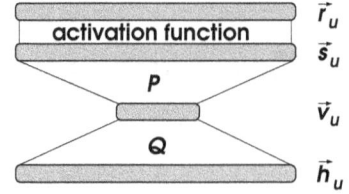

Figure 1: AMF viewed as a NN (see Section 2).

where $I(u)$ is the set of positive items in the feedback history of user u; we define matrix $Q = [\vec{q}_1, ..., \vec{q}_N]$ as well as the user's feedback vector $\vec{h}_u$, where $h_{u,j} = 1/\sqrt{N_u^{(+)}}$ if $j \in I(u)$, and 0 otherwise. Compared to an unconstrained latent user vector that has to be learned for each individual user in the basic MF model, the constraint in Eq. 2 results in a considerable reduction in the number of model parameters. Consequently, the parameters underlying the latent user vector $\vec{v}_u$ can be estimated more accurately from the sparse data, where $N_u^{(+)} \ll N$ for a typical user u. An additional advantage is the simplicity of the fold-in, ie computing $\vec{v}_u$ from the user's feedback history $\vec{h}_u$.

As to render notation in this paper independent of a particular MF model, we use θ as to refer to any model parameter, eg the elements in the matrices P and Q. More specifically, $\vec{\theta}_u$ refers to the vector of all parameters that determine the latent user vector $\vec{v}_u$, ie all $q_{j,k}$ where $j \in I(u)$; and $\vec{\theta}_i = \vec{p}_i$ refers to the parameters of item i.

In the remainder of this paper we will regularly refer to ideas from artificial neural networks (NN). Fig. 1 illustrates that AMF can be understood in terms of a NN: the user's feedback vector $\vec{h}_u$ corresponds to the input layer of the NN. The matrix Q maps $\vec{h}_u$ to the hidden layer in the NN, which corresponds to the user vector $\vec{v}_u$ in AMF. Multiplication with matrix P yields the values of the output layer $\vec{s}_u$, which are the scores of the items in AMF. Finally, as we will discuss in the remainder of this paper, a (non-linear) activation function is applied to the scores as to obtain the final output $\vec{r}_u$ of the NN. Note that the data points are indexed by the users u, while the observed dimensions within each data point are indexed by the items i.

3. DEFINITION OF RANKING PROBLEM

This section provides a formal definition of the ranking problem considered in this paper. While we use AMF in this paper, note that the presented learning-to-rank approach is also applicable to other MF models. Our objective is to minimize a rank loss function, like AUC or nDCG, denoted in general by

$$\sum_u L(\vec{y}_u, \vec{s}_u) \qquad (3)$$

where the losses L are summed over all users u (we use an unweighted sum for brevity of notation). The class label for negative and positive items is denoted by $y_{u,i} \in \{0, 1\}$, and the corresponding vector regarding all items as $\vec{y}_u$; $\vec{s}_u$ is the vector of predicted scores, as defined above. As to train the MF model, in the remainder of this paper we derive L as a function of the model parameters θ, based on the following assumptions:

1. binary labels: there are only *positive* items i (with label $y = 1$) and negative items (with label $y = 0$), as typical for implicit feedback data.

2. sparsity: for each user, the number of positive items is extremely small compared to the number of negative items: $N^{(+)} \ll N^{(-)}$. In recommender applications, the sparsity is typically $N^{(+)}/N < 1\%$, often by orders of magnitude.

3. for each user u, the distribution of the predicted scores $s_{u,i}$ follows a distribution $\mathcal{P}$. While the empirical estimate of $\mathcal{P}$ may be determined directly from the scores, we assume $\mathcal{P}$ to approximate a Gaussian, ie $\mathcal{N}(0, \text{std}_u^2)$ with zero mean and standard deviation std_u. This assumption is not only a useful working hypothesis in practice, as illustrated in Section 7, but it may also be motivated as follows: due to data sparsity, the vast majority of items belongs to the same (ie negative) class. Hence, the contribution of the positive items to the overall distribution of all items can be ignored in good approximation. Moreover, the score $s_{u,i}$ (as defined in Eq. 1) may be viewed as a sum of scores, ie $s_{u,i} = \sum_k s_{u,i,k}$ over the latent dimensions k, where $s_{u,i,k} = p_{i,k} v_{u,k}$. If the scores $s_{u,i,k}$ regarding different latent dimensions k are viewed as approximately independent random variables, then the central limit theorem implies that their summation (over k) results in scores $s_{u,i}$ that can be expected to be approximately normally distributed.

4. DECOMPOSED LOSS FUNCTION

The rank loss L is typically defined as a function of the ranks $r_{u,i}$, which themselves are determined by the scores $s_{u,i}$;[1] and $s_{u,i}$ are a function of the model parameters θ. As to minimize L by stochastic gradient descent (SGD), its partial derivative w.r.t. each model parameter θ is required. Using the chain rule, its derivative decomposes accordingly (where indices are omitted for brevity):

$$\frac{\partial L}{\partial \theta} = \frac{\partial L}{\partial r} \frac{\partial r}{\partial s^{(n)}} \frac{\partial s^{(n)}}{\partial s} \frac{\partial s}{\partial \theta} \quad (4)$$

where we have additionally inserted the normalized score $s^{(n)}$. Comments on each of the four terms are in order:

1. L as a function of the ranks rather than the scores is outlined in Section 4.1 in terms of two popular rank metrics, AUC and nDCG.

2. an item's rank $r_{u,i}$ depends on its normalized score $s_{u,i}^{(n)}$ according to

$$r_{u,i}(s_{u,i}^{(n)}) = \max\left\{1, N \cdot \left(1 - \text{CDF}(s_{u,i}^{(n)})\right)\right\}, \quad (5)$$

where N is the number of all items, and $\text{CDF}(s) = \int_{-\infty}^{s} \mathcal{P}(x)dx$ is the cumulative density function of the distribution $\mathcal{P}$ of the scores. This equation follows immediately as illustrated in Figure 2. Note that we treat the ranks $r \in [1, N]$ as continuous variables in this approach. For simplicity, we assume that $\mathcal{P}$ is a normalized Gaussian distribution, see Assumption 3 above, so that CDF is the *probit* function.

---
[1] Ranks are determined by sorting in descending order, ie the highest score results in the first rank.

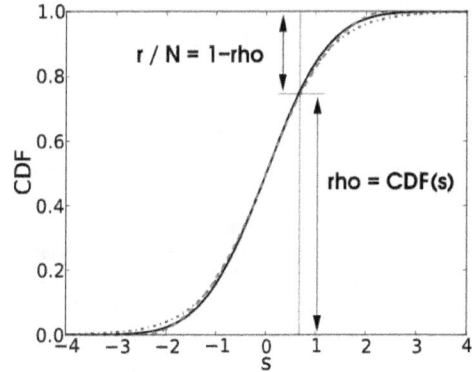

Figure 2: **Assuming a Gaussian distribution of the scores, the Gaussian CDF (black line) provides the mapping from score s to rank r via the 'normalized reverse' rank ρ. Also shown are approximations by the logistic function (blue dash-dotted line) and the piecewise quadratic function of Eq. 13 (red dashed).**

3. the normalized score depends on the (unnormalized) score $s_{u,i}$ according to $s_{u,i}^{(n)} = (s_{u,i} - \mu_u)/\text{std}_u$, where μ_u and std_u are the mean and standard deviation of the scores $s_{u,i}$ across all items i for a given user u. For simplicity, we assume that std_u does not change (noticeably) during a gradient descent update. Hence, we have $\partial s^{(n)}/\partial s = 1/\text{std}_u$. Moreover, we assume that std_u is the same for each user in the pointwise approach–this assumption is relaxed in Section 4.3.

4. the score $s_{u,i}$ depends on the model parameters $\vec{\theta}$; eg for $s_{u,i} = \vec{p}_i^{\top} \vec{v}_u$, we have $\partial s_{u,i}/\partial p_{i,k} = v_{u,k}$, see Eq. 1.

The first two terms of the chain rule in Eq. 4 are interesting and will be discussed in the following sections.

4.1 Rank-Loss Functions

This section discusses the rank loss L as a function of the ranks $r_{u,i}$, regarding the first term in Eq. 4. In the following, we consider the loss for a given user, and hence drop the index u in the notation. Note that the loss L is minimized by minimizing the *negative* of the following rank metrics. Here we outline the equations for AUC and nDCG, which–like many rank metrics–depend explicitly only on the ranks $r^{(+)}$ of the positive items, while the negative items enter only indirectly by affecting the ranks of the positives. Also other rank-loss functions may be used in this approach as long as they are differentiable with respect to the rank, when the rank is considered a continuous variable. Loss functions that *cannot* be used in this framework, are for instance, recall@n, precision@n etc, as they are not smooth at rank n.

4.1.1 Area under the Curve

The Area Under the ROC Curve (AUC) is commonly used for evaluating the ranking of the *entire* list of items (rather than the head of the ranked list). It can be defined as

$$\text{AUC} = \frac{1}{N^{(+)}N^{(-)}} \sum_{i=1}^{N^{(+)}} \sum_{j=1}^{N^{(-)}} \mathbf{I}\left(s_i^{(+)} > s_j^{(-)}\right) \quad (6)$$

with the indicator function $\mathbf{I}(\cdot) = 1$ if its argument is true, and 0 otherwise; $N^{(+)}$ and $N^{(-)}$ are the number of positive and negative items, respectively, and $N^{(+)} + N^{(-)} = N$. AUC determines the fraction of times when the score $s_i^{(+)}$ of a positive item i is correctly predicted to be larger than the score $s_j^{(-)}$ of a negative item j. AUC is equivalent to the Wilcoxon-Mann-Whitney statistic and to the fraction of concordant pairs. Replacing the indicator function by a smooth function immediately leads to a popular training method, Bayesian Personalized Ranking (BPR) [10].

Instead of evaluating $N^{(+)} \cdot N^{(-)}$ pairwise comparisons, however, it can be computationally more efficient to sort the N scores in time $\mathcal{O}(N \log N)$, and then use the ranks $r_i^{(+)}$ of the positive items:

$$\text{AUC} = \frac{1}{N^{(+)} N^{(-)}} \left[(N+1)N^{(+)} - \binom{N^{(+)}+1}{2} - \sum_{i=1}^{N^{(+)}} r_i^{(+)} \right] \tag{7}$$

It is easy to see the equivalence of Eqs. 6 and 7, eg see [3]. AUC is hence linear in the ranks $r_i^{(+)}$; the derivative of Eq. 7 is hence a constant for each positive item i,

$$\frac{\partial L}{\partial r_i^{(+)}} = -\frac{\partial \text{AUC}}{\partial r_i^{(+)}} = \frac{1}{N^{(+)} N^{(-)}}. \tag{8}$$

4.1.2 Normalized Discounted Cumulative Gain

The normalized Discounted Cumulative Gain (nDCG) emphasizes the head of the list. It is defined as

$$\text{nDCG} = \frac{DCG}{DCG^{(\text{opt})}}, \tag{9}$$

where $DCG^{(\text{opt})}$ is determined by the optimal ranking. While DCG can deal with graded relevance, it reads

$$\text{DCG} = \sum_{i=1}^{N^{(+)}} \frac{1}{\log(r_i^{(+)}+1)} \tag{10}$$

in the binary setting if negative items have zero relevance. The derivative of Eq. 9, which is needed in Eq. 4, reads

$$\frac{\partial L}{\partial r_i^{(+)}} = -\frac{\partial \text{nDCG}}{\partial r_i^{(+)}} = \frac{1}{DCG^{(\text{opt})}} \frac{1}{(r_i^{(+)}+1)\log^2(r_i^{(+)}+1)}. \tag{11}$$

4.2 Activation Functions

This section is concerned with the second term in Eq. 4, ie $\partial r/\partial s^{(n)}$. Eq. 5 provides the link between scores and ranks for a general CDF. The two most important special cases are: (1) if the scores follow a *uniform* distribution (on a finite interval), then the ranks are a *linear* function of the scores. This justifies the hinge loss of the scores as to optimize AUC, as discussed in more detail in [16]. In case (2), the scores $s_{u,i}$ (approximately) follow a *Gaussian* distribution. This was motivated in the third item in Section 3. In this case, the probit function provides the link between the scores and the ranks. It is well know that the probit is well approximated by the logistic or sigmoid function

$$\sigma(x) = \frac{1}{1 + \exp(-x)} \tag{12}$$

with appropriate scaling: $\text{probit}(s) \approx \sigma(s\sqrt{8/\pi})$, see eg [1]. Moreover, a computationally efficient approximation can be obtained by a piecewise quadratic function,

$$\text{quad}(x) = \begin{cases} 0 & \text{if } x \leq -1 \\ (1+x)^2/2 & \text{if } -1 < x \leq 0 \\ 1 - (1-x)^2/2 & \text{if } 0 < x < 1 \\ 1 & \text{if } 1 \leq x \end{cases} \tag{13}$$

when using the scaling: $\text{probit}(s) \approx \text{quad}(s/\sqrt{6})$. These approximations are illustrated in Fig. 2.

An even simpler approximation that we found to work well in practice, is obtained when we use the fact that among the positive items only those with a positive score matter (ie toward the top of the ranked list), while the (few) ones with negative scores can be ignored (ie toward the bottom of the ranked list): it is the *rank squared error*

$$\text{rankSE}(x) = [1 - ([1-x]_+)^2]_+, \tag{14}$$

where $[x]_+ = x$ if $x > 0$, and 0 otherwise. It is easy to see that $\text{quad}(x) = \text{rankSE}(x)$ for the relevant values, ie for $x > 0$.

4.3 Listwise Ranking

In this section, we consider listwise ranking, ie we take into account properties of the entire list of items for a given user. First, this allows us to overcome the assumption that the distribution of the scores has a fixed standard deviation $\text{std}_u = \text{const}$, independent of the user. Now we allow for different values of std_u for different users u. This can efficiently be estimated from the empirical distribution of the scores $s_{u,i}$ for a given user u.

Second, as discussed in Section 4.1, many rank losses depend explicitly on the ranks of only the *positive* items. Positive items typically have large scores and hence lie in the tail of the distribution of all the scores (of positive and negative items). Due to the sparsity in the tail, the mapping by means of the activation function may result in noisy estimates of their ranks as a function of their scores. In addition, the scores cannot be expected to follow exactly a Gaussian distribution in practice (as it is a simplifying assumption after all). For these two reasons, in the listwise variant, we simply sort all the items by their scores as to directly obtain their exact ranks, which are denoted by $\hat{r}_{u,i}$. Then, in Eq. 4, the derivative of the rank loss $\partial L(r)/\partial r$ can be evaluated immediately at $r = \hat{r}_{u,i}$. The second term in Eq. 4, ie $\partial r/\partial s^{(n)}$, can be approximated by mapping the rank $\hat{r}_{u,i}$ back to the corresponding score $\hat{s}_{u,i}^{(n)}$. This is analytically tractable if we assume a logistic activation function σ: given $\hat{r}_{u,i}$, we first compute the normalized reverse rank $\hat{\rho}_{u,i} = 1 - \hat{r}_{u,i}/N$, see Fig 2. Then, given that $\hat{\rho}_{u,i}$ and $\hat{s}_{u,i}^{(n)}$ are linked via $\hat{\rho}_{u,i} = \sigma(\hat{s}_{u,i}^{(n)})$, see Fig. 2, one obtains

$$\frac{\partial r}{\partial \hat{s}^{(n)}} = \sigma'(\hat{s}^{(n)}) = \sigma(\hat{s}^{(n)})(1 - \sigma(\hat{s}^{(n)})) = \hat{\rho}(1-\hat{\rho}), \tag{15}$$

where the indices are omitted for brevity. Note that this is computationally efficient as no logistic or exponential function has to be computed explicitly.

This is illustrated in Figure 3 when combined with AUC and nDCG: for the choice of AUC, one obtains

$$L'_{\text{AUC}}(\hat{\rho}) := \frac{\partial L}{\partial r} \cdot \frac{\partial r}{\partial \hat{s}^{(n)}} \propto \hat{\rho}(1-\hat{\rho}). \tag{16}$$

Note that, for the top half of the ranked list ($\hat{\rho} > 0.5$), the gradient $L'(\hat{\rho})$ monotonically *decreases* toward the top of the ranked list (ie toward $\hat{\rho} = 1$). In contrast, as illustrated by the other two curves in Figure 3, which show the behavior for nDCG, the derivative as a function of $\hat{\rho}$ reads

$$L'_{\text{nDCG}}(\hat{\rho}) := \frac{\partial L}{\partial r} \cdot \frac{\partial r}{\partial \hat{s}^{(n)}} \propto \frac{\hat{\rho}(1 - \hat{\rho})}{((1 - \hat{\rho})N + 1)\log^2((1 - \hat{\rho})N + 1)}. \tag{17}$$

as obtained by combining Eqs. 15 and 11. Note that $(1 - \hat{\rho})N = \hat{r} \in \{1, ..., N\}$. As shown in Figure 3, $L'_{\text{nDCG}}(\hat{\rho})$ *increases* with growing $\hat{\rho}$.

Between these two opposite behaviors (ie decreasing vs increasing derivatives for AUC vs nDCG), the *constant* gradient is a trivial but interesting case. It hence can be expected to optimize the ranking with emphasis that is partially on the head and partially on the entire list. Obviously the corresponding function has to be linear in the scores. The hinge loss and the linear rectifier are two functions that are linear unless they are zero. While the former is used as a loss in support vector machines, the latter is applied as an activation function in deep NN.

There is also another way of obtaining a nearly constant gradient, resulting in a partially head-heavy ranking loss: in our pointwise variant, one may choose an activation function with an associated standard deviation $\text{std}_{\text{activ}}$ that is considerably *larger* than std_u of the actual distribution of the scores. Then the resulting ranking loss is increasingly head-heavy as $\text{std}_{\text{activ}}$ becomes larger compared to std_u. The reason is that, for $\text{std}_{\text{activ}} \gg \text{std}_u$, the gradient decreases more slowly than the one resulting from the proper standard deviation (only if $\text{std}_{\text{activ}} = \text{std}_u$, the mapping from the scores to the ranks is correct in the sense of Eq. 5). In fact, we find this idea to work quite effectively in our experiments in Section 7: we use AUC as the loss function, but choose an activation function with $\text{std}_{\text{activ}} \gg \text{std}_u$ as to render the resulting loss head-heavy. This is indicated by probit$^{(w)}$, logistic$^{(w)}$ and rankSE$^{(w)}$ in Tables 1 and 2, which show that the resulting rankings are competitive toward the head of the ranked list, for the price of being degraded with respect to AUC.

5. TRAINING OBJECTIVE

Having discussed the rank loss L and several of its variants above, we now can add the regularization terms as to obtain the final training objective function to be minimized:

$$\sum_u \sum_{i \in I(u)} \left[L(s_{u,i}) + \lambda \cdot (\| \vec{\theta}_u \|^2 + \| \vec{\theta}_i \|^2) \right] + \sum_{j \in I} \gamma \cdot ([s_{u,j}]_+)^2 \tag{18}$$

The details are as follows. First, in the sum over the set $I(u)$ of positive items, we have the loss function L, which commonly is a function of the positive items only (see Section 4.1), as well as the usual ℓ_2-regularization terms for the model parameters $\vec{\theta}_u$ and $\vec{\theta}_i$ concerning the user u and items i, ie the parameters $p_{i,k}$ and $q_{i,k}$ with $i \in I(u)$ in AMF. The ℓ_2-regularization may be viewed as the logarithm of a Gaussian prior distribution with zero mean and variance $1/(2\lambda)$.

Second, the sum over all items $j \in I$ in Eq. 18 enforces the (approximately Gaussian) distribution of the scores $s_{u,j}$ about zero. This reflects our main assumption, as outlined in Section 3, namely that the scores follow approximately

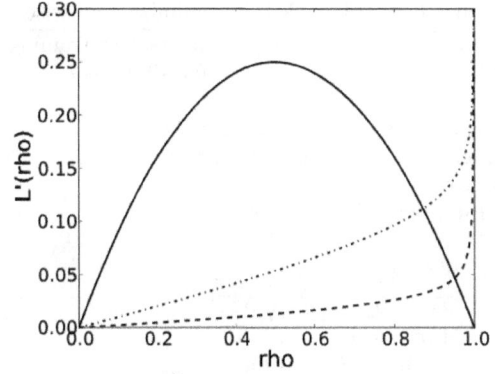

Figure 3: The derivative of the loss $\frac{\partial L}{\partial r} \frac{\partial r}{\partial s^{(n)}}$, ie the first two terms in Eq. 4, as a function of the 'normalized reverse' rank ρ: as ρ approaches the top of the list ($\rho \approx 1$), the gradient *decreases* for $L = -\text{AUC}$ (solid line), while it *increases* for $L = -\text{nDCG}$, for different lengths N of the ranked list, $N = 10,000$ (dashed line) and 10 million (dash-dotted line). The latter two curves are re-scaled along the y-axis. See Sections 4.3 and 4.1 for details.

the *posterior* distribution $s_{u,j} \sim \mathcal{N}(0, \text{std}_u^2)$. As to obtain such a posterior distribution with the desired variance std_u^2, one may use a *prior* distribution $s_{u,j} \sim \mathcal{N}(0, 1/(2\gamma))$, where γ is chosen appropriately. The logarithm of this prior immediately yields the additional term $\gamma \cdot s_{u,j}^2$. For simplicity, we have chosen γ to be independent of user u here.

The derivative of Eq. 18 may be interpreted as the force that pulls an item's score toward the target values 0 or 1 during training. This interpretation immediately originates from the perspective of physics when Eq. 18 is interpreted as an energy. In this picture, γ may be viewed as the degree with which an item's score is pulled toward *zero*. During training with the feedback data, this is counter-balanced by having the scores of the positive items being pulled toward a *positive* target value (like 1) due to the rank loss L. A proper choice of γ is hence crucial for the obtained results; the value of γ can be determined such that the desired rank metric on a validation set is optimized.

Note that there is no term in Eq. 18 that explicitly tries to pull scores toward a *negative* target value. For this reason, it is not necessary for the 'prior' to pull *negative* scores toward zero. In fact, it is beneficial to modify the last term in Eq. 18 from $\gamma \cdot s_{u,i}^2$ to $\gamma \cdot ([s_{u,i}]_+)^2$, where $[x]_+ = x$ if $x > 0$, and 0 otherwise; ie, an item's score $s_{u,i}$ is pulled toward zero only if it is positive. We found this modification to yield improved ranking results in our experiments.

Eq. 18 can efficiently be minimized by stochastic gradient descent (SGD). The necessary derivatives of the different variants of the rank loss are outlined in the previous sections. For computational efficiency, the sum over all items I in Eq. 18, and hence the iteration at line 11 in Algorithm 1, are sub-sampled, like eg in [8, 17]. Moreover, note that line 16 of Algorithm 1 refers to the negative items, while the last term in Eq. 18 refers to both positive and negative items—this difference is negligible in practice as $N^{(+)} \ll N^{(-)}$. The iterative training algorithm for AMF has the same structure as the one for training SVD++ [6]: for each user, one first

Algorithm 1 SGD for AMF to minimize pointwise loss L.

1: **Input::** learning rate η, parameters λ, γ, training data.
2: **Output**: latent vectors $\vec{p}_i$, $\vec{q}_i$ for all items i.
3: **do**:
4:   $\forall i: \vec{p}_i \leftarrow$ *random initialization*
5:   $\forall i: \vec{q}_i \leftarrow$ *random initialization*
6: **repeat**
7:   **for** *user u* **do**
8:     $\Lambda \leftarrow 0$
9:     $\vec{\epsilon} \leftarrow 0$
10:     $\vec{v}_u \leftarrow \sum_{j \in I_u} \vec{q}_j / \sqrt{N_u^{(+)}}$
11:     **for** *all items $i \in I(u)$* **do**
12:       **if** $i \in I(u)$ **then**
13:         $err \leftarrow -L'(\vec{p}_i^{\top} \vec{v}_u)$
14:         $\lambda_i \leftarrow \lambda$
15:         $\Lambda \leftarrow \Lambda + \lambda$
16:       **else**
17:         $err \leftarrow -\gamma [\vec{p}_i^{\top} \vec{v}_u]_+$
18:         $\lambda_i \leftarrow 0$
19:     $\vec{\epsilon} \leftarrow \vec{\epsilon} + err \cdot \vec{p}_i / \sqrt{N_u^{(+)}}$
20:     $\vec{p}_i \leftarrow \vec{p}_i + \eta \cdot (err \cdot \vec{v}_u - \lambda_i \cdot \vec{p}_i)$
21:     **for** $i \in I(u)$ **do**
22:       $\vec{q}_i \leftarrow \vec{q}_i + \eta \cdot (\vec{\epsilon} - \Lambda \cdot \vec{q}_i)$
23: **until** *convergence*

iterates through all the items i as to update the parameters $\vec{p}_i$, while the updates for the parameters $\vec{q}_i$ are aggregated in the temporary vector $\vec{\epsilon}$ and in the regularization value Λ. After that, in a second iteration at line 21 in Algorithm 1, the parameters $\vec{q}_i$ get updated based on the temporary vector. Algorithm 1 provides the pseudo code for pointwise ranking with AMF, using the derivative of the loss $L' = \frac{\partial L}{\partial r} \frac{\partial r}{\partial s^{(n)}} \frac{\partial s^{(n)}}{\partial s}$, which gets evaluated using score $s_{u,i} = \vec{p}_i^{\top} \vec{v}_u$, see also Eq. 4. The fourth derivative-term in Eq. 4 is included in lines 19 and 20 in Algorithm 1.

In the listwise training (see Section 4.3), there is an additional iteration over the items as to compute their scores, and then their ranks and the scores' standard deviation. Only after that, the SGD updates in line 11 and following are made analogous to the pointwise approach.

In addition, we use dropout learning [15]. It combines the random subspace method [4] with parameter sharing across the models in the (implicit) ensemble, which results in a reduced generalization error.

6. RELATED WORK

In the recommender literature, many learning-to-rank approaches are *pairwise* methods. The most well-known approach is perhaps BPR [10], which optimizes AUC. As to optimize head-heavy rank metrics, custom-tailored approaches to optimize mean-reciprocal-rank (MRR) and mean-average-precision (MAP) were presented in [13, 12]. Moreover, weighting schemes [19, 20] and sampling schemes for the negative items [21] were proposed, and may be viewed as extensions to BPR.

In contrast, the presented approach considers all items concerning a user u at once, rather than each user-item pair (u, i) separately. If we assume that the number of sampled negative items is the same as the number of positive items, ie $N_u^{(+)}$ for user u, then all the SGD updates for a

user u can be computed by first sorting the scores in time $\mathcal{O}(N_u^{(+)} \log(N_u^{(+)}))$ in the listwise approach (see Section 4.3). Note that this accounts for all pairwise comparisons between positive and negative items. In the pairwise approach, this would require much more time, ie $\mathcal{O}((N_u^{(+)})^2)$.

While minimizing RMSE on the observed ratings is associated with the 'rating prediction' problem in the recommender literature, minimizing the squared error with proper sampling and weighting of negatives [5, 8, 17] was also successfully used for ranking problems, and outperformed other ranking methods, like eg [2]. The presented approach essentially replaces the RMSE objective with a rank loss.

A listwise approach to training recommender systems has been proposed in [14]. It was motivated from top-1 recommendations, and was experimentally shown to outperform Cofi-rank [18] regarding nDCG for the top items. This approach uses the *softmax* activation function and the *cross entropy* as loss function. Interestingly, the same approach is also popular for training artificial neural networks. We included this approach as an additional baseline in our experiments.

7. EXPERIMENTS

This section outlines our results on the 10 million MovieLens data [7] and our proprietary Netflix data.

7.1 MovieLens Data

In the 10 million MovieLens data [7], 69,878 users have rated 10,677 movies. As to simulate binary 'play' data for use in our approach, we binarized the MovieLens data by retaining all ratings of 3 or higher as positives (which may indicate some user satisfaction), while discarding the lower ratings. This resulted in a data set of 8.2 million plays, with a sparsity of about 1%. All other user-movie pairs are considered as 'negative', as defined in Section 2. We split this data set into a training set (95%) and a disjoint test set (5%). We repeated this random split five times, and report mean and standard deviation. Given that the disjoint test set does not contain any movies played by the user in the training set, those movies are filtered out from the user's recommendations. We used AMF with $K = 50$ latent dimensions.

We evaluated the ranked list of items with respect to AUC and nDCG. Besides nDCG, there are various ranking metrics that summarize the ranking quality with a certain emphasis on the top of the list in a *single* number, like mean average precision (MAP), mean reciprocal rank (MRR), etc. Instead, we provide results w.r.t. recall@n for several n, which provides detailed insights in the ranking quality at different positions in the ranked list. In the interest of space, we do not report precision@n, as it is proportional to recall@n for the same test data and the same value n for each user, see eg [17].

When training the AMF model, we re-scaled the inputs of the activation functions such that their widths agreed with rankSE in Eq. 14 (rather than with the probit function)– this allowed as to use the target values 1 (instead of $\sqrt{6}$) and 0 for the positive and negative items in the pointwise approach, respectively. In the training objective function in Eq. 18 we used the parameters $\lambda = 10^{-7}$ and $\gamma = 0.3$ for this data set for the pointwise variants, as determined by a grid search. The step size in SGD was $\eta = 0.001$. Choosing

Table 1: Ranking results on the MovieLens data [7].[2] Based on five repetitions of the experiments, the standard deviation (std) is ≤ 0.002 for recall and nDCG, and ≤ 0.001 for AUC. Values within std of the best result are highlighted.

trained	loss	activ. fct.	recall@ 10	recall@ 30	recall@ 80	recall@ 500	recall@ 3000	AUC	nDCG
point-wise	'AUC'	probit$^{(w)}$	0.265	**0.432**	**0.602**	**0.883**	0.986	0.975	**0.426**
		logistic$^{(w)}$	0.266	**0.432**	**0.602**	**0.883**	0.986	0.976	**0.427**
		rankSE$^{(w)}$	0.265	**0.431**	**0.600**	**0.881**	0.986	0.975	**0.427**
list-wise	nDCG	logistic	**0.272**	**0.433**	0.592	0.820	0.891	0.901	0.421
	AUC	logistic	0.217	0.386	0.564	0.876	**0.993**	**0.978**	0.386
point-w.	RMSE	linear	0.250	0.410	0.579	0.867	0.988	0.974	0.413
list-w.	X ent.	softmax	0.256	0.420	0.589	0.872	0.989	0.975	0.417
pair-w.	AUC by BPR		0.241	0.404	0.577	0.877	**0.992**	**0.979**	0.408

that large a value for γ leads to an increased emphasis of the ranking quality at the head of the ranked list, as discussed at the end of Section 4.3. For this reason, we use probit$^{(w)}$, logistic$^{(w)}$ and rankSE$^{(w)}$ in Table 1, as to indicate that the AUC rank loss is combined with a *wide* activation function. Table 1 reflects this fact clearly, as 'AUC' with all three *wide* activation functions obtains high values with respect to recall toward the top as well as regarding nDCG. Moreover, these three variants of wide activation functions lead to very similar results, as expected from Figure 2.

The listwise variants of the proposed approach adapt the activation function to the width of the distribution of the scores of each user, ie $\text{std}_{\text{activ}} = \text{std}_u$. Consequently, the chosen rank loss, nDCG or AUC, determines whether the ranking is optimized regarding the head of the ranked list or concerning the entire list. Table 1 illustrates this flexibility of the presented approach, as either recall @ 10 and 30 is optimized, or AUC, depending on the chosen rank loss. Interestingly, Table 1 also shows that the presented approach trained with nDCG loss is much more head-heavy than expected: while it achieves high recall @ 10 and 30, the ranking quality deteriorates very quickly below the head of the ranked list, reflected by an extremely low AUC. This also degrades nDCG on the entire list. While not fully clear from the theoretical side, this behavior is actually desirable in real-world applications of recommender systems, where only a very limited number of items can be shown to the user due to space constraints.

7.2 Baseline Approaches

Table 1 also shows the results of three competing approaches for comparison, whose hyper-paramters were also optimized by grid search.[2] As to optimize the root mean squared error (RMSE)[2] on binary data we followed the ideas outlined in [5, 8, 17], ie we randomly sampled negative items in addition to using the positive items in the implicit feedback data. This is a crucial change to the popular approach used for 'rating prediction', eg [11, 6]. As a result, this approach is geared toward optimizing the ranking, and was found to outperform other ranking methods, like eg [2]. Table 1 shows that optimizing RMSE with sampled negative items yields solid ranking results.

BPR[2] [10] optimizes AUC in Table 1, as expected. Not surprisingly, as the head's contribution to the ranking of the entire list is small, the ranking at the top is rather unim-

portant, and consequently the head-heavy metrics are lower than for RMSE optimization.

As already outlined in Section 6, the approach that optimizes the cross-entropy and uses the softmax activation function[2] in Table 1 was motivated in [14] to optimize top-1 recommendations, and it was also shown to outperform Cofi-rank [18] concerning nDCG at the top. In Table 1 regarding the top of the ranked list, however, it only improves over the variants optimzied toward AUC and RMSE, while it is outperformed by all our pointwise and listwise variants that optimize the head.

7.3 Netflix Data

The results on our proprietary data agree with the insights from the MovieLens data above. We considered all movies and TV shows available in our US catalog (for simplicity, we ignored videos available on Netflix outside the US, as a global model that can deal with different availabilities of videos in different countries is beyond the scope of this paper). The split into disjoint training and test data was performed based on the time-stamp when a video was played, as to simulate the situation of the real-world system: we randomly picked a test-day in 2014, and the preceding 6 months as the training period. We used binary data that captured whether a user played a video or not during the training or test periods, respectively. If a user played the same video in the training and the test data, we removed it from the test data. We sampled a random subset of about 500,000 anonymized users. This was repeated five times, and we report the mean and standard deviation (std) of the test-metrics.

Table 2 depicts the results, where we focus on the very top of the recommended list, as this is crucial in the real-world application. We also provide AUC regarding the entire list as additional information. The hyper-parameters in the training objective were again determined by grid search for each model. The results are relative to the baseline model, for which we picked the one that optimizes RMSE regarding positive items combined with randomly sampled negative items, as described in the previous section. The proposed pointwise variants with a wide activation function, as well as the listwise optimization of nDCG again perform well at the top of the list. Regarding the AUC metric, BPR as well as our listwise optimization of AUC (and the RMSE baseline model itself) achieve the highest AUC (within the noise level).

---

[2]For fair comparisons, we also used the AMF (instead of the standard MF) model for all competing approaches.

Table 2: Ranking results on our proprietary Netflix data set, as a relative improvement over training toward RMSE with proper sampling of negative items.[2] The uncertainty (std) is 2 % for recall and 1% for AUC (percentage points). Values within std of the best result are highlighted.

loss fct.	activ. fct.	recall @				AUC
		1	5	10	30	
'AUC'	probit$^{(w)}$	28%	16%	9%	2%	-4%
	logistic$^{(w)}$	30%	15%	7%	-1%	-13%
	rankSE$^{(w)}$	28%	16%	9%	1%	-4%
nDCG	logistic	32%	17%	9%	2%	-5%
AUC	logistic	24%	9%	2%	-3%	0%
RMSE	linear	– –	– –	– –	– –	– –
X ent.	softmax	28%	14%	8%	0%	-1%
AUC by BPR		8%	-1%	-2%	-3%	1%

8. CONCLUSIONS

In this paper, we presented a novel learning-to-rank approach that takes advantage of two typical properties of implicit feedback data, namely that they are sparse and binary. This motivated us to make the approximation that the scores of the items, as predicted by a matrix factorization model, follow approximately a Gaussian distribution. Based on this assumption, we derived several non-linear activation functions. This enabled us to optimize toward different ranking metrics efficiently. In our experiments, we found that the presented approach is competitive with respect to the Area under the Curve, while it is particularly effective for optimizing the head of the ranked list.

Given that the used asymmetric matrix factorization model can be viewed as a shallow neural network, future work includes the extension of the presented learning-to-rank approach to deep neural networks.

9. ACKNOWLEDGMENTS

I would like to thank Caitlin Smallwood, Carlos Gomez-Uribe and Roelof van Zwol for their encouragement and support of this work.

10. REFERENCES

[1] C. Bishop. *Neural networks for pattern recognition*. Oxford, 1995.

[2] P. Cremonesi, Y. Koren, and R. Turrin. Performance of recommender algorithms on top-N recommendation tasks. In *ACM Conference on Recommender Systems*, pages 39–46, 2010.

[3] D. J. Hand and R. J. Till. A simple generalization of the area under the ROC curve for multiple class classification problems. *Machine Learning*, 45:171–86, 2001.

[4] T. Ho. The random subspace method for constructing decision forests. *IEEE Transactions on Pattern Analysis and Machine Learning*, 20:832–44, 1998.

[5] Y. Hu, Y. Koren, and C. Volinsky. Collaborative filtering for implicit feedback datasets. In *IEEE International Conference on Data Mining (ICDM)*, 2008.

[6] Y. Koren. Factorization meets the neighborhood: a multifaceted collaborative filtering model. In *ACM Conference on Knowledge Discovery and Data Mining (KDD)*, pages 426–34, 2008.

[7] MovieLens. Univ. of Minnesota, homepage: http://grouplens.org/datasets/movielens/.

[8] R. Pan, Y. Zhou, B. Cao, N. Liu, R. Lukose, M. Scholz, and Q. Yang. One-class collaborative filtering. In *IEEE International Conference on Data Mining (ICDM)*, 2008.

[9] A. Paterek. Improving regularized singular value decomposition for collaborative filtering. In *KDDCup*, 2007.

[10] S. Rendle, C. Freudenthaler, Z. Gantner, and L. Schmidt-Thieme. BPR: Bayesian personalized ranking from implicit feedback. In *Conference on Uncertainty in Artificial Intelligence (UAI)*, pages 452–61, 2009.

[11] R. Salakhutdinov and A. Mnih. Probabilistic matrix factorization. In *Advances in Neural Information Processing Systems (NIPS)*, 2008.

[12] Y. Shi, A. Karatzoglou, L. Baltrunas, M. Larson, A. Hanjalic, and N. Oliver. TFMAP: optimizing MAP for top-n context-aware recommendation. In *ACM SIGIR conference*, 2012.

[13] Y. Shi, A. Karatzoglou, L. Baltrunas, M. Larson, N. Oliver, and A. Hanjalic. CLiMF: Learning to maximize reciprocal rank with collaborative less-is-more filtering. In *ACM Conference on Recommender Systems (RecSys)*, 2012.

[14] Y. Shi, M. Larson, and A. Hanjalic. List-wise learning to rank with matrix factorization for collaborative filtering. In *ACM Conference on Recommender Systems (RecSys)*, 2010.

[15] N. Srivastava, G. Hinton, A. Krizhevsky, I. Sutskever, and R. Salakhutdinov. Dropout: A simple way to prevent neural networks from overfitting. *Journal of Machine Learning Research*, 15:1929–58, 2014.

[16] H. Steck. Hinge rank loss and the area under the ROC curve. In *Proceedings of the European Conference on Machine Learning (ECML)*, 2007.

[17] H. Steck. Training and testing of recommender systems on data missing not at random. In *ACM Conference on Knowledge Discovery and Data Mining*, pages 713–22, 2010.

[18] M. Weimer, A. Karatzoglou, Q. Le, and A. Smola. Cofi rank–maximum margin matrix factorization for collaborative ranking. In *Advances in Neural Information Processing Systems (NIPS)*, 2008.

[19] J. Weston, H. Yee, and R. Weiss. WSABIE: Scaling up to large vocabulary image annotation. In *Int. Joint Conference on Artificial Intelligence (IJCAI)*, 2011.

[20] J. Weston, H. Yee, and R. Weiss. Learning to rank recommendations with the k-order statistic loss. In *ACM Conference on Recommender Systems (RecSys)*, 2013.

[21] W. Zhang, T. Chen, J. Wang, and Y. Yu. Optimizing top-n collaborative filtering via dynamic negative item sampling. In *ACM SIGIR Conference*, 2013.

Context-Aware Event Recommendation in Event-based Social Networks

Augusto Q. Macedo
Dept. of Syst. and Computing
Fed. Univ. of Campina Grande
Campina Grande, Brazil
augusto@copin.ufcg.edu.br

Leandro B. Marinho
Dept. of Syst. and Computing
Fed. Univ. of Campina Grande
Campina Grande, Brazil
lbmarinho@dsc.ufcg.edu.br

Rodrygo L. T. Santos
Dept. of Computer Science
Fed. Univ. of Minas Gerais
Belo Horizonte, Brazil
rodrygo@dcc.ufmg.br

ABSTRACT

The Web has grown into one of the most important channels to communicate social events nowadays. However, the sheer volume of events available in event-based social networks (EBSNs) often undermines the users' ability to choose the events that best fit their interests. Recommender systems appear as a natural solution for this problem, but differently from classic recommendation scenarios (e.g. movies, books), the event recommendation problem is intrinsically cold-start. Indeed, events published in EBSNs are typically short-lived and, by definition, are always in the future, having little or no trace of historical attendance. To overcome this limitation, we propose to exploit several contextual signals available from EBSNs. In particular, besides content-based signals based on the events' description and collaborative signals derived from users' RSVPs, we exploit social signals based on group memberships, location signals based on the users' geographical preferences, and temporal signals derived from the users' time preferences. Moreover, we combine the proposed signals for learning to rank events for personalized recommendation. Thorough experiments using a large crawl of Meetup.com demonstrate the effectiveness of our proposed contextual learning approach in contrast to state-of-the-art event recommenders from the literature.

Categories and Subject Descriptors

H.3.3 [**Information Search and Retrieval**]: Information filtering; H.2.8 [**Database Applications**]: Data mining

General Terms

Algorithms; Experimentation

Keywords

Event-based social networks; recommender systems

RecSys'15, September 16–20, 2015, Vienna, Austria.
© 2015 ACM. ISBN 978-1-4503-3692-5/15/09 ...$15.00.
DOI: http://dx.doi.org/10.1145/2792838.2800187.

1. INTRODUCTION

Event-based social networks (EBSNs) are online social networks where users can create, promote and share upcoming events of any kind with other users. For instance, Meetup.com,[1] one of the largest EBSNs available today, registered 3,000 new groups and 330,000 users participating in events in the first week of January, 2015 alone.[2] In Meetup.com, users can create and join groups of like-minded people, promoting events (aka Meetups) that they are interested in. However, the sheer volume of available events, especially in large and touristic cities, often undermines the users' ability to find the ones that best match their interests.

Recommender systems appear as a natural solution to overcome such an information overload, as they help users discover relevant information in large data sets. Nonetheless, the event recommendation problem is arguably more challenging than classic recommendation scenarios (e.g. movies and books), since event recommenders need to deal with the new item cold-start problem that arises naturally in this setting [14]. Indeed, events published in EBSNs are typically short-lived and, by definition, are always in the future, having little or no trace of historical attendance. In this scenario, classic recommendation approaches may underperform, leaving the EBSN users unsatisfied.

To overcome this limitation, we propose a context-aware approach to event recommendation, by exploiting several contextual signals generally available in EBSNs. Besides content-based signals based on the events' description and collaborative signals derived from users' RSVPs,[3] we exploit social signals based on group memberships, location signals based on the users' home distance to each event, and temporal signals derived from the users' time preferences. In particular, our assumption is that each of these signals has a positive influence on the users' decision about attending an event. For example, a user may decide to attend an event not only because the event matches his or her interests and other like-minded users have RSVP'ed to the event, but also because the event is in the user's neighborhood.

To exploit the aforementioned contextual signals, we devise and meticulously analyse the behavior of a specialized recommendation model tailored to each signal. To combine the strengths of the various devised models, we further propose a hybrid contextual recommender for learning to rank upcoming events in an EBSN. Thorough experiments using

---

[1] http://www.meetup.com

[2] http://blog.meetup.com/chart

[3] RSVP stands for the French expression "répondez s'il vous plaît", meaning "please respond".

a large crawl of Meetup.com demonstrate the effectiveness of our proposed contextual learning approach in contrast to state-of-the-art event recommenders from the literature. To the best of our knowledge, this is the first attempt to conjointly exploit the aforementioned contextual evidence for the event recommendation problem. Our contributions can be summarized as follows:

- We compare and contrast several specialized event recommendation models based on multiple contextual signals available from EBSNs;

- We propose a hybrid recommendation approach that leverages multiple context-aware recommendation models as features for learning to rank events;

- We thoroughly evaluate our proposed approach on a large crawl of Meetup.com and demonstrate its effectiveness in contrast to state-of-the-art recommenders.

In the remainder of this paper, Section 2 formalizes our problem setting and the nomenclature used throughout the paper. Section 3 describes our proposed context-aware models for event recommendation. Section 4 presents the setup and the results of our experimental evaluation. Relevant related works are described in Section 5. Lastly, Section 6 provides our conclusions and directions for future work.

2. PROBLEM SETTING

Traditional recommender systems typically model an interaction between two types of entity, namely, users and items. Context-aware recommenders, on the other hand, exploit additional signals that help further define such an interaction, including the time, location, and social environment in which the interaction takes place [1]. As pointed out in Section 1, there is no interaction between users and candidate events in EBSNs, since the latter are always in the future.[4] Indeed, even when using positive RSVP data as a proxy for user-event attendance—as we do later in Section 3—this information is still missing for the majority of events (cf. Section 4). To overcome this problem, also known as the new item cold-start problem, we propose to use the rich contextual evidence available in EBSNs.

The problem that we address in this paper can be stated as follows: given a target user and a set of contextual signals, which of the available events are more likely to be attended (i.e. RSVP'ed "yes") by this user? We simulate this scenario by splitting the available RSVP data into two partitions, before and after a given time-stamp θ. The (user,events) pairs occurring before θ form the training partition, while those that occur after θ form the test partition. Formally, in addition to the set of users U and the set of events E, we consider as contextual signals users' temporal preferences T, the set of groups G that users can join, users' geographic distance preferences D, and the textual content of events C. In this paper, we only consider implicit feedback data, i.e., the set $S \subseteq U \times E \times T \times G \times D \times C \times D$ of relations between users, time, events, groups, distances and content. The task is then to find a scoring function of the form:

$$\hat{s} : U \times E \times T \times G \times C \times D \to \mathbb{R}, \qquad (1)$$

that assigns a preference score for candidate events. Thus, for a given target user $u \in U$ and the contextual signals

---

[4]Except for the events that occur periodically.

$t \in T$, $g \in G$, $c \in C$ and $d \in D$, the top-n recommendations can be computed by:

$$\text{top-}n(u,t,g,c,d) := \underset{e \in E \setminus E_u}{\arg\max^n} \hat{s}(u,e,t,g,c,d), \qquad (2)$$

where n denotes the number of events to be recommended and E_u the set of events that user u has attended in the past. In top-n recommendation settings, such as this, the goal is to minimize a ranking loss function of the form:

$$\ell : \mathcal{P}(E) \times \mathbb{R}^E \to \mathbb{R},$$

which quantifies the misfit between the recommended list (generated by $\hat{s} \in \mathbb{R}^E$) and the actual list (a subset of $\mathcal{P}(E)$) on test users whose actual events are unknown during training. In the sequel we will use $\hat{s}_X(u,e)$ to denote a context-aware recommender that computes the relevance score of $e \in E$ to user $u \in U$ based on context X.

3. CONTEXTUAL MODELS

Data sparsity can severely hamper the performance of traditional event recommenders based on a single strategy. To overcome this limitation, we propose a hybrid recommendation approach that leverages multiple context-aware recommenders as features for learning to rank events. In the following, we describe each of the proposed features as well as our learning approach for event recommendation.

3.1 Social-Aware

In some EBSNs, such as Meetup.com, users may join groups and interact with other users both online, through the communication tools available in the platform, and face-to-face, by means of the events promoted by the groups. Here we propose two models based on the social interactions in these two modes of communication.

3.1.1 Group Frequency Model

As we will see in Section 4, group membership has a strong influence on the users' decision on attending an event, specially when the user is a frequent attendant of the group events. The intuition here is that the likelihood of the target user $u \in U$ attending event $e \in E$ depends on the number of events this user attended in the group that e belongs to. In other words, the more events a user attends in a group, the higher is the probability that this user will continue to attend events of this group. More formally, assuming that g_e represents the group associated with the candidate event e, the relevance score of this event for the target user $u \in U$ is calculated as follows:

$$\hat{s}_{S_1}(u,e) := \frac{|E_{u,g_e}|}{|E_u|}, \qquad (3)$$

where E_u denotes the set of all events that the user $u \in U$ attended, E_{u,g_e} denotes the set of events attended by u that were created by group $g_e \in G$, and S_1 is the social context represented by this recommender.

3.1.2 Multi-Relational Model

Although simple and effective (cf. Section 4), the method described above does not consider two important interactions, namely, between users and all the groups they are affiliated to and between the groups and the events created by them. By using these two sources of interactions conjointly one might discover, for example, that users affiliated to the same or similar groups are prone to attend the same events created by these groups. The user-group relation is especially important because it enables the recommendation of cold-start events, i.e., events with zero RSVP.

To model and leverage these sources of interactions conjointly we propose to use Multi-Relational Factorization with Bayesian Personalized Ranking (MRBPR) [8], a state-of-art recommender that solves the top-n recommendation task by optimizing a personalized ranking function (aka BPR [16]) considering multiple binary relations. In our case, the idea is to reconstruct the target relation $R_{UE} \subseteq U \times E$ by considering a joint factorization approach that includes the auxiliary relations $R_{UG} \subseteq U \times G$ and $R_{GE} \subseteq G \times E$.

The parameters of the model $\Theta := \{\mathbf{U}, \mathbf{E}, \mathbf{G}\}$ are the latent matrices associated with each considered entity. For example, the set of users U is associated with the matrix $\mathbf{U} \in \mathbb{R}^{|U| \times k}$, where k is the number of latent factors considered. The objective function is then expressed as follows:

$$\underset{\Theta}{\arg\min} \; \alpha L(R_{UE}, \mathbf{UE}^T)$$
$$+ \beta L(R_{UG}, \mathbf{UG}^T)$$
$$+ \gamma L(R_{GE}, \mathbf{GE}^T)$$
$$+ \lambda_U \|\mathbf{U}\|^2 + \lambda_E \|\mathbf{E}\|^2 + \lambda_G \|\mathbf{G}\|^2, \quad (4)$$

where L is a loss function (in our case BPR [16]) measuring the reconstruction error of the relation under consideration, α, β, γ are application specific weights for the losses of the relations considered and $\lambda_U, \lambda_G, \lambda_E$ are regularization parameters. The intuition is that latent factors are shared between all relations that involve the same entities, i.e., information is propagated between relations sharing the same entities. The parameter learning is performed via stochastic gradient descent as proposed by [8].

Once the model is learned, predicting the relevance score of an event $e \in E$ for the target user $u \in U$ is done as follows:

$$\hat{s}_{S_2}(u, e) = \sum_{f=1}^{k} \vec{u}_f \vec{e}_f, \quad (5)$$

where $\vec{u}$ and $\vec{e}$ are the latent vectors of user u and event e respectively. The key difference from a standard matrix factorization (i.e. based on a single relation) is that now the latent factors of u and e also bear group aspects that may influence the users' decision on attending a future event.

3.2 Content-aware

Content-based filtering appears as a promising approach in EBSNs. In particular, besides its usual capacity of retrieving events with similar descriptions, it also captures recurrent events since these events tend to have similar or near-identical content. Thus, as content-based filtering approach, we use a classic bag-of-words model based on the textual description of events. Here, each user is represented as a TF-IDF vector of the words extracted from the past events the user attended. Additionally, each event is weighted by its time distance to the recommendation instant by means of a time value of money decay function [18]. More formally, the profile of the target user $u \in U$ is defined as follows:

$$\vec{u} := \sum_{e \in E_u} \frac{1}{(1+\alpha)^{\tau(e)}} \times \vec{e}, \quad (6)$$

where $\vec{e}$ is the TF-IDF representation of event e considering the terms that appear in the event's description, α is a time

decay factor and $\tau(e)$ returns the number of days from the RSVP to e until the moment of recommendation. In the end, the candidate events are ranked based on their cosine similarity with respect to the target user, such that:

$$\hat{s}_C(u, e) = \cos(\vec{u}, \vec{e}). \quad (7)$$

Other variations of this approach were also evaluated, such as Latent Dirichlent Allocation (LDA) [3], however, none of these variations outperformed the bag-of-words approach with time decay.

3.3 Location-aware

The mobility patterns of users within a city may vary from user to user. While someone may prefer to attend events in his neighborhood, others might like to attend events far away from their homes. Figure 3.3 depicts the estimated densities of two inhabitants of Phoenix, US, where the colored regions represent the density of attended events around their homes (depicted as map markers). Notice that while User 1 tends to concentrate his events in a single region with sporadic events in other regions, User 2 concentrates his events in two main regions.

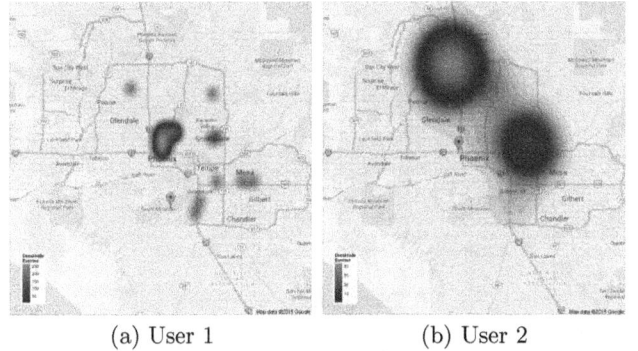

(a) User 1   (b) User 2

Figure 1: Geographical densities of two users.

Here we propose a kernel-based density estimation approach to model the mobility patterns of individual users as distributions of geographic distances between the attended events. The relevance of a new event for a user is based on the aggregated likelihood of this event being located in any of the regions the user attended events in the past.

More formally, let L_u be the sample of lat-long coordinates of the events the target user has attended in the past, i.e.,

$$L_u := \bigcup_{e \in E_u} l_e, \quad (8)$$

where l_e is the lat-long coordinate of event $e \in E_u$.

Assuming that L_u comes from an unknown distribution f, a kernel density function $\hat{f}$ is defined over L_u as follows:

$$\hat{f}(l) := \frac{1}{|L_u|} \sum_{l' \in L_u} K_{\mathbf{H}}(l - l'), \quad (9)$$

where l is a lat-long coordinate, $K_H(.)$ is the bivariate Gaussian kernel,

$$K_{\mathbf{H}}(\mathbf{x}) := \frac{1}{\sqrt{2\pi|\mathbf{H}|}} \epsilon^{-\frac{\mathbf{xx}^T}{2\sqrt{\mathbf{H}}}}, \quad (10)$$

and $\mathbf{H}$ is a 2×2 symmetric and positive definite matrix that represents the bandwidth defined as $\mathbf{H} = (h_1, h_2) \times \mathbb{I}$.

The geographical preferences of a given user are then represented by the sum of all Gaussian distributions centered at l_e, for all $e \in E_u$. The candidate events are now scored based on their distances to the events attended by the target user in the past as follows:

$$\hat{s}_D(u, e) := \hat{f}(l_e). \qquad (11)$$

3.4 Time-aware

Another important factor that might affect users' decision on attending an event is when the event occurs. Some users might prefer to attend events during the morning on weekends, while others prefer events occurring on Friday nights. We capture this intuition by assuming that users that attended events in the past at certain days of the week and at certain hours of the day will likely attend events with a similar temporal profile in the future. Figure 2 exposes two interesting cases. While User 1 tends to go to events every day, but mainly at night, User 2 attends events during the week and in the afternoon only.

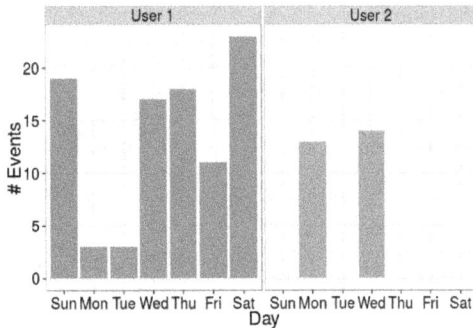

(a) Distribution per day.

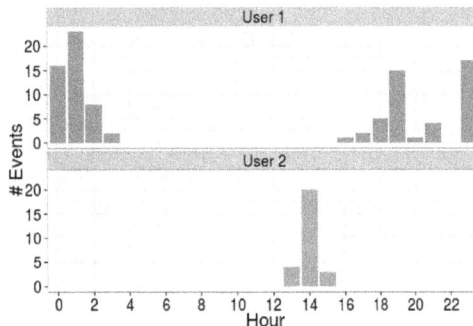

(b) Distribution per hour.

Figure 2: Temporal distribution of attended events.

To formalize this intuition, we represent each event e as a 24×7-dimensional vector $\vec{e}$ in the space of all possible days of the week and hours of the day, with a vector component set to 1 whenever the event happened at that particular day and hour. Accordingly, each user is represented as the centroid $\vec{u}$ of the events he attended in the past:

$$\vec{u} := \frac{1}{|E_u|} \sum_{e \in E_u} \vec{e}. \qquad (12)$$

Similarly to Equation (6), the temporal score for user u and event e can now be expressed as the cosine between their

vector representations, such that:

$$\hat{s}_T(u, e) := \cos(\vec{u}, \vec{e}). \qquad (13)$$

3.5 Learning to Rank Events with Contextual Features

To further improve the effectiveness of event recommendation, particularly for cold-start events, we use the aforementioned recommenders as features for learning to rank events. In particular, let $\mathcal{D} := \{(x_1, y_1), \ldots, (x_n, y_n)\}$ be the training set where $x_i := (\hat{s}_1(u, e), \ldots, \hat{s}_m(u, e), |U_e|)$ is a feature vector containing the normalized (i.e. z-score) scores generated for a given $(u \in U, e \in E)$ pair by each of the m context-aware recommenders plus the number of RSVPs $|U_e|$ the event e has received in the past. Notice that this last feature refers to the sparsity of this event. Also let $y_i = \{0, 1\}$ denote whether user u attended event e (class 1) or not (class 0) respectively. In a learning to rank setting, the classes are not nominal but ordinal (i.e. $0 < 1$). The goal is to learn a function $h(x)$ such that for any pair of training instances (x_i, y_i) and (x_j, y_j) the following implication holds:

$$h(x_i) > h(x_j) \Leftrightarrow y_i > y_j.$$

For learning $h(x)$, we have chosen Coordinate Ascent [12], a state-of-the-art listwise learning to rank approach. Coordinate Ascent directly optimizes a target ranking evaluation metric in an iterative fashion until convergence. As detailed in Section 4, in our experiments, we use NDCG@10 as the target optimization function. Once learned, we use function $h(x)$ to generate the final recommendation list. We will refer to this method as Multi-Contextual Learning to Rank Events (MCLRE for short).

4. EVALUATION

In this section, we thoroughly assess the effectiveness of our proposed context-aware learning approach for event recommendation. In Section 4.1, we describe the setup that supports our evaluation, including the EBSN dataset, the evaluation protocol and metrics, and the recommendation baselines used in our experiments. In Section 4.2, we discuss and analyse our experimental results.

4.1 Experimental Setup

4.1.1 Event Dataset

Meetup.com is an EBSN that promotes offline and face-to-face meetings, the so called Meetups. The network is formed by a Web-based structure of groups where like-minded people can plan, create, comment, share and advertise events. After the creation of a public event, any user can RSVP to it with "yes" or "no". We used the Meetup REST API[5] to crawl all public activity in the platform from January, 2010 to April, 2014, which comprises the dataset we used to evaluate the recommenders proposed in this paper.

Three cities located in the USA were selected for this investigation, namely Phoenix, Chicago and San Jose. We selected these cities for two main reasons: (i) they are among the most populous cities in the USA, which might indicate large event activity and (ii) the cities are located in different states, thus representing some degree of cultural diversity. The data collection procedure consisted of first collecting all

---

[5]http://www.meetup.com/meetup_api/

the groups of a given city. Next, for each group, its members and events were collected. Finally, from each group member, we collected his or her event's RSVPs. Table 4.1.1 summarizes salient statistics of this dataset, in terms of the number of groups ($|G|$), users ($|U|$), events ($|E|$), and RSVPs. We also report the sparsity of the dataset, as the percentage of missing links (i.e., RSVPs) between users and events.

City	$|G|$	$|U|$	$|E|$	RSVPs	Sparsity
Chicago	2,321	207,649	190,927	1,375,154	99.996%
Phoenix	1,661	117,458	222,632	1,209,324	99.995%
San Jose	2,589	242,143	206,682	1,607,985	99.996%

Table 1: Statistics of the Meetup.com dataset.

The statistics in Table 4.1.1 emphasize the extreme sparsity of RSVPs in our dataset. In addition, Figure 4.1.1 depicts the user and event RSVP distribution per sparsity level. We show all the users (as well as events) in the test set that are associated with a specific number of "yes" RSVPs. In both cases, we see that the most frequent level of sparsity is zero, which means that most of the users and events in the test partition have no history of "yes" RSVPs. It is worth noticing that collaborative-filtering algorithms based solely on RSVP data will not work on these cases.

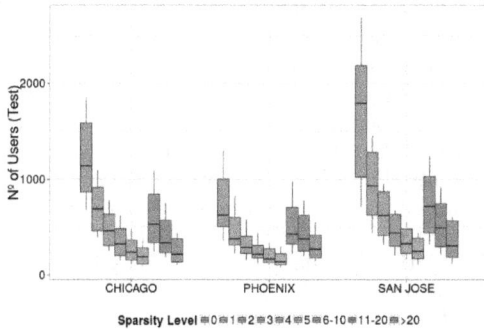

(a) Positive RSVPs per user.

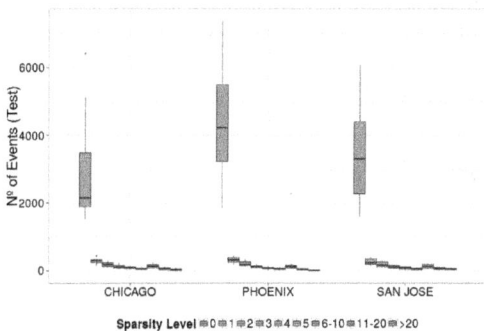

(b) Positive RSVPs per event.

Figure 3: Distribution of positive RSVPs per sparsity level for (a) users and (b) events.

4.1.2 Evaluation Protocol

In order to simulate a realistic event recommendation scenario in our evaluation, we select 12 timestamps equally spaced in time across the 52 months covered by our dataset.

By having multiple such timestamps, we can assess the effectiveness of each recommender through a sliding training window. In particular, each timestamp simulates a moment in time when an event recommendation must be generated. As illustrated in Figure 4, we consider as candidate events those created within the 6 months immediately *before* the target timestamp and that are scheduled to take place anytime *after* the timestamp. Accordingly, the RSVPs issued for a candidate event during the 6 months window preceding the target timestamp are used for training, whereas those issued after the timestamp form test instances to be recommended to the corresponding users. For each city, of the 12 train-test partitions induced by the chosen timestamps, the four initial partitions are used as validation sets for tuning the possible (hyper)parameters of the recommender models. The selected models are then tested by averaging their performance across the remaining eight partitions.

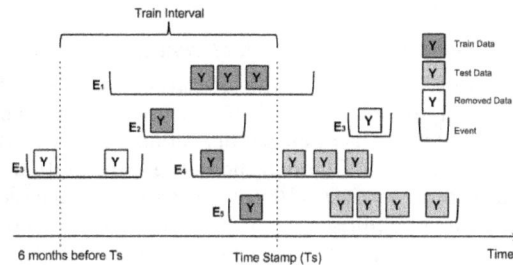

Figure 4: Example train-test partition.

Since the top-n item recommendation problem is usually related to personalized ranking (in our case, a ranked list of events to which a user is likely to RSVP "yes"), we use the well-known normalized discounted cumulative gain (NDCG) ranking evaluation metric truncated to the top 10 recommendations.

4.1.3 Recommendation Baselines

To assess the effectiveness of our MCLRE model, we compare it to the following state-of-the-art event recommenders:

- MP: A standard "most popular" baseline, which ranks events in descending order of the number of positive RSVPs that they received.

- BPR-MF: The Bayesian Personalized Ranking [17] is a state-of-the-art matrix factorization-based algorithm for top-n item recommendations.

- BPR-NET: This approach refers to the event recommender method proposed by [15]. The overall idea is to use two kinds of social networks as regularization terms of a BPR-MF model, namely, the social network based on the shared groups of users, and the social network inferred from the co-attended events.

The parameters used for all models were defined by a grid search on the validation sets. The following contextual model parameters were defined to Chicago, Phoenix and San Jose respectively: $\hat{s}_T$ (Equation (13)) considered 65, 50 and 100 neighbors; $\hat{s}_D$ (Equation (11)) used bandwidth parameters $h1$ and $h2$ set to 0.001, 0.00075, 0.00075; and the time decay factor α of $\hat{s}_C$ (Equation (7)) was set to 0.005, 0.01 and 0.005. The following models had the same parameter values for all cities: the MRBPR (Equation (5)) and BPR-MF parameters were set to $k = 300$ (number of latent factors), learn rate 0.1 (step size of gradient descent), number of iterations 1500 (stop criterion); MRBPR relation weights were defined as 0.1 to R_{UE}, 0.22 to the R_{UG} and 0.68 to R_{GE}; BPR-NET was set with $k = 200$, learn rate 0.1 and number of iterations 600.

4.2 Results and Discussion

In this section, we assess the effectiveness of our proposed MCLRE model for event recommendation. In particular, we aim to answer the following research questions:

Q1. How effective is MCLRE for event recommendation?

Q2. How robust is MCLRE to sparsity in the RSVP data?

Q3. Which contextual features are effective recommenders?

In the remainder of this section, we address each of these research questions in turn.

4.2.1 Recommendation Effectiveness

To address Q1, we assess the effectiveness of MCLRE by comparing it to three state-of-the-art event recommenders from the literature, as discussed in Section 4.1.3: MP, BPR-MF, and BPR-NET. Figure 5 shows the result of this comparison in terms of NDCG@10 for events recommended in the three cities comprised in our dataset (Chicago, Phoenix, and San Jose). In particular, the distribution of NDCG@10 figures for the test users considered in each case is represented in a boxplot, highlighting the 25th, 50th (i.e., the median), and 75th percentiles inside the box, and possible outliers outside the box.

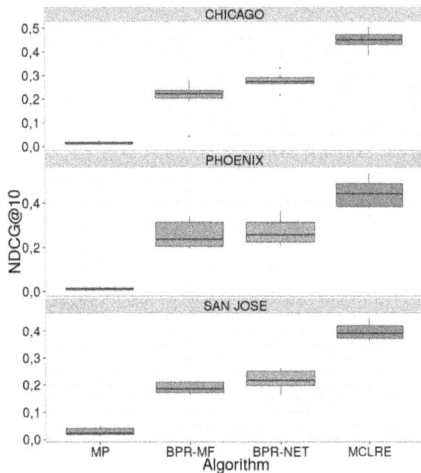

Figure 5: Event recommendation effectiveness.

From Figure 5, we first observe that MCLRE consistently outperforms all baselines in all three cities. Indeed, MCLRE improves upon the strongest baseline (BPR-NET) by 64% for Chicago, 72% for Phoenix, and 79% for San Jose in terms of the median NDCG@10. Recalling question Q1, this attests the effectiveness of our proposed model in contrast to state-of-the-art recommenders from the literature.

4.2.2 Robustness to Data Sparsity

One of the main reasons for the effective performance of our proposed model is that it is able to mitigate the cold-start problem for both users and events, which is intrinsic

to EBSNs. To further assess the robustness of our model to data sparsity and hence address question Q2, we evaluate the effectiveness of MCLRE compared to the aforementioned baselines for various user and event sparsity levels. Figure 6 shows the result of this comparison in terms of NDCG@10 for event recommendations in Phoenix.[6] Each sparsity level on the x-axis denotes the number of RSVPs available for events (resp. users) at that sparsity level.

From Figure 6, we observe that MCLRE shows a higher resilience to data sparsity for both users and events compared to the other event recommenders. Even in the extreme case, when users and events have absolutely no past RSVP (i.e., the sparsity level 0), our model is able to provide recommendations with reasonable accuracy. BPR-NET is the only approach, besides ours, that is able to recommend for cold-start users, which is explained by its ability to exploit user-user interactions in terms of the shared groups these users are affiliated to. On the other hand, MCLRE is the only method able to recommend for cold-start events, mainly due to the content, geographic, and time-aware methods used as features. Notice that both BPR-NET and BPR-MF (and in fact any other recommendation algorithm that relies on user-event interaction) are not able to recommend cold-start events. Recalling question Q2, these results attest the robustness of our approach to sparse RSVP data.

4.2.3 Contextual Feature Analysis

To address Q3, we further analyse the effectiveness of our proposed approach in terms of its constituent contextual features. In particular, Figure 7 shows the NDCG@10 performance of our proposed context-aware recommenders compared to MCLRE, which combines them for learning to rank events. From the figure, we first note that MCLRE outperforms all individual recommenders. Recalling Q3, the social context appears as the most informative signal, with the multi-relational model (Equation (5)) achieving the best result followed by the simple but efficient group frequency heuristic (Equation (3)). The content-aware recommender (Equation (7)) also achieves good results, probably due to its ability to recommend cold-start events. The least informative contexts are the geographical and temporal ones (Equations (11) and (13), respectively), which is somewhat expected since they capture less specific aspects of the user preferences for events. Notice however that they are still better than the MP baseline.

5. RELATED WORKS

In this section, we summarize the most relevant related works on event recommendation. Minkov et al. [13] proposed a hybrid approach for recommending future events. Because no direct feedback exists for such events, users' preferences for an event were inferred based upon their preference for past events with similar content. In addition, they proposed to distinguish content dimensions shared collaboratively among users from dimensions unique to individual users. In a small user study in the domain of academic events, they demonstrated the effectiveness of the proposed hybrid approach in contrast to a pure content-based recommender. Additionally to using historical data of events attendance and the content of events, we exploit other con-

---

[6]Results for Chicago and San Jose show similar trends and are omitted due to space constraints.

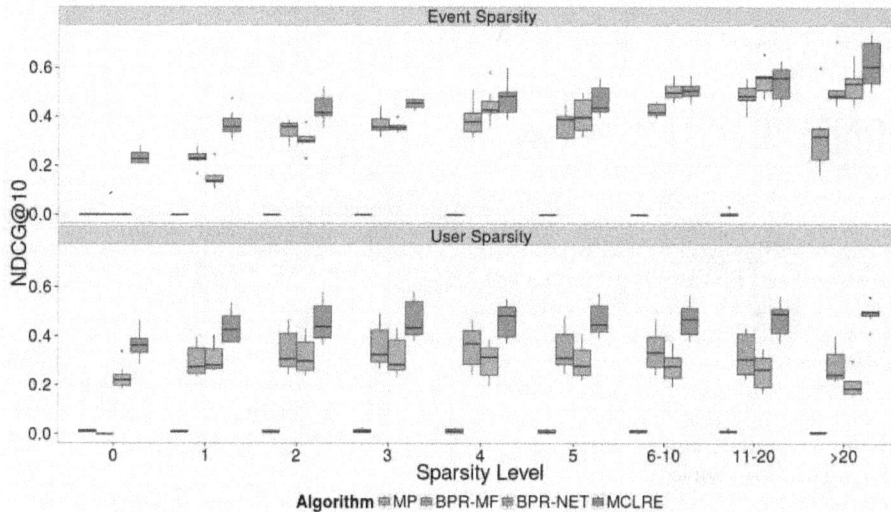

Figure 6: Recommendation effectiveness per sparsity level (Phoenix).

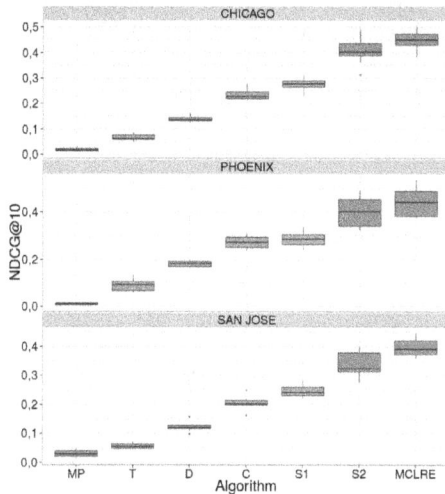

Figure 7: Per-feature recommendation effectiveness.

texts, such as the groups of users, location and temporal preferences. Moreover, we conduct a large scale experiment on data collected from a popular EBSN.

Another hybrid approach was proposed by Khrouf and Troncy [7] for recommending music-related events. In particular, their approach leveraged an enriched content-based representation of events by exploiting category information from DBPedia about the artists associated with each event. In addition, they modeled the cohesiveness of each user's content-based profile in order to avoid drifting from the user's core preferences. Lastly, this enriched content-based model was further combined with a collaborative model that exploited social interactions among users in an EBSN. Experiments on three music-oriented EBSNs demonstrated the effectiveness of the proposed extensions. Considering the multitude of domains found in general purpose EBSNs, such as Meetup.com, it may not be feasible to rely on DBPedia since many of these domains may not be covered. We do

not make this assumption and leverage only the data directly available in the EBSN under consideration.

Liu et al. [9] proposed to exploit online and offline patterns of interaction in EBSNs for recommending new events. By exploiting only the topological structure of an EBSN, they proposed different information flow models to infer a user's interest for a given event based upon the manifested interest of other EBSN users for the same event. They demonstrated that community-based diffusion models, which favor the flow of information within (as opposed to across) communities, are particularly effective signals for event recommendation. This approach was later extended by Qiao et al. [15], who proposed a Bayesian matrix factorization approach to event recommendation [16], by employing social regularization factors inspired by users' interactions in an EBSN. Zhang et al. [20] showed that the proposed model improves upon ordinary and non-regularized matrix factorization models. Our work is complementary to these, by exploiting, additionally to RSVP and group information, other contextual data. Furthermore, Zhang et al. [20] compared their approach only against matrix factorization methods, while some recent works (see [11]) have shown that pure matrix factorization (based only on user-event interactions) performs poorly on EBSN data in comparison to simpler methods due to the high level of sparsity of these data sets.

There is a large body of research on venue recommendation in location-based social networks (LBSNs) [2, 4, 5, 6, 19, 10]. LBSNs share similar properties with EBSNs, e.g., location information of users and venues. However, LBSNs do not suffer from the new item cold-start problem as EBSNs do, since venues usually do not have an expiration date.

In a previous study [11], we performed a large-scale analysis of several factors that impact a user's propensity to reply positively to future events in an EBSN. In particular, based upon two years worth of user, event, and RSVP (i.e., user-event interactions) data from three representative US cities on Meetup.com, we found that users tend to provide RSVPs close to the occurrence of the events. We also found that state-of-the-art matrix factorization algorithms for top-n recommendation did not perform better than simpler collaborative filtering algorithms such as user-based k-NN. This motivated us to try other approaches that consider explicit features instead of latent ones.

6. CONCLUSIONS AND OUTLOOK

In this paper, we tackled the event recommendation problem through a learning to rank approach that takes several context-aware recommenders as input features. Besides content-based signals based on the events' description and collaborative signals derived from RSVPs, we exploited social, geographic, and temporal signals. We used Coordinate Ascent, a state-of-the-art learning to ranking algorithm that learns a personalized ranking from the output scores of the context-aware recommenders by optimizing NDCG@10 directly. To the best of our knowledge, this is the first attempt to leverage, collectively, the aforementioned contextual signals for the event recommendation problem.

In a thorough evaluation on a large crawl of Meetup.com, we showed that our approach improves upon a state-of-the-art context-aware event recommender based on matrix factorization with social regularization by up to 79%. From our results, we can draw many interesting conclusions, such as:

- The use of multiple contexts pays off and can both lead to highly accurate recommendations and mitigate the new user and new item cold-start problem on EBSNs;

- In Meetup.com, events created by groups of which a user is a member are far more relevant than the content of the events or collaborative RSVP data.

We have several ideas to extend this work in the future. First, we will repeat the experiments with cities in different countries. Second, we will exploit other contexts and approaches to leverage these contexts. We also intend to exploit other kinds of EBSNs such as, e.g., Facebook events.

7. ACKNOWLEDGMENTS

This work is partially supported by the National Institute of Science and Technology for Software Engineering (INES), funded by CNPq and FACEPE, grants 573964/2008-4 and APQ-1037-1.03/08; and Hewlett-Packard Brasil Ltda., through the FRH-Analytics 2013 project, and used incentives from the Brazilian Informatics Law (n. 8.2.48/1991). We also want to thank Lucas Drumond for generously sharing the implementation of his MRBPR method.

8. REFERENCES

[1] G. Adomavicius and A. Tuzhilin. Context-aware recommender systems. In *Proc. of RecSys*, pages 335–336, 2008.

[2] J. Bao, Y. Zheng, and M. F. Mokbel. Location-based and preference-aware recommendation using sparse geo-social networking data. In *Proc. of SIGSPATIAL/GIS*, pages 199–208, 2012.

[3] D. M. Blei, A. Y. Ng, and M. I. Jordan. Latent dirichlet allocation. *J. Mach. Learn. Res.*, 3:993–1022, 2003.

[4] C. Cheng, H. Yang, I. King, and M. R. Lyu. Fused matrix factorization with geographical and social influence in location-based social networks. In *Proc. of AAAI*, pages 17–23, 2012.

[5] H. Gao, J. Tang, X. Hu, and H. Liu. Exploring temporal effects for location recommendation on location-based social networks. In *Proc. of RecSys*, pages 93–100, 2013.

[6] B. Hu and M. Ester. Spatial topic modeling in online social media for location recommendation. In *Proc. of RecSys*, pages 25–32, 2013.

[7] H. Khrouf and R. Troncy. Hybrid event recommendation using linked data and user diversity. In *Proc. of RecSys*, pages 185–192, 2013.

[8] A. Krohn-Grimberghe, L. Drumond, C. Freudenthaler, and L. Schmidt-Thieme. Multi-relational matrix factorization using bayesian personalized ranking for social network data. In *Proc. of WSDM*, pages 173–182, 2012.

[9] X. Liu, Q. He, Y. Tian, W.-C. Lee, J. McPherson, and J. Han. Event-based social networks: linking the online and offline social worlds. In *Proc. of SIGKDD*, pages 1032–1040, 2012.

[10] X. Liu, Y. Liu, K. Aberer, and C. Miao. Personalized point-of-interest recommendation by mining users' preference transition. In *Proc. of CIKM*, pages 733–738, 2013.

[11] A. Q. Macedo and L. B. Marinho. Event recommendation in event-based social networks. In *Proc. of Int. Work. on Social Personalization*, 2014.

[12] D. Metzler and W. Bruce Croft. Linear feature-based models for information retrieval. *Inf. Retr.*, 10(3):257–274, 2007.

[13] E. Minkov, B. Charrow, J. Ledlie, S. Teller, and T. Jaakkola. Collaborative future event recommendation. In *Proc. of CIKM*, pages 819–828, 2010.

[14] S.-T. Park and W. Chu. Pairwise preference regression for cold-start recommendation. In *Proc. of RecSys*, pages 21–28, 2009.

[15] Z. Qiao, P. Zhang, C. Zhou, Y. Cao, L. Guo, and Y. Zhang. Event recommendation in event-based social networks. In *Proc. of AAAI*, pages 3130–3131, 2014.

[16] S. Rendle, C. Freudenthaler, Z. Gantner, and L. Schmidt-Thieme. BPR: Bayesian personalized ranking from implicit feedback. In *Proc. of UAI*, pages 452–461, 2009.

[17] S. Rendle, C. Freudenthaler, Z. Gantner, and L. Schmidt-Thieme. Bpr: Bayesian personalized ranking from implicit feedback. In *Proc. of UAI*, pages 452–461, 2009.

[18] T. Sandholm and H. Ung. Real-time, location-aware collaborative filtering of web content. In *Proc. of CaRR*, pages 14–18, 2011.

[19] M. Ye, P. Yin, W.-C. Lee, and D. L. Lee. Exploiting geographical influence for collaborative point-of-interest recommendation. In *Proc. of SIGIR*, pages 325–334, 2011.

[20] W. Zhang, J. Wang, and W. Feng. Combining latent factor model with location features for event-based group recommendation. In *Proc. of SIGKDD*, pages 910–918, 2013.

It Takes Two to Tango: an Exploration of Domain Pairs for Cross-Domain Collaborative Filtering

Shaghayegh Sahebi
Intelligent Systems Program
University of Pittsburgh
Pittsburgh, PA, 15260
shs106@pitt.edu

Peter Brusilovsky
School of Information Sciences
University of Pittsburgh
Pittsburgh, PA, 15260
peterb@pitt.edu

ABSTRACT

As the heterogeneity of data sources are increasing on the web, and due to the sparsity of data in each of these data sources, cross-domain recommendation is becoming an emerging research topic in the recent years. Cross-domain collaborative filtering aims to transfer the user rating pattern from source (auxiliary) domains to a target domain for the purpose of alleviating the sparsity problem and providing better target recommendations. However, the studies so far have either focused on a limited number of domains that are assumed to be related to each other (such as books and movies), or a division of the same dataset (such as movies) into different domains based on an item characteristic (such as genre). In this paper, we study a broad set of domains and their characteristics to understand the factors that affect the success or failure of cross-domain collaborative filtering, the amount of improvement in cross-domain approaches, and the selection of best source domains for a specific target domain. We propose to use Canonical Correlation Analysis (CCA) as a significant major factor in finding the most promising source domains for a target domain, and suggest a cross-domain collaborative filtering based on CCA (CD-CCA) that proves to be successful in using the shared information between domains in the target recommendations.

1. INTRODUCTION

In the last five years, cross-domain recommendation has emerged as a hot topic in the field of recommender systems. The idea of cross-domain recommendation is to use rating information accumulated in one domain (known as a source or auxiliary domain) to improve the quality of recommendations in another domain (known as a target domain). The proponents of cross-domain recommendation argue that this technology might be especially helpful when the user has few or no ratings in the target domain or if the quality of recommendation in the target domain is low because of a lack of information. Modern users may have a solid user profile in a system that they have previously used, but may be required

RecSys'15, September 16–20, 2015, Vienna, Austria.
ⓒ 2015 ACM. ISBN 978-1-4503-3692-5/15/09 ...$15.00.
DOI: http://dx.doi.org/10.1145/2792838.2800188.

to start using a new domain or system, which would call for more research on cross-domain recommendations.

One of the important problems in cross-domain recommendation is the selection of source domains appropriate for a target domain. Previous work either assume that the best domain pairs can be decided by similarity of their nature (such as books and movies) [23, 17], or split the same dataset into multiple domains [1]. While the majority of early works have typically focused on one or two pairs of related domains (such as books and movies) and return quite positive results, which confirms the hopes of cross-domain enthusiasts [2, 17, 23], we argue that the success of cross-domain recommendations depends on domain characteristics, and specifically on shared (latent) information among domains. A recent work by Shapira et al. [19] has also delivered mixed results for cross-domain recommendations. Just as it takes two to tango, it takes two matching domains that are ready to work together (and not just a specific recommendation approach) to succeed in the context of cross-domain recommendation. This poses new questions: What makes a good auxiliary domain? How should we choose the best auxiliary domain for a specific target domain?

In this paper, we present our attempts to examine the success and failure of cross-domain collaborative filtering across a large number of domain pairs. Our goals are to broadly explore the added value of cross-domain recommendations in comparison with traditional within-domain recommendations by using two different cross-domain collaborative filtering approaches, and to achieve some progress in uncovering the main mystery of cross-domain recommendation: how can we determine whether a pair of domains is a good candidate for applying cross-domain recommendation techniques? In order to address our later goal, we pilot a canonical correlation approach as a possible predictor of successful domain pairs and examine a range of features of a single domain and domain pairs in order to see how they could be used to improve predictions.

In summary, our contribution in this paper is as follows:

- To the best of our knowledge, we present the first study that analyzes a large number of domain pairs (158) in cross-domain recommender systems.

- We propose a cross-domain recommendation approach based on Canonical Correlation Analysis (CD-CCA).

- We conduct a detailed study on both dataset characteristics and collaborative filtering approaches to find out

  - if the cross-domain recommendation results only

improve because of added information, or if the recommendation algorithm also matters;

- the data characteristics that affect the prediction error of approaches;
- the domain-pair characteristics that affect the amount of recommendation improvements;
- and the nature of suitable domain pairs.

The rest of the paper is structured as follows. In Section 2, we overview related work in the area of cross-domain recommendations. We propose a CCA-based cross-domain collaborative filtering approach in Section 3. Then, we conduct a detailed analysis of important factors in cross-domain collaborative filtering based on an extensive multi-domain dataset in Section 4. Finally, we summarize our findings and discuss future work in Section 5.

2. RELATED WORK

Although cross-domain recommendation has recently emerged, it has gained increasing attention and is a promising way to develop new methods to improve recommendations, especially in a cold-start setting [17]. Cross-domain recommender systems aim to take advantage of information among related source (auxiliary) domains to recommend items in a target domain [6]. According to [13], domains can be categorized as system, data, and temporal domains. These categories represent, respectively, different datasets that a recommender system is built upon, various representation of user preferences (explicit or implicit), and various time points in which the data is gathered.

Recent work on cross-domain recommendations has been focused on both collaborative filtering [7, 9, 10, 15, 17] and content-based approaches [2, 4, 11, 18, 21]. However, in this paper, we focus on cross-domain collaborative filtering approaches. Many cross-domain algorithms assume that the source and target domains share some of the users or items. However, in some of the cross-domain approaches, the assumption is that no shared users or items are available in the domains [3, 14]. In this paper, we assume the existence of shared users among domains.

In this paper, we propose a cross-domain collaborative filtering method, based on CCA. CCA has been used in different sources of the same domain recommenders or to find the correlation between the content (such as text or image) of the resources in cross-domain recommender systems. To the best of our knowledge, it has not yet been used in a pure, rating-based, cross-domain collaborative filtering setting. For example, in the area of recommender systems, Faridani has used CCA to predict hotel ratings from textual comments of the hotels and their sentiment analysis [5]. In [16], Ohkushi has used Kernel CCA to find the relationship between music pieces and human motion to recommend music to users. Yang et al. [24] have proposed a cross-domain feature learning algorithm that uses CCA for inferring features of semantic information in the data. However, Yang et al. have not yet used their model in recommender systems.

3. RECOMMENDATION BASED ON CCA

3.1 Regularized CCA

Canonical correlation analysis (CCA) is a multivariate statistical model that studies the interrelationships among sets of multiple dependent variables and multiple independent variables. It is the most generalized member of the family of multivariate statistical techniques [8]. It is related to factor analysis in the sense that it creates composites of variables, and is related to discriminant analysis in finding independent dimensions for each variable set. The goal of this analysis is to produce the maximum correlation between the dimensions. As a result, canonical correlation finds the optimum structure or dimensionality of each variable set that maximizes the relationship between independent and dependent variable sets. In other words, if we have $X \in \mathbb{R}^{m \times n}$ and $Y \in \mathbb{R}^{p \times n}$, CCA finds two projection vectors $w_x \in \mathbb{R}^m$ and $w_y \in \mathbb{R}^p$ that maximize the correlation coefficient:

$$\rho = \frac{w_x^T XY^T w_y}{\sqrt{(w_x^T XX^T w_x)(w_y^T YY^T w_y)}} \quad (1)$$

Since Equation 1 is not affected by re-scaling of w_x and w_y (namely, the multiplication of these vectors by a constant α does not change the value of ρ), we can maximize ρ as follows.

$$\max_{w_x, w_y} w_x^T XY^T w_y$$
$$\text{subject to } w_x^T XX^T w_x = 1, w_y^T YY^T w_y = 1 \quad (2)$$

It can be shown that solving Equation 2 is equivalent to finding the eigenvectors of top eigenvalues of the generalized eigenvalue problem in Equation 3, in which η is the eigenvalue that corresponds to the eigenvector w_x.

$$XY^T(YY^T)^{-1}YX^T w_x = \eta XX^T w_x \quad (3)$$

To compute multiple projection vectors, we can solve the optimization problem in Equation 4, in which matrix W consists of multiple projection vectors.

$$\max_{W} Trace(W^T XY^T(YY^T)^{-1}YX^T W)$$
$$\text{subject to } W^T XX^T W = I \quad (4)$$

To avoid the over-fitting of ρ and the singularity of XX^T, a term λI is added to Equation 3. We have the constraint $\lambda > 0$ in this regularization term. Eventually, the regularized CCA attempts to solve the generalized eigenvalue problem in Equation 5.

$$XY^T(YY^T)^{-1}YX^T w_x = \eta(XX^T + \lambda I)w_x \quad (5)$$

Sun et al. solve the regularized CCA problem, using a least squares formulation of it, with the Least Angle Regression algorithm [20].

3.2 CCA-based Cross-Domain Recommender

As explained in Section 3.1, CCA evaluates the latent linear correlations between two sets of variables. To draw an analogy between CCA and cross-domain recommender, we suppose that there are n common users between the source and target domains. We consider the source (auxiliary) domain in cross-domain recommender as the independent variable set X (with n users and m items), and the target domain as the dependent variable set Y (with n users and p items). Note that here we are working on $m \times n$ and $p \times n$ item-user matrices, as opposed to the usual user-item matrices in collaborative filtering. The value ρ in Equation 1 shows the maximum canonical correlation that can be achieved by rotating the X and Y spaces in direction of

w_x and w_y, respectively. In other words, CCA calculates the components of each domain, that are consisted of sets of items from each of the domains, which are most similar to each other based on user rating behavior. Also, it determines how much the two components are correlated to one another.

As a result, if we know the ratings in the source domain X and ratings in the target domain Y, we can find the w_x and w_y that maximize the canonical correlation between X and Y. In other words, with the projections vectors w_x and w_y, we know how the ratings of a combination of items in the source domain affect the ratings of an item in the target domain. Consequently, after adding the user ratings of the source domain X, we can understand how all of the ratings of a user in the source domain affect the same user's ratings in the target domain. Eventually, we can estimate the ratings of users in the target domain $\hat{Y}$ by using the projection vectors, the source domain ratings, and the canonical correlation value [22]. The calculation of estimated rating ($\hat{Y}$) is shown in Equation 6. Thus far, this approach only focuses on the first canonical component (projection vectors) that maximize the correlation (ρ or R-statistic). There are other components between the domains that can indicate different projection vectors and correlations (R-Statistics) for each pair of them. In this case of multiple projections, the estimated rating matrix $\hat{Y}$ is calculated as in Equation 7. Here, if we assume that c pairs of projection vectors are calculated, P is a diagonal $c \times c$ matrix, in which the diagonal elements are ρs for each canonical component; W_x is a $m \times c$ matrix consisted of c projection vectors of size $m \times 1$; and W_y is a $p \times c$ matrix of c projection vectors of size $p \ge 1$.

$$\hat{Y} = w_y \rho w_x^T X \qquad (6)$$

$$\hat{Y} = W_y P W_x^T X \qquad (7)$$

Eventually, if the target rating matrix ($\tilde{Y}$) is incomplete and has some missing values, we can estimate W_x and W_y ($\hat{W}_x$ and $\hat{W}_y$) by calculating the canonical correlations between the source rating matrix X and incomplete target matrix $\tilde{Y}$. Then, we can use the estimated projection vectors $\hat{w}_x$ and $\hat{w}_y$ to estimate a complete rating matrix $\hat{Y}$. More specifically, if we want to predict the unknown rating of user i on item j in the incomplete target domain ($\hat{y}_{j,i}$), we follow Equation 8 after finding $\hat{W}_x$ and $\hat{W}_y$ on matrices X and $\tilde{Y}$. Here, $X_{k,i}$ is the rating of user i on item k; $\hat{W}_{y_{j,l}}$ refers to the target projection element for the item j and component l; and $\hat{W}_{X_{k,l}}$ is the source projection element for the item k and component l.

$$\hat{y}_{j,i} = \Sigma_{l=1}^c \hat{W}_{y_{j,l}} P_{l,l} \Sigma_{k=1}^m \hat{W}_{X_{k,l}} X_{k,i} \qquad (8)$$

As an abbreviation, we use the name CD-CCA for this CCA-based cross-domain recommender.

4. ANALYSIS

In this section, we briefly describe our dataset, explain the approach of our analysis, and present our detailed analysis for each of our research questions.

4.1 Dataset

We used the Yelp Academic dataset[1] to run our experiments. The dataset contains user reviews on items from

---

[1] http://www.yelp.com/academic_dataset

Table 1: Summary of domain pair statistics

	Min	Max	Mean	Median
User Size	9	11013	1064.09	424
Item Size	8	4435	406.89	252.5
Rating Density	0.0017	0.1581	0.017	0.0084

various categories and subcategories. To obtain a better distinction between domains, we choose the 21 parent categories in the dataset. We also use the star ratings of reviews within each category. Each rating can be between 1 and 5. For each pair of categories, we find out the common users (the users who have rating reviews in both of the selected domains). To obtain more reliable results, we exclude the category pairs, within which the number of common users is smaller than the number of items in any of the two categories. For each pair of categories, we run the experiments twice: once with the first category as the source and the second category as the second domain, and once the other way around. Eventually, we end up with 158 category (domain) pairs. A summary of these data statistics is shown in Table 1.

We use a 5-fold user-stratified cross-validation on the target domain, in which 80% of the users are used in the training set and the rest is used as the test user set for each fold. We add 20% of each test user's target reviews to the training set, to obtain a partial profile for each user, and the rest of the reviews to the test set. We use 15% of the data as validation set for finding the best parameters. We use all of the source domain ratings of common users in the source training dataset for cross-domain recommendations.

4.2 Overview of Analysis

In our analysis, we aim to gain a more detailed understanding of cross-domain collaborative filtering and the factors that affect its performance. We use three algorithms: a cross-domain collaborative approach, a single-domain approach applied to the cross-domain data, and a single-domain recommendation only on the target dataset. Our dataset consists of various pairs with different data characteristics, such as number of users, items, data density, and others. The goal of our analysis is to understand the importance and scale of each of these factors on cross-domain recommendations, including the approach and dataset characteristics. Our first questions are: how do each of the algorithms perform on the data and how do they compare to each other? Are the RMSE of these approaches correlated? Is there any possibility that cross-domain recommendations harm the results that can be achieved by single-domain recommendation? Does the better performance of cross-domain algorithms occur only because of merging the two source and target datasets, or does it also depend on the ability of the cross-domain recommender to understand the common information among these datasets' ratings?

After analyzing the algorithm aspect of cross-domain collaborative filtering, we analyze its data aspect. In other words, we want to know the reason behind different results that we get for each of the approaches. The second question that we have in mind is about the data characteristics that affect the performance (RMSE) of each approach. Is there a data characteristic that significantly affects the results?

After finding the data characteristics that correlate with the results from each approach, we analyze the characteristics that affect the improvement of predictions in cross-domain collaborative filtering. Considering the domain pairs,

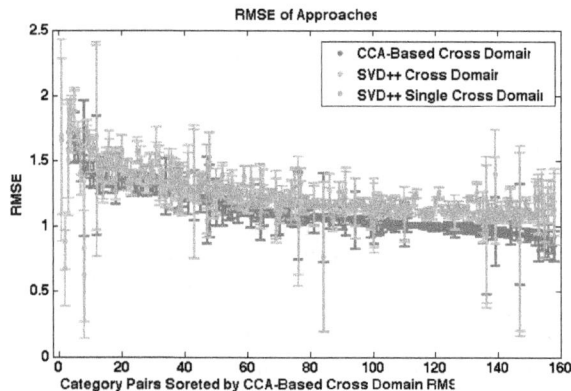

Figure 1: RMSE of algorithms on 158 domain pairs ordered by the RMSE of the CCA-based cross-domain algorithm

in which we have significantly better cross-domain recommendations, what can better explain this improvement? We examine the domain-pair characteristics in addition to the characteristics of each domain, and we study the correlation of the CCA's results with the improvement of cross-domain recommenders over the single-domain recommender.

In the final part of our analysis, we look at the specific samples of domain pairs to get a deeper understanding of the results of previous analyses. More specifically, we look at the domain pairs with a high CCA to see if they can obtain a higher improvement in cross-domain recommenders versus the single-domain recommender. We examine the domain-pairs with a high CCA and low improvement in a closer look to understand the reason behind this behavior. As a reverse look at these results, we look at the domain pairs with a high improvement ratio and their characteristics. More specifically, we look at the domain-pairs with a high improvement in cross-domain recommenders versus the single-domain recommender, and a low CCA, to understand the other factors that affect this result.

As baseline algorithms, in addition to CD-CCA, we run the SVD++ algorithm [12][2] in two single-domain and cross-domain modes. In the single domain SVD++ (SD-SVD), we only use the target domain ratings to predict the test user ratings in the target domain. For the cross-domain SVD++ (CD-SVD), we add the source domain item space to the target domain item space, as if the two categories are coming from the same (single) domain. This is done by concatenating the source and target domain rating matrices. We run the SVD++ algorithm on the joined domain matrices.

4.3 What is the Approach Effect on Recommendation Results?

We run CD-CCA, CD-SVD, and SD-SVD on the 158 domain pairs in the data. We evaluate the algorithms based on Root Mean Squared Error (RMSE). Figure 1 shows the RMSE of all three algorithms on the 158 domain pairs, including the 95% confidence interval. To better comprehend the difference between algorithms, we order the domain pairs based on RMSE of CD-CCA algorithm on them. Due to the visualization limitations, we cannot show the name of all domain pairs in the picture. However, it can be seen that in most of the domain pairs, CD-CCA has performed better than both CD-SVD and SD-SVD. Also, in most of the domain pairs, CD-SVD has performed better than SD-SVD.

---

[2]Using GraphChi Software (http://graphchi.org)

Table 2: Correlation of RMSE of algorithms with each other.
**: significant with $p - value < 0.01$

Correlation (R-Values)	CD-CCA	CD-SVD	SD-SVD
CD-CCA	–	0.7896**	0.7779**
CD-SVD	0.7896**	–	0.9550**
SD-SVD	0.7779**	0.9550**	–

CD-CCA performs significantly[3] different than SD-SVD in 77 domain pairs, and different than CD-SVD in 74 domain pairs. CD-SVD performs significantly different than SD-SVD in 9 domain pairs.

In some cases, the RMSE of cross-domain recommenders is more than the RMSE of the single-domain recommender. More specifically, the CD-CCA average RMSE is more than RMSE of SD-SVD in 8 domain pairs; the average RMSE of CD-CCA is more than the average RMSE of CD-SVD in 14 pairs; and the average RMSE of CD-SVD is more than SD-SVD in 51 domain pairs. However, these differences are not statistically significant in any of these domain pairs ($p - value < 0.05$). As a result, the cross-domain recommenders work at least as well as the single-domain recommender in our dataset. We can conclude that the CD-CCA works significantly better than the CD-SVD in 77 domain pairs; CD-CCA works significantly better than the CD-SVD in 74 domain pairs; and CD-SVD works better than SD-SVD in 9 domain pairs. In the rest of the domain pairs, CD-CCA and CD-SVD work similar to SD-SVD. As a result, we can see that cross-domain collaborative filtering approaches either improve the recommendation results, or will not significantly change them in our dataset. However, the CD-CCA method works better than CD-SVD method in many of these domain pairs. It means that there is some common information between the mentioned domain pairs that is only being captured by CD-CCA, although CD-SVD has the same information in its input data. Consequently, in addition to the improvement that we can obtain by adding the source data to the target domain, the CD-CCA approach shows an additional improvement. It means that performance of CD-CCA is not only because of the added data, but because of its ability to comprehend this additional data and use it to achieve better target recommendations.

We calculate the correlation between error rates of all algorithms in all of the domain pairs (Table 2). Based on these results, the RMSE of algorithms are highly and significantly correlated ($p - value < 0.01$). We can conclude that if the RMSE of single-domain recommender is low in the target domain, it is also most likely low for cross-domain recommenders, and vice versa.

4.4 What Data Characteristics Affect Prediction Error?

We investigate the domain characteristics to evaluate their effect on experiment results. These characteristics include user space and items space sizes in each domain, as well as domain densities. We define domain density as the ratio of known rating reviews to all possible reviews (number of items multiplied by number of users).

Figure 2 shows the RMSE results of each pair of domains, sorted based on number of items in target domain. The lines represent the least square lines of each set of data. Based on the picture it appears that by decreasing the target do-

---

[3]0.05 p-value

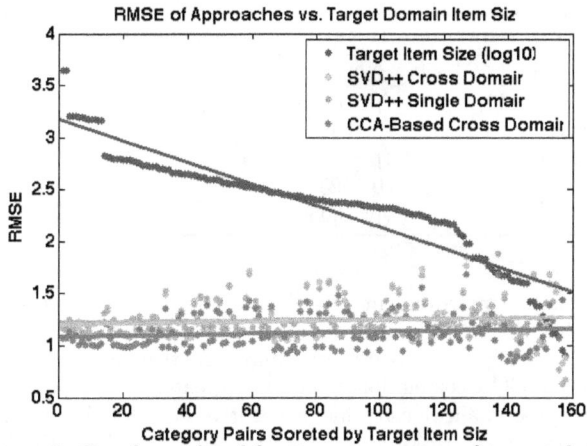

Figure 2: Results ordered by item space size of target domain

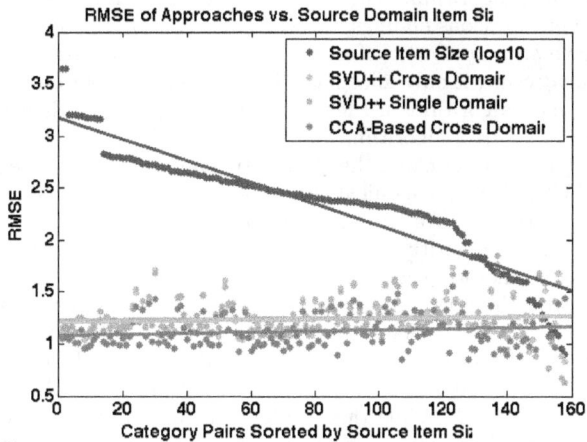

Figure 3: Results ordered by item space size of source domain

main's item space size (represented in logarithm to the base 10), the error rate increases slightly in all three algorithms. However, the correlation between size of the target domain's item size and the RMSE results is not statistically significant. In figure 3, we see the errors of each algorithm, sorted based on the item space size of the source domain. There is no significant correlation between this factor and the errors in any of the algorithms. Considering the common user size between the two domains, we sort the results based on this factor in Figure 4. Here, by increasing the number of users, we see a decrease in RMSE of both CD-CCA and CD-SVD. This correlation between RMSE of both algorithms on the 158 categories is significant, as shown in Table 3. Based on this finding, we can conclude that the more common users we have in the source and target domains, the better the cross-domain recommendations will be.

Looking at the error rates of algorithms ordered by target domain density (Figure 5), we see a slight increase of RMSE when the target domain density decreases. However, this correlation is not significant in any of the methods. The effect of source domain density on prediction error (Figure 6) is also insignificant.

Overall, we can see that the number of common users is the most significant factor among dataset characteristics in prediction error measured by RMSE. The more common users we have in the source and target domains, the better our prediction.

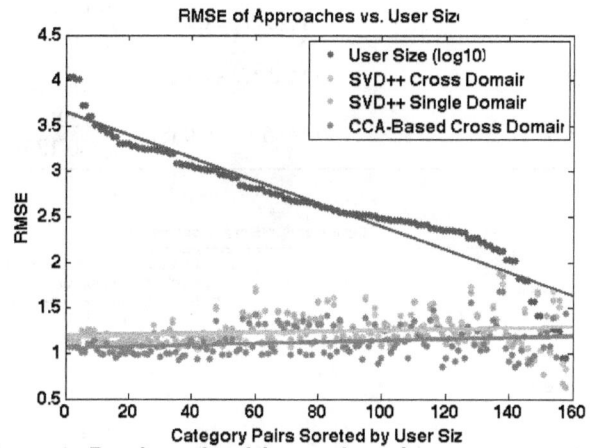

Figure 4: Results ordered by number of common users in pairs of domains

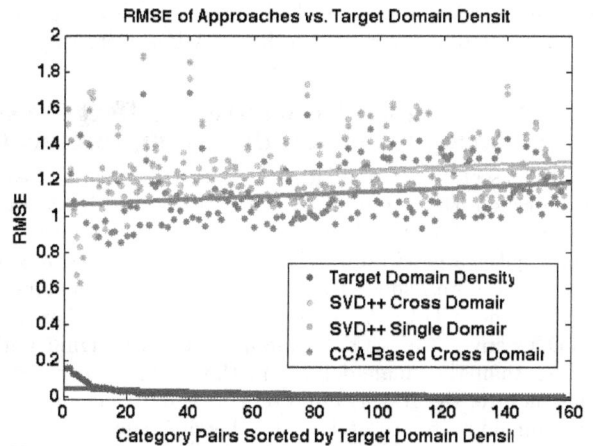

Figure 5: Results ordered by target domain's density

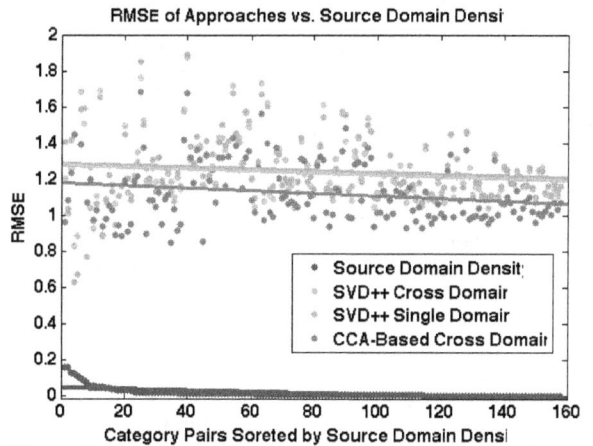

Figure 6: Results ordered by source domain's density

Table 3: Correlation of RMSE of algorithms with data characteristics. **: significant with $p - value < 0.01$, *: significant with $p - value < 0.05$

Correlation (R-Values)	User Size	Target Item Size	Source Item Size	Target Density	Source Density
CD-CCA	-0.1782*(p=0.026)	-0.1250 (p=0.121)	-0.1239 (p=0.1245)	-0.0502 (p=0.5352)	0.0515 (p=0.5246)
CD-SVD	-0.1745*(p=0.028)	-0.1445 (p=0.070)	-0.1274 (p=0.111)	-0.1346 (p=0.092)	-0.1161 (p=0.146)
SD-SVD	-0.1455 (p=0.068)	-0.1225 (p=0.125)	–	-0.1525 (p=0.056)	–

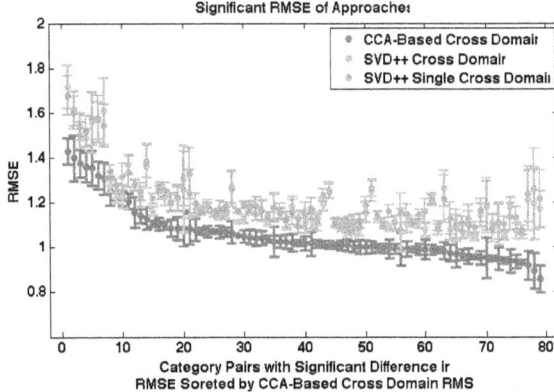

Figure 7: RMSE of algorithms on 79 significant domain pairs, ordered by the RMSE of the CCA-Based cross-domain algorithm

4.5 What Data Characteristics Affect Cross-Domain Recommendation Improvement?

In this section, we evaluate the improvement ratio of each pair of algorithms in each pair of domains and its correlation with each of the domain characteristics to understand what makes a good domain pair for a cross-domain recommender. Figure 7 shows the RMSE of all 79 domain pairs, in which either CD-CCA works significantly better than CD-SVD, or any of the cross-domain methods work significantly better than the single-domain method. As we can see in this picture, the RMSE improvement is different for different domain pairs. To understand this difference, we use the Improvement Ratio measure, which is defined as follows.

The improvement ratio of algorithm a_1 over algorithm a_2 with the source domain s_i and target domain d_j ($IR_{a_1,a_2}(s_i, d_j)$) is equivalent to the improvement of RMSE of algorithm a_1 over algorithm a_2, normalized by RMSE of algorithm a_2 in the source domain s_i and target domain d_j (Equation 9).

$$IR_{a_1,a_2}(s_i, d_j) = \frac{RMSE_{a_1}(s_i, d_j) - RMSE_{a_2}(s_i, d_j)}{RMSE_{a_2}(s_i, d_j)} \quad (9)$$

In addition to the domain characteristics that we evaluated in the previous section, we evaluate the correlation of improvement ratio with "user size to target item size ratio", "user size to source item size ratio", "source item size to target item size ratio", "source density to target density ratio", and "percentage of CCA correlation coefficients greater than 0.8, 0.9, and 0.95"[4]. The results are reported in Table 4. As we can see in these results, "user size to target item size ratio" is the only factor that has no significant correlation

---

[4]The factor "percentage of CCA correlation coefficients greater than λ" is equivalent to the number of CCA canonical components that are correlated with each other by $R - statistics > \lambda$ divided by the total number of components found by CCA.

with the improvement ratio in any of the three algorithm pairs. The two most important and significant factors in all the algorithm pairs are "source density" and "percentage of CCA correlation coefficients greater than 0.95". The source-domain density has a negative correlation with the improvement ratio: the denser the auxiliary data, the less the cross-domain algorithms perform better than the single-domain algorithm. This is an interesting finding, as based on our previous findings, the source domain density does not have any significant effect on the RMSE of each algorithm. As a result, it only affects the RMSE improvement of cross-domain algorithms if they are significantly better than the single-domain algorithm.

On the other hand, the more between-domain components of CCA have a canonical correlation of more than 0.95, the more the IR. We can see that this factor is significant in all of the algorithm pairs. However, the two other CCA-related factors ("percentage of CCA correlation coefficients greater than 0.9" and "percentage of CCA correlation coefficients greater than 0.8") are only significant for the improvement of CD-CCA versus CD-SVD and SD-SVD algorithms, and do not significantly affect the improvement of CD-SVD over SD-SVD. While this result might be due to the lower number of domain pairs (9), in which we have a significant improvement of RMSE in CD-SVD over SD-SVD, it might also be because the CD-CCA algorithm captures more relationships between the two domains that can be explained by CCA components and cannot be captured by the other two algorithms.

The next important factor presented in Table 4 is "target density". The same as "source density," this factor has a significant negative correlation with improvement factors for CD-CCA over both CD-SVD and SD-SVD. The correlation is not significant for CD-SVD over SD-SVD.

Among other factors, "target item size", "user size", and "source item size" have a positive correlation with IR for CD-CCA over both CD-SVD and SD-SVD. However, they do not have a significant correlation with IR for CD-SVD over SD-SVD. The reason might be a better performance of CD-CCA over CD-SVD (and SD-SVD) in the cases where we have more items in the target or source domain. It is interesting to see that even though "user size" is a significant factor in decreasing RMSE in both cross-domain algorithms in all domain pairs, it does not contribute to the improvement of RMSE of CD-SVD over SD-SVD, for the domain pairs in which cross-domain algorithms perform significantly better than the single-domain one.

Correlations for "user to source item ratio" and "source to target density ratio" factors are only significant for the IR of CD-CCA over CD-SVD. It means that the more users we have, as compared to source items, and the denser the source domain is, as compared to the target domain, the more improvement we can achieve by CD-CCA compared to

Table 4: Correlation of significant RMSE improvement (IR) with data characteristics. ***: significant with $p-value < 0.001$, **: significant with $p-value < 0.01$, *: significant with $p-value < 0.05$

Correlation (R-Values)	User Size	Source Item Size	Target Item Size	Source Density	Target Density	User to Target Item Ratio	User to Source Item Ratio	Percentage of CCA Correlation Co-efficients greater than 0.8	Percentage of CCA Correlation Co-efficients greater than 0.9	Percentage of CCA Correlation Co-efficients greater than 0.95	Source to Target Density Ratio	Source to Target Item Size Ratio
CD-CCA vs. CD-SVD	0.3924*** (p=0.0005)	0.3292** (p=0.0031)	0.4332*** (p<0.0001)	-0.4450*** (p<0.0001)	-0.7313*** (p<0.0001)	0.0565 (p=0.6325)	0.2805* (p=0.0155)	0.2603* (p=0.0251)	0.3563** (p=0.0018)	0.4000*** (p=0.0004)	0.2723* (p=0.0189)	-0.1711 (p=0.1450)
CD-CCA vs. SD-SVD	0.3287** (p=0.0035)	0.2825* (p=0.0128)	0.4206*** (p<0.0001)	-0.4031*** (p=0.0003)	-0.6973*** (p<0.0001)	-0.0659 (p=0.5691)	0.2207 (p=0.0537)	0.2503* (p=0.0281)	0.3633** (p=0.0012)	0.4155** (p=0.0002)	0.2096 (p=0.0673)	-0.2620* (p=0.0213)
CD-SVD vs. SD-SVD	0.3072 (p=0.4213)	0.3989 (p=0.2875)	0.916 (p=0.094)	-0.6881* (p=0.0405)	-0.2070 (p=0.5931)	0.0646 (0.8689)	-0.3506 (p=0.3549)	0.5999 (p=0.0877)	0.6579 (p=0.0541)	0.6701* (p=0.0483)	-0.4295 (p=0.2486)	0.1343 (p=0.7304)

CD-SVD. The factor "source to target item size ratio" has a negative significant correlation with IR of CD-CCA over SD-SVD. Note that the RMSE of CD-CCA is still significantly less than SD-SVD in the selected pairs of domains. However, the greater this ratio, the lesser the normalized difference of RMSEs. The reason behind this might be because the source item information dominates the target item information more and more in CD-CCA.

As we can see, the only negative significant correlations in Table 4 are source and target domain densities and ratio of source item size to target item size. Ten of all 12 factors have a significant effect on improvement ratio of CD-CCA over CD-SVD, nine of the factors are significantly correlated with improvement ratio of CD-CCA over SD-SVD, and only two of them are significantly responsible for improvement ratio of CD-SVD over SD-SVD. As mentioned before, this might be because of fewer number of domain pairs, in which the CD-SVD performs significantly better than SD-SVD.

4.6 What is the Nature of Good Domain-Pair Choices?

To have a better understanding of pairs of domains that have better prediction and higher improvement ratio, we look at some samples.

First, we look at the category pairs with a higher "percentage of CCA correlation coefficients greater than 0.8" factor to see if the domain pairs with high canonical correlation values are within the suitable cross-domain pairs. Looking at the domain pairs with higher CCA correlation (the higher ten percentile of all domain pairs), in three of these domain pairs, CD-CCA works better than both CD-SVD and SD-SVD, and CD-SVD works better than SD-SVD. It means that in these three domains, the large CCA correlation affects the improvement of cross-domain recommenders vs. the single-domain recommender, regardless of the method. However, the CD-CCA cross-domain recommender is better than the CD-SVD cross-domain recommender in capturing and using this information. These three domains are "Source: Food and Target: Arts and Entertainment", "Source: Arts and Entertainment and Target: Food", and "Source: Restaurants and Target: Food."

In some of the domain-pairs among the top ten CCA correlation percentile, only CD-CCA works better than CD-SVD and SD-SVD, and there is no significant difference between SD-SVD and CD-SVD. Some of these domains are "Source: Restaurants and Target: Nightlife" (and vice versa), "Source: Event Planning and Target: Hotels & Travel" (and vice versa), "Source: Shopping and Target: Arts & Entertainments", and "Source: Pets and Target: Nightlife". Although some of these domain pairs are inherently closer to each other (such as Restaurants and Nightlife), CD-SVD cannot express these relationships to produce better recommendations over SD-SVD. However, CD-CCA represents these relationships and their effect on the recommendation results. Notably, CD-CCA finds a correlation between some domains that do not seem very related by nature (for example, Pets and Nightlife) and can help to improve the recommendations in these domains.

However, there are some domain pairs, in which the CCA correlation is high, but we do not achieve a significant improvement of cross-domain recommendation over single-domain recommendation in them, neither in CD-CCA nor in CD-SVD. For example, "Source: Home Services and Target: Professional Services" (and vice versa) are two of these domain pairs that look naturally similar to each other. Looking into more details in these cases in the Appendix A, we can see that the "Home Services" and "Professional Services" domain densities are in the top 25 and 15 percentile of domain densities and their item sizes are in the low 15 and 20 percentile of items sizes. Also, the number of common users in the domains are in the low 15 percentile of the domain pairs. All of these characteristics work towards lowering the IR of CD-CCA and CD-SVD algorithms and the "user size" factor works towards increasing the RMSE of algorithms in general. It makes sense for the difference between the algorithms to be less significant.

Additionally, we look at the domain pairs with a high RMSE improvement ratio that do not have a very high CCA correlation factor, to understand other factors that affect IR. For example, CD-CCA has a high IR over CD-SVD and SD-SVD in the "Source: Education and Target: Local Flavor" domain pair is high (3 top percentile) while the CCA correlation factor of this domain pair is low (low 15 percentile). However, as reported in Appendix A, the source and target domains' item sizes and user sizes are low (10, 9, and 10 lower percentiles) and the source and target densities are high (13 and 8 high percentiles). Eventually, this result might not be reliable because of the small size of data. Also, we see a high IR for the "Source: Event Planning and Target: Active Life" domain pair in CD-CCA over SD-SVD with a low CCA (lower 28 percentile). In this pair, high user size (higher 28 percentile) and target item size (higher 25 percentile) ; and low source to target item size ratio (lower 29 percentile) and target and source sparsity (lower 29 and 32 percentiles) contribute to the high IR achievement. Again, we can see that low CCA correlations does not mean that we cannot have a good domain pair. Sometimes two sparse domains with more common users and high target item size, as compared to the source item size, can help to improve recommendations, even though they are not very correlated by CCA.

As a result, we can conclude that neither the natural similarity of the domains to us, nor the CCA correlation similarity, are enough to provide significant improvement of cross-domain recommenders over single domain recommenders. One should consider multiple factors together, including the

CCA correlation, source and target domains' densities, and item and user space sizes, in order to pick the best possible domain pairs.

5. CONCLUSIONS

In this paper we proposed a CCA-based cross-domain collaborative filtering (CD-CCA) method. We compared CD-CCA to an SVD++based recommender, on the joint source and target item spaces (CD-SVD++), and a single domain SVD++ recommender on the target domain (SD-SVD) on 158 domain pairs. Our results showed that, in our datasets, the cross-domain recommendations can be helpful in many of the domain pairs, and that they never harm the results, as compared to the single-domain recommender. These results indicate the ability of CD-CCA to capture the common information in the domain pairs and using them towards a better recommendation.

Additionally, we performed an extensive exploration of dataset characteristics and domain pair factors on the error results of each algorithm and error improvement of every pair of algorithms. Our experiments show that the number of common users in the domains is an important factor for the RMSE of cross-domain recommenders: the more common users in the domains, the lower the RMSE. Also, we explored the effect of canonical correlations between domains and concluded that it is a very important factor in increasing the error improvement ratio and determining suitable domain pairs. There are also other factors, such as source and target domain densities, number of common users, and number of items that affect the improvement ratio. We looked at domain pair samples in the data and their characteristics to get another viewpoint of the results and found out that although some domain pairs do not seem similar to each other by nature, they might share hidden and useful information that can be captured by CCA. We conclude that, even though CCA can be very helpful in a broad set of domains to determine the most suitable source domains for a given target domain, we should consider these other factors to achieve more reliable results.

In future work, we aim to consider more factors, such as each domain and domain pair's data distribution. Also, we plan to perform a multiple-factor analysis on these factors. This analysis can also be used to build a classifier to determine if a specific source domain can help recommendations in a specific target domain.

6. REFERENCES

[1] S. Berkovsky, T. Kuflik, and F. Ricci. Cross-domain mediation in collaborative filtering. In *Proc. 11th int'l conference on User Modeling*, UM '07, 2007.

[2] S. Berkovsky, T. Kuflik, and F. Ricci. Mediation of user models for enhanced personalization in recommender systems. *UMUAI*, 18(3), Aug. 2008.

[3] P. Cremonesi and M. Quadrana. Cross-domain recommendations without overlapping data: Myth or reality? In *Proc. 8th ACM Conference on Recommender Systems*, pages 297–300, 2014.

[4] A. Elkahky, Y. Song, and X. He. A multi-view deep learning approach for cross domain user modeling in recommendation systems. In *International World Wide Web Conference Committee (IW3C2)*, 2015.

[5] S. Faridani. Using canonical correlation analysis for generalized sentiment analysis, product recommendation and search. In *Proceedings of the fifth ACM conference on Recommender systems*, RecSys '11, New York, NY, USA, 2011. ACM.

[6] I. Fernández-Tobías, I. Cantador, M. Kaminskas, and F. Ricci. Cross-domain recommender systems: A survey of the state of the art. In *Spanish Conference on Information Retrieval*, 2012.

[7] S. Gao, H. Luo, D. Chen, S. Li, P. Gallinari, and J. Guo. Cross-domain recommendation via cluster-level latent factor model. In *Machine Learning and Knowledge Discovery in Databases*, pages 161–176. Springer, 2013.

[8] H. Hotelling. Relations Between Two Sets of Variates. *Biometrika*, 28(3/4), 1936.

[9] L. Hu, J. Cao, G. Xu, L. Cao, Z. Gu, and C. Zhu. Personalized recommendation via cross-domain triadic factorization. In *Proc. 22nd int'l conference on World Wide Web*, pages 595–606. 2013.

[10] M. Joshi, M. Dredze, W. W. Cohen, and C. P. Rosé. What's in a domain? multi-domain learning for multi-attribute data. In *Proceedings of NAACL-HLT*, pages 685–690, 2013.

[11] M. Kaminskas and F. Ricci. Location-adapted music recommendation using tags. In *UMAP*, pages 183–194. Springer, 2011.

[12] Y. Koren, R. Bell, and C. Volinsky. Matrix factorization techniques for recommender systems. *Computer*, (8):30–37, 2009.

[13] B. Li. Cross-domain collaborative filtering: A brief survey. In *Proc. 23rd IEEE Int'l Conference on Tools with Artificial Intelligence (ICTAI)*, pages 1085–1086. 2011.

[14] B. Li, Q. Yang, and X. Xue. Transfer learning for collaborative filtering via a rating-matrix generative model. In *Proc. 26th Annual International Conference on Machine Learning*, pages 617–624. ACM, 2009.

[15] B. Loni, Y. Shi, M. Larson, and A. Hanjalic. Cross-domain collaborative filtering with factorization machines. In *Advances in Information Retrieval*, pages 656–661. Springer, 2014.

[16] H. Ohkushi, T. Ogawa, and M. Haseyama. Kernel cca-based music recommendation according to human motion robust to temporal expansion. In *Proc. Int'l Symposium on Communications and Information Technologies (ISCIT)*, 2010.

[17] S. Sahebi and P. Brusilovsky. Cross-domain collaborative recommendation in a cold-start context: The impact of user profile size on the quality of recommendation. In *UMAP*, pages 289–295. Springer, 2013.

[18] S. Sahebi and T. Walker. Content-based cross-domain recommendations using segmented models. *CBRecSys 2014*, page 57, 2014.

[19] B. Shapira, L. Rokach, and S. Freilikhman. Facebook single and cross domain data for recommendation systems. *UMUAI*, 23(2-3):211–247, 2013.

[20] L. Sun, S. Ji, and J. Ye. A least squares formulation for canonical correlation analysis. In *Proceedings of the 25th international conference on Machine learning*, pages 1024–1031. ACM, 2008.

[21] S. Tan, J. Bu, X. Qin, C. Chen, and D. Cai. Cross domain recommendation based on multi-type media fusion. *Neurocomputing*, 127:124–134, 2014.

[22] D. Weenink. Canonical correlation analysis. In *Proc. Institute of Phonetic Sciences of the University of Amsterdam*, volume 25, pages 81–99, 2003.

[23] P. Winoto and T. Tang. If you like the devil wears prada the book, will you also enjoy the devil wears prada the movie? a study of cross-domain recommendations. *New Generation Computing*, 26, 2008. 10.1007/s00354-008-0041-0.

[24] X. Yang, T. Zhang, and C. Xu. Cross-domain feature learning in multimedia. *IEEE Transactions on Multimedia*, 17:64 – 78, 2015.

Recommending Fair Payments
for Large-Scale Social Ridesharing

Filippo Bistaffa,
Alessandro Farinelli
University of Verona
filippo.bistaffa@univr.it
alessandro.farinelli@univr.it

Georgios Chalkiadakis
Technical University of Crete
gehalk@intelligence.tuc.gr

Sarvapali D. Ramchurn
University of Southampton
sdr@ecs.soton.ac.uk

ABSTRACT

We perform recommendations for the Social Ridesharing scenario, in which a set of commuters, connected through a social network, arrange one-time rides at short notice. In particular, we focus on how much one should pay for taking a ride with friends. More formally, we propose the first approach that can compute fair coalitional payments that are also stable according to the game-theoretic concept of the *kernel* for systems with thousands of agents in real-world scenarios. Our tests, based on real datasets for both spatial (GeoLife) and social data (Twitter), show that our approach is significantly faster than the state-of-the-art (up to 84 times), allowing us to compute stable payments for 2000 agents in 50 minutes. We also develop a parallel version of our approach, which achieves a near-optimal speed-up in the number of processors used. Finally, our empirical analysis reveals new insights into the relationship between payments incurred by a user by virtue of its position in its social network and its role (rider or driver).

Categories and Subject Descriptors

H.4.0 [**Information Systems Applications**]: General; I.2.11 [**Distributed Artificial Intelligence**]: Intelligent Agents, Multiagent Systems

General Terms

Algorithms

Keywords

Algorithm Scalability; Innovative Applications; Coalition Formation; Social Networks; Ridesharing

1. INTRODUCTION

Real-time ridesharing, in which people arrange one-time rides at short notice, is rapidly changing the way people commute for their daily activities. Online services such as *Uber* or *Lyft*

RecSys'15, September 16–20, 2015, Vienna, Austria.
© 2015 ACM. ISBN 978-1-4503-3692-5/15/09 ...$15.00.
DOI: http://dx.doi.org/10.1145/2792838.2800177.

compete with standard transportation systems (such as taxis or public transport), allowing users to quickly share their positions and arrange rides with other people they know or trust. A clear tendency in such services is to embed a social network in their framework, favouring the formation of groups of users that are connected in such network. In fact, Uber[1] and Lyft[2] incentivise users to share rides with their friends, showing that social relationships play a fundamental role in the ridesharing scenario, which is consequently referred as *Social Ridesharing* (SR). Several works [20, 21] have focused on building recommendation mechanisms in the book-a-taxi domain, while recent research has shown that recommendation accuracy can be greatly improved by incorporating trust and geo-spatial information embedded in social networks that also encompass geographical data [14, 19]. However, recommendation systems research has never focused on the SR problem, as we do in this paper.

In more detail, the SR problem is, by and large, a *Coalition Formation* (CF) problem [13], requiring that the set of rides is partitioned in disjoint groups (i.e., *coalitions*) that minimise the overall transportation costs for the entire system. In addition, such a division must be computed assessing the constraints imposed by the social network (naturally modelled as a graph), in order to ensure that passengers are connected by *friends-of-friends* relationships. The most successful approach that tackles the SR problem from a real-world perspective is proposed by Bistaffa et al. [3], which define it as a *Graph-Constrained Coalition Formation* (GCCF) problem, and also provide a solution that scales to thousands of agents. That work, however, remains silent about the problem of distributing the travel expenses of each car among its passengers. Such a task, namely the *payoff distribution* task [15], represents a key challenge in the CF process and it is of utmost importance when offering ridesharing services, especially when considering commuters with rational behaviours. In fact, payoffs (corresponding to cash payments for sharing trip costs) to the commuters need to be computed given their distinct needs (e.g., shorter/longer trips), roles (e.g., drivers/riders, less/more socially connected) and opportunity costs (e.g., taking a bus, their car, or a taxi).

One key aspect of payment distribution in CF is the game-theoretic concept of *stability*, which measures how agents are keen to maintain the provided payments instead of deviating to a configuration deemed to be more rewarding from their individual point of view. Here, we induce stable payments in the context of the SR problem, employing *the kernel* [6]

---

[1]http://blog.uber.com/2013/07/15/faresplit.
[2]http://www.lyft.com/help/article/1637045.

stability concept. Kernel-stable payoffs are perceived as fair, since they ensure that agents do not feel compelled to claim part of their partners payoff (cf. Section 2 below). Kernel stability has been widely studied in cooperative game theory, and certain approaches have been proposed to compute kernel-stable payments [10, 16]. Specifically, Shehory and Kraus [16] adopt a transfer scheme that represents the state-of-the-art approach to compute kernel-stable payments. Despite having polynomial time complexity under certain assumptions, such an approach has some drawbacks that hinder its applicability in real-world scenarios, and especially in the SR one. First, it is designed for classic CF, failing to exploit the graph-constrained nature of this problem. Second, this algorithm assumes that coalitional values can be assessed at no computational cost (e.g., stored in memory or provided by an oracle). This hypothesis does not apply to SR, in which the value of a coalition is the solution of a routing problem and it cannot be stored in memory without limiting the scalability. These shortcomings lead to inefficiencies that prevent the application of the method proposed by Shehory and Kraus [16] in our case. Moreover, neither Klusch and Shehory [10] nor Shehory and Kraus [16] provide parallel solution algorithms, failing to take advantage of modern multi-core hardware. Finally, these papers have never been tested in realistic large-scale environments.

Against this background, we propose Paying for Rides with Friends (PRF), the first approach to compute kernel-stable payments for SR. In particular, we address the shortcomings of the state-of-the-art algorithm in real-world scenarios, we design a solution that scales up to systems of thousands of agents, and we also provide an efficient parallel version. PRF allows us to provide the first recommendation system for SR scenarios, as it can be used in conjunction with Bistaffa et al.'s approach to provide recommendations for the optimal groups to form, and also to define fair, stable payments that commuters should make as a compensation for their rides.

In more detail, this paper advances the state-of-the-art in the following ways: i) we present the first approach able to compute kernel-stable payments for systems with thousands of agents, ii) we benchmark our approach on real data (i.e., GeoLife from Microsoft Research for the geospatial data and Twitter for social networks), showing that our method computes payments for 2000 agents in less than an hour and it is 84 times faster than the state-of-the-art in the best case, iii) we develop new insights into the relationship between payments incurred by a user by virtue of its position in its social network and its role (rider or driver), and iv) we provide a parallel version of our method, providing a practical solution technique for large-scale systems thanks to a speed-up of 10.6 on a 12-core machine w.r.t. the serial approach.

2. BACKGROUND

In the following sections we provide the necessary background on Social Ridesharing and on the kernel, i.e., the stability concept we use to compute agents' payments.

2.1 The Social Ridesharing Problem

The *Social Ridesharing* (SR) problem [3] considers a set of n agents (or *commuters*) $\mathcal{A} = \{a_1, \ldots, a_n\}$ connected through a social network G, which arrange one-time rides at short notice in order to minimise the travel cost of the overall system. In the SR scenario, each commuter (which has a desired starting and destination point in the geographic map) can share a ride in one of the cars provided by the set of drivers $\mathcal{D} \subseteq \mathcal{A}$. We assume that each car has k seats, hence the maximum size of each group is at most k. To be part of a solution, each group of commuters must constitute a *feasible* coalition, i.e., it must satisfy the following constraints:

Constraint 1. *Its members must induce a $\hat{k}$-subgraph of G, where a $\hat{k}$-subgraph denotes a connected subgraph with at most k nodes.*

Constraint 2. *It must contain at least one driver.*[3]

The set of all feasible coalitions is referred as $\mathcal{FC}(G)$. Bistaffa et al. [3] tackle the SR problem casting it as a GCCF problem, in which each car represents a feasible coalition $C \in \mathcal{FC}(G)$, whose coalitional value $v(C)$, quantifying the total transportation cost for the group represented by C, is:

$$v(C) = \begin{cases} t(P_C) + c(P_C) + f(P_C), & \text{if } C \cap \mathcal{D} \neq \emptyset \\ \kappa(C), & \text{otherwise.} \end{cases}$$

where P_C is the optimal path for C, $t(\cdot)$, $c(\cdot)$ and $f(\cdot)$ are negative functions representing time, cognitive (i.e., the fatigue incurred by the driver during the trip) and fuel costs of driving through the path. The computation of $v(C)$ (and of P_C in particular) requires solving a routing problem. In general, this is a hard problem [12], which can be solved in this setting thanks to the limited[4] number of points in each path. Bistaffa et al. [3] only solve the optimisation problem of the SR scenario, which involves computing the optimal feasible *coalition structure* CS^* (i.e., a partition of $\mathcal{A}$ into disjoint feasible coalitions) that maximises the social welfare:

$$CS^* = \underset{CS \in \mathcal{CS}(G)}{\arg\max} \sum_{C \in CS} v(C),$$

where $\mathcal{CS}(G)$ refers to the set of all the feasible coalition structures. Such a problem is solved using a modified version of the state-of-the-art algorithm for the GCCF problem[5] (i.e., the CFSS algorithm [2]), providing optimal and approximate solutions with good quality guarantees.

Bistaffa et al.'s approach can be used to provide recommendations about the optimal groups to arrange from a joint cost perspective. However, such an approach does not address the payment computation problem for SR, as we do in this paper. In this context, a number of works have focused on computing incentives for ridesharing using mechanism design [8, 9] in order to promote *truthfulness* in the commuters. Nonetheless, in addition to such property, they do not address the stability of payments, which is crucial in selfish settings like ridesharing, but it has never been studied before. In addition, these works do not consider the role of the social network. Against this background, we introduce our payoff distribution scheme for SR, detailing the game-theoretic stability concept we employ, i.e., the kernel.

---

[3] Agents without a car can be in a singleton, which is considered a feasible coalition. If the total number of available seats is less than the total number of commuters in the system, an agent a_i might need to resort to public transport paying a cost $\kappa(\{a_i\})$ for the ticket.

[4] The points are at most $2 \cdot k$ (i.e., a starting and a destination point for each commuter). As an example, for $k=5$ only 2520 paths must be considered to compute the optimal one [3].

[5] Notice that, following the recent literature on optimisation in ridesharing [8], Bistaffa et al. maintain the assumption that all the request by the agents arrive at the same time, hence the solution can be computed offline in a static system.

2.2 The Kernel

Formally, the *payment computation* problem involves the computation of a *payoff allocation vector* x, which specifies a payoff x_i for each agent $a_i \in \mathcal{A}$ as a compensation of their contributions [15, 5]. As introduced above, computing payments that are *stable* (i.e., they incentivise agents to maintain the provided configuration) and *individually rational* (i.e., they guarantee that each agent receives at least the value of its singleton coalition) is of utmost importance in systems with selfish rational agents. As such, payoffs have to be distributed among agents to ensure that members get rewarded according to their bargaining power [5].

A number of recent papers have examined the computational complexity of reaching stable solutions in graph-restricted coalition formation scenarios [4, 7]. Nevertheless, these papers focus on the stability concept of *the core*, which denotes the set of payoff configurations that provide no incentives to players to deviate from the solution coalition structures. Unfortunately, the core might be empty, and its complexity makes it next to impossible to compute in real-world scenarios involving thousands of agents.

In this paper, we focus on *the kernel*, a stability concept introduced by Davis and Maschler [6] that is always non-empty and can be approximated in polynomial time when the size of coalitions is limited. The kernel provides stability within a given coalition structure, and under a given payoff allocation, by defining how payoffs should be distributed so that agents cannot *outweigh* (cf. below) their current partners. In order to define the kernel, we first define the *excess* of a coalition C as $e(C, x) = v(C) - x(C)$, where $x(C)$ refers to the sum of the payments of the members of C, i.e., $x(C) = \sum_{a_i \in C} x_i$. In the kernel, a positive excess is interpreted as a measure of threat: in the current payoff distribution, if some agents deviate by forming coalition with positive excess, they are able to increase their payoff by redistributing the coalitional excess among themselves. In more detail, the *surplus* s_{ij} of agent a_i over agent a_j with respect to a given payoff configuration x, is defined by $s_{ij} = \max_{C \in 2^{\mathcal{A}} | a_i \in C, a_j \notin C} e(C, x)$, where $2^{\mathcal{A}}$ denotes the powerset of $\mathcal{A}$. In other words, s_{ij} is the maximum of the excesses of all coalitions C that include a_i and exclude a_j, with C not in the current coalition structure (since under the current coalition structure agents a_i and a_j belong in the same coalition). We say that agent a_i outweighs agent a_j if $s_{ij} > s_{ji}$. When this is the case, a_i can claim part of a_j's payoff by threatening to walk away (or to expel a_j) from their coalition. When any two agents in a coalition cannot outweigh one another, the payoff vector lies *in the kernel* – i.e., it is stable. Importantly, the set of kernel-stable payoff vectors is always non-empty. Stearns [17] provides a *payoff transfer scheme* which converges to a vector in the kernel by means of payoff transfers from agents with less bargaining power to their more powerful partners, until the latter cannot claim more payoff from the former. Unfortunately, this may require an infinite number of steps to terminate. To alleviate this issue, the ϵ-kernel [10] has been introduced, in order to represent an allocation whose payoffs do not differ from an element in the kernel by more than ϵ. Note that an ϵ-kernel-stable payoff allocation can be computed in $O(n)$ iterations.[6]

---

[6]The number of iterations is also affected by ϵ. A more detailed discussion is provided by Shehory and Kraus [16].

2.3 Computing Payments in the ϵ-Kernel

The current state-of-the-art approach to compute an ϵ-kernel payoff allocation for classic CF is presented in Algorithm 1 [16]. Such an algorithm does not specify how x should be initialised, and assumes that a payoff vector is provided as an input. The first (and most expensive) phase is the computation of the *surplus matrix* s (lines 2–5), which iterates over the entire set of coalitions to assess the maximum excess (line 5) for each pair of agents in each coalition. Once the surplus matrix has been computed, a transfer between the pair of agents with the highest excess difference (i.e., $s_{ij} - s_{ji}$) is set up, while ensuring that each payment is individually rational. On the one hand, the maximisation at line 5 is a key bottleneck for classic CF, since it involves enumerating an exponential number of coalitions, i.e., $O(2^n)$. On the other hand, when the size of the coalitions is limited to k members as in our scenario, (denoted as k-CF in the remainder of the paper), such an algorithm has polynomial time complexity, since the coalitions are $O(n^k)$.

Algorithm 1 SHEHORYKRAUSKERNEL(x, CS, ϵ)

1: **repeat**
2:   **for all** $C \in CS$ **do**
3:     **for all** $a_i \in C$ **do**
4:       **for all** $a_j \in C - \{a_i\}$ **do**
5:         $s_{ij} \leftarrow \max_{R \in \mathcal{P}(\mathcal{A}) | a_i \in R, a_j \notin R} e(R, x)$
6:     {a_{i*} and a_{j*} have the maximum surplus difference δ}
7:     $\delta \leftarrow \max_{(a_i, a_j) \in \mathcal{A}^2} (s_{ij} - s_{ji})$
8:     $(a_{i*}, a_{j*}) \leftarrow \arg\max_{(a_i, a_j) \in \mathcal{A}^2} (s_{ij} - s_{ji})$
9:     {Ensure that payments are individually rational}
10:   **if** $x_{j*} - v(\{a_{j*}\}) < \delta/2$ **then**
11:     $d \leftarrow x_{j*} - v(\{a_{j*}\})$
12:   **else**
13:     $d \leftarrow \delta/2$
14:   $x_{j*} \leftarrow x_{j*} - d$ {Transfer payment from a_{j*}...}
15:   $x_{i*} \leftarrow x_{i*} + d$ {... to a_{i*}}
16: **until** $\delta/v(CS) \leq \epsilon$

Next, we discuss how this approach could be used to compute an ϵ-kernel payoff allocation for the SR problem.

3. COMPUTING PAYMENTS FOR SR

Algorithm 1 has been designed to compute payments for CF scenarios in which the set of coalition is *not* restricted by a graph. Such an approach can be readily applied also when the size of coalitions is limited to k members, in which the maximisation at line 5 has to be assessed among the coalitions of size up to k which include a_i but exclude a_j. This set, denoted as $\mathcal{R}$, can be easily obtained as $\mathcal{R} = \{\{a_i\} \cup R \mid R$ is a h-combination of $\mathcal{A} - \{a_i, a_j\}, \forall h \in \{1, \ldots, k-1\}\}$.

On the other hand, in GCCF scenarios like SR this simple approach would iterate over several unfeasible coalitions (i.e., which do not induce a connected subgraph of the social network), leading to inefficiency and reducing the scalability of the entire algorithm. In contrast, a better way to tackle this problem is to exploit the structure of the graph in order to consider *only* the coalitions that are indeed feasible, so to avoid any unnecessary computation.

a_i	a_j	Coalitions
a_1	a_2	$\{a_1\}$ $\{a_1,a_3\}$ $\{a_1,a_4\}$ $\{a_1,a_3,a_4\}$
a_1	a_3	$\{a_1\}$ $\{a_1,a_2\}$ $\{a_1,a_4\}$ $\{a_1,a_2,a_4\}$
a_1	a_4	$\{a_1\}$ $\{a_1,a_2\}$ $\{a_1,a_3\}$ $\{a_1,a_2,a_3\}$
a_2	a_1	$\{a_2\}$
a_2	a_3	$\{a_2\}$ $\{a_1,a_2\}$ $\{a_1,a_2,a_4\}$
a_2	a_4	$\{a_2\}$ $\{a_1,a_2\}$ $\{a_1,a_2,a_3\}$
a_3	a_1	$\{a_3\}$
a_3	a_2	$\{a_3\}$ $\{a_1,a_3\}$ $\{a_1,a_3,a_4\}$
a_3	a_4	$\{a_3\}$ $\{a_1,a_3\}$ $\{a_1,a_2,a_3\}$
a_4	a_1	$\{a_4\}$
a_4	a_2	$\{a_4\}$ $\{a_1,a_4\}$ $\{a_1,a_3,a_4\}$
a_4	a_3	$\{a_4\}$ $\{a_1,a_4\}$ $\{a_1,a_2,a_4\}$

Table 1: Coalitions considered at each iteration.

Moreover, Algorithm 1 considers many coalitions more than once at the maximisation in the loop at lines 2–5. We provide the following example to clarify why this redundancy exists. Consider the set of agent $\mathcal{A}=\mathcal{D}=\{a_1,a_2,a_3,a_4\}$ and a graph G that induces a set of feasible coalitions $\mathcal{FC}(G) = \{\{a_1\}, \{a_2\}, \{a_3\}, \{a_4\}, \{a_1,a_2\}, \{a_1,a_3\}, \{a_1,a_4\}, \{a_1,a_2, a_3\}, \{a_1,a_2,a_4\}, \{a_1,a_3,a_4\}, \{a_1,a_2,a_3,a_4\}\}$, and assume a coalition structure $CS = \{\{a_1,a_2,a_3,a_4\}\}$. In this case, such a loop requires 12 iterations, each looking at the coalitions reported in Table 1. Note that 23 (marked in bold) out of 33 coalitions (i.e., 70%) are evaluated more than once. This fact can substantially reduce the efficiency and the scalability of the computation of the surplus matrix in SR scenarios, where the computation cost required to assess coalitional values is not negligible and caching is not an option. In fact, storing all these values in memory is not affordable even for systems with hundreds of agents: since the number of feasible coalitions is $O(n^k)$, for $k = 5$ and $n = 100$, storing all coalitional values requires tens of GB of memory. Thus, each coalitional value must be computed only when needed, since computing them more than once significantly reduces efficiency and scalability, as shown in Section 4.1.

To overcome these issues, in the next section we present the PRF algorithm, an improved technique to calculate the surplus matrices in the SR scenario, allowing our payment scheme to scale up to systems with thousands of agents.

3.1 The PRF algorithm

We now present the PRF (Paying for Rides with Friends) algorithm, our method to compute an ϵ-kernel payoff allocation, given a coalition structure CS that is a solution to the SR problem. Our contribution improves on the k-CF version of Algorithm 1 by adopting a novel approach to calculate the surplus matrix s. Instead of computing each value s_{ij} using the maximisation at line 5 for each pair of agents in each $C \in CS$, we iterate over the set of $\hat{k}$-subgraphs of G (i.e., those satisfying Constraint 1 of the SR problem). Then, we update the appropriate values of the surplus matrix for each coalition with at least one driver (i.e., satisfying Constraint 1). By so doing, we ensure the exact coverage of the entire set of feasible coalitions $\mathcal{FC}(G)$, as ensured by Proposition 2.

PRF is detailed in Algorithm 2. After having initialised the payoff vector x by equally splitting each coalitional value among the members of the coalition, COMPUTEMATRIX computes the surplus matrix in each iteration of the main loop. In such a routine, UPDATEMAX is executed for each coalition that induces a $\hat{k}$-subgraph of G. These coalitions are computed with the SlyCE algorithm [18], which can list all the

---

Algorithm 2 PRF(CS, ϵ)

1: **for all** $C \in CS$ **do**
2:      **for all** $a_i \in C$ **do**
3:          $x_i \leftarrow {v(C)}/{|C|}$ {Equally split coalitional value}
4: **repeat**
5:      {Compute surplus matrix}
6:      $s \leftarrow$ COMPUTEMATRIX (CS, x)
7:      {a_{i*} and a_{j*} have the maximum surplus difference δ}
8:      $\delta \leftarrow \max_{(a_i,a_j)\in\mathcal{A}^2}(s_{ij} - s_{ji})$
9:      $(a_{i*}, a_{j*}) \leftarrow \arg\max_{(a_i,a_j)\in\mathcal{A}^2}(s_{ij} - s_{ji})$
10:      {Ensure that payments are individually rational}
11:      **if** $x_{j*} - v(\{a_{j*}\}) < {\delta}/{2}$ **then**
12:          $d \leftarrow x_{j*} - v(\{a_{j*}\})$
13:      **else**
14:          $d \leftarrow {\delta}/{2}$
15:      $x_{j*} \leftarrow x_{j*} - d$ {Transfer payment from a_{j*}....}
16:      $x_{i*} \leftarrow x_{i*} + d$ {... to a_{i*}}
17: **until** ${\delta}/{v(CS)} \leq \epsilon$

---

subgraphs of a given graph without redundancy (i.e., each subgraph is computed only once).

Algorithm 3 COMPUTEMATRIX(CS, x)

1: $s \leftarrow -\infty$ {Initialise the entire matrix with $-\infty$}
2: **for all** C that induce a $\hat{k}$-subgraph of G **do**
3:      $s \leftarrow$ UPDATEMAX (C, CS, s, x)
4: **return** s

Algorithm 4 UPDATEMAX(C, CS, s, x)

1: **if** $|C| = 1 \vee C \cap \mathcal{D} \neq \emptyset$ **then** {Constraint 2 of SR problem}
2:      $e_C \leftarrow e(C, x)$ {Compute the excess of coalition C}
3:      **for all** $a_i \in C$ **do** {For each agent a_i in coalition C}
4:          $C' \leftarrow$ the coalition in CS that contains a_i
5:          **for all** $a_j \in C' - C$ **do** {For each $a_j \in C'$ but $\notin C$}
6:              {s_{ij} is updated with the maximum between}
7:              {its old value and the excess of coalition C}
8:              $s_{ij} \leftarrow \max(s_{ij}, e_C)$
9: **return** s

UPDATEMAX only considers the coalitions that satisfy Constraint 2 of the SR problem (line 1), i.e., singletons or coalitions that contain at least one driver. For every coalition C that satisfies this property, lines 3–8 update all the values s_{ij} for which a_i is a member of C and a_j is part of C' (i.e., the coalition in CS that contains a_i) but is not part of C. The correctness of our approach is ensured by Proposition 1.

Proposition 1. *Algorithm 3 computes each s_{ij} correctly.*

Proof. Once the loop has ended, each s_{ij} stores the maximum excess among *all* feasible coalitions with a_i but without a_j, with both a_i and a_j part of the same coalition in CS. This matches line 5 of Algorithm 1. □

Moreover, our surplus matrix-calculating method has polynomial time complexity, while allowing to compute all feasible coalitions only once, as shown by Proposition 2.

Proposition 2. *Algorithm 3 lists all feasible coalitions only once and it has a worst-case time complexity of $O(n^k)$.*

Proof. Algorithm 3 lists all $\hat{k}$-subgraph of G exactly once [18]. Note that the number of $\hat{k}$-subgraphs is $O\left(n^k\right)$, since we only consider coalitions with up to k members [16]. Hence, Algorithm 3 makes at most $O\left(n^k\right)$ calls to UPDATEMAX. Finally, note that the time complexity of UPDATEMAX is constant w.r.t. n, since computing $e\left(C, x\right)$ requires the computation of $v\left(C\right)$ (which has constant time complexity [3]), and the loop at lines 3–8 requires $O\left(k^2\right)$ iterations. Moreover, UPDATEMAX only considers coalitions that satisfy Constraint 2 and it computes each coalitional value only once at line 2. Thus, Algorithm 3 computes all feasible coalitions only once and its worst-case time complexity is $O\left(n^k\right)$. □

Proposition 3. *Algorithm 2 has a polynomial worst-case time complexity w.r.t. n, i.e., $O\left(-\log_2\left(\epsilon\right) \cdot n^{k+1}\right)$.*

Proof. All the equations and lemmas referred in the following proof are provided by Stearns [17]. Each iteration of Algorithm 2 identifies the agents a_i and a_j with the maximum surplus difference $\delta = s_{ij} - s_{ij}$, performing a transfer of size d from a_j to a_i. Thus, by Lemma 1, in the following iteration these surpluses will be $s'_{ij} = s_{ij} - d$ and $s'_{ji} = s_{ji} + d$. Notice that $s'_{ij} - s'_{ji} = s_{ij} - s_{ji} - 2 \cdot d = \delta - 2 \cdot d$. Now, by definition of d (lines 11–14 of Algorithm 2), $d \leq \delta/2$, hence $s'_{ij} - s'_{ji} \geq 0$. Therefore, we can affirm that the transfer from a_j to a_i is indeed a *K-transfer*, since it satisfies Equation 4, 5, 6 and 7. Lemma 2 ensures the convergence of Algorithm 2, by affirming that a K-transfer *cannot* increase the larger surpluses in the system. Specifically, in the next iteration the difference between the surpluses between a_j to a_i will be half of what was in the previous one. After λ iterations, its value will be $\frac{1}{2^\lambda}$ of the original one. Thus, it will take approximately $\lambda = \log_2\left(\left[\delta_0/v(CS)\right]/\epsilon\right)$ iterations to ensure that $\left[\delta_0/v(CS)\right]/2^\lambda \leq \epsilon$, with δ_0 being the original maximum s_{ij} surplus. Since we have n agents into the setting, it will take approximately $\lambda \cdot n = O\left(-\log_2\left(\epsilon\right) \cdot n\right)$ iterations to convergence. Then, we know by Proposition 2 that COMPUTEMATRIX, which dominates the time complexity of each iteration, has a worst-case time complexity of $O\left(n^k\right)$. Given this, Algorithm 2 has a worst-case time complexity of $O\left(-\log_2\left(\epsilon\right) \cdot n^{k+1}\right)$. □

Given this, PRF provides a polynomial method to compute kernel-stable payments. Nonetheless, the $O\left(n^k\right)$ operations required for surplus matrix calculation may not be affordable in real-world scenarios with thousands of agents and $k = 5$, i.e., the number of seats of an average sized car. Hence, we next propose a parallel version of PRF, which allows us to distribute the computational burden among different threads, taking advantage of modern multi-core hardware.

3.2 P-PRF

We now detail P-PRF, the parallel version of our approach, in which the most computation-intensive task, i.e., the computation of s, is distributed among T available threads. In particular, Algorithm 5 details our parallel version of the COMPUTEMATRIX routine, obtained by having each thread t to compute a separate matrix s^t. Such a matrix is constructed considering the coalitions in $\mathcal{DIV}\left(G, t, k\right)$, i.e., the tth fraction of the set of all $\hat{k}$-subgraphs of G, computed using the D-SlyCE algorithm [18]. Specifically, this fraction is

obtained by splitting the first generation of children nodes in the search tree generated by the SlyCE algorithm [18] among the available threads, allowing a fair division of the set of the $\hat{k}$-subgraphs while ensuring that all feasible coalitions are computed exactly once (a more detailed discussion is provided by Voice et al. [18]). As such, it also distributes the computation of the coalitional values.

Algorithm 5 P-COMPUTEMATRIX(CS, x, T)

1: $s \leftarrow -\infty$ {Initialise all matrices with $-\infty$}
2: **for all** $t \in \{1, \ldots, T\}$ **do in parallel**
3:     **for all** $C \in \mathcal{DIV}\left(G, t, k\right)$ **do**
4:         $s^t \leftarrow$ UPDATEMAX $\left(C, CS, s^t, x\right)$
5: **for all** $i \in \{1, \ldots, n\}$ **do in parallel**
6:     **for all** $j \in \{1, \ldots, n\}$ **do in parallel**
7:         $s_{ij} \leftarrow \max_{t \in \{1, \ldots, T\}} s^t_{ij}$
8: **return** s

We provide the following example to clarify how this division is realised. Consider the same $\mathcal{FC}\left(G\right)$ of the example in Section 3, and assume $T = 4$. Then, the necessary coalitions are distributed by doing the following partitioning:

1. $\mathcal{DIV}\left(G, 1, k\right) = \{\{a_1\}, \{a_2\}, \{a_3\}\}$

2. $\mathcal{DIV}\left(G, 2, k\right) = \{\{a_4\}, \{a_1, a_2\}, \{a_1, a_3\}\}$

3. $\mathcal{DIV}\left(G, 3, k\right) = \{\{a_1, a_4\}, \{a_1, a_2, a_3\}\}$

4. $\mathcal{DIV}\left(G, 4, k\right) = \{\{a_1, a_2, a_4\}, \{a_1, a_3, a_4\}\}$

Note that, since each matrix s^t is modified only by thread t,[7] Algorithm 5 contains only one synchronisation point (i.e., at line 5), hence providing a full parallelisation. After that, the final surplus matrix s is computed with a maximisation on all the above matrices (lines 5–7), ensuring that the output of P-COMPUTEMATRIX is equal to the one of COMPUTEMATRIX, since each feasible coalition in $\mathcal{FC}\left(G\right)$ has been computed by a thread.

The effectiveness of our parallel approach will be demonstrated through the empirical evaluation, detailed below.

4. EMPIRICAL EVALUATION

Having described and analysed our approach to compute kernel-stable payments for the SR problem, we now benchmark our approach on a real-world dataset. We first present our evaluation methodology, then we discuss the achieved results. The main goals of the empirical analysis are:

1. To test the performance of our approach when computing payments for systems of thousands of agents.

2. To compare the efficiency of our algorithm w.r.t. the state-of-the-art approach proposed Shehory and Kraus.

3. To perform an analysis of the features that influence the payoff allocation.

4. To estimate the speed-up obtainable by using P-PRF w.r.t. PRF.

---

[7]Our parallel approach requires storing t separate surplus matrices, one per thread. Hence, its memory requirements are $O\left(t \cdot n^2\right)$, i.e., still polynomial in the number of agents.

Since there are no publicly available datasets which include *both* spatial and social data for the same users, in our empirical evaluation we consider two separate real-world datasets and we superimpose the first on the second one. This approach does not affect realism and, in our view, provides a far better experimental setting than using synthetic data. Moreover, since we are interested in evaluating the algorithmic performance of our approach, the specific datasets adopted are not crucial for the purposes of our analysis.

In particular, the spatial map is a realistic representation of the city of Beijing, derived from the GeoLife [22] dataset provided by Microsoft. These trajectories are also adopted to sample random paths used to provide the start and destination points to the riders in our tests. Moreover, in each instance the graph G is a subgraph of a large crawl of the Twitter network completed in 2010 by Kwak et al. [11].

In all our experiments we use $\epsilon = 0.05$. Since the coalition structure considered to compute the payments is obtained using the CFSS algorithm [3], we consider the same parameters with them in the definition of the cost model in the SR scenario. Specifically, we adopt a cost model that only considers fuel expenses (considering a fuel cost of 1 € per litre and an average consumption of 1 litre of fuel every 15 km). Moreover, we assume that each car has a capacity of 5 seats, i.e., $k = 5$. Our approach is executed on a machine with dual 8-core 2.60GHz processors and 32 GB of memory.

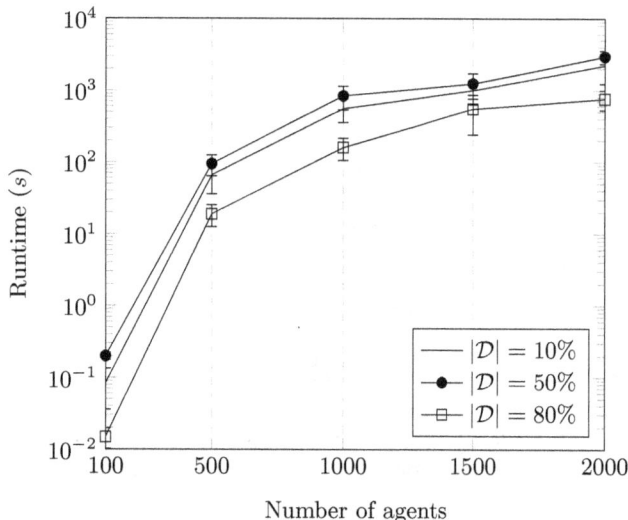

Figure 1: Runtime needed to compute payments.

Figure 1 shows the runtime needed to execute P-PRF on systems with a large number of agents, i.e., $n \in \{100, 500, 1000, 1500, 2000\}$. Our results show that P-PRF is able to compute payments for 2000 agents with a runtime ranging from 13 to 50 minutes, hence it can successfully scale to large systems. In particular, for each value of n, we consider $|\mathcal{D}| \in \{10\%, 50\%, 80\%\}$ with 20 repetitions for each n and $|\mathcal{D}|$, reporting the average and the standard error of the mean. In each test, the coalition structure has been computed using the approximate version of CFSS [3].

Our results also show the influence of the percentage of drivers on the complexity of the problem. On average, computing payments on an instance with $|\mathcal{D}| = 80\%$ is easier w.r.t. $|\mathcal{D}| = 10\%$ and $|\mathcal{D}| = 50\%$. Our findings are consistent with the results obtained by Bistaffa et al. [3], showing that the scenario with $|\mathcal{D}| = 50\%$ is more difficult to solve (i.e., requires a greater runtime), since more drivers are available, hence it is possible to form more cars, resulting in a larger search space. In fact, the number of feasible coalitions is determined by the number of available seats (reduced when such a percentage is low) and the number of riders without a car who can benefit from sharing their commutes (reduced when the majority of the agents owns a car).

4.1 Comparison with State-of-the-Art

Figure 2 shows the runtime needed by our approach to compute a kernel-stable payoff vector, comparing it with the state-of-the-art approach by Shehory and Kraus [16], i.e., Algorithm 1. In particular, we consider the runtime needed to solve random instances with $n \in \{30, 40, 50, 60, 70, 80, 90, 100\}$ and $|\mathcal{D}| = 50\%$,[8] with 20 repetitions for each n. To ensure a fair comparison, both algorithms have been run on the same set of instances. Moreover, for this comparison we employ the serial version of PRF, since Algorithm 1 is serial.

Our results show that PRF is at least one order of magnitude faster, outperforming the state-of-the-art by 27 times in the worst case, with an average improvement of 53 times, and a best case improvement of 84 times. Thus, our comparison has been run only up to $n = 100$, since the latter approach becomes impractical for instances with thousands of agents. In fact, with 1000 agents it requires over one day of computation, compared to a runtime of 2 hours required by PRF, and 14 minutes required by P-PRF. In particular, the approach proposed by Shehory and Kraus [16] is slower since it makes several redundant computations of many coalitional values, resulting in a significant impact on its runtime.

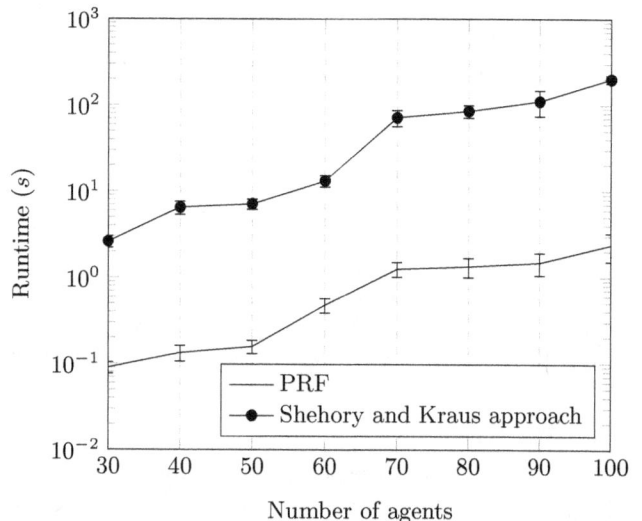

Figure 2: Runtime needed to compute payments.

---

[8]We benchmark both approaches in the most difficult scenario, i.e., the one with the largest search space. This is an intrinsic property of the instances, ensuring the fairness of our comparison.

4.2 Parallel Performance

Here we analyse the speed-up that can be achieved by using P-PRF w.r.t. PRF, i.e., its serial version. We ran the algorithms on 20 random instances with 500 agents and $|\mathcal{D}| = 50\%$, using a machine with 2 Intel® Xeon® E5-2420. For a fair comparison, both algorithms have been run on the same set of instances. The speed-up measured during these tests has been compared with the maximum theoretical one provided by Amdahl's Law [1], considering an estimated non-parallelisable part of 1%, due to memory allocation and thread initialisation. Our experiments show that the actual speed-up follows the theoretical one for up to 12 threads (i.e., the number of physical cores for this machine), reaching a final speed-up of 14.85 with all 24 threads active.

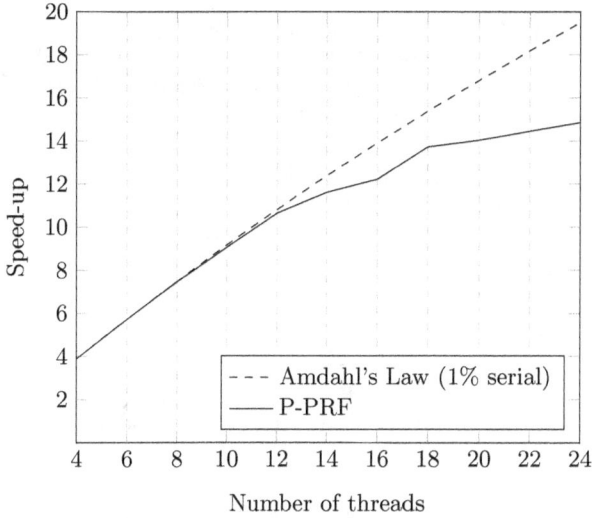

Figure 3: Multi-threading speed-up.

4.3 Costs and Network Centrality

The purpose of this section is to analyse the relationship between the cost incurred by a commuter and its importance in the environment, i.e., being a node with a high degree in the social network, or being driver or rider. To this end, we first compute the optimal solution of the SR problem on random instances with $n \in \{30, 40, 50, 60, 70, 80, 90, 100\}$ and $|\mathcal{D}| \in \{10\%, 50\%, 80\%\}$, with 20 repetitions for each pair of parameters, and we use our algorithm to compute a kernel-stable payoff vector. Then, to assess this correlation in a quantified manner, we define the *normalised cost* $\bar{c}_i$ and the *normalised degree* $\bar{d}_i$ for each agent a_i as follows:

- For any agent a_i in a coalition C with $|C| > 1$, we define its *normalised cost* $\bar{c}_i$ as

$$\bar{c}_i = \frac{|x_i| - \min_{|x|}^C}{\max_{|x|}^C - \min_{|x|}^C},$$

where $\min_{|x|}^C$ and $\max_{|x|}^C$ are the minimum and the maximum values of $|x_i|$ among the members of C. Note that we consider the absolute value of x_i since in our model, costs are represented by negative values for x_i.

- For any agent a_i in a coalition C with $|C| > 1$, we define its *normalised degree* $\bar{d}_i$ as

$$\bar{d}_i = \frac{deg(a_i) - \min_d^C}{\max_d^C - \min_d^C},$$

where $deg(a_i)$ represents the degree of a_i in the social network, and $\min_d^C$ and $\max_d^C$ are the minimum and the maximum degrees among the members of C.

When the denominator of $\bar{c}_i$ is 0, i.e, when $\max_{|x|}^C = \min_{|x|}^C$, it means that all the agents in C have the same payoff. In these cases, $\bar{c}_i$ is defined to be 0.5 as a middle point between 0 and 1 (the same discussion applies to $\bar{d}_i$).

Notice that, a direct comparison of the agents with respect to payments would not be appropriate for determining their overall power or benefits derived from participation in the SR setting. Nonetheless, it would definitely be interesting to have a way to measure and compare the power of the agents, regardless of the coalition to which each one belongs. To allow this comparison, both $\bar{c}_i$ and $\bar{d}_i$ are normalised between 0 (for the agents having the minimum costs/degrees in their coalitions) and 1 (similarly for the agents with maximum costs/degrees). The normalisation is done with respect to the coalition the agent belongs to because to reach kernel-stability, payment transfers only take place among agents within the same coalition. Finally, note that agents in singletons have been excluded from this analysis, as they do not have to split their coalitional value.

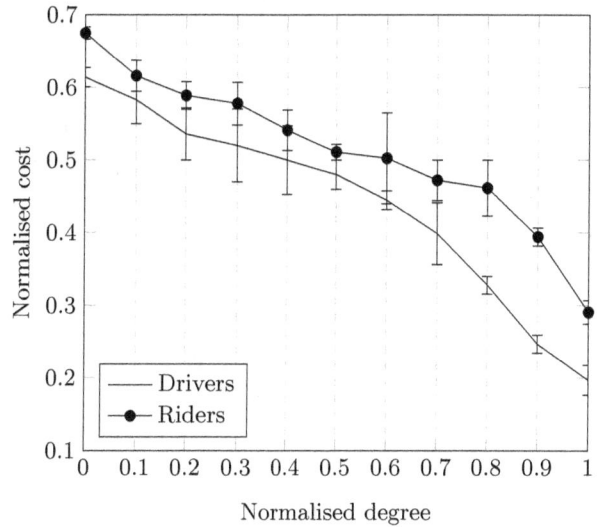

Figure 4: Normalised cost w.r.t. normalised degree.

In Figure 4 we report the average and the standard error of the mean for the normalised cost w.r.t. the normalised degree. Our results clearly show that costs are strongly influenced by the degree of the agents, and whether they are drivers or riders. Specifically, in our tests drivers had to pay costs that were on average 16% lower than riders. Moreover, agents with the minimum number of social connections in their coalition (i.e., with a normalised degree of 0) paid a cost 171% higher than the ones with the highest degree.

These findings allow us to discuss two interesting properties of our approach. On the one hand, our payment scheme *incentivises* commuters to be drivers, which is of utmost importance in SR scenarios with selfish rational agents. In fact, a rational user would not accept to join a ridesharing system as a driver (which requires her to deviate from the shortest path between its source and its destination, and to share its car with other people) without being appropriately rewarded for its service.

On the other hand, the social aspect of our ridesharing model introduces an additional degree of freedom that can be exploited by commuters to influence the distribution of payments. In fact, the more social connections they have, the more coalitions they can potentially join, the more bargaining power they obtain. Moreover, note that this fact is important for commuters that cannot choose to be drivers (e.g., they do not own a car), as it enables them to improve their payments by establishing new social relationships.

5. CONCLUSIONS

We perform recommendations for SR scenarios, developing a novel algorithm, PRF (Paying for Rides with Friends), to compute fair payments for large-scale systems. PRF can be used in conjunction with Bistaffa et al.'s approach to provide recommendations for the optimal groups to form, and also to define fair, stable costs that commuters should pay as a compensation for their rides. PRF avoids any redundancy by exploiting the structure of the social graph. Moreover, we parallelise PRF achieving a speed-up close to the maximum theoretical one. Our tests, based on real dataset for both spatial and social data, shows that our approach is up to 84 times faster than the state-of-the-art, allowing us to compute fair payments for 2000 agents in less than an hour. Finally, we identify a relationship between the ability of an agent to obtain a high payment and its degree in the social graph.

Future work will focus on studying the quality guarantees of payments when using approximate solutions (which have not been studied yet) and will aim to extend our parallel approach to different multi-threading models (e.g., General-Purpose Graphics Processing Units).

6. ACKNOWLEDGMENTS

This work was carried out as part of the ORCHID project funded by EPSRC (EP/I011587/1). We also acknowledge funding from the EPSRC-funded International Centre for Infrastructure Futures (ICIF) (EP/K012347/1).

References

[1] G. M. Amdahl. "Validity of the Single Processor Approach to Achieving Large Scale Computing Capabilities". In: *Spring Joint Computer Conference*. 1967, pp. 483–485.

[2] F. Bistaffa, A. Farinelli, J. Cerquides, J. Rodríguez-Aguilar, and S. D. Ramchurn. "Anytime Coalition Structure Generation on Synergy Graphs". In: *AAMAS*. 2014, pp. 13–20.

[3] F. Bistaffa, A. Farinelli, and S. D. Ramchurn. "Sharing Rides with Friends: a Coalition Formation Algorithm for Ridesharing". In: *AAAI*. 2015, pp. 608–614.

[4] G. Chalkiadakis, E. Markakis, and N. R. Jennings. "Coalitional stability in structured environments". In: *AAMAS*. 2012, pp. 779–786.

[5] G. Chalkiadakis, E. Elkind, and M. Wooldridge. *Computational Aspects of Cooperative Game Theory*. Synthesis Lectures on Artificial Intelligence and Machine Learning. 2011.

[6] M. Davis and M. Maschler. "The kernel of a cooperative game". In: *Naval Research Logistics Quarterly* 12.3 (1965), pp. 223–259.

[7] G. Greco, E. Malizia, L. Palopoli, and F. Scarcello. "On the complexity of the core over coalition structures". In: *IJCAI*. 2011, pp. 216–221.

[8] E. Kamar and E. Horvitz. "Collaboration and Shared Plans in the Open World: Studies of Ridesharing". In: *IJCAI*. 2009, pp. 187–194.

[9] A. Kleiner, B. Nebel, and V. A. Ziparo. "A mechanism for dynamic ride sharing based on parallel auctions". In: *IJCAI*. Vol. 11. 2011, pp. 266–272.

[10] M. Klusch and O. Shehory. "A Polynomial Kernel-Oriented Coalition Algorithm for Rational Information Agents". In: *International Conference on Multi-Agent Systems*. 1996.

[11] H. Kwak, C. Lee, H. Park, and S. Moon. "What is Twitter, a Social Network or a News Media?" In: *WWW*. 2010, pp. 591–600.

[12] J. K. Lenstra and A. Kan. "Complexity of vehicle routing and scheduling problems". In: *Networks* 11.2 (1981), pp. 221–227.

[13] R. B. Myerson. *Game Theory: Analysis of Conflict*. Harvard University Press, 1997.

[14] A. Papadimitriou, P. Symeonidis, and Y. Manolopoulos. "Geo-social recommendations". In: *RecSys 2011 Workshop on PeMA*. 2011.

[15] T. Sandholm, K. Larson, M. Andersson, O. Shehory, and F. Tohmé. "Coalition structure generation with worst case guarantees". In: *AIJ* 111.1 (1999), pp. 209–238.

[16] O. Shehory and S. Kraus. "Feasible Formation of Coalitions Among Autonomous Agents in Non-Super-Additive Environments". In: *Computational Intelligence* 15.3 (1999).

[17] R. E. Stearns. "Convergent Transfer Schemes for N-Person Games". In: *Transactions of the American Mathematical Society* 134.3 (1968), pp. 449–459.

[18] T. Voice, S. Ramchurn, and N. Jennings. "On coalition formation with sparse synergies". In: *AAMAS*. 2012, pp. 223–230.

[19] X. Yang, H. Steck, Y. Guo, and Y. Liu. "On top-k recommendation using social networks". In: *RecSys*. 2012, pp. 67–74.

[20] N. J. Yuan, Y. Zheng, L. Zhang, and X. Xie. "T-finder: A recommender system for finding passengers and vacant taxis". In: *TKDE* 25.10 (2013), pp. 2390–2403.

[21] X. Zheng, X. Liang, and K. Xu. "Where to Wait for a Taxi?" In: *ACM SIGKDD International Workshop on Urban Computing*. 2012, pp. 149–156.

[22] Y. Zheng, L. Zhang, X. Xie, and W.-Y. Ma. "Mining interesting locations and travel sequences from GPS trajectories". In: *WWW*. 2009, pp. 791–800.

Learning Distributed Representations from Reviews for Collaborative Filtering

Amjad Almahairi, Kyle Kastner, Kyunghyun Cho, Aaron Courville
Département d'Informatique et de Recherche Opérationelle
Université de Montréal
{amjad.almahairi, kyle.kastner, kyunghyun.cho, aaron.courville}@umontreal.ca

ABSTRACT

Recent work has shown that collaborative filter-based recommender systems can be improved by incorporating side information, such as natural language reviews, as a way of regularizing the derived product representations. Motivated by the success of this approach, we introduce two different models of reviews and study their effect on collaborative filtering performance. While the previous state-of-the-art approach is based on a latent Dirichlet allocation (LDA) model of reviews, the models we explore are neural network based: a bag-of-words product-of-experts model and a recurrent neural network. We demonstrate that the increased flexibility offered by the product-of-experts model allowed it to achieve state-of-the-art performance on the Amazon review dataset, outperforming the LDA-based approach. However, interestingly, the greater modeling power offered by the recurrent neural network appears to undermine the model's ability to act as a regularizer of the product representations.

Categories and Subject Descriptors

H.3.3 [**Information Search and Retrieval**]: Information filtering

Keywords

Recommender Systems; Neural Networks; Deep Learning

1. INTRODUCTION

Recommendation systems are a crucial component of many e-commerce enterprises, providing businesses with metrics to direct consumers to items they may find appealing. A general goal of these systems is to predict a user's preference for a certain product, often represented as an integer-valued rating, e.g., between 1 (unsatisfied) and 5 (satisfied).

In order to predict the user's preference for a product, it is often beneficial to consider as many sources of information as possible, including the preference of the user for other products, the preferences of other users, as well as any side information such as characteristics of each user and product. A data-driven approach based on this idea is called *collaborative filtering.*

Collaborative filtering has been successfully used for recommendation systems (see, e.g., [17]). A typical approach to using collaborative filtering for recommendation systems is to consider all the observed ratings given by a set of users to a set of products as elements in a matrix, where the row and column of this matrix correspond to users and products, respectively. As the observed ratings is typically only a small subset of the possible ratings (all users rating all products), this matrix is sparse. The goal of collaborative filtering is to fill in the missing values of this matrix: to predict, for each user, the rating of products the user has not rated. In this setting, collaborative filtering is usually cast as a problem of matrix factorization with missing values [10, 16, 18]. The sparse matrix is factorized into a product of two matrices of lower rank representing a user matrix and a product matrix. Once these matrices are estimated, a missing observation can be trivially reconstructed by taking a dot product of a corresponding user vector (or representation) and a product vector (or representation).

In this formulation of collaborative filtering, an important issue of data sparsity arises. For instance, the dataset provided as a part of the Netflix Challenge[1] had only 100,480,507 observed ratings out of more than 8 billion possible ratings[2] (user / product pairs) meaning that 99% of the values were missing. This data sparsity easily leads to naive matrix factorization overfitting the training set of observed ratings [10].

In this paper, we are interested in regularizing the collaborative filtering matrix factorization using an additional source of information: reviews written by users in natural language. Recent work has shown that better rating prediction can be obtained by incorporating this kind of text-based side information [13, 12, 1]. Motivated by these recent successes, here we explore alternative approaches to exploiting this side information. Specifically, we study how different models of reviews can impact the performance of the regularization.

We introduce two approaches to modeling reviews and compare these to the current state-of-the-art LDA-based approaches [13, 12]. Both models have previously been studied as neural-network-based document models. One is based on the Bag-of-Words Paragraph Vector [11]. This model is similar to the existing LDA-based model, but, as we argue, it offers a more flexible natural language model. The other is

RecSys'15, September 16–20, 2015, Vienna, Austria.
© 2015 ACM. ISBN 978-1-4503-3692-5/15/09 ...$15.00.
DOI: http://dx.doi.org/10.1145/2792838.2800192.

---

[1] http://www.netflixprize.com/
[2] 480,189 users and 17,770 movies

a recurrent neural network (RNN) based approach. RNNs have recently become very popular models of natural language for a wide array of tasks [11]. Here we will find that despite the considerable additional modelling power brought by the RNN, it does not offer better performance when used as a regularizer in this context.

The proposed approaches are empirically evaluated on the Amazon Reviews Dataset [13]. We observe that the proposed bag-of-words language model outperforms the existing approach based on latent Dirichlet allocation (LDA, [4]). We also confirm the use of an RNN language model does not lead to improved performance. Overall, our experiments demonstrate that, in this particular application where we rely on the document model to regularize the collaborative filtering matrix factorization, controlling the model flexibility is very important.

We also make methodological contributions in studying the effect of the train / test splits used in experimentation. Previous works on this subject (e.g. [13], [12] and [1]), do not clearly identify how the data was split into train and test sets. Here we empirically demonstrate the importance of doing so. We show that for a given fixed split, conclusions regarding the relative performance of competing approaches do generalize to other splits, but comparing absolute performance across difference splits is highly problematic.

2. MATRIX FACTORIZATION FOR COLLABORATIVE FILTERING

Let us assume that we are given a set $R = \{r_{u,i}\}_{(u,i) \in O_R}$ of observed ratings, where $r_{u,i} \in \{1, 2, \cdots, 5\}$ is the rating given by the user u to the product i. Collaborative filtering aims at building a model that is able to predict the rating of an unobserved user-product pair, i.e., $r_{u,i}$ where $(u, i) \notin O_R$.

In collaborative filtering based on matrix factorization, we estimate each user-product rating as

$$r_{u,i} \approx \hat{r}_{u,i} = \mu + \beta_u + \beta_i + \boldsymbol{\gamma}_u^\top \boldsymbol{\gamma}_i, \qquad (1)$$

where μ, β_i and β_u are a global bias, a user-specific bias for the user u and a product-specific bias for the product i, respectively. The vectors $\boldsymbol{\gamma}_u$ and $\boldsymbol{\gamma}_i$ are the latent factors of the user u and the product i respectively.

We estimate all the parameters in the r.h.s of Eq. (1) by minimizing the mean-squared error between the predicted ratings and the observed, true ratings:

$$C_R(\boldsymbol{\theta}) = \frac{1}{|O_R|} \sum_{(u,i) \in O_R} (\hat{r}_{u,i} - r_{u,i})^2, \qquad (2)$$

where $\boldsymbol{\theta} = \left\{ \mu, \{\beta_u\}_{u=1}^N, \{\beta_i\}_{i=1}^M, \{\boldsymbol{\gamma}_u\}_{u=1}^N, \{\boldsymbol{\gamma}_i\}_{i=1}^M \right\}$.

Once the parameters $\boldsymbol{\theta}$ are estimated by minimizing C_R, it is straightforward to predict the rating of an unobserved user-product pair (u, i) using Eq. (1).

2.1 Taming the Curse of Data Sparsity

It has been observed earlier, for instance in [10], that this matrix factorization approach easily overfits the observed ratings, leading to poor generalization performance on the held-out set, or unseen user-product pairs. This issue is especially serious in the case of recommendation systems, as it is highly likely that each user purchases/watches only a fraction of all the available products. For instance, in the

Amazon Reviews Dataset more than 99.999% of ratings, or elements in the rating matrix are missing.

The issue of overfitting is often addressed by adding a regularization term Ω to the cost C_R in Eq. (2). One of the most widely used regularization term is a simple weight decay

$$\Omega(\boldsymbol{\theta}) = \sum_{\theta \in \boldsymbol{\theta}} \|\theta\|^2.$$

Hence parameters are estimated by minimizing $C_R(\boldsymbol{\theta}) + \lambda\Omega(\boldsymbol{\theta})$, where λ is a regularization coefficient.

Another approach is to interpret matrix factorization in a probabilistic framework [10, 16, 18]. In this approach, all the parameters such as the user and product representations are considered as latent random variables on which the distribution of the rating, an observed random variable, is conditioned. This probabilistic matrix factorization can automatically regularize itself by maintaining the confidence of the estimates/predictions based on the observations.

On the other hand, we can improve generalization, hence reduce overfitting, by simultaneously estimating the parameters $\boldsymbol{\theta}$ of the matrix factorization to perform well on another related task [5]. With a model predicting a rating by a user on a product, we can consider letting the model also try to account for the product review given by the user. This seems like a useful side task as users often write reviews that justify their ratings and describe features that affected their opinions.

In this paper, we explore this approach of exploiting extra tasks to improve generalization performance of collaborative filtering based on matrix factorization.

3. REGULARIZING WITH EXTRA DATA

3.1 Reviews as Extra Data

In many e-commerce systems, each rating is often accompanied with a user's review of the product. As mentioned earlier, it is natural to expect that the accompanying review is used by the user to justify her/his rating or opinion, which suggests the possibility of improving the generalization performance of the prediction model for ratings [13]. As an illustrating example, a user, who wrote "this is a great adventure movie that children and adults alike would love!" for the movie "Free Willy", is likely to give a higher rating to this movie.[3]

In this section, we will propose two approaches to utilizing this type of review data for improving the generalization performance of a rating prediction model based on matrix factorization.

3.2 Natural Language Review Modeling

More technically, let us suppose that the set R of ratings (see Sec. 2) is accompanied with a set D of reviews $D = \{d_{u,i}\}_{(u,i) \in O_D}$. Each review $d_{u,i} = \left(w_{u,i}^{(1)}, \cdots, w_{u,i}^{(n_{u,i})} \right)$ is a piece of natural language text written by a user u about an item i, which we represent as a sequence of words.

Following the multitask learning framework [5], we build a model that jointly predicts the rating given by a user u to a product i and models the review written by the user u

---

[3]This is an actual sample from the Amazon Reviews dataset.

on the product i. The model has two components; matrix factorization in Eq. (1) and review modeling, which shares some of the parameters $\boldsymbol{\theta}$ from the rating prediction model.

Here, we follow the approach from [13] by modeling the conditional probability of each review given the corresponding product $\boldsymbol{\gamma}_i$:

$$p\left(d_{u,i} = \left(w_{u,i}^{(1)}, \cdots, w_{u,i}^{(n_{u,i})}\right) \mid \boldsymbol{\gamma}_i, \boldsymbol{\theta}_D\right),\qquad(3)$$

where $\boldsymbol{\theta}_D$ is a set of parameters for this review model.

We estimate the parameters of this review model ($\boldsymbol{\theta}_D$ and $\boldsymbol{\gamma}_i$'s) by minimizing the negative log-likelihood:

$$\underset{\boldsymbol{\theta}_D, \{\boldsymbol{\gamma}_i\}_{i=1}^{M}}{\arg\min} \ C_D(\boldsymbol{\theta}_D, \{\boldsymbol{\gamma}_i\}_{i=1}^{M}),$$

where

$$C_D(\boldsymbol{\theta}_D, \{\boldsymbol{\gamma}_i\}_{i=1}^{M}) =\qquad\qquad(4)$$
$$-\frac{1}{|O_D|} \sum_{(u,i) \in O_D} \log p\left(d_{u,i} = \left(w_{u,i}^{(1)}, \cdots, w_{u,i}^{(n_{u,i})}\right) \mid \boldsymbol{\gamma}_i\right).$$
$$(5)$$

We jointly optimize the rating prediction model in Eq. (1) and the review model in Eq. (3) by minimizing the convex combination of C_R in Eq. (2) and C_D in Eq. (4):

$$\underset{\boldsymbol{\theta}, \boldsymbol{\theta}_D}{\arg\min} \ \alpha \, C_R(\boldsymbol{\theta}) + (1-\alpha) C_D(\boldsymbol{\theta}_D, \{\boldsymbol{\gamma}_i\}_{i=1}^{M}),\qquad(6)$$

where the coefficient α is a hyperparmeter.

3.2.1 BoWLF: Distributed Bag-of-Word

The first model we propose to use is a distributed bag-of-words prediction. In this case, we represent each review as a bag of words, meaning

$$d_{u,i} = \left(w_{u,i}^{(1)}, \cdots, w_{u,i}^{(n_{u,i})}\right) \approx \left\{w_{u,i}^{(1)}, \cdots, w_{u,i}^{(n_{u,i})}\right\}.\qquad(7)$$

This leads to

$$p(d_{u,i} \mid \boldsymbol{\gamma}_i) = \prod_{t=1}^{n_{u,i}} p(w_{u,i}^{(t)} \mid \boldsymbol{\gamma}_i).$$

We model $p(w_{u,i}^{(t)} \mid \boldsymbol{\gamma}_i)$ as an affine transformation of the product representation $\boldsymbol{\gamma}_i$ followed by, so-called softmax, normalization:

$$p(w_{u,i}^{(t)} = j \mid \boldsymbol{\gamma}_i) = \frac{\exp\{y_j\}}{\sum_{l=1}^{|V|} \exp\{y_l\}},\qquad(8)$$

where

$$\mathbf{y} = \mathbf{W}\boldsymbol{\gamma}_i + \mathbf{b}$$

and V, $\mathbf{W}$ and $\mathbf{b}$ are the vocabulary, a weight matrix and a bias vector. The parameters $\boldsymbol{\theta}_D$ of this review model include $\mathbf{W}$ and $\mathbf{b}$.

When we use this distributed bag-of-words together with matrix factorization for predicting ratings, and we call this joint model the *bag-of-words regularized latent factor model* (BoWLF).

3.2.2 LMLF: Recurrent Neural Network

The second model of reviews we propose to use is a recurrent neural network (RNN) language model (LM) [14]. Unlike the distributed bag-of-words model, this RNN-LM does not make any assumption on how each review is represented, but takes a sequence of words as it is, preserving the order of the words.

In this case, we model the probability over a review which is a variable-length sequence of words by rewriting the probability as

$$p(d_{u,i} = (w_{u,i}^{(1)}, \cdots, w_{u,i}^{(n_{u,i})}) \mid \boldsymbol{\gamma}_i)$$
$$= p\left(w_{u,i}^{(1)} \mid \boldsymbol{\gamma}_i\right) \prod_{t=2}^{n_{u,i}} p\left(w_{u,i}^{(t)} \mid w_{u,i}^{(1)}, \cdots, w_{u,i}^{(t-1)}, \boldsymbol{\gamma}_i\right),$$

We approximate each conditional distribution with

$$p\left(w_{u,i}^{(t)} = j \mid w_{u,i}^{(<t)}, \boldsymbol{\gamma}_i\right) = \frac{\exp\left\{y_j^{(t)}\right\}}{\sum_{l=1}^{|V|} \exp\left\{y_l^{(t)}\right\}},$$

where

$$\mathbf{y}^{(t)} = \mathbf{W}\mathbf{h}^{(t)} + \mathbf{b}$$

and

$$\mathbf{h}^{(t)} = \phi\left(\mathbf{h}^{(t-1)}, w_{u,i}^{(t-1)}, \boldsymbol{\gamma}_i\right).$$

There are a number of choices available for implementing the recurrent function ϕ. Here, we use a long short-term memory (LSTM, [9]) which has recently been applied successfully to natural language-related tasks [7].

In the case of the LSTM, the recurrent function ϕ returns, in addition to its hidden state $\mathbf{h}^{(t)}$, the memory cell $\mathbf{c}^{(t)}$ such that

$$\left[\mathbf{h}^{(t)}; \mathbf{c}^{(t)}\right] = \phi\left(\mathbf{h}^{(t-1)}, \mathbf{c}^{(t-1)}, w_{u,i}^{(t-1)}, \boldsymbol{\gamma}_i\right),$$

where

$$\mathbf{h}^{(t)} = \mathbf{o}^{(t)} \odot \tanh(\mathbf{c}^{(t)})$$
$$\mathbf{c}^{(t)} = \mathbf{f}^{(t)} \odot \mathbf{c}^{(t-1)} + \mathbf{i}^{(t)} \odot \tilde{\mathbf{c}}^{(t)}.$$

The output $\mathbf{o}$, forget $\mathbf{f}$ and input $\mathbf{i}$ gates are computed by

$$\begin{bmatrix} \mathbf{o}^{(t)} \\ \mathbf{f}^{(t)} \\ \mathbf{i}^{(t)} \end{bmatrix} = \sigma(\mathbf{V}_g \mathbf{E}\left[w_{u,i}^{(t-1)}\right] + \mathbf{W}_g \mathbf{h}^{(t-1)} +$$
$$\mathbf{U}_g \mathbf{c}^{(t-1)} + \mathbf{A}_g \boldsymbol{\gamma}_i + \mathbf{b}_g),\quad(9)$$

and the new memory content $\tilde{\mathbf{c}}^{(t)}$ by

$$\tilde{\mathbf{c}}^{(t)} = \tanh(\mathbf{V}_c \mathbf{E}\left[w_{u,i}^{(t-1)}\right] + \mathbf{W}_c \mathbf{h}^{(t-1)} +$$
$$\mathbf{U}_c \mathbf{c}^{(t-1)} + \mathbf{A}_c \boldsymbol{\gamma}_i + \mathbf{b}_c),\quad(10)$$

where $\mathbf{E}$, $\mathbf{V}_g$, $\mathbf{W}_g$, $\mathbf{U}_g$, $\mathbf{b}_g$, $\mathbf{V}_c$, $\mathbf{W}_c$, $\mathbf{U}_c$, $\mathbf{b}_c$, $\mathbf{A}_g$ and $\mathbf{A}_c$ are the parameters of the RNN-LM. Note that $\mathbf{E}[w]$ denotes a row indexing by the word index w of the matrix $\mathbf{E}$.

Similarly to the BoWLF, we call the joint model of matrix factorization and this RNN-LM the *language model regularized latent factor model* (LMLF).

3.3 Related Work: LDA-based Approach

Similar approaches of modeling reviews to regularize matrix factorization have recently been proposed, however, with different review models such as LDA [13, 12] and non-negative matrix factorization [1]. Here, we describe "Hidden Factors as Topics" (HFT) recently proposed in [13], and discuss it with respect to the proposed approaches.

The HFT model is based on latent Dirichlet allocation (LDA, [4]), and similarly to the distributed bag-of-word model in Sec. 3.2.1, considers each review as a bag of words (see Eq. (7).) Thus, we start by describing how LDA models a review $d_{u,i}$.

LDA is a generative model of a review/document. It starts by sampling a so-called topic proportion τ from a Dirichlet distribution. τ is used as a parameter to a multinomial topic distribution from which a topic is sampled. The sampled topic defines a probability distribution over the words in a vocabulary. In other words, given a topic proportion, the LDA models a review with a mixture of multinomial distributions.

Instead of sampling the topic proportion from the top-level Dirichlet distribution in LDA, HFT replaces it with

$$\tau = \frac{1}{\|\exp\{\kappa\gamma_i\}\|_1}\exp\{\kappa\gamma_i\},$$

where κ is a free parameter estimated along with all the other parameters of the model. In this case, the probability over a single review $d_{u,i}$ given a product γ_i becomes

$$p(d_{u,i} \mid \gamma_i) = \prod_{t=1}^{n_{u,i}} \sum_{k=1}^{\dim(\gamma_i)} p(w_{u,i}^{(t)} \mid z_k = 1)p(z_k = 1 \mid \gamma_i)$$

$$\tag{11}$$

$$= \prod_{t=1}^{n_{u,i}} \sum_{k=1}^{\dim(\gamma_i)} \tau_k p(w_{u,i}^{(t)} \mid z_k = 1)$$

where z_k is an indicator variable of the k-th topic out of $\dim(\gamma_i)$, and τ_k is the k-th element of τ. The conditional probability over words given a topic is modeled with a stochastic matrix $\mathbf{W}^* = \left[w_{j,k}^*\right]_{|V|\times\dim(\gamma_i)}$ (each column sums to 1). The conditional probability over words given a product γ_i can be written as

$$p(w_{u,i}^{(t)} = j \mid \gamma_i) = \sum_{k=1}^{\dim(\gamma_i)} w_{j,k}^* \frac{\exp\{\kappa\gamma_{i,k}\}}{\|\exp\{\kappa\gamma_i\}\|_1}.\tag{12}$$

The matrix $\mathbf{W}^*$ is often parametrized by $w_{j,k}^* = \frac{\exp\{q_{j,k}\}}{\sum_l \exp\{q_{l,k}\}}$, where $\mathbf{Q} = [q_{j,k}]$ is an unconstrained matrix of the same size as $\mathbf{W}^*$. In practice, a bias term is added to the formulation above to handle frequent words.

3.4 Comparing HFT and BoWLF

From Eq. (8) and Eq. (12), we can see that the HFT and the proposed BoWLF (see Sec. 3.2.1) are closely related. Most importantly, both of them consider a review as a bag of words and parametrize the conditional probability of a word given a product representation with a single affine transformation (weight matrix plus offset vector).

The main difference is in how the product representation and the weight matrix interact to form a point on the $|V|$-dimensional simplex. In the case of HFT, both the product representation γ_i and the projection matrix $\mathbf{W}^*$ are separately stochastic (i.e. each γ_i and each column of $\mathbf{W}^*$ are interpretable as a probability distribution), while the BoWLF projects the result of the matrix-vector product $\mathbf{W}\gamma_i$ onto the probability simplex.

This can be understood as the difference between a mixture of experts and a product of experts [8]. On a per word basis, the BoWLF in Eq. (8) can be re-written as a (conditional) product of experts by

$$p(w = j \mid \gamma_i) = \frac{1}{Z(\gamma_i)}\prod_{k=1}^{\dim(\gamma_i)}\exp\{w_{j,k}\gamma_{i,k} + b_j\},$$

where $w_{j,k}$ and b_j are the element at the j-th row and k-th column of $\mathbf{W}$ and the j-th element of $\mathbf{b}$, respectively. On the other hand, an inspection of Eq. (11) reveals that, on a per word basis, the HFT model is clearly a mixture model, with the topics playing the role of the mixture components.

As argued in [8], a product of experts can more easily model a *peaky* distribution, especially, in a high-dimensional space.[4] The reviews of each product tend to contain a small common subset of the whole vocabulary, while those subsets vastly differ from each other depending on the product. In other words, the conditional distribution of words given a product puts most of its probability mass on only a few product-specific words, while leaving most other words with nearly zero probabilities. Product of experts are naturally better suited to modeling peaky distributions rather than mixture models.

A more concrete way of understanding the difference between HFT and BoWLF may be to consider how the product representation and the weight matrix interact. In the case of the BoWLF, this is a simple matrix-vector product with no restrictions on the weight matrix. This means that both the product representation elements as well as the elements of the weight matrix are free to assume negative values. Thus, it is possible that an element of the product representation could exercise a strong influence *suppressing* the expression of a given set of words. Alternatively, with HFT model, as the model interprets the elements of the product representation as mixture components, these elements have no mechanism of suppressing probability mass assigned to words by the other elements of the product representation.

We suggest that this difference allows the BoWLF to better model reviews compared to the HFT, or any other LDA-based model by offering a mechanism for negative correlations between words to be explicitly expressed by elements of the product representation. By offering a more flexible and natural model of reviews, the BoWLF model can improve the rating prediction generalization performance. As we will see in Sec. 4, our experimental results support this proposition.

The proposed LMLF takes one step further by modeling each review with a chain of products of experts taking into account the order of words. This may seem an obvious benefit at the first sight. However, it is not clear whether the order of the words is specific to a product or is simply a feature of language itself. In the latter case, we expect that LMLF will model reviews very well, but may not improve rating prediction.

4. EXPERIMENTS

4.1 Dataset

We evaluate the proposed approaches on the Amazon Reviews dataset [13].[5] There are approximate 35 million ratings and accompanying reviews from 6,643,669 users and

---

[4] Note that the size of a usual vocabulary of reviews is on the order of thousands.

[5] https://snap.stanford.edu/data/web-Amazon.html

2,441,053 products. The products are divided into 28 categories such as music and books. The reviews are on average 110 words long. We refer the reader to [12] for more detailed statistics.

4.2 Experimental Setup

Data Preparation.

We closely follow the procedure from [13] and [12], where the evaluation is done per category. We randomly select 80% of ratings, up to two million samples, as a training set, and split the rest evenly into validation and test sets, for each category. We preprocess reviews only by tokenizing them using a script from Moses[6], after which we build a vocabulary of 5000 most frequent words.

Evaluation Criteria.

We use mean squared error (MSE) of the rating prediction to evaluate each approach. For assessing the performance on review modeling, we use the average negative log-likelihood.

Baseline.

We compare the two proposed approaches, BoWLF (see Sec. 3.2.1) and LMLF (see Sec. 3.2.2), against three baseline methods; matrix factorization with L_2 regularization (MF, see Eqs. (1)–(2)), the HFT model from [13] (see Sec. 3.3) and the RMR model from [12]. In the case of HFT, we report the performance both by evaluating the model ourselves[7] and by reporting the results from [13] directly. For RMR, we only report the results from [12].

Hyper-parameters.

Both user γ_u and product γ_i vectors in Eq. (1) are five dimensional for all the experiments in this section. This choice was made mainly to make the results comparable to the previously reported ones in [13] and [12].

We initialize all the user and product representations by sampling each element from a zero-mean Gaussian distribution with its standard deviation set to 0.01. The biases, μ, β_u and β_i are all initialized to 0. All the parameters in BoWLF and LMLF are initialized similarly except for the recurrent weights of the RNN-LM in LMLF which were initialized to be orthogonal.

Training Procedure.

When training MF, BoWLF and LMLF, we use minibatch RMSProp with the learning rate, momentum coefficient and the size of minibatch set to 0.01, 0.9 and 128, respectively. We trained each model at most 200 epochs, while monitoring the validation performance. For HFT, we follow [13] which uses the Expectation Maximization algorithm together with L-BFGS. In all cases, we early-stop each training run based on the validation set performance.

In the preliminary experiments, we found the choice of α in Eq. (6), which balances matrix factorization and review modeling, to be important. We searched for the α that maximizes the validation performance, in the range of $[0.1, 0.01]$.

We used a CPU cluster of 16 nodes each with 8 cores and $8 - 16$ GB of memory to run experiments on BoWLF, MF,

and HFT. For LMLF, we used a cluster of K20 GPUs where we had up to 50 GPUs available.

4.3 Rating Prediction Results

We list results of the experiments in Table 1 for the 28 categories in terms of MSE with the standard error of mean shown in parentheses. From this table, we can see that except for a single category of "Jewelry", the proposed BoWLF outperforms all the other models with an improvement of 20.29% over MF and 5.64% over HFT across all categories.[8] In general, we note better performance of BoWLF and LMLF models over other methods especially as the size of the dataset grows, which is evident from Figs. 1 and 2.

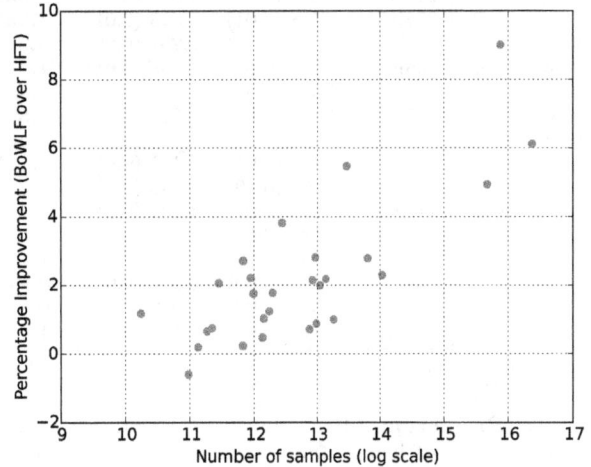

Figure 1: Scatterplot showing performance improvement over the number of samples. We see a performance improvement of BoWLF over HFT as dataset size increases.

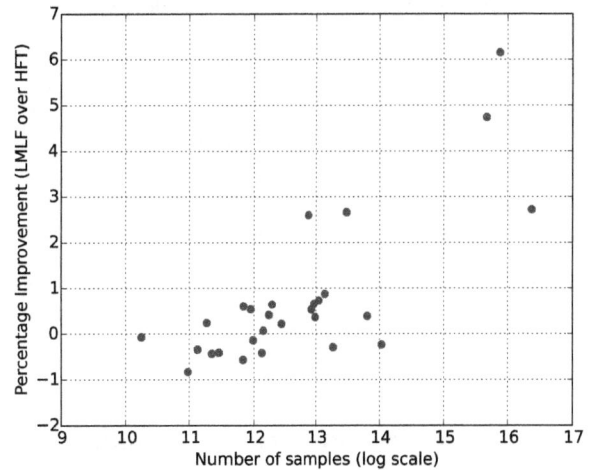

Figure 2: Scatterplot showing performance improvement over the number of samples. We see a modest performance improvement of LMLF over HFT as dataset size increases.

---

[6] https://github.com/moses-smt/mosesdecoder/
[7] The code was kindly provided by the authors of [13].

[8] Due to the use of different splits, the results by HFT reported in [13] and RMR in [12] are not directly comparable.

Dataset	Dataset Size	(a) MF	(b) HFT	(c) BoWLF	(d) LMLF	BoWLF improvement over (a)	over (b)	HFT*	RMR**
Arts	27K	1.434 (0.04)	1.425 (0.04)	**1.413** (0.04)	1.426 (0.04)	2.15%	1.18%	1.388	1.371
Jewelry	58K	1.227 (0.04)	**1.208** (0.03)	1.214 (0.03)	1.218 (0.03)	1.24%	-0.59%	1.178	1.160
Watches	68K	1.511 (0.03)	1.468 (0.03)	**1.466** (0.03)	1.473 (0.03)	4.52%	0.20%	1.486	1.458
Cell Phones	78K	2.133 (0.03)	2.082 (0.02)	**2.076** (0.02)	2.077 (0.02)	5.76%	0.66%	N/A	2.085
Musical Inst.	85K	1.426 (0.02)	1.382 (0.02)	**1.375** (0.02)	1.388 (0.02)	5.12%	0.75%	1.396	1.374
Software	95K	2.241 (0.02)	2.194 (0.02)	**2.174** (0.02)	2.203 (0.02)	6.70%	2.06%	2.197	2.173
Industrial	137K	0.360 (0.01)	0.354 (0.01)	**0.352** (0.01)	0.356 (0.01)	0.76%	0.24%	0.357	0.362
Office Products	138K	1.662 (0.02)	1.656 (0.02)	**1.629** (0.02)	1.646 (0.02)	3.32%	2.72%	1.680	1.638
Gourmet Foods	154K	1.517 (0.02)	1.486 (0.02)	**1.464** (0.02)	1.478 (0.02)	5.36%	2.22%	1.431	1.465
Automotive	188K	1.460 (0.01)	1.429 (0.01)	**1.419** (0.01)	1.428 (0.01)	4.17%	1.03%	1.428	1.403
Kindle Store	160K	1.496 (0.01)	1.435 (0.01)	**1.418** (0.01)	1.437 (0.01)	7.83%	1.76%	N/A	1.412
Baby	184K	1.492 (0.01)	1.437 (0.01)	**1.432** (0.01)	1.443 (0.01)	5.95%	0.48%	1.442	N/A
Patio	206K	1.725 (0.01)	1.687 (0.01)	**1.674** (0.01)	1.680 (0.01)	5.10%	1.24%	N/A	1.669
Pet Supplies	217K	1.583 (0.01)	1.554 (0.01)	**1.536** (0.01)	1.544 (0.01)	4.74%	1.78%	1.582	1.562
Beauty	252K	1.378 (0.01)	1.373 (0.01)	**1.335** (0.01)	1.370 (0.01)	4.33%	3.82%	1.347	1.334
Shoes	389K	0.226 (0.00)	0.231 (0.00)	**0.224** (0.00)	0.225 (0.00)	0.23%	0.72%	0.226	0.251
Tools & Home	409K	1.535 (0.01)	1.498 (0.01)	**1.477** (0.01)	1.490 (0.01)	5.78%	2.15%	1.499	1.491
Health	428K	1.535 (0.01)	1.509 (0.01)	**1.481** (0.01)	1.499 (0.01)	5.35%	2.82%	1.528	1.512
Toys & Games	435K	1.411 (0.01)	1.372 (0.01)	**1.363** (0.01)	1.367 (0.01)	4.71%	0.89%	1.366	1.372
Video Games	463K	1.566 (0.01)	1.501 (0.01)	**1.481** (0.01)	1.490 (0.01)	8.47%	2.00%	1.511	1.510
Sports	510K	1.144 (0.01)	1.137 (0.01)	**1.115** (0.01)	1.127 (0.01)	2.94%	2.19%	1.136	1.129
Clothing	581K	0.339 (0.00)	0.343 (0.00)	**0.333** (0.00)	0.344 (0.00)	0.60%	1.01%	0.327	0.336
Amazon Video	717K	1.317 (0.01)	1.239 (0.01)	**1.184** (0.01)	1.206 (0.01)	13.33%	5.47%	N/A	1.270
Home	991K	1.587 (0.00)	1.541 (0.00)	**1.513** (0.00)	1.535 (0.01)	7.41%	2.79%	1.527	1.501
Electronics	1.2M	1.754 (0.00)	1.694 (0.00)	**1.671** (0.00)	1.698 (0.00)	8.29%	2.30%	1.724	1.722
Music	6.3M	1.112 (0.00)	0.970 (0.00)	**0.920** (0.00)	0.924 (0.00)	19.15%	4.94%	0.969	0.959
Movies & Tv	7.8M	1.379 (0.00)	1.089 (0.00)	**0.999** (0.00)	1.022 (0.00)	37.95%	9.01%	1.119	1.120
Books	12.8M	1.272 (0.00)	1.141 (0.00)	**1.080** (0.00)	1.110 (0.00)	19.21%	6.12%	1.135	1.113
All categories	35.3M	1.289	1.143	1.086	1.107	20.29%	5.64%		

Table 1: Prediction Mean Squared Error results on test data. Standard error of mean in parenthesis. Dimensionality of latent factors $\dim(\gamma_i) = 5$ for all models. Best results for each dataset in bold. HFT* and RMR** represent original paper results over different data splits [13, 12].

Interestingly, BoWLF always outperforms LMLF. These results indicate that the complex language model, which the LMLF learns using an LSTM network, does not seem to improve over a simple bag-of-word representation, which the BoWLF learns, in terms of the learned product representations.

This can be understood from how the product representation, which is used *linearly* by the rating prediction model, is handled by each model. The word distribution modeled by the BoWLF depends linearly on the product representation, which requires the product-related structure underlying reviews be encoded linearly as well. On the other hand, LMLF *nonlinearly* manipulates the product representation to approximate the distribution over reviews. In other words, the LMLF does not necessarily encode the underlying product-related structure inside the product representation in the way the rating prediction model can easily decode [15].

4.4 Impact of Training / Test Data Split

Comparing the results of the original HFT paper with the results we get training over the same split, it becomes clear that models trained on different splits are not directly comparable. To further explore the importance of the chosen split for model selection, we perform experiments over five randomly selected folds and compare each model on every fold.

One of the challenges in pursuing empirical work on the Amazon review dataset is the current absence of a standard

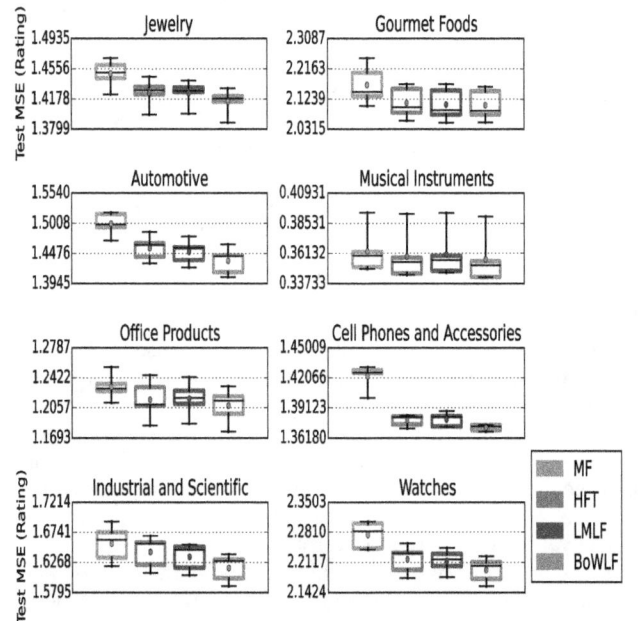

Figure 3: Box and whisker plot showing K-fold ($K = 5$) experiments. Point represents the mean over all folds. Center line represents median. Box extents represent 25th and 75th percentile. Whisker extents show minimum and maximum values.

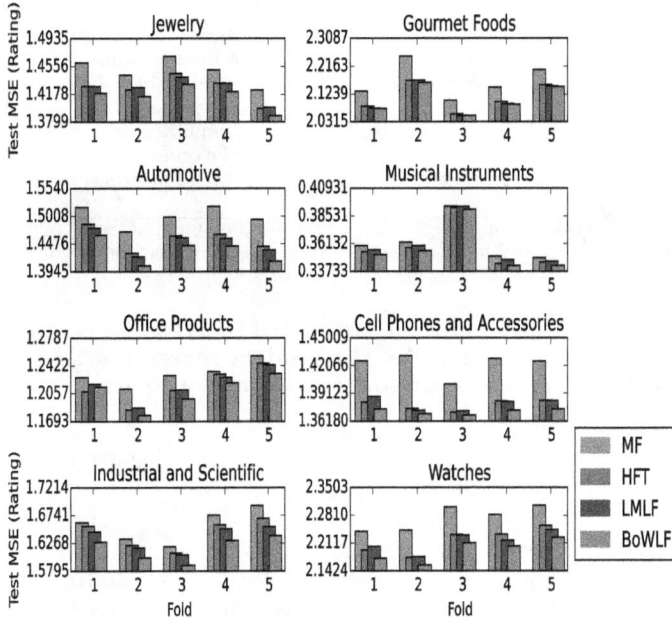

Figure 4: Bar chart showing showing K-fold ($K = 5$) experiments. Although values across folds vary, relative performance is consistent.

train / test split of the data. Here we evaluate the importance of establishing a standard data split.

Fig. 3 shows the results of experiments comparing the performance of each model over different splits. We perform 5-fold validation. That is, each model is trained 5 times, each on 80% of the data and we report performance on the remaining 20%. The result on the test reveal several important points. First, we note that the variance over splits can be large, meaning that comparing across different splits could be misleading when performing model selection. On the other hand, as shown in Fig 4, the relative performance of each model is consistent over the different splits. This implies that a single random split can be used for model selection and evaluation as long as this split is held constant over all evaluated models.

Taken together, Figs. 3 and 4 illustrate the importance of standardizing the dataset splits. Without standardization, performance measured between different research groups becomes incomparable and the use of this dataset as a benchmark is rendered difficult or even impossible.

4.5 Effect of Language Model

One way to analyze models which use text information is to compare their negative log-likelihood (NLL) scores on the same test dataset. We find BoWLF has a stronger language model than HFT, which is reflected in the NLL results, and in this case it appears to contribute to a better rating prediction. As shown in Fig. 5, LMLF has a much better language model than both HFT and BoWLF, but as discussed earlier, LMLF *does not* lead to better rating predictions than BoWLF. LMLF appears to be largely equivalent to HFT in prediction strength, despite having a much better language model. As discussed above in Sec. 4.3, this suggests that the strong nonlinearity in the LSTM helps modeling

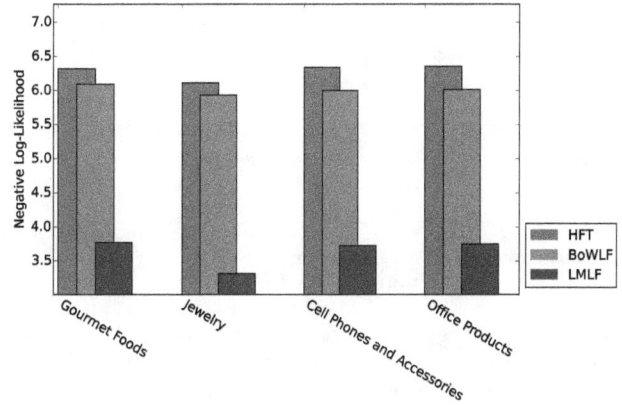

Figure 5: Bar chart showing showing negative log-likelihood (NLL) on test data for several datasets. LMLF is superior in NLL but does not improve rating prediction over BoWLF.

reviews, but not necessarily result in the linearly-decodable product representation, leading to less improvement in rating prediction.

Contrary to LDA-based approaches, the latent dimensions of the product representations learned by BoWLF do not necessarily have clear interpretations as topics. However, the neighborhoods learned by BoWLF are interpretable, where we use the cosine distance between two product representations, i.e., $1 - \frac{\gamma_i^\top \gamma_j}{\|\gamma_i\|_2 \|\gamma_j\|_2}$. The BoWLF product space neighbors seem qualitatively superior to the neighbors given by HFT as seen in Table 2. Note in particular the association of "MTR Simply Tomato Soup" with other soups by BoWLF, while HFT neighbors seem much broader, including crackers, noodles, and gummy bears. This observation is consistent with the interpretation of the differences in the mathematical form of HFT and BoWLF (as argued in Sec. 3.4). The ability of BoWLF to form peakier distributions over words, given the product representation, allows the model to be more discriminating and more closely group similar products. Furthermore, we can see that the neighbors based on the product representations from the LMLF are qualitatively worse than those from the BoWLF, which indirectly confirms that the underlying product-related structure encoded by the LMLF is more difficult to extract linearly.

While drawing firm conclusions from this small set of neighbors is obviously ill-advised, the general trend appears to hold in more extensive testing. Broadly speaking, this further strengthens the idea that stronger product representations lead to improvements in rating prediction.

5. DISCUSSION

We develop two new models (BoWLF and LMLF) which exploit text reviews to regularize rating prediction on the Amazon Reviews datasets. BoWLF achieves state of the art results on 27 of the 28 datasets, while LMLF outperforms HFT (but not BoWLF) as dataset size increases. Additionally, we explore the methodology behind the choice of data split, clearly demonstrating that models trained on different data subsets cannot be directly compared. Performing K-fold crossvalidation ($K = 5$), we confirm that BoWLF

Product	HFT	BoWLF	LMLF
Extra Spearmint Sugarfree Gum	Hong Kong Fu Xiang Yuan Moon Cakes French Chew - Vanilla Peck's Anchovette	Dubble Bubble Gum Trident Sugarless White Gum Gold Mine Nugget Bubble Gum	Gumballs Special Assorted Bazooka Bubble Gum Gourmet Spicy Beef Jerky
Dark Chocolate Truffle	Tastykake Kreamies Kakes Ceam .. Miko - Awase Miso Soyabean Paste Haribo Berries Gummi Candy	Ritter Sport Corn Flakes Chocolate Chocolate Dobosh Torte Sugar Free, Milk Chocolate Pecan Turtles	Fantis Grape Leaves Grape Flavoring Tutti Fruitti Flavoring
MTR Simply Tomato Soup	Wellington Cracked Pepper Crackers Maggi Instant Noodles Haribo Gummi Candy	MTR Mulligatawny Soup hai Kitchen Coconut Ginger Soup Miko - Awase Miso Soyabean Paste	Muir Glen Organic Soup Soy Ginger Saba Noodles Alessi Soup

Table 2: Nearest neighbors (cosine similarity) based on product representations estimated by HFT, BoWLF and LMLF, for Gourmet Foods dataset. Qualitatively, the ability to regularize the product representations seems to correlate well with the quality of the neighbourhoods formed in product representation space.

achieves superior performance across dataset splits. The resulting product neighborhoods measured by cosine similarity between product representations are intuitive, and correspond with human analysis of the data. Overall we find that BoWLF has a 20.29% average improvement over basic matrix factorization and a 5.64% average improvement over HFT.

We found that the proposed LMLF slightly lagged behind the BoWLF. As we discuss above, we believe this could be due to the nonlinear nature of language model based on a recurrent neural network. This nonlinearity results in the product-related structure underlying reviews being nonlinearly encoded in the product representation, which cannot be easily extracted by the linear rating prediction model. However, this will need to be further investigated in addition to analyzing the exact effect of language modeling on prediction performance.

Acknowledgements

We would like to thank the developers of Theano [3, 2] and Pylearn2 [6], for developing such a powerful tool for scientific computing. We are grateful to Compute Canada and Calcul Québec for providing us with powerful computational resources.

6. REFERENCES

[1] Y. Bao, H. Fang, and J. Zhang. TopicMF: Simultaneously exploiting ratings and reviews for recommendation. In *AAAI*, 2014.

[2] F. Bastien, P. Lamblin, R. Pascanu, J. Bergstra, I. J. Goodfellow, A. Bergeron, N. Bouchard, and Y. Bengio. Theano: new features and speed improvements. Deep Learning and Unsupervised Feature Learning NIPS 2012 Workshop, 2012.

[3] J. Bergstra, F. Bastien, O. Breuleux, P. Lamblin, R. Pascanu, O. Delalleau, G. Desjardins, D. Warde-Farley, I. J. Goodfellow, A. Bergeron, and Y. Bengio. Theano: Deep learning on gpus with python. In *Big Learn workshop, NIPS'11*, 2011.

[4] D. M. Blei, A. Y. Ng, and M. I. Jordan. Latent dirichlet allocation. *the Journal of machine Learning research*, 3:993–1022, 2003.

[5] R. Caruana. Multitask learning. *Machine learning*, 28(1):41–75, 1997.

[6] I. J. Goodfellow, D. Warde-Farley, P. Lamblin, V. Dumoulin, M. Mirza, R. Pascanu, J. Bergstra, F. Bastien, and Y. Bengio. Pylearn2: a machine learning research library. *arXiv preprint arXiv:1308.4214*, 2013.

[7] A. Graves. Generating sequences with recurrent neural networks. Technical report, arXiv:1308.0850, 2013.

[8] G. E. Hinton. Products of experts. In *Proceedings of the Ninth International Conference on Artificial Neural Networks (ICANN)*, volume 1, pages 1–6, Edinburgh, Scotland, 1999. IEE.

[9] S. Hochreiter and J. Schmidhuber. Long short-term memory. *Neural Computation*, 9(8):1735–1780, 1997.

[10] A. Ilin and T. Raiko. Practical approaches to principal component analysis in the presence of missing values. *The Journal of Machine Learning Research*, 11:1957–2000, 2010.

[11] Q. V. Le and T. Mikolov. Distributed representations of sentences and documents. *CoRR*, abs/1405.4053, 2014.

[12] G. Ling, M. R. Lyu, and I. King. Ratings meet reviews, a combined approach to recommend. In *Proceedings of the 8th ACM Conference on Recommender Systems*, RecSys '14, pages 105–112, New York, NY, USA, 2014. ACM.

[13] J. McAuley and J. Leskovec. Hidden factors and hidden topics: Understanding rating dimensions with review text. In *Proceedings of the 7th ACM Conference on Recommender Systems*, RecSys '13, pages 165–172, New York, NY, USA, 2013. ACM.

[14] T. Mikolov. *Statistical Language Models based on Neural Networks*. PhD thesis, Brno University of Technology, 2012.

[15] T. Mikolov, K. Chen, G. Corrado, and J. Dean. Efficient estimation of word representations in vector space. In *International Conference on Learning Representations: Workshops Track*, 2013.

[16] A. Mnih and R. Salakhutdinov. Probabilistic matrix factorization. In *Advances in neural information processing systems*, pages 1257–1264, 2007.

[17] F. Ricci, L. Rokach, B. Shapira, and P. B. Kantor. *Recommender systems handbook*, volume 1. Springer, 2011.

[18] R. Salakhutdinov and A. Mnih. Bayesian probabilistic matrix factorization using markov chain monte carlo. In *Proceedings of the 25th international conference on Machine learning*, pages 880–887. ACM, 2008.

Dynamic Poisson Factorization

Laurent Charlin
Columbia University
New York, NY
lcharlin@cs.columbia.edu

Rajesh Ranganath
Princeton University
Princeton, NJ
rajeshr@cs.princeton.edu

James McInerney
Columbia University
New York, NY
james@cs.columbia.edu

David M. Blei
Columbia University
New York, NY
david.blei@columbia.edu

ABSTRACT

Models for recommender systems use latent factors to explain the preferences and behaviors of users with respect to a set of items (e.g., movies, books, academic papers). Typically, the latent factors are assumed to be static and, given these factors, the observed preferences and behaviors of users are assumed to be generated without order. These assumptions limit the explorative and predictive capabilities of such models, since users' interests and item popularity may evolve over time. To address this, we propose dPF, a dynamic matrix factorization model based on the recent Poisson factorization model for recommendations. dPF models the time evolving latent factors with a Kalman filter and the actions with Poisson distributions. We derive a scalable variational inference algorithm to infer the latent factors. Finally, we demonstrate dPF on 10 years of user click data from arXiv.org, one of the largest repository of scientific papers and a formidable source of information about the behavior of scientists. Empirically we show performance improvement over both static and, more recently proposed, dynamic recommendation models. We also provide a thorough exploration of the inferred posteriors over the latent variables.

1. INTRODUCTION

The modern internet provides unprecedented access to products and information—examples include books, clothes, movies, news articles, social media streams, and academic papers—but these choices increasingly overwhelm its users. Recommender systems can alleviate this problem. Using historical behavior about what a user clicks (or purchases or watches), recommender systems can learn the users' preferences and form personalized suggestions for each.

Historical data accumulates. Today, services such as movie streaming websites and academic paper repositories have had the same customers for years, sometimes decades. During this time, user preferences evolve. For example, a long-time fan of sports biographies might read a science fiction novel that she finds inspiring, and then starts to read more science fiction in place of biographies. Similarly, items may serve different audiences at different times. For example, academic papers become popular in different fields

as one community discovers the techniques of another; a 1950s paper from signal processing might see renewed importance in the context of modern machine learning.

The problem is that most widely-used recommendation methods assume that user preferences and item attributes are static [20, 12, 5]. Such methods would continue to recommend sports biographies to the new fan of science fiction, and they might not notice that the 1950s paper is now relevant to a new kind of audience. This is the problem that we address in this paper. We develop a new recommendation method, dynamic Poisson factorization (dPF), that captures how users and items change over time.

DPF is a factorization approach. It represents users in terms of latent preferences; it represents items in terms of latent attributes; and it allows both preferences and attributes to change smoothly through time. As an example, we ran our algorithm on ten years of data from arXiv.org, containing users clicking on computer science articles. (ArXiv.org is a preprint server of scientific articles that has been serving users since 1991. Our data span 2003–2013.)

Figure 1 illustrates the kinds of representations that it finds. It shows the changing interests of an academic reader. Ten years ago, this user was interested in graph theory and quantum cryptography later the user was interested in data structures; now the user is interested in compressed sensing (For convenience we have named the latent factors with meaningful labels.) Note that a static recommendation engine would recommend graph theory papers as strongly as compressed sensing papers, even though this user lost interest in graph theory almost ten years ago. The figure also shows the latent attributes of the arXiv paper "The Google Similarity Distance", and how those attributes changed over the years. At first it was popular with graph theorists; since then it has found new audiences in math and quantum computing. Again, a static recommendation system would not capture this change in its audience. Further, for both the user and the paper, the click data alone (pictured on top in the figures) does not reveal the hidden structure at play.

Dynamic Poisson factorization efficiently uncovers sequences of user preferences and sequences of item attributes from large collections of sequential click data, i.e., implicit data. We used our algorithm to study two large real-world data sets, one from Netflix and one from arXiv.org. As we show in Section 3, the richer representation of dPF leads to significantly improved recommendations.

Technical approach. Formally, dynamic Poisson factorization is a new probabilistic model that builds on Poisson factorization (PF) [6]. PF is an effective model of implicit recommendation data, and leads to scalable algorithms for computation about large data sets. Dynamic PF extends PF to handle time series of clicks. It mimics PF within each epoch, but allows the representations of users and items to change across epochs.

While conceptually simple, this comes at the cost of some of the nice mathematical properties of PF, specifically "conditional conjugacy." Conditional conjugacy enables easy-to-derive algorithms for analyzing data, i.e., for performing approximate posterior inference with variational methods. Even without this property, we will derive an efficient algorithm for dPF (Section 2 and Appendix A). As with PF, our algorithm scales with the number of non-zero entries in the user behavior matrix, enabling large-scale analyses of sequential behavior data.

Related Work. Several authors emphasize the importance of time modeling in collaborative filtering. These approaches differ in how they incorporate time information and their use of implicit data.

Koren [11] presents an approach based on matrix factorization that models the ratings as a product of user and item factors. This factorization is augmented with a user-item-time bias and user evolving factors. Our work is similar, but we allow for item-evolving factors to capture the possibility that item traits change over time (see Figure 1 for an example). Further, we provide a probabilistic framework for our model with approximate Bayesian inference to handle the considerable uncertainty that arises when modeling time evolving user behaviors. Similarly, Chatzis posits that only user membership to a discrete *group* (or class of users) evolves at each time-step, with new groups being created over time [4].

Some methods propose factorization of the user-item-time tensor [10, 19]. The intuition behind these methods is to project user and item factors into click space using a time-specific factor. These methods, rather than modeling the evolution of users and items over time, quantify the activity of each dimension of the factor model over time. Thus comparing the trajectories of specific users and items is impossible.

Gultekin and Paisley [7] propose modeling both user and item evolution with a Gaussian state-space model. For computational reasons, they perform a single forward (filtering) pass in time. In our work we show that we can perform both filtering and smoothing on large datasets. Similarly, Li et al. [14] use Dirichlet distributed latent factors, though they take a sampling-based inference approach that is not practical for real world datasets.

All the aforementioned methods are for explicit data. Two additional methods focus on implicit data, though with only user evolving preferences. Sahoo et al. [16] proposes an extension to the hidden Markov model where clicks are drawn from a negative binomial distribution. This discrete class-based approach requires many more classes to represent the same size of space that our additive factors achieve. Acharya et al. [1], constructed from gamma processes, has the advantage of inferring the dimensionality of the latent space, but takes an approach to inference that is not scalable and does not allow for item evolution. Our work is the first model that considers implicit data where both the users and items can evolve over time.

It is worth noting that recommendation frameworks to model general attributes, including context such as location and time, have also been proposed [15, 8]. In principle our work could be used to provide predictions within the framwork of Hidasi and Tikk [8].

2. DYNAMIC POISSON FACTORIZATION

In this section we review matrix factorization methods, Poisson matrix factorization, and introduce dynamic Poisson factorization.

Background: Matrix Factorization and Poisson Matrix Factorization. The work of Koren [11] is based on matrix factorization

as are several of the other time-based methods highlighted at the start of this section. Matrix factorization aims at minimizing the distance between an approximation of the matrix, $U^T V$, and the original matrix Y ($\text{dist}(Y, U^T V)$). This distance often has a probabilistic interpretation. Therefore, obtaining a good approximation (a small distance) can be cast as a maximum likelihood problem. For example, obtaining an approximation to the user-item matrix in terms of $l2$-loss is equivalent to assuming Gaussian noise on the observations. Similarly, $l2$ regularization of the optimization variables is equivalent to assuming Gaussian noise on the equivalent variables of a probabilistic model [2].

Expressing a model in probabilistic terms can reveal previously hidden perspectives. For example, a Gaussian distribution is not appropriate for modelling discrete observations (implicit clicks or explicit ratings) because its support is $\mathbb{R}$ and it places zero probability mass at any discrete point. Furthermore, probabilistic models come with powerful inference techniques rooted in Bayesian statistics. Machine learning using probabilistic models (graphical models) can be understood as a sequence of three steps: 1) posit a generative model of how the observations are generated; 2) condition on the observed data to infer posterior distributions of model's unobserved (latent) variables; 3) use the posteriors according to the generative model to predict unobserved datum. In the context of matrix factorization, the Bayesian approach has been shown to produce superior predictions because it can average over many explanations of the data [17].

Poisson matrix factorization (PF) [6] addresses the mismatch between Gaussian models and the discrete observations. Poisson factorization assumes clicks are Poisson distributed[1] and user/item factors are gamma distributed. This is another difference with respect to Gaussian factorization where factors are typically Gaussian distributed and can therefore be negative. Additively combining non-negative factors can lead to models that are easier to interpret [13]. Poisson factorization has been shown to outperform several types of matrix factorization models, including Gaussian matrix factorization, on recommendation tasks [6]. Furthermore, properties of the Poisson distribution allows the model to easily scale to massive real-life recommendation datasets.

Dynamic Poisson Factorization. Poisson matrix factorization models users and items statically over time. This is unrealistic. For example, the preferences of the user in Figure 1 change from from "Graph Theory" and "Quantum Cryptography" to "Compressed Sensing". Similarly, the readership of the item in Figure 1 evolves from "Graph Theory" to "Quantum & Computational Complexity" and "Data Structures & Probability". To be able to capture both the changes of users and items over time, we introduce dynamic Poisson factorization (dPF).

DPF is a model of user-item clicks over time where time is assumed to be discrete (i.e., the modeler chooses a time window that aggregates clicks in chunks of 1 week, 1 month etc.). The aim is to capture the evolving preferences of users as well as the evolution of item popularity over time. Specifically, dPF models a set of users clicking, or rating, a set of items over time.[2]

We first give a high-level overview of dPF. The strengths of user preferences and item popularities are assumed to be a combination of static and dynamic processes. The static portion assigns each user and item a time-independent representation, while the dynamic

---

[1] In this context maximizing a Poisson likelihood is equivalent to minimizing the generalized-KL between the user-item matrix and its approximation.

[2] In the rest of the exposition we will refer to clicks and ratings interchangeably.

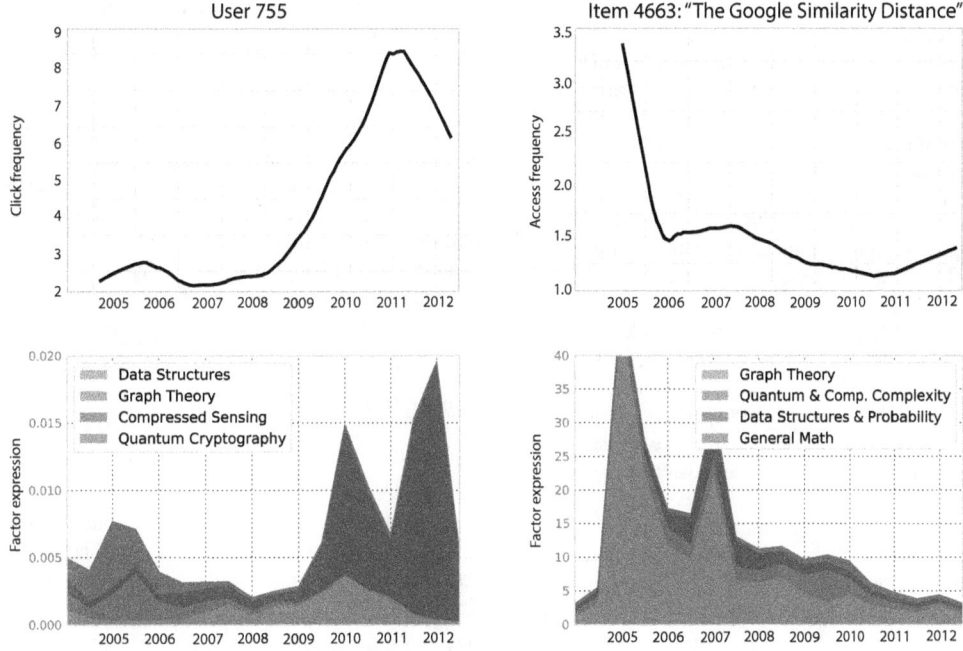

Figure 1: Our method, dPF, discovers evolving user interests and item audiences over time from raw click data. The top left plot shows the aggregate click frequencies for a user on arXiv.org for 8 years. dPF separates this aggregate data into a set of 20 interest groups with varying strengths over time (bottom left). This user was initially interested in quantum cryptography and graph theory; then, five years later, in compressed sensing and data structures. DPF decomposes raw access counts for items in a similar way. The top right plot shows the raw access frequencies for the paper "The Google Similarity Distance" (http://arxiv.org/pdf/cs/0412098.pdf). The bottom right plot indicates that the paper broadened its audience during its lifetime. It was initially popular only with graph theorists, then received attention from quantum physicists and computational complexity readers, perhaps explained by the fact that it was cited in "Google in a Quantum Network" (on arXiv and then in the *Nature* journal).

portion gives each user and item a time evolving model. The static representation is the same as in traditional matrix factorization approaches and captures the baseline interest of users and the baseline popularity of items, which is then modified by dynamic variables. In this respect, dPF is a generalization of PF [6].

We now give the mathematical details for how to capture this intuition in a model. To model time probabilistically, statisticians typically use Gaussian time series models called state space models [2]. In the simplest case, state space models draw the state at the next time step from a Gaussian with mean equal to the previous time step and fixed variance σ^2:

$$x_t | x_{t-1} \sim \mathcal{N}(x_{t-1}, \sigma^2).$$

We use state space models as the dynamic portion of dPF, where both the users and items evolve. Formally, $u_{nk,t}$, the kth component of the nth user at time t is constructed as

$$u_{nk,t} | u_{nk,t-1} \sim \mathcal{N}(u_{nk,t-1}, \sigma_u^2).$$

The state space process for items is symmetric. The static components associated with each user u_{nk} and item v_{mk} are also drawn from a normal distribution. They form the intercepts for a time evolving factorization with Poisson observations. That is, a user's expression of factor k at time t is the sum $\bar{u}_{nk} + u_{nk,t}$. In this sense, the state space model can be viewed as governing *correction factors* and thus capture the evolution of users' preferences through time, while static global factors capture the interest of users that are not influenced by time.

One issue in using Gaussian state space models is that Poisson observations have non-negative parameters (rates). Thus, we exponentiate the state-space models intercept sums for each user and item before combining them to form the mean of the observed rating. Concretely, the rating for user n, item m at time t, $y_{nm,t}$ has the following distribution

$$y_{nm,t} \sim \text{Poisson}(\sum_{k=1}^{K} e^{(u_{nk,t}+\bar{u}_{nk})} e^{(v_{mk,t}+\bar{v}_{mk})}).$$

Putting this all together, the observations are drawn as follows:

1. Draw user global factors: $\bar{u}_{nk} \sim \mathcal{N}(\mu_{\bar{u}}, \sigma_{\bar{u}}^2)$

2. Draw item global factors: $\bar{v}_{mk} \sim \mathcal{N}(\mu_{\bar{v}}, \sigma_{\bar{v}}^2)$

3. For each time step: $t = 1 \dots T$

   Draw user and item correction factors:
   if $t = 1$
   $$u_{nk,1} \sim \mathcal{N}(\mu_u, \sigma_u^2)$$
   $$v_{mk,1} \sim \mathcal{N}(\mu_v, \sigma_v^2)$$
   else
   $$u_{nk,t} | u_{nk,t-1} \sim \mathcal{N}(u_{nk,t-1}, \sigma_u^2)$$
   $$v_{mk,t} | v_{mk,t-1} \sim \mathcal{N}(v_{mk,t-1}, \sigma_v^2)$$
   Draw a click:
   $$y_{nm,t} \sim \text{Poisson}(\sum_{k=1}^{K} e^{(u_{nk,t}+\bar{u}_{nk})} e^{(v_{mk,t}+\bar{v}_{mk})})$$

Unlike Poisson matrix factorization [6] our model uses Gaussian-distributed (global) user and item factors. We could have also used Gamma-distributed factors [1] although the parametrization of Gaussians allows us to independantly control the mean and variance of each Gaussian in the chain. Further, even with this change, dPF can still model the long-tail of users and items, an important advantage of Poisson factorization over Gaussian matrix factorization [6].

Analysis and Predictions. We analyze data through the posterior, $p(u, \bar{u}, v, \bar{v}|Y)$. We use u to represent the set of all user factors and Y the observations. The posterior distribution places probability mass on the latent variables in proportion to how well they explain the observations. The posterior of standard Poisson factorization finds a single set of preferences and attributes, while the dPF posterior places high probability on the sequences of preferences and attributes that best describe the observed data. Figure 1 plots the expected value under the posterior distribution of the expression of factor k by user n, $u_{nk,t} + \bar{u}_{nk}$, and the similar posterior expectation for the items.

In recommendation applications, one wants to use the model to predict the value of unobserved clicks. We obtain predictions by taking the inner product of the expected value of the user factors and item factors under the posterior distribution:

$$\mathrm{E}[y_{nmt}|Y] \approx \sum_k \mathrm{E}_{\text{posterior}}[e^{(u_{nk,t}+\bar{u}_{n,k})}e^{(v_{mk,t}+\bar{v}_{m,k})}]. \quad (1)$$

In practice, recommender systems require rankings (e.g., to show users their top 10 most recommended items when they log on to a website, or to auto-play the most recommended video when the current video has finished). To calculate rankings we use the predictive distribution in Equation 1 as a score for each unobserved rating triplet (i.e., higher predictive probability results in a higher score) and sort the triplets by these scores.

Computation. We approximate the posterior distribution with variational inference, which transforms the posterior estimation problem into an optimization problem. In Appendix A we provide the variational inference algorithm for dPF. The per iteration complexity of performing posterior inference for dPF is $O(T(R + NK + MK))$ where R is the number of non-zero observations of the most populous time step ($R = \max_t R_t$), T the number of time steps, N and M the number of users and items, and K the number of latent components respectively.

The updates of each factor depend only on the other factors in its *Markov blanket* (a factor's parents, its children, and its children's parents). As a consequence, the updates to the variational parameters of each user are independent of all other users (and similarly for items). Hence we can easily parallelize the posterior inference computations. We implement dPF in C++ and use openMP for parallelization.[3] Empirically, we obtain a near linear speedup in the number of threads.

Implementation Details. We initialize hyperparameters ($\mu_u, \mu_v, \bar{\mu}_u, \bar{\mu}_v$) controlling the means to the priors to small random numbers close to 0 and variance hyperparameters ($\sigma_u, \sigma_v, \sigma_{\bar{u}}, \sigma_{\bar{v}}$) to 10. We found that these values work well across different datasets. We provide indications that the model is well-behaved under a wide range of hyperparameter settings (Section 3.4). We have found that for interpretability, it is important to use the same initialization for factors across time. We experimented with initializing the global factors with PF but that did not provide an advantage. We ran the

---

[3]Code is available: https://github.com/Blei-Lab/

the numerical optimization routines for up to 500 iterations or until convergence.

3. EXPERIMENTS

We now fit our model using datasets consisting of users consuming movies and scientists clicking on papers. As we describe in Section 2 we can use the expectation of the posterior distributions over user and item latent factors to provide item recommendations to users through time. In addition to measuring the performance of dPF against baselines we gain insights into the datasets and the model by exploring its posteriors. We highlight the following results:

1. dPF provides better recommendations across multiple datasets compared to several static and dynamic baselines.

2. dPF scales to large datasets.

3. dPF allows us to explore and gain interesting insights into the arXiv dataset.

In Section 3.1, we describe the two datasets used in our experiments. We then formalize the experimental methodology and the comparative metrics in Section 3.2. Finally, we provide comparative and explorative results in Sections 3.3, 3.4, and 3.5.

3.1 Datasets

We study two different datasets.

Netflix-time: First, we consider a movie dataset derived from the Netflix challenge. We follow a similar procedure as described in Li et al. [14] to obtain a subset of the original Netflix dataset focusing on users and movies that have been active over several years. The resulting dataset contains 7.5K users, 3.6K items, and 2 million non-zero observations over 14 time steps (with a granularity of 3 months). The validation and test sets are composed of all the clicks occurring in the final 9 months of the dataset (90K clicks). Since our focus is on the implicit data case, we binarize the data such that every observed rating is a "1" rating and all unobserved ratings are zeros.

Netflix-full: In addition to the Netflix-time dataset, we fit dPF on the whole Netflix dataset (with a granularity of 6 months) where we kept the last 1.5 years of click for validation and test. The resulting dataset contains over 225K users and 14K items and 6.9M observations. This dataset is more challenging for inference because it includes items in the long tail (i.e., a large number of items used by very few users) and very inactive users.

arXiv: DPF is also fit on a click data from the arXiv.org site. arXiv.org is a pre-print server for scientific papers. We have access to ten years of clicks from registered users of arXiv. We keep 75K papers with at least 20 clicks over the ten years and 5K users with clicks spanning at least five years (1.3M observations). We set the time granularity to be six months which seems reasonable to capture scientists' changing preferences. We verified that the results are similar with other time periods. The resulting dataset contains 19 time periods. We keep all observations of the last time step (the last six months) for validation and testing.

arXiv-cs-stats: Physicists were early adopters of the arXiv. As such, fits to the above dataset are dominated by that field. To gain insights into our model's discoveries we have found it useful to restrict our attention to subject areas that were closer to our computer science expertise. This dataset is a cut of the data with papers that are in either computer science (CS) or statistics (Stats) fields. The field(s) of each paper is selected by its authors when submitting. The resulting data has just under 1K users, 5K items and spans 7 years worth of clicks (58K observations). We use this data for explorative purposes (Section 3.5).

3.2 Baselines

We are able to compare to *BPTF*, a recently-proposed dynamic model based on tensor factorization approach. Xiong et al. [19] model the changing strengths of factors over time with a probabilistic tensor approach. In more detail, the observation matrix is assumed to decompose into a tensor product between user preferences, item popularities, and temporal trends. Their approach captures aggregate changes in behavior but is not specific enough to model the time-dependent shifts of individual users or items. They use Gibbs sampling to infer the latent factors given explicit data only, an approach that does not scale when considering implicit data on larger datasets. To adapt this method to the implicit data case we sampled a random subset of unobserved items such as to observe an equal number of zeros and ones.

Another natural benchmark to demonstrate the benefits of time modelling is Poisson matrix factorization, since our model builds on that approach.

An effective time model should be able to learn how to weight the different clicks based on recency and retain the information from older clicks only to the extent that it is useful to predict new ones. For example, in a system where user preferences quickly evolve, the system may rapidly forget about older preferences. To clearly demonstrate the benefits of time modelling we compare to two different PF models. The first is trained using all past ratings (*PF-all*) while the second is trained using only observations at the last (train) time period (*PF-last*).

We note that the implicit data case is significantly more challenging than the usual explicit data case. First, the observations are extremely imbalanced. For example in the datasets used in the experiments "0" observations outnumber "1" observations by a ratio of over 250 to 1 (arXiv). Second, implicit data methods train on exactly NM observations. Finding baselines that will scale to these data sizes is challenging. Furthermore, our focus on implicit data means that we cannot readily compare to previously published results.

We also fit the popular TimeSVD++ model [11]. It is not designed for the implicit data case and preliminary experiments (where we studied different methods of incorporating zero observations) on our Netflix-time dataset showed that it performed significantly worse than all baselines (including both static PF models).

For all experiments we set the number of components to $K = 20$. Our results generalize beyond this value.

3.3 Click prediction & Metrics

We simulate a realistic scenario where each method is given access to past user clicks and the models must predict items of future interest to the users. Further for each dataset we repeat this process for each time step. That is for each time step t we train with all observations before t (i.e., $1 \ldots t - 1$) and evaluate predictions on the observations at t. When reporting results we average over all time steps.

Evaluating the accuracy of a collaborative filtering model for implicit data is usually done using ranking-related error metrics. We consider user recall given K top-items to recommend ("recall@K" see below for details). However, we notice that on datasets containing many items, models often fail to place *any* of the user's consumed items in the top K. These metrics limit our ability to understand the merits of different models. As a remedy we turn to metrics which take into account all test items while discounting the contribution of an item as a function of its predicted rank. The popular NDCG, and mean reciprocal rank (MRR) both have this property. MRR linearly decays the relevance of an item as a function of its rank while NDCG logarithmically decays them. We also report the mean average rank (MAR) metric.

Formally, for binary data the four chosen metrics are:

- Recall@T: $\frac{1}{N} \sum_{i=1}^{N} \sum_{j \in \in \mathbf{y}_i^U} \frac{\mathbf{I}(\mathrm{rank}(i,j) \leqslant T)}{\min(T,|\mathbf{y}_i^U|)}$
  where $\mathbf{I}$ is the indicator function. In our experiments we set T to 50 for all datasets which is a reasonable number of items to present to a user. Results are consistent across other values of T that we have studied.

- Normalized discounted cumulative gain (NDCG):
  $\frac{1}{N} \sum_{i=1}^{N} \sum_{j \in \mathbf{y}_i^U} \frac{1}{\log(\mathrm{rank}(i,j)+1)}$.

- Mean reciprocal rank (MRR): $\frac{1}{N} \sum_{i=1}^{N} \sum_{j \in \mathbf{y}_i^U} \frac{1}{\mathrm{rank}(i,j)}$.

- Mean average rank (MAR): $\frac{1}{N} \sum_{i=1}^{N} \sum_{j \in \mathbf{y}_i^U} \mathrm{rank}(i,j)$.

$\mathbf{y}_i^U$ is the set containing user i's test observations and N the number of users. $\mathrm{rank}(i,j)$ is the predicted rank of item j for user i.

3.4 Results

The results across all datasets consistently show the superior performance of dPF according to all baselines. Below we examine these results in more detail.

We first turn our attention to the Netflix data. On the Netflix-time dataset dPF outperforms all baselines according to all metrics (Table 1). We note that the BPTF baseline mostly outperforms PF-all and PF-last. This indicates that while BPTF's time model is useful, modeling users' and items' individual evolutions is preferable.

The performance on Netflix-full is similar where dPF also outperforms all baselines. Other authors have shown that outperforming static models on Netflix is challenging [19]. As outlined in Koren [11], Netflix users who change at a very fine level of granularity (daily) may be hard to capture with a coarser granularity. Furthermore, we note that users who rarely use the service do not provide enough data to disambiguate between a small number of changing user interests and a wider number of *static* user interests that happen to be exhibited over many time steps (a similar argument applies to movies in the long tail). Nonetheless dPF is able to slightly outperform static methods by capturing evolving preferences and viewer ship where available.

Fitting BPTF to this larger dataset is prohibitively expensive even with our proposed subsampling approach. As such we could not report results on the larger Netflix dataset nor on the arXiv dataset.

The arXiv is a good testbed for our model since scientists and science evolve and we believe that it may be possible to capture such evolutions using arXiv's click data. We note that dPF outperforms all other methods on arXiv (Table 3). This further validates that dPF provides better recommendations by modelling the evolution of users and items.

From a methodological point of view it is also interesting to note that there is not always perfect correlation between all the metrics (that is the rank of the baselines change under different metrics). Amongst them MAR seems to be noisiest metric. It can probably be explained by the fact that it is less robust to outliers because it weights every test observation evenly.

Effect of hyperparameter values.

We have found that dPF is fairly robust to the values of its hyperparameters. We demonstrate it more formally for the variance hyperparameters (Figure 2). We note that except at the extremes the performance of dPF is good for a wide-range of variances. In our experimental setup the last time step is used for predictions. This can may explain the model's robustness.

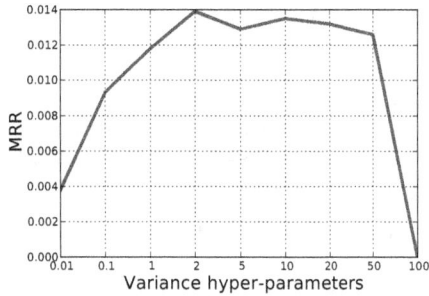

Figure 2: dPF performs well across a large range of variances (2–50) by MRR in a pilot study of a single timestep of the arXiv data.

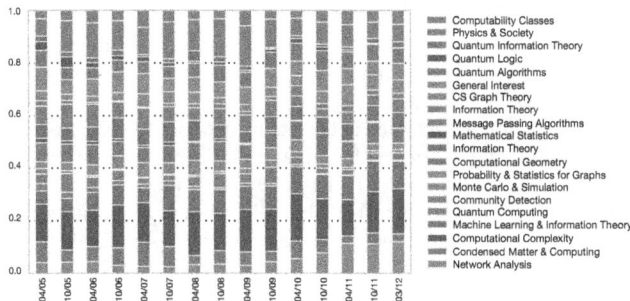

Figure 3: Evolution of latent factors, corresponding to research areas, as discovered by dPF from the raw click data. We see that network analysis has been a growing area of research in computer science over the past decade.

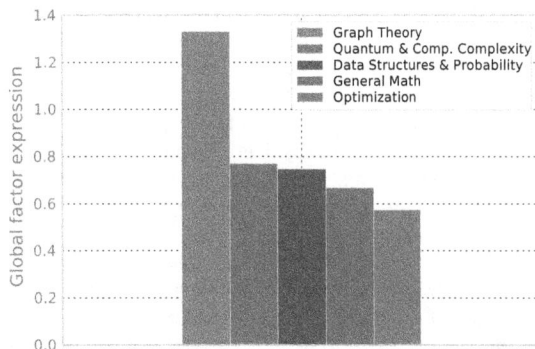

Figure 4: The expression level of five static factors of "The Google Similarity Distance" paper. When compared to the dynamic trend in Figure 1, we see that the static factors identify the paper's main field, graph theory. Moreover, dPF can use the local factors to express excursions to other fields.

	Recall@50	MAR	MRR	NDCG
dPF	**0.170**	**640**	**0.027**	**0.294**
BPTF [19]	0.148	668	0.020	0.277
PF-all [6]	0.145	691	0.021	0.280
PF-last [6]	0.065	807	0.019	0.268

Table 1: Performance of dPF versus baselines on Netflix-time. Bold numbers indicate the top performance for each metric. We were unable to obtain competitive performance from TimeSVD++[11].

	Recall@50	MAR	MRR	NDCG
dPF	**0.156**	**1605**	**0.021**	**0.358**
PF-all [6]	0.120	1807	0.015	0.338
PF-last [6]	0.138	1635	0.018	0.351

Table 2: Performance of dPF versus PF on the Netflix-full dataset. Bold numbers indicate the top performance for each metric. While dPF does best according to all metrics, PF-last slightly outperforms PF-all. The performance of PF-last seems to indicate that user preferences and movie popularities vary rapidly.

3.5 Exploration

There are various ways of evaluating a probabilistic model. While we have provided conclusive empirical results above we now turn to exploration of the model's posteriors. Exploring the posterior can be a useful diagnosis tool [3]. Here our aim is to further validate our modelling choices. We also want to better understand the arXiv-cs-stats dataset.

In Figure 1 we showed, using the local expected value of its factors under their posterior distribution, an item that garnered interest from different communities over time. We can also examine the model's global expected value under the posterior distribution (Figure 4). In addition to the four factors in Figure 1 we added an extra factor (labeled "Optimization") which is unused by this paper. The "Graph Theory" factor is the highest global factor, which is sensible since it expresses the paper's main field. The other three factors are expressed at levels which are in between "Graph Theory" and "Optimization". The global popularity of this paper in these four fields is the same. In particular, dPF can simply use local factors to explain ephemeral popularity in other fields.

In addition to looking at single users and items we can explore the model at the aggregate level to discover global patterns. For example, we can look at the evolution of different scientific fields over time. We plot the expected value of all 20 factors inferred using the arXiv-cs-stats dataset (Figure 3). We corrected for arXiv's growing popularity over time. Scientific fields on arXiv are all well established, and as such, their popularities are stable over time. Note that this does not mean that fields do not evolve. We also notice that according to dPF, some fields have gained in popularity (in particular "Machine Learning & Information Theory" as well as "Networks & Society").

4. CONCLUSIONS & FUTURE WORK

We examined the problem of modelling user-item clicks through time. Our main contribution is the dynamic Poisson factorization model (dPF). In addition to modeling both users and items changing through time and being able to scale to large datasets using implicit information, we showed the empirical advantages of modelling the evolution of users and items. Importantly we used this

	Recall@50	MAR	MRR	NDCG
dPF	**0.035**	**21822**	**0.0062**	**0.186**
PF-all [6]	0.032	22402	0.0056	0.182
PF-last [6]	0.023	25616	0.0040	0.168

Table 3: Performance of dPF versus baselines on arXiv. Bold numbers indicate the top performance for each metric.

model to explore and better understand the arXiv, an indispensable tool to many scientific fields.

There are several opportunities to extend this work. It would be interesting to model aggregate user trajectories to better understand how (scientific) communities evolve. It would also be worthwhile to allow users and items to be modelled at multiple different granularities. This would allow a model to understand both short and long-term evolutions. Although we can set the granularity in our current computation (and memory consumption) may become an issue as the granularity gets small. Continuous time models may offer interesting avenues to avoid specifying granularities.

Acknowledgements. We thank the reviewers for their helpful comments. RR is supported by an NDSEG fellowship. DMB is supported by NSF IIS-0745520, NSF IIS-1247664, ONR N00014-11-1-0651, and DARPA FA8750-14-2-0009.

References

[1] A. Acharya, J. Ghosh, and M. Zhou. Nonparametric bayesian factor analysis for dynamic count matrices. In *Proceedings of the 18th Conference on Artificial Intelligence and Statistics*, 2015.

[2] C. M. Bishop. *Pattern Recognition and Machine Learning*. Springer, 2006.

[3] D. M. Blei. Build, compute, critique, repeat: Data analysis with latent variable models. *Annual Review of Statistics and Its Application*, 1(1):203–232, 2014. doi: 10.1146/annurev-statistics-022513-115657.

[4] S. Chatzis. Dynamic bayesian probabilistic matrix factorization. In *Proceedings of the Twenty-Eighth AAAI Conference on Artificial Intelligence, 2014.*, pages 1731–1737, 2014.

[5] M. D. Ekstrand, J. T. Riedl, and J. A. Konstan. Collaborative filtering recommender systems. *Foundations and Trends in Human-Computer Interaction*, 4(2):81–173, 2011.

[6] P. Gopalan, J. Hofman, and D. Blei. Scalable recommendation with hierarchical poisson factorization. In *Proceedings of the Thirti-first Conference Annual Conference on Uncertainty in Artificial Intelligence (UAI-15)*. AUAI Press, 2015.

[7] S. Gultekin and J. Paisley. A collaborative kalman filter for time-evolving dyadic processes. In *2014 IEEE International Conference on Data Mining, ICDM, 2014*, pages 140–149, 2014.

[8] B. Hidasi and D. Tikk. General factorization framework for context-aware recommendations. *Data Mining and Knowledge Discovery*, pages 1–30, 2015. ISSN 1384-5810.

[9] M. I. Jordan, editor. *Learning in Graphical Models*. MIT Press, Cambridge, MA, USA, 1999. ISBN 0-262-60032-3.

[10] A. Karatzoglou, X. Amatriain, L. Baltrunas, and N. Oliver. Multiverse recommendation: n-dimensional tensor factorization for context-aware collaborative filtering. In *Proceedings of the fourth ACM conference on Recommender systems*, pages 79–86. ACM, 2010.

[11] Y. Koren. Collaborative filtering with temporal dynamics. *Commun. ACM*, 53(4):89–97, 2010.

[12] Y. Koren and J. Sill. Ordrec: an ordinal model for predicting personalized item rating distributions. In *Proceedings of the fifth ACM conference on Recommender systems*, pages 117–124, 2011.

[13] D. D. Lee and H. S. Seung. Learning the parts of objects by non-negative matrix factorization. *Nature*, 401(6755):788–791, 10 1999.

[14] B. Li, X. Zhu, R. Li, C. Zhang, X. Xue, and X. Wu. Cross-domain collaborative filtering over time. In *Proceedings of the Twenty-Second International Joint Conference on Artificial Intelligence - Volume Volume Three*, IJCAI'11, pages 2293–2298. AAAI Press, 2011.

[15] S. Rendle. Factorization machines. In *Proceedings of the 10th IEEE International Conference on Data Mining*. IEEE Computer Society, 2010.

[16] N. Sahoo, P. V. Singh, and T. Mukhopadhyay. A hidden markov model for collaborative filtering. *MIS Q.*, 36(4):1329–1356, Dec. 2012.

[17] R. Salakhutdinov and A. Mnih. Bayesian probabilistic matrix factorization using Markov chain Monte Carlo. In *Proceedings of the International Conference on Machine Learning*, volume 25, 2008.

[18] C. Wang and D. Blei. Variational inference in nonconjugate models. *Journal of Machine Learning Research*, 14:1005–1031, 2013.

[19] L. Xiong, X. Chen, T.-K. Huang, J. Schneider, and J. G. Carbonell. Temporal collaborative filtering with bayesian probabilistic tensor factorization. In *Proceedings of SIAM Data Mining*, 2010.

[20] X. Yi, L. Hong, E. Zhong, N. N. Liu, and S. Rajan. Beyond clicks: dwell time for personalization. In *Proceedings of the 8th ACM Conference on Recommender systems*, pages 113–120, 2014.

APPENDIX

A. INFERENCE

Performing Bayesian inference on the random variables of dPF requires calculating the posterior distribution. This is difficult due to the non-conjugacy (lack of analytic integrals) between the log-normal distribution of the factors and the Poisson-distributed observations. We therefore resort to approximate inference techniques (e.g., Markov chain Monte Carlo or variational methods).

Variational inference frames the posterior inference task as the problem of minimizing the KL-divergence between an approximate distribution and the true posterior. This optimization approach is orders of magnitudes faster than sampling-based approaches, at the cost of not being able to capture the full Bayesian posterior.

We assume that our approximating family (in variational inference) fully factorizes. The variational distribution of individual factors is normally-distributed:

$$
\begin{aligned}
q(\mathbf{u}_{nt}) &= \prod_k q(u_{nt,k}|\hat{\mu}_{unt,k}, \hat{\sigma}^2_{unt,k}) \\
&= \prod_k \mathcal{N}(u_{nt,k}|\hat{\mu}_{unt,k}, \hat{\sigma}^2_{unt,k})
\end{aligned}
$$

We treat the other time-independent (v) and time-dependent ($\bar{u}$ and $\bar{v}$) latent variables in a similar way. To differentiate the variables of the generative model from their variational counterparts we denote the latter with a circumflex (a "hat").

It is straightforward to show that minimizing the KL-divergence between the q distribution and the true posterior is equivalent to maximizing a lower bound on the model's log evidence [9].[4] We use the bold symbols to denote sets of factors, for example the set of all user factors: $\mathbf{u} \equiv \{u_{nt,k}\}_{n=0:N,t=1:T}$. ζ stands for the set of all hyperparameters: $\{\mu_u, \sigma_u, \mu_v, \sigma_v, \mu_{\bar{u}}, \sigma_{\bar{u}}, \mu_{\bar{v}}, \sigma_{\bar{v}}\}$. λ denotes all of the parameters to the variational distribution such as $\hat{\mu}_{unk,t}$ and $\hat{\sigma}^2_{unk,t}$. For our model, this evidence lower bound (ELBO) is

$$
p(\mathbf{y}|\zeta) \geqslant \mathcal{L}(\lambda) \tag{2}
$$
$$
:= \mathrm{E}_q[\log p(\mathbf{y}, \mathbf{u}, \mathbf{v}, \bar{\mathbf{u}}, \bar{\mathbf{v}}|\zeta)] - \mathrm{E}_q[\log q(\mathbf{u}, \mathbf{v}, \bar{\mathbf{u}}, \bar{\mathbf{v}})].
$$

The fully-factorized approximation allows us to expand the ELBO as follows:

$$
\sum_n^N \mathrm{E}_q[\log p(\bar{\mathbf{u}}_n|\boldsymbol{\mu}_{\bar{u}}, \sigma^2_{\bar{u}}\mathbf{I})] + \sum_m^M \mathrm{E}_q[\log p(\bar{\mathbf{v}}_m|\boldsymbol{\mu}_{\bar{v}}, \sigma^2_{\bar{v}}\mathbf{I})]
$$
$$
+ \sum_{t=2,n}^{T,N} \mathrm{E}_q[\log p(\mathbf{u}_{n,t}|\mathbf{u}_{n,t-1}, \sigma^2_u\mathbf{I})] + \sum_n^N \mathrm{E}_q[\log p(\mathbf{u}_{n,1}|\boldsymbol{\mu}_u, \sigma^2_u\mathbf{I})]
$$
$$
+ \sum_{t=2,m}^{T,M} \mathrm{E}_q[\log p(\mathbf{v}_{m,t}|\mathbf{v}_{m,t-1}, \sigma^2_v\mathbf{I})] + \sum_m^M \mathrm{E}_q[\log p(\mathbf{v}_{v,1}|\boldsymbol{\mu}_v, \sigma^2_v\mathbf{I})]
$$
$$
+ \sum_{n,m,t}^{N,M,T} \mathrm{E}_q[\log p(y_{nm,t}|\sum_k exp(u_{nk,t} + \bar{u}_{nk})^T exp(v_{mk,t} + \bar{v}_{mk}))]
$$
$$
+ H(q)
$$

where $H(q)$ is the entropy of the variational distribution.

To optimize the ELBO one typically expands the expectations in Equation 3. The variational parameters can then be optimized using coordinate or gradient ascent. The non-conjugacy in our model implies that further manipulations are required to express the expectations from Equation 3 in closed form. In particular the term requiring an additional approximation comes from the Poisson distribution. The Poisson pdf, with rate λ is $\frac{\lambda^k}{k!}e^{-\lambda}$. The first term

---

[4]The model evidence is also referred to as the marginal likelihood.

For $t = 1 \dots T$:

Update $\hat{\mu}_{unk,t}$ and $\hat{\sigma}_{unk,t}$ with L-BFGS using $\nabla_{\hat{\mu}_{unk,t}, \hat{\sigma}_{unk,t}} \mathcal{L}$ $\forall n, k$

Update $\hat{\mu}_{vmk,t}$ and $\hat{\sigma}_{vmk,t}$ with L-BFGS using $\nabla_{\hat{\mu}_{vmk,t}, \hat{\sigma}_{vmk,t}} \mathcal{L}$ $\forall m, k$

Update $\hat{\phi}_{nmk,t}$ $\forall n, m, k, t \mid y_{n,mt} > 0$ using Eq. 8

Update $\hat{\mu}_{\bar{u}n,k}$ and $\hat{\sigma}_{\bar{u}n,k}$ with L-BFGS using $\nabla_{\hat{\mu}_{\bar{u}n,k}, \hat{\sigma}_{\bar{u}n,k}}$ $\forall n, k$

Update $\hat{\mu}_{\bar{v}m,k}$ and $\hat{\sigma}_{\bar{v}m,k}$ with L-BFGS using $\nabla_{\hat{\mu}_{\bar{v}m,k}, \hat{\sigma}_{\bar{v}m,k}} \mathcal{L}$ $\forall m, k$

Repeat until convergence

Figure 5: Coordinate ascent algorithm for dPF. We first update the (variational) correction factors and subsequently we update the (variational) global factors. Prior to each update the corresponding vector ϕ_{nmt} must be evaluated.

in the ELBO as expressed in Equation 3 (the joint distribution over latent and observed variables) can be re-written using the product rule of probability as:

$$
\mathrm{E}_q[\log p(\mathbf{y}|\mathbf{u}, \mathbf{v}, \bar{\mathbf{u}}, \bar{\mathbf{v}}) + \log p(\mathbf{u}, \mathbf{v}, \bar{\mathbf{u}}, \bar{\mathbf{v}}|\zeta)].
$$

The first term corresponds to the Poisson distribution. It can be expanded into:

$$
\begin{aligned}
\mathrm{E}_q[\log \frac{\lambda^k}{k!} \exp^{-\lambda}] &= \mathrm{E}_q[k \log \lambda - k! - \lambda] \\
&= \mathrm{E}_q[k \log \lambda] - \mathrm{E}_q[\lambda] - k!
\end{aligned}
$$

where $\lambda = \sum_k \exp(u_{nk,t} + \bar{u}_{nk}) \exp(v_{mk,t} + \bar{v}_{mk})$. We do not know of a closed-form exact solution to the first expectation when k is non-zero. Fortunately several known techniques can be used to approximate this integral [18]. We re-use an idea from the recent Poisson factorization which consists of adding a set of auxiliary random variables. For dPF, this means adding auxilliary variables $\phi_{mnt,k}$ one for each user-item-timestep component for all of the non-zero ratings. Formally, this allows for the following manipulation:

$$
\log \sum_k \exp(u_{nk,t} + \bar{u}_{nk}) \exp(v_{mk,t} + \bar{v}_{mk}) \tag{3}
$$
$$
= \log \sum_k \frac{\phi_{nmk,t}}{\phi_{nmk,t}} \exp(u_{nk,t} + \bar{u}_{nk}) \exp(v_{mk,t} + \bar{v}_{mk}) \tag{4}
$$
$$
= \log \mathrm{E}_\phi[\frac{\exp(u_{nk,t} + \bar{u}_{nk}) \exp(v_{mk,t} + \bar{v}_{mk})}{\phi_{nmk,t}}] \tag{5}
$$
$$
\geqslant \mathrm{E}_\phi[u_{nk,t} + \bar{u}_{nk} + v_{mk,t} + \bar{v}_{mk} - \log \phi_{nmk,t}] \tag{6}
$$
$$
\tag{7}
$$

We obtain the last inequality by applying Jensen's inequality. We note that, unlike in Poisson factorization, the resulting model is not conditionally conjugate, which intuitively means the distribution of a variable given everything else has known form. As a result, the equations do not yield closed-form updates. We use numerical optimization and perform coordinate ascent on the ELBO using a quasi-Newton optimizer (L-BFGS). The update for $\phi_{nmt,k}$ can be solved for in expected value with respect to q of Eq. 7 as

$$
\phi_{nmk,t} \propto \exp(\hat{u}_{nk,t} + \hat{\bar{u}}_{nk} + \hat{v}_{mk,t} + \hat{\bar{v}}_{mk}) \tag{8}
$$

The algorithm used to infer the variational posteriors (i.e., train the model) is shown in Figure 5.

Blockbusters and Wallflowers: Accurate, Diverse, and Scalable Recommendations with Random Walks

Fabian Christoffel[a], Bibek Paudel[a], Chris Newell[b], Abraham Bernstein[a]
[a]Department of Informatics, University of Zurich, Zurich, Switzerland
[b]Research and Development, British Broadcasting Corporation, London, United Kingdom
fabian.christoffel@uzh.ch, {paudel, bernstein}@ifi.uzh.ch, chris.newell@bbc.co.uk

ABSTRACT

User satisfaction is often dependent on providing accurate and diverse recommendations. In this paper, we explore scalable algorithms that exploit random walks as a sampling technique to obtain diverse recommendations without compromising on accuracy. Specifically, we present a novel graph vertex ranking recommendation algorithm called RP^3_β that re-ranks items based on 3-hop random walk transition probabilities. We show empirically, that RP^3_β provides accurate recommendations with high long-tail item frequency at the top of the recommendation list. We also present scalable approximate versions of RP^3_β and the two most accurate previously published vertex ranking algorithms based on random walk transition probabilities and show that these approximations converge with increasing number of samples.

Categories and Subject Descriptors: H.3.3 [Information Search and Retrieval]: Information Filtering

Keywords: top-N recommendation; item ranking; diversity; long-tail; bipartite graph; random walks; sampling

1. INTRODUCTION

Users increasingly rely on recommender systems to choose movies, books, restaurants and other items. These systems are usually based on the assumption that users prefer items similar to those they previously liked or those liked by other users with similar preferences. However, this approach has some deficiences. Pariser [18] introduced the term "filter bubble" to describe how personalized recommendations can isolate people from diverse viewpoints or products. This has also led to the concern that recommender systems may reinforce the blockbuster nature of media [8] due to their promotion of already popular products. Also, the focus on the predictive accuracy of recommender systems can lead to a bias towards popular items over more specialized items. In other words, systems that are optimized for accuracy tend to produce unsurprising and boring recommendations.

User satisfaction depends on many factors such as variety, new experiences and serendipitous discovery which are

RecSys'15, September 16–20, 2015, Vienna, Austria.
Copyright is held by the owner/author(s). Publication rights licensed to ACM.
ACM 978-1-4503-3692-5/15/09 ...$15.00.
DOI: http://dx.doi.org/10.1145/2792838.2800180 .

not captured by accuracy metrics. These factors depend on finding suitable long tail items, which raise user satisfaction and, in turn, profitability [11]. Hence, a recent trend is to build recommender systems that do not only focus on optimizing the accuracy but also consider the diversity of recommendations [1, 2, 23, 24]. However, these can be conflicting goals as increasing diversity may produce irrelevant recommendations.

Recently, it was shown that approximations based on random graph walks can be used for accurate recommendations [6]. These algorithms are more accurate than previously presented vertex ranking methods (e.g., [9]) with the additional benefit of being computationally efficient and scalable. In this paper, we *explore scalable algorithms that exploit random walks as a sampling technique to obtain diverse recommendations without compromising on accuracy.*

Specifically, our contributions are: First, we introduce RP^3_β, a simple item popularity dependent re-ranking procedure of P^3 [6]. We show using three implicit feedback datasets (two public, one enterprise) that RP^3_β augments long-tail item recommendations while keeping accuracy high. Second, we empirically compare the performance of vertex ranking algorithms [9, 6, 23] including our own RP^3_β with traditional state-of-the-art methods. We find that some vertex ranking algorithms achieve comparable or better performance than the traditional ones. Third, we present scalable approximation algorithms for RP^3_β, P^3_α [6], as well as H_λ [23] based on random walk sampling. In a detailed evaluation we show that these methods converge to the performance scores of exact calculations. Last, we analyze the trade-off between sampling size (i.e., number of performed random walks) versus accuracy and diversity performance and find that RP^3_β provides a useful trade-off between accuracy, diversity, and sample size.

The remainder of this paper begins with a description of our data model and notations. We present a literature review in Section 3. We then describe our method RP^3_β and our approximations for P^3_α, RP^3_β, and H_λ. The experimental results are presented in Section 6 followed by conclusions.

2. MODEL

The recommendation algorithms studied in this paper try to rank the items in the training set for each user in the test set by decreasing appreciation. The algorithms are based on walks over the graph $G = (V, E)$ constructed from the users' feedback on items (*user-item-feedback graph*). The vertices V of G represent the union of the two entity sets users U and items I (i.e., $V = U \cup I$) in the training data.

If user $u \in U$ implicitly rated item $i \in I$ in the training phase (e.g., by accessing the item) then the graph's edge set $E \subseteq U \times I$ contains the edge $e = \{u, i\}$. As E contains no other edges, G is bipartite. All edges in the graph are unweighted/undirected and no parallel edges exist. Edge weights or parallel edges (e.g., based on rating values or the number of interactions) could be used for a more accurate representation of the users preference profile, but we do not consider this extension in the presented work.

The square matrix $A \in \{0, 1\}^{|V| \times |V|}$ is the *adjacency matrix* of G. Since edges of G are undirected, A is symmetric. The entry a_{ij} of A is 1 for two connected vertices i and j, and 0 otherwise. $D^{|V| \times |V|}$ is the diagonal *degree matrix* of G with $d_{ii} = \sum_{j=1}^{|V|} a_{ij}$. Assuming all diagonal elements of D are non-zero (i.e., no unconnected vertices), its inverse D^{-1} is given by (d_{ii}^{-1}), and hence cheap to compute.

A *random walk* process on G can be seen as a discrete Markov chain, where a walker starts on a vertex $v(0)$ and at each time step moves to one of its neighbors chosen randomly. After s steps, the sequence of vertices visited by the walker $\langle v(0), v(1), \ldots v(s) \rangle$ forms a Markov chain. The probability of transitioning from a vertex i to j is $p_{ij} = a_{ij}/d_{ii}$. Hence, the corresponding transition matrix $P^{|V| \times |V|}$ for one-step ($s = 1$) random walks is given by $P = D^{-1}A$. Furthermore, we obtain the s-step random walk transition probability matrix (we refer to its elements with p_{ij}^s) with

$$P^s = (D^{-1}A)^s. \tag{1}$$

Since we want to rank items i for users u, this paper considers random walks starting at user vertices and ending at item vertices (i.e., having an odd number of steps). To denote transition probabilities estimated using random walk samples (see Section 5), we write $\hat{p}_{ij}^s$. In general, an estimate of a random variable X is represented as $\hat{X}$.

3. RELATED WORK

In this section we discuss previous work on vertex ranking algorithms, sampling techniques, and diversity.

Graph based algorithms: The use of a graph-based model for recommendations was first introduced in [3]. To apply a bipartite user-item-feedback graph G was proposed in [14] and several projects [4, 5, 6, 9, 12, 15, 16, 22] extended this approach. We classify them as *vertex ranking algorithms* because their main idea is to rank the vertices in the graph based on their similarities with the target user and use the ranking to generate recommendations. Fouss *et al.* [9] introduced the idea of using random walks on G to rank the vertices. Vertices are ranked or scored based on quantities like hitting time, average commute time or the entries in the Moore-Penrose pseudo inverse of the Laplacian matrix of the graph (L^+). ItemRank [12] also scores vertices based on random walks on the graph, but uses a graph representing item correlations.

Random walk approximations: Cooper *et al.* [6] proposed three new methods called P^3, P^5, and P_{α}^3 based on random walks on G. They rank vertices based on transition probabilities after short random walks between users and items. P^3 and P^5 perform random walks of fixed length 3 and 5, respectively, starting from a target user vertex. P_{α}^3, which raises the transition probabilities to the power of α, is more accurate than the methods proposed in [9] and [12]. They also show that approximating the P^3 and P^5 rankings

with time- and memory-efficient random walk sampling is more scalable compared to methods based on matrix calculations, i.e., the methods can be applied to larger datasets.

Diversity in recommendations: The erstwhile focus of recommender systems research on improving accuracy (how well the system can predict future user behavior) was criticized as being detrimental to the goals of improving user experience and sales diversity [7, 17]. A recent trend, therefore, is to focus on the diversity of recommendations along with accuracy. Notions of novelty and diversity in recommender systems, as well as measures to quantify, and methods to improve them have been described by various authors [1, 2, 13, 21, 24]. Optimizing only for diversity will cause highly varied but irrelevant recommendations. Therefore it is necessary to find diverse recommendations that are also accurate. Zhou *et. al* [23] use vertex ranking algorithms to improve diversity and accuracy. Specifically, they describe a hybrid method (Hybrid or H_{λ}) that combines the ranking of an accurate with the ranking of a diverse algorithm.

In this work, we focus on the task of generating diverse and accurate recommendations with vertex ranking algorithms using scalable random walk sampling. To the best of our knowledge, this is the first work to bring together the three streams reviewed above: graph-based approaches, random walk approximation, and diversity. There are different notions of diversity in recommendation lists. Following [2, 23], we use three top-k measures to evaluate recommendation quality in terms of diversity: personalization, item-space coverage, and surprisal. Surprisal assures inclusion of long-tail items at the top of recommendation list, item-space coverage assures that varying long-tail items are considered, and personalization measures how much the recommendation list differs between users. We introduce RP_{β}^3, a novel algorithm to optimize the accuracy and diversity trade-off by re-ranking the P^3 item ranking. RP_{β}^3 benefits from the good scalability of approximating P^3 with random walk sampling. Also, we present approximations for H_{λ} and P_{α}^3 with the same sampling approach.

4. RP_{β}^3: POPULARITY-BASED RE-RANKING

In our experiments, we observed (see Section 6.3) that the ranking of items according to the transition probability matrix P^3 is strongly influenced by the popularity (i.e., vertex degree) of items. Hence, for most users the well known blockbuster (or high-degree) items dominate the recommendation lists. To compensate for the influence of popularity and to leverage recommendation of items from the long-tail, we introduce a simple re-ranking procedure dependent on item-popularity. The original score of item i for user u given by p_{ui}^3 (the transition probability after a random walk of length three from u to i). We re-weight the score with

$$\tilde{p}_{ui}^3 = \frac{p_{ui}^3}{d_{ii}^{\beta}} \text{ , where } \beta \in \mathbb{R} \text{ and } \beta > 0.0. \tag{2}$$

For two items i, j ($i \neq j$), a user u with $p_{ui}^3 = p_{uj}^3$ (equal probability of reaching the items from the user in a three-step random walk), and $d_{ii} < d_{jj}$ (i has a lower degree), the effect of our re-weighting is that i is ranked higher than j ($\tilde{p}_{uj}^3 < \tilde{p}_{ui}^3$). These items would have received equal scores without the re-weighting. We refer to this recommendation algorithm as RP_{β}^3. When we set the parameter $\beta = 0.0$, then RP_{β}^3 produces the same score as P^3 as $d_{ii}^{\beta=0} = 1$.

5. APPROXIMATING P_α^3, RP_β^3, AND H_λ

In a recent paper, Cooper *et al.* [6] compare two approaches to calculate vertex transition probabilities: by exact calculations using matrix algebra and by approximation via random walk sampling. It is shown that the latter approach is time- and memory-efficient, allowing the application on larger datasets with only limited impact on accuracy. However, they do not describe a sampling procedure for their algorithm P_α^3. Similarly, H_λ, a vertex-ranking algorithm that increases both recommendation accuracy and diversity [23], could also be made more scalable with a sampling procedure instead of exact calculations with matrix algebra.

This section introduces a novel random walk sampling procedure for both of these two algorithms as well as our reranking algorithm RP_β^3 .

5.1 Sampling as a Bernoulli Process

In order to estimate transition probabilities for user u using samples, we start multiple s-step random walks from u. We store the number of times each item i is visited by walks at the sth step. For reasons of efficiency, we would like to estimate the probabilities only based on these counts and the degrees of vertices traversed by the path. This sampling procedure can be modeled as a Bernoulli process as follows:

Denote the path traversed by the rth random walk of length s starting at u as $\pi_u^{r,s}$. Then define $I_r^s(u,i) = c_{rw}(\pi_u^{r,s})$ if i is the sth vertex in path $\pi_u^{r,s}$, i.e., if $\pi_u^{r,s}[s] = i$, and $I_r^s(u,i) = 0$ otherwise. The quantity $c_{rw}(\pi_u^{r,s})$ is a function of the vertices' degrees in the path (and varies for different algorithms). For simplicity, we use $I_r(u,i)$ for random walks of a fixed given length (e.g., $s \in \{3,5\}$). Next, define $\tau(u,i)$ as the score of item i for user u and $\hat{\tau}(u,i)$ as its estimator. When sampling N random walks starting from u, the estimator can be defined as $\hat{\tau}(u,i) = \frac{1}{N}\sum_{r=1}^{N} I_r(u,i)$. Given the law of large numbers, the expected value for $\hat{\tau}(u,i)$ is $E[\hat{\tau}(u,i)] = \tau(u,i)$. Also, walks are independent and $I_r \in [0,\psi]$ is i.i.d, where ψ is the maximum possible value for c_{rw}.

Similar to [20], we can use Hoeffding's inequality to show that the rate of convergence is exponential. Furthermore, using Union bound, the probability of the ϵ-approximate estimate for *any* user being less than δ is given as:
$$P(\exists u \in U, |\hat{\tau}(u,i) - \tau(u,i)| \geq \epsilon) \leq 2|U| \, exp(-\frac{2N\epsilon^2}{\psi^2}) \leq \delta$$
This provides a lower bound for N as $\frac{\psi^2}{2\epsilon^2}log\frac{2|U|}{\delta}$. For a fixed ϵ and δ, the number of walks required increases with ψ, which depends on the algorithm in use and degree distribution of the graph (due to different forms of c_{rw}).

For our method RP_β^3 (Section 4), $c_{rw}(\pi_u^{r,s})$ is simply $1/d_{ii}^\beta$, hence, $\psi = 1/argmin_i(d_{ii}^\beta)$ and the scores can be estimated as described above. For P_α^3 and H_λ, $c_{rw}(\pi_u^{r,s})$ takes more complicated forms, which we discuss below. Hereafter, we denote a path simply as π.

5.2 Approximating P_α^3 and RP_β^3

Ordering items in descending order according to the transition probabilities of random walks of length three (P^3, $s = 3$) is an accurate recommendation strategy, named P^3 in [6] and ProbS in [23]. The accuracy of this algorithm can be further improved by raising each entry of the transition probability matrix P^1 ($s = 1$) to the power of a parameter $\alpha \in \mathbb{R}$

resulting in an algorithm called P_α^3 by [6]. It follows from (1) that entries of the matrix P^1 raised to the power of α are calculated as $p_{ui_\alpha}^1 = (p_{ui}^1)^\alpha = (a_{ui}/d_{uu})^\alpha$, where $a_{ui} \in A$ (entry in adjacency matrix) and $d_{uu} \in D$ (entry in degree matrix). The transition probability $p_{ui_\alpha}^3 \in P_\alpha^3$ from user u to item i after a random walk of length three is obtained by:

$$p_{ui_\alpha}^3 = \sum_{v=1}^{|V|}\sum_{j=1}^{|V|} p_{uj_\alpha}p_{jv_\alpha}p_{vi_\alpha} = \sum_{v=1}^{|V|}\sum_{j=1}^{|V|} \left(\frac{a_{uj}}{d_{uu}}\right)^\alpha \left(\frac{a_{jv}}{d_{jj}}\right)^\alpha \left(\frac{a_{vi}}{d_{vv}}\right)^\alpha \quad (3)$$

Since the graph G defined in Section 2 is both bipartite (there are no edges from users to users or from items to items) and all entries in the adjacency matrix A are either 0 or 1, we can simplify (3) as:

$$p_{ui_\alpha}^3 = \sum_{v=1}^{|I|}\sum_{j=1}^{|U|} \frac{a_{uj}a_{jv}a_{vi}}{(d_{uu}d_{jj}d_{vv})^\alpha} \quad (4)$$

The term $a_{uj}a_{jv}a_{vi}$ in (4) is 1 if a path of length three starting from user u, through item j and user v, to item i exists in the graph G and is 0 otherwise. Hence, $p_{ui_\alpha}^3$ is the aggregate of all paths of length three between user u and item i, where each path $\pi = \langle U_u, I_j, U_v, I_i \rangle$ contributes $c_\pi^{P_\alpha^3} = \frac{1}{(d_{uu}d_{jj}d_{vv})^\alpha}$ to the total transition probability from user u to item i.

When approximating (4) with random walk sampling, one needs to take into account that some walks are more likely to be followed randomly than others. The probability of following the path from u via the item j and user v to item i in a random walk is dependent on three decisions. First, at user u, one needs to follow the edge that connects u to item j. The probability of randomly picking this edge is equal to the inverse of the degree of u: $\Pr(u \rightarrow j) = \frac{1}{d_{uu}}$. Next, the same procedure needs to be repeated at j and v, resulting in $\Pr(j \rightarrow v) = \frac{1}{d_{jj}}$ and $\Pr(v \rightarrow i) = \frac{1}{d_{vv}}$. Given that these three "choices" are independent, the probability $Pr(\pi)$ that one follows the path π is equal to

$$\Pr(\pi) = \Pr(u \rightarrow j)\Pr(j \rightarrow v)\Pr(v \rightarrow i) = \frac{1}{d_{uu}d_{jj}d_{vv}}. \quad (5)$$

Hence, when approximating with random walks, we are more likely to follow paths traversing vertices of low degrees than to follow paths traversing vertices of high degrees. Since an exact calculation of (4) requires following each path exactly once, random walk sampling needs to discount the contribution of paths with high probabilities (as we may by chance follow them many times), and boost the contribution of paths with low probabilities (as we may by chance follow them only few times). Consequently, to approximate the transition probability $\hat{p}_{ui_\alpha}^3$, we weigh a path contribution $c_\pi^{P_\alpha^3}$ with the inverse of its occurrence probability $(\Pr(\pi)^{-1})$ resulting in an overall weight $c_{rw}^{\hat{P}_\alpha^3}$ for a random walk:

$$c_{rw}^{\hat{P}_\alpha^3} = c_\pi^{P_\alpha^3} * \Pr(\pi)^{-1}$$
$$= \underbrace{\frac{1}{(d_{uu}d_{jj}d_{vv})^\alpha}}_{\substack{\text{path contribu-}\\\text{tion}}} * \underbrace{d_{uu}d_{jj}d_{vv}}_{\substack{\text{inverted path}\\\text{probability}}} = \underbrace{(d_{uu}d_{jj}d_{vv})^{1-\alpha}}_{\substack{\text{random walk}\\\text{contribution}}} \quad (6)$$

We can simplify $c_{rw}^{\hat{P}_\alpha^3}$ to $(d_{jj}d_{vv})^{1-\alpha}$ since d_{uu} takes the same value for all random walks of the target user u and, hence, does not influence the item ranking order.

Algorithm 1 Estimating item scores of $\hat{P}^3_\alpha$, $R\hat{P}^3_\beta$, or $\hat{H}_\lambda$ with random walk sampling.

Require: v_u is the vertex representing user u

1: **function** ESTIMATEITEMSCORES(v_u)
2:      $m \leftarrow$ an associative array with default value 0
3:      **while** !CONVERGED(m) **do**
4:          $v_c \leftarrow$ GETRANDOMNEIGHBOR(v_u)
5:          $d_{jj} \leftarrow$ GETDEGREE(v_c)
6:          $v_c \leftarrow$ GETRANDOMNEIGHBOR(v_c)
7:          $d_{vv} \leftarrow$ GETDEGREE(v_c)
8:          $v_c \leftarrow$ GETRANDOMNEIGHBOR(v_c)
9:          $d_{ii} \leftarrow$ GETDEGREE(v_c)
10:          $m[v_c] \leftarrow m[v_c] + c_{rw}$
11:      **end while**
12:      **return** m
13: **end function**

	MovieLens-M	iPlayer	BookCrossing
total ratings	1'000'047	4'703'471	369'195
total users	6'038	655'846	4'052
total items	3'706	808	18'280
Training: # ratings	700'047	4'691'493	258'436
min. / avg. ratings per user	10 / 115.9	1 / 7.2	15 / 63.8
min. / avg. ratings per item	1 / 188.9	5 / 5806.3	1 / 14.1
Sparsity	0.031	0.0089	0.0035
Graph Diameter (approx.*)	6	6	7
Test: # ratings	300'000	14'616	110'759
min. / avg. ratings per user	1 / 49.7	1 / 2.9	1 / 27.3
min. / avg. ratings per item	1 / 85.4	1 / 23.4	1 / 6.6
min. train-ratings for user	10	1	15
min. train-ratings for item	1	18	5

Table 1: Dataset Properties. *PseudoDiameter of *Mathematica 10*®.

Algorithm 1 shows the general principle of how to implement a random walk sampling approximation procedure. With this algorithm we obtain $\hat{P}^3_\alpha$ item scores by assigning $c^{\hat{P}^3_\alpha}_{rw}$ to the random walk contribution c_{rw} in line 10. Note that for $\alpha = 1$, the random walk contribution is $(d_{jj}d_{vv})^0$ and degenerates to 1. Hence, the sampling procedure $\hat{P}^3$ (same as $\hat{P}^3_{\alpha=1}$) is computationally less demanding, since updating the score of the destination item i of a random walk consists only of incrementing the count of i by one.

To estimate the item ranking of $R\hat{P}^3_\beta$ with random walk sampling, we can either first obtain $\hat{P}^3$ item scores and apply the re-ranking described in Section 4, or replace the random walk contribution $c^{\hat{P}^3}_{rw} = 1$ by $c^{R\hat{P}^3_\beta}_{rw} = 1/d^\beta_{ii}$ and omit the re-ranking. Hence, Algorithm 1 also fully describes $R\hat{P}^3_\beta$.

5.3 Approximation of H_λ

Zhou *et al.* [23] define H_λ as a scoring procedure of items using a weighted linear aggregation of scores from two algorithms: HeatS, which is analogous to heat diffusion across the user-item graph and ProbS, which is the same as P^3. W^{H+P} with dimension $|I| \times |I|$ is the transition matrix for H_λ and $f^u \in \{0,1\}^{|I|}$ is the preference profile of target user u, where f^u_i, the ith entry of f^u, is equal to the corresponding entry a_{iu} in the adjacency matrix A. Then, the item scores for user u are calculated as $\widetilde{f}^u = W^{H+P} f^u$. A single entry of W^{H+P} is calculated according to

$$w^{H+P}_{ij} = \frac{1}{d^{1-\lambda}_{ii} d^\lambda_{jj}} \sum_{v=1}^{|U|} \frac{a_{iv}a_{jv}}{d_{vv}} \qquad (7)$$

where $\lambda \in [0,1]$ is the hybridization parameter for the two basic methods. If we set $\lambda = 0$ or $\lambda = 1$, the ranking of H_λ is equal to the ranking of HeatS or ProbS, respectively. Furthermore, d_{ii} denotes the degree of item i and d_{vv} the degree of user v. The score of item i for the target user u can also be determined according to:

$$\widetilde{f}^u_i = \sum_{j=1}^{|I|} a_{ju} \frac{1}{d^{1-\lambda}_{ii} d^\lambda_{jj}} \sum_{v=1}^{|U|} \frac{a_{jv}a_{iv}}{d_{vv}} = \sum_{j=1}^{|I|} \sum_{v=1}^{|U|} \frac{a_{ju}a_{jv}a_{iv}}{d^{1-\lambda}_{ii} d^\lambda_{jj} d_{vv}} \qquad (8)$$

We can apply the same rationale for the deduction of a random walk simulation algorithm of H_λ as used for P^3_α: the term $a_{ju}a_{jv}a_{iv}$ in (8) is 1 if a path of length three from user u to item i exists in the graph G and 0 otherwise. Hence, $\widetilde{f}^u_i$ is the aggregate of all paths of length three between user u and item i, where a single path contributes $c^{H_\lambda}_\pi = \frac{1}{d^{1-\lambda}_{ii} d^\lambda_{jj} d_{vv}}$ to the score of item i for user u. Because (8) (similar to (4) for P^3_α) requires that each path contribution $c^{H_\lambda}_\pi$ is counted once, we need to weight $c^{H_\lambda}_\pi$ by the inverted path probability $\Pr(\pi)^{-1}$. The random walk path contribution $c^{\hat{H}_\lambda}_{rw}$ for the random walk sampling approximation algorithm ($\hat{H}_\lambda$) is calculated according to:

$$c^{\hat{H}_\lambda}_{rw} = c^{H_\lambda}_\pi * \Pr(\pi)^{-1} = \frac{d_{uu}d_{jj}d_{vv}}{d^{1-\lambda}_{ii} d^\lambda_{jj} d_{vv}} = \frac{d_{uu}d^{1-\lambda}_{jj}}{d^{1-\lambda}_{ii}} \qquad (9)$$

Again, we can further simplify $c^{\hat{H}_\lambda}_{rw}$ to $\frac{d^{1-\lambda}_{jj}}{d^{1-\lambda}_{ii}}$, since d_{uu} is the same value for all random walks for the target user u, and hence does not influence the item ranking order. With Algorithm 1 we obtain $\hat{H}_\lambda$ item scores by assigning $c^{\hat{H}_\lambda}_{rw}$ to c_{rw}.

6. EXPERIMENTS AND EVALUATION

This section provides a succinct introduction to the experimental methodology and then turns to the main questions of the paper: First, it explores if $R\hat{P}^3_\beta$ improves accuracy and diversity. Then it explores a general comparison between vertex ranking and traditional algorithms. It closes with a thorough comparison between P^3_α, $R\hat{P}^3_\beta$, and H_λ and our approximate versions $\hat{P}^3_\alpha$, $R\hat{P}^3_\beta$, and $\hat{H}_\lambda$.

6.1 Methodology

Datasets: We used the MovieLens-M[1], iPlayer, and Book-Crossing [24] datasets (see Table 1 for properties). Whilst Movie-Lens-M and BookCrossing are public, the iPlayer training dataset consists of the viewing logs of the BBC VoD system from the week of February 15-21, 2014, and the test data of the following week's logs, where only interactions with a single show longer than 5 minutes were considered. From the log data of the test week, we randomly selected 5'000 users that were also active during the training week. Since this work addresses recommendation generation based on implicit user feedback, we neglected the rating values available in MovieLens-M and BookCrossing for training and testing of the evaluated recommenders.

Set-Up: We extended the Java port of the MyMediaLite [10] recommender system framework[2] with (i) a set of metrics (see the following paragraphs) to measure recommendation performance according to the diversity dimensions

---

[1]MovieLens-M: grouplens.org/datasets/movielens
[2]Java port: github.com/jcnewell/MyMediaLiteJava

	Recommender	AUC	Prec@20	GiniD@20	Pers@20	Surp@20
MovieLens-M	Perfect	1.0000	0.835	0.218	0.927	4.01
	RP^3_β ($\beta = 0.8$)	**0.9287**	0.341	0.172	0.941	**3.79**
	RP^3_β ($\beta = 0.7$)	**0.9260**	**0.359**	0.080	0.862	2.80
	H_λ ($\lambda = 0.1$)	**0.9240**	0.338	0.100	0.913	**3.63**
	H_λ ($\lambda = 0.2$)	0.9214	0.347	0.052	0.831	2.58
	BPRMF ($d=50$)	0.9211	0.324	0.189	0.952	3.22
	BPRMF ($d=200$)	0.9197	0.333	0.145	0.932	2.96
	WI-kNN ($k=150$)	0.9180	**0.353**	0.090	0.918	2.75
	WI-kNN ($k=200$)	0.9178	**0.354**	0.085	0.912	2.71
	I-kNN ($k=150$)	0.9138	0.283	**0.221**	**0.973**	3.62
	I-kNN ($k=50$)	0.9056	0.295	**0.204**	**0.968**	3.47
	P^3_α ($\alpha = 1.8$)	0.9028	0.259	0.027	0.644	2.13
	P^3_α ($\alpha = 1.5$)	0.9011	0.263	0.015	0.565	1.96
	P^3	0.8910	0.252	0.011	0.497	1.88
	L^+	0.8811	0.215	**0.218**	**0.971**	**4.22**
	#3-Paths	0.8672	0.234	0.010	0.449	1.86
	P^5	0.8600	0.217	0.009	0.410	1.84
	MostPop	0.8514	0.210	0.009	0.401	1.84
	Random	0.5018	0.015	0.900	0.994	6.33
iPlayer	Perfect	0.9618	0.120	0.068	0.172	8.21
	H_λ ($\lambda = 0.2$)	**0.8972**	**0.059**	0.251	0.805	4.94
	RP^3_β ($\beta = 0.7$)	**0.8949**	**0.059**	**0.327**	0.848	5.29
	WI-kNN ($k=150$)	**0.8911**	0.058	0.195	0.734	4.55
	P^3_α ($\alpha = 1.5$)	0.8804	0.051	0.139	0.617	4.13
	P^3	0.8785	0.049	0.108	0.567	3.95
	BPRMF ($d=50$)	0.8756	0.056	0.211	0.734	4.54
	#3-Paths	0.8630	0.043	0.077	0.490	3.75
	I-kNN ($k=50$)	0.8560	0.033	**0.340**	**0.867**	**6.11**
	I-kNN ($k=10$)	0.8056	0.046	**0.309**	**0.869**	**5.89**
	MostPop	0.7506	0.024	0.038	0.163	3.31
	Random	0.4950	0.004	0.954	0.968	8.01
BookCrossing	Perfect	1.0000	0.663	0.266	0.828	7.80
	H_λ ($\lambda = 0.6$)	**0.8291**	**0.080**	0.109	0.854	5.83
	H_λ ($\lambda = 0.5$)	**0.8283**	**0.082**	0.158	0.913	6.42
	RP^3_β ($\beta = 0.3$)	**0.8271**	0.071	0.154	0.876	6.11
	P^3_α ($\alpha = 0.9$)	0.8255	0.059	0.010	0.610	4.44
	P^3	0.8248	0.060	0.015	0.652	4.56
	P^3_α ($\alpha = 1.1$)	0.8235	0.060	0.026	0.703	4.74
	L^+	0.8234	0.033	**0.318**	**0.996**	**9.19**
	P^5	0.8056	0.042	0.002	0.271	4.09
	BPRMF ($d=10$)	0.7985	0.035	0.100	0.966	6.39
	WI-kNN ($k=3200$)	0.7825	0.060	0.118	0.955	6.91
	#3-Paths	0.7783	0.048	0.002	0.436	4.14
	BPRMF ($d=200$)	0.7735	0.048	0.109	0.965	5.87
	I-kNN ($k=800$)	0.7535	0.048	0.148	**0.976**	**7.38**
	MostPop	0.7180	0.034	0.001	0.111	3.95
	WI-kNN ($k=50$)	0.6542	**0.083**	**0.236**	0.975	**7.09**
	I-kNN ($k=10$)	0.5911	0.078	**0.178**	**0.978**	6.97
	Random	0.5010	0.001	0.748	0.999	8.57

Table 2: Accuracy and diversity of all algorithms (ordered by decreasing AUC). Parameterized algorithms are represented by parameter values resulting in maximal AUC and Prec@20 performance. Top 3 numbers per metric highlighted (results from Perfect and Random recommender not considered).

introduced in Section 3 and (ii) a component implementing graph vertex ranking algorithms. Given our focus on implicit feedback we only employed the framework's positive-only feedback components. All computations where executed on a cluster of 16 machines running LINUX with 128 GB RAM and two Intel® Xeon® E5-2680V2 processors (25 MB Cache, 2.80 GHz base frequency, 10 cores, 20 threads).

Accuracy Metrics: We used both the Area Under the ROC curve (AUC) and precision at k (Prec@k). Referring to relevant items (in the test set) as *hits*, AUC is equal to the probability that randomly chosen items are ranked higher than non-hits. Prec@k counts the number of hits among the top-k items of the recommendation list divided by the cut-off level k. Given that users typically only see few recommendations, we chose $k = 20$. Higher values of AUC and Prec@k indicate better accuracy.

Diversity Metrics: We used coverage (Gini-Diversity, GiniD@k), personalization (Pers@k), and surprisal (Surp@k) as diversity metrics and extended the MyMediaLite framework accordingly. Given the already explained rationale, we used $k = 20$. Again, greater values indicate better diversity.

We measure coverage by calculating GiniD@k for the top-k recommendations of all test users [2]. In contrast to the original Gini coefficient, where greater values indicate a more

dispersed distribution, GiniD@k increases for a more uniform distribution. GiniD@k is equal to 1 if the frequency in the aggregated recommendation lists is the same for each item, indicating a good coverage.

Pers@k [23] measures the distinctness of the top-k recommendations based on the number of common items averaged over all pairs of generated recommendation sets. A value of Pers@k=1 indicates that none of the items appear more than once among the top-k items of any two recommendation lists, meaning greater personalization.

Surp@k [23] is calculated separately for each recommendation list and averaged over all users. This metric follows the rationale that recommendations of items of low popularity are perceived by the users as unexpected or surprising (unexpectedness given by the self-information of items).

Evaluated Recommendation Algorithms: We compared the performance of our methods with various algorithms proposed in the literature (and listed in Table 2, except for (iii)). These can be divided into the following categories: **(i) Parameter-free vertex ranking algorithms:** #3-Paths (ranks items by the number of paths of length 3 starting at the target user) [6, 14], L^+ (ranks items by the entries in the Moore-Penrose pseudoinverse of the Laplacian matrix) [9], P^3 [6, 23], and P^5 [6]. Due to computational limitations we could not obtain results for P^5 and L^+ for the iPlayer dataset. **(ii) Parameterized vertex ranking algorithms:** P^3_α [6], H_λ [23], and our RP^3_β. **(iii) Approximated/Sampled vertex ranking algorithms** $\hat{P}^3_\alpha$, $\hat{RP}^3_\beta$, and $\hat{H}_\lambda$. **(iv) Other algorithms:** MostPop (global item popularity), Random (random item ranking), weighted (WI-kNN) and unweighted (I-kNN) k-nearest neighbor item-based collaborative filtering using cosine distance as item similarity measure, and BPRMF [19] (a recommender based on a latent factor model obtained with matrix factorization) – all available in MyMediaLite. To facilitate performance comparison, we also calculated the performance of the perfect recommender (Perfect) that places all test items of a user in random order at the top of the recommendation list.

Parameter Tuning: We empirically tune the parameters for parameterized algorithms to maximize the two accuracy metrics. For I-kNN and WI-kNN with MovieLens-M and iPlayer we tested neighborhood sizes $k \in \{10, 50, 100, 150, 200\}$. For the BookCrossing I-kNN was tested for $k \in \{10, 50, 100, 150, 200, 400, 800, 1600\}$ and for WI-kNN we additionally tested $k = 3200$. Similarly, BPRMF was tested with the latent factors $d \in \{10, 50, 100, 150, 200\}$ for Movie-Lens-M and BookCrossing. Due to computational limitations, BPRMF could only be tested with $d \in \{10, 50\}$ for iPlayer.[3] For P^3_α, we tested values of $\alpha \in [-0.2, 4.5]$ in steps of 0.1. For RP^3_β, we tested values of $\beta \in [-0.2, 1.2]$ in steps of 0.1. H_λ was tested with values of $\lambda \in [0, 1]$ in steps of 0.1. The best performing parameters with respect to accuracy can be found in parentheses in the results Table 2.

6.2 RP^3_β increases Accuracy and Diversity

The goal of the first set of experiments is to evaluate our re-ranking procedure RP^3_β. To that end we compare it with

---

[3] Other parameters for BPRMF: 30 stochastic gradient ascent iterations for training, no item bias, iteration length of 5, learning rate α of 0.05, regularization parameter for positive item factors of 0.0025, regularization parameter for negative item factors of 0.00025, and regularization parameter for user factors of 0.0025.

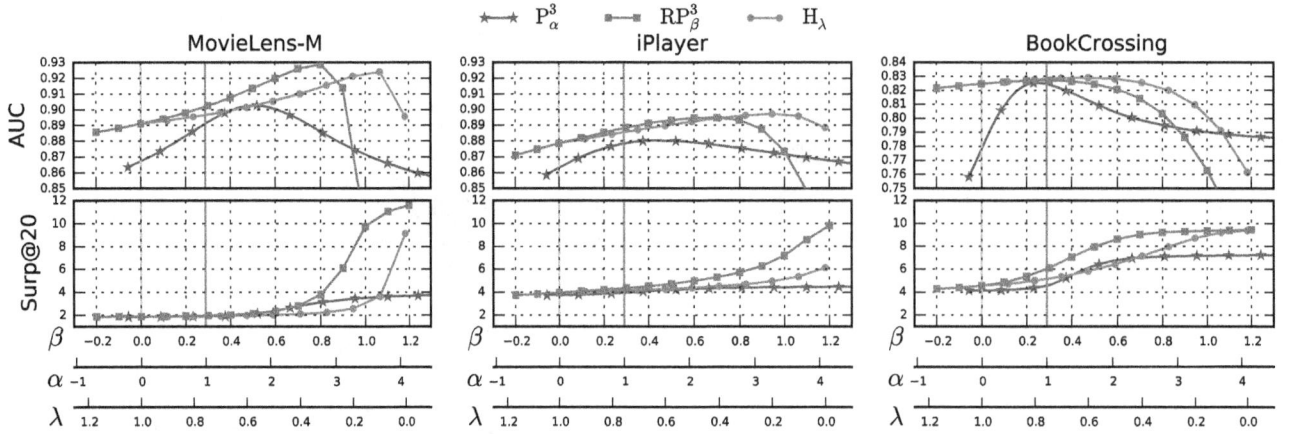

Figure 1: AUC and Surp@20 performance of P_α^3, RP_β^3, and H_λ at different parameter values. The left vertical line (cyan) at $\beta = 0.0$, $\alpha = 0.0$, and $\lambda = 1.0$ indicates the parameter values where RP_β^3 and H_λ give the same item ranking as P^3, and P_α^3 the ranking of #3-Paths. The right vertical line (magenta) at $\alpha = 1.0$ indicates the parameter value where P_α^3 gives the same item ranking as P^3.

the other algorithms evaluated and especially explore its performance compared to P_α^3 and H_λ.

As Table 2 shows, the RP_β^3 re-ranking increases both accuracy and diversity for all datasets compared to its P^3 basis. Measured by AUC, RP_β^3 is the most accurate algorithm for MovieLens-M and second most accurate algorithm after H_λ for iPlayer and BookCrossing. For Prec the results are less favorable: while the performance of RP_β^3 is best for MovieLens-M and second best for iPlayer, WI-kNN, I-kNN, and H_λ clearly outperform RP_β^3 for BookCrossing. This is possibly due to the lower number of average ratings per item, which may distort our boosting of low degree items.

Cooper *et al.* [6] show that P_α^3 improves accuracy over P^3. Our experiments confirm this claim but the accuracy improvements achieved with RP_β^3 are even greater than with P_α^3 for both AUC and Prec. Furthermore, at parameter values corresponding to maximum accuracy, RP_β^3 achieves better GiniD, Pers, and Surp scores than P_α^3. This shows that RP_β^3 gives a better trade-off between accuracy and diversity, i.e., at parameter values that achieve highest accuracy it produces more diverse results.

The results do not suggest a winner between RP_β^3 and H_λ. In terms of AUC and Prec, RP_β^3 has advantage over H_λ for MovieLens-M but not for iPlayer and BookCrossing. For BookCrossing the maximal achieved precision of H_λ is much better than that of RP_β^3. At parameter values corresponding to maximum accuracy, the diversity metric scores for RP_β^3 are better for H_λ for MovieLens-M and iPlayer. Again, RP_β^3 underperforms compared to H_λ on BookCrossing. Figure 1 graphs the AUC and Surp for P_α^3, RP_β^3, and H_λ for the whole parameter ranges. It shows that the maximally achieved Surp by RP_β^3 is better (for MovieLens-M and iPlayer) or comparable (for BookCrossing) to H_λ. The plots for the other accuracy and diversity metrics show similar results as AUC and Surp, respectively, but are omitted due to space considerations. Note that we measured the performance of H_λ only in the originally defined parameter interval ($\lambda \in [0, 1]$). We assume that the diversity performance of H_λ increases further for $\lambda < 0$ at the cost of accuracy.

We can conclude that the new method RP_β^3 is a vertex ranking algorithm with top-class accuracy and diversity per-

formance. Tuning of its parameter β allows the trade-off between recommendation accuracy and top-k long-tail item frequency to be controlled.

6.3 Performance of Vertex Ranking Algorithms

In this sub-section we compare the performance of vertex ranking to other recommendation algorithms.

As Table 2 shows, in accordance with [6], P^3 is the most accurate algorithm among the measured parameter-free recommenders (MostPop, P^3, P^5, #3-Paths, and L^+). In particular, P^3 is more accurate than the computationally more expensive L^+ algorithm, which was found to be the most accurate algorithm in an earlier study [9].

For AUC, the parameterized vertex ranking algorithms RP_β^3 and H_λ outperform the non-vertex ranking recommendation algorithms I-kNN, WI-kNN, and BPRMF. For Prec, the scores of RP_β^3 are high for the MovieLens-M dataset but low for the BookCrossing dataset; the opposite is true for H_λ. WI-kNN, the best performing non-vertex ranking algorithm, performs more consistently and archives comparable results to the best vertex ranking algorithm in terms of Prec.

The parameter free vertex ranking algorithms P^3, P^5, and #3-Paths clearly show lower diversity scores than I-kNN, WI-kNN, and BPRMF in all datasets. This is surprising considering the fact that I-kNN, WI-kNN, and BPRMF are more accurate for some of the datasets (e.g., MovieLens-M). Hence, the better diversity performance of the non-vertex recommenders is not explained by more randomness in their recommendations. Exploring the recommendation lists of P^3, P^5, and #3-Paths reveals that ranking is strongly biased by the item's degree (i.e., favoring blockbusters), resulting in rankings similar to MaxPop. The parameter free L^+ generates diverse recommendations at the cost of low Prec (worse than MostPop for BookCrossing). In terms of AUC it is almost as good as P^3.

Parameterized vertex ranking algorithms provide, besides better accuracy, improved diversity compared to parameter free algorithms. Comparing the diversity performance of the most precise vertex (RP_β^3 for MovieLens-M and iPlayer, H_λ for BookCrossing) and non-vertex (WI-kNN for all datasets) ranking recommendation algorithms reveals WI-kNN as the clear winner for BookCrossing: WI-kNN is not only slightly

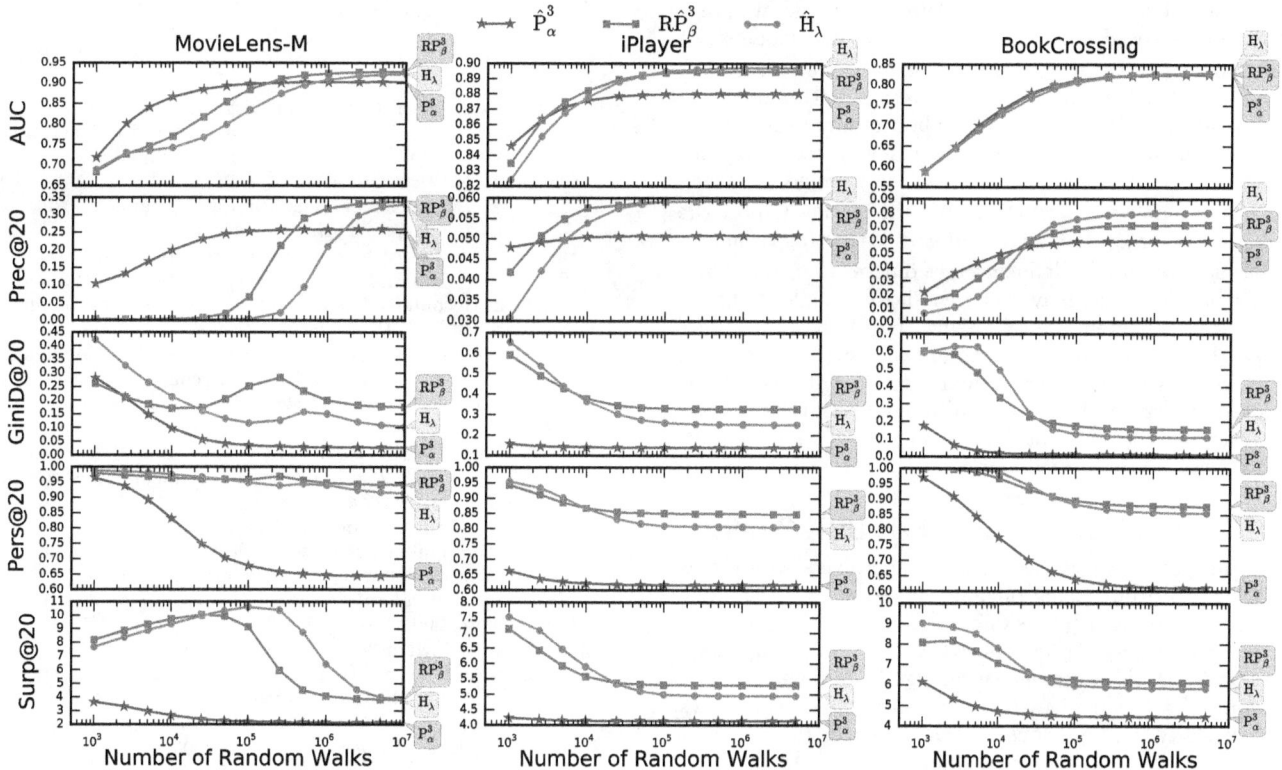

Figure 2: Accuracy and diversity performance of the sampling algorithms $\hat{P}_\alpha^3$, $\hat{RP}_\beta^3$, and $\hat{H}_\lambda$ for the parameter values of maximal AUC performance in dependency of the number of random walks per user. The annotations on the right-sided y-axis indicate the performance of the exact algorithms P_α^3, RP_β^3, and H_λ for the same parameter values.

Dataset	Recommender	AUC	Prec	GiniD	Pers	Surp
MovieLens-M (5 m walks)	$\hat{P}_\alpha^3$ ($\alpha = 1.8$)	0.013	0.054	2.256	0.127	0.221
	$\hat{RP}_\beta^3$ ($\beta = 0.8$)	0.089	1.188	2.813	0.148	1.190
	$\hat{H}_\lambda$ ($\lambda = 0.1$)	0.329	4.263	9.851	0.603	10.08
iPlayer (1 m walks)	$\hat{P}_\alpha^3$ ($\alpha = 1.5$)	0.014	0.138	0.050	0.011	0.008
	$\hat{RP}_\beta^3$ ($\beta = 0.7$)	0.012	0.169	0.076	0.029	0.031
	$\hat{H}_\lambda$ ($\lambda = 0.2$)	0.026	0.067	0.303	0.071	0.064
BookCrossing (1 m walks)	$\hat{P}_\alpha^3$ ($\alpha = 0.9$)	0.173	0.605	1.089	0.441	0.074
	$\hat{RP}_\beta^3$ ($\beta = 0.3$)	0.237	0.324	1.103	0.247	0.186
	$\hat{H}_\lambda$ ($\lambda = 0.6$)	0.359	0.125	1.527	0.436	0.287

Table 3: Percentage of performance deviation between P_α^3, RP_β^3, and H_λ and $\hat{P}_\alpha^3$, $\hat{RP}_\beta^3$, and $\hat{H}_\lambda$ after 1 m or 5 m random walks per user for parameter values of maximal AUC performance.

more precise than H_λ but also has higher diversity scores. For iPlayer RP_β^3 is slightly more precise than WI-kNN and achieves higher diversity scores. No clear winner can be found for the MovieLens-M dataset: RP_β^3 shows better precision and surprisal scores but WI-kNN succeeds in terms of GiniD and Pers performance.

6.4 Performance of Sampling Approximations

The goal of our second experiments is to investigate the performance of our sampling algorithms dependent on number of samples (i.e., number of random walks).

We determined the performance of our sampling algorithms $\hat{P}_\alpha^3$, $\hat{RP}_\beta^3$, and $\hat{H}_\lambda$ with parameter values of maximal AUC according to the non-sampling original algorithms whilst varying the number of random walks $N \in \{$ 1'000, 2'500, 5'000, 10'000, 25'000, 50'000, 100'000, 250'000, 500'000, 1 m, 2.5 m, 5 m$\}$ per user. Figure 2 shows the rate of convergence as well as the performance of the exact algorithms

as indicated by the callouts near right edge of each graph. As expected the sampled algorithms' performance converge to that of the exact ones with increasing N. To illustrate the closeness of the results we computed the percentage deviation $d = (|m - \hat{m}|) * 100 / m$ between the sampling procedures' $\hat{m}$ and exact calculations' m performance metrics for 5 million random walks for MovieLens-M and 1 m random walks for iPlayer and BookCrossing. The results of this procedure, listed in Table 3, show that the sampled algorithms usually deviate less than 1% from the exact ones, less than 3% in all cases but for $\hat{H}_\lambda$ for MovieLens-M. Despite the greater number of random walks, d is greater for the MovieLens-M dataset than for the iPlayer or BookCrossing datasets. We hypothesize that this is due to the greater number of distinct paths of length three starting at a given user existing in the graph G for MovieLens-M dataset as indicated by the high average vertex degree of 71.8 (compared to iPlayer: 7.1, BookCrossing: 11.6).

Furthermore, Figure 2 clearly indicates that $\hat{P}_\alpha^3$ requires less samples to converge than $\hat{RP}_\beta^3$, which in turn converges faster than $\hat{H}_\lambda$. Since these algorithms can be computed using Algorithm 1 and differ only in c_{rw}, we hypothesize that c_{rw} controls the efficiency of sampling. As a result $\hat{P}_\alpha^3$ is the most accurate sampling algorithm for small values of N. For slightly greater N, $\hat{RP}_\beta^3$ is more accurate than $\hat{P}_\alpha^3$ in the MovieLens-M and iPlayer datasets. If we increase N even further, $\hat{H}_\lambda$ becomes the most accurate recommender for the iPlayer and BookCrossing dataset.

Considering recommendation accuracy, diversity, and the sample size required to obtain acceptable accuracy, our results suggest the following: On data with moderate sparsity and balanced user and item degrees (MovieLens-M) one should use $\hat{P}^3_\alpha$ if computing resources are scarce, i.e., $N < 250'000$, because of the algorithm's better precision and otherwise $\hat{RP}^3_\beta$ which provides best accuracy and diversity (at comparable level of accuracy). For sparser data with more ratings per item than per user on average (iPlayer), $\hat{RP}^3_\beta$ is probably the best choice since it reaches almost the maximal accuracy but gives better diversity (at comparable level of accuracy) and converges quicker than $\hat{H}_\lambda$. For a sparse dataset with an average item degree smaller than the average user degree (BookCrossing) $\hat{H}_\lambda$ is the best choice given that computing resources are plenty ($N > 25'000$), since it gives better precision and diversity (at comparable level of accuracy). In the case of limited computing power however, the choice is not obvious due to the poor accuracy of $\hat{RP}^3_\beta$ and $\hat{H}_\lambda$ and very poor diversity of $\hat{P}^3_\alpha$.

7. CONCLUSIONS AND FUTURE WORK

In this paper, we studied accuracy and diversity of vertex ranking algorithms using random walk sampling techniques and thereby bring together three streams of earlier presented work. Specifically, we introduced RP^3_β, a novel graph random walk based recommendation algorithm based on a re-ranking of P^3 that gives better recommendation accuracy and diversity than previously proposed vertex ranking algorithms. We showed that re-ranking improves the accuracy performance over P^3 and its parameterized version P^3_α and pushes "wallflowers", i.e., long-tail items, closer to the top of the recommendation list. Our method is also competitive with another graph-based recommender H_λ that optimizes the accuracy diversity trade-off. We also showed that RP^3_β is competitive with traditional algorithms.

Additionally, we presented scalable random walk sampling implementations of the three best vertex ranking algorithms. We showed empirically that these algorithms converge to their exact counterparts with increasing number of samples. The sampling procedures have the favorable property of being anytime algorithms: a recommendation list of low accuracy can be generated after a short processing time, while longer computations, i.e., gathering more random walk samples, improve the accuracy of the recommendation list.

In future work we hope to investigate the sensitivity of the convergence of the sampling algorithms to domain characteristics and further explore convergence behavior for different datasets and algorithms. Also, we would like to take detailed run-time measurements to ascertain wall-clock time advantages and trade-offs.

Our results indicate that the goal of scalable, accurate, and surprising recommendations could be achieved with vertex ranking algorithms using random walk sampling.

Acknowledgements: We would like to thank the Hasler Foundation for their generous support under grant # 11072.

8. REFERENCES

[1] G. Adomavicius and Y. Kwon. Maximizing Aggregate Recommendation Diversity: A Graph-Theoretic Approach. In *Workshop on Novelty and Diversity in Recommender Systems, ACM RecSys*, 2011.

[2] G. Adomavicius and Y. Kwon. Improving Aggregate Recommendation Diversity Using Ranking-Based Techniques. *IEEE Transactions on Knowledge and Data Engineering*, 2012.

[3] C. C. Aggarwal, J. L. Wolf, K.-L. Wu, and P. S. Yu. Horting Hatches an Egg: A New Graph-Theoretich Approach to Collaborative Filtering. In *ACM SIGKDD*, 1999.

[4] S. Baluja, R. Seth, D. Sivakumar, Y. Jing, J. Yagnik, S. Kumar, D. Ravichandran, and M. Aly. Video Suggestion and Discovery for YouTube: Taking Random Walks Through the View Graph. In *WWW Conference*, 2008.

[5] T. Bogers. Movie Recommendation using Random Walks over the Contextual Graph. In *Workshop on Context-Aware Recommender Systems, ACM RecSys*, 2010.

[6] C. Cooper, S. H. Lee, T. Radzik, and Y. Siantos. Random Walks in Recommender Systems: Exact Computation and Simulations. In *WWW Conference*, 2014.

[7] P. Cremonesi, F. Garzotto, S. Negro, A. V. Papadopoulos, and R. Turrin. Looking for "Good" Recommendations: A Comparative Evaluation of Recommender Systems. In *INTERACT 2011*. Springer, 2011.

[8] D. M. Fleder and K. Hosanagar. Blockbuster Culture's Next Rise or Fall: The Impact of Recommender Systems on Sales Diversity. *Management science*, 2009.

[9] F. Fouss, A. Pirotte, and M. Saerens. A Novel Way of Computing Similarities between Nodes of a Graph, with Application to Collaborative Recommendation. In *IEEE/WIC/ACM International Conference on Web Intelligence*, 2005.

[10] Z. Gantner, S. Rendle, C. Freudenthaler, and L. Schmidt-Thieme. MyMediaLite: A Free Recommender System Library. In *ACM RecSys*, 2011.

[11] D. G. Goldstein and D. C. Goldstein. Profiting from the long tail. *Harvard Business Review*, 2006.

[12] M. Gori and A. Pucci. ItemRank: A Random-Walk Based Scoring Algorithm for Recommender Engines. In *IJCAI*, 2007.

[13] J. L. Herlocker, J. A. Konstan, L. G. Terveen, and J. T. Riedl. Evaluating Collaborative Filtering Recommender Systems. *ACM Transactions on Information Systems*, 2004.

[14] Z. Huang, H. Chen, and D. Zeng. Applying Associative Retrieval Techniques to Alleviate the Sparsity Problem in Collaborative Filtering. *ACM Transactions on Information Systems*, 2004.

[15] M. Jamali and M. Ester. TrustWalker: A RandomWalk Model for Combining Trust-based and Item-based Recommendation. In *ACM SIGKDD*, 2009.

[16] S. Lee, S. Park, M. Kahng, and S.-g. Lee. PathRank: A Novel Node Ranking Measure on a Heterogeneous Graph for Recommender Systems. In *CIKM*, 2012.

[17] S. M. McNee, J. Riedl, and J. A. Konstan. Being Accurate is Not Enough: How Accuracy Metrics have hurt Recommender Systems. In *CHI'06 extended abstracts*. ACM, 2006.

[18] E. Pariser. *The Filter Bubble: What the Internet is Hiding from You*. Penguin UK, 2011.

[19] S. Rendle, C. Freudenthaler, Z. Gantner, and L. Schmidt-Thieme. BPR: Bayesian Personalized Ranking from Implicit Feedback. In *UAI*, 2009.

[20] P. Sarkar, A. W. Moore, and A. Prakash. Fast Incremental Proximity Search in Large Graphs. In *ACM ICML*, 2008.

[21] S. Vargas and P. Castells. Rank and Relevance in Novelty and Diversity Metrics for Recommender Systems. In *ACM RecSys*, 2011.

[22] L. Xiang, Q. Yuan, S. Zhao, L. Chen, X. Zhang, Q. Yang, and J. Sun. Temporal Recommendation on Graphs via Long- and Short-term Preference Fusion. In *ACM SIGKDD*, 2010.

[23] T. Zhou, Z. Kuscsik, J.-G. Liu, M. Medo, J. R. Wakeling, and Y.-C. Zhang. Solving the apparent diversity-accuracy dilemma of recommender systems. *PNAS*, 2010.

[24] C.-N. Ziegler, S. M. McNee, J. A. Konstan, and G. Lausen. Improving Recommendation Lists Through Topic Diversification. In *WWW Conference*, 2005.

Fast Differentially Private Matrix Factorization

Ziqi Liu
MOEKLINNS Lab, Computer Science
Xi'an Jiaotong University
Xi'an, China
ziqilau@gmail.com

Yu-Xiang Wang
Machine Learning Department
Carnegie Mellon University
Pittsburgh, PA
yuxiangw@cs.cmu.edu

Alexander J. Smola
CMU Machine Learning
Marianas Labs Inc.
Pittsburgh, PA
alex@smola.org

ABSTRACT

Differentially private collaborative filtering is a challenging task, both in terms of accuracy and speed. We present a simple algorithm that is provably differentially private, while offering good performance, using a novel connection of differential privacy to Bayesian posterior sampling via Stochastic Gradient Langevin Dynamics. Due to its simplicity the algorithm lends itself to efficient implementation. By careful systems design and by exploiting the power law behavior of the data to maximize CPU cache bandwidth we are able to generate 1024 dimensional models at a rate of 8.5 million recommendations per second on a single PC.

Keywords

Differential Privacy; Collaborative Filtering; Scalable Matrix Factorization

1. INTRODUCTION

Privacy protection in recommender systems is a notoriously challenging problem. There are often two competing goals at stake: similar users are likely to prefer similar products, movies, or locations, hence sharing of preferences between users is desirable. Yet, at the same time, this exacerbates the type of privacy sensitive queries, simply since we are now not looking for aggregate properties from a dataset (such as a classifier) but for properties and behavior of other users 'just like' this specific user. Such highly individualized behavioral patterns are shown to facilitate provably effective user de-nonymization [25, 37].

Consider the case of a couple, both using the same location recommendation service. Since both spouses share much of the same location history, it is likely that they will receive similar recommendations, based on other users' preferences similar to theirs. In this context sharing of information is desirable, as it improves overall recommendation quality.

Moreover, since their location history is likely to be very similar, each of them will also receive recommendations to visit the place that their spouse visited (e.g. including places of ill repute), regardless of whether the latter would like to share this information or not. This creates considerable tension in trying to satisfy those two conflicting goals.

RecSys '15 September 16-20, 2015, Vienna, Austria
© 2015 ACM. ISBN 978-1-4503-3692-5/15/09 ...$15.00.
DOI: http://dx.doi.org/10.1145/2792838.2800191.

Differential privacy offers tools to overcome these problems. Loosely speaking, it offers the participants plausible deniability in terms of the estimate. That is, it provides guarantees that the recommendation would also have been issued with sufficiently high probability if another specific participant had not taken this action before. This is precisely the type of guarantee suitable to allay the concerns in the above situation [8].

Recent work, e.g. by Mcsherry and Mironov [20] has focused on designing *custom built* tools for differential private recommendation. Many of the design decisions in this context are hand engineered, and it is nontrivial to separate the choices made to obtain a differentially private system from those made to obtain a system that works well. Furthermore, none of these systems [20, 36] lead to very fast implementations.

In this paper we show that a large family of recommender systems, namely those using matrix factorization, are well suited to differential privacy. More specifically, we exploit the fact that sampling from the posterior distribution of a Bayesian model, e.g. via Stochastic Gradient Langevin Dynamics (SGLD) [35], can lead to estimates that are sufficiently differentially private [34]. At the same time, their stochastic nature makes them well amenable to efficient implementation. Their generality means that we *need not custom-design a statistical model for differential privacy* but rather that is possible to *retrofit an existing model* to satisfy these constraints. The practical importance of this fact cannot be overstated — it means that no costly re-engineering of deployed statistical models is needed. Instead, one can simply reuse the existing inference algorithm with a trivial modification to obtain a differentially private model.

This leaves the issue to performance. Some of the best reported results are those using GraphChi [15], which show that state-of-the-art recommender systems can be built using just a single PC within a matter of hours, rather than requiring hundreds of computers. In this paper, we show that by efficiently exploiting the power law properties inherent in the data (e.g. most movies are hardly ever reviewed on Netflix), one can obtain models that achieve peak numerical performance for recommendation. More to the point, they are 3 times faster than GraphChi on identical hardware.

In summary, this paper describes the by far the fastest matrix factorization based recommender system and it can be made differentially privately using SGLD without losing performance. Most competing approaches excel at no more than one of those aspects. Specifically,

1. It is efficient at the state of the art relative to other matrix factorization systems.

- we develop a cache efficient matrix factorization framework for general SGD updates.
- we develop a fast SGLD sampling algorithm with bookkeeping to avoid adding the Gaussian noise to the whole

parameter space at each updates while still maintaining the correctness of the algorithm.

2. And it is differentially private.

- We provably show that sampling from a scaled posterior distribution for matrix factorization system can guarantee user-level differential privacy.
- We present a personalized differentially private method for calibrating each user's privacy and accuracy.
- We only privately release V to public, and design a local recommender system for each user.

Experiments confirm that the algorithm can be implemented with high efficiency, while offering very favorable privacy-accuracy tradeoff that nearly matches systems without differential privacy at meaningful privacy level.

2. BACKGROUND

We begin with an overview of the relevant ingredients, namely collaborative filtering using matrix factorization, differential privacy and a primer in computer architecture. All three are relevant to the understanding of our approach. In particular, some basic understanding of the cache hierarchy in microprocessors is useful for efficient implementations.

2.1 Collaborative Filtering

In collaborative filtering we assume that we have a set of $\mathcal{U}$ users, rating $\mathcal{V}$ items. We only observe a small number of entries r_{ij} in the rating matrix R. Here r_{ij} means that user i rated item j. A popular tool [14] to deal with inferring entries in $R \in \mathbb{R}^{|\mathcal{U}| \times |\mathcal{V}|}$ is to approximate R by a low rank factorization, i.e.

$$R \approx UV^\top \text{ where } U \in \mathbb{R}^{|\mathcal{U}|k} \text{ and } V \in \mathbb{R}^{|\mathcal{V}|k} \quad (1)$$

for some $k \in \mathbb{N}$, which denotes the dimensionality of the feature space corresponding to each item and movie. In other words, (user,item) interactions are modeled via

$$r_{ij} \approx \langle u_i, v_j \rangle + b_i^u + b_j^m + b_0. \quad (2)$$

Here u_i and v_j denote row-vectors of U and V respectively, and b_i^u and b_j^m are scalar offsets responsible for a specific user or movie respectively. Finally, b_0 is a common bias.

A popular interpretation is that for a given item j, the elements of v_j measure the extent to which the item possesses those attributes. For a given user i the elements of u_i measure the extent of interest that the user has in items that score highly in the corresponding factors. Due to the conditions proposed in the Netflix contest, it is common to aim to minimize the mean squared error of deviations between true ratings and estimates. To address overfitting, a norm penalty is commonly imposed on U and V. This yields the following optimization problem

$$\min_{u,v} \sum_{i,j \in R} (r_{ij} - \langle u_i, v_j \rangle - b_i^u - b_j^m - b_0)^2 + \lambda(\|U\|_2^2 + \|V\|_2^2)$$

A large number of extensions have been proposed for this model. For instance, incorporating co-rating information [28], neighborhoods, or temporal dynamics [13] can lead to improved performance. Since we are primarily interested in demonstrating the efficacy of differential privacy and the interaction with efficient systems design, we focus on the simple inner-product model with bias.

Bayesian View. Note that the above optimization problem can be viewed as an instance of a Maximum-a-Posteriori estimation problem. That is, one minimizes

$$-\log p(U, V | R, \lambda_r, \Lambda_u, \Lambda_v) = -\log \mathcal{N}(R | \langle U, V \rangle, \lambda_r^{-1})$$
$$-\log \mathcal{N}(U | 0, \Lambda_u^{-1}) - \log \mathcal{N}(V | 0, \Lambda_v^{-1})$$

where, up to a constant offset

$$-\log p(r_{ij} | u_i, v_j) = \lambda_r (r_{ij} - \langle u_i, v_j \rangle - b_i^u - b_j^m - b_0)^2$$

and $-\log p(U) = U \Lambda_u U^\top$ and likewise for V. In other words, we assume that the ratings are conditionally normal, given the inner product $\langle u_i, v_j \rangle$, and the factors u_i and v_j are drawn from a normal distribution. Moreover, one can also introduce priors for $\lambda_r, \Lambda_u, \Lambda_v$ with a Gamma distribution $\mathcal{G}(\cdot | \alpha, \beta)$.

While this setting is typically just treated as an afterthought of penalized risk minimization, we will explicitly use this when designing differentially private algorithms. The rationale for this is the deep connection between samples from the posterior and differentially private estimates. We will return to this aspect after introducing Stochastic Gradient Langevin Dynamics.

Stochastic Gradient Descent. Minimizing the regularized collaborative filtering objective is typically achieved by one of two strategies: Alternating Least Squares (ALS) and stochastic gradient descent (SGD). The advantage of the former is that the problem is biconvex in U and V respectively, hence minimizing $U|V$ or $V|U$ are convex. On the other hand, SGD is typically faster to converge and it also affords much better cache locality properties. Instead of accessing e.g. all reviews for a given user (or all reviews for a given movie) at once, we only need to read the appropriate tuples. In SGD each time we update a randomly chosen rating record by:

$$u_i \leftarrow (1 - \eta_t \lambda) u_i + \eta_t v_j \left(r_{ij} - \langle u_i, v_j \rangle - b_i^u - b_j^m - b_0 \right)$$
$$v_j \leftarrow (1 - \eta_t \lambda) v_j + \eta_t u_i \left(r_{ij} - \langle u_i, v_j \rangle - b_i^u - b_j^m - b_0 \right) \quad (3)$$

One problem of SGD is that trivially parallelizing the procedure requires memory locking and synchronization for each rating, which could significantly hamper the performance. [27] shows that a lock-free scheme can achieve nearly optimal solution when the data access is sparse. We build on this *statistical* property to obtain a *fast system* which is suitable for differential privacy.

2.2 Differential Privacy

Differential privacy (DP) [7, 9] aims to provide means to cryptographically protect personal information in the database, while allowing aggregate-level information to be accurately extracted. In our context this means that we protect user-specific sensitive information while using aggregate information to benefit all users.

Assume the actions of a statistical database are modeled via a randomized algorithm $\mathcal{A}$. Let the space of data be $\mathcal{X}$ and data sets $X, Y \in \mathcal{X}^n$. Define $d(X, Y)$ to be the edit distance or Hamming distance between data set X and Y, for instance if X and Y are the same except one data point then we have $d(X, Y) = 1$.

Definition 1 (Differential Privacy). *We call a randomized algorithm $\mathcal{A}$ (ϵ, δ)-differentially private if for all measurable sets $S \subset Range(\mathcal{A})$ and for all $X, X' \in \mathcal{X}^n$ such that the hamming distance $d(X, X') = 1$,*

$$\mathbb{P}(\mathcal{A}(X) \in S) \leq \exp(\epsilon)\mathbb{P}(\mathcal{A}(X') \in S) + \delta$$

If $\delta = 0$ we say that $\mathcal{A}$ is ϵ-differential private.

The definition states that if we arbitrarily replace any individual data point in a database, the output of the algorithm doesn't change much. The parameter ϵ in the definition controls the maximum amount of information gain about an individual person in the database given the output of the algorithm. When ϵ is small, it prevents any forms of linkage attack to individual data record (e.g., linkage of Netflix data to IMDB data [25]). We refer readers to [8] for detailed interpretations of the differential privacy in statistical testing, Bayesian inference and information theory.

An interesting side-effect of this definition in the context of collaborative filtering is that it also limits the influence of so-called whales, i.e. of users who submit extremely large numbers of reviews. Their influence is also curtailed, at least under the assumption of an equal level of differential privacy per user. In other words, differential privacy confers robustness for collaborative filtering.

Wang et al. [34] show that posterior sampling with bounded log-likelihood is essentially exponential mechanism [21] therefore protecting differential privacy for free (similar observations were made independently in [23, 5]). Wang et al. [34] also suggests a recent line of works [35, 4, 6] that use stochastic gradient descent for Hybrid Monte Carlo sampling essentially preserve differential privacy with the same algorithmic procedure. The consequence for our application is very interesting: if we trust that the MCMC sampler has converged, i.e. if we get a sample that is approximately drawn from the posterior distribution, then we can use one sample as the private release. If not, we can calibrate the MCMC procedure itself to provide differential privacy (typically at the cost of getting a much poorer solution).

2.3 Computer Architecture

A key difference between generic numerical linear algebra, as commonly used e.g. for deep networks or generalized linear models, and the methods used for recommender systems is the fact that the access properties regarding users and items are highly nonuniform. This is a significant advantage, since it allows us to exploit the caching hierarchy of modern CPUs to benefit from higher bandwidth than what disks or main memory access would permit.

A typical computer architecture consists of a hard disk, solid-state drive (SSD), random-access memory (RAM) and CPU cache. A good algorithm design should be pushing the data flow to CPU cache level and *hide the latency* from SSD or even RAM and amplify the available bandwidth.

The key strategy in obtaining high throughput collaborative filtering systems is to obtain peak bandwidth on *each* of the subsystems by efficient caching. That is, if a movie is frequently reused, it is desirable to retain it in the CPU cache. This way, we will neither suffer the high latency (100ns per request) of a random read from memory, nor will we have to pay for the comparably slower bandwidth of RAM relative to the CPU cache.

3. DIFFERENTIALLY PRIVATE MATRIX FACTORIZATION

We start by describing the key ideas and algorithmic framework for differentially private matrix factorization. The method, which involves preprocessing data and then sampling from a scaled posterior distribution, is provably differentially private and has profound statistical implications. Then we will describe a specific Monte Carlo sampling algorithm: Stochastic Gradient Langevin Dynamics (SGLD) and justify its use in our setting. We then come up with a novel way to personalize the privacy protection for individual users. Finally, we discuss how to develop fast cache-efficient solvers to exploit bandwidth-limited hardware such that it can be used for general SGD-style algorithms.

Our differential privacy mechanism relies on a recent observation that posterior sampling preserves differential privacy, provided that the log-likelihood of each user is uniformly bounded [34]. This simple yet remarkable result suggests that sampling from posterior distribution is differentially private for free to some extent. In our context, the

claim is that, if[1] $\max_{U,V,R,i} \sum_{j \in R_i} (r_{ij} - \langle u_i, v_j \rangle)^2 \leq B$ then the method that outputs a sample from

$$P(U, V) \propto \exp\left(-\sum_{(i,j) \in R} (r_{ij} - \langle u_i, v_j \rangle)^2 + \lambda(\|U\|_F^2 + \|V\|_F^2)\right)$$

preserves $4B$-differential privacy. Moreover, when we want to set the privacy loss ϵ to another number, we can easily do this by simply rescaling the entire expression by $\epsilon/4B$.

The question now is whether $\max_{U,V,R,i} \sum_{j \in R_i} (r_{ij} - \langle u_i, v_j \rangle)^2$ is bounded. Since the ratings are bounded between $1 \leq r_{ij} \leq 5$ and we can consider a reasonable sublevel set $\{U, V \mid \max_{i,j} |u_i^T v_j| \leq \kappa\}$, we have every summand to be bounded by $(5 + \kappa)^2$. This does not affect the privacy claim as long as κ is chosen independent to the data.

B could still be large, if some particular users rated many movies. This issue is inevitable even if all observed users have few ratings, since differential privacy also protects users not in the database. We propose two theoretically-inspired algorithmic solutions to this problem:

Trimming: We may randomly delete ratings for those who rated a lot of movies so that the maximum number of ratings from a single user τ will not be too much larger than the average number of ratings. This procedure is the underlying gem that allows OptSpace (the very first provable matrix factorization based low-rank matrix completion method) [12] to work.

Reweighting: Alternatively, one can weight each user appropriately so that those who rated many movies will have smaller weight for each rating. Mcsherry and Mironov [20] used this reweighting scheme for controlling privacy loss. A similar approach is considered in the study of non-uniform and power-law matrix completion [22, 30], where the weighted trace norm has the same effect as if we reweight the loss-functions.

In addition, these procedures have their practical benefits for the robustness of the recommendation system, since they prevents any malicious user from injecting too much impact into the system, see e.g., Wang and Xu [33], Mobasher et al. [24]. Another justification of these two procedures is that, if the fully observed matrix is truly in a low-dimensional subspace, neither of these two procedures changes the underlying subspace. Therefore, the solutions should be similar to the non-preprocessed version.

The procedure for differentially private matrix factorization (DPMF) is summarized in Algorithm 1. Note that this is a *conceptual* sketch (we will discuss an efficient variant thereof later). The following theorem guarantees that our procedure is indeed differentially private.

Theorem 1. *Algorithm 1 obeys ϵ-differential privacy if the sample is exact and $(\epsilon, (1 + e^\epsilon)\delta)$-differential privacy if the sample is from a distribution δ-away from the target distribution in L_1 distance.*

The proof in [17] shows that this procedure uses in fact the exponential mechanism [21] with utility function being the negative MF objective and its sensitivity being $2B$. Note that this can be extended to considerably more complex models. This is the strength of our approach, namely that a large variety of algorithms can be adapted quite easily to differential privacy capable models.

---

[1] For convenience of notation we will omit the biases from the description below in favor of a slightly more succinct notation.

Algorithm 1 Differentially Private Matrix Factorization

Require: Partially observed rating matrix $R \in \mathbb{R}^{m \times n}$ with observation mask Ω. $m = \#$ of movies, $n = \#$ of users. Privacy parameter ϵ, a predefined positive parameter κ such that $\{U, V \mid u_i^T v_j \in [1 - \kappa, 5 + \kappa] \ \forall i, j\}$, rating range $[1, 5]$, max allowable number of ratings per-user τ, number of ratings of each user $\{m_1, ..., m_n\}$, weight of each user w, tuning parameter λ.

1: $B \leftarrow \max_{i=1,...,n} \min\{\tau, m_i\} w_i (5 - 1 + \kappa)^2$. ▷ Compute uniform upper bound.
2: Trim all users with ratings $> \tau$.
3: $F(U, V) := \sum_{i \in [i], j \in \Omega_i} w_i (R_{ij} - u_i^T v_j)^2 + \lambda(\|U\|_F^2 + \|V\|_F^2)$.
4: Sample $(U, V) \sim P(U, V) \propto e^{-\frac{\epsilon}{4B} F(U,V)}$
5: **while** $u_i^T v_j \notin [1 - \kappa, 5 + \kappa]$ for some i, j **do**
6: $\quad$ Sample $(U, V) \sim P(U, V) \propto e^{-\frac{\epsilon}{4B} F(U,V)}$
7: **return** (U, V)

3.1 Personalized Differential Privacy

Another interesting feature of the proposed procedure is that it allows us to calibrate the level of privacy protection for every user independently, via a novel observation that weights assigned to different users are linear in the amount of privacy we can guarantee for that particular user.

We will use the same sampling algorithm, and our guarantees in Theorem 1 still hold. The idea here is that we can customize the system so that we get a lower basic privacy protection for all users, say $\epsilon = 4B$. As we explained earlier this is the level of privacy that we can get more or less "for free". The protection of DP is sufficiently strong as to include even those users that are not in the database.

By adjusting the weight parameter, we can make the privacy protection stronger for particular users according to how much they set they want privacy. This procedure makes intuitive sense because if some user wants perfect privacy, we can set their weight to 0 and they are effectively not in the database anymore. For people who do not care about privacy, their ratings will be assigned default weight. Formally, we define personalized differential privacy as follows:

Definition 2 (Personalized Differential Privacy). *An algorithm $\mathcal{A}$ is (ϵ, δ)-personalized differentially private for User i in database X if for any measureable set S in the range of the algorithm $\mathcal{A}$*

$$\mathbb{P}(\mathcal{A}(X) \in S) \leq e^\epsilon \mathbb{P}(\mathcal{A}(X') \in S) + \delta.$$

for any $X \in \mathcal{X}^n$ and X' is either $X \cup \{x_i\}$ or $X \backslash \{x_i\}$.

Note that instead of replacing a user, we are now only adding or removing one specific user, such that the notion of personalized privacy is well-defined. We claim that

Theorem 2. *If we set w_i for User-i such that*

$$B_i := \min\{\tau, m_i\} w_i (4 + \kappa)^2 \leq B,$$

then Algorithm 1 guarantees $\frac{\epsilon B_i}{2B}$-personalized differential privacy for User i.

We show the proof in [17]. Note that if we set $\epsilon = 4B$ (so we are essentially sampling from the posterior distribution), we get $2B_i$-Personalized DP for user i.

In summary, if we simply set $\epsilon = 4B$, the method protects $4B$-differential privacy for everybody at very little cost and by setting the weight vector w, we can provide personalized service for users who demands more stringent DP protection. Also, personalized privacy offers a new perspective

in interpreting DP beyond the worst case scenario. For instance, users who are more predictable by the model will be likely to have stronger privacy protection. If a model fits the data well, even a large worst-case privacy loss ϵ could in fact provide meaningful protection to the large majority of users. Lastly, we recently become aware that personalized privacy (the exact same definition) has been independently developed in [10] along with a few basic properties that mirrors the standard DP. The difference is that we focus on the weighted posterior sampling aspect of it.

4. EFFICIENT SAMPLING VIA SGLD

Clearly, sampling from $\exp\left(-\frac{\epsilon}{4B} F(U, V)\right)$ is nontrivial. For a tractable approach we use a recent MCMC method named stochastic gradient Langevin dynamics (SGLD) [35], which is an annealing of stochastic gradient descent and Langevin dynamics that samples from the posterior distribution [26]. The basic update rule is

$$(u_i, v_j) = (u_i, v_j) - \eta_t \widehat{\nabla}_{(u_i, v_j)} F(U, V) + \mathcal{N}(0, \eta_t I) \quad (4)$$

where $\widehat{\nabla}_{(u_i, v_j)} F(U, V)$ is a stochastic gradient computed using only one or a small number of ratings. In other words, the updates are almost identical to those used in stochastic gradient descent. The key difference is that a small amount of Gaussian noise is added to the updates. This allows us to solve it extremely efficiently. We will describe our efficient implementation of this algorithm in Section 5.4.

The basic idea of SGLD is that when we are far away from the basin of convergence, the gradient of the log-posterior $\widehat{\nabla}_{(u_i, v_j)} F(U, V)$ is much larger than the additional noise so the algorithm behaves like stochastic gradient descent. As we approach the basin of convergence and η_t becomes small, $\sqrt{\eta_t} \gg \eta_t$ so the noise dominates and it behaves like a Brownian motion. Moreover, as η_t gets small, the probability of accepting the proposal in Metropolis-Hastings adjustment converges to 1, so we do not need to do this adjustment at all as the algorithm proceeds, as designed above.

This seemingly heuristic procedure was later shown to be consistent in [29, 31], where asymptotic "in-law" and "almost sure" convergence of SGLD to the correct stationary distribution are established. More recently, Teh et al. [32] further strengthens the convergence guarantee to include any finite iterations. This line of work justifies our approach in that if we run SGLD for a large number of iterations, we will end up sampling from the distribution that provides us (ϵ, δ)-differential privacy. By taking more iterations, we can make δ arbitrarily small.

5. SYSTEM DESIGN

The performance improvement over existing libraries such as GraphChi are due to both cache efficient design, prefetching, pipelining, the fact that we exploit the power law property of the data, and by judicious optimization of random number generation. This leads to a system that comfortably surpasses even moderately optimized GPU codes.

We primarily focus on the Stochastic Gradient Descent solver and subsequently we provide some details on how to extend this to SGLD. Inference requires a very large number of following operations on data:

- Read a rating triple (i, j, r_{ij}), possibly from disk, unless the data is sufficiently tiny to fit into RAM.
- For each given pair (i, j) of users and items fetch the vectors u_i and v_j from memory.
- Compute the inner product $\langle u_i, v_j \rangle$ on the CPU.
- Update u_i, v_j and write their new values to RAM.

To illustrate the impact of these operations consider training a $2,048$ dimensional model on the 10^8 rating triples of Netflix. Per iteration this requires over 3.2TB read/write operations to RAM. At a main memory bandwidth of 20GB/s and a latency of 100ns for each of the 200 million cache misses each pass would take over 6 minutes. Instead, our code accomplishes this task in approximately 10 seconds by using the steps outlined below.

5.1 Processing Pipeline

To deal with the dataflow from disk to CPU, we use a pipelined design, decomposing global and local state akin to [1]. This means that we process users sequentially, thus reducing the retrieval cost per user, since the operations are amortized over all of their ratings. This effectively halves IO. Moreover, since the data cannot be assumed to fit into RAM, we pipeline reads from disk. This hides latency and avoids stalling the CPUs. The writer thread periodically snapshots the model, i.e. U and V to disk.

Algorithm 2 Cache efficient Stochastic Gradient Descent

Require: parameters U, V; ratings R; P threads,
1: **preprocessing** Split R into B blocks;
2: **procedure** READ   ▷ Keep pipeline filled
3:     **while** #blocks in flight $\leq P$ **do**
4:        Read: block b from disk
5:        Sync: notify UPDATE about b
6: **procedure** UPDATE   ▷ Update U, V
7:     **while** at least one of P processors is available **do**
8:        Sync: receive a new block b from READ
9:        **for** user i in b **do**
10:           **for** each rating $r_{ij} \in b$ from user i **do**
11:              Prefetch next movie factor v_{j+1} from data stream
12:              $u_i \leftarrow u_i - \eta_t \widehat{\nabla}_{u_i}$
13:              $v_j \leftarrow v_j - \eta_t \widehat{\nabla}_{v_j}$
14:              ($\widehat{\nabla}$ is either the exact or private gradient)
15: **procedure** WRITE
16:     **if** B_t blocks processed **then** save U, V

5.2 Cache Efficiency

The previous reasoning discussed how to keep the data pipeline filled and how to reduce the user-specific cache misses by preaggregating them on disk. Next we need to address cache efficiency with regard to movies. More to the point, we need to exploit cache locality relative to the CPU *core* rather than simply avoiding cache misses. The basic idea is that each CPU core exactly reads a cache line (commonly 64 bytes) from RAM each time, so algorithm designers should not waste it until that piece of cache line is fully utilized.

We exploit the fact that movie ratings follow a power law [11], as is evident e.g. on Netflix in Figure 1. This means that if we succeed at keeping frequently rated movies in the CPU cache, we should see substantial speedups. Note that traditional matrix blocking tricks, as widely used for matrix multiplications operations are not useful, due to the sparsity of the rating matrix R. Instead, we decompose the movies into tiers of popularity. To illustrate, considering a decomposition into three blocks consisting of the Top 500, the Next 4000, and the remaining long tail.

Within each block, we process a batch of users simultaneously. This way we can preserve the associated user vectors u_i in cache and we are likely to cache the movie vectors, too (in particular for the Top 500 block). Also, parallelizing all the updates for multiple users does not require locks. Movie parameters are updated in a Hogwild fashion [27].

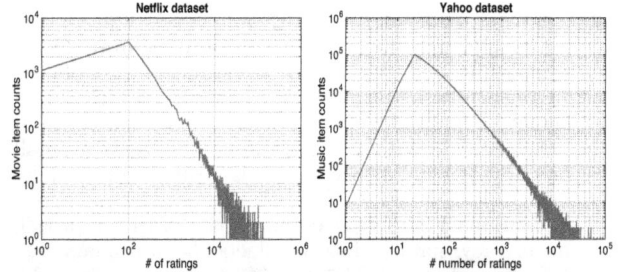

Figure 1: Distribution of items (Movies/Music pieces) as a function of their number of ratings. Many movies have 100 ratings or less, while the majority of ratings focuses on a small number of movies.

This design is particularly efficient for low-dimensional models since the Top 500 block fits into L1 cache (this amounts to 44% of all movie ratings in the Netflix dataset), the Next 4000 fits into L2, and ratings will typically reside in L3. Even in the extreme case of 2048 dimensions we can fit about 55% of all ratings into cache, albeit L3 cache.

5.3 Latency Hiding and Prefetching

To avoid the penalty for random requests we perform latency hiding by prefetching. That is, we actively request v_j in advance before the rating r_{ij} is to be updated. For dimensions less than 256, accurate prefetching leads to a dataflow of v_j into L1 cache. Beyond that, the size of the latent variables could be too big to benefit from the lowest level of caching due to limited size of caches in modern computers. We provide a detailed caching analysis in Section 6 to illustrate the effect of these techniques.

5.4 Optimizations for SGLD

The data flow of SGLD is almost analogous to that in SGD, albeit with a number of complications. First off, note that (4) applies to the whole parameter *matrix* U, V rather than just to a single vector. Following [3] we can derive an unbiased approximation of $\widehat{\nabla}_{u_i}$ in (4) which is nonzero only for (u_i, v_j) as follows:

$$\widehat{\nabla}_{u_i} = -N\lambda_r \left(r_{ij} - \langle u_i, v_j \rangle \right) v_j + \frac{N}{N_i} u_i^\top \Lambda_u u_i$$

where N, N_i denote number of rating data rated by all and rated by user i respectively. The parameters $\lambda_r, \Lambda_u, \Lambda_v$ do not incur any major cost — Λ_u, Λ_v are diagonal matrices with a Gamma distribution over them. We simply perform Gibbs sampling once per round. However, the most time-consuming part is to sample the remaining vectors, i.e. $P(U^{-i}, V^{-i} | R, \text{rest})$ since it both requires dense updates and moreover, it requires many random numbers, which adds nontrivial cost.

Dense Updates: Note that unless we encounter the triple (i, j, r_{ij}) all other parameters are only updated by adding Gaussian noise. This means that by keeping track of when a parameter was last updated, we can simply aggregate the updates (the Normal distribution is closed under addition). That is, c_i subsequent additions amount to a single draw from $\mathcal{N}(0, c_i \eta)$. The is possible since we only need to know the value of u_i, v_j whenever we encounter a new triple.

Table Lookup: Drawing iid samples from a Gaussian is quite costly, easily dominating all other floating point operations combined. We address this by pre-generating a large table of numbers [19] and then by performing random lookup within the table. More to the point, a lookup table of r random numbers is statistically indistinguishable from the truth until we draw $O(r^2)$ samples from it (this follows from the slow rate of convergence for two-sample tests), hence a few MB of data suffice. Finally, for cache efficiency, we read contiguous segments with random offset (this adds a small amount of dependence which is easily addressed by using a larger table).

A cautionary note is that the impact of this approach on privacy, namely how it affects the stationary distribution of the SGLD, is unknown. For readers who are interested in the impact of lookup table size vs. accuracy please refer to [17].

6. EXPERIMENTS AND DISCUSSION

We now investigate the efficiency and accuracy of our fast SGD solver and Stochastic Gradient Langevin Dynamics solver, compared with state-of-the-art available recommenders. We explore the differentially private accuracy by using our proposed method while varying different privacy budgets.

6.1 Comparisons

We compare the performance of both the SGD solver and the SGLD solver to other publicly available recommenders and one closed-source solver. In particular, we compare to both CPU and GPU solvers, since the latter tend to excel in massively parallel floating point operations.

GraphChi Most of our experiments focus on a direct comparison to GraphChi [15]. This is primarily due the fact that the code for GraphChi is publicly available as open source and its very good performance.

GraphLab Create is a closed source data analysis platform [18]. It is currently the fastest recommender system available, being slightly faster than GraphChi. We compared our system to GraphLab Create, albeit without fine-grained diagnostics that were possible for GraphChi.

BidMach is a GPU based system [48]. It reports runtimes of 90, 129 and 600 seconds respectively for 100, 200 and 500 dimensions using an Amazon g2.2xlarge instance for the Netflix dataset.[2] This is slower than the runtimes of 48, 63, and 83 seconds for 128, 256, and 512 that we achieve without GPU optimization on a c3.8xlarge instance.

Spark is a distributed system (Spark MLlib) for inferring recommendations and factorization. In recent comparison the argument has been made that it is somewhat slower[3] than GraphLab while being substantially faster than Mahout.

6.2 Data

We use two datasets — the well known Netflix Prize dataset, consisting of a training set of 99M ratings spanning 480k customers and their ratings on almost 18k, each movie being rated at a scale of 1 to 5 stars. Additionally, we use their released validation set which consists of 1.4M ratings for validation purposes.

Secondly, we use the Yahoo music recommender dataset, consisting of almost 263M ratings of 635k music items by 1M users. We also use the released validation set which consists of 6M ratings for validation. We re-scale each rating at a scale of 0 to 5.

---

[2] http://github.com/BIDData/BIDMach/wiki/Benchmarks
[3] http://stanford.edu/~rezab/sparkworkshop/slides/xiangrui.pdf, Slide 31

K	SC-SGD		GraphChi	
	L1 Cache	L3 Cache	L1 Cache	L3 Cache
16	2.84%	0.43%	12.77%	2.21%
256	2.85%	0.50%	12.89%	2.34%
2048	3.3%	1.7%	15%	9.8%

Table 1: Cache miss rates in C-SGD and GraphChi.

6.3 Runtime

We run all the experiments on an Amazon c3.8xlarge instance running Ubuntu 14.04 with 32 CPUs and 60GB RAM.

For SGD-based methods we grid search the best parameters [17] for initial learning rate η_0, decay rate γ and regularizer λ [17]. For our fast SGLD solver, in addition to previous paramters, practically we multiply learning rate by a temperature parameter ζ [4] in the Gaussian noise $\mathcal{N}(0, \zeta \cdot \eta_t)$ with $\sqrt{\zeta \cdot \eta_t} \gg \eta_t$ to speed up SGLD's burn-in procedure.

Since it is nontrivial to observe the test RMSE error in each epoch when using Graphlab Create, we only report the timing of Graphlab Create and all other methods in Figure 3. Note that we were unable to obtain performance results from BidMach for the Yahoo dataset, since Scala encountered memory management issues. However, we have no reason to believe that the results would be in any way more favorable to BidMach than the findings on the Netflix dataset. For reproducibility the results were carried out on an AWS g2.8xlarge instance.

To illustrate the convergence over time. We run all the methods in a fixed number of epochs. That is 15 epochs and 30 epochs respectively because we observe that our SGD solver can reach the convergence at that time. Figure 2 shows our timing results along with convergence while we vary dimensions of the models.

Both of our solvers, i.e. C-SGD and Fast SGLD benefit from our caching algorithm. C-SGD is around 2 to 3 times faster than GraphChi and Graphlab while simultaneously outperforming the accuracy of GraphChi.

Note that the algorithm required for Fast SGLD is rather more complex, since it performs sampling from the Bayesian posterior. Consequently, it is slower than plain SGD. Nonetheless, its speed is comparable to GraphChi in terms of throughput (despite the latter solving a much simpler problem). One problem of SGLD is that the more complex the models are, the worse its convergence becomes (even though generates good samples on small dimensions Figure 4), due to the fact that we are sampling from a large state space. This is possibly due to the slow mixing of SGLD, which is a known problem of SGLD [2]. Improving the mixing rate by considering a more advanced stochastic differential equation based sampler, e.g. [4, 6], while keeping the cache efficiency during the updates will be important future works. To our best knowledge we are the first to report the convergence results of SGLD at this scale.

6.4 Cache-efficient Design

We show the cache efficiency of C-SGD and Graphchi in this section. Our data access pattern can accelerate the hardware cache prefetching. In the meanwhile we also use software prefetching strategies (with prefetching stride set to 2) to prefetch movie factors in advance.

We set the experiments as follows. In each gradient update step given r_{ij}, once the parameters e.g. u_i and v_j in (3) been read they will stay in cache for a while until they be flushed away by new parameters. What we really care about in this section is if the first time each parameter be read by CPU is already staying in cache or not. If it is not in cache then there will be a cache miss and will push CPU to idle. We use Cachegrind [16] as a cache profiler and analyze

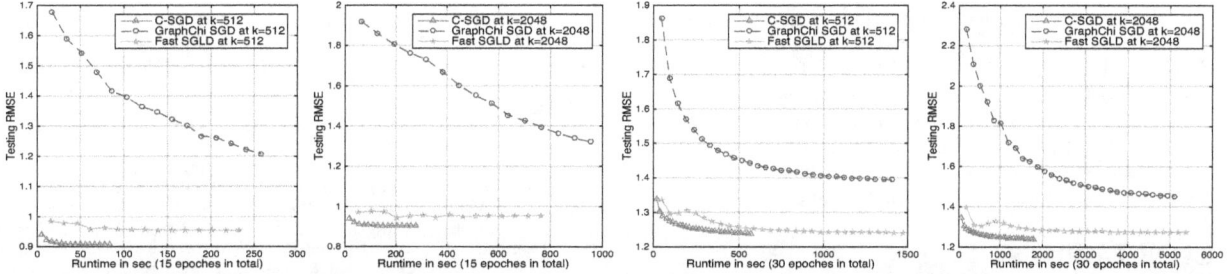

Figure 2: Runtime comparisons of the C-SGD solver, differentially private SGLD solver vs. non-private GraphChi/Graphlab on a identical Amazon AWS c3.8xlarge instance. (Left: Netflix, Right: Yahoo).

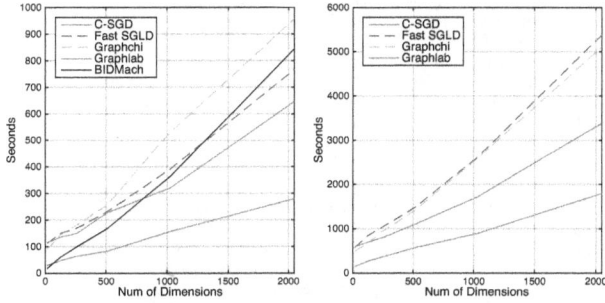

Figure 3: Timing comparisons on Netflix (left, 15 epochs) and Yahoo (right, 30 epochs).

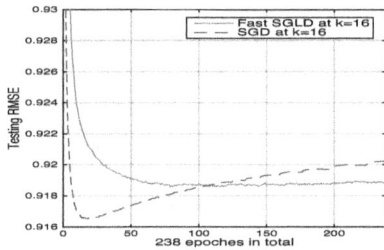

Figure 4: Convergence of SGLD for 16-dimensional models on Netflix.

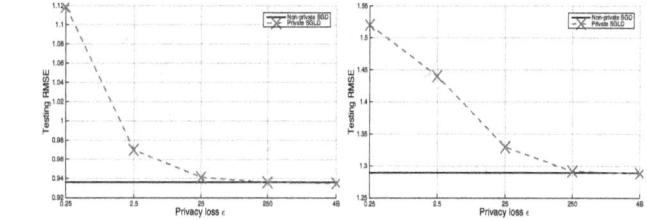

Figure 5: Test RMSE vs. privacy loss ϵ on Netflix (left) and Yahoo (right). A modest decrease in accuracy affords a useful gain in privacy.

cache miss (see Table 1 which shows it plays crucial effects on the final performance) for this purpose.

6.5 Privacy and Accuracy

We now investigate the influence of privacy loss on accuracy. As discussed previously, a small rescaling factor B can help us to get a nice bound on the loss function. For private collaborative filtering purposes, we first trim the training data by setting each user's maximum allowable number of ratings $\tau = 100$ and $\tau = 200$ for the Netflix competition dataset and Yahoo Music data respectively. We set $B = \tau(5 - 1 + \kappa)^2$ and weight of each user as $w_i = \min(\rho, \frac{B}{m_i(5-1+\kappa)^2})$ where κ is set to 1. According to different trimming strength we have $B = 2500$ and $B = 5000$ for Netflix data and Yahoo data respectively. As such we get a dataset with 33M ratings for Netflix and 100M ratings for Yahoo Music data. We study the prediction accuracy, i.e. the utility of our private method by varying the differential privacy budget ϵ for fixed model dimensionality $K = 16$. The parameters of the experiment are set as in [17].

While we are sampling (U, V) jointly, we essentially only need to release V. Users can then apply their own data to

get the full model and have a local recommender system:

$$u_i \approx \left(\lambda \mathbf{1} + \sum_{j|(i,j) \in \mathcal{S}} v_j v_j^\top \right)^{-1} \sum_j v_j r_{ij} \qquad (5)$$

The local predictions, i.e. in our context the utility of differentially private matrix factorization method, along with the different privacy loss ϵ are shown in Figure 5.

More specifically, the model (5) is a *two-stage* procedure which first takes the differentially private *item vectors* and then use the latter to obtain locally non-private user parameter estimates. This is perfectly admissible since users have no expectation of privacy with regard to their own ratings.

6.6 Rating privacy, user privacy and average personalized privacy

Interpreting the privacy guarantees can be subtle. A privacy loss of $\epsilon = 250$ as in Figure 5 may seem completely meaningless by Definition 1 and the corresponding results in Mcsherry and Mironov [20] may appear much better.

We first address the comparison to Mcsherry and Mironov [20]. It is important to point out that our privacy loss ϵ is stated in terms of user level privacy while the results in Mcsherry and Mironov [20] are stated in terms of rating level privacy, which offers exponentially weaker protection. ϵ-user differential privacy translates into ϵ/τ-rating differential privacy. Since $\tau = 200$ in our case, our results suggest that we almost lose no accuracy at all while preserving rating differential privacy with $\epsilon < 1$. This matches (and slightly improves) Mcsherry and Mironov [20]'s carefully engineered system.

On the other hand, we note that the plain privacy loss can be a very deceiving measure of its practical level of protection. Definition 1 protects privacy of an arbitrary user, who can be a malicious spammer that rates every movie in a completely opposite fashion as what the learned model would predict. This is a truly paranoid requirement, and arguably not the right one, since we probably should not protect these malicious users to begin with. For an average user, the personalized privacy (Definition 2) guarantee can be much stronger, as the posterior distribution concentrates around models that predict reasonably well for such users. As a result, the log-likelihood associated with these users will be bounded by a much smaller number with high probability. In the example shown in Figure 5, a typical user's personal privacy loss is about $\epsilon/25$, which helps to reduce the essential privacy loss to a meaningful range.

7. CONCLUSION

In this paper we described an algorithm for efficient collaborative filtering that is compatible with differential privacy. In particular, we showed that it is possible to accomplish all three goals: accuracy, speed and privacy without any significant sacrifice on either end.

Moreover, we introduced the notion of *personalized* differential privacy. That is, we defined (and proved) the notion of obtaining estimates that respect different degrees of privacy, as required by individual users. We believe that this notion is highly relevant in today's information economy where the expectation of privacy may be tempered by, e.g. the cost of the service, the quality of the hardware (cheap netbooks deployed with Windows 8.1 with Bing), and the extent to which we want to incorporate the opinions of users.

Our implementation takes advantage of the caching properties of modern microprocessors. By careful latency hiding we are able to obtain near peak performance. In particular, our implementation is approximately 3 times as fast as GraphChi, the next-fastest recommender system. In sum, this is a strong endorsement of Stochastic Gradient Langevin Dynamics to obtain differentially private estimates in recommender systems while still preserving good utility.

Acknowledgments: Parts of this work were supported by a grant of Adobe Research. Z. Liu was supported by Sience Fund for Creative Research Groups (61221063); Ministry of Education Innovation Research Team (IRT13035); NSF of China (91118005, 91218301, 61428206). Y.-X. Wang was supported by NSF Award BCS-0941518 to CMU Statistics and Singapore National Research Foundation under its International Research Centre @ Singapore Funding Initiative and administered by the IDM Programme Office.

References

[1] A. Ahmed, M. Aly, J. Gonzalez, S. Narayanamurthy, and A. Smola. Scalable Inference in Latent Variable Models. In *WSDM*, 2012.

[2] S. Ahn, A. Korattikara, and M. Welling. Bayesian posterior sampling via stochastic gradient fisher scoring. In *ICML'12*, pages 1591–1598, 2012.

[3] S. Ahn, A. Korattikara, N. Liu, S. Rajan, and M. Welling. Large scale distributed bayesian matrix factorization using stochastic gradient MCMC. 2015.

[4] T. Chen, E. B. Fox, and C. Guestrin. Stochastic Gradient Hamiltonian Monte Carlo. 32, 2014.

[5] C. Dimitrakakis, B. Nelson, A. Mitrokotsa, and B. I. Rubinstein. Robust and private bayesian inference. In *Algorithmic Learning Theory*, pages 291–305. Springer, 2014.

[6] N. Ding, C. Chen, R. D. Skeel, and R. Babbush. Bayesian Sampling Using Stochastic Gradient Thermostats. In *NIPS*, pages 1–14, 2014.

[7] C. Dwork. Differential privacy. In *Automata, Languages and Programming*, pages 1–12. Springer, 2006.

[8] C. Dwork and A. Roth. The Algorithmic Foundations of Differential Privacy. *Foundations and Trends in Theoretical Computer Science*, 9(3-4):211–407, 2013.

[9] C. Dwork, F. McSherry, K. Nissim, and A. Smith. Calibrating noise to sensitivity in private data analysis. In *Theory of cryptography*, pages 265–284. Springer, 2006.

[10] H. Ebadi, D. Sands, and G. Schneider. Differential privacy: Now it's getting personal. In *ACM Symposium on Principles of Programming Languages*, pages 69–81. ACM, 2015.

[11] A. Hartstein, V. Srinivasan, T. Puzak, and P. Emma. On the nature of cache miss behavior: Is it $\sqrt{2}$? *The Journal of Instruction-Level Parallelism*, 10:1–22, 2008.

[12] R. Keshavan, A. Montanari, and S. Oh. Matrix completion from noisy entries. In *NIPS'09*, pages 952–960, 2009.

[13] Y. Koren. Collaborative Filtering with Temporal Dynamics. In *KDD*, number 4, 2009.

[14] Y. Koren, R. Bell, and C. Volinsky. Matrix factorization techniques for recommender systems. *IEEE Computer Society*, pages 42–49, 2009.

[15] A. Kyrola, G. Blelloch, and C. Guestrin. GraphChi : Large-Scale Graph Computation on Just a PC Disk-based Graph Computation. In *OSDI*, 2012.

[16] N. P. Laptev. Analysis of cache architectures. *Department of Computer Science–University of California Santa Barbara*.

[17] Z. Liu, Y.-X. Wang, and A. J. Smola. Fast differentially private matrix factorization. *arXiv:1505.01419*, 2015.

[18] Y. Low, J. E. Gonzalez, A. Kyrola, D. Bickson, C. E. Guestrin, and J. Hellerstein. Graphlab: A new framework for parallel machine learning. *arXiv:1408.2041*, 2014.

[19] G. Marsaglia, W. W. Tsang, and J. Wang. Fast Generation of Discrete Random Variables. *Journal of Statistical Software*, 11, 2004.

[20] F. Mcsherry and I. Mironov. Differentially Private Recommender Systems : Building Privacy into the Netflix Prize Contenders. In *KDD*, 2009. ISBN 9781605584959.

[21] F. McSherry and K. Talwar. Mechanism design via differential privacy. In *Foundations of Computer Science, 2007. FOCS'07. 48th Annual IEEE Symposium on*, pages 94–103. IEEE, 2007.

[22] R. Meka, P. Jain, and I. S. Dhillon. Matrix completion from power-law distributed samples. In *NIPS*, 2009.

[23] D. J. Mir. *Differential privacy: an exploration of the privacy-utility landscape*. PhD thesis, Rutgers University-Graduate School-New Brunswick, 2013.

[24] B. Mobasher, R. Burke, R. Bhaumik, and C. Williams. Toward trustworthy recommender systems: An analysis of attack models and algorithm robustness. *ACM Transactions on Internet Technology (TOIT)*, 7(4):23, 2007.

[25] A. Narayanan and V. Shmatikov. Robust de-anonymization of large sparse datasets. In *Security and Privacy, 2008. SP 2008. IEEE Symposium on*, pages 111–125. IEEE, 2008.

[26] R. M. Neal. Mcmc using hamiltonian dynamics. *Handbook of Markov Chain Monte Carlo*, 2, 2011.

[27] F. Niu, B. Recht, R. Christopher, and S. J. Wright. Hogwild ! : A Lock-Free Approach to Parallelizing Stochastic Gradient Descent. In *NIPS*, pages 1–22, 2011.

[28] R. Salakhutdinov, A. Mnih, and G. Hinton. Restricted Boltzmann Machines for Collaborative Filtering. In *ICML*, 2007.

[29] I. Sato and H. Nakagawa. Approximation analysis of stochastic gradient langevin dynamics by using fokker-planck equation and ito process. In *ICML'14*, pages 982–990, 2014.

[30] N. Srebro and R. R. Salakhutdinov. Collaborative filtering in a non-uniform world: Learning with the weighted trace norm. In *NIPS'10*, pages 2056–2064, 2010.

[31] Y. W. Teh, A. Thiéry, and S. Vollmer. Consistency and fluctuations for stochastic gradient langevin dynamics. *arXiv preprint:1409.0578*, 2014.

[32] Y. W. Teh, S. J. Vollmer, and K. C. Zygalakis. (Non-) asymptotic properties of Stochastic Gradient Langevin Dynamics. *arXiv preprint:1501.00438*, 2015.

[33] Y.-X. Wang and H. Xu. Stability of matrix factorization for collaborative filtering. In *ICML'12*, pages 417–424, 2012.

[34] Y.-X. Wang, S. E. Fienberg, and A. Smola. Privacy for free: Posterior sampling and stochastic gradient monte carlo. In *ICML*, 2015.

[35] M. Welling and Y. W. Teh. Bayesian Learning via Stochastic Gradient Langevin Dynamics. In *ICML*, 2011.

[36] Y. Xin and T. Jaakkola. Controlling privacy in recommender systems. In *NIPS*, 2014.

[37] A. Zhang, N. Fawaz, S. Ioannidis, and A. Montanari. Guess who rated this movie: Identifying users through subspace clustering. *arXiv preprint arXiv:1208.1544*, 2012.

[38] H. Zhao and J. F. Canny. *High Performance Machine Learning through Codesign and Rooflining*. PhD thesis, EECS Department, University of California, Berkeley, Sep 2014.

Predicting Online Performance of News Recommender Systems Through Richer Evaluation Metrics

Andrii Maksai, Florent Garcin, and Boi Faltings
Artificial Intelligence Lab, Ecole Polytechnique Fédérale de Lausanne
Lausanne, Switzerland
{firstname.lastname}@epfl.ch

ABSTRACT

We investigate how metrics that can be measured offline can be used to predict the online performance of recommender systems, thus avoiding costly A-B testing. In addition to accuracy metrics, we combine diversity, coverage, and serendipity metrics to create a new performance model. Using the model, we quantify the trade-off between different metrics and propose to use it to tune the parameters of recommender algorithms without the need for online testing. Another application for the model is a self-adjusting algorithm blend that optimizes a recommender's parameters over time. We evaluate our findings on data and experiments from news websites.

Categories and Subject Descriptors

H.3.3 [**Information Storage and Retrieval**]: Information Search and Retrieval—*Information filtering*

Keywords

recommender system;online evaluation;evaluation metrics

1. INTRODUCTION

It was recognized early on in the history of recommender systems (recsys) that the most accurate recommendations were not always the best. The first approaches for diversifying recommendations were made by Zhang et al. [29] and Ziegler et al. [31]. Later, many different metrics - such as novelty, coverage, diversity, and serendipity [17] - have been introduced with the aim of enhancing the quality of recommendations. It has even been suggested that the focus on optimizing the accuracy of recsys has been detrimental to the field [13]. Ordering algorithms with respect to their offline accuracy can result in the exact inverse of ordering them with respect to the online click-through rate (CTR), which is the metric most site owners care about [6, 27].

The main reason for this is that recommending popular items is usually accurate – they are popular because peo-

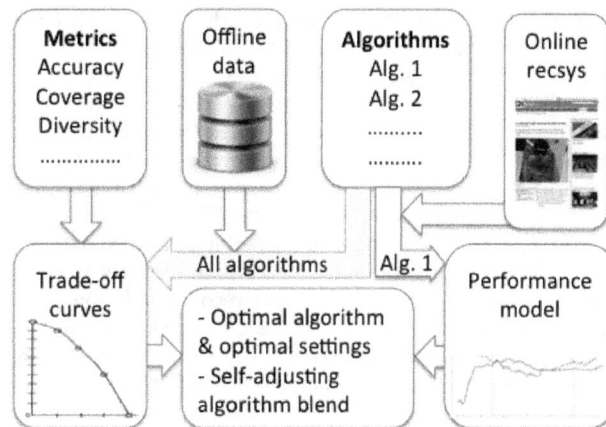

Figure 1: Workflow for selecting the best algorithm using a performance model with multiple metrics.

ple do indeed rate them highly – but such recommendations have little to no effect as people have already seen the items elsewhere. A contributing factor in the domain of news recommendations is that users are often interested in something entirely new. Finally, users often view recommendations concerning a variety of different topics more favorably than the ones concerning several interesting but similar items.

All of the above factors indicate that optimizing the accuracy of recommendations using offline data, gathered from past behavior without a running recommender algorithm, is neither an effective nor efficient way to select the best algorithm [13, 19]. The fairest way to compare algorithms is to launch them online and compare the actual reactions of users to the recommendations. However, this requires the existence of an online environment and a set of dedicated users, and it takes a long time. Another problem is the need of constant re-evaluation of algorithms, especially if they are sensitive to changes in the item or user set over time [2, 10]. Simulation of an online environment is a potential alternative [11, 27]. We discuss these solutions later in the paper.

In this work, we leverage recommendations from real news websites to model their CTR (Fig. 1). Our main contributions are threefold. First, in Sec. 2, we review the different metrics, find those that are most likely to affect online performance, and indicate the presence of a trade-off between them. Next, in Sec. 3, we combine a selected subset of metrics into a prediction model of online performance. Finally, in Sec. 4, using this model and the metric trade-offs, we show how to select the best version of an algorithm and its parameters using limited online evaluation, and how to create a blend of several recommender algorithms that adjusts over time for optimal performance. Results reported in Sec 5 show that given limited access to online environment, it is possible to model performance over time far better than by averaging performance over time.

2. EVALUATION METRICS

Over the years, various metrics have been suggested for evaluating recsys. In the approach presented here, we considered 17 metrics classified into five different groups [17].

2.1 Metric groups

Accuracy/Error metrics compute the quality of predictions (i.e., rating movies or a correct/incorrect guess of the next news item visited). Error metrics usually penalize errors, whereas accuracy metrics reward correct answers. We ignored metrics, such as RMSE or MAE, that penalize each item separately; we concentrated instead on metrics for the task of top-N recommendation. We investigated the following metrics: Precision, NDPM, Kendall's τ, Spearman's ρ [8], Success [6], Markedness, Informedness, and Matthew's Correlation [15]. All these metrics compute the accuracy of prediction and, for the case of top-1 recommendation, turn into binary indicators of the success of recommendation.

Diversity is usually defined as a measure of dissimilarity between items in the recommendation list with respect to a similarity metric. This "intra-list" diversity has been presented and used in several forms [29, 31, 28].

Lathia et al. [10] proposed a definition of the temporal diversity of a recsys which was dependent on the number of new items a user was shown during different visits. For news recommendations where users are often anonymous, we modified the definition to compute the amount of new items the system recommends to all users at a later time.

Zhou et al. [30] proposed a metric called "personalization" that is effectively the normalized pairwise Jaccard similarity between items recommended to each pair of users; it can be viewed as the "extra-list" diversity.

Novelty is the quality of an item of being new to a user (i.e., the recommendation of an item from the category that the user already likes is not novel). A variation of such a metric, called "surprisal", is a weighted sum of negative log frequencies of the items in the recommendation list [30].

Coverage is defined as the percentage of items that are ever recommended, and prediction coverage is the number of users for whom a recommendation can be made. We also considered the Gini Index and Shannon's Entropy [17].

Serendipity is the quality of being both unexpected and useful. One component penalizes the expectedness of the most popular items, whereas the other component measures usefulness – typically just accuracy [7, 14].

2.2 Metric correlations

We investigated the correlation between the metrics in each group by applying three different algorithms to the Swissinfo dataset, described later. Each data point was generated by averaging metric values for all the recommendations at equal time intervals. For metrics that are computed cumulatively over recommendations (i.e., temporal diversity) we computed the metric value at each point in time and used the cumulative difference as the metric value.

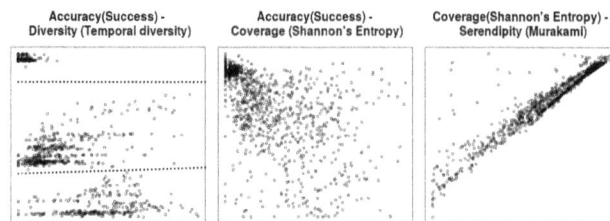

Figure 2: Pairwise plots between representative metrics from four groups (average over 10 minutes). Example of 3 clusters separated by the dotted lines.

The metrics in the Accuracy group (NDPM, Kendall's τ, Success, Spearman's ρ, Markedness, Informedness and Matthews correlation) showed correlations higher than 0.9 between all the pairs of metrics for the recommendation lists given by the algorithms. The same results were obtained for the other metric groups – Diversity (Intralist diversity, Personalization, and Temporal diversity), Coverage (Gini Index, Shannon's Entropy, and Coverage), and Serendipity (Serendipity by Ge [7], and Serendipity by Murakami [14]). We therefore examined correlation between pairs of "representative" metrics from each of these groups (Fig. 2). There was no strong agreement between metric groups (except for Coverage and Serendipity). This indicates that different metric groups all express different features of the recommendations and therefore at least one representative of each group should be used as a feature of the performance model.

Points often formed three distinct clusters. The clusters corresponded to recommendations given by the different algorithms, indicating that the relationship between metrics might be different for recommendations given by different algorithms.

The results in Fig. 2 were obtained from the recommendation lists comprising three items. We studied the effect of the length of recommendation lists on metric correlations (Fig. 3). For all metric pairs, we first observed a drop, and then almost no change in the absolute value of correlations. This indicates that different sets of metrics might be important for domains with different numbers of items to be recommended.

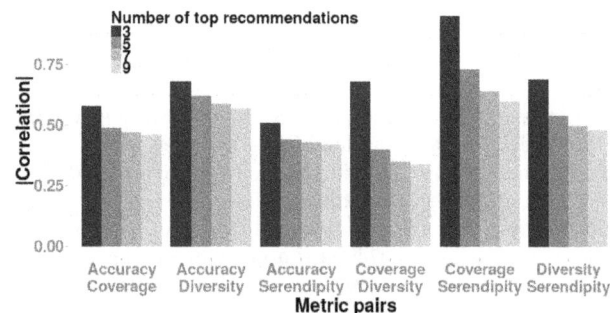

Figure 3: Absolute value of correlations between metrics in different groups for different numbers of recommendations.

2.3 Metric trade-off

Algorithms often have hyperparameters that affect their performance, and by varying the values of such hyperpa-

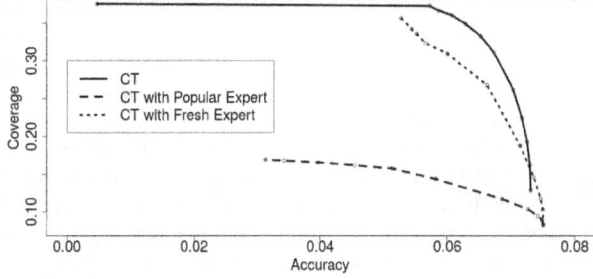

Figure 4: Coverage–accuracy trade-off curves for three variations of the CT algorithm [5]

rameters different sets of recommendations can be obtained. The average metric values for all the sets of recommendations given can be computed in order to observe how they change when varying a hyperparameter. The example shown in Fig. 4 was obtained using the Yahoo dataset and several variations of the Context Tree (CT) algorithm, described later in the paper. Each of the algorithms produced a curve that clearly indicated the trade-off between metrics – in this case, Accuracy and Coverage. We also observed these trade-offs using other datasets and algorithms. Getting the best performance requires selecting which metrics to optimize. The next section describes how we build a regression model of performance to achieve this.

3. PREDICTING ONLINE FROM OFFLINE

In this section, we first briefly describe the definitions of offline and online accuracy, and click-through rate. We then describe our method of feature selection for the regression model of online metrics, and finally the model itself.

Offline accuracy is the percentage of clicks predicted by the recsys when it is applied to a log of user browsing which occurred without the recommender system present.

Online accuracy is the percentage of clicks predicted by the recsys when it is online. If a recsys predicted that the user would browse to a particular page and she did so, but without clicking on its recommendations, this still counts towards online accuracy.

Click-through rate (CTR) is the percentage of clicks made on recommendations.

For any random user, the model assumes that all the items she visits without a recsys are included in the set of items she would visit with one. This means that if the user visits an item when using the recsys, that she would visit anyway when the recsys was absent, then that click should not be taken into account when measuring the impact of the recsys. A broader discussion of this topic is presented by Garcin et al. [6].

CTR and online accuracy are both important metrics for recsys. Therefore, we build a regression model for each of them. The regression model will use not only offline accuracy, as it is something different from the two above.

3.1 Feature selection

To verify the finding that multiple groups of metrics, such as Diversity and Coverage, are important for predicting on-

line performance metrics, we carried out feature selection using the Least Angle Regression (LAR, [4]). The LAR assumes a linear model of the relationship between independent variable y and n dependent variables $x = (x_1, \ldots, x_n)^\mathsf{T}$, with an L_1 regularizer:

$$y = \beta^\mathsf{T} x + \lambda \sum_{j=1}^{n} |x_j|$$

The L_1 regularizer promotes sparsity in β. By decreasing λ, it is possible to assign each predictor a value of λ at which it first enters the model with a non-zero weight. The order of the predictors given by these λ values serves as a proxy for their importance. The LAR allows efficient computation of this value for each regressor [4].

The average order position among folds was calculated using average metric values in time intervals of length Δt as predictors and average CTR as responses. Details of this approach are given in Alg. 1. Several Δt interval sizes were tested, but all values of ten minutes or longer were found to work reasonably well. Ten minute intervals were chosen as shorter intervals gave results with very high variance and longer intervals meant fewer data points and, therefore, less significant results. We used $F = 100$ folds.

Algorithm 1: Average model entering time for each metric. $t(i)$ indicates time when recommendation i was given.

input : Offline, online data D, D', metrics $M, \Delta t, F$
output: Average model entering time $T(m) \forall m \in M$

$T(m) \leftarrow 0 \ \forall m \in M$
for $f \leftarrow 1$ **to** F **do**
  $D_f \leftarrow$ Random 10% of D
  $D_f' \leftarrow$ Random 10% of D'
  Data $\leftarrow \emptyset$
  for $w = \min_{i \in D \cup D'} t(i) : \Delta t : \max_{i \in D \cup D'} t(i)$ **do**
    $\mathrm{F}_m^w \leftarrow \mathrm{Avg}(\{m(i)|i \in D_f, t(i) \in [w; w + \Delta t]\})$
    $\mathrm{R}^w \leftarrow \mathrm{Avg}(\{CTR(i)|i \in D_f', t(i) \in [w; w+\Delta t]\})$
    Data $\leftarrow$ Data $\cup (\mathrm{F}_1^w, \ldots, \mathrm{F}_m^w, R^w)$
  end
  $T(m)$ += LAREntryIdx(Data, m) / $F \ \forall m \in M$
end

3.2 Regression model

After identifying the best predictors, we used the multiple linear regression $y = \beta^\mathsf{T} x$. This simple model allowed us to interpret coefficients of β as trade-offs between different metrics for a particular model, or as derivatives of the performance with respect to metrics. We expand on this idea in Sec. 4. More complex models, such as Gaussian process regression or penalized linear regression, do not allow such a simple interpretation. Nevertheless, the results obtained using simple linear regression were compared to those of more complex methods. To build such a model, a limited amount of training data is required. Features should be collected simultaneously using the metrics from a recsys run on a log of offline data (user browsing without the recsys), and the online performance metric should be collected from the live website that is using a recsys.

4. ALGORITHM OPTIMIZATION

In this section we discuss two possible ways of using the model of online performance metric. The first allows an effective comparison between several variations of the algorithm, without the need for lengthy access to online data, and the selection of the optimal hyperparameters. The second describes an algorithm able to rebuild the model over time, continually aiming for optimal online performance.

4.1 Optimal algorithm selection

A typical task for recsys designers is the comparison of several variations of an algorithm, and the selection of the hyperparameter value and algorithm that perform best. An obvious solution would be to evaluate each of the algorithms online using several values of hyperparameter.

In our model, online performance can be approximated by a weighted combination of two offline metrics (i.e. Accuracy and Coverage). To simplify the argument below, we assume that weights are positive but approach trivially extends to the case when they are negative. Such a model is learned by evaluating one of the algorithm variations online and is assumed to be similar for other variations.

As described in Sec. 2.3, varying an algorithm's hyperparameter produces the metrics trade-off curve. When the curve for one algorithm is located above the curve for a second, the first algorithm is strictly better in terms of performance. Note that curves are produced using offline data.

Given the trade-off curves, there is no need for an online evaluation of all the combinations of algorithms and hyperparameters, but only those that produce points on the upper envelope of the curves. Furthermore, by inspecting the model coefficients it is possible to select an algorithm without evaluating it: if a model gives a much larger weight to one of the metrics, this can be used as a proxy for performance and the best algorithm is the one reaching the highest values for that metric.

Examples of real trade-off curves are shown in Fig. 4. We used several variations of the CT recommender as a source of recommendations ordered by Accuracy [5]. The standard CT algorithm makes predictions based on a count of the items viewed. CT with additional experts exploit the item click count and the last time an item was clicked. We used the items' Shannon's Entropy as a coverage score. Items were ordered by the weighted combinations of Accuracy and Coverage, and we varied the weight ratio, which was thus regarded as a hyperparameter for the algorithms. Curves were computed using the Yahoo dataset, described later.

Results such as these can be used for tuning a recommendation algorithm to a new site by picking the optimal value of a hyperparameter and the best algorithm. For example, for a site where the learned model gives a significant coefficient to coverage, the plain CT algorithm will be the best, whereas in cases where the accuracy coefficient dominates strongly, the "fresh" expert will be useful. Note also that the "popular" expert is never going to be best. The trade-off curves obtained from offline data can therefore be used to save on online experiments to determine the optimal algorithm and hyperparameter.

4.2 Self-adjusting algorithm blend

We applied the online performance model to a setting where we wanted to optimize the blend of several algorithms over time, given full access to the online environment. Let the algorithm give each item a rating based on the weighted combination of ratings assigned by several base recommenders: $F(i) = W^\mathsf{T}(F_1(i), \ldots, F_m(i))$. For each recommender F_a, we introduce a latent variable Z_a. $Z_a(t)$ measures how close the items, recommended at time t by the main algorithm, are to the top items recommended by $F_a(t)$. Alternatively, $Z_a(t)$ can measure how high this recommender rates them. We build a regression model of online performance at each time t, based on the regressors $Z_1(t), \ldots, Z_m(t)$. In this model, the positive weight of a regressor Z_a suggests that giving recommendations with increased Z_a in the future would improve online performance. Coefficients of linear regression β^T effectively form a gradient of online performance with respect to the latent variables. We can therefore perform a gradient descent, updating the weights, with which we mix different base recommenders: $W_{T+1} = W_T + \lambda * \beta_T$, with T and $T + 1$ corresponding to two consecutive time frames, and β_T being the coefficients of LR model, fitted on the data from frame T. This could be an effective alternative to A–B testing, which is analogous to a grid search in the space of all possible weight coefficients. In a simple case where Z_a are ratings given by base recommenders to the items recommended by the main algorithm, and recommenders F_a optimize a particular set of metrics, this approach is equivalent to modeling CTR using the set of metrics as regressors over time. This is especially important for sites with a dynamic user base, that, for example, prefers fresh news in the morning and a more diverse set in the evening.

5. RESULTS

In this section, the datasets used in the present experiments are described and then the results of several of those experiments are shown. First, feature selection showed that multiple groups of metrics were important for the prediction of online performance. Second, we demonstrate the regression model's performance using different feature sets on different datasets. We subsequently offer examples of the applications we described in the previous section. We finish by describing the results obtained using unbiased offline evaluation [11] and by discussing why this method is not generally applicable.

5.1 Datasets

We use two news datasets which have online and offline browsing logs and online evaluation on a news website.

Swissinfo dataset is a combination of three weeks' worth of offline and online browsing logs from the live news website *swissinfo.ch*. The offline data includes more than 227k clicks on 28,525 stories by around 188k users. The online data was gathered in the presence of three recommendation algorithms – random recommendations, most popular recommendations, and Context Tree (CT, [5]). 168k clicks were distributed almost equally between the three algorithms. Three recommendations were made to each user, and items to be recommended were selected from the pool of the last 200 unique articles visited. All users were identified solely by their browsing session, and the only information gathered about the users was from their browsing behavior.

Yahoo! Front page dataset is specifically tailored for unbiased offline evaluation [11]. It comprises 15 days' worth of clicks data from the main page of Yahoo!News. Each visit to the page was described by a binary vector of features. The item pool for recommendations always contains 20 items. The log consists of nearly 28M visits to a total of 653 items.

To make the dataset more suitable for news recommendations, we identified visits belonging to the same browsing session by selecting only visits with at least 50 binary features present. For visits with the same binary features, we assumed that visits were same session if the time between visits did not exceed 10 minutes. Otherwise, we assumed that these were visits from different sessions. This procedure decreased the total number of clicks in the log to ≈ 5.7M.

With sessions established, online browsing logs were generated using the algorithm from [11] (Section 5.5). For each algorithm, the number of clicks in the simulated browsing logs was around ≈ 285k. To generate offline browsing logs, we took a random 10% of user sessions; they contained 573k clicks by 401k users.

LePoint dataset contains 3.5 days worth of data from the live news website *lepoint.fr* (4.6M clicks and 3.3M users). Sessions that did not result in clicks on recommendations were used as offline data.

5.2 Feature selection

The procedure for feature selection described in Section 3 was applied to the Swissinfo dataset using the CT algorithm. Due to the nature of the LAR, if there are several correlated predictors, one of them will enter the model earlier, and the others will enter much later (as their contribution would be smaller after first correlated predictor was used). However, the order in which correlated predictors will enter the model, is unknown. As we are not interested in the predictors themselves, but rather in showing the importance of metric groups (Accuracy, Coverage, Diversity, Serendipity, and Novelty), we calculated the average time for the first metric of each metric group to enter the model (Tab. 1).

Table 1: Average index at which metrics entered the model. Second column shows the metric that typically entered the model first.

Metric group	First to enter	Avg. first entry±std
Diversity	Personalization	2.53±0.65
Serendipity	Serendipity [14]	2.71±0.58
Accuracy	Markedness	2.82±0.76
Coverage	Shannon's Entropy	5.94±0.80
Novelty	Novelty [24]	10.27±2.77

Metrics from the Serendipity, Accuracy and Diversity groups are usually the first three to enter the model. This is a strong indicator that these three groups relate to different parts of performance metric and are all important for predicting it.

We also noticed that if we removed the Diversity or Serendipity predictors, then Coverage metrics showed a low average first entry time. This indicates that two out of three groups from Diversity, Serendipity and Coverage might be enough. For Accuracy metrics, it did not matter which predictor was used, and Markedness was easily replaceable by precision or any of the other Accuracy metrics. A very strong correlation was seen to exist between different Accuracy group metrics.

The results obtained with the other two algorithms were similar to those above. In all of the results below, when we say that we have used a predictor from a certain metric group, we mean that we used the predictor that was first to enter in the LAR model from this metric group.

5.3 Regression model performance

We used the approach described in Section 2 to generate data points for the regression model. We divided the time interval into parts of 30%, 50% and 20%. The first 30% were used for training the algorithm itself and were not used in the regression model. The recommendations made by the algorithm on the next 50% were used to train the model, and the last 20% were used to test the model's performance.

Table 2: CTR prediction quality for different sets of features, reported values are RMSE×10^4. Lowest errors of linear regression models are in bold. Results per algorithm are shown for the Swissinfo dataset. S, Serendipity; C, Coverage; D, Diversity; A, Accuracy. Last three columns: averages for datasets.

Set of features	Most popular	Random	CT	Swiss-info	Yahoo	Le-Point
All	2.28	8.54	1.33	4.05	2.92	2.37
S+A+C+D	2.08	2.60	1.40	**2.03**	**1.79**	**2.35**
S+A+D	2.24	2.04	4.17	2.81	2.50	4.90
S+A+C	15.3	1.98	6.47	7.95	2.62	4.36
S+C+D	3.81	2.12	6.07	4.00	1.84	6.52
A+C+D	5.32	5.73	6.06	5.70	1.87	3.01
A	2.98	5.91	6.23	5.04	2.90	5.38
S	14.4	1.84	1.55	5.94	2.92	9.46
C	10.2	5.93	6.22	7.46	2.64	7.06
D	3.23	4.87	4.59	4.23	2.49	6.67
Const	1.75	5.99	6.01	4.58	2.45	10.01
All+L_2	1.97	2.30	1.17	1.81	1.67	2.15
GP+RBF	1.85	2.11	1.06	1.67	1.58	2.03

CTR prediction.

For CTR prediction (Tab. 2), the lowest average error was indeed obtained using one predictor from each of the four metric groups (we omitted novelty here and later on due to its poor results in feature selection). The error for the full set of metrics was much higher, probably due to overfitting. Diversity seemed to be very important in the first dataset, since it gave the best individual result as a predictor. Combinations of different groups including diversity also gave better results than combinations that did not. More complex models, such as penalized LR (All+L_2) or the Gaussian process with an RBF kernel (GP+RBF), gave even better results, however these models are more difficult to interpret and use. Note that results were consistent among datasets and that the best ones significantly outperformed the baseline model, which assumes constant CTR through time (Const).

Fig. 5 shows that the aforementioned metrics indeed have a predictive power. The shape of the curve of the performance metric over time was repeated in the predicted results, indicating that there was high probability that the model would be able to predict the behavior and approximate values of the performance metric over time.

The p-values associated with the regression coefficients of different metrics indicated that these predictors were significant for the model. A possible explanation for the only exception to this (Serendipity was not found to be an important predictor for Most Popular algorithm) is that all the Serendipity values for recommendations made by the Most

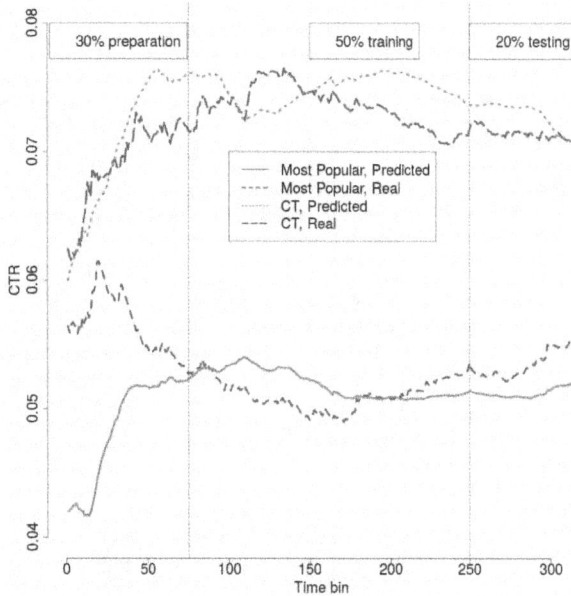

Figure 5: Performance metric prediction for the CT and Most Popular algoithms.

Popular algorithm were 0 or close to 0. According to definitions of Serendipity, its values are high for items not recommended by the "naive" recommender, which is precisely the Most Popular recommender.

Inspection of the coefficients revealed that the models were different for different datasets and algorithms. That is an expected indicator that a linear model made to predict the performance regardless of the algorithm, would perform worse than a set of models specifically trained for each algorithm.

Online accuracy prediction.

The results above were obtained assuming that the target online metric was CTR. We also trained a model to predict success, also called online accuracy (Tab. 3).

Table 3: Online success prediction quality for different sets of features, RMSE$\times 10^4$. Lowest errors are bold. Results per algorithm are shown for Swissinfo dataset. S, Serendipity; C, Coverage; D, Diversity; A, Accuracy. Last 3 columns: averages for datasets.

Sets of features	Most popular	Random	CT	Swiss-info	Yahoo	Le-Point
All	6.25	7.94	1.98	5.39	3.90	3.17
S+A+C+D	13.7	1.81	1.18	5.57	2.19	3.10
S+A+C	2.94	1.39	2.53	**2.28**	3.07	3.24
S+A+D	22.2	1.89	1.89	8.66	2.30	5.15
S+C+D	15.7	1.97	9.77	9.16	2.06	4.09
A+C+D	15.8	4.55	6.90	9.10	2.08	**2.15**
A	17.1	4.98	6.47	9.53	2.83	3.95
S	11.9	1.64	13.0	8.87	2.96	6.23
C	30.1	4.99	22.1	19.1	3.15	9.19
D	11.2	4.35	4.61	6.72	**1.95**	7.19

Prediction errors were less consistent among datasets, but a combination of Accuracy, Coverage, and Diversity predictors obtained high results for all datasets. On the Swissinfo dataset, best predictors came from three groups that did not include Diversity; on Yahoo, Diversity is the single best predictor (possibly due to the imperfect the visits were identified); and on the LePoint dataset the best predictors did not include Serendipity. Note that the predicted results for the Random algorithm are more accurate than for the Most Popular algorithm – an expected result, as Random performance does not change much over time.

5.4 Self-adjusting algorithm blend

For this experiment, we ran algorithms on a live news website. We used four algorithms based on the linear combination of recommendations given by the Context Tree and Most Popular recommenders, as described in Section 4.2. We had two latent metrics, Z_{CT} and Z_{pop}, that measured the closeness of the recommendation to that of the two algorithms. Weights for the recommendations from the Most Popular algorithm varied from 20% to 80% in steps of 20%. In each time frame and for each recommender, the updated weight increased or decreased the trade-off. We examined whether changing the algorithm weighting in the direction indicated by the gradient really did give higher CTR (Fig. 6).

In the third, fifth and seventh periods – during daytime – all coefficients suggested increasing the weight of the CT algorithm. At night, the algorithm with 20% of Most Popular was still best, but by a smaller margin, and the magnitude of the coefficients agreed with these results.

For the first two time periods the results were different, probably due to a lack of data. However, the changes suggested for increasing CTR were still consistent and correct – the regression coefficient for the algorithm using 40% of Most Popular was positive, suggesting an increase in weight, which lead to the algorithm using 60% of Most Popular, that did indeed obtain a higher CTR in this time frame.

The performance clearly changed over time, but followed a periodic pattern. This suggests that coefficients from the current time frame should provide suggestions to the same time frame next day, rather than the next chronological time frame.

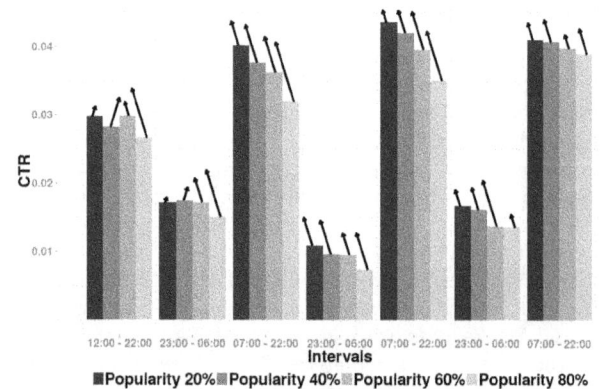

Figure 6: CTR for four different algorithms in three different time frames. Arrow indicates the sign and magnitude of popularity regression coefficient, suggesting the direction of trade-off change.

5.5 Unbiased offline evaluation

In this subsection, we discuss and apply the unbiased offline evaluation procedure [11]; this is another approach to predicting an algorithm's online performance. This procedure was developed for contextual bandit algorithms and requires the log of interaction with the world of an algorithm that recommends articles at random with equal probability. Based on this log, a simulation of online execution can be made for any other algorithm. If the original log from the random algorithm had I events, then the simulation will contain approximately $\frac{I}{H}$ events, where H is the number of items available for recommendation. In the Yahoo dataset, which is specifically tailored to this procedure, $H = 20$. However, in more realistic scenarios of news recommendations, such as the Swissinfo dataset, three out of 200 candidate items should be recommended, giving $H = 200^3 = 8M$. This does not produce enough events in the simulation to give significant results.

We used the Swissinfo dataset to test this algorithm. We used the output of the random algorithm to create a log and tested the CT algorithm on it. Due to the limitations described above, we were only able to compare algorithms for the task of top-1 recommendation. Even in the case of top-1 recommendation, after sampling we were left with only 266 points, compared to 55,587 points in the log. Fig. 7 (bottom part) shows the plot using the real and predicted CTR values. If we ignore a slight bias, probably due to the small number of points sampled, the shapes of the curves are quite similar, which proves the effectiveness of the unbiased offline evaluation for single-item recommendation. However, when we tried to use it for top-2 or top-3 recommendations, the number of sampled points decreased exponentially.

To overcome this problem, we applied the same technique in order to predict the third recommendation only: all the algorithms returned their third best prediction and we computed a CTR using this data. However, it is clearly visible that there was little correlation between real and predicted values (Fig. 7, top). This was caused by the fact that the presence or absence of clicks on the third item depends on

the first two items in the recommendation list, and this is not taken into consideration in this approach. Statistical tests showed the significance of our findings (Student's t-test, p-value < 0.05).

Other approaches for evaluating multiple recommendations by simulating clicks on the second and later items [23, 27] are not suitable for our task as they do not account for temporal effects in the data, and their hindsight models do not take into account parameters such as coverage, etc.

6. RELATED WORK

The work presented here concentrates on using different metrics to predict the online performance of news recommendations. Several recommender systems have been implemented and evaluated on live news websites [3, 12, 20, 21]. A number of previous works have advocated the use of multiple metrics for these evaluations [13, 17]. Below, we describe separately works that introduced and optimized new metrics, and works that combined existing metrics into multi-objective optimization.

Recommendations using multiple metrics.

The need to provide more diverse and unexpected recommendations that cover the items from the 'long tail' was identified early in the history of recsys. Zhang et al. [29, 28] proposed optimizing the trade-off between the average accuracy of the recommendations and the average diversity between each pair of recommended items. They pose this as a quadratic programming problem with binary variables that they relaxed by solving in the continuous domain. However, they only measured the results via their newly introduced novelty metric and, they performed neither an online evaluation nor a user study.

Ziegler et al. [31] proposed a greedy strategy for solving a similar problem, where each item was selected in a way that minimized the average similarity to previously selected items. The subsequent user survey and, as well as the regression model built on the top of it, indicated that both diversity and accuracy contributed positively to user satisfaction. To the best of our our knowledge, this work is the only one to have built a regression model to study how performance depends on metrics.

Two serendipity metrics [7, 14] have been proposed for the domains of music and TV show recommendation. The authors compared different algorithms with respect to a newly introduced metric, without any attempt to draw a relationship between the desired performance metric and the serendipity metric.

Vargas et al. [24] proposed multiple probabilistic definitions of novelty and diversity metrics that incorporate certain previous definitions. They showed how probabilities can be used as building blocks for metric definitions and compared several state-of-the-art algorithms. Although the authors clarified the reasoning behind the probabilistic definitions they used, they proposed no algorithm to optimize towards any particular metric, and they drew no relationships with the performance metrics.

Zhou et al. [30] proposed the concepts of "personalization" and "surprisal", and they used a heat diffusion model on a bipartite graph representing links between items and users in order to optimize a linear combination of Accuracy and Diversity. The actual selection of tuning parameters, however, was done by hand.

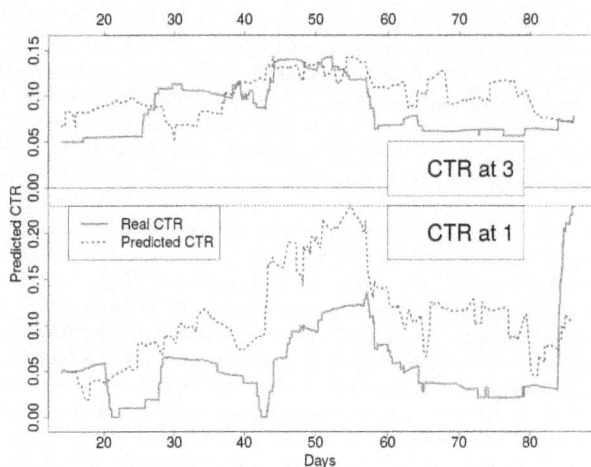

Figure 7: CTR, real and predicted by an unbiased evaluation: for the first (bottom part), and the third (top part) items in the list of recommendations.

Multi-objective optimization.

Multi-objective optimization of a list of items has been well investigated in the field of information retrieval [22, 25]. In the area of recsys, one of the first attempts at multi-objective optimization [28] used a quadratic objective function that involved a linear combination of Accuracy and Diversity. Jambor et al. [9] enhanced this idea by adding the variance of ratings to the objective function in order to promote items from the "long tail". Rodriguez et al. [18] optimized a smoothed version of the average precision and normalized discounted cumulative gain (NDCG) metrics by using gradient-based methods. Their framework optimized the trade-off between the quality of recommendations and the deviation between given recommendations and the expected ground truth, but did not consider competing objectives. Other works [1, 23] have expanded on ideas about optimizing a linear combination of metrics by using soft clustering of users. In [23], a linear combination of Variance and Accuracy for a contextual bandit algorithm was optimized and the recommendations were shared between different clusters through the similarity of clusters, expressed as a Gaussian kernel. Another line of research has been finding a Pareto-optimal frontier among multiple metrics, using genetic algorithms [16, 26].

7. CONCLUSION

We investigated predicting the online performance of news recommendation algorithms by a regression model using offline metrics. Our results confirmed that there is more to online performance than just offline Accuracy. Other metrics, such as Coverage or Serendipity, play important roles in predicting or optimizing online metrics such as click-through rates. The model can then be applied to trade-off curves for each algorithm constructed from offline data to select the optimal algorithm and parameters.

Regression models are best constructed for the particular user and item population; we did not find a universal formula for predicting online performance that would work for all settings. However, training a model separately from the algorithms still saves a lot of effort over blind A–B testing. Another application is to adapt parameters continuously in response to changes in user characteristics. In a setting where recommendations are obtained by mixing different algorithms, we proposed a method using latent metrics defined by the algorithms themselves, and showed that it correctly predicted the right adaptations in a live recommender system.

8. REFERENCES

[1] D. Agarwal, B.-C. Chen, P. Elango, and X. Wang. Click shaping to optimize multiple objectives. In *KDD*, 2011.

[2] R. Burke. Evaluating the dynamic properties of recommendation algorithms. In *RecSys*, 2010.

[3] A. S. Das, M. Datar, A. Garg, and S. Rajaram. Google news personalization: scalable online collaborative filtering. In *WWW*, 2007.

[4] B. Efron, T. Hastie, I. Johnstone, R. Tibshirani, et al. Least angle regression. *The Annals of statistics*, 32(2):407–499, 2004.

[5] F. Garcin, C. Dimitrakakis, and B. Faltings. Personalized news recommendation with context trees. In *RecSys*, 2013.

[6] F. Garcin, B. Faltings, O. Donatsch, A. Alazzawi, C. Bruttin, and A. Huber. Offline and online evaluation of news recommender systems at swissinfo. In *RecSys*, 2014.

[7] M. Ge, C. Delgado-Battenfeld, and D. Jannach. Beyond accuracy: evaluating recommender systems by coverage and serendipity. In *RecSys*, 2010.

[8] J. Herlocker, J. Konstan, L. Terveen, and J. Riedl. Evaluating collaborative filtering recommender systems. *Transactions on Information Systems*, 22(1):5–53, 2004.

[9] T. Jambor and J. Wang. Optimizing multiple objectives in collaborative filtering. In *RecSys*, 2010.

[10] N. Lathia, S. Hailes, L. Capra, and X. Amatriain. Temporal diversity in recommender systems. In *SIGIR*, 2010.

[11] L. Li, W. Chu, J. Langford, and X. Wang. Unbiased offline evaluation of contextual-bandit-based news article recommendation algorithms. In *WSDM*, 2011.

[12] J. Liu, P. Dolan, and E. R. Pedersen. Personalized news recommendation based on click behavior. In *IUI*, 2010.

[13] S. McNee, J. Riedl, and J. Konstan. Being accurate is not enough: how accuracy metrics have hurt recommender systems. In *CHI*, pages 1097–1101, 2006.

[14] T. Murakami, K. Mori, and R. Orihara. Metrics for evaluating the serendipity of recommendation lists. In *New frontiers in artificial intelligence*, pages 40–46. 2008.

[15] D. M. Powers. Evaluation: from precision, recall and f-measure to roc, informedness, markedness and correlation. In *Bioinfo Publications*, 2011.

[16] M. Ribeiro, A. Lacerda, E. de Moura, A. Veloso, and N. Ziviani. Multi-objective pareto-efficient approaches for recommender systems. *ACM Transactions on Intelligent Systems and Technology*, 9(1):1–20, 2013.

[17] F. Ricci, L. Rokach, and B. Shapira. *Introduction to recommender systems handbook*. Springer, 2011.

[18] M. Rodriguez, C. Posse, and E. Zhang. Multiple objective optimization in recommender systems. In *RecSys*, 2012.

[19] A. Said. *Evaluating the Accuracy and Utility of Recommender Systems*. PhD thesis, 2013.

[20] A. Said, A. Bellogín, J. Lin, and A. de Vries. Do recommendations matter?: news recommendation in real life. In *CSCW*, 2014.

[21] A. Said, J. Lin, A. Bellogín, and A. de Vries. A month in the life of a production news recommender system. In *CIKM-LL Workshop*, 2013.

[22] K. Svore, M. Volkovs, and C. Burges. Learning to rank with multiple objective functions. In *WWW*, 2011.

[23] H. Vanchinathan, I. Nikolic, F. De Bona, and A. Krause. Explore-exploit in top-n recommender systems via gaussian processes. In *RecSys*, 2014.

[24] S. Vargas and P. Castells. Rank and relevance in novelty and diversity metrics for recommender systems. In *RecSys*, 2011.

[25] H. Wang, A. Dong, L. Li, Y. Chang, and E. Gabrilovich. Joint relevance and freshness learning from clickthroughs for news search. In *WWW*, 2012.

[26] S. Wang, M. Gong, L. Ma, Q. Cai, and L. Jiao. Decomposition based multiobjective evolutionary algorithm for collaborative filtering recommender systems. In *Evolutionary Computation, IEEE Congress on*, pages 672–679, 2014.

[27] J. Yi, Y. Chen, J. Li, S. Sett, and T. W. Yan. Predictive model performance: Offline and online evaluations. In *KDD*, pages 1294–1302, 2013.

[28] M. Zhang and N. Hurley. Avoiding monotony: improving the diversity of recommendation lists. In *RecSys*, 2008.

[29] Y. Zhang, J. Callan, and T. Minka. Novelty and redundancy detection in adaptive filtering. In *SIGIR*, 2002.

[30] T. Zhou, Z. Kuscsik, J.-G. Liu, M. Medo, J. Wakeling, and Y.-C. Zhang. Solving the apparent diversity-accuracy dilemma of recommender systems. *Proceedings of NAS*, 107(10):4511–4515, 2010.

[31] C.-N. Ziegler, S. McNee, J. Konstan, and G. Lausen. Improving recommendation lists through topic diversification. In *WWW*, 2005.

Beyond "Hitting the Hits" – Generating Coherent Music Playlist Continuations with the Right Tracks

Dietmar Jannach
TU Dortmund, Germany
dietmar.jannach@tu-
dortmund.de

Lukas Lerche
TU Dortmund, Germany
lukas.lerche@tu-
dortmund.de

Iman Kamehkhosh
TU Dortmund, Germany
iman.kamehkhosh@tu-
dortmund.de

ABSTRACT

Automated playlist generation is a special form of music recommendation and a common feature of digital music playing applications. A particular challenge of the task is that the recommended items should not only match the general listener's preference but should also be coherent with the most recently played tracks. In this work, we propose a novel algorithmic approach and optimization scheme to generate playlist continuations that address these requirements. In our approach, we first use collections of shared music playlists, music metadata, and user preferences to select suitable tracks with high accuracy. Next, we apply a generic re-ranking optimization scheme to generate playlist continuations that match the characteristics of the last played tracks. An empirical evaluation on three collections of shared playlists shows that the combination of different input signals helps to achieve high accuracy during track selection and that the re-ranking technique can both help to balance different quality optimization goals and to further increase accuracy.

Keywords

Music Recommendation; Quality Factors; Evaluation

1. INTRODUCTION

The automated creation of music playlists – a special form of music recommendation – is a typical feature of modern digital music playing applications, and playlist generators are nowadays used both by online music platforms and by "offline" music applications that, e.g., run on smartphones. Over the last fifteen years, a variety of playlist generation approaches has been proposed in the literature [4, 12]. These next-track recommendation approaches differ from each other, e.g., with respect to the kinds of inputs they expect, which forms of additional data about the tracks they can process, or which quality criterion they seek to optimize.

A distinctive feature of music playlist generation is that the recommended items are immediately "consumed", usu-

ally in the specific order determined by the playlister. The problem is therefore not only to determine tracks that appeal to the general taste of the listener, but to generate playlists that obey additional constraints, e.g., with respect to the homogeneity of artist, genre, or tempo or the smoothness of track transitions [2, 13, 19, 21]. Furthermore, there are applications in which the generation of virtually endless playlists is required (radios). In such cases, the recommendations should not only be coherent in themselves but also match the most recently listened tracks.

In this work, we focus on such immediate next-track recommendations given a history of recent tracks. We apply a two-phase approach. In the first phase we determine a set of tracks that generally seem suitable to be combined with the most recent listening history. We base the selection and ranking of the tracks on a multi-faceted scoring method which combines track co-occurrence patterns in publicly shared playlists, music and meta-data features as well as personal user preferences. Similar to the approaches of [3, 4, 8, 14, 15], we aim to optimize the track selection accuracy in this phase. As a basis for the optimization, we use pools of music playlists that were manually created and shared by music enthusiasts. We use the track hit rate to assess to which extent the algorithms are capable of selecting tracks that were also chosen by the users.

In the second phase, we optimize the set of the immediate next tracks to be played. Optimizing for accuracy alone can be insufficient as the inclusion of a few wrong tracks can be easily detrimental to the perceived service quality as a whole [6]. The main idea is therefore to re-rank the tracks selected in the previous phase in a way that the resulting playlist continuation matches the characteristics of the recent history. Specifically, we use a generic optimization procedure that *minimizes the difference* between the history and the continuation in terms of one or more desired quality dimensions. Thereby, we avoid the definition of global quality levels to be achieved as these levels can depend on the "goals" of the playlist. Including, e.g., mostly popular tracks can be favorable for a party playlist. If the goal, in contrast, is track discovery, genre homogeneity and the inclusion of less popular tracks could be advisable.

To evaluate the optimization procedure, we compare the accuracy-optimized playlists from the first phase with the continuations obtained after the second phase in different dimensions. Specifically, we first evaluate to which extent the re-ranked continuations lists are more similar and thus coherent with the history. In addition, we determine the impact of the re-ranking process on track selection accuracy.

RecSys'15, September 16–20, 2015, Vienna, Austria.
© 2015 ACM. ISBN 978-1-4503-3692-5/15/09 ...$15.00.
http://dx.doi.org/10.1145/2645710.2645755.

2. FACETED TRACK SCORING

In this section, we present the details of our multi-faceted weighted scoring approach. The goal is to determine a relevance score for each possible next track given a playlist history h (sequence of tracks) using different input signals.

2.1 Baseline Scoring Approach

In [4], a number of playlisting algorithms based on patterns in publicly shared playlists were benchmarked. The results showed that a k-Nearest-Neighbor-based (kNN) approach worked best in terms of accuracy across all datasets in particular for the shorter list lengths that are relevant in our context. As we are interested in high-quality next-track recommendations, we will use kNN as a baseline. Given a history h and a set N_h of nearest neighbor playlists of h, we compute the kNN score of a target track t^* with $sim_{cosine}(h, n)$ as the binary cosine similarity of track occurrences in h and n. $1_n(t^*) = 1$ if n contains t^* and 0 otherwise.

$$score_{kNN}(h, t^*) = \sum_{n \in N_h} sim_{cosine}(h, n) \cdot 1_n(t^*) \quad (1)$$

kNN was also used as a baseline in [8]. Small hit rate increases were achieved at long list lengths by combining it with tag-based track information. The work also showed that the kNN method performs better than recent methods like BPR [17] for the given task. In [8] however, a very small value for $k = 10$ was used. Since our experiments show that larger values for k ($k = 300$) lead to significantly higher hit rates and to the best results, we will not use the tag-enhanced method of [8] as a baseline.

2.2 Computing Additional Suitability Scores

Playlist creators can have certain "themes", goals or quality criteria in mind when they design a playlist. The idea of our faceted scoring method is to combine the kNN approach with additional suitability scores. If we, for example, detect that the homogeneity of the tempo of the tracks is most probably a guiding quality criterion, we should give an extra relevance weight to tracks that are similar in tempo to those in the history; if we observe that several tracks in the history were annotated by users with certain tags, we should increase the relevance score of tracks with similar tags.

Generally, the combination of different scores shall serve two purposes: (1) increasing the hit rate as more relevant tracks receive a higher aggregated score and (2) making the playlist continuation more homogeneous, which is often a desirable goal in the Music Information Retrieval literature.

In our experiments, we tested the following scores as examples to validate our approach. The selection was based on the availability of track metadata in public sources.[1]

2.2.1 Measuring "Content-based" Similarity

There are several ways of determining the similarity of music tracks, e.g., by modeling the distribution of track features [2]. In our work, we retrieved the social tags[2] that were assigned to tracks by users on Last.fm as they are valuable indicators of what a certain playlist is about [8]. We removed irrelevant tags like "my favorite" or "like it", retained the 1,000 most frequent tags and computed TF-IDF (Term Frequency/Inverse Document Frequency) vectors for each track[3]. Given a history h consisting of tracks $t_i, \ldots, t_n$ with the TF-IDF vectors t_1^v to t_n^v, we compute the score of a target track t^* using its TF-IDF vector t^{*v} as follows.

$$score_{content}(h, t^*) = sim_{cosine}\left(\frac{\Sigma_{t_i^v \in h} t_i^v}{|h|}, t^{*v}\right) \quad (2)$$

2.2.2 Matching Numerical Features

Numerical track features can be music-related like the tempo or loudness or describe other aspects like the release year or track's general popularity. Such features can be relevant factors which determine the selection of tracks, e.g., for playlists like "Hits of the 90s", or "Best of" mixes.

The assumption of our scoring scheme for numerical values is that if a feature was actually relevant for the selection of tracks, the spread and variance of the values will be low. Given a history h and a feature value f_{ti} for a track t_i in the history, we therefore first compute the mean μ and standard deviation σ of the observed values. If there are too few values available – some might be unknown – or the standard deviation exceeds some threshold δ, the score is 0.

Otherwise, given the feature value f_t^* for a target track t^* we use the value of the probability density function of a Gaussian distribution as a score, where μ and σ are computed based on the value distributions in the history:

$$score_{numfeature}(h, t^*) = \frac{1}{\sigma_h \sqrt{2\pi}} e^{-\frac{(f_t^* - \mu_j)^2}{2\sigma_h^2}} \quad (3)$$

If the standard deviation is 0, e.g., because all tracks were released in the same year, we return a specific maximum score. In case the feature value f^* is too far away from the mean (e.g., more than 2 standard deviations), the score is again set to 0. The choice of the maximum score (after normalization) and the tolerance regarding the deviation from the mean can be made depending on the data.

2.2.3 Considering Personal Preferences

Personal preferences, e.g., regarding favorite artists, can influence what people add to their playlists. In our experiments we therefore also include an example of a personalized scoring scheme. We base the method on content features as only a limited number of playlists is available per user.

To build a "long-term" content-based profile for user u with the recent listening history h, we first compute an averaged TF-IDF vector CP_h from all playlists created by u. For a track t^* with a corresponding TF-IDF vector t^{*v}, the personalized score ($score_{contentpers}$) is then based on a weighted combination of the similarity of t^* with the current history $score_{content}(h, t^*)$ and the similarity of t^{*v} with the long-term profile CP_h, i.e.

$$score_{contentpers}(h, t^*) = \alpha \cdot score_{content}(h, t^*) + \\ (1 - \alpha) \cdot sim_{cosine}(CP_h, t^{*v}) \quad (4)$$

Other combination types are again possible, e.g., using a decay factor for older playlists, in case the playlist creation dates are available.

---

[1] Understanding the true theme of a playlist is in general challenging as it might be based on data like track lyrics or instrumentation aspects, which are not publicly available for most tracks.

[2] With "content", we refer to social tags and not to the audio signal, as is sometimes done in the field of Music Information Retrieval.

[3] Additional experiments using Probabilistic Latent Semantic Analysis (pLSA) for topic detection did not lead to better results.

2.3 Combining the Scores

Depending on the available data, various combinations of scores of different types can be used. In our experiments, we tested different configurations using a weighted scoring scheme. Given a set of scoring functions S, the score is

$$score_{overall}(h, t^*) = \Sigma_{score_i \in S} \; score_i(h, t^*) \cdot w_i \quad (5)$$

where w_i is a configurable weight term for each $score_i \in S$.

The selection of the scores as well as their corresponding weights depend on the goals that should be achieved. In this work, we systematically tested different values for the weight of each score and selected the best ones (listed in Table 2) with respect to accuracy.

2.4 Treatment of Single-Artist Histories

In particular on Last.fm, we can find playlists that contain tracks of only one single artist. If a history h has only one artist A, we apply an additional heuristic and compute a special artist score (AS) for tracks by A. In the experiments, we used a baseline AS value that is generally higher than the combined scores as computed in Equation 5. This ensures that the playlist continuation starts with the "right" artist. The tracks of artist A are then sorted according to their popularity, and we use a position-based decay function that assigns a lower AS value to less popular tracks of the artist and apply a minimum popularity threshold. The tracks of the other artists receive the usual combined score (Eq. 5).

3. NEXT-TRACK OPTIMIZATION

So far, we have designed a number of ways to score tracks with respect to a history of recent tracks. Given a specific dataset, our first goal is to find suitable weight factors and other parameters to optimize the prediction accuracy of the model, in our case in terms of the hit rate. Once this is done, our assumption is that the top-scoring tracks are generally well-suited for the given history.

The goal of the subsequent fine-tuning phase is to optimize the selection of the immediate next tracks. For that purpose, we will take a limited number of tracks from the top-scoring tracks and systematically re-rank them in order to better match one or more characteristics of the history. Since we limit the re-ranking to a smaller set at the top of the list, we (a) limit the computational complexity of the optimization process[4] and (b) can ensure that the potential accuracy losses are not too high.

3.1 Example and Design Rationale

Consider, as an example, that our optimization goal is to find a 10-track playlist continuation that maintains the tempo level of the recent history. In that situation, we pick, e.g., the top 30 tracks of the previously scored list and then systematically identify those 10 tracks among them which are most suitable in terms of the tempo. Note that the optimization goal here is *not* to find 10 tracks that all have the same tempo, but a set of tracks whose tempo distribution is as similar as possible to the current playlist. As another example, consider the diversity (of genres, artists, release years). Clearly, there is no global and context-independent optimum how diverse a playlist should be in general. In our approach, we therefore aim to find a set of tracks that mimics

the features of the current playlist as good as possible and our optimization goal is always to *minimize the difference* between the characteristics of a feature in the playlist and the recommended immediate next tracks.

In some sense, this approach helps to identify a possibly underlying theme and corresponding track-selection rationale of the history and recreate it with the recommendations. If the tempo, for example, is consistently very slow in the history we can consider this as a possible design criterion and a similar continuation. If there is a strong variation in the tempo, this can be a possible design criterion as well and could be captured by our approach. Finally, our method can be applied in situations in which more than one factor might be relevant.

3.2 Quantifying Track List Characteristics

Technically, in order to optimize the next-track list to match the characteristics of a given history, we first have to define a way to measure the characteristics and their differences. We therefore introduce a function $\mathcal{F}_c(l)$ that quantifies the characteristic c for a list of tracks l. In this work, we distinguish three types of list characteristics.

Mean and Standard Deviation. For numerical characteristics such as the release year, the loudness or the tempo of tracks, a simple way of assessing their "distribution" over a track history is to use the mean and the standard deviation. $\mathcal{F}_c(l)$ is therefore defined by a set of two values

$$\mathcal{F}_c(l) = \{\mu_c(l), \sigma_c(l)\}$$

which can be combined in different ways to obtain a single numerical score.

Aggregate Measures. Some playlist characteristics can be assessed based on more complex aggregate measures. One example is to determine the diversity of a list based on the average of the pairwise similarities. In our experiments, we use the "Intra-List-Similarity" measure [22], i.e.,

$$\mathcal{F}_c(l) = \sum_{i \in l} \sum_{j \in l} \frac{sim_c(i, j)}{|l|^2}$$

To compute the value of $sim_c(i, j)$ in our experiments, we use the cosine similarity between the TF-IDF vector representations of the social tags for each track.

Mixture Models. Another possible approach is to fit Gaussian Mixture Models (GMM) to the distribution of the values in the playlist history and use the Akaike Information Criterion (AIC) to assess the difference between the history and the playlist continuation[5].

3.3 Optimization Procedure

Optimization goal. The generic optimization goal of the subsequently described procedure is to minimize the value of a function $d(\mathcal{F}_c(h), \mathcal{F}_c(r_n))$ which captures the difference between the characteristics of a given playlist history h and the top-n next-track recommendations r_n.

How the difference between the history h and r_n is actually computed, depends on the way the list characteristics are captured. In our experiments we use the absolute difference for the aggregate ILS measure, i.e., $|\mathcal{F}_c(h) - \mathcal{F}_c(r_n)|$ and the pairwise absolute difference for mean and standard deviation characteristics, i.e., $|\mu_c(h) - \mu_c(r_n)| + |\sigma_c(h) - \sigma_c(r_n)|$.

---

[4] Optimization-based playlisting approaches such as [16] can be computationally demanding due to the large number of available tracks.

[5] We ran experiments using GMMs, but do not report the results here as these more complex models for our datasets did not lead to better results with respect to the measures reported in the paper.

Algorithm 1: Top-n optimization algorithm. All possible swapping combinations between r_n and x_m are evaluated. $r_n^{i\leftrightarrow j}$ denotes a swap of track i in r_n with j.

input : **int** $maxSteps$; **Array** h, r_n, x_m
output: The updated top-n list r_n

for 1 **to** $maxSteps$ **do**
   $\Delta_e \leftarrow 0$;
   $e_c \leftarrow d(\mathcal{F}_c(h), \mathcal{F}_c(r_n))$;
   for $i \in r_n$ *(backwards)*, $j \in x_m$ **do**
      $e'_c \leftarrow d(\mathcal{F}_c(h), \mathcal{F}_c(r_n^{i\leftrightarrow j}))$;
      if $e_c - e'_c > \Delta_e$ **then**
         $I_{best} \leftarrow i$; $J_{best} \leftarrow j$; $\Delta_e \leftarrow e_c - e'_c$;
   if $\Delta_e > 0$ **then**
      $r_n \leftarrow r_n^{I_{best}\leftrightarrow J_{best}}$
   else
      break;
return r_n;

Method. Let n be the length of the list of next tracks to be optimized. As a starting point, we take the first n recommendations of the list r produced by the faceted scoring method from Section 2 and determine the track list characteristics of the top-n list r_n as $\mathcal{F}_c(r_n)$. We then create an "Exchange List" x_m consisting of the m elements which immediately follow after r_n in r (e.g., tracks 11 to 30).

The optimization procedure shown in Algorithm 1 takes these lists – together with the history h – as an input and systematically exchanges elements from r_n with elements from x_m. In each iteration of the main loop, the best possible swap is determined. This is the one that leads to the largest reduction of e'_c. At the end, an exchange is only applied if it leads to a reduction of the difference between the characteristics of the history h and the updated top-n list. The algorithm stops when either no (measurable) improvement can be observed, all possible swaps are explored, or a maximum number of exchange steps were applied. The exact procedure is given in Algorithm 1.

Dealing with multiple goals. The general algorithm scheme can be used to optimize more than one goal at once, considering, e.g., both the tempo and the loudness in parallel. Instead of determining only one difference e_c, we would determine multiple difference values $e_{c1}, \ldots, e_{ck}$ and only perform a swap when the aggregated difference, e.g., the sum over all differences $e_{c1}, \ldots, e_{ck}$ (normalized to the same level), will be reduced. Weighted combinations of the individual error measures are possible as well.

4. EXPERIMENTAL EVALUATION

In the first part of the section, we analyze the effects of our faceted scoring method in terms of (a) accuracy, (b) homogeneity of the resulting lists, and (c) measure if the scoring methods help to generate list continuations that are coherent with the playlist histories. In the second part, we report the results of the re-ranking optimization procedure presented in the previous section. We use a significance level of $p = 0.05$ for all statistical tests throughout the section.

We used playlist collections from three different sources. One set of playlists was retrieved from Last.fm via their public API, one consists of playlists by music enthusiasts on

Table 1: Statistics of the used datasets.

	Last.fm	AotM	8tracks
Playlists	2,978	1,040	6,714
Users	451	142	996
Avg. Playlists/User	6.60	7.32	6.74
Tracks	18,083	11,413	39,875
Avg. Tracks/Playlist	11.68	16.98	12.97
Avg. Track Usage	1.93	1.55	2.18
Artists	3,272	2,770	9,122
Avg. Artists/Playlist	4.55	12.76	12.06
Avg. Artist Usage	10.65	6.38	9.54
Avg. Genres/Playlist	16.83	39.18	38.06
Avg. Tags/Playlist	94.88	140.62	123.07

Table 2: Set of evaluated algorithms.

Alg.	Description		
PopRank	Ranks tracks according to their popularity, i.e., their occurrence in the training playlists		
CAGH, SAGH	Recommend the greatest hits of the artists in the playlist (SAGH) or the similar (collocated) artists (CAGH) [3]		
kNN300	k-Nearest-Neighbors with k=300		
Content	Similarity-based ranking (Eq. 2)		
Content-Pers	Sim.-based ranking with personalization. Last.fm, AotM: α=0.6, 8tracks: α=0.8 (Eq. 4)		
kNN300*	Weighted combination of kNN300 (w=1.0) with other scores (Eq. 5)		
	Weight for w on:	Last.fm	AotM	8tracks
	RY=release year	0.7	2.0	0.3
	TMP=tempo	0.7	2.0	0.3
	LD=loudness	0.5	0.5	0.3
	ART=single-artist heuristic	4.0	2.0	2.0
	CP=ContentPers.	0.3	0.3	0.3
	CPA=ContentPers and ART (w as above)			
	ALL=all available scores (RY, TMP, LD and ContentPers, w as above)			

the Art-of-the-Mix (AotM) platform published by [15], and one was shared with us by the 8tracks music platform[6].

Table 1 shows basic statistics and the following additional observations can be made. In the Last.fm dataset, a number of playlists contain tracks of only one or very few artists. On the other hand, having several tracks of one artist in a playlist is forbidden for public playlists on 8tracks and uncommon for data from AotM. For each playlist, we know a dataset-dependent user ID of its creator. From each user, we have at least 4 playlists, which allows us to apply the content-based personalization score. Furthermore, information about features like tempo, release year, or social tags was retrieved with the public APIs of Last.fm, theechonest.com, and musicbrainz.org. However, the metadata is only 75% complete on average across all tracks.

Table 2 shows the algorithms, hybrid variants and parameter settings that were used in the experiments.

---

[6] http://last.fm, http://artofthemix.org, http://8tracks.com

4.1 Results – Faceted Scoring

4.1.1 Accuracy

Method. We use the following four-fold cross-validation setup to measure accuracy [3, 4, 8]: The available playlists are split into training and test sets. As usual, the algorithms learn their models on the training sets. From each playlist in the test set, we hide the last track (resulting in a history h) and let the algorithms recommend playlist continuations, i.e., predict the hidden track. A "hit" is registered whenever the generated top-n list contains the hidden element. Therefore, the hit rate is the fraction of playlists in the test set for which the hidden track was found. Beside the hit rate, we report the Mean Reciprocal Rank (MRR) measure, which takes the position of the hit into account[7].

Results. Table 3 shows hit rate and MRR at list length 100. Determining the accuracy for this list length gives us flexibility in setting the size of the Exchange Set later on. Note in addition that top-n lists of this and even much larger sizes are common in this domain [3, 4, 8]. The lowest and highest values are marked in light gray (lowest) and a bold font and a dark gray background (highest) respectively.

As expected, kNN300 has a competitive performance compared with the other baselines and recommending the most popular tracks to everyone can sometimes be a better strategy than using noisy tags alone (Content). The highest accuracy[8] across all three datasets can be achieved by combining kNN with the *personalized* content-based algorithm from Section 2.2.3 and the artist heuristic from Section 2.4 (kNN300CPA). The differences between the best performing hybrid method and the kNN baseline method are statistically significant on both measures and all three datasets. The results therefore indicate that different signals (track usage patterns, social annotations and personal long-term preferences) in combination with specific heuristics should be used to obtain high accuracy. While kNN300CPA consistently works best in absolute numbers, the differences to the second-best method for individual datasets and measures are not always significant.

Combining kNN with the numerical features from Section 2.2.2 (release year, tempo and loudness) can in some cases lead to modest accuracy improvements. On AotM, playlist creators seem to pay attention to aspects like a consistent loudness level in the playlists, which explains the improvement of kNN300LD over kNN300. For the other datasets and music features, no significant difference is observed when kNN300 is paired with a numerical feature.

The results so far show that combining different scores can help to increase the accuracy. In the next set of measurements, we assess if the combination of scores also impacts other possible quality factors like diversity and coherence of the playlist continuations, which are in the focus of the subsequent optimization process.

4.1.2 Diversity and Coherence - Tags and Artists

Method. Our first method to assess the diversity and coherence is based on the artists and the social tags of the tracks. We use the *inverse ILS* to quantify the diversity level and

Table 3: Recommendation accuracy results.

Playlist Algorithm	Accuracy @100 (hit rate | MRR)					
	Last.fm		AotM		8tracks	
PopRank	.029	.002	.048	.004	.050	.005
SAGH	.317	.100	.072	.014	.059	.008
CAGH	.334	.059	.081	.009	.061	.007
kNN300	.324	.067	.095	.010	.087	.007
Content	.236	.059	.078	.011	.048	.005
ContentPers	.236	.058	.079	.010	.048	.005
kNN300RY	.324	.064	.097	.011	.087	.007
kNN300TMP	.325	.067	.099	.010	.085	.007
kNN300LD	.323	.066	.099	.010	.086	.006
kNN300ART	.349	.072	.118	.011	.088	.007
kNN300CP	.347	.100	.116	.020	**.102**	**.009**
kNN300CPA	**.359**	**.102**	**.130**	**.022**	**.102**	**.009**
kNN300ALL	.356	.088	.111	.020	.099	**.009**

Table 4: Tag diversity and coherence.

Playlist Algorithm	Tag (inv. ILS | overlap)					
	Last.fm		AotM		8tracks	
PopRank	**.700**	.231	.548	.338	.651	.286
SAGH	.496	.357	.586	.405	.621	.385
CAGH	.482	.498	.579	.458	.621	.433
kNN300	.572	.477	**.706**	.475	**.726**	.523
Content	.116	.386	.153	.401	.144	.361
ContentPers	.117	.385	.149	.400	.143	.362
kNN300ART	.547	**.502**	.701	**.481**	.726	**.523**
kNN300CP	.321	.476	.334	.446	.479	.484
kNN300CPA	.339	.497	.343	.453	.479	.485

– as a proxy – the *overlap* of artists and tags in the history and the playlist continuation to assess the coherence level.

Results (Tags). Table 4 shows the results[9] for the diversity and coherence in terms of social tags. We can observe that the similarity-based methods (Content, ContentPers) by design lead to the lowest diversity (highest homogeneity). The most diverse (inhomogeneous) playlists were generated by the popularity-based method and the nearest-neighbor approach kNN300. Combining the kNN method with content information and the single-artist heuristic in kNN300CPA – the most accurate method – leads to values between these extremes and comparably high homogeneity[10].

kNN generally leads to good coherence results in terms of the tags. Adding the single-artist heuristics can help to further increase the coherence significantly for Last.fm and AotM. This indicates that tracks by the same artist receive the same tags (e.g., genres, album name), which is supported by the fact that CAGH also leads to high coherence. The content-based recommendations are homogeneous in themselves, but the overlap with the playlist beginning is comparably low. The most accurate kNN300CPA method yields comparable or slightly less coherent lists than kNN alone.

Results (Artists). Table 5 shows the artist diversity and coherence. The "greatest hits" methods (SAGH, CAGH) by design lead to the lowest diversity and PopRank to the high-

---

[7]Setups with more than one hidden track are possible. Another possible measure would be the "Average Log-Likelihood" [14]. We will not use it here because of the limitations discussed in [4].

[8]8tracks allows two songs from any artist per playlist. Thus the artist heuristic has no effect on the accuracy of kNN300CPA vs. kNN300CP.

[9]We only include the most relevant algorithms here and not hybrids which are optimized toward other goals like, e.g., kNN300RY.

[10]This is similar to the tendency of the commercial playlister of "The Echo Nest", which generates lists with lower diversity than kNN [10].

Table 5: Artist diversity and coherence.

Playlist Algorithm	Artist (inv. ILS | overlap)					
	Last.fm		AotM		8tracks	
PopRank	**.817**	.009	**.907**	.031	**.994**	.019
SAGH	.251	**.628**	.597	**.416**	.694	.402
CAGH	.319	.590	.623	.393	.711	**.413**
kNN300	.496	.427	.788	.230	.983	.274
Content	.614	.258	.763	.109	.780	.078
ContentPers	.619	.251	.758	.108	.778	.076
kNN300ART	.418	.508	.771	.244	.981	.276
kNN300CP	.453	.433	.759	.192	.961	.227
kNN300CPA	.385	.510	.741	.213	.960	.229

est diversity. All kNN-based methods exhibit a tendency to place a mix of different artists in their lists[11]. The content-based method leads to varying results. Sometimes, the artist diversity is higher than kNN (Last.fm), sometimes it is equal or lower (AotM, 8tracks). This phenomenon depends on the absolute diversity level achieved by the kNN method, which is comparably low for Last.fm, where users often only include popular tracks of a few artists in their playlists. The hybrid methods kNN300CP and kNN300CPA often lead to an even lower diversity than their components alone, which means that the individual components select tracks from an overlapping set of artists.

Discussion. Due to its hybrid nature the highly-accurate kNN300CPA method creates more homogeneous playlists than the pure kNN method in terms of tags and artists. At the same time, the playlist continuations generated by kNN300CPA are often less coherent than when using kNN alone, except for the Last.fm dataset. One possible explanation can be that the social tags used for tracks in the AotM and 8tracks datasets are more often related to the genre or mood and not to the artists. The content-based component would then push tracks that have the same genre but not necessarily the same artists as the history. In addition, the fact that the social tags for all datasets were obtained via the Last.fm API leads to a more sparse data situation for the other datasets.

4.1.3 Diversity and Coherence - Numerical Features

Method. For numerical features like the tempo, we analyze the effects of combining the kNN method with the respective scoring component, e.g., kNN300TMP. Specifically, we measure the *difference* between the mean value of the given feature in the history h and the generated playlist. To be successful, a method like kNN300TMP should result in smaller differences than when using kNN alone, i.e., the resulting playlist should match the tempo of the history better. Besides the mean value, we also report the change of the differences in the standard deviations to see if the distribution of the feature matches the history.

Results. Figures 1a to 1c show the results for the features tempo, loudness and release years. Across all dimensions and on all datasets, including a corresponding scoring component (significantly) helps to make the playlist continuation – in terms of mean – more coherent with the recent history than when using only the kNN scorer. At the same time, as shown in Table 3, adding the specific scoring method can furthermore often help to slightly increase the accuracy.

---

[11] A similar tendency is exhibited by "The Echo Nest" playlister [10].

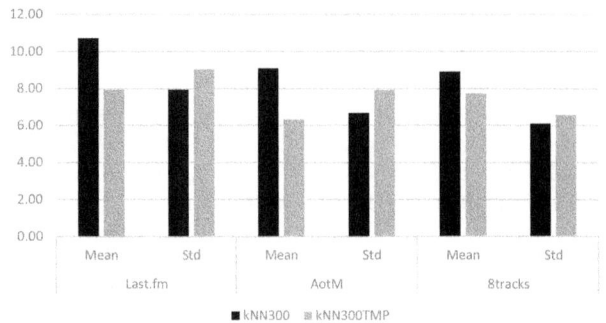

(a) Difference of mean and deviation: kNN300 vs. kNN300TMP

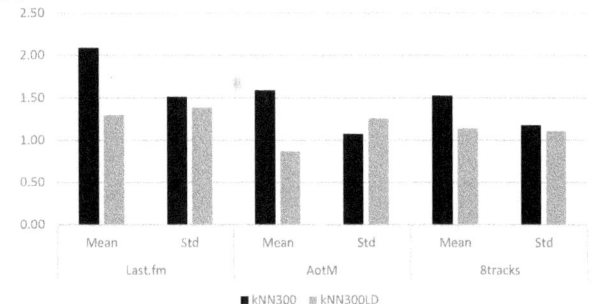

(b) Difference of mean and deviation: kNN300 vs. kNN300LD

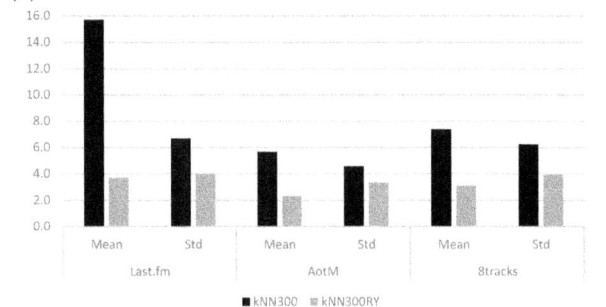

(c) Difference of mean and deviation: kNN300 vs. kNN300RY

Figure 1: Effects of combining the kNN-score with the scoring components for numerical feature.

The observations for the standard deviations (Std) are varying. The "error" for the release years and the loudness decreases – which means that we better match the feature's distribution in the history – or roughly remains the same. However, with respect to the tempo, we see that while the tempo scorer can better adapt to the average tempo, it varies more strongly than when we simply use the kNN method.

4.2 Results – Next-Track Optimization

Method. We applied the next-track optimization to the recommendations obtained with kNN300CPA, i.e., the approach with the best accuracy. Our goal is to analyze (a) if our method is effective in adapting the top-10 next-track list to the recent history and (b) how the adaptation affects the accuracy compared to kNN300CPA without optimization. The first aspect is assessed by measuring if the resulting playlists are "closer" to the history in different quality dimensions before and after optimization. For the latter aspect, we measured the accuracy before and after optimizing the result of kNN300CPA using Algorithm 1, this time at list length 10 to see possible effects for the immediate next tracks. We tested several individual and combined optimization goals and again applied four-fold cross-validation.

Results (AotM). The detailed results obtained for a set of selected configurations for the AotM are shown in Table 6 In the first column, we list the evaluation goal(s), e.g., artist (ART) or tag (TAG) diversity, or popularity (POP). In the following seven columns, we report the *relative improvement* of the deviation from the history with respect to the baseline method kNN300CPA. The value ".27" in the upper-left corner therefore means that after optimization for artists, the resulting playlist was 27% closer to the history (i.e., a better continuation) in terms of artist diversity than the playlist generated by the baseline method kNN300CPA. The last four columns refer to the *relative change* in accuracy and the absolute accuracy values after optimization. The value ".28" in the first row means that optimization not only helped to better match the artist diversity, but also led to a 28% improvement in the hit rate (HR).

In the first seven lines of Table 6, we report the results of single-goal optimization for the AotM dataset. All individual optimizations were (significantly) effective, which can easily be seen as all values on the diagonal are positive. The improvements range from 17% (tag diversity) to 35% (track popularity). Regarding the accuracy results we can observe for all single-goal optimizations except the tempo that the optimization did not negatively impact accuracy. In contrast, the optimization in fact led to *relative improvements* both in terms of the hit rate (between 3 and 28%) and the MRR (up to over 100%).

Optimizing for tempo in the playlist continuation is effective to reduce the deviation by 31%, but led to a modest relative degradation of the hit rate and the MRR (6% and 1%). Some of the single-objective optimizations furthermore have some side-effects, for instance, they all have a positive effect on the popularity aspect. In addition, the genre, tag, and artist optimization goals seem to be partially correlated.

In the last row of Table 6, we report the results of a multi-objective optimization run. We can observe that the results were improved in all dimensions – although to a smaller extent than with single-objective optimization – and again even helped to improve the accuracy. Other multi-objective combinations are possible, but are sometimes affected by optimization trade-offs and a loss in accuracy.

Observations - Other datasets. The results for the non-public 8tracks dataset are in line with AotM. All optimizations were effective and the relative improvements are in nearly all dimensions even stronger than for AotM. The hit rate improvements, for example, ranged between 7.8% and 39% and no negative effects on accuracy were observed.

On the Last.fm dataset, again all single-goal optimizations were effective. With respect to accuracy the effects of optimizing for one goal are in some but not all cases positive. In particular optimizing for the tempo and the loudness can lead to a degradation of the hit rate of up to 16%. The MRR value is also sometimes negatively affected. A trade-off between the goals can be observed for multiple-goal optimizations and therefore not all possible combinations lead to an increase in accuracy.

The conclusion that can be drawn from this phenomenon is that criteria other than tempo and loudness seem to be the driving factors for users of the Last.fm platform when they create their playlists. For the users of 8tracks, matching both quality factors seems important; for the AotM

Table 6: Next-Track optimization results (AotM). Target (= optimization target) can be ART = artist, TAG = tag, GNR = genre, POP = popularity, RY = release year, TMP = tempo, LD = loudness, [C] = Combination of [ART GNR POP RY]. Algorithm Parameters: Stopping criterion: Error reduction rate < 0.001, $maxSteps = 500$, $n = 10$, $m = 20$

| Target | Relative improvement w.r.t. baseline [kNN300CPA] | | | | | | | | | Absolute | |
| | diversity | | | average | | | | accuracy@10 | | accuracy@10 | |
	ART	TAG	GNR	POP	RY	TMP	LD	HR	MRR	HR	MRR
ART	.27	-.02	.14	.10	-.03	-.03	-.08	.28	1.17	**.072**	**.041**
TAG	.16	.17	.19	.16	-.02	-.06	-.09	.03	.65	.058	.031
GNR	.28	.04	.33	.12	-.02	-.04	-.07	.25	.61	.070	.030
POP	.02	-.04	.01	.35	-.07	-.06	-.06	.06	.70	.060	.032
RY	-.01	-.03	-.01	.10	.26	-.06	-.09	.19	.48	.070	.028
TMP	-.05	-.03	-.02	.11	-.10	.31	-.03	-.06	-.01	.053	.019
LD	-.03	-.02	.00	.11	-.08	-.04	.33	.16	.19	.063	.022
[C]	.22	.01	.22	.30	.01	-.05	-.07	.06	.75	.055	.021

users, an appropriate loudness seems more desirable. The observed differences between Last.fm and the other platforms are somehow expected, as 8tracks and AotM are platforms specifically designed for sharing playlists among music enthusiasts who consider various factors during playlist creation as analyzed in [7]. In contrast, users of Last.fm often seem to create recent "personal favorite tracks" playlists to be used by themselves.

5. RELATED WORK

A number of playlist generation techniques have been proposed over the last decade. They base their recommendations, e.g., on track co-occurrences and collaborative filtering, feature similarities and case-based reasoning, Markov models and sequential patterns, and various (discrete) optimization techniques [4]. In our work, we combine an unpersonalized co-occurrence based technique with content information as in [8] but furthermore (a) add personalization and feature-based scores in a weighted approach and (b) apply a post-processing procedure to match the characteristics of the immediate next tracks with the recent listening history.

From the evaluation perspective, we adopt a multi-metric and trade-off based evaluation approach as advised or applied for general and music-specific recommendation scenarios, e.g., in [1, 9, 11, 18], or [21]. In contrast to previous works, we however do not assume a "globally" desired level of diversity, novelty, or serendipity but aim to match the playlist continuation with the characteristics of a given listening history while maintaining accuracy.

Regarding our re-ranking approach, the work presented in [1] is similar to ours in that it tries to re-rank the first n items of an accuracy-optimized list in a way to increase or balance other quality factors. Their work however focuses on one single factor, "aggregate diversity", and aims to push items from the long tail. Diversity optimization – this time based on the ILS – was also done in [5] and [22] using techniques that reorder the recommendations based on their dissimilarity to each other. In [20], a binary optimization problem is used to model the trade-off between accuracy and diversity. Our approach can be used to achieve similar goals. It is however more generic in the sense that it is not limited to diversity-based measures and can deal with multiple goals at a time. Furthermore, we aim to match the diversity level of a given set of tracks or an individual user.

A comparable individualized "per-user" optimization technique for numerical quality factors was introduced in [9]. The authors employ a multi-objective linear optimization approach to re-rank the whole recommendation list by changing relevance scores of a baseline algorithms. Like our next-track optimization, the baseline algorithm is exchangeable, it however requires the existence of scores which might not be available if the underlying technique optimizes a rank measure as in learning-to-rank approaches. Furthermore, the focus of [9] lies on promoting long tail recommendations and does not cover aggregate measures. Finally, our re-ranking technique can be configured to exchange elements greedily from a comparably small exchange set x_m, thereby leading to a limited computational complexity.

In [21], music tracks are recommended by combining multiple algorithms through rank interpolation. Similar to our faceted scoring method, their goal is to increase the recommendation accuracy as well as other factors like novelty, diversity and serendipity. However, their main focus lies on creating more serendipitous recommendations and the technique is not based on exchangeable baseline methods but implements the optimizations inside the algorithms. In addition, their method aims to achieve globally defined quality levels whereas in our work we try to minimize the difference between the playlist history and the immediate next tracks.

6. CONCLUSIONS

Playlist generation is a special form of music recommendation which is particularly challenging as the recommended items are immediately "consumed", sequentiality and homogeneity aspects can be important, and the choice of a few wrong tracks within the sequence can easily be detrimental to the perceived service quality as a whole.

In our work, we have proposed a new multi-aspect scoring scheme which combines patterns in existing playlist with meta-data features and personal user preferences to achieve higher accuracy and, if desired, higher homogeneity than previous approaches. A post-processing procedure can furthermore help to match the characteristics of the playlist continuation with the most recent listening history. In our ongoing work we evaluate the application of these procedures to general recommendation settings, where, e.g., the most frequent user ratings are used as representatives for the recent user preferences to which the next item recommendations should be adapted. Conducting a user study to evaluate our approaches in terms of the perceived quality of the playlists and user satisfaction is part of our future work.

7. REFERENCES

[1] G. Adomavicius and Y. Kwon. Improving aggregate recommendation diversity using ranking-based techniques. *IEEE TKDE*, 24(5):896–911, 2012.

[2] W. Balkema and F. van der Heijden. Music Playlist Generation by Assimilating GMMs into SOMs. *Pattern Recognition Letters*, 31(11):1396–1402, 2010.

[3] G. Bonnin and D. Jannach. Evaluating the Quality of Playlists Based on Hand-Crafted Samples. In *Proc. ISMIR*, pages 263–268, 2013.

[4] G. Bonnin and D. Jannach. Automated generation of music playlists: Survey and experiments. *ACM Comput. Surv.*, 47(2):26:1–26:35, 2014.

[5] K. Bradley and B. Smyth. Improving Recommendation Diversity. In *Proc. AICS '01*, pages 75–84, 2001.

[6] P. Y. K. Chau, S. Y. Ho, K. K. W. Ho, and Y. Yao. Examining the effects of malfunctioning personalized services on online users' distrust and behaviors. *Decis. Support Syst.*, 56:180–191, 2013.

[7] S. Cunningham, D. Bainbridge, and A. Falconer. 'More of an Art than a Science': Supporting the Creation of Playlists and Mixes. In *Proc. ISMIR*, pages 240–245, 2006.

[8] N. Hariri, B. Mobasher, and R. Burke. Context-Aware Music Recommendation Based on Latent Topic Sequential Patterns. In *Proc. RecSys*, pages 131–138, 2012.

[9] T. Jambor and J. Wang. Optimizing multiple objectives in collaborative filtering. In *Proc. RecSys '10*, pages 55–62, 2010.

[10] D. Jannach, I. Kamehkhosh, and G. Bonnin. Analyzing the characteristics of shared playlists for music recommendation. In *RSWeb Workhop at ACM RecSys '14*, 2014.

[11] D. Jannach, L. Lerche, F. Gedikli, and G. Bonnin. What recommenders recommend - an analysis of accuracy, popularity, and sales diversity effects. In *Proc. UMAP 2013*, pages 25–37, 2013.

[12] M. Kaminskas and F. Ricci. Contextual music information retrieval and recommendation: State of the art and challenges. *Computer Science Review*, 6(2–3):89–119, 2012.

[13] B. Logan. Content-Based Playlist Generation: Exploratory Experiments. In *Proc. ISMIR*, pages 295–296, 2002.

[14] B. McFee and G. R. Lanckriet. The Natural Language of Playlists. In *Proc. ISMIR*, pages 537–542, 2011.

[15] B. McFee and G. R. Lanckriet. Hypergraph Models of Playlist Dialects. In *Proc. ISMIR*, pages 343–348, 2012.

[16] S. Pauws, W. Verhaegh, and M. Vossen. Music playlist generation by adapted simulated annealing. *Inf. Sci.*, 178(3):647–662, 2008.

[17] S. Rendle, C. Freudenthaler, Z. Gantner, and L. Schmidt-Thieme. BPR: Bayesian personalized ranking from implicit feedback. In *Proc. UAI '09*, pages 452–461, 2009.

[18] A. Said, B. J. Jain, and S. Albayrak. A 3D approach to recommender system evaluation. In *Proc. CSCW '13 Companion Volume*, pages 263–266, 2013.

[19] A. M. Sarroff and M. Casey. Modeling and Predicting Song Adjacencies In Commercial Albums. In *Proc. SMC*, 2012.

[20] M. Zhang and N. Hurley. Avoiding monotony: Improving the diversity of recommendation lists. In *RecSys '08*, pages 123–130, 2008.

[21] Y. C. Zhang, D. O. Séaghdha, D. Quercia, and T. Jambor. Auralist: Introducing serendipity into music recommendation. In *Proc. WSDM '12*, pages 13–22, 2012.

[22] C.-N. Ziegler, S. M. McNee, J. A. Konstan, and G. Lausen. Improving recommendation lists through topic diversification. In *Proc. WWW '05*, pages 22–32, 2005.

Content Driven User Profiling for Comment-Worthy Recommendations of News and Blog Articles

Trapit Bansal
trapitbansal@gmail.com

Mrinal Das
mrinal@csa.iisc.ernet.in

Chiranjib Bhattacharyya
chiru@csa.iisc.ernet.in

Department of Computer Science and Automation
Indian Institute of Science, Bangalore

ABSTRACT

We consider the problem of recommending *comment-worthy* articles such as news and blog-posts. An article is defined to be comment-worthy for a particular user if that user is interested to leave a comment on it. We note that recommending comment-worthy articles calls for elicitation of *commenting-interests* of the user from the *content* of both the articles and the past comments made by users. We thus propose to develop *content-driven* user profiles to elicit these latent interests of users in commenting and use them to recommend articles for future commenting. The difficulty of modeling comment content and the varied nature of users' commenting interests make the problem technically challenging.

The problem of recommending comment-worthy articles is resolved by leveraging article and comment content through topic modeling and the co-commenting pattern of users through collaborative filtering, combined within a novel hierarchical Bayesian modeling approach. Our solution, Collaborative Correspondence Topic Models (CCTM), generates user profiles which are leveraged to provide a personalized ranking of *comment-worthy* articles for each user. Through these *content*-driven user profiles, CCTM effectively handle the ubiquitous problem of *cold-start* without relying on additional meta-data. The inference problem for the model is intractable with no off-the-shelf solution and we develop an efficient Monte Carlo EM algorithm. CCTM is evaluated on three real world data-sets, crawled from two *blogs*, ArsTechnica (AT) Gadgets (102,087 comments) and AT-Science (71,640 comments), and a *news* site, DailyMail (33,500 comments). We show average improvement of **14%** (warm-start) and **18%** (cold-start) in AUC, and **80%** (warm-start) and **250%** (cold-start) in Hit-Rank@5, over state of the art [1, 2].

Categories and Subject Descriptors

G.3 [**Probability and Statistics**]: Probabilistic algorithms; H.4.m [**Information Systems Applications**]: Miscellaneous

Keywords

Comments; User Profiling; News; Blogs; Topic Modeling; Collaborative Filtering; Hybrid Recommendation Systems

RecSys'15, September 16–20, 2015, Vienna, Austria.
© 2015 ACM. ISBN 978-1-4503-3692-5/15/09 ...$15.00.
DOI: http://dx.doi.org/10.1145/2792838.2800186.

1. INTRODUCTION

Online news and blog portals have emerged as convenient tools to gather information and exchange thoughts. Facility of commenting on such news and blog sites have raised the experience of users and, through active user-engagement, play a pivotal role in the hosting site's popularity [1]. Comments have thus garnered much research interest, ranging from detecting spam [3] to summarization [4], ranking [5] and retrieval [6]. Instead of studying comments, in this paper we explore the key question of what stimulates a user to make a comment on such online media. We demonstrate that *content* can reveal a significant amount of knowledge about users' commenting interests which can be leveraged to elicit further commenting through specific and personalized recommendations of *comment-worthy* articles. This is a form of recommendation aimed at enhancing user engagement through commenting.

Consider a blog post reviewing *Samsung Galaxy S5*, dated Feb 25, 2014[1], with over 160 comments, shown in Fig. 1. The review discusses various features in different *segments* like the *cover material* (purple colored), the new features of *fingerprint scanner* (colored red), *heartbeat reader* (colored green), the *MicroUSB* support (colored blue), etc. Notice that some users commented almost entirely on the new feature of heartbeat scanner, like Carl (*..An inconspicuous way to check your pulse..*, colored green); while some commented on the *MicroUSB* aspect, like Bob (*..I do hope USB 3.0 C comes out soon..*, colored blue). In the same article, some users commented on the story solely for the purpose of replying to an existing comment, like Mark who replied to users Alice and Carl (*..it will only measure your pulse rate..*, colored green). This demonstrates the varied nature of *specific* interests of users in commenting.

Investigating the user-comments of such articles, we observe that a user can comment on an article mainly for four reasons, if he is interested in (1) the content of the article, (2) content of other users' comments on the article, (3) content of a specific part of the article or (4) if users with similar interests have commented on the article. While user-interest in existing comments and users is a well-known phenomenon which is realized in the form of explicit *reply-to* feature on most sites, the concept of commenting-interest in *specific* parts of articles is a recent finding [7]. Indeed, realizing the importance of this very behavior, recent blogging-platforms like Medium[2] and WordPress[2] have started to offer per-paragraph commenting facility, to wide-spread popularity.

---

[1] ArsTechnica Gadgets: http://tinyurl.com/ktlyv6x
[2] medium.com; wordpress.org/plugins/inline-comments

Explicitly modeling users' commenting interests is the key component in making comment-worthy recommendations. Realize that without modeling all the above interests explicitly, the user-article indicator matrix of comments is not fully indicative of commenting interest. Thus, traditional collaborative filtering (CF) methods [8, 9] used to recommend articles for viewing [10] are not very effective in recommending articles to users for commenting. Moreover, such CF methods [8, 9] are known to suffer from the problem of item *cold-start*, new content on which no user has commented. On the other hand, state of the art hybrid models like collaborative topic regression [2], do not model *comment-content* and the varied user interests, giving unsatisfactory performance. Recently, an attempt was made to recommend news articles to users *for commenting* [1]. However, due to the inability to leverage article and comment content, the approach is unable to distinguish users' specific interests in commenting, leading to sub-optimal results. Moreover, the reliance of the approach on less informative meta-data, like tags, causes unsatisfactory performance specially in cold-start scenario which is ubiquitous in the realm of online media.

Contributions.

We explore the role of content in recommending *comment-worthy* articles and propose content-driven user profiling aimed at elicitation of users' commenting interests. We identify that user profiles should depend on content of articles on which user previously commented, content of user's previous comments and the co-commenting pattern of users. The resulting problem (Section 2) turns out to be an instance of a correspondence problem between the article and comment content, and a collaborative filtering problem of finding co-commenting patterns. To this end, we propose (Section 3) a novel hierarchical Bayesian model, namely *Collaborative Correspondence Topic Models* (CCTM), which solve the problem by bringing together topic modeling [11], collaborative filtering [8] and Bayesian personalized ranking [9].

To tackle the challenge of modeling comment-content, we use the recently introduced concept of *multiple topic vectors* [7], to discover user interest in *specific* article segments and create topic profiles of users from previous *comment-content*. By associating each user and each *segment* of article with *latent offsets*, we show how the topic profiles can be leveraged to model users commenting interests through a Bayesian personalized ranking approach [9]. Through these content-driven profiles, CCTM naturally handles cold-start problem in recommendation without relying on meta-data.

The resulting inference problem becomes non-standard due to dependency among several variables introduced through the three different modeling components and there are no off-the-shelf solutions. We develop (Section 4) an efficient stochastic Monte Carlo expectation maximization (MCEM) inference algorithm for CCTM. CCTM is used to generate article recommendations for future commenting and is rigorously evaluated (Section 5) on *three real datasets*, consisting of crawled copies of 1 popular News sites and 2 popular Blogs. We find that, on average, CCTM achieves **16%** improvement in AUC and **165%** improvement in Hit-Rank@5 over state-of-the-art recommendation systems [1, 2].

Notation.

K is the number of topics and V is number of words in vocabulary. β_k is a V-dimension vector such that $\sum_{j=1}^{V} \beta_{kj} =$

Figure 1: Examples of various commenting interests of users. Article segments and comments are color coded so that they correspond to same topic. Dashed arrow indicates a reply-to comment.

1, popularly called as a *"topic"*. $x^T y$ is dot product of vectors x and y. *Dir* denotes Dirichlet distribution, *Ber* denotes Bernoulli distribution, and $\mathcal{N}$ denotes K dimension multivariate normal distribution. $[n] = \{1, 2, \ldots, n\}$ and $|R|$: cardinality of set R. $I[.]$ is the indicator function, $\sim$ means "distributed as" and 1_n is a n-dimension vector of ones.

2. THE PROBLEM OF RECOMMENDING COMMENT-WORTHY ARTICLES

We begin by introducing relevant notation to describe the data. An article A_d, indexed by d or $j \in [D]$, is composed of S_d segments (sentences or paragraphs), $A_d = \{s_{da}|a \in [S_d]\}$, with each segment being a bag-of-words $s_{da} = \{w_{dan}|n \in [N_{da}]\}$. Each article has a set of C_d comments denoted by $E_d = \{c_{de} \mid e \in [C_d]\}$, with comment $c_{de} = \{w'_{dem}|m \in [n_{de}]\}$ where w'_{dem} is the mth word of comment e on article d. Furthermore $w_{dan}, w'_{dem} \in [V]$, where V is vocabulary size. The unique set of U users is indexed by user-id $i \in [U]$. For each user i, $A_i^+ \subseteq [D]$ denotes the set of articles i commented on and $A_i^- \subseteq [D]$ denotes the set he did not comment on.

Commenting interests of users.

Analyzing commenting interests of users is a crucial step in achieving our goal. Commenting interest of user i can be on three aspects; (1) general content of article A_d, (2) a *specific* segment s_{da} ($a \in [S_d]$) or (3) a *subset* of existing comments ($\subseteq [C_d]$) and their corresponding users. The set $R_{di} \subseteq [S_d] \cup [C_d]$, for each user i, will be denoted as the set of his *commenting interests* in article d. If user i makes a comment being interested on any component of R_{di}, we say that user i has made a comment on article A_d.

Problem formulation.

Given article-comment pairs $\{(A_d, E_d)\}_{d=1}^{D}$, classify for every user $i \in [U]$, whether i will comment on A_d, by finding the set R_{di} of commenting interests for user i in article d.

As a glimpse of things to come, the model we propose will associate with each potential element of R_{di} a real-valued score for each user, which is then combined to give an overall *commenting-interest score* of that article for the user.

Key challenges.

The task of recommending comment-worthy articles is tightly bound with finding commenting interests. We describe some key challenges below.

(1) Inapplicability of supervised approaches. Explicit supervision about R_{di} is generally unavailable for the user's prior commenting history and creating such labeled data is costly, enforcing an unsupervised approach.

(2) Low correlation between user's interest and article's main topic. A user may be interested in a specific part of an article (see Fig. 1) denoted by R_{di}. The proportion over topics for R_{di} can be very different from that of the entire article and size of R_{di} can be as small as a sentence. That makes correlation between user's interest in the article and main content of the article very low, enhancing the difficulty for statistical models.

(3) Low correlation between user interest and majority of the comments. Most of the articles in a popular site will receive comments of varied topics. Although many of the comments will focus on main topic of the article, but a significant number of comments diverge from that [7], and a user may be interested in comments which are on different topic than most of the comments.

(4) Comments are short and diverse. A key observation we make here is that the information of a user's specific interests is hidden in his prior comment *content*, as can be seen in Fig. 1. However, simple textual overlap is unsuitable to discover this relation. Moreover, due to the short and noisy nature of comments, modeling comment-content is challenging and approaches often rely on external text enrichment [4, 12], which is impractical for ever-increasing datasets.

(5) Cold-Start conditions. New online articles are generated at a very rapid pace, leading to the problem referred to as *cold-start*. That is, finding user interest in fresh articles with no existing comments ($|C_d| = 0$). This prohibits use of vanilla matrix factorization [8, 9].

2.1 Related work

Our approach lies in the literature on correspondence topic models and recommendation systems. CorrLDA [11] was the first topic model to model correspondence between images and their annotations. Within user modeling, [13] apply the LDA model on user's view logs to predict which stories a user will view. [14] developed topic models to profile experts in community Q&A. Outside topic modeling, [6] developed language models incorporating comment content for retrieving related news stories, but ignores user-information and personalization. None of these [6, 13, 14] model commenting behavior or recommend articles for commenting.

Collaborative filtering (CF) is an active area of research with rich literature [15, 16]. The most common example is probabilistic matrix factorization (PMF) [8], which analyzes interdependencies between items and users. However, CF approaches are prone to the problem of *cold-start* which has led to research in *hybrid* CF methods. [5] developed a hybrid regression based latent factor model to rank comments on news articles, by leveraging meta-data. Recent research in hybrid CF methods, like collaborative topic re-

gression (CTR)[2], has combined LDA and PMF for generating article recommendations, by leveraging item content. Quite recently, [17] showed the advantage of using articles in users' libraries to generate relevant recommendations of scientific articles. These methods [2, 17] cannot model comment content and are unsuitable for the given task.

More germane to our work is the recent study of [1], who look at recommending news articles for commenting. They use a CF approach relying crucially on article *tags* as meta-data to handle cold-start. This has the following problems: *a)* Extensive editorial effort is required to ensure fine-grained tags with every new article. Indeed, the datasets that we crawled (5.1), only have generic *categories* like *Tennis*, making it impossible for the model to distinguish user's commenting interest on any two new articles on Tennis. *b)* It ignores both article and comment content, making it impossible to analyze commenting interests of users. As opposed to this, our model does not rely on meta-data by modeling article and comment content.

3. COLLABORATIVE CORRESPONDENCE TOPIC MODELS

In order to solve the problem of recommending comment-worthy articles, we propose in this section a novel hierarchical Bayesian modeling approach, namely *collaborative correspondence topic models* (CCTM). Full generative process is given in Fig. 2. We describe the modeling details below.

3.1 Modeling principle

Our objective in this paper is to analyze specific reasons behind commenting activity of users and apply that suitably to recommend articles for further commenting. Our approach is based on four key steps; (1) create *topic profiles*, (2) combine topic profile with *latent offsets*, (3) quantify commenting interests and (4) finally rank the preferences. CCTM thus brings in specific correspondence modeling (step 1), collaborative filtering (step 2 and 3) and Bayesian personalized ranking (step 4) together. We describe the steps below.

3.2 Modeling specific correspondence to capture topic profiles

As evinced by the example of Fig. 1, articles cover multiple topics in different segments and comment content can be related to such very specific segments, which in addition may not be contiguous. Due to this fact, proportion over topics should vary across the segments within an article and CorrLDA [11] fails to capture this aspect. We resort to the concept of multiple topic distributions (topic vectors) [7].

3.2.1 Multiple topic vectors (MTV) to vary proportion over topics

For every article, there are J_d topic vectors $\{\theta_{dt}\}$, representing its varied themes. For each word of a segment, a topic vector θ_{dt} is sampled from a multinomial ρ, and the topic assignment of the word is then sampled from θ_{dt}. Contrast this to CorrLDA, where a *single* θ_d is fixed for the article and any random segment has same distribution as the entire article (in expectation), whereas MTV allows it to be significantly different. Following [7], stick-breaking process (SBP) [18] is used as prior for ρ. MTV thus allows us to model low correlation in topic of a comment with an article but high correlation with topic of a *specific* article segment.

- For $k \in [K]$, sample topic $\beta_k \sim Dir(\eta\, 1_V)$

- For each user $i \in [U]$,
  - Sample $\vartheta_i \sim Dir(\alpha_u\, 1_K)$, $\epsilon_i \sim Beta(\lambda_1, \lambda_2)$

- For each article-comment pair, $d \in [D]$
  - For $t \in [J_d]$, draw topic vectors $\theta_{dt} \sim Dir(\alpha\, 1_K)$
  - For each article segment, $a \in [S_d]$
    * Sample $\rho_{da} \sim SBP(\tau, \iota)$
    * For each word $n \in [N_{da}]$,
      · Sample topic, $z_{dan} \sim \theta_{db_{dan}}$, $b_{dan} \sim \rho_{da}$
      · Sample word, $w_{dan} \sim \beta_{z_{dan}}$
    * Set topic profile $\tilde{s}_{da}$, $\tilde{s}_{dak} = \frac{|\{z_{dan}=k,\, n \in N_{da}\}|}{N_{da}}$
  - For each comment $e \in [C_d]$ by user $i \in [U]$
    * For each segment a, selector $\xi_{dea} \sim Ber(\pi_{de})$
    * Set $\varphi_{dek} = \frac{\#\{z_{dan}=k\ \forall(a,n)|\xi_{dea}=1\}}{\sum_{a=1}^{S_d} \xi_{dea} N_{da}}$
    * For each comment word $m \in [n_{de}]$,
      · Sample topic $y_{dem} \sim \epsilon_{de}\varphi_{de} + (1-\epsilon_{de})\vartheta_{de}$
      · Sample word, $w'_{dem} \sim \beta_{y_{dem}}$
    * Set topic profile $\tilde{c}_{de}$, $\tilde{c}_{dek} = \frac{|\{y_{dem}=k,\, m \in n_{de}\}|}{n_{de}}$

- For articles $d \in [D]$, sample $v_{d0} \sim \mathcal{N}(0, \lambda_v^{-1} I)$
  - For segment $a \in [S_d]$, sample $v_{da} \sim \mathcal{N}(0, \lambda_s^{-1} I)$,

- For users $i \in [U]$,
  - Set topic profile $\tilde{q}_i$, $\tilde{q}_{ik} = \frac{\sum_{(d,e) \in A_i^+} n_{de} c_{dek}}{\sum_{(d,e) \in A_i^+} n_{de}}$
  - Sample $u_i \sim \mathcal{N}(0, \lambda_q^{-1} I)$

- For each user-article pair, $(i,d) \in [U] \times [D]$,
  - Commenting interest, $r_{id} = r_{id}^{mf} + r_{id}^{art} + r_{id}^{cmnt}$,
  $r_{id}^{mf} = h_d + (\tilde{q}_i + u_i)^T v_{d0}$
  $r_{id}^{art} = \max_{1 \leq a \leq S_d} \{(\tilde{q}_i + u_i)^T(\tilde{s}_{da} + v_{da})\}$
  $r_{id}^{cmnt} = \sum_{e=1}^{C_d} (\tilde{q}_i + u_i)^T(\tilde{c}_{de} + u_{de}) p_{ide}$, where
  $p_{ide} = softmax\{(\tilde{q}_i + u_i)^T(\tilde{q}_{de} + u_{de})\}$

Figure 2: Generative Process of CCTM

3.2.2 Generating comment content

To relate comment content to specific segments of the article, topic assignment of comment words is sampled from subset of segments, rather than uniformly from entire article like CorrLDA. For every comment, the subset of article-segments is sampled through selector variable ξ. Then the topic assignment of each word in comment e is generated from a mixture distribution $\epsilon_{de}\varphi_{de} + (1-\epsilon_{de})\vartheta_{de}$; where φ_{de} is the uniform distribution over selected segments and ϵ_{de} is user's propensity to select from the article d or his own interests[3], ϑ_i. To capture commenting interests of users, each user is associated with topic interests defined by a distribution over topics, ϑ_i. ϑ_i relates user i's comment content

---

[3] we index user variables by comment-id for simplicity

across his commenting history and allows comment-topics to vary from the article distribution based on the user's other interests. Through this mechanism, we allow comments to exhibit content which is better modeled by the user's diverging interests from the current article. This is essential for modeling all the varied types of commenting activity and not ignore a substantial amount of comment content.

3.2.3 Creating topic profiles

After modeling the correspondence between article and comments, we create topic profiles. For each user i, we construct an empirical topic distribution $\tilde{q}_i$ from the topic assignment of all his prior comments which can be considered a summary of user's topic interests. Similarly, each article d's segment a and comment e get empirical topic distributions $\tilde{s}_{da}$ and $\tilde{c}_{de}$, respectively. These *topic profiles* will now be refined *collaboratively* to model users' commenting interests.

3.3 Complementing topic profiles with latent offsets

To model users' commenting interests, we introduce *latent offsets* to the topic profiles, much in the vein of [2, 19].

3.3.1 Latent offsets to model commenting interests

We introduce latent offsets for each *user i (u_i), each segment $a \in [S_d]$ (v_{da}) of article* d and a global offset for each article d (v_{d0}), in order to model the varied commenting interests. Following PMF approach [8], the latent offsets are drawn from zero-mean K-dimensional Gaussian distribution. These offsets will allow the topic profiles to change according to observed commenting interests.

Intuition behind latent offsets.

Suppose that the user *Mark* (in Fig. 1) has till now commented on *mobile apps* which gets reflected in his topic-profile. However, now his comments on the related topic of *health* app (green article-segment), cannot be explained by the content-model alone, due to lack of his prior comment-content on this topic. The latent offset will model this behavior by increasing the value for the *health* topic in the user's offset and *mobile app* topic in the corresponding segment's offset, due to the commenting activity of similar users like *Alice* who were also interested in mobile apps but also commented on health topic in this article and other articles.

The latent offsets, thus, will serve the purpose of allowing the topic profiles to deviate according to observed commenting patterns. The offsets are learned from the overall commenting activity, so the more comments users make, the better idea the model gets of the value of the offsets.

3.3.2 Content-driven user profiles

Latent offsets and topic profiles will be combined to give an overall *commenting-interest score*, $\hat{r}_{id}$, for each user i on article d, by taking into account interest in each element of R_{di}. To this end, we create content-driven user profiles, by combining topic profiles of users (content information) with the latent offset (co-commenting information) to obtain user i's profile, $(\tilde{q}_i + u_i)$. Following Bayesian approach, by associating (zero mean) latent offsets with topic profiles, we ensure good back-off estimates to the topic profile in sparse commenting scenarios. Similar profiles are considered for article segments and comments in the following section.

3.4 Quantifying commenting interests

A user can comment on the main article, a specific segment of the article or on some existing comments. We model interest in these aspects using scores r^{mf}, r^{art} and r^{cmnt}, respectively. The idea behind computing these scores is that, the closer the user's profile is to the profiles of these three aspects, the higher his interest is in that specific aspect.

3.4.1 Interest in article popularity

Users like *Anon* in Fig. 1 are interested in the main topic or popularity of article. Similar to PMF[8], we capture this:

$$r_{id}^{mf} = h_d + (\tilde{q}_i + u_i)^T v_{d0} \qquad (1)$$

where $h_d \sim \mathcal{N}(0, \lambda_h^{-1})$ is a popularity bias and v_{d0} is a global latent offset for article. Notice that unlike vanilla PMF (which would consider $u_i^T v_{d0}$), we use the complete user profile $(\tilde{q}_i + u_i)$ which allows the model to ensure that user's interest do not deviate much from his previous content interests. For a new article with no existing comments (i.e. cold-start), there is no contribution from this term.

3.4.2 Interest in article segments

The *segment's* latent profile is considered as $(\tilde{s}_{da} + v_{da})$, where $\tilde{s}_{da}$ is the topic-distribution of the segment. This profile is expected to capture the topic-level popularity of this segment among users. We thus set $r_{ida}^{art} = (\tilde{q}_i + u_i)^T (\tilde{s}_{da} + v_{da})$, for $a \in [S_d]$. Now considering the maximum value we get the score for the segment with highest interest as below.

$$r_{id}^{art} = \max_{1 \le a \le S_d} \{ (\tilde{q}_i + u_i)^T (\tilde{s}_{da} + v_{da}) \} \qquad (2)$$

3.4.3 Interest in existing comments and users

Consider a latent profile of existing comment e on A_d to be $(\tilde{c}_{de} + u_{de})$, where $\tilde{c}_{de}$ is the topic distribution of the comment and u_{de} is the latent offset associated with user of this comment. We thus consider the interest in comment e as $r_{ide}^c = (\tilde{q}_i + u_i)^T (\tilde{c}_{de} + u_{de})$. Note that $\tilde{c}_{de}$ is comment-specific but u_{de} is a global parameter for the user, avoiding explosion of the number of parameters to be learned (as quantity of comments can be high).

Main challenge in accounting for interest in $[C_d]$ is that users often don't respect the reply-to relations while commenting [12]. Moreover, such relations are unavailable for articles on which user has not yet commented. To model this, let γ_{ide} denote a Bernoulli random variable, with $\gamma_{ide} = 1$ if user i's comment on d is a *reply-to* comment to the comment e. Thus, the expected overall interest in existing comments:

$$r_{id}^{cmnt} = \mathbb{E}_{\gamma | u, \tilde{c}} \left[\sum_{e=1}^{C_d} r_{ide}^c I(\gamma_{ide} = 1) \right] = \sum_{e=1}^{C_d} r_{ide}^c p_{ide} \qquad (3)$$

where $p_{ide} = P(\gamma_{ide} = 1 | u_i, u_{de}, \tilde{c}_{de})$. The case of observed reply-to relations is trivial with $p_{ide} \propto 1$ for only the observed relations. Here we model the user as equally interested in all the users he replied to. For unobserved relations and uncommented articles, we use the intuition that a user i is interested in other comment if the user profiles are similar. Thus, for this case we consider $p_{ide} \sim softmax\{(\tilde{q}_i + u_i)^T (\tilde{q}_{de} + u_{de})\}$. Equation (3) and probability model p_{ide}, define the comment-interest part of the rating, r_{id}^{cmnt}. Apart from modeling *content*-relatedness, the cross-term of the latent offsets $(u_i^T u_{de})$ models user similar-

ity. Also note that r_{id}^{cmnt} causes the user's interest in an article d to evolve with new comments received on d.

3.4.4 Overall commenting interests of users

We take into account all the potential user-interests to consider an overall interest score of user i in article d:

$$\hat{r}_{id} = r_{id}^{mf} + r_{id}^{art} + r_{id}^{cmnt} \qquad (4)$$

where r_{id}^{mf} (1) is a popularity term for user interest in the topic popularity of the article (only for warm-start), r_{id}^{art} (2) accounts for the interest in specific segments of the article, and r_{id}^{cmnt} (3) accounts for the interest in the existing comment-content and co-commenters.

3.5 Ranking commenting preferences

With the interest score defined, we need to model users' personalized preferences for commenting. Note that the dataset consists of only positive item feedback, that is we only have access to information of which articles the user was interested in commenting on. This is a much harder problem of implicit feedback [9, 20]. We take recourse to Bayesian Personalized Ranking (BPR) [9, 21] which provides a Bayesian model for learning a personalized total ranking for each user. Given the predicted scores $\hat{r}_{id}$ and $\hat{r}_{ij}$, the probability of user i preferring article d over article j is $\sigma(\hat{r}_{id} - \hat{r}_{ij})$; where σ is the sigmoid function, $\sigma(x) = \frac{1}{1+e^{-x}}$.

4. INFERENCE AND PREDICTION

Our objective is to develop an efficient inference procedure to learn the model's latent offsets (denoted by Θ) and the latent content variables associated with articles, comments and users (denoted by Ω). The task is thus to maximize the log-posterior of the model parameters $p(\Theta, \Omega | R, W)$, where $R = \{(i, d) | i \in [U], d \in A_i^+\}$ is the observed commenting pattern and W are the words of the articles and comments. Inference is intractable and we resort to a stochastic MCEM algorithm [22], an inference method that alternates between Gibbs sampling for content variables Ω (keeping Θ fixed) and gradient ascent to estimate latent offsets Θ (Ω fixed).

4.1 Sampling content variables (E-step)

We develop an efficient *collapsed Gibbs sampling* inference for sampling the content-variables. The real-valued random variables $\beta, \vartheta, \epsilon, \theta, \rho, \pi$ (Fig. 2) are marginalized out, and only discrete variables b, z, y, and ξ are inferred, leading to accelerated convergence. Sampling of y requires introducing an auxiliary binary variable κ, with $\kappa = 0$ if comment-word topic is sampled from article-segments ϕ and $\kappa = 1$ if sampled from the user's topic vector ϑ. Note that unlike [2, 19], who add latent offsets to the document topic distributions θ, we add latent offset to *empirical* topic distributions $(\tilde{s}, \tilde{q})$, allowing us to collapse θ and ϑ, reducing the number of variables to be sampled. Derivation of conditional distributions is now conventional and we omit this due to space constraints. Refer to supplementary for more details.

4.2 Estimating latent offsets (M-step)

We seek to optimize the log-posterior of latent offsets given observed user preferences R and the content variables, that is: $\ln p(\Theta | R, \Omega) = \sum_{i \in U} \sum_{d \in A_i^+} \sum_{j \in A_i^-} \ln \sigma(\hat{r}_{id} - \hat{r}_{ij}) + \ln p(\Theta | \Omega)$. This requires computing $U \times D^2$ terms for the gradient, which is computationally infeasible. BPR [9], thus estimates the model parameters Θ by stochastic gradient ascent (SGA). In each step, a user i and a commented article d are sampled uniformly from R, an uncommented article j is sampled from A_i^- and a gradient step with respect to the associated terms in the log-posterior is performed.

However, a key challenge here is that $\hat{r}_{id}$ is *not differentiable* due to the use of the *max* function in the r_{id}^{art} (2), which explains users' interest in specific segments. We overcome this by a smooth approximation of the max function:

$$\underset{1 \leq k \leq K}{diffmax}\{a_k\} = \frac{1}{\sum_k e^{\psi a_k}} \sum_k a_k e^{\psi a_k} \qquad (5)$$

for some parameter $\psi \geq 0$. This is different from softmax but can be viewed as a weighted sum of the values a_k with weights given by the $softmax\{a_k\}$.

Note that $\lim_{\psi \to \infty} \underset{1 \leq k \leq K}{diffmax}\{a_k\} \equiv \underset{1 \leq k \leq K}{max}\{a_k\}$, and $\psi = 0$ corresponds to average of $\{a_k\}$.

Using *diffmax* allows us to carry out an efficient SGA algorithm. The computation of the gradients is now straightforward, details can be found in the supplementary[4].

Before concluding this section, we remark on our choice of BPR algorithm. Apart from its success for implicit feedback [21–23], we choose BPR as apposed to alternatives like weighted regularized matrix factorization (WRMF) [20], also used by CTR [2], due to practical considerations. The non-quadratic form of $\hat{r}$ (4), makes WRMF impractical, as an alternating least squares method like [2, 20] cannot be derived. Moreover, taking an SGA approach in WRMF is inferior to the SGA approach on BPR criterion which works with item-pair level as opposed to individual item level [9].

4.3 Predicting commenting interests

Given the learned latent offsets and topic profiles of articles, segments and comments, the predicted user interest in commenting on an article is given by equation (4). For an article with no comments, that is *cold-start*, this value is:

$$\mathbb{E}[r_{id}] = \mathbb{E}[r_{id}^{art}] \approx \underset{1 \leq a \leq S_d}{max}\{(\tilde{q}_i + u_i)^T(\tilde{s}_{da})\} \qquad (6)$$

5. EMPIRICAL EVALUATION

In this section, we evaluate the proposed model CCTM rigorously on three real datasets. We first show that CCTM is a good model of article-comment correspondence. Then we evaluate the main task of this paper, recommending articles to users *for commenting*.

5.1 Datasets

We crawled[4] live news and blog sites to collect article content, corresponding comments, user information of comments and reply-to relations (where available).

ATScience: We crawled 3 years of blog articles, from April 2011 to April 2014, from Science section of popular blog ArsTechnica[5]. This consists of $71,640$ comments by $3,581$ users on $2,500$ articles.

ATGadgets: We crawled $102,087$ comments by $4,872$ users on $3,000$ articles from Gadgets section of the site ArsTechnica[5], from June 2012 to April 2014.

DailyMail: We Crawled $33,468$ comments by $2,534$ users on $3,000$ articles from Sports section of this popular news

---

[4]Resources: http://mllab.csa.iisc.ernet.in/recsys15
[5]arstechnica.com/science; arstechnica.com/gadgets

site[6], going chronologically backwards from 1 July 2013. This crawl of the dataset did not have reply-to relations.

5.2 Experimental setup

5.2.1 Baselines

We consider three baselines: *a)* TagCF [1]: This is the state-of-art for recommending articles for commenting. It associates *tags* with latent factors and uses BPR criterion. This completely ignores article and comment content. *b)* Collaborative Topic Regression (**CTR**) [2]: State-of-the-art *hybrid* model which models the content of the articles along with the ratings. This approach ignores the content of the comments, but promises to handle *cold-start* by leveraging content of articles and does not rely on meta-data like tags. *c)* Content-Only Method (**CoTM**): This is the *content-only* part of our model (section 3.2), equivalent to setting the latent offsets $\{u_i, v_{d0}, v_{da}\} = 0$. We will refer to this as CoTM (Commenter Topic Model).

Improvement of CoTM over CTR will demonstrate the importance of modeling *comment content* and its correspondence to article content. Improvement of CCTM over both CoTM and CTR will demonstrate importance of modeling commenting interests explicitly. Note that all baselines ignore modeling of commenting interests of users.

5.2.2 Implementation details

We remove standard stop words and restrict vocabulary to $15k$ words using term-frequency. Articles and users with less than 2 comments were removed since they cannot be evaluated. We used uninformative hyperparameter values for the content variables[7]: $\alpha, \alpha_u, \eta = 0.1$; $\tau = 1$, $\iota = 0.1$; $\lambda_1, \lambda_2 = 1$; and $J_d = 5$. For all models, $K = 150$. The precision parameters for latent-offsets $\lambda_v, \lambda_s, \lambda_q, \lambda_h$, similar parameters for baselines, were tuned on the first fold of DailyMail and the same value used for all other folds and datasets. The *diffmax* parameter ψ was tuned same way and found to be $\psi = 10$. We observed the estimation procedure for CTR to be sensitive to initialization, and initialized CTR with the output from LDA. We initialize CCTM randomly. CCTM is trained by 1000 EM-iterations, with 1k SGA updates per iteration. Due to unavailability of tags on articles, for TagCF we follow the advice of [1] to extract entities. We extract 10k entities by frequency (more entities did not improve performance) and do 1000k SGA updates.

5.2.3 Methodology

We test the performance of all the models in both warm-start and cold-start scenarios, following the approach of [2].

Warm-Start: In this case every test article had at least one comment in training data. For each user we do a stratified 5-fold split of articles (both 1's and 0's). For each fold, we fit the models on training data and test on within-fold articles of each user (users have different sets of within-fold articles).

Cold-Start: This is the task of predicting user interest in commenting on a new article with no existing comments. Articles are split into 5 folds. For each fold in turn, we remove all comments on the articles in that fold forming the test-set and keep the other folds as training-set. The models are fitted on the training set and tested on within-fold articles (same for each users).

---

[6]dailymail.co.uk/sport

Table 1: **AUC for recommending comment-worthy articles (higher is better). CCTM outperforms CTR & TagCF in both warm (14% better) and cold start (18% better). † means statistical significance over baselines, at 1% using paired t-test. CoTM is a content-only restriction of proposed CCTM (see section 5.2.1 for details).**

Dataset	Warm-Start				Cold-Start			
	TagCF	CTR	CoTM	CCTM	TagCF	CTR	CoTM	CCTM
DailyMail	0.723	0.739	0.767	**0.860**†	0.601	0.693	0.725	**0.751**†
ATScience	0.658	0.643	0.628	**0.723**†	0.555	0.572	0.620	**0.646**†
ATGadgets	0.635	0.636	0.615	**0.721**†	0.514	0.571	0.602	**0.622**†

5.2.4 Evaluation

We perform our evaluation broadly on two aspects. First we validate CCTM's ability to model correspondence between articles and comments. Then, we focus on the main task of the paper, to recommend comment-worthy articles. For the second task, each model is allowed to present (hypothetically) each user with a ranked list of articles for commenting in the test set. The quality of the ranking thus presented is evaluated for each user through AUC (Area Under ROC Curve) metric [9], using the articles in the held-out set that the user actually commented on. AUC $\in (0,1]$, measures the probability that a randomly chosen article on which user commented is ranked higher than one he didn't comment on. Eventually we averaged the AUC score for each user to get an overall performance score.

5.3 Evaluating content correspondence

Ability to effectively model correspondence relationship between the content of an article and its comments is crucial in detecting commenting interests of users. We first evaluate the ability of CCTM to model this aspect. For this purpose, we randomly select 20% articles in each dataset as test articles and remove all comments on the articles. The model is then fitted on the remaining set of article-comments, and the perplexity [11] of comment words in test-set is evaluated. We compare with CorrLDA [11], which also models correspondence but ignores specificity and user information. CCTM achieved perplexity measure (lower is better) of **459** (Daily-Mail), **998** (AT-Science), **843** (ATGadgets); while CorrLDA achieved 647 (DailyMail), 1324 (ATScience), 1100 (ATGadgets). This shows that CCTM is a better model of comment-content and article-comment correspondence.

5.4 Evaluating recommendations

We now evaluate CCTM on the main objective of recommending *comment-worthy* articles. Table 1 shows the performance for both warm-start and cold-start conditions. Under warm-start condition, note that a content-only approach (CoTM) gives almost similar performance to TagCF and state-of-art hybrid method CTR. This shows the importance of leveraging prior *comment-content* and article content through topic profiles. CCTM, by modeling *commenting interests* of users through content-driven profiles, gives significant improvements over all of these methods on all the datasets, showing that modeling commenting interest of users explicitly is crucial to generate relevant recommendations for commenting.

Cold-start recommendation is a much harder problem, as evinced by the relatively lower AUC values of all models. As explained earlier, TagCF particularly suffers in cold-start, with performance only slightly better than random guessing. Whereas the content-only approach (CoTM) it-

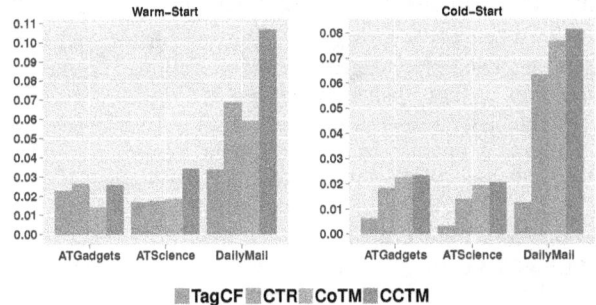

Figure 3: **Average reciprocal Hit-Rank@5. CCTM is 165% better (average) than [1, 2]**

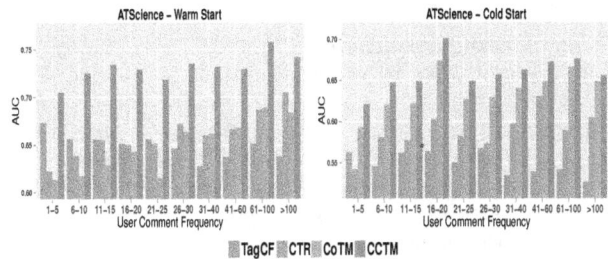

Figure 4: **AUC by users' comment frequency.**

self gives significant gains over CTR and TagCF. CoTM gives almost similar performance for both warm-start and cold-start which is expected as it is a content-only approach. Performance is further improved through CCTM which uses a latent offset to model user profile. Note, the only difference in this scenario between CoTM and CCTM is the presence of a latent-offset in user topic profile.

5.5 Evaluating quality of ranking

To test which model ranks comment-worthy articles much higher in the ranked list of articles, we evaluate *average reciprocal hit-rank* (HR). Given a list of M ranked articles for user i with n_i test comments, let $c_1, c_2, \ldots, c_h$ denote the ranks of h articles in $[M]$ on which the user actually commented. HR is then defined as $\frac{1}{n_i} \sum_{t=1}^{h} \frac{1}{c_t}$ and tests whether top ranked articles are correct. Fig. 3 shows the results for both warm and cold start with $M = 5$, a realistic scenario where users can only be shown 5 articles. CCTM is significantly better than CTR and TagCF in both warm (**80%** better) and cold-start (**250%** better), establishing that relevant articles are ranked much higher. TagCF performs similar to CTR for warm-start but suffers severely in cold-start.

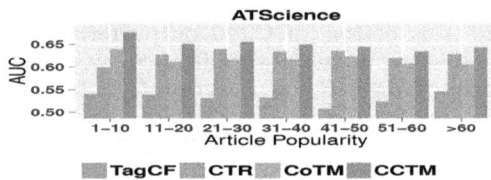

Figure 5: AUC by article's commenting popularity.

5.6 Evaluation in sparse commenting scenario

Ability of CCTM to model comment content and users latent interests should give CCTM advantage in extreme conditions such as when a user has made few comments or an article has received very few comments so far. We evaluate our approach on such cases here. In the following, we focus on ATScience, other results are similar (see supplementary).

Recommending to tail users.

In Fig. 4 we study performance by number of comments made by users in the training data. CCTM is superior in performance for all kinds of users and largest improvements are observed for tail-users, i.e. users with 1-5 comments in the training data. This shows that modeling commenting interests gives significant information about a user's commenting activity with as few as 5 comments made by the user.

Recommending tail articles.

We group articles by comment volume in training data (for warm-start) and evaluate AUC for each group. Average across these groups is the *stratified AUC* metric [1]. Fig. 5 shows the results. While CCTM is substantial superior throughout, largest improvements are observed for tail-articles, i.e. articles with 1-10 comments in the training data. This shows that modeling commenting interests gives significant information about users commenting activity with as few as 10 comments received on the article. CCTM is also substantially superior to the content-only model (CoTM) in this respect. CoTM, performs better than CTR for tail-items but worse for highly popular items. CTR's performance improves over CoTM for popular articles, showing that collaborative information dominates for high comment-volume, but CCTM is still significantly better than either.

6. CONCLUSIONS

We study a novel problem of eliciting *content-driven* user profiles to recommend articles which are *comment-worthy* of a particular user. We propose a novel hierarchical Bayesian model CCTM to solve this problem and demonstrate significant advancement in generating comment-worthy recommendations over state of art recommendation systems [1, 2], on three real life datasets using various metrics. There are many avenues for future work – incorporating comment sentiment, users' social information, modeling temporal nature of commenting preferences, and developing distributed and streaming inference [13] for web-scale deployment.

7. ACKNOWLEDGMENTS

We are thankful to all the reviewers for their valuable comments. The authors were partially supported by DST grant (DST/ECA/CB/1101).

References

[1] E. Shmueli, A. Kagian, Y. Koren, and R. Lempel. Care to comment?: Recommendations for commenting on news stories. In *WWW*, pages 429–438. ACM, 2012.

[2] C. Wang and D. Blei. Collaborative topic modeling for recommending scientific articles. In *SIGKDD*, pages 448–456. ACM, 2011.

[3] R. Kant, S. Sengamedu, and K. Kumar. Comment spam detection by sequence mining. In *WSDM*, pages 183–192. ACM, 2012.

[4] Z. Ma, A. Sun, Q. Yuan, and G. Cong. Topic-driven reader comments summarization. In *CIKM*, pages 265–274. ACM, 2012.

[5] D. Agarwal, B. Chen, and B. Pang. Personalized recommendation of user comments via factor models. In *EMNLP*, pages 571–582. ACL, 2011.

[6] Q. Li, J. Wang, Y. Chen, and Z. Lin. User comments for news recommendation in forum-based social media. *Information Sciences*, 180(24):4929–4939, 2010.

[7] M. Das, T. Bansal, and C. Bhattacharyya. Going beyond Corr-LDA for detecting specific comments on news & blogs. In *WSDM*, pages 483–492. ACM, 2014.

[8] R. Salakhutdinov and A. Mnih. Probabilistic matrix factorization. In *NIPS*, pages 1257–1264, 2007.

[9] S. Rendle, C. Freudenthaler, Z. Gantner, and L. Schmidt-Thieme. BPR: Bayesian personalized ranking from implicit feedback. In *UAI*, pages 452–461. AUAI Press, 2009.

[10] J. Liu, P. Dolan, and E. Pedersen. Personalized news recommendation based on click behavior. In *IUI*, pages 31–40. ACM, 2010.

[11] D. Blei and M. Jordan. Modeling annotated data. In *SIGIR*, pages 127–134. ACM, 2003.

[12] J. Wang, C. Yu, P. Yu, B. Liu, and W. Meng. Diversionary comments under political blog posts. In *CIKM*, pages 1789–1793. ACM, 2012.

[13] A. Ahmed, Y. Low, M. Aly, V. Josifovski, and A. Smola. Scalable distributed inference of dynamic user interests for behavioral targeting. In *SIGKDD*, pages 114–122. ACM, 2011.

[14] T. Zhao, N. Bian, C. Li, and M. Li. Topic-level expert modeling in community question answering. In *SDM*, pages 776–784. SIAM, 2013.

[15] X. Su and T. Khoshgoftaar. A survey of collaborative filtering techniques. *Advances in artificial intelligence*, 2009:4, 2009.

[16] F. Ricci, L. Rokach, and B. Shapira. *Introduction to recommender systems handbook*. Springer, 2011.

[17] L. Charlin, R. Zemel, and H. Larochelle. Leveraging user libraries to bootstrap collaborative filtering. In *SIGKDD*, pages 173–182. ACM, 2014.

[18] H. Ishwaran and L. James. Gibbs sampling methods for stick-breaking priors. *Journal of the American Statistical Association*, 96(453):161–173, 2001.

[19] W. Neiswanger, C. Wang, Q. Ho, and E. Xing. Modeling citation networks using latent random offsets. In *UAI*, 2014.

[20] Y. Hu, Y. Koren, and C. Volinsky. Collaborative filtering for implicit feedback datasets. In *ICDM*, pages 263–272. IEEE, 2008.

[21] S. Rendle and L. Schmidt-Thieme. Pairwise interaction tensor factorization for personalized tag recommendation. In *WSDM*, pages 81–90. ACM, 2010.

[22] A. Ahmed, B. Kanagal, S. Pandey, V. Josifovski, L. Pueyo, and J. Yuan. Latent factor models with additive and hierarchically-smoothed user preferences. In *WSDM*, pages 385–394. ACM, 2013.

[23] L. Hong, A. Doumith, and B. Davison. Co-factorization machines: modeling user interests and predicting individual decisions in Twitter. In *WSDM*, pages 557–566. ACM, 2013.

Selection and Ordering of Linear Online Video Ads

Wreetabrata Kar
Adobe Research
Adobe
345 Park Avenue
San Jose, 95110, U.S.A.
wkar@adobe.com

Viswanathan
Swaminathan
Adobe Research
Adobe
345 Park Avenue
San Jose, 95110, U.S.A.
vishy@adobe.com

Paulo Albuquerque
Insead
Boulevard de Constance
77305 Fontainebleau, France
paulo.albuquerque@insead.edu

ABSTRACT

This paper studies the selection and ordering of in-stream ads in videos shown in online content publishers. We propose an allocation algorithm that uses a collective measure of price and quality for each ad and factors in slot-specific continuation probabilities to maximize publisher revenue. The algorithm is based on cascade models and uses a dynamic programming method to assign linear (video) ads to slots in an online video. The approach accounts for the negative externality created by lower quality ads placed in a video, leading to viewer exit and thereby preventing the publisher from showing the subsequent ads scheduled in that session. Our algorithm is scalable and suited for real-time applications. A large log of viewer activity from a video ad platform is used to empirically test the algorithm. A series of simulations show that our algorithm, when compared to other algorithms currently practiced in industry, generates more revenue for the publisher and increases viewer retention.

Categories and Subject Descriptors

Information systems [**World Wide Web**]: Online advertising; Theory of computation [**Algorithm design techniques**]: [dynamic programming]; Information systems applications [**Multimedia information systems**]: [Multimedia streaming]

Keywords

Linear online video ads; Revenue maximization; Viewer retention; Dynamic program; Scalable real-time algorithm.

1. INTRODUCTION

In this paper, we study the linear ad allocation problem in an online video. A linear ad is an in-stream interactive advertising medium, in which the ads appear before, during, and after an online video. According to the 2013 annual revenue report from the Interactive Advertising Bureau, digital video has grown into a $2.8 billion industry and remains the

RecSys'15, September 16–20, 2015, Vienna, Austria.
ⓒ 2015 ACM. ISBN 978-1-4503-3692-5/15/09 ...$15.00.
DOI: http://dx.doi.org/10.1145/2792838.2800194.

one of the fastest growing format of the display market [1]. The rise of online video has motivated the rapid growth of video ads in this medium.

We approach the allocation process of linear ads by considering the externality that each ad imposes on subsequent ads. An inferior ad can make the viewer leave the session or even the publisher's site or application [2]. This externality on the publisher reduces the opportunities to show ads because unlike other types of in-stream ads, like overlay and companion ads, linear ads interrupt the video. When a viewer quits a session due to linear ad, subsequent ads in that video are not watched and need to be rescheduled to a different video session. Therefore, decisions related to the choice and positioning of ads in these videos should account for this externality.

In this paper we propose an algorithm that selects and orders linear ads for a video session through a dynamic programming approach that accounts for ad prices, ad quality, and externalities from other ads. Our algorithm also considers the slot-specific continuation probabilities, i.e. the effect of slot (or the position of the ad in the video) on viewer retention. It is assumed that ads are non-skippable and each slot has only one ad. The objective of this algorithm is to select ads for each slot so that publisher revenue is maximized and retention is increased. Our paper is the first empirical work on the ad allocation problem in linear ads. Methodologically, we contribute to the existing body of work on Internet ads, by proposing an algorithm that accounts for slot-specific continuation probabilities, but still maintains a compute-time and scalability fit for real-time applications.

We apply the proposed approach to data from a video ad platform that manages the selection and positioning of ads for online video publishers. A series of simulations are done to determine the effectiveness of the proposed algorithm over the existing system. We show that our algorithm improves the revenue of the publisher by nearly 9% compared to alternative common practices and increases average retention in the video by nearly 14%.

The paper continues with a literature review in Section 2. The description of the industry and dataset is presented in Section 3; Section 4 explains the ad allocation model and the dynamic programming algorithm, Section 5 discusses the relative performance of our algorithm compared to other methods, and Section 6 concludes.

2. RELATED WORK

In the last two decades, there has been substantial volume of work done on online advertising, particularly in revenue management through ad allocation. In sponsored search, advertisers participate in auctions for slots and search engines use these bids to allocate slots [2, 3, 4, 5, 6, 7]. A comprehensive summary of sponsored search auctions could be found in Qin *et al.* [8]. Methods have also been explored to optimize allocation with respect to target number of impressions for each ad, by using linear programming [9, 10] or dynamic programming [11, 12, 13]. Further, authors have proposed ad allocation algorithms along with new pricing structures, for broadcasting media and online media [12, 13, 14, 15, 16].

In order to measure ad quality, which affects the efficiency of allocation, researchers have suggested using click-through rates as a metric of ad quality, and consequently proposed showing online ads based on the decreasing order of the product of bid values and click-through rates [17, 18, 19, 20]. Other measures of ad quality have been conversion rate and bounce rate [21]. Since none of these measures of quality are known *a priori*, scheduling ads must balance exploration with exploitation [22]. With the probability of clicks or conversions being very low in video ads, few recent papers have explored statistical models based on logistic regressions to evaluate ad quality of video ads [2, 23, 24, 25].

Besides its own quality, an ad in a video session is also affected by the externality imposed by other ads shown before it. Kempe and Mahdian, in [12], and Aggarwal *et al.*, in [13], addressed this issue by extending the work of Craswell *et al.*, in [26], on cascade models and proposed a theoretical cascade model for search advertising that accounts for price bids and externalities created by the ad quality on total viewership. In their models, they design an optimal algorithm to assign the ads to different slots of sponsored search through a dynamic program where a viewer makes independent decisions with ad specific probabilities whether to continue scanning or to exit. But the optimality of the above algorithms is lost when slot-specific effects on viewer retention are considered. A similar problem is studied by Wilbur *et al.* in the context of television, where they solve the assignment of TV ads in a commercial break for heterogeneous viewer segments to maximize the audience value to the advertiser [2]. However, this algorithm cannot be implemented for real-time applications.

More recently, models proposing contextual advertising, and calculating optimal number of ad slots in online videos have been studied [27, 28]. In this paper we assume slots are pre-determined by publishers. We extend the analytical work on cascade models in sponsored search to an allocation algorithm for linear ads in digital videos. Our work adds to this literature by proposing a real-time, scalable algorithm which accounts for slot-specific ad tune-away propensities along with ad prices, ad quality and the externality experienced by each ad from other ads.

3. DATASET AND ANALYSIS

With the significant growth in viewership of digital content, linear ads have become a major source of revenue for online publishers. These ads are generally shown at the beginning of the video (pre-roll), during the video (mid-roll), or at the end of the video (post-roll). The position of an ad in a particular video becomes very significant as the rate of completion of the ad vary based on the slot in which it is placed. Although absent in our data set, each break can have multiple ads for some publishers.

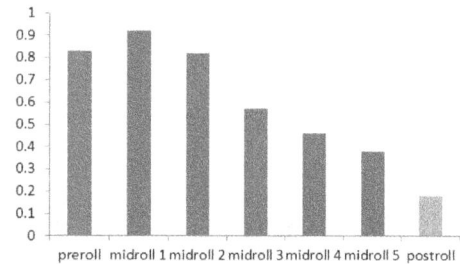

Figure 1: Completion Rate by Ad Position.

Traditionally, the target impressions for an ad is determined by dividing the budget of the ad campaign (set by the advertiser) with the cost per mille (one thousand) impressions or CPM (set by negotiation between publisher and advertiser). An advertiser, at a premium, also has the option of selecting priority levels, where an ad with higher priority gets higher preference in selection and slot-positions in a video session.

There are often intermediate video ad platforms who embed and select ads in the video stream for different publishers, and are also responsible for meeting the target impressions for each ad. Our data comes from one such video ad platforms. The data has information on viewer activity during linear ads shown in online videos on a popular publisher. We use log data collected over a period of one month, with the volume of the data running into billion of events per day.

In our dataset, we chose ads for which we have complete information. We further restrict our data set to heavy users who has at least 10 sessions per month and a maximum of 20 sessions per day. This kind of selection also helped us to create state dependence variables for each user, which we use in calculating ad quality. We limit the dataset to the US viewers given that this was the largest geographic group in our dataset. With this selection, we have 19 ads shown in 19.09 million video sessions accessed by 650,000 users.

Figure 1 shows the slot-specific continuation probabilities for the ads in our data set and highlights an interesting viewing behavior. The continuation rates of ads in pre-roll (83%) is less than that in the first mid-roll (92%). However after the first mid-roll, the continuation rates monotonically decrease, almost linearly, until the post-roll (19%), where there is a sharp decline. Thus the effect of slot on continuation becomes an important factor in the measurement of ad quality. We note that there is a selection issue since a viewer can only reach a mid-roll ad if she has watched the pre-roll ad. Similar selection issue stands for post-roll ads.

For each ad placed in a video, we have information on video characteristics (genre, duration), ad characteristics (industry of the advertiser, duration), session characteristics (when the video was viewed, weekday/weekend, whether the ad was clicked on, slot of the ad) and viewer characteristics (how many times a viewer has watched the ad before, and ad viewing propensity). We utilize this information to construct a quality measure of an ad based on viewer retention. This measure, called the *continuation rate*, is defined as the probability that a viewer will watch an ad completely and will continue to the rest of the video [2, 24]. Continuation rate of an ad is estimated by an econometric model proposed in Kar *et al.* [24], where along with the ad-intrinsic

Ads	CPM (in $)	Cont. Rates
Ad 1	59	0.68
Ad 2	150	0.71
Ad 3	83	0.72
Ad 4	90	0.75
Ad 5	120	0.76
Ad 6	60	0.79
Ad 7	48	0.83
Ad 8	158	0.84
Ad 9	59	0.85
Ad 10	113	0.86
Ad 11	105	0.87
Ad 12	90	0.87
Ad 13	48	0.88
Ad 14	143	0.89
Ad 15	128	0.90
Ad 16	135	0.91
Ad 17	120	0.92
Ad 18	120	0.92
Ad 19	128	0.94

Note: Real CPMs have been scaled for data confidentiality.

Table 1: Ad Characteristics.

features, factors like video characteristics, ad characteristics, session information, and viewer behavior are factored in to create the quality metric. In Table 1, we show the CPM of the ads and their estimated continuation rates. Constructing ad continuation rates specific to users and videos would further enrich the efficiency of our proposed algorithm and could be pursued in future research.

Please note that the dataset has some limitations: it is limited regarding viewer demographics, capturing only geographical information and the platform (e.g., Windows, Mac OS, etc.). Further, the data in our sample covers only those videos in which ads cannot be skipped and where users cannot start a video from the middle without going through the pre-roll. Finally, in our sample data we observe that, on an average, fifteen percent of viewers have watched only one video in fifteen days. We overcome this limitation by restricting our data to only heavy users.

4. AD SELECTION MODEL

In our framework, we have three agents: the viewer, the advertisers, and the publisher. Once a video is selected by a viewer, the publisher's decision is to define the number and position of the slots in that video, and choose ads to show in those slots. The viewer's decision is whether or not to watch through an ad and continue to the rest of the video. A publisher chooses ads from a set of N ads to display in J slots in an online video session (assume, without loss of generality $N \geq J$). Linear ads could be placed in slots before, during, or at the end of a video. Each advertiser i - with a certain campaign budget - negotiates with the publisher a CPM, b_i, for its ad a_i and also a target number of times t_i that the ad needs to be shown. Therefore $b_i \times t_i$ is the campaign budget of the advertiser. Any ad shown beyond the target impressions is not paid by the advertiser. The publisher's revenue from each video comes from the cumulative price of the ads watched by the viewer in the video. In our model, each ad, a_i, has a continuation rate c_i. If the viewer decides not to watch the ad, she starts a different video or moves to a different website, with a probability of $1 - c_i$.

In our model, we assume the following:

1. Each video starts with a pre-roll ad and ends with a post-roll ad, with one or more mid-roll ads in between.

2. The model assumes that none of the ads can be skipped.

3. The model also assumes that only one ad is placed in each slot.

4. The viewer decides to continue watching the video beyond this ad with a probability c_i;

5. In addition to a continuation rate (c_i) of an ad, the retention is significantly affected depending on the slot the ad is placed (as shown in Figure 1). To account for this, we assume that there is a slot-specific continuation probability. This probability represented as λ_j, for slot j, is independent of the quality of the ad in that slot. Since ad continuation rates (c_i) are not calculated specific to slots, we need these slot-specific continuation probabilities (λ_j) to scale each c_i and to form continuation rates of ads specific to each slot.

4.1 Publisher's Revenue Maximization Problem

We build our model as a cascade model [12, 13, 26]. Cascade models have been previously used to solve ad assignment problems in search ads. In both search ads and linear ads, a publisher is trying to determine which ads to pick and in what sequence to show them.

We first illustrate how the expected revenue is calculated with two ads in a video and then extend that to a generic form. Let a_i and $a_{i'}$ be two ads selected for two consecutive slots in a video. The CPM and continuation rates of each ad is given by (b_i, c_i) and $(b_{i'}, c_{i'})$. For each slot j, the slot-specific continuation probability is λ_j. The expected revenue from ad a_i in slot 1 would be $b_i.c_i.\lambda_1$. For the second slot, the expected revenue from ad $a_{i'}$ is also influenced by the probability of reaching that slot, given by the continuation rate of ad a_i. So the overall expected revenue from second slot is $b_{i'}.c_{i'}.c_i.\lambda_2$. Therefore the total expected revenue from ads a_i and $a_{i'}$ placed consecutively in the first two slots is given by $b_i.c_i.\lambda_1 + b_{i'}.c_{i'}c_i.\lambda_2$. In a generic form, given an assignment $(a_1, ..., a_j)$ of ads to J slots, the overall expected revenue is given by:

$$R = b_1.c_1.\lambda_1 + b_2.c_2.c_1.\lambda_2 + ... + b_j.c_j.c_{j-1}...c_1.\lambda_j. \quad (1)$$

As shown in Equation 1, the probability of reaching a slot j is affected by the continuation rates of the previous ads. We express this as a *Cascade Probability* for slot j, i.e.

$$C_j = \prod_{i=1}^{j-1} c_i, \quad (2)$$

where c_i is the estimated continuation probability of ad a_i and C_j is the estimated cascade probability of reaching slot j starting from slot 1. In order to maximize revenue, the publisher has the following objective function:

$$max \left(\sum_{j=1}^{J} b_i^j.c_i^j.C_j.\lambda_j \right) \ subject \ to \ \sum_{1}^{t-1} n(a_i) < t_i. \quad (3)$$

At each slot j, b_i^j - the price b_i for ad a_i placed in slot j, is scaled by three factors: c_i^j (which is the continuation rate c_i of ad a_i placed in slot j), the slot-specific continuation probability (λ_j) and a cascade probability C_j carried over from the ads shown before it. An ad a_i is valid for selection at time t only when the total number of impressions ($\sum_1^{t-1} n(a_i)$) shown for that ad till time $t-1$ has not reached the target impressions t_i as specified by the advertiser i. Since impressions shown beyond the target are not paid by the advertiser, the target impressions is used as a constraint for the revenue maximization function. To maximize this function, we require the values b_i, λ_j, c_i and C_j for each slot j. While b_i is decided through negotiation between the advertiser and the publisher; c_i and λ_j are estimated from log data of viewer activity; and C_j is calculated from the product of continuation rates (c_i) of ads placed before slot j.

In our model the revenue function, as described in Equation 3, is dependent on the characteristics of the ad as well as on the slot-specific continuation rates. We solve the revenue maximization problem in two stages:

Stage 1: We consider the case where the slot-specific probability (λ_j) is linearly decreasing in j. Under this restrictive assumption, we find an optimal solution to the maximize revenue by using a dynamic programming algorithm.

Stage 2: We relax the assumption that slot-specific continuation probabilities linearly decrease as the video session progresses. We assume that the slot-specific continuation probability increases from pre-roll to the first mid-roll, and decreases linearly after that (see Figure 1). Further, we give a near-optimal heuristic solution to the revenue maximization problem.

4.2 Dynamic Programming for Linearly Decreasing λ

Before we describe the algorithm, we describe some properties of the optimal assignment.

4.2.1 Linearly Decreasing λ

As shown in Figure 1, other than the pre-roll, the retention in ads drops almost linearly through the mid-roll till it reaches the post-roll. Let us assume that the retention is linearly decreasing across all the slots. This assumption allows us to create a constant, α, which is the ratio between the slot-specific continuation probability of the next slot compared to the present slot, i.e. $\alpha = \lambda_{j+1}/\lambda_j$.

4.2.2 Slot-adjusted CPM

Extending the proposal given by Aggarwal *et al.* [13], we further define a *slot-adjusted CPM* for each ad a_i, which is expressed as $\frac{b_i.c_i}{1-\alpha.c_i}$. Intuitively, it is the price of the impression multiplied by the inverse of the negative effect of the ad. Therefore, slot-adjusted CPM is a combined measure of price and quality of the ad. We explain the importance of this quantity through *Lemma 1*.

Lemma 1: In the most efficient assignment, the selected ads are placed in the decreasing order of slot-adjusted CPM ($\frac{b_i.c_i}{1-\alpha.c_i}$), where $\alpha = \frac{\lambda_{j+1}}{\lambda_j}$ and $\alpha \in (0,1]$.[1]

---

[1] Aggarwal *et al.* [13] proposed that selected ads are placed in the decreasing order of ($\frac{b_i.c_i}{1-c_i}$) under efficient assignment. However, this order does not account for slot-specific continuation probability (λ_j). Once λ_j is considered, the order does not hold when extended to more than two ads.

Proof: Suppose that the optimal assignment is (a_i, $a_{i'}$). The CPM and continuation rates of each ad is given by (b_i, c_i) and ($b_{i'} c_{i'}$); and the slot-specific continuation probabilities are λ_1, λ_2. The corresponding expected revenue, as explained in Equation 1, is given by

$$R = b_i.c_i.\lambda_1 + b_{i'}.c_{i'}.c_i.\lambda_2.$$

Since the above arrangement is optimal, then the alternate sequence, i.e. where ad $a_{i'}$ is shown before ad a_i would generate a sub-optimal revenue (R').

$$R' = b_{i'}.c_{i'}.\lambda_1 + b_i.c_i.c_{i'}.\lambda_2.$$

Since $R \geq R'$, algebraic manipulation yields,

$$\Rightarrow \frac{b_i.c_i}{\lambda_1 - \lambda_2.c_i} \geq \frac{b_{i'}.c_{i'}}{\lambda_1 - \lambda_2.c_{i'}}. \tag{4}$$

Dividing both sides of Equation 4 by λ_1, implies

$$\frac{b_i.c_i}{1 - (\lambda_2/\lambda_1).c_i} \geq \frac{b_{i'}.c_{i'}}{1 - (\lambda_2/\lambda_1).c_i}. \tag{5}$$

Since the ratio of λ_{j+1}/λ_j will vary between every pair of slots, the above order between two ads cannot be generalized to all ads in J slots.

But if we assume that the continuation rates are decreasing linearly across the slots, then λ_{j+1}/λ_j is a constant. Let $\alpha = \lambda_{j+1}/\lambda_j$.

Substituting α in Equation 5, implies

$$\frac{b_i.c_i}{1 - \alpha.c_i} \geq \frac{b_{i'}.c_{i'}}{1 - \alpha.c_{i'}}. \tag{6}$$

This assumption of linearity allows us to extend the above order between a pair of ads to any number of ads in our inventory, i.e. for J chosen ads the following relationship would be maintained: $\frac{b_1.c_1}{1-\alpha.c_1} > ... > \frac{b_j.c_j}{1-\alpha.c_j}$. $\square$

Lemma 1 ensures that an ad with higher slot-adjusted CPM will always come before an ad with lower slot-adjusted CPM under the most efficient assignment. This property helps to reduce the number of combinations of ads to be compared to find the optimal allocation. Thus, Lemma 1 provides an important simplification to the algorithm needed to solve Equation 3. However, Lemma 1 does not tell us which ads to choose. Selecting top J ads from the decreasing order of slot-adjusted CPMs would not necessarily give the optimal assignment, as that selection does not account for the externalities imposed on an ad by ads shown before it.

4.2.3 Dominance of CPM

Usual allocation of linear ads in online video is based on a simple ranking system, i.e. an ad a_i dominates ad $a_{i'}$ over a specific slot j, by having a higher CPM, i.e. ad a_i will always appear whenever ad $a_{i'}$ appears and in an earlier position. However as shown in Lemma 1, whether an ad a_i is shown before $a_{i'}$ will also depend on the order of the slot-adjusted CPM. So higher CPM alone is not sufficient to guarantee selection and an earlier slot. But, as proved in Aggarwal et al (2008), if a_i has a higher CPM as well as a higher slot-adjusted CPM then it does ensure the selection and positioning of a_i before $a_{i'}$. So an ad a_i is dominant over ad $a_{i'}$ when both $b_i > b_{i'}$ and $\frac{b_i.c_i}{1-\alpha.c_i} \geq \frac{b_{i'}.c_{i'}}{1-\alpha.c_{i'}}$.

4.2.4 Publisher's Revenue Maximization Algorithm

To maximize publisher's revenue from a video session, a dynamic programming method is used, which finds the optimal allocation by iterating over all possible combinations after arranging ads according to decreasing order of slot-adjusted CPM. Given N ads and J slots, the problem of assigning ads to slots translates to a problem of optimal selection of J ads out of N. This problem boils down to selecting ads based on whether the selection improves the total revenue.

First, we sort ads according to slot-adjusted CPM as described in Lemma 1. Let $R[i, j]$ be the optimal solution (the maximum expected revenue) of assigning ads from the set $\{a_i, a_{i+1}, ..., a_N\}$ ads into slots $j, j+1, .., J$, where $1 \leq i \leq N$ and $1 \leq j \leq J$. The dynamic program is solved in a backward recursive way. If ad a_i has been selected in slot j, then the optimal value of $R[i, j]$ accrues values from ad a_i as well as from the ads in the subsequent slots. Otherwise, $R[i, j]$ should be assigned the value of $R[i + 1, j]$. Assuming that $R[i+1, j]$ is computed optimally, $R[i, j]$ would also yield the optimal value. So, $R[i, j]$ can be recursively defined as

$$R[i, j] = max \left\{ R[i+1, j], b_i.c_i.\lambda_j + R[i+1, j+1].c_i \right\}. \tag{7}$$

The above recursive equation represents an optimal selection of J ads. For $N = J$, there is only one selection possible - all ads must be selected. For $N > J$, for each i and j, $R[i, j]$ can be computed based on whether the selection of ad a_i in slot j increases the total value. So, a_i should be selected in slot j if $b_i.c_i.\lambda_j + c_i.R[i+1, j+1]$ has higher value than $R[i+1, j]$. On the other hand, if $R[i+1, j]$ is greater that signifies that an ad which is lower in the order is adding more value to the allocation - therefore ad a_i must not be selected for slot j. Since this recursive function is solved backwards, the maximum expected revenue is given by the entry in $R[1, 1]$.

While the R matrix stores the maximum expected revenue for every ad-slot combination, it does not store the ad allocation. For that we define a selection matrix S with dimensions $i \times j$ where each cell represents whether ad a_i is a viable candidate for selection in slot j. If ad a_i could be selected in slot j, then $(S[i, j] = 1)$, otherwise $(S[i, j] = 0)$. Then, $S[i, j]$ can be defined as –

$$S[i, j] = \begin{cases} 1 & for\ all\ i\ and\ j\ if\ N == J \\ 1 & if\ b_i.c_i.\lambda_j + c_i.R[i+1, j+1] \geq R[i+1, j] \\ 0 & if\ R[i+1, j] > b_i.c_i.\lambda_j + c_i.R[i+1, j+1] \end{cases}. \tag{8}$$

Intuitively, an ad a_i is suitable for slot j, only if its inclusion in the ad sequence adds more to the accrued revenue (from ads in subsequent slots) than the revenue accrued at the $(i+1)^{th}$ position. Once $S_{i,j}$ is calculated for every ad-slot combination, we know which ads are viable for selection in each slot. Beginning with the first slot, we choose the one with the highest slot-adjusted CPM among all viable ads for each slot. Please note that once an ad has been chosen for any slot, it cannot be chosen again for any of the subsequent slots even if the selection matrix S shows it as a viable candidate for one or more of the following slots.

The above algorithm runs in time $O(n \log n + nj)$ and brings down the computational complexity from exponential $(O(n^j))$ to linear. As the dynamic programming uses a backward recursion, an ad could be selected for a slot only after the ads for subsequent slots have been selected. So the entire allocation needs to be done before the video is played, and thus the algorithm needs to be run in real-time.

4.3 Heuristic Algorithm for the Revenue Maximization Problem

In this section we consider an extension of the publisher's revenue maximization problem. Specifically, we relax the assumption that the slot-specific continuation probability is monotonically decreasing over the course of the video. This is a much harder problem to solve than what we addressed in Section 4.2. The key to solving the optimization problem in Section 4.2 was Lemma 1 which does not hold in this case (as α is no longer constant). As exhibited in Figure 1, the decreasing monotonicity is broken by the fact that the first mid-roll has a higher continuation probability than pre-roll.

However, we note that the mid-roll slots tend to exhibit decreasing monotonicity. This leads to a 2-step heuristic algorithm (2SHA) which we describe in more detail below. The basic idea is to first solve the sub-problem of which ads to place in the mid-roll slots. We will solve this problem by exploiting the decreasing monotonicity of the slot-specific probabilities in the mid-roll slots. Then in the second step, we find the best ads to show in the pre-roll and post-roll.

Step 1: Here we introduce a sub-problem that will aide us in selecting the mid-roll ads. Our original optimization problem is as shown in Equation 3. In our sub-problem, we define a new optimization problem as

$$max \left(\sum_{j=2}^{J-1} b_i^j.\lambda_j . \prod_{m=2}^{j} c_m^i \right), \tag{9}$$

where our decision variable is to allocate ads only in the mid-roll. Our approach is to use dynamic programming, in a way similar to Section 4.2.4.

We define the function a as the configuration of ads to be shown, i.e. a_j gives the ad that is shown in the jth slot of the video, for $j \in \{1, 2, \ldots, J\}$. Now we run the following sequence:

i. Let N be the set of all available ads and denote the configuration of this sub-problem as $a_s = \{a_2, \ldots, a_{j-1}\}$, and denote the set of all ads shown as $\mathcal{A} = \{a_2, \ldots, a_{j-1}\}$.

ii. Solve sub-problem again with $\mathcal{N} - \mathcal{A}$ ads and define the sequence of ads chosen as $a'_s = \{a'_2, \ldots, a'_j\}$, and let $\mathcal{A}' = \{a'_2, \ldots, a'_j\}$.

Step 2: With the selected allocation for mid-roll spots from Step 1, in this step we find the ads for pre-roll and post-roll as follows:

i. Exhaustively try all combinations of ads in pre-roll. For each ad a that is selected in the first slot (pre-roll), if $a \notin \mathcal{A}$ then the ad with maximum revenue in the set $\mathcal{N} - \mathcal{A} - \{a\}$ is assigned as a_j (post-roll ad), otherwise if $a \in \mathcal{A}$ then the ad with maximum revenue in the set $\mathcal{N} - \mathcal{A}' - \{a\}$ is assigned as a_j (post-roll ad).

ii. For every ad a in pre-roll, the configuration chosen is given by $(a, a_2, \ldots, a_{j-1}, a_j)$ if $a \notin \mathcal{A}$, otherwise the configuration is given by $(a, a'_2, \ldots, a'_{j-1}, a_j)$ if $a \in \mathcal{A}$, and denote the resulting expected revenue by R_a.

iii. Select the configuration with the maximum revenue.

4.4 Intuition

In Step 1 of 2SHA, we select the top two configurations (a_s and $a_{s'}$) for the mid-roll slots. Assuming there is a huge repository of ads, then the top two candidates should give similar expected revenue. Next, we exhaustively try all ads in pre-roll. For each ad that is selected in pre-roll, we use the configuration a_s in mid-rolls if possible. However, it might be possible that the ad that is selected for pre-roll has already been selected in mid-roll. In that case for mid-roll we choose to show the alternative configuration a'_s. This does not change the expected revenue significantly. Finally, in the last slot, from the ads which are not yet selected, we select the one that gives the maximum revenue, since the continuation probability at this point is irrelevant.

5. 2SHA PERFORMANCE

The primary objective of 2SHA was to maximize the expected revenue for the publisher and increase viewer retention. In this section, we present a series of simulations to assess the performance of 2SHA toward achieving these goals. To run the simulations we need the CPM of each ad, target impressions for each ad, continuation rates for each ad and the slot-specific continuation probabilities. Ad continuation rates and slot-specific continuation probabilities are estimated from our dataset; CPMs and target impressions are deduced from the data we have on advertisers' campaigns.

5.1 Comparing 2SHA to Enumeration

As explained in Section 4.3, 2SHA assumes that the slot-specific continuation probabilities are linearly decreasing in mid-rolls. This approximation will always provide an allocation whose expected revenue would be sub-optimal compared to the one where we enumerate over all possible combinations of ads. In this section we run simulations to see if the loss in having a sub-optimal allocation by 2SHA is substantial to render this algorithm ineffective. We also highlight how the computation time required to find the global maximum makes it impractical for real-time application.

To run this simulation, we set $J = 4, 5$ and the inventory of ads $N = 20, 25, 30$. We run 50 simulations for each combination of J and N where we vary the CPM of the ads between \$100 to \$500. In order to have a greater variance between retentive and less retentive ads, we vary the continuation rates between 0.5 and 0.95. The cost of finding the global optimum increases exponentially as we increase the slots (J) and inventory of ads (N). Therefore the comparison is made only for smaller values of J and N.

Table 2 shows that difference in average revenue between allocation by 2SHA and by enumeration is less than 5% in all the simulations. But most importantly when an ad inventory reaches 30, computation time by enumeration is to the order of one hour and thirty minutes and increases exponentially as J and N increase - which makes it infeasible for real-time application. However the computation time in 2SHA never exceeds 0.1 seconds on an Intel Core $i7$ 2.7 GHz processor with 16 GB RAM.

5.2 Comparing 2SHA to Other Alternatives

In this section, we compare 2SHA with two other methods. The objective of this simulation is to quantify the increase in revenue and audience retention by implementing 2SHA. The publisher has two goals to accomplish through the ad allocation process: monetization and audience retention. The former goal can be achieved by choosing the ad with highest CPM for a slot; and the later by choosing the ad with highest continuation rate for the slot. However these two goals can often be in conflict with each other and can be viewed as a trade-off. Ideally, to maximize revenue, the publisher would want the trade-off between these two goals to change as the video progresses. At the beginning of the video, retention is most important and toward the end of the video monetization is more critical. The dynamic program in 2SHA ensures that the best possible trade-off is made in selecting ad in every slot. The two alternatives that we compare with 2SHA are:

i. *Sorting based on CPM*: In this method, ads are arranged according to the descending order of their CPMs and the publisher chooses the top J ads to fill the slots in a video session. The objective behind this method is to maximize the immediate revenue available from a single slot by showing the ad with the highest CPM first. This method completely ignores the continuation rates of the selected ads. In this situation, it is possible that an ad placed earlier on in the video has a low continuation probability and the viewer quits the video during that ad. Therefore the publisher might maximize revenue from that particular slot, but might lose overall revenue expected from ads in the subsequent slots. This is the most common method practiced in this industry.

ii. *Sorting based on Slot-Adjusted CPM*: In this paper we have defined slot-adjusted CPM as $\frac{b_i c_i}{1 - \alpha . c_i}$ which is a collective measure of the price and the quality of the ad. In this rule, the ads are sorted based on slot-adjusted CPM and the top J ads are selected for J slots in a video session. This method provides a trade-off between monetization and retention, but the trade-off does not change as the video progresses.

5.2.1 Simulation Characteristics

To compare the three algorithms described above, we run the following simulation 100 times. For each simulation, we assume that the publisher needs to design an allocation of ads for 50 video sessions. Each video session is assumed to have 5 slots and in each slot only one ad can be inserted. Showing the same ad more than once is not allowed within a video session, maintaining conformity with the publisher's practice. With 50 video sessions and 5 spots in each session, publisher now has the opportunity to show 250 impressions. We choose a cumulative target impressions for the focal 19 ads as 300. Individual target impression of these ads are computed from the original ratios between target impressions of these ads as provided in the data. The total target has been set as 300 so that during allocation the individual target of some of the ads are reached and thereby identical sets of ads are not selected for all video sessions. For 2SHA, we also need to have an estimate of α - the factor by which the slot-specific continuation rates decreases in consecutive mid-rolls. For our algorithm, we use $\alpha = 0.8$ which was calculated from the ratios of the mean drop in viewer population during successive mid-rolls in our data. The CPMs and ad continuation rates used for these 19 ads are the ones presented in Table 1. For every ad in a video session, we randomly draw from uniform distribution $[0, 1]$ to simulate the continuation rate for a viewer to continue with the ad. If the simulated rate is higher than the estimated ad continuation rate, the viewer exits the session.

5.2.2 Simulation Results

Three algorithms were compared: sorting based on CPM, sorting based on slot-adjusted CPM, and 2SHA. Table 3

N	J	Opt. Ave. Rev. ($)	Opt. Ave. Run-time (secs)	2SHA Ave. Rev. ($)	2SHA Ave. Run-time (secs)
20	4	777 (21)	26 (1.2)	743 (15.3)	0.01 (0.002)
20	5	832 (13.5)	737 (3.8)	793 (12.9)	0.01 (0.003)
25	4	763 (9.8)	107 (2.6)	739 (14.7)	0.02 (0.005)
25	5	822 (16.9)	2303 (7.9)	803 (17.2)	0.04 (0.005)
30	4	768 (15.4)	133 (2.67)	755 (10.4)	0.06 (0.006)
30	5	836 (11.3)	5713 (8.1)	815 (10.6)	0.07 (0.005)

Note: Standard deviations are shown in parenthesis.

Table 2: Comparing 2SHA Performance to Enumeration.

Algorithm	Selection Criterion	Average Rev.($)	Average % Retn.
Sort by CPM	Order by CPM b_i. Select top j ads.	9827 (583)	38 (8.90)
Sort by Slot-Adjusted CPM	Order by $\frac{b_i \cdot c_i}{(1-\alpha \cdot c_i)}$, Select top j ads.	9058 (449)	39 (12.7)
2SHA	Order by $\frac{b_i \cdot c_i}{(1-\alpha \cdot c_i)}$, Run DP.	10761(497)	44 (10.4)

Note: Standard deviations are shown in parenthesis.

Table 3: Relative Performance Metrics.

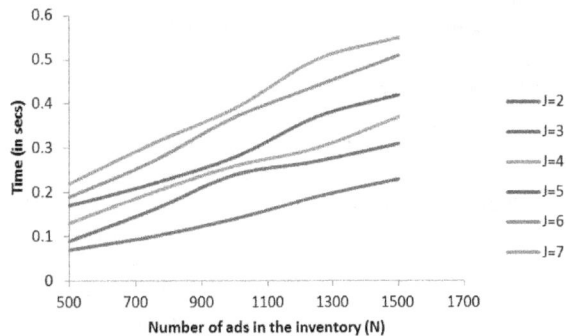

Figure 2: Computation Time for 2SHA.

presents the performance statistics of these algorithms in terms of publisher revenue and audience retention. Revenue is calculated by the sum of cpms of ads seen by viewers and retention is calculated by the ads seen divided by the ads scheduled. On average, 2SHA outperforms the other two algorithms, both in terms of revenue and viewer retention. Sorting based on slot-adjusted CPM does the worst in terms of revenue. This essentially shows that a constant trade-off between monetization and retention is not optimal and the weightage needs to shift from retention to monetization as the video progresses - as achieved by the dynamic program proposed in 2SHA. 2SHA generates 9% more average revenue and 14% more audience retention than the sorting based on CPM. This shows that maximizing revenue from each slot may not maximize overall revenue, and that the continuation rates of ads and their externality should be also considered for optimal allocation.

5.3 Feasibility of 2SHA

Table 3 shows that 2SHA generates more revenue and increases retention compared to the other algorithms investigated. However, unlike the other sorting based algorithms which are not iterative, 2SHA is more complex as it needs to explore several combinations of ads to find the optimal sequence. However, we claim that it is still suitable for real-time applications.

To prove this, we run simulations where we vary the number of ads (N) available for selection, and the number of slots (J) in a video and register the computation time for each simulation. We assume that on a daily basis, a publisher needs to select ads from an inventory that varies between 500 ads to 1500 ads. In our simulation we vary the number of slots from 2 to 7.

As shown in Figure 2, the computation time of 2SHA increases almost linearly with the number of ads (N) and in the number of slots (J). The results show that the maximum computation time registered is 0.55 secs which 2SHA

requires to find the allocation for 7 slots (J) from an inventory (N) of 1500 ads. Therefore we can see that 2SHA is highly scalable and well suited for real time applications.

6. CONCLUSION

Viewership of online video has grown tremendously in the last decade and linear ads have become a potential source of revenue. Our paper develops an allocation mechanism for linear ads in a single video session. For this allocation, we account for ad prices and target impressions provided by the advertisers. Subsequently, we estimate ad and slot-specific continuation rates from a large log dataset of viewer activity. We employ a cascade model in which our dynamic program accounts for slot-specific tune-away probabilities and proposes a scalable algorithm which would run in real-time.

Our results highlight several significant insights. We show that publishers, by accounting for externalities imposed by the ads, generate more revenue than their current practice of selecting based on decreasing order of CPM. In our method, the revenue is maximized by changing the trade-off between monetization and retention at every slot, i.e. placing highly retentive ads in the early slots and gradually shifting to costlier ads at the later slots of the video. Further, we show that our algorithm, compared to alternate algorithms, increases viewer retention which helps in building publisher loyalty. Our approach can be generalized for allocation of ads on any digital media.

We conclude with a few comments on the limitations of our model and possible extensions. In our paper we have only accounted for ad externalities for a single video session. It would be interesting to model the impact of ad externality on the viewership during multiple video sessions watched by a viewer. Further, our model addresses the target number of impressions as a constraint in the maximization function i.e. an ad could only be considered if the target is not yet met. Additionally, ads with low continuation rates would never be picked. This could lead to underachieving the target and potential loss of clients. So one could explore how the target could be included in the maximization function. Further, algorithms to allocate skippable ads could be explored, which would make the model less restrictive (although prohibitively more complex) and increase its applicability. Finally, while the linearity assumption significantly reduces the run-time of the algorithm and makes it suitable for real-time applications, it would be useful to explore other algorithms that could relax this assumption and still generate an allocation close to the global optimum.

7. REFERENCES

[1] Internet Advertsing Bureau. Iab internet advertising revenue report 2013 conducted by PricewaterhouseCoopers (pwc). Accessed: 2015-04-10.

[2] Kenneth C Wilbur, Linli Xu, and David Kempe. Correcting audience externalities in television advertising. *Marketing Science*, 32(6):892–912, 2013.

[3] Hal R Varian. Position auctions. *International Journal of Industrial Organization*, 25(6):1163–1178, 2007.

[4] Benjamin Edelman, Michael Ostrovsky, and Michael Schwarz. Internet advertising and the generalized second price auction: Selling billions of dollars worth of keywords. Technical report, National Bureau of Economic Research, 2005.

[5] Gagan Aggarwal, Ashish Goel, and Rajeev Motwani. Truthful auctions for pricing search keywords. In *Proceedings of the 7th ACM conference on Electronic commerce*, pages 1–7. ACM, 2006.

[6] Sébastien Lahaie, David M Pennock, Amin Saberi, and Rakesh V Vohra. Sponsored search auctions. *Algorithmic game theory*, pages 699–716, 2007.

[7] Li Liang and Qi Qi. Cooperative or vindictive: Bidding strategies in sponsored search auction. In *Internet and Network Economics*, pages 167–178. Springer, 2007.

[8] Tao Qin, Wei Chen, and Tie-Yan Liu. Sponsored search auctions: Recent advances and future directions. *ACM Transactions on Intelligent Systems and Technology (TIST)*, 5(4):60, 2015.

[9] David Maxwell Chickering and David Heckerman. Targeted advertising on the web with inventory management. *Interfaces*, 33(5):71–77, 2003.

[10] John Turner, Alan Scheller-Wolf, and Sridhar Tayur. Or practice-scheduling of dynamic in-game advertising. *Operations research*, 59(1):1–16, 2011.

[11] Guillaume Roels and Kristin Fridgeirsdottir. Dynamic revenue management for online display advertising. *Journal of Revenue & Pricing Management*, 8(5):452–466, 2009.

[12] David Kempe and Mohammad Mahdian. A cascade model for externalities in sponsored search. In *Internet and Network Economics*, pages 585–596. Springer, 2008.

[13] Gagan Aggarwal, Jon Feldman, S Muthukrishnan, and Martin Pál. Sponsored search auctions with markovian users. In *Internet and Network Economics*, pages 621–628. Springer, 2008.

[14] VF Araman and K Fridgeirsdottir. Online advertising: Revenue management approach. Technical report, Working paper. London Business School, 2008.

[15] Alf Kimms and Michael Muller-Bungart. Revenue management for broadcasting commercials: the channel's problem of selecting and scheduling the advertisements to be aired. *International Journal of Revenue Management*, 1(1):28–44, 2007.

[16] Victor F Araman and Ioana Popescu. Stochastic revenue management models for media broadcasting. Technical report, Working paper, 2007.

[17] Thorsten Joachims, Laura Granka, Bing Pan, Helene Hembrooke, Filip Radlinski, and Geri Gay. Evaluating the accuracy of implicit feedback from clicks and query reformulations in web search. *ACM Transactions on Information Systems (TOIS)*, 25(2):7, 2007.

[18] Kinshuk Jerath, Liye Ma, Young-Hoon Park, and Kannan Srinivasan. A "position paradox" in sponsored search auctions. *Marketing Science*, 30(4):612–627, 2011.

[19] Susan Athey and Glenn Ellison. Position auctions with consumer search. Technical report, National Bureau of Economic Research, 2009.

[20] Matthew Richardson, Ewa Dominowska, and Robert Ragno. Predicting clicks: estimating the click-through rate for new ads. In *Proceedings of the 16th international conference on World Wide Web*, pages 521–530. ACM, 2007.

[21] D. Sculley, Robert G. Malkin, Sugato Basu, and Roberto J. Bayardo. Predicting bounce rates in sponsored search advertisements. In *Proceedings of the 15th ACM SIGKDD International Conference on Knowledge Discovery and Data Mining*, KDD '09, pages 1325–1334, New York, NY, USA, 2009. ACM.

[22] Paat Rusmevichientong and David P Williamson. An adaptive algorithm for selecting profitable keywords for search-based advertising services. In *Proceedings of the 7th ACM Conference on Electronic Commerce*, pages 260–269. ACM, 2006.

[23] Peter McCullagh, John A Nelder, and P McCullagh. *Generalized linear models*, volume 2. Chapman and Hall London, 1989.

[24] Wreetabrata Kar, Viswanathan Swaminathan, and Paulo Albuquerque. Measuring Quality of Linear Ads in Online Videos. Working Paper, 2015.

[25] Dan Zigmond, Sundar Dorai-Raj, Yannet Interian, and Igor Naverniouk. Measuring advertising quality based on audience retention. *Journal of Advertising Research*, 49(4):419–428, 2009.

[26] Nick Craswell, Onno Zoeter, Michael Taylor, and Bill Ramsey. An experimental comparison of click position-bias models. In *Proceedings of the 2008 International Conference on Web Search and Data Mining*, pages 87–94. ACM, 2008.

[27] Tao Mei, Xian-Sheng Hua, and Shipeng Li. Videosense: A contextual in-video advertising system. *Circuits and Systems for Video Technology, IEEE Transactions on*, 19(12):1866–1879, 2009.

[28] Karthik Yadati, Harish Katti, and Mohan Kankanhalli. Cavva: Computational affective video-in-video advertising. *Multimedia, IEEE Transactions on*, 16(1):15–23, 2014.

Adaptation and Evaluation of Recommendations for Short-term Shopping Goals

Dietmar Jannach
TU Dortmund, Germany
dietmar.jannach@tu-dortmund.de

Lukas Lerche
TU Dortmund, Germany
lukas.lerchet@tu-dortmund.de

Michael Jugovac
TU Dortmund, Germany
michael.jugovac@tu-dortmund.de

ABSTRACT

An essential characteristic in many e-commerce settings is that website visitors can have very specific short-term shopping goals when they browse the site. Relying solely on long-term user models that are pre-trained on historical data can therefore be insufficient for a suitable next-basket recommendation. Simple "real-time" recommendation approaches based, e.g., on unpersonalized co-occurrence patterns, on the other hand do not fully exploit the available information about the user's long-term preference profile.

In this work, we aim to explore and quantify the effectiveness of using and combining long-term models and short-term adaptation strategies. We conducted an empirical evaluation based on a novel evaluation design and two real-world datasets. The results indicate that maintaining short-term *content-based* and *recency-based* profiles of the visitors can lead to significant accuracy increases. At the same time, the experiments show that the choice of the algorithm for learning the long-term preferences is particularly important at the beginning of new shopping sessions.

Categories and Subject Descriptors

H.3.3 [**Information Search and Retrieval**]: Information filtering

Keywords

E-Commerce; Algorithms; Context; Evaluation

1. INTRODUCTION

Modern online shops are no longer static catalogs of items, but meet the user's interest by providing personalized product recommendations. In the best case, these recommendations should match both the users' long-term preferences as well as their current shopping goals. On Amazon.com, for example, each product page contains multiple personalized recommendation lists with different purposes. They comprise complements or alternatives to the currently viewed product, remind the user of recently viewed items, or represent recommendations that should appeal to the general taste of the user (Figure 1). Therefore, the displayed content not only depends on the features of the currently viewed article, like the product category, but can also be influenced, e.g., by a combination of the user's past shopping behavior (long-term preferences) and his most recent navigation actions (short-term shopping goals).

Research in recommender systems (RS) has made impressive advances over the last decade in particular with respect to algorithms capable of modeling long-term user preferences. Note, however, that the first four recommendation lists of the real-world site shown in Figure 1 actually appear to be non-personalized and merely depend on the currently viewed item. The last list, in contrast, is based on recent navigation actions and furthermore seems to integrate recommendations that are based on a longer-term user profile. Overall, relying solely on long-term models seems to be insufficient in this situation, as these models cannot easily adapt to the user's short-term shopping goals.

The goal of our work is to explore, quantify, and compare the effectiveness of using such short-term and long-term user profiles in online shopping scenarios. We will therefore first design and evaluate three different "real-time" recommendation strategies that can be found on real shops and that are based on item co-occurrence patterns, content-based similarity and recent item views. We will then compare these approaches with state-of-the-art long-term recommendation models and finally test hybrids that combine short-term and long-term models.

We will base our evaluations on real-world navigation log data from two real-world shopping sites. Since the standard evaluation approaches from the literature [13] do not cover our specific situation, we first propose a general and domain-independent time-based and session-based evaluation protocol which can in particular help us to assess how quickly the different recommendation strategies can adapt their recommendations to the visitor's short-term goals.

Generally, our work is related to recent works in context-aware recommendation approaches, which try to consider information about the user's current situation, environment, as well as temporal dynamics in the recommendation process [1, 7]. However, only limited works exist that use navigation logs to estimate the user's shopping goals as the recommendation context and to our knowledge no work exists to date that aims to compare and quantify the individual and combined effects of short-term and long-term profiles using real-world navigation log data.

RecSys'15, September 16–20, 2015, Vienna, Austria.
ⓒ 2015 ACM. ISBN 978-1-4503-3692-5/15/09 ...$15.00.
DOI: http://dx.doi.org/10.1145/2792838.2800176.

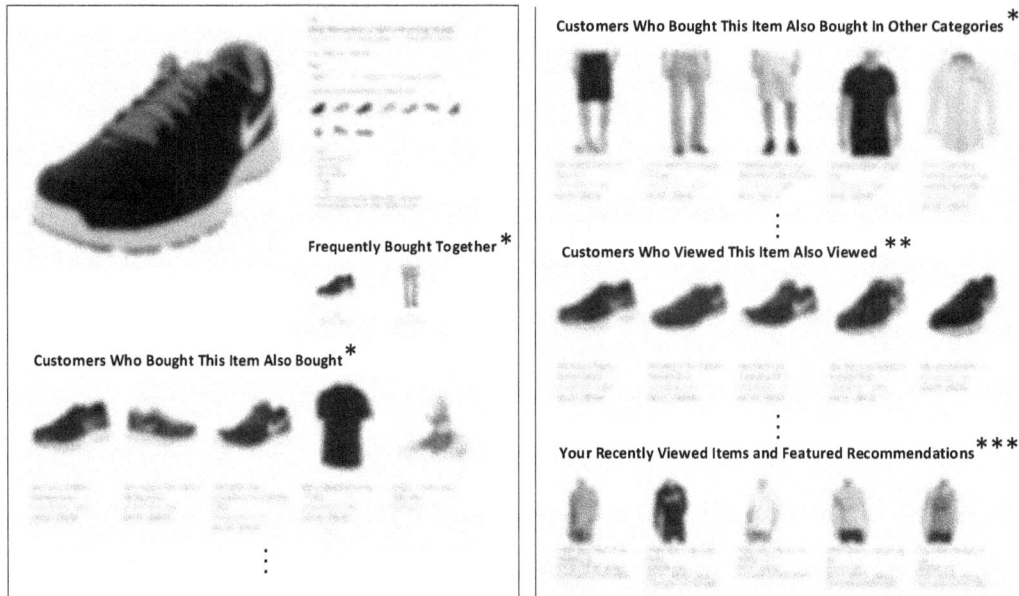

Figure 1: Simplified structure of an Amazon.com product detail page as of 2014, which contains personalized recommendations for *complements, **alternatives and ***reminders.

In the next section, we present the details of the proposed evaluation protocol, which is inspired by the protocol used by our industrial partner. The evaluated recommendation schemes and the results of an empirical evaluation on two real-world datasets are described in later sections.

2. EVALUATION PROTOCOL

The proposed protocol is designed to help us evaluate both the prediction accuracy and the capability of algorithms to adapt to short-term shopping goals in a realistic way. The general goal is that it can be used with various types of time-ordered implicit feedback signals which can be acquired, e.g., from web shop navigation logs. Such information is typically available on e-commerce platforms and furthermore corresponds to what is sometimes shared by companies for research purposes as in the RecSys 2015 challenge[1]. Regarding the long-term models, state-of-the-art recommendation algorithms – in particular those relying on implicit feedback – can be applied and evaluated with standard accuracy measures like precision, recall, or the mean reciprocal rank (MRR).

Figure 2 visualizes the main idea and the different steps of the protocol. We first split the available data (i.e., the sequence of log actions) into a training and a test set. Since the time and the sequence of the actions is important when considering short-term and long-term interests, we use a time-related splitting criterion. We can, for example, put all but the last two shopping *sessions*[2] of each user in the training set, which serves as a basis to learn a long-term user model.

Then, instead of using an RS algorithm to recommend one single ranked list of items given the training set, the task is rather to predict user actions, e.g., purchases, *for each session* in the test set. The underlying idea is that the user's shopping goals can be different for each session. In order to assess how quickly different strategies adapt their recommendations to the session-specific goals, the protocol furthermore provides the means to "reveal" a defined number of very *recent* user actions.

These most recent actions – which we will call *context* from here on – are, for example, "view" actions during the currently evaluated session or actions from a limited number of preceding sessions. Since no k-fold cross-validation is possible due to the time-based split, we propose to apply repeated random sub-sampling to avoid random effects.

Generally, as an alternative to hiding only the last n sessions, the proposed protocol can be varied to implement a "sliding window" technique, e.g., in order to vary the amount of available training data for the long-term models. Such analyses are however not in the focus of our current work.

The steps of the protocol can be summarized as follows.

Training phase.

1. Create a time-ordered list of user sessions and their actions from the log data.

2. Split the session list into training and test sessions while retaining the sequence. Splitting criteria could be, e.g., "retain the last session containing a purchase", or "retain the last 20% of the sessions". Remove users with session lists that are too short to be split (e.g., the user only visited the shop once).

3. Use an arbitrary recommendation algorithm to learn a long-term user model from the training data.

---

[1]http://2015.recsyschallenge.com/
[2]A session is a set of user actions identified by the *session ID* of each action assigned by the system of the dataset provider. In general, a session represents actions of a user within a particular time period or for completing a particular task.

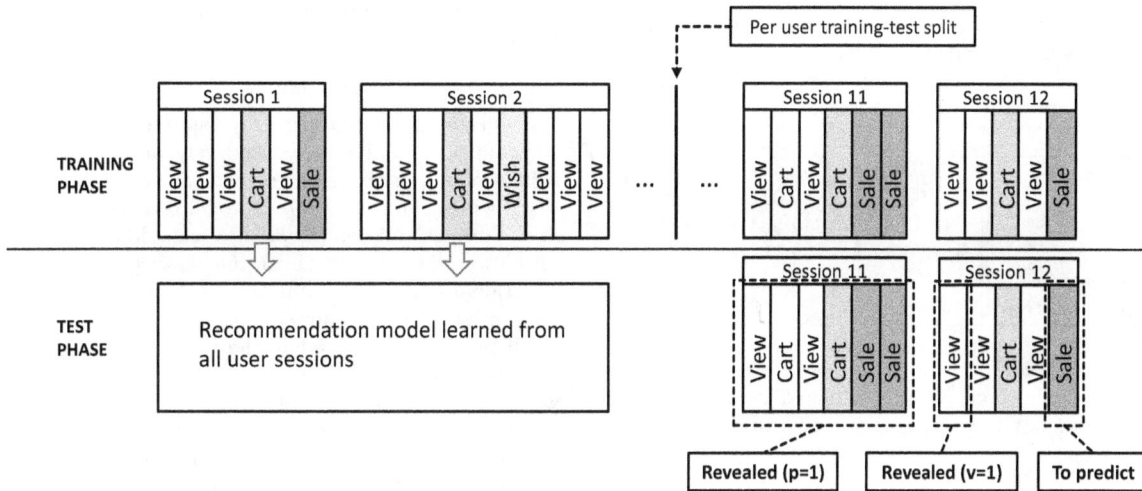

Figure 2: Protocol sketch: training phase and evaluation of the 12th session of a user.

Recommendation and evaluation.

1. Predict the next user action, e.g., purchase, for each session in the test set that contains at least one action of the desired type.

2. To allow a given algorithm to adapt its strategy to short-term goals, reveal a set of recent actions (the user's context) in addition to the training data. Here, two different types of information are used.

   - Parameter v determines up to how many *views* of the *currently evaluated* session – e.g., session 12 in Figure 2 – are revealed. This parameter helps us to assess how many clicks it takes for an adaptive recommendation strategy to guess the user's shopping goal.

   - Parameter p determines up to how many *previous* sessions – with respect to the currently evaluated one – are revealed. By changing the parameter a potential recent interest drift of the visitor during the last few sessions can be determined.

3. Use hit rates or rank-based measures to assess the quality of the predictions.

Discussion.

The general question in offline experimental designs is whether the chosen evaluation procedure and the performance metrics represent a good approximation of the *true quality* of an information system. Recent studies for example indicate that algorithms that achieve lower RMSE values are not necessarily favorable when we look at the specific business or application goals to be achieved (see, e.g., [9, 15, 18]). Overall, we are confident that the proposed form of predicting user actions is a realistic way to asses the effectiveness and accuracy of different algorithms. First, our protocol is similar to one protocol used by our research partner Zalando for offline performance evaluations[3]. In addition, recent RS

competitions held by industrial sponsors, e.g., the *Tmall Prize* competition[4] and the 2015 ACM RecSys Challenge, use protocols that share several similarities with our protocol. The main difference to these existing protocols is that our approach is more generic in terms of compatible algorithms and that the simulation of short-term information is more parameterizable.

3. EXPERIMENTAL SETUP

In the following sections, we propose a number of adaptation strategies and report the results of a series of experiments which we conducted using two datasets: a larger one provided by the online fashion retailer Zalando, and a smaller one from the Tmall competition.

3.1 Details of the Zalando dataset

The "raw" dataset from Zalando comprises nearly 1 million purchases, 1.6 million cart actions and about 20 million item view events in about 170,000 sessions. The data was sampled from the shop's web log in a way that no conclusions about the visitors or the business numbers can be drawn. There are 800,000 anonymized user IDs in the dataset; however, more than 500,000 of the visitors have never made a purchase but only viewed items. The product catalog is huge and comprises over 150,000 different items.

Data sparsity represents a major problem in our application scenario. The average number of purchases per user, for example, is about 3.5 when only counting those users which have ever made a purchase. Each item ever purchased was sold on average about 6 times. Finally, a major fraction of the users visited the shop only once.

Personalization based on past behavior is therefore only reasonable for the subset of "heavy" users. Following a common practice in research, we not only used the full dataset but created subsets with higher data density by applying constraints on the minimum number of purchases per user and per item. In Table 1 we show the resulting characteristics of the data subsamples called *Sparse*, *Medium*, and

---

[3] Zalando is a major European online retailer of fashion products, see http://www.zalando.com

[4] http://102.alibaba.com/competition/addDiscovery/index.html

Table 1: Characteristics of Zalando evaluation data sets with different density constraints. The datasets are still sparse; note that users in typical movie datasets have rated at least 20 items.

	Sparse	Medium	Dense
Users	121,018	38,447	1,869
Items	40,526	19,061	2,208
Purchases	680,787	344,684	43,079
Views	9,807,282	3,929,813	117,734
Min. purchases/user	3	5	10
Min. purchases/item	3	5	10

Dense. In our evaluation, we only retained view and purchase actions but not the cart actions; we will discuss this decision later on.

3.2 Algorithms

We differentiate between (i) non-contextualized *baseline strategies* used to learn the long-term user models and (ii) *contextualization strategies* that rely on the additionally revealed user actions to adapt the recommendations to the short-term shopping goals.

Non-contextualized baseline strategies

Any existing recommendation algorithm capable of building a model from the given implicit rating data can be used as a baseline. The task of the baseline strategy is to compute a ranked list of items for a given user based on the training data. We chose the following algorithms in the experiments to generate long-term models.

BPR: Matrix factorization (MF) and learning-to-rank techniques represent the most successful classes of methods to build highly accurate recommender systems in the recent literature, especially for implicit feedback domains. Therefore, and since only implicit user feedback is available, we use BPR (Bayesian Personalized Ranking) [25] in combination with an MF model of 100 features as a state-of-the-art baseline in our experiments. The model was learned in 100 training steps with learning rate $\alpha = 0.05$ and regularization parameters $\lambda_W = 0.0025$, $\lambda_{H+} = 0.0025$, $\lambda_{H-} = 0.00025$. The optimal parameters for BPR and the next algorithm (FCTMCH) were manually fine-tuned.

FctMch: Factorization Machines [24] combine feature engineering and factorization models and can be applied for general prediction tasks. Markov Chain Monte Carlo optimization (MCMC) was used in the experiments with the parameters stddev = 0.3, steps = 50.

PopRank: Depending on the evaluation setting, simple popularity-based approaches can represent a quite hard baseline [10]. We implemented an unpersonalized baseline strategy which ranks the items based on the number of times they have been viewed or purchased in the training set.

Random: A method that recommends random items to users. We include this baseline to assess the effects when only short-term techniques are applied (and the resulting lists are filled up with random elements).

We do not recommend items to users that they already purchased in the past. We also do not differentiate between item views and purchases in the training phase, since contextualization is our main focus. In more elaborate schemes, a graded relevance feedback technique could be used as in [20] or [30] and more weight could, for example, be given to purchase actions.

Contextualization strategies

The following approaches are inspired by those of Amazon.com and similar shops and rely on the additional information about the user's recent navigation behavior (*context*), which the evaluation protocol reveals to them. In one of the proposed schemes, we also use additional content information. The contextualization strategies are of low computational complexity and therefore suitable for real-time adaptation of the recommendations. The general strategy of all techniques is to refine the results returned by a *baseline recommender* – which reflects the long-term model – with the help of the current context. This can be considered as a form of contextual post-filtering.

CoOccur: In this method, the recommendable items are ranked by the *conditional probability* of co-occurring with the items in the user's context (which corresponds to association rules of size two and the "Customers who viewed ..." strategy shown in Figure 1). Items for which no scores can be computed are appended to the list in the order in which they were ranked by the baseline method.

CoOccur-Filter: The method again combines co-occurrence scores with the item ranking of the baseline method. The recommendation list again starts with items for which co-occurrence scores can be computed. However, the ordering of the baseline method is used for ranking the items. Again, the list is then filled up with the remaining items using the order of the baseline method.

FeatureMatching (FM): This method re-ranks the items returned by a baseline recommender based on *content features*. Specifically, a short-term content-based user profile is created that contains the brand and category information of items that the user has recently viewed. Each recommendable item is compared with this short-term profile and re-ranked with a weight factor based on the number of overlapping feature values.

RecentlyViewed (RV): This technique places the recently viewed items on the top of the recommendation list and appends the remaining items. The internal ranking of both parts of the list is based on the baseline method's score. This strategy was designed in analogy to the last set of recommendations shown in Figure 1 used on Amazon.com.

3.3 Evaluation measures

Since the data only contains unary (positive) feedback, we use the protocol variant of [10] to determine the *recall* by measuring the relative position of the recommended items in a given set of items. Each target item t is combined with k random items unknown to the user. The resulting list of $k + 1$ items is then ranked by the algorithm. A "hit" occurs when t was in the top n items. The recall for each ranking problem is therefore either 0 or 1. Precision can be computed as $1/(k + 1) \cdot recall$ and is thus proportional to the recall. We report the results obtained using $k = 100$ and Recall@10.

We additionally measured the MRR, and the results were in line with the results for Recall@10. Varying the protocol parameters k and n led to different absolute results but did not change the overall ranking of the algorithms.

Table 2: Recall for the *Dense* Zalando data set

	v=0, p=2	v=2, p=2	v=5, p=2	v=10, p=2	v=5, p=0
BPR			0.40		
FctMch			0.20		
PopRank			0.21		
Random			0.09		
CoOccur +					
BPR	0.38	0.47	0.49	0.52	0.48
FctMch	0.38	0.46	0.48	0.52	0.42
PopRank	0.37	0.45	0.48	0.51	0.41
Random	0.31	0.44	0.48	0.50	0.40
CoOccur-Filter +					
BPR	0.39	0.47	0.48	0.50	0.48
FctMch	0.31	0.37	0.39	0.41	0.40
PopRank	0.29	0.36	0.38	0.39	0.38
Random	0.23	0.34	0.35	0.37	0.36
FeatureMatching +					
BPR	0.41	0.65	0.71	0.76	0.71
FctMch	0.37	0.61	0.68	0.73	0.63
PopRank	0.38	0.62	0.68	0.72	0.64
Random	0.31	0.60	0.66	0.73	0.61
RecentlyViewed +					
BPR	0.40	0.55	0.64	0.72	0.63
FctMch	0.36	0.53	0.61	0.70	0.51
PopRank	0.36	0.53	0.62	0.71	0.52
Random	0.27	0.47	0.57	0.67	0.47
RecentlyViewed + FeatureMatching +					
BPR	0.41	**0.66**	**0.73**	**0.79**	**0.71**
FctMch	**0.42**	0.65	0.72	**0.79**	0.63
PopRank	0.40	0.65	0.72	**0.79**	0.64
Random	0.32	0.63	0.70	0.78	0.62

4. RESULTS

We report the results of different configurations, where the maximum number of revealed views v and previous sessions p was varied to determine the importance of the recent actions and sessions. The setting $v = 0$, $p = 0$ corresponds to the non-contextualized evaluation shown in the second row of Table 2. We randomly selected 80% of the users and repeated the measurements 5 times using different samples. For each user, the recommendation task was to predict the purchases of the last session in which a purchase was observed. Table 2 shows the results on the *Dense* dataset for the baseline strategies and the effects when adding the contextualization strategies. The standard deviations across the different measurements were between 0.003 and 0.015 for the recall, i.e., the results are quite stable.

Observations for baseline strategies.

Regarding the baseline strategies, the BPR learning-to-rank technique for implicit feedback unsurprisingly – see also [16] – leads to the best results for recall (and all other measures) as shown in the first data rows of Table 2. Beating the popularity-based baseline is generally hard in this specific setup as discussed in [10], in particular when only implicit feedback is available, for which techniques like FctMch are not optimized[5]. While using FctMch alone is not better than PopRank in this setup, we will see in the following that FctMch can be a better suited baseline strategy when contextualization is applied.

General observations regarding contextualization.

All contextualization strategies lead to better recall (and MRR) values than when using the baselines alone in case the navigation actions of the current session ($v \geqslant 2$) are taken into account. The differences are statistically significant ($p < 0.01$). The accuracy of all techniques also consistently increases when more views of the current session are revealed, i.e., all techniques are able to adapt their recommendations to the current short-term goals based on the navigation behavior. Revealing more previous sessions (e.g., $p = 0$ vs. $p = 2$ with $v = 5$) has a much lower impact on the performance, especially for BPR[6]. Combining these two findings indicates not only that the most recent actions reflect the user's short-term shopping goals, but also that these goals can vary quickly from session to session.

Using short-term content-based profiles.

The content-enhanced FeatureMatching method works very well in terms of recall with any of the baseline techniques. This indicates that many users arrive at the web site with a specific shopping goal and focus their navigation on items of a certain category in which they finally make a purchase. In addition, brand loyalty seems to be a relevant domain-specific aspect.

Users who viewed ... also viewed ....

The co-occurrence based and non-personalized "standard" technique of modern shops leads to comparably high recall values, even if the lists are combined (continued) with random elements and only little is known about the current session (e.g., $v = 2$). Combinations with other baseline methods lead to further statistically significant improvements ($p < 0.01$) for all cases except for BPR with $v = 0$.

This observation indicates that co-occurrence based short-term models can significantly contribute to the overall accuracy of a system. Combining these models with stronger baselines helps to further increase the accuracy, in particular when nothing is known about what the user was interested in during previous sessions ($v = 5$, $p = 0$).

The CoOccur-Filter leads to similar results when BPR is used as a baseline but exhibits lower absolute recall values when the baseline is weaker.

Recently viewed items.

Recommending what users have recently viewed leads to very good results with respect to recall, independent of the chosen baseline strategy. Note that in our application scenario a purchase action for an item is in most cases preceded by a view action in the current or one of the previous sessions. This explains the comparably high values for recall because it is not unlikely that the user viewed the purchased item at the beginning of a session or has slept on his decision since the last session.

Reminding users of items they have recently looked at generally seems to be a reasonable strategy. However, our rank measures unfortunately do not tell us if focusing on such items supports the business strategy of a company in the best possible way. Recommending only items that the visitor already knows will, e.g., not help to stimulate them to purchase items from other parts of the product catalog. At the same time, visitors might find such recommendations

---

[5] An evaluation using the traditional item-to-item nearest-neighbor scheme led to even worse results, which we omit here for space reasons.

[6] Results when using $p = 1$ (not shown) are almost identical to $p = 2$.

Table 3: Recall for the *Medium*, *Sparse* and *"Raw"* (complete) Zalando datasets

	$v=0$, $p=2$	$v=2$, $p=2$	$v=5$, $p=2$	$v=10$, $p=2$	$v=5$, $p=0$
Medium: RecentlyViewed + FeatureMatching +					
BPR	**0.53**	**0.69**	**0.73**	**0.78**	**0.72**
FCTMCH	0.52	0.68	0.72	0.77	0.73
POPRANK	0.51	0.68	0.72	0.77	0.65
RANDOM	0.36	0.59	0.65	0.72	0.55
Sparse: RecentlyViewed + FeatureMatching +					
BPR	**0.59**	**0.75**	**0.79**	**0.83**	**0.77**
FCTMCH	0.58	0.73	0.77	0.82	0.73
POPRANK	0.58	0.73	0.78	0.82	0.72
RANDOM	0.36	0.63	0.69	0.76	0.60
Raw dataset: RecentlyViewed + FeatureMatching +					
BPR	**0.64**	**0.74**	**0.77**	**0.81**	**0.74**
FCTMCH	0.63	**0.74**	**0.77**	**0.81**	0.72
POPRANK	0.63	**0.74**	**0.77**	**0.81**	0.71
RANDOM	0.36	0.59	0.64	0.70	0.54

Table 4: Recall for the *Tmall* data set

	$v=0$, $p=2$	$v=2$, $p=2$	$v=5$, $p=2$	$v=10$, $p=2$	$v=5$, $p=0$
BPR			0.49		
FCTMCH			0.21		
POPRANK			0.24		
RANDOM			0.10		
CoOccur +					
BPR	**0.45**	0.43	0.45	0.46	0.42
FCTMCH	0.43	0.44	0.44	0.46	0.27
POPRANK	0.41	0.40	0.43	0.43	0.25
RANDOM	0.39	0.39	0.43	0.42	0.21
CoOccur-Filter +					
BPR	**0.45**	0.45	0.45	0.46	0.42
FCTMCH	0.37	0.35	0.37	0.37	0.27
POPRANK	0.36	0.32	0.34	0.33	0.23
RANDOM	0.31	0.27	0.30	0.30	0.20
RecentlyViewed +					
BPR	0.40	**0.78**	**0.88**	**0.92**	**0.88**
FCTMCH	0.38	0.77	0.87	0.92	0.80
POPRANK	0.36	0.75	0.85	0.91	0.80
RANDOM	0.33	0.72	0.83	0.91	0.75

to be of limited value. Still, Amazon.com, for example, also recommends items under the "recently viewed" label that were viewed in the current session.

Finally, combining the recency-based approach with the content-based technique and the strongest baseline BPR leads to the best overall results as shown in the last rows of Table 2. Compared to RECENTLYVIEWED and FEATUREMATCHING individually, the improvements obtained with the hybrid of both strategies can be significant if enough context information is available (e.g., $p = 2$ and $v \geqslant 2$). Otherwise, the combination is about as good as FEATUREMATCHING alone.

Results for lower-density datasets.

Table 3 shows results for the best performing strategy on the larger, low-density datasets. On the *raw* dataset we only made predictions for users that had at least 5 purchases in the test set. Overall, the same trends can be observed as with the dataset of higher density. Again, the combination of the different contextualization techniques and using BPR as a baseline leads to the best results. Although comparing the absolute recall values across the different datasets

should be done with care, we can, to some surprise, see that the absolute values are similar or even better for the lower-density datasets. The reasons for this can be (a) that the contextualization strategies are responsible for a major fraction of the hits and (b) that some of the baseline methods profit from a much larger training data set.

Validation on an additional dataset.

We repeated the experiments on another real-world dataset of the recommender competition held by the Chinese online retailer *Tmall*[7]. The published dataset is smaller but has similar characteristics as the Zalando dataset and comprises about 175,000 time-stamped view actions and 7,000 purchase actions organized in sessions. There were about 750 users, who on average purchased around 8 items of the about 2,000 different products. It contains, however, no content information about the items.

Therefore, we could only use the RECENTLYVIEWED and COOCCUR strategies. The results corroborate most of our previous observations, see Table 4. BPR generally leads to higher and statistically significant recall and MRR values than the popularity-based and FCTMCH approaches. The non-contextualized recall for BPR was about 0.49 and 0.24 for POPRANK. Focusing on recently viewed items expectedly leads to strong improvements. The recall with BPR as a baseline increased to 0.78 and to 0.75 when using POPRANK ($p = 2$, $v = 2$). The COOCCUR contextualization strategy, however, only leads to significant improvements when the popularity-based scheme is used. COOCCUR with the BPR baseline performs worse than using BPR without contextualization. Furthermore, the item-to-item method again did not reach the performance level of the popularity-based method in this setup. These effects are most probably caused by the small size of the dataset.

5. DISCUSSION

Implications. Our results support the assumption that taking the short-term interests of visitors into account and combining them with long-term preference models can help to significantly increase the recommendation accuracy. Specifically, even comparably simple, "real-time"-enabled techniques based on content-similarity, item co-occurrence or recent user behavior can be helpful, even in cases in which only limited information about the current shopping session is revealed. At the same time, the choice of a good baseline technique can be essential and our analysis has revealed that recent methods like BPR lead to good results in the explored domains. Optimizing for accuracy measures through offline experiments as done in the research literature is therefore important. In practice, however, these recommendations should be paired with complementary techniques.

Another observation was that the consideration of domain-specific aspects can be crucial. In particular brand loyalty seems to be a common phenomenon as well as the tendency of users to make repeated purchases from a restricted set of product categories. This tendency to purchase "more of the same" was also observed in the real-world study in [15].

Open questions. From a methodological perspective, we see our work as a step towards more realistic and complementary research designs for recommender systems. However, while our protocol allows us to assess the role of short-

---

[7] http://www.tmall.com

term interests to some extent using an offline experimental design, some questions remain to be explored in future works. One specific aspect to consider is, how certain recent user actions should be considered in the recommendation process. Should items be recommended that the user has already viewed before? Should we remind the users of an item that they have placed in the cart some time ago and never purchased? In which specific ways should we incorporate other types of user actions? These decisions often depend on the application domain and cannot easily be generalized or answered through offline experiments.

A more general issue is that relying on established measures like recall and MRR alone to predict the effectiveness of an RS can be misleading as these measures do not take alternate objectives and business goals into account. Recommending only recently viewed items can, for example, result in comparably high hit rates but perhaps not in additional purchases. Such an approach is also not suited for directing users to additional item categories of the online shop or non-mainstream products as shown in [11] or [32]. Traditional accuracy measures should therefore be paired and contrasted with other possible quality aspects like diversity, serendipity or domain-specific measures to obtain a more realistic picture of the potential effectiveness of a method. Additionally, given that the different recommendation and contextualization strategies can lead to quite different recommendation lists corresponding, e.g., to short-term or long-term interests, a multi-list approach could be advisable to clearly distinguish the purpose of the recommendations. Research in this direction is unfortunately very limited so far.

Dataset limitations. The used dataset from Zalando only contains log data from a comparably limited time frame and only certain types of information about the items. In practice, however, additional factors like visitor demographics or seasonal aspects could be relevant for the success of the recommendation system. Furthermore, since our data was collected from a real-world web shop, the behavior of the users might be at least to some extent biased by unknown external factors. Nonetheless, since we could validate our findings on an additional dataset, we are confident that the effects of such unknown factors, if they exist, must be very limited.

6. RELATED WORK

Implicit ratings. Fueled by the existence of publicly available data sets, most of today's RS research is based on explicit rating information [17]. There are, however, a number of recent approaches that focus on processing implicit unary or binary relevance feedback, e.g., [14] or [26]. In our work, we use Rendle et al.'s BPR method [25] as a baseline technique in particular because it has characteristics of recent learning-to-rank methods.

Context-aware and time-aware recommendations (CARS). The goal of CARS is to incorporate information about the user's recent situation – such as short-term shopping goals – or other environmental conditions into the recommendation process. As discussed in [6], the connection between contextual factors and item selection can be hard to assess. According to the classification from [1] our methods fall in the category of "post-filtering" approaches. Context-enriched benchmark datasets are rare and time-stamp information is often the only additional source of context. Existing works that rely on time-stamp information in web log

data include [5] and [19]. For a recent overview on various forms to evaluate such time-aware RS, see [7]. In our work, the log entries are sorted in chronological order but no explicit time-stamps are available. Therefore, we can only reason about possible effects related to the relative recency of the events. With the availability of explicit time-stamps, additional behavioral patterns could potentially be detected in the data using the above-mentioned methods.

Short-term interests. Information about the user's short-term interests is typically not explicitly given and has to be estimated based on the recent actions as done in our work. While short-term interests seem to play a minor role in RS research – some exceptions are [22] or [27] – there exists a number of recent works in the information retrieval field. Especially for news recommendation, short-term interests are a current research topic. Similar to our approach, the news recommender in [21] adapts the results of a collaborative filtering approach to the user's current interests with the content-based information of the recent search behavior. Some approaches, e.g., [2] or [3], use clustering to identify common navigation patterns in the log data and apply CF or association rule mining to match the recent history of a target user. In our work, a combination of short- and long-term interests is used to generate recommendation. Alternative combination methods are discussed in [4] and [23]. The domain of fashion products is explicitly addressed in [29] with a scenario-based modeling technique. The recent approach in [31] also focuses on fashion products and aims to identify the theme of a user's session by using factored Markov decision processes (fMDPs). In [12], short-term goals are modeled by a multi-armed bandit algorithm that detects a shift in the user's interest based on implicit feedback signals. In contrast to our work, these two approaches focus only on the short-term user goals whereas our method combines long-term user model with short-term interests.

Evaluation aspects. A number of factors determine the success of an RS in practice, e.g., the quality perceived by users [8, 9] or the correspondence of the recommendations with the application goals [16]. In fact, some studies suggest that methods that are optimized for high predictive accuracy on historical data do not always work best with regard to the desired effects on the users [15, 18]. [28] frames this evaluation challenge as a multi-objective decision problem where user requirements, business models, and technical constraints should all be taken into account in parallel. Our evaluations so far are limited to the usual accuracy metrics. In order to obtain a better assessment of the actual effectiveness, a multi-dimensional analysis has to be done provided that suitable data for such an evaluation is available.

7. SUMMARY

The goal of this work was to analyze the importance and quantify the effects of issuing recommendations according to long- and short-term shopping goals in e-commerce sites. We evaluated different short-term recommendation strategies which can be found on modern e-commerce sites and combined them with state-of-the-art techniques for long-term user profiling. Our experiments were based on a time-based and session-based evaluation protocol to show that short-term adaptations can be crucial to be able to make accurate recommendations according to short-term shopping goals. Furthermore, the results indicate that combining optimized long-term models with short-term strategies leads to the best overall results, i.e., long-term user models are not only suitable for generating non-contextualized recommendations on a shop's landing page but encode valuable knowledge that can be exploited for matching immediate short-term shopping goals. Our ongoing works include the analysis of additional characteristics of the recommendation lists – like diversity, catalog coverage, or popularity biases – and the development of additional algorithmic approaches for short-term adaptations.

8. REFERENCES

[1] G. Adomavicius and A. Tuzhilin. Context-aware recommender systems. In *Recommender Systems Handbook*, pages 217–253. 2011.

[2] S. R. Aghabozorgi and T. Y. Wah. Recommender systems: Incremental clustering on web log data. In *Proc. ICIS '09*, pages 812–818, 2009.

[3] Y. AlMurtadha, N. B. Sulaiman, N. Mustapha, N. I. Udzir, and Z. Muda. ARS: Web page recommendation system for anonymous users based on web usage mining. In *Proc. ECS '10*, pages 115–120, 2010.

[4] S. Anand and B. Mobasher. Contextual recommendation. In *From Web to Social Web*, volume 4737 of *LNCS*, pages 142–160. 2007.

[5] L. Baltrunas and X. Amatriain. Towards time-dependant recommendation based on implicit feedback. In *Proc. CARS WS at RecSys '09*, 2009.

[6] L. Baltrunas, B. Ludwig, and F. Ricci. Context relevance assessment for recommender systems. In *Proc. IUI '11*, pages 287–290, 2011.

[7] P. G. Campos, F. Díez, and I. Cantador. Time-aware recommender systems: a comprehensive survey and analysis of existing evaluation protocols. *UMUAI*, 24(1-2):67–119, 2014.

[8] P. Cremonesi, F. Garzotto, S. Negro, A. Papadopoulos, and R. Turrin. Looking for "good" recommendations: A comparative evaluation of recommender systems. In *Proc. Interact '11*, pages 152–168, 2011.

[9] P. Cremonesi, F. Garzotto, and R. Turrin. Investigating the persuasion potential of recommender systems from a quality perspective: An empirical study. *ACM TIST*, 2(2):11:1–11:41, 2012.

[10] P. Cremonesi, Y. Koren, and R. Turrin. Performance of algorithms on top-n recommendation tasks. In *Proc. RecSys '10*, pages 39–46, 2010.

[11] M. B. Dias, D. Locher, M. Li, W. El-Deredy, and P. J. Lisboa. The value of personalised recommender systems to e-business: A case study. In *Proc. RecSys '08*, pages 291–294, 2008.

[12] N. Hariri, B. Mobasher, and R. Burke. Context adaptation in interactive recommender systems. In *Proc. RecSys '14*, pages 41–48, 2014.

[13] J. L. Herlocker, J. A. Konstan, L. G. Terveen, and J. T. Riedl. Evaluating collaborative filtering recommender systems. *ACM TOIS*, 22(1):5–53, 2004.

[14] Y. Hu, Y. Koren, and C. Volinsky. Collaborative filtering for implicit feedback datasets. In *Proc. ICDM '08*, pages 263–272, 2008.

[15] D. Jannach and K. Hegelich. A case study on the effectiveness of recommendations in the mobile internet. In *Proc. RecSys '09*, pages 205–208, 2009.

[16] D. Jannach, L. Lerche, F. Gedikli, and G. Bonnin. What recommenders recommend - an analysis of accuracy, popularity, and sales diversity effects. In *Proc. UMAP '13*, pages 25–37, 2013.

[17] D. Jannach, M. Zanker, M. Ge, and M. Gröning. Recommender systems in computer science and information systems - a landscape of research. In *Proc. EC-Web '12*, pages 76–87, 2012.

[18] E. Kirshenbaum, G. Forman, and M. Dugan. A live comparison of methods for personalized article recommendation at Forbes.com. In *Proc. ECML/PKDD '12*, pages 51–66, 2012.

[19] Y. Koren. Collaborative filtering with temporal dynamics. In *Proc. KDD '09*, pages 447–456, 2009.

[20] L. Lerche and D. Jannach. Using graded implicit feedback for bayesian personalized ranking. In *Proc. RecSys '14*, pages 353–356, 2014.

[21] J. Liu, P. Dolan, and E. R. Pedersen. Personalized news recommendation based on click behavior. In *Proc. IUI '10*, pages 31–40, 2010.

[22] B. Mobasher, H. Dai, T. Luo, and M. Nakagawa. Using sequential and non-sequential patterns in predictive web usage mining tasks. In *Proc. ICDM '02*, pages 669–672, 2002.

[23] Q. N. Nguyen and F. Ricci. Long-term and session-specific user preferences in a mobile recommender system. In *Proc. IUI '08*, pages 381–384, 2008.

[24] S. Rendle. Factorization machines with libFM. *ACM Transactions on Intelligent Systems Technology*, 3(3):57:1–57:22, 2012.

[25] S. Rendle, C. Freudenthaler, Z. Gantner, and L. Schmidt-Thieme. BPR: Bayesian personalized ranking from implicit feedback. In *Proc. UAI '09*, pages 452–461, 2009.

[26] S. Rendle, C. Freudenthaler, and L. Schmidt-Thieme. Factorizing personalized markov chains for next-basket recommendation. In *Proc. WWW '10*, pages 811–820. ACM, 2010.

[27] F. Ricci, A. Venturini, D. Cavada, N. Mirzadeh, D. Blaas, and M. Nones. Product recommendation with interactive query management and twofold similarity. In *Proc. ICCBR '03*, pages 479–493, 2003.

[28] A. Said, D. Tikk, K. Stumpf, Y. Shi, M. Larson, and P. Cremonesi. Recommender systems evaluation: A 3D benchmark. In *Proc. RUE WS at RecSys '12*, pages 21–23, 2012.

[29] E. Shen, H. Lieberman, and F. Lam. What am I gonna wear?: Scenario-oriented recommendation. In *Proc. IUI '07*, pages 365–368, 2007.

[30] Y. Shi, A. Karatzoglou, L. Baltrunas, M. Larson, and A. Hanjalic. xCLiMF: optimizing expected reciprocal rank for data with multiple levels of relevance. In *Proc. RecSys '13*, pages 431–434, 2013.

[31] M. Tavakol and U. Brefeld. Factored MDPs for detecting topics of user sessions. In *Proc. RecSys '14*, pages 33–40, 2014.

[32] M. Zanker, M. Bricman, S. Gordea, D. Jannach, and M. Jessenitschnig. Persuasive online-selling in quality & taste domains. In *Proc. EC-Web '06*, pages 51–60, 2006.

E-commerce Recommendation with Personalized Promotion

Qi Zhao[†], Yi Zhang[†], Daniel Friedman[‡], Fangfang Tan[‡]
† School of Engineering ‡ Economics Department
University of Calfornia, Santa Cruz, CA, 95060
qzhao2@ucsc.edu, yiz@soe.ucsc.edu,dan@ucsc.edu, tfangfan@ucsc.edu

ABSTRACT

Most existing e-commerce recommender systems aim to recommend the right products to a consumer, assuming the properties of each product are fixed. However, some properties, including price discount, can be personalized to respond to each consumer's preference. This paper studies how to automatically set the price discount when recommending a product, in light of the fact that the price will often alter a consumer's purchase decision. The key to optimizing the discount is to predict consumer's willingness-to-pay (WTP), namely, the highest price a consumer is willing to pay for a product. Purchase data used by traditional e-commerce recommender systems provide points below or above the decision boundary. In this paper we collected training data to better predict the decision boundary. We implement a new e-commerce mechanism adapted from laboratory lottery and auction experiments that elicit a rational customer's exact WTP for a small subset of products, and use a machine learning algorithm to predict the customer's WTP for other products. The mechanism is implemented on our own e-commerce website that leverages Amazon's data and subjects recruited via Mechanical Turk. The experimental results suggest that this approach can help predict WTP, and boost consumer satisfaction as well as seller profit.

Categories and Subject Descriptors

H.3.3 [**INFORMATION STORAGE AND RETRIEVAL**]: [Information filtering]

General Terms

Algorithms, Experimentation

Keywords

recommender system; e-commerce; consumer; promotion; crowdsourcing

1. INTRODUCTION

RecSys'15, September 16–20, 2015, Vienna, Austria.
ⓒ 2015 ACM. ISBN 978-1-4503-3692-5/15/09 ...$15.00.
DOI: http://dx.doi.org/10.1145/2792838.2800178.

Recommender systems have achieved much commercial success and are becoming increasingly popular in a wide variety of practical applications. For example, online stores such as Amazon, iTunes and Walmart.com provide customized recommendations for additional products or services based on a consumer's history. Since it is widely believed that even minor improvements in recommender systems can boost the profitability of e-commerce companies, these systems have been studied intensively by researchers in industry and in academia.

An important limitation of existing studies is that they assume that the properties of items (i.e. products) are static. However, an e-commerce company could tailor some properties of a product for a particular customer, and that could dramatically improve the effectiveness of a recommendation. In particular, we argue that price is a controllable property that the recommender system should incorporate. A consumer might like a recommended product, but may reject it because the price is too high, and the purchasing decision could be changed by a personalized promotion. Of course, outside of the literature on recommender systems, the crucial role of pricing is widely recognized. Researchers in marketing, for example, have shown the importance of personalized promotion for increasing sales volume [17].

In this paper, we introduce personalized promotion into e-commerce recommender systems. The objective is to improve the effectiveness of product recommendations through customizing product price on an individual basis.

To achieve this goal, we create a novel auction/lottery mechanism to elicit consumer willingness to pay (WTP) for relevant products in an e-commerce setting. Using an online shopping website with products from Amazon, we recruit experimental subjects via Mechanical Turk and use responses elicited for some chosen products to predict a individual's WTP on other products. The predicted WTP and the given production cost enable us to find profitable personalized prices. The data indicate that the new approach achieves nearly 200% improvement in gross profit when compared with Amazon's default pricing strategy.

Our contribution is three-fold. First, to the best of our knowledge, our work is the first attempt to add personalized promotion to e-commerce recommender systems, and we measure recommendation performance with metrics of direct interest to industry. Second, we introduce a novel WTP elicitation procedure that is adapted to e-commerce systems. Most previous WTP elicitation studies are conducted in settings that are very different from an e-commerce website — typically only a handful of products in a narrow category are pre-selected by the experimenters — and so the applicability to e-commerce is unclear. Third, we have several methodological observations that could be very useful for further research on personalized pricing in e-commerce.

2. RELATED WORK

Despite the complexity of recommender systems, the most common approach is to reduce the problem to predicting the user's ratings or purchasing decision of items, and recommending items based on the prediction. In early work, the Grundy system built stereotypes for recommendation [28]. The Tapestry system let users identify similar users manually and made recommendations based on these similar users [16]. The advent of the internet resulted in large sets of user data. Consequently, manual constructions have been largely replaced by automatic recommendation algorithms, such as collaborative filtering algorithms, content-based filtering algorithms, and hybrid algorithms. **Collaborative filtering** is based on the assumption that users with similar tastes for previous items will have similar preferences for new items, so the algorithm recommends items ranked highly by users deemed similar to the current user. Such algorithms fall into two main categories [18] [10, 20, 21, 27]. **Content based filtering** is based on the assumption that the features (meta data, words in description, price, tags, etc.) used to describe the items that a user likes or dislikes tell much about the user's preferences. It usually recommends new items similar to previous items the user liked. The underlying research focuses on estimating a user's profile from explicit feedback on whether she liked previous items. State of the art text classification algorithms, such as Support Vector Machine (SVM), K nearest neighbors (K-NN), neural networks, logistic regression, and Winnow, have been used to solve this binary classification task [29, 36, 37, 30, 25, 35]. **Hybrid recommendation algorithms** combine collaborative filtering with content based filtering, and usually perform better than either filtering method alone [7].

Most existing research in recommender systems overlooks a factor that is extremely important in a consumer's decision making: the product price. One notable exception is [12], who show that price is a factor that is transferrable across categories to help recommendation system predictions. Another exception, [34], explores price's marginal net utility role in E-commerce recommendation. However, these works still assume price is given and are focusing on boosting recommendation prediction performance with price as additional information; they do not treat prices a as controllable factors to influence user decisions.

Two recent pilot studies examine pricing strategies in recommendation systems. Backhaus et al. [6] ask consumers questions over the phone, cluster consumers into different groups, use conjoint analysis to estimate customers' WTP, and then use the estimates to price a small set of intangible value-added services on B2B market when making recommendations. Massoud and Abo-Rizka[24] proposed a conceptual model of personalized pricing recommender systems. However, no experiments were done to implement or study the proposed conceptual model. Kamishma and Akaho [19] went a little further and proposed a method for adding price personalization to standard recommendation algorithms based on customer preference data and purchasing history. However, only artificially generated data (based on the Movie-Lens dataset) are used. It's not clear how the approaches proposed by these pilot studies can be applied in a real e-commerce system with a large and varied set of users and many products of different types, brands and price ranges.

There is an established literature in economics and marketing showing that personalized promotion is an important marketing tactic for increasing sales volume [17]. Especially important for our paper is prior research, also in economics and marketing, on estimating a consumer's WTP for a particular product. Roughly speaking, there are four empirical approaches: estimating WTP from transactions data, direct surveys, indirect surveys or laboratory auctions. Transaction data is incentive compatible in that it represents actual purchase decisions. However, the transaction price is only the lower bound on WTP, and equally relevant non-purchase decisions are missing from transactions data. Direct surveys (see, e.g., [31, 15]) estimate a consumer's WTP by directly asking indicate their maximum acceptable price for a given product [1]. However, as pointed out by Breidert et al. [9], direct surveys are not incentive compatible — the respondent is not motivated to reveal his or her true WTP, and often is motivated to understate it substantially. Indirect surveys offer respondents a list of alternative products (often hypothetical products with their properties varied independently) and ask them to either to rank them according to personal preference [23] as in conjoint analysis, or simply to choose the most favored alternative as in choice-based conjoint analysis (CBC)[22][2, 3, 4, 5, 13, 14]. Similar to direct surveys, the conjoint analysis and CBC are not incentive compatible. To overcome this problem, Ding et.al in [13] proposed an ICBC - incentive aligned choice-based conjoint method, which applies the BDM mechanism described below to the WTP inferred from conjoint analysis. Dong et al. [14] proposed ranking revealed products based on the WTP inferred from conjoint analysis data. The authors argue their proposed approach is incentive aligned as subjects will receive top ranked products.

The remaining empirical approach is WTP elicitation via laboratory auction. The famous Vickrey auction [33], requires each bidder to a submit sealed bid (not seen by other bidders); the bidder with highest bid wins the auction and pays a price equal to the second highest bid. This procedure is incentive compatible. The intuition is that a person's own bids only determine whether or not she wins the auction but never affects the price that she pays, and therefore she has no incentive to understate (or overstate) her WTP. Closely related to the Vickrey auction is the Becker-DeGroot-Marschak (BDM) mechanism to elicit WTP [8]. Under BDM, each bidder submits a bid to purchase a product. A sales price is randomly drawn from an interval which covers all plausible bids. If that sales price is lower than a participant's bid, then she receives the product and pays the sales price. The BDM is theoretically incentive compatible for the same reason as the Vickrey auction; indeed (although it was invented independently) it is equivalent to a Vickrey auction with two bidders, one human and the other an automaton who bids randomly. Our own approach exploits the fact that BDM is easier to operate in an e-commerce setting since, unlike the Vickrey auction, it does not require gathering all participants' bids in order to determine the winner.

Despite considerable research on WTP elicitation [26] and existing pilot research on pricing strategies when recommending, we still face several challenges when adapting existing approaches to real world e-commerce settings. Existing approaches often require an artificial laboratory setting with only a handful of products preselected by researchers, and/or with product data generated artificially. In e-commerce systems, however, consumers are exposed to a much larger number of products of different types and price ranges, and the system needs to estimate WTP for products that might be of interest to an individual user. The gaps between the settings makes it unclear whether the conclusions derived from laboratory experiments generalize to e-commerce settings.

3. METHODS

We envision a recommender system that not only predicts whether a consumer likes a product, but also predicts a consumer's *willingness-to-pay* (WTP) for it. WTP is the highest price the consumer is willing to pay for a product [32]. If the WTP is lower than the default product price, the system might give a personalized promotion to the consumer to increase the possibility of accepting the recommendation.

We propose that the e-commerce system run a lottery (related to the BDM mechanism just described) for customers to collect WTP for a small number of recommended products, and then use machine learning on each customer's lottery data to build a WTP prediction model. The WTP predictions then allow the recommender system to set personalized promotion prices automatically, potentially enhancing customer satisfaction as well as seller profit.

The rest of this section details this approach.

3.1 Bidding & Lottery Procedures

Our procedure elicits WTP for N products. To describe it clearly, we begin with the case of a single product ($N = 1$). The participant's true WTP, denoted y, is unknown to us. We endow her with a large amount of cash C that likely exceeds y, and tell her that the mechanism will draw a random price r uniformly from the range $[R_L, R_U]$, which is chosen to include all plausible values of her WTP. She is asked to state her actual WTP by entering a bid $y' \in [R_L, R_U]$, and told that the mechanism will sell her the product at price r only if that price is less than her bid.

Using the symbol P to denote probability, her payoff is

$$\mathcal{M} = \begin{cases} C & \text{if } r > y', P = \frac{R_U - y'}{R_U - R_L}, \\ C + y - r & \text{if } r \leq y', P = \frac{y' - R_L}{R_U - R_L}. \end{cases} \quad (1)$$

That is, she keeps the cash if the random price r exceeds her stated WTP y', and otherwise she purchases (and gains true benefit y) at the random price, which is lower (and hence a better deal) than her her stated WTP y'.

To see that this BDM procedure is incentive compatible, first note that the expected payoff is:

$$\begin{aligned} E\left[\mathcal{M}|y',y\right] &= P(r > y')C + P(r \leq y')E[C + y - r|r \leq y'] \\ &= C + P(r \leq y')(y - E[r|r \leq y']). \end{aligned} \quad (2)$$

Use the convenient property of the uniform distribution that the last conditional expectation is $E[r|r \leq y'] = \frac{R_L + y'}{2}$ to simplify the equation to:

$$E\left[\mathcal{M}|y',y\right] = C + \frac{2yy' - y'^2 - 2R_L y + R_L^2}{2(R_U - R_L)} \quad (3)$$

Equation 3 shows that the participant's expected payoff is a quadratic function of her decision variable y' whose unique global optimum is reached when $y' = y$. In other words, it is in the subject's best interest to state her WTP truthfully.

Note for later reference that when the participant indeed sets $y' = y$, her expected payoff can be written as

$$E\left[\mathcal{M}|y,y\right] = C + \frac{(y - R_L)^2}{2(R_U - R_L)} > C \quad (4)$$

In our experiment we set $R_L = 0$ and $R_U = p$, where p is the known outside (undiscounted) market price for the product. In this case,

$$E\left[\mathcal{M}|y,y\right] = C + \frac{1}{2}k^2 p \quad (5)$$

where $y = k * p$, and we refer to k as the normalized bidding price.

What if the subject wants to bid above R_U or below R_L? In principle, there is no problem; in the first case she obtains the object for sure and reveals that her true WTP exceeds R_U, and in the second case she keeps the cash for sure and reveals that her true WTP is below R_L.

A potential problem does arise when the number of products $N > 1$. Running a separate BDM elicitation for several products that are substitutes for each other will motivate participants to underbid, since the probability of winning at least one of several bids is higher than winning a single bid. We eliminate this problem by having each participant enter a bid for each product, but only drawing a random bid for one of the products chosen randomly. That is, we conduct a lottery over which of the products will actually be available to the participant. The expected payoff (or $1/N$ of the expected payoff) is still maximized by truthfully reporting WTP for each product.

An extension of this lottery approach enables us to economize payments in the experiment. We can also conduct a lottery over which participants actually get the cash C and perhaps one of the products. Again, that attenuates the expected payoff but doesn't change where it is maximized.

3.2 Personalized Promotion

Our lottery/auction procedure gives us training data for predicting a consumer's WTP on a range of products that might be recommended. Given the values of y elicited from consumer u for product i, we run the regression

$$y_{ui} = b_0 + b_u + f(\mathbf{x_{ui}}, \mathbf{w}), \quad (6)$$

where b_0 is the global bias and b_u is the user bias, $\mathbf{x}_{ui}$ is a feature vector representing information about consumer u, product i and their relationships. The functional form of the regression function f depends on the machine learning algorithm used, such as linear regression or gradient boosted trees. We used *linear regression* (LR) in our experiments. Thus our model parameters are:

$$(b_0, b_u, \mathbf{w}^*) = \underset{b_0, b_u, \mathbf{w}}{\arg\min} \sum_{u,i} L(y_{ui} - b_u - b_0 - f(\mathbf{x_{ui}}, \mathbf{w})) \quad (7)$$

where in our implementation the loss function L is quadratic.

Given the model parameters learned from the training dataset, we use Equation 6 to predict WTP for any user u and item i pair. To capture the uncertainty in our estimation, we assume that the true WTP value follows a Gaussian

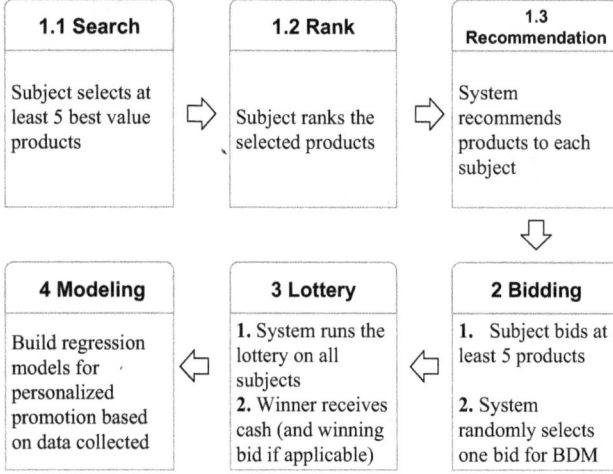

Figure 1: Overview of the experiment flow.

distribution centered on the predicted WTP:

$$Y_{ui} \sim \mathcal{N}(\mu_{ui}, \sigma^2) \tag{8}$$

where $\mu_{ui} = b_u + b_0 + f(\mathbf{x}_{ui}, \mathbf{w})$. The parameter σ^2 could be estimated, but for simplicity we assume that is the same for all user item pairs and approximate it using the variance of y on the training dataset in our experiments.

Based on the distribution of Y_{ui}, we can find the optimal price t^* that maximizes the expected seller profit as follows:

$$t^* = \arg\max_t (t - c) P(Y_{ui} \geq t) \tag{9}$$

where c is the production cost of product i and

$$
\begin{aligned}
P(Y_{ui} \geq t) &= \int_t^\infty \frac{1}{\sigma\sqrt{2\pi}} \exp^{-\frac{(x-\mu_{ui})^2}{2\sigma^2}} dx \\
&= \frac{1}{2} - \frac{1}{2} erf\left(\frac{t - \mu_{ui}}{\sqrt{2}\sigma}\right)
\end{aligned}
\tag{10}
$$

where $erf(x)$ is Gauss error function encountered in integrating the normal distribution. Equation 9 is solved numerically using standard optimization techniques.

4. EXPERIMENTAL PROCEDURES

Can the proposed lottery-auction mechanism and the prediction model actually work with normal e-commerce customers? Are those methods of practical value to sellers and customers? To begin to answer these questions we ran an experiment as follows.

4.1 Data collection

We first developed a website that links to amazon.com, a leading online shopping website. Our website implements a full fledged product search engine and displays the product information in a similar way to Amazon. The website hosts about 120k skin care products. We chose skin care products as they have short repurchase cycle, reducing problems that arise from unknown current holdings of the participants. The products are from amazon.com and the product information is synchronized with amazon.com at real time. For each product, Amazon provided both its list price and sales price.

Subjects recruited from Amazon Mechanical Turk were paid a participation fee of \$0.50 for around 10 minutes to complete the experiment. Figure 1 is an overview of the procedure. First, the subject sees a set of recommended products produced by a standard recommendation algorithm. This step would be straightforward for a typical e-commerce system, which can find relevant products based on subject's past purchasing or click data. Since our custom website don't have the recruited subject's purchasing history, we just let each subject search and identify at least 5 products which he or she thinks are worth buying; these are referred to as *best value* products. Then the subject proceeds to next step to rank their best value products in decreasing order of interest. Next, the system recommends a list of products using Amazon's "consumer who bought this also bought these" recommendations.

Having completed the steps labelled 1.1-1.3 in Figure 1, the recruited subject then participates in N BDM lotteries. That is, she enters a bid on each of $N \geq 5$ products that she chooses from those recommended in the previous step, knowing that at most one of the products will be randomly selected to go through the BDM procedure. Finally, one of the subjects recruited that day is randomly selected as the lottery winner, and one of her chosen N products is randomly selected. If her bid on that product exceeds the random buyout price r, then she receives the product and \$100 minus r. Otherwise she gets \$100 cash.

4.2 Subjects' training and selection

We showed earlier that truth telling (bidding one's actual WTP) is the unique optimal strategy in BDM. However, earlier empirical research has shown that people may have misconceptions about the game and may not use the optimal bidding strategy [11]. Guided by the earlier research, we provided detailed explanations about the game rule and encouraged our subjects to practice with a bidding simulator to see how the outcome changes with different bids. Then each subject was required to take a quiz to check whether the participant understands the optimal bidding strategy. Only the 79 subjects who passed the quiz (out of 130 who responded initially) were allowed to participate in the game.

4.3 Data collection

To clean the data, records with normalized bidding prices either below 10% or more than two times higher than the Amazon sale price are filtered out, as are the bids of subjects who took less than 5 minutes to complete the experiment. After cleaning, we ended up with 339 product bids from 54 subjects. The bid price is normalized using the product's Amazon sale price, as k in Equation 5.

To construct $\mathbf{x}_{ui}$, we used the 9 features described in Table 1. The features are based on information collected from each experiment step.

4.4 Evaluation Metrics

RMSE (Root Mean Square Error) is the most commonly used metric and is naturally adopted in our experiments. However, to understand the commercial value of personalized promotion based on the estimation of consumer's WTP, we go beyond RMSE and introduce *seller profit* to measure the effectiveness of WTP prediction. Seller profit of a single product purchase is simply the purchase price minus the cost of producing the product. For the proposed WTP prediction method in Section 3.2, the profit is expected profit given pricing via Equation 9. Hence

$$\text{Profit}_{ui} = \begin{cases} t_{ui}^* - c_i & \text{if } y_{ui} \geq t_{ui}^* \\ 0 & otherwise \end{cases} \quad (11)$$

where t_{ui}^* is the optimal personalized promotion price from Equation 9, y_{ui} is the consumer's true WTP and c_i is the unit production cost of product i.

5. EXPERIMENTAL RESULTS

We compared the proposed approach with Amazon sale price with 0, 10% and 20% discounts and ZeroR. The Amazon sale price methods serve as baselines. ZeroR algorithm is a simple learning based method that find the mean value of y on the training data and simply set the price at the learned mean value, which means a fixed discount rate. In our experiment, the normalized bidding price for product i by ZeroR is 0.72 (i.e. the learned discount rate is 0.28). Our proposed algorithm LR sets the price at the point where the expected profit is maximized (Equation 9). All algorithms are evaluated by 10 fold cross validation.

In our experiments, we don't know the production cost of each product. Because retail businesses commonly set price using a fixed markup on cost, we assume that production cost is a certain percentage of the sale price. We varied the percentage from 0 to 50% with an incremental step of 10%. Table 2 reports the corresponding profit and conversion rate for each algorithm at different production costs level.

Table 2 shows that our proposed method (i.e. LR) significantly outperforms Amazon's pricing strategy and simple learning method (i.e. ZeroR). All improvements are statistically significant (p < 5%). The LR algorithm maximizes expected profit as in Equation 9, using $\sigma = 0.22$ based on the training dataset. Is it important to model the *uncertainty* of WTP and set the price by maximizing the expected profit? The answer is yes. We compared the proposed method with simply setting the price at the most likely WTP (i.e. $b_0 + b_i + f(x_{ui}, w)$), and we found the simple method is statistically significantly worse.

5.1 Further Analysis

The feature weights of normalized bidding price k in the LR model may be of interest. Table 1 indicates that:

List price: normalized WTP decreases slightly as product's list price increases.

Number of reviews: normalized WTP decreases as the number of reviews increases. This is counter intuitive, as consumers presumably would tend to perceive goods with more reviews as more valuable. Of course, the expression is reduced form and for normalized (not direct) WTP, so future work may be able to find an explanation.

Discount: Products with larger Amazon discounts have higher normalized WTP. Like the list price impact, this effect probably also works mainly through the normalization (again recall Equation 5) but it is much stronger.

Average rating: Consumers are willing to pay more for products rated higher.

User rank: Not surprisingly, a consumer is willing to pay more for products she ranks more highly.

Switch brand: A consumer switching to a new brand tends to have lower WTP. This seems closely related to the

Name	Description	Weight
list price	Amazon list price of the product	−0.0013
number of reviews	number of reviews on Amazon	−0.001
brand variety	the variety of the brands of consumer's best value products, measured by entropy. The larger value of this feature, the more variety.	0.018
discount	Amazon promotional discount	0.399
Amazon recommendation rank	rank in Amazon product recommendation list	0.02
average rating	Amazon average rating	0.044
user rank	rank in consumer's best value products	−0.0017
switch brand	whether product(s) of the same brand as the bidding product have been identified by consumer as best value products	−0.059
brand popularity	the number of times getting bidded	0.054
intercept	*intercept term of the LR model*	−0.058

Table 1: The features used to predict WTP modeling, and their weight coefficients learned by Equation 7.

Algorithm	RMSE	Profit ($) w.r.t production cost (percent of product price)					
		None	10%	20%	30%	40%	50%
Amazon price	0.4549	784.69	675.73	566.76	457.79	348.82	239.85
90% Amazon price	0.4012	1267.18	1091.21	915.24	739.27	563.30	387.33
80% Amazon price	0.3674	1884.11	1622.47	1360.83	1099.18	837.54	575.90
ZeroR	0.3586	2358.13	2030.66	1703.19	1375.72	1048.25	720.78
LR	**0.2200**	**2734.14**	**2260.44**	**1831.22**	**1442.21**	**1104.83**	**818.60**

Table 2: Performance of different WTP prediction algorithms in 10-fold cross validation setting. Profit is evaluated w.r.t production cost as percentage of sale price. Note that the flat discount rate is applied to Amazon market price (after promotion discount off the list price).

brand variety effect, as variety seekers are more likely to switch brand than loyal customers.

Brand popularity: Not surprisingly, the more popular the brand, the more consumer is willing to pay.

6. CAVEATS

The analysis above noted many technical simplifications (e.g., normally distributed estimation errors for normalized WTP with constant variance), most of which can be relaxed in future work. This may be a good juncture to mention more general complications that we have put to one side.

- Most products have substitutes (and complements); and we mostly sidestepped the resulting complications. As this line of research matures it may be useful to consider bundles of goods and sets of alternatives explicitly.

- Personalized discounts, if not properly framed, can provoke customer backlash. Large scale application of our suggestions must tread carefully to avoid causing resentment.

- Our profit metric only took into account unit production costs. These could easily include handling and shipping, and researchers with access to cost data should have no problem extending our approach. However, a different treatment would be required to account for the costs of running a recommender system, or the costs of eliciting WTP. Presumably these are an order of magnitude smaller than production costs but they still could be important.

- Our Mechanical Turk subjects were convenient and turned out to quite useful. There is no reason to believe that naturally occurring e-commerce customers will behave in qualitatively different ways, but that remains an empirical question to be tested by researchers with access to large numbers of such customers. True A/B testing on that subject pool would be the gold standard.

7. CONCLUSION

This paper proposes including personalized promotion in e-commerce recommender systems. We developed a lottery-auction mechanism to elicit consumers' willingness to pay on a small subset of products, and a machine learning model to predict each consumer's WTP on a wide range of other products. We demonstrated the feasibility of the proposed approach in an experiment with real world products from Amazon and subjects recruited from Amazon Mechanical Turks. The results suggest that personalized promotion leads to significantly higher profits for sellers compared to the baseline pricing.

Our work also shows the viability of doing e-commerce experiments via crowdsourcing; our Mechanical Turk subjects turned out to be quite useful. Besides recommender systems, the proposed approach also has practical implication for managerial marketing.

The work just presented is only first step; much remains to be done. First and foremost, personalized promotion and recommendation should be considered jointly within a unified framework, and not remain as separate problems. Second, we focused on seller's profit as the evaluation metric. However, we believe it is crucial to include consumer surplus into the objective function and we see no conceptual obstacles in doing so. Finally, as alluded to in the caveats, it will be crucial to study the longer term effects on consumer satisfaction with personalized promotion. We hope that researchers in industry, with better access to normal e-commerce consumers, will be inspired to do so.

8. ACKNOWLEDGMENTS

Part of this work is sponsored by the National Science Foundation under grant CCF-1101741 and IIS-0953908. Any opinions, findings, conclusions or recommendations expressed in this paper are the authors, and do not necessarily reflect those of the sponsors.

9. REFERENCES

[1] J. Abrams. A new method for testing pricing decisions. *The Journal of Marketing*, pages 6–9, 1964.

[2] G. M. Allenby, N. Arora, and J. L. Ginter. Incorporating prior knowledge into the analysis of conjoint studies. *Journal of Marketing Research*, pages 152–162, 1995.

[3] G. M. Allenby, N. Arora, and J. L. Ginter. On the heterogeneity of demand. *Journal of Marketing Research*, pages 384–389, 1998.

[4] N. Arora, G. M. Allenby, and J. L. Ginter. A hierarchical bayes model of primary and secondary demand. *Marketing Science*, 17(1):29–44, 1998.

[5] N. Arora and J. Huber. Improving parameter estimates and model prediction by aggregate customization in choice experiments. *Journal of Consumer Research*, 28(2):273–283, 2001.

[6] K. Backhaus, J. Becker, D. Beverungen, M. Frohs, O. Müller, M. Weddeling, R. Knackstedt, and M. Steiner. Enabling individualized recommendations and dynamic pricing of value-added services through willingness-to-pay data. In *Electronic Markets*, 2010.

[7] J. Basilico and T. Hofmann. A joint framework for collaborative and content filtering. In *27th Annual International ACM SIGIR Conference*, 2004.

[8] G. M. Becker, M. H. DeGroot, and J. Marschak. Measuring utility by a single-response sequential method. *Behavioral science*, 9(3):226–232, 1964.

[9] C. Breidert, M. Hahsler, and T. Reutterer. A review of methods for measuring willingness-to-pay. *Innovative Marketing*, 2(4):8–32, 2006.

[10] J. Canny. Collaborative filtering with privacy via factor analysis. In *SIGIR '02: Proceedings of the 25th annual international ACM SIGIR conference on Research and development in information retrieval*, pages 238–245, New York, NY, USA, 2002. ACM.

[11] T. N. Cason and C. R. Plott. Misconceptions and game form recognition of the bdm method: challenges to theories of revealed preference and framing. 2014.

[12] J. Chen, Q. Jin, S. Zhao, S. Bao, L. Zhang, Z. Su, and Y. Yu. Does product recommendation meet its waterloo in unexplored categories?: No, price comes to help. In *Proceedings of the 37th International ACM SIGIR Conference on Research & Development in Information Retrieval*, SIGIR '14, pages 667–676, New York, NY, USA, 2014. ACM.

[13] M. Ding. An incentive-aligned mechanism for conjoint analysis. *Journal of Marketing Research*, pages 214–223, 2007.

[14] S. Dong, M. Ding, and J. Huber. A simple mechanism to incentive-align conjoint experiments. *International Journal of Research in Marketing*, 27(1):25–32, 2010.

[15] A. Gabor, C. W. Granger, and A. P. Sowter. Real and hypothetical shop situations in market research. *Journal of Marketing Research*, pages 355–359, 1970.

[16] D. Goldberg, D. Nichols, B. M. Oki, and D. Terry. Using collaborative filtering to weave an information tapestry. *Commun. ACM*, 35(12):61–70, 1992.

[17] S. Gupta. Impact of sales promotions on when, what, and how much to buy. *Journal of Marketing research*, pages 342–355, 1988.

[18] T. Hofmann and J. Puzicha. Latent class models for collaborative filtering. In *Proceedings of the International Joint Conference in Artificial Intelligence*, 1999.

[19] T. Kamishima and S. Akaho. Personalized pricing recommender system: Multi-stage epsilon-greedy approach. In *Proceedings of the 2Nd International Workshop on Information Heterogeneity and Fusion in Recommender Systems*, HetRec '11, pages 57–64, New York, NY, USA, 2011. ACM.

[20] Y. Koren, R. Bell, and C. Volinsky. Matrix factorization techniques for recommender systems. *Computer*, 42(8):30–37, 2009.

[21] Y. J. Lim and Y. W. Teh. Variational Bayesian approach to movie rating prediction. In *Proceedings of KDD Cup and Workshop*, 2007.

[22] J. J. Louviere and G. Woodworth. Design and analysis of simulated consumer choice or allocation experiments: an approach based on aggregate data. *Journal of marketing research*, pages 350–367, 1983.

[23] Y. Marbeau. What value pricing research today. *Journal of the Market Research Society*, 29(2):153–182, 1987.

[24] M. Massoud and M. Abo-Rizka. A conceptual model of personalized pricing recommender system based on customer online behavior. 2012.

[25] P. McNamee, C. Piatko, and J. Mayfield. JHU/APL at TREC 2002: Experiments in filtering and arabic retrieval. In *Proceeding of the Eleventh Text REtrieval Conference (TREC-11)*, 2002.

[26] K. M. Miller, R. Hofstetter, H. Krohmer, and Z. J. Zhang. How should consumers' willingness to pay be measured? an empirical comparison of state-of-the-art approaches. *Journal of Marketing Research*, 48(1):172–184, 2011.

[27] A. Paterek. Improving regularized singular value decomposition for collaborative filtering. In *Proceedings of KDD Cup and Workshop*, 2007.

[28] E. Rich. User modeling via stereotypes. *Cognitive Science*, 3(4):329 – 354, 1979.

[29] S. Robertson and I. Soboroff. The TREC-10 filtering track final report. In *Proceeding of the Tenth Text REtrieval Conference (TREC-10)*, pages 26–37. National Institute of Standards and Technology, special publication 500-250, 2002.

[30] M. Srikanth, X. Wu, and R. Srihari. UB at TREC 11: Batch and adaptive filtering. In *Proceeding of the Eleventh Text REtrieval Conference (TREC-11)*, 2002.

[31] R. G. Stout. Developing data to estimate price-quantity relationships. *The Journal of Marketing*, pages 34–36, 1969.

[32] H. R. Varian and W. Norton. *Microeconomic analysis*, volume 2. Norton New York, 1992.

[33] W. Vickrey. Counterspeculation, auctions, and competitive sealed tenders. *The Journal of finance*, 16(1):8–37, 1961.

[34] J. Wang and Y. Zhang. Utilizing marginal net utility for recommendation in e-commerce. In *SIGIR 2011*. ACM.

[35] L. Wu, X. Huang, J. Niu, Y. Xia, Z. Feng, and Y. Zhou. FDU at TREC 2002: Filtering, Q&A, web and video tasks. In *Proceeding of the Eleventh Text REtrieval Conference (TREC-11)*, 2002.

[36] Y. Yang, S. Yoo, J. Zhang, and B. Kisiel. Robustness of adaptive filtering methods in a cross-benchmark evaluation. In *Proceedings of the 28th Annual International ACM SIGIR Conference on Research and Development in Information Retrieval*, 2005.

[37] Y. Zhang. Using bayesian priors to combine classifiers for adaptive filtering. In *SIGIR '04: Proceedings of the 27th annual international ACM SIGIR conference on Research and development in information retrieval*, pages 345–352, New York, NY, USA, 2004. ACM Press.

Personalized Catch-up & DVR:
VOD or Linear, That is the Question

Pancrazio Auteri
ContentWise, CTO
Milan, Italy
pancrazio.auteri@contentwise.tv

Roberto Turrin
ContentWise, R&D
Milan, Italy
roberto.turrin@contentwise.tv

ABSTRACT

The expansion of TV services such as DVR and, more recently, Catch-up have removed the temporal constraint typical of the Linear "appointment" TV enabling users to watch content they love at any time and on-demand. However, the DVR and Catch-up TV libraries, while providing a convenient time-shifted "on-demand" consumption, are indeed composed by content previously aired on the Linear TV, so that they have more in common with Linear TV than they have with VOD.

In this talk we will present and discuss the main challenges and some possible solutions to personalize the user experience with content from DVR and Catch-up TV, such as:

(i) The consumption pattern is strongly affected by the context (e.g., time and device used to access the video service).

(ii) Some content is consumed serially and follows seasonal dynamics (e.g., TV Series).

(iii) The system is fed with a massive and very dynamic stream of data (e.g., new content right after broadcast, signals of user interactions).

(iv) The same piece of content may coexist across multiple services provided by the same operator (e.g., linear schedule, network-DVR, Catch-up TV, subscription VOD, rental VOD).

Categories and Subject Descriptors

H.3.3 [**Information storage and retrieval**]: Information Search and Retrieval—*Information filtering, Relevance feedback*

Keywords

TV; catch-up; VOD; video on demand; DVR; linear TV; context; personalization; recommender systems; predictive analytics; content lifecycle

RecSys'15, September 16–20, 2015, Vienna, Austria.
ACM 978-1-4503-3692-5/15/09.
DOI: http://dx.doi.org/10.1145/2792838.2799493.

Recommendations for Live TV

Jan Neumann
Comcast Labs
1110 Vermont Ave NW
Washington, DC 20005
Jan_Neumann@cable.comcast.com

Hassan Sayyadi
Comcast Labs
1110 Vermont Ave NW
Washington, DC 20005
hassan.sayyadi@cable.comcast.com

ABSTRACT

Despite the rise in video-on-demand consumption, live TV is still the most popular way to consume video entertainment. At Comcast we are developing novel ways to make it easy for our customers to access the live TV content that is interesting and relevant for them at the current moment. In this talk, we will describe some of the latest research at Comcast Labs on learning the favorite stations and programs for a customer at a given time of day, personalizing their TV guide, and informing our customers of what is trending on TV and social media at that moment, so that they can participate in the shared experience of live TV. We will explain how usage data is processed using both batch and real-time approaches to personalize the experience for Comcast's customers

Categories and Subject Descriptors

H.2.8 [**Database Management**]: Database Applications – *data mining.* I.2.10 [**Artificial Intelligence**]: Vision and Scene Understand – *video analysis,* Implementation - *interactive systems.*

General Terms

Algorithms, Measurement, Performance, Design, Experimentation, Human Factors.

Keywords

Recommendations; big data; television, movies; video-on-demand.

Jan Neumann is a senior manager at Comcast Labs Washington DC where he leads the big data and multi-media content analysis research teams. Before Comcast, he worked for Siemens Corporate Research on various computer vision related projects. He holds a Ph.D. in Computer Science from the University of Maryland, College Park.

Hassan Sayyadi is a Lead Researcher at the Comcast Research Lab in Washington DC. His research interests lie in the general field of machine learning with a special focus on recommendation and ranking problems in the TV and video domain. At Comcast, he is leading the personalization research team that develops novel personalized search, browse, and recommendation solutions to improve the experience for Comcast's customers. He holds a Ph.D. in Computer Science from the Univ. of Maryland, College Park.

RecSys'15, September 16–20 2015, Vienna, Austria
ACM 978-1-4503-3692-5/15/09.
http://dx.doi.org/10.1145/2792838.2799494.

The Application of Recommender Systems in a Multi Site, Multi Domain Environment

Steven Bourke
Schibsted Media Group
Barcelona, Spain
steve@schibsted.com

ABSTRACT

Recommender systems have cemented themselves in the daily experiences of most online users. In this work we will elaborate on the different challenges faced when creating recommendations in the following domains

- Online marketplaces: Two sided marketplaces where buyers and sellers can interact and sell items with each other.

- Online News: Online news sites where users consume the latest news articles related to current affairs.

- Generic Recommendations: Sites which create generic recommendations based on generalised algorithms.

We will review how we address these different challenges in Schibsted. Schibsted is an international media company with over 200 million unique users a month, split across 39 countries across the world.

Concretely we will review, and compare the primary challenges between the different domains mentioned as well as the commonalities and general lessons we have learnt. For example in a two sided marketplace, it is important that both actors in the interaction are considered when creating recommendations. Constraints such as price sensitivity and geographical location become important when identifying good quality recommendations for our users.

Alternatively, in online news we need to consider issues such as freshness and topical relevance when creating recommendations for users, while also striving to ensure we have editorial satisfaction. Finally we can look to generic recommendation solutions where we provide simple recommendation API end points. In this case it is important to ensure good quality recommendations while ensuring a generic enough solution that it can be used in many different scenarios.

What makes these challenges particularly interesting is that we approach these different challenges with a holistic view of for improving the overall user experience for our users in Schibsted.

Steven Bourke is a data scientist in Schibsted. He is a member of the recently formed Schibsted product and technology group where he works on building out and researching personalisation techniques to be used across Schibsted?s online properties. Previous to that he performed research in the field of recommender systems in the University of Dublin, under the supervision on Prof. Barry Smyth.

Categories and Subject Descriptors

H.3.3 [**Information Search and Retrieval**]: Information Filtering; J.0 [**Computer Applications**]: General

General Terms

Experimentation, Human Factors

Keywords

Recommender System; E-Commerce; News; Real world deployments

RecSys'15, September 16–20, 2015, Vienna, Austria.
ACM 978-1-4503-3692-5/15/09.
DOI: http://dx.doi.org/10.1145/2792838.2799495 .

We Know Where You Should Work Next Summer: Job Recommendations

Fabian Abel
XING AG
fabian.abel@xing.com

ABSTRACT

Business-oriented social networks like LinkedIn[1] or XING[2] support people in discovering career opportunities. In this talk, we will focus on the problem of recommending job offers to Millions of XING users. We will discuss challenges of building a job recommendation system that has to satisfy the demands of both job seekers who have certain wishes concerning their next career step and recruiters who aim to hire the most appropriate candidate for a job. Based on insights gained from a large-scale analysis of usage data and profile data such as curriculum vitae, we will study features of the recommendation algorithms that aim to solve the problem.

Job advertisements typically describe the job role that the candidate will need to fill, required skills, the expected educational background that candidates should have and the company and environment in which candidates will be working. Users of professional social networks curate their profile and curriculum vitae in which they describe their skills, interests and previous career steps. Recommending jobs to users is however a non-trivial task for which pure content-based features that would just match the aforementioned properties are not sufficient. For example, we often observe that there is a gap between what people specify in their profiles and what they are actually interested in. Moreover, profile and CV typically describe the past and current situation of a user but do not reflect enough the actual demands that users have with respect to their next career step. Therefore, it is crucial to also analyze the behavior of the users and exploit interaction data such as search queries, clicks on jobs, bookmarks, clicks that similar users performed, etc.

Our job recommendation system exploits various features in order to estimate whether a job posting is relevant for a user or not. Some of these features rather reflect social aspects (e.g. does the user have contacts that are living in the city in which the job is offered?) while others capture to what extent the user fulfills the requirements of the role that is described in the job advertisement (e.g. similarity of user's skills and required skills). To better understand appropriate next career steps, we mine the CVs of the users and learn association rules that describe the typical career paths. This information is also made publicly available via FutureMe[3]—a tool that allows people to explore possible career opportunities and identify professions that may be interesting for them to work in.

One of the challenges when developing the job recommendation system is to collect explicit feedback and thus understanding (i) whether a recommended job was relevant for a user and (ii) whether the user was a good candidate for the job. We thus started to stronger involve users in providing feedback and build a feedback cycle that allows the recommender system to automatically adapt to the feedback that the crowd of users is providing. By displaying explanations about why certain items were suggested, we furthermore aim to increase transparency of how the recommender system works.

Categories and Subject Descriptors

H.3.3 [**Information Systems**]: Information Search and Retrieval—*Information filtering*

General Terms

Algorithms, Design

Keywords

recommender systems, social networks

Short Bio

Fabian Abel is a Data Science team lead at XING. He enjoys solving large-scale data mining problems and delivering data products that do something meaningful. Before he joined XING in 2012, he was working as a postdoc at TU Delft, the Netherlands, and as PhD student at L3S Research Center in Hanover, Germany, researching user behavior and personalized information retrieval on the Social Web.

Acknowledgments

The work leading to these results has received funding from the EU's Seventh Framework Programme (FP7/2007-2013) under CrowdRec Grant Agreement no. 610594.

[1] http://linkedin.com

[2] http://xing.com

RecSys'15, September 16–20, 2015, Vienna, Austria.
ACM 978-1-4503-3692-5/15/09.
DOI: http://dx.doi.org/10.1145/2792838.2799496.

[3] http://futureme.xing.com

Assessing Expertise in the Enterprise: The Recommender Point of View

Aleksandra (Saška) Mojsilović, Kush R. Varshney

IBM Research

Abstract:

Some of the largest worldwide employers today are knowledge-based enterprises whose most important asset is human capital. Knowledge workers are unique, each having individualized skills, competencies and expertise, which constantly evolve and expand. Managing and planning for such a workforce critically depends on the ability to construct complete, accurate, and real-time representation and inventory of the expertise of employees in a form that integrates with business processes. In this session Saška will describe how enterprise expertise assessment process can be posed as predictive modeling and recommendation problem, and will present results and lessons learned from an actual deployment of IBM Expertise, a corporate-wide expertise recommendation and management system.

ACM Classification:

J.4 Computer Applications: SOCIAL AND BEHAVIORAL SCIENCES

Keywords:

recommender systems; expertise; social; predictive modeling

Bio:

Aleksandra (Saška) Mojsilović manages Data Science Group at the IBM T. J. Watson Research Center in Yorktown Heights, New York. Saška is one of the pioneers of business analytics at IBM an in the industry; throughout her career she championed innovative uses of analytics for business decision support: from the early identification of client risk via predictive modeling, to the estimation of outsourcing benefits via signal analysis in support of IBM marketing campaigns, retention analytics, and identifying and recommending experts in the enterprise. For her technical contributions and the business impact of her work, Saška was appointed an IBM Fellow, the company's highest technical honor. Saška received her PhD in Electrical Engineering in 1997 from the University of Belgrade, Belgrade, Serbia. She has worked at Bell Laboratories (1998-2000) and IBM Research (2000-present). Her main research interests include multidimensional signal processing, pattern recognition and machine learning, with applications to business analytics, healthcare, financial modeling, multimedia and social systems. She is the author of over 100 publications and holds 14 patents. Saška received a number of awards for her work, including the IEEE Young Author Best Paper Award, INFORMS Wagner Prize, IEEE International Conference on Service Operations and Logistics and Informatics Best Paper Award, European Conference on Computer Vision Best Paper Award, IBM Gerstner Award, IBM Market Intelligence Award and several IBM Outstanding Technical Achievement Awards.

Kush R. Varshney was born in Syracuse, NY in 1982. He received the B.S. degree (magna cum laude) in electrical and computer engineering with honors from Cornell University, Ithaca, NY, in 2004. He received the S.M. degree in 2006 and the Ph.D. degree in 2010, both in electrical engineering and computer science at the Massachusetts Institute of Technology (MIT), Cambridge. He is a research staff member in the Data Science Group of the Mathematical Sciences and Analytics Department at the IBM T. J. Watson Research Center, Yorktown Heights, NY. He is also a data ambassador with DataKind, New York, NY. His research interests include statistical signal processing, machine learning, data mining, and image processing. Dr. Varshney is a member of Eta Kappa Nu, Tau Beta Pi and ACM, and a senior member of IEEE. He has received a Best Student Paper Travel Award at the 2009 International Conference on Information Fusion, the Best Paper Award at the 2013 IEEE International Conference on Service Operations and Logistics, and Informatics, the Best Social Good Paper Award at the 2014 ACM SIGKDD Conference on Knowledge Discovery and Data Mining, a Best Research Paper Honorable Mention at the 2015 SIAM International Conference on Data Mining, and several IBM awards for contributions to analytics projects. He is on the editorial board of Digital Signal Processing and a member of the IEEE Signal Processing Society's Machine Learning for Signal Processing Technical Committee and Signal Processing Theory and Methods Technical Committee.

RecSys'15, September 16–20 2015, Vienna, Austria
ACM 978-1-4503-3692-5/15/09.
http://dx.doi.org/10.1145/2792838.2799497

Large-Scale Real-Time Product Recommendation at Criteo

Romain Lerallut, Diane Gasselin, Nicolas Le Roux
Criteo Labs
{r.lerallut, d.gasselin, n.leroux}@criteo.com

ABSTRACT

Performance retargeting consists of displaying online advertisements that are personalized according to each user's browsing history. We show close to three billion personalized ads a day, each of them optimized to generate the best post-click sales performance for our clients. Within this time frame, Criteo's recommender system must choose a dozen relevant products from billions of candidates in a few milliseconds. Our main challenge is to balance the amount of data we use with the processing speed and low-latency requirements of a web-scale environment.

Criteo has about ten thousand clients, each with a catalog of products that usually run in millions, sometimes more. Product-to-product similarities are computed by analyzing billions of product events (view, sales) spread over several weeks. The backend part must therefore crunch dozens of terabytes of data in a few hours.

On the other hand, retargeting is a business that requires very up-to-date recommendations. We show targetted ads that depend both on long-term user behavior as well as events that occurred a few seconds ago. Building an architecture that can accomodate such a large amount of data and yet provide accurate recommendations using almost realtime data is a major challenge.

Metrics are also a difficult topic. Finding the metrics that will accurately predict offline the performance a model would have online is a hard problem. Constant improvements of our systems require a lot of trial-and-error. In our environment, online A/B testing can be a costly solution. Can we do better ?

In this talk, we will expose the way we have built our system to provide optimal recommendations under these constraints, as well as the many challenges we have in front of us.

Keywords

Real-time, Large-Scale, Low-latency

RecSys'15, September 16–20, 2015, Vienna, Austria.
ACM 978-1-4503-3692-5/15/09
DOI: http://dx.doi.org/10.1145/2792838.2799498 .

BIOS
Romain Lerallut

Romain Lerallut is a Senior Engineering Manager at Criteo in the Engine department, in charge of applying large-scale machine learning algorithms to actual problems such as product recommendation or graphical layout optimization. Romain has been working on building up the Engine since 2011, first as devlead and then as manager. Before joining Criteo, he was teaching computers how to read cursive handwriting at A2iA. He has an engineering degree from "Ecole des Ponts-Paristech" and a PhD in Computer Science from "Ecoles des Mines-Paristech".

Diane Gasselin

Diane Gasselin is a Software Engineer at Criteo, since 2011. She worked at first on the infrastructure and algorithms for predicting a banner profitability and is now part of the recommendation team, responsible of selecting the best products to display on the banner considering the context and user features. She graduated from the computer science and applied mathematics engineering school ENSIMAG.

Nicolas Le Roux

Nicolas Le Roux is the head of the Criteo Research Team in Paris, working on improving the Machine Learning systems at the heart of the Criteo Engine since 2012. Before joining Criteo, Nicolas was a researcher with expertise in machine learning, computer vision, neural networks, deep learning, optimization, large-scale learning and statistical modeling in general. He held a position at INRIA/ENS and before that in Microsoft Research, Cambridge, UK. He has a PhD from the University of Montreal under Yoshua Bengio, working on theoretical and practical advances on neural networks and kernel methods.

Scaling up Recommendation Services in Many Dimensions

Bottyán Németh

Gravity Research&Development
Mészáros u. 58/b
1016 Budapest, Hungary
bottyan@gravityrd.com

ABSTRACT

Gravity R&D has been providing recommendation engines as SaaS solutions since 2009. The company has a strong research focus and recommendation quality has always been their primary differentiating factor. Widely used or open source recommendation algorithms are of little use to our technology team as a result of the superiority of our in-house developed, proprietary algorithms.

Gravity R&D experienced many challenges while scaling up their services. The sheer quantity of data handled on a daily basis increased exponentially. This presentation will cover how overcoming these challenges permanently shaped our algorithms and system architecture used to generate these recommendations.

Serving personalized recommendations requires real-time computation and data access for every single request. To generate responses in real-time, current user inputs have to be compared against their history in order to deliver accurate recommendations. We then combine this user information with specific details about available items as the next step in the recommendation process.

It becomes more difficult to provide accurate recommendations as the number of transactions and items increase. It also becomes difficult because this type of analysis requires the combination of multiple heterogeneous algorithms that all require different inputs.

Initially, the architecture was designed for MF based models and serving huge numbers of requests but with a limited number of items. Now, Gravity is using MF, neighborhood based models and metadata based models to generate recommendations for millions of items within their databases. This required a shift from a monolithic architecture with in-process caching to a more service oriented architecture with multi-layer caching. As a result of an increase in the number of components and number of clients, managing the infrastructure can be quite difficult.

Even with these challenges, we don't believe that it is worthwhile to use a fully distributed system. It adds unneeded complexity, resources, and overhead to the system. We prefer an approach of firstly optimizing current algorithms and architecture and only moving to a distributed system when no other options are left.

RecSys'15, September 16–20, 2015, Vienna, Austria.
ACM 978-1-4503-3692-5/15/09.
DOI: http://dx.doi.org/10.1145/2792838.2799499

Categories and Subject Descriptors

E.0 [**General**]

General Terms

Performance

Keywords

recommendation engine; performance; scalability

Short Bio

Bottyán Németh started research on recommendation systems while participating the Netflix Prize with the Gravity team. After successes in the Netflix Prize competition, the research team transformed into a company providing recommendation and personalization solutions on a Software as a Service basis for companies all over the world. As one of the founders of the company, he has been working at Gravity R&D since its origination and has been continuously nurturing the development of its recommendation engine from the beginning.

In the last couple of years the company scaled up exponentially. This occurred not only in the number of recommendations served per day, from several million to more than 100 million, but also in the number of recommendable items stored in their database, which went from a couple thousand to tens of millions. Simultaneously, the company increased the number of recommendation and personalization related features. A new focus has been undertaken, focusing on the quality of the user experience and also improving the quality of the proprietary algorithmic features. Bottyán has contributed in this evolution in several ways from developing the data mining tools, designing the system architecture, and development of the operation workflow. Currently he is focused on how to apply state of the art recommendation algorithms in real world problems to help Gravity's clients deliver more engaging and relevant user experiences, which will result in an increase in their business's KPIs.

Recommendations in Travel

Onno Zoeter
Booking.com
Onno.Zoeter@Booking.com

ABSTRACT

Recommender systems have received much attention in recent years, and they have been successfully applied in many different domains. With each domain come new constraints that require system designers to make choices about how to apply and extend generic algorithms in their context. Booking.com is planet earth's number one accommodation reservation site. The accommodation recommendation problem that it needs to solve has several interesting and unique challenges that make that a straightforward matrix factorization or a basic bi-linear model are not sufficient to provide the required predictions.

A concrete challenge is the high-stakes nature of selecting accommodations. Whereas, say, a movie can be stopped after a few minutes, a holiday is more costly to stop. And whereas, say, an expensive television can often be returned, cancelling a reservation upon arrival leaves you with significantly less choice for alternatives. Because of this, users will interact with the recommendation system more and will require guidance in understanding a market and preferences before making a decision. This effect is clearly visible in the data for instance by the number of re-rankings users make before making a final decision.

Another concrete challenge is that the inventory is not static and all decisions are made in a very specific context. For example when a particular user makes a selection not all properties might be available and the price of both the selected and alternative properties will vary through time. This requires model components that describe the choice process and keeps track of the context of each decision.

Other challenges include the mix of business and leisure bookings by the same person, the sparsity and long-tail effects in all dimensions, the multi-level nature of recommendations that span from destination to dates and to hotels, the anonymity of users in many browsing sessions continued on different devices, and more.

In this talk, we will discuss several of the challenges we have encountered and solutions we have developed.

Categories and Subject Descriptors

G.3 [**Probability and Statistics**]: Multivariate statistics

Keywords

Recommender Systems

Bio

Dr. Onno Zoeter is principal data scientist at Booking.com where he works on designing and improving prediction, collaborative filtering and ranking models. Before joining Booking.com, Dr. Zoeter led the research on transportation demand management at Xerox's European Research Lab and worked on large scale click-through rate prediction problems at Microsoft Research in Cambridge. His research received numerous awards. Among them the OECD International Transport Forum Innovation Award and the International Parking Institute Award of Excellence. The large scale system for advertisement relevance prediction he co-developed won Microsoft's adPredict competition and was adopted as part of the Bing search engine. Fortune selected him among their 20 Big Data All-Stars in 2014.

RecSys'15, September 16–20, 2015, Vienna, Austria.
ACM 978-1-4503-3692-5/15/09.
DOI: http://dx.doi.org/10.1145/2792838.2799500.

Making Meaningful Restaurant Recommendations At OpenTable

Sudeep Das
OpenTable Inc.
1 Montgomery Street
San Francisco, CA, USA
sdas@opentable.com

ABSTRACT

At OpenTable, recommendations play a key role in connecting diners with restaurants. The act of recommending a restaurant to a diner relies heavily on aligning everything we know about the restaurant with everything we can infer about the diner. Our methods go beyond using the diner-restaurant interaction history as the sole input - we use click and search data, the metadata of restaurants, as well as insights gleaned from reviews, together with any contextual information to make meaningful recommendations. In this talk, I will highlight the main aspects of our recommendation stack built with Scala using Apache Spark.

Categories and Subject Descriptors

H.2.8 [**Database Management**]: Database applications—*Data Mining*

Keywords

Recommendation Systems, Natural Language Processing

RecSys'15, September 16–20, 2015, Vienna, Austria.
ACM 978-1-4503-3692-5/15/09.
DOI: http://dx.doi.org/10.1145/2792838.2799501 .

The Role of User Location in Personalized Search and Recommendation

Ido Guy
Yahoo Labs Israel
idoguy@acm.org

ABSTRACT

With mobile devices, users no longer access the web from specific locations, but virtually from anywhere. How does this affect our ability to provide personalized information for users? In this talk, I will discuss the influence of location activity on users' information needs and how a better understanding of these needs can help enhance web applications in which personalization plays a central role.

Categories and Subject Descriptors

H.3.3 Information Search and Retrieval – *Information filtering*

General Terms

Algorithms, Measurement, Human Factors.

Keywords

Context-based recommendation; location-aware search; recommender systems; search personalization; user modeling.

1. INTRODUCTION

Mobile devices have led to a paradigm shift from web use that is mainly performed in specific locations to web use that is being done virtually anywhere and is frequently related to the geographic environment. Considering user location therefore becomes fundamental to many web applications, in order to provide a better service for their users. In this talk, I will discuss the importance of understanding user location in order to enhance personalized search and recommendation. I will describe a model we developed to distinguish between web search in familiar places, which the user frequently visits, and unfamiliar places, which are seldom visited by the user [14]. I will demonstrate how this model can contribute to the understanding of both users and locations and how it can benefit applications such as search auto-completion. I will also discuss how user location can enhance research areas I have previously studied, including people search and expertise location [1,9,17], relationship analysis [12,13,15], crowdsourcing [2,4], people recommendation [6,8], content recommendation [10,11,16], and social stream filtering [3,5,7].

2. Bio

Ido Guy is a Principal Research Engineer at Yahoo Labs, where he focuses on data science for Yahoo products in search, questions answering, and email. Prior to joining Yahoo Labs, Ido was a senior technical staff member and manager of the Social Technologies group, an area that he established and managed in 2007-2014, as part of the IBM Haifa Research Lab. Recommender systems are a key part of Ido's research, with focus on the social media domain. He served as program co-chair for RecSys 2012.

3. REFERENCES

[1] Guy, I., Avraham, U., Carmel, D., Ur, S., Jacovi, M., and Ronen, I. 2013. Mining expertise and interests from social media. *Proc. WWW '13*, 515-526.

[2] Guy, I., Hashavit, A., and Corem, Y. 2015. Games for crowds: A crowdsourcing game platform for the enterprise. *Proc. CSCW '15*, 1860-1871.

[3] Guy, I., Levin, R., Daniel, T., and Bolshinsky, E. 2015. Islands in the Stream: A study of item recommendation within an enterprise social stream. *Proc. SIGIR '15*.

[4] Guy, I., Perer, A., Daniel, T., Greenshpan, O., and Turbahn, I. 2011. Guess who? Enriching the social graph through a crowdsourcing game. *Proc. CHI '11*, 1373-1382.

[5] Guy, I., Ronen, I., and Raviv, A. 2011. Personalized activity streams: Sifting through the "river of news". *Proc. RecSys '11*, 181-188.

[6] Guy, I., Ronen, I., and Wilcox, E. 2009. Do you know? Recommending people to invite into your social network. *Proc. IUI '09*, 77-86.

[7] Guy, I., Steier, T., Barnea, M., Ronen, I., and Daniel, T. 2012. Swimming against the streamz: Search and analytics over the enterprise activity stream. *Proc. CIKM '12*, 1587-1591.

[8] Guy, I., Ur, S., Ronen, I., Perer, A., and Jacovi, M. 2011. Do you want to know? Recommending strangers in the enterprise. *Proc. CSCW '11*, 285-294.

[9] Guy, I., Ur, S., Ronen, I., Weber, S., and Oral, T. 2012. Best faces forward: A large-scale study of people search in the enterprise. *Proc. CHI '12*, 1775-1784.

[10] Guy, I., Zwerdling, N., Carmel, D., Ronen, I., Uziel, E., Yogev, S., and Ofek-Koifman, S. 2009. Personalized recommendation of social software items based on social relations. *Proc. RecSys '09*, 53-60.

[11] Guy, I., Zwerdling, N., Ronen, I., Carmel, D., and Uziel, E. 2010. Social media recommendation based on people and tags. *Proc. SIGIR '10*, 194-201.

[12] Jacovi, M., Guy, I., Kremer-Davidson, S., Porat, S., and Aizenbud-Reshef, N. 2014. The perception of others: Inferring reputation from social media in the enterprise. *Proc. CSCW '14*, 756-766.

[13] Jacovi, M., Guy, I., Ronen, I., Perer, A., Uziel, E., and Maslenko, M. 2011. Digital traces of interest: Deriving interest relationships from social media interactions. *Proc. ECSCW '11*, 21-40.

[14] Kravi, E., Agichtein, E., Guy, I., Kanza, Y., Mejer, A., and Pelleg, D. 2015. Searcher in a strange land: Understanding web search from familiar and unfamiliar locations. *Proc. SIGIR '15*.

[15] Perer, A., Guy, I., Uziel, E., Ronen, I., and Jacovi, M. 2011. Visual social network analytics for relationship discovery in the enterprise. *Proc. VAST '11*, 71-79.

[16] Ronen, I., Guy, I., Kravi, E., and Barnea, M. 2014. Recommending social media content to community owners. *Proc. SIGIR '14*, 243-252.

[17] Yogev, A., Guy, I., Ronen, I., Zwerdling, N., and Barnea, M. 2015. Social media-based expertise evidence. *Proc. ECSCW '15*.

RecSys '15, September 16-20, 2015, Vienna, Austria
ACM 978-1-4503-3692-5/15/09.
http://dx.doi.org/10.1145/2792838.2799502

A Study of Priors for Relevance-Based Language Modelling of Recommender Systems

Daniel Valcarce, Javier Parapar, Álvaro Barreiro
Information Retrieval Lab
Department of Computer Science
University of A Coruña, Spain
{daniel.valcarce, javierparapar, barreiro}@udc.es

ABSTRACT

Probabilistic modelling of recommender systems naturally introduces the concept of prior probability into the recommendation task. Relevance-Based Language Models, a principled probabilistic query expansion technique in Information Retrieval, has been recently adapted to the item recommendation task with success. In this paper, we study the effect of the item and user prior probabilities under that framework. We adapt two priors from the document retrieval field and then we propose other two new probabilistic priors. Evidence gathered from experimentation indicates that a linear prior for the neighbour and a probabilistic prior based on Dirichlet smoothing for the items improve the quality of the item recommendation ranking.

Categories and Subject Descriptors

H.3.3 [**Information Search and Retrieval**]: Information filtering

General Terms

Algorithms, Experimentation

Keywords

Recommender Systems; Collaborative Filtering; Relevance-Based Language Models; prior probability

1. INTRODUCTION

Recommender systems aim to find relevant pieces of information which may be of interest to the users. Since this objective can be modelled as a personalised item ranking task, the use of techniques from the Information Retrieval (IR) field is becoming more and more popular. An effective approach to recommendation is Collaborative Filtering (CF). This family of algorithms exploits the past interaction between users and items to generate personalised suggestions.

Loosely speaking, CF algorithms analyse the users' taste in a system and intend to recommend relevant items.

Relevance-Based Language Models (RM) were conceived for expanding queries automatically [6]. However, they can be effectively applied to CF recommendation [8, 2, 10]. The task of recommending items to a user can be assimilated to the task of expanding a query with new terms. In this case, the user profile plays the role of the query. This approach has been proved to be notably effective in terms of ranking quality, surpassing other state-of-the-art algorithms such as nearest neighbours or matrix factorisation methods [8].

Information Retrieval algorithms often include the notion of a *document prior* which encodes the importance of a document independently of the user's query. These priors can be used for improving the performance of the document ranking. Therefore, they were thoroughly studied in the IR field [5, 4, 9, 3].

The use of probabilistic models such as RM for recommendation provides several advantages. One of them is the possibility of introducing prior probabilities into the recommendation process. In fact, the most effective estimation of the Relevance-Based Language Models for CF is RM2 whose formulation includes a user prior and an item prior. Previous works on the relevance modelling of recommender systems considered those priors uniform [8, 2] leaving open the possibility of further studying this aspect. Thus, in this paper, we analyse the effects of the user and the item priors in the RM2 model. First, we adapt two effective document length priors from IR to the CF task [5, 3]. Next, we propose two new variants of the probabilistic length prior devised in [3]. Finally, we conduct a series of experiments that show that the use of a linear length prior for the users and a probabilistic length prior based on Dirichlet smoothing for the items leads to significant improvements in terms of ranking accuracy.

2. RELEVANCE MODELLING OF RECOMMENDER SYSTEMS

Recommender systems help users with the finding of relevant items. The set of users of the system is denoted by $\mathcal{U}$ and the set of items by $\mathcal{I}$. When a user u rate an item i, we refer to that rating with the notation $r_{u,i}$. We use the term $\mathcal{I}_u$ to represent the set of items that were rated by the user u. Likewise, the set of users that rated the item i is denoted by $\mathcal{U}_i$. The goal of the recommender is to generate, for each user u, a personalised list of k items L_u^k ordered in decreasing order of estimated relevance.

Relevance-Based Language Models [6] are a probabilistic

pseudo-relevance feedback technique for text retrieval. Their goal is to expand the user's query with new relevant terms to improve the retrieval performance. In order to achieve so, an initial retrieval is computed and relevance over the first top results is assumed (this set of documents is called pseudo-relevant set). Recently, RM have been adapted to CF showing high accuracy figures [8]. Under this scenario, users' profiles play the role of both documents and queries and the items are equivalent to the terms. In this way, instead of expanding queries with new terms, we can use RM to expand users' profiles with new relevant items. The pseudo-relevant set in the CF task is the neighbourhood of the target user. These neighbourhoods can be determined using, for instance, the traditional k-NN algorithm.

There exist two estimates of Relevance Models that were proposed for recommendation. In this paper, we focus on RM2 since it was reported to provide the best results. This algorithm computes a Relevance Model for each user u calculates the relevance of each item i under it, $p(i|R_u)$:

$$p(i|R_u) \propto p(i) \prod_{j \in \mathcal{I}_u} \sum_{v \in V_u} \frac{p(i|v)p(v)}{p(i)} p(j|v) \quad (1)$$

where V_u refers to the set of neighbours of the user u. The conditional probability of an item given a user, $p(i|u)$, is computed by smoothing the maximum likelihood estimate. The original papers used Jelinek-Mercer smoothing [8]; however, in this paper, we employ Absolute Discounting smoothing which consists in subtracting a constant δ from each rating. The rationale behind this decision is that this smoothing method models the user bias yielding better recommendations. The reason is that the amount of smoothing applied from the background collection $p(i|\mathcal{C})$ is inversely proportional to the average rating of the user [10]:

$$p(i|u) = \frac{\max(r_{u,i} - \delta, 0)}{\sum_{j \in \mathcal{I}_u} r_{u,j}} + \delta \frac{|\mathcal{I}_u|}{\sum_{j \in \mathcal{I}_u} r_{u,j}} p(i|\mathcal{C}) \quad (2)$$

Finally, we need to specify how to compute the user prior $p(v)$ and the item prior $p(i)$. In the original paper uniform distributions were used [8]. Our proposed priors are described next.

3. PROPOSED PRIORS

The recommendation formula that results from applying Relevance Models to the CF task (see Eq. 1) involves the use of a user prior for each of the neighbours, $p(v)$, and an item prior for each of the candidate items to be recommended, $p(i)$. Next, we introduce the user priors; from these, the deviation of the item priors is straightforward.

We will use the following priors to compute the prior probability of a neighbour in the RM2 algorithm.

Uniform (U).

This prior is drawn from a uniform distribution. That is to say, every user in the population has the same prior probability. We use this prior as our baseline.

$$p_u(u) = \frac{1}{|\mathcal{U}|} \quad (3)$$

Linear (L).

The linear document length prior was previously used in Information Retrieval [5, 3]. Its adaptation to recommen-

dation boosts those users with larger rating profiles. In this way, we are promoting the recommendations that came from the power users of the system.

$$p_L(u) = p(u|\mathcal{C}) = \frac{\sum_{i \in \mathcal{I}_u} r_{u,i}}{\sum_{v \in \mathcal{U}} \sum_{j \in \mathcal{I}_v} r_{v,j}} \quad (4)$$

Probabilistic using Jelinek-Mercer (PJM).

An effective prior for Information Retrieval is the probabilistic document length prior proposed in [3]. It is indirectly based on the document length. For the CF task, this method computes the users' priors as a function of the statistics of the items they rated. The original formulation of this prior employs Jelinek-Mercer smoothing:

$$\begin{aligned} p_{PJM}(u) &\propto \sum_{i \in \mathcal{I}_u} p(i|u) \\ &= \sum_{i \in \mathcal{I}_u} \left[(1 - \lambda) \frac{r_{u,i}}{\sum_{j \in \mathcal{I}_u} r_{u,j}} + \lambda p(i|\mathcal{C}) \right] \\ &= (1 - \lambda) + \lambda \sum_{i \in \mathcal{I}_u} p(i|\mathcal{C}) \end{aligned} \quad (5)$$

Probabilistic using Dirichlet (PD).

In this work, we also propose to explore the previous Probabilistic prior using Dirichlet smoothing:

$$\begin{aligned} p_{PD}(u) &\propto \sum_{i \in \mathcal{I}_u} p(i|u) \\ &= \sum_{i \in \mathcal{I}_u} \frac{r_{u,i} + \mu p(i|\mathcal{C})}{\mu + \sum_{j \in \mathcal{I}_u} r_{u,j}} \\ &= \frac{\sum_{i \in \mathcal{I}_u} r_{u,i} + \mu \sum_{i \in \mathcal{I}_u} p(i|\mathcal{C})}{\mu + \sum_{i \in \mathcal{I}_u} r_{u,i}} \end{aligned} \quad (6)$$

Probabilistic using Absolute Discounting (PAD).

Finally, the same applying Absolute Discounting:

$$\begin{aligned} p_{PAD}(u) &\propto \sum_{i \in \mathcal{I}_u} p(i|u) \\ &= \sum_{i \in \mathcal{I}_u} \frac{\max(r_{u,i} - \delta, 0) + \delta |\mathcal{I}_u| p(i|\mathcal{C})}{\sum_{j \in \mathcal{I}_u} r_{u,j}} \\ &= \frac{\sum_{i \in \mathcal{I}_u} \max(r_{u,i} - \delta, 0) + \delta |\mathcal{I}_u| \sum_{i \in \mathcal{I}_u} p(i|\mathcal{C})}{\sum_{j \in \mathcal{I}_u} r_{u,j}} \end{aligned} \quad (7)$$

The straightforward item-based counterparts of the proposed priors are not showed here for brevity.

4. EVALUATION

Next, we describe the collections, methodology, experiments and the results analysing the priors proposed in the previous section.

The experiments were conducted in three collections: *MovieLens 100k*[1] (films), *R3-Yahoo! Webscope Music*[2] (music) and LibraryThing[3] (books). Their details can be found in Table 1.

---

[1] http://grouplens.org/datasets/movielens/
[2] http://webscope.sandbox.yahoo.com/catalog.php
[3] http://www.macle.nl/tud/LT/

Table 1: Datasets statistics

Dataset	Users	Items	Ratings	Density
MovieLens 100k	943	1682	100,000	6.305%
R3-Yahoo!	15,400	1,000	365,703	2.375%
LibraryThing	7,279	37,232	749,401	0.277%

We performed five-fold cross-validation using the splits provided by MovieLens 100k to train the prior parameters and choose the best priors. Then, we applied these priors and their parameters to the R3-Yahoo! and LibraryThing collections. Since LibraryThing does not include a default split, we randomly selected 80% of the ratings of each user as training subset and the rest as test subset. Thus, the splits of the MovieLens collection were used for tuning parameters whilst the splits of other datasets were employed solely for evaluation purposes, that is, the training split was used as seed data for the recommender system and the testing split was used for assessing the performance.

We followed the *TestItems* approach described in [1] for estimating the ranking quality of the recommendations. For each user in the test subset, we compute recommendations including all the items in the test subset. Although this methodology underestimates the true value of the precision-oriented metrics (because it considers that non-rated items are irrelevant), it provides more reliable results.

We decided to use nDCG (Normalised Discounted Cumulative Gain) at a cut-off value of 10 for assessing the quality of the top ranking. We employed the *standard formulation* [11] using the ratings in test as graded relevance judgements.

For computing the neighbourhoods, we utilised k-NN with Pearson's correlation coefficient as similarity metric. We fixed the value of k to 400 neighbours. We used the optimal smoothing method (Absolute Discounting with $\delta = 0.1$) reported in [10].

Regardless the fact that we tested all possible combinations of priors (and their parameters), we decided to present the results in two steps for the sake of the discussion. First, we introduce the results of tuning only the user prior and, second, we show the results of tuning the item prior using the best user prior. We denote that we use the prior X for users and the prior Y for items with the following notation X-Y.

4.1 Tuning the User Prior

Taking a uniform distribution for the item prior, we tested all the priors proposed in Sec. 3. Figure 1 illustrates the results, in terms of nDCG@10, of this experiment.

We can observe that using a uniform distribution is the worst scenario: any of the others user priors improves the ranking quality. In spite of the fact that the Probabilistic priors improve the nDCG figures, the Linear prior is the one that provides the best results implying that we should rely on neighbours with a high number of ratings. This finding suggests that users with a tiny rating profile are not very reliable for computing recommendations since we have few data about them.

An advantage of this finding is that the Linear prior is a parameter-free technique. This allows to improve the performance of a RM2 recommender without introducing more complexity into the model.

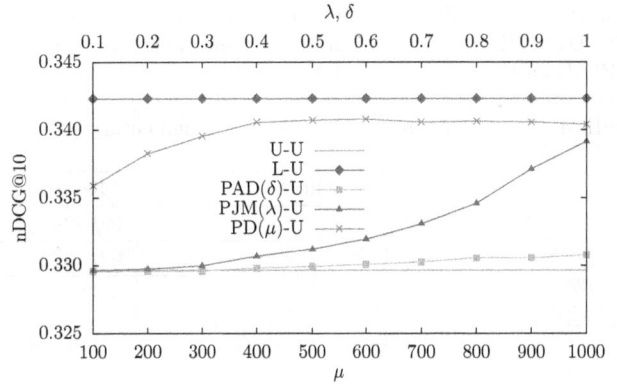

Figure 1: Values of nDCG@10 for RM2 varying the user prior and taking a uniform distribution for the item prior. We show Uniform (U) and Linear (L) priors as well as Probabilistic priors using Jelinek-Mercer (PJM), Dirichlet (PD) and Absolute Discounting (PAD) smoothings.

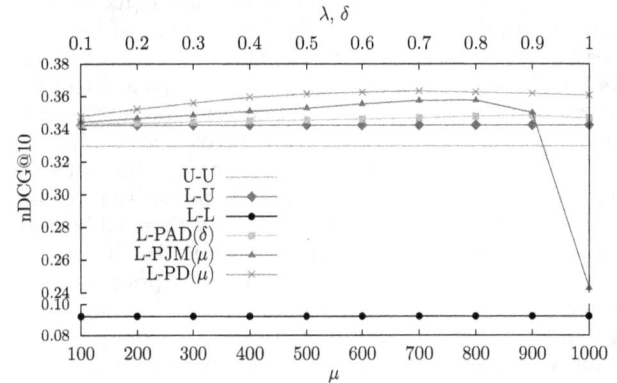

Figure 2: Values of nDCG@10 for RM2 varying the item prior and taking a Linear prior (L) for the user prior. We show Uniform (U) and Linear (L) priors as well as Probabilistic priors using Jelinek-Mercer (PJM), Dirichlet (PD) and Absolute Discounting (PAD) smoothings. We also present the baseline consisting in using both uniform priors.

4.2 Tuning the Item Prior

Now that we have the optimal user (neighbour) prior, we fixed it and we focus on finding the best item prior. We show the values of nDCG@10 obtained for each item prior in Fig. 2. For the sake of comparison, we also present the main baseline which consists in using uniform distributions for users and items (U-U).

In contrast to the previous scenario, we can appreciate that the performance of the Linear prior is very poor. We should note that the item prior divides the RM2 estimate. Thus, the Linear prior is demoting items that have a high number of ratings. Intuitively, lowering the importance of popular items is not a good idea if we want to generate recommendations although it may promote more novel and diverse suggestions.

On the other hand, the results show that the use Probabilistic priors affects the ranking quality positively. It is interesting to observe that Jelinek-Mercer with the parameter $\lambda = 1$ degrades the performance of the recommender.

Table 2: Test values of nDCG@10 using the classic user-based CF neighbour algorithm (UB), Single Value Decomposition (SVD), RM2 with uniform priors (U) and RM2 with Linear prior (L) for the neighbours and Probabilistic Prior with Dirichlet (PDP) for the items. Bolded cells correspond to the best tested method for each dataset. Statistically significant improvements according to the two-sided Wilcoxon test ($p < 0.01$) with respect to UB, SVD, RM2-U-U and RM2-L-PD are superscripted with a, b, c and d, respectively. The complementary statistically significant decreases are subscripted in the same way.

Method	MovieLens 100k	R3-Yahoo!	LibraryThing
UB	0.0468_{bcd}	0.0106_{cd}	0.0055^{b}_{cd}
SVD	0.0936^{a}_{cd}	0.0103_{cd}	0.0014_{acd}
RM2-U-U	0.3296^{ab}_{d}	0.0205^{ab}	0.0900^{ab}_{d}
RM2-L-PD ($\mu = 700$)	$\mathbf{0.3632}^{abc}$	$\mathbf{0.0207}^{ab}$	$\mathbf{0.0942}^{abc}$

This is expected because in this extreme case since the effect of this prior in the denominator would demote items that were rated by power users. In contrast, if we lower λ too much, we are obtaining a uniform prior.

The Probabilistic prior based on Absolute Discounting smoothing produces worse results than the other Probabilistic priors because of the counterintuitiveness in its formulation. Although this method normalises the bias of the users (see Sec. 2), when we amplify the effect of the power users we are also decreasing the importance of popular items because we discount a constant δ from each rating (i.e., the more ratings an item has, the more discount we apply).

Finally, the Probabilistic prior based on Dirichlet presents the best figures, with $\mu = 700$ as the optimal value of the parameter. Dirichlet smoothing has been thoroughly studied in Information Retrieval [7] concluding that it demotes large documents. In this case, as the item prior is in the denominator, we are promoting, in a controlled way, items with a larger number of ratings. Moreover, it shows a quite stable performance with respect to the parameter μ.

4.3 Testing on the Other Collections

To assess if the previous findings generalise to other collections, we apply those priors to the R3-Yahoo! and the LibraryThing datasets. We also report the results of the standard user-based Collaborative Filtering algorithm (using the 50 nearest neighbours according to Pearson's correlation) denoted by UB and a standard matrix factorisation algorithm (using 350 latent factors) denoted by SVD. We present the nDCG@10 values of these recommendation methods in Table 2.

From this data, it can be seen that the use of the Linear prior for modelling neighbour prior probabilities and Probalistic prior (with Dirichlet smoothing) for items improves the ranking precision in the three collections. Nevertheless, the results obtained for the R3-Yahoo! dataset are not statistically significant according to the Wilcoxon test ($p < 0.01$).

5. CONCLUSIONS AND FUTURE WORK

In this paper, we have studied the effect that the user and item priors play in the RM2 algorithm, the most effective Relevance-Based Language Model estimate for Collaborative Filtering recommendation. This study has identified the Linear prior as the optimal one for modelling neighbourhoods. Additionally, the Probabilistic prior based on Dirichlet smoothing is a good choice for computing the item prior probability. We have found that the correct modelling of these prior probabilities can significantly improve the ranking accuracy in two out of three collections.

As future work, it would be interesting to analyse if the combination of different priors can lead to better results as it was shown in Information Retrieval [9]. Moreover, future research may study priors such as PageRank [4].

Acknowledgments

This work was funded by grant TIN2012-33867 from the Spanish Government and grants GPC2013/070, R2014/034 and R2014/002 from the Galician Government.

6. REFERENCES

[1] A. Bellogín, P. Castells, and I. Cantador. Precision-Oriented Evaluation of Recommender Systems. In *RecSys '11*, page 333, Oct. 2011.

[2] A. Bellogín, J. Parapar, and P. Castells. Probabilistic Collaborative Filtering with Negative Cross Entropy. In *RecSys '13*, pages 387–390, 2013.

[3] R. Blanco and A. Barreiro. Probabilistic Document Length Priors for Language Models. In *ECIR '08*, pages 394–405, 2008.

[4] S. Brin and L. Page. The Anatomy of a Large-scale Hypertextual Web Search Engine. In *WWW '98*, volume 30, pages 107–117, 1998.

[5] W. Kraaij, T. Westerveld, and D. Hiemstra. The Importance of Prior Probabilities for Entry Page Search. In *SIGIR '02*, pages 27–34, 2002.

[6] V. Lavrenko and W. B. Croft. Relevance-Based Language Models. In *SIGIR '01*, pages 120–127, Sept. 2001.

[7] D. E. Losada and L. Azzopardi. An Analysis on Document Length Retrieval Trends in Language Modeling Smoothing. *Inf. Retr.*, 11(2):109–138, Dec. 2008.

[8] J. Parapar, A. Bellogín, P. Castells, and A. Barreiro. Relevance-based language modelling for recommender systems. *Inf. Process. Manage.*, 49(4):966–980, July 2013.

[9] J. Peng, C. Macdonald, B. He, and I. Ounis. Combination of Document Priors in Web Information Retrieval. In *RIAO '07*, pages 596–611, 2007.

[10] D. Valcarce, J. Parapar, and A. Barreiro. A Study of Smoothing Methods for Relevance-Based Language Modelling of Recommender Systems. In *ECIR '15*, volume 9022, pages 346–351, 2015.

[11] Y. Wang, L. Wang, Y. Li, D. He, W. Chen, and T.-Y. Liu. A Theoretical Analysis of NDCG Ranking Measures. In *COLT '13*, pages 1–30, 2013.

Adapting Recommendations to Contextual Changes Using Hierarchical Hidden Markov Models

Mehdi Hosseinzadeh
Aghdam
DePaul University
Chicago, IL 60604, USA
maghdam@depaul.edu

Negar Hariri
DePaul University
Chicago, IL 60604, USA
nhariri@cs.depaul.edu

Bamshad Mobasher
DePaul University
Chicago, IL 60604, USA
mobasher@cs.depaul.edu

Robin Burke
DePaul University
Chicago, IL 60604, USA
rburke@cs.depaul.edu

ABSTRACT

Recommender systems help users find items of interest by tailoring their recommendations to users' personal preferences. The utility of an item for a user, however, may vary greatly depending on that user's specific situation or the context in which the item is used. Without considering these changes in preferences, the recommendations may match the general preferences of a user, but they may have small value for the user in his/her current situation. In this paper, we introduce a hierarchical hidden Markov model for capturing changes in user's preferences. Using a user's feedback sequence on items, we model the user as a hierarchical hidden Markov process and the current context of the user as a hidden variable in this model. For a given user, our model is used to infer the maximum likelihood sequence of transitions between contextual states and to predict the probability distribution for the context of the next action. The predicted context is then used to generate recommendations. Our evaluation results using Last.fm music playlist data, indicate that this approach achieves significantly better performance in terms of accuracy and diversity compared to baseline methods.

1. INTRODUCTION

Traditional recommender systems recommend items based on users' history of preferences and interactions. In general, however, users' preferences can change because of the natural evolution of their tastes, changes in their current context, or the emergence of new items. As a result of these preference changes, a static set of recommendations generated based on the full set of past preferences does not always provide the most utility for a user. In particular, in domains where there may be frequent changes in user's context during the course of interaction with the system, failure to consider these changes may result in considerable performance degradation. For example, the user of a music recommender may have different interests in music depending on her/his current activity (such as exercising, relaxing, driving, etc.).

To address this issue context-aware recommender systems (CARSs) have been introduced [1]. Compared to the traditional systems that mainly utilize users' preference history, CARSs provide more relevant results by generating recommendations that match the current interests of each user. In some applications, the current context of the user might be explicitly given to the system as a set of factors affecting the recommendations. On the other hand, if the contextual factors explaining the preference changes are not directly observed, it might still be possible to infer them as a set of latent variables and use them to generate recommendations during the course of a user's interactions with the system.

In this paper, we focus on a setting where users' feedback on items is revealed sequentially. Based on the feedback data in the current session and also the user's history of preferences, the recommender predicts the next item that would be interesting for the user. For example, based on the sequence of songs that a user has listened to in her current playing session, the recommender suggests other songs that might be of interest.

We propose a context-aware recommendation algorithm based on hierarchical hidden Markov modeling (HHMM) [4]. Our model captures common patterns of contextual changes in users' preferences, represented as hidden variables in the model, and use them to produce personalized recommendations matching the current interests of the user. Also, the proposed approach increases diversity of recommendations while maintaining an acceptable level of accuracy. The ability to capture user preferences at a more aggregate level of latent variables representing contexts, enables our approach to produce more diverse recommendation lists.

We evaluated our approach using an off-line cross validation strategy. In our experiments we used Last.fm dataset containing time-stamped sequences of users' listening activities. Our evaluation results indicate that our proposed approach achieves significantly better performance in terms of accuracy and diversity of the recommendations compare to other baseline methods.

RecSys'15, September 16–20, 2015, Vienna, Austria.
© 2015 ACM. ISBN 978-1-4503-3692-5/15/09 ...$15.00.
DOI: http://dx.doi.org/10.1145/2792838.2799684.

2. RELATED WORK

Many of the existing conventional recommendation methods, such as matrix factorization or neighborhood-based methods, don't take into account the users' change of interests. Time-aware recommendation approaches such as [6] consider the drift in users' preferences over time and model the temporal dynamics within the data. However, these methods assume that time is the only factor that can impact users' interests while ignoring other possible contextual factors.

Recommendation based on pattern-mining [7][5], can be one possible approach for context-adaptation in sequential recommenders. This technique relies on discovering frequent patterns of items based on sequence of items in the training data and using these patterns to generate recommendations.

Recommendation based on a Markov chain model [8] is another method that can utilize such sequential data by predicting users' next actions based on their previous preferences. For an mth order model, the recommendations are generated based on only the last m recent observations from each user. So, if m is a small value, then the recommender is not generating personalized recommendations as the algorithm is ignoring a large part of the information in a user's profile. On the other hand, setting m to a large value increases the number of model parameters exponentially which makes it impractical to learn the model in many situations.

Another alternative is the hidden Markov modeling (HMM) approach [11], where the states are latent variables and the items liked by the user in that state are observed variables. Each state has a probability distribution over the set of items. The learning process includes estimating the transition probabilities between the states as well as the probability distribution of observing items at each hidden state. The distribution of current state changes as result of changes in a user's behavior. Therefore, these latent states can be used as a representation of the current context of the user.

Many of the recommendation algorithms are biased toward recommending a few popular items. These algorithms often can achieve good precision and recall levels in comparison to more complex methods. In fact, according to the analysis in [3], the recommendation accuracy captured based on precision and recall can be increased when an additional popularity bias is introduced. However, it has been shown that these popular items are not extremely exciting for the users and do not help with increasing the sales revenue as much as more niche and new items. Similar studies (e.g., [2]) have shown that recommendation in the long tail has special value in increasing the sales revenue and producing more useful and diverse recommendations.

3. HIERARCHICAL HIDDEN MARKOV MODEL

In this paper, we focus on a setting where users' preferences are revealed as a time-stamped sequence of positive feedback on items, such as playing songs or clicking on Web pages. The goal of the recommender is to predict the future interests of the user. We introduce a context-aware recommender that models the changing contextual states of the user based on the feedback sequence collected from that user. The recommender system monitors variations in users' preferences and dynamically adapts to these changes.

Our approach is based on training an HHMM for modeling context as a latent variable affecting the users' feedback

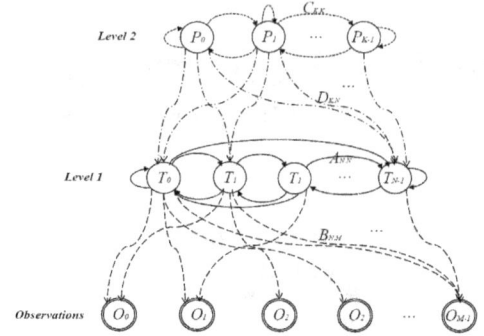

Figure 1: Graphical model of HHMM.

Table 1: Model Parameters

N = Number of states in the first level.
M = Number of items.
A = State transition probabilities in the first level.
B= Observation probability matrix between the first level of hidden states and items.
C = State transition probabilities in the second level.
D = Observation probability matrix between second and first levels.
π = Initial state distribution.
$O = < O_0, O_1, \cdots, O_{L-1} >$ = observation sequence.
L =Length of the observation sequence.

behaviors. Hierarchical hidden Markov model is a type of structured hierarchical stochastic process. HHMM extends the original hidden Markov model by training two levels of hidden variables. The hidden variables at the first level are used as observations for training the second level.

In our system, we used users' sequences of positive feedback on items as the set of observations to train the first level of hidden states. The first level of hidden variables, represent our model of the latent contextual states affecting users' preferences over time. The second level of hidden variables, captures the common patterns of transition between different contextual states and correspond to our latent model of users' interests. Figure 1 presents the overall process of HHMM in our system. Table 1 describes the notation used in the presented graphical model.

3.1 Inference and Recommendation

Algorithm 1 presents the general process of training the HHMM in our system and using it for producing context-aware recommendations [4]. The model parameters that need to be inferred are shown as $\lambda(A, B, C, D, \pi)$ and are described in table 1. At the beginning, each of these parameters is randomly initialized. Let $O =< o_1, o_2, \cdots, o_l >$ represent a feedback sequence with size l where o_i indicates the ith item in the sequence that received positive feedback from the user. Given each user feedback sequence, parameters A and B are first updated. In other words, for each input sequence, the state distribution, the first-level state

Algorithm 1: HHMM for context-aware recommendation
1- Initialize $\lambda = (A, B, C, D, \pi)$ to small random values.
2- For each user:
3-   For each user's feedback sequence:
4-   Re-estimate $\lambda(A, B, \pi)$.
5-   Find the most likely first-level state sequence.
6-   Re-estimate $\lambda(C, D, \pi)$ based on first-level state sequence inferred in the previous step.
7-   Find the most likely second-level state sequence based on first-level sequence.
8-   Predict next context using $\lambda(C, D, \pi)$.
9-   Predict next observation using $\lambda(A, B, C, D, \pi)$.

transition probabilities, and the observation probability matrix (between the first-level latent variables and the items) are updated. These parameters are updated as follows:

> **for** $i=0..N\text{-}1$ **do**
> $\pi_i = \gamma_0(i)$
> **for** $i=0..N\text{-}1$ **do**
>   **for** $j=0..N\text{-}1$ **do**
> $a_{ij} = \sum_{l=0}^{L-2} \gamma_l(i,j) / \sum_{l=0}^{L-2} \gamma_l(i)$
> **for** $j=0..N\text{-}1$ **do**
>   **for** $k=0..M\text{-}1$ **do**
> $b_j(k) = \sum \gamma_l(j) / \sum_{l=0}^{L-2} \gamma_l(j)$
> $l\in\{0,...,L-2\}$, $o_l=k$

Where $\gamma_l(i,j) = P(x_l = s_i, x_{l+1} = s_j | O, \lambda)$ is the transition probability from state s_i to state s_j at time $l+1$, and $\gamma_l(i) = \sum_{j=0}^{N-1} \gamma_l(i,j)$. In the next step, the first-level state sequence with maximum likelihood is discovered. This corresponds to the most likely transition sequence between contextual states that explains the user feedback sequence. We applied Viterbi algorithm to solve this problem [10].

The first-level state sequence discovered in the previous step is then used to update matrices C and D. The procedure we used in this step is similar to the method used for updating the matrices A and B. The only difference is in the type of input: the parameters C and D are updated based on the discovered first-level state sequences while A and B are re-estimated based on the observed item sequences.

In the next step, the second-level state sequence with maximum likelihood is determined. This sequence is the most likely transition sequence between the second-level hidden variables that explains the contextual changes. Based on the trained context transition probabilities (parameters C and D), our model predicts the context of the next action of the user. By using the predicted context and having the observation probability matrix B, our model then generates the recommendations that match the predicted context. These recommendations are chosen as the set of items that have the highest probability given the predicted context.

After training the model, we used the multiplication of C and D to predict the next context for a given user. In the next step, by multiplication A and B, we compute the probability of each item for the recommendation based on the contexts. Finally, by using these probabilities and having predicted context, we predict the top-N recommendations with the highest probability that correspond to predicted context.

4. EXPERIMENTS

This section describes our experiments for evaluating our sequential recommendation approach against a number of other popular baseline methods. We did our experiments based on users' music listening activities collected from Last.fm Website between 2009/01/01 to 2009/05/31. This dataset contained the time-stamped sequence of artists that each user had listened to during the specified time period. We used the first four months of the data for training the models and the last month (2009/05) for evaluation of the recommendations. The training set contained 837 users, with at least one artist in the test and train partitions, and the number of unique artists was 51759. The test data contained 462 users. Given a user, each of the competing algorithms

produced a set of N recommendations which were then evaluated based on the test data.

4.1 Evaluation Metrics

All the recommendation methods were compared based on the *precision* and *recall* metrics. These two measures are among the common metrics used for off-line evaluation of recommendation algorithms where binary type of feedback is available. Given a set of recommendations, let TP represent the number of correct recommendations, and FP indicate the number of incorrect recommendations. A recommendation is assumed to be correct only if it appears in the test data. The precision and recall are computed as:

$$Precision = \frac{TP}{TP + FP}, Recall = \frac{TP}{TP + FN} \qquad (1)$$

Where FN indicates the number of relevant items that are not included in the recommendation list. Another metric used in our experiments was F-measure that is defined as:

$$F - Measure = \frac{2 \times Precision \times Recall}{Precision + Recall} \qquad (2)$$

Popularity Bias was used in our evaluations to compare the diversity of different recommendation methods. We followed the same approach as in [3] to compute this metric. The items were first sorted based on their overall frequencies in all users' profiles and were then grouped into $I = 10$ bins such that the items in the same bin were similar in popularity. For each baseline method, the top $N = 10$ recommendations generated for each test case were then analyzed to compute the normalized distribution of each category.

4.2 Baseline Recommendation Algorithms

This section focuses on comparing the performance of HHMM against other baseline approaches. We used AIC criterion ($AIC=ML_\lambda - P_\lambda$) to determine the optimal number of latent states for HMM and HHMM. Where ML_λ is the maximum likelihood of the model, and P_λ is the number of parameters in the model. Based on this criterion, the number of latent states in the first level was set to 20 and the number of states in the second level was set to 10. The baseline methods used in our evaluations are as followed:

HMM: Recommendation algorithm based on the standard HMM model [11]. Similar to HHMM, we used 20 hidden states for training the HMM model.

Sequential Pattern Mining: Recommendation based on contiguous sequential patterns [7][5] was used as one of the baselines in our evaluations. In our evaluations, the support value of sequential patterns was tuned and set to 0.01.

Item-based Markov Modeling: As another baseline sequential recommender, a kth-order Markov model was built where states corresponded to all item subsequences of length k observed in the training data, and actions corresponded to different items. For each user, the last k items were used to produce recommendations. The transition probability for state s_i and action a_j was computed based on the training sequence database and as the normalized frequency of times a_j occurred after s_j. The order of the model was to $k = 3$.

User-Based kNN: This method was used as one of the baseline approaches. The cosine metric was used to compute the similarity of users and the size of neighborhood for each user was set to 100.

Table 2: Recall and precision for various recommendation methods.

Method	Top 5			Top 10		
	Precision	Recall	F-Measure	Precision	Recall	F-Measure
HHMM	0.3272	0.00655	0.01284	0.27995	0.01125	0.02163
HMM	0.3644	0.0054	0.01064	0.3228	0.0102	0.01977
Sequential Pattern Mining	0.1036	3.56E-05	7.12E-05	0.0812	3.63E-05	7.26E-05
Item-based Markov Modeling	0.0342	8.69E-05	1.73E-04	0.0281	1.23E-04	2.45E-04
User-Based kNN	0.0350	0.0035	6.36E-03	0.0297	0.007	1.13E-02
BPRMF	0.0273	0.0047	8.02E-03	0.0247	0.006	9.65E-03
Most Popular	0.02188	0.006	9.42E-03	0.0179	0.008	1.11E-02
Random	0.0004	5.74E-06	1.13E-05	0.0004	2.76E-05	5.16E-05

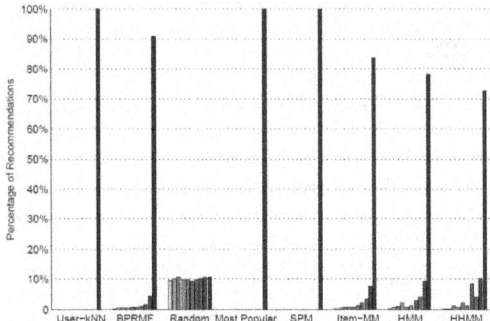

Figure 2: Comparison of popularity bias of different recommendation methods

BPRMF: Matrix Factorization using Bayesian Personalized Ranking (BPRMF) [9] was used as another baseline in our evaluations. This model was trained for 30 factors.

Most Popular: This baseline ranks the items based on popularity.

Random: This recommender, randomly selects N items as the recommendation list for each given user.

4.3 Evaluation Results

Table 2 presents the recall and precision at ranks 5, and 10 for each of the competing algorithms. According to this table, HMM has slightly better precision in comparison to HHMM and also has a significantly higher precision compare to the rest of the baseline methods. However, HHMM has the highest recall and achieves the best overall F-score.

Figure 2 compares the popularity bias of HHMM and other methods. As expected, the random recommender has the lowest popularity bias as the recommendations are almost uniformly distributed over the 10 bins. On the other hand, user-based kNN, most-popular recommender, and recommendation based on sequential pattern mining have the highest popularity bias. All the recommendations generated by these three algorithms belong to a single bin (most popular items) while the items in the remaining bins are not selected for recommendation. Although BPRMF and Item-based Markov model have better diversity than user-based kNN, both HMM and HHMM achieve better performance with respect to lower popularity bias while HHMM has slightly better diversity compare to HMM.

5. CONCLUSIONS

This paper proposes a recommendation method based on Hierarchical Hidden Markov Models for adapting to users' varying interests as a result of contextual changes. We model context as a latent variable affecting the likelihood that a user likes a given item. Our model captures the probability of transition between different contextual states and uses these probabilities to predict the context of the next interaction of the user with the system. The predicted context is then used to generate the recommendations that are most relevant to the current interests of the user as well as his/her history of preferences. Our evaluation results indicate that using the predicted context can improve the diversity of the recommendations.

6. REFERENCES

[1] G. Adomavicius, B. Mobasher, F. Ricci, and A. Tuzhilin. Context-aware recommender systems. *AI Magazine*, 32(3):67–80, 2011.

[2] O. Celma. *Music Recommendation and Discovery - The Long Tail, Long Fail, and Long Play in the Digital Music Space*. Springer, 2010.

[3] F. G. D. Jannach, L. Lerche and G. Bonnin. What recommenders recommend - an analysis of accuracy, popularity, and sales diversity effects. In *User Modeling, Adaptation, and Personalization*. Springer, 2013.

[4] S. FINE, Y. SINGER, and N. TISHBY. The hierarchical hidden markov model: analysis and applications. *Machine Learning*, 32, 1998.

[5] N. Hariri, B. Mobasher, and R. Burke. Context-aware music recommendation based on latenttopic sequential patterns. In *In Proc. of the sixth ACM conference on Recommender systems*, pages 131–138. ACM, 2012.

[6] Y. Koren. Collaborative filtering with temporal dynamics. *Communications of the ACM*, 53(4):89–97, 2010.

[7] B. Mobasher, H. Dai, T. Luo, and M. Nakagawa. Using sequential and non-sequential patterns for predictive web usage mining tasks. In *Proc.of the IEEE International Conference on Data Mining*, 2002.

[8] J. Pitkow and P. Pirolli. Mining longest repeating subsequences to predict world wide web surfing. In *Proc. USENIX Symp. On Internet Technologies and Systems*, page 1, 1999.

[9] S. Rendle, C. Freudenthaler, Z. Gantner, and L. Schmidt-Thieme. Bpr: Bayesian personalized ranking from implicit feedback. In *In Proc. of the Twenty-Fifth Conference on Uncertainty in Artificial Intelligence*.

[10] M. S. Ryan and G. R. Nudd. The viterbi algorithm. 1993.

[11] N. Sahoo, P. V. Singh, and T. Mukhopadhyay. A hidden markov model for collaborative filtering. *MIS Quarterly*, 36(4):1329–1356, 2012.

Are Real-World Place Recommender Algorithms Useful in Virtual World Environments?

Leandro Balby Marinho
Federal University of Campina Grande
Campina Grande, Brazil
lbmarinho@dsc.ufcg.edu.br

Christoph Trattner
NTNU & Know-Center
Trondheim, Norway & Graz, Austria
ctrattner@know-center.at

Denis Parra
Pontificia Universidad Católica de Chile
Santiago, Chile
dparra@ing.puc.cl

ABSTRACT

Large scale virtual worlds such as massive multiplayer online games or 3D worlds gained tremendous popularity over the past few years. With the large and ever increasing amount of content available, virtual world users face the information overload problem. To tackle this issue, game-designers usually deploy recommendation services with the aim of making the virtual world a more joyful environment to be connected at. In this context, we present in this paper the results of a project that aims at understanding the mobility patterns of virtual world users in order to derive place recommenders for helping them to explore content more efficiently. Our study focus on the virtual world SecondLife, one of the largest and most prominent in recent years. Since SecondLife is comparable to real-world Location-based Social Networks (LBSNs), i.e., users can both check-in and share visited virtual places, a natural approach is to assume that place recommenders that are known to work well on real-world LBSNs will also work well on SecondLife. We have put this assumption to the test and found out that (i) while collaborative filtering algorithms have compatible performances in both environments, (ii) existing place recommenders based on geographic metadata are not useful in SecondLife.

Categories and Subject Descriptors

H.3.3 [**Information Storage and Retrieval**]: Information Search and Retrieval—*Information filtering*

Keywords

virtual environments; location-based recommendations

1. INTRODUCTION

Location-based social networks (LBSN) enable users to check-in and share places and relevant content, such as photos, tips and comments that help others in exploring novel and interesting places they might not have been before. Foursquare[1], for example, is a popular LBSN with millions of subscribers doing millions of check-ins everyday all over the world. This vast amount of check-in data, publicly available through Foursquare's data access APIs, has recently inspired many researchers to investigate human mobility patterns and behavior with the aim of assisting users, by means of personalized recommendation services, in exploring their surroundings more efficiently [19, 20, 9].

Problem Statement. Virtual world environments, on the other hand, are interactive 3D worlds where millions of users all around the globe spend a lot of time every day to create and explore new content. Rules are typically drawn from reality, such as gravity, topography, locomotion, real-time actions, and communication. These systems gained tremendous popularity over the past few years and are poised for continued growth. Facebook, for example, recently bought Oculus VR that produces virtual reality headsets for allowing game players to immerse themselves in virtual worlds, which indicates that there are big plans for virtual worlds on the table[2]. With the massive amount of content available all the time, virtual world users, especially newbies and the inexperienced ones, typically suffer from the information overload problem which undermines their ability to find relevant and exciting content. To tackle this issue content suggestion services are typically provided to help people in exploring content more efficiently [17].

While there are many works on recommender systems for virtual worlds that focus on economical [6, 16] and social aspects of these systems [12, 11, 13], only a few of them try to understand mobility patterns in virtual worlds (see e.g., [15, 1]). These latter works indicate a strong correlation between virtual and real world movement patterns and although they suggest that existing real world LBSN recommender approaches would perform similarly in virtual worlds, to the best of our knowledge there are no studies yet showing explicitly if this assumption really holds. The findings with this respect have important implications for recommender systems designers, because if this assumption holds, a whole suite of place recommendation algorithms can be transferred from the LBSN domain to virtual worlds. If not, new algorithms need to be devised for characterizing the specificities of virtual world users mobility patterns.

RecSys '15, September 16 – 20, 2015, Vienna, Austria.
ACM 978-1-4503-3692-5/15/09.
DOI: http://dx.doi.org/10.1145/2792838.2799674 .

---

[1] http://www.foursquare.com
[2] http://www.theguardian.com/technology/2014/jul/22/facebook-oculus-rift-acquisition-virtual-reality

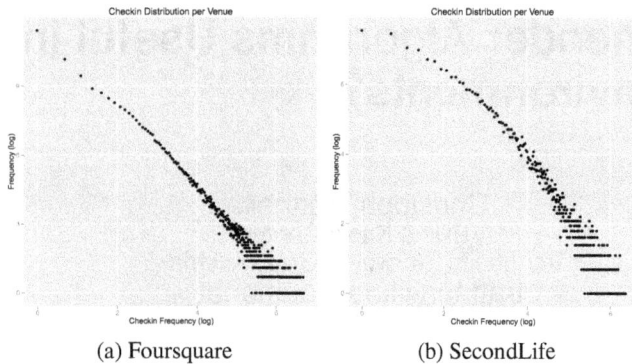

(a) Foursquare   (b) SecondLife

Figure 1: Distribution of Check-Ins per Venue in Foursquare and SecondLife (log-log scale).

In this paper we compared the check-in behavior of users in the virtual world of SecondLife[3] (with over 7 million active users one of the largest virtual eviroments world wiede) and the real-world LBSN Foursquare and explored in detail the extent to which place recommender systems that are known to work well on real-world LBSNs are applicable to virtual worlds.

Research Question. The research question that this research was driven by is the following: Knowing that Foursquare and the virtual world of SecondLife are comparable environments, to what extent are current real-world LBSN place recommender algorithms applicable to SecondLife?

Results. Based on a number of experiments, we find that while both worlds are indeed comparable in some aspects, such as the check-in distributions of Foursquare and SecondLife users, recommender algorithms purely based on a distance function however are not suitable for the virtual world of SecondLife, i.e., they do not have comparable performances. We also evaluated state-of-the-art collaborative-filtering algorithms based on user-based k-nearest neighbors (KNN) and matrix factorization and found out that these algorithms have comparable performances in Foursquare and SecondLife.

Contributions. The main contributions of this work are: (i) the study of current real-world LBSN recommender algorithms in the virtual world context and (ii) the insight that, although comparable in some aspects as suggested by related works, some of the assumptions upon which location recommenders of real-world LBSN recommenders operate, does not seem to hold in SecondLife. Another contribution of this work is the introduction and provision of a novel data set that allows the study of human mobility patterns in virtual worlds.

2. EXPERIMENTAL SETUP

In this section we describe in detail our experimental setup, i.e., the data sets and recommender approaches, as well as the evaluation protocol used to investigate our research question.

2.1 Datasets

Our study relies on data from Foursquare containing the check-in history of 11,326 users collected from January 2011 to December 2011. This data set was collected and used by the authors of [5] and is publicly available under request at [4]. The SecondLife data[4]

[3]http://www.secondlife.com
[4]The data set can be obtained for free per request.

Data	#users	#venues	#checkins	Sparsity
Foursquare	11,326	176,452	537,877	99.9%
SecondLife	4,771	17,167	120,078	99.8%

Table 1: Basic statistics of the datasets.

was collected from October 2014 to November 2014 containing the check-in history of 34,277 users[5]. Figure 1 depicts the distribution of check-ins per venue in Foursquare (a) and SecondLife (b) in log-log scale. Please note that they are very similar to each other, i.e., some venues are very popular and receive most of the check-ins, whereas the rest lies in the long tail of the distribution. The distributions of check-ins per user in both worlds follow a similar pattern, which we omitted due to space constraints.

2.2 Place Recommender Approaches

A key feature of LBSNs is the availability of geographic meta-data about checked-in places. In Foursquare and SecondLife, for example, the lat-long coordinates of the checked-in places are available. Several place recommender approaches have appeared that exploits geographic metadata of users and venues in order to improve the recommendation quality, under the assumption that users prefer to check-in venues that are nearby the venues they have visited in the past [8, 2, 9, 19].

To test whether this assumption holds in SecondLife, we have chosen two state-of-the-art place recommenders, purely based on geographic distance (aka location-aware), proposed in [19] and [9]. Given that such recommenders work well in Foursquare, as demonstrated in the aforementioned works, it should also work in SecondLife, assuming that the check-in behavior of users in both systems are comparable.

The approaches proposed at [19, 9] assign higher weights to candidate places that are nearby the places that the target user has already checked-in. Ye at al. [19] assume that the pairwise distance distribution of check-ins per user follows a power-law and propose to learn the parameters of the distribution by a simple linear regression on a log-log transformation of the distribution. Thus, the probability of any pair of places x and y being checked-in is computed as follows:

$$P(dist(x,y)) = a * dist(x,y)^b$$
$$\log P(dist(x,y)) = w_0 + w_1 * \log dist(x,y)$$

where $a = 2^{w_0}$, $b = w_1$ and $dist$ returns the distance between x and y (Great-Circle on Foursquare and Euclidian in SecondLife). Now, the probability that a given user u will check-in venue l is modelled as the conditional probability $P(l|L_u)$, where L_u is the set of all venues checked-in by user u, computed as follows:

$$P(l|L_u) = \prod_{l' \in L_u} P(dist(l, l')) \qquad (1)$$

A ranked list of venues is then generated using Equation 1 above and the top-N are recommended. We will refer to this method as *LinearRegression*.

A similar approach was proposed by [9] where Gaussian kernels were used for modeling the check-in behavior of users. The probability that a given user u will check-in place l is then modeled

[5]Similar to the real world, SecondLife offers since 2009 a location-based service which allows users to check-in places and share this information with friends in a Facebook-like social network called mySecondLife (see [12, 11] for more information).

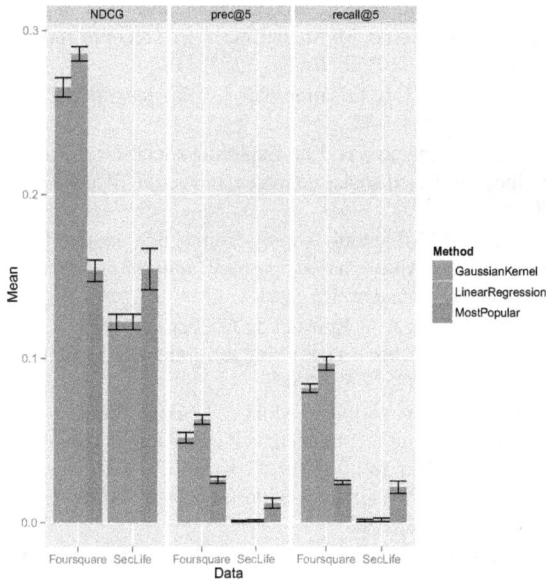

Figure 2: Results of the compared algorithms in terms or precision, recall and NDCG.

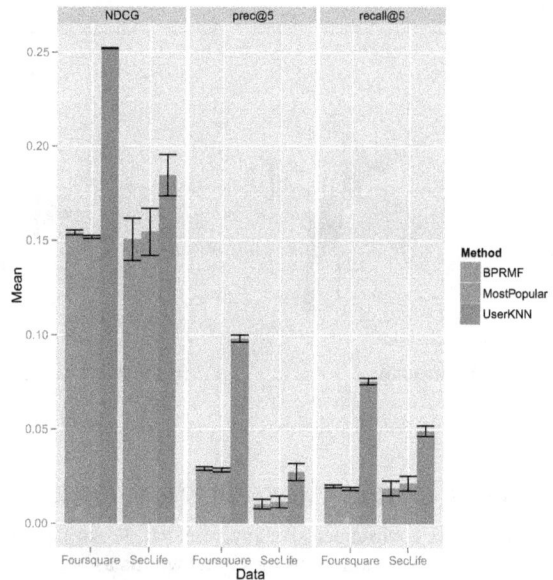

Figure 3: Comparison of pure CF-based algorithms for place recommendations in SecondLife and Foursquare.

as:

$$P(l|L_u) = \frac{1}{|L_u|} \sum_{l' \in L_u} \frac{1}{\sqrt{2\pi}} e^{-\frac{1}{2} dist(l,l')^2} \qquad (2)$$

We will refer to this method as *GaussianKernel*.

The algorithms above achieve better performance when combined with collaborative filtering-based algorithms such as the classic user-based KNN or matrix factorization [2, 19]. These algorithms operate under the assumption that users who checked-in the same places in the past tend to check-in the same places in the future. Therefore, we also considered in our study two collaborative filtering algorithms that are solely based on the check-in history of users (i.e. do not use geographic information, but only the user-place interactions in terms of check-ins) observed in the training data, namely, the user-based KNN and a state-of-the-art based on matrix factorization known as BPRMF (Bayesian Personalized Ranking Matrix Factorization) [10].

To run the collaborative-filtering algorithms we have used the recommender systems library MyMediaLite [3] adopting the default settings for the collaborative-filtering recommenders. The location-aware algorithms were implemented on top of MyMediaLite in order to reuse the evaluation functions available.

2.3 Evaluation Protocol

For computing the recommendations we considered only the users with 10 or more check-ins in distinct venues. We split the data randomly keeping 90% of users' check-ins for training and the rest for testing. We repeated this process 5 times in order to measure some variability in the results. Table 1 summarizes the training data after this pre-processing. To evaluate the recommenders we have used prec@5, recall@5 and NDCG (Normalized Discounted Cumulative Gain), which are typical evaluation metrics in the recommender systems field [7].

3. RESULTS

Figure 2 shows the results of the location-aware recommenders in comparison to the most popular recommender on both data sets.

The most popular simply recommend the most frequently checked-in venues for all users and is usually used as a baseline for testing new recommender algorithms. Please note that while in Foursquare the location-aware recommender is clearly better than the Most-Popular, in SecondLife the location-aware has worse or equal performance than the most popular approach.

In general, location algorithms based on geographic distances alone, like the ones we are using here, do not produce highly accurate recommendations. Instead, they are used as additional contextual signals on an ensemble of recommenders that usually include collaborative-filtering algorithms.

The fact that such location-aware algorithm is better than the most popular recommender in Foursquare provides a clear indication about the importance of this kind of signal for predicting users' check-in behavior, in contrast to SecondLife where this does not seem to be the case.

In order to better understand the aforementioned results, we plotted the pairwise distance distribution between the users' check-ins in Figure 4. In the case of the Foursquare distribution (Figure 4.a), there is a clear pattern indicating that users prefer to check-in venues within a small distance from his/her past check-ins. Please note that such pattern does not appear in the SecondLife distribution (Figure 4.b). In fact, in SecondLife users seem to prefer visiting places that are farther apart from each other. A possible explanation to this lies in the fact that SecondLife users can easily teleport anywhere in the virtual world map, thus diminishing their distance dependence when deciding to visit a new place.

Figure 3 shows the results of the collaborative-filtering algorithms. Note that in this case the recommender performances are comparable. The best result comes from UserKNN, whereas BPRMF and the MostPopular have comparable performance. In case of Foursquare, the performance can be improved by combining the location-aware and collaborative filtering recommenders. As for SecondLife, this would probably not work, which suggests that new approaches for modeling the mobility patterns of SecondLife users are needed, putting, for instance, a higher preference to places which are farther away from each other.

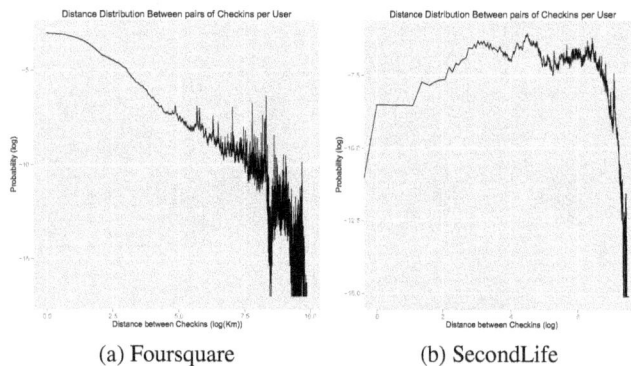

(a) Foursquare   (b) SecondLife

Figure 4: Distribution of pairwise check-in distances per user.

4. CONCLUSIONS & FUTURE WORK

Being rich data environments, many research works have appeared recently with the aim of using virtual worlds as proxies for studying and predicting real world social and behavioral characteristics of humans. But for this to work, it is required that human behaviors in virtual spaces and their counterparts in the offline world are similar. This requirement is known as the Mapping Principle and has to be established on a case-by-case basis, i.e., not all virtual worlds and virtual behaviors map to the offline world [18]. In this paper, we also contribute to this strand of research by (i) comparing the check-in behavior of SecondLife and Foursquare users and (ii) evaluating the extent to which real-world LBSN recommender systems are useful in virtual worlds such as SecondLife. Our main findings are summarized below:

- The check-in distribution, per venue and user, of SecondLife and Foursquare are very similar.

- While Foursquare users tend to check-in places that are nearby the places they visited in the past, SecondLife users present the opposite behavior, tending to check-in places far apart from one another.

- Most popular and collaborative-filtering algorithms, based on KNN and matrix factorization, have comparable performances considering both environments.

For future work we plan to investigate alternative approaches for modeling the distance dependence of users in virtual worlds, as well as other factors that influence virtual world users' decision on checking-in a new place. In this context we plan to investigate recommender models for other interesting entities such as events [14] and along other virtual environments.

Acknowledgments. This work was carried out during the tenure of an ERCIM "Alain Bensoussan" fellowship program. This work is also supported by the National Institute of Science and Technology for Software Engineering (INES), funded by CNPq and FACEPE, grants 573964/2008-4 and APQ-1037-1.03/08.

5. REFERENCES

[1] M. Ahmad, C. Shen, J. Srivastava, and N. Contractor. *Predicting Real World Behaviors from Virtual World Data.* Springer Proceedings in Complexity. Springer International Publishing, 2014.

[2] C. Cheng, H. Yang, I. King, and M. R. Lyu. Fused matrix factorization with geographical and social influence in location-based social networks. In *Proc. AAAI'12*, 2012.

[3] Z. Gantner, S. Rendle, C. Freudenthaler, and L. Schmidt-Thieme. MyMediaLite: A free recommender system library. In *Proc. RecSys'11*, 2011.

[4] H. Gao and H. Liu. Location-based social network data repository, 2014.

[5] H. Gao, J. Tang, and H. Liu. Exploring social-historical ties on location-based social networks. In *Proc. ICWSM'12*, 2012.

[6] G. Guo and M. Elgendi. A new recommender system for 3d e-commerce: An eeg based approach. *Journal of Advanced Management Science*, 1(1), 2013.

[7] J. L. Herlocker, J. A. Konstan, L. G. Terveen, and J. T. Riedl. Evaluating collaborative filtering recommender systems. *ACM TOIS*, 22(1):5–53, 2004.

[8] B. Jie, Y. Zheng, and M. F. Mokbel. Location-based and preference-aware recommendation using sparse geo-social networking data. In I. F. Cruz, C. Knoblock, P. Kroeger, E. Tanin, and P. Widmayer, editors, *SIGSPATIAL/GIS*, pages 199–208. ACM, 2012.

[9] I. Nunes and L. Marinho. A gaussian kernel approach for location recommendations, 2013.

[10] S. Rendle, C. Freudenthaler, Z. Gantner, and L. Schmidt-Thieme. BPR: Bayesian personalized ranking from implicit feedback. In *Proc. UAI '09*, pages 452–461, Arlington, Virginia, United States, 2009. AUAI Press.

[11] M. Steurer and C. Trattner. Acquaintance or partner?: predicting partnership in online and location-based social networks. In *Proc. ASONAM'13*, pages 372–379. ACM, 2013.

[12] M. Steurer and C. Trattner. Predicting interactions in online social networks: an experiment in second life. In *Proc. MSM'13*, page 5. ACM, 2013.

[13] M. Steurer and C. Trattner. Who will interact with whom? a case-study in second life using online social network and location-based social network features to predict interactions between users. In *Ubiquitous Social Media Analysis*, pages 108–127. Springer, 2013.

[14] M. Steurer, C. Trattner, and F. Kappe. Success factors of events in virtual worlds a case study in second life. In *Proc. NetGames'12*, pages 1–2. IEEE, 2012.

[15] M. Szell, R. Sinatra, G. Petri, S. Thurner, and V. Latora. Understanding mobility in a social petri dish. *Scientific reports*, 2, 2012.

[16] C. Trattner, D. Parra, L. Eberhard, and X. Wen. Who will trade with whom?: Predicting buyer-seller interactions in online trading platforms through social networks. In *Proc. WWW'14*, pages 387–388. ACM, 2014.

[17] C. V. D. Weth, V. Hegde, and M. Hauswirth. Virtual location-based services: Merging the physical and virtual world. In *Proc. ICWS'14*, pages 113–120. IEEE, 2014.

[18] D. Williams. The mapping principle, and a research framework for virtual worlds. *Communication Theory*, 20(4):451–470, 2010.

[19] M. Ye, P. Yin, W.-C. Lee, and D. L. Lee. Exploiting geographical influence for collaborative point-of-interest recommendation. In *Proc. SIGIR'11*, pages 325–334. ACM, 2011.

[20] H. Yin, Y. Sun, B. Cui, Z. Hu, and Chen. Lcars: a location-content-aware recommender system. In *Proc. KDD'13*, pages 221–229. ACM, 2013.

Asymmetric Recommendations: The Interacting Effects of Social Ratings' Direction and Strength on Users' Ratings

Oded Nov
New York University
onov@nyu.edu

Ofer Arazy
University of Haifa
University of Alberta
ofer.arazy@gmail.com

ABSTRACT

In social recommendation systems, users often publicly rate objects such as photos, news articles or consumer products. When they appear in aggregate, these ratings carry social signals such as the direction and strength of the raters' average opinion about the product. Using a controlled experiment we manipulated two central social signals – the direction and strength of social ratings of five popular consumer products – and examined their interacting effects on users' ratings. The results show an asymmetric user behavior, where the direction of perceived social rating has a negative effect on users' ratings if the direction of perceived social rating is negative, but no effect if the direction is positive. The strength of perceived social ratings did not have a significant effect on users' ratings. The findings highlight the potential for cascading adverse effects of small number of negative user ratings on subsequent users' opinions.

Categories and Subject Descriptors

H.1.2 [Models and Principles]: User/machine systems —Human Factors; H.5 Information interfaces and presentation

Keywords

Anchoring; recommender systems; social influence; social signals; theory-driven design.

1. INTRODUCTION

Extant research ihas demonstrated that people's expressed opinions online can be influenced by what they perceive to be the behavior or opinions of others [11, 17]. In social recommender systems, where users can express opinions about objects they come across (e.g., photos, news articles, consumer products), the basic social information provided to users about others' opinions, is the number of others as well as their "average" rating. Examples include information about up/down or like/dislike votes made by others. These basic elements of information – or social signals – often influence the signals' viewers, who in turn often express their own opinions by rating, voting, or liking. Presented together, these social signals can be thought of as representing the *direction* of the social rating (i.e. whether, on average, others have positive or negative opinion about the object), and the social rating *strength* (i.e. how many personal ratings the average social rating is based on).

RecSys'15, September 16–20, 2015, Vienna, Austria.
© 2015 ACM. ISBN 978-1-4503-3692-5/15/09…$15.00.
DOI: http://dx.doi.org/10.1145/2792838.2799667

Our objective in this study was to identify and quantify the interacting effects of social ratings' direction and strength on user behavior. We addressed the following research question: can we describe the mechanisms by which social influence shapes users' ratings of objects online? And more specifically, what are the interacting roles of the social influence's direction and its strength? Using a web-based randomized controlled experiment, we sought to identify social influence patterns that are consistent across objects and user opinions.

2. INFLUENCE AND ANCHORING

Social influence its underlying mechanisms have been studied extensively in a variety of online settings [4, 7]. For example, [18], [16] and [14] showed that experimental manipulations arbitrarily signaling the seeming prior "success" of products on Kickstarter, downloadable songs, and articles on a social news aggregation website, respectively, led users to favorable online behavior toward these perceived "successes". Furthermore, higher ratings on Yelp were found to lead to increased restaurants' sales [3]. Social influence is often explained by a conformity effect, whereby people form or change their judgment when presented with a consensus, even when such consensus contradicts their own perception or opinion [19]. Therefore, good understanding of the mechanisms that determine social influence online is important for effective design and management of social recommendation systems.

By design, social recommender systems often give way to *anchoring* – users' bias towards information that is available to them [13]. In numerous studies, anchoring was shown to influence people's behavior. For example, exposure to high and low prices can influence the prices consumers would be willing to pay for products in related and unrelated categories [1]. Similarly, studies in law have found that among judges, anchors influence judicial decisions [9]. Similar findings were reported in other areas such as finance [12] and visual perception [10].

Researchers have largely focused on either the direction of the social signals – for example, whether the social ratings anchor users to a certain value or direction (e.g. positive vs. negative) – or alternatively, on the strength of these social signals, such as how strong the social consensus is, or how many others downloaded the song. For example, [7] found that when users of a movie recommender system were asked to re-rate movies while (experimentally manipulated) "predicted" rating were presented to them, they tended to change their rating toward the "prediction" anchor. More recently, [2] showed that users' ratings are often influenced by a recommender system's (experimentally manipulated) anchors, and that the effects of anchoring can be separated from the effects of the system's perceived reliability.

However, social recommender systems often present simultaneously to users both the direction of the social signal (i.e. the average opinion of others, represented by their average ratings), and its strength (i.e. the number of others on which the average rating is based). Therefore, to examine the interacting effects of the social signals' direction and strength on users' ratings, we used a randomized experiment in which we manipulated the social ratings' direction and strength attributed to a number of popular consumer products the experiment participants were exposed to, and compared the product ratings provided by these participants. Our hypothesis, based on the prior research reviewed above, was that both the strength and the direction of the social signals will affect users' opinions. In particular, our hypothesis was that the interaction between strength and direction will work such that the signals' strength will moderate the effect of their direction. In other words, a strong positive social signal about an object will lead user to express, on average, a more positive opinion about the same object than when a weak positive signal is associated with it. Similarly, a strong negative social signal would have a more negative effect than a weak negative signal.

3. METHOD

Using a between-subjects experimental design (see Table 1), we explored behavior patterns that are consistent across different objects and different social rating levels.

Table 1. Experimental conditions: social signals' direction and strength.

Social signal strength	Social signal direction	
	Negative	*Positive*
Weak	Weak-Negative: Negative social opinion based on few "others"	Weak-Positive: Positive social opinion based on few "others"
Strong	Strong-Negative: Negative social opinion based on many "others"	Strong-Positive: Positive social opinion based on many "others"

3.1 Participants and Data

Participants in the experiment were recruited from Amazon Mechanical Turk (MTurk) and asked about their opinions on a number of popular consumer products. Participants were paid $1.00 for their taking part in the study. All participants had at least 100 prior HITs of which at least 99% were approved, and were all from the US, based on the MTurk filter.

Participants were presented with images and names of five online and offline consumer products, one at a time and in a random order. The products included Cheerios, Gmail, Starbucks coffee, Twitter, and WhatsApp, selected for their popularity. Once they were presented with the products' names and images, participants were asked to rate their familiarity with the product on a 1-10 scale, using a slider ranging between "Not at all familiar with it." and "Extremely familiar with it." The default value of the familiarity question was set at 5 and users could move the slider to the right (more familiar), to the left (less familiar), or leave it unchanged. The users then needed to click the Submit button to move to the next screen in which they rated products (see Figure 1). The familiarly question served two purposes: first, as an honesty check to screen out participants who might quickly click through the task without attempting to answer honestly. To screen

out such data, in the analysis of each product we moved all product ratings from users who indicated a familiarity rating of 5 for the analyzed product. This way, we ensured that users had to make a deliberate choice. Second, the familiarity question helped us make sure that the products presented to users were across a wide range of familiarity levels.

Familiarity in itself was not part of our hypotheses, since causal relationship between familiarity and opinion are difficult to disentangle: it's unclear if, for example, positive opinion leads to greater familiarity (I have a good opinion so I use it more) or if familiarity leads to positive opinion (by using it more I get used to it and develop a positive opinion on it).

3.2 Experimental Design

Participants could only take part in the experiment once, and were asked to rate each product in a separate product page, using a 1-5 star ratings (see Figure 2). In each product page, the participants were assigned to one of five experimental conditions: four were manipulated social signals, assigned randomly, in which information about the average rating of the product was presented next to the product image, together the number of ratings received by previous viewers (along the lines of UI design that are common to popular recommender systems such as Amazon or Netflix). A fifth experimental treatment served as a control condition, in which no social rating was presented to users. The ratings provided by users in the control condition served as a baseline against which to compare the effects of the social signaling experimental interventions.

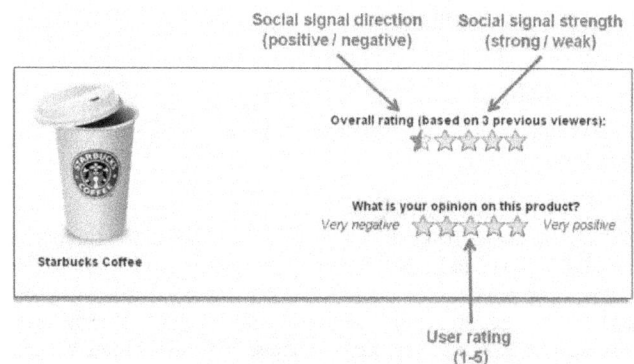

Figure 1. Social signals and user expressed opinion

Social anchoring was used to represent to users the direction of the social ratings. To achieve this, we presented to the users consumer products next to their experimentally manipulated average ratings made by "other" participants in the study. These perceived ratings of "others" signaled the direction of social ratings, and were anchored in two opposing directions: a negative signal was represented by values ranging between randomly assigned 0.5-1 star (out of five possible), and a positive signal represented by values ranging between 4.5-5 stars randomly assigned for each product (see Figure 2).

The strength of the social ratings was manipulated by varying the number of "others" who seemingly rated the product (see Figure 2): the number of others was set at either a single-digit number of other raters, ranging between 3-7, representing a weak social signal, or a random high number (ranging between 3,000-7,000), representing a strong social signal. The difference in the strength of these chosen social signals values was shown in prior research to be perceived by users as representing significantly different numbers of raters [15].

We wanted all participants to interpret the social signals in a similar way. Therefore, the text "overall rating (based on N previous viewers)" was placed above the social rating (see Figure 2). The value of N presented to users changed between products and users, based on the experimental condition assigned.

In order to increase the perceived authenticity of the social rating the users viewed, we increased the variety of social opinions users we exposed to throughout their experiment interaction: we added two popular products (Colgate toothpaste and Diet Coke) for which all values of the social signals' direction and strength were different from the values assigned to the products included in the experiment. The social signal direction of these dummy products was set at 1, 2, 3 or 4 stars, and the signal's strength at around 50 and 500 prior raters (non-rounded numbers were used). This addition ensured that under any experimental condition combination, no user will see the same social signals for all products.

In summary, for each product they rated, users were exposed to one of five experimental conditions - four interventions combining signal direction and strength (see Table 1), and a control condition.

4. RESULTS

Overall, 1040 people took part in this study. Their age ranged between 18 and 79, with the average at 34.7 (stdev = 11.7). 54.1% of the participants were women. Since ratings in which the users chose the default level of 5 as their familiarity level were removed from the statistical analysis, different products were analyzed using different sample sizes.

To explore the simultaneous effects of the direction and strength of social ratings, Analysis of Variance (ANOVA) was performed followed by Bonferroni corrections, to compare user ratings across the five experimental conditions for each product (see Figure 3). Specifically, we compared users' rating in the four intervention conditions with the control conditions.

The following product-specific differences in user rating were found: for Starbucks coffee, we found a significant effect of Direction-Strength on user ratings (F (4, 962) = 4.24, p < 0.01). User ratings in the Weak-Negative condition were significantly lower than user ratings in the control condition (p<0.05). For Gmail, we also found a significant effect of Direction-Strength on user ratings (F (4, 880) = 6.81, p < 0.001). User rating in the Strong-Negative condition were significantly lower than ratings in the control condition (p<0.01). For Whatsapp, we found a significant effect of Direction-Strength on user ratings (F (4, 816) = 19.27, p < 0.001). Here, user ratings in both the Strong-Negative and Weak-Negative conditions were significantly different lower than ratings in the control condition (p<0.01 in both comparisons). Similarly, for Cheerios, we found a significant effect of Direction-Strength on user ratings (F (4, 1000) = 5.25, p < 0.001). User rating in the Weak-Negative were significantly lower than the ratings in the control conditions (p<0.05). Finally, for Twitter we found a significant effect of Direction-Strength on user ratings (F (4, 874) = 7.03, p < 0.001). The Strong-Negative condition was significantly different from the control condition with the average ratings in it lower than ratings in the control condition (p<0.01). To ensure that the effects observed were not a result of different levels of familiarity with the products, we examined the interactions between familiarity and signal direction, and found no significant effect on users' ratings.

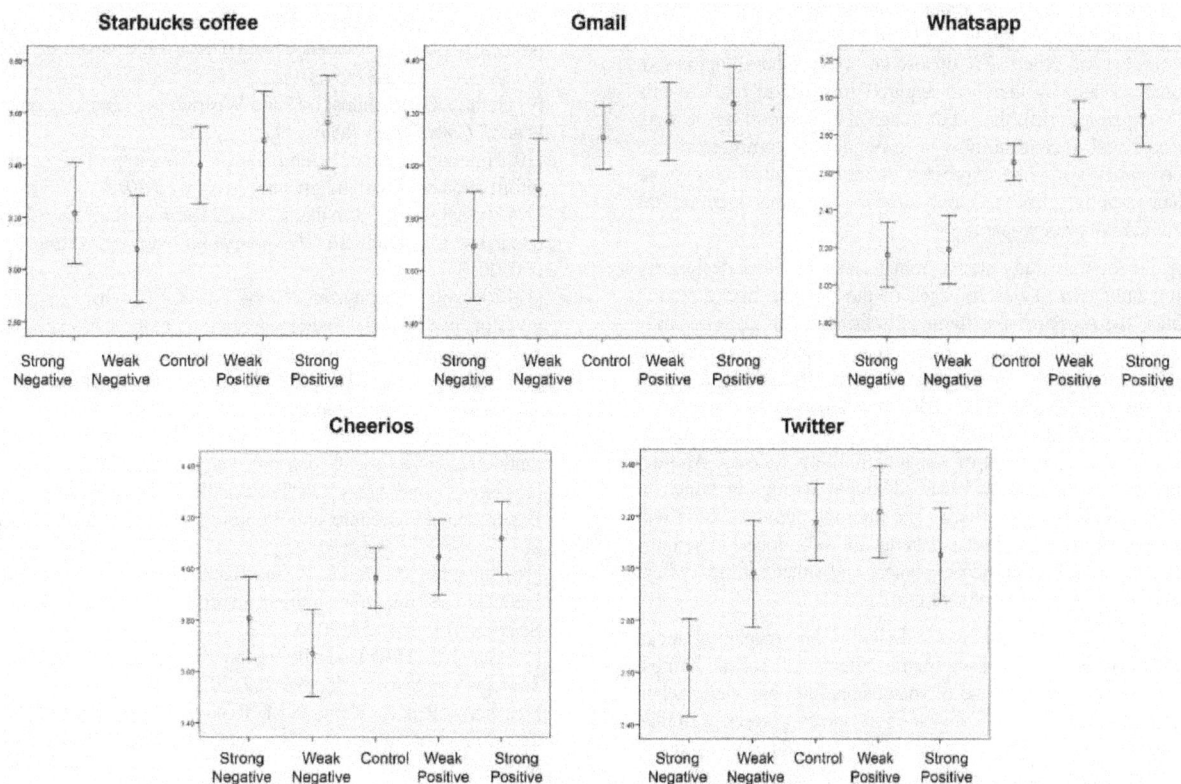

Figure 1. User ratings in the five experimental conditions. Error bars indicate 95% confidence intervals.

In summary, in all five products negative social signals led to significantly lower user ratings, whereas positive signals did not have any significant effect on user ratings. The size of the social signal was not found to effect user ratings.

5. DISCUSSION

By comparing users' rating in the experimental conditions, we examined the simultaneous effects of perceived social ratings' direction and strength on users' ratings (Figure 3). The findings point to two aspects of the relationship between direction and strength and their influence. First, there is an asymmetry between the effects of the positive and negative direction signal: a negative signal influences users' expressed opinions in the expected direction (downward), but a positive signal did not lead to a similar effect in the opposite direction. This asymmetry was consistent across different products and varying levels of average product ratings. Second, the social signals' strength did not have an effect on users' ratings: none of the ten Strong-Weak positive and Strong-Weak negative pairs (i.e. two per product) exhibited significant differences between the weak and strong signals.

A possible interpretation of the asymmetry found between the effects of positive and negative social signals is that negative signals may be more persuasive than positive signals. Such a finding is consistent with prior research, and extends the research about the effectiveness of framing (i.e. the presentation of the positive or negative consequences of adhering to message recommendations), which found negative frames to be more persuasive than positive ones in the contexts of health behavior communication [6] and political campaigns [8]. It is also consistent with research showing that negative framing of messages can be more effective than positive one when the level of elaboration is low [5], as it is in many product rating settings.

The mixed findings of the effects of social signals' strength may reflect the weight people attribute to the social signals' strength. While somewhat surprising, it may be that users pay little attention to the number of others (as oppose to these others' opinions). Additional research is therefore required in order to explore this possible explanation further, but more data supporting it may demonstrate that a small number of responders or commenters can relatively easily sway the expressed opinions of other users who view their responses. Some supporting evidence in this direction has been provided in prior research [14].

A limitation of this study stems from its experimental design: by exploring only two values for each of the strength and direction treatments, the scope of the findings is limited. Future work may address this limitation by examining a larger number of interventions, and in particular, additional combinations of signal direction-strength levels. This study nonetheless demonstrates the importance of considering both of these factors, simultaneously, in the design and management of social computing systems. Another direction for future work involves additional settings in which to explore direction-strength effects. The findings presented here will be more generalizable if similar patterns are to be found in settings such as news article comments, photos, and other settings where both social signals are presented to users.

Our findings have implications for designing and managing social computing systems. The asymmetric effects of social ratings' direction call for a careful use of social signaling, especially when such signaling is at the early stages of an object's presence online. Initial negative social signaling may create a cascade of increasingly negative opinions. With respect to presenting social signals' strength, the findings provide little support for the utility of presenting to users the number of prior raters.

6. CONCLUSION

In this work we examined the simultaneous effects social ratings' direction and strength. We showed that the direction signal is influential, but only when negative, and that social ratings' strength does not affect users' behavior. The findings highlight the potential effects negative social signals carry, and stress the need for designers of social computing systems to consider the risk of cascading negative input which may be self-reinforcing.

7. ACKNOWLEDGMENTS

This work was partially supported by NSF Award IIS 1149745.

8. REFERENCES

[1] Adaval, R. and Wyer R., "Conscious and Nonconscious Comparisons with Price Anchors," *Journal of Marketing Research,* 48, 355-365, 2011.

[2] Adomavicius, G., Bockstedt, J., Curley, S., and Zhang, J., "Recommender systems, consumer preferences, and anchoring effects," in *Proc. Decisions@ RecSys 2011.*

[3] Anderson, M. and Magruder, J., "Learning from the crowd: Regression discontinuity estimates of the effects of an online review database*," *The Economic Journal,* 122, 957-989, 2012.

[4] Arazy, O., Nov, O., and Kumar, N., "Personalityzation: UI Personalization, Theoretical Grounding in HCI and Design Research," *AIS Transactions on Human-Computer Interaction* 7, 43-69 2015.

[5] Baba , S, Britton, J., and Payne, J. "Does Elaboration Increase or Decrease the Effectiveness of Negatively versus Positively Framed Messages?," *J. of Consumer Research,* 31, 199-208, 2004.

[6] Block, L. and Keller, P., "When to accentuate the negative," *J. of Marketing Research,* 192-203, 1995.

[7] Cosley, D., Lam, S. K., Albert, I., Konstan, J. A., and Riedl, J., "Is seeing believing?: how recommender system interfaces affect users' opinions," *Proc. CHI 2003.*

[8] Enikolopov, R., Petrova, M., and Zhuravskaya, E., "Media and political persuasion: Evidence from Russia," *The American Economic Review,* 101, 3253-3285, 2011.

[9] Guthrie, C., Rachlinski, J., and Wistrich, A., "Blinking on the bench," *Cornell Law Review,* 93, p. 1, 2007.

[10] Hullman, J., Adar, E., and Shah, P., "The impact of social information on visual judgments," *Proc. CHI 2011.*

[11] Hysenbelli, D., Rubaltelli, E., and Rumiati, R., "Others' opinions count, but not all of them," *Judgment and Decision Making,* 8, 678-690, 2013.

[12] Johnson, J., Schnytzer, A., and Liu, S., "To what extent do investors in a financial market anchor their judgments excessively?," *J. Behavioral Dec. Making,* 22, 410-434, 2009.

[13] McElroy, T. and Dowd, K., "Susceptibility to anchoring effects," *Judgment and Decision Making,* 2, 48-53, 2007.

[14] Muchnik, L., Aral, S., and Taylor, S. J., "Social influence bias: A randomized experiment," *Science,* 341, 647-651, 2013.

[15] Nov, O. and Arazy, O., "Personality-Targeted Design: Theory, Experimental Procedure, and Preliminary Results," in *Proc. CSCW,* 2013.

[16] Salganik, M., Dodds, P., and Watts, D., "Experimental study of inequality and unpredictability in an artificial cultural market," *Science,* 311, 854-856, 2006.

[17] Sun, M., "How Does the Variance of Product Ratings Matter?," *Management Science,* 58, 696-707, 2012.

[18] van de Rijt, A., Kang, S. M., Restivo, M., and Patil, A., "Field experiments of success-breeds-success dynamics," *PNAS,* 111, 6934-6939, 2014.

[19] Zhu, H., Huberman, B., and Luon, Y., "To switch or not to switch," *Proc. CHI 2012.*

Crowd Sourcing, with a Few Answers: Recommending Commuters for Traffic Updates

Elizabeth M. Daly, Michele Berlingerio
Smart Cities Technology Centre
IBM Research - Ireland
dalyeliz, mberling@ie.ibm.com

François Schnitzler
Technion - Israel Institute of Technology
Haifa, Israel
francois@ee.technion.ac.il

ABSTRACT

Real-time traffic awareness applications are playing an ever increasing role understanding and tackling traffic congestion in cities. First-hand accounts from drivers witnessing an incident is an invaluable source of information for traffic managers. Nowadays, drivers increasingly contact control rooms through social media to report on journey times, accidents or road weather conditions. These new interactions allow traffic controllers to engage users, and in particular to query them for information rather than passively collecting it. Querying participants presents the challenge of which users to probe for updates about a specific situation. In order to maximise the probability of a user responding and the accuracy of the information, we propose a strategy which takes into account the engagement levels of the user, the mobility profile and the reputation of the user. We provide an analysis of a real-world user corpus of Twitter users contributing updates to LiveDrive, a Dublin based traffic radio station.

Keywords: Recommender Systems; Crowd-sourcing; Traffic.

1. INTRODUCTION

Crowd sourcing of urban information is becoming increasingly important in the context of smarter cities. For example, Waze[1] provides crowd sourced traffic monitoring. FixMyStreet supports reporting information such as noise pollution, potholes and general repairs for the attention of city councils[2]. Social media analysis has already been used for incident or emergency detection or monitoring, such as earthquakes [9] or floods [5, 12]. It has been used also for traffic monitoring in the city of Dublin [4]. In order to move from passive crowd sourcing to active crowd sourcing, such systems need to actively identify and engage users to provide the right information at the right time, thus encouraging contributions.

Specific solutions have also been developed to estimate user reliability in the context of spatial crowd sourcing, and in particular traffic monitoring. Crowd sourcing can be used to resolve conflicting reports from physical sensors, and these reports can be used as an initial estimate of the true answer [2]. Spatial models have been

developed to detect unreliable crowd sourced sensors to measure radioactivity in Japan [11]. When monitoring social media, a related challenge is to detect individuals that are located in the area affected by a problem and these merely talking about it [10].

Sensor or user selection based on space and time constraints have also been considered. In order to maximise the usefulness of the answers received, one can construct probability distributions over sensor locations and optimise the queries based on this distribution [8]. Generic location aware crowd sourcing platforms have also been developed. These platforms distribute tasks to users based on their location [1, 6, 7]. These platforms are different from our setting. Indeed, they either use a pull-based system, where users request tasks based on their current location, continuously monitor the location of users or expect users to move to complete tasks. We, on the other hand, expect our queries to be generated mostly during peak hours, and for users commuting. In our opinion, such users are unlikely to take a detour in a traffic jam to answer a question. However, they can report on a location they've been through recently. We expect a user to provide information only if they have a history of reporting on this particular location of interest.

Our contribution is an algorithm to recommend, based on predicted user engagement, which users to follow or to query to obtain traffic updates around the city. Our algorithm takes into account:

- the engagement level and reputation of the user;
- the time and mobility profile of the user, based on the time of day and locations a user typically communicate about;
- the number of queries previously directed at the user, in order to distribute the load across users;

We evaluate this proposed strategy using a real-world collection of user contributed tweets and traffic related updates of LiveDrive, a Dublin based traffic radio station.

2. EXPERIMENTAL SETUP

LiveDrive[3] CityFM is a radio station run by Dublin County Council. The radio station broadcasts during the morning and evening peak traffic times. Listeners are incentivised to provide real-time updates to the station by the possibility to receive free parking vouchers, request a song of their choice and the general understanding that if they contribute useful information that benefits others, they too may benefit from the contributions of others. The team consists primarily of three members, the radio presenter who communicates the updates to the listeners, the producer who monitors incoming alerts and a camera controller who has access to a number of the traffic cameras in the city when trying to clarify reported issues. Incoming alerts are sent to the team via email, phone calls, text messages and Twitter.

---

[1] https://www.waze.com/

[2] https://www.fixmystreet.ie/

[3] http://dublincityfm.ie/livedrive

We collected the tweets both originating from and directed to the LiveDrive Twitter account using the public API[4] from October 2012 until February 2014 resulting in 38637 tweets from 2240 accounts. As most of the tweets are not geo-located, we generate for each tweet an approximate location based on specific words used, mostly street names, abbreviations of these names or specific area in the city. To do so, we follow the methodology of [4].

Example LiveDrive tweet:

```
Source: LiveDrive
Message: There has been an incident on Nassau St
at the junction of Dawson St. Nassau St is blocked
and the left turn from Dawson St is also blocked
Date: Fri Feb 14 07:06:29
Location Keywords:  nassau junction dawson
Approx. Location: 53.341297, -6.2582927
```

Example tweet from user:

```
Source: @BeastyBoy_
Message: Pedestrian knocked down on Nassau st at
house of frasier - no traffic getting past.
@LiveDrive  @aaroadwatch @gardainfo @GardaTraffic
Date: Fri Feb 14 07:04:03
Location Keywords: nassau
Approx. Location: 53.342697,-6.256634
```

For a broader analysis, we also collected another 943703 tweets geo-located in Dublin, not related to the LiveDrive account.

2.1   Tweet validation

To build the reputation of a user, we must decide whether a tweet sent to LiveDrive is related to a valid incident or not. There are two typical crowd sourcing methods to assess the quality of a tweet: compare to other tweets, or to a gold standard. Since the majority of incidents were reported by a single user or a very small number of users, majority voting strategies are of limited use. Therefore, we rely on a gold standard: the warnings about incidents on the LiveDrive Twitter account.

We first assign an approximate location to both the user tweets and the LiveDrive tweets. We then try to match each single user tweet with a LiveDrive one, based on a spatio-temporal distance. For the spatial dimension, we tried increasing distances from 0km to 5km, and we saw a sharp increase of matches up to 1km, while little difference was noted after that. We therefore selected 1km as spatial threshold. For time, we noticed that there is a linear correlation between temporal distance and number of matched tweets. We arbitrarily chose 2 hours as temporal threshold, based on our personal estimates of how long a traffic problem may last.

2.2   User Reputation

In order to take into account the reputation of a user, we wish to reward users who provide actionable information. If a user consistently provides content that is rebroadcast and shared by the LiveDrive team and therefore of benefit to other users, then this user can be considered a reputable contributor. The reputation of a user is initialised to an input parameter $R_{init} \in [0, 1]$. For every additional informative tweet sent by the user, the value is updated with a reward constant R_{reward}

$$R_{new} = R_{old} + (1 - R_{old}) \times R_{reward}. \qquad (1)$$

In order to capture the time dynamics and take into account that the last time a user has contributed information also plays a role in the probability as to whether the user will tweet, or respond, about an incident, the reputation value is decayed over time. As a result, users who are continuously providing valuable updates are

[4]http://www.twitter.com

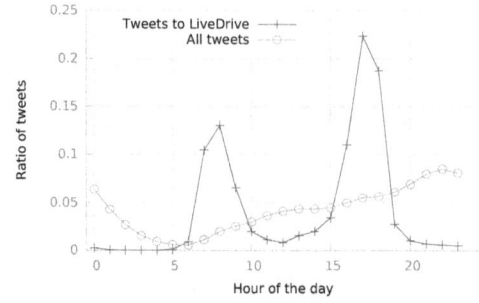

Figure 1: Probability Distribution of User Contributed Tweets over Time

rewarded, and inactive users are degraded by:

$$R_{new} = R_{old} \times \gamma^k \qquad (2)$$

where γ is the decay coefficient and k is the number of elapsed time units since the user last contributed an update. The selection of the decay coefficient, γ, and time unit, k, should be based on the importance of recency. For the purposes of this paper we use the following values: R_{init}=0.5, R_{reward}=0.1, γ=0,98 and k = number of weeks.

2.3   Time Profile

We seek information updates that can be provided in an opportunistic manner, so we need to take into account the time of day we believe the user may be travelling, based on the previous updates provided by the user. Figure 1 shows the probability distribution of when messages are received by the LiveDrive team (crossed red line). The peak hours for the LiveDrive related tweets are in the morning between 7 and 10 followed by an afternoon peak between the hours of 4 and 7. We also report the probability distribution of all other tweets not related to LiveDrive (circled green line) to give a perspective of the relative effects and volume of the LiveDrive service compared to generic Twitter accounts and topics.

In order to compute the time profile of the users we discretise the time of day the users were observed into hourly intervals $t \in [1, 2, \cdot, 24]$. We then bin the frequencies a user has been observed in the respective hourly intervals $c_u(t)$ and compute the corresponding maximum likelihood estimate as:

$$P_u(t) = \frac{c_u(t)}{\sum_t c_u(t)}. \qquad (3)$$

2.4   Location Profile

We also need to take into account the locations each user may be travelling through based on his previous tweets. Figure 2 shows the locations associated to all tweets we use. We construct individual users' location profiles by looking at the location keywords used for the geo-coding of tweets rather than at the coordinates. We believe that these words provide more information about the trajectory of a user than point-wise coordinates. For example, a user reporting a problem on the N4 on the way to the M50 motorway (big road circling Dublin) may be able to report on a problem on the N4 or the M50 far from the crossroad, but not be able to do so for a problem on a road parallel to these even if the incident is closer to the N4-M50 junction.

We compute the location profile in a similar manner as before. We bin the frequencies of a user's observations across all location keywords assuming location keywords are not necessarily dependent on each other. Given an input location query $\mathbf{l} = \{l_i\}$ that gives potentially multiple location keywords is now used to compute the probability that the user has information about those input location keywords:

$$P_u(\mathbf{l}) = \frac{\sum_{l \in \mathbf{l}} c_u(l)}{\sum_l c_u(l)} . \qquad (4)$$

Figure 2: Locations in Dublin that were associated to tweets. The radius of the circles is proportional to the number of tweets at each location.

3. STRATEGY FOR RECOMMENDATIONS

The criteria we consider include the number of tweets contributed by the user, the time profile of the user, the location profile of the user and the reputation. Each of these criteria has a different scale and therefore mapping these objectives to a single utility scale can be problematic, since it may be difficult to provide precise trade-offs between objectives [3]. As a result, it is natural to consider multi-attribute or multi-criteria utility functions to cope with multiple and non-commensurate utility scales on which the decision maker's preferences are expressed. Therefore we propose using Pareto optimisation to determine the non-dominant solution set.

Given p attributes, a *multi-attribute utility value* is characterised by a vector $\vec{u} = (u_1, \ldots, u_p) \in \mathbb{R}^p$, where u_i represents the utility with respect to attribute $i \in \{1, \ldots, p\}$. Given $\vec{u}, \vec{v} \in \mathbb{R}^p$, we say that $\vec{u}$ *Pareto dominates* $\vec{v}$ (denoted $\vec{u} \succcurlyeq \vec{v}$) iff $\forall i \in \{1, \ldots, p\}$ $u_i \geq v_i$. As usual, the symbol $\succ$ refers to the asymmetric part of $\succcurlyeq$, namely $\vec{u} \succ \vec{v}$ iif $\vec{u} \succcurlyeq \vec{v}$ and it is not the case that $\vec{v} \succcurlyeq \vec{u}$. Given a finite set of utility vectors $\mathcal{U} \subseteq \mathbb{R}^p$, we define the *maximal set*, denoted by $\max_{\succcurlyeq}(\mathcal{U})$, to be the set consisting of the undominated elements in $\mathcal{U}$, i.e., $\max_{\succcurlyeq}(\mathcal{U}) = \{\vec{v} \in \mathcal{U} \mid \nexists \vec{v} \in \mathcal{U}, \vec{v} \succ \vec{u}\}$. Computing $\max_{\succcurlyeq}(\mathcal{U})$ is quadratic in the size of $\mathcal{U}$.

4. APPLICABILITY STUDY

Our goal here is to study how the main strategy described above performs in an hypothetical application for recommending users to follow, or to query about a specific incident. We imagine to have to query a number of users under budget constraints to maximize the likelihood of their reply, while ensuring load balance across users. Further validation of this methodology involving actual queries is part of our future work in this direction.

We utilise the LiveDrive messages to simulate the workload for the users. This results in 2124 queries about "incidents" (LiveDrive messages) where we try to predict users that contributed tweets about the incident, that is, tweets that were a) geo-coded and contained usable location keywords and b) validated as described in the previous section. User contributions up until the query time (i.e. time of the LiveDrive "incident" tweet) are used to build user profiles. Note that this includes tweets that were not validated by a LiveDrive event and did not necessarily contain location keywords. Users sometimes signal there is no problem (anymore) at a particular location, and while these tweets are usually not validated by LiveDrive, they still provide information about the typical location and time a user is active. User contributed tweets that have been validated are withheld until after the given LiveDrive message has been processed in order to not unfairly advantage the algorithm.

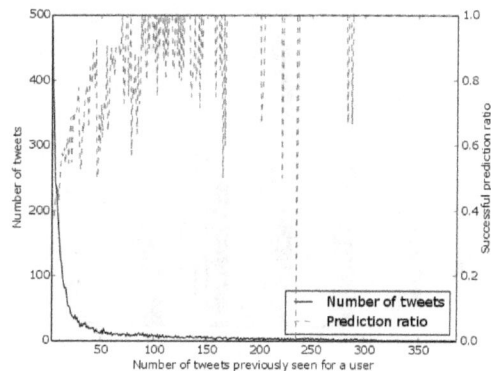

Figure 3: The frequency of a contributing user to be included in the Pareto optimal set of selected users without budget constraint increases with the number of tweets previously seen for that user.

4.1 User Candidate Selection

We first include four metrics as selection criteria: number of tweets, time probability, location probability and the reputation of the user. Our goal is to accurately recommend which users to query based on the time of day and the location keywords of interest. A recommendation is a success if a user who actually did contribute a validated tweet is included in the Pareto optimal solution set.

We achieved an accuracy of 77.16% with an infinite budget. We only consider contributing users who have a history of at least 4 tweets, as with fewer tweets the system may not know enough about a user. Indeed, the accuracy for any particular user increases with the number of tweets from that user that the system as seen before, as shown by Figure 3 (dashed green line). The accuracy starts at 40% and increases to above 60% after the first 20 tweets. This indicates our approach is able to capture the behaviour of users. Depending on the accuracy required from the system, it may be beneficial to increase the minimum number of tweets that must be observed from a user before considering it for a query.

Figure 3 also shows the number of users that have received a query with a given number of previously observed tweets. That curve is not monotonically decreasing because no query is emitted for non-validated tweets. Because users emit tweets at different rates, the overall accuracy does not increase much over time.

4.2 Budget Constraints

We now investigate the performance of our approach under a budget constraint. The initial candidates are selected using the Pareto optimisation approach and users are then ranked based on three possible strategies. Figure 4 shows the performance with a decreasing budget ranking the candidates based on time probability, location probability and reputation. As can be seen the budget does not have an impact until it drops below 50 queries. The reputation ranked strategy however, only drops 2% when the budget is reduced to 25 and still maintains a success rate of 65.34% with a budget of 10. The success rate drops to only 21.56% with a budget of one, however it should be noted that this measure of success is whether we accurately predicted which user contributed a relevant tweet. Our end goal is to identify users who are good candidates to poll for updates taking into account the time of day and location, meaning those recommended with a budget of 1 may still be valid candidates who could respond if probed with a high probability. Ranking based on location and time on the other hand suffer a large drop in performance as the budget available decreases, demonstrating that once users with a reasonable probability based on time and location profiles are identified, taking into account the reputation of the user becomes the more successful strategy.

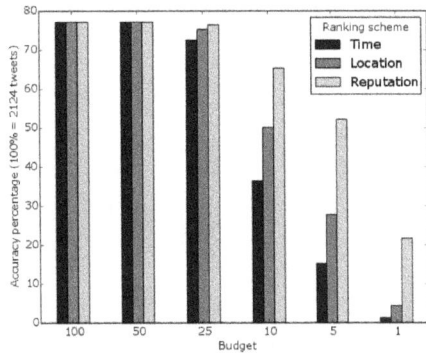

Figure 4: Success Rate for varying budget and candidates ranking schemes

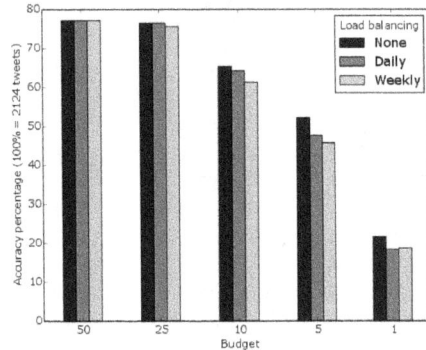

Figure 5: Success Rate with varying budget and load balancing constraints

4.3 User Query Load

Figure 6 shows a violin plot[5] demonstrating the distribution of queries across the user population with varying budget constraints. As can be seen, when no load balancing strategy is in place, a single user could potentially be queried 2124 times when considering a budget of 25 over the course of the 15 month experiment. This is clearly too much load to place on a single user in the system and has the potential to cause this user to opt out of the system. As a result we introduce an additional decay factor in the user reputation as proposed in equation 2, however the value of k is determined by the number of times the user was queried in the given time unit. Figure 6 shows the impact on load distribution when considering the number of queries the user has received that day, or that week. Depending on the budget constraints the additional decay factor helps to distribute the load more evenly across the available users.

Figure 5 shows the impact on accuracy when predicting the exact user who contributed the tweet when employing the load balancing schemes. As can be seen, there is only a small reduction in accuracy due to the decision to distribute the load across users. When considering a budget of 5 the accuracy drops from 52.11% to 47.55% and 45.66% when considering the number of queries a user has already been given that day and that week respectively.

5. CONCLUSION AND FUTURE WORK

We present a strategy to recommend users who may be probed in order to provide crowd-sourced traffic updates. We evaluate our strategy using a novel dataset consisting of real user-service interactions over the course of 15 months. We demonstrate the ability to accurately predict which user is appropriate to provide information depending on the time of day and location of interest. We study the behaviour of our algorithm with a budget of maximum users that can be queried. We also consider different load balancing ap-

[5]http://www.itl.nist.gov/div898/software/dataplot/refman1/auxillar/violplot.htm

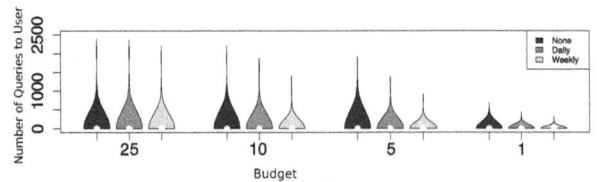

Figure 6: Effect of load balancing on the number of queries per users

proaches to better spread queries between users. While this can lead to a decrease in accuracy, it can both keep medium users engaged in the system and avoid sending too many queries to good users, which may make them leave our crowd sourcing scheme. Using real tweets addressed to a Dublin traffic radio, our empirical evaluation shows our approach can accurately predict who will contribute tweets about an incident at a particular place and time. While these first results are promising, we believe there is room for improvement. From an algorithmic point of view, more advanced method from reinforcement learning could increase accuracy or the learning rate. From a practical point of view, we hope to test our approach by actively querying users. Human traffic controllers could trigger the queries. However, automatically sending queries based on sensor measurements may be a more promising approach.

Acknowledgements

This work is partly funded by the EU FP7 INSIGHT project (project number 318225).

6. REFERENCES

[1] Alt, F., Shirazi, A.S., Schmidt, A., Kramer, U., Nawaz, Z.: Location-based crowdsourcing: extending crowdsourcing to the real world. In: NordCHI'10. pp. 13–22. ACM (2010)

[2] Artikis, A., Weidlich, M., Schnitzler, F., Boutsis, I., Liebig, T., Piatkowski, N., Bockermann, C., Morik, K., Kalogeraki, V., Marecek, J., Gal, A., Mannor, S., Gunopulos, D., Kinane, D.: Heterogeneous stream processing and crowdsourcing for urban traffic management. In: EDBT. pp. 712–723 (2014)

[3] Brink, T., Keeney, R., Raiffa, H.: Decisions with multiple objectives, preferences and value tradeoffs. Behavioral Science 39(2), 169–170 (1994), http://dx.doi.org/10.1002/bs.3830390206

[4] Daly, E.M., Lecue, F., Bicer, V.: Westland row why so slow?: Fusing social media and linked data sources for understanding real-time traffic conditions. In: IUI '13. pp. 203–212 (2013)

[5] Fuchs, G., Andrienko, N., Andrienko, G., Bothe, S., Stange, H.: Tracing the german centennial flood in the stream of tweets: First lessons learned pp. 31–38 (2013)

[6] Kakantousis, T., Boutsis, I., Kalogeraki, V., Gunopulos, D., Gasparis, G., Dou, A.: Misco: A system for data analysis applications on networks of smartphones using mapreduce. In: MDM '12. pp. 356–359 (2012)

[7] Kazemi, L., Shahabi, C.: Geocrowd: enabling query answering with spatial crowdsourcing. In: SIGSPATIAL '12. pp. 189–198 (2012)

[8] Krause, A., Horvitz, E., Kansal, A., Zhao, F.: Toward community sensing. In: IPSN '08. pp. 481–492 (2008)

[9] Sakaki, T., Okazaki, M., Matsuo, Y.: Earthquake shakes twitter users: real-time event detection by social sensors. In: WWW '10. pp. 851–860 (2010)

[10] Starbird, K., Muzny, G., Palen, L.: Learning from the crowd: Collaborative filtering techniques for identifying on-the-ground twitterers during mass disruptions. In: Proc. 9th Int. Conf. Inf. Syst. Crisis Response Manag. Iscram (2012)

[11] Venanzi, M., Rogers, A., Jennings, N.R.: Crowdsourcing spatial phenomena using trust-based heteroskedastic gaussian processes. In: HCOMP. pp. 182–189 (2013)

[12] Victorino, J.N.C., Estuar, M.J.E.: Profiling flood risk through crowdsourced flood level reports. In: ICITCS'14. pp. 1–4 (2014)

Data Quality Matters in Recommender Systems

Oren Sar Shalom*
Microsoft, Israel and
Bar Ilan University, Israel
t-orens@microsoft.com

Shlomo Berkovsky
CSIRO, Australia
shlomo.berkovsky@csiro.au

Royi Ronen
Microsoft, Israel
royir@microsoft.com

Elad Ziklik
Microsoft, USA
eladz@microsoft.com

Amir Amihood[†]
Bar Ilan University, Israel and
Johns Hopkins University
amir@esc.biu.ac.il

ABSTRACT

Although data quality has been recognized as an important factor in the broad information systems research, it has received little attention in recommender systems. Data quality matters are typically addressed in recommenders by ad-hoc cleansing methods, which prune noisy or unreliable records from the data. However, the setting of the cleansing parameters is often done arbitrarily, without thorough consideration of the data characteristics. In this work, we turn to two central data quality problems in recommender systems: sparsity and redundancy. We devise models for setting data-dependent thresholds and sampling levels, and evaluate these using a collection of public and proprietary datasets. We observe that the models accurately predict data cleansing parameters, while having minor effect on the accuracy of the generated recommendations.

1. INTRODUCTION

Data quality is an important practical consideration in many information systems. It can have a strong effect on the performance of the system and the level of user satisfaction. Data quality received significant attention in the general context of information systems, but it has yet to be thoroughly investigated through the recommender systems' prism. For instance, what dimensions of data quality are particularly important for recommenders and what methods can address these? Although there exists some evidence that data quality issues do matter [2, 3, 8], little work has looked into the application of data quality methods to recommenders. These are typically addressed through an ad-hoc data cleansing, such as "prune users with less than X ratings" or "consider data from the recent period Y". But the setting of the data cleansing parameters is often arbitrary and asks for more methodical solutions.

This work addresses two data quality problems in recommender systems. The first refers to the well-established *data sparsity* problem. To this end, we devise a novel model for setting data-dependent threshold for filtering of cold items or users, not having enough data

to facilitate generation of reliable recommendations. The second considers the *data redundancy* problem, which may lead to significant overheads at the recommendation model training stages. We propose a method for adaptive sampling of users that can decrease the model training overheads, while still facilitating the construction of accurate recommendation models. This paradigm is used successfully by Azure Machine Learning recommendations [7].

We propose heuristic models for setting the item threshold and user sampling rate, both *without building the recommendation models*. These heuristic models are evaluated using a large collection of public and proprietary recommender system datasets from a range of domains. We observe that the models accurately predict the data cleansing parameters, while having only minor effect on the accuracy of the generated recommendations.

In summary, the contribution of our work is twofold. First, we highlight and demonstrate the importance of data quality matters in recommender systems. Second, we address two practical data quality issues of sparsity and redundancy, by proposing and validating models for adaptive setting of the data cleansing parameters.

2. RELATED WORK

Wang and Strong developed a framework encapsulating the fundamental dimensions of data quality [10]. They derived more than 100 data quality attributes and split these into four dimensions. The *intrinsic quality* dimension refers to the core data characteristics, e.g., accuracy, objectivity, and reputation. *Contextual quality* considers the data in the context of the task at hand and includes attributes like relevancy, completeness, and timeliness. *Representational quality* refers to the format (representation and consistency) and meaning (interpretability) of the data. Finally, the *accessibility* dimension primarily considers data security. Pipino et al. turned to the assessment and metrics of data quality [6]. With the attributes proposed in [10] in mind, they presented a methodology for developing objective metrics communicating the fit of data regardless of the application and task at hand.

Specifically in recommender systems, it has been observed that the rating data can be noisy, imprecise, or outdated [2, 8]. Amatriain et al. demonstrated that offering users to re-rate previously rated items would lead to somewhat different ratings, which substantially change the accuracy of the generated recommendations [2]. Marlin and Zemel questioned the assumption of uniformity in user rating distribution, and showed that this assumption deteriorated the accuracy of collaborative recommendations [4]. Said et al. evaluated the stability of user ratings over time and offered users to re-rate already rated items [8]. It was found that this omnipresent white noise in user ratings poses "the magic barrier" to the accuracy attainable by recommender systems.

---

*This paper is part of the author's PhD thesis.

[†]Partially supported by ISF grant number 571/14.

To the best of our knowledge, little work has studied the recommenders' data sparsity and redundancy from the data quality perspective. In this work, we systematically address these two data quality attributes and propose methods for dataset-dependent setting of sparsity- and redundancy-related data cleansing parameters.

3. DATA SPARSITY

3.1 Threshold model

Most rating-based recommender system datasets contain a considerable portion of cold users and items. The small number of ratings for these is not sufficient to build a reliable recommendation model, such that the common practice is to omit such items and users outright, as part of the data cleansing process. The real problem, however, is to determine the appropriate cleansing thresholds for a given dataset. A too-low threshold may result in noisy training data and imprecise recommendation models, whereas a too-high threshold may lead to overlooked rating patterns and preclude the system from generating recommendations for these users/items.

A brute-force solution to determining the cleansing threshold could be to exhaustively evaluate all the plausible combinations of item and user thresholds. Even for a small dataset, the number of such combinations is in the thousands, which rules the brute-force solution out for practical business cases. Thus, our aim is to develop a heuristic method that predicts the optimal thresholds for a given user-item rating matrix, without building the model. In this work we focus on the optimization of one – either item or user – threshold, and leave the concurrent optimization of the two for the future. Without the loss of generality, we discuss below the method applied to the item threshold.

We assume that the target threshold value for items is correlated with the average length of the item vectors in the dataset, $\overline{r_i}$, i.e., average number of ratings assigned to an item. However, this feature alone is not sufficient for achieving accurate threshold predictions. Hence, another feature we exploit stems from the parameterization of the power-law distribution of ratings. Let H be the distribution of the item vector lengths. We fit H to a power-law distribution Ax^{-m}, where x is the length of the item vector. Since, typically, there is a small number of popular items with many ratings and a large number of items with a few ratings, m is positive.

We model the item threshold value as a function of $\overline{r_i}$ and m, and assume positive correlation between $\overline{r_i}$ and the item threshold. This is explained by the more robust nature of longer item profiles. Also, we assume negative correlation between the value of m and the threshold. This is due to the observation that when m increases, the weight of the tail of the power-law distribution decreases and there are fewer items with many ratings. Hence, for high m the sparsity of the data is higher and the item threshold is lower. We parameterize the model by a linear multiplier γ. In summary, we model[1] the item threshold IT_d of a dataset d as

$$IT_d = \gamma \cdot \frac{\log(\overline{r_i})}{m^2} \qquad (1)$$

3.2 Evaluation

We use 24 public and proprietary datasets with either implicit or explicit item ratings. Among the public datasets are Movielens, Million Songs, Flixster, Moviepilot, Filmtipset, Yelp, Yahoo! Music (broken down into albums, artists, and tracks), and BookCrossing. The 14 proprietary datasets (referred to as PD) were obtained

---

[1]We experimented with several other models of IT and the model in Equation 1 yielded the most accurate performance.

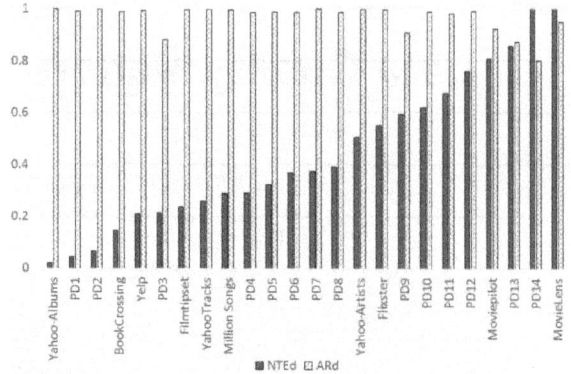

Figure 1: Item threshold predictions of the 24 datasets.

from various companies and sites, and belong to application domains of eCommerce, car sales, real estate, books, software purchases, grocery shopping, app downloads, video games, and more.

Each dataset was partitioned into the training and test sets using the 90-10 ratio. In order to assess the accuracy of the predictions, we used the *Precision@K* metric [9]. Since the datasets are fairly different, the value of K was set dynamically to 10% of the dataset item set size. The split was repeated ten times, as per the N-fold validation methodology, and the reported precision scores are the averages computed across the ten splits.

We first exhaustively found the optimal item threshold IT_d^{opt} for each dataset d. For this, we gradually increased the value of the item threshold IT, filtered from the data items having less than IT ratings, trained the Matrix Factorization (MF) recommendation model [5, 7] on the cleansed data, and measured the precision score obtained for a fixed test set. The threshold, for which the highest precision was obtained, is referred to as IT_d^{opt}, while the corresponding precision score is P_d^{opt}.

Then, we applied the threshold model in Equation 1 to compute the predicted item threshold IT_d^{pred}. This was done using leave-one-out cross-validation. That is, one dataset d was withheld, the threshold model was trained on the other 23 datasets, and we applied the model to predict the IT_d^{pred} threshold for d. Having set the item threshold to IT_d^{pred}, we trained the recommendation model on the data, with items having less than IT_d^{pred} ratings being filtered out. Given this model, we computed the precision P_d^{pred} of the predictions generated by the model for the fixed test set.

This allows us to derive two performance metrics of the threshold predictions. The first, referred to as the normalized threshold error (NTE), is computed by $NTE_d = |IT_d^{opt} - IT_d^{pred}|/IT_d^{opt}$, and communicates the error of the item threshold predictions. The second quantifies the impact of NTE on the predictions of the recommendation model for the test set. This is referred to as the accuracy ratio (AR) and is computed by $AR_d = P_d^{pred}/P_d^{opt}$. Note that although the threshold model is trained to predict the item threshold IT_d^{pred}, our objective is to cleanse the data in a way that maximizes AR, i.e., $\sum_d(P_d^{pred}/P_d^{opt})$, across the 24 datasets.

We present in Figure 1 the individual NTE and AR scores obtained for the 24 datasets. Each dataset is represented by two bars: the left represents NTE_d and the right – AR_d. The datasets are sorted in an increasing order of NTE_d. As can be seen, the first 14 datasets achieve $NTE_d \leq 0.4$, whereas the next 8 achieve $0.5 \leq NTE_d \leq 1$, and for the last 2 datasets we observe $NTE_d \geq 2$ (these bars are truncated). Overall, the average NTE score across the 24 datasets is 0.632.

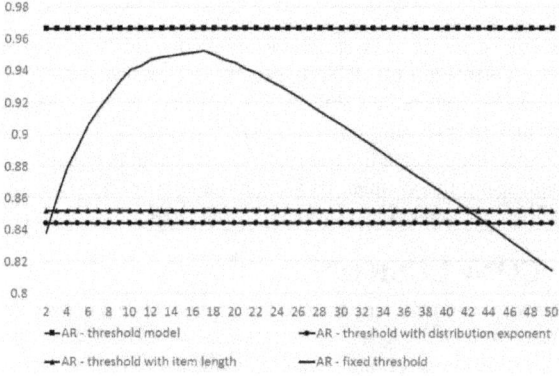

Figure 2: Fixed item threshold experiment.

However, of a greater interest is the impact of NTE on AR. All the datasets demonstrate $AR_d \geq 0.8$, whereas 19 out of the 24 datasets achieve remarkably high $AR_d \geq 0.95$. The overall average AR value across all the datasets is 0.966. Thus, despite the observed threshold prediction errors, the recommendation models built using the cleansed data generate predictions *comparable* to those of the models using the optimal threshold values. We observe correlation of -0.540 between the values of NTE_d and AR_d. This aligns with the intuition that lower errors in the item threshold predictions yield more accurate recommendation models.

To better understand the setting of the item threshold, we carry out another experiment, in which we fix the item threshold IT for all the datasets. We compute the AR, averaged for various values of IT across the 24 datasets. The average AR is compared to three baseline AR using the following IT setting: (i) computed by the model in Equation 1; (ii) computed by a model using only the average item length $\overline{r_i}$; and (iii) computed by a model using only the exponent m of the item length distribution. The results are shown in Figure 2, where the horizontal axis stands for the value of the IT threshold and vertical – for the average AR across the 24 datasets.

As expected, the three baselines are independent of IT and their AR scores are constant. We observe that the model in Equation 1 outperforms the individual models using either $\overline{r_i}$ or m by 13.4% and 14.4%, respectively. The fixed threshold model demonstrates an inverse-curve behavior: for low IT the data is noisy, while for high IT too much data is filtered, such that in both cases the predictions are inaccurate. The highest AR is achieved for $IT = 17$, but this is still 1.5% lower than that of the model in Equation 1. Consider also that such a-priori parameterization may not be feasible for recommenders with dynamic user/item sets and the superiority of our parameter-free model becomes evident.

4. DATA REDUNDANCY

4.1 Model

Another important data quality problem is to identify cases, where some data available in the dataset is redundant, and the recommendation model can be built using a sample of the data. Focusing on random sampling, our target is to pick the lowest sampling rate that will still result in the recommendation model as close as possible to the model that would have been built using the complete data. This is particularly important for practical recommenders and very large scale datasets, where building the complete model may be costly and time consuming. Again, the challenge is to predict the sampling rate, without building the recommendation model.

Unlike in the item cleansing threshold case, there is no optimal sampling rate, because the recommendation model built using the complete data is always superior to, i.e., more accurate than, the one built using the sampled data. Hence, we define the target sampling rate SR as the lowest rate, for which the similarity between the complete recommendation model and the sampled model is greater than a pre-determined parameter Δ. The similarity of the two models is established by comparing the predictions generated by the models for a fixed test set.

In more detail, let us denote by U_d, I_d, and R_d the number of users, items, and ratings, respectively, in a dataset d. We first build the recommendation model using the complete d. As usual in recommender systems, we sample the users in d [1]. Given a sampling rate SR, we retain in the dataset $SR \cdot U_d$ randomly chosen users. Then, we build the recommendation model using the sampled data and generate predictions for a fixed test set. Given a performance metric, we can finally compare the predictions generated by the recommendation model using the sampled data with the ones generated by the model using the complete data.

Since the sampling is done on the users, we assume the level of redundancy to be positively correlated with U_d. We also assume positive correlation with the density of the rating matrix, computed by $\frac{R_d}{U_d \cdot I_d}$. We also incorporate another feature characterising the data, which we denote by *V-structure*. Intuitively, *V-structure* is the relative increase in the similarity of two users given that they have at least one commonly rated item. We compute *V-structure* as the ratio between the average pair-wise similarity of users having at least one jointly rated item and the overall average pair-wise user similarity. Since high *V-structure* of a dataset reflects a greater amount of common rating patterns observed, we posit that the redundancy is positively correlated with *V-structure*.

We model the redundancy level of a dataset d as a combination of three parameters: number of users, density, and *V-structure*. Note that the redundancy is inversely correlated with the sampling rate. That is, when the data is redundant, we sample a small portion of users to build a reliable recommendation model. Also, we need to clamp the sampling rate to the $[0, 1]$ range and keep the function monotonic increasing. We use the hyperbolic tangent function for normalization purposes. In summary, we model[2] the minimal sampling rate SR_d of a dataset d as

$$SR_d = \tanh\left(\frac{1}{\textit{V-structure}_d \cdot \sqrt{U_d} \cdot \frac{R_d}{U_d \cdot I_d}}\right) \qquad (2)$$

4.2 Evaluation

For the evaluation of the sampled models, we used 19 proprietary datasets with implicit and explicit ratings. Each dataset d was partitioned again into the training and test sets using the 90-10 ratio. Also in this experiment the split was repeated ten times and the reported performance was averaged across the ten splits.

We exhaustively found the optimal sampling rate SR_d^{opt} for each dataset d. For this, we first trained MF recommendation model [5, 7] using the complete training dataset and applied this model to generate predictions for a fixed test set. We denote these predictions generated by the model using the complete data as *complete predictions*. Then, we gradually decreased SR by steps of 0.1.[3] For each value of SR we randomly sampled the training data, built the recommendation model using the sampled data, and generated predictions for the same fixed test set.

---

[2]Here, we also experimented with several other models of SR, and the best performance was achieved by the model in Equation 2.

[3]More fine-grained steps of SR were not sufficiently sensitive.

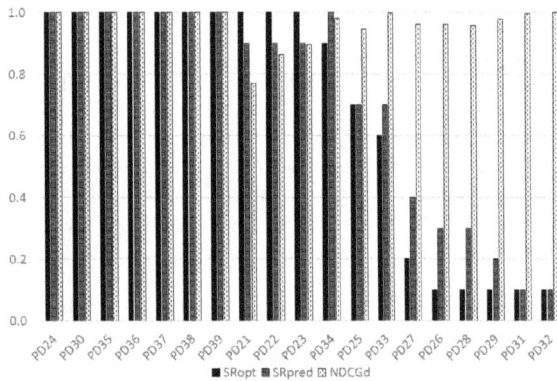

Figure 3: Sampling rate predictions of the 19 datasets.

We used the $NDCG$ metric [9], where the gain of each item was proportional to its rank in the complete predictions, to quantify the predictions generated by the sampled models[4]. We considered the complete model and the sampled model to be sufficiently similar, as long as the $NDCG$ computed by the sampled model for the fixed test set was greater than $\Delta = 0.95$. Thus, we decreased the sample rate SR by steps of 0.1 as long as we managed to obtaine $NDCG \geq 0.95$. The minimal SR, for which this $NDCG$ had been obtained, was considered the optimal sampling rate SR_d^{opt}.

On top of this, we applied the model in Equation 2 to predict the sampling rate SR_d^{pred} for each d. Since the optimal sampling rate SR_d^{opt} was an approximation found by search with steps of 0.1, also SR_d^{pred} was rounded to the closest 0.1 mark. Having set the sampling rate of d to SR_d^{pred}, we created the sampled dataset, then built the sampled MF recommendation model, and generated predictions for the fixed test set. Finally, we evaluated the performance, $NDCG_d^{pred}$, of the recommendation model built using the predicted sampling rate SR_d^{pred}.

Figure 3 presents the results of the sampling rate predictions for the 19 datasets. Each dataset is represented by three bars: namely, SR_d^{opt}, SR_d^{pred}, and $NDCG_d^{pred}$. The datasets are sorted in a decreasing order of SR_d^{opt}. As can be seen, the values of SR_d^{opt} vary across the datasets from 1 (no sampling is needed, all the users are necessary) to 0.1 (only 10% of users are necessary). For 10 datasets out of the 19 we observe $SR_d^{opt} = 1$, which aligns with the established sparsity problem in recommender systems. However, for 6 datasets we observe $SR_d^{opt} \leq 0.2$, indicating that some datasets have high degree of redundancy in the data.

Overall, the predicted sampling rates produced by the model in Equation 2 are close to the optimal ones. We observe that SR_d^{opt} and SR_d^{pred} are identical for 10 datasets out of the 19 (note that for 7 datasets, we observe $SR_d^{opt} = SR_d^{pred} = 1$, i.e., no sampling needed), for 6 datasets the difference is 0.1 (3 over-sampled and 3 under-sampled), and for 6 datasets the difference is 0.2 (SR_d^{pred} over-samples). The average difference between SR_d^{opt} and SR_d^{pred} across the 19 datasets is 0.063. Note that when $SR_d^{opt} \neq SR_d^{pred}$, we prefer to over-sample, i.e., $SR_d^{pred} > SR_d^{opt}$, as in this case, despite keeping unnecessary users, the recommendation model still achieves the desired degree of similarity to the complete model.

We also observe high $NDCG_d^{pred}$ scores, such that for 15 datasets we achieve $NDCG_d^{pred} \geq 0.95$. These include the 7 datasets with $SR_d^{opt} = SR_d^{pred} = 1$, where no sampling is performed and we

---

[4]As $NDCG$ combines ranking and predictive accuracy metrics, we deem it to be a reliable model performance indicator.

obviously achieve $NDCG_d^{pred} = 1$. The average $NDCG_d^{pred}$ obtained across the 19 datasets stands at 0.964. Finally, we observe negative correlation of -0.382 between the obtained $NDCG_d^{pred}$ scores and the absolute value of the difference between the predicted and optimal sampling rate, $|SR_d^{opt} - SR_d^{pred}|$. This result is not surprising, since the accuracy of the recommendation models built using the sampled data deteriorates with the error in the sampling rate predictions generated by the model in Equation 2.

5. CONCLUSIONS

Our work was driven by the need to instantiate data quality models for recommender systems. To this end, we addressed two practical considerations of large-scale recommenders: sparsity of user ratings and redundancy of users in the datasets. We developed two models for predicting the data cleansing parameters and demonstrated their validity using a large collection of datasets. Notably, these models capitalize only on the parameters of the datasets and do not require the costly recommendation model building.

This work paves the way for future works on data quality in recommender systems. First, the proposed predictive models for data cleansing parameters were evaluated using the MF recommendation model. However, our models should be evaluated with other recommendation techniques, as, for instance, the item threshold may depend on the underlying recommendation model. Second, the impact of data cleansing on other performance metrics. The filtering of cold users/items and the sampling of users can affect the coverage and the diversity of the generated recommendations. Hence, there is a need to strike the balance between data quality assurance and these metrics. Third, we will consider the ways to incorporate content features of the items and demographic features of the users in the proposed predictive models.

6. REFERENCES

[1] X. Amatriain, A. Jaimes, N. Oliver, and J. M. Pujol. Data mining methods for recommender systems. In *Recommender Syst. Handbook*. 2011.

[2] X. Amatriain, J. M. Pujol, N. Tintarev, and N. Oliver. Rate it again: increasing recommendation accuracy by user re-rating. In *Recommender Syst. Conf.*, pages 173–180, 2009.

[3] S. Berkovsky, T. Kuflik, and F. Ricci. The impact of data obfuscation on the accuracy of collaborative filtering. *Expert Syst. Appl.*, 39(5):5033–5042, 2012.

[4] B. M. Marlin and R. S. Zemel. Collaborative prediction and ranking with non-random missing data. In *Recommender Syst. Conf.*, pages 5–12, 2009.

[5] U. Paquet and N. Koenigstein. One-class collaborative filtering with random graphs. In *Int. World Wide Web Conf.*, pages 999–1008, 2013.

[6] L. L. Pipino, Y. W. Lee, and R. Y. Wang. Data quality assessment. *Commun. of the ACM*, 45(4):211–218, 2002.

[7] R. Ronen, N. Koenigstein, E. Ziklik, M. Sitruk, R. Yaari, and N. Haiby-Weiss. Sage: recommender engine as a cloud service. In *Recommender Syst. Conf.*, pages 475–476, 2013.

[8] A. Said, B. J. Jain, S. Narr, and T. Plumbaum. Users and noise: The magic barrier of recommender systems. In *Int. Conf. on User Modeling, Adaptation, and Personalization*, pages 237–248, 2012.

[9] G. Shani and A. Gunawardana. Evaluating recommendation systems. In *Recommender Syst. Handbook*. 2011.

[10] R. Y. Wang and D. M. Strong. Beyond accuracy: What data quality means to data consumers. *Journal of Management Information Systems*, pages 5–33, 1996.

Elsevier Journal Finder:
Recommending Journals for your Paper

Ning Kang
Research Management, Elsevier
Radarweg 29, 1043 NX Amsterdam,
The Netherlands

n.kang@elsevier.com

Marius Doornenbal
Research Management, Elsevier
Radarweg 29, 1043 NX Amsterdam,
The Netherlands
+31 20 4583255

m.doornenbal@elsevier.com

Bob Schijvenaars
Research Management, Elsevier
Radarweg 29, 1043 NX Amsterdam,
The Netherlands

b.schijvenaars@elsevier.com

ABSTRACT

Rejection is the norm in academic publishing. One of the main reasons for rejections is that the topics of the submitted papers are not relevant to the scope of the journal, even when the papers themselves are excellent. Submission to a journal that fits well with the publication may avoid this issue. A system that is able to suggest journals that have published similar articles to the submitted papers may help authors choose where to submit. The Elsevier journal finder, a freely available online service, is one of the most comprehensive journal recommender systems, covering all scientific domains and more than 2,900 per-reviewed Elsevier journals. The system uses natural language processing for feature generation, and Okapi BM25 matching for the recommendation algorithm. The procedure is to paste text, such as an abstract, and get a list of recommend journals and relevant metadata. The website URL is http://journalfinder.elsevier.com.

Categories and Subject Descriptors

H.3.3 [**Information Search and Retrieval**]: Clustering; I.2.7 [**Natural Language Processing**]: Text analysis; I.5.3 [**Clustering**]: Similarity measures

General Terms

Algorithms, Measurement, Experimentation, OKAPI BM25.

Keywords: Natural language processing, Recommender system, Noun phrase, TF-IDF, Okapi BM25

1. INTRODUCTION

Finding the right journal to submit a paper is one of the most important steps during the process of paper publishing. For most authors, this job is difficult because many journals have a very wide diversity of topics, and many articles involve several academic disciplines or professional specializations.

According to the records from the Scopus database [2], from 1992 to 2002, 12 million peer-reviewed papers have been published. This number has doubled between 2003 and 2013. With the rapid growth of new journals and papers each year, the task to select a correct journal to submit a paper becomes more and more difficult.

In this study, we present the Elsevier journal finder, a comprehensive journal recommender system that covers all major scientific domains and more than 2,900 peer-reviewed Elsevier journals, to help authors easily find relevant journals for their paper.

2. BACKGROUND

Recommender systems have become quite common in recent years, and are applied in a variety of applications [10][1].

In the field of journal recommendation, there are already some systems that search for similar articles [7]. For example, PubMed [6] offers the function to search similar records from Medline records, but only existing Medline records can be used as queries. eTBLAST [3] accepts full abstracts search for journal recommendation, and Jane [12] also provides similar functions. However, these systems only cover the biomedical domain. Some cross domain tools such as Mendeley [9] search for similar articles based on articles that have already been published, but do not recommend journals.

3. METHOD

3.1 Source of journals and papers

The Scopus database [2] is used as the source of journals and papers for the Elsevier journal finder. The Scopus database is the largest abstract and citation database of peer-reviewed literature from scientific journals, books and conference proceedings. It contains more than 55 million records and 5000 publishers, and covers all major scientific domains: Agriculture, Chemistry, Economics, Geo-Sciences, Humanities and Arts, Life and Health Sciences, Materials Science and Engineering, Mathematics, Physics, and Social Sciences.

For our system, we only use the papers that are published after 2008, for the reason that the scope of the journals may change over time, and newer papers reflect the current scope of journals more accurately. Also, the system's response time improves when it includes less sample papers. We also filter out all papers from non-Elsevier journals because our system only recommends Elsevier journals. The remaining 1.98 million paper records from the Scopus database are used as the sample papers set.

3.2 Noun phrase annotations

The Elsevier journal finder uses noun phrases [5] as features for the paper matching and journal ranking algorithm. The noun phrases are annotated and normalized by the Elsevier Fingerprint Engine [14]. The Elsevier Fingerprint Engine (EFE) applies a variety of Natural Language Processing (NLP) techniques to mine the input text and generates all relevant annotations, including sentence boundaries, tokenization, part-of-speech tags, and phrase chunking. Noun phrases are extracted based on a relatively simple pattern of part-of-speech (POS) tag sequences. We employed a simple noun phrase syntax, sketched in Backus-Naur-form:

$$<NP> ::= <Pre> <NN> \mid <NN> \mid <NP> \text{ "in" } <NP>$$
$$<Mod> ::= \text{ "jj" } \mid \text{ "nn" } \mid \text{ "nn\$" } \mid \text{ "np" }$$
$$<Pre> ::= <Mod> \mid <Pre> <Mod>$$
$$<NN> ::= \text{ "nn" } \mid \text{ "np" } \mid \text{ "nns" }$$

In this noun phrase grammar, POS tags are used as terminals (*jj* is 'adjective', *nn* is 'noun', *np* is 'proper noun', *nn$* is 'possessive noun', *nns* is 'plural noun', and *in* is 'preposition'). To improve feature generation however, we made the algorithm to select sub-phrases of full noun phrases, in order to avoid a very sparse vector space containing only very specific noun phrases. The feature set consists of noun phrases in normalized form, meaning that plural forms translate to singular variants, and spelling variations, e.g. British to American, are normalized away.

We preprocess the 1.98 million sample papers from the Scopus database to generate normalized noun phrases as weighted features (vector-dimensions) for each paper published in the target journals. For each query input text submitted, we use the EFE to generate normalized noun phrases as a query vector for the paper matching algorithm. We remove all noun phrases that occur only once and the top 300 noun phrases that occur most frequently (e.g., study, method, data, analyse, paper, conclusion, model, system, etc. ....). These noun phrases are too commonly used to contribute to the ranking algorithm. By testing the accuracy, these optimization parameters give the highest accuracy.

3.3 Ranking algorithm

The journal recommendation ranking algorithm is divided into two parts. The first part is matching the submitted query to existing papers in the database. For this purpose, we use the Okapi BM25 algorithm [11]. The Okapi BM25 algorithm is widely used in the domain of information retrieval. It ranks matching documents according to their relevance to a given search query. Normally, the input is a bag-of-words, and the output is a set of documents with scores and ranks based on the query words appearing in each document, regardless of the inter-relationship between the query terms within a document (e.g., their relative proximity).

In our case, instead of using the whole text as input for the retrieval function, we use the normalized noun phrase annotations of the input text as input for the algorithm. By our estimate, this feature selection may account for part of the improved accuracy of our system relative to other recommender systems.

The Okapi BM25 can be described as below: Given an input text Q, containing noun phrases $q_1, ..., q_m$, the BM25 score of a paper D is:

$$score(D, Q) = \sum_{i=1}^{n} IDF(q_i) \cdot \frac{f(q_i, D) \cdot (k_1 + 1)}{f(q_i, D) + k_1 \cdot (1 - b + b \cdot \frac{|D|}{avgdl})}$$

where $f(q_i, D)$ is q_i's frequency in paper D, |D| is the length of the paper D in noun phrases, and *avgdl* is the average paper length in noun phrases in the sample paper set. The parameters k_1 and b allow for adapting the algorithm to different use cases. In our case, we used 1.5 for k_1, 0.6 for b (experimentally), and measured 68 for *avgdl* as the average document length.

IDF q_i is the IDF (inverse document frequency) [12] weight of the noun phrase q_i. It is usually computed as:

$$IDF(q_i) = \log \frac{N - n(q_i) + 0.5}{n(q_i) + 0.5}$$

where N is the total number of papers in the sample paper set, and $n(q_i)$ is the number of papers containing q_i.

After the first step, we get a ranked paper list with a BM25 score for each paper that has already been published in a journal [5]. The top paper in this list is the paper most similar to the input text.

The second part of the journal recommendation ranking algorithm translates the scores for individual papers to scores for journals. This step is divided into the following sub-steps:

1. Keep the top 1 million papers with the highest BM25 score from the ranked paper list, and find the journal and the journal's scientific domains of the journal that each paper belongs to. Given the size of the data set we have no reason to expect that articles outside the top 1 million will contribute to the aggregated score per journal (see below, 3);

2. If the end-user has already selected a domain, then remove all documents that do not belong to this domain. This step is skipped if the end-user did not select a domain for the input text. (See the section of system overview for more information about the input from end-users);

3. Compute an average BM25 score per journal by averaging the scores of all papers published in the same journal:

$$score(J, Q) = \frac{\sum_{i=1}^{N_J} score(D_i, Q)}{N_J}$$

Where N_J is the number of papers published in journal J, $score(D_i, Q)$ is the BM25 score of paper D_i in journal J. We take the average to correct for journal size.

3.4 System overview

In Figure 1, we show the system overview of the Elsevier journal finder. When an end-user inputs an abstract, the EFE first generates the normalized noun phrases, which are then used by the paper matching algorithm to find the related papers from the Scopus database, and then these papers are used by the journal ranking algorithm to get the recommended journals list.

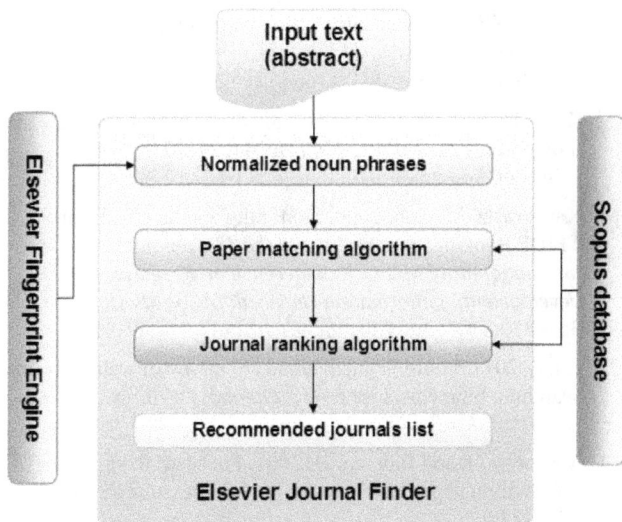

Figure 1: System overview of the Elsevier journal finder

From Figure 2, we can see the input interface of the Elsevier journal finder. The end users can simply input the paper title and abstract, or even just a few keywords, and then select one or more scientific domains that the input text belongs to (this step can also be skipped if the end-user is not sure about which domain(s) the input text belongs to).

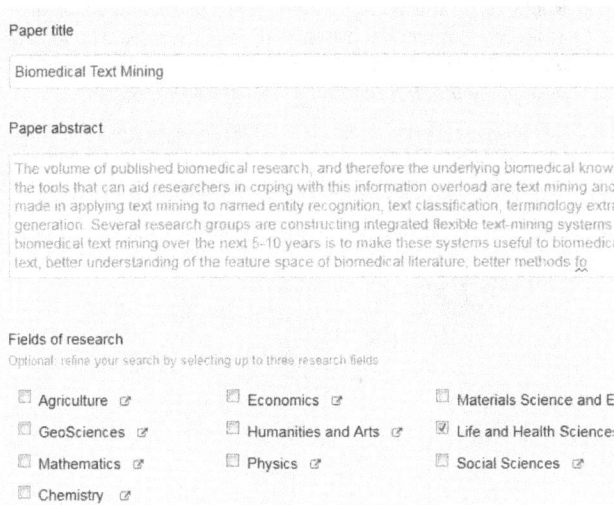

Figure 2: Screenshot of the input interface

Figure 3 shows the list of recommended Elsevier journals, together with some important metadata of the recommended journals, such as matching score, impact factor, open access, editorial times, acceptance rate, and production times. By clicking each journal title, user can also see the scope and more information about this journal. This information can help the authors to decide to which journal to submit their papers, and may reduce the probability of rejection.

Figure 3: Screenshot of the recommended journal list.

4. EXPERIMENTS AND RESULTS

To evaluate the accuracy of our system, we applied a strategy similar to leave-one-out cross-validation: we randomly selected 10 to 100 (depending on the number of papers published in each journal) already published papers from each Elsevier journal as the input documents, and removed these input documents from the source database. If the top three or top ten recommended journals contained the journal in which the input paper was published, then this is counted as a correct recommendation, otherwise it is counted as a false recommendation.

Table 1 shows the performance of each optimization. By changing the features from concepts to noun phrases, the performance is improved by more than 10%. By optimizing the noun phrases (normalize and filter the noun phrases) and the algorithm (tuning the parameters of the paper matching algorithm and the journal ranking algorithm), the performance is further improved by another 5%. The best performance is 42.6% for the top 3, and 64.6% for the top 10.

Table 1. The performance of each optimization step

Features	Performance	
	Top 3	Top 10
Concepts	26.7%	47.8%
Noun phrases	36.3%	59.8%
Optimized noun phrases	38.1%	61.2%
Optimized noun phrases and algorithm	42.6%	64.6%

5. DISCUSSION

We use normalized noun phrases as the features for our ranking algorithm, and do not use advanced annotations such as concepts as thesaurus-defined entities. Although the EFE can generate high quality concept annotations, these are not suitable for this use case. Using concept annotations results in a sparse feature set, particularly as a comprehensive, good-coverage thesaurus spanning all disciplines is not readily available. Furthermore, considering the diverse nature of the data (texts from multiple science domains), using noun phrase annotations as features is better than using concept annotations. For an extensive discussion of the best feature sets, cf. [4].

The ranking algorithm only works well if there are enough sample papers (at least more than 100) in each journal. However, for some new journals, there are not enough published papers. To solve this problem, we asked the editors to select some papers from other journals that are relevant to the scope of the new journals, and then used these selected papers as the sample papers for the ranking algorithm.

The performance of the Elsevier journal finder is better than Jane (42% for top 3 and 58% for top 10) [13] and eTBLAST (35% for top 3 and 50% for top 10) [3] that use the same evaluation method of leave-one-out cross-validation. Besides that, the Elsevier journal finder is the only system that covers all major scientific domains (including the biomedical domain), whereas the other two systems only cover the biomedical domain.

However, the performance figures of these systems are based on different test document sets. They could be changed if we use the same test document set. This is difficult to do because the leave-one-out cross-validation method needs to change the training document set, which is impossible if we do not have the source code of Jane and eTBLAST.

Theoretically, the Elsevier journal finder can recommend any journal in the Scopus database. Although the recommended journals are limited to Elsevier journals only, the system can always recommend highly relevant journals to the authors for their papers, since Elsevier has more than 2900 peer-reviewed journals that cover almost all major scientific domains.

6. REFERENCES

[1] Bobadilla, J. et al. 2013. Recommender systems survey. *Knowledge-Based Systems.* 46, (2013), 109–132. DOI= http://dx.doi.org/10.1016/j.knosys.2013.03.012

[2] Burnham, J.F. 2006. Scopus database: a review. *Biomedical digital libraries.* 3, (2006), 1. DOI= http://dx.doi.org/10.1186%2F1742-5581-3-1

[3] Errami, M. et al. 2007. ETBLAST: A web server to identify expert reviewers, appropriate journals and similar publications. *Nucleic Acids Research 35(S2).*

[4] Jimeno Yepes, A.J., Plaza, L., Carrillo-de-Albornoz, J., Mork, J.G., Aronson, A.R. Feature engineering for MEDLINE citation categorization with MeSH. *BMC Bioinformatics, 16 (1), 113* (2015), DOI=http://dx.doi.org/10.1186/s12859-015-0539-7

[5] Kang, N. et al. 2011. Comparing and combining chunkers of biomedical text. *J Biomed Inform.* 44, 2 (2011), 354–60. DOI=http://dx.doi.org/10.1016/j.jbi.2010.10.005

[6] Kantrowitz, M. et al. 2000. Stemming and its effects on TFIDF Ranking. *Proceedings of the 33st annual international ACM SIGIR conference on Research and development in information retrieval, (ACM SIGIR 2000),* 357–359. DOI=http://dx.doi.org/10.1145/345508.345650

[7] Lu, Z. 2011. PubMed and beyond: A survey of web tools for searching biomedical literature. *Database.* (2011). DOI=http://dx.doi.org/10.1093/database/baq036

[8] McEntyre, J. and Lipman, D. 2001. PubMed: Bridging the information gap. *Canadian Medical Association Journal. 164, 1317-1319.*

[9] Reiswig, J. 2010. Mendeley. *Journal of the Medical Library Association.* 98, (2010), 193–194. DOI= http://dx.doi.org/10.3163%2F1536-5050.98.2.021

[10] Ricci, F. et al. 2011. Introduction to Recommender Systems Handbook. *Recommender Systems Handbook* 1-35

[11] Robertson, S.E. 1990. On term selection for query expansion. *Journal of Documentation. 46(4),* 359-364 DOI= http://dx.doi.org/10.1108/eb026866

[12] Roelleke, T. and Wang, J. 2008. TF-IDF uncovered: a study of theories and probabilities. *Proceedings of the 31st annual international ACM SIGIR conference on Research and development in information retrieval* (2008), 435–442.

[13] Schuemie, M.J. and Kors, J.A. 2008. Jane: Suggesting journals, finding experts. *Bioinformatics.* 24, (2008), 727–728. DOI=http://dx.doi.org/10.1093/bioinformatics/btn006

[13] Vestdam, T.V. et al. 2014. Black magic meta data - Get a glimpse behind the scene. *Procedia Computer Science* (2014), 239–244. DOI=http://dx.doi.org/10.1016/j.procs.2014.06.038

Evaluating Tag Recommender Algorithms in Real-World Folksonomies: A Comparative Study

Dominik Kowald
Know-Center
Graz University of Technology
Graz, Austria
dkowald@know-center.at

Elisabeth Lex
Knowledge Technologies Institute
Graz University of Technology
Graz, Austria
elisabeth.lex@tugraz.at

ABSTRACT

To date, the evaluation of tag recommender algorithms has mostly been conducted in limited ways, including p-core pruned datasets, a small set of compared algorithms and solely based on recommender accuracy. In this study, we use an open-source evaluation framework to compare a rich set of state-of-the-art algorithms in six unfiltered, open datasets via various metrics, measuring not only accuracy but also the diversity, novelty and computational costs of the approaches. We therefore provide a transparent and reproducible tag recommender evaluation in real-world folksonomies. Our results suggest that the efficacy of an algorithm highly depends on the given needs and thus, they should be of interest to both researchers and developers in the field of tag-based recommender systems.

Categories and Subject Descriptors

H.2.8 [**Database Management**]: Database Applications—*Data mining*; H.3.3 [**Information Storage and Retrieval**]: Information Search and Retrieval—*Information filtering*

Keywords

tag recommender; recommender evaluation; social tagging systems; accuracy; diversity; novelty; computational costs

1. INTRODUCTION

Since social tagging has become an essential Web 2.0 tool for collaborative content annotation, research on tag recommenders has significantly expanded over the past years. Tag recommender algorithms process folksonomy data in order to assist people in finding descriptive tags for their bookmarked resources. Although a number of tag recommender evaluation studies have been performed (e.g., [6, 5, 13, 11]), most of them have only involved a limited view of the tag recommender evaluation process with respect to the algorithms, datasets and evaluation metrics included. Furthermore, most of these evaluations were conducted only on

RecSys'15, September 16–20, 2015, Vienna, Austria.
ⓒ 2015 ACM. ISBN 978-1-4503-3692-5/15/09 ...$15.00.
DOI: http://dx.doi.org/10.1145/2792838.2799664.

p-core pruned datasets which does not reflect a real-world folksonomy setting as shown by Doerfel et al. [2]. With that regard, this study aims to provide a transparent and reproducible evaluation of various tag recommender algorithms in real-world folksonomies. Our contributions are as follows:

- We compare the performance not only of classic tag recommender algorithms, such as Collaborative Filtering, FolkRank and Pairwise Interaction Tensor Factorization, but also of novel time-based and cognitive-inspired approaches.

- We conduct our evaluation using unfiltered dataset samples (i.e., no p-cores) gathered from six folksonomies (Flickr, CiteULike, BibSonomy, Delicious, LastFM and Delicious) to demonstrate the performance of the algorithms in real-world settings.

- We investigate the performance of the algorithms via a wide range of evaluation metrics measuring not only the accuracy, ranking, diversity and novelty of the recommended tags but also the computational costs (runtime and memory) of the approaches.

- We calculate all of our results using the open-source tag recommender evaluation framework TagRec [8], which contains implementations of the tag recommender algorithms, evaluation metrics and the protocol used in this study.

In summary, this study may help researchers in the area of tag-based recommender systems and especially tag recommenders to obtain an overview of the performance of state-of-the-art approaches as well as developers of live recommender systems to achieve an understanding of which algorithm could best fit their needs. To the best of our knowledge, this is the first tag recommender study of this kind, which provides a transparent overview of such a wide range of algorithms, datasets and metrics in real-world folksonomy settings.

2. METHODOLOGY

This section describes the methodology used in our study, including descriptions of the algorithms, datasets, metrics and the evaluation protocol. All the evaluations have been conducted via the open-source Java framework TagRec[1] (2015-01-21) [8], except for the results for the Pairwise Interaction Tensor Factorization (PITF) algorithm that were calculated

---

[1]https://github.com/learning-layers/TagRec/

using the C++ code provided by the University of Konstanz[2] (2011-07-14). Unless stated otherwise in the text, we applied the default parameter settings for the algorithms specified in the frameworks.

2.1 Algorithms

In this study, we used a wide range of folksonomy-based tag recommender algorithms. We focused on folksonomy-based rather than content-based approaches for two reasons: first, freely available social tagging datasets typically do not contain content data about the resources (e.g., title or description) and second, Rendle et al. [13] proved that personalized folksonomy-based approaches outperform the theoretically best unpersonalized method (to which content-based algorithms typically belong). The algorithms for our comparative study were chosen based on their novelty, popularity and effect in the field. Since previous tag recommender studies mostly employed classic approaches, we attempted to expand the coverage by also including novel time-based and cognitive-inspired algorithms.

The simplest approaches that we utilized are the frequency-based *MostPopular$_r$ (MP$_r$)* and *MostPopular$_{u,r}$ (MP$_{u,r}$)* algorithms [5] and *Collaborative Filtering (CF)* [12] with a neighborhood size of 20. As for algorithms that apply latent factor models, we chose two types of algorithms: *Latent Dirichlet Allocation (LDA)* [10] with 1000 latent topics and *Pairwise Interaction Tensor Factorization (PITF)* [14] with 256 dimensions of factorization. Another well-known tag recommender approach we chose for this study was *Folk-Rank (FR)* [5]. With regard to time-dependent tag recommenders, we included four algorithms: *Temporal Tag Usage Patterns (GIRPTM)* [15] that works in a more data-driven way and three that are inspired by models of cognitive science. The first one of this kind, BLL$_{AC}$ [7], is the only algorithm in our study that works solely on the individual level and thus, can only recommend tags used by the target user in the past. Furthermore, we also included BLL$_{AC}$+MP$_r$, which extends BLL$_{AC}$ by also recommending tags that were assigned by other users to the target resource [7]. The third cognitive-inspired algorithm (and last one in this study) is the 3LT+MP$_r$ approach [9].

2.2 Datasets

In this section, we describe the datasets used in our study. We chose a set of six freely available folksonomy datasets: Flickr[3] (2010-01-07), CiteULike[4] (2015-02-03), BibSonomy[5] (2015-01-01), Delicious[3] (2010-01-07), LastFM[6] (2011-05-12) and MovieLens[7] (2009-01-05). These datasets differ in terms of their domain type (i.e., images, URLs, citations, music and movies), size and narrowness degree. For the purposes of this study, we defined the degree of narrowness as the average number of posts assigned to a resource which also correlates with the commonly known definition of narrow and broad folksonomies [4].

[2] http://www.informatik.uni-konstanz.de/rendle/software/ tag-recommender/

[3] https://www.uni-koblenz.de/FB4/Institutes/IFI/ AGStaab/Research/DataSets/PINTSExperimentsDataSets

[4] http://www.citeulike.org/faq/data.adp

[5] http://www.kde.cs.uni-kassel.de/bibsonomy/dumps

[6] http://files.grouplens.org/datasets/hetrec2011/ hetrec2011-lastfm-2k.zip

[7] http://files.grouplens.org/datasets/movielens/ml-10m.zip

Dataset	$|U|$	$|R|$	$|T|$	$|P|$	$|P|/|R|$
Flickr	9,590	856,755	125,119	856,755	1.000
CiteULike	18,474	811,175	273,883	900,794	1.110
BibSonomy	10,179	683,478	201,254	772,108	1.129
Delicious	15,980	963,741	184,012	1,447,267	1.501
LastFM	1,892	12,522	9,748	71,062	5.674
MovieLens	4,009	7,601	15,238	55,484	7.299

Table 2: Summary of the real-world folksonomy datasets used in this study where $|U|$ is the number of users, $|R|$ is the number of resources, $|T|$ is the number of tags, $|P|$ is the number of posts and $|P|/|R|$ accounts for the degree of narrowness.

As outlined in Section 1 above, it was crucial for us to benchmark the algorithms in the unfiltered datasets without *p*-core pruning to avoid a biased evaluation and to simulate a real-world folksonomy setting (see also [2]). This is especially important for the development of live recommender services. The narrowness degrees of the datasets used (see the last column of Table 2) justifies this approach since the average number of posts assigned to a resource is lower than two in four of the six datasets (Flickr, CiteULike, BibSonomy and Delicious). This means that even a small *p*-core of two would delete a lot of posts and so, substantially distort the natural structures of these datasets. Hence, the only filtering techniques we applied to our datasets were decapitalizing the tags and excluding all automatically generated tags (e.g., "no-tag" or "bibtex-import"). In order to be able to process the data of Flickr, CiteULike and Delicious, we had to use samples of the whole datasets. Thus, we randomly chose 3% of the complete user profiles (i.e., all posts of a user) in Flickr and Delicious and 15% in CiteULike (see [3]) to maintain the original characteristics of the data. The final properties of our datasets after these steps are summarized in Table 2.

2.3 Metrics

We used a wide set of evaluation metrics known from field of recommender systems to assess the performance of the algorithms. Specifically, we measured the accuracy, ranking, diversity and novelty of the recommended tags, as well as the computational costs in terms of runtime and memory consumption of the algorithms.

Accuracy. In terms of metrics that measure recommender accuracy [11], we report *F1-Score (F1@5)*, which was the main performance metric in the PKDD Discovery Challenge 2009[8], and the ranking-dependent metrics *Mean Reciprocal Rank (MRR@10)*, *Mean Average Precision (MAP@10)* and *Normalized Discounted Cumulative Gain (nDCG@10)*.

Diversity. We measure tag recommender diversity by means of the *Average IntraList Distance (AILD@10)* metric as defined in [1]. In this metric, the dissimilarity of two tags is given by the relative difference between the sets of resources to which the tags were applied. This means that a set of tags is diverse if the tags were used for different sets of resources.

Novelty. The novelty of the recommended tag list is calculated using the *Average Inverse Popularity (AIP@10)* metric. Similarly to [1], we define a recommended tag as novel if it was not previously used to annotate the target resource. Thus, the lower the popularity of a tag for a resource is, the higher its novelty.

[8] http://www.kde.cs.unikassel.de/ws/dc09/

Dataset	Metric	MP_r	$MP_{u,r}$	CF	LDA	PITF	FR	GIRPTM	BLL_{ac}	$BLL_{ac}+MP_r$	$3LT+MP_r$
Flickr	F1@5	-	.371	.453	.178	.350	.365	.455	.470	.470	**.482**
	MRR@10	-	.392	.474	.184	.366	.387	.488	.512	.512	**.525**
	MAP@10	-	.509	.631	.216	.469	.501	.647	.680	.680	**.698**
	nDCG@10	-	.569	.666	.280	.535	.561	.686	.711	.711	**.727**
	AILD@10	-	.789	.975	**.980**	**.980**	**.980**	.789	.789	.789	.670
	AIP@10	-	-	-	-	-	-	-	-	-	-
	Runtime [s]	-	1	4,342	1,227	228,868	18,090	2	5	5	10,594
	Memory [MB]	-	4,672	8,488	9,652	**2,502**	9,190	4,974	6,053	6,053	6,942
CiteULike	F1@5	.042	.249	.231	.089	.178	.250	.262	.259	.273	**.277**
	MRR@10	.043	.277	.263	.086	.207	.276	.303	.312	.319	**.321**
	MAP@10	.054	.329	.311	.094	.233	.327	.359	.367	.380	**.383**
	nDCG@10	.063	.392	.359	.138	.294	.392	.420	.422	.438	**.440**
	AILD@10	.152	.916	.961	**.991**	**.991**	**.991**	.916	.902	.916	.893
	AIP@10	.142	.952	.960	.983	**.991**	.958	.953	.985	.951	.953
	Runtime [s]	1	2	6,315	10,673	343,181	27,305	3	1,290	1,424	10,796
	Memory [MB]	5,725	5,913	9,301	11,943	**3,030**	9,347	6,631	8,177	8,789	9,474
BibSonomy	F1@5	.068	.281	.260	.145	.215	.279	.291	.279	.298	**.307**
	MRR@10	.054	.268	.248	.143	.218	.269	.282	.278	.289	**.298**
	MAP@10	.073	.337	.310	.162	.257	.337	.356	.346	.365	**.378**
	nDCG@10	.091	.407	.369	.219	.327	.408	.425	.409	.434	**.445**
	AILD@10	.199	.916	.941	.990	**.991**	**.991**	.916	.901	.916	.889
	AIP@10	.182	.939	.954	.966	.973	.944	.940	**.976**	.937	.941
	Runtime [s]	1	2	2,797	9,847	219,573	12,549	2	502	601	9,316
	Memory [MB]	4,811	4,972	9,405	14,012	**2,432**	9,494	5,567	8,078	8,307	9,137
Delicious	F1@5	.135	.238	.243	.182	.199	.196	.261	.243	.283	**.284**
	MRR@10	.117	.232	.241	.171	.193	.184	.258	.261	.290	**.291**
	MAP@10	.153	.279	.296	.204	.229	.226	.314	.312	**.358**	.357
	nDCG@10	.187	.358	.356	.271	.302	.292	.393	.374	**.431**	.430
	AILD@10	.353	.968	.972	**.999**	**.999**	**.999**	.968	.955	.968	.946
	AIP@10	.256	.882	.874	.887	.895	.877	.873	**.938**	.863	.874
	Runtime [s]	1	3	9,645	15,373	324,737	44,747	4	395	396	12,869
	Memory [MB]	12,198	12,596	35,090	11,894	**3,075**	7,381	13,672	16,469	17,620	59,425
LastFM	F1@5	.199	.258	.226	.258	.276	.270	.263	.251	**.283**	.279
	MRR@10	.186	.251	.208	.254	.276	.257	.255	.260	**.283**	.277
	MAP@10	.226	.301	.252	.306	.336	.313	.310	.312	**.344**	.338
	nDCG@10	.283	.386	.317	.388	.414	.399	.397	.375	**.425**	.421
	AILD@10	.722	.902	.855	.918	**.919**	**.919**	.902	.840	.902	.900
	AIP@10	.604	.730	.761	.741	.797	.728	.736	**.866**	.711	.722
	Runtime [s]	1	1	6	265	8,657	101	1	1	1	225
	Memory [MB]	80	92	214	593	87	237	155	204	301	3,332
MovieLens	F1@5	.135	.153	.124	.141	.156	.153	.159	.086	**.160**	.162
	MRR@10	.211	.260	.198	.233	.264	.243	.251	.183	**.265**	.263
	MAP@10	.223	.269	.209	.242	.275	.253	.262	.188	**.276**	.274
	nDCG@10	.271	.328	.254	.296	.324	.319	.326	.203	**.338**	.336
	AILD@10	.910	.954	.935	**.958**	.957	.957	.954	.726	.954	.954
	AIP @10	.787	.741	.861	.785	.816	.777	.751	**.976**	.756	.755
	Runtime [s]	1	1	11	206	6,091	90	1	1	1	120
	Memory [MB]	365	375	1,043	761	**96**	833	434	500	501	3,297

Table 1: Summary of the tag recommender results showing the accuracy, diversity, novelty, runtime and memory consumption estimates of the algorithms in the six datasets (bold numbers indicate the best results).

Computational Costs. Since recommendations should not only be accurate, diverse and novel but also be provided in (near) real-time, we determined the computational costs of the algorithms in terms of *Runtime* (in seconds) and *Memory* (in megabytes) required. Both runtime and memory are measured for the complete workflow of the algorithms (including training and testing) using an IBM System x3550 M4 Server with one Intel(R) Xeon(R) CPU E5-2640 v2 @ 2.00GHz and 256GB RAM.

2.4 Evaluation Protocol

We followed a standard evaluation procedure in tag recommender research (e.g., [5]) to split our datasets mentioned in Section 2.2 into training and test sets. To that end, for each user, the set of tags in her most recent post in time were put it into the test set and the remaining posts were then used to train the algorithms. This protocol is a promising simulation of a real-world social tagging environment since it preserves the chronological order of the data and predicts the user's future tag assignments based on the past tag assignments. To compute the metrics from Section 2.3, we compared the top-10 tags an algorithm suggested for a given user and resource pair in the test set with the set of relevant tags actually used in the corresponding post.

3. RESULTS AND DISCUSSION

Table 1 shows an overview of the exact accuracy (F1@5, MRR@10, MAP@10 and nDCG@10), diversity (AILD@10), novelty (AIP@10) and computational cost (runtime in seconds and memory consumption in megabytes) estimates of all the algorithms for the six datasets (highest values per dataset and metric are shown in bold). We merged the results across the datasets and metrics in Table 3 to make it easier to determine the usefulness of the algorithms in respect to the various user needs. The merged results indicate that the two cognitive inspired algorithms $BLL_{AC}+MP_r$ and $3LT+MP_r$ were the best (in the narrow and broad settings) with regard to recommender accuracy.

Algorithm	Accuracy narrow	broad	Div	Nov	Runtime	Memory
MP_r	-		-	-	++	+
$MP_{u,r}$					++	+
CF			+			
LDA	-		++		-	-
PITF	-	+	++	+	-	++
FR		+	++			
GIRPTM	+	+			++	+
BLL_{AC}	+		-	++	+	
$BLL_{AC}+MP_r$	++	++			+	
$3LT+MP_r$	++	++			-	-

Table 3: Summary of the performance of the algorithms in real-world folksonomies showing tag recommender accuracy in narrow and broad settings, diversity (Div), novelty (Nov), runtime and memory consumption. "++" indicates best, "+" good, "-" poor and an empty space average performance.

The difference between the narrow and broad settings are especially of interest when comparing our results with previous studies (e.g., [6, 5, 13, 11]), in which FR and PITF typically had the best recommender accuracy in p-core pruned (i.e., very broad) folksonomies. Our results also indicate a good performance of FR and PITF in broad folksonomies but a fairly poor one in the narrow settings. The opposite is the case for the BLL_{AC} approach, which strictly operates on the individual level and thus, performs well in the narrow setting but is only average in the broad setting.

Furthermore, the most diverse tag recommendations are provided via the classic approaches LDA, PITF and FR. With regard to novelty, the strictly individual BLL_{AC} approach outperforms all the other algorithms (which operate also on the collective level). As for the computational costs, the best runtime results are delivered by the frequency-based methods MP_r, $MP_{u,r}$ and GIRPTM and the lowest memory is required by the PITF approach. One reason for the low memory consumption of PITF is surely the fact that it was developed in C++ (the other approaches were implemented in Java). Additionally, the cognitive-inspired $BLL_{AC}+MP_r$ approach that has the highest recommender accuracy also provides fair results in terms of the other metrics. Interestingly, this is not the case for the other cognitive-inspired algorithm $3LT+MP_r$ which has poor runtime and memory consumption estimates since it requires a computationally expensive topic calculation step (see [9]).

4. CONCLUSION

Providing helpful tag recommendations in real-world folksonomies is not a trivial task, which greatly depends on the given user needs, as our results suggest. If recommender accuracy is mostly important, cognitive-inspired algorithms, such as $BLL_{AC}+MP_r$, provide the best results. If runtime is crucial, simple frequency-based methods, such as $MP_{u,r}$, should be applied. Although the classic approaches (CF, LDA, PITF and FR) known from most previous studies do not seem to be the best choice in terms of accuracy in these (mostly narrow) real-world settings, they provide the most diverse recommendations. The most novel tags, however, can be recommended via strictly individual methods, such as the cognitive-inspired BLL_{AC} algorithm.

Thus, we believe that our results should be of interest to both researchers and developers in the field of tag-based rec-

ommender systems. In the future, we plan to verify these results with an online user study in a live recommender system (e.g., BibSonomy), which would also allow us to assess the real user acceptance of the recommendations.

Acknowledgments: This work is funded by the Know-Center and the EU-IP Learning Layers (Grant Agreement: 318209). The Know-Center is funded within the Austrian COMET Program - Competence Centers for Excellent Technologies - under the auspices of the Austrian Ministry of Transport, Innovation and Technology, the Austrian Ministry of Economics and Labor and by the State of Styria. COMET is managed by the Austrian Research Promotion Agency (FFG).

5. REFERENCES

[1] F. Belém, E. Martins, J. Almeida, and M. Gonçalves. Exploiting novelty and diversity in tag recommendation. In *Advances in Information Retrieval*, pages 380–391. Springer, 2013.

[2] S. Doerfel and R. Jäschke. An analysis of tag-recommender evaluation procedures. In *Proc. of RecSys'13*, pages 343–346. ACM, 2013.

[3] J. Gemmell, T. Schimoler, M. Ramezani, L. Christiansen, and B. Mobasher. Improving folkrank with item-based collaborative filtering. *Recommender Systems & the Social Web*, 2009.

[4] D. Helic, C. Körner, M. Granitzer, M. Strohmaier, and C. Trattner. Navigational efficiency of broad vs. narrow folksonomies. In *Proc. of HT'12*, pages 63–72. ACM, 2012.

[5] R. Jäschke, L. Marinho, A. Hotho, L. Schmidt-Thieme, and G. Stumme. Tag recommendations in folksonomies. In *Knowledge Discovery in Databases: PKDD 2007*, pages 506–514. Springer, 2007.

[6] R. Jäschke, L. Marinho, A. Hotho, L. Schmidt-Thieme, and G. Stumme. Tag recommendations in social bookmarking systems. *Ai Communications*, 21(4):231–247, 2008.

[7] D. Kowald, S. Kopeinik, P. Seitlinger, T. Ley, D. Albert, and C. Trattner. Refining frequency-based tag reuse predictions by means of time and semantic context. In *Mining, Modeling, and Recommending'Things' in Social Media*, pages 55–74. Springer, 2015.

[8] D. Kowald, E. Lacic, and C. Trattner. Tagrec: towards a standardized tag recommender benchmarking framework. In *Proc. of HT'14*, pages 305–307. ACM, 2014.

[9] D. Kowald, P. Seitlinger, S. Kopeinik, T. Ley, and C. Trattner. Forgetting the words but remembering the meaning: Modeling forgetting in a verbal and semantic tag recommender. In *Mining, Modeling, and Recommending'Things' in Social Media*, pages 75–95. Springer, 2015.

[10] R. Krestel, P. Fankhauser, and W. Nejdl. Latent dirichlet allocation for tag recommendation. In *Proc. of RecSys'09*, pages 61–68. ACM, 2009.

[11] M. Lipczak. *Hybrid tag recommendation in collaborative tagging systems*. PhD thesis, Dalhousie University Halifax, 2012.

[12] L. B. Marinho and L. Schmidt-Thieme. Collaborative tag recommendations. In *Data Analysis, Machine Learning and Applications*, pages 533–540. Springer, 2008.

[13] S. Rendle, L. Balby Marinho, A. Nanopoulos, and L. Schmidt-Thieme. Learning optimal ranking with tensor factorization for tag recommendation. In *Proc. of KDD'09*, pages 727–736. ACM, 2009.

[14] S. Rendle and L. Schmidt-Thieme. Pairwise interaction tensor factorization for personalized tag recommendation. In *Proc. of WSDM'10*, pages 81–90. ACM, 2010.

[15] L. Zhang, J. Tang, and M. Zhang. Integrating temporal usage pattern into personalized tag prediction. In *Web Technologies and Applications*. Springer, 2012.

Good Times Bad Times: A Study on Recency Effects in Collaborative Filtering for Social Tagging

Santiago Larrain
Pontificia Universidad Católica de Chile
Santiago, Chile
slarrain@uc.cl

Christoph Trattner
NTNU & Know-Center
Trondheim Norway & Graz,
Austria
ctrattner@know-center.at

Denis Parra
Pontificia Universidad Católica de Chile
Santiago, Chile
dparra@ing.puc.cl

Eduardo Graells-Garrido
Telefónica I+D
Santiago, Chile

Kjetil Nørvåg
NTNU
Trondheim, Norway
noervaag@idi.ntnu.no

ABSTRACT

In this paper, we present work-in-progress of a recently started project that aims at studying the effect of time in recommender systems in the context of social tagging. Despite the existence of previous work in this area, no research has yet made an extensive evaluation and comparison of time-aware recommendation methods. With this motivation, this paper presents results of a study where we focused on understanding (i) "when" to use the temporal information into traditional collaborative filtering (CF) algorithms, and (ii) "how" to weight the similarity between users and items by exploring the effect of different time-decay functions. As the results of our extensive evaluation conducted over five social tagging systems (Delicious, BibSonomy, CiteULike, MovieLens, and Last.fm) suggest, the step ($when$) in which time is incorporated in the CF algorithm has substantial effect on accuracy, and the type of time-decay function (how) plays a role on accuracy and coverage mostly under pre-filtering on user-based CF, while item-based shows stronger stability over the experimental conditions.

Categories and Subject Descriptors

H.3.3 [**Information Storage and Retrieval**]: Information Search and Retrieval—*Information filtering*

Keywords

time-aware recommendations; collaborative filtering; social tagging.

1. INTRODUCTION

Time-Aware recommender systems have been extensively studied in the past and have proven to be more effective than traditional un-contextualized recommender systems [1]. Although there is a huge body of research in this context, few studies have investigated to what extent time can help to improve implicit feedback recom-

RecSys '15, September 16 – 20, 2015, Vienna, Austria.
ACM 978-1-4503-3692-5/15/09.
http://dx.doi.org/10.1145/2792838.2799682 .

mender systems relying on data such as social tags [19, 5, 10]. Also there seems to be a gap in the literature on *how* and *when* to incorporate the variable of time in the recommendation process, *i.e.*, which type of decay functions to choose and where to incorporate the variable of time, before or after the filtering step in a Collaborative Filtering (hereinafter *CF*) setting.

Problem Statement. We try to find the best way to incorporate temporal information in a *CF* item recommender for social tagging systems. Our notion of temporal information is related to *recency* considering this argument: if users u and v have bookmarked items using the same tag t they might have some degree of similarity, but if u have used the tag recently and v used it long ago, their similarity might have weaken as a consequence of concept drift [7]. Based on this intuition, we address the following challenges (i) "when" to use the temporal information into traditional *CF* algorithms for time-aware item predictions, since these algorithms consist of two steps where similarity calculations play a role, and (ii) "how" to weight the similarities between users and items exploring the effect of different time-decay functions .

Research Questions. Our study was henceforth driven by the following two research questions:

- **RQ1.** Being aware of different ways of incorporating the variable of time in a *CF* time-aware item recommender system, formally known as pre- or post-filtering, what is the most efficient approach?

- **RQ2.** Being aware of different types of decay functions to model recency effects in recommender systems, which of those functions provides the best approximation in the context of item recommendation in social tagging systems?

Results. Our results indicate that the step (pre- or post-filtering) in which temporal information is incorporated in the recommendation algorithm has a substantial effect on the performance of the algorithms. On the other side, the decay function affects in different ways the version of the *CF* method: item-based is very stable while user-based is affected by the decay function. In addition, combining both user- and item-based recommendation has a small but regular improvement on ranking accuracy.

2. DATASET AND APPROACHES

Since users' preferences drift over time [7], some works on tag-based recommenders have investigated how to incorporate temporal information into *CF* approaches [5, 10, 19]. These works consider

Dataset	|B|	|U|	|R|	|T|	|TAS|
BIB	82,539	2,437	28,000	30,919	339,337
CUL	10,533	7,182	42,320	46,060	373,271
ML	53,607	3,983	3,983	14,883	92,387
DEL	379,667	8,377	82,557	44,280	1,205,018
LFM	66,353	1,798	8,190	8,378	172,051

Table 1: Descriptive statistics of our datasets. B: Bookmarks, U: users, T: Tags, TAS: Tag Assignments.

Decay	Param.	BIB	CUL	ML	DEL	LFM
-	$T_0 = median(\Delta t)$	417	482	92	184	273
Exp.	$\lambda = \frac{\beta}{T_0}$	.0016	.0014	.0075	.0037	.0025
Power	$\lambda = \frac{\beta}{\ln(T_0)}$	.1148	.1121	.1532	.1329	.1235
Linear	$\lambda = \beta * T_0$	834	964	184	368	546
Log.	$\lambda = \frac{\beta}{T_0}$	.0026	0022	.0119	.0059	.0040

Table 2: Decay function parameters for each data set. The parameter β is optimized according to each dataset and decay function.

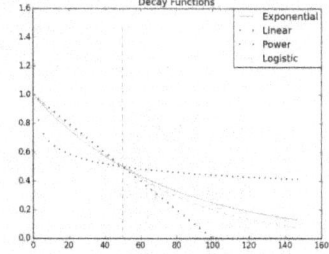

Figure 1: The figure compares the different decay functions at the step of parameter fitting. The x-axis represents temporal data (days since a bookmark was set) and the vertical blue dashed line is a median set on x=50 for representation purposes. BLL is not shown because its parameters are set based on literature.

that user-similarity is conditioned not only on the common items they have consumed, but how recently both users have consumed them [14]. For instance, Zheng et al. [19] improved the performance of a tag-based recommender after filtering their data based on recency of tagging interactions by applying a power decay function. Likewise, Huang et al. [5] improved a tag-based recommender relying on a two-step filtering process which modelled the recency effect of interactions as a linear decay function. More recently, Lacic et al. [11] outperformed state-of-the-art tag-based recommendation methods by decaying the similarity of users and items considering the recency of their tagging actions using the Base-Level Learning function [10]. Although these results are certainly promising, there is no consensus in current literature about which is the best approach to incorporate the variable of time.

2.1 Datasets

For reproducibility, we focused on five well-known and freely-available folksonomy datasets in our experiments. In particular, we used datasets of the social bookmark and publication sharing system BibSonomy[1] (BIB), the reference management system CiteULike[2] (CUL), the movie recommendation website MovieLens[3] (ML), the social bookmarking system Delicious[4] (DEL) and the online music platform LastFM[5] (LFM). As suggested by related work in the field (e.g., [6]), we excluded all automatically imported and generated tags. In the case of CiteULike we randomly selected 10% of the user profiles and in the case of Delicious 2% for reasons of computational effort (see also [3]). The final dataset statistics can be found in Table 1.

2.2 Pre- and Post-Filtering

First, we briefly introduce the traditional versions of CF: user-based [15] and item-based [16]. User-based CF is made of two steps: (i) given a center user u, find a neighborhood N of the k most similar users (K-nearest neighbors or K-NN) to u by a similarity function $sim(u, v), u \in U \wedge v \in U \wedge u \neq v$, and then (ii) given the items consumed by users in N, which have not yet been consumed by u, recommend items after ranking them by a score function that predicts the value $\hat{v}_{u,i}$ that user u will give to item i:

$$\hat{v}_{u,i} = \bar{v}_u + \alpha \sum_{n \in N} sim(u, n)(v_{n,i} - \bar{v}_n), \quad (1)$$

where $\bar{v}_u$ is the average value that user u has given to items in the dataset, $sim(u, n)$ is a similarity function (usually Cosine or Jaccard), $v_{n,i}$ is the value that user n gave to item i, $\bar{v}_n$ is the average value that user n has given to items in the dataset, and α is a normalization constant. Traditionally, $v_{x,y}$ represents an ordinal rating, e.g. 1–5, but in our model it represents a binary value (user

[1] http://www.kde.cs.uni-kassel.de/bibsonomy/dumps
[2] http://www.citeulike.org/faq/data.adp
[3] http://files.grouplens.org/datasets/movielens/
[4] https://www.uni-koblenz.de/FB4/Institutes/IFI/AGStaab/Research/DataSets/PINTSExperimentsDataSets/
[5] http://grouplens.org/datasets/hetrec-2011/

bookmarked the item or not). Then, Eq. 1 is adapted as shown in [19] to:

$$\hat{v}_{u,i} = \frac{\sum_{n \in N} sim(u, n) \times v_{n,i}}{\sum_{n \in N} sim(u, n)} \quad (2)$$

Since we are interested in studying the recency effect by applying time-decay functions during the K-NN step or at the moment of picking the relevant items, we call our approaches pre-filtering and post-filtering. In order to implement a pre-filtering approach we update each user vector with the decay function, $f(\Delta t_{u,i})$, where $\Delta t_{u,i}$ is the amount of time between a reference time t_{u_0} and the moment where user u interacted with item i. If our similarity function is cosine-based, we change it to:

$$cos'(u, n) = \frac{\sum_{i \in I_{u,n}} f(\Delta t_{u,i}) v_{u,i} f(\Delta t_{n,i}) v_{n,i}}{\sqrt{\sum_{i \in I_{u,n}} (f(\Delta t_{u,i}) v_{u,i})^2 \sum_{i \in I_{u,n}} (f(\Delta t_{n,i}) v_{n,i})^2}}, \quad (3)$$

where $I_{u,n}$ is the set of common items that both users u and n have consumed, and $v_{u,i}$ is the value given by user u to item i. Similar to [2] we apply post-filtering as a decay factor $f(\Delta t_{n,i})$ when doing the recommendation on the CF:

$$\hat{v}_{u,i} = \alpha \sum_{n \in N} f(\Delta t_{n,i}) cos'(u, n) v_{n,i}, \quad (4)$$

where α is a normalizing constant, similar to Eq. 1. In the case of item-based collaborative filtering, the method has two steps: (i) create a user model $items(u)$ as a vector of items that user u has consumed with the respective values or ratings that u has given to those items, and then (ii) using a similarity function between items $sim(i, j)$, select the items which are most similar to those in $items(u)$. In this case, pre-filtering is implemented by weighting the rating or value of each item in $items(u)$ with the decay function $f(\Delta t_{u,i})$, and post-filtering is accomplished by decaying the similarity between two items in a similar fashion to Eq. 3, but considering pairs of items rather users.

2.3 Decay Functions

We have identified five approaches that make use of decay functions to model the recency of user interactions. These approaches

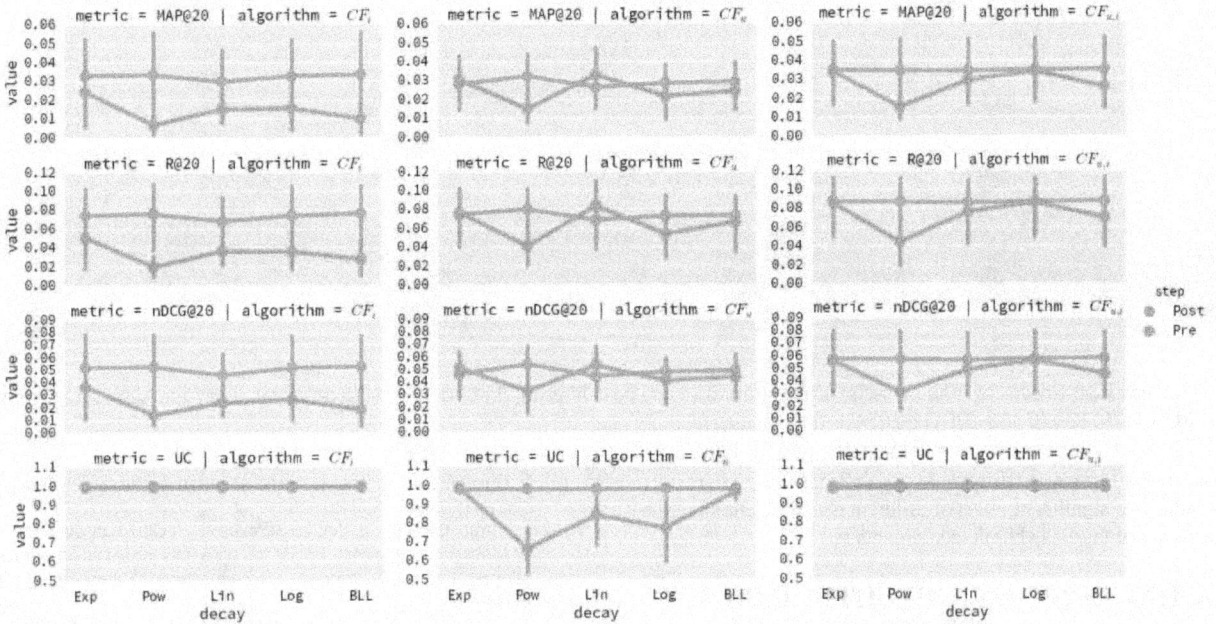

Figure 2: The figure summarizes the results averaged over the five datasets in a 4 x 3 plot matrix. Rows are metrics (MAP@20, R@20, nDCG@20 and User Coverage), columns represent the methods (CF_i, CF_u, $CF_{u,i}$), and the x-axis of each plot shows the 5 decay-functions studied (Exponential, Power, Linear, Logistic, and BLL).

decay the similarity between a pair of users if they have interacted with the same item at different times, what we denote in the following functions as $f(\Delta t)$.

Exponential. This type of decay function has been used in several works (*e.g.*, [2, 13]), $f(\Delta t) = e^{-\lambda \times \Delta t}$.

Power. The power decay function was used by Wu et al. [18] in a user-based CF approach for a social tagging system in a digital library, $f(\Delta t) = (\Delta t)^{-\lambda}$.

Linear. A linear decay function was used by Lee and Park [12], where they use the time variable in a user-based CF approach before calculating the user similarity, $f(\Delta t) = \max(0, 1 - \frac{\Delta t}{\lambda})$.

Logistic. Suggested by Ding and Li [2] as alternative to exponential decay but disregarded without empirical support since it would be less representative of users' latest preferences. We test it in our experiments as $f(\Delta t) = \frac{2}{1 + e^{\lambda \times \Delta t}}$.

BLL. Finally, we employed the Base-Level learning function that was introduced by Kowald et al. [10], $f(\Delta t) = \ln(\sum_{i=1}^{n} \Delta t_i^{-\lambda})$.

Parameters. Ding and Li [2] achieved the best performance by applying a half-life decay, i.e., setting a parameter T_0 in such a way that $f(\Delta t)$ reduces by $1/2$ in T_0 days. The effect of this parameter fitting in the different distributions can be seen in Figure 1. The relation between T_0 and and λ, the parameter we set in the aforementioned decay functions, follows the procedure in [2] and Table 2 shows the relation and values for each dataset and decay function in our experiments. To set T_0, we analyzed the distribution of Δt at each dataset and we tested setting T_0 at their mean and median, obtaining better results with $T_0 = median(\Delta t)$. The parameter β in Table 2 was optimized after performing a 5-fold cross-validation on each dataset. The only exception was taken on the BLL approach, where we set $\lambda = .5$ based Kowald et al.'s recommendation [10].

3. EXPERIMENTAL SETUP

Evaluation Methodology. We used a training and test-set split method as proposed by popular and related work in this area [19, 17]. Hence, for each user we sorted her bookmarks in chronological or-

der and used the 20% most recent bookmarks for testing and the rest for training [1]. To quantify the performance of each of our recommender methods, we used a diverse set of well-established metrics in recommender systems. In particular, we report Normalized Discounted Cumulative Gain (nDCG@20), Mean Average Precision (MAP@20), Recall (R@20) and User Coverage (UC) [4, 9].

Recommendation Methods. The approaches we utilized were User- (CF_u) [15], Item- (CF_i) [16] and User-Item-based ($CF_{u,i}$) collaborative filtering (without time as introduced before). The size of the neighborhood for the User-based KNN calculations was K=20, based on the results of [10].

4. RESULTS

RQ1. Pre- and post-filtering. Among all results, this one had the clearest effect, but the size of the effect depends on the method used, as seen in Figure 2. We observe that the largest performance difference between post- and pre-filtering is seen when using the item-based *CF* method, where the only decay function that results in comparable performance for the pre-filtering is the exponential decay. For the other decay functions, there is a large gap in favor of post-filtering. Now, under the user-based *CF* the pre-filtering works better than post-filtering under linear decay, but this improvement in performance is obtained at the cost of user coverage, dropping to barely over 80%. We can also observe the stability of the post-filtering method independent of the decay function. Finally when combining user- and item-based *CF* we see an improvement of pre-filtering with respect to the logistic decay, but the power decay combined with pre-filtering still results in poor performance over MAP@20, R@20 and nDCG@20, though the user coverage problem is alleviated.

RQ2. Decay functions. The recency effect was investigated through different decay functions. If we consider post-filtering, there are no significant differences among decay functions in average, but the power decay function $f(\Delta t) = (\Delta t)^{-b}$ was the one resulting in the top accuracy results as seen in the bottom row of plots in Figure 3, and also in the table of the appendix. On the other hand, the power-decay was the one performing the worst under pre-filtering,

271

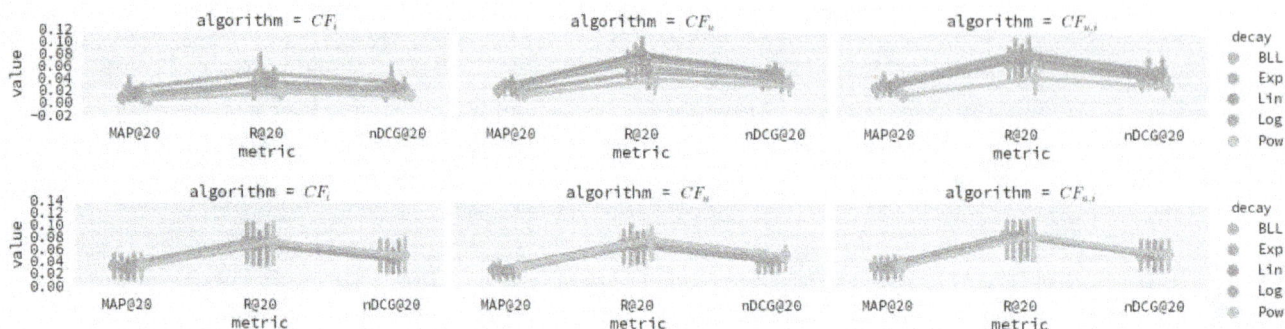

Figure 3: The effect (means over all datasets) of pre- (top row) and post-filtering (bottom row) with different decay functions and algorithms on the MAP@20, R@20 and nDCG@20 performance metric.

as seen in the top row of Figure 3. Apart from that, our results don't indicate a significant effect of different decay functions in the performance of tag-based item recommenders.

5. CONCLUSIONS AND FUTURE WORK

In this paper we have shown that it is worthwhile to study the effect of time in recommender systems. We focused in our analysis on the effect on the weighting step and five different decay functions proposed in the literature. As our experimental results conducted over five different social tagging datasets suggest, there is a strong effect on the weighting procedure (pre- and post-filtering) as well on the decay function used but mostly when using pre-filtering, challenging the results obtained by previous published work in the area (e.g., [5, 10, 19]). Though there are differences in the optimal combination of variables to obtain the optimal values at each dataset, our general results suggest using post-filtering with a power decay function. In terms of the algorithm, using user- and item-based combined helps to overcome the weaknesses of each method and performs consistently well, but the improvement over item-based CF is actually minimal.

In future work, we will include a more detailed analysis on parameter tuning, to study the relations between graph properties and optimal metric performance, and the use of matrix factorization techniques. First, although we tested two ways of tuning the parameters for the different decay functions, we used the same values for all users (mean vs. median of the Δt distributions) and we can explore further by setting parameter values for each user based on their tagging habits. Second, although post-filtering with power decay had the most consistent results in general, we realized important differences among datasets. It might be interesting to study graph properties of each dataset and a relation with their performance with combinations of algorithms, filtering step and decay function. Finally, matrix factorization techniques are usually cited as state-of-art techniques in recommender systems in terms of accuracy, and previous works have studied how to incorporate time, implicit feedback, and contextual variables [8]. Nevertheless, no previous work have yet explored how to integrate time-decay functions into the matrix factorization recommendation framework of social tagging systems.

Acknowledgments. This work was carried out during the tenure of an ERCIM "Alain Bensoussan" fellowship program by CT.

6. REFERENCES

[1] P. G. Campos, F. Díez, and I. Cantador. Time-aware recommender systems: a comprehensive survey and analysis of existing evaluation protocols. *UMUAI*, pages 67–119, 2014.

[2] Y. Ding and X. Li. Time weight collaborative filtering. In *Proc. CIKM'05*, pages 485–492, 2005.

[3] J. Gemmell, T. Schimoler, M. Ramezani, L. Christiansen, and B. Mobasher. Improving FolkRank with item-based collaborative filtering. In *Proc. Workshop on Recommender Systems and the Social Web*, 2009.

[4] J. L. Herlocker, J. A. Konstan, L. G. Terveen, and J. T. Riedl. Evaluating collaborative filtering recommender systems. *ACM TOIS*, 22(1):5–53, 2004.

[5] C.-L. Huang, P.-H. Yeh, C.-W. Lin, and D.-C. Wu. Utilizing user tag-based interests in recommender systems for social resource sharing websites. *Knowledge-Based Systems*, 56:86–96, 2014.

[6] R. Jäschke, L. Marinho, A. Hotho, L. Schmidt-Thieme, and G. Stumme. Tag recommendations in folksonomies. In *Proc. PKDD'2007*, pages 506–514. 2007.

[7] Y. Koren. Collaborative filtering with temporal dynamics. In *Proc. KDD'09*, pages 447–456, 2009.

[8] Y. Koren, R. Bell, and C. Volinsky. Matrix factorization techniques for recommender systems. *Computer*, 42(8):30–37, 2009.

[9] D. Kowald, E. Lacic, and C. Trattner. Tagrec: Towards a standardized tag recommender benchmarking framework. In *Proc. HT '14*, 2014.

[10] D. Kowald, P. Seitlinger, C. Trattner, and T. Ley. Long time no see: The probability of reusing tags as a function of frequency and recency. In *Proc. WWW'14*. ACM, 2014.

[11] E. Lacic, D. Kowald, P. Seitlinger, C. Trattner, and D. Parra. Recommending items in social tagging systems using tag and time information. *arXiv preprint arXiv:1406.7727*, 2014.

[12] T. Q. Lee, Y. Park, and Y.-T. Park. A time-based approach to effective recommender systems using implicit feedback. *Expert systems with applications*, 34(4):3055–3062, 2008.

[13] D. Li, P. Cao, Y. Guo, and M. Lei. Time weight update model based on the memory principle in collaborative filtering. *Journal of Computers*, 8(11):2763–2767, 2013.

[14] D. Parra and X. Amatriain. Walk the talk: Analyzing the relation between implicit and explicit feedback for preference elicitation. In *Proc. UMAP'11*, pages 255–268, 2011.

[15] P. Resnick, N. Iacovou, M. Suchak, P. Bergstrom, and J. Riedl. GroupLens: an open architecture for collaborative filtering of netnews. In *Proc. CSCW'94*, pages 175–186, 1994.

[16] B. Sarwar, G. Karypis, J. Konstan, and J. Riedl. Item-based collaborative filtering recommendation algorithms. In *Proc., WWW'01*, pages 285–295, 2001.

[17] C. Trattner, D. Kowald, and E. Lacic. Tagrec: towards a toolkit for reproducible evaluation and development of tag-based recommender algorithms. *ACM SIGWEB Newsletter*, (Winter):3, 2015.

[18] D. Wu, Z. Yuan, K. Yu, and H. Pan. Temporal social tagging based collaborative filtering recommender for digital library. In *Proc. ICADL'2012*, pages 199–208. 2012.

[19] N. Zheng and Q. Li. A recommender system based on tag and time information for social tagging systems. *Expert Syst. Appl.*, 38:4575–4587, 2011.

Improving the User Experience during Cold Start through Choice-Based Preference Elicitation

Mark P. Graus
Eindhoven University of Technology
IPO 0.20
5600 MB Eindhoven, Netherlands
+31 40 247 8420
m.p.graus@tue.nl

Martijn C. Willemsen
Eindhoven University of Technology
IPO 0.17
5600 MB Eindhoven, Netherlands
+31 40 247 2561
m.c.willemsen@tue.nl

ABSTRACT

We studied an alternative choice-based interface for preference elicitation during the cold start phase and compared it directly with a standard rating-based interface. In this alternative interface users started from a diverse set covering all movies and iteratively narrowed down through a matrix factorization latent feature space to smaller sets of items based on their choices. The results show that compared to a rating-based interface, the choice-based interface requires less effort and results in more satisfying recommendations, showing that it might be a promising candidate for alleviating the cold start problem of new users.

Categories and Subject Descriptors

H.1.2 [**Information Systems**]: User/Machine Systems — *Human information processing*; H.5.2 [**Information interfaces and presentation**]: User Interfaces — *Evaluation / methodology*

General Terms

Algorithms, Measurement, Performance, Design, Reliability, Experimentation, Human Factors, Theory.

Keywords

User-Centric Evaluation, Diversification, Preference Elication, Matrix Factorisation, Choice, Rating

1. INTRODUCTION

1.1 Cold Start

Recommender systems face a cold start problem when insufficient data is available to make personalized recommendations. This can occur when a new system is starting, when a new user enters the system or when a new item is entered into the system.

For new users in particular the cold-start problem can be an issue, as they are often asked to submit a number of ratings to overcome the cold-start problem, which is a tedious task. In addition users typically do not get any feedback from the recommender system during such a training task. For these reasons user dropout can occur as the task takes too much effort.

RecSys '15, September 16 - 20, 2015, Vienna, Austria.
© 2015 ACM. ISBN 978-1-4503-3692-5/15/09...$15.00
DOI: http://dx.doi.org/10.1145/2792838.2799681

Adaptive elicitation strategies have been developed to reduce the effort during the cold start phase by collect ratings as efficiently as possible, requesting ratings for items that are predicted to provide the most information. This can be done from both a system-perspective [3], minimizing the duration of the cold-start for the system, and a user perspective [4], minimizing the duration of the cold-start for users.

1.2 Ratings versus Choice

Ratings are the main data used as input for recommender systems. They are expressions of how a user evaluates an item along an absolute scale (like a star rating). Research in marketing and decision making psychology demonstrates the challenges and drawbacks of these separate evaluations instead of relative, joint evaluations. Jameson et al. [5] argue that preferences are by nature relative expressions and that absolute ratings thus might not might not measure the preference of the user in the best way possible. Because ratings are collected separately they have more noise due to inconsistencies in the data, while the scales lead to limited granularity; in addition users of recommender systems have indicated that choices (joint evaluations) instead of ratings (separate evaluations) are easier and faster [6]. Nguyen et al. investigated how these problems can be reduced by providing rating support by showing exemplars (previously rated movies) as anchor values on the rating scale [11]. However, rather than improving the rating task, perhaps a better approach would be to use a choice task that would allow for relative preference expressions.

Decision trees can provide a way to leverage the advantages of choices compared to ratings in recommender systems [4]. By repetitively asking a user of a system to pick her favorite from a set of items extracted from a decision tree, a system can quickly remove irrelevant subtrees and narrow down the recommendations to a set that is likely to contain the best items. We argue that such a decision tree could be improved by making it dynamic rather than static, using the latent features underlying Matrix factorization algorithms.

1.3 Latent Features

Matrix factorization is a family of collaborative filtering algorithms that is used to predict unobserved ratings. It does so by performing a dimensionality reduction similar to singular value decomposition over the matrix R, where $R_{i,u}$ corresponds to the rating given by user u for item i. The matrix is decomposed into two submatrices of dimensionality k describing users and items on these k latent features [8].

These latent features are said to describe attributes of movies that relate to the preferences. Previous research has demonstrated that these features can be used for reducing choice overload in recommender systems by providing lists with more diverse items in terms of latent feature scores [12] or to increase control in recommendations by allowing users to fine-tune their recommendations through choosing between candidate sets based on these latent feature scores [9].

1.4 Latent Feature Based Navigation

We propose a way to alleviate the cold start problem by combining adaptive preference elicitation based on the latent feature space with the advantages of choices over ratings.

In this solution a user is assigned a null-vector as user vector when entering the system. In order to establish the actual user vector, the user is asked to make choices from a number of sets of 10 items. The initial choice set is randomly selected from all available items. After which in an iterative fashion, for every choice 1) the user vector is moved in the direction of the item vector corresponding to the chosen item, 2) rating predictions are calculated based on the new user vector, 3) a proportion of items with the lowest predicted ratings is discarded, and 4) a list of the previously chosen item together with maximally diversified (in terms of latent features) candidate items is calculated following the algorithm described by Minack[10] and presented as the next choice set.

In this way, the user vector slowly traverses the latent feature space in the direction of the evolving user vector, narrowing down the set of movies to that part of the space where the ideal movie(s) might be located. Maximizing diversity ensures that a user has the full set of choices and that each choice step can maximally learn from the choice made.

The goal of the alternative choice interface is to improve the user experience with a recommender system (and in particular the cold start), while ensuring that the quality of recommender output does not deteriorate. This leads to the following research question:

RQ: Can choice-based preference elicitation improve the training phase of a recommender over rating-based elicitation, enhancing the user experience and reducing effort while maintaining the perceived quality of recommendation sets?

2. Study

An online experiment was implemented to compare the proposed interface with the conventional way of preference elicitation during the training phase (i.e. asking users to rate the movies they know from lists of randomly selected movies until 15 ratings are collected). The experiment used a within-subjects design, so each participant evaluated both preference elicitation tasks.

The recommendations were predicted through a matrix factorization model trained on ratings for the 2500 most rated movies in the 10M MovieLens dataset. The final dataset consisted of 69k users, 2500 items and 8.82M ratings. The performance metrics of the used model were up to standards (MAE: 0.61358, RMSE: 0.79643, measured through 5-fold cross-validation).

2.1 Procedure

The study started after participants agreed to the informed consent and read the basic instructions, when they were provided with either the choice-based interface or the conventional rating based interface (the order was counter-balanced over users). Once sufficient information was provided (i.e. 10 choices or 15 ratings), the participant was asked to complete a questionnaire measuring the usability of the interface. Subsequently the same would be done

for the other interface. Both interfaces provided users additional information for the movies consisting of a picture of the movie cover, a synopsis and the names of cast and director for all titles to allow them to make better choices.

Two recommendation lists were generated, each using the input data of one of the two preference elicitation tasks. To measure differences in the perception of these lists, participants were asked to compare the two recommendation sets side by side[1] on perceived differences in diversity, novelty and satisfaction (c.f. [2]). After this list comparison was made, participants were again presented with the recommendations based on one task (in the same order as the interfaces were originally presented) and asked to pick their favorite from the list. After choosing they were asked to complete a final questionnaire for list accuracy, choice difficulty and choice satisfaction (c.f. [7]). Finally participants would choose from and evaluate the other list of recommendations. Note that in questionnaires we did not reveal from which interface the recommendation list was generated.

2.2 Participants

Participants were gathered through an online panel and were rewarded with €5 compensation for their participation. Some participants were excluded from our analysis for unreliability from being either exceptionally fast or slow (e.g. more than an hour on an elicitation task) or from providing contradictory responses. In total data from 103 participants was used in the analysis. Average age was 27.22 years ($SD = 12.68$), with 54 female and 49 male participants.

2.3 Measures

2.3.1 Subjective Measures

The three questionnaires were based on Knijnenburg et al. [7] and Ekstrand et al. [2]. The first 'interface usability' questionnaire was aimed to measure interaction usability in terms of ease of use (e.g. "It was easy to let the system know my preferences") and effort (e.g. "Using the interface was effortful."). The second 'list comparison' questionnaire was aimed to compare the two recommendation lists in terms of diversity, satisfaction and novelty. The final 'list perception' questionnaire was aimed to measure recommendation output in terms of accuracy (e.g. "Each of the recommended movies in the list was relevant."), satisfaction (e.g. "I like the movie I have chosen.") and choice difficulty (e.g. "It was easy to select a movie.").

Items from the 'list perception' and 'interface usability' questionnaires were formulated as statements to which the user was asked to express to what extent they agreed to them on a 5-point Likert scale (from 'Completely Disagree' to 'Completely Agree'). Per questionnaire all items were submitted to a confirmatory factor analysis (CFA). The CFA used ordinal dependent variables and a weighted least squares estimator. Items with low factor loadings, high cross-loadings, or high residual correlations were removed from the analysis. For the 'list comparison' questionnaire the scales ranged from ("List A much more than B" to "List B much more than A") and these questions were averaged and directionally coded, rather than submitted to a CFA.

2.3.2 Algorithmic Measures

The subjective experience can be checked against objective properties of the recommendation sets [2]. Relevant features of the output recommendations are the novelty and the diversity of the set. Ekstrand et al.[2] also calculated retrospective accuracy but this was not possible as we had no prior ratings from our participants.

---

[1] Due to a coding error, our first batch of participants (50% of the total) received one fixed order (rating-based recommendations left, choice-based right). The second batch (sampled from the same population) was therefore given the opposite order, to have all possible counterbalancing orders of the preference elicitation and comparisons tasks.

2.4 Results

2.4.1 Descriptive results

A number of metrics were gathered or calculated from the data to provide insight in how participants completed the study and the type of recommendations they received. First we inspect (like Ekstrand et al. [2]) the algorithmic measures of novelty and diversity of the recommendations sets calculated from input from the two tasks as depicted below in Fig 1. It shows that recommendation sets for the choice task are more popular and less diverse than recommendations based on the rating task.

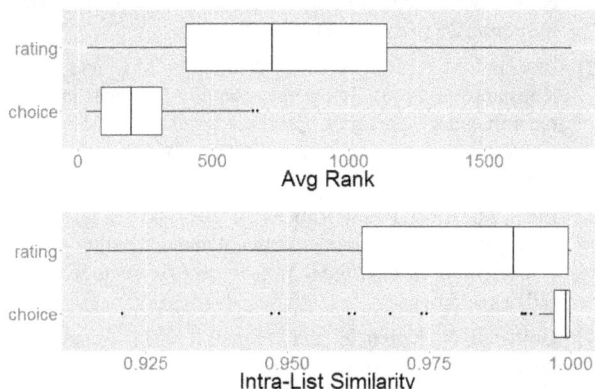

Figure 1. Boxplots for Popularity (top) and Diversity (bottom)

When looking at the choice task, interesting aspects are the moment where users encounter their favorite movie and stop picking other movies and the number of unique items that is chosen throughout the task. If the first list already contains the perfect item we would expect a user to choose that item and stick with it, whereas if the lists are not perfect we expect more unique choices. We see that most users only find their perfect item around the 8th / 9th item (upper left chart of Fig. 2), and that they inspect quite some unique items along the way (upper right chart of Fig. 2), suggesting our parameterization of the choice task was adequate.

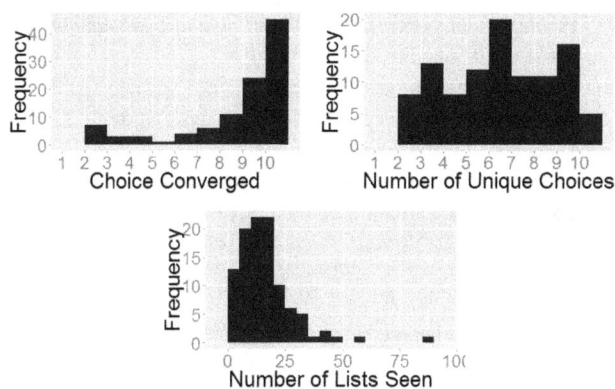

Figure 2. Histograms Describing Choice Task (top) and Rating Task (bottom)

When looking at the rating task, the main metric of interest is the number of lists (of 10 movies each) a user sees before enough ratings (15) are provided to continue. Users need to inspect a large number of these lists (median = 13, see bottom graph in Fig. 2) suggesting high effort in the rating task. This effort is consistent with the large differences in the duration of completing the two tasks (rating 15 items versus choosing 10 movies). Participants needed more time on average for the rating task (388sec) than for the choice task (280 sec). The log of the duration (correcting for skewness) was compared in a paired t-test and found to be significantly higher for the rating task ($D=0.533$) with t(102) = 6.024, p < .001.

2.4.2 Interaction Usability

After each preference elicitation interface, participants were asked to answer 12 questions regarding the usability (ease of use) of the interface and the effort required to perform the task. This gives two sets of responses per user, one for each task. These were submitted to a CFA (clustered per participant), resulting in 5 items loading on the construct 'usability' and 3 items on 'effort'. Using structural equation modeling we related the two factors to each other and the independent variables (task and order factors). We also related these subjective perceptions to the durations for both tasks. The resulting model shows that effort and usability are highly related (correlation of 0.62) and that only effort is affected by the independent variables. This indicates that we cannot really sufficiently distinguish effort from usability and consequently we fitted a model for effort only, as it was affected more by the independent variables.

The resulting model shows a reasonable fit ($\chi^2(4) = 11.8$, $p = .01$, CFI = .97, TLI = .93, RMSEA = 0.098, 90% CI: [.036, .165]) in which subjective effort is perceived to be higher in rating than in choice ($\beta = -.242$, SE = .141, $p < .1$) and perceived effort increases with the log-transformed duration of the task ($\beta = .401$, SE = .113, $p < .001$).

2.4.3 List Comparison

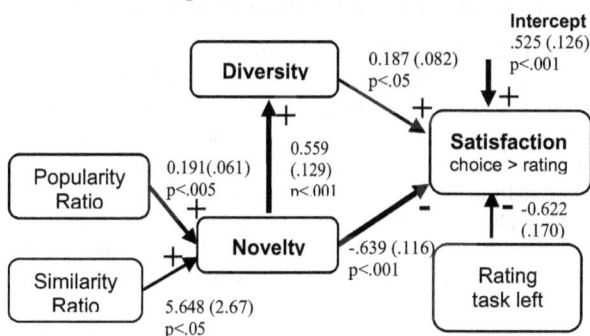

Figure 3. Path Model of Comparison Questionnaire

The path model produced from the questionnaires in which participants were asked to compare the lists from both tasks side by side is shown in Fig. 3. Participants are more satisfied with the choice lists than the rating lists in general (as can be seen from the statistically significant positive intercept). Satisfaction is further positively affected when the choice list is more diverse and less novel than the rating list. The advantage of the choice task on satisfaction is reduced if the rating list is presented left. This reflects a well-known phenomenon in decision psychology for comparison tasks [1], by which the first (left) item in a comparison receives the focus in the comparison and therefore gets an advantage. We also find that differences in perceived novelty between lists increases with differences in the (log) ratio of popularity rank (similar to Ekstrand et al.) and the similarity ratio (which interestingly was related to novelty more than diversity as in Ekstrand et al [2]: however, they found this measure to have small differences and to be strongly dependent on the size of the item set).

2.4.4 List Perception

As a final task, participants made a choice from each recommendation list and rated the lists in terms of perceived accuracy, choice satisfaction and choice difficulty. The items from the questionnaires were submitted to a CFA, clustered per participant. Accuracy was discarded from the remainder of the analysis as it correlated very strongly with choice satisfaction. The resulting constructs of choice difficulty and choice satisfaction were combined with the independent measures (order/task) and the algorithmic measures for novelty and diversity in a SEM model. The model shows a good fit ($\chi^2(41) = 44.26$, $p = .34$, CFI = 1.00, TLI = 0.999, RMSEA =.02, 90% CI: [0, .053]).

The resulting model (Fig. 4) shows that choice satisfaction decreases with choice difficulty and less popular items. As a result choices from the recommendations based on the choice-based interface are perceived to be more satisfactory than those by the rating task, as these lists are less difficult to choose from and contain more popular items.

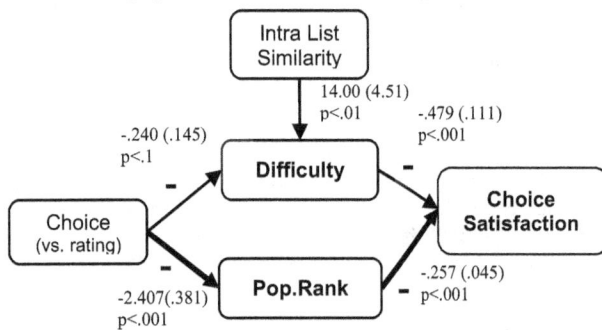

Figure 4. Path Model of List Perception Questionnaire

3. Conclusion and Discussion

Using choices for preference elicitation reduced the effort for participants in our study compared to rating-based elicitation. The recommendation sets generated from both interfaces were perceived to be quite different, with mainly the higher popularity of the items from the choice task leading to participants being more satisfied with their choice-based recommendations than their rating-based recommendations. Moreover, the recommendations calculated from the choice interface resulted in a higher choice satisfaction, again mostly because these were less difficult to choose from and had a higher popularity. These results indicate that a choice-based elicitation might indeed be a way to alleviate the cold start problem of new users of systems. This new interface seems promising given that recommendations calculated from it were perceived as better than those from a conventional interface.

Further research is needed. For example, the parameterization of the choice task, as well as the strong effect of choice on the popularity of the resulting list requires additional research. Furthermore, choice and rating required different instructions. For example, we instructed participants to choose the movie they would like to watch in the choice based interface, but in the rating interface we asked to express to what extent they liked the movies presented. In addition a choice based interface reduces the number of ratings a system receives and recommender performance in terms of prediction accuracy may be harmed over time compared to an interface that uses ratings only. The extent of these effects will have to be investigated.

3.1 Limitations

There are some limitations to our study. The number of participants, while enough for the study as performed, did not allow for optimizing the parameters used in the choice-based interface.

Furthermore, novelty effects can play a role especially when investigating alternative interfaces. Recommender systems and ratings can be found anywhere, leading to assumptions against which a new interface is compared. Especially the effects in terms of interface usability can diminish over time as people get used to the new way of interacting.

4. Acknowledgments
We would like to thank Johannes Sanders for programming the study and collecting the data.

5. References

[1] Dhar, R. and Simonson I. 1992, The Effect of the focus of comparison on consumer preferences, *Journal of Marketing Research*, 29 (November), 430-440.

[2] Ekstrand, M.D., Harper, F.M., Willemsen, M.C. and Konstan, J. a. 2014. User perception of differences in recommender algorithms. *Proceedings of the 8th ACM Conference on Recommender systems - RecSys '14*. (2014), 161–168.

[3] Elahi, M., Ricci, F. and Rubens, N. 2013. Active learning strategies for rating elicitation in collaborative filtering. *ACM Transactions on Intelligent Systems and Technology*. 5, 1 (2013), 1–33.

[4] Golbandi, N., Koren, Y. and Lempel, R. 2011. Adaptive bootstrapping of recommender systems using decision trees. *Proceedings of the fourth ACM international conference on Web search and data mining - WSDM '11*. (2011), 595.

[5] Jameson, A., Willemsen, M.C., Felfernig, A., Gemmis, M. de, Lops, P., Semeraro, G. and Chen, L. (in press). Human Decision Making and Recommender Systems. In F. Ricci et al. (Eds.), *Recommender Systems Handbook* (2nd ed.).

[6] Jones, N., Brun, A. and Boyer, A. 2011. Comparisons instead of ratings: Towards more stable preferences. *Proceedings - 2011 IEEE/WIC/ACM International Conference on Web Intelligence, WI 2011*. 1, (2011), 451–456.

[7] Knijnenburg, B., Willemsen, M., Gantner, Z., Soncu, H. and Newell, C. 2012. Explaining the user experience of recommender systems. *User Modeling and User-Adapted Interaction*. 22, 4-5 (2012), 441–504.

[8] Koren, Y., Bell, R. and Volinsky, C. 2009. Matrix Factorization Techniques for Recommender Systems. *IEEE Computer*. (2009), 42–49.

[9] Loepp, B., Hussein, T., & Ziegler, J. (2014). Choice-based preference elicitation for collaborative filtering recommender systems. In *Proceedings of the 32nd annual ACM conference on Human factors in computing systems - CHI '14* (pp. 3085–3094). http://doi.org/10.1145/2556288.2557069

[10] Minack, E., Siberski, W. and Nejdl, W. 2011. Incremental diversification for very large sets. *Proceedings of the 34th international ACM SIGIR conference on Research and development in Information - SIGIR '11* (2011), 585.

[11] Nguyen, T.T., Kluver, D., Wang, T.-Y., Hui, P.-M., Ekstrand, M.D., Willemsen, M.C. and Riedl, J. 2013. Rating support interfaces to improve user experience and recommender accuracy. *Proceedings of the 7th ACM conference on Recommender systems - RecSys '13*. (2013), 149–156.

[12] Willemsen, M.C., Knijnenburg, B.P., Graus, M.P., Velter-bremmers, L.C.M. and Fu, K. 2011. Using latent feature diversification to reduce choice difficulty in recommendation lists. *Decisions@RecSys 11* (2011), 14–20.

Incremental Matrix Factorization via Feature Space Re-learning for Recommender System

Qiang Song, Jian Cheng, Hanqing Lu
National Laboratory of Pattern Recognition
Institute of Automation, Chinese Academy of Sciences
Beijing, China
{qiang.song, jcheng, luhq}@nlpr.ia.ac.cn

ABSTRACT

Matrix factorization is widely used in Recommender Systems. Although existing popular incremental matrix factorization methods are effectively in reducing time complexity, they simply assume that the similarity between items or users is invariant. For instance, they keep the item feature matrix unchanged and just update the user matrix without re-training the entire model. However, with the new users growing continuously, the fitting error would be accumulated since the extra distribution information of items has not been utilized. In this paper, we present an alternative and reasonable approach, with a relaxed assumption that the similarity between items (users) is relatively stable after updating. Concretely, utilizing the prediction error of the new data as the auxiliary features, our method updates both feature matrices simultaneously, and thus users' preference can be better modeled than merely adjusting one corresponded feature matrix. Besides, our method maintains the feature dimension in a smaller size through taking advantage of matrix sketching. Experimental results show that our proposal outperforms the existing incremental matrix factorization methods.

Categories and Subject Descriptors

H.3.3 [**Information Systems**]: Information Search and Retrieval—*Information Filtering*

Keywords

Recommender Systems, Matrix Factorization, Sketching

1. INTRODUCTION

Recommender Systems have become ubiquitous in our lives, helping us filter out the huge amount of useless information by preference learning. The most widely used recommendation technique is matrix factorization which factorizes the ratings matrix into two smaller matrices. Traditional matrix factorization methods have been proved to be effective, but most of them are designed for stationary data. However, in real-world online applications, users and items grow continuously, which can rarely meet the stationary condition. One strategy to tackle this rapid data expansion is to re-train the model if the data growth exceeds a predefined threshold. But the key challenge lies in that the factorization process is very time-consuming. Therefore, it is crucial and challenging on addressing the problem towards high complexity of factorization model and the rapid expansion of data.

A feasible way to deal with such situation is the use of incremental model updating. Recent works [6][7][8] perform incremental matrix factorization by adopting locally updating strategies which only modify a small fraction of feature matrix at a time. For instance, sarwar [7] proposed a novel incremental SVD algorithm to locally update the user feature matrix while keep the item feature matrix invariant. Rendel [6] also put forward an online regularized kernel matrix factorization(RKMF) method through merely updating one of feature matrices. These locally updating strategies are based on an underlying assumption that the similarity between items (users) is invariant to the new-user(new-item) problem. For instance, as for the new-user problem, supposed that the category of items is invariant, and the amount of coming new users in one round is much smaller than the existing users, then these strategies reduce the time cost through keeping the item feature matrix invariant. In other words, they omit the new ratings' influence on the item features so as to speed up the calculation. However, with the new users growing continuously, the fitting error would be accumulated since the extra distribution information of items has not been utilized. Therefore, the item feature matrix should also be modified in each round. Here, we raise a relaxed and reasonable assumption which considers the similarity between items (users) is relatively stable after updating. The projection of items in feature space will be modified, since these new users in one round may bring with some extra information of items. But the similarity between items still remains relatively stable.

In this paper, we propose an incremental matrix factorization method via feature space re-learning strategy(IMF-FSR). The feature space is re-learnt via auxiliary feature learning and matrix sketching strategies. Concretely, 1) we exploit matrix extension to induce an auxiliary feature learning strategy for better modeling the new preferences, in which the residual error of new data is normalized and added to the existing factorized matrices as auxiliary features. 2) We try to address the increasing feature size issue

RecSys'15, September 16–20, 2015, Vienna, Austria.
© 2015 ACM. ISBN 978-1-4503-3692-5/15/09 ...$15.00.
DOI: http://dx.doi.org/10.1145/2792838.2799668.

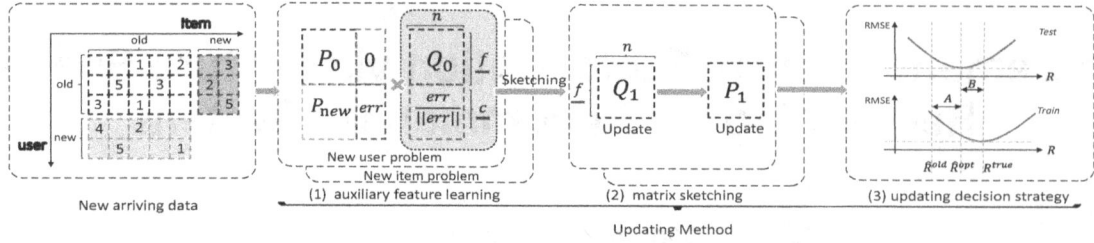

Figure 1: A flow chart of our incremental matrix factorization. The updating method consists of 3 parts: (1) auxiliary feature learning (2) matrix sketching (3) updating decision strategy

by modifying the item feature matrix(user feature matrix) so as to maintain a sketch with a smaller feature size.

2. OUR APPROACH

Given a rating matrix $R \in \mathbb{R}^{m \times n}$, the goal of regularized matrix factorization(RMF) is to construct a low rank decomposition of it. Let f denote the dimension of the feature space, $P \in \mathbb{R}^{m \times f}$ and $Q \in \mathbb{R}^{f \times n}$ denote the user as well as item feature matrix respectively. And the approximation of the rating by user u on item i can be confined to $\hat{r}_{ui} = p_u q_i$, where p_u and q_i stand for the uth row of P and ith column of Q. Studies show that incorporating bias can further improve the prediction performance. Based on[3], the modified equation is expressed as:

$$\min_{p,q} \sum_{(u,i) \in D} (r_{ui} - b_{avg} - b_u - b_i - p_u q_i)^2 + \lambda(b_u^2 + b_i^2 + ||p_u||^2 + ||q_i||^2) \quad (1)$$

where b_{avg}, b_u, b_i stand for the average rating bias, the user average bias and the item average bias respectively. λ stands for the regularized factor.

2.1 Problem Definition

Suppose the online Recommender System has an initial dataset R_0, which consists of a group of users U_0 and items I_0, then in each round there will be a series of new users signing in and giving ratings. We denote the set of new users as U_{new} and the rating set as R_{new}. Symmetrically, in each round there will be a series of new items being added to the system. We denote the set of new items as I_{new}. The task is to predict the missing ratings for these new data.

2.2 Scheme

In this paper, we propose a novel incremental matrix factorization to address the above problem, considering taking advantage of the coming new data as auxiliary information to partly update another invariant factorized matrix Q. Without loss of generality, we describe the detailed method in terms of the new-user problem. While everything can be applied to the new-item problem as well since the RMF models are symmetric. Our idea is demonstrated in Figure 1, which consists of three stages: 1) auxiliary feature learning, 2) matrix sketching, 3) updating decision strategy.

2.2.1 Stage 1: Auxiliary Feature Learning

In real-world online applications, data arrives in a stream. Re-training the entire model in each round is impractical since the factorization process is very time-consuming. A feasible way to deal with such situation is the use of incremental model updating. In this paper, we exploit online

matrix extension to induce an auxiliary feature strategy for faster modeling the new preferences. Similar to the method of online matrix completion for streaming data[1], the residual error of new data is normalized and added to the existing factorized matrices as auxiliary features. A particular expression is given in lemma 2.1.

LEMMA 2.1. *As for new-user problem, where $R_{new} \in \mathbb{R}^{c \times n}$, let R_1 be R_{new} appended into the initial matrix R_0. We can obtain P_1, Q_1 such that $R_1 = P_1 Q_1$ without computing the full factorization. Let $w = R_{new}Q_0^{\dagger}$ and $err = R_{new} - wQ_0$ be the least-squares weights and associated residual. The matrix R_1 can be factorized as*

$$R_1 = \begin{bmatrix} R_0 \\ R_{new} \end{bmatrix} = \begin{bmatrix} P_0 & 0 \\ P_{new} & ||err|| \end{bmatrix} \begin{bmatrix} Q_0 \\ \frac{err}{||err||} \end{bmatrix} \quad (2)$$

where $Q_0^{\dagger}$ denotes the pseudo-inverse of Q_0, $||err||$ is vector norm of err. Different from those locally updating strategies in related work, this step not only adjusts the user feature matrix P, but also makes an extension of item feature matrix Q. The residual error contains a distribution of new data that can not be well modeled by existing factorization. In a consequence, this auxiliary strategy can efficiently fit the new users' preferences. It is worth pointing out two issues: *1)* The feature size gradually increases along with the coming new data . *2)* The feature size extension step may also introduce some over-fitting as well. Thus, designing a feasible method to address these issues is essential.

2.2.2 Stage 2: Matrix Sketching

Due to the sparseness of data, the feature dimension f of matrix factorization in Recommender Systems is often set to much smaller than that of data. But the auxiliary feature learning brings with a side-effect that the feature dimension continuously increases, resulting in a worse performance. Therefore, we try to address this issue via modifying the item feature matrix and maintaining a sketch with a smaller feature size. A strict definition is given in Theorem 2.2.

THEOREM 2.2. **Low Rank Matrix Sketching:** *Suppose $A \in \mathbb{R}^{m \times n}$ is a large row-wise matrix. It maintains a sketch $B \in \mathbb{R}^{l \times n}$ containing only $l \ll m$ rows but still guarantees that $A^T A \approx B^T B$. More accurately,*

$$B^T B \prec A^T A \text{ and } ||A^T A - B^T B|| \leqslant 2||A||_f^2/l \quad (3)$$

In this paper, we make use of the low rank matrix sketching algorithms[5][4] to compress the factorized feature matrix Q_1 into a smaller feature size. Our foundations are as follows: In accordance with our proposed comprehensive view of space projection, Q can be viewed as the coefficient

Algorithm 1 IMF-FSR for New-User Problem

Input: $R_{k-1}, Q_{k-1}, b_{avg_{k-1}}, R_k, D_k$
Output: $P_k, Q_k, b_{avg_k}, b_{u_k}, b_{i_k}$

1: Update biases $b_{avg_k}, b_{u_k}, b_{i_k}$ by the new arriving data R_k.
2: **for** $(u, i) \in R_k$ **do**
3:     $r_{u,i}^{residual} \leftarrow r_{u,i} - (b_{avg_k} + b_{i_k} + b_{u_k})$
4: **end for**
5: **repeat**
6:     random select $u \in |U_k|$
7:     $w_u \leftarrow w_u + \eta((r_{ui}^{residual} - w_u q_i)q_i - \lambda w_u)$
8: **until** convergence
9: $err \leftarrow R^{residual} - WQ_{k-1}$
10: $Q_k \leftarrow \begin{bmatrix} Q_{k-1} \\ \frac{err}{\|err\|} \end{bmatrix}$
11: $Q_k \leftarrow Sketching(Q_k)$
12: $P_k, b_{i_k}, b_{u_k} \leftarrow RMF(R_k, Q_k, b_{avg_k}, b_{i_k}, b_{u_k})$
13: $Y \leftarrow \left| \|R_k - \hat{R}_k^{new}\|_F^2 - \|R_k - \hat{R}_k^{old}\|_F^2 \right|$
14: **if** $Y > L_k$ **then**
15:     $Q_k \leftarrow Q_{k-1}$
16:     $P_k, b_{i_k}, b_{u_k} \leftarrow RMF(R_k, Q_k, b_{avg_k}, b_{i_k}, b_{u_k})$
17: **end if**
---

matrix, in which each column represents an item's coordinate, consisting of a series of coefficients corresponding to the base vectors of P. $Q_1 \in \mathbb{R}^{(f+c) \times n}$ is viewed as the large row-wise matrix. We try to maintain a sketch $\hat{Q}_1 \in \mathbb{R}^{f \times n}$ that retains most of the information. Here, we have to guarantee that $Q_1^T Q_1 \approx \hat{Q}_1^T \hat{Q}_1$. Based on equation 3, the more accurately formula can be expressed as:

$$\hat{Q}_1^T \hat{Q}_1 \prec Q_1^T Q_1 \ and \ \|Q_1^T Q_1 - \hat{Q}_1^T \hat{Q}_1\| \leqslant 2\|Q_1\|_f^2 / l \quad (4)$$

where $Q_1^T Q_1 \in \mathbb{R}^{n \times n}$ can be viewed as a similarity metric matrix of item-item pairs, while the compressed matrix $\hat{Q}_1$ still maintains the similarity metric of Q_1, which is in line with the assumption that the similarity of items in one round on new-user problem is relatively stable. We then re-learn the rest features through the function RMF.

2.2.3 *Stage 3: Updating Decision Strategy*

The residual error err in each round may contain not only the model updating bias $err_m = |r_{ij}^{old} - r_{ij}^{new}|$, but also the real predictive bias $err_p = |r_{ij} - r_{ij}^{opt}|$, where r_{ij}^{opt} stands for the rating prediction by the best modified model. Thus, we should consider whether it is worth of updating the model. Based on model selection in Figure 1(3), the updating model should fall into region A. An optional strategy is to make constraints on the updating degree. We put forward two different strategies as follows:

$$\|\hat{R}_k^{new} - \hat{R}_k^{old}\|_F^2 \leqslant L_k, k \in \mathbb{N}^+ \quad (5)$$

$$\left| \|R_k - \hat{R}_k^{new}\|_F^2 - \|R_k - \hat{R}_k^{old}\|_F^2 \right| \leqslant L_k, k \in \mathbb{N}^+ \quad (6)$$

where L_k is a variable determined by the number of new users in each round, representing the upper bound limit. The former makes constraints on the prediction difference between the new and old model, while the latter focuses on the difference of prediction error. We reject updating if the model does not satisfy the above constraint condition. Here, we simply select the difference of prediction error as our updating decision strategy.

We apply the above scheme to our incremental matrix factorization. Alg.1 describes the kth updating.

2.3 Time Complexity Analysis

The total time complexity of our method in one updating period consists of several parts and the primary cost is summarized as follows: 1) The matrix sketching algorithm has time complexity near $O(|T_m|(f + c)nf)$ where $|T_m|$ is the total number of iteration in sketching, f is the feature size, c is the number of new users per round, n is the sum of items. 2) The incremental matrix factorization without the matrix sketching algorithm has time complexity near $O(|T||D_{new}|f^2)$ where $|T|$ is the total iteration of SGD algorithm, $|D_{new}|$ is the number of new ratings. Since $|T_m|(f + c)n \ll |T||D_{new}|f$, the final time complexity is near $O(|T||D_{new}|f^2)$. Since the number of new ratings $|D_{new}|$ is much smaller than the total ratings size, the proposed method is efficient.

3. EXPERIMENTS

3.1 Datasets

Two real-world datasets used here are MovieLens[1] and Douban [2]. MovieLens is widely used in related work. Douban is real-world dataset crawled from the publicly available website Douban. For experiments, we obtain 1,000,209 observations from 6040 users and 3900 items in MovieLens1M, 2,152,962 observations from 6000 users and 14648 items in Douban.

3.2 Experimental Setup

We set the experiments as follows: The experiments are started with a fixed ratings size of R_0 and the initial factorized matrices were given. After each round, a set of new users signing in (new items added) and ratings are given. Here, for simplicity, we just use a fixed number of new data. e.g. U_{new} or $I_{new} = 20$ per round. While for each new user(item) i in $U_{new}(I_{new})$, we randomly select $D_{new}^i \in [20\%, 80\%]$ observed ratings as the train set so as to model the variety of signing new data. Then we update the models and evaluate the new-user(new-item) problem based on a standard metric, namely Root Mean Square Error($RMSE$). All the experiments were run on machines with the same hardwares (an Intel Core i7 CPU and 16GB RAM, WIN7 64 OS).

3.3 Compared Methods

SVD++(Fully and Partly) [3]: A well known matrix factorization model proposed by Koren et al. Here, "Fully" and "Partly" represent re-training the model entirely or partly.
Online-updating RKMF(Non-negative with linear kernel) [6]: Non-negative with linear kernel achieves the highest performance in the experiments.
Incremental Non-negative Matrix Factorization [2]: An incremental learning algorithm for matrix factorization.
IMF-FSR: IMF-FSR(w) and IMF-FSR denote our method without and with the updating strategy respectively.

3.4 Recommendation results

Table 1 shows the quality of evaluation metrics on the MovieLens as well as Douban dataset for both the new-user and new-item problem respectively. For each problem, we

---
[1] http://grouplens.org/datasets/movielens/
[2] http://www.douban.com

Table 1: The upper is the $RMSE$ metric of different methods on two datasets.($mean \pm std$). The lower is the running time in average round.

Metric	Datasets	Methods					
		IMF-FSR(w)	IMF-FSR	SVD++(f)[3]	SVD++(p)[3]	Non-neg[6]	INMF[2]
New-user	MovieLens	0.9097±0.0985	**0.9018±0.1057**	0.9129±0.0953	1.1366±0.1255	0.9336±0.0979	0.9506±0.1097
	Douban	0.7808±0.1210	**0.7806±0.1210**	0.7981±0.1235	0.9776±0.1543	0.8482±0.1825	0.8599±0.1870
New-item	MovieLens	0.8689±0.1324	**0.8678±0.1347**	0.8682±0.1332	1.2346±0.1890	0.8891±0.1330	0.9393±0.1444
	Douban	0.7441±0.1364	**0.7429±0.1361**	0.7548±0.1386	1.0733±0.2363	0.7576±0.1393	0.7796±0.1425
New-user	MovieLens	0.64s	0.66s	118.82s	0.37s	0.39s	1.17s
	Douban	0.51s	0.53s	193.98s	0.29s	0.32s	1.01s

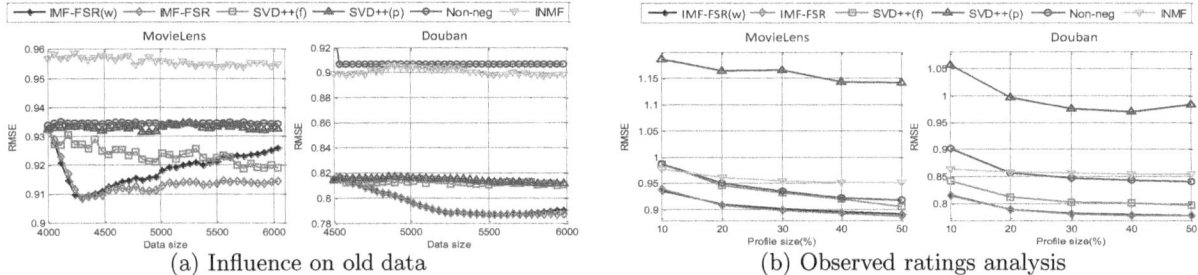

(a) Influence on old data

(b) Observed ratings analysis

Figure 2: Influence on old data and observed ratings analysis

randomly sample the train and test set and implement the same experiments 4 times. Based on cross validation, we set $\lambda = 0.05$, the learning rate $\eta = 0.005$, total iterations $T = 400$ for MovieLens. We set $\lambda = 0.04$, $\eta = 0.002$, $T = 100$ for Douban. We set the feature size $f = 20$, the update limit $L_k = \frac{4}{5}U_{new}$ or $\frac{4}{5}I_{new}$ in each round.

Our proposed methods, which take advantage of the matrix sketching algorithm, are superior to those incremental baselines. This may contribute to our methods effectively demonstrating the assumption. It is also interesting to find that our methods even outperform SVD++(f) on new-user problem. This may be related to the facts that 1) if we regard the auxiliary features as a prior information, then the re-learning step can take advantage of this prior potentially. 2) Matrix sketching algorithm compresses the feature dimension into a smaller size while still maintains a stable similarity.

We also learn that the incremental updates are much faster than the full re-train model in each round. Our methods are proved to have the same time complexity as those incremental baselines. Although the time cost is slightly lower than Non-neg, the $RMSE$ performance greatly outperforms the latter. We omit the new-item running time.

3.5 Case Studies

Updating influence on old data: It is shown in Figure 2 (a) that along with the dataset increases, the $RMSE$ of old data by our methods falls down quickly, even better than that by SVD++(f). Besides, it is also worth pointing out that the IMF-FSR is superior to IMF-FSR(w) since the former has the capability of preventing from over-fitting.

Observed ratings analysis: Figure 2 (b) shows the relationship between the $RMSE$ metric and the observed ratings of new users. We draw a conclusion that $RMSE$ decreases along with the amount of observed data increases and our methods still work well when comes to few observed ratings.

4. CONCLUSION

We propose an incremental matrix factorization algorithm, which updates both the feature matrices based on a set of new users (items). Empirical results on different datasets show that our approach gains satisfactory consequences.

5. ACKNOWLEDGMENTS

This work was supported in part by National Natural Science Foundation of China (Grant No. 61170127).

6. REFERENCES

[1] M. Brand. Fast online svd revisions for lightweight recommender systems. In *SDM*, pages 37–46. SIAM, 2003.

[2] S. Han, Y. Yang, and W. Liu. Incremental learning for dynamic collaborative filtering. *Journal of Software*, 6(6):969–976, 2011.

[3] Y. Koren, R. Bell, and C. Volinsky. Matrix factorization techniques for recommender systems. *Computer*, (8):30–37, 2009.

[4] C. Leng, J. Wu, J. Cheng, X. Bai, and H. Lu. Online sketching hashing. In *Proceedings of the IEEE Conference on Computer Vision and Pattern Recognition*, pages 2503–2511, 2015.

[5] E. Liberty. Simple and deterministic matrix sketching. In *Proceedings of the 19th ACM SIGKDD international conference on Knowledge discovery and data mining*, pages 581–588. ACM, 2013.

[6] S. Rendle and L. Schmidt-Thieme. Online-updating regularized kernel matrix factorization models for large-scale recommender systems. In *Proceedings of the 2008 ACM conference on Recommender systems*, pages 251–258. ACM, 2008.

[7] B. Sarwar, G. Karypis, J. Konstan, and J. Riedl. Incremental singular value decomposition algorithms for highly scalable recommender systems. In *Fifth International Conference on Computer and Information Science*, pages 27–28. Citeseer, 2002.

[8] G. Takács, I. Pilászy, B. Németh, and D. Tikk. Scalable collaborative filtering approaches for large recommender systems. *The Journal of Machine Learning Research*, 10:623–656, 2009.

Latent Trajectory Modeling: A Light and Efficient Way to Introduce Time in Recommender Systems

Elie Guardia-Sebaoun
Sorbonne Universites,
UPMC, LIP6, UMR 7606,
4 place Jussieu,
F-75005 Paris, France
elie.guardia-
sebaoun@lip6.fr

Vincent Guigue
Sorbonne Universites,
UPMC, LIP6, UMR 7606,
4 place Jussieu,
F-75005 Paris, France
vincent.guigue@lip6.fr

Patrick Gallinari
Sorbonne Universites,
UPMC, LIP6, UMR 7606,
4 place Jussieu,
F-75005 Paris, France
patrick.gallinari@lip6.fr

ABSTRACT

For recommender systems, time is often an important source of information but it is also a complex dimension to apprehend. We propose here to learn item and user representations such that any timely ordered sequence of items selected by a user will be represented as a trajectory of the user in a representation space. This allows us to rank new items for this user. We then enrich the item and user representations in order to perform rating prediction using a classical matrix factorization scheme. We demonstrate the interest of our approach regarding both item ranking and rating prediction on a series of classical benchmarks.

1. INTRODUCTION

During the last decade, the emergence of collaborative filtering has demonstrated the interest of exploiting past ratings to establish relevant profiles for both users and items in various application fields [17, 10]. Recent works has focused on profile enrichment: the better we understand users' tastes, the more accurate our suggestions will be. Several directions have been investigated for this: global ratings of reviews have been manually split into different aspects [7], then [11] has proposed to automate this process by learning a common latent space to represent the items, the users and the reviews they wrote. Yet another approach directly exploits tokens extracted from those reviews in order to improve user characterization [15]. Time is another important dimension since the perception of a user may change with time or be time dependent. There are different ways to handle time, for example one can consider the temporal evolution of items perception [9] or model the evolution of the user's way of thinking [12]. Considering the time dimension usually considerably increases the complexity of recommendation models. Instead of time, we propose to consider the ordering of user actions and to embed this information into the users and the items representations for recommendation tasks. Ordered sequences convey less information than full time sequences of user actions, but allow for a compromise between the information provided to the system and the system complexity needed to handle this information. More precisely, we consider ordered sequences of items corresponding to sequences of user actions. We learn a representation -a vector in a multidimensional euclidean space- of individual items in the context of the sequences where they appear. Each item will then have a unique vector representation in a vector space. A user representation will be a function operating on this item representation space that allows to move from one item to the next one, or said otherwise to infer the next item from the current one. In this paper, we consider a simple vectorial operator corresponding to a translation. Given a sequence of items, this allows us to infer the future sequence and then to recommend at each step an ordered list of items to a user. We then enrich this representation by additional dimensions and use a classical matrix factorization scheme in order to learn this new representation for learning to predict item ratings like in classical collaborative filtering.

This approach offers two advantages: it models the dynamical aspects of the user profile while keeping the number of parameters low. We demonstrate the effectiveness of our approach on classical review datasets through two evaluation schemes: item ranking and rating prediction.

The paper is structured as follows: related work is reviewed in Section 2, then we describe the model and the training algorithm in Section 3. In Section 4, we describe the datasets and our results.

2. RELATED WORK

Recommender systems can be evaluated in two different setups, one consists in recommending a set of items (ranking) [3, 13] while the other aims at estimating how a user would rate a given item (rating prediction) [17, 2, 8].

In the recommendation literature, time is often considered as a relevant contextual information as it facilitates detecting the changes in users preferences [18]. A better understanding of these changes allow the recommender systems to capture periodicity in users interests [5] or simply to improve its performance [9].

However, capturing temporal dynamics in a recommender engine is not straightforward. For example using an exponential decay to downweight older reviews either improve [6] or degrade [9] the system performance. As another example, while in [1], the authors used a time-dependent data partition to learn context-aware user profiles, they found best results for a random split. [4] surveys different ways to handle time inthe recommender literature like using temporal drift, heuristics or splits. Two recent interesting contributions for introducing time in recommender systems are [19] who uses Kalman filters to represent a transition between the latent representations of the users over time and [12] who represents this evolution as user experience gained over time.

RecSys'15, September 16–20, 2015, Vienna, Austria.
Copyright is held by the owner/author(s). Publication rights licensed to ACM.
ACM 978-1-4503-3692-5/15/09...$15.00.
DOI: http://dx.doi.org/10.1145/2792838.2799676.

3. CONTRIBUTION

We will use the following notations: Items (resp. users) are indexed using i (resp. u) and gathered in a set: $I = \{i_k\}_{k=1,\dots,N}$ (resp. $U = \{u_k\}_{k=1,\dots,M}$). To each user corresponds a trace θ_u, i.e. an ordered sequence of items he rated: $\theta_u = \{(i,r)|i \in I\}$ where r is the rating ; those traces are gathered in a set $\Theta = \{\theta_u | u \in U\}$.

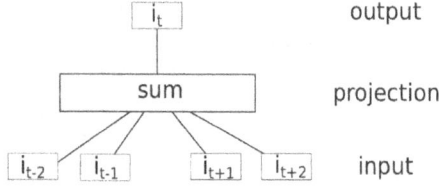

Figure 1: The *Mikolov et al.* [14] architecture predicts the current item based on the context

Item Latent Representation

Mikolov et al. Word2Vec model [14], as illustrated in Fig.1, uses a neural network to build a latent representation of words depending on the surrounding words in a sentence, by optimizing a word prediction criterion. In this paper we used the same neural net architecture for learning from item sequences corresponding to user traces $\{\theta_u, u \in U\}$, a contextualized item representations. For every item i, we build a representation ϕ_i (in blue in Fig.2) that considers the items order in all the sequences corresponding to user traces.

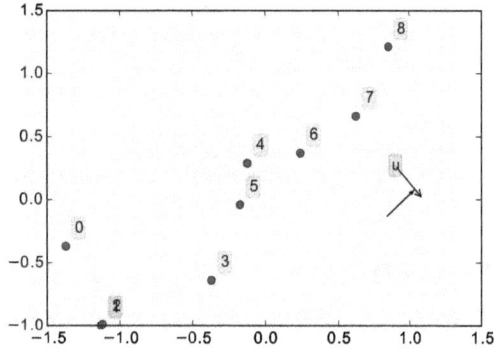

Figure 2: Representation for d=2 of an extract of a user trace (numbered items in blue) and the user representation as a vector (in green) for the RateBeer dataset.

Ranking Function Optimisation

For every user u, we learned a representation ϕ_u (u in Fig. 2) modeling the way u moves from an item to the next one in the sequence representation in the latent space, by performing a gradient descent on the following ranking loss:

$$\mathcal{L}_{ranking}(\Theta) = \sum_{u \in U} \sum_{i \in \theta_u} \sum_{j \in I \setminus x_n} \left[1 - |\phi_u + \phi_{x_n} - \phi_i|^2 - |\phi_u + \phi_{x_n} - \phi_j|^2 \right]^+ \quad (1)$$

In equation 1, the $^+$ sign indicates that we used a hinge loss function. This means that during the learning phase, we only updated the parameter values when $\mathcal{L}_{ranking}(u,i,e) > 0$.

ϕ_u is a vector which represents the mean of the translations needed to move from one item in the representation space to the next one in a sequence corresponding to a user trace. From these representation, we can - by applying the ϕ_u translation from an item representation- compute the nearest neighbors of the resulting point and thus produce ordered list of items to recommend. Given a user u and i the most recent item he reviewed, the item recommendation is given by:

$$rec(u,i) = argmin_{j \in I} \left\| (\phi_i + \phi_u) - \phi_j \right\| \quad (2)$$

Rating Function Optimisation

In a second step, we construct new representations γ_u and γ_i by enriching ϕ_u and ϕ_i, in order for our model to tackle the rating task.

- $\gamma_u = [\bar{\gamma}_u, \phi_u], \forall u \in U$
- $\gamma_i = [\phi_i, \bar{\gamma}_i], \forall i \in I$

Where $\{\bar{\gamma}_u, u \in U\}$ and $\{\bar{\gamma}_i, i \in I\}$ are initialized randomly and learned by performing a gradient descent for optimizing the following mean square rating loss:

$$\mathcal{L}_{rating}(\Theta) = \sum_{u \in U} \sum_{(i,r) \in \theta_u} [\mu + \mu_u + \mu_i + \langle \gamma_u, \gamma_i \rangle - r]^2 + \lambda \Omega(\bar{\gamma}_u, \bar{\gamma}_i) \quad (3)$$

We added the regularization term $\lambda \Omega(\bar{\gamma}_u, \bar{\gamma}_i)$ in order to avoid overfitting [16].

Given a user u and an item i, the rating score is computed using the classical matrix factorization formula proposed in [8]. Let μ, μ_u and μ_i denote respectively the overall bias, the user bias and the item bias:

$$score(u,i) = \mu + \mu_u + \mu_i + \langle \gamma_u, \gamma_i \rangle \quad (4)$$

4. EXPERIMENTS

In this section, we evaluate our model performance regarding two different tasks, item ranking and rating prediction.

Baselines

In order to evaluate our rating prediction, we implemented a matrix factorization (MF) as presented in [10] and the model presented by *McAuley et al.* (EXP) in [12] as baselines. To evaluate our model in an item ranking paradigm we used the popularity function that always return the most popular result (POP) as a prediction.

Datasets

In order to perform our experiments, we used five time-labeled datasets: *BeerAdvocate* and *RateBeer* datasets from [12] contain reviews on beers, MovieLens10m and Flixster datasets contain reviews on movies and FineFoods from [12] contains reviews from the fine foods category from Amazon. The characteristics of each dataset can be found in Table 1.

As the ratings were on different scales, we normalized them all to be on the scale $[0,5]$. Then, we used the settings presented in [19]: only the users with more than 20 reviews were kept, and every dataset has been divided in time windows, each representing a year period (except for the Flixster dataset which is divided bimonthly regarding its smaller timespan).

In order to perform the evaluation, the last three time windows were selected as test $\mathcal{U}$ and for each $\mathcal{U}$, we used all the previous windows for training $\mathcal{T}$. We ran each experiment 5 times on each window and report the average results for reliability.

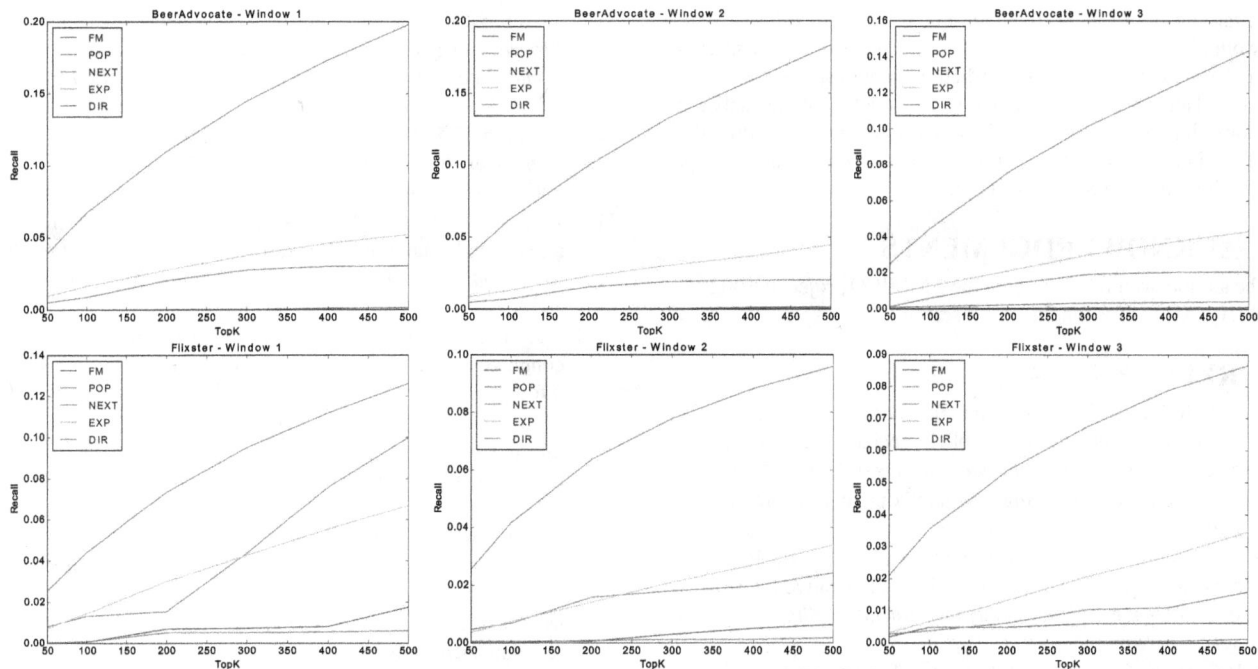

Figure 3: Results regarding the item prediction for each inference model given for K = 50, 100, 200, 300, 400 and 500 and expressed in recall.

Dataset	# items	# users	# reviews
BeerAdvocate	66051	33387	1586259
RateBeer	110419	40213	2924127
MovieLens	10000	72000	10000000
Flixster	49000	1000000	8200000
FineFoods	74258	256059	568454

Table 1: Datasets characteristics.

Evaluation

Item ranking

We evaluated our model by computing the Recall@K measure for K=300 and compared them to the baselines. The results are presented in Table 2. A plot of the evolution of recall@K for K varying between 50 and 500 on the BeerAdvocate and Flixster datasets is also available in Fig.3.

Dataset	MF	POP	EXP	DIR
BeerAdvocate	0.001	0.022	0.033	**0.126**
RateBeer	0.001	0.008	0.021	**0.106**
MovieLens	0.118	0.027	0.12	**0.15**
Flixster	0.005	0.024	0.028	**0.08**
FineFoods	0.042	0.027	0.054	**0.156**

Table 2: Ranking Results averaged over all three time windows, given in Recall@300 for the matrix factorization (MF), the experience based model (EXP), the popularity model (POP) and the directional vector based model (DIR)

Our model (DIR) clearly outperforms all other models. This corroborates the relevance of taking into account the sequential structure of the user-item interaction as a core feature. Furthermore, the

MF and EXP baselines show that the rating prediction is not a good indicator for item prediction ; this validates the idea that using the same representations to compute both rating and ranking values requires some sort of tradeoff. The DIR model uses two different yet intertwined representations, freeing it from the aforementioned tradeoff constraint.

Rating prediction

The results of our experiments expressed in MSE can be found in Table 3. We compared our items to a classic Matrix factorization as described in [10] and to the EXP model.

Dataset	MF	EXP	DIR
BeerAdvocate	0.4	0.366	**0.361**
RateBeer	0.343	0.307	**0.292**
MovieLens	0.691	0.684	**0.661**
Flixster	0.892	0.892	**0.817**
FineFoods	1.365	1.337	**1.06**

Table 3: Rating Results averaged over all three time windows, given in MSE for the matrix factorization (MF), the experience based model (EXP) and the directional vector based model (DIR)

Here also, the proposed model significantly outperforms both models, showing that incorporating the order information allows learning better user and item representations.

5. CONCLUSION AND FUTURE WORK

In this paper, we have proposed a light and scalable latent method for recommendation using item sequence information which has been shown to be also efficient as we performed evaluations regarding two different tasks: rating prediction and item ranking.

Regarding future work, there are many paths to explore. First, we would like to find better ways to model the user representation *e.g.* using a more sophisticated prediction functions. We would also like to add an expertise notion in order to model more precisely the temporal dimension. Last, we think that touristic data follow the same kind of temporal evolution as web data and we plan to adapt this method to visit recommendation.

6. ACKNOWLEDGEMENTS

The authors would like to thank the AMMICO project (F1302017 Q - FUI AAP 13) for funding our research.

7. REFERENCES

[1] L. Baltrunas and X. Amatriain. Towards time-dependant recommendation based on implicit feedback. In *In Workshop on context-aware recommender systems (CARS09*, 2009.

[2] J. Bennett and S. Lanning. The netflix prize. In *KDD Cup Workshop 2007*, pages 3–6, 2007.

[3] J. S. Breese, D. Heckerman, and C. Kadie. Empirical analysis of predictive algorithms for collaborative filtering. In *Conference on Uncertainty in Artificial Intelligence*, pages 43–52, 1998.

[4] P. Campos, F. Díez, and I. Cantador. Time-aware recommender systems: a comprehensive survey and analysis of existing evaluation protocols. *User Modeling and User-Adapted Interaction*, 24(1-2):67–119, 2014.

[5] P. G. Campos, F. Diez, and A. Bellogin. Temporal rating habits: A valuable tool for rating discrimination. In *Proceedings of the 2Nd Challenge on Context-Aware Movie Recommendation*, CAMRa '11, pages 29–35, New York, NY, USA, 2011. ACM.

[6] Y. Ding and X. Li. Time weight collaborative filtering. In *Proceedings of the 14th ACM International Conference on Information and Knowledge Management*, CIKM '05, pages 485–492, New York, NY, USA, 2005. ACM.

[7] G. Ganu, N. Elhadad, and A. Marian. Beyond the stars: Improving rating predictions using review text content. In *WebDB*, 2009.

[8] Y. Koren. Factorization meets the neighborhood: A multifaceted collaborative filtering model. In *ACM SIGKDD*, pages 426–434, 2008.

[9] Y. Koren. Collaborative filtering with temporal dynamics. In *Proceedings of the 15th ACM SIGKDD International Conference on Knowledge Discovery and Data Mining*, KDD '09, pages 447–456, New York, NY, USA, 2009. ACM.

[10] Y. Koren, R. Bell, and C. Volinsky. Matrix factorization techniques for recommender systems. *Computer*, 42(8):30–37, Aug. 2009.

[11] J. McAuley and J. Leskovec. Hidden factors and hidden topics: Understanding rating dimensions with review text. In *ACM Conference on Recommender Systems*, pages 165–172, 2013.

[12] J. J. McAuley and J. Leskovec. From amateurs to connoisseurs: modeling the evolution of user expertise through online reviews. In *World Wide Web*, 2013.

[13] M. R. McLaughlin and J. L. Herlocker. A collaborative filtering algorithm and evaluation metric that accurately model the user experience. In *ACM SIGIR*, pages 329–336, 2004.

[14] T. Mikolov, K. Chen, G. Corrado, and J. Dean. Efficient estimation of word representations in vector space. *CoRR*, abs/1301.3781, 2013.

[15] M. Poussevin, V. Guigue, and P. Gallinari. Extended recommendation framework: Generating the text of a user review as a personalized summary. *CoRR*, abs/1412.5448, 2014.

[16] S. Rendle and L. Schmidt-Thieme. Online-updating regularized kernel matrix factorization models for large-scale recommender systems. In *Proceedings of the 2008 ACM conference on Recommender systems*, pages 251–258. ACM, 2008.

[17] P. Resnick, N. Iacovou, M. Suchak, P. Bergstrom, and J. Riedl. Grouplens: An open architecture for collaborative filtering of netnews. In *ACM Conference on Computer Supported Cooperative Work*, 1994.

[18] L. Xiang, Q. Yuan, S. Zhao, L. Chen, X. Zhang, Q. Yang, and J. Sun. Temporal recommendation on graphs via long- and short-term preference fusion. In *Proceedings of the 16th ACM SIGKDD International Conference on Knowledge Discovery and Data Mining*, KDD '10, pages 723–732, New York, NY, USA, 2010. ACM.

[19] C. Zhang, K. Wang, H. Yu, J. Sun, and E. Lim. Latent factor transition for dynamic collaborative filtering. In *Proceedings of the 2014 SIAM International Conference on Data Mining, Philadelphia, Pennsylvania, USA, April 24-26, 2014*, pages 452–460, 2014.

Making the Most of Preference Feedback by Modeling Feature Dependencies

S Chandra Mouli
Indian Institute of Technology Madras
schandra@cse.iitm.ac.in

Sutanu Chakraborti
Indian Institute of Technology Madras
sutanuc@cse.iitm.ac.in

ABSTRACT

Conversational recommender systems help users navigate through the product space by exploiting feedback. In conversational systems based on preference-based feedback, the user selects the most preferred item from a list of recommended products. Modelling user's preferences then becomes important in order to recommend relevant items. Several existing recommender systems accomplish this by assuming the features to be independent. Here we will attempt to forego this assumption and exploit the dependencies between the features to build a robust user preference model.

Categories and Subject Descriptors

H.3.4 [**Information Storage and Retrieval**]: Systems and Software

General Terms

Algorithms, Experimentation, Performance

Keywords

Conversational recommendation systems, Preference-based feedback, User preference model

1. INTRODUCTION

Conversational recommendation is a knowledge-based approach to recommendation where the system engages in a chat with the user about his requirements from the product much like a human shopkeeper. Since most users do not have complete information about the domain, they do not know the product that is best suited for them. Conversational systems improve their recommendations by requesting for some sort of feedback on them from the user. Preference-based feedback is one way to elicit feedback in which the user is asked to choose the product that she prefers from a small set of recommendations.

In order to recommend relevant products, the system needs to understand the priorities of the user. It needs to know which of the features the user is willing to compromise to get an improvement in the others. We demonstrate in this paper how this can be achieved by abandoning the feature independence assumption. We shall see later that the proposed algorithm results in a significant reduction in the number of interactions to reach the desired product.

2. BACKGROUND AND RELATED WORK

In this section, we shall look at a few conversational recommender systems that use preference-based feedback to recommend a better set of products in the subsequent iterations.

2.1 More-Like-This based approaches

The MLT (*More Like This*) approach proposed by McGinty et al. [3] modifies the query for the next iteration by simply selecting all the features of the chosen product. In the subsequent iteration, the system returns products that are most similar to the modified query. The obvious drawback of the MLT approach is that it assumes every feature in the chosen product to be important to the user which, in general, is not true.

The wMLT (*weighted More Like This*) approach attempts to solve this by assigning weights to the features such that if a feature value is present in the rejected products along with the chosen product, it is given a lower weight. These weights are used in calculating similarity between the products as given by the *weighted similarity model*,

$$Similarity(P, q) = \sum_i w_i \cdot sim_i(P_i, q_i) \qquad (1)$$

where, sim_i is the similarity between the ith features of the products and w_i is the weight associated to the ith feature. Smyth et al. [5] provide a novel way of including diversity in the recommendations without compromising on similarity and their algorithm MLT-AS (*Adaptive Selection*) was shown to perform better than other MLT based approaches.

2.2 Critique-MAUT

Zhang and Pu [6] introduced a method based on Multi Attribute Utility Theory (MAUT) to generate compound critiques. One of the simplest ways to calculate utility of a product is given by,

$$U(< x_1, ..., x_n >) = \sum_{i=1}^{n} w_i \cdot V_i(x_i) \qquad (2)$$

where n is the number of features, w_i is the weight associated with each feature and V_i is the value function of the feature value x_i.

In each cycle of Critique-MAUT, the critiques are generated based on the products with maximal utility. Chen and Pu [1] also used MAUT-based preference model but introduced a novel critique generation approach using Apriori algorithm. The weights of the features in both these methods are adjusted for the next cycle by a factor β according to the difference between the old and the chosen value of the feature.

The recommender systems discussed above assume the features to be independent while forming the new query or while updating the feature weights. The proposed method addresses this fundamental issue with these systems. While there have been past efforts to model constraints made explicit by the user in the context of example critiquing [4], this paper presents a novel and practical approach to model user preferences by exploiting feature tradeoffs implicit in preferences expressed by the user. Both similarity based approaches like wMLT and utility based approaches like Critique-MAUT can be extended with our algorithm.

3. PROPOSED IDEA

Let us assume that the set of cameras shown in Table 1 is recommended in a particular iteration to a user. For the sake of this discussion, we consider only three features for each camera - Price, Zoom and Resolution. Now, say the user chooses product 1 over the products 2 and 3. Our aim is to learn about the preferences of the user based on this choice.

Table 1: Cameras shown to the user in an iteration

Product	Price ($)	Zoom (X)	Resolution (M pixels)
1	1000	4	3
2	400	3	2
3	800	5	2

For illustration, values in Table 1 are not normalized. For the rest of the discussion assume that all values are range normalized.

3.1 Constraints

Consider products 1 and 2 in Table 1. The user prefers product 1 over product 2 thereby compromising price for getting better zoom and resolution. Lets denote the difference in the normalized feature values by $\Delta_{12}P$, $\Delta_{12}Z$ & $\Delta_{12}R$ (where, $\Delta_{12}f = f_{product1} - f_{product2}$). An important point to note here is that Zoom and Resolution are "more-is-better" (MIB) features whereas Price is a "less-is-better" (LIB) feature. Thus, we consider a positive difference in Zoom and Resolution a gain but a positive difference in Price a loss. In order to make it consistent, we negate the Δ's that correspond to LIB features.

In a uniform scenario, we would expect that the net gain (i.e., simple addition of the gains and losses) the user obtains by choosing product 1 is positive. This might not be true in general as different users have different priorities over features. In order to model such priorities, we assign, for every user, a set of preference weights corresponding to the feature set. Now, we hypothesize that the net gain weighted with these preference weights should be positive, given that the

user prefers one product over the other. Mathematically,

$$w_p \cdot (-\Delta_{12}P) + w_z \cdot \Delta_{12}Z + w_r \cdot \Delta_{12}R \geq 0 \qquad (3)$$

where w_p, w_z and w_r are the preference weights associated to Price, Zoom and Resolution respectively. Although it is possible to combine the user preferences in a more flexible way, we adopt a linear combination in order to limit the number of weights to a feasible total. Notice that there is a negative sign in front of $\Delta_{12}P$ in the above equation since Price is an LIB feature. In our example, $\Delta_{12}P > 0, \Delta_{12}Z > 0, \Delta_{12}R > 0$. Let us rewrite inequality (3) as,

$$w_z \cdot \Delta_{12}Z + w_r \cdot \Delta_{12}R \geq w_p \cdot \Delta_{12}P \qquad (4)$$

representing the fact that the compensation obtained from Zoom and Resolution is higher than what the user is compromising in Price. Now, if the difference in price is very high, then we can infer that the weight associated with price should be low so that the above inequality is satisfied.

Similarly, another inequality can be obtained from the fact that the user has chosen product 1 over product 3 as well. In general, we can obtain $k - 1$ inequalities where k is the number of products recommended in each iteration.

Since these weights represent the user's priority over the features, we require them to be such that,

$$\sum_i w_i = 1 \qquad \text{and} \qquad w_i \geq 0 \qquad (5)$$

where w_i refers to the ith feature (w_p, w_z and w_r in our example).

3.2 Objective Function

Our aim now is to obtain the preference weights from these inequalities. In order to choose one among infinite sets of weights, we need to make some assumption about the general behaviour of users. One possible assumption is that a user's preferences do not change substantially over multiple interactions. Hence, we assume that the optimal set of weights lies close to the one obtained from the previous iteration. This gives way for an appropriate objective function.

$$\text{minimize} \sum_i (w_i - f_i)^2$$

subject to constraints on $\tilde{w}$ as identified in §3.1 (6)

(where $\tilde{f}$ is the vector of old weights)

We use Augmented Lagrangian method [2] to solve the nonlinear optimization problem described above. It adds the constraints along with a penalty factor to the original objective function giving rise to a new unconstrained objective function. In case the inequalities have no common solution, the algorithm will try to satisfy as many inequalities as possible.

Now, using this kind of an objective function has a key limitation. If the set of weights obtained from previous iterations already satisfy the current set of inequalities, then there is no change in the weights for the next cycle. Consequently, the products recommended in the next cycle are very similar to the products recommended in the current cycle. Hence, the system is likely to get stuck with the same set of weights for several iterations. Another drawback arises when the user wishes to change his priorities during the course of his interactions. In this case, it might take a few cycles just to abandon the weights from previous interactions.

Algorithm 1: CDPM-Util and CDPM-Sim

Data: DB : Database
Result: Desired Product
1   query ← GetInitialUserPreferences ();
2   currWts ← GenInitialWeights ();
3   Rec ← FindClosestKProducts (DB, query, currWts) ;
4   DB ← DB - Rec;
5   **while** *not* UserAccept *(Rec)* **do**
6   id ← chooseBest (Rec);
7   choice ← Rec_{id};
8   ineqConst ← GenInequalities (choice, Rec);
9   objFunc ← GenObjFunc (currWts) ;
10   currWts ← Optimize (objFunc, ineqConst, normConst) ;
11   **if** recommendationType *is Utility* **then**
12   Rec ← GenKMaxUtilityProducts (DB, currWts);
13   **else**
14   newQuery ← choice;
15   Rec ← FindClosestKProducts (DB, newQuery,
16   currWts);
17   **end**
18   DB ← DB - Rec;
19 **end**

We call our approach Compromise Driven Preference Model (CDPM) since it attempts to exploit dependencies between features and learn weights that provide explanations for compromises the user may have made in the course of making preferences.

3.3 Preference Weights

The user preference weights obtained after optimization can be used as feature weights either in the *weighted similarity model* defined by (1) or in the MAUT based model defined by (2). We will refer to the resulting algorithms as *CDPM-Sim* and *CDPM-Util* respectively. Algorithm 1 provides a condensed description of these two methods.

Now we shall see how our approach makes use of the dependencies between the features to obtain better preference weights. Consider the example given in Table 2.

Table 2: Example : Importance of feature dependencies

Product	Price ($)	Zoom (X)	Resolution (M pixels)
1	100	1	1
2	200	1	1.2

Say a particular user chooses product 2 over product 1. This should, intuitively, increase the weight of Resolution to a large value because the user is willing to spend 100$ for just 0.2MP increase in Resolution, which is what happens in our approach. The weight of a particular feature obtained from our approach is not just dependent on the difference in value of that feature but on that of every other feature as well. In the above example, the weight of the feature Resolution is affected by every other feature including Price. Here we took an extreme example to illustrate our point but the same is true for a general scenario as well.

4. EVALUATION

We evaluate our system on three datasets - **Camera**, **PC** and **Used Cars**. The **Camera** dataset consists of 210 cameras with 6 numeric features and 4 categorical features. The

PC dataset consists of 120 PCs with 5 numeric features and 3 categorical features. The **Used Cars** dataset is a larger dataset consisting of 960 cars with 6 numeric features and 5 categorical features.

We use a utility function for each categorical attribute that assigns a normalized numeric value for every attribute value. Every iteration, the utility of the attribute value present in the chosen product is boosted. Hence, the value of the categorical attribute that is preferred by the user is given a higher utility than others. These utilities can be used in the inequalities described in §3.1, effectively handling categorical features.

We evaluate our solution by employing the approach commonly used to analyse the effectiveness of preference-based feedback recommender systems [3, 5]. We simulate the interaction with the recommender system using an artificial agent. We start with a random product, remove it from the database and form a partial query by eliminating values for some of the features. Three types of queries were formed containing value for 1 feature (Q1), 3 features (Q3) and 5 features (Q5) respectively.

In an intermediate cycle the artificial agent chooses a product from the k products recommended. We experimented with two selection strategies - Optimal and Noisy. In the Optimal strategy, the agent chooses the product with highest similarity to the original product. In the noisy strategy, the similarity values to the original product are perturbed to some extent. Here, the agent might choose suboptimal products, mimicking the way real users behave. We define the target product as the one still in the database with highest similarity with the original product. Thus, the job of the recommendation system is to reach this target product from the partial query and the intermediate interactions in as few cycles as possible.

We repeat this process multiple times with different initial products and record the number of cycles taken to reach the target product. We generated 3000 random queries for each dataset and compared the performance of our algorithms with MLT, wMLT and Critique-MAUT.

5. EMPIRICAL EVALUATION

The average number of cycles taken by the algorithms to reach the target product for the three datasets is shown in Figure 1. In Camera dataset, *CDPM-Util* takes only 16.77 cycles on average for query type Q1 whereas Critique-MAUT takes 21.18 cycles. Similarly, in query types Q3 and Q5, there is 22.2% and 26.4% reduction in the number of cycles respectively. There is upto 35.2% and 53% reduction in cycles as compared to Critique-MAUT in PC and Used Cars datasets respectively.

CDPM-Sim outperforms the other similarity-based algorithms like MLT and wMLT by a significant margin. In Camera dataset, *CDPM-Sim* takes 7.47 and 2.12 cycles on average for query type Q3 and Q5 whereas wMLT takes 9.52 and 4.55 cycles respectively. This translates to 21.5% and 53.35% reduction in cycles for Q3 and Q5 types when compared with wMLT. Similar improvements can be observed for PC and Used Cars datasets as well. It was observed that these trends were preserved in the Noisy selection strategy (the deviations with respect to Optimal selection in improvement percentages were of the order of 1%-4% for the Camera dataset, 3%-8% for the PC dataset and 3%-5% for the Used Cars dataset).

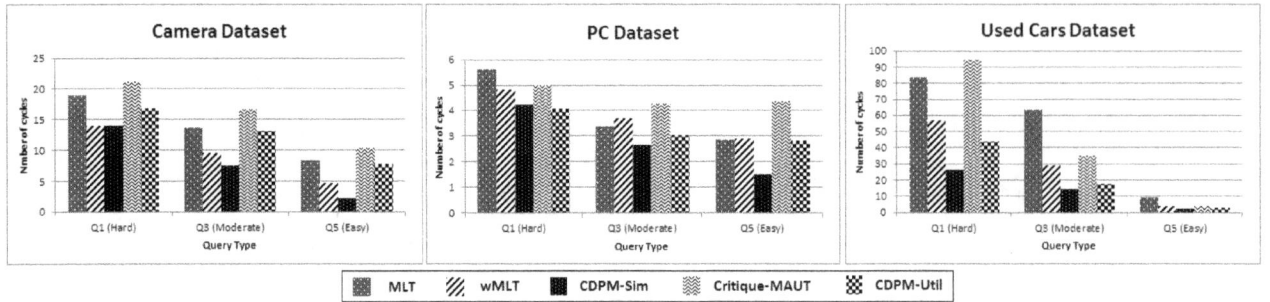

Figure 1: Performance of the algorithms on Camera, PC and Used Cars datasets for Optimal selection strategy.

The experiments were done on a system with Intel i5 processor, 2.53GHz clock speed, 3MB cache and 6GB memory using R environment. On an average, MLT, wMLT and Critique-MAUT take 8-16ms per iteration whereas *CDPM-Util* and *CDPM-Sim* take around 136ms and 345ms per iteration respectively. This increase in time is adequately compensated by CPDM's reduction in number of cycles, since each cycle involves manual screening which not only adds to cognitive load but is slower by orders of magnitude. Having said this, we need to devise faster optimization schemes to improve CPDM's current time performance.

As discussed before, the present objective function might cause the system to remain stuck with the same weights for several iterations. Let us look at two variations of our approach that attempt to solve this issue.

5.1 Confidence Parameter

We hypothesized, in §3.1, that if a product is chosen over the other, then the weighted net gain should be positive. Now, we propose that the net gain should be greater than a small positive value (δ) that represents the user's confidence while choosing one product over the other. This reduces the feasible region for the optimization algorithm thereby lowering the chances of the old set of weights satisfying the new constraints.

Table 3: Impact of confidence for Camera dataset

Confidence (δ)	CDPM-Util-C			CDPM-Sim-C		
	Q1	Q3	Q5	Q1	Q3	Q5
0.00	16.77	13.05	7.76	13.89	7.47	2.12
0.01	16.59	12.99	7.12	13.44	6.84	2.07
0.05	14.94	**11.07**	**6.51**	**9.82**	**6.19**	**1.93**
0.10	**14.5**	11.10	7.17	12.12	8.41	2.11

Improvements obtained for different values of the confidence parameter, δ, is presented in Table 3. A confidence value of 0.05 performs best in almost all cases. We observe close to 20% and 30% further reduction in number of cycles for *CDPM-Util-C* and *CDPM-Sim-C* when compared with their respective counterparts with no confidence factor. A further increase in the confidence parameter leads to over-pruning of the search space and hence, adversely affects performance.

5.2 Diversity

Diversity in recommendation ensures that the user's choice provides more information about his preferences. We use the *Adaptive Selection* approach mentioned in [5] to construct two new algorithms - *CDPM-Util-AS* and *CDPM-Sim-AS*. These algorithms recommend the product chosen in the previous iteration again along with the new set of recommendations. If the user selects the same product again, it is assumed that the user is not being given enough alternatives and the strategy is modified to include more diverse

products. The scores for products is calculated by a linear combination of the diversity introduced by the product and its utility/similarity value with weights α and $1 - \alpha$ respectively. The improvements obtained for different values of α are shown in Table 4.

Table 4: Impact of Diversity for Camera dataset

Diversity (α)	CDPM-Util-AS			CDPM-Sim-AS		
	Q1	Q3	Q5	Q1	Q3	Q5
0.0	16.77	13.05	7.76	13.89	7.47	2.12
0.3	16.72	12.99	7.71	11.95	5.51	1.53
0.5	16.70	12.97	7.71	11.74	5.39	1.52
0.7	16.69	12.99	7.78	11.31	5.35	1.52
1.0	**16.16**	**12.94**	**7.59**	**10.32**	**4.64**	**1.43**

CDPM-Util-AS performs only marginally better than *CDPM-Util*. On the other hand, *CDPM-Sim-AS* takes 30-40% fewer cycles than *CDPM-Sim* across different query types. This is because, unlike *CDPM-Util-AS*, *CDPM-Sim-AS* also uses the diversified recommendation as query for the next iteration along with the updated weights.

6. CONCLUSION

Many recommender systems based on preference-based feedback like Critique-MAUT and wMLT assume the product attributes to be preferentially independent of each other. In this paper, we presented a recommender system that exploits the dependencies between the features and reported empirical findings that suggest significant performance improvements over these recommender systems.

7. REFERENCES

[1] L. Chen and P. Pu. Preference-based organization interfaces: aiding user critiques in recommender systems. In *User Modeling 2007*, pages 77–86. Springer, 2007.

[2] M. R. Hestenes. Multiplier and gradient methods. *Journal of optimization theory and applications*, 4(5):303–320, 1969.

[3] L. Mc Ginty and B. Smyth. Evaluating preference-based feedback in recommender systems. In *Artificial Intelligence and Cognitive Science*, pages 209–214. Springer, 2002.

[4] P. Pu and B. Faltings. Decision tradeoff using example-critiquing and constraint programming. *Constraints*, 9(4):289–310, 2004.

[5] B. Smyth and L. McGinty. The power of suggestion. In *IJCAI*, pages 127–132, 2003.

[6] J. Zhang and P. Pu. A comparative study of compound critique generation in conversational recommender systems. In *Adaptive Hypermedia and Adaptive Web-Based Systems*, pages 234–243. Springer, 2006.

Nudging Grocery Shoppers to Make Healthier Choices

Elizabeth Wayman
PARC, a Xerox Company
800 Phillips Road
Webster, NY 14580, USA
ElizabethDWayman@gmail.com

Sriganesh Madhvanath
PARC, a Xerox Company
800 Phillips Road
Webster, NY 14580, USA
smadhvan@parc.com

ABSTRACT

Despite the rampant increase in obesity rates and concomitant increases in rates of mortality from heart disease, cancer and diabetes, getting the general public to adopt a healthy diet has proven to be challenging for a variety of reasons. In this paper, we describe Foodle, a research project aimed at providing automated, personalized and goal-driven dietary guidance to users based on their grocery receipt data, by leveraging the availability of digital receipts for grocery store purchases. We discuss challenges faced, the current state of the project, and directions for future work.

Categories and Subject Descriptors

H.3.3 [Information Storage and Retrieval]: Information Search and Retrieval

Keywords

Nutrition; Diet; Recommender Systems

1. INTRODUCTION

Obesity is a health problem that has assumed epidemic proportions not only in the US but also in large parts of the world, and has been related to increased risk of serious health problems, including diabetes, heart disease, stroke, arthritis and some cancers. Obesity is a consequence of a number of factors [7] but clearly an important one is the poor choice of foods. Despite several public health attempts over the years to specify guidelines for an "ideal diet" and communicate it in simple terms (e.g. the "food pyramid" [1], Dietary Reference Intake (DRIs) [4]), getting the general public to adopt a healthy diet has proven difficult.

In this paper we describe Foodle, a research project aimed at bridging what we see as a vital gap in the present landscape of available tools and aids to promote healthier diets. Foodle is based on the analysis of users' grocery purchase data that is now increasingly available for example, through "shoppers club" accounts. The distinguishing objectives of Foodle are (i) *automation*, to address the tedium and inaccuracy of self-reporting; (ii) *personalization*, to address issues of information overload and relevance; and (iii) *goal-directedness*, to motivate users to achieve dietary goals.

2. RELATED WORK

There are a vast number of nutritional scoring systems for foods [2] accessible either through websites or prominently displayed on

food packages in stores, that attempt to relieve the burden of understanding package food labels. For example, Heart Check, developed by the American Heart Association, guides consumers in choosing heart healthy products. The glycemic index, a relative measure of the carbohydrate content of a food [11], is used by diabetics. The Healthy Eating Index (HEI) [12] assesses diet quality by measuring consumption of the various food groups. Aggregate Nutrient Density Index (ANDI) from Whole Foods Markets, ShopWell.com, NutritionFacts.org, Kraft's Sensible Solutions and NuVal are all examples of privately promoted scoring systems developed in conjunction with nutritionists and physicians. While well intentioned, these scoring systems are inconsistent and occasionally of questionable accuracy [2]. While some nutrition scoring sites attempt personalization by requesting data about users' current diets and dietary restrictions, they are tedious to use and do not convey to users the changes they must make to their current diets in practical terms. A personalized diet plan requires the services of a dietician, who may not be accessible or affordable to most individuals and families.

Food recommendations are a relatively nascent area of research. Phanich et al [8] describe a food recommendation system for diabetics that uses clustering to group foods categorized by nutritionists to recommend diabetes friendly alternatives to a food item specified by a user. Other systems attempt to match users to foods they may like. A content-based recommendation system that recommends foods by computing a cosine similarity score between foods and a user profile is described in [9]. The user rates randomly chosen ingredients of foods served at various types of restaurants to build a profile. M. A. El-Dosuky et al [5] propose a semantic food recommendation framework based on matching foods to user supplied profiles from an ontology of foods classified into categories. The system incorporates nutrition heuristics to bias recommendations toward healthy eating patterns.

Work on linking grocery receipt data with nutrition databases is very recent [3] and has been driven primarily by the desire to understand nutritional intake from a public health perspective. Tracking supermarket grocery purchases has been shown to be good proxy for understanding dietary habits and much better than relying on self-reporting [10].

3. THE FOODLE PROJECT

The objective of Foodle was to explore the feasibility of providing personalized food recommendations from a direct understanding of user nutrition. It differs from previous research and existing tools and aids for food recommendations in its emphasis on *automation, personalization* and *goal-directedness*. Automation refers to relying on an analysis of the user's grocery receipts instead of self-reporting to understand the user's current diet. Digital receipts are increasingly common, especially in association with customer loyalty programs, and provide a better estimate of a family's diet than any other available method. Personalization refers to food recommendations based on the user's actual purchases, which may be further customized using a user profile containing information such as height, weight, age, activity level, dietary restrictions and food preferences. Finally, unlike other efforts, Foodle's recommendations are not meant to be solely foods that have high nutritional scores and are generally "good for you", but suggestions that will gradually move the user towards a nutritional goal, such as the USDA Dietary Reference Intake values [4].

As a first step in this exploration, and in order to study the various technical and research challenges involved, we have implemented a prototype, comprised of a user interface and a set of web services. The user interface enables users to visualize their current state of nutrition, set dietary goals, receive food recommendations, and track their progress towards their goals as they implement the recommendations and make other dietary changes. These are supported by a set of web services that ingest grocery receipts, compute the user's state of nutrition from receipt data, support interactive visualization of the current state and historical trends, evaluate the current nutritional state against the user's goals, and compute specific food recommendations. Key aspects of the prototype are detailed below.

3.1 User Interface

Fig. 1 shows the web user interface of the initial Foodle prototype. Once logged in, the user is provided access to several charts that summarize her state of nutrition. The most important of these is a "scorecard" that shows, in the form of bar charts, how the nutrient content of the user's food purchases compares with the recommended amounts. Nutrient content is computed for a temporal window, e.g. the most recent 60 days. The scorecard is divided into three charts corresponding to meets target, excess, and insufficient nutrients. The values are presented as percentages of the recommended daily amounts.

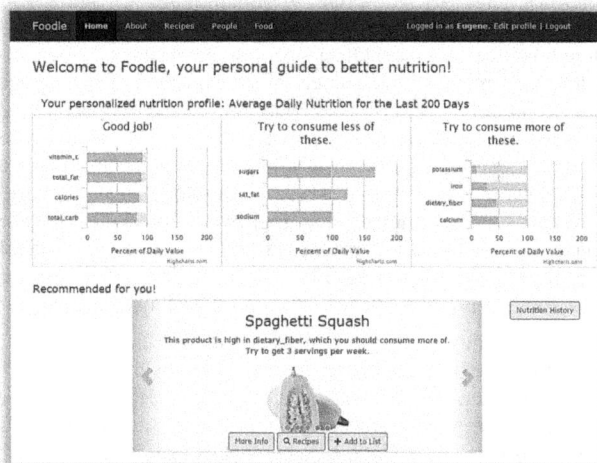

Figure 1. Foodle user interface

The excess or shortfall in nutrient content of food purchases is shown using different colors. Hovering over a bar provides the actual data for that nutrient, as well as the 2-3 food items (and their portions) that substantially contributed that nutrient. The central idea of the visualization is to allow the user to focus on what she needs to work on, as opposed to overwhelming her with information.

Also provided are recommendations of foods that will help the user fill the gaps in the nutritional content of her purchases, as well as a suggestion of how many servings per week are needed (Fig. 1). These recommendations are shown on a carousel that the user can click to advance. For each recommendation, the user is able to see a more complete nutritional description by clicking on

the 'More Info' button just below the item. This information includes the percent Daily Value per serving of each of the nutrients contained in the item. The 'Recipes' button takes the user to a recipe site showing results for a search on that item. The 'Add to list' button conveniently adds the item to the user's digital grocery list, accessible through the user profile.

The user interface also provides a Nutrition History chart showing a detailed historical view of the scorecard by plotting nutrient content of food purchases as percentages of their recommended quantities against the time axis (Fig. 2).

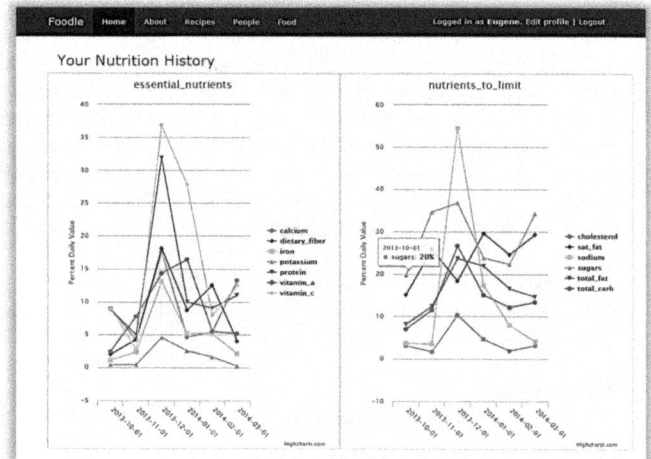

Figure 2. Nutrition History

The chart includes all nutrients currently shown on food labels and groups them into essential nutrients or nutrient to limit. Nutrient values are estimated using overlapping sliding windows of 60 days. The main purpose of this chart is to show the user how she is progressing towards her final goal, and to help identify trends in nutrient content. Hovering over a nutrient in the chart shows detailed information for that nutrient.

3.2 Databases

3.2.1 Receipt Database

The receipt data used for our prototype corresponds to grocery purchases at a local grocery chain that supports a shopper loyalty card. The chain's website allows its customers to view their own grocery receipts and download them in electronic form. The data for the prototype was donated by 15 volunteers and de-identified. The data contains purchase date, product name, department, UPC, quantity, and price information for each product purchased over a period ranging from 6 months to 1.5 years. Products from non-food departments, such as pet food and paper products were excluded from the analysis. The total number of food product purchases across all users was 16123, and the total number of distinct products was 5120.

3.2.2 Nutrition Databases

One of the significant challenges faced in this research was finding nutrition information for the products in the receipt database. The prototype eventually used nutrition data from three sources: (i) a commercial database with an open access API, (ii) nutrition datasheets available from the grocery chain, and (iii) a USDA public database. The preferred source for nutrition data was the commercial database, since it was indexed by UPC and allowed us to unambiguously identify a product based on UPC.

However, while the database claimed to provide nutrition information for as many as 700,000 products, the coverage of food products from our receipt database was poor. One of the contributing factors was the significant fraction of house brand products purchased by our users. In addition, some products were missing nutrition information.

The next source of nutrition data was nutrition datasheets provided by the grocery chain on its website. While these datasheets provided nutrition data for almost 4000 products carried by the chain, not all products carried by the chain were covered, and only about 9% of the products that were covered were identified by UPC. We therefore also explored the use of a USDA public database, the Food and Nutrition Database for Dietary Studies (FNDDS) [6]. This database contains nutrient information for 64 nutrients for over 8,000 food descriptions. However, this database also has no UPC information and the food descriptions are in a form (*<base product>*, *<comma separated modifiers>*) that made matching product names difficult and ambiguous. For example, in the FNDDS, there are 31 distinct entries for "carrots," including "carrots, raw," "carrots, cooked, from fresh," and "carrots, canned, low sodium." However, the grocery store receipts show product descriptions such as "[store name] cleaned and cut triple washed peeled baby carrots," "[store name] carrots, organic," and "[store name] carrots, sliced, no salt added." When a product from the receipt database was not matched by UPC in either the commercial or the grocery chain database, we used string-matching algorithms and heuristics to match product names between receipts and all three databases, and this proved especially valuable for house brand products.

In addition to these food nutrition databases, we used a database containing the recommended daily values of consumption, or dietary reference intake values (DRI) of certain nutrients, available from the USDA [4]. This is a set of tables that captures average recommended consumption amounts of over 20 nutrients, determined by the Food and Nutrition Board, Institute of Medicine, National Academies. These may be customized based on the age, gender and weight of the individual.

3.2.3 Recommendable Foods Database
This database identifies the set of food items from which to select recommendations to users. There are several choices for this. For the prototype, we restricted the recommendations to the food items listed in the nutrition datasheets provided by the grocery chain, since (i) we wish to recommend items that are easily accessible to users, and (ii) the datasheets provided good coverage of produce and other healthy foods. The commercial database, on the other hand, focused on packaged foods, many of which may not have been accessible to our users.

3.3 Nudging Recommendations

3.3.1 Nutritional Gap
We chose to use the nutritional gap between the current state of nutrition and a target state (corresponding to a dietary goal) to guide food recommendations as the initial research approach. The prototype used the DRI values as the dietary goal. The current nutritional intake was estimated over a sliding temporal window such as the most recent 30, 60 or 90 days, by aggregating the nutritional contents of different food products purchased during this window (obtained from the nutrition databases), and scaled by the quantity purchased. Scaling is complicated by the fact that the purchased quantity reported on the receipt varies from mass units (e.g. for produce items) to number (for packaged goods), whereas nutrition databases typically report nutrition per *serving*, and the

definition of a serving typically varies both across food products within a database, as well as across databases.

The current nutrition is represented as a vector in *n*-space, where *n* is the number of nutrients. For the prototype, we used a core set of 12 nutrients commonly found on food package labels (and therefore found in most nutrition databases), including, for example, calcium, sodium, and protein. The target nutrition is similarly represented as a vector in this space. This vector uses the DRI values, scaled for the number of days in the period under consideration. The nutritional gap is represented as a vector describing the difference between the amounts of nutrients in the food the user is purchasing and the recommended consumption for the nutrients. The values in the vector represent the percentage gap (or excess) of each nutrient.

In order to speed up computation, a nutrition profile vector, N_p, describing the nutrient content of each recommendable food product was pre-computed. This vector is also in *n*-space, as the nutritional gap vector above.

3.3.2 Computing Recommendations
Food recommendations that nudge the user towards a nutritional goal (in this case, the DRI) are generated by identifying food items (along with the number of servings) that best fill the gap in nutrition described by the nutrition gap vector. To do this, we compute the cosine similarity between N_g, the user's nutrition gap vector and N_p, the nutrition profile vector for each food product in the recommendable foods database.

The 12 nutrients used fall into two categories - *nutrients to limit* (e.g. fat and sodium), and *nutrients to meet* (e.g. calcium, iron, and vitamin C). Elements of the "gap" vector may actually be negative, especially due to an excess of the former category of nutrients. This first exploratory implementation uses a weighted form of the nutrition gap vector N_g, to control the relative importance of the nutrients, as shown below. In particular, nutrients to limit are assigned a weight of 0, which effectively excludes them from the computation.

$$N_{g\text{-weighted}}[i] = N_g[i] * \begin{cases} 0, i \in \{nutrients\ to\ limit\} \\ 2, i = nutrient\ with\ largest\ gap \\ 1, i \in \{all\ other\ nutrients\} \end{cases}$$

The cosine similarity is thus given by

$$Similarity\ (food_i) = \frac{Ng\text{-}weighted \cdot Np(foodi)}{\|Ng\text{-}weighted\|\|Np(foodi)\|}$$

The five highest scoring foods are presented as recommendations. We also present to the user the number of servings for a given time interval that would be needed to fill the gap *for the nutrient with the largest gap*. The number of servings needed is computed as the nutrition gap value for this nutrient divided by the corresponding value in the nutrition profile vector for that food, and displayed as part of the recommendation.

4. RESULTS AND DISCUSSION
The initial Foodle prototype allowed us to demonstrate our research objective of providing automated, personalized and goal driven food recommendations to users. The recommendations are driven by the gap in nutrition between the present state (defined by a sliding temporal window) and the target state corresponding to DRIs. It is expected that these recommendations will be reflected in a user's grocery purchases when adopted, and the nutrition gap will change, as will the recommendations, constantly narrowing the gap. Thus a feedback loop is built into the system. We observed that for users with sufficient grocery data, the recommendations delivered by Foodle are sensible and address

significant nutrient shortages in their diets. For user "Eugene" who showed a 50% deficiency in dietary fiber, the top three recommendations were spaghetti squash (3 servings/week), green beans (3 servings/week) and vegetable bean medley (1 serving/week), all rich sources of dietary fiber.

In this process, we also identified several conceptual and practical challenges:

Under-estimating nutritional intakes: The percentage of food purchases that we were able to match to nutrition information varied between 30 and 60%, depending on the particular user's purchase habits. This resulted primarily from the difficulty in matching product names of purchased foods with their nutrition data, and was particularly significant in the case of house brands, which represented a significant fraction of purchases. Semantic analysis of product descriptions to identify brand names, adjectives (e.g. "fresh", "organic") and ingredients would help increase the accuracy of matching. Other options include screen scraping and crowdsourcing to capture nutrient information from product pages found online. More fundamentally however, nutritional intakes are under-estimated because users may shop at farmer's markets, eat at restaurants or forget to use their loyalty cards. There may be ways to mitigate these effects, such as providing the user a capability to enter that information, either manually, or automatically e.g. by processing restaurant receipts and matching them with nutrition information provided by restaurant chains. Despite these gaps, grocery purchase data has been shown to be a reliable indicator of nutrition, and useful recommendations for nudging may be obtained by making some assumptions about the fraction of consumption going unrecorded (perhaps input by the user) and scaling the available nutrient data.

Individual vs. family purchases: We observed significant excess of all nutrients for some users, and these turned out to be users purchasing groceries for their families. Capturing information about members of the family would allow more accurate estimation of the *aggregate* target nutrition for family units. The recommendations provided would be "personalized" at the level of these family units.

Recommendation algorithms: The algorithm used in the prototype for recommending foods works only for gaps caused by insufficient nutrients. To compute recommendations for excess nutrients, for example, salt or sugar, currently purchased products that contribute high amounts of these nutrients could be identified, and recommended for reduced purchase. However, it is not guaranteed that this process would converge since a food product contains several nutrients. We have developed an alternative formulation of the problem as an unbounded Knapsack problem. Intuitively, the objective is to fill the knapsack with different servings of available food items such that the total "nutritional value" of the knapsack is maximized, subject to the constraint that the net calories from the selected items does not exceed the recommended caloric intake for the individual user, given their profile. But in doing so, our solution attempts to make the least possible change to the current diet.

5. SUMMARY & FUTURE DIRECTIONS

In this paper, we described our research in using grocery receipt purchase data to generate recommendations of foods to nudge the user to a healthier diet. The initial prototype has several advantages over available tools and aids to promote healthier diets, and shows considerable promise for generating highly personalized recommendations that directly address nutritional deficiencies in users' diets. The persuasiveness and adoption of these recommendations needs to be validated using longitudinal user studies.

Beyond addressing the shortcomings of the initial prototype as described, there are several interesting directions for future research: (i) User profiles: The user can specify dietary restrictions or preferences; there may also be ways to learn some of these through data analysis (ii) With a larger population of users, other recommender system architectures can be explored, such as user-user collaborative filtering. This may have the benefit of recommending food items the user is more likely to adopt. (iii) New ways of delivering recommendations can be explored, e.g. in the context of the grocery shopping experience through mobile app, shopping list integration, or even as part of a "smart" grocery cart. (iv) Social navigation may be useful to help users select and adopt food recommendations (v) The scope of recommendations could be extended to school boards, nursing homes and SNAP (food stamp) programs to improve public health outcomes.

6. REFERENCES

[1] A Brief History of USDA Food Guides: 2011.

[2] Armstrong, K. 2010. *Stumped at the Supermarket*. Technical Report. Public Health Law Center, William Mitchell College of Law, St. Paul, Minnesota.

[3] Carol Byrd-Bredbenner, C.A.B. 2010. Assessing the home food environment nutrient supply using mobile barcode (Universal Product Code) scanning technology. *Nutrition & Food Science*. 40, 3 (2010), 305–313.

[4] DRI Tables and Application Reports: *http://fnic.nal.usda.gov/dietary-guidance/dietary-reference-intakes/dri-tables-and-application-reports*.

[5] El-Dosuky, M.A., Rashad, M.Z., Hamza, T.T. and EL-Bassiouny, A.H. 2012. Food Recommendation using Ontology and Heuristics. *Advanced Machine Learning Technologies and Applications* (Cairo, 2012), 423–429.

[6] Food Surveys : FNDDS 5.0: *http://www.ars.usda.gov/Services/docs.htm?docid=22370*.

[7] Obesity Epidemic "Astronomical": *http://www.webmd.com/diet/obesity-epidemic-astronomical*.

[8] Phanich, M., Pholkul, P. and Phimoltares, S. 2010. Food Recommendation System Using Clustering Analysis for Diabetic Patients. *International Conference on Information Science and Applications* (Seoul, Korea, 2010), 1–8.

[9] Tatli, I. 2009. Food Recommendation System Project Report 1- Introduction and Problem Definition (2009).

[10] Tin, S.T., Mhurchu, C.N. and Bullen, C. 2007. Supermarket Sales Data : Feasibility and Applicability in Population Food and Nutrition Monitoring. 65, 1 (2007), 20–30.

[11] Atkinson, Fiona S., R., Kaye Foser-Powell, Kaye, R. and Brand- Miller, Jennie C., P. 2008. International Tables of Glycemic Index and Glycemic Load Values : 2008. Diabetes Care. 31, 12 (2008), 2281–2283.

[12] Guenther, P.M., Kirkpatrick, S.I., Reedy, J., Krebs-smith, S.M., Buckman, D.W., Dodd, K.W., Casavale, K.O. and Carroll, R.J. 2014. The Healthy Eating Index-2010 Is a Valid and Reliable Measure of Diet Quality According to the 2010 Dietary Guidelines for Americans 1 – 3. (2014), 399–407.

Nuke 'Em Till They Go: Investigating Power User Attacks to Disparage Items in Collaborative Recommenders

Carlos E. Seminario and David C. Wilson
Software and Information Systems Department
College of Computing and Informatics
University of North Carolina at Charlotte
Charlotte, NC 28223 USA
cseminar@uncc.edu   davils@uncc.edu

ABSTRACT

Recommender Systems (RSs) can be vulnerable to manipulation by malicious users who successfully bias recommendations for their own benefit or pleasure. These are known as *attacks* on RSs and are typically used to either promote ("push") or disparage ("nuke") targeted items contained within the recommender's user-item dataset. Our recent work with the Power User Attack (PUA) model, determined that attackers disguised as *influential power users* can mount successful (from the attacker's viewpoint) *push attacks* against user-based, item-based, and SVD-based recommenders. However, the success of push attack vectors may not be symmetric for *nuke attacks*, which target the opposite effect — *reducing* the likelihood that target items appear in users' top-N lists. The asymmetry between push and nuke attacks is highlighted when evaluating these attacks using traditional robustness metrics such as Rank and Prediction Shift. This paper examines the PUA attack model in the context of nuke attacks, in order to investigate the differences between push and nuke attack orientations, as well as how they are evaluated. In this work we show that the PUA is able to mount successful nuke attacks against commonly-used recommender algorithms highlighting the "nuke vs. push" asymmetry in the results.

Categories and Subject Descriptors

H.3.3 [**Information Storage and Retrieval**]: Information Search and Retrieval–*Information filtering*

Keywords

Recommender Systems; Power Users; Attacks; Evaluation

1. INTRODUCTION

As with many online systems, recommenders are subject to attack by devious or self-interested users who enter false information to either promote items (push), disparage their competition (nuke), or simply to disrupt the RS results [7, 5, 6]. Although system operators do not usually disclose detailed information about attacks on their systems, we know that real attacks on RSs are not uncommon,

the most popular being the use of fake reviews known as opinion spam.[1] The problem with attacks on ratings-based Collaborative Filtering (CF) recommenders is that they can corrupt the system dataset and cause users to distrust the recommendations provided.

We have previously studied a novel category of RS attacks based explicitly on measures of influence, in particular the potential impact of high-influence, or *power users* [13]. Power users in the RS context are those that are able to influence the largest group of RS users; influence is indicated by the ability of power user i to change (positively or negatively) the RS prediction for another user j, or for power user i's target item to appear in user j's top-N list. We found that Power User Attacks (PUAs) impacted user-based, item-based, and SVD-based recommenders [13, 10, 14, 11] for *push attacks*.

For this study, we turned our attention to the complementary notion of *nuke attacks* to determine whether the PUA could also be successful nuking selected target items. Nuke attacks are designed to reduce the likelihood that a target item is recommended; their objective is to impact RS robustness metrics[2] by increasing Rank and causing negative Prediction Shift [5, 6]. However, while they may employ similar mechanisms for attack, the goals for push and nuke attacks are really asymmetric. Push attacks attempt to move items from a large pool not being presented to the user into the viewed recommendation list. Nuke attacks attempt to move items from the small pool of viewed recommendations into the great unshown. And these contextual differences have implications for evaluating the attacks. For example, if a nuke attack effectively shifts target items down the list, but all of the movement is below the threshold of visibility to the user, is that a good measure of effectiveness? In the nuke attack context, and using robustness metrics, the objectives of this paper are to study (1) the effectiveness of the PUA against common RSs, and (2) the effectiveness of various power user selection methods on attack results.

2. RELATED WORK

Attacking RSs by entering false ratings has been termed a *profile injection attack* [6] or *shilling attack* [5]. Burke et al provide a summary overview of RS attack models, attack detection, and algorithm robustness [1]. Most of the attack research has targeted the use of similarity-focused attack models that generate synthetic at-

---

[1] Example nuke attack: http://www.dailymail.co.uk/travel/article-2059000/TripAdvisor-controversy-Reviews-website-launches-complaints-hotlines.html

[2] *Rank* indicates the ordinal position of a target item in a user's top-N list sorted descending based on predicted rating value, *Prediction Shift* indicates the average shift in predicted values of specified target items, before and after the attack. Traditionally used for evaluating only push attacks, *Hit Ratio* is percentage of users that have a target item in their top-N list,

tack user profiles using random or average item ratings or a variant of these two approaches [5, 6]. Nuke attack models developed and explored in [5, 6], indicated that user-based recommenders were more vulnerable to nuke attacks than item-based.

Our research has investigated using explicit measures of influence to create attack models based on the notion of *influential power users* [13]. In earlier work, we defined the *Power User Attack* model as a set of power user profiles with biased ratings that influence the results presented to other users [13, 14]. The PUA demonstrated that influential users can impact common recommender approaches [13, 10, 14, 11] with push attacks. However, the PUA model has not yet been tested in the nuke attack context.

To evaluate nuke attacks, researchers [5, 6] have used Prediction Shift metrics to measure impacts on prediction values before and after the attack, and metrics such as Rank and Expected top-N Occupancy (ExpTopN)[3] that measure the effect an attack will have on top-N recommendation lists. *These studies, however, have not explicitly indicated whether or not the target items were in the top-N lists before the attack.* This is important to note because, while Rank (or ExpTopN) and Prediction Shift can indicate the impact that the nuke attack has on the target items, *they only really matter to an attacker if the target items are actually removed from users' top-N lists as a result of the attack.* In this study, we evaluate the asymmetric aspect of the nuke PUA and, extending prior research approaches, use Hit Ratio to explicitly indicate the extent to which target items appear in the top-N lists before and after the attack.

3. POWER USER NUKE ATTACKS

Nuke attacks using various attack models have previously been evaluated [6] by measuring Rank and Prediction Shift of the target items. Rank was measured before the attack (as a baseline) and after the attack to measure the impact; negative Prediction Shift indicated that the predicted values decreased as a result of the attack. Lam and Riedl [5] used ExpTopN and Prediction Shift in their evaluation. Results of those studies indicated that (1) user-based recommenders were more vulnerable than item-based, and (2) effective attacks are those that increase target item Rank beyond top-N or have a negative ExpTopN, and have a negative Prediction Shift.

For this study, we introduce the use of the Hit Ratio metric in the evaluation of the nuke attacks[4], i.e., using Hit Ratio, we measure the extent to which target items appear in top-N lists BEFORE the attack and then observe their top-N status AFTER the attack. A successful nuke attack would reduce Hit Ratio and increase Rank, in contrast to push attacks where the objective is to increase Hit Ratio and decrease Rank. To evaluate the impact of a nuke attack on users' top-N lists, we chose Most Popular (highest number of ratings) and Most Liked (highest average rating) items as target items because they would most likely appear in top-N lists before the nuke attack, and they would be more challenging to nuke than either new or new and established items. We chose a top-N list size of 40 based on analysis in [5] that the median recommendation search ends within the first 40 items displayed.

To study the impacts of the PUA, we use power user selection methods to generate synthetic power user (SPU) profiles [14]:

InDegree or ID: Based on in-degree centrality [12], power users are those who participate in the highest number of similarity neighborhoods. We developed this method in previous work [13, 14].

---

[3]*ExpTopN* is the expected number of occurrences of target items in a top-N recommendation list [5].

[4]In prior research, Hit Ratio was not used because of concerns that nuked items would drop out of the retrieval windows, making Hit Ratio differences insignificant [6].

Number of Ratings (NumRatings or NR): Power users were defined in [4] as users with the highest number of item ratings.

Random (Rand): To contrast with InDegree and NumRatings power users, this method selects users randomly from the entire set of users in the RS dataset.

Two experiments were used to evaluate power user nuke attacks:
Experiment 1 (E1): To compare with previous work in [6], we select new and established target items, mount the nuke attack against CF RS algorithms, inject the dataset with SPU attack profiles, and evaluate the impact of the PUA using Rank and Prediction Shift.

Experiment 2 (E2): To evaluate the effect of a nuke attack on top-N recommendation lists, we select Most Popular and Most Liked target items, mount the nuke attack against various CF RS algorithms, inject the dataset with SPU attack profiles, and evaluate the attack impact using Hit Ratio, Rank, and Prediction Shift metrics. For this experiment, Rank after attack and Prediction Shift are based on target items that were in the top-N list before the attack.

For these experiments, we test two hypotheses:

H1: *A PUA with relatively small number of attackers (<=5% of all users) can have significant effects on RS predictions and top-N recommendations, as measured with Hit Ratio, Rank, Prediction Shift.*
H2: *Attackers identified using InDegree power user selection will have a higher level of impact, compared to attackers identified using NumRatings or Rand, on RS predictions and top-N recommendations, as measured with Hit Ratio, Rank, Prediction Shift.*

4. EXPERIMENTAL DESIGN

Evaluation Metrics: Evaluations were performed before and after the attacks using the Apache Mahout platform[5]. For robustness metrics [6], we use Hit Ratio (HR), Average HR ($\overline{HR}$), Prediction Shift (PS), Average PS ($\overline{PS}$), Rank (R), and Average R ($\overline{R}$); the Average metrics are averaged over all users and target items. After a nuke attack, low $\overline{HR}$, high $\overline{R}$, and negative $\overline{PS}$ indicate that the attack was successful (from the attacker's viewpoint).

Datasets and Algorithms: We used the public MovieLens[6] ML100K[7] dataset. The RS algorithms used were provided in Apache Mahout and customized (except SVD) for this study. The CF user-based algorithms (user-based weighted or UBW [2], and user-based mean-centered or UMCP [8]) use Pearson similarity with a threshold of 0.0 (positive correlation), neighborhood size of 50, and significance weighting of n/50 where n is the number of co-rated items [3]. The item-based weighted algorithm (IBW) [9] uses Pearson similarity with a threshold of 0.0 and significance weighting of n/50. For the SVD-based algorithm (SVD), we used RatingStochasticGradient-Descent (RSGD); run-time parameter settings, number of features (=100) and number of iterations (=50), were determined empirically to optimize recommender accuracy.

Attack User Profiles: To mount the Power User Nuke Attack, SPU profiles were generated as described in [14] and converted to attack user profiles by setting target item ratings to reflect a nuke attack.

Power User Selection: Methods used for power user selection are described in § 3. Randomly-selected SPU attackers (Rand) had the following average number of ratings, average rating, and average rating entropy, respectively: 10 SPUs: 133.00, 3.451, 2.014; 50 SPUs: 126.68, 3.454, 1.964; 100 SPUs: 129.94, 3.281, 2.161.

Target Item Selection: For E1, we used "new and established" items, i.e., 50 target items were selected randomly and had the following average number of ratings, average rating, and average rating entropy for ML100K: 73.78, 3.133, 1.769. For E2, we used

---

[5]http://www.mahout.apache.org
[6]http://www.grouplens.org
[7]nominal 100,000 ratings, 1,682 movies, and 943 users.

Most Liked items (top-50 items with highest average rating) and Most Popular items (top-50 items with highest number of ratings). Most Liked and Most Popular items had the following average number of ratings, average rating, and average rating entropy, respectively, for ML100K: 130.56, 4.471, 1.109 for Most Liked and 356.82, 3.864, 1.859 for Most Popular.

Attack Parameter Selection: The Attack Intent is Nuke, i.e., target item ratings are set to the minimum rating (= 1) at run time. The Attack Size, or number of SPU attackers, was varied for these experiments: 1% (10 SPUs), 5% (50 SPUs), and 10% (100 SPUs).

Test Variations: Three power user selection methods, 4 CF algorithms, 3 attack sizes. In E1 we used one target type, and in E2 we used 2 target types. Each variation was run multiple times[8].

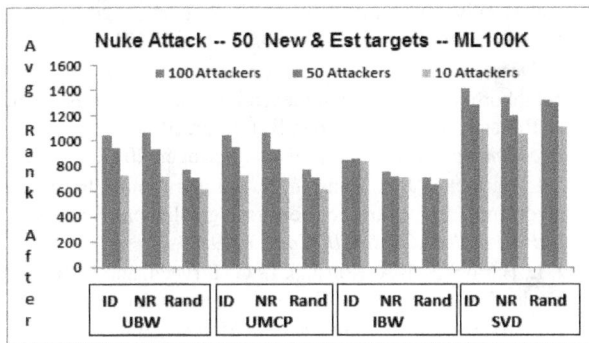

Figure 1: Experiment 1: Average Rank Results (After Attack) for New and Established Target Items, ML100K

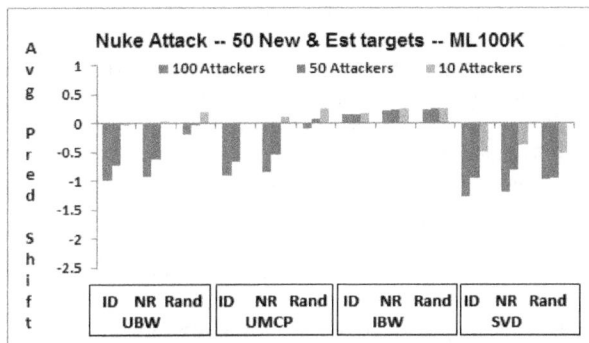

Figure 2: Experiment 1: Average Prediction Shift Results for New and Established Target Items, ML100K

5. EXPERIMENTS AND RESULTS

5.1 E1: Nuking New and Established Items

In this experiment, we select 50 new and established target items from the ML100K dataset. Attacks are conducted for three levels of attack size (1%, 5%, and 10%) for each of the three power user types (ID, NR, and Rand) and using each of the four recommender algorithms (UBW, UMCP, IBW, SVD). For each variation, we run multiple attacks[8]. The $\overline{R}$ results after attack are shown in Figure 1. Before the attack (not shown), $\overline{R}$ for UBW and UMCP ranges from 500 to 600, for IBW about 700, and for SVD about 800. In most

---

[8]Each attack is run 50 times, each with a different target item; then the results are averaged over all 50 targets.

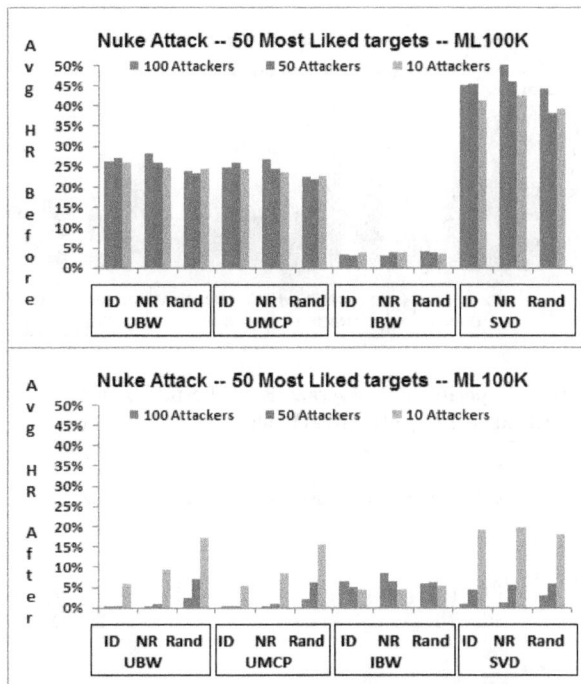

Figure 3: Experiment 2: Average Hit Ratio Results (Before and After Attack) for Most Liked Target Items, ML100K

cases after the attack, the differences in impacts between 1%, 5%, and 10% attack sizes are significant. The increase in $\overline{R}$ for each power user type varies between 1.2X to 1.75X between before and after attack, compared to 2X increase using various attack models reported by ([6] who used only UMCP. The IBW algorithm showed the least amount of $\overline{R}$ increase, indicating its robustness to this attack. Results for $\overline{PS}$ in Figure 2 indicate that UBW, UMCP, and SVD algorithms are vulnerable to this attack showing strong negative impacts, whereas, IBW is robust to attack showing a positive shift (this positive shift in IBW was also reported by [6] for various attack models). Thus, for new and established target items, a prediction shift of -1.0 would reduce the average rating from 3.13 to 2.13, which could discourage some users from watching those recommended movies. Hypothesis H1 is accepted for UBW, UMCP, and SVD recommenders, meaning that a relatively small number of power users (5% or less of the user base on a given dataset) can have significant effects on RS predictions and top-N lists of recommendations regardless of power user selection method. Hypothesis H2 is accepted for UBW, UMCP, and SVD recommenders, with In-Degree having a slight advantage over NumRatings as indicated in the $\overline{R}$ and $\overline{PS}$ results; and both methods are superior to Random.

5.2 E2: Nuking Likable and Popular Items

The motivation for Experiment 2 was to evaluate the nuke attack in a manner consistent with push attacks, i.e., showing the impact that the attack has on the top-N list of recommendations provided to the users. In the case of nuke attacks, however, the attacker's goal is to remove the target items from the top-N list of recommendations. Figure 3 indicates that Most Liked items appearing in the top-N lists before the attack did not remain after the attack for UBW, UMCP, and SVD; results also show that IBW is minimally affected by this attack. Results for Most Popular items (not shown) are similar albeit not as impactful: before the attack $\overline{HR}$ was 7% for UBW and UMCP, 10% for SVD, and slightly above 0% for IBW;

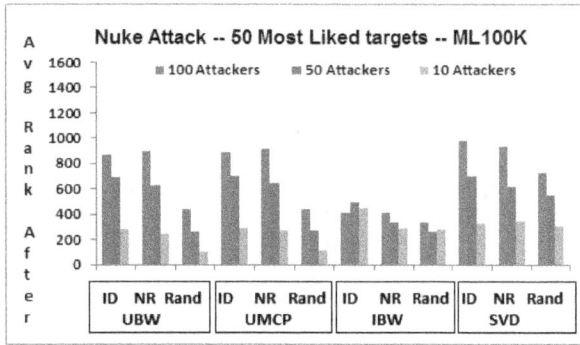

Figure 4: Experiment 2: Average Rank Results (After Attack) for Most Liked Target Items, ML100K

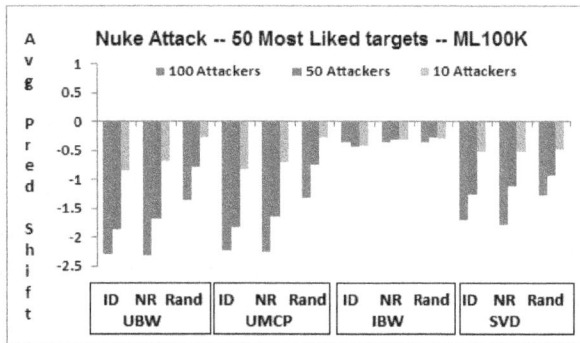

Figure 5: Experiment 2: Average Prediction Shift Results for Most Liked Target Items, ML100K

after the attack $\overline{HR}$ was close to 0% across algorithms and attack sizes except for the 1% attacks. For Most Liked and Most Popular targets, the 1% attacks show relatively higher $\overline{HR}$ values after attack indicating that the attack was not as successful as the 5% and 10% attacks (as expected). Although not shown, $\overline{R}$ before the attack was relatively stable and averaged 21.4 for Most Liked and 27.1 for Most Popular across all algorithms and attack sizes. Figure 4 shows $\overline{R}$ results after the attack for Most Liked indicating a significant rise in $\overline{R}$; results for Most Popular (not shown) also rise albeit not to the same high levels. Average Most Liked high $\overline{R}$ values using 10% attacks for UBW, UMCP, IBW, and SVD were 734, 747, 386, 879, respectively; they were 381, 527, 375, and 345 for Most Popular. Figure 5 shows $\overline{PS}$ results after the attack for Most Liked indicating strong results for UBW, UMCP, and SVD; results for Most Popular (not shown) also show $\overline{PS} < 0$ albeit not to the same levels of reduction. Average Most Liked low $\overline{PS}$ values using 10% attacks for UBW, UMCP, IBW, and SVD were -1.99, -1.93, -0.36, -1.59, respectively; they were -0.88, -0.94, -0.25, -0.46 for Most Popular. Based on these results, we see that Most Liked targets are significantly more vulnerable to attack than Most Popular targets. With InDegree and NumRatings selection methods, prediction values can be reduced by about 2 points, e.g., from a 4 rating down to 2 compared to a 0.5 point reduction for Most Popular target items. We also see that IBW is more robust to attack for both Most Liked and Most Popular targets. Hypothesis H1 is accepted for UBW, UMCP, and SVD recommenders. Hypothesis H2 is partially accepted for UBW and UMCP, and SVD recommenders. Although the InDegree and NumRatings both perform well at a high level, NumRatings occasionally shows slightly better results; and both methods are superior to Random.

6. CONCLUSION AND FUTURE WORK

This study evaluated power user nuke attacks mounted against various CF RS algorithms as measured by traditional robustness metrics. User-based and SVD-based algorithms are shown to be vulnerable, while item-based is more robust to nuke attacks. We showed that Most Liked target items are more vulnerable to attack than Most Popular targets, and that a relatively few NumRatings and InDegree synthetic user profiles can have significant effects on RS predictions and top-N recommendation lists. Future work includes evaluation with larger datasets and other domains.

7. REFERENCES

[1] R. Burke, M. P. O'Mahony, and N. J. Hurley. Robust collaborative recommendation. In F. Ricci et al., editors, *Recommender Systems Handbook*. Springer, 2011.

[2] C. Desrosiers and G. Karypis. A comprehensive survey of neighborhood-based recommendations methods. In F. Ricci, L. Rokach, B. Shapira, and P. B. Kantor, editors, *Recommender Systems Handbook*. Springer, 2011.

[3] J. L. Herlocker, J. A. Konstan, A. Borchers, and J. Riedl. An algorithmic framework for performing collaborative filtering. In *Proc of the ACM SIGIR Conf*, 1999.

[4] J. L. Herlocker, J. A. Konstan, L. G. Terveen, and J. Riedl. Evaluating collaborative filtering recommender systems. *ACM Transactions on Information Systems*, 2004.

[5] S. K. Lam and J. Riedl. Shilling recommender systems for fun and profit. In *Proceedings of the 13th international conference on World Wide Web*. ACM, 2004.

[6] B. Mobasher, R. Burke, R. Bhaumik, and C. Williams. Toward trustworthy recommender systems: An analysis of attack models and algorithm robustness. *ACM Trans. Internet Technol.*, 2007.

[7] M. P. O'Mahony, N. Hurley, and G. C. M. Silvestre. Promoting recommendations: An attack on collaborative filtering. In *Proceedings of DEXA'02*, 2002.

[8] P. Resnick, N. Iacovou, M. Suchak, P. Bergstrom, and J. Riedl. GroupLens: an open architecture for collaborative filtering of netnews. In *Proceedings of CSCW'94*, 1994.

[9] B. Sarwar, G. Karypis, J. Konstan, and J. Riedl. Item-based collaborative filtering recommendation algorithms. In *Proceedings of the World Wide Web Conference*, 2001.

[10] C. E. Seminario and D. C. Wilson. Assessing impacts of a power user attack on a matrix factorization collaborative recommender system. In *Proceedings of the 27th Florida Artificial Intelligence Research Society Conf.*, 2014.

[11] C. E. Seminario and D. C. Wilson. Attacking item-based recommender systems with power items. In *Proceedings of the 8th ACM Conference on Recommender Systems*, RecSys '14. ACM, October 2014.

[12] S. Wasserman and K. Faust. *Social Network Analysis: Methods and Applications*. Cambridge University Press, New York, NY, 1994.

[13] D. C. Wilson and C. E. Seminario. When power users attack: assessing impacts in collaborative recommender systems. In *Proceedings of the 7th ACM conference on Recommender Systems*, RecSys '13. ACM, 2013.

[14] D. C. Wilson and C. E. Seminario. Evil twins: Modeling power users in attacks on recommender systems. In *Proceedings of the 22nd Conference on User Modelling, Adaptation and Personalization*, 2014.

"Please, Not Now!" A Model for Timing Recommendations

Nofar Dali Betzalel, Bracha Shapira, Lior Rokach
Ben-Gurion University of the Negev
and Telekom Innovation Laboratories at BGU
P.O box 84105
Beer Sheva, Israel
972-8-6473947
dalinof@post.bgu.ac.il, {bshapira, liorrk}@bgu.ac.il

ABSTRACT

Proactive recommender systems push recommendations to users without their explicit request whenever a recommendation that suits a user is available. These systems strive to optimize the match between recommended items and users' preferences. We assume that recommendations might be reflected with low accuracy not only due to the recommended items' suitability to the user, but also because of the recommendations' timings. We therefore claim that it is possible to learn a model of good and bad contexts for recommendations that can later be integrated in a recommender system. Using mobile data collected during a three week user study, we suggest a two-phase model that is able to classify whether a certain context is at all suitable for any recommendation, regardless of its content. Results reveal that a hybrid model that first decides whether it should use a personal or a non-personal timing model, and then classifies accordingly whether the timing is proper for recommendations, is superior to both the personal or non-personal timing models.

Categories and Subject Descriptors

H.2.8 **[Database Management]**: Database Applications - *Data Mining*; H.4.0 **[Information Systems Applications]**: General

General Terms

Algorithms, Measurement, Performance, Experimentation

Keywords

Recommender Systems; Proactivity; Mobile; Personalization; Data Mining

1. INTRODUCTION

Proactive recommender systems (RSs) push recommendations to the user without explicit user request, trying to optimize the recommendation to the user's current needs and preferences. Recent studies [16, 17, 13, 11] report that adding contextual information such as the user's current location, weather, and time of the day into the recommendation process improves the system's accuracy. However, we claim that situations exist during which the most accurately predicted recommendation will not be appreciated by the user as she may not prefer to receive any recommendations at that moment. Examples of such situations include: while driving, watching a movie, talking on the phone, chatting with a friend, and so on. In these cases, the accuracy of an RS that provides proactive

RecSys '15, September 16-20, 2015, Vienna, Austria
© 2015 ACM. ISBN 978-1-4503-3692-5/15/09...$15.00
DOI: http://dx.doi.org/10.1145/2792838.2799672

recommendations will be low regardless of their content. In this paper, we propose to explore the feasibility of improving RSs for mobile devices by identifying such situations. We propose considering the user's context not only in order to determine the most accurate recommendation's content but also in order to decide whether the user's context is suitable at all for providing any recommendation. None of the previous studies that mention the importance of timing proactive recommendations have implemented a model for doing so, nor have they evaluated such a model's capabilities using data collected by real users.

In our work, we trained models that classify users' contexts that are suitable for recommendations (henceforth referred to as "now" contexts) and user contexts in which users are highly likely to refuse any recommendations (henceforth referred to as "not now" contexts). These models can be easily integrated into a proactive RS to improve its recommendations' timings. In a large scale user study, we collected data using users' mobile devices' sensors, and inferred behavioral patterns of "now" and "not now" contexts based on users' explicit feedback. The feedback and sensors sampling were obtained through an application that proactively recommended nearby POIs to users. The application enabled users to use a "not now" button if the recommendation's timing was not suitable, before providing a recommendation. We used the data collected to generate personal models which used only the user's training data, and non-personal models that used all users' training data. Preliminary tests revealed that personal models obtained higher accuracy when classifying the user's context in some cases while the non-personal model dominated in others. Thus, we propose an integration of the two to a hybrid classification model. The suggested model first decides whether it is more beneficial to use the user's personal or the non-personal model and then classifies the given context as "now" or "not now" using the chosen model. Results indicate that in nearly all cases the suggested hybrid model is able to achieve higher precision than both the personal and the non-personal models.

Our contribution in this work is twofold: first we show the feasibility of inferring a model that can classify between "now" and "not now" contexts. Secondly, we present a hybrid model for such tasks and show its superiority over two other considered options.

2. RELATED WORK

Context Aware Proactive RSs - Recent studies in the field of proactive RSs mention the importance of context awareness for recommendations in mobile applications. Some of these works suggest mobile applications that proactively recommend different items or services, e.g., an RS for mobile applications [5], Points of Interest (POIs) RSs for tourists [3, 14], and an RS for leisure activities [4], incorporate context into their recommendations. While these works incorporate context in order to choose items that best suit users given their current context, we use the user's context in order to decide whether the RS should make recommendations to the user at all, regardless of the recommendation's content.

Interruptions Management - Proactive recommendations can be referred to as interruptions for the user, since they pop up during the user's daily routine. The field of interruption management aims to define "good" and "bad" interruptions. Recent studies in the field [12] focused on computer-based interruption technologies investigating various interruption modes. Various studies concluded that applications that interrupt a user at an inopportune moment have had bad effects on the user's performance and satisfaction compared to interruption at a more opportune moment [1, 6, 10]. These findings strengthen our argument that addressing the right timing for a recommendation may greatly benefit the performance of RSs.

Finding the Right Timing for a Recommendation - Few studies in the field of proactive RSs mention the importance of timing recommendations. Lerchenmueller and Woerndl [11] present an algorithm that is implemented for a Smartphone application and analyzes the user's current context based on GPS data. The authors focus on correctly classifying the user's activity online. They report that they plan to use these results in order to determine the best point in time for a recommendation, while we already implemented and evaluated the feasibility of inducing models of the right contexts for recommendations. In addition, the authors use mainly GPS data and infer users' explicit activity that might be defined as suitable or not for recommendations, while we take a variety of different sensors under consideration and infer implicit contexts (rather than activities) for "now" and "not now" scenarios.

In [15], the authors present a new model for proactivity in mobile CARSs. Their model periodically assesses whether the current context is proper for recommendations. If assessed positively, candidate items were rated to decide which recommendations would be suggested. They implemented a prototype for recommending gas stations. Their prototype used parameters such as fuel level and detour to the nearest gas station. The different parameters used in their model were in part derived from an earlier study investigating gas station selection [2] and building the model itself was done in previous work [8]. Their current work focused on assessing the model's first phase's abilities using an online questionnaire. Users were asked to enter demographic data and then rate the usefulness and convenience of recommendations for 13 different scenarios presented for them. The scenarios were composed of various features that the model took under consideration while deciding whether the timing was proper for recommendations (e.g. fuel level, the driver's stress level, etc.). The authors found that in most cases their model's results were close to the users' feedback. Our work differs from this in various aspects. First, their model uses a set of explicit features chosen in accordance with the domain used in the presented prototype, while we use mostly implicit features that are not domain specific. Secondly, we examined our suggested model using real data collected in a user study, while their work used literal scenarios in an online questionnaire.

In summary, works presented in this section deal with proactive RSs and realize the importance of timing such recommendations. Our work, as opposed to those presented here, uses mostly implicit features that are not domain specific in order to define user context—which in turn assists in deciding whether the user is available for recommendations and acts accordingly. Our work is the first to assess this challenge, provide a solution and test it with real user data.

3. RECOMMENDERPRO USER STUDY

We conducted a user study in which the main goal was to develop a machine learning based classification model that will learn the right contexts for recommendations. In order to collect the needed data, we designed and developed an application that generates proactive recommendations of POIs for users and collects data from their mobile devices.

3.1 Participants

We recruited 90 students between the ages of 20-45 for our user study. 53 (58%) of them were male and 37 (41%) were female. They were all students from one of two academic institutions.

3.2 POIs

The collection of POIs was generated using the Foursquare API.[1] We selected POIs from Foursquare that covered the cities in which participants lived and studied. The selected POIs were categorized as "Food" or "Nightlife Spots" and gained at-least 10 check-ins by Foursquare users.

3.3 RecommenderPro Application

We developed *RecommenderPro*, an Android application that collects data and provides recommendations about POIs nearby to the user. The application collects sensors' data every 30 minutes for 10 seconds. This is followed by a pop-up dialog box accompanied by a notification sound, that asks whether the user is available for recommendations, as shown in Figure 1a. The user might select the "not now" option, signaling that the current timing is not suitable for recommendations. If the user responds positively, the application presents the three most highly rated recommendations by the RS for the user to rate, as presented in Figure 1b. The participants recruited for the user study watched a short introductory video that explained how to use the application. One of our main focuses while making the video was to properly explain the meaning of the different rating options. The "Like" rating means that the user finds the recommended POI a good recommendation for his or her *current context*, while a "Dislike" rating means the opposite. An additional "Check-in" option enabled the users to signal that they are currently at the recommended POI. After each dialog is presented, the user has two minutes to answer it before it disappears, assuming that she is not available. The user's response, i.e. rating, pressing "not now," or simply not answering the dialog and missing it (an action labeled as "not available"), is immediately sent to the server with the sampled sensors data. The application constantly runs in the background and the described mechanism repeats itself with no need of user action to invoke recommendations. The application was designed to avoid repeating the same recommendations in consecutive recommendations timings.

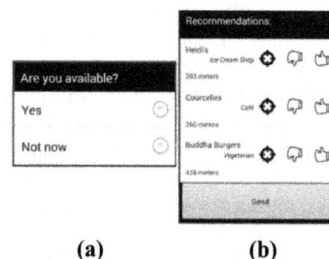

(a)   (b)

Figure 1: *RecommenderPro*'s (a) Per-Recommendation dialog and (b) POIs rating dialog.

---

[1] https://developer.foursquare.com/

3.4 The Recommendation Algorithm

The application used a popularity-based RS algorithm. Since the users answer the question *"Are you available?"* before seeing the recommended POIs, the recommending algorithm is not the main focus of the current work; rather, we focus on modeling the correct timings for recommendations. When attempting to generate a recommendation, the RS gathers all POIs that are at most 500 meters away from the user's current location. If less than five POIs are found, the RS will extend its search and will gather all POIs that are at most 1,000 meters away from the user's current location. In order to generate popularity-based recommendations, the RS granted each POI with a rate that reflected the amount of "Like" and "Check-in" actions it received, relative to the other candidate POIs. It then randomized three POIs, taking under consideration the POI's rate as its probability to be chosen. In order to handle the cold-start problem, we allowed the RS to recommend randomly during the first two weeks. During this period of time participants were exposed to, and subsequently rated, a large number of the filtered POIs (1,186 of them), enabling us to generate popularity-based recommendations during the third week of the user study.

3.5 Context Features

As mentioned above, the application periodically collects a set of sensors. This set consists of the nine following sensors: accelerometer, Wi-Fi, battery, light, orientation, magnetic field, gravity, audio level, and location. Additional information was derived as well, such as the sampling timestamp, day of the week, time of day, activity recognition, screen-log, call-log, and traffic statistics of certain applications installed on the user's mobile device (i.e. Facebook, WhatsApp, Waze, Chrome, Moovit, and Ynet). Raw data collected by the sensors and the additional information listed above were aggregated, analyzed and engineered to generate 479 features. These features define the user's context. Due to limited space, we will only give limited examples of the feature processing.

Accelerometer, magnetic field, orientation, and gravity are sensors that produce raw data in the form of a 3D axis and sample nearly 100 records per second for each axis. We calculated the average, median, standard deviation, correlation, minimum and maximum values, the range, the first and third quarters, RMS, and entropy for each axis. From the timestamp, we calculated the time of the week (midweek, weekend) and time of day (dawn, morning, afternoon, night). We also added information regarding the device's screen mode. To do so, we constantly sampled the timestamps in which the user turned on and off her mobile device's screen and the action that was made (i.e. "screen turned on" and "screen turned off"). Our *screen log* kept this type of information for the last 20 minutes at any point of time. The screen-log was processed to three features. The first feature indicates the percent of the time the screen was on during the last 20 minutes, the second was analyzed during the last 10 minutes and the third was analyzed for the past minute.

4. METHOD

RecommenderPro was installed and used by the users for three weeks, followed by an offline analysis of the collected data. The data collected consists of 22,697 records, each one describing a labeled user context. 6,158 of the contexts were labeled as "now," 2,363 were labeled as "not now" and 14,176 were labeled as "not available." For the work discussed in this paper, we treated "not available" actions as "not now." We split the data by the record's timestamp using 80% of it for training and the remaining 20% for testing. We aimed to train a model that would be able to classify a test-set context as "now" or "not now." First, we used the training set for feature-selection. We performed Gain Ratio (GR) feature-selection [9], which granted a rate higher than zero to 413

features, and Correlation Feature Selection (CFS) [7], that chose four features only. We decided to examine the following sets of features: (1) the top 50 features rated by GR, (2) the top 30 features rated by GR, and (3) the features chosen by CFS. The features that dominated mostly in these feature-sets are Wi-Fi, screen-log, and orientation.

We generated a personal classification model for each user, training it by using data collected only by her own mobile device. A single non-personal model was generated for all of the users and thus trained using the entire training set. Both types of models were trained using RandomForest learning algorithm. Preliminary evaluations of these models' performances showed that the personal model might be more accurate in some cases and the non-personal in others. These results led us to generate a third type of model, a hybrid one, which uses both the personal and the non-personal models. This model was built gradually. First, we generated a duplication of the training set, but for this version, the class-attribute was not "now" or "not now," but the type of model that better classified the context: either "personal" or "non-personal." Specifically, we classified each context in the training set using the user's personal model and using the non-personal model. We then let each one of the classification models generate a distribution that was composed of probabilities for each one of the possible classifications, "now" and "not now." If the personal model generated a distribution that was closer to the context's actual classification, the context was labeled as "personal," otherwise, it was labeled as "non-personal." At this point, we trained a learning algorithm and generated a model that was meant to classify whether a given context is better classified using the user's personal classification model or the non-personal model, and finally, used the chosen model for the "now" or "not now" classification. To conclude, given a user's context for classification, the suggested hybrid model will first decide whether it is better classified by the user's personal model or the non-personal model and then use the chosen model to classify the context either as "now" or "not now."

The measure used to evaluate the classification models described above was the models' precision for a version of the top N recommendations task. We let each model classify contexts in the test set and choose the top N contexts that are classified as most likely to be "now" contexts, for each user. Precision was evaluated for each model type, using the features-sets detailed above for different N values (N=5, 10, 15, 20, 25).

5. EVALUATIONS AND RESULTS

Precision for the different values of N was evaluated using the suggested models for top 50 features rated by GR (Figure 2a), top 30 features rated by GR (see Figure 2b) and features selected by CFS (see Figure 2c). The precisions presented in this section are the average precision for the different users that had at least one context in the test set labeled "now" (81 users).

One can see that as the amount of features increases, all models managed to achieve higher precisions. Lower values of N result in substantial advantage for the non-personal models compared to the personal models, for two of the examined features-sets (features selected by GR). This advantage fades as the value of N increases. For these two feature-sets, the suggested hybrid model managed to perform better than both the personal and the non-personal models for all examined values of N but N=5, for which it performed second best after the non-personal model. For the third feature-set (features selected by CFS) the hybrid model performed better than the non-personal model, alongside the personal model, for every examined value of N. Similar trends were seen for additional learning algorithms, i.e. Bagging and Vote (Ensemble of J48 and Decision Stump). These results are excluded from this paper, due to limited space.

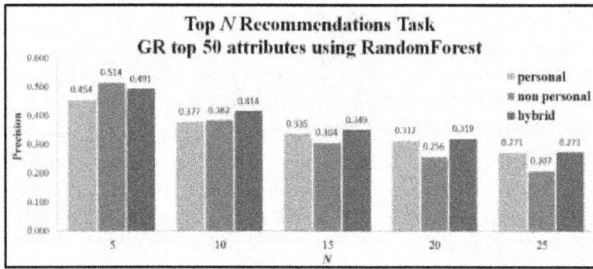

(a)

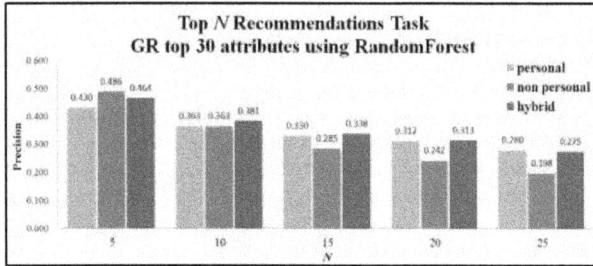

(b)

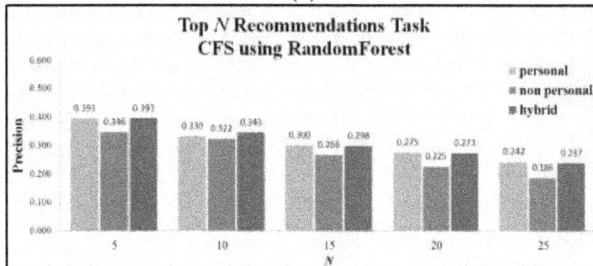

(c)

Figure 2: Average precision for the top *N* recommendations task using personal, non-personal and hybrid models for (a) the 50 most highly rated features by GR, (b) the 30 most highly rated features by GR and (c) the features selected by CFS.

6. CONCLUSIONS AND FUTURE WORK

In this paper, we suggested the integration of a pre-recommending phase in proactive RSs that classifies users' contexts as either suitable or unsuitable for any recommendation. We tested three types of models for such a task: (1) a personal model, (2) a non-personal model and (3) a hybrid model combining the first two. While testing the three models' precisions for different values of *N*, given a top *N* recommendations task, we found that the hybrid model was able to achieve better results than the personal and the non-personal models. A single exception was noticed for the lowest value of *N* among two of the examined data sets, for which the non-personal model tended to perform better. It is worth mentioning that even though our test set did not contain new users, a significant advantage of the hybrid model is that it could easily choose the non-personal model for such cases and thus be able to handle new users as well as familiar ones.

We are currently conducting the final part of our user study, using the same users that participated in the first part, detailed in the current work. We used the data collected in order to generate models that are currently used to classify, online, whether a certain context is suitable for a recommendation. Meaning, the application decides whether it should recommend or not and responds accordingly, online. We hope to be able to show that recommending only at times that seem appropriate can positively affect the accuracy of the RS.

7. REFERENCES

[1] Adamczyk, P. and Bailey, B. 2004. If not now, when?: the effects of interruption at different moments within task execution. *Proceedings of the SIGCHI conference on Human factors in computing systems. ACM.*

[2] Bader, R., Neufeld, E., Woerndl, W. and Prinz, V. 2011. Context-aware POI recommendations in an automotive scenario using multi-criteria decision making methods. *Proceedings of the 2011 Workshop on Context-awareness in Retrieval and Recommendation. ACM.*

[3] Baltrunas, L., Ludwig, B., Peer, S. and Ricci, F. 2012. Context relevance assessment and exploitation in mobile recommender systems. *Workshops at the Twenty-Sixth AAAI Conference on Artificial Intelligence.*

[4] Bellotti, V., Begole, B. and Chi, E. 2008. Activity-based serendipitous recommendations with the Magitti mobile leisure guide. *Proceedings of the SIGCHI Conference on Human Factors in Computing Systems. ACM.*

[5] Böhmer, M., Bauer, G. and Krüger, A. 2010. Exploring the design space of context-aware recommender systems that suggest mobile applications. *2nd Workshop on Context-Aware Recommender Systems.*

[6] Dey, A. 2001. Understanding and using context. *Personal and ubiquitous computing.*

[7] Hall, M. 1999. Correlation-based feature selection for machine learning. *Diss. The University of Waikato.*

[8] Hong, J., Suh, E.H., Kim, J. and Kim, S. 2009. Context-aware system for proactive personalized service based on context history. *Expert Systems with Applications.* 36, 4 (2009), 7448–7457.

[9] Karegowda, A. 2010. Comparative study of attribute selection using gain ratio and correlation based feature selection. *International Journal of Information Technology and Knowledge Management 2.2.*

[10] Kwapisz, J., Weiss, G. and Moore, S. 2011. Activity recognition using cell phone accelerometers. *ACM SigKDD Explorations Newsletter 12.2*, 74–82.

[11] Lerchenmueller, B. and Woerndl, W. 2012. Inference of User Context from GPS Logs for Proactive Recommender Systems. *Workshops at the Twenty-Sixth AAAI Conference on Artificial Intelligence.*

[12] McFarlane, D. and Latorella, K. 2002. The scope and importance of human interruption in human-computer interaction design. *Human-Computer Interaction.*

[13] Parsons, J., Ralph, P. and Gallagher, K. 2004.Using viewing time to infer user preference in recommender systems.

[14] Setten, M. Van, Pokraev, S. and Koolwaaij, J. 2004. Context-aware recommendations in the mobile tourist application COMPASS. *Adaptive hypermedia and adaptive web-based systems.*

[15] Woerndl, W. and Huebner, J. 2011. A model for proactivity in mobile, context-aware recommender systems. *Proceedings of the fifth ACM conference on Recommender systems. ACM.*

[16] Zheng, Y., Chen, Y., Li, Q., Xie, X. and Ma, W.-Y. 2010. Understanding transportation modes based on GPS data for web applications. *ACM Transactions on the Web.* 4.1, 1-36.

[17] Zimmermann, A., Lorenz, A. and Oppermann, R. 2007. An operational definition of context. *Modeling and using context.* 558–571.

POI Recommendation: Towards Fused Matrix Factorization with Geographical and Temporal Influences

Jean-Benoît Griesner
Télécom ParisTech
UMR CNRS LTCI, Paris,
France
griesner@telecom-
paristech.fr

Talel Abdessalem
Télécom ParisTech, UMR
CNRS LTCI, Paris, France
School of Computing, National
University of Singapore
UMI CNRS IPAL
talel.abdessalem@telecom-
paristech.fr

Hubert Naacke
Sorbonne Universités
UPMC Univ Paris 06, LIP6
Paris, France
Hubert.Naacke@lip6.fr

ABSTRACT

Providing personalized point-of-interest (POI) recommendation has become a major issue with the rapid emergence of location-based social networks (LBSNs). Unlike traditional recommendation approaches, the LBSNs application domain comes with significant geographical and temporal dimensions. Moreover most of traditional recommendation algorithms fail to cope with the specific challenges implied by these two dimensions. Fusing geographical and temporal influences for better recommendation accuracy in LBSNs remains unexplored, as far as we know. We depict how matrix factorization can serve POI recommendation, and propose a novel attempt to integrate both geographical and temporal influences into matrix factorization. Specifically we present GeoMF-TD, an extension of geographical matrix factorization with temporal dependencies. Our experiments on a real dataset shows up to 20% benefit on recommendation precision.

Categories and Subject Descriptors

H.3.3 [**Information Search and Retrieval**]: Retrieval models; Information filtering—*matrix factorization; kernel density estimation; accuracy measures*

1. INTRODUCTION

The last years have witnessed the emergence of location-based social networks (LBSNs) such as Foursquare, Flickr, Weibo, Facebook places and so on. The success of these LBSNs has promoted the advent of new forms of online services. One of the main goals of these services is to offer to users the possibility to interact with each other and to explore new sets of points-of-interest (or POIs) by sharing their personal experiences and feelings on POIs they have visited in the past.

RecSys '15 September 16 - 20, 2015, Vienna, Austria
© 2015 ACM. ISBN 978-1-4503-3692-5/15/09 ...$15.00
DOI: http://dx.doi.org/10.1145/2792838.2799679.

By collecting the mobility records of users, LBSNs constitute a rich and large-scale check-in data source. These data considered as an abundant implicit feedback of the travel experiences of the user, give a significant opportunity to improve POI recommendation performances. POI recommendation is the task of making personalized recommendations of the best POIs fitting the user preferences. Today this task has become an essential component of the LBSN domain since it allows users to have better user experiences, and POI owners as well to get more targeted customers. The traditional way to realize this task is to use classical collaborative filtering (CF) algorithms. CF algorithms are usually distributed into model-based and memory-based approaches. They derive from the check-in data the classical *user-POI rating* matrix in which a rating corresponds to the visit frequency of a user at a given POI.

A recent study showed [7] that weighted matrix factorization was the most adapted method to CF problems with implicit feedback. This method has been exploited and augmented by the authors of [9] to include the geographical influence of POI by the modeling of the spatial clustering phenomenon [14, 15] directly into the factorization process. However LBSN data comes with much more than only geographical information. Notably we have also access to the recorded timestamp of each check-in.

Our work aims at integrating time dependencies into geographical matrix factorization. In this paper, we investigate the idea of augmenting matrix factorization model with both geographical and temporal influences. This leads to the GeoMF-TD algorithm we present in the following.

2. RELATED WORK

Many methods have been proposed to solve POI recommendation. Most of these approaches try to adapt traditional recommendation algorithms to the specific problem of POI recommendation. One important line of research includes matrix factorization models. Matrix factorization techniques have demonstrated since the Netflix challenge [8] to be one of the most accurate recommendation methods many previous works use [2, 12]. Zhang et al. in [16] have proposed Collaborative Location Activity Filtering (CLAF) algorithm for generic recommendation. CLAF is a collective matrix factorization close to the method presented by Singh et al. in [13] based on the exploitation of the correlations existing between the features of the locations and the POIs.

Differently Regularized Matrix Factorization presented in [1] apply CF personalized methods on dimensionally reduced user-POI matrices aiming at minimizing squared regularized errors. In [11] Sattari et al. proposed Improve Feature Combination (IFC), which is based on an extended matrix factorization model that integrates additional data resources before applying Singular Value Decomposition technique to the extended model. It has been proven in several studies that IFC performs better than CLAF in terms of prediction accuracy.

Since each POI comes with a significant geographical dimension, many works have tried to integrate this geographical information into the recommendation model. Recently Ye et al. showed in [14] how to integrate geographical influence with classical CF approaches. More precisely Ye et al. have studied the geographical influence of POI assuming a power-law distribution of the visited POIs. On another hand, Cheng et al. [2] have recently proposed a multi-center gaussian model as a model of the spatial clustering phenomenon. Differently Zhang et al. in [15] proposed a personalized fusion framework based on kernel density estimation of the distances distribution between POIs of each user.

In addition to the geographical dimension, the temporal dimension is another important factor leveraging the accuracy of the model. Exploring temporal dimension into matrix factorization is not a new idea. Recently in [4] Gao et al. have proposed a location recommendation framework with temporal effects (LRT). Specifically they showed how to model two main temporal properties of data (i.e. non uniformness and consecutiveness) with matrix factorization. The experiments conducted showed that LRT outperforms traditional recommendation algorithms.

3. POI RECOMMENDATION IN LBSNS

Let $\mathbf{u} = \{u_1, u_2, ..., u_m\} \subset U^m$ be a subset of users and $\mathbf{p} = \{p_1, p_2, ..., p_n\} \subset P^n$ a subset of POIs. Then let $\mathbf{C} \in \mathbb{R}^{m \times n}$ be a user-POI matrix containing m users and n POIs. Value $c_{u,j}$ in $\mathbf{C}$ refers to the visit frequency of user u to the POI i.

3.1 Weighted Matrix Factorization

Basically the goal of matrix factorization is to approximate matrix $\mathbf{C}$ by the product of two matrices $\mathbf{P} \in \mathbb{R}^{m \times k}$, and $\mathbf{Q} \in \mathbb{R}^{n \times k}$ of latent factors with dimension $k \ll \min(m, n)$ by solving the following classical optimization problem,

$$\min_{\mathbf{P},\mathbf{Q}} \left\| \mathbf{C} - \mathbf{P}\mathbf{Q}^T \right\|^2 + \gamma \left(\|\mathbf{P}\|^2 + \|\mathbf{Q}\|^2 \right) \quad (1)$$

with γ a non-negative parameter to avoid overfitting by controling the capability of $\mathbf{P}$ and $\mathbf{Q}$. Then it becomes possible to approximate the missing value $\widetilde{c_{u,j}}$ in $\mathbf{C}$ by computing the inner product between corresponding latent factors $\widetilde{c_{u,j}} = \mathbf{P}_u \mathbf{Q}_j^T$. However, the application domain of LBSNs is different from traditional recommendation domains. Indeed the check-in datasets in LBSNs provide only indication of *confidence* but no information about *preferences* of users. This property refers to the recommendation problems with *implicit feedback*. Specifically Hu et al. have proven in [7] that weighted matrix factorization (WMF) gives the best results with implicit feedback datasets. Weighted matrix factorization takes into account of the asymmetry existing between *confidence* and *preference* and creates two new vari-

ables for formalizing this asymmetry. Then WMF turns the problem of Eq(1) into the following new optimization problem,

$$\min_{\mathbf{P},\mathbf{Q}} \left\| \mathbf{W} \odot \left(\mathbf{R} - \mathbf{P}\mathbf{Q}^T \right) \right\|^2 + \gamma \left(\|\mathbf{P}\|^2 + \|\mathbf{Q}\|^2 \right) \quad (2)$$

where $\odot$ is the element-wise matrices multiplication (i.e. the Hadamard product) and where the only differences with Eq (1) is the presence of the matrix $\mathbf{W}$, and the binary 0/1 matrix $\mathbf{R}$ whose each entry $r_{u,i}$ indicates if user u has visited POI i. The idea of WMF is to assume a minimum confidence for all POI, visited or not. This minimum confidence is encoded within the $\mathbf{W}$ matrix, setted as follows,

$$w_{u,i} = \begin{cases} 1 + \alpha(c_{u,i}) & \text{if } c_{u,i} > 0 \\ 1 & \text{otherwise} \end{cases} \quad (3)$$

where $\alpha()$ is a monotonically increasing function.

3.2 Modeling Geographical Influence

The modeling of geographical influence for POI recommendation in LBSNs has been widely studied in previous works [14, 2, 15, 10]. Recently Lian et al. in [9] have proposed a geographical matrix factorization (GeoMF) to integrate this influence directly into the factorization model of WMF. The idea of the authors was to distinguish for each user the unvisited but interesting POIs among the negative ones. The intuition is that if a user visits a POI without visiting the other closely located POIs then these "ignored" POIs may not be interesting enough for the user. Consequently these POIs become *negative* for the factorization model. This approach divides the space into L even grids $\mathbb{L} = \{g_1, g_2, ..., g_L\}$ and computes for each POI its influence area onto each one of these L grids based on the normal distribution of distances. Specifically they augmented the traditional matrix of latent factors $\mathbf{P}$ and $\mathbf{Q}$ with two matrices of latent geographical factors $\mathbf{X} \in \mathbb{R}^{m \times L}$ and $\mathbf{Y} \in \mathbb{R}^{n \times L}$. With these new latent factors, Eq(2) is modified as follows,

$$\min_{\mathbf{P},\mathbf{Q},\mathbf{X}} \left\| \mathbf{W} \odot \left(\mathbf{R} - \mathbf{P}\mathbf{Q}^T - \mathbf{X}\mathbf{Y}^T \right) \right\|^2 + \gamma \left(\|\mathbf{P}\|^2 + \|\mathbf{Q}\|^2 \right) + \lambda \|\mathbf{X}\|^2 \quad (4)$$

where λ controls the sparsity constraint over the mobility behavior of each user through the L grids. A row $\mathbf{x}_u$ of $\mathbf{X}$ refers to the activities areas of user u i.e. the distribution of his visit frequencies in each grid g_l of the map, while a row $\mathbf{y}_i$ of $\mathbf{Y}$ refers to the influence area of POI i. More precisely we compute for each POI i and for each grid g_l the gaussian geographical influence i has on g_l:

$$\mathbf{y}_i^l = \frac{1}{\sigma} K\left(\frac{d(i,l)}{\sigma}\right) \quad (5)$$

where $K()$ is the standard normal distribution and σ the standard deviation. With this augmented geographical model we get the recommendation ranking score for user u and POI i as follows,

$$\widetilde{c_{u,i}} = \mathbf{P}_u \mathbf{Q}_i^T + \mathbf{X}_u \mathbf{Y}_i^T \quad (6)$$

One of the most significant advantage of this approach is that it encompasses both preferences of user from latent factors and preferences from geographical factors.

4. GEOMF WITH TIME DEPENDENCIES

The GeoMF model assumes that the space is an isotropic homogeneous space without physical constraints. Especially this model assumes that the influence area of each POI follows a normal distribution fixed in advance and only based on distances over space. However the influence areas of two distinct POIs can be very different in reality by considering different parameters other than the distances. Notably the temporal effects in POIs visit sequences play also a significant role [4]. Particularly these effects can reflect that a POI j can be in the influence area of another POI i but not being really negative.

Following the GeoMF approach, our basic idea is to integrate these temporal influences into the GeoMF model. Actually, we propose to modify the values of the influence area of each POI i through the grid $g_{l \in \mathbb{N}^L}$ to take into account the time spent by a user to go from the POI i to the other POIs collocated in g_l. More precisely, for each POI i, we compute the average time that each user spend to reach j (j is in g_l) from i. We compute this for every user that has at least one check-in at i and another (more recent) check-in at j into g_l. Then, we average the per-user values to get a single value related to POI i. Let $t_i^{g_l}$ be the average time computed between i and collocated POIs existing in g_l. We introduce temporal coefficients $\theta_l(t_i^{g_l})$ as follows,

$$\theta_l(t_i^{g_l}) = \begin{cases} \alpha * \mathbf{y}_i^l & \text{if } t_i^{g_l} > \sigma^i \text{ and } \mathbf{y}_i^l < 0.1 \\ \mathbf{y}_i^l & \text{otherwise} \end{cases} \quad (7)$$

where σ^i refers to the standard variation of time intervals for POI i and $\mathbf{y}_i^l$ has been computed from Eq(5). Then we fuse these coefficients with influence vector $\mathbf{y}_i$ for POI i,

$$\mathbf{y}_i = [\theta_1(t_i^{g_1}), ..., \theta_L(t_i^{g_L})] \quad (8)$$

The idea of these temporal coefficients is to decrease the *negativeness* of potential negative POIs when no user has checked-in them during a certain time. That is why these coefficients let unchanged the influence area value when this value is low. We use these coefficients as a fusion output between geographical gaussian influence over space, and temporal dependencies existing into the dataset.

5. EXPERIMENTS

In our experiments, we compared the accuracy of our approach with GeoMF. This section describes the dataset we used, the evaluation metrics we chose, and the results we obtained.

5.1 Dataset and Experimental Setup

We evaluated the algorithms on check-ins crawled from Gowalla[1] and publicly available [3]. Gowalla was a famous LBSN closed in 2012. Gowalla dataset has already been used in several works on POI recommendation [2, 3, 15]. Table 1 presents the main statistics concerning this LBSN. In order to reduce matrix sparsity in the dataset we keep only users with at least 50 check-ins and for practical purposes we use only check-ins localized in France. Figure 1 presents the spatial distribution of check-ins over the France area. Finally it remains 161 users, 7697 distincts POIs for 12418 distinct check-ins, which is very few but enough for an initial evaluation. Then we organize this dataset as a user-POI matrix.

[1]The Gowalla check-ins dataset can be downloaded here: http://snap.stanford.edu/data/loc-gowalla.html

Number of users	196,591
Number of check-in	6,442,890
Number of social links	950,327
Matrix density	2.9×10^{-5}
Average No. of visited POIs per user	37.18
Average No. of check-ins per POI	3.11

Table 1: Statistics of the Gowalla data set

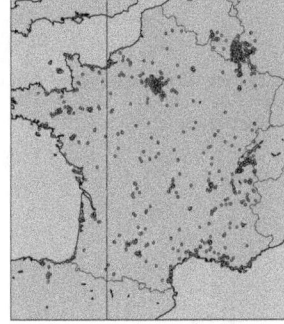

Figure 1: Check-in distribution from Gowalla users during 21 months of the most visited POIs in France.

5.2 Evaluation Metrics

It is traditional for each user $u_i \in U$ to mark off between 20% and 40% of all POIs he has checked-in in the past for testing, while the rest remains for training the model. Basically a recommendation algorithm estimates a ranking score for each candidate POI $i_{cand} \in P$ and returns the top-k highest ranked POIs $p_1, p_2, ..., p_k \in P^k$ as recommendation results for the targeted user. Then we evaluate the recommendation accuracy by finding out how many recommended POIs are effectively present into the test set of this targeted user. More precisely we compute *precision@N* and *recall@N*. The former refers to the ratio of recovered POIs to the N recommended POIs, while the latter refers to the ratio of recovered POIs to the set of previously visited POIs as follows,

$$precision@N = \frac{\sum_{u_i \in U} |TopN(u_i) \cap L(u_i)|}{\sum_{u_i \in U} |TopN(u_i)|} \quad (9)$$

$$recall@N = \frac{\sum_{u_i \in U} |TopN(u_i) \cap L(u_i)|}{\sum_{u_i \in U} |L(u_i)|} \quad (10)$$

where $TopN(u_i)$ represents the set of top-N POIs recommended to user u_i and $L(u_i)$ represents the set of POIs from the test set checked-ins by u_i. We have evaluated *precision@N* and *recall@N* with N ranging from 1 to 20 for precision, and from 1 to 100 for recall. We provide the results we obtained on the average after cross-validation with 5 folds in the next section.

5.3 Results and Discussions

For comparison purpose, we implemented the GeoMF approach using the LibRec Java library[2]. Figure 2 and Figure 3

[2]LibRec library can be downloaded here: http://www.librec.net/

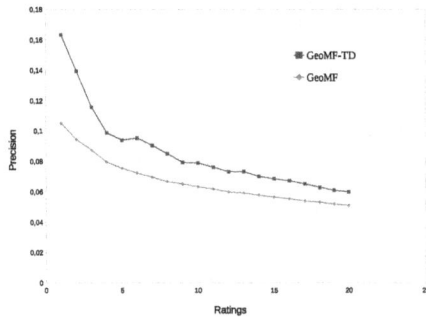

Figure 2: Precision comparison between GeoMF and GeoMF-TD

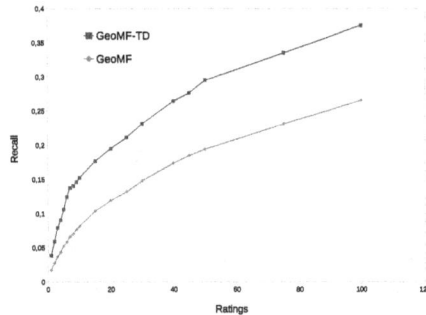

Figure 3: Recall comparison between GeoMF and GeoMF-TD

depict a comparative analysis of respectively the *precision@N* and the *recall@N* results of GeoMF and our approach (GeoMF-TD) with N ranging from 1 to 20 for the precision, and with N ranging from 1 to 100 for the recall. As expected the temporal coefficients we introduce allowed to take into account the temporal dependencies existing between POIs and thus improve the global accuracy. Figures 2 and 3 show an average benefit of 60% for recall and 20% for precision. This overall performance comparison does not integrate the study of the influence of the threshold parameter, but gives promising results for the future.

6. CONCLUSIONS AND FUTURE WORKS

In this paper, we have focused on the problem of POI recommendation in LBSNs. Specifically we have investigated matrix factorization algorithms based on geographical influence. Our goal was to try to leverage the factorization model of GeoMF by considering the temporal influences of POIs checked-ins. To this end we have provided GeoMF-TD algorithm as a first proposal of an extension of GeoMF and we have presented accuracy comparisons. Our experimental evaluation shows that GeoMF-TD presents better accuracy performances than GeoMF.

Considering the preferences of the user will change over time, a future line of work we should investigate will be to take into account of the online integration of user's preferences changes and to capture this evolution into our model. This problem refers to the recommendation *dynamicity* challenge widely studied in recent studies [5, 6]. Additionally, one of our future goal will be to include POI categories into the model, and to cope with the scalability issues.

7. ACKNOWLEDGMENTS

This work has been partly funded by the Télécom Paris-Tech Research Chair on Big Data and Market Insights.

8. REFERENCES

[1] B. Berjani and T. Strufe. A recommendation system for spots in location-based online social networks. SNS '11, 2011.

[2] C. Cheng, H. Yang, I. King, and M. R. Lyu. Fused matrix factorization with geographical and social influence in location-based social networks. AAAI, 2012.

[3] E. Cho, S. A. Myers, and J. Leskovec. Friendship and mobility: User movement in location-based social networks. KDD '11, 2011.

[4] H. Gao, J. Tang, X. Hu, and H. Liu. Exploring temporal effects for location recommendation on location-based social networks. RecSys '13, 2013.

[5] M. Gueye, T. Abdessalem, and H. Naacke. Technique de factorisation multi-biais pour des recommandations dynamiques. EGC'13, 2013.

[6] M. Gueye, T. Abdessalem, and H. Naacke. Dynamic recommender system : using cluster-based biases to improve the accuracy of the predictions. *Advances in Knowledge Discovery and Management - Volume 5*, 2015.

[7] Y. Hu, Y. Koren, and C. Volinsky. Collaborative filtering for implicit feedback datasets. ICDM '08, 2008.

[8] Y. Koren, R. Bell, and C. Volinsky. Matrix factorization techniques for recommender systems. 2009.

[9] D. Lian, C. Zhao, X. Xie, G. Sun, E. Chen, and Y. Rui. Geomf: Joint geographical modeling and matrix factorization for point-of-interest recommendation. KDD '14, 2014.

[10] B. Liu and H. Xiong. Point-of-interest recommendation in location based social networks with topic and location awareness. ICDM'13, 2013.

[11] M. Sattari, M. Manguoglu, I. H. Toroslu, P. Symeonidis, P. Senkul, and Y. Manolopoulos. Geo-activity recommendations by using improved feature combination. UbiComp '12, 2012.

[12] H. Shan and A. Banerjee. Generalized probabilistic matrix factorizations for collaborative filtering. ICDM '10, 2010.

[13] A. P. Singh and G. J. Gordon. Relational learning via collective matrix factorization. KDD '08, 2008.

[14] M. Ye, P. Yin, W.-C. Lee, and D.-L. Lee. Exploiting geographical influence for collaborative point-of-interest recommendation. SIGIR '11, 2011.

[15] J.-D. Zhang and C.-Y. Chow. igslr: Personalized geo-social location recommendation: A kernel density estimation approach. SIGSPATIAL'13, 2013.

[16] V. W. Zheng, Y. Zheng, X. Xie, and Q. Yang. Collaborative location and activity recommendations with gps history data. WWW '10, 2010.

The Recommendation Game [*]

Using a Game-with-a-Purpose to Generate Recommendation Data

Sam Banks[†], Rachael Rafter, Barry Smyth
Insight Centre for Data Analytics
School of Computer Science
University College Dublin
Dublin, Ireland
firstname.lastname@insight-centre.org

ABSTRACT

This paper describes a casual Facebook game to capture recommendation data as a side-effect of gameplay. We show how this data can be used to make successful recommendations as part of a live-user trial.

Categories and Subject Descriptors

H.3.3 [**Information Search and Retrieval**]: Information Filtering; H.3.5 [**Online Information Services**]: Web-Based Services

Keywords

Recommender Systems; Games-with-a-Purpose; Human Computation; Crowdsourcing

1. INTRODUCTION

Recommender systems suggest items to users. Most rely on user preferences, such as past ratings [1]. Many use matrix factorization methods to find hidden patterns within these preferences [9]. Yet others harness inter-user similarity to identify groups of like-minded users [2]. And some leverage social network data to infer trust relationships between users [6]. Collecting this information at scale is the subject of much research. Many approaches have been considered, from using explicit feedback such as transaction histories to inferring interest from implicit signals such as read-times or sharing [8]. More recently, crowdsourcing ideas have been considered (e.g. [11]); see also *CrowdRec* workshops[1]. In this paper we consider a crowdsourcing approach by developing a so-called game-with-a-purpose (GWAP) for soliciting recommendation data as a by-product of gameplay.

GWAPs are games that are simple and fun to play with gameplay contributing to some secondary problem solving goal; e.g. the ESP Game, arguably the original of the species, invites pairs of players to guess words for images [15] to improve indexing in image search. Other games have been developed to index audio and video [5,10,14]. GWAPs have also been developed for object segmentation [12] and even protein folding [3]. The power of a GWAP stems from its ability to attract many players who collectively contribute to a greater goal through their gameplay. Can GWAPs also be used for recommender systems? This question has been asked by [16] in the context of the Curator system, a game-with-a-purpose for recommending collections of items that go together; see also [4, 7]. In this paper we focus on a complementary set of recommendation matters related to user-user tie strength and user-item relevance.

2. THE RECOMMENDATION GAME

Our game is a Facebook app wherein a player p is tasked with matching a set of movies with their friends $Friends(p)$. We know movies each friend likes ($Likes(f)$) from their FaceBook 'likes'. Figure 1 shows the game in action. Movie posters float across the screen, becoming more erratic as the game progresses. By dragging a movie m to a friend $f \in Friends(p)$, player p *matches* m with f ($match(p, m, f)$) if they believe that f will like m. The more matches a player generates the more we learn their beliefs about the preferences of their friends; the set of matches that p generates is $Matches(p)$ (Equation 1). But how can we decide if these matches are correct? And, if we can decide, then doesn't this confirm recommendation data that we already know?

$$Matches(p) = \bigcup_{\forall f \in Friends(p)} \{(p, m, f) : match(p, m, f)\}$$

$$(1)$$

2.1 Resolving the Matching Paradox

For a match we either know that f likes m (a *known match*) or we have no such knowledge (an *unknown match*). Either way, we can infer recommendation data as follows.

2.1.1 From Known Matches to Tie Strength

In the case that f is known to like m ($m \in Likes(f)$) then we learn something about p's understanding of f's (movie)

[*]This work is supported by Science Foundation Ireland through the Insight Centre for Data Analytics under grant number SFI/12/RC/2289.

[†]Sam Banks completed this work as a final-year Computer Science student in University College Dublin.

[1]http://crowdrecworkshop.org/

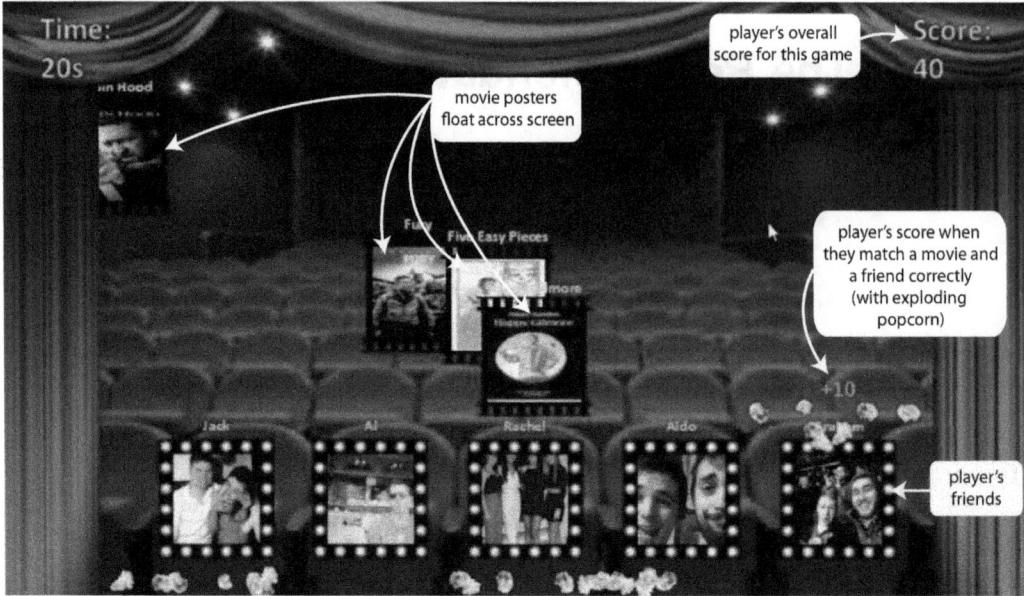

Figure 1: The Recommendation Game in action.

interests. The more such known matches, the better p seems to know f; useful recommendation data in itself. For example, we can estimate this as the proportion of known matches that p generates for f relative to all matches p generates for f in a given set of games; see Equations 2 – 4.

$$FriendMatches(p, f) =$$
$$\{(p', m', f') \in Matches(p) : p = p' \wedge f = f'\} \quad (2)$$

$$KnownMatches(p, f) =$$
$$\{(p, m, f) \in FriendMatches(p, f) : m \in Likes(f)\} \quad (3)$$

$$knows(p, f) = \frac{|KnownMatches(p, f)|}{|FriendMatches(p, f)|} \quad (4)$$

2.1.2 Unknown Matches → Recommendations

Even when we have no information about f's interest in m ($m \notin Likes(f)$) this does not mean it is a poor match; $Likes(f)$ is not exhaustive. And the fact that p assigns the match suggests that p believes that f will be interested in m, establishing m as a plausible, novel recommendation candidate for f. If other players also match m with f then this strengthens the possible interest of f in m. Equation 5 captures this as an interest score based on the number of players who have matched some unknown m with f, and their tie strength with f.

$$interest(m, f) = \sum_{\forall p:match(p,m,f) \wedge m \notin Likes(f)} knows(p, f) \quad (5)$$

2.2 Game Mechanics

The game is implemented as a Facebook app to gain access to the social graph and likes of players; this way friends can be chosen and (known) matches can be verified. The game has been developed in PHP and is responsible for storing all player data, friendship links, movie data, and game

sessions. The game uses the Rotten Tomatoes API to collect additional movie data (poster graphics, trailers etc.) for the purpose of enhancing gameplay. On the client-side the front-end is written in Javascript using jQuery and some task specific libraries for animation and image manipulation.

Game mechanics are simple and enjoyable. At the start of the game the player p is presented with a subset of friends; currently 5 friends are picked who have at least 10 movie likes. Each game comprises 18 movies which are chosen from a mixture of the friends' profiles/likes and the Rotten Tomatoes most popular movie list. This ensures a mix of known movies, with which to validate matches and infer tie strength, plus unknown movies to generate novel recommendation candidates.

During the game a graphic of a movie's poster floats across the screen following a particular trajectory and speed. As the game continues the screen becomes more cluttered and the trajectory of movies more erratic thereby making the matching process more frenetic and challenging. And when a player matches a movie by dragging its icon over a friend's avatar, the player is rewarded by an audio and graphical flourish and a score.

Scoring is more challenging than might first appear. It seems intuitive to award a score if the player matches a known (liked) movie with a friend. But if they match an unknown movie should they miss out, given how these matches are potentially valuable, novel recommendation candidates? If we only score known matches then players may avoid making more novel matches. And what if a novel match has been made often during other games? How should it effect the scoring?

In the end we chose the scoring metric shown in Equation 6 which combines scores for known and unknown matches; we set $\alpha = 0.5$ in this work but this could be adjusted to give more or less weight to each match type. This returns a score between up to 10 for each match. For example, if p matches m with f, such that $m \in Likes(f)$, and 3 other players have made the same match before, then p will receive a score 6.25. If on the other hand $m \notin Likes(f)$ and p is the first to make such a match then p receives a score of 5. There are no doubt many possible variations on this scoring metric that could (and should) be tested in the future.

$$score(p,m,f) =$$
$$10 \bullet \left(\alpha \bullet 1[m \in Likes(f)] + \frac{1 - \alpha}{1 + PastMatches(m,f)} \right) \quad (6)$$

3. EVALUATION

To test the data generated by gameplay we ran a small two-part, live-user trial based on 27 mutual friends and friends-of-friends; a mixture of male and female undergraduates and postgraduates. Participants acted as both players and friends during gameplay. During each game a subset of 5 friends was chosen at random for a given p; the number of friends per participant varied from 5 to 12. For each participant we also had an initial set of movie likes from Facebook (on average, 27 movies per participant).

3.1 Methodology

The evaluation took place in two phases. Phase 1 focused on collecting data by asking participants to play the game a few times; in fact players played an average of 9 games each, suggesting many found it at least somewhat enjoyable. On average 11.69 matches were made per game. These data were then used in phase 2 to generate recommendations for each of the 27 users. We generated 6 movie recommendations per user from 3 different recommendation strategies and asked each participant to rate all 18 recommendations as either satisfactory or unsatisfactory; a simple binary rating per movie. We were careful to interleave the order of recommendations from each strategy to avoid any positional bias.

3.2 Recommendation Strategies

As to the recommendation strategies used: we distinguish each in terms of the candidate items they consider for recommendation and how these are ranked to produce a *top-6* for the target user u_t, as follows.

3.2.1 Crowdsourced Recommendations (CS)

Here we rely purely on gameplay data to generate and rank our recommendations. The candidates are those movies matched with u_t (but unknown to u_t) by player-friends of u_t during gameplay; see Equation 7. These candidates are then ranked in terms of $interest(m, u_t)$ as per Equation 5.

$$CS\_Candidates(u_t) =$$
$$\bigcup_{\forall p \in Friends(u_t)} \{m : match(p,m,u_t) \wedge m \notin Likes(u_t)\}$$
$$(7)$$

Thus, movies that are often matched with u_t, by many players who know u_t's preferences well, will rank higher than movies less often matched with u_t by less familiar players.

3.2.2 Collaborative Filtering Recommendations (CF)

Next we implemented a version of collaborative filtering by choosing movies from the profiles (likes) of u_t's friends;

	Satisfaction	Diversity
CS	90%	21%
CF	79%	37%
CB	77%	50%

Table 1: Satisfaction and diversity results.

see Equation 8. Collaborative filtering usually ranks recommendations based on the similarity between u_t and the friends/neighbours from where they originate; similarity is usually based on some form of ratings correlation. In our small trial we instead use the $knows(f, u_t)$ metric as a proxy for user similarity and rank the candidates according to $interest(m, u_t)$. In this way the CS and the CF techniques differ primarily in the source of the candidates (gameplay vs. profiles, respectively).

$$CF\_Candidates(u_t) =$$
$$\bigcup_{\forall f \in Friends(u_t)} Likes(f) - Likes(u_t) \quad (8)$$

3.2.3 Content-based Recommendations (CB)

Finally, as a content-based strategy we used the Rotten Tomatoes API call, $movie\_similar(m)$, to obtain a set of 5 movies that are similar (based on meta-data) to each $m \in Likes(u_t)$. The candidate movies for u_t are the collection ($\bigoplus$)) of all movies returned by Rotten Tomatoes for each of the movies in $Likes(u_t)$.

$$CB\_Candidates(u_t) = \bigoplus_{\forall m \in Likes(u_t)} movie\_similar(m) \quad (9)$$

At recommendation time 6 content-based candidates are selected from these candidates at random. Since these collections may contain duplicates, if the same movies are returned by Rotten Tomatoes for different seeds, then this approach will tend to recommend movies that are more frequently represented in the candidate list, giving priority to movies that are considered similar to many of u_t's likes.

3.3 Results

Satisfaction results are shown in Figure 1 and indicate a benefit to the CS approach compared to CF or CB. 90% of users found the CS recommendations to be satisfactory compared to only 79% and 77% for CF and CB, respectively. This speaks to the quality of the recommendation data being created as part of the gameplay; remember the difference between CS and CF is only a matter of how the movies were sourced (gameplay vs. profiles).

It is also interesting to examine the diversity of recommendations made by the different approaches; diversity speaks to the ability of the recommender to offer the user more or less variety through its suggestions [13]. As a simple measure of diversity we compared the percentage of unique recommendations made by each of the 3 approaches in Figure 1. CS presents with lower levels of diversity than either CF or CB. Only 21% of the movies recommended by CS were unique compared to 37% and 50% for CF and CB.

One explanation for this is that the CS approach tends to skew towards popular movies because players recognise their posters more quickly and naturally gravitate towards these during gameplay. Moreover, because these movies are popular they may also be easier to match with friends leading to a greater likelihood that they will be liked, hence the improved satisfaction scores. The higher level of diversity using the CB approach on the other hand, can be partially attributed to the fact that it can draw recommendations from a larger pool of candidates.

It is a matter for future work to consider this relationship between satisfaction and diversity further. It may be possible to guide gameplay towards more novel items by manipulating the size and speed of items according to the item popularity. For example, perhaps unusual movies could be presented with a larger icon and/or a slower trajectory, making them more attractive gameplay targets; scoring could also be adapted with respect to inverse item popularity.

4. CONCLUSIONS

The purpose of this paper has been to explore the use of a GWAP to collect recommendation data as a side-effect of casual gameplay. We have implemented and tested a simple movie matching game and described the different types of recommendation data that we can collect from its gameplay. We have shown how this data can be useful in a recommendation context as part of a live-user trial. And, it should be noted that, as a practical matter, the approach is not limited to movie preferences because similar ideas could be used for many other types of items.

This work is of course limited in many ways. The system is a working prototype and the small scale of our evaluation offers little more than a proof-of-concept for what we are trying to achieve. Nevertheless we believe it serves as a first-step to highlight the potential for new ways to think about recommendation data and recommender systems while contributing to a growing interest in the role of crowdsourcing in recommender systems research.

5. REFERENCES

[1] G. Adomavicius and A. Tuzhilin. Toward the Next Generation of Recommender Systems: A Survey of the State-of-the-Art and Possible Extensions. *IEEE Transactions on Knowledge and Data Engineering*, 17(6):734–749, June 2005.

[2] G. K. Christian Desrosiers. A Comprehensive Survey of Neighborhood-based Recommendation Methods. In F. Ricci, L. Rokach, B. Shapira, and P. B. Kantor, editors, *Recommender Systems Handbook*, pages 107–144. 2011.

[3] S. Cooper, F. Khatib, A. Treuille, J. Barbero, J. Lee, M. Beenen, A. Leaver-Fay, D. Baker, Z. Popović, and F. Players. Predicting Protein Structures with a Multiplayer Online Game. *Nature*, 466(7307):756–760, 2010.

[4] A. Felfernig, M. Jeran, M. Stettinger, T. Absenger, T. Gruber, S. Haas, E. Kirchengast, M. Schwarz, L. Skofitsch, and T. Ulz. Human computation based acquisition of financial service advisory practices. In *Proceedings of the 1st International Workshop on Personalization & Recommender Systems in Financial Services, Graz, Austria, April 16, 2015.*, pages 27–34, 2015.

[5] R. Gligorov, M. Hildebrand, J. van Ossenbruggen, G. Schreiber, and L. Aroyo. On the Role of User-Generated Metadata in Audio Visual Collections. *Proceedings of the 6th International Conference on Knowledge Capture (K-CAP '11)*, pages 145–151, June 2011.

[6] J. Golbeck. In K. Stølen, W. H. Winsborough, F. Martinelli, and F. Massacci, editors, *Proceedings of the 4th International Conference on Trust Management (iTrust'06)*, pages 93–104, Pisa, Italy, May. Springer Berlin Heidelberg.

[7] S. Hacker and L. von Ahn. Matchin: eliciting user preferences with an online game. In *Proceedings of the 27th International Conference on Human Factors in Computing Systems, CHI 2009, Boston, MA, USA, April 4-9, 2009*, pages 1207–1216, 2009.

[8] D. Kelly and J. Teevan. Implicit Feedback for Inferring User Preference: A Bibliography. *ACM SIGIR Forum*, 37(2):18 – 28, 2003.

[9] Y. Koren, R. Bell, and C. Volinsky. Matrix Factorization Techniques for Recommender Systems. *Computer*, 42(8):30–37, Aug. 2009.

[10] E. Law and L. von Ahn. Input-Agreement: A New Mechanism for Collecting Data using Human Computation Games. In *Proceedings of the 27th International Conference on Human Factors in Computing Systems - CHI 09*, pages 1197–1206, Boston, Massachusetts, USA, Apr. 2009. ACM Press.

[11] P. Organisciak, J. Teevan, S. Dumais, R. C. Miller, and A. T. Kalai. A Crowd of Your Own: Crowdsourcing for On-Demand Personalization. *Proceedings of the 2nd AAAI Conference on Human Computation and Crowdsourcing (HCOMP-2014)*, Nov. 2014.

[12] A. Salvador, A. Carlier, X. Giro-i Nieto, O. Marques, and V. Charvillat. Crowdsourced Object Segmentation with a Game. *Proceedings of the 2nd ACM International Workshop on Crowdsourcing for Multimedia - CrowdMM '13*, pages 15–20, Oct. 2013.

[13] B. Smyth and P. McClave. Similarity vs. diversity. In *Case-Based Reasoning Research and Development, 4th International Conference on Case-Based Reasoning, ICCBR 2001, Vancouver, BC, Canada, July 30 - August 2, 2001, Proceedings*, pages 347–361, 2001.

[14] R. van Zwol, L. Garcia, G. Ramirez, B. Sigurbjornsson, and M. Labad. Video Tag Game. In H. Jinpeng, R. Chen, H.-W. Hon, Y. Liu, W.-Y. Ma, A. Tomkins, and X. Zhang, editors, *Proceedings of the 17th International World Wide Web Conference (WWW Developer Track)*, Beijing, China, Apr. 2008. ACM Press.

[15] L. von Ahn and L. Dabbish. Labeling Images with a Computer Game. *Proceedings of The ACM Conference on Human Factors in Computing Systems*, pages 319 – 326, Apr. 2004.

[16] G. Walsh and J. Golbeck. Curator: a Game with a Purpose for Collection Recommendation. In *Proceedings of the 28th International Conference on Human Factors in Computing Systems - CHI '10*, pages 2079–2082, Atlanta, Georgia, USA, Apr. 2010. ACM Press.

Top-N Recommendation with Missing Implicit Feedback

Daryl Lim
Univ. of California, San Diego
dklim@ucsd.edu

Julian McAuley
Univ. of California, San Diego
jmcauley@ucsd.edu

Gert Lanckriet
Univ. of California, San Diego
gert@ece.ucsd.edu

ABSTRACT

In implicit feedback datasets, non-interaction of a user with an item does not necessarily indicate that an item is irrelevant for the user. Thus, evaluation measures computed on the observed feedback may not accurately reflect performance on the complete data. In this paper, we discuss a missing data model for implicit feedback and propose a novel evaluation measure oriented towards Top-N recommendation. Our evaluation measure admits unbiased estimation under our missing data model, unlike the popular Normalized Discounted Cumulative Gain (NDCG) measure. We also derive an efficient algorithm to optimize the measure on the training data. We run several experiments which demonstrate the utility of our proposed measure.

Categories and Subject Descriptors:
H.3.3 [Information Search and Retrieval]

Keywords: Recommender Systems; Ranking; Evaluation

1. INTRODUCTION

Personalized recommendation of relevant content is a common task in many retrieval systems. Many collaborative filtering approaches [3] attempt to identify user preferences based on *explicit feedback* such as user ratings. However, *implicit feedback*[1], in which a user's preferences are expressed through item interactions such as views or purchases, is often more common than explicit feedback.

In both explicit and implicit feedback systems, the presence of missing data poses a challenge to the evaluation of a recommendation system. In explicit feedback datasets, ratings can be Missing-not-at-Random (MNAR)[8], so systems trained only on observed ratings may give biased predictions. On the other hand, in implicit feedback datasets, non-interaction of a user with an item does not necessarily indicate that the item is irrelevant for the user. If we view unobserved but relevant user-item pairs as missing data, then measures which do not take the missing data mechanism into consideration may also exhibit bias when evaluated on the complete data.

To address the MNAR problem in explicit feedback systems, a missing data model was proposed in [8], and it was shown that the Top-N recall and the Area-under-the-Top-N-curve(ATOP) measures evaluated on the observed data provided an unbiased estimate of performance on the complete data under the missing data model. Due to the close relationship between ATOP and AUC, surrogate loss functions to minimize AUC on the training data were proposed.

However, the Top-N recall is known to be difficult to maximize directly, while it has been shown in several recent works ([10, 7, 4]) that optimizing for AUC may not yield the best results on performance measures such as NDCG or MAP which focus on the top of the ranking. Thus, there is a need for a performance measure which admits efficient optimization and is aligned with top-of-the-ranking metrics.

In this work, we first present a missing observation model for implicit feedback data. Next, we present a new performance measure, the Average Discounted Gain (ADG), which focuses on top-of-the-ranking performance and can be estimated without bias on the observed relevance data under our missing data model. Finally, we present an efficient optimization algorithm to optimize the ADG, and evaluate our proposed method on several datasets.

2. DATA MODEL

In our setting, we assume that we are given a set of users $\mathcal{U} = \{u_1, u_2 \cdots u_m\}$ and a set of candidate items $\mathcal{I} = \{i_1, i_2 \cdots i_n\}$. We are also given implicit feedback in the form of a user-item relevance matrix $X \in \mathbb{R}^{|\mathcal{U}| \times |\mathcal{I}|}$ where

$$X(j,k) = \begin{cases} 1, & i_k \text{ is relevant to } u_j \\ 0, & \text{otherwise} \end{cases}$$

Accordingly, we can define the lists of *relevant* and *irrelevant* items for each user:

$$\mathcal{O}_u^+ = \{i_k : X(u, i_k) = 1\}; \quad \mathcal{O}_u^- = \mathcal{I} \setminus \mathcal{O}_u^+.$$

2.1 Generation of observed ratings

Due to the scarcity of resources (for example, time, money or both), users may not be able to consume all items in $\mathcal{I}$ in which they are interested. We therefore assume that each user has a partially observed *prior relevant* set $\mathcal{P}_u^+ \subseteq \mathcal{I}$, which contains *all* items in $\mathcal{I}$ which are relevant to the user. We can then view $\mathcal{O}_u^+ \subseteq \mathcal{P}_u^+$ as a subset of items that a user has chosen to consume (i.e., interact sufficiently with so that it is identified as relevant). In our model, we will assume that the observed items $\mathcal{O}_u^+$ are a simple random sample of unknown size drawn from $\mathcal{P}_u^+$. Equivalently, for a given user

u, each item in $\mathcal{P}_u^+$ has the same (but unknown) probability of being in $\mathcal{O}_u^+$. It may be argued that in real-world settings, such a missing data model may be unrealistic; however, selecting test-set items uniformly from $\mathcal{O}_u^+$ to evaluate implicit feedback methods is a common practice (e.g. [6, 1]).

Our model has close connections to the model in [8] which was originally proposed for explicit data. In fact, when the non-relevant explicit feedback is discarded, the model in [8] is mathematically equivalent to our model, albeit with a different underlying interpretation.

3. AVERAGE DISCOUNTED GAIN (ADG)

In this section, we will present the Average Discounted Gain, a new evaluation measure which can give us an unbiased estimate of performance on $\mathcal{P}_u^+$ under our missing data model. We first assume that we are given user and item sets $\mathcal{U}$ and $\mathcal{I}$, and for each user are given relevant/irrelevant item sets $\mathcal{R}_u^+$ and $\mathcal{R}_u^-$. We also assume a prediction function $f_\theta(u, i)$ parameterized by θ which assigns a score to each user-item pair (u, i). In this paper, we learn a k-dimensional vector for each user and item, as well as a per-item bias:

$$\theta = \{\theta^{user} \in \mathbb{R}^{|\mathcal{U}| \times k}, \theta^{item} \in \mathbb{R}^{|\mathcal{I}| \times k}, \theta^{bias} \in \mathbb{R}^{|\mathcal{I}|}\}$$

and define

$$f_\theta(u, i) = \theta_u^{user} \cdot \theta_i^{item} + \theta_i^{bias}. \quad (1)$$

For a given user u, we define the *rank* of item i under the prediction function $f_\theta(u, i)$ as

$$\text{rank}(i) = \sum_{i' \in \mathcal{I} \setminus i} \mathbf{I}(f_\theta(u, i') - f_\theta(u, i)),$$

where $\mathbf{I}(k) = 1$ if $k > 0$ and 0 otherwise. Essentially, $\text{rank}(i)$ is the number of items (both relevant and irrelevant) with a higher predicted score than item i for a given u. Then, we can define the ADG:

Definition 1. The Average Discounted Gain (ADG) is defined as

$$\frac{1}{|\mathcal{R}_u^+|} \sum_{i^+ \in \mathcal{R}_u^+} \frac{1}{\log_2(\text{rank}(i^+) + 2)} \quad (2)$$

where $\mathcal{R}_u^+$ is the set of all relevant items to the user u.

Using this definition, we define the ADG on the observed and complete data respectively:

$$\text{ADG}^{obs} = \frac{1}{|\mathcal{O}_u^+|} \sum_{i^+ \in \mathcal{O}_u^+} \frac{1}{\log_2(\text{rank}(i^+) + 2)}$$

$$\text{ADG}^{comp} = \frac{1}{|\mathcal{P}_u^+|} \sum_{i^+ \in \mathcal{P}_u^+} \frac{1}{\log_2(\text{rank}(i^+) + 2)}$$

THEOREM 1. *Under the assumption that $\mathcal{O}_u^+$ is a simple random sample from $\mathcal{P}_u^+$, ADG^{obs} is an unbiased estimator of ADG^{comp}.*

PROOF. Given a fixed θ, each relevant item $i_p \in \mathcal{P}_u^+$ is associated with a discounted gain value $\frac{1}{\log_2(\text{rank}(i_p)^+) + 2)}$, which depends *only* on the rank of i_p. Now note that every observed item $i_o \in \mathcal{O}_u^+$ has the same rank, and therefore the same discount value, as the corresponding item in $\mathcal{P}_u^+$. Thus if $\mathcal{O}_u^+$ is a random sample from $\mathcal{P}_u^+$, then the mean discounted gain (i.e. ADG) can be estimated without bias. □

In the next section, we show how ADG is related to the NDCG measure, and also show that under our missing data model, NDCG^{obs} is a biased estimator of NDCG^{comp}.

3.1 Comparison with NDCG

The (binary) NDCG with logarithmic discount factor for a user u can be defined as

$$\frac{1}{\text{IDCG}(\mathcal{R}_u^+)} \sum_{i^+ \in \mathcal{R}_u^+} \frac{1}{\log_2(\text{rank}(i^+) + 2)}$$

where $\text{IDCG}(k) = \sum_{j=1}^{k} \frac{1}{\log_2(j+2)}$. We can see that the ADG is equivalent to the NDCG with a different per-user weighting function; thus, we expect that the ADG will focus on the top of the ranking just like the NDCG.

THEOREM 2. *Under the assumption that $|\mathcal{O}_u^+|$ is a simple random sample from $\mathcal{P}_u^+$, NDCG^{obs} is an unbiased estimator of NDCG^{comp} only when $|\mathcal{O}_u^+| = |\mathcal{P}_u^+|$.*

PROOF. First note that

$$\text{NDCG}^{comp} = \frac{1}{\text{IDCG}(|\mathcal{P}_u^+|)} \sum_{i^+ \in \mathcal{P}_u^+} \frac{1}{\log_2(\text{rank}(i^+) + 2)},$$

then

$$\mathbb{E}\left[\text{NDCG}^{obs}\right] = \frac{|\mathcal{O}_u^+| \cdot \mathbb{E}\left[\frac{1}{|\mathcal{O}_u^+|} \sum_{i \in \mathcal{O}_u^+} \frac{1}{\log_2(\text{rank}(i^+)+2)}\right]}{\text{IDCG}(|\mathcal{O}_u^+|)}$$

$$= \frac{|\mathcal{O}_u^+|}{\text{IDCG}(|\mathcal{O}_u^+|)} \text{ADG}^{comp} \quad \text{(from Theorem 1)}$$

$$= \frac{|\mathcal{O}_u^+| \cdot \text{IDCG}(|\mathcal{P}_u^+|)}{|\mathcal{P}_u^+| \cdot \text{IDCG}(|\mathcal{O}_u^+|)} \text{NDCG}^{comp}$$

which is only unbiased when $|\mathcal{O}_u^+| = |\mathcal{P}_u^+|$. □

Since $\mathcal{O}_u^+ \subseteq \mathcal{P}_u^+$, this means that NDCG^{obs} will always be a biased estimate of NDCG^{comp} unless the user consumes *all* items in $\mathcal{P}_u^+$.

4. OPTIMIZATION

We now present an efficient algorithm to optimize the ADG for a given dataset. Since the ADG is bounded between 0 and 1, instead of maximizing the ADG, we will minimize $(1 - \text{ADG})$. First, we note that

$$1 - \text{ADG} = 1 - \frac{1}{|\mathcal{O}_u^+|} \sum_{i^+ \in \mathcal{O}_u^+} \frac{1}{\log_2(\text{rank}(i^+) + 2)}$$

$$= \frac{1}{|\mathcal{O}_u^+|} \sum_{i^+ \in \mathcal{O}_u^+} \mathcal{C}(\text{rank}(i^+)) \quad (3)$$

where

$$\mathcal{C}(k) = 1 - \frac{1}{\log_2(k + 2)}. \quad (4)$$

It can be shown (omitted for brevity) that $\forall k \in \{1 \cdots |\mathcal{I}|\}$,

$$\mathcal{C}(k) = \sum_{1}^{k} \alpha_k, \ \exists \vec{\alpha} \in \{\vec{\alpha} \in \mathbb{R}^{|\mathcal{I}|} : \alpha_1 > \alpha_2 \cdots > \alpha_{|\mathcal{I}|} > 0\}.$$

Thus, we can transform $\text{rank}(i^+)$ into a loss, and use the approximation

$$\mathcal{C}(\text{rank}(i^+)) \approx \sum_{i^- \in \mathcal{V}_{u,i^+}} \mathcal{C}(|\mathcal{V}_{u,i^+}|) \frac{f_\theta(u, i^-) - f_\theta(u, i^+) + 1}{|\mathcal{V}_{u,i^+}|} \quad (5)$$

(see [10] for a related derivation) where

$$\mathcal{V}_{u,i^+} = \{i^- \in (\mathcal{I} \setminus i^+) : f_\theta(u,i^-) - f_\theta(u,i^+) + 1 > 0\}.$$

Finally, we substitute Eq. (5) into Eq. (3), to get the final optimization problem:

$$\min_\theta \frac{1}{|\mathcal{U}|} \sum_U \sum_{\substack{i^+ \in \mathcal{O}_u^+ \\ i^- \in \mathcal{V}_{u,i^+}}} \mathcal{C}(|\mathcal{V}_{u,i^+}|) \frac{f_\theta(u,i^-) - f_\theta(u,i^+) + 1}{|\mathcal{O}_u^+||\mathcal{V}_{u,i^+}|}.$$

We follow a similar procedure to [10] to derive a stochastic gradient descent algorithm, and also use the early-stopping technique in [4] to speed up the optimization process. The pseudocode for the full algorithm is given in Algorithm 1.

Algorithm 1 The OPT-ADG algorithm

Input: user set $\mathcal{U}$, item set $\mathcal{I}$, relevance sets $\{\mathcal{O}_u^+ : u \in \mathcal{U}\}$
1: **repeat**
2:     Sample u uniformly from $\mathcal{U}$, i^+ uniformly from $\mathcal{O}_u^+$
3:     $N = 0$
4:     violatorFound = False
5:     **repeat**
6:         Sample i^- uniformly from $\mathcal{I} \setminus i^+$
7:         **if** $f_\theta(u,i^+) - f_\theta(u,i^-) < 1$ **then**
8:             violatorFound = True; $v = i^-$
9:             **break**
10:        **end if**
11:        $N = N + 1$
12:    **until** $N >= \frac{|\mathcal{I}|-1}{\gamma}$
13:    **if** violatorFound **then**
14:        Take gradient step on

$$\mathcal{C}\left(\left\lfloor \frac{|\mathcal{I}|-1}{N} \right\rfloor\right)(f_\theta(u,v) - f_\theta(u,i^+) + 1) \quad \text{(Eq. (4))}$$

15:    **end if**
16: **until** max iterations exceeded

---

5. DISCUSSION

One purported advantage of measures like the ATOP and the ADG is that their performance on $\mathcal{O}_u^+$ gives us an unbiased estimate of performance on $\mathcal{P}_u^+$ (henceforth, we shall refer to them as unbiased-to-missing-data (UBM) measures).

However, in practice, we cannot directly make use of this property if the ranking model to be evaluated is trained on data in $\mathcal{O}_u^+$, since items in $\mathcal{O}_u^+$ are no longer a random sample with respect to the ranking model. Thus, we cannot extrapolate performance on $\mathcal{P}_u^+$ by measuring performance on $\mathcal{O}_u^+$, as this is analogous to guessing test set performance based on training performance in a classification setting.

Nevertheless, we note that UBM measures still retain a nice property: if *a priori*, some relevant items per user are held out (i.e. not used for training by the ranking model) in disjoint test and validation sets which are both uniform random samples from $\mathcal{O}_u^+$, then we can expect the validation and test set performance to be similar *regardless of the number of validation or test items held out*.

Our claim is easy to prove: If we denote the relevant items in the validation set as $\mathcal{R}_{u,\text{val}}^+$ and the relevant items in the test set as $\mathcal{R}_{u,\text{test}}^+$, then we can view both $\mathcal{R}_{u,\text{val}}^+$ and $\mathcal{R}_{u,\text{test}}^+$ as uniform random samples from the set $\mathcal{R}_{u,\text{val}}^+ \cup \mathcal{R}_{u,\text{test}}^+$. Therefore from Theorem 1, we can expect that if we evaluate the validation and test sets with respect to any UBM

measure, they would both yield unbiased estimates of performance on $\mathcal{R}_{u,\text{val}}^+ \cup \mathcal{R}_{u,\text{test}}^+$, *regardless of* $|\mathcal{R}_{u,\text{val}}^+|$ and $|\mathcal{R}_{u,\text{test}}^+|$. Using the same logic, if we are given an observation set $\mathcal{O}_u^+$ and prior observation set $\mathcal{P}_u^+$, then splitting $\mathcal{O}_u^+$ into $\mathcal{O}_{u,train}$ and $\mathcal{O}_{u,test}$, training a ranker on $\mathcal{O}_{u,train}$ then evaluating $\mathcal{O}_{u,test}$ on any UBM measure should yield similar performance to the same UBM measures given to $\{\mathcal{P}_u^+ \setminus \mathcal{O}_u^+\}$, which are exactly the unknown but relevant items we want to predict. Here, the intuition is somewhat analogous to the generalization ability of classifiers in classical machine learning settings when the validation and test set come from the same distribution.

Another desirable property of UBM methods is allowing us to make statements about the *absolute performance* of ranking models: For example, ADG can be interpreted as the mean discounted gain of relevant items. In contrast, we cannot predict the absolute performance of a ranking model on non-UBM measures such as NDCG on $\{\mathcal{P}_u^+ \setminus \mathcal{O}_u^+\}$ without knowing $|\{\mathcal{P}_u^+ \setminus \mathcal{O}_u^+\}|$.

6. EXPERIMENTS

To evaluate the performance of our proposed measure, we conducted experiments on 3 datasets: *Amazon Games*, a subset of customer reviews from the Video Games category on Amazon, MovieLens 10M data, and *last.FM* listening data for 110000 users from the Million Song Dataset Challenge hosted on Kaggle. For the Amazon Games and MovieLens data, we binarized the data and treated the 4 and 5 star reviews as relevant and the rest as irrelevant. For the last.FM data, we considered a song relevant to a user if the user listened to it at least 3 times, and irrelevant otherwise. Due to the sparsity of each dataset, we also densified the data by retaining the most popular items and users with the most reviews. Our datasets are summarized below.

Dataset	Users	Items	Interactions	Sparsity
last.FM	10000	10000	97727	0.097%
MovieLens	9888	5000	711084	1.44%
Amazon Games	17437	17915	201154	0.064%

To show the utility of optimizing for ADG over AUC, we implemented two similar matrix factorization methods, MF-ADG and MF-AUC, both with $f_\theta(u,i)$ defined as in Eq. (1). MF-ADG uses Algorithm 1, while MF-AUC tries to optimize the empirical AUC for each user by solving

$$\min_\theta \frac{1}{|\mathcal{U}|} \sum_U \frac{1}{|\mathcal{O}_u^+||\mathcal{O}_u^-|} \sum_{i+\in\mathcal{O}_u^+} \sum_{i-\in\mathcal{O}_u^-} [f_\theta(u,i^-) - f_\theta(u,i^+) + 1]_+$$

where $[\cdot]_+ = \max(0, \cdot)$.

For each user, 10% of the relevant items were used for the validation set, while 20% of the relevant items were used for the test set, and both were uniformly sampled from $\mathcal{O}_u^+$. This process was repeated four times to create four folds and the mean performance was reported. For fairness, both methods were initialized with the same random parameters, and each algorithm was run for 1000000 iterations. We regularized the ℓ_2−norms of both the user and item latent vectors, and used a single regularization parameter λ whose optimal value was determined by performance on the validation set. The number of latent factors per item and user was fixed at 50, and for MF-ADG, the value of γ was fixed at 100. For each method, we report three UBM measures,

ATOP, ADG, Recall@10) and also two popular ranking measures, Mean Average Precision (MAP) and NDCG. As there was negligible difference between ATOP and AUC in our experiments ($<0.1\%$) we chose to only report ATOP in the paper. As a baseline, we also computed the rank-k SVD on the user-item relevance matrix for different values of k for each dataset, but do not report the results as the performance even for the best value of k was significantly worse than both MF-ADG and MF-AUC on all metrics.

6.1 Results

Table 1 shows the performance of both methods on all experiments. For each dataset, MF-ADG performed better than MF-AUC on all ranking measures except ATOP, which is expected because of the close link between the ATOP objective and AUC optimization. This supports our claim that optimizing ADG on the training set improves performance at the top of the ranking.

	Amazon Games		last.FM		MovieLens	
	MF-AUC	MF-ADG	MF-AUC	MF-ADG	MF-AUC	MF-ADG
ATOP	0.7584 (0.0014)	0.7546 (0.0049)	0.7490 (0.0064)	0.7449 (0.0028)	0.8855 (0.0018)	0.8821 (0.0042)
MAP	0.0104 (0.0003)	**0.0124** **(0.0003)**	0.0242 (0.0006)	**0.0281** **(0.0006)**	0.0775 (0.0007)	**0.0858** **(0.0003)**
NDCG	0.1460 (0.0006)	**0.1501** **(0.0004)**	0.1701 (0.0007)	**0.1750** **(0.0008)**	0.3718 (0.0010)	**0.3820** **(0.0002)**
rec@10	0.0170 (0.0004)	**0.0211** **(0.0007)**	0.0473 (0.0010)	**0.0539** **(0.0019)**	0.0945 (0.0011)	**0.1025** **(0.0013)**
ADG	0.1080 (0.0005)	**0.1110** **(0.0003)**	0.1294 (0.0005)	**0.1332** **(0.0006)**	0.1714 (0.0004)	**0.1768** **(0.0001)**

Table 1: Mean performance on all datasets across 4 folds. The number in brackets is the standard error of the mean. Methods which performed significantly better are bolded.

Table 2 shows the mean performance of both methods on the test and validation subsets of the MovieLens dataset respectively. As discussed in Section 5, we can see that the UBM measures (ATOP, REC@10 and ADG) show broadly consistent performance across the test and validation sets, while the MAP and NDCG measures vary greatly. Similar observations were made for the other two datasets which we have omitted due to space constraints. This supports our claim that measuring these performance measures on a validation set can allow us to make confident predictive statements about the performance of the model on the unseen test data, even when the number of test items is unknown.

7. RELATED WORK

Many predictive models have been proposed for both explicit feedback [3] and implicit feedback [1, 6]. [5, 2] have studied the MNAR assumption in terms of model fitting with different missing data models but the evaluations do not take the missing data models into account. Furthermore, to the best of our knowledge, no one has formally proposed a missing data model for implicit feedback models. Our work is most closely related to [8, 9].

8. CONCLUSION

In this work, we proposed a missing data model for implicit feedback and a novel evaluation measure which allows unbiased estimation with respect to our missing data model.

We also showed that ranking models trained to maximise our evaluation measure have improved performance on top-of-the-ranking measures. In future work, we plan to explore different models of missing data generation.

Measure	MF-AUC			MF-ADG		
	Test	Valid	Diff%	Test	Valid	Diff%
ATOP	0.8855	0.8849	-0.06	0.8821	0.8817	-0.05
ADG	0.1714	0.1709	-0.29	0.1768	0.1768	-0.00
REC@10	0.0945	0.0945	0.00	0.1025	0.1030	0.49
MAP	0.0775	0.0586	-24.38	0.0858	0.0657	-23.43
NDCG	0.3718	0.2957	-20.47	0.3820	0.3046	-20.42

Table 2: Test vs. validation performance on MovieLens dataset. Performance on UBM measures is consistent across test and validation sets.

9. ACKNOWLEDGMENTS

The authors acknowledge support from Yahoo!, Inc., the Sloan Foundation, and NSF Grants CCF-0830535 and IIS-1054960. Daryl Lim was supported by a fellowship from the Agency for Science, Technology and Research (A*STAR), Singapore.

10. REFERENCES

[1] Y. Hu, Y. Koren, and C. Volinsky. Collaborative filtering for implicit feedback datasets. In *Proc. IEEE ICDM (2008)*, pages 263–272, 2008.

[2] Y. Kim and S. Choi. Bayesian binomial mixture model for collaborative prediction with non-random missing data. In *RecSys '14*, pages 201–208, 2014.

[3] Y. Koren, R. M. Bell, and C. Volinsky. Matrix factorization techniques for recommender systems. *IEEE Computer*, 42(8):30–37, 2009.

[4] D. Lim and G. Lanckriet. Efficient learning of mahalanobis metrics for ranking. In *Proc. ICML 2014*, pages 1980–1988, 2014.

[5] B. M. Marlin and R. S. Zemel. Collaborative prediction and ranking with non-random missing data. In *RecSys '09*, pages 5–12, 2009.

[6] S. Rendle, C. Freudenthaler, Z. Gantner, and L. Schmidt-Thieme. BPR: bayesian personalized ranking from implicit feedback. In *UAI 2009*, pages 452–461, 2009.

[7] Y. Shi, A. Karatzoglou, L. Baltrunas, M. Larson, A. Hanjalic, and N. Oliver. Tfmap: optimizing map for top-n context-aware recommendation. In *Proc. ACM SIGIR*, 2012.

[8] H. Steck. Training and testing of recommender systems on data missing not at random. In *Proc. ACM SIGKDD*, pages 713–722, 2010.

[9] H. Steck. Evaluation of recommendations: rating-prediction and ranking. In *RecSys '13*, pages 213–220, 2013.

[10] J. Weston, S. Bengio, and N. Usunier. Large scale image annotation: learning to rank with joint word-image embeddings. *Machine Learning*, 81:21–35, 2010.

Towards Automatic Meal Plan Recommendations for Balanced Nutrition

David Elsweiler
University of Regensburg
Regensburg, Germany
david@elsweiler.co.uk

Morgan Harvey
Northumbria University
Newcastle, UK
pwhq2@northumbria.ac.uk

ABSTRACT

Food recommenders have been touted as a useful tool to help people achieve a healthy diet. Here we incorporate nutrition into the recommender problem by examining the feasibility of algorithmically creating daily meal plans for a sample of user profiles (n=100), combined with a diverse set of food preference data (n=64) collected in a natural setting. Our analyses demonstrate it is possible to recommend plans for a large percentage of users which meet the guidelines set out by international health agencies.

Keywords

Health; Recommender Systems; Planning; Prevention

1. INTRODUCTION AND MOTIVATION

Poor dietary habits are a major cause of today's world health problems. Evidence shows that issues such as obesity and diabetes, as well as other lifestyle-related illnesses, can be prevented and sometimes even reversed through good nutrition [3]. People are often very poor at judging the healthiness of their own diet [2] and need support to implement positive changes [5]. Nutritionalists can create long-term plans and help people learn to make better choices, however this solution is neither practical nor economically feasible for everyone. As a result, food recommender systems (RS) have been touted as a potential means to assist people in nourishing themselves more healthily [4, 6, 11].

Food recommenders make sense as part of a strategy for behavioural change as suggesting a change that is less painful, i.e. based on something the user might like, is more likely to be accepted and followed. Recommenders are likely to be effective at predicting which changes will be painful or not but they have a serious drawback when aiming for positive change: they learn user preferences for ingredients and food styles. This leads to users who like fat- and calorie-laden meals being recommended fat- and calorie-laden meals [6] - an outcome not conducive to improving nutritional habits. Here we begin to address a fundamental question: to which

RecSys'15, September 16–20, 2015, Vienna, Austria.
© 2015 ACM. ISBN 978-1-4503-3692-5/15/09 ...$15.00.
DOI: http://dx.doi.org/10.1145/2792838.2799665.

extent is it possible to recommend users recipes they will like, but at the same time fit into a balanced diet?

Our approach is to automatically create daily meal plans by first calculating the nutritional requirements of the user based on their personal *personas* (age, gender, height,etc.). We then take the top recommendations, as estimated by a state-of-the-art recipe recommendation algorithm [6], and attempt to combine these algorithmically such that each plan corresponds to guidelines published by international health agencies.

2. RELATED WORK

Early work on recommending recipes include JULIA [7], which used case-based planning to generate a meal plan to satisfy multiple, interacting constraints. More recent efforts try to better understand the user's tastes [4] and how various factors in the rating process influence a user's choice [6]. Although food RS has been mooted as a potential tool to assist users in achieving good nutrition, to our knowledge no published work has explained exactly how to achieve this. We therefore present a first approach to integrating nutrition in the RS by moving beyond recommending individual items - which alone may be considered "unhealthy" - to groups of items, which together may represent a more balanced whole.

Recommending groups of items requires a balance to be struck between the items with the highest individual utility and those which, while they may have lower predicted ratings in isolation, join together to give a better combination. Examples include recommending complete, complementary playlists of music tracks [8] or combining recommended tourist attractions into a plan for a user's stay [9].

Schaller et al. [12] combine event recommendations given defined start and end times and locations, as well as the user's preferences. A schedule is built such that the user can visit as many of their preferred events as possible, whilst adhering to time constraints imposed by the duration of each event and travelling times. In many ways this is analogous to our situation where we are trying to combine a user's preferred meals given a number of nutritional constraints.

Little literature exists dealing with combined meal recommendations. JULIA [7] creates meal plans, although not for health or nutritional reasons. A second exception is an interface allowing users to manually combine recommendations into a food plan [1]. This work is interesting as it provides an example situation where our algorithms could be used. Our goal is slightly different. We wish to produce plans which are both pleasing to the user and, at the same time, meet the user's daily nutritional needs.

3. METHOD

To collect food preferences data we created a food portal website, http://www.quizine.me, where users could upload, browse, share and search recipes, calculate the nutritional properties of a recipe and receive recipe recommendations based on their profile. Users can rate recipes from 1 (strongly dislike) to 5 stars (strongly like). Over 3 years 148 users gave 4,549 ratings (median 8 per user) of 957 recipes, consisting of diverse styles of food. The median number of ratings per recipe is 4 and each recipe is classified as being either a main meal, a side dish, a breakfast or a dessert.

To investigate meal planning we needed a number of varied user *personas* describing quantities like height, weight, gender, age, nutritional goal (lose/gain/maintain weight) and activity level (from sedentary to highly active). Due to the general variability of the human form, we decided not to randomly generate body measurements. Instead we randomly sampled 50 male and 50 female subjects from a large survey of the US population [1] which reports general demographic information as well as detailed information about weights, heights, BMIs and ages at the time of the survey. Activity levels and goals were assigned to each subject at random assuming unconditional uniform distributions.

The 100 personas have a mean weight of 82.24kg and a mean height of 167.4 cm - an average BMI of 27.44 - meaning 3 are underweight, 27 overweight, 40 obese and the remaining 30 have a healthy weight. Ages vary almost uniformly from 18 to 80 with a median age of 46. This represents the US population well, serving to highlight the obesity present in modern human populations and providing us with a realistic and varied set of data points, allowing us to test the effect individual differences have on our planning approaches.

3.1 Creating Meal plans

For each persona-profile combination we combine meals, which the user has told us he likes and others that we predict he will like based on his profile, such that the combination meets his daily nutritional requirements. This requires several steps: 1) establishing the nutritional requirements for the persona 2) estimating recipe ratings based on each profile 3) combining recipes and establishing if the combination meets the requirements.

We calculate nutritional requirements for a given persona using a version of the Harris-Benedict equation revised by Roza and Shizgal [10] which estimates an individual's basal metabolic rate (BMR) and daily calorie requirements. The estimated BMR value is multiplied by a number between 1.2 and 1.9 corresponding to the individual's activity level giving a recommended daily energy intake to maintain current body weight. We add or remove 500 kilocalories for individuals who wish to gain or lose weight. This is a crude mechanism which would result in the safe gain or loss of 0.45 kgs in 7 days. We assume that 20% of the required energy will come form drinks and between-meal snacks.

Nutritional scientists have established generally-accepted ranges for carbohydrates, fat and protein intake ensuring that a person maintains a balanced diet with sufficient intake of essential nutrients, vitamins, and minerals. 45% to 65% of calories eaten should come from carbohydrates, 20% to 35% from fat and 10% to 35% from protein [2]. As a met-

---

[1] NHANES - http://www.cdc.gov/nchs/nhanes.htm
[2] https://www.nrv.gov.au/chronic-disease/summary

ric to optimise we target the central value of each of these ranges and set a fixed acceptable error margin of 10%. By accounting for the rate of calories per gram we can calculate how many calories should come from each energy source.

The diversity of user taste profiles can be estimated from the variety of ingredients in rated recipes. A user who has rated recipes with a wide variety of different ingredients likely has a wider range of tastes than another user who sticks to a smaller set. *Simple diversity* is the number of distinct ingredients in the recipes rated by a given user divided by the sum of all ingredients in the same set of recipes. Given a set N of integer counts, *Simpson diversity* is: $D(N) = 1 - \frac{\sum_{n \in N} n(n-1)}{\sum_{n \in N} n(\sum_{n \in N} n - 1)}$ and measures the probability that two elements randomly selected from a sample will belong to the same class (in this case ingredient). For both metrics 1 is infinite diversity and 0 is no diversity.

Omitting users with very few (< 10) ratings, leaving 64, both diversity metrics show an approximately normal distribution (*Simple diversity* mean = 0.57, sd=0.21; *Simpson diversity* mean = 0.98, sd = 0.004). Therefore most users had a good degree of ingredient diversity with few cases of low diversity. There is a strong linear relationship between ingredient diversity of rated recipes and the ingredient diversity of those recommended by the system ($r = 0.716$), meaning users with very narrow tastes will continue to have narrow tastes if they follow the recommendations.

Most users only have a relatively small number of their rated recipes from the top 50 most popular ($^3/_4$ of users drew less than 12% of their recipes from this set). The prevalence of top 50 recipes is negatively correlated with the diversity of the rated recipes ($r = -0.558$), meaning that people who have a preponderance towards popular recipes have a less diverse taste range.

We can create plans for a given user (persona-profile combination) by first taking the top x recommendations from the RS for the taste profile. This set of recipes is then split into two separate sets, one for breakfasts and one for main meals. A full search is performed to find **every combination** of these recipes in the sequence [breakfast, main meal, main meal] which meets the target nutritional requirements defined above. Combinations with the same meals cannot be repeated, e.g. [R1, R2, R3] and [R1, R3, R2] are treated as only one plan.

This elementary approach is sensible as 1) we are analysing the feasibility of creating plans and this provides all combinations meeting the set criteria and 2) we are dealing with small sets of recommendations so efficiency is not an issue.

4. RESULTS

For the following analyses (except in Section 4.3) the number of top recommendations used for planning, x, is set to 100. Combining taste profiles for users who have rated 10 or more recipes (n=64) with the 100 sampled personas yields 6400 simulated users. The method outlined above was able to generate plans for 4025/6400 cases (63%) and at least 1 plan was generated for 58 out of the 64 (91%) user profiles and for all 100 personas. On a per-persona basis, the total number of plans generated and the number of profiles for which any plans can be generated are related. As the number of "easy" profiles increases, the number of plans that can be generated from those profiles increases polynomially, thus increasing the number of recipes users rate will quickly improve coverage of the planning algorithm.

For the majority of people to eat in a way conforming to nutritional guidelines, we do not have to change what they eat, rather just when they eat what they like and how they combine meals. That said, there was still a number of user combinations for whom plans could not be generated. To understand why we defined features describing each profile and used these to compare the difference between the profiles for which we can generate plans and those we can't. Comparing these groups statistically showed that profiles are "difficult" if:

- They tend to only rate highly calorific and fatty recipes
- They rate very few breakfasts, which is a potential bottleneck in our algorithm
- They rate recipes with a lower diversity of ingredients
- The number of recipes they have rated is low

These insights point to a general theme - difficult profiles exhibit less diversity than the easier ones, meaning the set of recipes used by the planning algorithm is itself less diverse.

To understand how good the generated plans are we need to define a quality metric. We use a normalised linear combination of the expected rating from the RS (i.e. whether the user will like the recipe) and the inverse of the error compared to the user's ideal nutritional profile (i.e. distance from what the user should be eating). For a plan i this is:

$$score(i) = \lambda \cdot \left(1 - \frac{\epsilon_i}{\forall i Max(\epsilon_i)}\right) + (1 - \lambda) \cdot \frac{\hat{\mu}_i}{\forall i Max(\hat{\mu}_i)}$$

where ϵ_i is the error for plan i and $\hat{\mu}_i$ is its expected rating. λ is set to 0.5 to apply equal weighting to both nutrition and taste. As each plan is actually composed of three recipes (a breakfast, lunch and dinner), the error and expected ratings in the above equation are the average of these values over the three items. The error distribution is normal with mean 0.048 (4.8% of the total) and σ^2 0.015. The distribution of ratings is approximately normal with peaks at 4 and 5 (due to the presence of the actual ratings).

To understand what features of profiles and personas have the greatest impact on the plans generated we identified the top ("easy") and bottom ("hard") quartiles of each based on their mean scores. Note that for all of the comparisons in the following section we first assessed the normality of each distribution using the Shapiro-Wilk test and then performed the appropriate statistical test to compare the two distributions: Student's t-test for normal data (parametric) and the Wilcoxon signed-rank test (non-parametric) otherwise.

4.1 Personas

	mean		significance	
	easy	diff.	test	p value
age	47.8	43.9	t	0.43
weight	83.2	99.4	t	0.013*
height	166	173	t	0.011*
energy	1826	2536	wilcox	≪ 0.001*
nutrition goal	0.68	1.32	wilcox	≪ 0.037*

Table 1: Summary statistics for personas.

Table 1 shows the differences between the easy and difficult groups of personas (the physical attributes of the sampled people as well as their nutritional goals and activity

levels). A person's physical dimensions play a crucial role in the difficulty of generating plans; in general the larger someone is, the more nutrition they need to consume. This is difficult for the planning algorithm as it is constrained by the need to fulfil all nutritional requirements from just 3 meals and does not have the ability to adjust the portion sizes. Similarly, the person's goal also has an effect on food intake and, in turn, the difficulty of planning. Of the 25 difficult personas, 16 wish to gain weight whereas only 4 personas from the easy group had this goal.

Linear models shows that all of the features in table 1 are able to significantly explain the variance when predicting the score. Gender is also a significant feature with male personas more likely to belong to the difficult group.

4.2 Profiles

	median		significance	
	easy	diff.	test	p value
# rated recipes	71	14	wilcox	≪ 0.001*
# rated ingr.	378	56	wilcox	≪ 0.001*
ingr. diversity	0.711	0.393	wilcox	≪ 0.001*
# in top 50	7	2	wilcox	0.003*

Table 2: Summary statistics for profiles.

Table 2 displays statistics for the easy and difficult groups of profiles which describe the user's tastes based on the recipes they rated. Recall that recipes returned by the RS to be used for planning also include those already rated 4 or 5 by the user (indicating strong approval of the recipe). The number of rated recipes has an influence on the difficulty of planning, primarily because it increases the number of recipes the planner has at its disposal and also slightly increases the mean rating score and, therefore, the outcomes of the combined score. This is because the mean *predicted* rating (over all users) is 3.38 whereas the mean of all of the 4 and 5 star ratings is 4.43.

4.3 Varying the parameter x

x	# plans	# profiles	plans/comb	score
25	204,523	41	124	0.703
50	273,071	54	97	0.694
75	375,371	56	105	0.681
100	539,818	58	134	0.667

Table 3: Change in performance when varying x.

To make plans, the algorithm takes the recipes each user had liked previously as well as the top x suggested recipes from the recommender system. In the above analyses we set x to 100, however it is interesting to consider what effect varying this parameter has on the number of plans that can be generated as well as the "quality" of those plans. As x increases, the number of plans that can be created increases, albeit not linearly. As x increases so does the number of profiles for which plans can be generated with a particularly large jump between 25 and 50. The average number of plans generated per user profile-persona combination does not monotonically increase or decrease as either extreme of the parameters values have the highest outputs for this metric. In the case of $x = 25$ this is likely because there are relatively few profiles for which it can generate plans at all that the ones it can generate for are quite easy. In terms of average plan score, this decreases almost linearly with the value of x. This is because as x is increased the average score of the ratings decreases, causing a corresponding decrease in the scores.

5. DISCUSSION AND LIMITATIONS

We have shown that even with a simple algorithm and a recipe collection of modest size, it possible to create balanced meal plans for many users by combining recipes that they like or which a recommender predicts they will like. For other users the task is more challenging. The results of our analyses suggests ways that we can make changes to our approach in order to increase the number of situations where plan generation is possible.

A simple change that we can make is to encourage users to rate more recipes to increase the pool of potential combinations for the system to work with. Our analyses show that the users who rated the most recipes tended to have more possible plans and even small increases helped. In particular if users can rate recipes with diverse ingredients this can be beneficial as diverse taste profiles were also correlated with the number of the possible plans. It may be helpful to employ a recommender algorithm specifically designed to recommend diverse recommendations as increasing diversity is a popular research topic in RS e.g. [13]. However, this may come at a cost to ratings.

Another specific bottleneck in our approach was the lack of breakfasts. It may be of benefit therefore to use separate lists of top x breakfasts and top y main meals as input to the algorithm, although, again, this may come at the cost of lower ratings and hurt quality scores overall.

We have also shown that it is often difficult to generate high quality plans conforming to nutritional guidelines when the user requires large numbers of calories per day. For example when the user wishes to gain weight or they are very tall. It also seems more challenging to create plans for males than for females. These results suggest that for difficult cases what is needed are planning methods with more flexibility, such as the ability to alter portion sizes, the number of meals per day or to consider side dishes. Greater flexibility will require more complicated algorithms to deal with a larger search space and efficiency issues. The methods and metrics we provide here, however, offer a framework and a baseline to study such algorithms in the future.

6. CONCLUSIONS AND FUTURE WORK

Previous work has proposed food RS as a valuable tool for assisting people achieve a healthy diet. In this paper we have provided a first attempt at incorporating health and nutrition into the food recommendation problem. We have shown that it is possible to combine recommended recipes into balanced meal plans according to guidelines from nutritional agencies. By analysing situations where it was difficult or impossible to generate plans we have gained clues as to how to design better planning algorithms in the future.

There are several other aspects of this work that open up future research questions. We wish to build on our contributions here by experimenting with more complicated planning algorithms using the methodology and metrics we have developed here to understand the costs and benefits of dif-

ferent approaches. We are, moreover, looking for nutritional experts to collaborate with to evaluate and refine the approach from this perspective. Such an expert would also be able to evaluate how truly healthy the meal plans are, as just because they fit the various nutritional constraints does not necessarily mean they are balanced. The number of recommendations used has an impact on both the number of plans that can be generated as well as the quality of those plans. In future work it would be useful to investigate in more detail which value or range of values are optimal and how this is influenced by factors such as the total number of ratings available to the system and the quality of the recommender system used. Finally, we want to better understand how to combine recipes and what makes a good plan from the user's perspective. To achieve this we plan to perform a further user study where complete daily plans are rated and not just recipes, in addition to analysing how the planner, already embedded in our food portal, is actually used.

7. REFERENCES

[1] S. Berkovsky, J. Freyne, and G. Smith. Personalized network updates: increasing social interactions and contributions in social networks. In *UMAP*, pages 1–13. Springer, 2012.

[2] E. Brunner, D. Stallone, M. Juneja, S. Bingham, and M. Marmot. Dietary assessment in whitehall ii: comparison of 7 d diet diary and food-frequency questionnaire and validity against biomarkers. *British J. of Nutrition*, 86(3):405–14, 2001.

[3] D. Ornish et al. Can lifestyle changes reverse coronary heart disease?: The lifestyle heart trial. *The Lancet*, 336(8708):129 – 133, 1990.

[4] J. Freyne and S. Berkovsky. Intelligent food planning: personalized recipe recommendation. In *IUI*, pages 321–324, 2010.

[5] J. F. Guthrie, B. M. Derby, and A. S. Levy. *America's Eating Habits: Changes and ConsequencesAgriculture Information Bulletin No. (AIB750)*, pages 243–280. US Dept. for Agriculture, 1999.

[6] M. Harvey, B. Ludwig, and D. Elsweiler. You are what you eat: Learning user tastes for rating prediction. In *SPIRE*, pages 153–164, 2013.

[7] T. Hinrichs. Strategies for adaptation and recovery in a design problem solver. In *Workshop on Case-Based Reasoning*, 1989.

[8] J.C. et al. Platt. Learning a gaussian process prior for automatically generating music playlists. In *NIPS*, pages 1425–1432, 2001.

[9] F. Ricci, B. Arslan, N. Mirzadeh, and A. Venturini. Itr: a case-based travel advisory system. In *Advances in Case-Based Reasoning*, pages 613–627. Springer, 2002.

[10] A.M. Roza and H.M. Shizgal. The harris benedict equation reevaluated: resting energy requirements and the body cell mass. *Am Jour. of clinical nutrition*, 40(1):168–182, 1984.

[11] A. Said and A. Bellogín. You are what you eat! tracking health through recipe interactions. *Proc. of RSWeb*, 14, 2014.

[12] R. Schaller, M. Harvey, and D. Elsweiler. Entertainment on the go: Finding things to do and see while visiting distributed events. In *IIiX*, pages 90–99. ACM, 2012.

[13] S. Vargas and P. Castells. Rank and relevance in novelty and diversity metrics for recommender systems. In *ACM RecSys*, pages 109–116, 2011.

Uncovering Systematic Bias in Ratings across Categories: a Bayesian Approach

Fangjian Guo
Department of Computer Science
Duke University
Durham, NC 27708, USA
guo@cs.duke.edu

David B. Dunson
Department of Statistical Science
Duke University
Durham, NC 27708, USA
dunson@duke.edu

ABSTRACT

Recommender systems are routinely equipped with standardized taxonomy that associates each item with one or more categories or genres. Although such information does not directly imply the quality of an item, the distribution of ratings vary greatly across categories, e.g. animation movies may generally receive higher ratings than action movies. While it is a natural outcome given the diversity and heterogeneity of both users and items, it makes directly aggregated ratings, which are commonly used to guide users' choice by reflecting the overall quality of an item, incomparable across categories and hence prone to fairness and diversity issues. This paper aims to uncover and calibrate systematic category-wise biases for discrete-valued ratings. We propose a novel Bayesian multiplicative probit model that treats the inflation or deflation of mean rating for a combination of categories as multiplicatively contributed from category-specific parameters. The posterior distribution of those parameters, as inferred from data, can capture the bias for all possible combinations of categories, thus enabling statistically efficient estimation and principled rating calibration.

Categories and Subject Descriptors

H.2.8 [**Database Applications**]: Data Mining

General Terms

Algorithms, Human Factors

Keywords

Bayesian model; category; genre; taxonomy; bias

1. INTRODUCTION

Recent studies in recommender systems have primarily focused on personalization, where different sets of items are recommended to users with different tastes and preferences [1]. Yet, a related but seemingly simple task, namely how to aggregate ratings to reflect the overall quality of an item, has

been somewhat overlooked [4]. As an indicator believed to reflect the population level perception of an item, aggregated ratings, such as the rating or number of stars accompanying each rated movie or product appearing on IMDB and Amazon.com, are commonly adopted to guide users' choice when they browse a variety of items [2, 6]. The impact of these overall evaluations are substantial given that they are part of the first impression when a user browses an unseen item. It has been shown that the average ratings shown previously to users may influence their own ratings through a "social influence bias", namely inducing users to bias their assessment towards the average ratings given by the bigger community [2, 6]. Aggregated ratings from one platform are also useful for personalized recommendation in another platform as an external source of information [9]. For example, a movie recommender may augment its data with aggregated ratings from IMDB to provide more accurate predictions.

Direct or weighted averaging are most commonly used methods to aggregate ratings, but their truthfulness and robustness are shown to be problematic [4]. Alternative aggregation strategies have been recently proposed, including using median or mode for aggregation to guard against malicious users or users with extreme opinions [4], and other methods based on reputation of users [7, 3].

These issues with aggregated ratings arise from the increased heterogeneity of *users*, with malicious attackers as an extreme case. In this paper, we instead examine the issue related to the increased diversity of *items*, which to our knowledge has received little attention. In particular, we focus on diversity structured by a predefined taxonomy system, such as genres for movies and music, and "departments" and "sub-departments" for products on Amazon. We ask the question — are averaged ratings comparable across genres (and combinations of genres)? If not, can we extract the systematic biases and calibrate the ratings accordingly so that they are comparable? Note that we will use "categories" and "genres" interchangeably throughout the paper.

Although the comparison of "overall quality" between products from different categories may not always seem well-posed, it is a daily task faced by users. For example, they need to decide between spending time and/or money on a comedy movie versus a documentary. Besides, the websites that run a marketplace for third party sellers (e.g. eBay) face the same task when they judge the performance of sellers based on ratings given to different types of products or services. In both cases, adopting aggregated ratings without removing systematic category-wise biases may impair the fairness and diversity of the ecosystem.

2. BACKGROUND

2.1 Empirical analysis

To motivate our study, in this section, we show how the average rating levels vary across different combinations of categories with empirical observations. We perform our analysis on the MovieLens 1M dataset[1], which contains about 1 million ratings from 6,000 users on 4,000 movies. All ratings are on a $1 - 5$ discrete scale. Each movie is categorized into at least one genre from a list of 18 *basic genres*. Typically, a movie is assigned to $1 - 3$ genres.

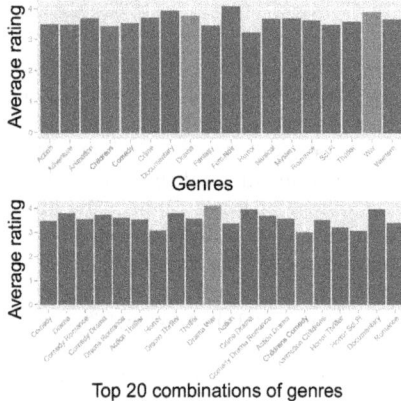

Figure 1: Top: the average rating for each genre; Bottom: the average ratings for the top 20 combinations of genres.

Figure 1 shows the average ratings for all 18 genres and for the 20 combinations of genres having the largest number of rated movies in the dataset. It is clear that the average ratings do not align across genres, as well as their combinations. Given the large number of ratings, most of the differences are statistically significant: among all the pairs of genre combinations with at least 5 movies in each, 92.4% of them are found to reject the equal-mean null hypothesis with a t-test at a significance level of 0.05. The figure also shows that a combination of genres being underrated/overrated is related to one or more of its component genres being *marginally* underrated/overrated.

Besides, given 18 basic genres, there are an exponential number of possible combinations. We also find the number of ratings vary greatly among combinations, as shown in Figure 2. Similar observation has been reported for the Netflix dataset [10].

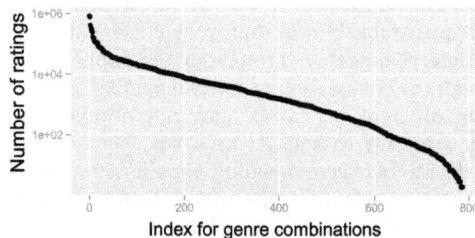

Figure 2: The number of ratings available (plotted in decreasing order) vary greatly across combinations of genres.

[1]http://grouplens.org/datasets/movielens/

2.2 Why Bayesian modeling

We briefly summarize the challenges implied by empirical studies before we move on to the modeling part. The estimation for systematic bias across genres should address the following issues.

1. Jointly estimating the bias for an exponential number of combinations of basic genres/categories, which are non-independent.

2. Efficiently borrowing information across combinations that share a subset of basic genres.

3. Good interpretability that relates a combination to its constituent basic genres.

3. BAYESIAN MULTIPLICATIVE PROBIT MODEL

3.1 Model and prior specification

Suppose that we have N items and each item i receives n_i ratings, which are denoted by R_{ij} ($j = 1, 2, \cdots, n_i$). Note that $\{R_{ij}\}$ for the same j do not necessarily correspond to the same user. Each rating is on a discrete scale with K levels, i.e. $R_{ij} \in \{1, 2, \cdots, K\}$. Suppose we have T basic categories/genres and every item is associated with a combination of them. The categorization for item i is encoded by $\{G_{it}\}$ ($t = 1, 2, \cdots, T$), where each component is binary: $G_{it} = 1$ indicates that the item is within category t and $G_{it} = 0$ otherwise. Our task is to model the distribution of the rating for item i depending on its categorization, namely $P(R_{ij} \mid \{G_{it}\})$.

The probit model is widely used for describing ratings and other ordered categorical data [5]. The probit model assumes a continuous latent variable Z_{ij} underlying every discrete-valued R_{ij}. By introducing thresholds $-\infty = g_0 < g_1 < \cdots < g_{K-1} < g_K = +\infty$ that partition the real line into non-overlapping intervals, R_{ij} is recovered by looking at which interval Z_{ij} falls into, i.e.

$$R_{ij} = r(Z_{ij}) = \sum_{k=1}^{K} k\mathbf{1}(g_{k-1} < Z_{ij} \le g_k), \qquad (1)$$

where we use $r(\cdot)$ to denote the transform from the latent variable to the observed data.

Commonly, the latent Z_{ij} is set to be a Gaussian random variable with mean value *linearly* related to the features, such as $Z_{ij} \mid \{G_{it}\} \overset{\text{iid}}{\sim} \mathcal{N}(\mu_i, 1)$ with $\mu_i = \sum_{t=1}^{T} G_{it}\beta_t$, where β_t is the coefficient that measures the *additive* effect on the average rating contributed from category t. However, we find this model unsatisfactory in interpretability. For example, it would be of interest to know how much higher the users tend to rate for animations. Yet, a coefficient of value 0.18, for example, is not so straightforward to interpret.

In the Bayesian multiplicative probit model, Z_{ij} is still a Gaussian latent variable associated with every observed rating R_{ij}, i.e. $Z_{ij} \mid \{G_{it}\} \overset{\text{iid}}{\sim} \mathcal{N}(\mu_i, \sigma_i^2)$. The categorical dependence is characterized by modulating μ_i and σ_i according to categorization given by $\{G_{it}\}$. For each category $t = 1, 2, \cdots, T$, we define γ_t and η_t, both being positive parameters around 1, as multiplicative factors adjusting the mean and the variance respectively. We have the mean for item i as the baseline mean μ_0 multiplied by inflation/deflation factors contributed from the categories it belongs to; the variance is modeled similarly to allow for bigger flexibility:

$$\mu_i = \mu_0 \gamma^{(i)} = \mu_0 \prod_{t=1}^{T} \gamma_t^{G_{it}}, \quad \sigma_i^2 = \sigma_0^2/\eta^{(i)} = \sigma_0^2 \prod_{t=1}^{T} \eta_t^{-G_{it}},$$

where σ_0^2 is fixed to the empirical variance of $\{R_{ij}\}$.

We put a conjugate Gaussian prior on the baseline mean centering around the empirical mean of all ratings, given by

$$\mu_0 \sim \mathcal{N}(\theta_\mu, \sigma_\mu^2), \quad \theta_\mu = \text{mean of } \{R_{ij}\}. \qquad (2)$$

We explicitly align the center and spread for Z_{ij} and R_{ij} to increase the interpretability of $\{\gamma_t\}$, so that the inflation/deflation of ratings from the t-th category can be directly reflected by γ_t.

The category-specific parameters $\{\gamma_t\}$ and $\{\eta_t\}$ should take positive values centered around 1. We put unit-mean conjugate gamma priors on $\{\eta_t\}$ and truncated conjugate Gaussian priors on $\{\gamma_t\}$, namely

$$\pi(\eta_t \mid a_\eta) = \text{Gamma}(\eta_t \mid a_\eta, a_\eta), \qquad (3)$$

$$\pi(\gamma_t \mid \sigma_\gamma) \propto N(\gamma_t \mid 1, \sigma_\gamma^2) \mathbf{1}(\gamma_t > 0) \quad (t = 1, 2, \cdots, T). \quad (4)$$

The priors for thresholds $\{g_k\}$ are chosen to be uninformative subject to the ordering constraint, given by

$$\pi(g_1, g_2, \cdots, g_{K-1}) \propto \mathbf{1}(g_1 < g_2 < \cdots < g_{K-1}). \qquad (5)$$

4. POSTERIOR INFERENCE

4.1 MCMC sampling algorithm

The posterior distribution of the parameters can be obtained with Markov Chain Monte Carlo (MCMC). Algorithm 1 illustrates a Gibbs sampler for drawing S posterior samples: each round, one parameter is sampled from its full conditional given the latest sample values of all other parameters. The thresholds $\{g_k\}$ are updated directly on the observed data $\{R_{ij}\}$ by integrating out the latent variables $\{Z_{ij}\}$ to improve mixing [5].

4.2 Rating calibration

To get the calibrated ratings, we can impute the latent variables Z_{ij} from the posterior distribution, rescale its mean value by those $\{\gamma_t\}$ involved and finally threshold the rescaled latent variable to get the calibrated rating. To form a single calibrated rating R'_{ij} corresponding to each raw rating R_{ij}, we use the posterior mean as a point estimate, i.e.

$$R'_{ij} = \mathbb{E}[r(Z'_{ij}) \mid \{R_{ij}\}], \qquad (6)$$

where $Z'_{ij} = Z_{ij} \prod_{t=1}^{T} \gamma_t^{-G_{it}}$. The transform $r(\cdot)$ is given by (1) and it depends on the thresholds $\{g_k\}$. The calibrated ratings given above can be easily approximated with MCMC samples for $\{Z_{ij}\}$, $\{\gamma_t\}$ and $\{g_k\}$.

5. RESULTS

In all the following experiments, the hyperparameters are chosen as $\sigma_\mu = 0.05$, $\sigma_\gamma = 0.1$ and $a_\eta = 20$. We performed the posterior inference using an HMC-based sampler implemented with *Stan* [8]. All the results below are obtained from 10,000 MCMC samples on the MovieLens dataset after first discarding 10,000 burn-in samples.

5.1 Predictive evaluation

Admittedly, we are faced with an obvious obstacle in evaluation — it is impossible to obtain a "ground truth" rating that consistently maps an item to its "intrinsic quality" regardless of categories. Instead, since we explicitly model the way systematic biases distribute, we evaluate our model on its *predictive ability*, namely how accurately it captures the distribution of ratings corresponding to different combinations of categories from data.

Again, the "true" distributions are missing here. Therefore, we compare the prediction of our model fitted with a *tiny* subset to empirical histograms (an inefficient but consistent estimator) from the full dataset, assuming that the latter is close enough to the truth for those combinations with large sample size. Our posterior is inferred from a randomly sampled training set consisting of 10,000 ratings, which accounts for 1% in size of the full dataset.

We adopt the KL-divergence to measure the difference between two distributions. Figure 3 plots the metric $\Delta_{\text{KL}} = \text{KL}(P_{\text{true}} \| P_{\text{histogram}}) - \text{KL}(P_{\text{true}} \| P_{\text{model}})$ (P_{true} and $P_{\text{histogram}}$ are the empirical histograms from the full set and training set respectively) for each combination of genres (with at least 5 movies) against the number of samples available in the training set. A bigger positive Δ_{KL} suggests that the predicted distribution is closer to the true distribution compared to the empirical histogram in the training set.

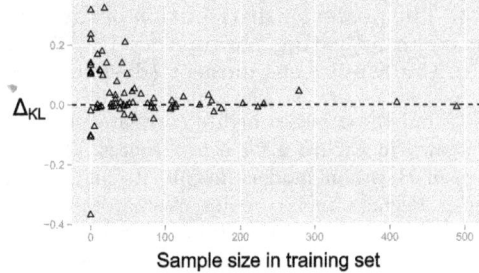

Figure 3: Δ_{KL} for combination of genres with more than 5 movies in the dataset.

Movie	Genres	n_i	Before	After
Flubber (1997)	Childrens Comedy Fantasy	53	2.75	3.28
Jumanji (1995)	Action Fantasy Sci.Fi Adventure Childrens	96	3.31	3.77
The Grifters (1990)	Crime Drama Film.Noir	89	3.48	2.94
L.A. Confidential (1997)	Crime Thriller Film.Noir Mystery	297	4.16	3.69

Table 1: Most heavily under/overrated movies and their aggregated ratings before/after calibration.

5.2 Uncovering biases

The posterior distributions estimated from the MCMC samples for the mean adjusting parameters $\{\gamma_t\}$ are plotted in Figure 4. The most overrated genre is "Film Noir", then followed by "Animation", while the most underrated genre is "Fantasy", then followed by "Childrens". γ_t for either the most overrated or the most underrated genre amounts to 10% above or below 1, which roughly means an inflation or deflation of involved ratings by 10%. Therefore, the systematic bias is not negligible if we use the raw ratings without calibration. We also showcase two most underrated and two most overrated movies in Table 1, along with their aggregated ratings before/after calibration.

Algorithm 1 MCMC inference algorithm

1: Randomly initialize parameters.
2: **for** each $l = 1, 2, \cdots, S$ **do**
3:    Sample $P(\mu_0 \mid -) = \mathcal{N}(\mu_0 \mid \tilde{\theta}_\mu, \tilde{\sigma}_\mu^2)$, with $\tilde{\sigma}_\mu^{-2} = \sigma_\mu^{-2} + \sigma_0^{-2} \sum_{i=1}^N n_i \gamma^{(i)2} \eta^{(i)}$ and $\tilde{\theta}_\mu / \tilde{\sigma}_\mu^2 = \theta_\mu / \sigma_\mu^2 + \sigma_0^{-2} \sum_{i=1}^N \sum_{j=1}^{n_i} Z_{ij} \gamma^{(i)} \eta^{(i)}$.
4:    Sample $P(Z_{ij} \mid -) \propto \mathcal{N}(Z_{ij} \mid \mu_i, \sigma_i^2) \mathbf{1}(g_{R_{ij}-1} < Z_{ij} < g_{R_{ij}})$.
5:    Sample $P(\eta_t \mid -) = \text{Gamma}(\eta_t \mid \tilde{a}_t, \tilde{b}_t)$, with $\tilde{a}_t = a_\eta + \frac{1}{2} \sum_{i:G_{it}=1} n_i$ and $\tilde{b}_t = a_\eta + \frac{1}{2} \sum_{i:G_{it}=1} \sum_{j=1}^{n_i} (Z_{ij} - \mu_i)^2 / (\sigma_i^2 \eta_t)$.
6:    Sample $P(\gamma_t \mid -) \propto \mathcal{N}(\gamma_t \mid \tilde{\mu}_t, \tilde{\sigma}_t^2) \mathbf{1}(\gamma_t > 0)$, with $\tilde{\sigma}_t^{-2} = \sigma_\gamma^{-2} + \sum_{i:G_{it}=1} n_i \sigma_i^{-2} \phi_{it}^2$, $\tilde{\mu}_t / \tilde{\sigma}_t^2 = 1/\sigma_\gamma^2 + \sum_{i:G_{it}=1} \phi_{it} (\sum_{j=1}^{n_i} Z_{ij}) / \sigma_i^2$,
     and $\phi_{it} = \mu_0 \prod_{l \neq t} \gamma_l^{G_{il}}$.
7:    Sample $P(\{g_k\} \mid -) \propto \mathbf{1}(g_1 < \cdots < g_{K-1}) \prod_{i=1}^N \prod_{j=1}^{n_i} \left[\Phi(\frac{g_{R_{ij}} - \mu_i}{\sigma_i}) - \Phi(\frac{g_{R_{ij}-1} - \mu_i}{\sigma_i}) \right]$, where Φ is the standard Gaussian CDF.
8: **end for**

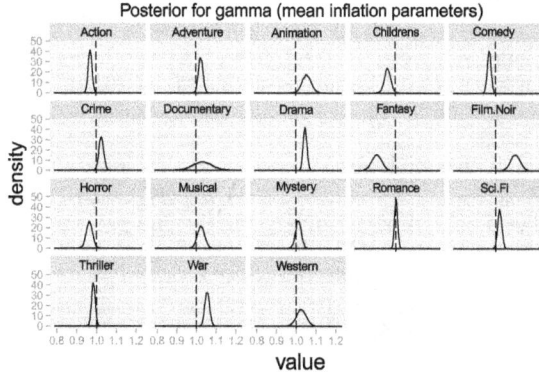

Figure 4: The posterior distribution of the category-specific mean adjusting parameters $\{\gamma_t\}$ for all the genres in the MovieLens dataset (dashed line=1).

We also find these biases highly correlated in the posterior, as shown in Figure 5 for a few genres. This justifies the usage of Bayesian models despite its higher computational cost, because merely point estimators of $\{\gamma_t\}$ cannot correctly calibrate combinations of genres by accounting for their correlations. For example, because "Childrens" and "Animation" are negatively correlated, corrections based on the multiplication of their point estimators will tend to "over-correct".

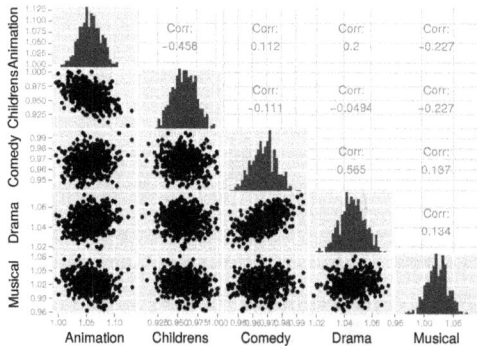

Figure 5: The category-specific mean adjusting parameters $\{\gamma_t\}$ are highly correlated in the posterior.

6. CONCLUSIONS AND FUTURE WORK

We present a Bayesian multiplicative probit model to uncover and calibrate category-wise bias in ratings, by efficiently borrowing information across a vast number of combinations of categories/genres. Future directions include modeling bias in a hierarchical taxonomy and comparing the Bayesian model with matrix-factorization-based methods.

7. ACKNOWLEDGMENTS

This work was partly supported by grant NIH R01-ES017436 from National Institute of Environmental Health Sciences.

8. REFERENCES

[1] G. Adomavicius and A. Tuzhilin. Toward the next generation of recommender systems: A survey of the state-of-the-art and possible extensions. *IEEE Transactions on Knowledge and ata Engineering*, 17(6):734–749, 2005.

[2] D. Cosley, S. K. Lam, I. Albert, J. A. Konstan, and J. Riedl. Is seeing believing?: how recommender system interfaces affect users' opinions. In *roceedings of the SIG I conference on uman factors in computing systems*, pages 585–592. ACM, 2003.

[3] F. Garcin, B. Faltings, and R. Jurca. Aggregating reputation feedback. In *roceedings of the First International onference on Reputation: Theory and Technology*, volume 1, pages 62–74, 2009.

[4] F. Garcin, B. Faltings, R. Jurca, and N. Joswig. Rating aggregation in collaborative filtering systems. In *roceedings of the third A M conference on Recommender systems*, pages 349–352. ACM, 2009.

[5] V. E. Johnson and J. H. Albert. *Ordinal data modeling*. Springer, 1999.

[6] S. Krishnan, J. Patel, M. J. Franklin, and K. Goldberg. A methodology for learning, analyzing, and mitigating social influence bias in recommender systems. In *roceedings of the 8th A M onference on Recommender Systems*, RecSys '14, pages 137–144. ACM, 2014.

[7] B. Mobasher, R. Burke, R. Bhaumik, and C. Williams. Toward trustworthy recommender systems: An analysis of attack models and algorithm robustness. *A M Transactions on Internet Technology*, 7(4):23, 2007.

[8] Stan Development Team. Stan: A C++ library for probability and sampling, version 2.1, 2013.

[9] A. Umyarov and A. Tuzhilin. Improving rating estimation in recommender systems using aggregation-and variance-based hierarchical models. In *roceedings of the third A M conference on Recommender systems*, pages 37–44. ACM, 2009.

[10] S. Vargas, L. Baltrunas, A. Karatzoglou, and P. Castells. Coverage, redundancy and size-awareness in genre diversity for recommender systems. In *roceedings of the 8th A M onference on Recommender systems*, pages 209–216. ACM, 2014.

User Churn Migration Analysis with DEDICOM

Rafet Sifa, César Ojeda, Christian Bauckhage
Fraunhofer IAIS
Sankt Augustin, Germany
{rafet.sifa|cesar.ali.ojeda.marin|christian.bauckhage}@iais.fraunhofer.de

ABSTRACT

Time plays an important role regarding user preferences for products. It introduces asymmetries into the adoption of products which should be considered in the context of recommender systems and business intelligence. We therefore investigate how temporally asymmetric user preferences can be analyzed using a latent factor model called Decomposition Into Directional Components (DEDICOM). We introduce a new scalable hybrid algorithm that combines projected gradient descent and alternating least squares updates to compute DEDICOM and imposes semi-nonnegativity constraints to better interpret the resulting factors. We apply our model to analyze user churn and migration between different computer games in a social gaming environment.

Categories and Subject Descriptors

H.2.8 [**Database Applications**]: Data mining

Keywords

Latent Factor Models; Preference Learning; Churn Migration Analysis;

1. INTRODUCTION

Recommender systems play two crucial roles in the modern information age. On the one hand, they aid users in decision making when confronted with massive amounts of data. On the other hand, they allow companies to capitalize on the purchasing patterns of users. Especially w.r.t. the latter, it is important to understand *migration* patterns between products. Traditional recommender systems, however, focus on the former and try to establish similarities between items based on explicit or implicit user feedback. Latent factor models [9] extend this notion by studying similarities between users and items. Such similarities are defined trough latent factors resulting from a factorization of, say, a rating matrix in which user preference for different items are encoded. Contrary to this, we here consider a latent

RecSys'15, September 16–20, 2015, Vienna, Austria.
Copyright is held by the owner/author(s). Publication rights licensed to ACM.
ACM 978-1-4503-3692-5/15/09 ...$15.00.
DOI: http://dx.doi.org/10.1145/2792838.2799680

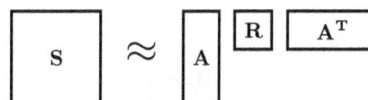

Figure 1: A pictorial representation of *Two Way DEDICOM* partitioning. Asymmetrical relationships in $\mathbf{S} \in \mathbb{R}^{n \times n}$ are decomposed into a latent factor matrix $\mathbf{A} \in \mathbb{R}^{n \times k}$ and an asymmetric mode transition matrix $\mathbf{R} \in \mathbb{R}^{k \times k}$.

factor model that attempts to reveal latent migration patterns between products. This requires us to consider asymmetric matrices encoding ownership histories or movements between different items.

Our contribution relies on the *decomposition into directional components (DEDICOM)* model due to Harshman [6] who introduced it to analyze asymmetric relationships in social connections. We propose a new scalable hybrid algorithm composed of projected gradient descent and alternating least squares methods for DEDICOM partitioning. Our approach is easy to implement and computationally less intensive than previously proposed algorithms. Moreover, while traditional DEDICOM may produce negative mode transitions which might be difficult to interpret, our approach forces them to be nonnegative. In doing so, latent migrations habits are expressed in terms of proportions. We illustrate the use of our approach in the context of analyzing churn migration of players of computer games.

2. THE DEDICOM MODEL

Matrix and tensor factorization techniques have become popular tools to analyze large and complex data sets for they can reveal hidden structures and provide interpretable and actionable results [1,4,9]. Often, data matrices are asymmetric, for instance if they express relationships between members of a community, movements between places, or item-to-item relationships [1,2,6,8]. In this paper, we are thus concerned with DEDICOM which is a latent factor model for asymmetric matrices. DEDICOM and its variants have been used in variety of contexts including network analysis, game data mining, natural language processing, and information retrieval [1,2,4,7]. Given a matrix $\mathbf{S} \in \mathbb{R}^{n \times n}$ which expresses asymmetric relations between n objects and an integer $k \ll n$, DEDICOM attempts to factorize $\mathbf{S}$ as

$$\mathbf{S} \approx \mathbf{A}\mathbf{R}\mathbf{A}^T \qquad (1)$$

where $\mathbf{A} \in \mathbb{R}^{n \times k}$ and $\mathbf{R} \in \mathbb{R}^{k \times k}$. Fig. 1 illustrates this idea. The columns $\mathbf{a}_{\cdot j}$ of matrix $\mathbf{A}$ are understood to represent *latent factors* causing the structures represented in **S** and the relations between these factors are encoded by the asymmetric affinity matrix **R**. DEDICOM thus approximates individual relationships in s_{ij} as

$$s_{ij} \approx \mathbf{a}_{i:}\mathbf{R}\mathbf{a}_{j:}^T = \sum_{b=1}^{n}\Big(a_{ib}\mathbf{r}_{b:}\Big)\mathbf{a}_{j:}^T = \sum_{b=1}^{n}\sum_{c=1}^{n}a_{ib}r_{bc}a_{jc} \quad (2)$$

where $\mathbf{a}_{i:}$ and $\mathbf{a}_{j:}$ represent the ith and jth row of **A**, respectively, and $\mathbf{r}_{b:}$ represents the bth row of **R**.

Computing DEDICOM can be cast as a matrix norm minimization problem where the objective is to minimize the following loss function with respect to **A** and **R**

$$E(\mathbf{A}, \mathbf{R}) = \left\| \mathbf{S} - \mathbf{A}\mathbf{R}\mathbf{A}^T \right\|^2. \quad (3)$$

A variety of constrained and unconstrained methods have been proposed to solve (3) [1, 2, 7]. In this work we introduce a hybrid algorithm composed of projected gradient descent and alternating least squares methods for Orthogonal DEDICOM. Our algorithm updates **A** using projected gradient descent and thereafter it updates **R** in an alternating least squares fashion. The main difference of our approach to previous solutions [1, 2, 7] is in the update for **A**. Unlike in [1,2], our method takes each occurrence of **A** into account when minimizing (3) w.r.t. **A**. Compared to previously introduced methods it provides a computationally efficient approach including a reduced number of factor parameters for the updates which makes the update step straightforward to implement. Furthermore, we propose a new way of interpreting DEDICOM factorizations in an additive fashion which is realized through constraining **R** to be nonnegative.

3. AN ALGORITHM FOR ORTHOGONAL TWO WAY DEDICOM

In this section, we derive our Hybrid Orthogonal (HO) DEDICOM model and present two algorithms to find such a decomposition. Starting with the derivation of the update step for **A**, we write (3) in terms of matrix traces to have

$$E(\mathbf{A}) = \text{tr}\Big[\mathbf{S}^T\mathbf{S} - 2\mathbf{S}^T\mathbf{A}\mathbf{R}\mathbf{A}^T + \mathbf{A}\mathbf{R}^T\mathbf{A}^T\mathbf{A}\mathbf{R}\mathbf{A}^T\Big]. \quad (4)$$

Since traces are linear mappings and the term $[\mathbf{S}^T\mathbf{S}]$ does not depend on **A**, minimizing E in (4) is equivalent to minimizing E' which is defined as

$$E'(\mathbf{A}) = \text{tr}\Big[\mathbf{A}\mathbf{R}^T\mathbf{A}^T\mathbf{A}\mathbf{R}\mathbf{A}^T\Big] - 2\,\text{tr}\Big[\mathbf{S}^T\mathbf{A}\mathbf{R}\mathbf{A}^T\Big]. \quad (5)$$

The solution can be now simplified if we introduce an orthogonality constraint. Since traces are invariant under cyclic permutations, we cast (5) as

$$E'(\mathbf{A}) = \text{tr}\Big[\mathbf{A}^T\mathbf{A}\mathbf{R}^T\mathbf{A}^T\mathbf{A}\mathbf{R}\Big] - 2\,\text{tr}\Big[\mathbf{S}^T\mathbf{A}\mathbf{R}\mathbf{A}^T\Big]. \quad (6)$$

Restricting the columns of **A** to be orthogonal unit vectors in $\mathbb{R}^n$ yields the equality $\mathbf{A}^T\mathbf{A} = \mathbf{I_k}$. This simplifies (6) to

$$E'(\mathbf{A}) = \text{tr}\Big[\mathbf{R}^T\mathbf{R}\Big] - 2\,\text{tr}\Big[\mathbf{S}^T\mathbf{A}\mathbf{R}\mathbf{A}^T\Big]. \quad (7)$$

Considering the gradient of E' with respect to **A**, we have

$$\frac{\partial E'}{\partial \mathbf{A}} = -2\frac{\partial}{\partial \mathbf{A}}\,\text{tr}\Big[\mathbf{S}^T\mathbf{A}\mathbf{R}\mathbf{A}^T\Big] \quad (8)$$

$$= -2\Big(\mathbf{S}^T\mathbf{A}\mathbf{R} + \mathbf{S}\mathbf{A}\mathbf{R}^T\Big). \quad (9)$$

Algorithm 1 Hybrid Orthogonal DEDICOM

Randomly initialize **A** and **R**
while Stopping condition is not satisfied **do**
  //Compute the gradient
  $\frac{\partial E'}{\partial \mathbf{A}_t} \leftarrow -2\Big(\mathbf{S}^T\mathbf{A}_t\mathbf{R}_t + \mathbf{S}\mathbf{A}_t\mathbf{R}_t^T\Big)$
  //Update **A** in the opposite direction of the gradient
  $\mathbf{A_{t+1}} \leftarrow \mathbf{A}_t - \eta_A\frac{\partial E'}{\partial \mathbf{A}_t}$
  //Project $\mathbf{A}_{t+1}$ by means of QR-Decomposition
  $\mathbf{A_{t+1}}, \mathbf{U} \leftarrow QR\Big(\mathbf{A_{t+1}}\Big)$
  //Update **R** in ALS manner
  $\mathbf{R_{t+1}} \leftarrow \mathbf{A}_{t+1}^T\mathbf{S}\,\mathbf{A}_{t+1}.$
end while

Using the gradient in (9) we can define an update for **A** that adapts the current solution as follows

$$\mathbf{A} \leftarrow \mathbf{A} + 2\eta_A\Big(\mathbf{S}^T\mathbf{A}\mathbf{R} + \mathbf{S}\mathbf{A}\mathbf{R}^T\Big) \quad (10)$$

where η_A is a learning rate that might be static or dynamically adapted using inexact line search methods or annealing techniques. Similar to [2], as the update might lead to solutions that are not orthogonal, we enforce orthogonality using the QR-Decomposition $\mathbf{A} = \mathbf{QU}$ where **Q** is orthogonal and **U** is upper triangular and set $\mathbf{A} = \mathbf{Q}$.

Fixing **A**, the problem of minimization (3) becomes a matrix regression problem w.r.t. **R**. That is, as **A** has full rank and $k < n$, we multiply both sides of **S** by the left- and right generalized inverses. Owing to the orthogonality of **A** we have

$$\Big(\mathbf{A}\Big)_{left}^{-1} = \Big(\mathbf{A}^T\mathbf{A}\Big)^{-1}\mathbf{A}^T = \mathbf{A}^T \quad (11)$$

and

$$\Big(\mathbf{A}^T\Big)_{right}^{-1} = \mathbf{A}\Big(\mathbf{A}^T\mathbf{A}\Big)^{-1} = \mathbf{A}. \quad (12)$$

Accordingly, an alternating least square update for **R** can be defined as

$$\mathbf{R} \leftarrow \mathbf{A}^T\mathbf{S}\mathbf{A}. \quad (13)$$

The essential steps of this procedure are summarized in Algorithm 1. Compared to the existing approaches our method is straightforward to implement and does not require computationally expensive operations such as matrix inversion in the update step.

4. SEMI-NONNEGATIVE DEDICOM

Revisiting (2), we can interpret DEDICOM as a soft clustering method that accounts for asymmetric similarities between *loadings*, i.e. entries in **A**. In this case, the relation between two objects will be determined as a weighted combination of the global relations between clusters that are scaled by the latent factors. This interpretation might be misleading when the global relations between clusters that are encoded in **R** are negative. This leaves us with a situation where we can only interpret entries where each of the factors in $a_{ib}r_{bc}a_{jc}$ is positive. To address this issue, we impose nonnegativity constraints on the affinity matrix **R**. The advantages of having nonnegative affinities in DEDICOM consist in an interpretability of both the affinity matrix **R** as a compressed version of the data matrix **S** and

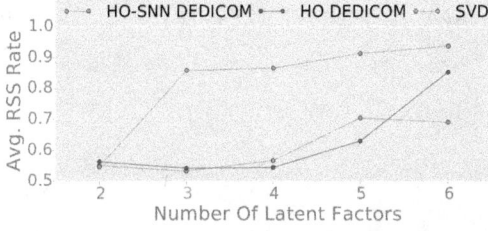

Figure 2: Average reconstruction error for missing link estimation through cross-validation.

the estimation in (2). In other words, when $\mathbf{R}$ contains only nonnegative values, they will scale the *additive cluster-ranking* assigned through the loadings. For instance, given two entities i and j and a nonnegative matrix $\mathbf{R}$, when approximating the similarity from i to j: the loadings with the same sign will have an additive effect whereas the loadings with opposite signs will have a subtractive effect.

Keeping the above alternating least squares approach, a nonnegative $\mathbf{R}$ can be found by making sure that its values are nonnegative and do not increase the error defined in (3). Formally, in each iteration, we are thus required to solve for $\mathbf{R}$ with a nonnegativity constraint

$$E''(\mathbf{R}) = \left\| \mathbf{S} - \mathbf{A}\mathbf{R}\mathbf{A}^T \right\|^2 \wedge r_{ij} \geq 0 \; \forall \; i,j \in [1,\ldots,k]. \quad (14)$$

The error in (14) remains the same if we vectorize the matrices as

$$E''(\mathbf{R}) = \left\| \text{vec}(\mathbf{S}) - \text{vec}(\mathbf{A}\mathbf{R}\mathbf{A}^T) \right\|^2 \quad (15)$$

where vec vectorizes (flattens) a matrix $\mathbf{C} \in \mathbb{R}^{n \times m}$ as follows

$$\text{vec}(\mathbf{C}) = [c_{11}, \ldots, c_{1m}, \ldots, c_{n1}, \ldots, c_{nm}]^T. \quad (16)$$

Considering our special case of $\mathbf{A}\mathbf{R}\mathbf{A}^T$, we can write

$$\text{vec}(\mathbf{A}\mathbf{R}\mathbf{A}^T) = \left(\mathbf{A} \otimes \mathbf{A} \right) \text{vec}(\mathbf{R}) \quad (17)$$

where $\otimes$ denotes the Kronecker product. Substituting (17) in (15) we obtain

$$E''(\mathbf{R}) = \left\| \text{vec}(\mathbf{S}) - \left(\mathbf{A} \otimes \mathbf{A} \right) \text{vec}(\mathbf{R}) \right\|^2. \quad (18)$$

We can then reformulate (14) as

$$E'''(\mathbf{x}) = \left\| \mathbf{y} - \mathbf{B}\mathbf{x} \right\|^2 \wedge x_i \geq 0 \; \forall \; i \in [1,\ldots,k^2] \quad (19)$$

where $\mathbf{y} = \text{vec}(\mathbf{S})$, $\mathbf{B} = \left(\mathbf{A} \otimes \mathbf{A} \right)$ and $\mathbf{x} = \text{vec}(\mathbf{R})$. With the latest derivation in (19), we have reformulated the problem of obtaining semi-nonnegative affinities in DEDICOM as a nonnegative least-squares problem [10] for which fast methods are available [3]. Therefore, keeping the updates of matrix $\mathbf{A}$ as in Alg. 1 and finding $\mathbf{R}$ by solving (19) provides us with an optimal Semi-Nonnegative (SNN) DEDICOM partitioning.

5. GAME MIGRATION ANALYSIS

Churn and retention analysis in virtual environments consists of analyzing factors affecting the dynamics of global user preferences [5,11]. As a use case, we consider an application of semi-nonnegative DEDICOM to analyze the churn

migration behavior among computer game players. Churn analysis has been previously studied in the context of game behavior analysis in [5,11] where a player is considered to be churning when there is no player activity present in a particular time window. Generalizing this notion to multiple games, we define that a migration occurs between any two different games i and j from time t to $t+1$ when a player *quits* playing game i that they played at t and *starts* playing game j at $t+1$. In the study presented here, we analyze migration between games in a data set of two consecutive snapshots each covering two months of game activity logs in 2014. That is, our data set contains information as to whether players played a game or not. In total our data shows the game-play activities of 79,695 individual players on a social gaming platform with 2,257 games. We define a churn migration matrix as described above by accumulating the frequencies of migrations for each player, between the snapshots. We compare the generalization capabilities of Hybrid Orthogonal DEDICOM with and without semi-nonnegativity constraint to *pure*-SVD due to the latter's popularity in research and industry. Our results indicate outcomes after 5-fold block-based cross validation.

In Fig. 2 we show how the rate of residual sum of squares (RSS) [4] which can be defined as

$$RSSR = \left\| \mathbf{S} - \mathbf{A}\mathbf{R}\mathbf{A}^T \right\| \Big/ \left\| \mathbf{S} \right\| \quad (20)$$

changes for different numbers of latent factors determined by the algorithms. Within the given settings, we observed that semi-nonnegative DEDICOM yields the lowest average error rate and obtained a value of 53% for the unseen game migration entries with three latent factor partitioning.

Analyzing the semi-nonnegative partitioning with three latent factors, we obtain different characteristics describing the migration behavior among the analyzed players (summarized in Fig. 3a). The first behavioral group represents the migration among highly rated games (a.k.a. *AAA* games) and the largest interactions that occur in this group show that the majority of users actually prefers to stay within this group of games. The second group, which we labeled *F2P-Indie*, represents player interactions between Free-to-play (F2P) games and so called indie games (released by independent developers) in comparison to the *AAA*-group and the *Platformer*-group; here we do not observe any self transitions. The third group, i.e. the *Platformer*-group, represents player activity within a genre of games called two- and two-and-a-half-dimensional or *oblique rotated games*; here we observe only a strong self affinity which indicates that players of this genre like to stay within the genre. Additionally, we use distributions of user generated game tags that describe the content, difficulty and the genres of games to have more insight about the types of games contributing to the groups. Since the games we are analyzing mostly contain more than one tag, in Fig. 3b, we compare loading-weighted user generated game tag distributions for each cluster as defined by the columns of $\mathbf{A}$ where we observe a clear distinction among game genres. Furthermore, comparing the high negative loadings for each cluster we observe no negative loadings for the *AAA* group specifically whereas the famous games that belong to this group do show rather high negative values in the *F2P-Indie*-group indicating a weak relationship between games within these two groups. Similarly the high negative loadings for the *Platformer*-group are distributed

323

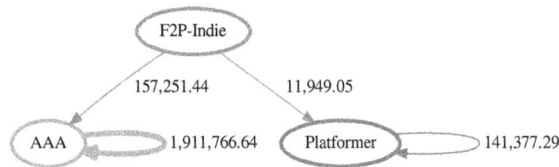

(a) Game Affinity Map

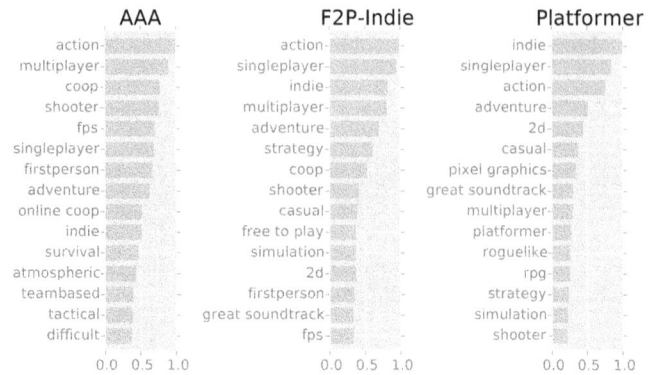

(b) Game Tag Distribution

Figure 3: Game affinity map and normalized weighted game tag distributions for churn based migration analysis resulting from Semi-nonnegative Hybrid Orthogonal DEDICOM. The game affinity map reveals the overall migration behavior among games and indicates the importance of game genres for each activity group. The group *AAA* contains activities mostly from distributor's flagship games which are dominant in the population we analyzed. The *F2P-Indie* group contains player activities from F2P-Indie games that rather move to the other two groups. The *Platformer* group indicates the group of player activities among 2d platform-like games which is a conservative group mainly containing interactions with itself.

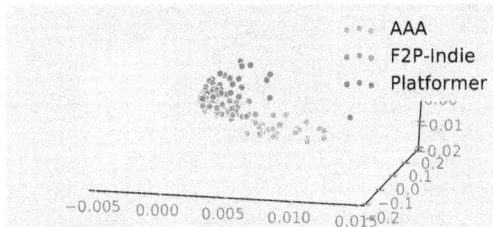

Figure 4: Low dimensional embeddings of games with high loadings. We observe a clear separation among the groups of games with different genres.

among games that have the highest loadings for the other groups. Moreover similar to other latent factor models, we can study the low dimensional embeddings of games with high loadings in Fig. 4 where we observe a clear separation between the group of games with different genres.

6. CONCLUSION

Asymmetric similarity-based latent factor models reveal actionable user preferences and provide descriptive explanations as to complex item-related user activities over time. In this paper, we have shown how a semi-nonnegativity constrained DEDICOM model can reduce the dimensionality of asymmetric data matrices and reveal hidden structure in an interpretable manner to help build advanced analytics systems. The presented use case of analyzing churn migration behavior of the users of a social gaming environment is of considerable practical interest for the gaming industry which is currently adopting their business models towards *freemium* games in which players pay for game content. In this business environment player churn must be avoided at all cost and a better understanding of player migration between games helps developers improve their designs. Our future work involves incorporating DEDICOM models to user- and item-based recommender systems, as well as, analyzing different forms of item-to-item relations.

7. REFERENCES

[1] B. Bader, R. Harshman, and T. Kolda. Temporal Analysis of Semantic Graphs using ASALSAN. In *Proc. IEEE ICDM*, 2007.

[2] C. Bauckhage, R. Sifa, A. Drachen, C. Thurau, and F. Hadiji. Beyond Heatmaps: Spatio-Temporal Clustering using Behavior-Based Partitioning of Game Levels. In *Proc. IEEE CIG*, 2014.

[3] R. Bro and S. De Jong. A Fast Non-negativity constrained Least Squares Algorithm. *J. of Chemometrics*, 11(5), 1997.

[4] P. A. Chew, B. W. Bader, and A. Rozovskaya. Using DEDICOM for Completely Unsupervised Part Of Speech Tagging. In *Proc. Workshop on Unsupervised and Minimally Supervised Learning of Lexical Semantics*, 2009.

[5] F. Hadiji, R. Sifa, A. Drachen, C. Thurau, K. Kersting, and C. Bauckhage. Predicting Player Churn in the Wild. In *Proc. IEEE CIG*, 2014.

[6] R. Harshman. Models for Analysis of Asymmetrical Relationships among N Objects or Stimuli. In *Proc. Joint Meeting of the Psychometric Society and the Society for Mathematical Psychology*, 1978.

[7] H. Kiers. DESICOM: Decomposition of Asymmetric Relationships Data into Simple Components. *Behaviormetrika*, 24(2), 1997.

[8] N. Koenigstein and Y. Koren. Towards Scalable and Accurate Item-oriented Recommendations. In *Proc. ACM RecSys*, 2013.

[9] Y. Koren, R. Bell, and C. Volinsky. Matrix Factorization Techniques for Recommender Systems. *IEEE Computer*, 42(8), 2009.

[10] C. L. Lawson and R. J. Hanson. *Solving Least Squares Problems*. SIAM, 1974.

[11] J. Runge, P. Gao, F. Garcin, and B. Faltings. Churn Prediction for High-value Players in Casual Social Games. In *Proc. IEEE CIG*, 2014.

A Personalised Reader for Crowd Curated Content

Gabriella Kazai, Daoud Clarke,
Iskander Yusof
Lumi
{gabs,daoud,iskander}@lumi.do

Matteo Venanzi
Lumi and University of Southampton
matteo@lumi.do

ABSTRACT

Personalised news recommender systems traditionally rely on content ingested from a select set of publishers and ask users to indicate their interests from a predefined list of topics. They then provide users a feed of news items for each of their topics. In this demo, we present a mobile app that automatically learns users' interests from their browsing or twitter history and provides them with a personalised feed of diverse, crowd curated content. The app also continuously learns from the users' interactions as they swipe to like or skip items recommended to them. In addition, users can discover trending stories and content liked by other users they follow. The crowd is thus formed of the users, who as a whole act as the curators of the content to be recommended.

Categories and Subject Descriptors

H.4.m [**Information Systems Applications**]: Miscellaneous

Keywords

Recommender system, crowd curation, social filter, mobile

1. INTRODUCTION

Online content is growing at an unprecedented rate, with millions of news stories, blogs, videos, and a wide range of publisher and user generated content being added every day. Users typically navigate this space with the help of search engines, via social media, or through services like RSS feeds, content aggregators or recommender systems. With the proliferation of smart phones, access to this content is shifting away from search engines to consuming content directly within apps. As a result, a number of mobile content apps have been developed, including well known commercial systems like Feedly, Prismatic or Pinterest[1], as well as research prototypes like Focal [2], PEN [1] and others, e.g., [4, 3]. However, these apps rely on users manually defining their topics of interest, based on which articles from selected publishers can be pushed to them.

---

[1] feedly.com, getprismatic.com/news, uk.pinterest.com

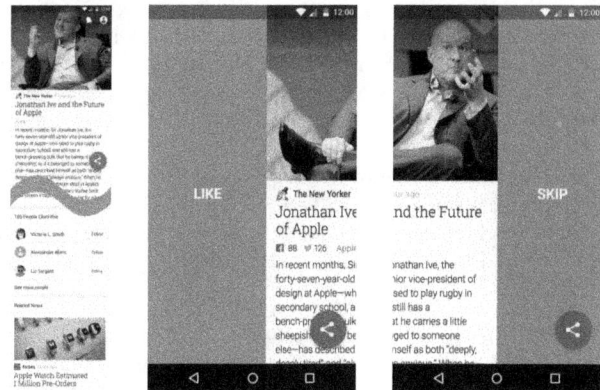

Figure 1: Full view of a recommended article and screenshots of user swipe actions to like or skip

Our system, called Lumi Social News[2], is not limited to specific publishers, but aims to provide users a personalised feed of diverse, crowd curated content, including long tail and user generated content. It automatically learns users' interests either from their public Twitter feed or from public pages in their browsing history. The generated user model is then matched against the stream of incoming content, consisting of public pages visited or tweeted by the crowd (the community of users) or ingested via RSS.

Instead of showing the user a list of recommendations that is typical in recommender systems, Lumi displays a single recommended item at any given time. This item is picked from a given time window of ingested content, where the selection is based on the item's relevance to the user as well as its popularity on social media, i.e., Twitter and Facebook. Figure 1 shows an example recommended article.

The header image is picked based on image quality and positioning in the original text, which is followed by the title and the full text of the article. In the case of a video, the video itself is positioned at the top, followed by the title and any textual description if available on the original site. The top three users who liked the recommended item are listed below the content, ordered by similarity to the user. Finally a list of related articles are shown, based on content similarity.

To get to the next recommendation, the user needs to either like or skip the current item by swiping left or right on the screen, respectively (see Figure 1). All liked items are

---

[2] android.lumi.do

saved by the system and can be accessed through the user's profile area. The liked/skipped actions are used to continually update the user's model, thus learning more about the user's evolving interests and filtering or boosting recommendations based on the user's feedback actions.

Lumi also supports a social network, where users can follow each other and discover interesting content that was liked by those they follow. Recommendations on who to follow are based on the relevance of the suggested user's liked items to the current user's interests as well as based on existing social links in the user's Twitter network.

2. SYSTEM OVERVIEW

The system uses a graph processing architecture, similar to that of Twitter's Storm, where each node is a process and data is passed around from node to node. This is driven by a need for real-time processing, as opposed to processing offered by Hadoop-like tools. The topology of a graph is specified dependent on its function. For example, a bootstrapping graph is designed for real-time processing of large-scale browsing or twitter data at signup in order to create a user model as quickly as possible. The front-end is implemented for Android phones in Java, which connects to the back-end via an API. The main system components are:

- *Ingestion*: Ingestion nodes process a number of incoming streams of content from RSS, Twitter and public pages from user visits. The content is rendered, passed through a quality filter and subsequently a range of features and media are extracted. An SVM classifier is used to assign a category label, e.g., business or technology. Named entities are extracted using multiple open-source tools, e.g., NLTK and OpenNLP[3]. Top ranking entities are assigned as topic tags. Data is stored in Cassandra[4] and Elasticsearch[5]. Note that for additional privacy, user's browsing data are stored completely anonymously and separately from their Twitter data, and no link is made between the two.

- *Bootstrapping*: At signup, the public pages in a new user's browsing history or Twitter feed are analysed and an initial user model is built. We build separate models for their browsing data and for their Twitter data. The only time the two sets of data can be connected is when the user is online and makes a request for recommendations, thus to maintain this level of privacy we need to generate separate models.

- *User model update*: Users' models are updated based on their ongoing online activities, e.g., Twitter feed, as well as based on their in-app actions, e.g., when they read, swipe to like or swipe to skip a recommended item, and when they share a recommendation.

- *Trending content*: Trending content is identified by monitoring social media, e.g., likes on Facebook and tweets on Twitter. In addition, we use clustering to detect breaking stories, i.e., when the same story is being published across multiple outlets.

- *Offline recommender*: Ingested content is passed through a Content Based (CB) and a Collaborative Filtering (CF) based recommender, which calculates relevance

scores for each user model and stores their top recommendations. This is run as a background process which generates recommendations for users even when they are not online, so that they don't miss out on interesting content.

- *Online recommender*: When an Android client requests new recommendations, the top ranking items are returned from across a number of different sources, including the offline recommendations store, the latest trending stories as well as the freshest content ingested in the last few hours. The ranking function then takes into account both the relevance of an item, its freshness and its popularity.

- *Related content*: Same stories from multiple outlets are clustered together and can be served to the user as related items. Articles based on broader topical similarity are also linked together. Other articles from the same site may also be of interest to the user and may also be shown below the recommended article.

- *Suggested user to follow*: We recommend users to follow based on the relevance of the items they liked to the current user or based on existing links between them on Twitter.

At the time of writing, we are conducting online experiments with real users, using an A/B testing framework. Among others, we are experimenting with different recommender algorithms and trending story detection methods and different UI features. We are tracking the quality of our recommendations as reflected in likes, skips and reading times, averaged across users and plotted over time.

3. CONCLUSIONS

The presented system is the first in its class to provide personalised feeds by non-intrusively learning users' interests and responding to their feedback actions when reading recommended items. The assessment of how recommender systems may perform in this setting with noisy and sparse data and online user feedbacks is the key challenge to deliver this service.

4. ACKNOWLEDGMENTS

Lumi is a result of the efforts of a great team, see https://lumi.do/about/team.

5. REFERENCES

[1] F. Garcin and B. Faltings. Pen recsys: A personalized news recommender systems framework. NRS '13, pages 3–9. ACM, 2013.

[2] F. Garcin, F. Galle, and B. Faltings. Focal: A personalized mobile news reader. RecSys'14, pages 369–370. ACM, 2014.

[3] A. Said, J. Lin, A. Bellogín, and A. de Vries. A month in the life of a production news recommender system. In *Proc. Workshop on Living Labs for IR Evaluation*, pages 7–10. ACM, 2013.

[4] M. Tavakolifard, J. A. Gulla, K. C. Almeroth, J. E. Ingvaldesn, G. Nygreen, and E. Berg. Tailored news in the palm of your hand: A multi-perspective transparent approach to news recommendation. WWW'13 Companion, pages 305–308, 2013.

---

[3] github.com/nltk, opennlp.apache.org/
[4] cassandra.apache.org/
[5] elastic.co/products/elasticsearch

Automated Recommendation of Healthy, Personalised Meal Plans

Morgan Harvey[1]   David Elsweiler[2]
[1]Northumbria University, Newcastle, United Kingdom
[2]University of Regensburg, Germany
e-mail: morgan.harvey@northumbria.ac.uk, david@elsweiler.co.uk

ABSTRACT

Poor health due to a lack of understanding of nutrition is a major problem in the modern world, one which could potentially be addressed via the use of recommender systems. In this demo we present a system to generate meal plans for users which they will not only like, based on their taste preferences, but will also conform to daily nutritional guidelines. The interface allows the selection of recipes for breakfast, lunch and dinner and can automatically complete a daily meal plan or can generate entire plans itself.

Keywords

Health, Recommender Systems, Planning, Prevention

1. INTRODUCTION AND MOTIVATION

Poor dietary habits are a major cause of today's world health problems, however lifestyle-related illnesses can be prevented and sometimes even reversed through good nutrition [1]. Since people often lack the requisite knowledge to implement positive changes [2] food recommender systems (RS) have been touted as a potential means to assist people in nourishing themselves more healthily [3].

Food RS make sense as part of a strategy for behavioural change as suggesting a change that is less painful, i.e. based on something the user might like, is more likely to be accepted and followed. Recommenders are likely to be effective at predicting which changes will be painful or not but they have a serious drawback when aiming for positive change: they learn user preferences for ingredients and food styles. This leads to users who like fat- and calorie-laden meals being recommended fat- and calorie-laden meals [3] - an outcome not conducive to improving nutritional habits.

This demo presents a web-based system able to automatically create daily meal plans for users. It does so by calculating the nutritional requirements of the user based on their personal *personas* (age, gender, height,etc.) and, using the top recommendations given by a state-of-the-art recipe recommendation algorithm [3], attempts to generate a plan

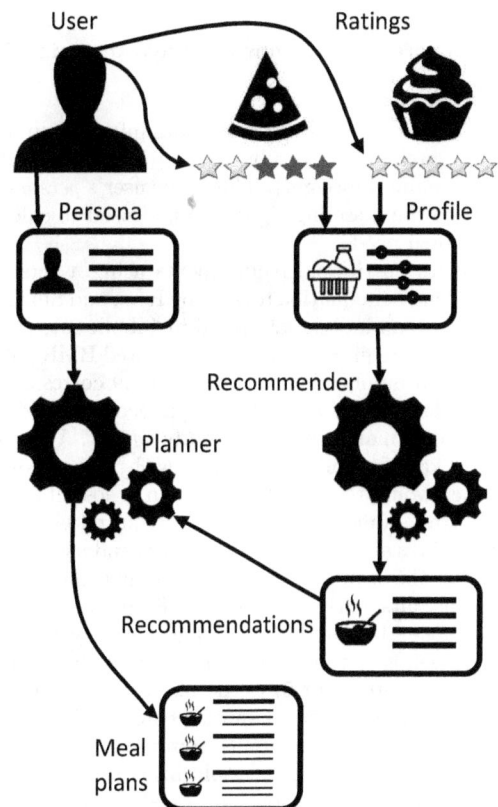

Figure 1: Diagram of system architecture.

which corresponds to guidelines published by international health agencies. The planner is designed to form part of a larger web site where users can share, rate, search and browse recipes. After rating recipes, the user can receive recommendations of other recipes they might like and can even submit their own. The nutritional properties of the recipes are automatically estimated by the system using a state-of-the-art algorithm [4].

2. SYSTEM ARCHITECTURE

Figure 1 shows the main components of, and flow of data within, the meal planning system. The user first provides information about their tastes by rating a number of recipes in the system via a typical 5 star rating paradigm. These are used to build the user's taste *profile* which is fed into the

Figure 2: Screenshots showing meal planning interface (centre and right) and user *persona* creation (left).

RS detailed in [3]. The user also provides information about their height, weight, age, daily activity level and goal (to lose, gain or maintain weight). This is the user's *persona* and is an input to the planning algorithm and used to calculate their nutritional needs.

We calculate nutritional requirements using a version of the Harris-Benedict equation revised by Roza and Shizgal [5] which estimates an individual's basal metabolic rate (BMR) and daily calorie requirements. The estimated BMR value is multiplied by a number between 1.2 and 1.9 corresponding to the individual's activity level giving a recommended daily energy intake to maintain current body weight. We add or remove 500 kcal for individuals who wish to gain or lose weight which would result in the safe gain or loss of 0.45 kgs per week. We assume that 20% of the required energy will come form drinks and between-meal snacks and use standard measures for the proportion of calories that should come from proteins, fats, carbohydrates and fibres [1].

The RS generates predicted ratings for as yet unrated recipes and sends a ranked list of these (along with the recipes the user rated 4 or 5) to the planner. We can create plans for a given user (persona-profile combination) by first taking the top x recommendations from the RS for the taste profile. This set of recipes is then split into two separate sets, one for breakfasts and one for main meals. A full search is performed to find **every combination** of these recipes in the sequence [breakfast, main meal, main meal] which meets the target nutritional requirements defined above. Combinations with the same meals cannot be repeated, e.g. [R1, R2, R3] and [R1, R3, R2] are treated as only one plan.

The planner calculates the nutritional needs of the user based on the *persona* and attempts to build plans from the top x recommended recipes that can combine to provide all of the user's daily needs within an error margin of 10%. These plans are outputted for the user to evaluate and use. Note that it is also possible for the user to directly choose 1 or 2 meals for a plan and in this case the planner must complete the plan by filling in the blank meals (not shown).

2.1 Demo System

Figure 2 shows screenshots of the demo application. On the left is the interface for creating a user *persona*. The centre screenshot shows a list of recipes that can be dragged and

dropped into the planning interface on the right. The system also provides a number of features for searching, sorting and browsing recipes which (not shown). The user has already chosen a lunch and dinner and can either have their plan automatically completed by clicking the "complete this plan" link (dashed line) or can try dragging another recipe of their choice into the breakfast slot (solid line). The screenshot on the extreme right shows one of the 18 generated meal plans for this example in which the system has chosen a breakfast which fits in to the existing meal plan. The table near the bottom summarises the nutritional properties of the plan and compares this to the target values for the user. The final column shows a colour-coded percentage indicating how far away from the ideal value the current plan is.

3. SUMMARY

This demo presents a first attempt at incorporating health and nutrition into the food recommendation problem by generating meal plans. This shows it is possible to combine recommended recipes into balanced meal plans according to nutritional guidelines.

4. REFERENCES

[1] D. Ornish et al. Can lifestyle changes reverse coronary heart disease?: The lifestyle heart trial. *The Lancet*, 336(8708):129 – 133, 1990.

[2] J. F. Guthrie, B. M. Derby, and A. S. Levy. *America's Eating Habits: Changes and ConsequencesAgriculture Information Bulletin No. (AIB750)*, pages 243–280. US Dept. for Agriculture, 1999.

[3] M. Harvey, B. Ludwig, and D. Elsweiler. You are what you eat: Learning user tastes for rating prediction. In *SPIRE*, pages 153–164, 2013.

[4] M. Müller, M. Harvey, D. Elsweiler, and S. Mika. Ingredient matching to determine the nutritional properties of internet-sourced recipes. In *PervasiveHealth Conference*, pages 73–80, 2012.

[5] A.M. Roza and H.M. Shizgal. The harris benedict equation reevaluated: resting energy requirements and the body cell mass. *Am Jour. of clinical nutrition*, 40(1):168–182, 1984.

---

[1]https://www.nrv.gov.au/chronic-disease/summary

CNARe: Co-authorship Networks Analysis and Recommendations

Guilherme A. de Sousa, Matheus A. Diniz, Michele A. Brandão, Mirella M. Moro
Universidade Federal de Minas Gerais, Belo Horizonte, Brazil
{guilhermeaugusto,matheusad,micheleabrandao,mirella}@dcc.ufmg.br

ABSTRACT

We present CNARe, an easy-to-use online system that shows personalized collaboration recommendations to researchers. It also provides visualizations and metrics that allow to investigate how the recommendations affect a co-authorship social network and other analyses.

Categories and Subject Descriptors

H.4 [**Information Systems Applications**]: Miscellaneous

Keywords

Social Network Analysis; Co-authorship Recommendation

1. INTRODUCTION

In science, usually, research is done through collaboration. However, searching for collaborators (other researchers to work with) is not an easy task and has become an important obstacle to many researchers. The intense concern with innovation and productivity is one main reason for such phenomenon. Indeed, Lopes et al. [3] show that productive researchers are more inclined to collaborating, and prolific research groups have better connected academic social networks (given by researchers and their co-authorships). Other examples include finding people to work with in a new institution and to participate in collaborative grant proposals. Then, the recommendation of collaborators is key to increase the interactions among researchers and, consequently, to rise their productivity and research quality.

Driven by such motivation, there are recent advances in proposing collaboration recommendation algorithms [1, 2, 4]. Each algorithm recommends collaborators using different strategies, such as network topological analysis, semantic of the relationship between researchers, and mathematical formalization. In general, such algorithms consider the co-authorship among researchers to capture their collaborations. These relationships can be found in co-authorship social networks, a specific type of social network (SN) where

RecSys '15, September 16-20, 2015, Vienna, Austria
ACM 978-1-4503-3692-5/15/09.
http://dx.doi.org/10.1145/2792838.2796553

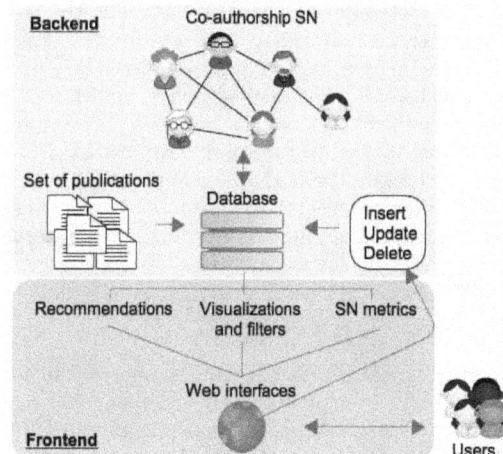

Figure 1: CNARe architecture.

the nodes are researchers and edges represent their connections through publication authorships.

Here, we propose an online tool called *CNARe*[1] (*scenery*). It provides better ways to help researchers in: choosing collaborators, visualizing recommendations, and contrasting results given by different recommendation algorithms. So far, we focus on three recommendation algorithms that combine topological properties of co-authorship social networks and academic metrics: *Affin* [1] considers the shortest path between researchers and the researchers' institutional affiliation; *CORALS* [2] combines the shortest path between researchers and their research area; and *MVCWalker* [4] uses a random walk model with three academic metrics (co-author order, latest collaboration time, and number of collaboration). Another unique feature is to show how the recommended collaborations may impact a co-authorship network. Finally, CNARe provides different visualizations that allow important social networks analyses.

2. SYSTEM ARCHITECTURE

A brief overview of CNARe's main components on both backend and frontend is illustrated in Figure 1. Specifically at the backend, CNARe stores sets of researchers' publications in a SQL database (see CNARe's webpage for information on its database modeling). The database is initially populated with publications from Computer Science. Users

---

[1]CNARe information webpage: http://goo.gl/rn5lud

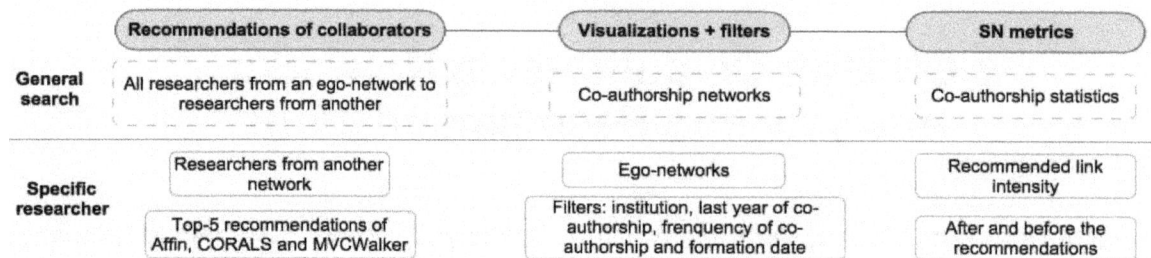

	Recommendations of collaborators	Visualizations + filters	SN metrics
General search	All researchers from an ego-network to researchers from another	Co-authorship networks	Co-authorship statistics
Specific researcher	Researchers from another network	Ego-networks	Recommended link intensity
	Top-5 recommendations of Affin, CORALS and MVCWalker	Filters: institution, last year of co-authorship, frenquency of co-authorship and formation date	After and before the recommendations

Figure 2: CNARe main features: general ones in dashed lines, and specific for researchers in full lines.

may also upload other sets of researchers and their publications. Then, CNARe uses such publications to generate co-authorship social networks (which will also be stored in the database). In turn, at the frontend, users benefit from three major features: recommendations, visualizations with filters, and social networks metrics analyzes. It is important to note that the last two features aim to improve the presentation and understanding of the recommendations. Finally, on the online interface, users may also insert a co-authorship SN through comma separated values files, edit researchers' information, and edit the research area of a researcher.

3. DESIGN AND INTERFACES

The main features of CNARe are summarized in Figure 2. Some of them are for specific researchers, i.e. a user must choose a researcher before accessing them. Different rectangle line styles indicate whether it is necessary to select a researcher (continuous line) or not (dashed line). Next, we detail each of the main features.

Recommendations of collaborators. CNARe provides a researcher search interface. By selecting a researcher, the user is able to compare the top-5 recommendations given by the algorithms. Specifically, the comparison is done through pairs (i.e., three combinations: *Affin* and *CORALS*, *Affin* and *MVCWalker*, *CORALS* and *MVCWalker*). Besides the resulting recommendations of collaborators, the tool presents their institution and research areas, which allows the user to know a little bit more about the researcher. There are also other pages showing the recommendations, and they differ by the visualizations of the social networks and recommendations, quantity of researchers, and SN metrics.

Visualizations and filters. CNARe provides two main visualizations: co-authorship ego-networks and global co-authorship networks. The ego-networks focus on a researcher and show his/her direct co-authorships, with current collaborations and the recommended ones. The global co-authorship networks show all co-authorships from an institution, a researcher (the co-authors of the researcher's co-authors), or an uploaded network. Such global SNs provide a general view of the co-authorships, and allow to better analyze the context of the ego-networks. For example, a user can see the global co-authorship social network of an institution of a recommended researcher.

In order to personalize the visualizations, there are four filters that can be applied to the co-authorships. They are: (*i*) by institution, showing only the links of co-authors from the selected institution; (*ii*) the last time of co-authorship, by focusing on the co-authorships within a period of years (for

example, last 2 years); (*iii*) the frequency of co-authorship, presenting the links between researchers that publish together a selected number of times (for instance, 2 to 5 publications in common); and (*iv*) the date of the last academic formation, allowing to consider researchers from similar academic "generation". This last one is important to filter, for example, researchers who have retired or are too young.

Social networks metrics. CNARe also shows social networks metrics. Considering the ego-networks, it is hard to find relevant metrics, because such networks are relatively small, with not enough information. Thus, for such networks, CNARe applies neighborhood overlap, clustering coefficient, and affiliation homophily. Specifically, the neighborhood overlap presents the strength of the recommended link, which allows to analyze if the recommend link will be a bridge (i.e., an edge responsible for linking different and unconnected communities) or not. The other metrics show how the recommendations affect the networks. CNARe also presents statistics of the global co-authorship social network. For instance, the number of authors, number of links, frequency of co-authorship, and so on.

4. CONCLUDING REMARKS

We presented CNARe, a friendly online tool for contrasting the collaboration recommendations of three different algorithms. It also uses visualizations and SN metrics to show how the recommendations change a researcher ego-network. Besides, the visualizations present how new recommended links can work as bridges to another researchers' co-authorship network. All such visualizations represent a step forward in recommending collaboration tools, which have focused on the recommendation algorithms rather than visualizing their results. As future steps, we plan to integrate more recommendations algorithms and SN metrics.

Acknowledgments to CAPES and CNPq - Brazil.

5. REFERENCES

[1] M. A. Brandão et al. Using link semantics to recommend collaborations in academic social networks. In *WWW Workshops*, 2013.

[2] G. R. Lopes et al. Collaboration recommendation on academic social networks. In *ER Workshops*, 2010.

[3] G. R. Lopes et al. Ranking strategy for graduate programs evaluation. In *ICITA*, 2011.

[4] F. Xia et al. Mvcwalker: Random walk based most valuable collaborators recommendation exploiting academic factors. *IEEE Transactions on Emerging Topics in Computing*, 2(3):364–375, 2014.

Event Recommendation using Twitter Activity

Axel Magnuson [*]
Dept. of Computer Science,
Boise State University,
1910 University Drive,
Boise, ID
axelmagnuson@u.boisestate.edu

Vijay Dialani
Dept. of Computer Science,
Boise State University,
1910 University Drive,
Boise, ID
vijaydialani@boisestate.edu

Deepa Mallela
Dept. of Computer Science,
Boise State University,
1910 University Drive,
Boise, ID
deepamallela@u.boisestate.edu

ABSTRACT

User interactions with Twitter (social network) frequently take place on mobile devices - a user base that it strongly caters to. As much of Twitter's traffic comes with geo-tagging information associated with it, it is a natural platform for geographic recommendations. This paper proposes an event recommender system for Twitter users, which identifies twitter activity co-located with previous events, and uses it to drive geographic recommendations via item-based collaborative filtering.

General Terms

Recommender Systems; Geographic Information Systems

Keywords

Point of Interest; geo tagging; event identification; opinion mining

1. INTRODUCTION

With the rise of geotagged users data being available through both mobile applications and social media, it is possible to detect events where multiple users congregate. In the case of social media, additional "timeline" information is available in the form of messages posted by users. Together, these features provide a rich feature space informing us about the preferences of users towards certain events, that can be used to generate recommendations looking forward for upcoming events they might find interesting.

Several approaches to event recommendation have been explored in the past, using many different data sources. Similarly, many works explore techniques for detecting real-world events on social networks such as Twitter [6, 1, 3]. However, to our knowledge no solution yet exists which recommends events for users based on their Twitter activity.

---

[*]Corresponding Author

RecSys'15, September 16–20, 2015, Vienna, Austria.
ACM 978-1-4503-3692-5/15/09.
DOI: http://dx.doi.org/10.1145/2792838.2796556.

In this paper we propose a system which associates a user's tweets with real-world events via their geo-location tags in order to create a users interest profile about the events. A list of events are extracted from a web crawl of Eventbrite, a popular event organization website which contains a database of previous and upcoming events. These events are cross-referenced with geotagged twitter traffic to identify users who have attended these events. From the tweets that the user created or received or retweeted we mine the users opinion about the event using sentiment analysis. The intensity of user sentiment about an event is translated into a rating about the event. A user model generated from above data is used to provide geographic recommendation based on time and geo-location of the user.

2. DEMO OVERVIEW

The demo system allows the user to provide their social media activity by sharing their twitter handle and permission to access their immediate social graph. Tweets from the user and their immediate neighbors is used to create a topic model that represents the users interests. We use labelled LDA [4] to represent the users interests and also identify the tweets in their historic feed that can provide a qualitative assessment about the user opinions of past "public events". We use this data to identify the people and events that are similar to the user social network and past experiences. A web application allows user to specify a future date-time, sentiment profile and geographic locations to recommend potential events of interest. To provide a real-time experience we undertake a number of data collection and pre-processing steps described in the rest of this section.

2.1 Data Processing

Twitter data is collected from the twitter public streaming API, and stored on a hadoop file system. It is filtered down to high-activity areas of interest such as New York and Chicago. Tweet geolocations and timestamps are extracted for use in the user model described in Subsection 2.3.

Apache Nutch is used to crawl the event organizing sites mentioned above to extract the event content. Event related information mentioned earlier is extracted. The bounding box around the event location is identified. The time span of which the event is going to last around and key words related to the event are analyzed using the topic modeling tools.

2.2 Event Item Model

Similarity between two different events is calculated based on event description, user participation and social media interaction during and about the event. In addition, to the description from Eventbrite, a bounding box is inferred from geotagged data in tweets discussing the the event. The social media traffic is monitored for prior during and after the duration of the event the combined duration is referred to as event life time. As we do not have access to complete twitter firehose, we use historic event data to predict the interval and the geographic area to subscribe for events on the social network. The event database and the associated tweets is used to create a non-personalized model of events attractiveness to attendees.

2.3 User Model

Twitter incorporates rich metadata, among which we are going to use two fields. They are geo-location and time associated with tweet posted. These two fields help us in identifying the past events user has visited.

In order to identify if user has been to an event, we look for two aspects. One: if the user appears in the event bounding box and the other, does he appear in the bounding box within time bounds of event life time. If both the conditions are satisfied, then we identify him as the visitor to the event. Once the user was Identified in the previous/history events, we build the user's previous event activity.

2.4 Recommendation

Event recommendation presents a unique challenge because we cannot measure user interaction with the event until it has already occurred. In order to recommend events to users, we use item-based collaborative filtering to recommend upcoming events similar to ones previously attended by the user [5]. In this case events are interpreted as items, and the event model from Subsection 2.2 provides item features. User twitter activity is associated with previous events as described in Subsection 2.3, which we interpret as an implicit preference of a user towards that event. Recommendations themselves are performed using the LensKit implementation of Collaborative Filtering, which enables this system to be easily included in other applications and recommendation frameworks[2].

3. CONCLUSION AND DEMO DESCRIPTION

This event recommendation can be applied to any other social network user activity that has ties with geo-location and time of the activity.

In this system we consider if the user had attended the event, but we are not showing concern about analyzing their opinion. Learning about their opinion help us in making better recommendations.

A detailed description of our demo can be found at: http://cs.boisestate.edu/ vijaydialani/recsys/demo.html

4. REFERENCES

[1] Hila Becker, Mor Naaman, and Luis Gravano. Beyond trending topics: Real-world event identification on twitter. *I WSM*, 11:438–441, 2011.

[2] Michael D. Ekstrand, Michael Ludwig, Joseph A. Konstan, and John T. Riedl. Rethinking the recommender research ecosystem: Reproducibility, openness, and lenskit. In *roceedings of the Fifth A M onference on Recommender Systems*, RecSys '11, pages 133–140, New York, NY, USA, 2011. ACM.

[3] Ryong Lee and Kazutoshi Sumiya. Measuring geographical regularities of crowd behaviors for twitter-based geo-social event detection. In *roceedings of the 2nd A M SIGS ATIAL international workshop on location based social networks*, pages 1–10. ACM, 2010.

[4] Daniel Ramage, David Hall, Ramesh Nallapati, and Christopher D Manning. Labeled lda: A supervised topic model for credit attribution in multi-labeled corpora. In *roceedings of the 2 9 onference on Empirical Methods in Natural Language rocessing: Volume 1-Volume 1*, pages 248–256. Association for Computational Linguistics, 2009.

[5] Badrul Sarwar, George Karypis, Joseph Konstan, and John Riedl. Item-based collaborative filtering recommendation algorithms. In *roceedings of the 1 th International onference on World Wide Web*, WWW '01, pages 285–295, New York, NY, USA, 2001. ACM.

[6] Qiankun Zhao, Prasenjit Mitra, and Bi Chen. Temporal and information flow based event detection from social text streams. In *AAAI*, volume 7, pages 1501–1506, 2007.

Health-aware Food Recommender System

Mouzhi Ge
Free University of
Bozen-Bolzano
Bolzano, Italy
mouzhi.ge@unibz.it

Francesco Ricci
Free University of
Bozen-Bolzano
Bolzano, Italy
fricci@unibz.it

David Massimo
Free University of
Bozen-Bolzano
Bolzano, Italy
david.massimo@unibz.it

ABSTRACT

With the rapid changes in the food variety and lifestyles, many people are facing the problem of making healthier food decisions to reduce the risk of chronic diseases such as obesity and diabetes. To this end, our recommender system not only offers recipe recommendations that suit the user's preference but is also able to take the user's health into account. It is developed on a mobile platform by considering that our application may be directly used in the kitchen. This demo paper summarizes the complete human-computer interaction design, the implemented health-aware recommendation algorithm and preliminary user feedback.

Categories and Subject Descriptors

H.4.2 [**Information Systems Applications**]: Types of Systems—*Decision support*

Keywords

Recommender systems; smart health; food, utility

1. INTRODUCTION

Nowadays, food, healthy eating and new recipes have become central subjects in our daily life. In fact, there is an extensive growth of food variety and ingredient combinations, and more and more recipes are created, even by IBM supercomputers[1]. Therefore, it can be time-consuming to make better and healthier recipe choices and, notwithstanding this increase in choice options, for many people food selection is driven by bad habits that lead to poor healthy conditions [1]. Still, many people are not aware of the potential health problems that can be caused by improper eating habits. Therefore, it is valuable to conduct research on food recommender systems by taking both user preference and nutritional factors into account [2].

---

[1]http://www-03.ibm.com/innovation/ca/en/cognitivecooking/

RecSys 2015, Vienna Austria
© 2015 ACM. ISBN 978-1-4503-3692-5/15/09 ...$15.00.
DOI: http://dx.doi.org/10.1145/2792838.2796554.

To further explore the demand of healthy food recommendations, we have conducted a survey about the user's opinion on recipe recommendations. 20 subjects from different countries such as Italy, Germany, France, China, USA, Spain and India, were involved in the survey. Their ages were in the range of 22-50 years old, 65% of them were male and 35% were female. In the survey, we asked "would you like to have healthier recipe recommendations by adapting or yielding your personal taste?" The possible answers were *yes*, *yes but to some extend*, and *absolutely not*. Futher, we provided the following descriptions for the three answers. *Yes* means the user prefers healthier recipe recommendation, the healthier the better. *Yes but to some extent* means the user would like to receive the recommendation that balances his taste and health. *Absolutely not* means the user only wants the food recommendation that suits his taste.

The survey results show that 10% users selected yes, 85% users selected yes but to some extent, and 5% users selected absolutely not. That means 95% of the surveyed users would like to somehow adapt their taste in order to obtain healthier food recommendations. This confirms that in the food domain recommendations that only consider user preference do not suffice. When obtaining recipe recommendations, people would like to take the health factor into account. Therefore in addition to using traditional recommendation technologies, our demo system proposes a health-aware recommendation algorithm by including calorie balance.

In this demo paper, we firstly summarize the user and recommender interaction procedure. Further, we describe the key aspects of the implemented health-aware recommender algorithm. Then, we highlight the novelties of our system and conclude the paper by reporting the preliminary user feedback and future works.

2. SYSTEM DESCRIPTION

The system demo is illustrated by a video, which can be found at http://goo.gl/R3PDYd. We have designed a complete interaction process that includes preference elicitation, recommendation generation and presentation, user support for browsing and critiquing the given recommendations as well as for providing the user alternative recommendations.

The interaction begins with a regular login interface, if the user is new to the system, the user needs to register in the system. In this step, the system will ask the user to provide some personal profile data such as height, weight and routine activities. The user profile data are then used to estimate the daily calories the user needs.

Afterwards, it begins the long-term (stable) preference elicitation. This is to collect what the user generally likes to cook or eat. The user can browse a full catalog of recipes and mark those that he has used before. This is to let the user find the recipes that she can actually evaluate. Different categories of recipes such as fish or meat are presented to the user. Users can easily navigate through the categorization to find a concrete recipe, for example, Meat -> Beef -> Roasted Beef with Salad.

After the user has marked some recipes, these are presented to the user for rating and tagging. If the user has not marked enough recipes, the system provides some additional recipes that are selected by guessing what the user may have used but not marked. In order to find such recipes, an active learning technique, which is called Binary Prediction, is used. Details can be found in [2].

The rating interface uses a 5-star Likert scale. When the user tags a recipe, she can her own tags or use suggested tags. These tags (normally between 5 and 10) are identified by the system on the base of their relevance to the recipe. While tagging, the user also can mark whether the selected tags indicate positive or negative aspects of the recipe. Positive and negative aspects are clearly shown by different colors of the tags.

Until this point, the user registration is finished. During the registration, we have collected the user profile and her long-term preferences. This process is only done once when the user registers to the system. It is then followed by session-based preference elicitation.

Session-based preference elicitation is to ask the user which ingredients she would like to use for cooking. It enables the user to cook recipes that are based on what she has. In this step, the user can enter the ingredient (e.g., tuna fish) or specify a feature of the recipe (e.g., Italian dish) that she wants to cook. If the user already registered before, after logging in, the session-based preference elicitation is the first interface that the user interacts with.

Based on the user profile, the long-term and the session-based preferences, the system generates a set of recipe recommendations and present them, one by one, to the user. The user can evaluate the recommendations to find the most suitable recipe. When the user is satisfied with a recommendation, she can select it and its detailed cooking instruction are shown. The user can also "critique" a recommendation. When the user clicks the critique button on one recommended recipe, a list of tags related to this recipe is shown for critiquing. The user can choose the option of more or less towards certain tag. For example, more spicy and less garlic, in which spicy and garlic are the given tags. After the critique, alternative recommendations are given based on the adjusted factors. This is similar to the critiquing function implemented in [4].

3. HEALTH-AWARE RECOMMENDER ALGORITHM

In our recommendation algorithm we have considered both the user's preference and health requirements. For the user u, the utility $util$ of the recipe rp is computed as:

$$util(u, rp) = w_p * pref(u, rp) + w_h * health(u, rp)$$

Regarding the preference component $pref(u, rp)$, we have proposed an algorithm that extends matrix factorization by including additional parameters that are used for modelling the dependencies between assigned tags and ratings. The details of this algorithm can be found in [2].

We have now extended this algorithm by including the health component $health(u, rp)$. This is based on a calorie balance function of the difference between the calories the user still needs and the calories of the recipe. The smaller the difference is, the healthier the recipe is estimated. This assumes that calorie balance is one indicator for health. The calories that the user needs are calculated using the typical user activity (profile data) [3], while calories of the recipe are determined by the nutritional values of the recipe.

The weight w_p and w_h can be manually adjusted by the user. The user can define if the recommendations should be more taste-oriented or more health-oriented.

4. NOVELTIES IN THE SYSTEM

Many food recommendation algorithms are lacking a precise real-world application context, and many of them have not been coupled with a precise interaction design. We have provided a complete user/recommender interaction design from preference elicitation, to recommendation presentation and critique. Compared to our recent work [2], we have added to the supported interaction: user profile collection and recommendation critiquing. Further, most food recommendation applications provide just non-personalized suggestions and without considering the health factor. Compared to other systems such as [1] and [2], this new system has taken into account the health concerns and also provides to the users the possibility of adjusting the relative importance of personal taste and health.

5. CONCLUSION

The application of recommender system to the food domain is emerging. We have implemented a new system that allows users to balance their tastes and health. The described demo system has been developed on the Android platform. Users can easily access the applications in a ubiquitous way. After using our application, users commented that the system is easy to use and the quality of the recommendations is high. As future work, we will take into account in the utility function the cooking effort and recipes' diversity (between recommendation sessions). Beside the calorie balance, we will also construct healthy recommendations by leveraging domain knowledge from nutritionists.

6. REFERENCES

[1] J. Freyne and S. Berkovsky. Intelligent food planning: personalized recipe recommendation. In *Proceedings of the 15th International Conference on Intelligent User Interfaces*, pages 321–324. ACM, 2010.

[2] M. Ge, M. Elahi, I. Fernández-Tobías, F. Ricci, and D. Massimo. Using tags and latent factors in a food recommender system. In *Proceedings of the 5th International Conference on Digital Health*. ACM, 2015.

[3] W. McArdle, F. Katch, and V. Katch. *Exercise Physiology: Energy, Nutrition, and Human Performance*. Lippincott Williams and Wilkins, 2001.

[4] J. Vig, S. Sen, and J. Riedl. The tag genome: Encoding community knowledge to support novel interaction. *ACM Transactions on Interactive Intelligent Systems*, 2(3):13:1–13:44, 2012.

Kibitz: End-to-End Recommendation System Builder

Quanquan Liu
MIT CSAIL
32 Vassar Street
Cambridge, MA
quanquan@mit.edu

David R. Karger
MIT CSAIL
32 Vassar Street
Cambridge, MA
karger@mit.edu

ABSTRACT

Kibitz (kibitz.csail.mit.edu) is a web application and recommendation system framework that helps inexperienced and novice programmers to build recommenders without the need to program the back end for the system. The author uploads a table of items, and Kibitz produces a collaborative-filtering recommender for the uploaded items. The recommender can be hosted by Kibitz or downloaded and customized as a set of static pages hosted on the author's personal web domain. Developers who want to avoid the hassle of writing their own recommender back end may choose to link their websites to our service through our easy to use API. A demo of our system can be found at kibitz.csail.mit.edu/video_demo/.

1. INTRODUCTION

Personalized recommendation systems that provide users with recommendations based on ratings are becoming increasingly popular among many websites and online services. To implement a recommendation system, one may choose from a few implementations such as *Apache Mahout* or *Lenskit* [1, 4]. But the labor involved in installing and configuring such a system can be a deterrent for experienced developers and an impassable barrier for novice users, which unnecessarily limits the adoption of recommender systems in places where they would be useful such as small businesses and startups, organization websites, and student researchers.

Our Kibitz system aims to reduce or eliminate barriers to the incorporation of recommender systems for both developers and novices. Kibitz provides an easy to use web interface for creating a recommendation service–both back end and front end. It also provides a simple API for linking the recommender back end to any front-end web page that an author provides. Novice users can deploy a hosted recommender service (both back and front end) on the Kibitz server or can download and customized front-end HTML to place on their own site. Developers can host their back end on Kibitz while connecting any front end they write to it via a simple API.

2. KIBITZ SYSTEM OVERVIEW

We now present a more detailed description of Kibitz's components. Kibitz supports the typical workflow of collaborative filter-

RecSys'15, September 16–20, 2015, Vienna, Austria.
ACM 978-1-4503-3692-5/15/09
DOI: http://dx.doi.org/10.1145/2792838.2796557.

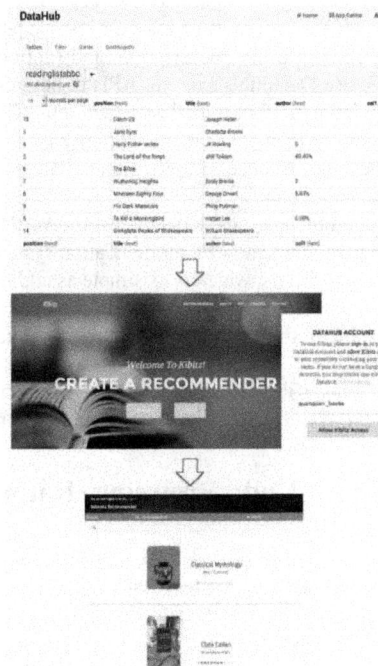

Figure 1: The content creator first creates an account on Datahub and uploads their list of items to create a table. Then, they enter the information about their table into Kibitz. Kibitz will take that information and output a front end listing the items that the creator uploaded.

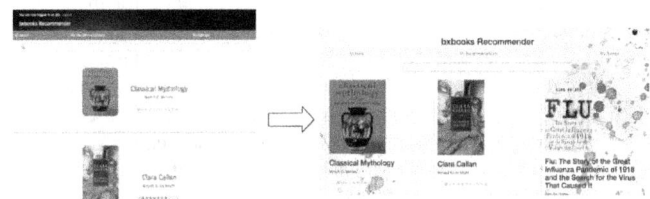

Figure 2: Simple alterations to the main CSS file downloaded in the Kibitz front-end package can result in a recommender with a very different look.

ing:

1. The creater selects a set of items that will be rated and recommended.
2. Users rate items from this set.
3. Collaborative filtering computations are used to recommend items from the set to users.

2.1 Back End: Item Data and Collaborative Filtering System

The Kibitz back end maintains a database of items and set of user accounts, receives and stores user ratings, and runs collaborative filtering algorithms to predict other ratings. We leverage our own separate project, Datahub [3], which provides a hosted SQL database, to store item information and user accounts. Kibitz assumes that items will be stored as rows of a database table with at least columns providing a title, description, and (optional) image for the items. We use Datahub's existing APIs to help users create accounts and upload data items. The user then tells Kibitz which Datahub table contains their set of items. If they have a file of previous ratings, they may choose to upload those ratings for initial training of the recommender.

To compute recommendations, Kibitz uses *Apache Mahout* [1]. In the future, we plan to add new recommendation systems such as *LensKit* and new algorithms, which is as simple as adding another `makeNewAlgorithmRecommendations` method to our API.

Fig. 1 shows some of the steps a creator takes to create a recommender on Kibitz.

In addition to items, Kibitz uses Datahub to store user rating data as its input (see Fig. 3). This permits developers to use rating data for other purporses.

2.2 Web Front End: Browsing, Rating, Recommending

After creating a table of items on Datahub and completing the relevant info in the Kibitz form, we generate a default recommender front end containing the items in the table and methods for the user to rate the item. This basic front end allows users to browse items, search for items, rate, and receive recommendations based on ratings. Content creators may choose to enable certain types of recommendations such as most popular items and random. Fig. 1 shows the front end that is output by Kibitz based on information provided by the content creator. This front end is a simple HTML page with a small amount of JavaScript that uses calls to the (Thrift-based [2]) Kibitz API to let users log in to the recommender, to collect user ratings, and to deliver lists of recommended items based on ratings.

2.3 Customization

Kibitz allows creators who want a different look for their recommender to download the HTML document providing the basic recommnder and customize it. The creator can define templates for presenting items and modify CSS to change the look of the recommender. Fig. 2 shows some simple alterations to the CSS file `main.css` downloaded from Kibitz. Content creators may also choose to host their new front end under the Kibitz domain by uploading their CSS files on the site.

2.4 API

A creator with web programming skills can create arbitary front ends, for example, embedding rating and recommendation functionality in any web application over a set of items, by directly making API calls to the Kibitz back end. Fig. 4 illustrates some calls made to the Kibitz server via JavaScript.

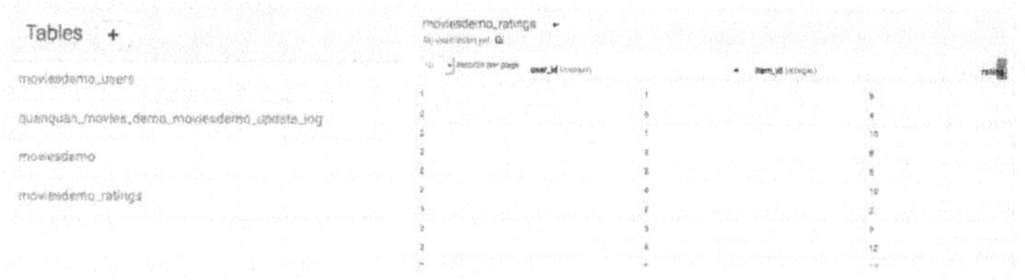

Figure 3: Tables created by Kibitz containing user information. One such table created is a table containing user ratings so creators may use the information to their benefit.

```
/*
 * Kibitz API
 */

//Creates a recommender server with the correct client key
client.createNewIndividualServer(client_key);

client.initiateModel(client_key, recommender_name, creator_name, repo_name);

//gets a list of items to display
var items = client.getPageItems(client_key, page_num, 10, display_items);

//gets a list of recommendations
items = client.makeRecommendation(client_key, userId, num_recs, false, display_items);

//gets a list of user rated items
items = client.getUserRatedItems(client_key, userId, display_items);
```

Figure 4: Example API calls in JavaScript that can be made to the Kibitz server.

The API returns the relevant strings and objects that are queried. The API includes methods to obtain information about the items that are stored in the database (`getPageItems`, `getUserRatedItems`, `getItemCount`) as well as to obtain a list of recommendations by calling individual recommenders (`makeRecommendation`).

3. FUTURE WORK

Because of the flexibility of our system, we plan to add more recommendation algorithms to Kibitz. This may be done simply by creating a new API call for the algorithm and including that algorithm in the current list of recommendation algorithms. We also plan to add more customization options for the recommenders hosted on our server (such as drag-and-drop widgets for customizing the front end). The added functionality supports our intent for our recommender builder system to support a wide variety of items.

4. REFERENCES

[1] Apache Mahout, http://mahout.apache.org.

[2] Apache Thrift, https://thrift.apache.org.

[3] A. P. Bhardwaj, S. Bhattacherjee, A. Chavan, A. Deshpande, A. J. Elmore, S. Madden, and A. G. Parameswaran. Datahub: Collaborative data science & dataset version management at scale. In *CIDR 2015, Seventh Biennial Conference on Innovative Data Systems Research, Asilomar, CA, USA, January 4-7, 2015, Online Proceedings*, 2015.

[4] M. D. Ekstrand, M. Ludwig, J. A. Konstan, and J. T. Riedl. Rethinking the recommender research ecosystem: Reproducibility, openness, and lenskit. In *Proceedings of the Fifth ACM Conference on Recommender Systems*, RecSys '11, pages 133–140, New York, NY, USA, 2011. ACM.

5. ACKNOWLEDGMENTS

We would like to thank Anant Bhardwaj for support of this project by adding new functionality to Datahub that allows Kibitz to communicate effectively and efficiently with it.

OSMRec Tool for Automatic Recommendation of Categories on Spatial Entities in OpenStreetMap

Nikos Karagiannakis
IMIS Institute, ATHENA R.C.

Giorgos Giannopoulos
IMIS Institute, ATHENA R.C.

Dimitrios Skoutas
IMIS Institute, ATHENA R.C.

Spiros Athanasiou
IMIS Institute, ATHENA R.C.

ABSTRACT

In this demonstration, we present OSMRec, a command line utility and JOSM plugin for automatic recommendation of tags (categories) on newly created spatial entities in OpenStreetMap (OSM). JOSM allows downloading parts of OSM, editing the map (e.g. inserting, deleting, annotating with tags spatial entities) and re-uploading the updated part back on OSM. OSMRec plugin exploits already annotated entities within OSM to train category classification models and utilizes these models in order to recommend OSM categories for newly inserted spatial entities in OSM.

Categories and Subject Descriptors

[**Information systems**]: [Recommender systems]

Keywords

Category recommendation, spatial entities, OSM

1. INTRODUCTION

Over the past years, in parallel to geospatial data created and collected by authoritative sources, such as governmental organizations, there has been an increasingly large volume of geospatial data contributed directly or indirectly by casual users. An example of this is OSM[1], a community initiative for the crowdsourced production of open global maps. Through various authoring tools, users contribute several spatial entities, such as roads, buildings or administrative areas. One of the most prominent tools of OSM is JOSM[2], a graphical tool that allows users to (a) download all the entities of a geographic area from OSM, (b) visualize them on a map overlay, (c) add, change or delete entities and (d) reload the changed dataset into the publicly accessible OSM

[1] https://www.openstreetmap.org/
[2] https://josm.openstreetmap.de/

RecSys'15, September 16–20, 2015, Vienna, Austria.
ACM 978-1-4503-3692-5/15/09.
DOI: http://dx.doi.org/10.1145/2792838.2796555 .

map dataset. These spatial entities can also be annotated by categories (classes, tags) that assign semantics to them. Each entity may belong to multiple classes; for example, a building can be further characterized as school or bar.

In this demonstration, we present OSMRec, focusing on its JOSM plugin version. OSMRec facilitates the contribution of new spatial features (entities) into OSM, by recommending to users already existing OSM categories, in order to annotate newly inserted spatial entities. This is important for two reasons. First, users may not be familiar with the OSM categories; thus searching and browsing the OSM category hierarchy to find appropriate categories for the entity they wish to insert may often be a time consuming and frustrating process, to the point of users neglecting to add this information. Second, if an already existing category that matches the new entity cannot be found quickly and easily (although it exists), the user may resort instead to using his/her own term, resulting in synonyms that later need to be identified and dealt with.

To the best of our knowledge, this is the first approach on recommending annotation categories for spatial entities in OSM. Another existing work on a similar problem [1] focuses on classifying road segments in OSM, thus it specializes only on geometrical and topological features of the specific entities and reduces the space of recommendation categories from more than 1000 to only 21. Next, we briefly describe the recommendation model we implemented and then we demonstrate the usage of the tool. The experimental results demonstrate that the proposed methodology can recommend annotation categories for new spatial features with high accuracy (achieving from 79% to 92% recommendation precision, using 5-fold cross validation in a set of 111,491 geospatial entities and 1421 OSM categories).

2. RECOMMENDATION MODEL

We apply multiclass SVM classification, using LIBLINEAR[3], and considering as training items the geospatial entities themselves and as labels the categories that characterize them. The method maps the training entities into a multi-dimensional feature space and aims at finding the optimal hyperplanes that discriminates the entities belonging to different categories. The optimality of the hyperplane depends on the selected parameter C, which adjusts the trade-off

[3] http://www.csie.ntu.edu.tw/~cjlin/liblinear/

between misclassified training entities and optimal discrimination of correctly classified entities.

Since the same entity might be annotated with more than one class, we consider, for each entity, as many training items as its classes. The items are represented uniformly, with the exception of the different label that corresponds to the different class. Each item is represented as a feature vector, with each feature corresponding to a property of the item. Next, we present the features we define and implement:

Geometry type. Six distinct geometry types are identified: Point, LineString, Polygon, LinearRing, Circle and Rectangle.

Number of geometry points. In total, we define (based on a statistical analysis of the frequencies of entities having certain numbers of points) 13 ranges, thus mapping this integer characteristic into 13 boolean features: [1-10], (10-20], ..., (200-300], (300-500], (500-1000], (1000-...). So, according to the number of points of an entity's geometry, the proper position is set to 1, while the rest positions are set to 0.

Area of geometry. We define intuitively (and considering that in this problem setting we are mainly interested in entities that are buildings) 24 ranges with increasing length in square meters, until the area of 4000m2, where we consider the 25th range of (4000-...).

Mean edge length. In our case, we define 23 ranges, starting from length less than 2meters and ending with length more than 200meters.

Variance of edge lengths. Likewise, we define 36 ranges.

Textual features. For each entity of the training set, we extract the textual description of its name. We consider each word separately and count their frequency within the dataset. Then, we sort the list of words in descending frequency and filter out words with frequency less than 20. Finally, we apply a stopword list and remove words without any particular meaning. What remains are special meaning identifiers, such as avenue, church, school, park, etc. Each of these special keywords is used as a separate boolean feature.

Category features. This is a set of 1421 boolean features, each one corresponding to one of the OSM categories. Of course, since in this case OSM categories are used both as training labels and as training features, it is impossible to be used for entities that are not already annotated with at least one category. That is because, we would essentially use information that we want to predict as a means to predict (training features). So, these features are not included the first time the algorithm runs; however, each time a new category is assigned to an entity, the respective training feature is utilized and the category recommendation is updated.

3. TOOL DEMONSTRATION

OSMRec[4] is implemented in Java, as a command line application and as a JOSM plugin. It consists of two core components: the Training Module and the Recommendations Module. The former runs an offline process that takes as training input an OSM dataset and produces as output a classification model. The latter takes as input a set of geospatial entities, formatted according to the OSM XML format[5], as well as the trained model, and produces a set of categories that are the model's recommendation for tagging each geospatial entity from the input set.

Next, we demonstrate the usage of the software through the graphical user interface provided in the plugin version. A screencast video is also available at [6]. OSMRec plugin is accessed from Tools -> OSM Recommendation tab in JOSM menu bar. Due to lack of space, we omit the description of the offline training phase, and we focus on the actual automatic category recommendation process.

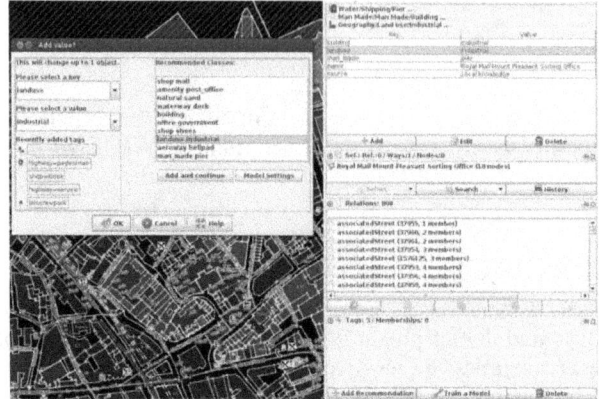

Figure 1: Recommendation Panel

The user can select an entity or draw a new entity on the map and ask for recommendations by clicking the "Add Recommendation" button. The recommendation panel opens (Fig. 1) and provides a list with the top-10 recommended categories and the user can select from this list and click "Add and continue". As a result, the selected category is added to the OSM tags. By the time the user adds a new tag at the selected object, a new vector is computed for that OSM instance in order to re-calculate the predictions and display an updated list of recommendations (taking into account the previously selected categories/tags, as extra training information).

Further, OSMRec provides functionality for allowing the user to combine several recommendation models, based on (a) a selected geographic area, (b) user's past editing history on OSM and (c) combination of (a) and (b). By clicking the "Model Settings" button the model settings panel opens and the user can choose to use a single model or combine several SVM models.

4. CONCLUSIONS

In this demonstration, presented OSMRec tool and especially the JOSM plugin version. OSMRec exploits historical annotations of spatial entities with OSM categories in order to train classification models, based on problem-specific training features. Then, it utilizes these models to recommend categories for newly inserted geometries in OSM.

5. ACKNOWLEDGEMENTS.

This research is conducted as part of the EU project Geo-Know[7] FP7-ICT-2011-8, 318159.

6. REFERENCES

[1] Jilani, M. and Corcoran, P. and Bertolotto, M. Automated Highway Tag Assessment of OpenStreetMap Road Networks. In *Proceedings of SIGSPATIAL'14*, 2014.

---

[4]https://github.com/GeoKnow/OSMRec
[5]http://wiki.openstreetmap.org/wiki/OSM_XML

[6]https://vimeo.com/126477260
[7]http://geoknow.eu/

Second Workshop on New Trends in Content-based Recommender Systems (CBRecSys 2015)

Toine Bogers
Department of Communication and Psychology
Aalborg University Copenhagen
2450 Copenhagen, Denmark
toine@hum.aau.dk

Marijn Koolen
Institute for Logic, Language and Computation
University of Amsterdam
Amsterdam, The Netherlands
marijn.koolen@uva.nl

ABSTRACT

While content-based recommendation has been applied successfully in many different domains, it has not seen the same level of attention as collaborative filtering techniques have. However, there are many recommendation domains and applications where content and metadata play a key role, either *in addition to* or *instead of* ratings and implicit usage data. For some domains, such as movies, the relationship between content and usage data has seen thorough investigation already, but for many other domains, such as books, news, scientific articles, and Web pages we still do not know *if* and *how* these data sources should be combined to provided the best recommendation performance. The *CBRecSys 2015* workshop aims to address this by providing a dedicated venue for papers dedicated to all aspects of content-based recommendation.

Categories and Subject Descriptors

H.3.3 [**Information Storage and Retrieval**]: Information Search and Retrieval—*information Filtering*

General Terms

Algorithms, Experimentation, Human Factors, Theory

Keywords

recommender systems; content-based recommendation; semantics; user-generated content; text reviews; implicit feedback; context

1. INTRODUCTION

Content-based recommendation has been applied successfully in many different domains [5], yet it has not seen the same level of attention as collaborative filtering techniques have. In recent years, competitions like the Netflix Prize[1], CAMRA[2], and the Yahoo! Music KDD Cup 2011 [4] have spurred on advances in collaborative filtering and how to utilize ratings and usage data. However,

[1] http://www.netflixprize.com/
[2] http://www.dai-labor.de/camra2010/

there are many recommendation domains and applications where content and metadata play a key role, either *in addition to* or *instead of* ratings and implicit usage data. For some domains, such as movies, the relationship between content and usage data has seen thorough investigation already (e.g. [6]) , but for many other domains, such as books, news, scientific articles, and Web pages we still do not know *if* and *how* these data sources should be combined to provided the best recommendation performance.

2. FORMAT, AUDIENCE AND TOPICS

The *CBRecSys 2015* workshop is the follow-up to the successful first edition of the workshop in Silicon Valley in 2014 [1, 2], which featured a varied high-quality program and was attended by over 60 participants.

CBRecSys 2015 will be organized as a full-day workshop. The workshop starts with a keynote by Frank Hopfgartner (University of Glasgow) on the challenges of news recommendation and the NEWSREEL living lab at CLEF 2015. The accepted papers are presented in 30-minute talks. The workshop will close with an interactive break-out session, with attendees split into smaller groups to discuss current and future challenges in content-based recommendation, and reporting back in a final plenary session.

The CBRecSys 2015 workshop aims to address this by providing a venue for papers dedicated to all aspects and new trends of content-based recommendation. This would include both recommendation in domains where textual content is abundant (e.g. books, news, scientific articles, jobs, educational resources, and Web pages) as well as dedicated comparisons and combinations of content-based techniques with collaborative filtering approaches.

2.1 Topics of Interest

Relevant topics of the workshop include:

- Developing novel recommendation approaches
  - Hybrid strategies combining content-based and collaborative filtering recommendations
  - Content-based approaches to cross-system and cross-domain recommendation
  - Latent factor models for content-based recommendation
- Exploiting user-generated content for recommendation
  - Mining microblogging data in recommender systems
  - Social tag-based recommender systems
  - Exploiting Semantic Web and Linked Open Data in content-based recommender systems

- Processing text reviews

  – Estimating (implicit) ratings associated with text reviews

  – Opinion mining and sentiment analysis of text reviews to support content-based recommendation

  – Extracting user personality traits and factors from text reviews for recommendation

- Mining contextual data from content

  – Extraction of contextual signals from textual content for recommendation

  – Incorporating the temporal dimension in content-based recommendation

  – Mood-based recommender systems

- Addressing limitations of recommender systems

  – Addressing the cold-start problem with content-based recommendation approaches

  – Increasing diversity of content-based recommendations

  – Providing novelty in content-based recommendations

3. SUBMISSIONS

A total of 12 full papers were submitted, focused on the following topics. Several papers present hybrid systems combining collaborative filtering and content-based recommendation, finding them complementary, with content-based recommendation components especially suitable for tackling the cold-start problem. Other papers investigate how different content features can be used for similarity measures and explore ways to identify which features are the most relevant for a given context. Some papers present approaches to mine user reviews for inferring user preferences on specific attributes of items, essentially deriving more structured feature information from unstructured text. Finally, several papers look at semantic frameworks and Linked Open Data to measure item similarity across different domains. All submitted papers were reviewed by a program committee of international experts in the field.

4. WEBSITE AND PROCEEDINGS

The workshop material (list of accepted papers, invited talk, and the workshop schedule) can be found on the CBRecSys 2015 workshop website at http://humanities.uva.nl/~mkoolen1/CBRecSys15. The proceedings are published as a CEUR Workshop Proceedings volume. Similar to last year's workshop [3], we will also look into publishing a summary of the workshop in venues like the SIGIR Forum, to increase cross-disciplinary awareness of recommender systems research.

5. REFERENCES

[1] T. Bogers, M. Koolen, and I. Cantador, editors. *Proceedings of the 1st Workshop on New Trends in Content-based Recommender Systems, co-located with the 8th ACM Conference on Recommender Systems, CBRecSys@RecSys 2014, Foster City, Silicon Valley, California, USA, October 6, 2014*, volume 1245 of *CEUR Workshop Proceedings*. CEUR-WS.org, 2014.

[2] T. Bogers, M. Koolen, and I. Cantador. Workshop on New Trends in Content-based Recommender Systems: (CBRecSys 2014). In *Eighth ACM Conference on Recommender Systems, RecSys '14, Foster City, Silicon Valley, CA, USA - October 06 - 10, 2014*, pages 379–380, 2014.

[3] T. Bogers, M. Koolen, and I. Cantador. Report on RecSys 2014 Workshop on New Trends in Content-Based Recommender Systems. *ACM SIGIR Forum*, 2015.

[4] G. Dror, N. Koenigstein, Y. Koren, and M. Weimer. The Yahoo! Music Dataset and KDD-Cup '11. In *JMLR Workshop and Conference Proceedings*, volume 18 of *Proceedings of KDD Cup 2011*, pages 3–18. Springer, 2012.

[5] P. Lops, M. de Gemmis, and G. Semeraro. Content-based Recommender Systems: State of the Art and Trends. In *Recommender Systems Handbook*, pages 73–105. Springer, 2011.

[6] I. Pilászy and D. Tikk. Recommending New Movies: Even a Few Ratings Are More Valuable Than Metadata. In *RecSys '09: Proceedings of the Third ACM Conference on Recommender Systems*, pages 93–100. ACM, 2009.

Overview of ACM RecSys CrowdRec 2015 Workshop:

Crowdsourcing and Human Computation for Recommender Systems

Martha Larson
Delft University of Technology
Delft, Netherlands
m.a.larson@tudelft.nl

Domonkos Tikk
Gravity R&D
Budapest, Hungary
domi@gravityrd.com

Roberto Turrin
ContentWise R&D
Milan, Italy
roberto.turrin@moviri.com

ABSTRACT

CrowdRec 2015 provides the recommender system community with a forum at which to discuss crowdsourcing and human computation. Systems that explicitly collect information from human annotators to improve recommendations are becoming more widespread. At this year's workshop, we highlight incentivization and the issue of avoiding bias. We take a special look at how recommender systems can influence collective behavior, and the contribution that the crowd can make to recommender system evaluation.

Categories and Subject Descriptors

H.3.3 [**Information Storage and Retrieval**]: Information Filtering

Keywords

human computation; human intelligence; crowdsourcing; recommender systems

1. INTRODUCTION

The success of recommender systems arises from their ability to make use of explicit or implicit information about user preferences for items. Under conventional approaches, a recommender system is passive, waiting for users to contribute information or collecting it from existing sources. A crowdsourcing approach to recommendation changes the assumption that passivity is a given. Instead, systems actively approach users to ask for information that is needed in order to improve recommendations. Alternatively, information can be elicited from crowdworkers on a commercial crowdsourcing platform, or contributed by dedicated experts.

The ACM RecSys 2015 CrowdRec Workshop[1] is the third in a series of workshops on crowdsourcing and human computation for recommender systems. Since the series began in 2013, it has been clear that crowdsourcing is a permanent

---

[1]http://crowdrecworkshop.org

RecSys'15, September 16–20, 2015, Vienna, Austria.
ACM 978-1-4503-3692-5/15/09.
DOI: http://dx.doi.org/10.1145/2792838.2798719.

fixture in the recommender system community. The growing profile of crowdsourcing techniques at ACM RecSys is evidence of its importance. A key is example was 'Crowd recommendations' as discussed at ACM RecSys 2014 by Hector Garcia-Molina in his keynote at ACM RecSys 2014 entitled "The Future of Recommender Systems" [5]. Further, last year's CrowdRec workshop [7] covered a diverse array of topics including recommender systems that use input from the crowd, best practices for crowdsourcing, and also recommender systems that recommend tasks to crowdworkers on crowdsourcing platforms.

In commercial systems, humans make important contributions. Well known examples include Pandora's Music Genome Project in which music is labeled by analysts [1] and also Netflix' use of taggers to annotate content [3]. June 2015 saw the release of Apple Music [2], which brought the importance of curation again into the public eye. Curation is the process by which human experts make a selection of items. The emphasis on curation reflects the growth of the idea that recommender system algorithms do not provide the ultimate best consumption experience for users, but that human decisions should enter the process.

The goal of the CrowdRec Workshop series is to provide a venue where members of the recommender system community can exchange information and develop new approaches that make use of crowd input to improve recommender systems. In the following, we briefly discuss issues and applications highlighted at the 2015 workshop.

2. CROWD IN RECOMMENDER SYSTEMS

It is useful to distinguish three types of human contributions that can be made to recommender systems. First, information collected from domain experts. Second, information collected from crowdworkers, without particular expertise. Third, information collected from users who also, ultimately, receive recommendations themselves from the recommender system. The three groups of contributors can be differentiated with respect to their motivations to contribute. Domain experts might contribute to recommender systems as part of a conventional career. The other two groups require more careful and creative consideration in order to ensure that they are both motivated to contribute and compensated for their efforts.

For crowdworkers, payment is often a major component of the motivation. Recommender systems that take advantage of crowdworkers must offer crowdworkers more than money, however. In the longterm, crowdsourcing is sustainable only it contributes to, rather than detracts from, crowdworkers' ability to support themselves, and to their quality of life. The needs and wishes of crowdworkers are various, and difficult to understand without careful study. Work such as [10] is an important step towards taking the preferences of crowdworkers into account. Recommender systems themselves are an important tool for the personalization of crowdsourcing tasks to crowdmember needs.

In order to motivate users to contribute to recommender systems, special mechanisms must be deployed. There can be as simple as reminding users of the connection between their contributions and improvements in the recommendations that they receive. Games and gamification are other ways in which users can be incentivized.

Human contributors must not only be motivated to contribute, but they must make contributions in good faith. Making use of information collected from crowdworkers or users may open a recommender system to a collusion attack. Under such an attack, human contributors work together to bias the outcome of recommendation technology. However, if appropriate design of crowdsourcing mechanisms, this probability can be reduced. We also mention the possibility that human contributions may have an important contribution to make, as the recommender system community becomes increasingly aware of the dangers of biased recommendations [8]. Human contributors have the ability to act as guards to ensure that recommendations remain at the level of helpful personalization, and do not disadvantage particular groups of users (e.g., low income, or living in certain geographic regions).

3. NEW CROWD APPLICATIONS

In addition to contributing information that addresses the *knowledge acquisition bottleneck*, as in [4], connecting the crowd to recommender systems opens up the possibility of new applications. Here, we mention two.

3.1 Shaping collective behavior

A recommender system helps users to make choices, but also has a net influence on their decisions. As such, recommender systems can be used to steer the behavior of a community in a manner that benefits all its members. An example is *Commutastic* [6], which rewards users for avoiding traffic. It recommends alternate afterwork activities, which gives it the potential to guide collective behavior. It is critical that users remain aware and informed of the purpose of the application. By choosing to adopt its suggestions, they are also choosing to improve the conditions of the community at large.

3.2 Evaluating recommender systems

Finally, we mention the potential of using feedback of the crowd to help evaluate recommender systems. A basic example is a recommender system that asks its users for feedback on their perceptions of recommendations. The power of using the crowd for help in evaluation is that it is possible to collect fine-grained information about preferences, which would not have otherwise been available, i.e., as in [9].

4. SUMMARY AND OUTLOOK

Crowdsourcing platforms benefit from, and also provide benefit to, recommender systems. The information provided by the crowd can fill in important gaps that help to address

the cold start problem, and allow recommendations to be more precisely targeted. Crowdsourcing opens up new opportunities for evaluating recommender systems. Finally, recommender systems can help to coordinate the behavior of the crowd, creating improved situations for the members of a community.

As we move forward to take advantage of the benefits that the crowd has to offer, we should remember that the crowd is not a nameless, faceless hoard. Rather crowdmembers have individual preferences, needs, and rights. The most effective crowd-enhanced recommender systems, are those that develop sustainable, rather than exploitative, relationships with human contributors.

5. ACKNOWLEDGMENTS

We would like to thank the authors, presenters, and reviewers, whose efforts made the workshop possible. The organizers are supported in part by the European Union's Seventh Framework Programme (FP7/2007-2013) under grant agreement 610594, CrowdRec.

6. REFERENCES

[1] About the music genome project, https://www.pandora.com/about/mgp.

[2] Introducing Apple Music—all the ways you love music. all in one place. https://www.apple.com /pr/library/2015 /06/08Introducing-Apple-Music-All-The-Ways-You-Love-Music-All-in-One-Place-.html.

[3] J. Elker. Netflix tagging: Yes, it's a real job, http://www.washingtonpost.com/blogs/style-blog/wp/2015/06/11/netflix-tagging-yes-its-a-real-job Washington Post, June 11, 2015.

[4] A. Felfernig, T. Ulz, S. Haas, M. Schwarz, S. Reiterer, and M. Stettinger. Peopleviews: Human computation for constraint-based recommendation. In *ACM RecSys 2015 CrowdRec Workshop*, 2015.

[5] H. Garcia-Molina. "Crowd Recommendations" in The Future of Recommender Systems ACM RecSys 2014 keynote https://www.youtube.com/watch?v= khodcjwp1us& feature=youtu.be&t=39m22s.

[6] M. Kracheel. Commutastic—a mobile application that rewards you for avoiding traffic http://www.innovation.public.lu/en/actualites/2015/ 06/snt-commutastic/index.html.

[7] M. Larson, P. Cremonesi, and A. Karatzoglou. Overview of ACM RecSys CrowdRec 2014 Workshop: Crowdsourcing and human computation for recommender systems. In *Proceedings of the 8th ACM Conference on Recommender Systems*, RecSys '14, pages 381–382, New York, NY, USA, 2014.

[8] C. C. Miller. When algorithms discriminate, http://www.nytimes.com/2015/07/10/upshot/when-algorithms-discriminate.html, New York Times July 9, 2015.

[9] M. Nasery, M. Elahi, and P. Cremonesi. PoliMovie: a feature-based dataset for recommender systems. In *ACM RecSys 2015 CrowdRec Workshop*, 2015.

[10] S. Schnitzer, C. Rensing, S. Schmidt, K. Borchert, M. Hirth, and P. Tran-Gia. Demands on task recommendation in crowdsourcing platforms—the worker's perspective. In *ACM RecSys 2015 CrowdRec Workshop*, 2015.

EMPIRE 2015: Workshop on Emotions and Personality in Personalized Systems

Marko Tkalčič
Johannes Kepler University,
Linz, Austria
Department of computational
Perception
marko.tkalcic@jku.at

Berardina DeCarolis
University of Bari Aldo Moro
Italy
nadja@di.uniba.it

Marco de Gemmis
University of Bari Aldo Moro
Italy
marco.degemmis@uniba.it

Ante Odić
Outfit7 (Slovenian subsidiary
Ekipa2 d.o.o.)
Ljubljana, Slovenia
ante.odic@gmail.com

Andrej Košir
University of Ljubljana
Faculty of Electrical
Engineering
Slovenia
andrej.kosir@fe.uni-lj.si

ABSTRACT

The EMPIRE workshop focuses on recommender systems (and other personalized systems) that take advantage of user-centric properties, such as emotions and personality. The workshop is organized as a focused mini-conference with technical and position papers. The goal is to gather the scattered work under a common umbrella and take advantage of the discussion time to draw future research opportunities.

Categories and Subject Descriptors

H.1.2 [**MODELS AND PRINCIPLES**]: User/Machine Systems; H.3.4 [**INFORMATION STORAGE AND RETRIEVAL**]: Systems and Software —*User profiles and alert services*; I.2.0 [**ARTIFICIAL INTELLIGENCE**]: General; I.2.1 [**ARTIFICIAL INTELLIGENCE**]: Applications and Expert Systems

General Terms

Algorithms, Human Factors, Experimentation, Theory, Design

Keywords

Emotions, Personality, Recommender Systems

Workshop Summary

The 3rd EMPIRE workshop is held in conjunction with the ACM RecSys 2015 conference in Vienna (Austria) on 19. September 2015. The previous editions of the workshop have been held in conjunction with UMAP 2013 in Rome and with UMAP 2014 in Aalborg.

The RecSys research community has done a tremendous job in the last decade on exploiting various data sources to improve recommendations of all kinds through sophisticated algorithms. The workshop complements these core RecSys activities by pushing the agenda of taking into account user-centric aspects, such as emotions and personality, into the RecSys framework. In fact, personality and emotions shape our daily lives by having a strong influence on our preferences, decisions and behaviour in general. In recent years, emotions and personality have shown to play an important role in various aspects of recommender systems, such as implicit feedback, contextual information, affective content labeling, cold-start problem, diversity, cross-domain recommendations, group recommendations etc. With the development of robust techniques for the unobtrusive acquisition of emotions (e.g. from various modalities, such as video or physiological sensors) and personality (e.g. from social media) the time is right to take advantage of these possibilities to collect massive datasets and improve recommender systems.

The topics include the usage of affect and personality to improve personalized systems, as contextual factors, as implicit feedback, in cross domain recsys, for calculating user and item similarities, in applications, for supporting human decision making, in group recsys, for addressing the cold-start problem, the implicit detection of affect/personality for personalized systems, computational models of emotion and personality and evaluation methods.

The workshop has a hybrid format; it accepts either (i) technical papers (long: 12 pages max, short: 8 pages max) or (ii) white papers/position statements (6 pages max).

For more information about the workshop, consult the webpage `https://empire2015recsys.wordpress.com/`.

RecSys'15, September 16–20, 2015, Vienna, Austria.
ACM 978-1-4503-3692-5/15/09.
DOI: http://dx.doi.org/10.1145/2792838.2798716

3rd International Workshop on News Recommendation and Analytics (INRA 2015)

Jon Atle Gulla
Department of Computer and
Information Science
NTNU
Trondheim, Norway
jag@idi.ntnu.no

Bei Yu
School of Information Studies
Syracuse University, USA
byu@syr.edu

Özlem Özgöbek
Computer Engineering
Department
Balikesir University
Balikesir, Turkey
ozlemozgobek@gmail.com

Nafiseh Shabib
Department of Computer and
Information Science
NTNU
Trondheim, Norway
shabib@idi.ntnu.no

ABSTRACT

The 3rd International Workshop on News Recommendation and Analytics (INRA 2015) is held in conjunction with RecSys 2015 Conference in Vienna, Austria. This paper presents a brief summary of the INRA 2015. This workshop aims to create an interdisciplinary community that addresses design issues in news recommender systems and news analytics, and promote fruitful collaboration opportunities between researchers, media companies and practitioners. We have a keynote speaker and an invited demo presentation in addition to 4 papers accepted in this workshop.

Categories and Subject Descriptors

H.0 [**Information Systems**]: General

Keywords

Recommender systems; news recommendation; analytics

1. INTRODUCTION

The motivation for news recommender systems is the tremendous amount of news articles available online and the dynamic nature of news domain. For a user it is getting harder to reach the relevant news items according to her personal interests and preferences. News recommender systems aim to bring the most relevant news items to the users.

Each domain in recommender systems has different characteristics and requires different approaches to make successful recommendations. Compared to other recommender system domains like books, music and movies, news recommender systems have particular challenges which requires a deeper analysis of both the user, content and their relationships. The news domain is characterized by a constant flow of unstructured, fragmentary, and unreliable news stories from numerous sources and different perspectives. Some important challenges of news domain are:

- Dynamic environment: Every hour hundreds of new articles is published by different sources,

- Faster changing user interests compared to other domains. User interests in movies, music or books change much slower than news,

- Willingness to read news articles that are independent from user interests like breaking news,

- Recency issues of news articles (people tend to read recent news, not the old ones),

- Unstructured subjective content that create content analysis problems and may turn recommendations unreliable.

This workshop addresses primarily news recommender systems and news analytics, with a particular focus on user profiling and techniques for dealing with and extracting knowledge from large-scale news streams. The news streams may originate in large media companies, but may also come from social sites, where user models are needed to decide how user-generated content is to be taken into account. As part of news recommendation and analytics, Big Data architectures and large-scale statistical and linguistic techniques are used to extract aggregated knowledge from large news streams and prepare for personalized access to news.

2. TOPICS OF INTEREST

Topics of interests for this workshop include but are not limited to:

- News semantics and ontologies,

- News summarization, classification and sentiment analysis,

RecSys '15 September 16-20, 2015, Vienna, Austria
ACM 978-1-4503-3692-5/15/09
http://dx.doi.org/10.1145/2792838.2798721.

- Recommender systems and news personalization,

- Group recommendation for news,

- User profiling and news context modeling,

- News evolution and trends,

- Large-scale news mining and analytics,

- Evaluation methods,

- News from social media,

- Big Data technologies for news streams,

- News recommendation and analytics on mobile platforms.

3. WORKSHOP DETAILS

In INRA 2015 we have received 6 submissions, of which 4 were accepted for presentation. The submissions to our workshop includes good quality of works for user profiling, social network analysis, hybrid methods and deep learning for news recommendation. This year we have the acceptance rate of 66%. In INRA 2015 we have a keynote speaker who has a very good background of industrial and academic work on data analytics and news research. INRA also includes a demo session with a full-fledged news recommender system that has been developed as part of the SmartMedia program at NTNU in Trondheim. This system integrates numerous Norwegian news sources and demonstrates how the use of context can improve the quality of personalized mobile news aggregators.

3.1 Keynote Speaker

Dr. Bahareh Heravi is the keynote speaker of INRA 2015. She is a Research Fellow at Insight Centre for Data Analytics @ NUI Galway and the founder and Leader of the Insight News Lab [1] (Digital Humanities and Journalism). She is an Adjunct Lecturer and a programme board member of Journalism Studies at the National University of Ireland, Galway. Dr Heravi's research and teaching are at the nexus of data, technology and journalism. She has worked with and within various news organizations. Her main research interests are in the areas of Data and Computational Journalism, Information Science, Social Media & Citizen Sensing, Semantic Web and Linked Data. She leads a number of projects at the Insight News Lab, including RTE News360, Newswire 2.0, VeritaWire, Social Semantic Journalism and the Social Repository of Ireland. Dr Heravi is the founder of Irish Times Data [2] and also the founder and organizer of Hacks/Hackers Dublin. She is the former Lead Data Scientist at The Irish Times, where she lead the Irish Times'R&D programme and pioneered data innovation in the newsroom. Dr. Heravi's talk is about data journalism as a practice, the new directions and challenges in news organizations.

3.2 Previous Workshops

3rd International Workshop on News Recommendation and Analytics (INRA 2015) is based on the following previous workshops:

- International News Recommender Systems Workshop and Challenge (NRS)[3] held in conjunction with the 7th ACM Recommender Systems Conference in 2013. This workshop had a very limited scope, which restricted the number of submissions and led to an acceptance rate of 75%.

- International Workshop on News Recommendation and Analytics (NRA) 2014 [4] held in conjunction with 22nd Conference on User Modelling, Adaptation and Personalization (UMAP) in 2014. The workshop scope was extended with news analytics, which is closely lined with the field of news recommendation. The acceptance rate was 50%.

4. ORGANIZERS

4.1 Workshop Chairs

Jon Atle Gulla, Professor at Department of Computer and Information Science, Norwegian University of Science and Technology (NTNU), Norway

Bei Yu, Assistant Professor at School of Information Studies, Syracuse University, USA

4.2 Organizing Committee Co-Chairs

Özlem Özgöbek, Computer Engineering Department, Balikesir University, Turkey

Xiaomeng Su, Department of Informatics and eLearning, Sør-Trøndelag University College, Norway

4.3 Program Committee Co-Chairs

Nafiseh Shabib, Norwegian University of Science and Technology (NTNU), Department of Computer and Information Science, Norway

Jon Espen Ingvaldsen, Norwegian University of Science and Technology (NTNU), Department of Computer and Information Science, Norway

---

[1]http://newslab.insight-centre.org/
[2]http://irishtimes.com/data

[3]http://recsys.acm.org/recsys13/nrs
[4]http://research.idi.ntnu.no/nra2014

RecSys'15 Joint Workshop on Interfaces and Human Decision Making for Recommender Systems

John O'Donovan
Dept. of Computer Science,
University of California,
Santa Barbara, USA
jod@cs.ucsb.edu

Nava Tintarev
Dept. of Computer Science,
University of Aberdeen, UK
n.tintarev@abdn.ac.uk

Alexander Felfernig
Institute for Software Technology,
Graz University of Technology, Austria
alexander.felfernig@ist.tugraz.at

Peter Brusilovsky
School of Information Sciences,
University of Pittsburgh, USA
peterb@pitt.edu

Giovanni Semeraro
Dept. of Computer Science,
University of Bari "Aldo Moro", Italy
giovanni.semeraro@uniba.it

Pasquale Lops
Dept. of Computer Science, University
of Bari "Aldo Moro", Italy
pasquale.lops@uniba.it

ABSTRACT

As an interactive intelligent system, recommender systems are developed to give recommendations that match users' preferences. Since the emergence of recommender systems, a large majority of research focuses on objective accuracy criteria and less attention has been paid to how users interact with the system and the efficacy of interface designs from users' perspectives. The field has reached a point where it is ready to look beyond algorithms, into users' interactions, decision making processes, and overall experience. Following from the success of the joint IntRS 2014 workshop and previous workshops on Interfaces and Decisions in Recommender Systems, this workshop will focus on the aspect of integrating different theories of human decision making into the construction of recommender systems. It will focus particularly on the impact of interfaces on decision support and overall satisfaction, and on ways to compare and evaluate novel techniques and applications in this area.

Categories and Subject Descriptors

H3.3 **[Information Search and Retrieval]**; H.4.2 **[Decision Support Systems]** H5.2 **[Information Interfaces and Presentation]**

General Terms

Algorithms, Experimentation, Human Factors, Human-Computer Interaction

Keywords

Recommender Systems; Decision Making; User Interfaces; Interaction; Decision Psychology; Recommender Algorithms; Decision Biases

RecSys '15, September 16–20, 2015, Vienna, Austria
ACM 978-1-4503-3692-5/15/09.
http://dx.doi.org/10.1145/2792838.2798714

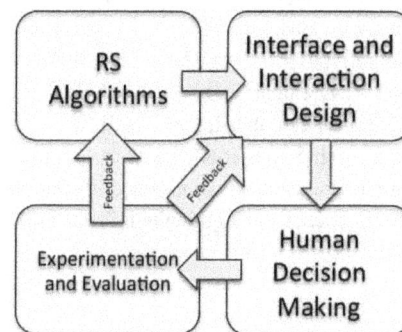

Fig 1: Overview of interactions between key workshop themes.

1. OVERVIEW AND MOTIVATION

The aim of the workshop is to bring together researchers and practitioners around the topics of designing and evaluating novel intelligent interfaces for recommender systems in order to: (1) share research and techniques, including new design technologies and evaluation methodologies (2) identify next key challenges in the area, and (3) identify emerging topics. This workshop aims at establishing an interdisciplinary community with a focus on the interface design issues for recommender systems and promoting the collaboration opportunities between researchers and practitioners. We particularly encourage demos and mock-ups of systems to be used as a basis of a lively and interactive discussion in the workshop

This workshop is a follow up on five previous successful workshops at RecSys:

- Joint Workshop on Interfaces and Decision Making in Recommender Systems (IntRS)
  2014: http://recex.ist.tugraz.at/intrs2014/
- Workshop on Human Decision Making in Recommender Systems (Decisions)
  2013: http://recex.ist.tugraz.at/RecSysWorkshop/

2012: http://recex.ist.tugraz.at/RecSysWorkshop2012
2011:
http://recex.ist.tugraz.at:8080/RecSysWorkshop2011
- Workshop on Interfaces for Recommender Systems (InterfaceRS)
2012:
https://homepages.abdn.ac.uk/n.tintarev/pages/InterfaceRS/

2. TOPICS OF INTEREST

The following list outlines core topics of interest.

User Interfaces

- Visual interfaces for recommender systems
- Explanation interfaces for recommender systems
- Collaborative multi-user interfaces (e.g., group decision making in e-tourism)
- Spoken and natural language interfaces
- Trust-aware interfaces
- Social interfaces
- Context-aware interfaces
- Ubiquitous and mobile interfaces
- Conversational interfaces
- Example- and demonstration-based interfaces
- New approaches to designing interfaces for recommender systems
- User interfaces for decision making (e.g., decision strategies and user ratings)

Interaction, user modeling and decision-making

- Cognitive Modeling for recommender systems
- Human-recommender interaction
- Controllability, transparency and scrutability
- Decision theories in recommender systems (e.g., priming, framing, and decoy effects)
- Preference detection (e.g., eye tracking for automated preference detection)
- The role of emotions in recommender systems (e.g., emotion-aware recommendation)
- Trust inspiring recommendation (e.g., explanation-aware recommendation

- Argumentation and Persuasive recommendation (e.g., argumentation-aware recommendation)
- Cultural differences (e.g., culture-aware recommendation)
- Mechanisms for effective group decision making (e.g., group recommendation heuristics)
- Decision theories for effective group decision making (e.g., hidden profile management)
- Detection and avoidance of decision biases (e.g., in item presentations)

Evaluation

- Case studies
- Empirical studies and evaluations of new interfaces
- Empirical studies and evaluations of new interaction designs
- Evaluation methods and metrics (e.g., evaluation questionnaire design)
- Benchmarking for Interactive Recommender Systems
- Challenge Competitions

3. WORKSHOP FORMAT

The workshop format consists of a short general introduction to the workshop themes by the organizers. This is to be followed by oral presentation of accepted papers listed at the link below. Presentations will be grouped into sessions based on the subthemes of the workshop. One keynote presentation will be given. After each presentation and session, time will be allocated for general discussion and feedback.

4. FURTHER INFORMATION

The workshop material including list of accepted papers, invited talk and workshop schedule are available at the IntRS@RecSys 2015 webpage: http://intrs.ist.tugraz.at/intrs/ and via the workshops section on the main conference website: http://recsys.acm.org/recsys15/intrs/

LSRS'15: Workshop on Large-Scale Recommender Systems

Tao Ye
Pandora Inc.
2101 Webster St., 16th Fl
Oakland, CA 94612
(+1) 510-451-4100
tye@pandora.com

Danny Bickson
Dato Inc.
Suite 208, 936 North 34th Street,
Seattle, WA 98195
(+1) 206-494-3383
bickson@dato.com

Nicholas Ampazis
University of the Aegean
41 Kountouriotou Street
82100, Chios, Greece
(+30) 2271 0 35467
n.ampazis@fme.aegean.gr

Andras Benczur
Hungarian Academy of Sciences
13-17 Kende u, Budapest H-1111,
Hungary
(+36) 1 279 6172
benczur@info.ilab.sztaki.hu

ABSTRACT

With the increase of data collected and computation power available, modern recommender systems are ever facing new challenges. While complex models are developed in academia, industry practice seems to focus on relatively simple techniques that can deal with the magnitude of data and the need to distribute the computation. The workshop on large-scale recommender systems (LSRS) is a meeting place for industry and academia to discuss the current and future challenges of applied large-scale recommender systems.

Categories and Subject Descriptors

H.2.8 [Database Management]: Database Applications – *data mining*. H.3.4 [Database Management]: System and Software – *distributed systems*.

Keywords

Recommendation systems; big data; scalability; machine learning

1. BACKGROUND AND MOTIVATION

As we enter the era of Big Data, the modern Recommender System faces greatly increased data volume and complexities. Previous computational models and experience on small data may not hold today, thus, how to build an efficient and robust system has become an important issue for many practitioners. Meanwhile, there is an increasing gap between academia research of recommendation systems focusing on complex models, and industry practice focusing on solving problems at large scale using relatively simple techniques.

RecSys'15, September 16–20, 2015, Vienna, Austria.
ACM. ISBN 978-1-4503-3692-5/15/09
DOI: http://dx.doi.org/10.1145/2792838.2798715

Chances favor connected minds. The motivation of this workshop is to bring together researchers and practitioners working on large-scale recommender system in order to: (1) share experience, techniques and methodologies used to develop effective large-scale recommender, from architecture, algorithm, programming model, to evaluation (2) identify key challenges and promising trends in the area, and (3) identify collaboration opportunities among participants.

2. OBJECTIVES

This workshop aims to foster discussions in several fields that are of interest to our growing community of recommendation system builders. On the practical side, we would like to encourage sharing of architecture best practices in large-scale recommender systems as they are practiced in industry, as well as particular challenges and pain points. We hope this will guide future research that is system aware. On the research side, we focus on bringing in ideas and evaluations on scaling beyond the current generation of big data systems, with improved recommendation metrics. We believe the brightest minds from both sides will mutually benefit from the discussions and accelerate problem solving.

3. TOPICS OF INTEREST

We solicited submissions from industrial level recommendation system practitioners in either a short paper or slides format on large scale system practice, as well as from recommendation systems researchers on their new research related to system aspect of recommendation with Big Data.

We focused on the following topics:

Systems of Large-scale RS:

- Architecture
- Programming Model
- Distributed systems
- Real-time recommendation

- Online learning for recommendation
- Scalability and Robustness

Data & Algorithms in Large-scale RS:
- Big data processing in offline/near-line/online modules
- Streaming data for recommendation
- Data platforms for recommendation
- Large, unstructured and social data for recommendation
- Heterogeneous data fusion
- Sampling techniques
- Parallel algorithms
- Incremental algorithms
- Algorithm validation and correctness checking

Application & Evaluation of Large-scale RS:
- Recommendation on mobile devices
- Explanations in Large-scale RS
- Anti-attack of Large-scale RS
- Large data and privacy issue
- Evaluation methodology
- Large user studies
- Measurement platforms
- Visualization

4. PROGRAM COMMITTEE

We are grateful for the help of our program committee to review submissions:

Srikrishna Sridhar, Dato
Noam Koenigstein, Microsoft
Sebastian Schelter, Dato Inc

Andy Twigg, C9 Inc.
David Zibriczky, ImpressTV
Barak Chizi, Deutsche Telekom
Andreas Lommatzsch, Technische Universität Berlin
Fabian Abel
Dominik Ryzko
Denis Parra, Pontificia Universidad Catolica de Chile
Roberto Turrin, Moviri
Domonkos Tikk, Gravity
Udi Weinsberg, Facebook
Edo Liberty, Yahoo! Labs
Dionysios Logothetis, Facebook
Ranjit Desai, Nook Media
Royi Ronen, Microsoft
Steffen Rendle, Google
Jeremy Schiff, OpenTable
Andres Arpteg, Spotify
Vijay Bharadwaj, Netflix
Lior Rokach, BGU
Gianmarco De Francisci Morales, Aalto University

5. WORKSHOP FORMAT

The workshop will feature one keynote and three presentation sessions. We expect a mix of peer reviewed contributions one presentation session to be 4 peer reviewed papers and the other two shorter sessions to be invited talks.

6. ACKNOWLEDGMENTS

We thank the RecSys 2015 organizing committee for giving us the opportunity to host this workshop in conjunction with RecSys 2015 in Vienna, Austria.

LocalRec'15: Workshop on Location-Aware Recommendations

Panagiotis Bouros
Humboldt-Universität zu
Berlin, Germany
bourospa@informatik.hu-
berlin.de

Neal Lathia
University of Cambridge,
United Kingdom
neal.lathia@cl.cam.ac.uk

Matthias Renz
Ludwig-Maximilians
Universität München,
Germany
renz@dbs.ifi.lmu.de

Francesco Ricci
Free University of
Bozen-Bolzano, Italy
fricci@unibz.it

Dimitris Sacharidis
Technische Universität Wien,
Austria
dimitris@ec.tuwien.ac.at

ABSTRACT

The amount of available geo-referenced data has seen a dramatic explosion over the past few years. Human activities now generate digital traces that are annotated with location data, enabling the collection of rich information about people's interests and habits. This torrent of geo-referenced data provides a tremendous potential to augment recommender systems. The LocalRec'15 workshop brings together scholars from location-based services and recommender systems, and seeks to set out new trends and research directions.

Categories and Subject Descriptors

H.3.3 [**Information Storage and Retrieval**]: Information Search and Retrieval—*Information Filtering*

General Terms

Algorithms, Design, Experimentation

Keywords

recommender systems; location-based services

1. MOTIVATION

Driven by technological advances in hardware (positioning systems, environmental sensors), software (standards, tools, network services), and aided by various open movements (open, linked, government data) and the ever-growing trend of sharing for the greater good (crowdsourcing, crowdfunding, collaborative and volunteered geographic information), the amount of available geo-referenced data has seen dramatic explosion over the past few years. Human activities

generate data and traces that are now often transparently annotated with location and contextual information. At the same time, it has become easier than ever to collect and combine rich and diverse information about locations. Exploiting this torrent of geo-referenced data provides a tremendous potential to materially improve existing and offer novel types of recommendation services, with clear benefits in many domains, including social networks, marketing, and tourism.

Fully exploiting the potential of location-aware recommendations, requires addressing many core challenges and combining ideas and techniques from various research communities, such as recommender systems, data management, geographic information systems, social network analytics, and text mining. Bringing together scholars and practitioners from these communities, the aim of the LocalRec'15 workshop was to provide a unique forum for discussing in depth and collecting feedback about the challenges, opportunities, novel techniques and applications of location-aware recommendations, in order to fuel better and novel recommender systems beyond the current research frontiers.

The non-exhaustive list of topics relevant to LocalRec'15 was the following.

- Location-based social networks
  - friend/communities recommendations
  - event, venue, and other location-aware recommendations
  - extracting preferences, tips, ratings, patterns, habits
  - modeling geo-social influence of users and locations
- Location-based marketing
  - viral campaigning
  - event planning
  - location-based advertising
- Tourism and mobile commerce
  - trip planning and recommendations
  - automatic guide and tour generation
  - exhibition arrangement
- Evaluation of location-aware recommender systems
  - collaborative filtering vs. content-based recommendations
  - case and empirical studies
  - evaluation methods and metrics
  - datasets and benchmarks
- Security and privacy implications

RecSys'15, September 16–20, 2015, Vienna, Austria.
ACM 978-1-4503-3692-5/15/09.
DOI: http://dx.doi.org/10.1145/2792838.2798720 .

- spatial anonymization and cloaking
- attack and threat scenarios

Further information can be found at the website of the LocalRec'15 workshop.[1]

2. WORKSHOP PROGRAM

We received ten submissions and we selected seven papers that are shortly summarized in the following.

Del Carmen Rodríguez-Hernández et al. [2] survey location-aware recommender systems (LARS). The authors describe LARS as a kind of context-aware recommender system that focuses on the spatial properties of the items that can be recommended; they discuss a number of studies that have been published, categorizing them as domain-independent (i.e., about generic spatial-ratings) and domain-dependent (recommending POIs, tourist routes, news, and shopping). The authors close with a comprehensive table of open challenges in this domain, that range from acquiring location data, evaluation, and security issues.

Giannopoulos et al. [3] present an approach to the recommendation of categories for geospatial entities annotation that leverages knowledge of previously annotated entities. They identify features that represent geospatial entities and capture their relation with the categories they are annotated with. These features involve spatial and textual properties of the entities. They evaluate two different learning approaches (SVM and kNN) and show that the best algorithm (SVM) can generate high precision category recommendations.

Kumar et al. [4] argue that close geographical distance does not necessarily imply increased similarity in users' preferences. This reasoning is in contrast to popular location-aware recommender systems that assume similarity decreases with distance. In the movie domain, the authors find that nearby locations are more similar than slightly more distant one, but average similarity does not generally decrease as distance increases. In fact, there are many cases where the average similarity of locations separated by thousands of kilometers exceeds the average similarity of nearby locations. Therefore, their approach is to cluster users taking into account the similarity, instead of the proximity, of their locations, which leads to accuracy improvements compared to proximity-based and randomized clustering.

Lamche et al. [5] design a context-aware recommendation system for mobile shopping. The goal is to employ user's mobile context for recommending clothing items in shops close to her position. Compared to existing mobile recommender systems, the challenge is to deal with frequent updates on the items list. The proposed framework extends a critique-based recommender system with a pre and a post-filtering stage. During pre-filtering, items relevant to the user context are determined based on factors such as the distance to or the opening hours of a shop and time of the day. Post-filtering employs a nearest neighbor algorithm to select the best-fits out of the items returned by the core recommender.

Lu et al. [6] introduce a location recommendation framework providing personalized recommendations. The proposed solution combines results from various recommenders that consider different factors. In a nutshell, the framework estimates, for each individual user, the underlying influence of each factor and aggregates suggestions from different recommenders based on this estimation. The paper shows how to learn individual user preferences over different recommenders and how to aggregate the resulting recommendations.

Palovics et al. [7] present a solution for Twitter hashtag recommendation for users retrieved from a stream of geotagged tweets. The proposed solution leverages the combination of local hashtag popularity, geographical hierarchy information and temporal context to learn the Twitter hashtag recommendations online. They use two models to recommend hashtags at a given location, one based on the estimated probability of the hashtag appearance based on its recency, and another based on its temporal popularity. Their proposed tree based method strongly outperforms state-of-the-art online matrix factorization solutions.

Sen and Larson [8] introduce a system that uses data from sensors (such as location) to model the user's situational context and recommend songs, with focus on achieving surprising and delightful recommendations. The authors conducted a focus group to support their design. The rest of the paper introduces the system: the list of smartphone/smartwatch sensors that data will be drawn from, how these will be modelled into context (e.g. from a location reading to "home"), and finally how the situational context tags are used to retrieve songs from SoundCloud; this system is currently being developed as a mobile app.

3. ACKNOWLEDGMENTS

The organizers would like to thank the program committee members and the authors for making this workshop possible, as well as the ACM RecSys'15 organizers for giving us the opportunity to host the workshop.

4. REFERENCES

[1] P. Bouros, N. Lathia, M. Renz, F. Ricci, and D. Sacharidis, editors. *Proceedings of the 1st Workshop on Location-Aware Recommendations (LocalRec'15), in ACM RecSys Conference*, number 1405 in CEUR Workshop Proceedings, Aachen, 2015. URL: http://ceur-ws.org/Vol-1405/.

[2] M. del Carmen Rodríguez-Hernández, S. Ilarri, R. Trillo-Lado, and R. Hermoso. Location-aware recommendation systems: Where we are and where we recommend to go. In Bouros et al. [1]. URL: http://ceur-ws.org/Vol-1405/paper-01.pdf.

[3] G. Giannopoulos, N. Karagiannakis, D. Skoutas, and S. Athanasiou. Automatic recommendations of categories for geospatial entities. In Bouros et al. [1]. URL: http://ceur-ws.org/Vol-1405/paper-02.pdf.

[4] V. Kumar, D. Jarratt, R. Anand, J. A. Konstan, and B. Hecht. "Where Far Can Be Close": Finding distant neighbors in recommender systems. In Bouros et al. [1]. URL: http://ceur-ws.org/Vol-1405/paper-03.pdf.

[5] B. Lamche, Y. Rödl, and W. Wörndl. Context-aware recommendations for mobile shopping. In Bouros et al. [1]. URL: http://ceur-ws.org/Vol-1405/paper-04.pdf.

[6] Z. Lu, H. Wang, N. Mamoulis, W. Tu, and D. W. Cheung. Personalized location recommendation by aggregating multiple recommenders in diversity. In Bouros et al. [1]. URL: http://ceur-ws.org/Vol-1405/paper-05.pdf.

[7] R. Palovics, P. Szalai, L. Kocsis, J. Pap, E. Frigo, and A. A. Benczur. Location-aware online learning for top-k hashtag recommendation. In Bouros et al. [1]. URL: http://ceur-ws.org/Vol-1405/paper-06.pdf.

[8] A. Sen and M. Larson. From sensors to songs: A learning-free novel music recommendation system using contextual sensor data. In Bouros et al. [1]. URL: http://ceur-ws.org/Vol-1405/paper-07.pdf.

2nd Workshop on Recommendation Systems for Television and Online Video (RecSysTV 2015)

Jan Neumann
Comcast Labs
1110 Vermont Ave NW
Washington, DC 20005
jan_neumann@
cable.comcast.com

Danny Bickson
Dato Inc
4000 Mason Rd
Seattle, WA 98195
bickson@dato.com

Hassan Sayyadi
Comcast Labs
1110 Vermont Ave NW
Washington, DC 20005
hassan.sayyadi@
cable.comcast.com

Roberto Turrin
Moviri S.p.A. - ContentWise R&D
Via Schiaffino, 11- Milan, Italy
Roberto.turrin@moviri.com

John Hannon
Zalando IE
Dublin, Ireland
john.hannon@zalando.ie

ABSTRACT

For many households the television is the central entertainment hub in their home, and the average TV viewer spends about half of their leisure time in front of a TV. At any given moment, a costumer has hundreds to thousands of entertainment choices available, which makes some sort of automatic, personalized recommendations desirable to help consumers deal with the often overwhelming number of choices they face. The 2nd Workshop on Recommendation Systems for Television and Online Video aims to offer a place to present and discuss the latest academic and industrial research on recommendation systems for this challenging and exciting application domain.

Categories and Subject Descriptors

H.2.8 [**Database Management**]: Database Applications – *data mining*. I.2.6 [**Artificial Intelligence**]: Learning – *Parameter learning*.

General Terms

Algorithms, Measurement, Performance, Design, Experimentation, Human Factors.

Keywords

Recommendations; big data; television; movies; video-on-demand.

1. BACKGROUND AND MOTIVATION

For many households the television is still the central entertainment hub in their home and the average TV viewer spends about half of their leisure time in front of a TV (3-5 hours/day).

The choice of what to watch becomes more overwhelming though because the entertainment options are scattered across various channels, such as on-demand video, digital recorders (on premise or in the cloud) and the traditional linear TV. In addition, consumers can also access the content not just on the big screen, but also on their computers, phones, and tablet devices.

Recommendation systems provide TV users with suggestions about both online video-on-demand and broadcast content and help them to search and browse intelligently for content that is relevant to them. While many open questions in video-on-demand recommendations have already been solved, recommendation systems for broadcast content (e.g., linear channels and catch-up TV) still experience a number of unique challenges due to the peculiarity of such domain. For example, the content available on linear channels is constantly changing and often only available once which leads to severe cold start problems and we often consume TV in groups of varying compositions (household vs individual) which makes building taste profiles and modeling consumer behavior very challenging.

Finally, recommendation systems have to address a number of very different consumption patterns, such as actively browsing through a list of personalized Video on Demand choices that match our current mood, compared to enjoying a "lean back experience" where a recommendation systems playlists a stream of TV shows from our favorite channels for us.

The unique challenges and wide-ranging applications of recommender systems in this domain motivated us to organize this workshop to bring together researchers from industry and academy in order to identify and share the key challenges, approaches and solutions of the field.

2. OBJECTIVES

The objective of this workshop is to encourage discussions among the researchers in the field, disseminate the latest approaches and encourage future collaboration among the participants. We believe that all participants will mutually benefit from the workshop activities and hopefully this will accelerate progress towards creating better recommendation systems for television and online video in the future.

3. TOPICS OF INTEREST

We solicited contributions from industrial and academic researchers on novel approaches to challenges found in the TV and online video recommendations space. Authors submitted both long and short papers focused on the following topics:

Context-aware TV and online video recommendations

- Leveraging contextual viewing behavior, e.g. device specific recommendations
- Mood based recommendations
- Group recommendations

User modeling & leveraging user viewing and interaction behavior

- How can social media improve TV recommendations
- Cross-domain recommendation algorithms (linear TV, video on demand, DVR, gaming consoles)
- Multi-viewer profile separation
- Evaluation metrics for TV and online video recommendations

Content-based TV and online video recommendations

- Analysis techniques for video recommendations based on video, audio, or closed caption signals
- Utilization of external data sources (movie reviews, ratings, plot summaries) for recommendations

Other topics related to TV and online video recommendations

- Video play listing
- Linear TV usage and box office success prediction
- Catch-up TV recommendations
- Personalized advertisement recommendations
- Recommendations of 2nd screen web content
- Recommendations of short form videos (previews, trailers, music videos)

4. PROGRAM COMMITTEE

We thank the program committee for their help with reviewing the submissions:

Balázs Hidasi, GravityR&D

Justin Basilico, Netflix

Craig Carmichael, Rovi

Emanuele Coviello, Keevio

Paolo Cremonesi, Politecnico di Milano

Joaquin Delgado, OnCue TV (Verizon)

Diana Hu, OnCue TV (Verizon)

Brendan Kitts, Adap.tv (AOL)

Gert Lanckriet, UC San Diego

Royi Ronen, Microsoft

Barry Smyth, Insight Centre for Data Analytics

Esti Widder, Viaccess-Orca

Dávid Zibriczky, ImpressTV

Jiayu Zhou, Samsung Research

5. WORKSHOP FORMAT

The workshop will consist of several key note and presentation sessions with contributions from both academic and industrial researchers. We will also have an industrial demo session to demonstrate the latest state of the art systems in the area of TV and online video recommendations.

6. ACKNOWLEDGEMENTS

We thank the RecSys 2015 organizing committee for giving us the opportunity to host this workshop in conjunction with RecSys 2015 and our companies Comcast, Dato, Moviri and Zalando for supporting this event.

TouRS'15: Workshop on Tourism Recommender Systems

Antonio Moreno
Universitat Rovira i Virgili
Av.Països Catalans, 26
Tarragona, Spain
+34-977559681
antonio.moreno@urv.cat

Laura Sebastiá
Univ. Politécnica de Valencia
Camino de Vera, s/n
Valencia, Spain
+34-963877000
lstarin@dsic.upv.es

Pieter Vansteenwegen
KU Leuven
Celestijnenlaan 300
Leuven, Belgium
+32-16321669
pieter.vansteenwegen@kuleuven.be

ABSTRACT
Tourism has been one of the most prominents fields of application of recommender systems in the last ten years.This summary gives an overview of the latest advances in the area, which have been presented in the RecSys 2015 workshop on Tourism Recommender Systems.

Categories and Subject Descriptors
H.3.3 [**Information Search and Retrieval**]: Information Filtering. H.4.2 [**Information Systems Applications**]: Types of Systems – Decision Support.

General Terms
Algorithms, Performance.

Keywords
Recommender systems; tourism; diversification; planning; personalization; group recommendation; ontologies

1. INTRODUCTION
The huge amount of information about tourism and leisure activities available on the Web has turned the action of preparing a trip into a very challenging task, ripe for the application of recommender systems. Travellers are very keen on using tools that may support their decision making processes when they are planning a travel, including the choice of destination, the selection of attractions to visit, the construction of a multi-day plan, the suggestion of appropriate accommodations and restaurants, etc. Complex problems such as automated planning, semantic knowledge management, group recommendation or context-awareness are now been heavily studied in this area [2]. The works reported at the RecSys-2015 workshop on Tourism Recommender Systems, briefly commented in the next section, provide a glimpse of the state of the art in the field and its main current challenges.

RecSys '15, September 16–20, 2015, Vienna, Austria
ACM978-1-4503-3692-5/15/09.
http://dx.doi.org/10.1145/2792838.2798713

2. MAIN LINES OF WORK
Tourism Recommender Systems (TRS) usually employ a combination of diverse types of recommendation techniques: content-based, knowledge-based, collaborative filtering, demographic, etc. However, the particular characteristics of this domain provoke the appearance of novel problems and the need of developing new techniques (which, in turn, could be later adopted in other domains). In the following subsections we comment some of the most relevant areas of this work in this field and the proposals made in the TouRS workshop.

2.1 Group Recommendation
Classical recommender systems try to filter the domain items that may be more relevant for a particular user, given her demographic data, her past ratings or purchasing history and her preferences. This approach can be very suitable to recommend specific items such as books, songs or films. However, travelling is an activity that is usually carried out in groups of people (couple, family, friends, colleagues); thus, it is necessary to take into account the tastes of all the travellers when providing recommendations [4].

Two works presented in the workshop addressed this issue. In the system *TravelWithFriends*, the first step is to build a recommendation list for each user and to merge them (using the *average without misery* strategy) to obtain a destinations shortlist. Afterwards, each group member rates these options and a Borda count is used to determine the best five destinations to be recommended. The second work dealing with group recommendation is the system *CLG-REJA*, which is an extension of the *REJA* restaurant recommender [8]. In this case the first step is also the construction of a list of recommendations for each group member, taking into account her ratings. In a second step, an automatic consensus-reaching process is applied [3]. This is an iterative process in which individual preferences are updated until a high degree of agreement between all the group members is reached.

2.2 Planning
Planning the order in which recommended tourist activities have to be visited is a complex problem that has received a great deal of attention in the last years [10]. Kurata et al. have presented in the workshop *CT-Planner5*, the latest version of the well-known *CT-Planner* [6]. The system engages with the user in a collaborative process to construct a route. The user keeps refining her constraints iteratively, until the system can build a satisfying plan. Genetic algorithms are employed in the planning procedure.

2.3 Use of Semantic Information
The use of semantic domain knowledge in the recommendation process, usually represented in the form of an ontology, has

heavily increased in recent years [11] as exemplified by three of the works presented in the workshop. Borràs et al. propose to improve the diversity of the results provided by the *SigTur* recommender [9] using a semantic clustering procedure. The items to be recommended are clustered according to their semantic similarity and the recommendation procedure iteratively selects the best item from random clusters. It is shown that this procedure increases the diversity of the results while keeping their accuracy and an acceptable computational cost. The system *Troovel* also contains an ontology with information about the different kinds of tourist activities. The degree of relationship of each item with respect to each category has been automatically computed from TripAdvisor ratings. The user profile, which is continuously updated through the analysis of the interaction of the user with the recommended items, stores a preference degree with respect to each category, which is used by a hybrid recommender system to provide the appropriate suggestions to the users. Semantic information can also be used to determine the items to be recommended in a personalized visit to a museum [1]. More concretely, Lo Bue et al. have presented in the workshop a mobile guide in which both the user profile and the domain items are represented with bags of DBpedia topic categories [7]. A shortest-path semantic distance is used to determine the museum objects that should be recommended to the user.

2.4 Theoretical results

Sánchez-Vilas et al. show in their contribution to the workshop a surprising result: the performance of recommenders systems based on k-Nearest Neighbours improves when user profiles which are quite different to the current user are considered. This result is explained in terms of the *diversity prediction theorem* [5], which says that a higher diversity of the items considered in the recommendation leads to a smaller global error.

3. CONCLUSIONS

Tourism is a very exciting field of application of recommender systems [2]. The TouRS workshop, held at the RecSys-2015 conference, has witnessed the presentation of both theoretical and practical works which have highlighted some of the most relevant areas of current work in this field, including planning, group recommendation and the management of semantic knowledge.

4. ACKNOWLEDGMENTS

A.Moreno has been supported by the Spanish research project *SHADE: Semantic Hierarchical Attributes for Decision Aid* (TIN2012-34369). L.Sebastiá acknowledges the support of the Spanish project TIN-2014-55637-C2-2-R and the Valencian project PROMETEOII/2013/019.

5. REFERENCES

[1] Ardisono, L., Kuflik, T. and Petrelli, D. 2011. Personalization in cultural heritage: the road travelled and the one ahead. *User Modeling and User-Adapted Interaction* 22, 1-27.

[2] Borràs, J., Moreno, A. and Valls, A. 2014. Intelligent tourism recommender systems: A survey. *Expert Systems with Applications* 41(16), 7370-7389.

[3] Castro, J., Quesada, F.J., Palomares, I. and Martínez, L. 2015. A consensus-driven group recommender system. International Journal of Intelligent Systems 30 (8), 887-906.

[4] García, I., Sebastiá, L. and Onaindia, E. 2011. On the design of individual and group recommender systems for tourism. *Expert systems with applications* 38, 7683-7692.

[5] Hong, L. and Page, S.E. 2011. The foundations of Wisdom. In *Collective Wisdom: Principles and Mechanisms*, 1-22.

[6] Kurata, Y. and Hara, T. 2014. CT-Planner4: towards a more user-friendly interactive day-tour planner. In *Proceedings of the 21st International Conference on Information Technology and Travel and Tourism*. ENTER-2014, 73-86.

[7] Lehmann, J., Isele, R., Jakob, M., Jentzsch, A., Kontokostas, D., Mendes, P., Hellmann, S., Morsey, M., van Kleef, P., Auer, S. and Bizer, C. 2014. DBpedia-a large-scale, multilingual knowledge base extracted from Wikipedia. *Semantic Web Journal* 5, 1-29.

[8] Martínez, L., Rodríguez, R.M. and Espinilla, M. 2009. REJA: a geo-referenced hybrid recommender system for restaurants. In *Proceedings of the IEEE/WIC/ACM International Joint Conference on Web Intelligence and Intelligent Agent Technology*. WI-IAT'09, 187-190.

[9] Moreno, A., Valls, A., Isern, D., Marin, L. and Borràs, J. 2013. Sigtur/e-destination: ontology-based personalized recommendation of tourism and leisure activities. *Engineering Applications of Artificial Intelligence* 26 (1), 633-651.

[10] Souffriau, W. and Vansteenwegen, P. 2010. Tourist trip planning functionalities: state-of-the-art and future. In *Current Trends in Web Engineering* (Lecture Notes in Computer Science 6385), 474-485.

[11] Valls, A., Moreno, A. and Borràs, J. 2013. Preference representation with ontologies. In *Multicriteria Decision Aid and Artificial Intelligence: Links, Theory and Applications*. Eds: M. Doumpos, E. Grigoroudis. John Wiley and Sons, 77-100.

RecSys Challenge 2015 and the YOOCHOOSE Dataset

David Ben-Shimon
YOOCHOOSE Labs Ltd
Omer, Israel
david.ben-shimon@yoochoose.com

Alexander Tsikinovsky
YOOCHOOSE Labs Ltd
Omer, Israel
alexander.tsikinovsky@yoochoose.com

Michael Friedmann
YOOCHOOSE GmbH
Cologne, Germany
michael.friedmann@yoochoose.com

Bracha Shapira
Ben-Gurion University of the Negev
Beer-Sheva, Israel
bshapira@bgu.ac.il

Lior Rokach
Ben-Gurion University of the Negev
Beer-Sheva, Israel
liorrk@bgu.ac.il

Johannes Hoerle
YOOCHOOSE GmbH
Cologne, Germany
johannes.hoerle@yoochoose.com

ABSTRACT

The 2015 ACM Recommender Systems Challenge offered the opportunity to work on a large-scale e-commerce dataset from a big retailer in Europe which is accepting recommender system as a service from YOOCHOOSE. Participants tackled the problem of predicting what items a user intends to purchase, if any, given a click sequence performed during an activity session on the e-commerce website.

The challenge ran for seven months and was very successful, attracting 850 teams from 49 countries which submitted a total of 5,437 solutions. The winners of the challenge scored approximately 50% of the maximum score, which we considered as an impressive achievement. In this paper we provide a brief overview of the challenge and its results.

Categories and Subject Descriptors

H.2.8 [**Database Applications**]: Data mining

General Terms

Algorithms, Performance, Experimentation

Keywords

Recommender Systems, RecSys Challenge 2015, E-Commerce, YOOCHOOSE

1. INTRODUCTION

Traditionally, the annual ACM Conference on Recommender Systems features a related challenge designed to test participants' skills and algorithms [2][3]. The 2015 RecSys Challenge presented here is associated with ACM RecSys 2015 and organized by the recommender system (RC) provider, YOOCHOOSE[1].

Many small and mid-sized e-commerce businesses outsource the implementation and operation of their RSs. As part of the services offered, RS providers record users' activities and compute statistical models in order to deliver top-N recommendations. In e-businesses the task of delivering the top-N recommendations is more pertinent than the task of rating items, because e-businesses

---

[1] www.yoochoose.com

RecSys '15, September 16-20, 2015, Vienna, Austria
ACM 978-1-4503-3692-5/15/09.
http://dx.doi.org/10.1145/2792838.2798723

strive to present interesting items to the user. YOOCHOOSE is a RS provider [1] specializing in the calculation of top quality (best matching) top-N recommendations for a variety of purposes, such as generating cross or up-sell, exploiting long tail items, etc., while keeping the user engaged and satisfied.

In this challenge[2], YOOCHOOSE provides a collection of sequence of click events (click sessions) as a training set. Some of the sessions also include buying events. Given a new sequence of clicks, the goal is to predict what items the user will buy, if any. Such information is highly valuable to e-businesses, since it can indicate not only what items to suggest to the user but also how to encourage the user to become a buyer. For example, if the recommender system is able to determine that the user doesn't intend to make a purchase during the current session, it may try to change this behavior by offering the user dedicated promotions, discounts, and the like.

2. DATASET & TASK DESCRIPTION

The data represents six months of user activities for a large European e-commerce business that sells a variety of consumer goods including garden tools, toys, clothes, electronics, and more. The training data is comprised of two different files: yoochoose-clicks.dat and yoochoose-buys.dat. Each record in yoochoose-clicks.dat represents a click event and includes the following four fields: Session ID, Time stamp, Item ID, and Item category. Each record in yoochoose-buys.dat represents a purchase and includes the following five fields: Session ID, Time Stamp, Item ID, Item Price, and Quantity. There were 33,040,175 records in the clicks file and 1,177,769 records in the buys file. Together these 9,512,786 unique sessions form the training set. Participants are required to run algorithms on the training data in order to predict which items will be bought during each session in a testing data. The yoochoose-test.dat file consists of 2,312,432 click sessions and is structured identically to the training data's yoochoose-clicks.dat file.

For every item in each of the test file's click sessions the task is to predict whether an item will be purchased during a given session or not. Upon completion of this task, participants must upload their solution/predictions to the challenge website, which in turn calculates a score to this solution immediately and updates the leaderboard online. The solution file to be submitted is comprised of records that have exactly two fields: 1) Session ID and, 2) Comma separated list of item IDs that have been purchased during this session. If a Session ID exists in the test file but does not exist in the uploaded solution file, it means that the challenger predicts that the session ends without a buying event. It should be noted

---

[2] http://recsys.yoochoose.net/

that approximately 95% of the sessions in the training set end without a buying event, a distribution was also maintained in the test set.

3. EVALUTION

The task of the challenge can be divided into two sub-goals, first to determine whether a session ends with buying event or not, and if so, to identify what items will be bought. Consequently, we developed a unique measure to emphasize the two sub-goals, as well as to maintain the balance of the importance between the two. Let's note the following:

- Sl – number of sessions in the submitted solution file
- S – number of sessions in the test set
- s – a session in test set
- Sb – set of sessions in test set which end with buy
- As – set of predicted bought items in session s
- Bs – set of actual bought items in session s

Then, equation (1) represents the score of a solution.

$$Score(Sl) = \sum_{\forall s \in Sl} \begin{cases} if\ s \in Sb \rightarrow \frac{Sb}{S} + \frac{|As \cap Bs|}{|As \cup Bs|} \\ else \rightarrow -\frac{Sb}{S} \end{cases} \quad (1)$$

For each session included in the solution file, we add the value of $|Sb|/|S|$ to the overall score in cases which actually includes a buying event. Additionally, the Jaccard score $|As \cap Bs|/|As \cup Bs|$ / is computed between the predicted and actual set of bought items and is later added to the overall score.

If the challenger predicts that the session will end with buying events but lists the wrong items, he still gets a positive score. However, if the participant incorrectly predicts that a session ends with a buying event there is a penalty of $-|Sb|/|S|$ which is subtracted from the overall score for each wrong prediction. The score for a perfect and optimal solution on the test set is 135,176. The winning team achieved a score of 63,102.

4. SCHEDULE, PRIZES, AND PAPERS

The challenge was launched on November 15, 2014, with a final submission deadline of June 15, 2015. The challenge was announced during the 2014 ACM Conference on Recommender Systems, along with monetary prizes in the amounts of 3000€, 1500€, and 500€ for first, second, and third teams respectively.

The winners were determined based on the final ranking of the scores at the end of the challenge. Furthermore, in order to receive a monetary prize, the winners were required to have an accepted workshop paper detailing the applied algorithms, and attend the conference on the day of the challenge workshop. The papers went through a review process taking into account performance, as well as various other aspects such as simplicity, novelty, clarity, sophistication, and the like. Seven papers, out of twenty one submissions, accepted and published in a special volume of ACM SIG proceedings, dedicated to the challenge.

5. CHALLENGE RESULTS

The challenge was very popular primarily because it focused on tackling a current and real e-commerce problem, and also due to its early announcement, incentives, publication of the submitted papers, and the online evaluation system that enabled participants to receive their score upon submission. Figure 1 present distribution by country, figure 2 includes the number of submissions by month throughout the challenge, and figure 3 indicates the maximum score achieved by month.

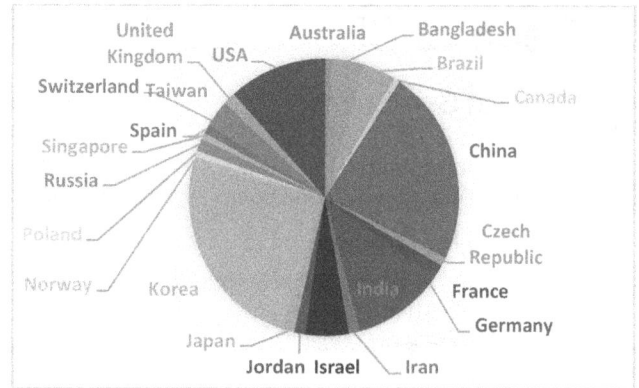

Figure 1. Distribution by Country (for countries with more than 5 teams). 850 teams from 49 countries participated.

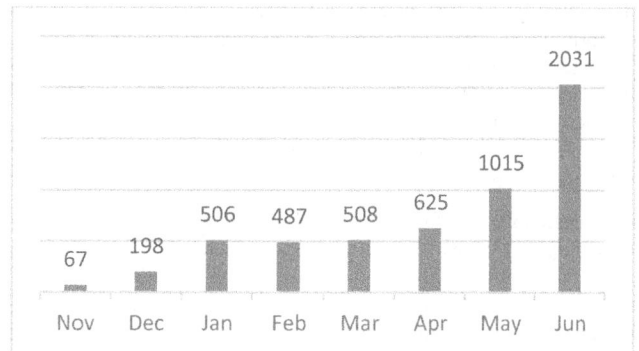

Figure 2. Number of submissions by month. Total of 5,437 solutions submitted during the 7 month challenge.

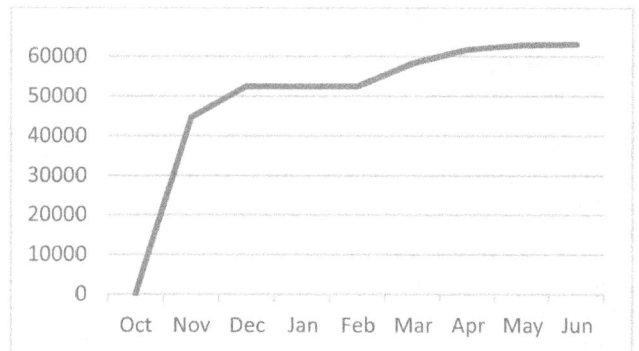

Figure 3. Maximum score achieved by month.

6. REFERENCES

[1] Ben-Shimon D., Friedman M., Hoerle J., Tsikinovsky A., Gude R., Aluchanov R. (2014). "Deploying recommender system for the masses." In Proceedings of the companion publication of the 19th international conference on Intelligent User Interfaces, pp. 1-4. ACM IUI 2014, Haifa, Israel

[2] Blomo, J., Ester, M., Field, M., 'Recsys challenge 2013', in Proceedings of the 7th ACM Conference on Recommender Systems, RecSys '13, pp. 489–490, New York, NY, USA, (2013). ACM..d

[3] Said, A., Dooms, S., Loni, B., & Tikk, D. (2014, October). Recommender systems challenge 2014. In Proceedings of the 8th ACM Conference on Recommender Systems. ACM

Interactive Recommender Systems

[Tutorial]

Harald Steck
Netflix Inc.
Los Gatos, California
hsteck@netflix.com

Roelof van Zwol
Netflix Inc.
Los Gatos, California
roelofvanzwol@netflix.com

Chris Johnson
Spotify Inc.
New York, New York
cjohnson@spotify.com

ABSTRACT

In this tutorial we will explore the field of interactive video and music recommendations (eg [1, 6, 3, 2]) and their application at Netflix and Spotify. Interactive recommender systems enable the user to steer the received recommendations in the desired direction through explicit interaction with the system. In this tutorial, we outline the various aspects that are crucial for a smooth and effective user experience. In particular, we present our insights from several A/B tests. The tutorial will help researchers and practitioners in the RecSys community to gain a deeper understanding of the challenges related to the application of recommender systems in the online video and music entertainment business.

Categories and Subject Descriptors

H.2.8 [**Database Management**]: Database Applications—*Data Mining*

Keywords

Interactive Recommender Systems; Personalization

1. INTRODUCTION

In the larger ecosystem of recommender systems used on a website, interactive recommender systems are positioned between a lean-back recommendation experience of the user and an active search for a specific piece of content. They adapt to the user's current interests based on instantaneous explicit feedback, steering the recommendations in the desired direction, or to discover new titles in a certain niche of the catalog.

In this tutorial, we will discuss several aspects that are especially important for interactive recommender systems, including the following: design of the user interface and its tight integration with the algorithm in the back-end; computational efficiency of the recommender algorithm; as well as choosing the right balance between exploiting the feedback from the user as to provide relevant recommendations,

and enabling the user to explore the catalog and steer the recommendations in the desired direction.

In particular, we will explore the field of interactive video and music recommendations and their application at Netflix and Spotify. We outline some of the user-experiences built, and discuss the approaches followed to tackle the various aspects of interactive recommendations. We will discuss lessons learned from our user studies and A/B tests.

2. CHALLENGES

In this tutorial, we will first discuss challenges that are specific to building an *interactive* recommender system.

2.1 Clear and Transparent User-Guidance

In an interactive setting, where recommendations adjust based on the user's feedback, it is quite easy to confuse the users so that they cannot clearly follow what and why recommendations are changing. We will discuss different variants of guiding the user in an intuitive way through an interactive experience.

2.2 Exploration vs Exploitation

While an interactive system has to yield relevant recommendations by exploiting the user's feedback, it is equally important that the provided recommendations allow the user to navigate / explore and to interactively steer the recommendations in the desired direction. As to ensure navigability, diversity in the recommendation list as well as the popularity of the recommended items has to be adapted on a continuous basis according the user's sequence of actions.

The degree of *diversity* (eg [8]), as opposed to focused / relevant recommendations, varies dependent on the user's sequence of actions. Beginning with a vastly diverse set, diversity may be reduced as long as the user continues to zoom into a certain niche of similar items. In contrast, when the sequence of a user's actions indicates that she intends to navigate out of a certain niche, or from one niche to a neighboring one, the algorithm has to automatically increase the degree of diversity.

Additionally, the balance between *popularity* and relevance/similarity of items (eg [7]) varies according to the user's actions as well: as the user zooms into a niche area, popularity may be reduced. As to aid navigation to a neighboring niche or to a completely different genre, it is helpful to recommend increasingly popular titles.

RecSys'15, September 16–20, 2015, Vienna, Austria.
© 2015 ACM. ISBN 978-1-4503-3692-5/15/09.
DOI: http://dx.doi.org/10.1145/2792838.2792840.

3. SOLUTIONS

In the second part of the tutorial, we will discuss the implications of the above challenges on the user interface as well as the recommendation algorithm of interactive recommender systems. We will illustrate the various points based on the two systems that we have built.

3.1 User Interface

There are several important properties of the user interface (UI). First, it has to be easy and intuitive to use, requiring minimal effort by the user. Moreover, the UI has to be tightly integrated with the recommendation algorithm in the back-end. For one, the UI has to allow the user to provide informative feedback data to the algorithm. Conversely, the UI has to allow for instantaneous updates of the recommendations by the algorithm, while making these updates transparent and easy to understand. For instance, we found it to be less confusing to the user when the UI updates the recommendations only slowly, so that the user can understand and follow them. It is also crucial to understand the user's intent when they come to the site as to determine as to when and how to invite the user to provide feedback in an interactive mode.

3.2 Algorithm

Specific to algorithms used in an interactive setting, we will discuss the following important properties.

While explicit feedback is provided by the user in an interactive setting, we found it useful to train the algorithm on implicit feedback data, as these data better reflect what users actually prefer to play (as opposed to what they think they like).

The algorithm has to be flexible as to combine relevance, popularity and diversity in varying degrees as to capture the user's intent and allow them to receive useful recommendations while also enabling effective navigation at the same time, as discussed above. For instance, through matrix factorization (eg [5, 4]) one can derive a compact representation for each item in the catalog in the form of a latent vector. While the orientations of the vectors reflect similarity, their norms reflect the items' popularity. These are important properties to derive a scoring function that allows for dynamic modification of the norms of the vectors, as well as incorporating a notion of diversity based on item similarity. In addition to the recommender algorithm, we used a second algorithm as to predict the optimal balance (ie weights) between relevance, popularity and diversity based on the sequence of a user's actions.

Moreover, the algorithms for interactive recommender systems have to be sufficiently efficient as to compute recommendations in real time based on the user's current actions.

3.3 Music Domain

Spotify's radio service allows users to start an interactive music session seeded by an artist, track, album, genre, or playlist. The service will then play music similar to the seed. Additionally, the radio service provides users the opportunity to explicitly "tune" their station using positive and negative "thumbs". The underlying recommendation engine powering the radio service jointly optimizes for seed similarity, artist and album diversity, user taste personalization, as well as station personalization based on the explicit thumbs feedback user has provided. An important difference to note

between the music and movie domains is that music is consumed more quickly and there is less of a commitment to evaluate recommendations. This means that explicit interactive feedback can be gathered more quickly and there is less of a cost in exploring new content to gather taste and intent.

3.4 Video Domain

Interactive recommendations can help the user find videos to watch in various scenarios that are not well covered by the Netflix homepage or search. For instance, a user may like to actively explore certain sub-genres of movies or TV shows in the Netflix catalog, before settling on a video to watch. To this end, we built two user experiences. In the first one, a single title is shown at a time and the user can navigate with positive and negative "thumbs" to the next title. In the second experience, several relevant but diverse titles are shown simultaneously, and the user is able to select the subset of interest. Based on the chosen titles, the recommendations are refreshed, which enables the user to iteratively refine the set of selected titles and hence to explore parts of the catalog. We conducted several user studies as well as A/B tests, where we experimented with various user interfaces as well as algorithms tuned in different ways.

4. ACKNOWLEDGMENTS

H.S. and R.v.Z. would like to thank Caitlin Smallwood and Carlos Gomez-Uribe for their encouragement and support of this work.

5. REFERENCES

[1] S. Bostandjiev, J. O'Donovan, and T. Höllerer. Tasteweights: A visual interactive hybrid recommender system. In *ACM Conference on Recommender Systems (RecSys)*, 2012.

[2] N. Hariri, B. Mobasher, and R. Burke. Context Adaptation in Interactive Recommender Systems. In *ACM Conference on Recommender Systems (RecSys)*, 2014.

[3] E. Gansner, Y. Hu, S. Kobourov, and C. Volinsky. Putting recommendations on the map – visualizing clusters and relations, 2009. AT&T Technical Report.

[4] C. Johnson. Logistic Matrix Factorization for Implicit Feedback Data. In *NIPS Workshop on Distributed Matrix Computations*, 2014.

[5] Y. Koren, R. Bell, and C. Volinsky. Matrix factorization techniques for recommender systems. *IEEE Computer*, pages 30–7, 2009.

[6] B. N. Miller, I. Albert, S. K. Lam, J. A. Konstan, and J. Riedl. MovieLens unplugged: Experiences with an occasionally connected recommender system. In *International Conference on Intelligent User Interfaces (IUI)*, 2003.

[7] H. Steck. Item popularity and recommendation accuracy. In *ACM Conference on Recommender Systems (RecSys)*, 2011.

[8] S. Vargas, L. B. , A. Karatzoglou, and P. Castells. Coverage, redundancy and size-awareness in genre diversity for recommender systems. In *ACM Conference on Recommender Systems (RecSys)*, 2014.

Real-time Recommendation of Streamed Data

Frank Hopfgartner
University of Glasgow, UK
frank.hopfgartner@
glasgow.ac.uk

Benjamin Kille
TU Berlin, Germany
benjamin.kille@dai-
labor.de

Tobias Heintz
plista GmbH, Germany
thz@plista.com

Roberto Turrin
ContentWise, Italy
roberto.turrin@contentwise.tv

ABSTRACT

This tutorial addressed two trending topics in the field of recommender systems research, namely A/B testing and real-time recommendations of streamed data. Focusing on the news domain, participants learned how to benchmark the performance of stream-based recommendation algorithms in a live recommender system and in a simulated environment.

Categories and Subject Descriptors

H.4 [**Information Systems Applications**]: Miscellaneous

General Terms

Experimentation

Keywords

Stream Recommendation; A/B testing; Offline Evaluation

1. INTRODUCTION

1.1 Evaluation Paradigms

The release of the Netflix dataset and the associated challenge was a key event that resulted in *offline evaluation* [11] being the most commonly used methodology for the evaluation of recommender systems. Although it comes with clear advantages such as the ability to compare the performance in predicting user ratings with state-of-the-art techniques, it has been criticized for its inability to incorporate the user in the evaluation process. An alternative evaluation paradigm is *online evaluation*, also referred to as A/B testing [1]. Online evaluation aims to benchmark varieties of a recommender system by a larger group of users. It is increasingly adopted for the evaluation of commercial systems with a large user base as it provides the advantage of observing the efficiency of recommendation algorithms under real conditions. However, while online evaluation is the de-facto standard evaluation methodology in Industry, university-based researchers often do not have access to either infrastructure or user base to perform online evaluation on a larger scale. Addressing this deficit, participants learned in this tutorial how they can join a living lab on news recommendation that allows them to perform A/B testing. The living lab and its recommendation scenario are described further in Section 2.

1.2 Recommendations of Streamed Data

Offline evaluation allows for the evaluation of research hypotheses that center around modeling recommendation as user-specific selection from static collections of items. While this might be suitable in some domains where the content does not change too often (e.g., in movie databases), it fails in more dynamic domains where items continuously emerge and extend collections, and where existing items become less and less relevant. Examples include news, microblog, or advertisement recommendations [3, 4, 5, 7, 6, 10] where content comes in the form of a constant stream of data.

Streamed data triggers specific challenges for recommender systems. For example, it challenges collaborative filtering as this imposes that the sets of users and items rapidly fluctuate. This tutorial focused on stream-based recommenders which reflect these dynamics. It concentrates on the domain of new recommendation as addressed NewsREEL. The scenario is described in the following section.

2. NEWS ARTICLE RECOMMENDATION

News content published on news portals represents a typical example for streamed data as new content is constantly added to the data corpus. At the same time, the more users visit a news portal, the more requests for providing news recommendations are triggered, resulting in a constant stream of requests. This recommender scenario is realized in the News REcommendation Evaluation Lab (NewsREEL)[1], a campaign style evaluation lab that focuses on benchmarking stream-based recommenders. The NewsREEL challenge consists of two subtasks: In the first subtask, the idea of *living laboratories* is implemented, i.e., researchers gain access to the resources of a company to evaluate different information access techniques using A/B testing. The infrastructure is provided by plista GmbH, a company that provides a recommendation service for online publishers. Whenever a user requests an article from one of their customers' web portals, plista recommends further articles that the user might be interested in. In NewsREEL, plista outsourced this rec-

RecSys'15, September 16–20, 2015, Vienna, Austria.
ACM 978-1-4503-3692-5/15/09.
DOI: http://dx.doi.org/10.1145/2792838.2792839.

---

[1] http://clef-newsreel.org/

ommendation task to interested researchers via their Open Recommendation Platform (ORP) [2]. As users visit selected news publishers, ORP randomly forwards recommendation requests to registered participants [8]. The tutorial will detail the idea, technologies, and existing SDK to use ORP. Hence, participants will be able to evaluate their recommendation algorithms in a live system. We argue that this use case represents a unique opportunity for researchers in the area of recommender systems.

The second subtask of NewsREEL focuses on simulating a constant data stream as provided by ORP. In contrast to the first scenario, performing an offline evaluation allows us to issue the same request to different algorithms and subsequently compare them. Additionally, it allows to measure factors such as time and space complexity. In NewsREEL, the Idomaar framework[2] is employed to simulate this data stream. Idomaar is a novel reference framework that was developed in the context of the European project CrowdRec [9]. It adopts open-source technologies widely known by the research community to allow handling of large-scale streams of data (e.g., Apache Kafka, Apache Spark, etc.). Focusing on the news scenario, participants learned how to use this technology to simulate constant data streams.

3. TARGETED AUDIENCE

This tutorial was designed for researchers and practitioners in the field of recommender algorithms. Researchers learned the steps required to setup a recommendation server, connect to ORP and evaluate recommendation algorithms. Practitioners learned about the special characteristics of streamed data for recommender systems. Further, they got to know recommendation algorithms able to deal with such conditions. Participants learned how to use ORP and the reference framework Idomaar to evaluate their recommendation algorithms in an authentic and a simulated setting, respectively.

4. IMPORTANCE OF THIS TOPIC

In recent years, a significant number of papers focused on improving the accuracy when predicting ratings. Typically, rating prediction evaluation starts by partitioning available data into training and test sets. However, commercial recommender systems face dynamics disregarded by this methodology as they often meet an endless stream of interactions between two fluctuating sets.

This tutorial supported researchers to start focusing on streams as recommender systems' input. We showed how participants can approximate an authentic way to evaluate their recommendation algorithms. This can help the community to better distribute their attention to problems urging industrial recommender systems.

5. OBJECTIVES

Having attended the tutorial, participants learned how to tackle the specific challenges of stream-based recommendations, in particular news recommendation. The tutorial highlighted differences between living lab scenarios and stream simulation. The following aspects were covered:

- recommenders operating on streamed data as opposed to static sets of users, items, and interactions

<hr>

[2] http://rf.crowdrec.eu/

- living laboratories and A/B testing as evaluation methodologies

- specificities of news challenging recommender systems

- comparing recommendation algorithms on streamed data

- frameworks and tools to evaluate news recommenders, in particular ORP and Idomaar

- current trends in the field of real-time recommender systems

As a result, users learned how to implement, evaluate, and continuously improve recommenders for streamed data in general, and news in particular.

Acknoledgments

The second and fourth authors are funded by European Union's Seventh Framework Programme (FP7/2007-2013) under CrowdRec Grant Agreement n.610594.

6. REFERENCES

[1] X. Amatriain. Beyond data: from user information to business value through personalized recommendations and consumer science. In *CIKM'13*, pages 2201–2208, 2013.

[2] T. Brodt and F. Hopfgartner. Shedding light on a living lab: the CLEF NEWSREEL open recommendation platform. In *IIiX'14*, pages 223–226, 2014.

[3] J. Chen, R. Nairn, L. Nelson, M. Bernstein, and E. Chi. Short and tweet: Experiments on recommending content from information streams. In *CHI'10*, pages 1185–1194. ACM, 2010.

[4] Y. Chen, P. Berkhin, B. Anderson, and N. R. Devanur. Real-time bidding algorithms for performance-based display ad allocation. In *KDD '11*, pages 1307–1315. ACM, 2011.

[5] E. Diaz-Aviles, L. Drumond, L. Schmidt-Thieme, and W. Nejdl. Real-time top-n recommendation in social streams. In *RecSys'12*, pages 59–66, 2012.

[6] D. Doychev, R. Rafter, A. Lawlor, and B. Smyth. News recommenders: Real-time, real-life experiences. In *UMAP'15*, pages 337–342, 2015.

[7] F. Garcin, B. Faltings, O. Donatsch, A. Alazzawi, C. Bruttin, and A. Huber. Offline and online evaluation of news recommender systems at swissinfo.ch. In *RecSys'14*, pages 169–176. ACM, 2014.

[8] F. Hopfgartner, B. Kille, A. Lommatzsch, T. Plumbaum, T. Brodt, and T. Heintz. Benchmarking news recommendations in a living lab. In *CLEF'14*, pages 250–267, 2014.

[9] B. Kille, A. Lommatzsch, R. Turrin, A. Sereny, M. Larson, T. Brodt, J. Seiler, and F. Hopfgartner. Stream-based recommendations: Online and offline evaluation as a service. In *CLEF'15*, 2015.

[10] A. Lommatzsch. Real-time recommendations for user-item streams. In *SAC'15*, pages 1039–1046, 2015.

[11] G. Shani and A. Gunawardana. Evaluating recommendation systems. In *Recommender Systems Handbook*, pages 257–297. 2011.

Replicable Evaluation of Recommender Systems

Alan Said
Recorded Future
Sweden
alansaid@acm.org

Alejandro Bellogín
Universidad Autónoma de Madrid
Spain
alejandro.bellogin@uam.es

ABSTRACT

Recommender systems research is by and large based on comparisons of recommendation algorithms' predictive accuracies: the better the evaluation metrics (higher accuracy scores or lower predictive errors), the better the recommendation algorithm. Comparing the evaluation results of two recommendation approaches is however a difficult process as there are very many factors to be considered in the implementation of an algorithm, its evaluation, and how datasets are processed and prepared.

This tutorial shows how to present evaluation results in a clear and concise manner, while ensuring that the results are comparable, replicable and unbiased. These insights are not limited to recommender systems research alone, but are also valid for experiments with other types of personalized interactions and contextual information access.

Categories and Subject Descriptors

H.3.3 [**Information Search and Retrieval**]: information filtering, relevance feedback, retrieval models, search process, selection process.

General Terms

Algorithms; Design; Experimentation; Measurement; Performance

Keywords

Evaluation; Replicability; Reproducibility; Experimental Design; Experimental Methodology

1. INTRODUCTION

The Recommender System community strives towards improving the quality of recommendation algorithms, in order to do so, it is imperative that comparisons across recommendation approaches can be performed in an accurate and unbiased fashion. Assuming the assumption "the higher the evaluation scores, the better the recommender algorithm", which is usually taken for granted, it is important for both researchers and practitioners that their evaluations are fair. However, it is difficult to compare the results from

RecSys'15, September 16–20, 2015, Vienna, Austria.
ACM 978-1-4503-3692-5/15/09.
DOI: http://dx.doi.org/10.1145/2792838.2792841 .

a given evaluation of a recommender system, mainly because the very many alternatives that exist in designing and implementing an evaluation strategy. At the ACM RecSys conferences, every year there usually are several papers on evaluation, additionally there have been a number of workshops (UCERSTI [5, 8], RUE [2], RepSys [4], REDD [1]) and tutorials on related topics. However, there has been little focus on the reproducibility and replicability of the evaluation and results themselves; hence, this tutorial aims to provide a broader view that integrates also this aspect into a general evaluation methodology.

A related tutorial was given at ACM Hypertext 2014 [3].

2. TUTORIAL DESCRIPTION

This tutorial aims to give an introduction to clear and concise reporting of evaluation methodologies and results, while at the same time ensuring that the results of the evaluation are comparable, replicable and unbiased to allow for fair comparisons with related work. The tutorial defines and presents evaluation metrics, methodologies, and experimental configurations used in the recommender systems literature. Using these definitions, we present specific guidelines towards reporting experimental results in the recommender systems area. As a particular focus of interest, in the tutorial we address the commons datasets and benchmarking frameworks available, and how they can be applied in future publications in the recommender systems field in order to overcome limitations related to the lack of reproduction and reproducibility of the experiments and results.

2.1 Tutorial Structure

Introduction. This part of the tutorial focuses on the basics of recommendation and evaluation: core recommendation concepts, definitions of metrics and methodologies.

Evaluation. This section provides the necessary setting to understand how recommender systems are evaluated. A brief introduction to the basic evaluation concepts (metrics, data splits, etc.) allows participants on all levels to understand the basic setting. Following this, more specific concepts related to evaluation will be presented, e.g. data splitting criteria, biases that can arise from incorrectly configured algorithms, and calculations of metrics. We also discuss advanced evaluation concepts, such as subjective evaluation criteria (novelty, diversity) as well as methods used in in situ evaluation, e.g. A/B testing, significance testing, etc.

Replication. This section focuses on replication itself, i.e. how to best plan, perform, and report evaluation results in order to allow for others to grasp the objective quality of an experiment without necessarily having to reproduce it themselves. We seek to present in a clear way specific guidelines towards reporting experimental results. Particular focus is put on common datasets and frameworks available, and show how they can be put to use in research publications in order to overcome limitations related to the lack of reproduction and reproducibility of the experiments.

Replication by example. This is an interactive session which presents results where several of the discussed configurations are tested with real data. The audience is invited to a discussion on expected results vs. obtained outcomes. The feedback obtained during the discussion is used to improve and augment the aforementioned experiments to other recommendation-related areas, such as contextual search or personalized mobile services. For this session, code examples are available on GitHub[1]. These code examples show the necessary steps in order to make the evaluation of recommender systems replicable and build on the recommender system evaluation toolkit RiVal [6, 7][2]. The demonstration combines common recommendation frameworks with RiVal in order to present an evaluation comparable across recommendation framework.

Conclusions and wrap-up. This session concludes the tutorial and iterates the most important factors to consider while planning and performing evaluation, not only for the sake of reproducibility by others, but also for the sake of correct and objective comparison within the same recommendation setting.

Q&A. This session gives the participants the opportunity to ask questions on the topics presented.

2.2 Intended Audience

The tutorial is designed to be useful for researchers, students, and practitioners in the Recommender Systems and personalization communities, and in related areas such as Information Retrieval, Data Mining, Machine Learning and Human-Computer Interaction, working in different application domains, and concerned with implementation, reproduction, evaluation, research and practice.

3. PRESENTERS

Alan Said is a Machine Learning engineer at Recorded Future in Gothenburg, Sweden. Prior to this he was a postdoctoral researcher at TU Delft, and Marie Curie (ERCIM ABCDE) Fellow at Centrum Wiskunde & Informatica in Amsterdam, The Netherlands. He obtained a doctorate at Technische Universität Berlin. His research interests include evaluation, benchmarking, user modeling and different aspects of recommender systems. He has served as PC member of international conferences and workshops (e.g. RecSys, UMAP, HT, IIiX, ECIR, ECMLPKDD, IUI) and as reviewer for journals (e.g. UMUAI, TIST, TKDD, TWEB). In 2010, 2011, 2012 and 2014 he co-organized the CAMRa and RecSys Challenge benchmarking challenges at ACM RecSys. At the 2012 ACM RecSys conference, Alan co-presented a tutorial on *Best Practices in Recommender System Challenges*. The tutorial outlined the necessary steps to be taken in order to achieve comparable results in the context of a competition or a challenge.

Alejandro Bellogín is a Lecturer at the Autónoma University of Madrid. Previously, he was an ERCIM Post-doctoral fellow at

Centrum Wiskunde & Informatica in The Netherlands. His research is focused on recommender systems, in particular, adaptations from the information retrieval area, such as performance prediction techniques, evaluation methodologies, and probabilistic models. He has authored papers on national and international conferences, journals, and workshops in the aforementioned areas. He has co-organized a workshop on the topic of reproducibility in evaluation at the ACM RecSys conference. He has served as PC member of international conferences and workshops (such as CIKM, ECIR, and RecSys) and as reviewer for journals (e.g., IRJ, IPM, INS, TIST). At the 2014 ACM Hypertext conference, Alejandro Bellogín gave a tutorial on *Evaluating Recommender Systems - Ensuring Replicability of Evaluation*. The tutorial was tailored to a broad audience from other fields than recommendation.

4. ACKNOWLEDGMENTS

Supported in part by the Ministerio de Educación y Ciencia (TIN2013-47090-C3-2).

5. REFERENCES

[1] ADAMÓPOULOS, P., BELLOGÍN, A., CASTELLS, P., CREMONESI, P., AND STECK, H. REDD 2014 - international workshop on recommender systems evaluation: dimensions and design. In *Eighth ACM Conference on Recommender Systems, RecSys '14, Foster City, Silicon Valley, CA, USA - October 06 - 10, 2014* (2014), pp. 393–394.

[2] AMATRIAIN, X., CASTELLS, P., DE VRIES, A. P., AND POSSE, C. Workshop on recommendation utility evaluation: beyond RMSE - RUE 2012. In *Sixth ACM Conference on Recommender Systems, RecSys '12, Dublin, Ireland, September 9-13, 2012* (2012), pp. 351–352.

[3] BELLOGÍN, A. Evaluating recommender systems:ensuring replicability of evaluation. http://ir.ii.uam.es/ alejandro/2014/ht.pdf, 2014.

[4] BELLOGÍN, A., CASTELLS, P., SAID, A., AND TIKK, D. Workshop on reproducibility and replication in recommender systems evaluation: Repsys. In *Seventh ACM Conference on Recommender Systems, RecSys '13, Hong Kong, China, October 12-16, 2013* (2013), pp. 485–486.

[5] KNIJNENBURG, B. P., SCHMIDT-THIEME, L., AND BOLLEN, D. G. F. M. Workshop on user-centric evaluation of recommender systems and their interfaces. In *Proceedings of the 2010 ACM Conference on Recommender Systems, RecSys 2010, Barcelona, Spain, September 26-30, 2010* (2010), pp. 383–384.

[6] SAID, A., AND BELLOGÍN, A. Comparative recommender system evaluation: benchmarking recommendation frameworks. In *Eighth ACM Conference on Recommender Systems, RecSys '14, Foster City, Silicon Valley, CA, USA - October 06 - 10, 2014* (2014), pp. 129–136.

[7] SAID, A., AND BELLOGÍN, A. Rival: a toolkit to foster reproducibility in recommender system evaluation. In *Eighth ACM Conference on Recommender Systems, RecSys '14, Foster City, Silicon Valley, CA, USA - October 06 - 10, 2014* (2014), pp. 371–372.

[8] WILLEMSEN, M. C., BOLLEN, D. G. F. M., AND EKSTRAND, M. D. UCERSTI 2: second workshop on user-centric evaluation of recommender systems and their interfaces. In *Proceedings of the 2011 ACM Conference on Recommender Systems, RecSys 2011, Chicago, IL, USA, October 23-27, 2011* (2011), pp. 395–396.

---

[1] http://github.com/recommenders/evaltutorial
[2] http://rival.recommenders.net

Scalable Recommender Systems:
Where Machine Learning Meets Search!

Si ying Diana Hu, Joaquin Delgado
Verizon Communications
375 W. Trimble Rd
San Jose, CA 95131, USA
{diana.hu, joaquin.a.delgado} @verizon.com

ABSTRACT

This tutorial provides an overview of how search engines and machine learning techniques can be tightly coupled to address the need for building scalable recommender or other prediction-based systems. In particular, we will review ML-Scoring, an open source framework, created by the authors that tightly integrates machine-learning models into Elasticsearch, a popular search engine that is distributed, scalable, highly available with real-time search and analytic functionalities.

The fundamentals and basic methods in information retrieval and machine learning will be explained. Accompanying the theory, practical examples will illustrate their applications with a series of hands-on exercises. These will demonstrate how to load a dataset into Elasticsearch [5], how to train a model in an external software framework such as Spark [13], Weka [6], or R [7], and finally how to load the trained models as a ML-Scoring plugins created for Elasticsearch.

Categories and Subject Descriptors

D.2.11 [**Software**]: Software Architecture – *data abstraction, domain-specific architectures;* H.3.3 [**Information Storage and Retrieval**]: Information Search and Retrieval – *information filtering, query formulation, relevance feedback, retrieval process, search process, selection process;* I2.6 [**Artificial Intelligence**]: Learning – *parameter learning.*

Keywords

Search engines; large-scale recommender systems.

1. INTRODUCTION

The recommender systems and search engine problems are similar. Both can be formulated as prediction based systems with roots in data mining that comprises the following stages in:

1. *Data preparation* (i.e. text analysis, feature selection, dimensionality reduction, and normalization)

2. *Data mining* (i.e. clustering, classification, rule mining, indexing, relevance ranking and scoring)

3. *Post-processing* (i.e. filtering, visualization, and re-ranking)

In the early days of their development, their communities diverged. One focused on the problem of information retrieval (IR) and another one on information filtering (IF). Consequently, different avenues of research were followed that produced different technologies and areas of expertise.

Modern search engines use distributed computing for both indexing and serving of results to provide scalable and speedy data retrieval. This can be of great value in applications such as e-commerce, online advertising and recommender systems [10, 12]. In these applications, the search space may be large and results need to be determined within just a small fraction of a second. To achieve speed and scalability, the IR community has developed techniques to represent items, such as products, movies or advertisements, as semi-structured documents that are indexed. In most cases, these systems require the results to be scored and ranked in order to determine the top set of items. These will match a particular serving opportunity while satisfying the constraints that are expressed as a query (e.g. keyword, user and context as input).

Relevance ranking of results by search engines is modeled after the early days of IR, primarily dealing with keywords and text. These are represented as queries in the term document vector space. Overtime as search engines became widely adopted, more complex ranking and scoring functionalities were implemented, such as multi-field document structures, and ways to "tweak" the basic TF-IDF weights used in the $(\vec{Q} \circ \vec{D})$ dot product to compute the similarity score between a query expression and a document [1, 3, 9].

On the other hand, the recommender systems community has concentrated on solving the information filtering aspect with successes on methods developed in collaborative filtering to predict ratings [8]. Overtime as the number of users and the size of items' catalog have multiplied, the need to build scalable recommender system is becoming a fast growing priority. Typically, such scalable systems architect retrieval and prediction in two phases. In Phase I, a search engine returns the top-k results based on constraints expressed as a query. In Phase II, the top-k results are re-ranked in another system according to an optimization function that uses a supervised trained model. However this approach presents several issues, such as the possibility of returning sub-optimal results due to the top-k limits during query, as well as the presence of some inefficiencies in the system due to the decoupling of retrieval and ranking [2, 4, 11].

To address this issue the authors created ML-Scoring, an open source framework that tightly integrates machine-learning models

RecSys '15, September 16-20, 2015, Vienna, Austria
ACM 978-1-4503-3692-5/15/09.
http://dx.doi.org/10.1145/2792838.2792842

into Elasticsearch. ML-Scoring replaces the default information retrieval ranking function with a custom supervised model that is trained through Spark, Weka, or R and loads the model as a plugin into Elasticsearch. Once a learning-to-rank model has been created, the customized Elasticsearch plugin can be used to write *function_score* queries to perform both constraint-based retrieval of candidate items and relevance ranking of those items according to the learnt model. As a result, the scoring of the model happens during query time as a single step process in a single system within the search engine. Models can also be updated and loaded periodically to reflect the changes in the data as parameters are updated with new observations.

2. TUTORIAL DESCRIPTION
2.1 Structure and Length
This tutorial is broken down into three sections

1. **Explanation of Index-based techniques**: How to build scalable recommender systems using Elasticsearch as a base search engine

   a. Introduction: What is a recommender system? What is Elasticsearch?

   b. Representing recommended products/services as documents and user/context as search queries.

   c. Content based similarity using "More Like This" (MLT) functionality.

   d. Filters and Caching Controls.

   e. Introduction on controlling how scores for documents are generated.

2. **Review of Machine Learning techniques**:

   a. Using historical selection ratings paired with recommendation serving constraints to train a feature-based machine-learning model. The model will predict ratings associated with new or unobserved instances.

   b. Learning-to-rank through supervised learning

   c. Constructing a matrix that includes query associated rows and item-associated columns. This will include content feature-based information as well as predicted rating features in each cell.

3. **Querying and Re-writing the ranking function**:

   a. Demonstrating how to write a new similarity (ranking/scoring) module in Elasticsearch.

   b. Demonstrating how to train a model through Spark, Weka, R and write a custom Elasticsearch plugin to replace the scoring function.

   c. Writing a query using the new scoring function.

   d. Re-scoring within Elasticsearch to address tight response-time SLA constraints.

2.2 Intended Audience
This tutorial is intended for researchers and software practitioners that wish to build scalable recommender systems using search engines. No prior experience is required in any system listed (Elasticsearch, Spark, Weka, R), though some information retrieval, machine learning background and programming experience is recommended.

3. REFERENCES
[1] Baeza-Yates, R., & Ribeiro-Neto, B. 2011. *Modern information retrieval*. New York: ACM press.

[2] Chirita, P. A., Firan, C. S., & Nejdl, W. 2007. Personalized query expansion for the web. In *Proceedings of the 30th annual international ACM SIGIR conference on Research and development in information retrieval* (pp. 7-14). ACM.

[3] Croft, W. B., Metzler, D., & Strohman, T. 2010. *Search engines: Information retrieval in practice*. Reading: Addison-Wesley.

[4] Dunning, T. 1993. Accurate methods for the statistics of surprise and coincidence. *Computational linguistics*, *19*(1), 61-74.

[5] Elastic, Elasticsearch: RESTful, Distributed Search & Analytics. 2015. https://www.elastic.co/products/elasticsearch.

[6] Hall, M., Frank, E., Holmes, G., Pfahringer, B., Reutemann, P., & Witten, I. H. 2009. The WEKA data mining software: an update. *ACM SIGKDD explorations newsletter*, *11*(1), 10-18.

[7] Ihaka, R., & Gentleman, R. 1996. R: a language for data analysis and graphics. *Journal of computational and graphical statistics*, *5*(3), 299-314.

[8] Kantor, P. B., Rokach, L., Ricci, F., & Shapira, B. 2011. *Recommender systems handbook*. Springer.

[9] Manning, C. D., Raghavan, P., & Schütze, H. 2008. *Introduction to information retrieval*. Cambridge: Cambridge university press.

[10] Qiu, F., & Cho, J. 2006. Automatic identification of user interest for personalized search. In *Proceedings of the 15th international conference on World Wide Web* (pp. 727-736). ACM.

[11] Sun, J. T., Zeng, H. J., Liu, H., Lu, Y., & Chen, Z. 2005. Cubesvd: a novel approach to personalized web search. In *Proceedings of the 14th international conference on World Wide Web* (pp. 382-390). ACM.

[12] Xing, B., & Lin, Z. 2006. The impact of search engine optimization on online advertising market. In *Proceedings of the 8th international conference on Electronic commerce: The new e-commerce: innovations for conquering current barriers, obstacles and limitations to conducting successful business on the internet* (pp. 519-529). ACM.

[13] Zaharia, M., Chowdhury, M., Franklin, M. J., Shenker, S., & Stoica, I. 2010. Spark: cluster computing with working sets. In *Proceedings of the 2nd USENIX conference on Hot topics in cloud computing* (Vol. 10, p. 10).

A Hybrid Recommendation System Based on Human Curiosity

Alan Menk dos Santos[*]
Universitat Politecnica de Valencia
Valencia, Spain
amenkdossantos@dsic.upv.es

ABSTRACT

Traditional recommendation systems use multiple computational techniques to perform personalized recommendations, and can consider the interests of users and even the context in which they live. However, they usually ignore each individual's personality factors, and hence, the recommendations generated overwhelmingly consider that all the users are identical psychologically. They ignore, for example, the curiosity level of each user, which may indicate that individuals with a high level of curiosity seek visit exotic locations and/or not yet visited by them, or even individuals with a low curiosity level tend to do the same things they did in the past, uninterested in new or different areas.

Our paper presents a complete hybrid recommendation system considering the curiosity level of each individual as a decisive factor to recommend sites of South America. In order to prove the efficiency of our system in contrast to traditional recommendation systems, as well as to measure the satisfaction of users about the recommendations, we performed some preliminary experiments with the participation of 105 Brazilian volunteers. The first results indicate that considering the level of curiosity of a user increases the satisfaction with the recommendations.

Categories and Subject Descriptors

Data [**Miscellaneous**]:

Keywords

Recommendation System, Curiosity, Data Mining, Social Media

1. INTRODUCTION AND MOTIVATIONS

Nowadays, recommendation systems are facing challenges to generate recommendation of contents with low rejection rates and high performance, besides to overcome already known obstacles in the area of content recommendation, for example: limited content analysis, super-specialization and cold start problem [1]. Hence, in these last few years, several lines of study have been developed, in order to consider the psychological characteristics of users, giving a greater weight to what people feel and think, instead of simply consider their previous purchases or people with similar profiles.

In the literature we can find a wide variety of academic papers related to recommendation systems for individuals and groups, using both traditional methods and hybrid applications. However, papers that use psychology in recommendation systems are still rarely found.

We can highlight the work in [6]. It describes three algorithms to model and predict the satisfaction experienced by individuals using a recommender system for groups, which recommends sequences of items. By analysing the impact on satisfaction of the following item after visualize the previous one, they could model the wearing-off effect and the assimilation effect, in order to select the next item. Another research presented in [8], proposes a new method of performing recommendations for groups bearing in mind the personality of the group members and how they deal with conflicts.

This work introduces a complete recommendation system that combines theoretical psychological models with the contemporary idea of positive psychology to enhance the performance of traditional recommendation systems for tourist domains. This system presents two important features. First, data collected from a social network is analysed in order to calculate the level of curiosity of a given user. Then, through an online recommendation system, we show the user the recommended sites of South America, in order to assess the level of satisfaction of volunteers and, consequently, analyse the efficiency/accuracy of our technique.

This way, we aim to demonstrate that the combination of traditional recommendation techniques by taking into account psychological characteristics of individuals can improve the user satisfaction with respect to the recommendation. It is expected that this way, we can generate a more "humanized" recommendation, according to the psychological characteristics of the individual, being able to positively surprise the users.

This paper is organized as follows. First, we introduce the definition of curiosity and how it can be measured, after we present the architecture of our system and we describe the different modules that compose our system. Next, we detail the performed experiments and the feedback obtained from

*CAPES Foundation, Ministry of Education of Brazil, Brasilia - DF, Zip Code 70.040-020.

the volunteers when the recommendations were presented. We finish with some conclusions and further work.

2. CURIOSITY

Why some people tend to always travel to the same places while others do not? Why do individuals explore the unknown? What makes people curious? From the publication of the paper "A theory of human curiosity" by Berlyne in 1954 [2] the word "curiosity" starts to gain a higher visibility in psychology, and a number of researches have been developed since then, so questions like those can be measured and answered. Curiosity is defined as a desire for acquiring new knowledge and new sensory experience which motivates exploratory behavior [4]. Recent studies have introduced different scales to measure the curiosity of an individual, and one of those is the model Curiosity and Exploration Inventory (CEI-II) by Kashdan et al. [3], which we have adopted in this project.

This scale is considered one of the most reliable and practical today, consisting by only 10 items (Figure 1). It offers empirical support for two curiosity dimensions: motivation to seek out knowledge and new experiences (Stretching; five items) and a willingness to embrace the novel, uncertain, and unpredictable nature of everyday life (Embracing; five items).

Curiosity and Exploration Inventory (CEI-II) Instructions: Rate the statements below for how accurately they reflect the way you generally feel and behave. Do not rate what you think you should do, or wish you do, or things you no longer do. Please be as honest as possible.	Very Slightly	A Little	Moderately	Quite a Bit	Extremely
1	I actively seek as much information as I can in new situations.	1	2	3	4	5
2	I am the type of person who really enjoys the uncertainty of everyday life.	1	2	3	4	5
3	I am at my best when doing something that is complex or challenging.	1	2	3	4	5
4	Everywhere I go, I am out looking for new things or experiences.	1	2	3	4	5
5	I view challenging situations as an opportunity to grow and learn.	1	2	3	4	5
6	I like to do things that are a little frightening.	1	2	3	4	5
7	I am always looking for experiences that challenge how I think about myself and the world.	1	2	3	4	5
8	I prefer jobs that are excitingly unpredictable.	1	2	3	4	5
9	I frequently seek out opportunities to challenge myself and glow as a person.	1	2	3	4	5
10	I am the king of person who embraces unfamiliar people, events, and places.	1	2	3	4	5

Figure 1: CEI-II Form applied to the participants

3. THE HYBRID RECOMMENDER BASED ON CURIOSITY

This section describes the main aspects of our recommendation system. We formulate three hypothesis: (H1) The level of curiosity of a given user may influence his decisions about what places to visit; (H2) It is possible to use data available on social networks like Facebook[1] to measure the level of curiosity; And (H3) the level of curiosity of an individual may play a crucial role in the choice of the recommendation technique.

To prove our hypothesis, we have developed a hybrid recommendation system based on human curiosity. Figure 2

[1]Facebook <https://www.facebook.com/>.

shows the architecture of our system which was divided into two main parts: The first one, "Model Generation", is devoted to generate a model of curiosity by using information available in Facebook and the CEI-II psychological test and, the second one, the "Model Execution" applies this model to new users to measure the curiosity level and it is also responsible for the recommendation itself.

3.1 Model Generation

The "Model Generation" phase works in 3 stages, with the aim of generating a curiosity model. For this purpose, we recruited 105 Brazilian volunteers that participated in the project. This set of volunteers is composed by 50% of men and 50% women, from different regions of Brazil, between ages from 18 to 56, whose level of study is: 60% Postgraduate, 31% Graduate, 3% High School and 6% Basic Level.

At the first stage (represented by circles in Figure 2) we obtained three types of different information. The first one (Profile) obtains basic data from Facebook in an implicit way (age, gender, marital status, etc). The second one (Survey test) calculates the level of curiosity of each volunteer through the CEI-II questionnaire. And the third type of information (Access to database) consists in implicitly obtaining Facebook data as likes, groups, visited places, photo tagging etc.

The second stage (represented by squares in Figure 2) comprises Search System for Social Network (SSSN) and Knowledge Discovery in Databases (KDD) modules. The SSSN (square in Figure 2) aims "to clean" data obtained in the previous process, i.e remove repeated, incomplete or inconsistent data, but also SSSN is responsible for classifying the "likes" of a given user, in order to better capture his interests. This is performed by selecting the "name" field in table "likes". In Table 1, we can observe an example of the results obtained with the fan pages classification and groupings performed by category and subcategory.

Table 1: Sample of Fan Pages classification grouping by category and subcategory

Like Name	Category	Subcategory	Method
Gloria Alegria	Temple	Religion	Deduction
Assassin's Creed	Game	Fiction	Wikipedia
Bar do Ze	Place	Bar	Deduction
Caetano Veloso	Music	MPB	Wikipedia
Gigante acordou	Forum	Politic	Deduction

In the KDD module (square in Figure 2), we receive the data from the survey test and the data previously processed by SSSN, in order to generate the curiosity model through the application of a data mining algorithm. We have performed some experiments with three different algorithms: Apriori, J48 and K-means [5].

In our simulations, we obtained better reliability values with the J48 algorithm, the results were: 32.24% for Extremely curious, 64.57% for Moderately curious, 91.03% for Quite a Bit curious and 38.56% for A Little curious. In other words, when introducing a new user (Model Execution) to our system without answering the Survey test, we can infer his curiosity level with the values of reliability mentioned above. Although we think that these values are not good enough, they are promising with respect to the Moderately and Quite a Bit curious users.

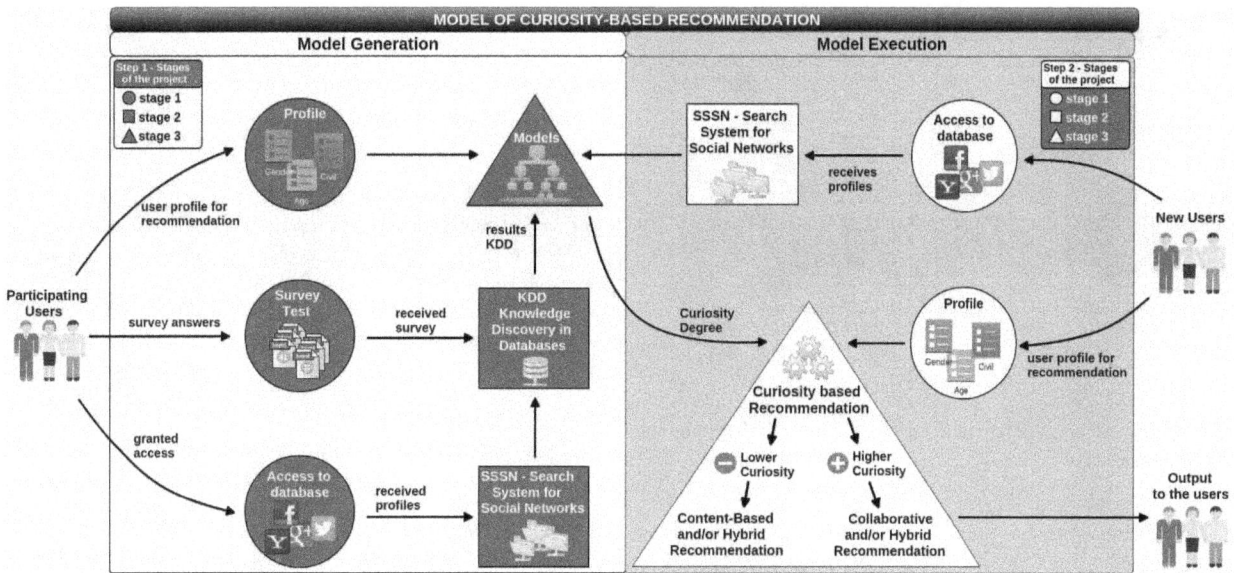

Figure 2: Architecture of our Recommendation System Based on Curiosity

3.2 Model Execution

The "Model Execution" is also divided in 3 stages. At stage 1, the system analyses the Facebook data of the user to infer, through the generated model, his level of curiosity (stage 2).

The stage 3, called "Curiosity-based recommendation", consists in our hybrid recommendation system. It uses two basic recommendation techniques: content-based (CB) and collaborative filtering (CF). Then, two lists of recommendations are computed. The first list corresponds to the CB recommendation technique, which uses travelling history to make a list of sites with similar features to those that the user visited in the past. The second list is generated by means of the CF recommendation technique, which makes a new list of sites from similar profiles to the user. The final list of recommendations is obtained by combining both lists in a weighted way, which depends on the level of curiosity of the user.

Specifically, for users with a lower level of curiosity a higher percentage of items from the CB recommendation list is used, and for those who have a higher level of curiosity a higher percentage of items from recommendation lists based on CF is used.

Table 2 shows the relationship between the level of curiosity and the percentage of items of each list that is used in the hybrid system to build the final lists of recommendations. Let's consider for instance a user with a level of curiosity "1 - A Little"; the hybrid algorithm will create a new list with 80% of recommendation items from the CB list and 20% from the CF list, whose results will be ordered according to their estimated rating.

To derive the values presented in Table 2, we consider the premise of positive psychology stated by Peterson & Seligman [7], which says that curious people are willing to explore the unknown before judge it. Thus, curious people are not apathetic to uncertain things or new ideas. Face to unexpected or unknown, the curious feel excited to seek, unveil, know. Therefore, curiosity and novelty often go hand in hand.

Table 2: Weights Hybrid Recommendation System based on Curiosity

	Degree of Curiosity	% CB	% CF
1	A Little	80%	20%
2	Moderately	60%	40%
3	Quite a Bit	40%	60%
4	Extremely	20%	80%

By applying this theory in recommendation systems, we realized that, the more curious an individual, the more will be his seek for sites different of those he already knows so the recommendation based on CF fits optimally in this situation. On the contrary, little curious people tend to visit the same or similar places, so the CB recommendation becomes the best option to those individuals.

4. EVALUATIONS

This section summarizes the experiments we have performed in order to test our hybrid recommendation system. Given that we were interested in making some preliminary tests, only 26 out of 105 volunteers were asked to participate.

They received a recommendation of sites of South America through photos, allowing us to meet two objectives: first, analysing the level of the satisfaction of volunteers regarding to the recommendation and second, comparing possible gains of the hybrid system we developed to traditional recommendation systems. For this purpose, we developed an online system (Figure 3) called "Points of Interest in Latin America" which, integrated to the Flickr[2] platform, shows photos of sites of South America corresponding to the recommended places.

By accessing the online system (through a web page), the three recommendation lists were presented to the users, with 3 photos of sites in each page (10 pages in total), and they could rate each sight as: Little Interesting, Moder-

---

[2]Flickr <https://www.flickr.com/>.

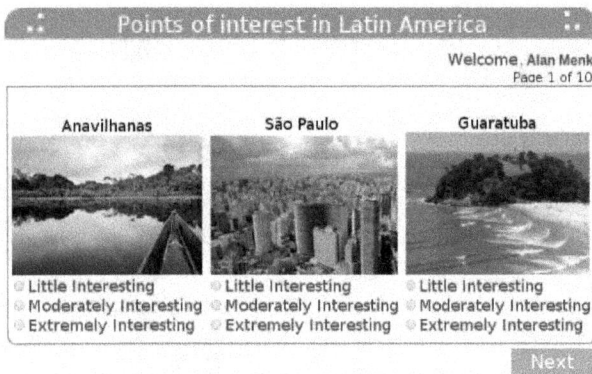

Figure 3: Main page online system Points of Interest in Latin America

ately Interesting and Extremely Interesting, according to their tastes. The system generates three lists of 10 recommendations for each volunteer, and the level of curiosity that we have considered is the one obtained by the CEI-II questionnaire.

The first results we have obtained with real users are shown in Figure 4. It can be observed that both CB and CF techniques had 86 and 81 votes, respectively, of "uninteresting" recommendations, whereas the recommendation based on curiosity obtained only 76 votes, which represents a reduction in the rejection rate of approximately a 18%. When analysing the second aspect, "Moderately Interesting," we can see that the curiosity-based recommended achieved a gain in relation to the CB technique of 20% and 25% compared to the CF technique, so an average gain of about 23% in relation to traditional recommendation systems. Finally the number of sites that the volunteers found "Extremely Interesting" remains stable regardless the recommendation system.

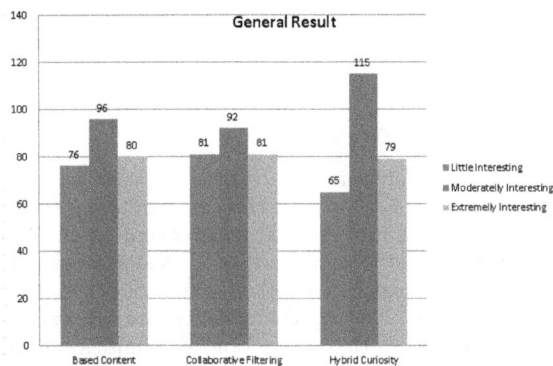

Figure 4: Comparison of traditional and hybrid recommendation systems.

Therefore, we can conclude that the use of our hybrid recommender is able to increase the user satisfaction. In other words, the use of curiosity can aid recommendation systems to achieve better prediction rates and also decrease rejection rate if compared to traditional recommendation systems.

5. CONCLUSIONS AND FUTURE WORK

In this work, we have presented a curiosity-based recommendation system. By means of the data available in the social network Facebook, our system is able to measure the curiosity level of a given user and to provide recommendations based on this level. In the experiments we performed, we proved that human curiosity defined in Psychology can aid recommendation systems to be more efficient.

Regarding to future researches, we intend to use a larger amount of personal characteristics by means of other data sources like the social networks Linkedin and Twitter, thus getting data like: history of previous jobs, skills, certifications, courses, content of tweets, etc., always looking for variables which can identify the personal characteristics of the individuals.

We also intend to use the database from MyPersonality[3] project, which currently has approximately 4,000,000 individual Facebook profiles, so we could test the curiosity generated models here. Finally, we will perform new experiments with a bigger amount of volunteers. We will also generate lists with different weights between the content-based and collaborative-filtering lists and, moreover, we will present the results (photos) in a scrambled way, so that the user is not influenced by the order in which they are shown.

6. ACKNOWLEDGMENTS

Supported by CAPES Foundation, bolsista da CAPES - Proc. 6394-13-2 (Alan Menk dos Santos) and Spanish Government Project TIN2014-55637-C2-2-R (Laura Sebastia).

7. REFERENCES

[1] G. Adomavicius and A. Tuzhilin. Toward the next generation of recommender systems: a survey of the state-of-the-art and possible extensions. *IEEE Transactions on Knowledge and Data Engineering*, 17(6):734–749, June 2005.

[2] D. E. Berlyne. A theory of human curiosity.

[3] T. B. Kashdan, P. Rose, and F. D. Fincham. Curiosity and exploration: facilitating positive subjective experiences and personal growth opportunities. *Journal of personality assessment*, 82(3):291–305, June 2004.

[4] J. A. Litman and C. D. Spielberger. Measuring epistemic curiosity and its diversive and specific componets. *Journal of personality assessment*, (80):75–86, August 2003.

[5] J. MacQueen. Some methods for classification and analysis of multivariate observations. proceedings of the fifth berkeley symposium on mathematical statistics and probability. *University of California Press*, 1:281–297, 1967.

[6] J. Masthoff. The pursuit of satisfaction: Affective state in group recommender systems. *User Modeling 2005*, 3538(80):297–306, July 2005.

[7] C. Peterson and M. E. P. Seligman. *Character Strengths and Virtues: A Handbook and Classification*. American Psychological Association, 750 First Street, NE, Washington, DC 20002-4242, 2004.

[8] J. G. Recio-Garcia, A. Jimenez-Diaz, Sanchez-Ruiz, and B. Diaz-Agudo. Personality aware recommendations to groups. *ACM RecSys*, pages 325–328, 2009.

[3]Mypersonality <http://mypersonality.org/>.

Context-aware Preference Modeling with Factorization

Balázs Hidasi
balazs.hidasi@gravityrd.com

Gravity Research and Development Inc.
Mészáros utca 58/B.
1016 Budapest
Hungary

Budapest University of Technology and Economics
Magyar Tudósok krt. 2
1117 Budapest
Hungary

ABSTRACT

This work focuses on solving the context-aware implicit feedback based recommendation task with factorization and is heavily influenced by the practical considerations. I propose context-aware factorization algorithms that can efficiently work on implicit data. I generalize these algorithms and propose the General Factorization Framework (GFF) in which experimentation with novel preference models is possible. This practically useful, yet neglected feature results in models that are more appropriate for context-aware recommendations than the ones used by the state-of-the-art. I also propose a way to speed up and enhance scalability of the training process, that makes it viable to use the more accurate high factor models with reasonable training times.

Categories and Subject Descriptors

I.2.6 [[**Artificial Intelligence**]]: Learning - Parameter Learning

General Terms

Algorithms, Experimentation

Keywords

recommender systems; context-awareness; factorization; preference modeling; implicit feedback; scalability

1. INTRODUCTION

Recommender systems are more and more widely used in e-commerce and on multimedia sites. My work focuses on advanced algorithms that can be used in practical recommender system. One of the biggest distinction between practice and academic research is that the latter focuses on explicit feedback and the prediction of ratings, while the former uses implicit feedback and requires top N recommendations. Although there has been a shift towards this more practical setting in the last few years, the majority of research still focuses on ratings.

Implicit feedback is collected via monitoring the behaviour of users while they use a service (e.g. a web shop). User interaction is not required in order to get the feedback, therefore it is available in large quantity. This is of key importance in practical scenarios. Explicit feedback on the other hand is usually either not available or its amount is negligible compared to implicit feedback. The primary challenge of implicit feedback is that it does not explicitly encode user preferences. These preferences must be inferred from the interactions. The presence of an user action on an item (e.g. purchase) is considered to be a noisy sign of positive preference. However it is much harder to infer negative feedback as the absence of an event can be traced back to multiple causes, the most common being that the user does not know about the item. Although there are some ways to infer negative feedback in special cases, it is generally assumed to be missing and the absence of positive feedback is considered as a very week sign of negative preference.

Context-aware recommender systems (CARS) consider additional information (termed context) besides user–item interactions. Any information can be considered as context, however I argue that it is useful to distinguish event context from other types of data, such as item metadata, sociodemographic information or social network of the user. The common property of latter categories is that they are bound either to the item or to the user. Also, they are thoroughly examined in specific research topics, such as content based or hybrid recommenders. On the other hand, event context is associated with the interaction of the users and items and can not be bounded to either one. Typical examples are the time or the location of the event. The hypothesis of context-aware recommendations is that they can significantly improve recommendation accuracy, because (1) context related effects can be handled during training; (2) recommendation lists can be tailored according to the actual value of the context, which may influence the users' needs.

One of the most extensive data models for representing context-enhanced data is the Multidimensional Dataspace Model (MDM) [1] in which the dataspace is the Cartesian product of several dimensions, and each dimension is the Cartesian product of one or more attributes. Attributes are atomic and nominal and their value comes from a finite set of values. Almost all practically used context-enhanced data can be expressed in a more simple dataspace model,

The work leading to these results has received partial funding from the European Union's Seventh Frame work Programme (FP7/2007-2013) under CrowdRec Grant Agreement n° 610594

where each dimension consist of exactly one attribute. I refer to this dataspace model as single attribute MDM or SA-MDM. Note that if data is representable in SA-MDM it is also representable in a tensor. The SA-MDM representation is powerful enough for commonly used context dimensions, such as time or location[1].

Latent feature based collaborative filtering methods—such as matrix factorization—have gained popularity in the last decade due to their high accuracy and good scalability. My work focuses on factorization methods for implicit feedback that also incorporate context dimensions.

2. PREFERENCE MODELS & CONTEXT

In my early work I proposed a context-aware tensor factorization algorithm—iTALS (implicit Tensor Alternating Least Squares) [6]—for the implicit feedback problem. The algorithm works with SA-MDM. The presence of an event (i.e. a combination of attributes is in the training data) is considered to be strong positive preference, while the absence of an event is considered to be weak negative preference. The method uses pointwise ranking by optimizing for weighted root mean squared error (wRMSE). The value of the target is 1 for positive and 0 for negative feedback; the weight for positive feedback is much higher than for negative. Interaction data is inherently sparse and the usage of additional context dimension makes it even sparser; thus majority of the values in the tensor are zeros. However, contrary to explicit problems, there are no missing values in the tensor that makes the direct application of explicit algorithms inefficient. In iTALS, each dimension is assigned with a feature matrix that contains feature vectors of K length for all of the possible attribute values in that dimension. For the prediction of preferences iTALS uses the N-way model, i.e. the "dot product" of one feature vector from every dimension, corresponding to the user–item–context(s) configuration on which the prediction is requested.

The iTALSx algorithm [4][5] is a variation of iTALS. The difference is in the prediction model for which iTALSx uses a variant of the pairwise model, i.e. the sum of dot products between pairs of feature vectors. iTALSx considers only the user–item, user–context(s) and item–context(s) pairs[2]. The change in the model affects the optimization procedure.

Generalizing the idea of factorization, preference models—i.e. the expression with which the preference (or rating) is approximated—can be considered as the sum of various interactions. An interaction type is the dot product of feature vectors from selected dimensions, one vector per dimension (e.g. the user and the item feature vector for the given user and item). With only the user and item dimensions, there is only one possible interaction type: the user–item interaction (UI). This results in one possible factorization model. Adding one context dimension (S) gives the following new interaction types. USI is a reweighted user–item interaction where the weight is dependent on the value of the context. US and IS are context-dependent user and biases. The number of different models with 3 dimensions is 15. Adding another context (Q) further increases the number of interaction types. Besides UQI, UQ and IQ, there is $USQI$ (the

user–item interaction whose reweighting depends on both context dimensions); USQ, ISQ and SQ in which there is some kind of interaction between context dimensions. The number of possible models with 4 dimensions is 2047.

However, not all of the interaction types are of equal importance. Generally items are recommended to users, therefore these two dimensions are more important. Also, users are the only entities which act and the target of these actions are the items. Context on the other hand is not a direct participant in the transactions, but may influence behaviour.

Despite of the large number of models, only two of them are used widely in the literature: the N-way and the full pairwise interaction model. Both of these models are symmetric, thus all dimensions are considered to be equal.

The choice of the model affects the optimization, but it is ineffective to implement a new version of an algorithm for every one of them. Therefore I created the General Factorization Framework (GFF) [7], which is a single flexible algorithm that takes the preference model as an input and does the computations accordingly. GFF allows its user to easily experiment with various linear models on any context-aware recommendation task. The following properties were important at the design of GFF.

1. No restriction on context[3]: GFF works on any context-aware recommendation problem independently of the number and the meaning of context dimensions.

2. Large preference model class: the only restriction on the preference model is that it must be linear in the dimensions of the problem[4]. This restriction does not restrict the applicability to real-world problems.

3. Data type independence: the implicit case is in the focus, but explicit problems can be also addressed by simply changing the weighting scheme in the loss function.

4. Flexibility: the weighting scheme of GFF is very flexible, enabling to incorporate extra knowledge through the weights such time decay, dwell time dependent weighting, missing not at random hypotheses and more.

5. Scalability: GFF scales well both in terms of the number of interactions in the training set and in the number of features. This makes it applicable in real life recommender systems. (See Section 3.)

Along with the users (U) and items (I), I used two context dimensions—seasonality (S) and sequentiality (Q)—that are available with every implicit datasets as long as the timestamp of the events is recorded. Their availability and usefulness makes these dimensions suitable for the experiment.

Seasonality: Many application areas of recommender systems exhibit the seasonality effect, because periodicity can be observed in many human activities. Thus seasonal data is an obvious choice for context [9]. First, the length of the season has to be defined. No repetitions are expected in the aggregated behavior of users within a season, and similar aggregated behaviour is expected at the same time offset in different seasons. Next, *time bands* need to be created within the seasons that are the context-states. Time bands specify the time resolution of a season. The length of time

---

[1]Even context dimensions that contain more than one attribute can be represented in SA-MDM, but less effectively.
[2]Other methods, such as Factorization Machines [11] also use context–context pairs in their variation of the this model.

[3]The basic GFF builds on SA-MDM, but the algorithm also has an extension that is compatible with the full MDM.
[4]Meaning that a dimension can not directly interact with itself in the model.

bands can be equal or different. In the final step, events are assigned to time bands according to their time stamp.

Sequentiality: In some domains, like movies or music, users consume similar items. In other domains, like electronic gadgets or e-commerce in general, they avoid items similar to what they already consumed and look for complementary products. Sequential patterns can be observed on both domain types. Sequentiality was introduced in [6] and uses the previously consumed item of the user as a context for the actual item. This information helps in the characterizations of repetitiveness related usage patterns and sequential consumption behavior.

Besides the traditional N-way and pairwise models, I selected the following preference models for experimentation.

- **Interaction model ($UI + USI + UQI$):** The model is the composite of the base behavior of the users (UI) and the context-influenced modification of this behavior (USI and UQI). This model assumes that the preferences of the users can be divided into context independent and dependent parts.
- **Context interaction model ($USI + UQI$):** Preferences in this model are modeled by solely context dependent parts, i.e. it assumes that user–item interactions strongly depend on the context and this dependency affects the whole interaction.
- **Reduced pairwise model** ($UI + US + IS + UQ + IQ$): This model is a minor variation of the traditional pairwise model with the exclusion of the interaction between context dimensions (SQ). The interaction with context is done separately by users and items.
- **User bias model ($UI + US + UQ$):** Here it is assumed that only the user interacts with the other dimensions. This results in a model where the user–item relation is supported by context dependent user biases. Note that during recommendation the user biases are constant, thus do not affect the ranking. But they filter out some context related noise during training.
- **Item bias model ($UI + IS + IQ$):** This model assumes that the effect of context can described by context dependent item biases (e.g. items are popular under certain conditions). The item biases affect the ranking as well as filter context related noise.
- **A complex model** ($UI + US + IS + UQ + IQ + USI + UQI$): This model is the composite of the reduced pairwise and the interaction model. It can be also treated as a reduced 3-way interaction model from which the context-context interactions are omitted.

2.1 Evaluation of models

I used five genuine implicit feedback data sets to evaluate the models in GFF. Three of them are public (LastFM 1K, [2]; TV1, TV2, [3]), the other two are proprietary (Grocery, VoD). The properties of the data sets are summarized in Table 1. The train–test splits are time-based: the first event in the test set falls chronologically after the last event of the training set. Artists were used as items in LastFM.

The primary evaluation metric is recall@20. The reason for using recall@N is threefold: (1) in live recommender systems recall correlates well with click-through rate (CTR), an important metric for recommendation success. (2) Recall@20 is a good proxy of estimating recommendation accuracy offline for real-world applications[6][10]. (3) Recall is event based, while ranking based metrics like MAP and NDCG are query based. The inclusion of context changes the query set of the test data, therefore the comparison by query based metrics is unfair.

The hyperparameters of the algorithms, such as regularization coefficients were optimized on a part of the training data (validation set). Then the algorithm was trained on the whole training data (including the validation set) and recall was measured on the test set. The number of epochs was set to 10, because all methods converge in at most 10 epochs. The number of features was set to $K = 80$ that is a good trade-off between accuracy and training time in practice.

Table 1: Main properties of the data sets

| Dataset | Domain | Training set | | | Test set | |
		#Users	#Items	#Events	#Events	Length
Grocery	E-grocery	24947	16883	6238269	56449	1 month
TV1	IPTV	70771	773	544947	12296	1 week
TV2	IPTV	449684	3398	2528215	21866	1 day
LastFM	Music	992	174091	18908597	17941	1 day
VoD	IPTV/VoD	480016	46745	22515406	1084297	1 day

Table 2: Recall@20 values for models within GFF. Grey: traditional models. Bold: best results.

Model	Grocery	TV1	TV2	LastFM	VoD
$USI + UQI$	0.1504	**0.1551**	0.2916	0.1984	0.1493
$UI + USI + UQI$	**0.1669**	0.1482	**0.3027**	**0.2142**	**0.1509**
$USQI$	0.1390	0.1315	0.2009	0.1906	0.1268
$UI + US + IS + UQ + IQ$	0.1390	0.1352	0.2388	0.1884	0.0569
$UI + US + UQ$	0.1619	0.0903	0.1399	0.1993	0.0335
$UI + IS + IQ$	0.1364	0.1266	0.2819	0.1871	0.1084
$UI + US + IS + UQ + IQ + SQ$	0.1388	0.1344	0.2323	0.1873	0.0497
$UI + US + IS + UQ + IQ + USI + UQI$	0.1389	0.1352	0.2427	0.1866	0.0558

Table 2 shows the accuracy of two traditional models and six novel models. There exists a novel model with all five datasets that performs better than both traditional models. 4 out of 5 cases the interaction model ($UI + USI + UQI$) is the best and it is the second best in the remaining one case. Thus this model is not only intuitively sound but also performs well that underpins its assumptions.

3. SCALABILITY IMPROVEMENT

GFF, iTALS and iTALSx use Alternating Least Squares (ALS) during training. In ALS, feature matrices are computed in an alternating fashion and all but the currently computed matrix are fixed. The efficient usage of ALS with implicit problems is not straightforward, although it is possible with the smart separation of computations. The computation of one feature matrix can be divided into three phases[6][5]: (1) computing common statistics[5] that are the same for all feature vectors; (2) feature vector specific update of the statistics using the training events; (3) solving a $K \times K$ sized system of linear equations per feature vector.

This way, the complexity of one epoch (computing each feature matrix once) is $O(N_D|O|N^+K^2 + \sum_{i=1}^{N_D} S_i K^3)$, where N^+, K, N_D, S_i are the number of events, features, dimensions, different values of the attribute in the ith dimension and $|O|$ is the complexity of the preference model. The method scales linearly with the number of events, which is very important in practice. It scales cubically with the number or features, but since $N_D|O|N^+ \gg \sum_{i=1}^{N_D} S_i$ the first

---

[5]A $K \times K$ sized matrix and a vector of K length.

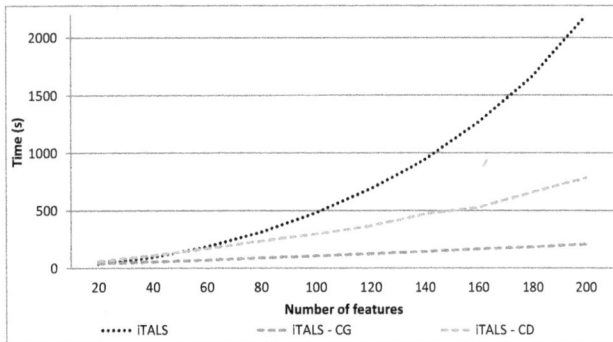

Figure 1: Time of one epoch of ALS, CD & CG with iTALS w.r.t. different number of features, using one CPU core

term is dominant in the range of practically used feature numbers an thus it scales quadratically with K in practice. This scaling property is fine for smaller K values but the training takes a lot of time for high factor models. For practical applicability, the training time of the algorithms is a key aspect. Faster training allows to (1) capture a more recent state of the system modeled; (2) retrain the models more frequently; (3) apply trade-off between running times and accuracy by using more features or running more epochs.

I created two approximate solutions that scale better in the number of features than ALS, but achieve similar recommendation accuracy[8]. The first uses Coordinate Descent (CD), an ALS variant in which each feature is computed separately while the others are fixed. The application of CD to this problem requires the efficient handling of the large amounts of "missing" feedback. CD does not approximate the ALS solution and has a complexity of $O(N_D|O|N_I N^+ K + \sum_{i=1}^{N_D} S_i K^2 N_I + N_D K^3)$ (linear in K in practice for the lower range of practical K values), where N_I is the number of inner iterations. The second method uses Conjugate Gradient (CG). CG is a fast way to approximate the solution of a system of linear equations with a symmetric coefficient matrix. The efficiency of CG depends on the efficiency of the matrix–vector multiplication between the coefficient matrix and a vector. In my methods the feature vector specific update is done by adding a dyadic sum to the common statistics. This allows the multiplication to be done in $K^2 + N_j^+ K$ time for the jth feature vector. The complexity of one epoch can be reduced to $O(N_D|O|N_I N^+ K + \sum_{i=1}^{N_D} S_i K^2 N_I)$, that is linear in the number of features for the range of practical K values. CG approximates the ALS solution and yields the exact solution if the number of inner iterations equals to K.

Experimentation showed that ALS-CD and ALS-CG performs similarly to ALS in terms of recommendation accuracy. ALS-CD was found to be unstable with N-way components in the model if the number of features is high and one of the interacting dimensions is small. The speed up achieved by ALS-CG and ALS-CD is significant: for the commonly used $K = 80$ the speed up to ALS is ~ 3.5 and ~ 1.3 respectively; for $K = 200$ it increases to ~ 10.6 and ~ 2.9. Figure 1 shows the scaling of ALS, ALS-CG and ALS-CD with the number of features.

Overall, ALS-CG seems to be the better of the two approximation methods, due to its stability, speed, better approximation of ALS and other properties.

4. CONCLUSION & FUTURE WORK

My research is heavily influenced by practical considerations. It focuses on the implicit feedback problem and tackles it using context-awareness and factorization. The iTALS and iTALSx algorithms solve this task efficiently. These algorithms use different preference models and are better for different datasets. The preference modeling has been unjustly neglected in recommender related research. Therefore I created GFF, a single flexible algorithm that takes the preference model as an input and computes the latent feature matrices accordingly. Novel models were examined for a 4 dimensional context-aware problem using GFF. Novel models outperformed traditional ones and the *interaction model* performs well generally. Scalability is another important aspect in practice, therefore I proposed two solutions that enable the usage of high factor models for the implicit context-aware task. The ALS-CG method scales linearly in the number of features in practice that results in significant speed up compared to the basic ALS.

In future research I aim to add an automatic model learning feature to GFF. While the flexibility of GFF is a great asset for finding new models, the users of the framework may be overwhelmed by the possible preference models, especially with novel context dimensions. Although the intuitively sound interaction model is a good starting point, it may not be the best model for all context-aware problems. Therefore it would be useful if GFF could propose a good model for any context-aware recommendation problems.

5. REFERENCES

[1] Adomavicius, G., Sankaranarayanan, R., Sen, S., and Tuzhilin, A. Incorporating contextual information in recommender systems using a multidimensional approach. *ACM Trans. Inf. Syst. 23*, 1 (2005), 103–145.

[2] Celma, O. *Music Recommendation and Discovery in the Long Tail*. Springer, 2010.

[3] Cremonesi, P., and Turrin, R. Analysis of cold-start recommendations in IPTV systems. In *Recsys'09: ACM Conf. on Recommender Systems* (2009).

[4] Hidasi, B. Technical report on iTALSx. Tech. Report Series 2012-2, Gravity R&D Inc., 2012.

[5] Hidasi, B. Factorization models for context-aware recommendations. *Infocommunications Journal VI*, 4 (2014), 27–34.

[6] Hidasi, B., and Tikk, D. Fast ALS-based tensor factorization for context-aware recommendation from implicit feedback. In *ECML-PKDD'12, Part II*, no. 7524 in LNCS. Springer, 2012, 67–82.

[7] Hidasi, B., and Tikk, D. General factorization framework for context-aware recommendations. *Data Mining and Knowledge Discovery* (2015), 1–30.

[8] Hidasi, B., and Tikk, D. Speeding up ALS learning via approximate methods for context-aware recommendations. *Knowledge and Information Systems* (2015), 1–25.

[9] Liu, N. N., Zhao, B. C. M., and Yang, Q. Adapting neighborhood and matrix factorization models for context aware recommendation. In *CAMRa'10: Workshop on Context-Aware Movie Recommendation* (2010), 7–13.

[10] Liu, Q., Chen, T., Cai, J., and Yu, D. Enlister: Baidu's recommender system for the biggest Chinese Q&A website. In *RecSys-12: Proc. of the 6th ACM Conf. on Recommender Systems* (2012), 285–288.

[11] Rendle, S. Factorization machines with libFM. *ACM Transactions on Intelligent Systems and Technology (TIST) 3*, 3 (2012), 57.

Exploring Statistical Language Models
for Recommender Systems

Daniel Valcarce
Information Retrieval Lab
Department of Computer Science
University of A Coruña, Spain
daniel.valcarce@udc.es

ABSTRACT

Even though there exist multiple approaches to build recommendation algorithms, algebraic techniques based on vector and matrix representations are predominant in the field. Notwithstanding the fact that these algebraic Collaborative Filtering methods have been demonstrated to be very effective in the rating prediction task, they do not generally provide good results in the top-N recommendation task. In this research, we return to the roots of recommender systems and we explore the relationship between Information Filtering and Information Retrieval. We think that probabilistic methods taken from the latter field such as statistical Language Models can be a more effective and formal way for generating personalised ranks of recommendations. We compare our improvements against several algebraic and probabilistic state-of-the-art algorithms and pave the way to future and promising research directions.

Categories and Subject Descriptors

H.3.3 [**Information Search and Retrieval**]: Information filtering

Keywords

Recommender systems; Language Models.

1. INTRODUCTION

The goal of an Information Retrieval (IR) system is to retrieve the relevant pieces of information according to an information need, typically in the form of a query. Prior to the arrival of the Web, IR was a narrow area of research —only the small part of the society that had access to digital libraries, librarians and information experts, were interested on IR techniques [1]. Nevertheless, nowadays, IR has become a vital part of the Web: the difficulty of finding relevant information in the largest repository of knowledge makes imperative the use of specialised techniques.

On the other hand, Information Filtering (IF) consists in selecting relevant items for the users from an information stream [9]. Passive IF system remove unwanted pieces of information. For example, anti-spam techniques are passive filters that keep only useful messages. In contrast, active IF systems push relevant information to the users. Nowadays, recommenders are probably the most prominent type of active information filters. Recommenders deliver suggestions to the users based on their profiles. There exist several approaches to build recommenders system. Traditionally, they are classified in three main categories: Collaborative Filtering (CF), Content-Based (CB) and hybrid techniques [14]. CB methods use the features of the items that are part of the user's profile to find similar items that may be of interest. On the other hand, CF algorithms exploit the recorded data about the interactions betweens users and items (ratings, clicks, etc.). Finally, hybrid methods are the fruit of the combination of techniques from the previous approaches.

In the end, both IR and IF have the same objective: provide relevant information to the users. The main difference lies largely in the representation of the information need: a traditional IR system employs an explicit query prompted by the user while an IF system uses the user's profile. Therefore, some authors consider IF as a part of IR [3], meanwhile others think that they are two sibling fields [9]. In any case, in spite of the similarities between IR and IF, there has been little research about applying classic IR techniques to recommender systems, specially to Collaborative Filtering recommenders.

Many CF algorithms rely on finding neighbours using vector similarities [8], in a similar way to the Vector Space Model from IR [1]. However, matrix factorisation methods, such as SVD, are the most popular techniques in the recommender systems literature [11, 6]. These algebraic approaches rely on computing low-rank approximations of the user-item matrix. SVD was already used in text retrieval under the name of Latent Semantic Indexing [7], however its effectiveness is now surpassed by other techniques [1].

The introduction of probabilistic models represented a breakthrough in IR. In particular, statistical Language Models have become a state-of-the-art technique for the text retrieval task [20]. We consider that these models with a solid statistical foundation may bring significant improvements to the field of Recommender Systems as it did in IR.

In our work, we aim to explore different probabilistic IR techniques (specially statistical Language Models) for recommendation tasks. Mostly, but not exclusively, we would want to investigate the following questions:

- Are probabilistic IR models suitable to tackle Collaborative Filtering tasks such as neighbourhood finding or item ranking?
- Can probabilistic IR models be adapted to deal with temporal and/or extra contextual information?
- Is there a principled formulation of statistical Language Models that effectively merges Content-Based and Collaborative Filtering approaches?

2. RELATED WORK

It was acknowledged that rating prediction does not model effectively the recommendation task since users are interested in obtaining a short list of relevant items, they are not particularly concerned about the predicted rating values [10, 6]. This is known as the top-N recommendation task [6]. An advantage of the Information Retrieval methods is that they are traditionally focused on generating a ranked list of items. Thus, there exists an emerging interest in applying IR techniques to the field of Recommender Systems [18, 17, 5, 13].

Recently, the performance of probabilistic graphical models for Collaborative Filtering tasks has been analysed [2] showing better results than other algebraic state-of-the-art recommenders [6].

Aiming to unify IR with recommenders systems, Bellogín et al. presented a general framework that is able to employ any IR system for generating CF recommendations [5]. These methods showed better figures than traditional CF algorithms in terms of precision and ranking metrics.

Another approach is the proposal of Wang et al. based on the probability ranking principle [18]. Wang also derived a CF method utilising Language Models using a risk-averse model that penalises less reliable scores [17]. Nevertheless, these methods are intended to employ implicit feedback.

An idea that showed very satisfactory results is to define the CF task as a Pseudo-Relevance Feedback problem using a specific analogy between IR and IF and applying Relevance-Based Language Models [13]. Following this line of research, we plan to continue to explore the relationship between these fields.

3. RELEVANCE-BASED LANGUAGE MODELS FOR CF

Parapar et al. adapted the Pseudo-Relevance Feedback framework to the Collaborative Filtering recommendation task [13]. Pseudo-Relevance Feedback is a family of methods for expanding the user's query with new terms to improve the performance of a retrieval system. The terms are extracted from a set of documents that are assumed to be relevant. This pseudo-relevant set is obtained from the top documents of an initial retrieval. A second retrieval is performed using the new expanded query and its results are the ones presented to the user.

The Pseudo-Relevance Feedback scheme can be tailored to Collaborative Filtering as follows. Users have a dual role: they act as queries when they are the target user of the recommendations but they also act as documents. On the other hand, items are modelled as terms (they can be query terms as well as document terms). The neighbourhood of the target user is modelled as the pseudo-relevant set. In this way, the problem of recommending items to users becomes the task of expanding queries with novel terms taken from their neighbours.

In the original paper, they applied Relevance-Based Language Models to CF recommendation outperforming the state of the art [13]. Relevance-Based Language Models (or RM for short) [12] are a very effective method for Pseudo-Relevance Feedback. In particular, RM2 model presents high figures in accuracy:

$$p(i|R_u) \propto p(i) \prod_{j \in \mathcal{I}_u} \sum_{v \in V_u} \frac{p(i|v)p(v)}{p(i)} p(j|v) \qquad (1)$$

Given a set of $\mathcal{U}$ users and $\mathcal{I}$ items, a relevance model R_u is computed for each user $u \in \mathcal{U}$ and the relevance of each item $i \in \mathcal{I} \setminus \mathcal{I}_u$ in this model is estimated, $p(i|R_u)$. $\mathcal{I}_u$ is used for representing the set of items the user u rated. Also, V_u refers to the neighbourhood of the user u. Additionally, the prior probabilities, the neighbour prior $p(v)$ and the item prior $p(i)$, should be estimated. Finally, the conditional probability estimations, $p(i|v)$ and $p(j|v)$, are obtained smoothing the Maximum Likelihood Estimate (MLE) with the probability in the collection. The MLE is calculated as follows:

$$p_{ml}(i|u) = \frac{r_{u,i}}{\sum_{j \in \mathcal{I}_u} r_{u,j}} \qquad (2)$$

whereas the probability in the collection is:

$$p(i|\mathcal{C}) = \frac{\sum_{v \in \mathcal{U}} r_{v,i}}{\sum_{j \in \mathcal{I}, v \in \mathcal{U}} r_{v,j}} \qquad (3)$$

The notation $r_{u,i}$ denotes the rating that the user u gave to the item i.

4. ONGOING WORK

In this section, we present our current work on the Relevance-Based Language Modelling of recommender systems. The previous RM2 formula (see Eq. 1) contains different probabilities that should be estimated. First, we describe our findings about smoothing methods for estimating the conditional probabilities of RM2 and, then, we explore some prior estimates.

4.1 Smoothing Methods

We started by analysing different smoothing methods for estimating the conditional probabilities of RM2 [16]. We considered three smoothing techniques.

Jelinek-Mercer.

It performs a linear interpolation between the MLE (see Eq. 2) and the collection model (see Eq. 3) controlled by the parameter λ. This method was used in the original work of RM2 for recommendation [13].

$$p_\lambda(i|u) = (1 - \lambda) p_{ml}(i|u) + \lambda p(i|\mathcal{C}) \qquad (4)$$

Dirichlet priors.

It utilises Dirichlet priors for Bayesian analysis yielding the following expression with parameter μ:

$$p_\mu(i|u) = \frac{r_{u,i} + \mu p(i|\mathcal{C})}{\mu + \sum_{j \in \mathcal{I}_u} r_{u,j}} \qquad (5)$$

Absolute Discounting.

This method subtracts a constant, δ, from each rating.

$$p_\delta(i|u) = \frac{\max(\mathrm{r}_{u,i} - \delta, 0) + \delta\,|\mathcal{I}_u|\,p(i|\mathcal{C})}{\sum_{j \in \mathcal{I}_u} \mathrm{r}_{u,j}} \quad (6)$$

In previous experiments [16], we found out that Absolute Discounting is the best smoothing method. Not only does it yield better rankings but it is also a very stable technique: different values of the parameter barely modify the performance of the recommendation algorithm. Moreover, Absolute Discounting effectively tackles the user bias taking into account the average rating of each user.

4.2 Prior Probabilities

One advantage of the RM2 probabilistic algorithm over other algebraic proposal is its interpretability. The modelling of prior probabilities provide a principled way of introducing business rules into the recommendation algorithm. The original proposal of RM2 for Collaborative Filtering employed uniform priors [13]; however, it would be interesting to explore another approaches. Next, we describe the standard uniform prior and a new proposal for user priors. More work in this line of research is being performed.

Uniform Prior.

This classic prior is drawn from a uniform distribution: we assign the same probability to each user.

Linear Prior.

This prior promotes those users with larger rating profiles. The rationale behind this decision is that we should rely more on the users for which we have more information about.

$$p_L(u) = p(u|\mathcal{C}) = \frac{\sum_{i \in \mathcal{I}_u} r_{u,i}}{\sum_{v \in \mathcal{U}} \sum_{j \in \mathcal{I}_v} r_{v,j}} \quad (7)$$

5. EVALUATION AND RESULTS

The evaluation of recommender systems is crucial in order to choose between models or to tune parameters. In this section, we present the evaluation methodology followed in our experiments that we plan to apply during the development of the PhD thesis. In addition, we performed a series of experiments to analyse the performance RM2-based methods against other recommendation approaches. We chose to report these experiments only on the *MovieLens 100k*[1] dataset, a well-known film collection for Collaborative Filtering, because of space reasons.

5.1 Evaluation methodology

We aim to analyse the performance of recommender systems in the top-N recommendation task, that is, measuring how well recommenders put relevant items in the top of the list [6]. Consequently, we are interested in precision-oriented metrics that analyse only the top N recommendations. With that purpose in mind, we followed the *TestItems* approach described in [4] consisting in scoring, for each user, every item included in the test set. We considered a recommendation relevant if the item is rated by the user in the test set. Although this methodology is very restrictive and may underestimate the true value of the metric, it provides comparable and trustworthy results [4].

[1]http://grouplens.org/datasets/movielens

Table 1: Values of nDCG@10, Gini@10 and MSI@10 on the MovieLens 100k collection for different CF algorithms.

Algorithm	nDCG@10	Gini@10	MSI@10
SVD	0.09456	0.01094	14.61295
SVD++	0.11126	0.01264	14.95739
NNCosNgbr	0.17710	0.03440	16.82222
UIR-Item	0.21876	0.01242	5.23371
PureSVD	0.35946	0.13645	11.88408
RM2-DP	0.29226	0.01760	6.05446
RM2-JM	0.31748	0.02323	6.69447
RM2-AD	0.32964	0.02561	6.82732
RM2-AD-L	0.34232	0.02644	6.78484

Not only ranking accuracy but also novelty and diversity are crucial aspects in recommendation [10]. We used nDCG (Normalised Discounted Cumulative Gain) for assessing the quality of the ranking [19], we employed the complement of the Gini index as a measure of recommendation diversity [15] and, finally, we utilised MSI (Mean Self-Information) as a tool for quantifying novelty [21]. These metrics can be measured at a given cut-off, that is, considering only the top results which are the ones presented to the user.

5.2 Experiments

We compared the performance of RM2-based methods against several state-of-the-art recommendation algorithms. All of these techniques were tuned to optimise the values of nDCG@10. First, we describe the baselines and, then, the proposed algorithms. The results are presented in Table 1.

We used the common SVD and SVD++ approaches to rating prediction with 400 dimensions [11]. We also used NNCosNgbr, a nearest neighbour approach oriented to top-N ranking recommendation [6]. For this method, we used cosine similarity with a shrinking factor of 100 and a L2 regularization factor of 0.9 for computing the user and item biases. Additionally, we implemented the probabilistic approach (UIR-Item) proposed in [18] with $\lambda = 0.5$. Finally, we tested PureSVD (with 50 dimensions) because Cremonesi et al. in [6] showed that it is a very effective matrix factorisation algorithm for top-N recommendation. It computes a global factorisation using the well-known SVDLIBC, in contrast with SVD and SVD++ methods that only minimise the error on the known ratings.

Turning to our probabilistic approaches, we analysed the performance of RM2-based methods using the 400 nearest neighbours according to the Pearson's correlation coefficient. We tested RM2 using Dirichlet Priors (RM2-DP) with $\mu = 100$, Jelinek-Mercer (RM2-JM) with $\lambda = 0.1$ and Absolute Discounting (RM2-AD) with $\delta = 0.1$. In addition, we chose the best smoothing method, Absolute Discounting, and we used a linear prior for estimating $p(v)$ in Eq. 1. We denoted this approach by RM2-AD-L.

All the differences in nDCG@10 reported in Table 1 are statistically significant according to the Wilcoxon signed-rank test ($p < 0.01$). As it was expected, rating prediction methods (SVD and SVD++) performed poorly compared to the rest of the techniques. It can be pointed out that RM2 methods provided higher figures in nDCG@10 than the rest of the baselines expect for PureSVD. This latter method is still the best algorithm in terms of nDCG. These findings confirmed the precision and recall results presented in [6].

Additionally, PureSVD also showed great figures of diversity and novelty. Nevertheless, it is important to note that RM2 provide another advantages such as interpretability and a principled way of introducing business rules into the model using prior probabilities.

It is interesting to remark that there is still room for improvement in the Relevance-Based Language Modelling framework where we plan to work on. The use of the correct smoothing method or the adequate prior estimate can boost significantly the quality of the recommendations. With regard to diversity and novelty, we can notice that PureSVD provides very good values. Thus, it would be worthwhile to explore how to improve RM2 in those aspects.

6. CONCLUSIONS AND FUTURE WORK

The probabilistic modelling of recommender systems is a broad area that has reached little attention. Probabilistic models provided significant improvements to the IR task. Since IR and IF are two closed fields, we think that probabilistic approaches may also lead to important improvements to the recommendation task. In this paper, we explore the performance of Relevance-Based Language Models against several state-of-the-art algorithms. We discovered that RM2 is superior to all baselines except for PureSVD, a recent matrix factorisation approach designed for top-N recommendation.

The experiments showed that different smoothing methods can lead to significant improvements. Moreover, we devised a prior estimate that enhanced the quality of the recommendations. We intend to further study this topic.

Additionally, as future work, we also envision to study other clustering techniques for computing neighbourhoods. In this work, we employed the simple k-NN algorithm using Pearson's correlation coefficient. Further investigation on clustering algorithms may shed light on how to increase the diversity and novelty figures of this probabilistic approach. Aspects such as user and item biases, temporal dynamics or modelling item content and user context information are still open research lines in this probabilistic modelling approach of the recommendation task. We think it is feasible to merge CF and CB approaches in a principle manner using a probabilistic framework.

Acknowledgments

This work was funded by grant TIN2012-33867 from the Spanish Government and grants GPC2013/070, R2014/034 and R2014/002 from the Galician Government.

7. REFERENCES

[1] R. Baeza-Yates and B. Ribeiro-Neto. *Modern Information Retrieval: The Concepts and Technology Behind Search*. Addison Wesley, 2011.

[2] N. Barbieri and G. Manco. An Analysis of Probabilistic Methods for Top-N Recommendation in Collaborative Filtering. In *ECML PKDD '11*, pages 172–187, 2011.

[3] N. J. Belkin and W. B. Croft. Information Filtering and Information Retrieval: Two Sides of the Same Coin? *Commun. ACM*, 35(12):29–38, Dec. 1992.

[4] A. Bellogín, P. Castells, and I. Cantador. Precision-oriented Evaluation of Recommender Systems. In *RecSys '11*, page 333, Oct. 2011.

[5] A. Bellogín, J. Wang, and P. Castells. Bridging Memory-Based Collaborative Filtering and Text Retrieval. *Inf. Retr.*, 16(6):697–724, Nov. 2013.

[6] P. Cremonesi, Y. Koren, and R. Turrin. Performance of Recommender Algorithms on Top-n Recommendation Tasks. In *RecSys '10*, pages 39–46. ACM, Sept. 2010.

[7] S. Deerwester, S. T. Dumais, G. W. Furnas, T. K. Landauer, and R. Harshman. Indexing by Latent Semantic Analysis. *JASIST*, 41(6):391–407, 1990.

[8] C. Desrosiers and G. Karypis. A Comprehensive Survey of Neighborhood-based Recommendation Methods. In F. Ricci, L. Rokach, B. Shapira, and P. B. Kantor, editors, *Recommender Systems Handbook*, pages 107–144. Springer, 2011.

[9] U. Hanani, B. Shapira, and P. Shoval. Information Filtering: Overview of Issues, Research and Systems. *User Model. User-Adapt. Interact.*, 11(3):203–259, 2001.

[10] J. L. Herlocker, J. A. Konstan, L. G. Terveen, and J. T. Riedl. Evaluating Collaborative Filtering Recommender Systems. *ACM Transactions on Information Systems*, 22(1):5–53, Jan. 2004.

[11] Y. Koren and R. Bell. Advances in Collaborative Filtering. In F. Ricci, L. Rokach, B. Shapira, and P. B. Kantor, editors, *Recommender Systems Handbook*, pages 145–186. Springer, 2011.

[12] V. Lavrenko and W. B. Croft. Relevance-Based Language Models. In *SIGIR '01*, pages 120–127, Sept. 2001.

[13] J. Parapar, A. Bellogín, P. Castells, and A. Barreiro. Relevance-based language modelling for recommender systems. *Inf. Process. Manage.*, 49(4):966–980, July 2013.

[14] F. Ricci, L. Rokach, B. Shapira, and P. B. Kantor. *Recommender Systems Handbook*. Springer-Verlag New York, Inc., 1st edition, 2010.

[15] G. Shani and A. Gunawardana. Evaluating Recommendation Systems. In F. Ricci, L. Rokach, B. Shapira, and P. B. Kantor, editors, *Recommender Systems Handbook*, pages 257–297. Springer US, 2011.

[16] D. Valcarce, J. Parapar, and A. Barreiro. A Study of Smoothing Methods for Relevance-Based Language Modelling of Recommender Systems. In *ECIR '15*, volume 9022, pages 346–351. Springer, 2015.

[17] J. Wang. Language Models of Collaborative Filtering. In *AIRS '09*, pages 218–229. Springer-Verlag, 2009.

[18] J. Wang, A. P. de Vries, and M. J. Reinders. A User-Item Relevance Model for Log-based Collaborative Filtering. In *ECIR '06*, volume 3936, pages 37–48. Springer-Verlag, 2006.

[19] Y. Wang, L. Wang, Y. Li, D. He, W. Chen, and T.-Y. Liu. A Theoretical Analysis of NDCG Ranking Measures. In *COLT '13*, pages 1–30. JMLR.org, 2013.

[20] C. Zhai. *Statistical Language Models for Information Retrieval*. Synthesis lectures on human language technologies. Morgan & Claypool, 2009.

[21] T. Zhou, Z. Kuscsik, J.-G. Liu, M. Medo, J. R. Wakeling, and Y.-C. Zhang. Solving the Apparent Diversity-Accuracy Dilemma of Recommender Systems. *PNAS*, 107(10):4511–5, Mar. 2010.

Factorization Machines for Hybrid Recommendation Systems Based on Behavioral, Product, and Customer Data

Stijn Geuens

IESEG School of Management – Université Catholique de Lille (LEM-CNRS (UMR 9221))
3 Rue de la Digue
F-59000 Lille, France
s.geuens@ieseg.fr

ABSTRACT

This study creates a hybrid recommendation system for online offer personalization of an e-commerce company. The system goes beyond existing literature by combining four different data sources, i.e. customer data, product data, implicit and explicit behavioral data, in a single algorithm. Factorization machines are employed as model-based algorithm and have as advantage that the four data sources are incorporated in a single model by feature combination. Results show that hybridization of the four distinct data sources improves accuracy compared to (i) factorization machines based on a single data source and (ii) a real-life company benchmark model using collaborative filtering.

Categories and Subject Descriptors

Information Systems - Information retrieval - Retrieval tasks and goals - Recommender systems

General Terms

Algorithms, Performance, Experimentation

Keywords

Recommendation System, Factorization Machine, Hybrid Algorithm, Feature Combination

1. INTRODUCTION

Recommendation systems are nowadays commonly used to personalize a company's online offer and communication. They take many forms and numerous typologies exist. A typical classification based on input data is proposed by [5] and [4]. These two studies identify four main system types. First, recommendation systems can be based on customer data (CD). These systems are called *demographic recommendation systems*. Second, *content-based systems* use product data (PD) and make recommendations based on similarity between product characteristics of items bought and other products not yet purchased by the customer. Third, *knowledge-based systems* use (real-time) information to recommend products. Fourth, *collaborative filtering algorithms (CF)* use prior explicit or implicit customer behavioral data (BD). CF identifies customers who exhibit the same behavior (nearest

neighbors), then suggest products based on the actions of their peers. Explicit BD refers to evaluations explicitly given by the customers e.g. a star-rating or a like on Facebook. This kind of data has the advantage that it clearly represents customer interest [12], but has as drawback that it demands customer effort and time to rate items which leads often to insufficient data to recommend products [11]. In addition, people have difficulties expressing their interest which results in biased information [14]. To overcome these problems, implicit BD can be used. In contrast to explicit ratings, implicit ratings do not require direct user feedback, but derive affinity with items from actual user behavior like purchase, views, click, etc. The collection of implicit feedback is objective, non-intrusive and often readily available in the customer database [14], but has as disadvantage that the observed action not always correctly represents the user's interest [11].

All types of recommendation systems have advantages and disadvantages. The need for only behavioral data, adaptability, and ability to recommend across niches are clear advantages of CF [5], while the cold-start problem and scalability are disadvantages of CF [1]. Content-based systems tend to be less accurate compared to CF models, have also the new user problem and lead to overspecialization [4]. Demographic systems tend to be less accurate compared to CF and need collection of customer data, but do not require the collection product data [5]. Finally knowledge based systems need knowledge engineering and are therefore more subjective [5].

To resolve the issues related to single data source systems, hybrid algorithms are developed. These systems combine multiple data sources and/or prediction techniques. Combining different data sources is very popular in the recommender literature [4]. The main advantages of these systems are mainly the improved prediction accuracy and the fact that they overcome issues related to techniques based on a single data source [5].

This study combines different data sources, PD, CD, and implicit and explicit BD in a single state-of-the-art, linear scalable recommendation algorithm, factorization machines (FM) [17]. Based on the setup of this study, all four data sources can be deployed in a single algorithm which is never done before in the feature combination literature. Additionally, from an algorithmic point of view, FM is a very promising technique with the ability to include all kinds of real valued feature vectors [17]. Nevertheless, combining different data sources, as done in this study, is never investigated in the specific FM literature.

The proposed hybrid FM algorithm is compared to three single data source FMs and a company-used benchmark algorithm based on

CF. Added value of combining different data sources is analyzed in terms of recall and computation time.

The remainder of the study is divided as follows. In the related research section a brief overview of hybrid algorithms and an introduction to FMs is given. A third section discusses the components of the conducted analysis focusing on the data used and the algorithms calculated. Section 4 shows the results of the analysis. Finally section 5 concludes and identifies paths for future research.

2. RELATED RESEARCH

2.1 Hybrid Algorithms

In recent years, a lot of studies successfully focus on creating hybrid models combining different data sources. Overviews are given by [5], [1], and [4].

Most contributions to literature combine BD and PD, or CF and content-based systems [3; 6; 15; 19], but hybridization of BD and CD is investigated as well [15; 19]. Combination of CD and PD [7], without BD is less investigated in literature. Combinations of two out of four different identified data sources are already investigated in literature, nevertheless the hybridization of all four data sources remains uninvestigated. Therefore this study incorporates the four distinct data sources and shows the added value of this unique combination.

Next to data sources used, hybrid algorithms are characterized by the hybridization method. Burke [5] distinguishes between seven combination methods; weighting, switching, mixing, cascading, feature augmentation, meta-level, and feature combination. Whereas the first six techniques calculate distinct models for each data source and combine results afterwards, feature combination includes different data sources in a single algorithm. Many different algorithms using feature combination are developed to integrate two out of the four identified data sources [3; 16; 18]. In this study we integrate all four data sources using feature combination. More specific a factorization machine, as discussed in the next section, is proposed to incorporate the four distinct data sources.

2.2 Factorization Machines

In recent years many new state-of-the-art model-based algorithms are created [2; 8]. One of these techniques, 'factorization machines' (FM), first introduced by [17], is based on Support Vector Machines (SVM) and factorization models and combines the advantages of both. Like SVMs, FMs are a general predictor working with any real valued feature vector. In contrast to SVMs, FMs are able to estimate interactions even in problems with huge sparsity (like recommender systems) where SVMs fail. Main reason of this interesting property is the fact that variable interaction is calculated based on factorized parameters. This allows to calculate the model in linear time.

Compared to factorization models, like SVD++ [13], FM works with any real valued feature vector. This advantage gives the opportunity to include different types of BD, PD, and CD as predictors.

The general model equation of a FM of degree 2 is formulated as follows:

$$f(x) = w_0 + \sum_{i=1}^{n} w_i x_i + \sum_{i=1}^{n} \sum_{j=i=1}^{n} \langle v_i, v_j \rangle x_i x_j. \quad (1)$$

In equation 1 x_i represent the predictors being BD, PD, and/or CD. w_0 is the global bias and w_i are the parameters related to first degree effect of the n predictors. $\langle v_i, v_j \rangle$ represents the dot product of v_i and v_j where these two terms are low dimensionality vector representations of rank k of the predictors.

3. COMPONENTS

This study employs four different FMs including different data sources, i.e. different sets of predictors, and a benchmark model based on item-based CF. The results of these algorithms are used to target customers by personalized direct e-mailing. More specific, if a customer visits at least one product in a product category on the e-commerce site, the customer receives an e-mail with product recommendations in the same product category. In the remainder of this section, the used data and algorithms are discussed in more detail.

3.1 Data

The data used in this study are real-life data sets of a large European e-commerce company specialized in home decoration and clothing. The analyses are conducted on two distinct data sets, containing information about the furniture and children's clothing product categories. The furniture product category consists of 5,368 users and 2,601 items and the children's clothing product category comprises 5,999 users and 4,372 items. In the tested algorithms three distinct data sources, BD, PD, and CD, are incorporated for the two product categories.

Five types of BD divided in two categories are included. First, explicit ratings of customers on a five-point scale are gathered. Second, four types implicit BD are collected, being, purchase, view, addition to cart, and internal search engine data. Table 1 gives an overview of the different BD sources.

Table 1: Overview of different BD sources

	Users (Furniture / Children's clothing)	Items (Furniture / Children's clothing)	Hits (Furniture / Children's clothing)
Explicit Ratings	1,159 / 1,545	2,218 / 3,482	3,140 / 5,202
Purchases	952 / 1,384	2,482 / 3,942	3,241 / 6,040
Internal Search	3,519 / 3,741	21,667 / 30,260	524,476 / 841,672
Add to Cart	4,564 / 5,225	17,930 / 24,066	721.774 / 1,706,773
Views	5,368 / 5,999	58,221 / 75,186	4,068,151 / 10,531,876

Next to BD, CD is gathered. Main variables in this category are:

- socio-demographic information
  - age, gender, place of residence, and children information
- RFM (Recency – Frequency – Monetary) variables:
  - Total value of purchases
  - Number of total purchases
  - Time since last purchase
- Relationship variables
  - Length of relationship
  - Value-based segmentation
- Mean product rating of the customer

Finally, PD is included. Three main product divisions are used as well as brand, mean product rating, availability on the web, and a dummy indicating internal or external product.

FMs need a target to make predictions, as further explained in the next section. The target in this study will be a binary purchase variable. If customer X buys product Y, this combination gets value 1, 0 otherwise.

Keeping the volume of data and customer purchase cycles in mind, data is gathered on different time periods for different input data sources, as depicted in Figure 1. The time periods are based on internal analysis of purchase cycles by the company. For explicit ratings we include a history of two years, while for implicit rating